A SELECT LIBRARY

OF

NICENE AND POST-NICENE FATHERS

OF

THE CHRISTIAN CHURCH

𝔖𝔢𝔠𝔬𝔫𝔡 𝔖𝔢𝔯𝔦𝔢𝔰

TRANSLATED INTO ENGLISH WITH PROLEGOMENA AND EXPLANATORY NOTES

UNDER THE EDITORIAL SUPERVISION OF

PHILIP SCHAFF, D.D., LL.D.,   AND   HENRY WACE, D.D.,

Professor of Church History in the Union Theological   *Principal of King's College,*
Seminary, New York.   *London.*

IN CONNECTION WITH A NUMBER OF PATRISTIC SCHOLARS OF EUROPE
AND AMERICA.

VOLUME V

GREGORY OF NYSSA :

DOGMATIC TREATISES, ETC.

T&T CLARK
EDINBURGH

WM. B. EERDMANS PUBLISHING COMPANY
GRAND RAPIDS, MICHIGAN

British Library Cataloguing in Publication Data

Nicene & Post-Nicene Fathers. — 2nd series
1. Fathers of the church
I. Schaff, Philip   II. Mace, Henry
230'.11   BR60.A62

T&T Clark ISBN 0 567 09414 6

Eerdmans ISBN 0-8028-8119-X

Reprinted, January 1994

PHOTOLITHOPRINTED BY EERDMANS PRINTING COMPANY
GRAND RAPIDS, MICHIGAN, UNITED STATES OF AMERICA

EDITOR'S PREFACE

THESE translations from the works of St. Gregory of Nyssa have involved unusual labour, which the Editor hopes will be accepted as a sufficient apology for the delay of the volume. The difficulty has been extreme of conveying with correctness in English the meaning of expressions and arguments which depend on some of the most subtle ideas of Greek philosophy and theology; and, in addition to the thanks due to the translators, the Editor must offer a special acknowledgment of the invaluable help he has received from the exact and philosophical scholarship of the Rev. J. H. Lupton, Surmaster of St. Paul's School. He must renew to Mr. Lupton, with increased earnestness, the expression of gratitude he had already had occasion to offer in issuing the Translation of St. Athanasius. From the careful and minute revision which the volume has thus undergone, the Editor ventures to entertain some hope that the writings of this important and interesting Father are in this volume introduced to the English reader in a manner which will enable him to obtain a fair conception of their meaning and value.

HENRY WACE

King's College, London, 6th November, 1892.

SELECT WRITINGS AND LETTERS

OF

GREGORY, BISHOP OF NYSSA

TRANSLATED, WITH PROLEGOMENA, NOTES, AND INDICES,

BY

WILLIAM MOORE, M.A.

RECTOR OF APPLETON,
LATE FELLOW OF MAGDALEN COLLEGE, OXFORD;

AND

HENRY AUSTIN WILSON, M.A.

FELLOW AND LIBRARIAN OF MAGDALEN COLLEGE, OXFORD.

PREFACE

THAT none of the Treatises of S. Gregory of Nyssa have hitherto been translated into English, or even (with one exception long ago) into French, may be partly due to the imperfections, both in number and quality, of the MSS., and by consequence of the Editions, of the great majority of them. The state of the MSS., again, may be owing to the suspicion diligently fostered by the zealous friends of the reputation of this Father, in ages when MSS. could and should have been multiplied and preserved, that there were large importations into his writings from the hands of the Origenists—a statement which a very short study of Gregory, whose thought is *always* taking the direction of Origen, would disprove.

This suspicion, while it resulted in throwing doubts upon the genuineness of the entire text, has so far deprived the current literature of the Church of a great treasure. For there are two qualities in this Gregory's writings not to be found in the same degree in any other Greek teacher, namely, a far-reaching use of philosophical speculation (quite apart from allegory) in bringing out the full meaning of Church doctrines, and Bible truths; and excellence of style. With regard to this last, he himself bitterly deplored the days which he had wasted over the study of style; but we at all events need not share that regret, if only for this reason, that his writings thereby show that patristic Greek could rise to the level of the best of its time. It is not necessarily the thing which it is, too easily, even in other instances, assumed to be. Granted the prolonged decadence of the language, yet perfects are not aorists, nor aorists perfects, the middle is a middle, there are classical constructions of the participle, the particles of transition and prepositions in composition have their *full* force in Athanasius; much more in Basil; much more in Gregory. It obscures facts to say that there was good Greek only in the age of Thucydides. There was good and bad Greek of its kind, in every epoch, as long as Greek was living. So far for mere syntax. As for adequacy of language, the far wider range of his subject-matter puts Gregory of Nyssa to a severer test; but he does not fail under it. What could be more dignified than his letter to Flavian, or more choice than his description of the spring, or more richly illustrated than his praises of Contemplation, or more pathetic than his pleading for the poor? It would have been strange indeed if the Greek language had not possessed a Jerome of its own, to make it speak the new monastic devotion.

But the labours of J. A. Krabinger, F. Oehler, and G. H. Forbes upon the text, though all abruptly ended, have helped to repair the neglect of the past. They in this century, as the scholars of Paris, Ghent, and Basle, though each working with fewer or more imperfect MSS., in the sixteenth and seventeenth, have been better friends to Gregory than those who wrote books in the sixth to defend his orthodoxy, but to depreciate his writings. In this century, too, Cardinal Mai has rescued still more from oblivion in the Vatican—a slight compensation for all the materials collected for a Benedictine edition of Gregory, but dispersed in the French Revolution.

The longest Treatise here translated is that *Against Eunomius* in 13 Books. The reproduction of so much ineffectual fencing in logic over a question which no longer can trouble the Church might be taken exception to. But should men like Gregory and Basil, pleading for the spirit and for faith and. for mystery against the conclusions of a hard logician, be an indifferent spectacle to us? The interest, too, in the contest deepens when we know that their opponent not only proclaimed himself, but was accepted, as a martyr to the Anomœan cause; and that he had large congregations to the very end. The moral force of Arianism was stronger than ever as its end drew near in the East, because the Homœans were broken up and there was no more complicity with the court and politics. It was represented by a man who had suffered and had made no compromises; and so the life-long work, previous to his, of Valens the bishop at last bore fruit in conversions; and the Anomœan teaching came to a head in the easily understood formula that the Ἀγεννησία was the essence of the Father—an idea which in the Dated Creed Valens had repudiated.

What, then, was to be done? Eunomius seemed by his parade of logic to have dug a gulf for ever between the Ungenerate and the Generate, in other words between the Father and the Son. The merit and interest of this Treatise of Gregory consists in showing this logician as making endless mistakes in his logic; and then, that anything short of the "eternal generation" involved unspeakable absurdities or profanities; and lastly, that Eunomius was fighting by means of distinctions which were the mere result of mental analysis. Already, we see, there was floating in the air the Conceptualism and Realism of the Middle Ages, invoked for this last Arian controversy. When Eunomius retorted that this faculty of analysis cannot give the name of God, and calls his opponents atheists for not recognizing the more than human source of the term Ἀγέννητος, the last word of Nicene orthodoxy has to be uttered; and it is, that God is really incomprehensible, and that here we can never know His name.

This should have led to a statement of the claims of the Sacraments as placing us in heart and spirit, but not in mind, in communion with this incomprehensible God. But this would have been useless with such opponents as the Eunomians. Accuracy of doctrine and clearness of statement was to them salvation; mysteries were worse than nothing. Only in the intervals of the logical battle, and for the sake of the faithful, does Gregory recur to those moral and spiritual attributes which a true Christianity has revealed in the Deity, and upon which the doctrine of the Sacraments is built.

Such controversies are repeated now; *i. e.* where truths, which it requires a certain state of the affections to understand, should be urged, but cannot be, on the one side; and truths which are logical, or literary, or scientific only, are ranged on the other side; as an instance, though in another field, the arguments for and against the results of the "higher criticism" of the Old Testament exhibit this irreconcilable attitude.

Yet in one respect a great gain must have at once resulted to the Catholic cause from this long work. The counter opposition of Created and Uncreate, with which Gregory met the opposition of Generate and Ungenerate, and which, unlike the latter, is a dichotomy founded on an *essential* difference, must have helped many minds, distracted with the jargon of Arianism, to see more clearly the preciousness of the Baptismal Formula, as the casket which contains the Faith. Indeed, the life-work of Gregory was to defend this Formula.

The Treatise *On Virginity* is probably the work of his youth; but none the less Christian for that. Here is done what students of Plato had doubtless long been asking for, *i. e.* that his "love of the Beautiful" should be spiritualized. Beginning with a bitter accusation of marriage, Gregory leaves the reader doubtful in the end whether celibacy is necessary or not for the contemplative life; so absorbed he becomes in the task of showing the blessedness of those who look to the source of all visible beauty. But the result of this seeing is not, as in Plato, a mere enlightenment as to the real value of these visible things. There are so many more beautiful things in God than Plato saw; the Christian revelation has infinitely enriched the field of contemplation; and the lover of the beautiful now must be a higher character, and have a more chastened heart, not only be a more favoured child of light, than others. His enthusiasm shall be as strong as ever; but the model is higher now; and even an Aristotelian balance of moral extremes is necessary to guide him to the goal of a successful Imitation.

It was right, too, that the Church should possess her *Phædo*, or Death-bed Dialogue; and it is Gregory who has supplied this in his *On the Soul and the Resurrection.* But the copy becomes an original. The dialogue is between a sister and a brother; the one a saintly Apologist, the other, for argument's sake, a gainsayer, who urges all the pleas of Greek materialism. Not only the immortality of the soul is discussed, but an exact definition of it is sought, and that in the light of a truer psychology than Plato's. His "chariot" is given up; sensation, as the basis of all thought, is freely recognized; and yet the passions are firmly separated from the actual essence of the soul; further, the "coats of skins" of fallen humanity, as symbolizing the *wrong* use of the passions, take the place of the "sea-weed" on the statue of Glaucus. The grasp of the Christian philosopher of the traits of a perfect humanity, so conspicuous in his *Making of Man*, give him an advantage here over the pagan. As for the Resurrection of the flesh, it was a novel stroke to bring the beliefs of Empedocles, Pythagoras, Plato, and the later Platonists, into one focus as it were, and to show that the teaching of those philosophers as to the destinies of the soul recognized the possibility, or even the necessity, of the reassumption of *some* body. Grotesque objections to the Christian Resurrection, such as are urged nowadays, are brought forward and answered in this Treatise.

The appeal to the Saviour, as to the Inspiration of the Old Testament, has raised again a discussion as to the Two Natures; and will probably continue to do so. But before the subject of the "communication of attributes" can be entered upon, we must remember that Christ's mere humanity (as has been lately pointed out [1]) is, to begin with, sinless. He was perfect man. What the attributes of a perfect, as contrasted with a fallen, humanity are, it is not given except by inference to know; but no Father has discussed this subject of Adam's nature more fully than Gregory, in his treatise *On the Making of Man*.

The reasons for classing the *Great Catechism* as an Apologetic are given in the Prolegomena: here from first to last Gregory shows himself a genuine pupil of Origen. The plan of Revelation is made to rest on man's free-will; every objection to it is answered by the fact of this free-will. This plan is unfolded so as to cover the whole of human history; the beginning, the middle, and the end are linked, in the exposition, indissolubly together. The Incarnation is the turning-point of history; and yet, beyond this, its effects are for all Creation. Who made this theology? Origen doubtless; and his philosophy of Scripture, based on a few leading texts, became, one point excepted, the property of the Church: she at last possessed a *Théodicée* that borrowed nothing from Greek ideas. So far, then, every one who used it was an Origenist: and yet Gregory alone has suffered from this charge. In using this *Théodicée* he has in some points surpassed his master, *i. e.* in showing in details the skilfulness ($\sigma o \phi \iota a$) which effected the real "touching" of humanity; and how the "touched" soul and the "touched" body shall follow in the path of the Redeemer's Resurrection.

To the many points of modern interest in this Gregory should be added his eschatology, which occupies a large share of his thoughts. *On Infants' Early Deaths* is a witness of this. In fact, when not occupied in defending, on one side or another, the Baptismal Formula, he is absorbed in eschatology. He dwells continually on the agonizing and refining processes of Purgatory. But to claim him as one who favours the doctrine of "Eternal Hope" in a universal sense is hardly possible, when we consider the passage in *On the Soul and the Resurrection* where he speaks of a Last Judgment as coming after the Resurrection and Purgatory.

So much has been said in a Preface, in order to show that this Volume is a step at least towards reinstating a most interesting writer, doubtless one of the most highly educated of his time, and, let it be observed as well, a canonized saint (for, more fortunate than his works, he was never branded as a heretic), in his true position.

In a first English translation of Treatises and Letters most of which (notably the books against Eunomius) have never been illustrated by a single translator's note, and by but a handful of scholia, a few passages remain, which from the obscurity of their allusion, local or historical, are unexplained. In others the finest shades of meaning in one Greek word, insisted on in some argument, but which the best English equivalent fails to represent, cause the appearance of obscurity. But, throughout, the utmost clearness possible without unduly straining the literal meaning has been aimed at; and in passages too numerous to name, most grateful acknowledgment is here made of the invaluable suggestions of the Rev. J. H. Lupton.

It is hoped that the Index of Subjects will be of use, in lieu of an analysis, where an analysis has not been provided. The Index of Texts, all of which have been strictly verified, while it will be found to prove Gregory's thorough knowledge of Scripture (nothwithstanding his somewhat classical training), does not attempt to distinguish between citation and reminiscence; care, however, has been taken that the reminiscence should be undoubted.

The Index of Greek words (as also the quotations in foot-notes of striking sentences) has been provided for those interested in the study of later Greek.

W. M.

July, 1892.

[1] *Christus Comprobator*, p. 99, sq.

CONTENTS OF VOLUME V

---

[1] The Chapters, Translations, Notes, Analysis, &c., are by Rev. W. Moore, except where otherwise stated.

WORKS ON ANALYTICAL CRITICISM, HISTORY, AND BIBLIOGRAPHY, CONSULTED.

Rupp (Dr. Julius), Gregors des Bischofs von Nyssa Leben und Meinungen. Leipzig, 1834.

Möller (E. W.) Gregori Nysseni doctrinam de hominis naturâ et illustravit et cum Origenianâ comparavit. Halle, 1854.

Denys (J.), De la Philosophie d'Origéne. Paris, 1884.

Dorner (Dr. J. A.), Doctrine of the Person of Christ. Clark's English translation. Edinburgh.

Heyns (S. P.), Disputatio Historico-Theologica de Gregorio Nysseno. Leyden, 1835.

Alzog (Dr. J.), Handbuch d. Patrologie. 3rd ed. 1876.

Ceillier (Rémi), Histoire Générale des Auteurs Sacrés et Ecclésiastiques. Paris, 1858 sqq.

Tillemont (Louis Sebastien Le Nain De), Mémoires pour servir à l'Histoire Ecclésiastique des six premiers Siècles, Vol. IX. Paris, 1693-1712.

Fabricius (J. A.), Bibliotheca Græca. Hamburg, 1718-28.

Prolegomena to the Paris edition of all Gregory's Works, with notes by Father Fronto Du Duc, 1638.

Cave (Dr. W.), Historia Literaria. London, 1688. (Oxford, 1740.)

Du Pin (Dr. L. E.) Library of Ecclesiastical Authors. Paris, 1686.

Fessler (Joseph), Institutiones Patrologiæ: Dr. B. Jungmann's edition. Innsbruck, 1890.

DATES OF TREATISES, &c., HERE TRANSLATED.

(*Based on Heyns and Rupp.*)

331. Gregory born.
360. *Letters x. xi. xv.*
361. Julian's edict. Gregory gives up rhetoric.
362. Gregory in his brother's monastery.
363. *Letter vi.* (probably).
368. *On Virginity.*
369. Gregory elected a Reader.
372. Gregory elected Bishop of Nyssa early in this year.
374. Gregory is exiled under Valens.
375. *On the Faith. On "Not three Gods."*
376. *Letters vii. xiv. On the Baptism of Christ.*
377. *Against Macedonius.*
378. Gregory returns to his See. *Letter iii.*
379. *On Pilgrimages.*[1]
       Letter ii.
380. *On the Soul and the Resurrection.*
       On the Making of Man.
       On the Holy Trinity.
381. Gregory present at the Second Council. *Oration on Meletius.*
382-3. *Against Eunomius*, Books I—XII.
       Letter to Eustathia.
383. Present at Constantinople. *Letter xii.*
384. *Answer to Eunomius' Second Book.*
385. *The Great Catechism.*
386. *Letter xiii.*
390. *Letter iv.*
393. *Letter to Flavian.*
394. Present for Synod at Constantinople.
395. *On Infants' Early Deaths.*

---

[1] Rupp places this after the Council of Constantinople, 381.
Letters i., v., viii., ix., xvi. are also probably after 381.

THE LIFE AND WRITINGS OF

GREGORY OF NYSSA

CHAPTER I.

A Sketch of the Life of S. Gregory of Nyssa.

In the roll of the Nicene Fathers there is no more honoured name than that of Gregory of Nyssa. Besides the praises of his great brother Basil and of his equally great friend Gregory Nazianzen, the sanctity of his life, his theological learning, and his strenuous advocacy of the faith embodied in the Nicene clauses, have received the praises of Jerome, Socrates, Theodoret, and many other Christian writers. Indeed such was the estimation in which he was held that some did not hesitate to call him 'the Father of Fathers' as well as 'the Star of Nyssa [1].'

Gregory of Nyssa was equally fortunate in his country, the name he bore, and the family which produced him. He was a native of Cappadocia, and was born most probably at Cæsarea, the capital, about A.D. 335 or 336. No province of the Roman Empire had in those early ages received more eminent Christian bishops than Cappadocia and the adjoining district of Pontus.

In the previous century the great prelate Firmilian, the disciple and friend of Origen, who visited him at his See, had held the Bishopric of Cæsarea. In the same age another saint, Gregory Thaumaturgus, a friend also and disciple of Origen, was bishop of Neo-Cæsarea in Pontus. During the same century, too, no less than four other Gregories shed more or less lustre on bishoprics in that country. The family of Gregory of Nyssa was one of considerable wealth and distinction, and one also conspicuously Christian.

During the Diocletian persecution his grandparents had fled for safety to the mountainous region of Pontus, where they endured great hardships and privations. It is said that his maternal grandfather, whose name is unknown, eventually lost both life and property. After a retirement of some few years the family appear to have returned and settled at Cæsarea in Cappadocia, or else at Neo-Cæsarea in Pontus, for there is some uncertainty in the account.

Gregory's father, Basil, who gave his name to his eldest son, was known as a rhetorician. He died at a comparatively early age, leaving a family of ten children, five of whom were boys and five girls, under the care of their grandmother Macrina and mother Emmelia. Both of these illustrious ladies were distinguished for the earnestness and strictness of their Christian principles, to which the latter added the charm of great personal beauty.

All the sons and daughters appear to have been of high character, but it is only of four sons and one daughter that we have any special record. The daughter, called Macrina, from her grandmother, was the angel in the house of this illustrious family. She shared with her grandmother and mother the care and education of all its younger members. Nor was there

---

[1] Ὁ τῶν Πατέρων Πατήρ; ὁ τῶν Νυσσαέων φωστήρ, Council. Nic. II. Act. VI. Edition of Labbe, p. 477.—Nicephor. Callist. *H.E.* xi. 19.

one of them who did not owe to her religious influence their settlement in the faith and consistency of Christian conduct.

This admirable woman had been betrothed in early life, but her intended husband died of fever. She permitted herself to contract no other alliance, but regarded herself as still united to her betrothed in the other world. She devoted herself to a religious life, and eventually, with her mother Emmelia, established a female conventual society on the family property in Pontus, at a place called Annesi, on the banks of the river Iris.

It was owing to her persuasions that her brother Basil also gave up the worldly life, and retired to lead the devout life in a wild spot in the immediate neighbourhood of Annesi. Here for a while he was an hermit, and here he persuaded his friend Gregory Nazianzen to join him. They studied together the works of Origen, and published a selection of extracts from his Commentaries, which they called "Philocalia." By the suggestions of a friend Basil enlarged his idea, and converted his hermit's seclusion into a monastery, which eventually became the centre of many others which sprung up in that district.

His inclination for the monastic life had been greatly influenced by his acquaintance with the Egyptian monks, who had impressed him with the value of their system as an aid to a life of religious devotion. He had visited also the hermit saints of Syria and Arabia, and learnt from them the practice of a severe asceticism, which both injured his health and shortened his days.

Gregory of Nyssa was the third son, and one of the youngest of the family. He had an elder brother, Nectarius, who followed the profession of their father, and became rhetorician, and like him died early. He had also a younger brother, Peter, who became bishop of Sebaste.

Besides the uncertainty as to the year and place of his birth it is not known where he received his education. From the weakness of his health and delicacy of his constitution, it was most probably at home. It is interesting, in the case of one so highly educated, to know who, in consequence of his father's early death, took charge of his merely intellectual bringing up : and his own words do not leave us in any doubt that, so far as he had a teacher, it was Basil, his senior by several years. He constantly speaks of him as the revered ' Master : ' to take but one instance, he says in his *Hexaemeron (ad init.)* that all that will be striking in that work will be due to Basil, what is inferior will be the ' pupil's.' Even in the matter of style, he says in a letter written in early life to Libanius that though he enjoyed his brother's society but a short time yet Basil was the author of his oratory (λόγου) : and it is safe to conclude that he was introduced to all that Athens had to teach, perhaps even to medicine, by Basil : for Basil had been at Athens. On the other hand we can have no difficulty in crediting his mother, of whom he always spoke with the tenderest affection, and his admirable sister Macrina, with the care of his religious teaching. Indeed few could be more fortunate than Gregory in the influences of home. If, as there is every reason to believe, the grandmother Macrina survived Gregory's early childhood, then, like Timothy, he was blest with the religious instruction of another Lois and Eunice.

In this chain of female relationship it is difficult to say which link is worthier of note, grandmother, mother, or daughter. Of the first, Basil, who attributes his early religious impressions to his grandmother, tells us that as a child she taught him a Creed, which had been drawn up for the use of the Church of Neo-Cæsarea by Gregory Thaumaturgus. This Creed, it is said, was revealed to the Saint in a vision. It has been translated by Bishop Bull in his "Fidei Nicænæ Defensio." In its language and spirit it anticipates the Creed of Constantinople.

Certain it is that Gregory had not the benefit of a residence at Athens, or of foreign travel. It might have given him a strength of character and width of experience, in which he was certainly deficient. His shy and retiring disposition induced him to remain at home without choosing a profession, living on his share of the paternal property, and educating himself by a discipline of his own.

He remained for years unbaptized. And this is a very noticeable circumstance which meets us in the lives of many eminent Saints and Bishops of the Church. They either delayed baptism themselves, or it was delayed for them. Indeed there are instances of Bishops baptized and consecrated the same day.

Gregory's first inclination or impulse to make a public profession of Christianity is said to have been due to a remarkable dream or vision.

His mother Emmelia, at her retreat at Annesi, urgently entreated him to be present and take part in a religious ceremony in honour of the Forty Christian Martyrs. He had gone unwillingly, and wearied with his journey and the length of the service, which lasted far into the night, he lay down and fell asleep in the garden. He dreamed that the Martyrs appeared to him and, reproaching him for his indifference, beat him with rods. On awaking he was filled with remorse, and hastened to amend his past neglect by earnest entreaties for mercy and forgiveness. Under the influence of the terror which his dream inspired he consented to undertake the office of reader in the Church, which of course implied a profession of Christianity. But some unfitness, and, perhaps, that love of eloquence which clung to him to the last, soon led him to give up the office, and adopt the profession of a rhetorician or advocate. For this desertion of a sacred for a secular employment he is taken severely to task by his brother Basil and his friend Gregory Nazianzen. The latter does not hesitate to charge him with being influenced, not by conscientious scruples, but by vanity and desire of public display, a charge not altogether consistent with his character.

Here it is usual to place the marriage of Gregory with Theosebeia, said to have been a sister of Gregory Nazianzen. Certainly the tradition of Gregory's marriage received such credit as to be made in after times a proof of the non-celibacy of the Bishops of his age. But it rests mainly on two passages, which taken separately are not in the least conclusive. The first is the ninety-fifth letter of Gregory Nazianzen, written to console for a certain loss by death, i. e. of "Theosebeia, the fairest, the most lustrous even amidst such beauty of the ἀδελφοὶ ; Theosebeia, the true priestess, the yokefellow and the equal of a priest." J. Rupp has well pointed out that the expression 'yokefellow' (σύζυγον), which has been insisted as meaning 'wife,' may, especially in the language of Gregory Nazianzen, be equivalent to ἀδελφός. He sees in this Theosebeia 'a sister of the Cappadocian brothers.' The second passage is contained in the third cap. of Gregory's treatise On Virginity. Gregory there complains that he is "cut off by a kind of gulf from this glory of virginity" (παρθενία). The whole passage should be consulted. Of course its significance depends on the meaning given to παρθενία. Rupp asserts that more and more towards the end of the century this word acquired a technical meaning derived from the purely ideal side, i. e. virginity of soul : and that Gregory is alluding to the same thing that his friend had not long before blamed him for, the keeping of a school for rhetoric, where his object had been merely worldly reputation, and the truly ascetic career had been marred (at the time he wrote). Certainly the terrible indictment of marriage in the third cap. of this treatise comes ill from one whose wife not only must have been still living, but possessed the virtues sketched in the letter of Gregory Nazianzen : while the allusions at the end of it to the law-courts and their revelations appear much more like the professional reminiscence of a rhetorician who must have been familiar with them, than the personal complaint of one who had cause to depreciate marriage. The powerful words of Basil, de Virgin. I. 610, a. b., also favour the above view of the meaning of παρθενία : and Gregory elsewhere distinctly calls celibacy παρθενία τοῦ σώματος, and regards it as a means only to this higher παρθενια (III. 131). But the two passages above, when combined, may have led to the tradition of Gregory's marriage. Nicephorus Callistus, for example, who first makes mention of it, must have put upon παρθενια the interpretation of his own time (thirteenth century,)

i. e. that of continence. Finally, those who adopt this tradition have still to account for the fact that no allusion to Theosebeia as his wife, and no letter to her, is to be found in Gregory's numerous writings. It is noteworthy that the Benedictine editors of Gregory Nazianzen (ad Epist. 95) also take the above view.

His final recovery and conversion to the Faith, of which he was always after so strenuous an asserter, was due to her who, all things considered, was the master spirit of the family. By the powerful persuasions of his sister Macrina, at length, after much struggle, he altered entirely his way of life, severed himself from all secular occupations, and retired to his brother's monastery in the solitudes of Pontus, a beautiful spot, and where, as we have seen, his mother and sister had established, in the immediate neighbourhood, a similar association for women.

Here, then, Gregory was settled for several years, and devoted himself to the study of the Scripture and the works of his master Origen. Here, too, his love of natural scenery was deepened so as to find afterwards constant and adequate expression. For in his writings we have in large measure that sentiment of delight in the beauty of nature of which, even when it was felt, the traces are so few and far between in the whole range of Greek literature. A notable instance is the following from the *Letter to Adelphus*, written long afterwards:— "The gifts bestowed upon the spot by Nature, who beautifies the earth with an impromptu grace, are such as these: below, the river Halys makes the place fair to look upon with his banks, and glides like a golden ribbon through their deep purple, reddening his current with the soil he washes down. Above, a mountain densely overgrown with wood stretches, with its long ridge, covered at all points with the foliage of oaks, more worthy of finding some Homer to sing its praises than that Ithacan Neritus which the poet calls 'far-seen with quivering leaves.' But the natural growth of wood as it comes down the hill-side meets at the foot the plantations of human husbandry. For forthwith vines, spread out over the slopes and swellings and hollows at the mountain's base, cover with their colour, like a green mantle, all the lower ground: and the season also was now adding to their beauty with a display of magnificent grape-clusters." Another is from the treatise *On Infants' Early Deaths:* —"Nay look only at an ear of corn, at the germinating of some plant, at a ripe bunch of grapes, at the beauty of early autumn whether in fruit or flower, at the grass springing unbidden, at the mountain reaching up with its summit to the height of the ether, at the springs of the lower ground bursting from its flanks in streams like milk, and running in rivers through the glens, at the sea receiving those streams from every direction and yet remaining within its limits with waves edged by the stretches of beach, and never stepping beyond those fixed boundaries: and how can the eye of reason fail to find in them all that our education for Realities requires?" The treatise *On Virginity* was the fruit of this life in Basil's monastery.

Henceforward the fortunes of Gregory are more closely linked with those of his great brother Basil.

About A. D. 365 Basil was summoned from his retirement to act as coadjutor to Eusebius, the Metropolitan of Cæsarea in Cappadocia, and aid him in repelling the assaults of the Arian faction on the Faith. In these assaults the Arians were greatly encouraged and assisted by the proclivities of the Emperor Valens. After some few years of strenuous and successful resistance, and the endurance of great persecution from the Emperor and his Court, a persecution which indeed pursued him through life, Basil is called by the popular voice, on the death of Eusebius, A. D. 370, to succeed him in the See. His election is vehemently opposed, but after much turmoil is at length accomplished.

To strengthen himself in his position, and surround himself with defenders of the orthodox Faith, he obliges his brother Gregory, in spite of his emphatic protest, to undertake the Bishopric of Nyssa [1], a small town in the west of Cappadocia. When a friend expressed his surprise that he had chosen so obscure a place for such a man as Gregory, he replied, that

---

[1] Now Nirse.

he did not desire his brother to receive distinction from the name of his See, but rather to confer distinction upon it.

It was with the same feeling, and by the exercise of a like masterful will, that he forced upon his friend Gregory Nazianzen the Bishopric of a still more obscure and unimportant place, called Sasima. But Gregory highly resented the nomination, which unhappily led to a life-long estrangement.

It was about this time, too, that a quarrel had arisen between Basil and their uncle, another Gregory, one of the Cappadocian Bishops. And here Gregory of Nyssa gave a striking proof of the extreme simplicity and unreflectiveness of his character, which without guileful intent yet led him into guile. Without sufficient consideration he was induced to practise a deceit which was as irreconcileable with Christian principle as with common sense. In his endeavours to set his brother and uncle at one, when previous efforts had been in vain, he had recourse to an extraordinary method. He forged a letter, as if from their uncle, to Basil, earnestly entreating reconciliation. The inevitable discovery of course only widened the breach, and drew down on Gregory his brother's indignant condemnation. The reconciliation, however, which Gregory hoped for, was afterwards brought about.

Nor was this the only occasion on which Gregory needed Basil's advice and reproof, and protection from the consequences of his inexperienced zeal. After he had become Bishop of Nyssa, with a view to render assistance to his brother he promoted the summoning of Synods. But Basil's wider experience told him that no good would come of such assemblies under existing circumstances. Besides which he had reason to believe that Gregory would be made the tool of factious and designing men. He therefore discouraged the attempt. At another time Basil had to interpose his authority to prevent his brother joining in a mission to Rome to invite the interference of Pope Damasus and the Western Bishops in the settlement of the troubles at Antioch in consequence of the disputed election to the See. Basil had himself experience of the futility of such application to Rome, from the want of sympathy in the Pope and the Western Bishops with the troubles in the East. Nor would he, by such application, give a handle for Rome's assertion of supremacy, and encroachment on the independence of the Eastern Church. The Bishopric of Nyssa was indeed to Gregory no bed of roses. Sad was the contrast to one of his gentle spirit, more fitted for studious retirement and monastic calm than for controversies which did not end with the pen, between the peaceful leisure of his retreat in Pontus and the troubles and antagonisms of his present position. The enthusiasm of his faith on the subject of the Trinity and the Incarnation brought upon him the full weight of Arian and Sabellian hostility, aggravated as it was by the patronage of the Emperor. In fact his whole life at Nyssa was a series of persecutions.

A charge of uncanonical irregularity in his ordination is brought up against him by certain Arian Bishops, and he is summoned to appear and answer them at a Synod at Ancyra. To this was added the vexation of a prosecution by Demosthenes, the Emperor's *chef de cuisine*, on a charge of defalcation in the Church funds.

A band of soldiers is sent to fetch him to the Synod. The fatigue of the journey, and the rough treatment of his conductors, together with anxiety of mind, produce a fever which prevents his attendance. His brother Basil comes to his assistance. He summons another Synod of orthodox Cappadocian Bishops, who dictate in their joint names a courteous letter, apologising for Gregory's absence from the Synod of Ancyra, and proving the falsehood of the charge of embezzlement. At the same time he writes to solicit the interest of Astorgus, a person of considerable influence at the Court, to save his brother from the indignity of being dragged before a secular tribunal.

Apparently the application was unsuccessful. Demosthenes now obtains the holding another Synod at Gregory's own See of Nyssa, where he is summoned to answer the same charges. Gregory refuses to attend. He is consequently pronounced contumacious, and deposed from his Bishopric. His deposition is followed immediately by a decree of banishment from the Emperor, A.D. 376. He retires to Seleucia. But his banishment did not secure him from the malice and persecution of his enemies. He is obliged frequently to shift his quarters, and is subjected to much bodily discomfort and suffering. From the consoling answers of his friend Gregory of Nazianzen (for his own letters are lost), we learn the crushing effects of all these troubles upon his gentle and sensitive spirit, and the deep despondency into which he had fallen.

At length there is a happier turn of affairs. The Emperor Valens is killed, A.D. 378, and with him Arianism 'vanished in the crash of Hadrianople.' He is succeeded by Gratian, the friend and disciple of St. Ambrose. The banished orthodox Bishops are restored to their Sees, and Gregory returns to Nyssa. In [2] one of his letters, most probably to his brother Basil, he gives a graphic description of the popular triumph with which his return was greeted.

But the joy of his restoration is overshadowed by domestic sorrows. His great brother, to whom he owed so much, soon after dies, ere he is 50 years of age, worn out by his unparalleled toils and the severity of his ascetic life. Gregory celebrated his death in a sincere panegyric. Its high-flown style is explained by the rhetorical fashion of the time. The same year another sorrow awaits him. After a separation of many years he revisits his sister Macrina, at her convent in Pontus, but only to find her on her death-bed. We have an interesting and graphic account of the scene between Gregory and his dying sister. To the last this admirable woman appears as the great teacher of her family. She supplies her brother with arguments for, and confirms his faith in, the resurrection of the dead; and almost reproves him for the distress he felt at her departure, bidding him, with St. Paul, not to sorrow as those who had no hope. After her decease an inmate of the convent, named Vestiana, brought to Gregory a ring, in which was a piece of the true Cross, and an iron cross, both of which were found on the body when laying it out. One Gregory retained himself, the other he gave to Vestiana. He buried his sister in the chapel at Annesi, in which her parents and her brother Naucratius slept.

From henceforth the labours of Gregory have a far more extended range. He steps into the place vacated by the death of Basil, and takes foremost rank among the defenders of the Faith of Nicæa. He is not, however, without trouble still from the heretical party. Certain Galatians had been busy in sowing the seeds of their heresy among his own people. He is subjected, too, to great annoyance from the disturbances which arose out of the wish of the people of Ibera in Pontus to have him as their Bishop. In that early age of the Church election to a Bishopric, if not dependent on the popular voice, at least called forth the expression of much popular feeling, like a contested election amongst ourselves. This often led to breaches of the peace, which required military intervention to suppress them, as it appears to have done on this occasion.

But the reputation of Gregory is now so advanced, and the weight of his authority as an eminent teacher so generally acknowledged, that we find him as one of the Prelates at the Synod of Antioch assembled for the purpose of healing the long-continued schisms in that distracted See. By the same Synod Gregory is chosen to visit and endeavour to reform the Churches of Arabia and Babylon, which had fallen into a very corrupt and degraded state. He gives a lamentable account of their condition, as being beyond all his powers of reformation. On this same journey he visits Jerusalem and its sacred scenes: it has been conjectured that the Apollinarian heresy drew him thither. Of the Church of Jerusalem he can give no better account than of those he had already visited. He expresses himself as greatly scandalized at the conduct of the Pilgrims who visited the Holy City on the plea of religion. Writing to three ladies, whom he had known at Jerusalem, he takes occasion, from what he had witnessed there, to speak of the uselessness of pilgrimages as any aids to

---

[2] Epist. III. (Zacagni's collection).

reverence and faith, and denounces in the strongest terms the moral dangers to which all pilgrims, especially women, are exposed.

This letter is so condemnatory of what was a common and authorized practice of the mediæval Church that [3] Divines of the Latin communion have endeavoured, but in vain, to deny its authenticity.

The name and character of Gregory had now reached the Imperial Court, where Theodosius had lately succeeded to the Eastern Empire. As a proof of the esteem in which he was then held, it is said that in his recent journey to Babylon and the Holy Land he travelled with carriages provided for him by the Emperor.

Still greater distinction awaits him. He is one of the hundred and fifty Bishops summoned by Theodosius to the second Œcumenical Council, that of Constantinople, A.D. 381. To the assembled Fathers he brings an [4] instalment of his treatise against the Eunomian heresy, which he had written in defence of his brother Basil's positions, on the subject of the Trinity and the Incarnation. This he first read to his friend Gregory Nazianzen, Jerome, and others. Such was the influence he exercised in the Council that it is said, though this is very doubtful, that the explanatory clauses added to the Nicene Creed are due to him. Certain, however, it is that he delivered the inaugural address, which is not extant; further that he preached the funeral oration, which has been preserved, on the death of Meletius, of Antioch, the first President of the Council, who died at Constantinople; also that he preached at the enthronement of Gregory Nazianzen in the capital. This oration has perished.

Shortly before the close of the Council, by a Constitution of the Emperor, issued from Heraclea, Gregory is nominated as one of the Bishops who were to be regarded as the central authorities of Catholic Communion. In other words, the primacy of Rome or Alexandria in the East was to be replaced by that of other Sees, especially Constantinople. Helladius of Cæsarea was to be Gregory's colleague in his province. The connexion led to a misunderstanding. As to the grounds of this there is much uncertainty. The account of it is entirely derived from Gregory himself in his *Letter to Flavian*, and from his great namesake. Possibly there were faults on both sides.

We do not read of Gregory being at the Synod, A.D. 382, which followed the great Council of Constantinople. But we find him present at the Synod held the following year.

This same year we have proof of the continued esteem and favour shown him by the Imperial Court. He is chosen to pronounce the funeral oration on the infant Princess Pulcheria. And not long after that also on the death of the Empress Flaccilla, or Placidia, herself. This last was a magnificent eulogy, but one, according to Tillemont, even surpassed by that of Theodoret. This admirable and holy woman, a saint of the Eastern Church, fully warranted all the praise that could be bestowed upon her. If her husband Theodosius did not owe his conversion to Christianity to her example and influence, he certainly did his adherence to the true Faith. It is one of the subjects of Gregory's praise of her that by her persuasion the Emperor refused to give an interview to the 'rationalist of the fourth century,' Eunomius.

Scarcely anything is known of the latter years of Gregory of Nyssa's life. The last record we have of him is that he was present at a Synod of Constantinople, summoned A.D. 394, by Rufinus, the powerful præfect of the East, under the presidency of Nectarius. The rival claims to the See of Bostra in Arabia had to be then settled; but perhaps the chief reason for summoning this assembly was to glorify the consecration of Rufinus' new Church in the suburbs. It was there that Gregory delivered the sermon which was probably his last, wrongly entitled ' *On his Ordination.*' His words, which heighten the effect of others then preached, are humbly compared to the blue circles painted on the new walls as a foil to the gilded dome above. " The whole breathes a calmer and more peaceful spirit; the deep sorrow over heretics

---

[3] Notably Bellarmine: Gretser, the Jesuit, against the Calvinist Molino.
[4] See Note 1 to the Introductory Letter to the Treatise.

who forfeit the blessings of the Spirit changes only here and there into the flashes of a short-lived indignation." (J. Rupp.)

The prophecy of Basil had come true. Nyssa was ennobled by the name of its bishop appearing on the roll of this Synod, between those of the Metropolitans of Cæsarea and Iconium. Even in outward rank he is equal to the highest. The character of Gregory could not be more justly drawn than in the words of Tillemont (IX. p. 269). "Autant en effet, qu' on peut juger de lui par ses écrits, c'étoit un esprit doux, bon, facile, qui avec beaucoup d'élevation et de lumière, avoit néanmois beaucoup de simplicité et de candeur, qui aimoit plus le repos que l'action, et le travail du cabinet que le tumulte des affaires, qui avec cela étoit sans faste, disposé à estimer et à louer les autres et à se mettre à dessous d'eux. Mais quoiqu' il ne cherchât que le repos, nous avons vû que son zèle pour ses frères l'avoit souvent engagé à de grands travaux, et que Dieu avait honoré sa simplicité en le faisant regarder comme le maitre, le docteur, le pacificateur et l'arbitre des églises."

His death (probably 395) is commemorated by the Greek Church on January 10, by the Latin on March 9.

CHAPTER II.

His General Character as a Theologian.

"The first who sought to establish by rational considerations the whole complex of orthodox doctrines." So Ueberweg (History of Philosophy, p. 326) of Gregory of Nyssa. This marks the transition from ante-Nicene times. Then, at all events in the hands of Origen, philosophy was identical with theology. Now, that there is a ' complex of orthodox doctrines' to defend, philosophy becomes the handmaid of theology. Gregory, in this respect, has done the most important service of any of the writers of the Church in the fourth century. He treats each single philosophical view only as a help to grasp the formulæ of faith ; and the truth of that view consists with him only in its adaptability to that end. Notwithstanding strong speculative leanings he does not defend orthodoxy either in the fashion of the Alexandrian school or in the fashion of some in modern times, who put forth a system of philosophy to which the dogmas of the Faith are to be accommodated.

If this be true, the question as to his attitude towards Plato, which is one of the first that suggests itself, is settled. Against polytheism he does indeed seek to defend Christianity by connecting it apologetically with Plato's system. This we cannot be surprised at, considering that the *definitions* of the doctrines of the Catholic Church were formed in the very place where the last considerable effort of Platonism was made ; but he by no means makes the New Life in any way dependent on this system of philosophy. "We cannot speculate," he says (*De Anim. et Resurrect.*), . . . "we must leave the Platonic car." But still when he is convinced that Plato will confirm doctrine he will, even in polemic treatises, adopt his view ; for instance, he seeks to grasp the truth of the Trinity from the Platonic account of our internal consciousness, i.e. ψυχή. λόγος, νοῦς ; because such a proof from consciousness is, to Gregory, the surest and most reliable.

The "rational considerations," then, by which Gregory would have established Christian doctrine are not necessarily drawn from the philosophy of the time : nor, further, does he seek to rationalize entirely all religious truth. In fact he resigns the hope of comprehending the Incarnation and all the great articles. This is the very thing that distinguishes the Catholic from the Eunomian. " Receiving the *fact* we leave untampered with the *manner* of the creation of the Universe, as altogether secret and inexplicable [1]." With a turn resembling the view of Tertullian, he comes back to the conclusion that for us after all Religious Truth consists in mystery. "The Church possesses the means of demonstrating these things : or rather,

---

[1] Cp. *Or. Cat.* c. xi.

she has faith, which is surer than demonstration [1]." He develops the truth of the Resurrection as much by the fulfilment of God's promises as by metaphysics: and it has been considered as one of the proofs that the treatise *What is being 'in the image of God'?* is not his that this subordination of philosophical proof to the witness of the Holy Spirit is not preserved in it.

Nevertheless there was a large field, larger even than in the next century, in which rationalizing was not only allowable, but was even required of him. In this there are three questions which Gregory has treated with particular fulness and originality. They are:—1. Evil; 2. The relation between the ideal and the actual Man; 3. Spirit.

I. He takes, to begin with, Origen's view of evil. Virtue and Vice are not opposed to each other as two Existencies: but as Being is opposed to not-Being. Vice exists only as an absence. But how did this arise?

In answering this question he seems sometimes to come very near Manicheism, and his writings must be read very carefully, in order to avoid fixing upon him the groundless charge that he leaves evil in too near connexion with Matter. But the passages [2] which give rise to this charge consist of comparisons found in his homilies and meditations; just as a modern theologian might in such works make the Devil the same as Sin and Death. The only imperfection in his view is that he is unable [3] to regard evil as not only suffered but even *permitted* by God. But this imperfection is inseparable from his time: for Manicheism was too near and its opposition too little overcome for such a view to be possible for him; he could not see that it is the only one able thoroughly to resist Dualism.

Evil with Gregory is to be found in the spontaneous proclivity of the soul towards Matter: but not in Matter itself. Matter, therefore, in his eschatology is not to be burnt up and annihilated: only soul and body have to be *refined*, as gold (this is a striking comparison) is refined. He is very clear upon the relations between the three factors, body, matter, and evil. He represents the mind as the mirror of the Archetypal Beauty: then below the mind comes body (φύσις) which is connected with mind and pervaded by it, and when thus transfigured and beautified by it becomes itself the mirror of this mirror: and then this body in its turn influences and combines Matter. The Beauty of the Supreme Being thus penetrates all things: and as long as the lower holds on to the higher all is well. But if a rupture occurs anywhere, then Matter, receiving no longer influence from above, reveals its own deformity, and imparts something of it to body and, through that, to mind: for matter is in itself 'a shapeless unorganized thing [4].' Thus the mind loses the image of God. But evil began when the rupture was made: and what caused that? When and how did the *mind* become separated from God?

Gregory answers this question by laying it down as a principle, that *everything created is subject to change*. The Uncreate Being is changeless, but Creation, since its very beginning was owing to a change, i.e. a calling of the non-existent into existence, is liable to alter. Gregory deals here with angelic equally as with human nature, and with all the powers in both, especially with the will, whose virtual freedom he assumes throughout. That, too, was created; therefore that, too, could change.

It was possible, therefore, that, first, one of the created spirits, and, as it actually happened, he who was entrusted with the supervision of the earth, should choose to turn his eyes away from the Good; he thus looked at a lower good; and so began to be envious and to have πάθη. All evil followed in a chain from this beginning; according to the principle that the beginning of anything is the cause of all that follows in its train.

---

[1] *In verba 'faciamus hominem,'* I. p. 140.

[2] *De Perf. Christiani Forma,* III. p. 294, he calls the 'Prince of darkness' the author of sin and death: *In Christi Resurrect.* III. p. 386, he calls Satan 'the heart of the earth:' and p. 387 identifies him with sin. 'And so the real wisdom visits that arrogant heart of the earth, so that the thought great in wickedness should vanish, and the darkness should be lightened, &c.'

[3] As expressed by S. Thomas Aquinas Summ. I. Qu. xix. Art. 9, Deo nec nolente, nec volente, sed permittente. . . . Deus neque vult fieri, neque vult non fieri, sed vult permittere mala fieri.

[4] *De Virginit.* c. xi.

So the Devil fell: and the proclivity to evil was introduced into the spiritual world.   Man, however, still looked to God and was filled with blessings (this is the 'ideal man' of Gregory). But as when the flame has got hold of a wick one cannot dim its light by means of the flame itself, but only by mixing water with the oil in the wick, so the Enemy effected the weakening of God's blessings in man by cunningly *mixing wickedness in his will*, as he had mixed it in his own.   From first to last, then, evil lies in the προαίρεσις and in nothing else.

God knew what would happen and suffered it, that He might not destroy our freedom, the inalienable heritage of reason and therefore a portion of His image in us.   [1] He 'gave scope to evil for a nobler end.'   Gregory calls it a piece of " little mindedness " to argue from evil either the weakness or the wickedness of God.

II.   His remarks on the relation between the ideal and the actual Man are very interesting. It is usual with the other Fathers, in speaking of man's original perfection, to take the moment of the first man's residence in Paradise, and to regard the *whole* of human nature as there represented by the first two human beings.   Gregory is far removed from this way of looking at the matter.   With him human perfection is the 'idea' of humanity : he sees already in the bodily-created Adam the fallen man.   The present man is not to be distinguished from that bodily Adam ; both fall below the ideal type.   Gregory seems to put the Fall beyond and before the beginning of history.   'Under the form of narrative Moses places before us mere doctrine [2].' The *locus classicus* about the idea and the reality of human nature is *On the Making of Man*, I. p. 88 f.   He sketches both in a masterly way.   He speaks of the division of the human race into male and female as a 'device' (ἐπιτέχνησις), implying that it was not the first 'organization' (κατασκευή).   He hints that the irrational element was actually provided by the Creator, Who foresaw the Fall and the Redemption, for man to sin in ; as if man immediately upon the creation of the perfect humanity became a mixed nature (spirit and flesh), and his fall was not a mere accident, but a *necessary consequence of this mixed nature.*   Adam must have fallen : there was no perfect humanity in Paradise.   In man's mixed nature of spirit and flesh nutrition is the basis of his sensation, and sensation is the basis of his thought ; and so it was inevitable that sin through this lower yet vital side of man should enter in.   So ingrained is the spirit with the flesh in the whole history of actual humanity that all the varieties of all the souls that ever have lived or ever shall, arise from this very mixture ; i.e. from the varying degrees of either factor in each.   But as Gregory's view here touches, though in striking contrast, on Origen's, more will be said about it in the next chapter.

It follows from this that Gregory, as Clement and Basil before him, did not look upon Original Sin as the accidental or extraordinary thing which it was afterwards regarded. 'From a man who is a sinner and subject to passion of course is engendered a man who is a sinner and subject to passion : sin being in a manner born with him, and growing with his growth, and not dying with it.'   And yet he says elsewhere, " An infant who is just born is not culpable, nor does it merit punishment ; just as he who has been baptized has no account to give of his past sins, since they are forgiven ; " and he calls infants ἀπόνηροι, 'not having in the least admitted the disease into their soul.'   But these two views can of course be reconciled ; the infant at the moment of its physical birth starts with sins *forgotten*, just as at the moment of its spiritual birth it starts with sins *forgiven*. No actual sin has been committed.   But then its nature has lost the ἀπαθεία ; the inevitable weakness of its ancestry is in it.

III.   'Spirit.'   Speaking of the soul, Gregory asks, 'How can that which is incomposite be dissolved ?'   i.e. the soul is spirit, and spirit is incomposite and therefore indestructible.

But care must be taken not to infer too much from this his favourite expression 'spirit' in connexion with the soul.   'God is spirit' too ; and we are inclined to forget that this

---

[1] *On Infants' early Deaths*, III. p. 336.   [2] *Or. Cat.* c. viii. D.

is no more than a negative definition, and to imagine the human spirit of equal prerogative with Deity. Gregory gives no encouragement to this; he distinctly teaches that, though the soul is incomposite, it is not in the least independent of time and space, as the Deity is.

In fact he almost entirely drops the old Platonic division of the Universe into Intelligible (spiritual) and Sensible, which helps to keep up this confusion between human and divine 'spirit,' and adopts the Christian division of Creator and Created. This difference between Creator and Created is further figured by him as that between

1. The Infinite.	The Finite.
2. The Changeless.	The Changeable.
3. The Contradiction-less.	The Contradictory.

The result of this is that the Spirit-world itself has been divided into Uncreate and Created.

With regard, then, to this created Spirit-world we find that Gregory, as Basil, teaches that it existed, i. e. it had been created, *before* the work of the Six Days began. 'God made all that is, at once' (ἀθρόως). This is only his translation of the verse, 'In the beginning God created the heaven and the earth;' the material for 'heaven' and 'earth,' i.e. spirits and chaos, was made in a moment, but God had not yet spoken the successive Words of creation. The souls of men, then, existed from the very beginning of creation, and in a *determinate* number; for this is a necessary consequence of the 'simultaneous creation.' This was the case with the Angels too, the other portion of the created Spirit-world. Gregory has treated the subject of the Angels very fully. He considers that they are perfect: but their perfection too is contingent: it depends on the grace of God and their own wills; the angels are free, and therefore changeable. Their will necessarily moves towards something: at their first creation the Beautiful alone solicited them. Man 'a little lower than the Angels' was perfect too; deathless, passionless, contemplative. 'The true and perfect soul is single in its nature, intellectual, immaterial[1].' He was 'as the Angels' and if he fell, Lucifer fell too. Gregory will not say, as Origen did, that human souls had a body when *first* created: rather, as we have seen, he implies the contrary; and he came to be considered the champion that fought the doctrine of the pre-existence of *embodied* souls. He seems to have been influenced by Methodius' objections to Origen's view. But his magnificent idea of the first man gives way at once to something more Scriptural and at the same time more scientific; and his ideal becomes a downright forecast of Realism.

Taking, however, the human soul as it is, he still continues, we often find, to compare it with God. In his great treatise *On the Soul and the Resurrection*, he rests a great deal on the parallel between the relation of man to his body, and that of God to the world.—'The soul is as a cord drawn out of mud; God draws to Himself what is His own.'— He calls the human spirit 'an influx of the divine in-breathing' (*Adv. Apollin.* c. 12). Anger and desire do not belong to the essence of the soul, he says: they are only among its varying states. The soul, then, as separable from matter, is *like* God. But this likeness does not extend to the point of identity. Incomprehensible, immortal, it is not uncreated. The distinction between the Creator and the Created cannot be obliterated. The attributes of the Creator set down above, i.e. that He is infinite, changeless, contradictionless, and so always good, &c., can be applied only *catachrestically* to some men, in that they resemble their Maker as a copy resembles its original: but still, in this connexion, Gregory does speak of those 'who do not need any cleansing at all[2],' and the context forces us to apply these words to men. There is no irony, to him or to any Father of the fourth century, in the words, 'They that are whole need not a physician.' Although in the treatise *On Virginity*,

---

[1] *On the Making of Man.* c. xiv.   [2] *Or. Cat.* c. xxvi.

where he is describing the development of his own moral and religious life, he is very far from applying them to himself, he nevertheless seems to recognize the fact that since Christianity began there are those to whom they might apply.

There is also need of a certain amount of 'rational considerations' in advancing a Defence and a Theory of Christianity. He makes this according to the special requirements of the time in his *Oratio Catechetica*. His reasonings do not seem to us always convincing; but the presence of a living Hellenism and Judaism in the world required them. These two phænomena also explain what appears to us a great weakness in this work: namely, that he treats Hellenism as if it were all speculation; Judaism as if it were all facts. These two religions were too near and too practically opposed to each other for him to see, as we can now, by the aid of a sort of science of religions, that every religion has its *idea*, and every religion has its *facts*. He and all the first Apologists, with the spectacle of these two apparently opposite systems before them, thought that, in arriving at the True Religion as well, all could be done by considering *facts;* or all could be done by *speculation*. Gregory chose the latter method. A Dogmatic in the modern sense, in which both the idea and the facts of Christianity flow into one, could not have been expected of him. The *Oratio Catechetica* is a mere philosophy of Christianity in detail written in the philosophic language of the time. Not only does he refrain from using the historic proofs, i.e. of prophecy and type (except very sparingly and only to meet an adversary), but his defence is insufficient from another point of view also; he hardly uses the moral proofs either; he wanders persistently in metaphysics.

If he does not lean enough on these two classes of proofs, at all events that he does not lean entirely on either, may be considered as a guarantee of his excellence as a theologian pure and simple. But he is on the other hand very far from attempting a philosophic construction of Christianity, as we have seen. Though akin to modern theologians in many things, he is unlike those of them who would construct an *a priori* Christianity, in which the relationship of one part to another is so close that all stands or falls together. Philosophic deduction is with him only 'a kind of instruction' used in his apologetic works. On occasion he shows a clear perception of the historic principle. "The supernatural character of the Gospel miracles bears witness to their divine origin[1]." He points, as Origen did, to the continued possession of miraculous powers in the Church. Again, as regards moral proof, there had been so much attempted that way by the Neo-Platonists that such proof could not have exactly the same degree of weight attributed to it that it has now, at least by an adherent of the newer Hellenism. Philostratus, Porphyry, Iamblichus had all tried to attract attention to the holy lives of heathen sages. Yet to these, rough sketches as they were, the Christian did oppose the Lives of the Saints: notably Gregory himself in the *Life of Gregory Thaumaturgus:* as Origen before him (c. Celsum, passim) had shewn in detail the difference *in kind* of Christian holiness.

His treatment of the Sacraments in the *Oratio Catechetica* is noteworthy. On Baptism he is very complete: it will be sufficient to notice here the peculiar proof he offers that the Holy Spirit is actually given in Baptism. It is the same proof, to start with, as that which establishes that God came in the flesh when Christ came. Miracles prove this; (he is not wanting here in the sense of the importance of History). If, then, we are persuaded that God is here, we must allow also that truth is here: for truth is the mark of Deity. When, therefore, God has said that He will come in a particular way, if *called in a particular way*, this must be true. He is so called in Baptism: therefore He comes. (The vital importance of the doctrine of the Trinity, upon which Gregory laboured for so many years, thus all comes from Baptism.) Gregory would not confine the entire force of Baptism to the

---

[1] *Or. Cat.* c. iii.

one ritual act. A resurrection to a new immortal life is begun in Baptism, but owing to the weakness of nature this complete effect is separated into stages or parts. With regard to the necessity of Baptism for salvation, he says he does not know if the Angels receive the souls of the unbaptized; but he rather intimates that they wander in the air seeking rest, and entreat in vain like the Rich Man. To him who wilfully defers it he says, 'You are out of paradise, O Catechumen!'

In treating the Sacrament of the Eucharist, Gregory was the first Father who developed the view of transformation, for which transubstantiation was afterwards substituted to suit the mediæval philosophy; that is, he put this view already latent into actual words. There is a *locus classicus* in the *Oratio Catechetica*, c. 37.

"Therefore from the same cause as that by which the bread that was transformed in that Body was changed to a divine potency, a similar result takes place now. For as in that case, too, the grace of the Word used to make holy the Body, the substance of which came of the bread and was in a manner itself bread, so also in this case the bread, as says the Apostle, 'is sanctified by the word of God and prayer:' not *that it advances by the process of eating to the stage of passing into the body of the Word, but it at once is changed into the Body by the Word, as the Word Himself said, 'This is My Body;'*" and just above he had said: "Rightly do we believe that now also the bread which is consecrated by the word of God is changed into the body of God the Word." This way of explaining the mystery of the Sacrament, i.e. from the way bread was changed into the Word when Christ was upon earth, is compared by Neander with 'another way Gregory had of explaining it, i.e. the heightened efficacy of the bread is as the heightened efficacy of the baptismal water, the anointing oil [1], &c., a totally different idea. But this, which may be called the *metabatic view*, is the one evidently most present to his mind. In a fragment of his found in a Parisian MS.[2], quoted with the Liturgies of James, Basil, Chrysostom, we also find it; "The consecrated bread is changed into the body of the Word; and it is needful for humanity to partake of that."

Again, the necessity of the Incarnation, drawn from the words "it was necessary that Christ should suffer," receives a rational treatment from him. There must ever be, from a meditation on this, two results, according as the physical or the ethical element in Christianity prevails, i.e. 1. Propitiation; 2. Redemption. The first theory is dear to minds fed upon the doctrines of the Reformation, but it receives no countenance from Gregory. Only in the book in which Moses' Life is treated allegorically does he even mention it. The sacrifice of Christ instead of the bloody sacrifices of the Old Testament is not his doctrine. He develops his theory of the Redemption or Ransom (i.e. from the Devil), in the *Oratio Catechetica*. Strict justice to the Evil One required it. But in his hands this view never degenerates, as with some, into a mere battle, e.g. in Gethsemane, between the Rescuer and Enslaver.

So much has been said about Gregory's inconsistencies, and his apparent inconsistencies are indeed so many, that some attempt must be made to explain this feature, to some so repulsive, in his works. One instance at all events can show how it is possible to reconcile even the most glaring. He is not a one-sided theologian: he is not one of those who pass always the same judgment upon the same subject, no matter with whom he has to deal. There could not be a harsher contradiction than that between his statement about human generation in the *Oratio Catechetica*, and that made in the treatises *On Virginity* and *On the Making of Man*. In the *O. C.* everything hateful and undignified is removed from the idea of our birth; the idea of πάθος is not applied; "only evil brings disgrace." But in the other two Treatises he represents generation as a consequence of the Fall. This contradiction arises simply from the different standpoint in each. In the one case he is

---

[1] In Sermon *On the Baptism of Christ*.   A. 1560 fol.; also Antwerp, p. 1562 (Latinè).

apologetic; and so he adopts a universally recognised moral axiom. In the other he is the Christian theologian; the natural process, therefore, takes its colouring from the Christian doctrine of the Fall. This is the standpoint of most of his works, which are polemical, not apologetic. But in the treatise *On the Soul and the Resurrection* he introduces even a third view about generation, which might be called that of the Christian theosophist; i.e. generation is the means in the Divine plan for carrying Humanity to its completion. Very similar is the view in the treatise *On Infants' Early Deaths;* "the design of all births is that the Power which is above the universe may in all parts of the creation be glorified by means of intellectual natures conspiring to the same end, by virtue of the same faculty operating in all; I mean, that of looking upon God." Here he is speaking to the purely philosophic instinct. It may be remarked that on this and all the operations of Divine foreknowledge in vast world-wide relations he has constantly striking passages, and deserves for this especially to be studied.

The style of Gregory is much more elegant than that of Basil: sometimes it may be called eloquent. His occasional digressions did not strike ancient critics as a fault. To them he is "sweet," "bright," "dropping pleasure into the ears." But his love for splendour, combined with the lateness of his Greek, make him one of the more difficult Church writers to interpret accurately.

His similes and illustrations are very numerous, and well chosen. A few exceptions must, perhaps, be made. He compares the mere professing Christian to the ape, dressed like a man and dancing to the flute, who used to amuse the people in the theatre at Alexandria, but once revealed during the performance its bestial nature, at the sight of food. This is hardly worthy of a great writer, as Gregory was [1]. Especially happy are his comparisons in the treatise *On the Soul and Resurrection*, by which metaphysical truths are expressed; and elsewhere those by which he seeks to reach the due proportions of the truth of the Incarnation. The chapters in his work against Eunomius where he attempts to depict the Infinite, are striking. But what commends him most to modern taste is his power of description when dealing with facts, situations, persons: he touches these always with a colour which is felt to be no exaggeration, but the truth.

CHAPTER III.

His Origenism.

A TRUE estimate of the position and value of Gregory as a Church teacher cannot be formed until the question of his 'Origenism,' its causes and its quality, is cleared up. It is well known that this charge began to be brought against his orthodoxy at all events after the time of Justinian: nor could Germanus, the Patriarch of Constantinople in the next century, remove it by the device of supposed interpolations of partizans in the interests of the Eastern as against the Western Church: for such a theory, to be true, would still require some hints at all events in this Father to give a colour to such interpolations. Moreover, as will be seen, the points in which Gregory is most like Origen are portions of the very groundwork of his own theology.

The question, then, remains why, and how far, is he a follower of Origen?

I. When we consider the character of his great forerunner, and the kind of task which Gregory himself undertook, the first part of this question is easily answered. When Christian doctrine had to be set forth philosophically, so as to be intelligible to any cultivated mind of that time (to reconcile Greek philosophy with Christian doctrine was a task which Gregory never dreamed of attempting), the example and leader in such an attempt was Origen; he

---

[1] His comparison of the hidden meaning of the proverb or parable (III. c. Eunom. p. 236) to the 'turned up' side of the peacock's feather is beautiful in itself for language (e.g. 'the varied painting of nature,' 'the half-circle shining in the midst with its dye of purple,' 'the golden mist round the circle'): but it rather fails as a simile, when applied to the other or the literal side, which cannot in the case of parables be said to 'lack beauty and tint.'

occupied as it were the whole horizon. He was the founder of theology; the very vocabulary of it, which is in use now, is of his devising. So that Gregory's language must have had, necessarily, a close connexion with that of the great interpreter and apologist, who had explained to his century the same truths which Gregory had to explain to his: this must have been the case even if his mind had not been as spiritual and idealizing as Origen's. But in some respects it will be seen Gregory is even more an idealist than Origen himself. Alike, then, from purpose and tradition as from sympathy he would look back to Origen. Though a gulf was between them, and, since the Council of Nicæa, there were some things that could come no more into controversy, Gregory saw, where the Church had not spoken, with the same eyes as Origen: he uses the same keys as he did for the problems which Scripture has not solved; he uses the same great weapon of allegory in making the letter of Scripture give up the spiritual treasures. It could not have been otherwise when the whole Christian religion, which Gregory was called on to defend as a philosophy, had never before been systematically so defended but by Origen; and this task, the same for both, was presented to the same type of mind, in the same intellectual atmosphere. It would have been strange indeed if Gregory had not been a pupil at least (though he was no blind follower) of Origen.

If we take for illustration of this the most vital point in the vast system, if system it can be called, of Origen, we shall see that he had traced fundamental lines of thought, which could not in that age be easily left. He asserts the virtual freedom of the human will, in every stage and condition of human existence. The Greek philosophy of the third century, and the semi-pagan Gnosticism, in their emanational view of the world, denied this freedom. With them the mind of man, as one of the emanations of Deity itself, was, as much as the matter of which the world was made, regulated and governed directly from the Source whence they both flowed. Indeed every system of thought, not excepting Stoicism, was struck with the blight of this fatalism. There was no freedom for man at all but in the system which Origen was drawing from, or rather reading into, the Scriptures. No Christian philosopher who lived amongst the same counter-influences as Origen could overlook this starting-point of his system; he must have adopted it, even if the danger of Pelagianism had been foreseen in it; which could not have been the case.

Gregory adopted it, with the other great doctrine which in the mind of Origen accompanied it; i.e., that evil is caused, not by matter, but by the act of this free will of man; in other words, by sin. Again the fatalism of all the emanationists had to be combated as to the nature and necessity of evil. With them evil was some inevitable result of the Divine processes; it abode at all events in matter, and human responsibility was at an end. Greek philosophy from first to last had shewed, even at its best, a tendency to connect evil with the lower φύσις. But now, in the light of revelation, a new truth was set forth, and repeated again and again by the very men who were inclined to adopt Plato's rather Dualistic division of the world into the intelligible and sensible. 'Evil was due to an act of the will of man.' Moreover it could no longer be regarded *per se*: it was relative, being a 'default,' or 'failure,' or 'turning away from the true good' of the will, which, however, was always free to rectify this failure. It was a στέρησις,—loss of the good; but it did not stand over against the good as an independent power. Origen contemplated the time when evil would cease to exist; 'the non-existent cannot exist for ever:' and Gregory did the same.

This brings us to yet another consequence of this enthusiasm for human freedom and responsibility, which possessed Origen, and carried Gregory away. The ἀποκατάστασις τῶν πάντων has been thought[1], in certain periods of the Church, to have been the only piece of Origenism with which Gregory can be charged. [This of course shows ignorance of the kind of influence which Gregory allowed Origen to have over him; and which did not require him to

---

[1] Cf. Dallæus, *de pœnis et satisfactionibus*, I. IV. c. 7, p. 368.

select even one *isolated* doctrine of his master.] It has also brought him into more suspicion than any other portion of his teaching. Yet it is a direct consequence of the view of evil, which he shares with Origen. If evil is the non-existent, as his master says, a στέρησις, [1] as he says, then it must pass away. It was not made by God; neither is it self-subsisting.

But when it has passed away, what follows? That God will be "all in all." Gregory accepts the whole of Origen's explanation of this great text. Both insist on the impossibility of God being in 'everything,' if evil still remains. But this is equivalent to the restoration to their primitive state of all created spirits. Still it must be remembered that Origen required many future stages of existence before all could arrive at such a consummation: with him there is to be more than one 'next world;' and even when the primitive perfection is reached, his peculiar view of the freedom of the will, as an absolute balance between good and evil, would admit the possibility of another fall. 'All *may* be saved; and all *may* fall.' How the final Sabbath shall come in which all wills shall rest at last is but dimly hinted at in his writings. With Gregory, on the other hand, there are to be but two worlds: the present and the next; and in the next the ἀποκατάστασις τῶν πάντων must be effected. Then, after the Resurrection, the fire ἀκοίμητος, αἰώνιος, as he continually calls it, will have to do its work. 'The avenging flame will be the more ardent the more it has to consume' (*De Animâ et Resurr.*, p. 227). But at last the evil will be annihilated, and the bad saved by nearness to the good.' There is to rise a giving of thanks from *all* nature. Nevertheless [2] passages have been adduced from Gregory's writings in which the language of Scripture as to future punishment is used without any modification, or hint of this universal salvation. In the treatise, *De Pauperibus Amandis*, II. p. 240, he says of the last judgment that God will give to each his due; repose eternal to those who have exercised pity and a holy life; but the eternal punishment of fire for the harsh and unmerciful: and addressing the rich who have made a bad use of their riches, he says, 'Who will extinguish the flames ready to devour you and engulf you? Who will stop the gnawings of a worm that never dies?' Cf. also *Orat.* 3, *de Beatitudinibus*, I. p. 788: *contra Usuarios*, II. p. 233: though the hortatory character of these treatisés makes them less important as witnesses.

A single doctrine or group of doctrines, however, may be unduly pressed in accounting for the influence of Origen upon a kindred spirit like Gregory. Doubtless fragments of Origen's teaching, mere details very often, were seized upon and appropriated by others; they were erected into dogmas and made to do duty for the whole living fabric; and even those details were sometimes misunderstood. '[3] What he had said with a mind full of thought, others took in the very letter.' Hence arose the evil of 'Origenism,' so prevalent in the century in which Gregory lived. Different ways of following him were found, bad and good. Even the Arians could find in his language now and then something they could claim as their own. But as Rupp well says, 'Origen is not great by virtue of those particular doctrines, which are usually exhibited to the world as heretical by weak heads who think to take the measure of everything with the mere formulæ of orthodoxy. He is great by virtue of one single thought, i.e. that of bringing philosophy into union with religion, and thereby creating a theology. With Clement of Alexandria this thought was a mere instinct: Origen gave it consciousness: and so Christendom began to have a science of its own.' It was this single purpose, visible in all Origen wrote, that impressed itself so deeply upon Gregory. He, too, would vindicate the Scriptures as a philosophy. Texts, thanks to the labours of Origen as well as to the councils of the Church, had now acquired a fixed meaning and an importance that all could acknowledge. The new spiritual philosophy lay within them; he would make them speak its language. Allegory was with him, just as with Origen, necessary, in order to find the Spirit which inspires them. The letter must not impose itself upon us and stand for more than it is worth; just as the practical experience of evil in the world must not blind us to the fact that

---

[1] Cf. *De An. et Resurr.*, 227 C.D.   [2] Collected by Ceillier in his Introduction (Paris, 1860).   [3] Bunsen.

it is only a passing dispensation. If only the animus and intention is regarded, we may say that all that Gregory wrote was Origenistic.

II. But nevertheless much had happened in the interval of 130 years that divides them ; and this leads us to consider the limits which the state of the Church, as well as Gregory's own originality and more extended physical knowledge, placed upon the complete filling in of the outlines sketched by the master. First and chiefly, Origen's doctrine of the pre-existence of the soul could not be retained ; and we know that Gregory not only abandoned it, but attacked it with all his powers of logic in his treatise, *De Animâ et Resurrectione:* for which he receives the applause of the Emperor Justinian. Souls, according to Origen, had pre-existed from eternity : they were created certainly, but there never was a time when they did not exist : so that the procession even of the Holy Spirit could in thought only be prior to their existence. Then a failure of their free wills to grasp the true good, and a consequent cooling of the fire of love within them, plunged them in this material bodily existence, which their own sin made a suffering one. This view had certainly great merits : it absolved the Deity from being the author of evil, and so was a 'théodicée ;' it entirely got rid of the two rival principles, good and evil, of the Gnostics ; and it avoided the seeming incongruity of what was to last for ever in the future being not eternal in the past. Why then was it rejected ? Not only because of the objection urged by Methodius, that the addition of a body would be no remedy but rather an increase of the sin ; or that urged amongst many others by Gregory, that a vice cannot be regarded as the precursor of the birth of each human soul into this or into other worlds ; but more than that and chiefly, because such a doctrine contravened the more distinct views now growing up as to what the Christian creation was, and the more careful definitions also of the Trinity now embodied in the creeds. In fact the pre-existence of the soul was wrapped up in a cosmogony that could no longer approve itself to the Christian consciousness. In asserting the freedom of the will, and placing in the will the cause of evil, Origen had so far banished emanationism ; but in his view of the eternity of the world, and in that of the eternal pre-existence of souls which accompanied it, he had not altogether stamped it out. He connects rational natures so closely with the Deity that each individual λόγος seems almost, in a Platonic way, to lie in the Divine Λόγος, which [1] he styles οὐσία οὐσιῶν, ἰδέα ἰδεῶν. They are 'partial brightnesses (ἀπαυγάσματα) of the glory of God.' He [2] allows them, of course, to have been created in the Scriptural sense of that word, which is certainly an advance upon Justin ; but his creation is not that distinct event in time which Christianity requires and the exacter treatment of the nature of the Divine Persons had now developed. His creation, both the intelligible and visible world, receives from him an eternity which is unnatural and incongruous in relation to his other speculations and beliefs : it lingers, Tithonus-like, in the presence of the Divine Persons, without any meaning and purpose for its life ; it is the last relic of Paganism, as it were, in a system which is otherwise Christian to the very core. His strenuous effort to banish all ideas of time, at all events from the intelligible world, ended in this eternal creation of that world ; which seemed to join the eternally generated Son too closely to it, and gave occasion to the Arians to say that He too was a κτίσμα. This eternal pre-existence in fact almost destroyed the idea of creation, and made the Deity in a way dependent on His own world. Athanasius, therefore, and his followers were roused to separate the divinity of the Son from everything created. The relation of the world to God could no longer be explained in the same terms as those which they employed to illustrate the relations between the Divine Persons ; and when once the doctrine of the consubstantiality of the Father and Son had been accepted and firmly established there could be no more favour shown by the defenders of that doctrine to the merely Platonic view of the nature and origin of souls and matter.

Amongst the defenders of the Creed of Nicæa, Gregory, we know, stands well-nigh foremost.

---

[1] *c. Cels.* VI. 64. [2] *In Joann.*, tom. 32, 18.

In his long and numerous treatises on the Trinity he employs every possible argument and illustration to show the contents of the substance of the Deity as transcendent, incommunicable to creation *per se*.   Souls cannot have the attributes of Deity.   Created spirits cannot claim immediate kindred with the Λόγος.   So instead of the Platonic antithesis of the intelligible and sensible world, which Origen adopted, making *all equal* in the intelligible world, he brings forward the antithesis of God and the world.   He felt too that that antithesis answers more fully not only to the needs of the Faith in the Trinity daily growing more exact and clear, but also to the facts of the Creation, i.e. its variety and differences.   He gives up the pre-existence of the rational soul; it will not explain the infinite variety observable in souls.   The variety, again, of the material world, full as it is of the miracles of divine power, cannot have been the result of the chance acts of created natures embodying themselves therein, which the theory of pre-existence supposes.   God and the created world (of spirits and matter) are now to be the factors in theology; although Gregory does now and then, for mere purposes of illustration, divide the Universe still into the intelligible and the sensible.

When once pre-existence was given up, the parts of the soul could be more closely united to each other, because the lower and higher were in their beginning no longer separated by a gulf of ages.   Accordingly Gregory, reducing the three parts of man which Origen had used to the simpler division into visible and invisible (sensible and intelligible), dwells much upon the intimate relation between the two and the mutual action of one upon the other. Origen had retained the trichotomy of Plato which other Greek Fathers also, with the sanction, as they supposed, of S. Paul (1 Thess. v. 23), had adopted.   'Body,' 'soul,' and 'spirit,' or Plato's 'body,' 'unreasoning' and 'reasoning soul,' had helped Origen to explain how the last, the pre-existent soul (the spirit, or the conscience [1], as he sometimes calls it) could ever have come to live in the flesh.   The second, the soul proper, is as it were a mediating ground on which the spirit can meet the flesh.   The celestial mind, 'the real man fallen from on high,' rules by the power of conscience or of will over this soul, where the merely animal functions and the natural appetites reside; and through this soul over the body.   How the celestial mind can act at all upon this purely animal soul which lies between it and the body, Origen leaves unexplained.   But this division was necessary for him, in order to represent the spirit as remaining itself unchanged in its heavenly nature, though weakened by its long captivity in the body.   The middle soul (in which he sometimes places the will) is the scene of contamination and disorder; the spirit is free, it can always rejoice at what is well done in the soul, and yet is not touched by the evil in it; it chooses, convicts, and punishes.   Such was Origen's psychology.   But an intimate connexion both in birth and growth between *all* the faculties of man is one of Gregory's most characteristic thoughts, and he gave up this trichotomy, which was still, however, retained by some Greek fathers, and adopted the simpler division mentioned above in order more clearly and concisely to show the mutual play of spirit and body upon each other.   There was soon, too, another reason why this trichotomy should be suspected. It was a second time made the vehicle of error.   Apollinaris adopted it, in order to expound that the Divine Λόγος took the place, in the tripartite soul of Christ, of the 'reasonable soul' or spirit of other men.   Gregory, in pressing for a simpler treatment of man's nature, thus snatched a vantage-ground from a sagacious enemy.   His own psychology is only one instance of a tendency which runs through the whole of his system, and which may indeed be called the dominating thought with which he approached every question; he views each in the light of form and matter; spirit penetrating and controlling body, body answering to spirit and yet at the same time supplying the nutriment upon which the vigour and efficacy of spirit, in this world at least, depends.   This thought underlies his view of the material universe and of Holy Scripture, as well as of man's nature.   With

---

[1] *Comment. in Rom.* ii. 9, p. 486.

regard to the last he says, 'the intelligible cannot be realized in body at all, except it be commingled with sensation;' and again, 'as there can be no sensation without a material substance, so there can be no exercise of the power of thought without sensation[1].' The spiritual or intelligent part of man (which he calls by various names, such as 'the inner man,' the ψυχὴ λογικὴ, νοῦς or διάνοια, τὸ ζωοποιὸν αἴτιον, or simply ψυχὴ as throughout the treatise *On the Soul*), however alien in its essence from the bodily and sentient part, yet no sooner is united with this earthly part than it at once exerts power over it. In fact it requires this instrument before it can reach its perfection. 'Seeing, then, man is a reasoning animal of a certain kind, it was necessary that the body should be prepared as an instrument appropriate to the needs of his reason[2].' So closely has this reason been united with the senses and the flesh that it performs itself the functions of the animal part; it is the 'mind' or 'reason' itself that sees, hears, &c.; in fact the exercise of mind depends on a sound state of the senses and other organs of the body; for a sick body cannot receive the 'artistic' impressions of the mind and, so, the mind remains inoperative. This is enough to show how far Gregory had got from pre-existence and the 'fall into the prison of the flesh.'

His own theory of the origin of the soul, or at least that to which he visibly inclines, is stated in the treatise, *De Animâ et Resurrectione*, p. 241. It is that of Tertullian and some Greek Fathers also: and goes by the name of 'traducianism.' The soul is transmitted in the generating seed. This of course is the opposite pole to Origen's teaching, and is inconsistent with Gregory's own spiritualism. The other alternative, Creationism, which a number of the orthodox adopted, namely that souls are created by God at the moment of conception, or when the body of the fœtus is already formed, was not open to him to adopt; because, according to him, in *idea* the world of spirits was made, and in a determinate number, along with the world of unformed matter by the one creative act 'in the beginning.' In the plan of the universe, though not in reality as with Origen, all souls are already created. So the life of humanity contains them: when the occasion comes they take their beginning along with the body which enshrines them, but are not created then any more than that body. Such was the compromise between spiritualism and materialism to which Gregory was driven by the difficulties of the subject. Origen with his eye unfalteringly fixed upon the ideal world, and unconscious of the practical consequences that might be drawn from his teaching, cut the knot with his eternal pre-existence of souls, which avoided at once the alleged absurdity of creationism and the grossness of traducianism. But the Church, for higher interests still than those of pure idealism, had to reject that doctrine; and Gregory, with his extended knowledge in physic and his close observation of the intercommunion of mind and body, had to devise or rather select a theory which, though a makeshift, would not contradict either his knowledge or his faith.

Yet after admitting that soul and body are born together and attaching such importance to the 'physical basis' of life and thought, the influence of his master, or else his own uncontrollable idealism, carries him away again in the opposite direction. After reading words in his treatise which Locke might have written we come upon others which are exactly the teaching of Berkeley. There is a passage in the *De Animâ et Resurrectione* where he deals with the question how an intelligent Being could have created matter, which is neither intelligent or intelligible. But what if matter is only a concourse of qualities, ἔννοιαι, or ψιλὰ νοήματα as he elsewhere calls them? Then there would be no difficulty in understanding the manner of creation. But even about this we can say so much, i.e. that not one of those things which we attribute to body is itself body: neither figure, nor colour, nor weight, nor extension, nor quantity, nor any other qualifying notion whatever: but every one of them is a *thought*: it is the combination of them all into a single whole that constitutes body. Seeing, then, that these

---

[1] *De Hom. Op.* c. viii.; *De An. et Resurr.* 205. [2] *De Hom. Op.* c. viii.

several qualifications which complete the particular body are grasped by thought alone, and not by sense, and that the Deity is a thinking being, what trouble can it be to such a thinking agent to produce the thoughts whose mutual combination generate *for us* the substance of that body? and in the treatise, *De Hom. Opif.*, c. 24, the intelligible φύσις is said to produce the intelligible δυνάμεις, and the concourse of these δυνάμεις brings into being the material nature. The body itself, he repeats (*contra Fatum*, p. 67), is not a real substance; it is a soulless, unsubstantial thing. The only real creation is that of spirits. Even Origen did not go so far as that. Matter with him, though it exists by concomitance and not by itself, nevertheless *really* exists. He avoided a rock upon which Gregory runs; for with Gregory not only matter but created spirit as well vanish in idealism. There remain with him only the νοούμενα and God.

This transcendent idealism embarrasses him in many ways, and makes his theory of the soul full of inconsistency. (1) He will not say unhesitatingly whether that pure humanity in the beginning created in the image of God had a body or not like ours. Origen at all events says that the eternally pre-existing spirits were invested with a body, even before falling into the sensible world. But Gregory, while denying the pre-existence of souls in the sense of Origen, yet in many of his treatises, especially in the *De Hom. Opificio*, seems to point to a primitive humanity, a predeterminate number of souls destined to live in the body though they had not yet lived, which goes far beyond Origen's in its ideal character. "When Moses," Gregory says, "speaks of the soul as the image of God, he shows that all that is alien to God must be excluded from our definition of the soul; and a corporal nature is alien to God." He points out that God first 'made man in His own image,' and *after that* made them male and female; so that there was a double fashioning of our nature, ἥ τε πρὸς τὸ θεῖον ὁμοιωμένη, ἥ τε πρὸς τὴν διαφορὰν ταύτην (i.e. male and female) διῃρημένη. On the other hand, in the *Oratio Catechetica*, which contains certainly his more dogmatic statement on every point, this ideal and passionless humanity is regarded as still in the future: and it is represented that man's double-nature is actually the very centre of the Divine Councils, and not the result of any mistake or sin; man's soul from the very first was commingled (ἀνάκρασις is Gregory's favourite word) with a body, in order that in him, as representing every stage of living things, the whole creation, even in its lowest part, might share in the divine. Man, as the paragon of animals, was necessary, in order that the union might be effected between two otherwise irreconcilable worlds, the intelligible and the sensible. Though, therefore, there was a Fall at last, it was not the occasion of man's receiving a body similar to animals; that body was given him at the very first, and was only preparatory to the Fall, which was foreseen in the Divine Councils and provided for. Both the body and the Fall were necessary in order that the Divine plan might be carried out, and the Divine glory manifested in creation. In this view the "coats of skins" which Gregory inherits from the allegorical treasures of Origen are no longer merely the human body itself, as with Origen, but all the passions, actions, and habits of that body after the Fall, which he sums up in the generic term πάθη. If, then, there is to be any reconciliation between this and the former view of his in which the pure unstained humanity, the 'image of God,' is differentiated by a second act of creation as it were into male and female, we must suppose him to teach that immediately upon the creation in God's image there was added all that in human nature is akin to the merely animal world. In that man was God's image, his will was free, but in that he was created, he was able to fall from his high estate; and God, foreseeing the Fall, at once added the distinction of sex, and with it the other features of the animal which would befit the fall; but with the purpose of raising thereby the whole creation. But two great counter-influences seem always to be acting upon Gregory; the one sympathy with the speculations of Origen, the other a tendency to see even with a modern insight into the closeness of the intercommunion between soul and body. The results of these two influences cannot be altogether reconciled. His ideal and his actual man, each sketched wit a skilful and discriminating hand, represent the interval that divides his aspirations from his observations: yet both are present to his mind when he writes about the soul. (2) He does not alter, as Origen does, the traditional belief in the resurrection of the body, and yet his idealism, in spite of his actual and strenuous defence of it in the carefully argued treatise *On the Soul and Resurrection*, renders it unnecessary, if not impossible. We know that his faith impelled Origen, too, to [1] contend for the resurrection of the flesh: yet it is an almost forced importation into the rest of his system. Our bodies, he teaches, will rise again: but that which will make us the same persons we were before is not the sameness of our bodies (for they will be ethereal, angelic, uncarnal, &c.) but the sameness of a λόγος within them which never dies (λόγος τις ἔγκειται τῷ σώματι, ἀφ' οὗ μὴ φθειρομένου ἐγείρεται τὸ σῶμα ἐν ἀφθαρσίᾳ, c. Cels. v. 23). Here we have the λόγοι σπερματικοί, which Gregory objected to as somehow connected in his mind with the infinite plurality of worlds. Yet his own account of the Resurrection of the flesh is nothing but Origenism, mitigated by the suppression of these λόγοι. With him, too, matter is nothing, it is a negative thing that can make and effect nothing: the soul, the ζωτικὴ δύναμις, does everything; it is gifted by him with a sort of ubiquity after death. 'Nothing can break its sympathetic union with the particles of the body.' It is not a long and difficult study for it to discern in the mass of elements that which is its own from that which is not its own. 'It watches over its property, as it were, until the Resurrection, when it will clothe itself in them anew[2].' It is only a change of names: the λόγος has become this ζωτικὴ δύναμις or ψυχή, which seems itself, almost unaided, to effect the whole Resurrection. Though he teaches as against Origen that the 'elements' are the same 'elements,' the body the same body as before, yet the strange importance both in activity and in substance which he attaches to the ψυχή even in the disembodied state seems to render a Resurrection of the flesh unnecessary. Here, too, his view of the plan of Redemption is at variance with his idealistic leanings. While Origen regarded the body, as it now is, as part of that 'vanity' placed upon the creature which was to be laid aside at last, Gregory's view of the design of God in creating man at all absolutely required the Resurrection of the flesh [3] (ὡς ἂν συνεπαρθείη τῷ θείῳ τὸ γήϊνον). Creation was to be saved by man's carrying his created body into a higher world: and this could only be done by a resurrection of the flesh such as the Church had already set forth in her creed.

Again, however, after parting with Origen upon this point, he meets him in the ultimate contemplation of Christ's glorified humanity and of all glorified bodies. Both steadily refuse at last 'to know Christ according to the flesh.' They depict His humanity as so absorbed in deity that all traces of His bodily nature vanish; and as with Christ, so finally with His true followers. This is far indeed from the Lamb that was slain, and the vision of S. John. In this heaven of theirs all individual or generic differences between rational creatures necessarily cease.

Great, then, as are their divergences, especially in cosmogony, their agreements are maintained throughout. Gregory in the main accepts Origen's teaching, as far as he can accommodate it to the now more outspoken faith of the Church. What [4] Redepenning summarises as the groundplan of Origen's whole way of thinking, Gregory has, with the necessary changes, appropriated. Both regard the history of the world as a movement between a beginning and an end in which are united every single spiritual or truly human nature in the world, and the Divine nature. This interval of movement is caused by the falling away of the free will of the creature from the divine: but it will come to an end, in order that the former union may be restored. In this summary they would differ only as to the closeness of the original union. Both, too, according to this, would regard 'man' as the final cause, and the explanation, and the centre of God's plan in creation.

---

[1] He does so *De Principiis* I. præf. 5. *C. Cels.* II. 77, VIII. 49 sq.
[2] *De Anim. et Resurrectione*, p. 198, 199, 213 sq.   [3] *Oratio Cat.* 55 A.   [4] Orig. II. 314 sq.

Even in the special sphere of theology which the later needs of the Church forced into prominence, and which Gregory has made peculiarly his own, that of the doctrine of the Trinity, Gregory employs sometimes a method which he has caught from Origen. Origen supposes, not so much, as Plato did, that things below are images of things above, as that they have certain secret analogies or affinities with them. This is perhaps after all only a peculiar application for his own purpose of Plato's theory of ideas. There are mysterious sympathies between the earth and heaven. We must therefore read within ourselves the reflection of truths which are too much beyond our reach to know in themselves. With regard to the attributes of God this is more especially the case. But Origen never had the occasion to employ this language in explaining the mystery of the Trinity. Gregory is the first Father who has done so. He finds a key to it in the [1] triple nature of our soul. The νοῦς, the λόγος, and the soul, form within us a unity such as that of the Divine hypostases. Gregory himself confesses that such thoughts about God are inadequate, and immeasurably below their object: but he cannot be blamed for employing this method, as if it was entirely superficial. Not only does this instance illustrate trinity in unity, but we should have no contents for our thought about the Father, Son, and Spirit, if we found no outlines at all of their nature within ourselves. Denis [2] well says that the history of the doctrine of the Trinity confirms this: for the advanced development of the theory of the λόγος, a purely human attribute in the ancient philosophy, was the cause of the doctrine of the Son being so soon and so widely treated: and the doctrine of the Holy Spirit came into prominence only when He began to be regarded as the principle of the purely human or moral life, as Love, that is, or Charity. Gregory, then, had reason in recommending even a more systematic use of the method which he had received from Origen: 'Learn from the things within thee to know the secret of God; recognise from the Triad within thee the Triad by means of these matters which you realise: it is a testimony above and more sure than that of the Law and the Gospel[3].'

He carries out elsewhere also more thoroughly than Origen this method of reading parables. He is an actual Mystic in this. The mysterious but real correspondences between earth and heaven, upon which, Origen had taught, and not upon mere thoughts or the artifices of language, the truth of a parable rests, Gregory employed, in order to penetrate the meaning of the whole of external nature. He finds in its facts and appearances analogies with the energies, and through them with the essence, of God. They are not to him merely indications of the wisdom which caused them and ordered them, but actual symptoms of the various energies which reside in the essence of the Supreme Being; as though that essence, having first been translated into the energies, was through them translated into the material creation; which was thus an earthly language saying the same thing as the heavenly language, word for word. The whole world thus became one vast allegory[4]: and existed only to manifest the qualities of the Unseen. Akin to this peculiar development of the parable is another characteristic of his, which is alien to the spirit of Origen; his delight in natural scenery, his appreciation of it, and power of describing it.

With regard to the question, so much agitated, of the Ἀποκατάστασις, it may be said that not Gregory only but Basil and Gregory Nazianzen also have felt the influence of their master in theology, Origen. But it is due to the latter to say that though he dwells much on the "all in all" and insists much more on the sanctifying power of punishment than on the satisfaction owed to Divine justice, yet no one could justly attribute to him, as a doctrine, the view of a Universal Salvation. Still these Greek Fathers, Origen and 'the three great Cappadocians,' equally showed a disposition of mind that left little room for the discussions that were soon to agitate the West. Their infinite hopes, their absolute confidence in the goodness of God,

---

[1] This is an independent division to that mentioned above. [2] *De la Philosophie D'Origène* (Paris, 1884).
[3] *De eo quod immut.*, p. 30. [4] See *De iis qui præmature abripiuntur*, p. 231, quoted above, p. 4.

who owes it to Himself to make His work perfect, their profound faith in the promises and sacrifice of Christ, as well as in the vivifying action of the Holy Spirit, make the question of Predestination and Grace a very simple one with them. The word Grace occurs as often in them as in Augustine: but they do not make original sin a monstrous innovation requiring a remedy of a peculiar and overwhelming intensity. Passion indeed seems to Gregory of Nyssa himself one of the essential elements of the human soul. He borrows from the naturalists many principles of distinction between classes of souls and lives: he insists incessantly on the intimate connexion between the physical growth and the development of the reason, and on the correlation between the one and the other: and we arrive at the conclusion that man in his eyes, as in Clement's, was not originally perfect, except in possibility; that being at once reasoning and sentient he must perforce feel within himself the struggle of reason and passion, and that it was inevitable that sin should enter into the world: it was a consequence of his mixed nature. This mixed nature of the first man was transmitted to his descendants. Here, though he stands apart from Origen on the question of man's original perfection, he could not have accepted the whole Augustinian scheme of original sin: and Grace as the remedy with him consists rather in the purging this mixed nature, than in the introduction into it of something absolutely foreign. The result, as with all the Greek Fathers, will depend on the co-operation of the free agent in this remedial work. Predestination and the 'bad will' are excluded by the Possibility and the 'free will' of Origen and Gregory.

CHAPTER IV.

HIS TEACHING ON THE HOLY TRINITY.

To estimate the exact value of the work done by S. Gregory in the establishment of the doctrine of the Trinity and in the determination, so far as Eastern Christendom is concerned, of the terminology employed for the expression of that doctrine, is a task which can hardly be satisfactorily carried out. His teaching on the subject is so closely bound up with that of his brother, S. Basil of Cæsarea,—his "master," to use his own phrase,—that the two can hardly be separated with any certainty. Where a disciple, carrying on the teaching he has himself received from another, with perhaps almost imperceptible variations of expression, has extended the influence of that teaching and strengthened its hold on the minds of men, it must always be a matter of some difficulty to discriminate accurately between the services which the two have rendered to their common cause, and to say how far the result attained is due to the earlier, how far to the later presentment of the doctrine. But the task of so discriminating between the work of S. Basil and that of S. Gregory is rendered yet more complicated by the uncertainty attaching to the authorship of particular treatises which have been claimed for both. If, for instance, we could with certainty assign to S. Gregory that treatise on the terms οὐσία and ὑπόστασις, which Dorner treats as one of the works by which he "contributed materially to fix the uncertain usage of the Church [1]," but which is found also among the works of S. Basil in the form of a letter addressed to S. Gregory himself, we should be able to estimate the nature and the extent of the influence of the Bishop of Nyssa much more definitely than we can possibly do while the authorship of this treatise remains uncertain. Nor does this document stand alone in this respect, although it is perhaps of more importance for the determination of such a question than any other of the disputed treatises. Thus in the absence of certainty as to the precise extent to which S. Gregory's teaching was directly indebted to that of his brother, it seems impossible to say how far the "fixing of the uncertain usage of the Church" was due to either of them singly. That together they did contribute very largely to

---

[1] See Dorner, *Doctrine of the Person of Christ*, Div. I. vol. ii. p. 314 (English Trans.).

that result is beyond question : and it is perhaps superfluous to endeavour to separate their contributions, especially as there can be little doubt that S. Gregory at least conceived himself to be in agreement with S. Basil upon all important points, if not to be acting simply as the mouth-piece of his "master's" teaching, and as the defender of the statements which his "master" had set forth against possible misconceptions of their meaning. Some points, indeed, there clearly were, in which S. Gregory's presentment of the doctrine differs from that of S. Basil ; but to these it may be better to revert at a later stage, after considering the more striking variation which their teaching displays from the language of the earlier Nicene school as represented by S. Athanasius.

The council held at Alexandria in the year 362, during the brief restoration of S. Athanasius, shows us at once the point of contrast and the substantial agreement between the Western school, with which S. Athanasius himself is in this matter to be reckoned, and the Eastern theologians to whom has been given the title of "Neo-Nicene." The question at issue was one of language, not of belief; it turned upon the sense to be attached to the word ὑπόστασις. The Easterns, following a use of the term which may be traced perhaps to the influence of Origen, employed the word in the sense of the Latin "Persona," and spoke of the Three Persons as τρεῖς ὑποστάσεις, whereas the Latins employed the term "hypostasis" as equivalent to "substantia," to express what the Greeks called οὐσία,—the one Godhead of the Three Persons. With the Latins agreed the older school of the orthodox Greek theologians, who applied to the Three Persons the phrase τρία πρόσωπα, speaking of the Godhead as μία ὑπόστασις. This phrase, in the eyes of the newer Nicene school, was suspected of Sabellianism [1], while on the other hand the Westerns were inclined to regard the Eastern phrase τρεῖς ὑποστάσεις as implying tritheism. The synodal letter sets forth to us the means by which the fact of substantial agreement between the two schools was brought to light, and the understanding arrived at, that while Arianism on the one hand and Sabellianism on the other were to be condemned, it was advisable to be content with the language of the Nicene formula, which employed neither the phrase μία ὑπόστασις nor the phrase τρεῖς ὑποστάσεις [2]. This resolution, prudent as it may have been for the purpose of bringing together those who were in real agreement, and of securing that the reconciled parties should, at a critical moment, present an unbroken front in the face of their common and still dangerous enemy, could hardly be long maintained. The expression τρεῖς ὑποστάσεις was one to which many of the orthodox, including those who had formerly belonged to the Semi-Arian section, had become accustomed : the Alexandrine synod, under the guidance of S. Athanasius, had acknowledged the phrase, as used by them, to be an orthodox one, and S. Basil, in his efforts to conciliate the Semi-Arian party, with which he had himself been closely connected through his namesake of Ancyra and through Eustathius of Sebastia, saw fit definitely to adopt it. While S. Athanasius, on the one hand, using the older terminology, says that ὑπόστασις is equivalent to οὐσία, and has no other meaning [3], S. Basil, on the other hand, goes so far as to say that the terms οὐσία and ὑπόστασις, even in the Nicene anathema, are not to be understood as equivalent [4]. The adoption of the new phrase, even after the explanations given at Alexandria, was found to require, in order to avoid misconstruction, a more precise definition of its meaning, and a formal defence of its orthodoxy. And herein consisted one principal service rendered by S. Basil and S. Gregory ; while with more precise definition of the term ὑπόστασις there emerged, it may be, a more precise view of the relations of the Persons, and with the defence of the new phrase as expressive of the Trinity of Persons a more precise view of what is implied in the Unity of the Godhead.

---

[1] It is to be noted further that the use of the terms "Persona" and πρόσωπον by those who avoided the phrase τρεῖς ὑποστάσεις no doubt assisted in the formation of this suspicion. At the same time the Nicene anathema favoured the sense of ὑπόστασις as equivalent to οὐσία, and so appeared to condemn the Eastern use.

[2] S. Athanasius, Tom. ad Antioch, 5.

[3] Ad Afr. Episc. § 4. S. Athanasius, however, does not shrink from the phrase τρεῖς ὑποστάσεις in contradistinction to the μία οὐσία : see the treatise, In illud, 'Omnia mihi tradita sunt.' § 6.

[4] S. Bas. Ep. 125 (being the confession of faith drawn up by S. Basil for the subscription of Eustathius)

The treatise, *De Sancta Trinitate* is one of those which are attributed by some to S. Basil, by others to S. Gregory: but for the purpose of showing the difficulties with which they had to deal, the question of its exact authorship is unimportant. [1] The most obvious objection alleged against their teaching was that which had troubled the Western theologians before the Alexandrine Council,—the objection that the acknowledgment of Three Persons implied a belief in Three Gods. To meet this, there was required a statement of the meaning of the term ὑπόστασις, and of the relation of ὀυσία to ὑπόστασις. Another objection, urged apparently by the same party as the former, was directed against the "novelty," or inconsistency, of employing in the singular terms expressive of the Divine Nature such as "goodness" or "Godhead," while asserting that the Godhead exists in plurality of Persons [2]. To meet this, it was required that the sense in which the Unity of the Godhead was maintained should be more plainly and clearly defined.

The position taken by S. Basil with regard to the terms ὀυσία and ὑπόστασις is very concisely stated in his letter to Terentius [3]. He says that the Western theologians themselves acknowledge that a distinction does exist between the two terms: and he briefly sets forth his view of the nature of that distinction by saying that ὀυσία is to ὑπόστασις as that which is common to individuals is to that in respect of which the individuals are naturally differentiated. He illustrates this statement by the remark that each individual man has his being τῷ κοίνῳ τῆς ὀυσίας λόγῳ, while he is differentiated as an individual man in virtue of his own particular attributes. So in the Trinity that which constitutes the ὀυσία (be it "goodness" or be it "Godhead") is common, while the ὑπόστασις is marked by the Personal attribute of Fatherhood or Sonship or Sanctifying Power [4]. This position is also adopted and set forth in greater detail in the treatise, *De Diff. Essen. et Hypost.* [5], already referred to, where we find once more the illustration employed in the Epistle to Terentius. The Nature of the Father is beyond our comprehension; but whatever conception we are able to form of that Nature, we must consider it to be common also to the Son and to the Holy Spirit: so far as the ὀυσία is concerned, whatever is predicated of any one of the Persons may be predicated equally of each of the Three Persons, just as the properties of man, *quâ* man, belong alike to Paul and Barnabas and Timothy: and as these individual men are differentiated by their own particular attributes, so each Person of the Trinity is distinguished by a certain attribute from the other two Persons. This way of putting the case naturally leads to the question, "If you say, as you do say, that Paul and Barnabas and Timothy are 'three men,' why do you not say that the Three Persons are 'three Gods?'" Whether the question was presented in this shape to S. Basil we cannot with certainty decide: but we may gather from his language regarding the applicability of number to the Trinity what his answer would have been. He [6] says that in acknowledging One Father, One Son, One Holy Spirit, we do not enumerate them by computation, but assert the individuality, so to say, of each hypostasis—its distinctness from the others. He would probably have replied by saying that strictly speaking we ought to decline applying to the Deity, considered as Deity, any numerical idea at all, and that to enumerate the Persons as "three" is a necessity, possibly, imposed upon us by language, but that no conception of number is really applicable to the Divine Nature or to the Divine Persons,

---

[1] It appears on the whole more probable that the treatise is the work of S. Gregory; but it is found, n a slightly different shape, among the Letters of S. Basil. (Ep. 189 in the Benedictine Edition.)

[2] In what sense this language was charged with "novelty" is not very clear. But the point of the objection appears to lie in a refusal to recognize that terms expressive of the Divine Nature, whether they indicate attributes or operations of that Nature, may be predicated of each ὑπόστασις severally, as well as of the ὀυσία, without attaching to the terms themselves that idea of plurality

which, so far as they express attributes or operations of the ὀυσία, must be excluded from them. [3] S. Bas. Ep. 214, § 4.

[4] The *differentia* here assigned to the Third Person is not, in S. Basil's own view, a *differentia* at all: for he would no doubt have been ready to acknowledge that this attribute is common to all Three Persons. S. Gregory, as it will be seen, treats the question as to the differentiation of the Persons somewhat differently, and rests his answer on a basis theologically more scientific. [5] S. Bas. Ep. 38 (Benedictine Ed.).

[6] De Spir. Sancto, § 18.

which transcend number [1].   To S. Gregory, however, the question did actually present itself as one demanding an answer, and his reply to it marks his departure from S. Basil's position, though, if the treatise, *De Diff. Essen. et Hyp.* be S. Basil's, S. Gregory was but following out and defending the view of his "master" as expressed in that treatise.

S. Gregory's reply to the difficulty may be found in the letter, or short dissertation, addressed to Ablabius (*Quod non sunt tres Dei*), and in his treatise περὶ κοινῶν ἐννοιῶν. In the latter he lays it down that the term θεός is a term οὐσίας σημαντικόν, not a term προσώπων δηλωτικόν: the Godhead of the Father is not that in which He maintains His differentiation from the Son : the Son is not God because He is *Son*, but because His essential Nature is what it is. Accordingly, when we speak of "God the Father, God the Son, and God the Holy Ghost," the word *and* is employed to conjoin the terms expressive of the Persons, not the repeated term which is expressive of the Essence, and which therefore, while applied to each of the Three Persons, yet cannot properly be employed in the plural. That in the case of three individual "*men*" the term expressive of essence *is* employed in the plural is due, he says, to the fact that in this case there are circumstances which excuse or constrain such a use of the term "man" while such circumstances do not affect the case of the Holy Trinity. The individuals included under the term "man" vary alike in number and in identity, and thus we are constrained to speak of "men" as more or fewer, and in a certain sense to treat the essence as well as the persons numerically. In the Holy Trinity, on the other hand, the Persons are always the same, and their number the same. Nor are the Persons of the Holy Trinity differentiated, like individual men, by relations of time and place, and the like ; the differentiation between them is based upon a constant causal relation existing among the Three Persons, which does not affect the unity of the Nature : it does not express the Being, but the *mode* of Being [2]. The Father is the Cause ; the Son and the Holy Spirit are differentiated from Him as being from the Cause, and again differentiated *inter se* as being immediately from the Cause, and immediately through that which is from the Cause. Further, while these reasons may be alleged for holding that the cases are not in such a sense parallel as to allow that the same conclusion as to modes of speech should be drawn in both, he urges that the use of the term "men" in the plural is, strictly speaking, erroneous. We should, in strictness, speak not of "this or that man," but of "this or that hypostasis of man"—the "three men" should be described as "three hypostases" of the common οὐσία "man." In the treatise addressed to Ablabius he goes over the same ground, clothing his arguments in a somewhat less philosophical dress ; but he devotes more space to an examination of the meaning of the term θεός, with a view to showing that it is a term expressive of operation, and thereby of *essence*, not a term which may be considered as applicable to any one of the Divine Persons in any such peculiar sense that it may not equally be applied also to the other two [3]. His argument is partly based upon an etymology now discredited, but this does not affect the position he seeks to establish (a position which is also adopted in the treatise, *De S. Trinitate*), that names expressive of the Divine Nature, or of the Divine operation (by which alone that Nature is known to us) are employed, and ought to be employed, only in the singular. The unity and inseparability of all Divine operation, proceeding from the Father, advancing through the Son, and culminating in the Holy Spirit, yet setting forth one κίνησις οι the Divine will, is the reason why the idea of plurality is not suffered to attach to these names [4],

---

[1] On S. Basil's language on this subject, see Dorner, Doctrine of the Person of Christ, Div. I. vol. ii. pp. 309—11. (Eng. Trans.)

[2] This statement strikes at the root of the theory held by Eunomius, as well as by the earlier Arians, that the ἀγεννησία of the Father constituted His Essence. S. Gregory treats His ἀγεννησία as that by which He is distinguished from the other Persons, as an attribute marking His hypostasis. This subject is treated more fully, with special reference to the Eunomian view, in the *Ref. alt. libri Eunomii*

[3] S. Gregory would apparently extend this argument even to the operations expressed by the names of "Redeemer," or "Comforter;" though he would admit that in regard of the mode by which these operations are applied to man, the names expressive of them are used in a special sense of the Son and of the Holy Spirit, yet he would argue that in neither case does the one Person act without the other two.

[4] See Dorner, *ut sup.*, pp. 317-18.

while the reason for refusing to allow, in regard to the three Divine Persons, the same laxity of language which we tolerate in regard to the case of the three "men," is to be found in the fact that in the latter case no danger arises from the current abuse of language : no one thinks of "three human natures ;" but on the other hand polytheism is a very real and serious danger, to which the parallel abuse of language involved in speaking of "three Gods" would infallibly expose us.

S. Gregory's own doctrine, indeed, has seemed to some critics to be open to the charge of tritheism. But even if his doctrine were entirely expressed in the single illustration of which we have spoken, it does not seem that the charge would hold good, when we consider the light in which the illustration would present itself to him. The conception of the unity of human nature is with him a thing intensely vivid : it underlies much of his system, and he brings it prominently forward more than once in his more philosophical writings[1]. We cannot, in fairness, leave his realism out of account when we are estimating the force of his illustration : and therefore, while admitting that the illustration was one not unlikely to produce misconceptions of his teaching, we may fairly acquit him of any personal bias towards tritheism such as might appear to be involved in the unqualified adoption of the same illustration by a writer of our own time, or such as might have been attributed to theologians of the period of S. Gregory who adopted the illustration without the qualification of a realism as determined as his own[2]. But the illustration does not stand alone : we must not consider that it is the only one of those to be found in the treatise, *De Diff. Essen. et Hypost.*, which he would have felt justified in employing. Even if the illustration of the rainbow, set forth in that treatise, was not actually his own (as Dorner, ascribing the treatise to him, considers it to have been), it was at all events (on the other theory of the authorship), included in the teaching he had received from his "master :" it would be present to his mind, although in his undisputed writings, where he is dealing with objections brought against the particular illustration from human relations, he naturally confines himself to the particular illustration from which an erroneous inference was being drawn. In our estimate of his teaching the one illustration must be allowed to some extent to qualify the effect produced by the other. And, further, we must remember that his argument from human relations is professedly *only* an illustration. It points to an *analogy*, to a resemblance, not to an identity of relations ; so much he is careful in his reply to state. Even if it were true, he implies, that we are warranted in speaking, in the given case, of the three human persons as "three men," it would not follow that we should be warranted thereby in speaking of the three Divine Persons as "three Gods." For the human personalities stand contrasted with the Divine, at once as regards their being and as regards their operation. The various human πρόσωπα draw their being from many other πρόσωπα, one from one, another from another, not, as the Divine, from One, unchangeably the same : they operate, each in his own way, severally and independently, not, as the Divine, inseparably : they are contemplated each by himself, in his own limited sphere, κατ' ἰδίαν περιγραφήν, not, as the Divine, in mutual essential connexion, differentiated one from the other only by a certain mutual relation. And from this it follows that the human πρόσωπα are capable of enumeration in a sense in which number cannot be considered applicable to the Divine Persons. Here we find S. Gregory's teaching brought once more into harmony with his "master's :" if he has been willing to carry the use of numerical terms rather further than S. Basil was prepared to do, he yet is content in the last resort to say that number is not in strictness applicable to the Divine ὑποστάσεις, in that they cannot be contemplated κατ' ἰδίαν περιγραφήν, and therefore cannot be enumerated by way of addition. Still the distinction of the ὑποστάσεις remains ; and if there is no other way (as he seems to have considered there was

---

[1] Especially in the treatise, *De Anima et Resurrectione,* and in that *De Conditione Hominis.* A notable instance is to be found in the former (p. 242 A.).   [2] See Dorner, *ut sup.*, p. 315, and p. 319, note 2.

none), of making full acknowledgment of their distinct though inseparable existence than to speak of them as "three," he holds that that use of numerical language is justifiable, so long as we do not transfer the idea of number from the ὑποστάσεις to the οὐσία, to that Nature of God which is Itself beyond our conception, and which we can only express by terms suggested to us by what we know of Its operation.

Such, in brief, is the teaching of S. Gregory on the doctrine of the Holy Trinity, as expressed in the treatises in which he developed and defended those positions in which S. Basil appeared to diverge from the older Nicene theologians. That the terminology of the subject gained clearness and definiteness from his exposition, in that he rendered it plain that the adoption of the Eastern phraseology was a thing perfectly consistent with the Faith confessed alike by East and West in varying terms, seems beyond doubt. It was to him, probably, rather than to S. Basil, that this work was due; for he cleared up the points which S. Basil's illustration had left doubtful; yet in so doing he was using throughout the weapons which his " master " had placed in his hands, and arguing in favour of his "master's" statements, in language, it may be, less guarded than S. Basil himself would have employed, but in accordance throughout with the principles which S. Basil had followed. Each bore his own part in the common work : to one, perhaps, is due the credit of greater originality; to the other it was given to carry on and to extend what his brother had begun : neither, we may well believe, would have desired to claim that the work which their joint teaching effected should be imputed to himself alone.

So far, we have especially had in view those minor treatises of S. Gregory which illustrate such variations from Athanasian modes of expression as are to be found in the writers of the " Neo-Nicene " school. These are perhaps his most characteristic works upon the subject. But the doctrine of the Trinity, as he held it, is further set forth and enforced in other treatises which are, from another point of view, much more important than those with which we have been dealing—in his *Oratio Catechetica*, and his more directly polemical treatises against Eunomius. In both these sections of his writings, when allowance is made for the difference of terminology already discussed, we are less struck by the divergencies from S. Athanasius' presentment of the doctrine than by the substantial identity of S. Gregory's reasoning with that of S. Athanasius, as the latter is displayed, for example, in the " Orations against the Arians."

There are, of course, many points in which S. Gregory falls short of his great predecessor ; but of these some may perhaps be accounted for by the different aspect of the Arian controversy as it presented itself to the two champions of the Faith. The later school of Arianism may indeed be regarded as a perfectly legitimate and rigidly logical development of the doctrines taught by Arius himself; but in some ways the task of S. Gregory was a different task from that of S. Athanasius, and was the less formidable of the two. His antagonist was, by his own greater definiteness of statement, placed at a disadvantage : the consequences which S. Athanasius had to extract from the Arian statements were by Eunomius and the Anomœans either openly asserted or tacitly admitted : and it was thus an easier matter for S. Gregory to show the real tendency of Anomœan doctrine than it had been for S. Athanasius to point out the real tendency of the earlier Arianism. Further, it may be said that by the time of S. Basil, still more by the time when S. Gregory succeeded to his brother's place in the controversy, the victory over Arianism was assured. It was not possible for S. Athanasius, even had it been in his nature to do so, to treat the earlier Arianism with the same sort of contemptuous criticism with which Eunomius is frequently met by S. Gregory. For S. Gregory, on the other hand, it was not necessary to refrain from such criticism lest he should thereby detract from the force of his protest against error. The crisis in his day was not one which demanded the same sustained effort for which the contest called in the days of S. Athanasius. Now and then, certainly, S. Gregory also rises to a white heat of indignation against his adversary : but it is hardly too much to say that his work appears to lack just those qualities which seem, in the writings of S. Athanasius, to have been called forth by the author's sense of the weight of the force opposed to him, and of the "life and death" character of the contest. S. Gregory does not under-estimate the momentous nature of the questions at issue : but when he wrote, he might feel that to those questions the answer of Christendom had been already given, that the conflict was already won, and that any attempt at developing the Arian doctrine on Anomœan lines was the adoption of an untenable position,—even of a position manifestly and evidently untenable: the doctrine had but to be stated in clear terms to be recognized as incompatible with Christianity, and, that fact once recognized, he had no more to do. Thus much of his treatises against Eunomius consists not of constructive argument in support of his own position, but of a detailed examination of Eunomius' own statements, while a further portion of the contents of these books, by no means inconsiderable in amount, is devoted not so much to the defence of the Faith as to the refutation of certain misrepresentations of S. Basil's arguments which had been set forth by Eunomius.

Even in the more distinctly constructive portion of these polemical writings, however, it may be said that S. Gregory does not show marked originality of thought either in his general argument, or in his mode of handling disputed texts. Within the limits of an introductory essay like the present, anything like detailed comparison on these points is of course impossible ; but any one who will take the trouble to compare the discourses of S. Gregory against Eunomius with the "Orations" of S. Athanasius against the Arians,—the Athanasian writing, perhaps, most closely corresponding in character to these books of S. Gregory,—either as regards the specific passages of Scripture cited in support of the doctrine maintained, and the mode of interpreting them, or as to the methods of explanation applied to the texts alleged by the Arian writers in favour of their own opinions, can hardly fail to be struck by the number and the closeness of the resemblances which he will be able to trace between the earlier and the later representatives of the Nicene School. A somewhat similar relation to the Athanasian position, as regards the basis of belief, and (allowing for the difference of terminology) as regards the definition of doctrine, may be observed in the *Oratio Catechetica*.

Such originality, in fact, as S. Gregory may claim to possess (so far as his treatment of this subject is concerned) is rather the originality of the tactician than that of the strate-gist: he deals rather with his particular opponent, and keeps in view the particular point in discussion more than the general area over which the war extends. S. Athanasius, on the other hand (partly, no doubt, because he was dealing with a less fully developed form of error), seems to have more force left in reserve. He presents his arguments in a more concise form, and is sometimes content to suggest an inference where S. Gregory proceeds to draw out conclusions in detail, and where thereby the latter, while possibly strengthening his presentment of the truth as against his own particular adversary,— against the Anomœan or the polytheist on the one side, or against the Sabellian or the Judaizer on the other,—renders his argument, when considered *per se* as a defence of the orthodox position, frequently more diffuse and sometimes less forcible. Yet, even here, originality of a certain kind does belong to S. Gregory, and it seems only fair to him to say that in these treatises also he did good service in defence of the Faith touching the Holy Trinity. He shows that alike by way of formal statement of doctrine, as in the *Oratio Catechetica*, and by way of polemical argument, the forces at the command of the defenders of the Faith could be organized to meet varied forms of error, without abandoning, either for a more original theology like that of Marcellus of Ancyra, or for the compromise which the Homœan or Semi-Arian school were in danger of being led to accept, the weapons with which S. Athanasius had conquered at Nicæa.

CHAPTER V.

MSS. AND EDITIONS.

FOR the 13 Books *Against Eunomius*, the text of F. Oehler (S. Greg. Nyss. Opera. Tom. I. Halis, 1865) has in the following translations been almost entirely followed.

The 1st Book was not in the 1st Paris Edition in two volumes (1615); but it was published three years afterwards from the 'Bavarian Codex,' i.e. that of Munich, by J. Gretser in an Appendix, along with the *Summaries* (these headings of the sections of the entire work are by some admirer of Gregory's) and the two introductory Letters. Both the Summaries and the letters, and also nearly three-quarters of the 1st Book were obtained from J. Livineius' transcript of the Vatican MS. made at Rome, 1579. This Appendix was added to the 2nd Paris Edition, in three volumes (1638).

In correcting these Paris Editions (for MSS. of which see below), Oehler had access, in addition to the identical Munich MS. (paper, 16th century) which Gretser had used, to the following MSS. :—

1. Venice (Library of S. Mark; cotton, 13 Cent., No. 69). This he says 'wonderfully agrees' with the Munich (both, for instance, supply the lacunæ of the Paris Edition of Book I : he concludes, therefore, that these are not due to Gretser's negligence, who gives the Latin for these passages, but to that of the printers).
2. Turin (Royal Library; cotton, 14 Cent., No. 71).
3. Milan (Library of S. Ambrose; cotton, 13 Cent., No. 225, Plut. 1; its inscription says that it was brought from Thessaly).
4. Florence (Library Medic. Laurent.; the oldest of all; parchment, 11 Cent., No. 17, Plut. vi. It contains the *Summaries*).

These, and the Munich MS., which he chiefly used, are "all of the same family :" and from them he has been able to supply more than 50 lacunæ in the Books against Eunomius. This family is the first of the two separated by G. H. Forbes (see below). The Munich MS. (No. 47, on paper, 16 Cent.), already used by Sifanus for his Latin version (1562), and by Gretser for his Appendix, has the corrections of the former in its margin. These passed into the two Paris Editions; which, however, took no notice of his critical notes. When lent to Sifanus this MS. was in the Library of J. J. Fugger. Albert V. Duke of Bavaria purchased the treasures of Greek literature in this library, to found that in Munich.

For the treatise *On the Soul and the Resurrection*, the *Great Catechetical Oration*, and the *Funeral Oration on Meletius*, John George Krabinger's text has been adopted. He had MSS. 'old and of a better stamp' (Oehler) than were accessible to the Paris editors. Krabinger's own account of them is this :—

On the Soul. 5 MSS. of 16th, 14th, and 11th Cent. All at Munich. In one of them there are scholia, some imported into the text by J. Naupliensis Murmureus the copyist; and Sifanus' corrections.

The 'Hasselman,' 14th Cent. J. Christopher Wolf, who annotated this treatise (*Aneedota Græca*, Hamburgh, 1722), says of this MS. "very carefully written." It was lent by Zach. Hasselman, Minister of Oldenburgh.

The 'Uffenbach,' 14th Cent., with var. lect. in margin. Lent to Wolf by the Polish ambassador at Frankfort on Main, at the request of Zach. Uffenbach.

Catechetical Oration. 4 MSS. of 16th Cent., 1 *of 13th Cent., 'much mutilated.'* All at Munich.

On Meletius. 2 MSS. of 16th Cent., 1 of 10th Cent. All at Munich.

His edition of the former appeared, at Leipzic, 1837; of the two latter, at Munich, 1838; all with valuable notes.

For the treatise *Against Macedonius*, the only text available is that of Cardinal Angelo Mai (Script. Vet. Nova Collectio, Rome, 1833). It is taken from the Vatican MS. ' on silk.' The end of this treatise is not found in Mai. Perhaps it is in the MS. of Florence.

For fourteen of the *Letters*, Zacagni (Præfect of the Vatican Library, 1698—1713) is the only editor. His text from the Vatican MS., No. 424, is printed in his Collectan. Monument. ret. (pp. 354—400), Rome, 1698.

He had not the use of the Medicean MS. which Caraccioli (see below) testifies to be much superior to the Vatican; there are lacunæ in the latter, however, which Zacagni occasionally fills by a happy guess with the very words supplied by the Medicean.

For the *Letter to Adelphius*, and that (on Church Architecture) *to Amphilochius*, J. B. Caraccioli (Professor of Philosophy at Pisa) furnishes a text (Florence, 1731) from the Medicean MS. The Letters in this collection are seven in all. Of the last of these (including that to Amphilochius) Bandinus says *non sincerâ fide ex Codice descriptas*, and that a fresh collation is necessary.

For the treatise *On the Making of Man*, the text employed has been that of G. H. Forbes, (his first Fasciculus was published in 1855; his second in 1861; both at Burntisland, at his private press), with an occasional preference for the readings of one or other of the MSS. examined by him or by others on his behalf. Of these he specifies twenty : but he had examined a much larger number. The MSS. which contain this work, he considers, are of two families.

Of the first family the most important are three MSS. at Vienna, a tenth-century MS. on vellum at S. Mark's, Venice, which he himself collated, and a Vatican MS. of the tenth century. This family also includes three of the four Munich MSS. collated for Forbes by Krabinger.

The other family displays more variations from the current text. One Vienna MS. "pervetustus" "initio mutilus," was completely collated. Also belonging to this family are the oldest of the four Munich MSS., the tenth-century Codex Regius (Paris), and a fourteenth-century MS. at Christ Church, Oxford, clearly related to the last.

The Codex Baroccianus (Bodleian, perhaps eleventh century) appears to occupy an independent position.

For the *other Treatises and Letters* the text of the Paris Edition of 1638 ('plenior et emendatior' than that of 1615, according to Oehler, probably following its own title, but "much inferior to that of 1615" Canon Venables, *Dict. Christ. Biog.*, says, and this is the judgment of J. Fessler) and of Migne have been necessary as the latest *complete* editions of the works of Gregory Nyssene. (All the materials that had been collected for the edition of the Benedictines of St. Maur perished in the French Revolution.)

Of the two Paris Editions it must be confessed that they are based 'for the most part on inferior MSS.' (Oehler.) The frequent lacunæ attest this. Fronto Ducæus aided Claude, the brother of F. Morel, in settling the text, and the MSS. mentioned in the notes of the former are as follows :

1. Pithoeus' "not of a very ancient hand," "as like F. Morel's (No. 2.) as milk to milk" (so speaks John the Franciscan, who emended 'from one corrupt mutilated manuscript,' i.e. the above, the Latin translation of the Books against Eunomius made by his father N. Gulonius.)
2. F. Morel's. ("Dean of Professors" and Royal Printer.)
3. The Royal (in the Library of Henry II., Paris), on vellum, tenth century.
4. Canter's ("ingens codex" sent from Antwerp by A. Schott; it had been written out for T. Canter, Senator of Utrecht).
5. Olivar's. "Multo emendatius" than (2.)
6. J. Vulcobius', Abbot of Belpré.
7. The Vatican.
8. Bricman's (Cologne).
9. Œgidius David's, I. C. Paris. ⎱ for the treatise *On Virginity*. (The Paris Editors used Livineius' Edition, based on (7) and (8).)

10. The Bavarian (Munich) for Books II.—XIII. Against Eunomius and other treatises; only after the first edition of 1615.

Other important MSS. existing for treatises here translated are

On Pilgrimages:
   MS. Cæsareus (Vienna): "valde vetustus" (Nessel, on the Imperial Library), vellum, No. 160, burnt at beginning.
   MSS. Florence (xx. 17 : xvi. 8).
   MS. Leyden (not older than fifteenth century).
On the Making of Man:
   MS. Augsburgh, with twelve Homilies of Basil,

the two last being wrongly attributed to Gregory (Reizer).
   MS. Ambrosian (Milan). See Montfaucon, Bibl. Bibliothec. p. 498.
On Infants' Early Deaths:
   MS. Turin (Royal Library).
On the Soul and Resurrection:
   MSS. Augsburgh, Florence, Turin, Venice.
Great Catechetical:
   MSS. Augsburgh, Florence, Turin, Cæsareus.

Many other MSS., for these and other treatises, are given by S. Heyns (*Disputatio de Greg. Nyss.* Leyden, 1835). But considering the mutilated condition of most of the oldest, and the still small number of treatises edited from an extended collation of these, the complaint is still true that 'the text of hardly any other ancient writer is in a more imperfect state than that of Gregory of Nyssa.'

VERSIONS OF SEVERAL TREATISES.

Latin.

1. Of Dionysius Exiguus (died before 556): *On the Making of Man.* Aldine, 1537. Cologne, 1551. Basle, 1562. Cologne, 1573. Dedicated to Eugippius.' This Dedication and the Latin of Gregory's Preface was only once printed (i.e. in J. Mabillon's Analecta, Paris, 1677).

   This ancient Latin Version was revised by Fronto Ducæus, the Jesuit, and Combeficius. There is a copy of it at Lèyden.

   It stimulated J. Leünclaius (see below), who judged it "fœda pollutum barbariâ planeque perversum," to make another. Basle, 1567.

2. Of. Daniel Augentius: *On the Soul.* Paris 1557.

3. Of Laurent. Sifanus, I. U. Doct.: *On the Soul* and many other treatises. Basle, 1562 Apud N. Episcopum.

4. Of Pet. Galesinius: *On Virginity* and *On Prayer.* Róme, 1563, ap. P. Manutium.

5. Of Johann. Leünclaius: *On the Making of Man.* Basle, 1567, ap. Oporinum.

6. Of Pet. Morelius, of Tours: *Great Catechetical.* Paris, 1568.

7. Of Gentianus Hervetus, Canon of Rheims, a diligent translator of the Fathers: *Great Catechetical,* and many others. Paris, 1573.

8. Of Johann. Livineius, of Ghent: *On Virginity.* Apud Plantinum, 1574.

9. Of Pet. Fr. Zinus, Canon of Verona, translator of Euthymius' Panoplia, which contains the *Great Catechetical.* Venice, 1575.

10. Of Jacob Gretser, the Jesuit: *I. e. Eunom.* Paris, 1618.

11. Of Nicolas Gulonius, Reg. Prof. of Greek: *II.—XIII. c. Eunom.* Paris, 1615. Revised by his son John, the Franciscan.

12. Of J. Georg. Krabinger, Librarian of Royal Library, Munich: *On the Soul, Great Catechetical, On Infants' Early Deaths,* and others. Leipzic, 1837.

German.

1. Of Glauber: *Great Catechetical,* &c. Gregorius von Nyssa und Augustinus über den ersten Christlichen Religions-unterricht. Leipzic, 1781.

2. Of Julius Rupp, Königsberg: *On Meletius.* Gregors Leben und Meinungen. Leipzic, 1834.

3. Of Oehler: *Various treatises.* Bibliothek der Kirchenväter I. Theil. Leipzic, 1858—59.

4. Herm. Schmidt, paraphrased rather than translated: *On the Soul.* Halle, 1864.

5. Of H. Hayd: *On Infants' Early Deaths : On the Making of Man,* &c. Kempton, 1874.

GREGORY OF NYSSA AGAINST EUNOMIUS

LETTER I.

GREGORY to his brother Peter, Bishop of Sebasteia.

Having with difficulty obtained a little leisure, I have been able to recover from bodily fatigue on my return from Armenia, and to collect the sheets of my reply to Eunomius which was suggested by your wise advice ; so that my work is now arranged in a complete treatise, which can be read between covers. However, I have not written against both his pamphlets [1] ; even the leisure for that was not granted ; for the person who lent me the heretical volume most uncourteously sent for it again, and allowed me no time either to write it out or to study it. In the short space of seventeen days it was impossible to be prepared to answer both his attacks.

Owing to its somehow having become notorious that we had laboured to answer this blasphemous manifesto, many persons possessing some zeal for the Truth have importuned me about it : but I have thought it right to prefer you in your wisdom before them all, to advise me whether to consign this work to the public, or to take some other course. The reason why I hesitate is this. When our saintly Basil fell asleep, and I received the legacy of Eunomius' controversy, when my heart was hot within me with bereavement, and, besides this deep sorrow for the common loss of the church, Eunomius had not confined himself to the various topics which might pass as a defence of his views, but had spent the chief part of his energy in laboriously-written

abuse of our father in God. I was exasperated with this, and there were passages where the flame of my heart-felt indignation burst out against this writer. The public have pardoned us for much else, because we have been apt in showing patience in meeting lawless attacks, and as far as possible have practised that restraint in feeling which the saint has taught us ; but I had fears lest from what we have now written against this opponent the reader should get the idea that we were very raw controversialists, who lost our temper directly at insolent abuse. Perhaps, however, this suspicion about us will be disarmed by remembering that this display of anger is not on our own behalf, but because of insults levelled against our father in God ; and that it is a case in which mildness would be more unpardonable than anger.

If, then, the first part of my treatise should seem somewhat outside the controversy, the following explanation of it will, I think, be accepted by a reader who can judge fairly. It was not right to leave undefended the reputation of our noble saint, mangled as it was by the opponent's blasphemies, any more than it was convenient to let this battle in his behalf be spread diffusely along the whole thread of the discussion ; besides, if any one reflects, these pages do really form part of the controversy. Our adversary's treatise has two separate arms, viz. to abuse us and to controvert sound doctrine ; and therefore ours too must show a double front. But for the sake of clearness, and in order that the thread of the discussion upon matters of the Faith should not be cut by parentheses, consisting of answers to their personal abuse, we have separated our work into two parts, and devoted ourselves in the first to refute these charges : and then we have grappled as best we might with that which they have advanced against the Faith. Our treatise also contains, in addition to a refutation of their heretical views, a dogmatic exposition of our own teaching ; for it would be a most shameful want of spirit, when our foes make no concealment of their blasphemy, not to be bold in our statement of the Truth

---

[1] *both his pamphlets.* The 'sheets' which Gregory says that he has collected are the 12 Books that follow. They are written in reply to Eunomius' pamphlet, 'Apologia Apologiæ,' itself a reply to Basil's Refutation. The other pamphlet of Eunomius seems to have come out during the composition of Gregory's 12 Books : and was afterwards answered by the latter in a second 12th Book, but not now, because of the shortness of the time in which he had a copy of the 'heretical volume' in his hands. The two last books of the five which go under the title of Basil's Refutation are considered on good grounds to have been Gregory's, and to have formed that short reply to Eunomius which he read, at the Council of Constantinople, to Gregory of Nazianzen and Jerome (*d. vir. illust.* c. 128). Then he worked upon this longer reply. Thus there were in all three works of Gregory corresponding to the three attacks of Eunomius upon the Trinity.

LETTER II.

To his most pious brother Gregory.　Peter greeting in the Lord.

Having met with the writings of your holiness and having perceived in your tract against this heresy your zeal both for the truth and for our sainted father in God, I judge that this work was not due simply to your own ability, but was that of one who studied that the Truth should speak, even in the publication of his own views.　To the Holy Spirit of truth I would refer this plea for the truth; just as to the father of lies, and not to Eunomius, should be referred this animosity against sound faith. Indeed, that murderer from the beginning who speaks in Eunomius has carefully whetted the sword against himself; for if he had not been so bold against the truth, no one would have roused you to undertake the cause of our religion.　But to the end that the rottenness and flimsiness of their doctrines may be exposed, He who " taketh the wise in their own craftiness " hath allowed them both to be headstrong against the truth, and to have laboured vainly on this vain speech.

But since he that hath begun a good work will finish it, faint not in furthering the Spirit's power, nor leave half-won the victory over the assailants of Christ's glory; but imitate thy true father who, like the zealot Phineas, pierced with one stroke of his Answer both master and pupil.　Plunge with thy intellectual arm the sword of the Spirit through both these heretical pamphlets, lest, though broken on the head, the serpent affright the simpler sort by still quivering in the tail.　When the first arguments have been answered, should the last remain unnoticed, the many will suspect that they still retain some strength against the truth.

The feeling shewn in your treatise will be grateful, as salt, to the palate of the soul.　As bread cannot be eaten, according to Job, without salt, so the discourse which is not savoured with the inmost sentiments of God's word will never wake, and never move, desire.

Be strong, then, in the thought that thou art a beautiful example to succeeding times of the way in which good-hearted children should act towards their virtuous fathers.

BOOK I

§ 1. *Preface.—It is useless to attempt to benefit those who will not accept help.*

IT seems that the wish to benefit all, and to lavish indiscriminately upon the first comer one's own gifts, was not a thing altogether commendable, or even free from reproach in the eyes of the many; seeing that the gratuitous waste of many prepared drugs on the incurably-diseased produces no result worth caring about, either in the way of gain to the recipient, or reputation to the would-be benefactor. Rather such an attempt becomes in many cases the occasion of a change for the worse. The hopelessly-diseased and now dying patient receives only a speedier end from the more active medicines; the fierce unreasonable temper is only made worse by the kindness of the lavished pearls, as the Gospel tells us. I think it best, therefore, in accordance with the Divine command, for any one to separate the valuable from the worthless when either have to be given away, and to avoid the pain which a generous giver must receive from one who 'treads upon his pearl,' and insults him by his utter want of feeling for its beauty.

This thought suggests itself when I think of one who freely communicated to others the beauties of his own soul, I mean that man of God, that mouth of piety, Basil; one who from the abundance of his spiritual treasures poured his grace of wisdom into evil souls whom he had never tested, and into one among them, Eunomius, who was perfectly insensible to all the efforts made for his good. Pitiable indeed seemed the condition of this poor man, from the extreme weakness of his soul in the matter of the Faith, to all true members of the Church; for who is so wanting in feeling as not to pity, at least, a perishing soul? But Basil alone, from the abiding[2] ardour of his love, was moved to undertake his cure, and therein to attempt impossibilities; he alone took so much to heart the man's desperate condition, as to compose, as an antidote of deadly poisons, his refutation of this heresy[3], which aimed at saving its author, and restoring him to the Church.

He, on the contrary, like one beside himself with fury, resists his doctor; he fights and struggles; he regards as a bitter foe one who only put forth his strength to drag him from the abyss of misbelief; and he does not indulge in this foolish anger only before chance hearers now and then; he has raised against himself a literary monument to record this blackness of his bile; and when in long years he got the requisite amount of leisure, he was travailling over his work during all that interval with mightier pangs than those of the largest and the bulkiest beasts; his threats of what was coming were dreadful, whilst he was still secretly moulding his conception: but when at last and with great difficulty he brought it to the light, it was a poor little abortion, quite

---

[1] **This** first Book against Eunomius was not in the 1st Paris Edition of Gregory's works, 1615: but it was published three years later from the 'Bavarian Codex,' i.e. that of Munich, by J. Gretser, in an Appendix, along with the Summaries (i.e. the headings of the sections, which appear to be not Gregory's) and the two Introductory Letters. These Summaries and the Letters, and nearly three quarters of the 1st Book were found in J. Livineius' transcript from the Codex Vaticanus made 1579, at Rome. This Appendix was added to the 2nd Paris Edit. 1638. F. Oehler, whose text has been followed throughout, has used for the 1st Book the Munich Codex (on paper, xvi th Cent.); the Venetian (on cotton, xiiith Cent.); the Turin (on cotton, xivth Cent.), and the oldest of all, the Florentine (on parchment, xith Cent.).

[2] Reading,—
τὸ μόνιμον . . . ἐπιτολμῶντα. This is the correction of Oehler for τὸν μόνον . . . ἐπιτολμῶν which the text presents. The Venetian MS. has ἐπιτολμῶντι.

[3] *his refutation of this heresy.* This is Basil's Ἀνατρεπτικὸς τοῦ ἀπολογητικοῦ τοῦ δυσσεβοῦς Εὐνομίου. 'Basil,' says Photius, 'with difficulty got hold of Eunomius' book,' perhaps because it was written originally for a small circle of readers, and was in a highly scientific form. What happened next may be told in the words of Claudius Morellius (Prolegomena to Paris Edition of 1615): 'When Basil's first essay against the fœtus of Eunomius had been published, he raised his bruised head like a trodden worm, seized his pen, and began to rave more poisonously still as well against Basil as the orthodox faith.' This was Eunomius' 'Apologia Apologiæ:' of it Photius says, 'His reply to Basil was composed for many Olympiads while shut up in his cell. This, like another Saturn, he concealed from the eyes of Basil till it had grown up, i.e. he concealed it, by devouring it, as long as Basil lived.' He then goes on to say that after Basil's death, Theodore (of Mopsuestia), Gregory of Nyssa, and Sophronius found it and dealt with it, though even then Eunomius had only ventured to show it to some of his friends. Philostorgius, the ardent admirer of Eunomius, makes the amazing statement that Basil died of despair after reading it.

prematurely born. However, those who share his ruin nurse it and coddle it; while we, seeking the blessing in the prophet ("Blessed shall he be who shall take thy children, and shall dash them against the stones [4]") are only eager, now that it has got into our hands, to take this puling manifesto and dash it on the rock, as if it was one of the children of Babylon; and the rock must be Christ; in other words, the enunciation of the truth. Only may that power come upon us which strengthens weakness, through the prayers of him who made his own strength perfect in bodily weakness [5].

§ 2. *We have been justly provoked to make this Answer, being stung by Eunomius' accusations of our brother.*

If indeed that godlike and saintly soul were still in the flesh looking out upon human affairs, if those lofty tones were still heard with all their peculiar [6] grace and all their resistless utterance, who could arrive at such a pitch of audacity, as to attempt to speak one word upon this subject? that divine trumpet-voice would drown any word that could be uttered. But all of him has now flown back to God; at first indeed in the slight shadowy phantom of his body, he still rested on the earth; but now he has quite shed even that unsubstantial form, and bequeathed it to this world. Meantime the drones are buzzing round the cells of the Word, and are plundering the honey; so let no one accuse me of mere audacity for rising up to speak instead of those silent lips. I have not accepted this laborious task from any consciousness in myself of powers of argument superior to the others who might be named; I, if any, have the means of knowing that there are thousands in the Church who are strong in the gift of philosophic skill. Nevertheless I affirm that, both by the written and the natural law, to me more especially belongs this heritage of the departed, and therefore I myself, in preference to others, appropriate the legacy of the controversy. I may be counted amongst the least of those who are enlisted in the Church of God, but still I am not too weak to stand out as her champion against one who has broken with that Church. The very smallest member of a vigorous body would, by virtue of the unity of its life with the whole, be found stronger than one

that had been cut away and was dying, however large the latter and small the former.

§ 3. *We see nothing remarkable in logical force in the treatise of Eunomius, and so embark on our Answer with a just confidence.*

Let no one think, that in saying this I exaggerate and make an idle boast of doing something which is beyond my strength. I shall not be led by any boyish ambition to descend to his vulgar level in a contest of mere arguments and phrases. Where victory is a useless and profitless thing, we yield it readily to those who wish to win; besides, we have only to look at this man's long practice in controversy, to conclude that he is quite a word-practitioner, and, in addition, at the fact that he has spent no small portion of his life on the composition of this treatise, and at the supreme joy of his intimates over these labours, to conclude that he has taken particular trouble with this work. It was not improbable that one who had laboured at it for so many Olympiads would produce something better than the work of extempore scribblers. Even the vulgar profusion of the figures he uses in concocting his work is a further indication of this laborious care in writing [7]. He has got a great mass of newly assorted terms, for which he has put certain other books under contribution, and he piles this immense congeries of words on a very slender nucleus of thought; and so he has elaborated this highly-wrought production, which his pupils in error are lost in the admiration of;—no doubt, because their deadness on the vital points deprives them of the power of feeling the distinction between beauty and the reverse:—but which is ridiculous, and of no value at all in the judgment of those, whose hearts' insight is not dimmed with any soil of unbelief. How in the world can it contribute to the proof (as he hopes) of what he says and the establishment of the truth of his speculations, to adopt these absurd devices in his forms of speech, this new-fangled and peculiar arrange-

---

4 Psalm cxxxvii. 9.
5 'He asks for the intercession of Saint Paul' (Paris Edit. in marg.).
6 ἀποκληρωθεῖσαν. This is probably the meaning, after the analogy of ἀποκλήρωσις, in the sense (most frequent in Origen), of 'favour,' 'partiality,' passing into that of 'caprice,' 'arbitrariness,' cf. below, cap. 9, τίς ἡ ἀποκλήρωσις, κ.τ.λ. 'How arbitrarily he praises himself.'

7 Photius reports very much the same as to his style, i.e. he shows a 'prodigious ostentation:' uses 'words difficult to pronounce, and abounding in many consonants, and that in a poetic, or rather a dithyrambic style:' he has 'periods inordinately long:' he is 'obscure,' and seeks 'to hide by this very obscurity whatever is weak in his perceptions and conceptions, which indeed is often.' He 'attacks others for their logic, and is very fond of using logic himself:' but 'as he had taken up this science late in life, and had not gone very deeply into it, he is often found making mistakes.'
The book of Eunomius which Photius had read is still extant: it is his 'Apologeticus' in 28 sections, and has been published by Canisius (*Lectiones Antiquæ*, I. 172 ff.). His ἔκθεσις τῆς πίστεως, presented to the emperor Theodosius in the year 383, is also extant. This last is found in the Codex Theodosius and in the MSS. which Livineius of Ghent used for his Greek and Latin edition of Gregory, 1574: it follows the Books against Eunomius. His 'Apologia Apologiæ,' which he wrote in answer to Basil's 5 (or 3) books against him, is *not* extant: nor the δευτερὸς λόγος which Gregory answered in his second 12th Book.
Most of the quotations, then, from Eunomius, in these books of Gregory cannot be verified, in the case of a doubtful reading, &c.

ment, this fussy conceit, and this conceited fussiness, which works with no enthusiasm for any previous model? For it would be indeed difficult to discover who amongst all those who have been celebrated for their eloquence he has had his eye on, in bringing himself to this pitch; for he is like those who produce effects upon the stage, adapting his argument to the tune of his rhythmical phrases, as they their song to their castenets, by means of parallel sentences of equal length, of similar sound and similar ending. Such, amongst many other faults, are the nerveless quaverings and the meretricious tricks of his Introduction; and one might fancy him bringing them all out, not with an unimpassioned action, but with stamping of the feet and sharp snapping of the fingers declaiming to the time thus beaten, and then remarking that there was no need of other arguments and a second performance after that.

§ 4. *Eunomius displays much folly and fine writing, but very little seriousness about vital points.*

In these and such like antics I allow him to have the advantage; and to his heart's content he may revel in his victory there. Most willingly I forego such a competition, which can attract those only who seek renown; if indeed any renown comes from indulging in such methods of argumentation, considering that Paul[8], that genuine minister of the Word, whose only ornament was truth, both disdained himself to lower his style to such prettinesses, and instructs us also, in a noble and appropriate exhortation, to fix our attention on truth alone. What need indeed for one who is fair in the beauty of truth to drag in the paraphernalia of a decorator for the production of a false artificial beauty? Perhaps for those who do not possess truth it may be an advantage to varnish their falsehoods with an attractive style, and to rub into the grain of their argument a curious polish. When their error is taught in far-fetched language and decked out with all the affectations of style, they have a chance of being plausible and accepted by their hearers. But those whose only aim is simple truth, unadulterated by any misguiding foil, find the light of a natural beauty emitted from their words.

But now that I am about to begin the examination of all that he has advanced, I feel the same difficulty as a farmer does, when the air is calm; I know not how to separate his wheat from his chaff; the waste, in fact, and the chaff in this pile of words is so enormous, that it makes one think that the residue of facts and real thoughts in all that he has said is almost nil. It would be the worse for speed and very irksome, it would even be beside our object, to go into the whole of his remarks in detail; we have not the means for securing so much leisure so as wantonly to devote it to such frivolities; it is the duty, I think, of a prudent workman not to waste his strength on trifles, but on that which will clearly repay his toil.

As to all the things, then, in his Introduction, how he constitutes himself truth's champion, and fixes the charge of unbelief upon his opponents, and declares that an abiding and indelible hatred for them has sunk into his soul, how he struts in his 'new discoveries,' though he does not tell us what they are, but says only that an examination of the debateable points in them was set on foot, a certain 'legal' trial which placed on those who were daring to act illegally the necessity of keeping quiet, or to quote his own words in that Lydian style of singing which he has got, " the bold law-breakers —in open court—were forced to be quiet;" (he calls this a "proscription" of the conspiracy against him, whatever may be meant by that term);—all this wearisome business I pass by as quite unimportant. On the other hand, all his special pleading for his heretical conceits may well demand our close attention. Our own interpreter of the principles of divinity followed this course in *his* Treatise; for though he had plenty of ability to broaden out his argument, he took the line of dealing only with vital points, which he selected from all the blasphemies of that heretical book[9], and so narrowed the scope of the subject.

If, however, any one desires that our answer should exactly correspond to the array of his arguments, let him tell us the utility of such a process. What gain would it be to my readers if I were to solve the complicated riddle of his title, which he proposes to us at the very commencement, in the manner of the sphinx of the tragic stage; namely this 'New Apology for the Apology,' and all the nonsense which he writes about that; and if I were to tell the long tale of what he dreamt? I think that the reader is sufficiently wearied with the petty vanity about this newness in his title already preserved in Eunomius' own text, and with the want of taste displayed there in the account of his own exploits, all his labours and his trials, while he wandered over every land and every sea, and was 'heralded' through the whole world. If all that had to be written down over again,—and with additions, too, as the refuta-

---

[8] Cf. 1 Corinth. ii. 1—5.

[9] *that heretical book*, i.e. the first 'Apology' of Eunomius in 28 parts: a translation of it is given in Whiston's *Eunomianismus Redivivus*.

tions of these falsehoods would naturally have to expand their statement,—who would be found of such an iron hardness as not to be sickened at this waste of labour? Suppose I was to write down, taking word by word, an explanation of that mad story of his; suppose I were to explain, for instance, who that Armenian was on the shores of the Euxine, who had annoyed him at first by having the same name as himself, what their lives were like, what their pursuits, how he had a quarrel with that Armenian because of the very likeness of their characters, then in what fashion those two were reconciled, so as to join in a common sympathy with that winning and most glorious Aetius, his master (for so pompous are his praises); and after that, what was the plot devised against himself, by which they brought him to trial on the charge of being surpassingly popular: suppose, I say, I was to explain all that, should I not appear, like those who catch opthalmia themselves from frequent contact with those who are already suffering so, to have caught myself this malady of fussy circumstantiality? I should be following step by step each detail of his twaddling story; finding out who the " slaves released to liberty" were, what was " the conspiracy [1] of the initiated" and " the calling out [2] of hired slaves," what ' Montius and Gallus, and Domitian,' and ' false witnesses,' and ' an enraged Emperor,' and ' certain sent into exile' have to do with the argument. What could be more useless than such tales for the purpose of one who was not wishing merely to write a narrative, but to refute the argument of him who had written against his heresy? What follows in the story is still more profitless; I do not think that the author himself could peruse it again without yawning, though a strong natural affection for his off-spring *does* possess every father. He pretends to unfold there his exploits and his sufferings; the style rears itself into the sublime, and the legend swells into the tones of tragedy.

§ 5. *His peculiar caricature of the bishops, Eusta-thius of Armenia and Basil of Galatia, is not well drawn.*

But, not to linger longer on these absurdities in the very act of declining to mention them, and not to soil this book by forcing my subject through all his written reminiscences, like one who urges his horse through a slough and so gets covered with its filth, I think it is best to leap over the mass of his rubbish with as high and as speedy a jump as my thoughts are capable of, seeing that a quick retreat from what is disgusting is a considerable advantage; and let us hasten on [3] to the finale of his story, lest the bitterness of his own words should trickle into my book. Let Eunomius have the monopoly of the bad taste in such words as these, spoken of God's priests [4], "curmudgeon squires, and beadles, and satellites, rummaging about, and not suffering the fugitive to carry on his concealment," and all the other things which he is not ashamed to write of grey-haired priests. Just as in the schools for secular learning [5], in order to exercise the boys to be ready in word and wit, they propose themes for declamation, in which the person who is the subject of them is nameless, so does Eunomius make an onset at once upon the facts suggested, and lets loose the tongue of invective, and without saying one word as to any actual villainies, he merely works up against them all the hackneyed phrases of contempt, and every imaginable term of abuse: in which, besides, incongruous ideas are brought together, such as a ' dilettante soldier,' ' an accursed saint,' ' pale with fast, and murderous with hate,' and many such like scurrilities; and just like a reveller in the secular processions shouts his ribaldry, when he would carry his insolence to the highest pitch, without his mask on, so does Eunomius, without an attempt to veil his malignity, shout with brazen throat the language of the waggon. Then he reveals the cause why he is so enraged; ' these priests took every precaution that many should not' be perverted to the error of these heretics; accordingly he is angry that they could not stay at their convenience in the places they liked, but that a residence was assigned them by order of the then governor of Phrygia, so that most might be secured from such wicked neighbours; his indignation at this bursts out in these words; ' the excessive severity of our trials,' ' our grievous sufferings,' ' our noble endurance of them,' ' the exile from our native country into Phrygia.' Quite so: this Oltiserian [6] might well be proud of what occurred, putting an end as it did to all his family pride, and casting such a slur upon his race that that far-renowned Priscus, his grand-father, from whom he gets those brilliant and most remarkable heirlooms, " the mill, and the

---

[1] σχέσιν. [2] τάξιν. We have no context to explain these allusions, the treatise of Eunomius being lost, which Gregory is *now* answering, i.e. the Apologia Apologiæ.

[3] Reading πρός τε τὸ πέρας.
[4] This must be the ' caricature' of the (Greek) Summary above. Eustathius of Sebasteia, the capital of Armenia, and the Galatian Basil, of Ancyra (Angora), are certainly mentioned, c. 6 (end). Twice did these two, once Semi-Arians, oppose Aetius and Euno-mius, before Constantius, at Byzantium. On the second occasion, however (Sozomen, H.E. iv. 23, Ursacius and Valens arrived with the proscription of the Homoousion from Ariminum: it was then that " the world groaned to find itself Arian " (Jerome). The ' accursed saint' ' pale with fast,' i.e. Eustathius, in his Armenian monastery, gave Basil the Great a model for his own.
[5] τῶν ἐξωθεν λόγων.
[6] Oltiseris was probably the district, as Corniaspa was the village, in which Eunomius was born. It is a Celtic word: and probably suggests his half-Galatian extraction.

leather, and the slaves' stores," and the rest of his inheritance in Chanaan [7], would never have chosen this lot, which now makes him so angry. It was to be expected that he would revile those who were the agents of this exile. I quite understand his feeling. Truly the authors of these misfortunes, if such there be or ever have been, deserve the censures of these men, in that the renown of their former lives is thereby obscured, and they are deprived of the opportunity of mentioning and making much of their more impressive antecedents; the great distinctions with which each started in life; the professions they inherited from their fathers; the greater or the smaller marks of gentility of which each was conscious, even before they became so widely known and valued that even emperors numbered them amongst their acquaintance, as he now boasts in his book, and that all the higher governments were roused about them and the world was filled with their doings.

§ 6. *A notice of Aetius, Eunomius' master in heresy, and of Eunomius himself, describing the origin and avocations of each.*

Verily this did great damage to our declamation-writer, or rather to his patron and guide in life, Aetius; whose enthusiasm indeed appears to me to have aimed not so much at the propagation of error as to the securing a competence for life. I do not say this as a mere surmise of my own, but I have heard it from the lips of those who knew him well. I have listened to Athanasius, the former bishop of the Galatians, when he was speaking of the life of Aetius; Athanasius was a man who valued truth above all things; and he exhibited also the letter of George of Laodicæa, so that a number might attest the truth of his words. He told us that originally Aetius did not attempt to teach his monstrous doctrines, but only after some interval of time put forth these novelties as a trick to gain his livelihood; that having escaped from serfdom in the vineyard to which he belonged,—how, I do not wish to say, lest I should be thought to be entering on his history in a bad spirit,—he became at first a tinker, and had this grimy trade of a mechanic quite at his fingers' end, sitting under a goat's-hair tent, with a small hammer, and a diminutive anvil, and so earned a precarious and laborious livelihood. What income, indeed, of any account could be made by one who mends the shaky places in coppers, and solders holes up, and hammers sheets of tin to pieces, and clamps with lead the legs of pots?

We were told that a certain incident which befell him in this trade necessitated the next change in his life. He had received from a woman belonging to a regiment a gold ornament, a necklace or a bracelet, which had been broken by a blow, and which he was to mend: but he cheated the poor creature, by appropriating her gold trinket, and giving her instead one of copper, of the same size, and also of the same appearance, owing to a gold-wash which he had imparted to its surface; she was deceived by this for a time, for he was clever enough in the tinker's, as in other, arts to mislead his customers with the tricks of trade; but at last she detected the rascality, for the wash got rubbed off the copper; and, as some of the soldiers of her family and nation were roused to indignation, she prosecuted the purloiner of her ornament. After this attempt he of course underwent a cheating thief's punishment; and then left the trade, swearing that it was not his deliberate intention, but that business tempted him to commit this theft. After this he became assistant to a certain doctor from amongst the quacks, so as not to be quite destitute of a livelihood; and in this capacity he made his attack upon the obscurer households and on the most abject of mankind. Wealth came gradually from his plots against a certain Armenius, who being a foreigner was easily cheated, and, having been induced to make him his physician, had advanced him frequent sums of money; and he began to think that serving under others was beneath him, and wanted to be styled a physician himself. Henceforth, therefore, he attended medical congresses, and consorting with the wrangling controversialists there became one of the ranters, and, just as the scales were turning, always adding his own weight to the argument, he got to be in no small request with those who would buy a brazen voice for their party contests. But although his bread became thereby well buttered he thought he ought not to remain in such a profession; so he gradually gave up the medical, after the tinkering. Arius, the enemy of God, had already sown those wicked tares which bore the Anomœans as their fruit, and the schools of medicine resounded then with the disputes about that question. Accordingly Aetius studied the controversy, and, having laid a train of syllogisms from what he remembered of Aristotle, he became notorious for even going beyond Arius, the father of the heresy, in the novel character of his speculations; or rather he perceived the consequences of all that Arius had advanced, and so got this character of a shrewd discoverer of truths not obvious; revealing as he did that the Created,

---

[7] This can be no other than the district Chammanene, on the east bank of the Halys, where Galatia and Cappadocia join.

even from things non-existent, was *unlike* the Creator who drew Him out of nothing.

With such propositions he tickled ears that itched for these novelties; and the Ethiopian Theophilus [8] becomes acquainted with them. Aetius had already been connected with this man on some business of Gallus; and now by his help creeps into the palace. After Gallus [9] had perpetrated the tragedy with regard to Domitian the procurator and Montius, all the other participators in it naturally shared his ruin; yet this man escapes, being acquitted from being punished along with them. After this, when the great Athanasius had been driven by Imperial command from the Church of Alexandria, and George the Tarbasthenite was tearing his flock, another change takes place, and Aetius is an Alexandrian, receiving his full share amongst those who fattened at the Cappadocian's board; for he had not omitted to practice his flatteries on George. George was in fact from Chanaan himself, and therefore felt kindly towards a countryman: indeed he had been for long so possessed with his perverted opinions as actually to dote upon him, and was prone to become a godsend for Aetius, whenever he liked.

All this did not escape the notice of his sincere admirer, our Eunomius. This latter perceived that his natural father—an excellent man, except that he had such a son—led a very honest and respectable life certainly, but one of laborious penury and full of countless toils. (He was one of those farmers who are always bent over the plough, and spend a world of trouble over their little farm; and in the winter, when he was secured from agricultural work, he used to carve out neatly the letters of the alphabet for boys to form syllables with, winning his bread with the money these sold for.) Seeing all this in his father's life, he said goodbye to the plough and the mattock and all the paternal instruments, intending never to drudge himself like that; then he sets himself to learn Prunicus' skill [10] of

short-hand writing, and having perfected himself in that he entered at first, I believe, the house of one of his own family, receiving his board for his services in writing; then, while tutoring the boys of his host, he rises to the ambition of becoming an orator. I pass over the next interval, both as to his life in his native country and as to the things and the company in which he was discovered at Constantinople.

Busied as he was after this 'about the cloke and the purse,' he saw it was all of little avail, and that nothing which he could amass by such work was adequate to the demands of his ambition. Accordingly he threw up all other practices, and devoted himself solely to the admiration of Aetius; not, perhaps, without some calculation that this absorbing pursuit which he selected might further his own devices for living. In fact, from the moment he asked for a share in a wisdom so profound, he toiled not thenceforward, neither did he spin; for he is certainly clever in what he takes in hand, and knows how to gain the more emotional portion of mankind. Seeing that human nature, as a rule, falls an easy prey to pleasure, and that its natural inclination in the direction of this weakness is very strong, descending from the sterner heights of conduct to the smooth level of comfort, he becomes with a view of making the largest number possible of proselytes to his pernicious opinions very pleasant indeed to those whom he is initiating; he gets rid of the toilsome steep of virtue altogether, because it is not a persuasive to accept his secrets. But should any one have the leisure to inquire what this secret teaching of theirs is, and what those who have been duped to accept this blighting curse utter without any reserve, and what in the mysterious ritual of initiation they are taught by the reverend hierophant, the manner of baptisms [1], and the 'helps of nature,' and all that, let him question those who feel no compunction in letting indecencies pass their lips; we shall keep silent. For not even though we are the accusers should we be guiltless in mentioning such things, and we have been taught to reverence purity in word as well as deed, and not to soil our pages with equivocal stories, even though there be truth in what we say.

But we mention what we then heard (namely that, just as Aristotle's evil skill supplied

---

[8] Probably the 'Indian' Theophilus, who afterwards helped to organize the Anomœan schism in the reign of Jovian.

[9] Gallus, Cæsar 350—354, brother of Julian, not a little influenced by Aetius, executed by Constantius at Flanon in Dalmatia. During his short reign at Antioch, Domitian, who was sent to bring him to Italy, and his quæstor Montius were dragged to death through the streets by the guards of the young Cæsar.

[10] The same phrase occurs again: Refutation of Eunomius' Second Essay, p. 844: οἱ τῇ προυνίκου σοφίᾳ ἐγγυμνασθέντες· ἐξ ἐκείνης γὰρ δοκεῖ μοι τῆς παρασκευῆς τὰ εἰρημένα προενηνοχέναι· In the last word there is evidently a pun on προυνίκου; προφερής, in the secondary sense of 'precocious,' is used by Iamblichus and Porphyry, and προύνικος appears to have had the same meaning. We might venture, therefore, to translate *that* knowing trick' of short-hand: but why Prunicus is personified, if it *is* personified, as in the Gnostic Prunicos Sophia, does not appear. See Epiphanius Hæres. 253 for the feminine Proper name.

The other possible explanation is that given in the margin of the Paris Edition, and is based on Suidas, i.e. Prunici sunt cursores celeres; hic pro *celer scriba*. Hesychius also says of the word; οἱ μισθοῦ κομίζοντες τὰ ὤνια ἀπὸ τῆς ἀγορᾶς, οὕς τινες παιδαριωνας καλοῦσιν, δρομεῖς, τραχεῖς, ὀξεῖς, εὐκίνητοι, γοργοί, μισθωτοί.

Here such 'porter's' skill, easy going and superficial, is opposed to the more laborious task of tilling the soil.

[1] For the baptisms of Eunomius, compare Epiphanius Hær. 765. Even Arians who were not Anomœans he rebaptized. The 'helps of nature' may possibly refer to the 'miracles' which Philostorgius ascribes both to Aetius and Eunomius.

Sozomen (vi. 26) says, "Eunomius introduced, *it is said*, a mode of discipline contrary to that of the Church, and endeavoured to disguise the innovation under the cloak of a grave and severe deportment." . . . His followers "do not applaud a virtuous course of life . . . so much as skill in disputation, and the power of triumphing in debates."

Aetius with his impiety, so the simplicity of his dupes secured a fat living for the well-trained pupil as well as for the master) for the purpose of asking some questions. What after all was the great damage done him by Basil on the Euxine, or by Eustathius in Armenia, to both of whom that long digression in his story harks back? How did they mar the aim of his life? Did they not rather feed up his and his companion's freshly acquired fame? Whence came their wide notoriety, if not through the instrumentality of these men, supposing, that is, that their accuser is speaking the truth? For the fact that men, themselves illustrious, as our writer owns, deigned to fight with those who had as yet found no means of being known naturally gave the actual start to the ambitious thoughts of those who were to be pitted against these reputed heroes; and a veil was thereby thrown over their humble antecedents. They in fact owed their subsequent notoriety to this,—a thing detestable indeed to a reflecting mind which would never choose to rest fame upon an evil deed, but the acme of bliss to characters such as these. They tell of one in the province of Asia, amongst the obscurest and the basest, who longed to make a name in Ephesus; some great and brilliant achievement being quite beyond his powers never even entered his mind; and yet, by hitting upon that which would most deeply injure the Ephesians, he made his mark deeper than the heroes of the grandest actions; for there was amongst their public buildings one noticeable for its peculiar magnificence and costliness; and he burnt this vast structure to the ground, showing, when men came to inquire after the perpetration of this villany into its mental causes, that he dearly prized notoriety, and had devised that the greatness of the disaster should secure the name of its author being recorded with it. The secret motive[2] of these two men is the same thirst for publicity; the only difference is that the amount of mischief is greater in their case. They are marring, not lifeless architecture, but the living building of the Church, introducing, for fire, the slow canker of their teaching. But I will defer the doctrinal question till the proper time comes.

§ 7. *Eunomius himself proves that the confession of faith which He made was not impeached.*

Let us see for a moment now what kind of truth is dealt with by this man, who in his Introduction complains that it is because of his telling the truth that he is hated by the unbelievers; we may well make the way he

handles truth outside doctrine teach us a test to apply to his doctrine itself. " He that is faithful in that which is least is faithful also in much, and he that is unjust in the least is unjust also in much." Now, when he is beginning to write this "apology for the apology " (that is the new and startling title, as well as subject, of his book) he says that we must look for the cause of this very startling announcement nowhere else but in him who answered that first treatise of his. That book was entitled an Apology; but being given to understand by our master-theologian that an apology can only come from those who have been accused of something, and that if a man writes merely from his own inclination his production is something else than an apology, he does not deny—it would be too manifestly absurd—[3] that an apology requires a preceding accusation; but he declares that his 'apology' has cleared him from very serious accusations in the trial which has been instituted against him. How false this is, is manifest from his own words. He complained that "many heavy sufferings were inflicted on him by those who had condemned him "; we may read that in his book.

But how could he have suffered so, if his 'apology' cleared him of these charges? If he successfully adopted an apology to escape from these, that pathetic complaint of his is a hypocritical pretence; if on the other hand he really suffered as he says, then, plainly, he suffered because he did *not* clear himself by an apology; for every apology, to be such, has to secure this end, namely, to prevent the voting power from being misled by any false statements. Surely he will not now attempt to say that at the time of the trial he produced his apology, but not being able to win over the jury lost the case to the prosecution. For he said nothing at the time of the trial 'about producing his apology;' nor was it likely that he would, considering that he distinctly states in his book that he refused to have anything to do with those ill-affected and hostile dicasts. " We own," he says, "that we were condemned by default: there was a packed [4] panel of evil-disposed persons where a jury ought to have sat." He is very labored here, and has his attention diverted by his argument, I think, or he would have noticed that he has tacked on a fine solecism to his sentence. He affects to be imposingly Attic with his phrase 'packed panel;' but the correct in language use these words, as those familiar with the forensic

---

[3] The μὴ is redundant and owing to οὐκ.

[4] Εἰσφρησάντων. A word used in Aristophanes of ' letting into court,' probably a technical word: it is a manifest derivation from εἰσφορεῖν. What the solecism is, is not clear; Gretser thinks that Eunomius meant it for εἰσπηδᾶν.

vocabulary know, quite differently to our new Atticist.

A little further on he adds this; " If he thinks that, because I would have nothing ·to do with a jury who were really my prosecutors he can argue away my apology, he must be blind to his own simplicity." When, then, and before whom did our caustic friend make his apology? He had demurred to the jury because they were ' foes,' and he did not utter one word about any trial, as he himself insists. See how this strenuous champion of the true, little by little, passes over to the side of the false, and, while honouring truth in phrase, combats it in deed. But it is amusing to see how weak he is even in seconding his own lie. How can one and the same man have ' cleared himself by an apology in the trial which was instituted against him,' and then have ' prudently kept silence because the court was in the hands of the foe?' Nay, the very language he uses in the preface to his Apology clearly shows that no court at all was opened against him. For he does not address his preface to any definite jury, but to certain unspecified persons who were living then, or who were afterwards to come into the world; and I grant that to such an audience there was need of a very vigorous apology, not indeed in the manner of the one he has actually written, which requires another still to bolster it up, but a broadly intelligible one[5], able to prove this special point, viz., that he was not in the possession of his usual reason when he wrote this, wherein he rings[6] the assembly-bell for men who never came, perhaps never existed, and speaks an apology before an imaginary court, and begs an imperceptible jury not to let numbers decide between truth and falsehood, nor to assign the victory to mere quantity. Verily it is becoming that he should make an apology of that sort to jurymen who are yet in the loins of their fathers, and to explain to them how he came to think it right to adopt opinions which contradict universal belief, and to put more faith in his own mistaken fancies than in those who throughout the world glorify Christ's name.

Let him write, please, another apology in addition to this second; for this one is not a correction of mistakes made about him, but rather a proof of the truth of those charges. Every one knows that a proper apology aims at disproving a charge; thus a man who is accused of theft or murder or any other crime either denies the fact altogether, or transfers the blame to another party, or else, if neither of these is possible, he appeals to the charity or to the compassion of those who are to vote upon his sentence. But in his book he neither denies the charge, nor shifts it on some one else, nor has recourse to an appeal for mercy, nor promises amendment for the future; but he establishes the charge against him by an unusually labored demonstration. This charge, as he himself confesses, really amounted to an indictment for profanity, nor did it leave the nature of this undefined, but proclaimed the particular kind; whereas his apology proves this species of profanity to be a positive duty, and instead of removing the charge strengthens it. Now, if the tenets of our Faith had been left in any obscurity, it might have been less hazardous to attempt novelties; but the teaching of our master-theologian is now firmly fixed in the souls of the faithful; and so it is a question whether the man who shouts out contradictions of that about which all equally have made up their minds is defending himself against the charges made, or is not rather drawing down upon him the anger of his hearers, and making his accusers still more bitter. I incline·to think the latter. So that if there are, as our writer tells us, both hearers of his apology and accusers of his attempts upon the Faith, let him tell us, how those accusers can possibly compromise[7] the matter now, or what sort of verdict that jury must return, now that his offence has been already proved by his own 'apology.'

§ 8. *Facts show that the terms of abuse which he has employed against Basil are more suitable for himself.*

But these remarks are by the way, and come from our not keeping close to our argument. We had to inquire not how he ought to have made his apology, but whether he had ever made one at all. But now let us return to our former position, viz., that he is convicted by his own statements. This hater of falsehood first of all tells us that he was condemned because the jury which was assigned him defied the law, and that he was driven over sea and land and suffered much from the burning sun and the dust. Then in trying to conceal his falsehood he drives out one nail with another nail, as the proverb says, and puts one falsehood right by cancelling it with another. As every one knows as well as he does that he never uttered one word in court, he declares that he begged to be let off coming into a hostile court and was condemned by default. Could there

---

5 γενικῆς.　　6 συνεκρότει. The word has this meaning in Origen. In Philo (*de Vitâ Mosis*, p. 476, l. 48, quoted by Viger.), it has another meaning, συνεκρότουν ἄλλος ἄλλον, μὴ ἀποκάμνειν, i.e. ' cheered.'

7 καθυφήσουσιν. This is the reading of the Venetian MS. The word bears the same forensic sense as the Latin prævaricari. The common reading is καθυβρίσουσιν.

be a plainer case than this of a man contradicting both the truth and himself? When he is pressed about the title of his book, he makes his trial the constraining cause of this 'apology;' but when he is pressed with the fact that he spoke not one word to the jury, he denies that there was any trial and says that he declined[8] such a jury. See how valiantly this doughty champion of the truth fights against falsehood! Then he dares to call our mighty Basil 'a malicious rascal and a liar;' and besides that, 'a bold ignorant parvenu[9],' 'no deep divine,' and he adds to his list of abusive terms, 'stark mad,' scattering an infinity of such words over his pages, as if he imagined that his own bitter invectives could outweigh the common testimony of mankind, who revere that great name as though he were one of the saints of old. He thinks in fact that he, if no one else, can touch with calumny one whom calumny has never touched; but the sun is not so low in the heavens that any one can reach him with stones or any other missiles; they will but recoil upon him who shot them, while the intended target soars far beyond his reach. If any one, again, accuses the sun of want of light, he has not dimmed the brightness of the sunbeams with his scoffs; the sun will still remain the sun, and the fault-finder will only prove the feebleness of his own visual organs; and, if he should endeavour, after the fashion of this 'apology,' to persuade all whom he meets and will listen to him not to give in to the common opinions about the sun, nor to attach more weight to the experiences of all than to the surmises of one individual by 'assigning victory to mere quantity,' his nonsense will be wasted on those who can use their eyes.

Let some one then persuade Eunomius to bridle his tongue, and not give the rein to such wild talk, nor kick against the pricks in the insolent abuse of an honoured name; but to allow the mere remembrance of Basil to fill his soul with reverence and awe. What can he gain by this unmeasured ribaldry, when the object of it will retain all that character which his life, his words, and the general estimate of the civilized world proclaims him to have possessed? The man who takes in hand to revile reveals his own disposition as not being able, because it is evil, to speak good things, but only "to speak from the abundance of the heart," and to bring forth from that evil treasure-house. Now, that his expressions are merely those of abuse quite divorced from actual facts, can be proved from his own writings.

§ 9. *In charging Basil with not defending his faith at the time of the 'Trials,' he lays himself open to the same charge.*

He hints at a certain locality where this trial for heresy took place; but he gives us no certain indication where it was, and the reader is obliged to guess in the dark. Thither, he tells us, a congress of picked representatives from all quarters was summoned; and he is at his best here, placing before our eyes with some vigorous strokes the preparation of the event which he pretends took place. Then, he says, a trial in which he would have had to run for his very life was put into the hands of certain arbitrators, to whom our Teacher and Master who was present gave his charge[1]; and as all the voting power was thus won over to the enemies' side, he yielded the position[2], fled from the place, and hunted everywhere for some hearth and home; and he is great, in this graphic sketch[3], in arraigning the cowardice of our hero; as any one who likes may see by looking at what he has written. But I cannot stop to give specimens here of the bitter gall of his utterances; I must pass on to that, for the sake of which I mentioned all this.

Where, then, was that unnamed spot in which this examination of his teachings was to take place? What was this occasion when the best men were collected for a trial? Who were these men who hurried over land and sea to share in these labours? What was this 'expectant world that hung upon the issue of the voting?' Who was 'the arranger of the trial?' However, let us consider that he invented all that to swell out the importance of his story, as boys at school are apt to do in *their* fictitious conversations of this kind; and let him only tell us who that 'terrible combatant' was whom our Master shrunk from encountering If this also is a fiction, let him be the winner again, and have the advantage of his vain words. We will say nothing: in the useless fight with shadows the real victory is to decline conquering in *that*. But if he speaks of the events at Constantinople and means the assembly there, and is in this fever of literary indignation at tragedies enacted there, and means himself by that great and redoubtable athlete, then we would display the reasons why, though present on the occasion, we did not plunge into the fight.

---

8 ἀπαξιοῖ.
9 παρέγγραπτον: for the vox nihili παράγραπτον. Oehler again has adopted the reading of the Ven. MS.

1 ὑποφωνεῖν.
2 Sozomen (vi. 26): "After his (Eunomius) elevation to the bishopric of Cyzicus he was accused by his own clergy of introducing innovations. Eudoxius obliged him to undergo a public trial and give an account of his doctrines to the people: finding, however, no fault in him, Eudoxius exhorted him to return to Cyzicus. He replied he could not remain with people who regarded him with suspicion, and it is said seized this opportunity to secede from communion."
3 ὑπογραφῇ; or else 'on the subject of Basil's charge.'

Now let this man who upbraids that hero with his cowardice tell us whether *he* went down into the thick of the fray, whether *he* uttered one syllable in defence of his own orthodoxy, whether *he* made any vigorous peroration, whether *he* victoriously grappled with the foe? He cannot tell us that, or he manifestly contradicts himself, for he owns that by his default he received the adverse verdict. If it was a duty to speak at the actual time of the trial (for that is the law which he lays down for us in his book), then why was he then condemned by default? If on the other hand he did well in observing silence before such dicasts, how arbitrarily [4] he praises himself, but blames us, for silence at such a time! What can be more absurdly unjust than this! When two treatises have been put forth since the time of the trial, he declares that his apology, though written so very long after, was in time, but reviles that which answered his own as quite too late! Surely he ought to have abused Basil's intended counter-statement before it was actually made; but this is not found amongst his other complaints. Knowing as he did what Basil was going to write when the time of the trial had passed away, why in the world did he not find fault with it there and then? In fact it is clear from his own confession that he never made that apology in the trial itself. I will repeat again his words:—'We confess that we were condemned by default;' and he adds why; 'Evil-disposed persons had been passed as jurymen,' or rather, to use his own phrase, 'there was a packed panel of them where a jury ought to have sat.' Whereas, on the other hand, it is clear from another passage in his book that he attests that his apology was made 'at the proper time.' It runs thus:— "That I was urged to make this apology at the proper time and in the proper manner from no pretended reasons, but compelled to do so on behalf of those who went security for me, is clear from facts and also from this man's words." He adroitly twists his words round to meet every possible objection; but what will he say to this? 'It was not right to keep silent during the trial.' Then why was Eunomius speechless during that same trial? And why is his apology, coming as it did after the trial, in good time? And if in good time, why is Basil's controversy with him not in good time?

But the remark of that holy father is especially true, that Eunomius in pretending to make an apology really gave his teaching the support he wished to give it; and that genuine emulator of Phineas' zeal, destroying as he does with the sword of the Word every spiritual fornicator, dealt in the 'Answer to his blasphemy' a sword-thrust that was calculated at once to heal a soul and to destroy a heresy. If he resists that stroke, and with a soul deadened by apostacy will not admit the cure, the blame rests with him who chooses the evil, as the Gentile proverb says. So far for Eunomius' treatment of truth, and of us: and now the law of former times, which allows an equal return on those who are the first to injure, might prompt us to discharge on him a counter-shower of abuse, and, as he is a very easy subject for this, to be very liberal of it, so as to outdo the pain which he has inflicted: for if he was so rich in insolent invective against one who gave no chance for calumny, how many of such epithets might we not expect to find for those who have satirized that saintly life? But we have been taught from the first by that scholar of the Truth to be scholars of the Gospel ourselves, and therefore we will not take an eye for an eye, nor a tooth for a tooth; we know well that all the evil that happens admits of being annihilated by its opposite, and that no bad word and no bad deed would ever develope into such desperate wickedness, if one good one could only be got in to break the continuity of the vicious stream. Therefore the routine of insolence and abusiveness is checked from repeating itself by long-suffering: whereas if insolence is met with insolence and abuse with abuse, you will but feed with itself this monster-vice, and increase it vastly.

§ 10. *All his insulting epithets are shewn by facts to be false.*

I therefore pass over everything else, as mere insolent mockery and scoffing abuse, and hasten to the question of his doctrine. Should any one say that I decline to be abusive only because I cannot pay him back in his own coin, let such an one consider in his own case what proneness there is to evil generally, what a mechanical sliding into sin, dispensing with the need of any practice. The power of becoming bad resides in the will; one act of wishing is often the sufficient occasion for a finished wickedness; and this ease of operation is more especially fatal in the sins of the tongue. Other classes of sins require time and occasion and co-operation to be committed; but the propensity to speak can sin when it likes. The treatise of Eunomius now in our hands is sufficient to prove this; one who attentively considers it will perceive the rapidity of the descent into sins

---

[4] τίς ἡ ἀποκλήρωσις: this is a favourite word with Origen and Gregory.

in the matter of phrases: and it is the easiest thing in the world to imitate these, even though one is quite unpractised in habitual defamation. What need would there be to labour in coining our intended insults into names, when one might employ upon this slanderer his own phrases? He has strung together, in fact, in this part of his work, every sort of falsehood and evil-speaking, all moulded from the models which he finds in himself; every extravagance is to be found in writing these. He writes " cunning," " wrangling," "foe to truth," "high-flown ⁵," "charlatan," " combating general opinion and tradition," "braving facts which give him the lie," " careless of the terrors of the law, of the censure of men," " unable to distinguish the enthusiasm for truth from mere skill in reasoning;" he adds, "wanting in reverence," "quick to call names," and then "blatant," "full of conflicting suspicions," " combining irreconcileable arguments," " combating his own utterances," " affirming contradictories;" then, though eager to speak all ill of him, not being able to find other novelties of invective in which to indulge his bitterness, often in default of all else he reiterates the same phrases, and comes round again a third and a fourth time and even more to what he has once said; and in this circus of words he drives up and then turns down, over and over again, the same racecourse of insolent abuse; so that at last even anger at this shameless display dies away from very weariness. These low unlovely street-boys' jeers do indeed provoke disgust rather than anger; they are not a whit better than the inarticulate grunting of some old woman who is quite drunk.

Must we then enter minutely into this, and laboriously refute all his invectives by showing that Basil was not this monster of his imagination? If we did this, contentedly proving the absence of anything vile and criminal in him, we should seem to join in insulting one who was a 'bright particular star' to his generation. But I remember how with that divine voice of his he quoted the prophet [6] with regard to him, comparing him to a shameless woman who casts her own reproaches on the chaste. For whom do these reasonings of his proclaim to be truth's enemy and in arms against public opinion? Who is it who begs the readers of his book not 'to look to the numbers of those who profess a belief, or to mere tradition, or to let their judgment be biassed so as to consider as trustworthy what is only suspected to be the stronger side?' Can one and the same man write like this, and then make those charges, scheming that his readers should follow his own novelties at the very moment that he is abusing others for opposing themselves to the general belief? As for 'brazening out facts which give him the lie, and men's censure,' I leave the reader to judge to whom this applies; whether to one who by a most careful self-restraint made sobriety and quietness and perfect purity the rule of his own life as well as that of his entourage, or to one who advised that nature should not be molested when it is her pleasure to advance through the appetites of the body, not to thwart indulgence, nor to be so particular as that in the training of our life; but that a self-chosen faith should be considered sufficient for a man to attain perfection. If he denies that this is his teaching, I and any right-minded person would rejoice if he were telling the truth in such a denial. But his genuine followers will not allow him to produce such a denial, or their leading principles would be gone, and the platform of those who for this reason embrace his tenets would fall to pieces. As for shameless indifference to human censure, you may look at his youth or his after life, and you would find him in both open to this reproach. The two men's lives, whether in youth or manhood, tell a widely-different tale.

Let our speech-writer, while he reminds himself of his youthful doings in his native land, and afterwards at Constantinople, hear from those who can tell him what they know of the man whom he slanders. But if any would inquire into their subsequent occupations, let such a person tell us which of the two he considers to deserve so high a reputation; the man who ungrudgingly spent upon the poor his patrimony even before he was a priest, and most of all in the time of the famine, during which he was a ruler of the Church, though still a priest in the rank of presbyters [7]; and afterwards did not hoard even what remained to him, so that he too might have made the Apostles' boast, 'Neither did we eat any man's bread for nought [8]:' or, on the other hand, the man who has made the championship of a tenet a source of income, the man who creeps into houses, and does not conceal his loathsome affliction by staying at home, nor considers the natural aversion which those in good health must feel for such, though according to the law of old he is one of those who are banished from the inhabited camp because of the contagion of his unmistakeable [9] disease.

---

⁵ σοφιστης.

6 Jeremiah iii. 3.

7 ἔτι ἐν ᾧ κλήρῳ τῶν πρεσβυτέρων ἱερατεύων.
8 2 Thess. iii. 8.
9 According to Ruffinus (Hist. Eccl. x. 25), his constitution was poisoned with jaundice within and without

GREGORY OF NYSSA

Basil is called 'hasty' and 'insolent,' and in both characters 'a liar' by this man who 'would in patience and meekness educate those of a contrary opinion to himself;' for such are the airs he gives himself when he speaks of him, while he omits no hyperbole of bitter language, when he has a sufficient opening to produce it. On what grounds, then, does he charge him with this hastiness and insolence? Because 'he called me a Galatian, though I am a Cappadocian;' then it was because he called a man who lived on the boundary in a.n obscure corner like Corniaspine[1] a Galatian instead of an Oltiserian; supposing, that is, that it is proved that he said this. I have not found it in my copies; but grant it. For this he is to be called 'hasty,' 'insolent,' all that is bad. But the wise know well that the minute charges of a faultfinder furnish a strong argument for the righteousness of the accused; else, when eager to accuse, he would not have spared great faults and employed his malice on little ones. On these last he is certainly great, heightening the enormity of the offence, and making solemn reflections on falsehood, and seeing equal heinousness in it whether in great or very trivial matters. Like the fathers of his heresy, the scribes and Pharisees, he knows how to strain a gnat carefully and to swallow at one gulp the hump-backed camel laden with a weight of wickedness. But it would not be out of place to say to him, 'refrain from making such a rule in our system; cease to bid us think it of no account to measure the guilt of a falsehood by the slightness or the importance of the circumstances.' Paul telling a falsehood and purifying himself after the manner of the Jews to meet the needs of those whom he usefully deceived did not sin the same as Judas for the requirement of his treachery putting on a kind and affable look. By a falsehood Joseph in love to his brethren deceived them; and that too while swearing 'by the life of Pharaoh[2];' but his brethren had really lied to him, in their envy plotting his death and then his enslavement. There are many such cases: Sarah lied, because she was ashamed of laughing: the serpent lied, tempting man to disobey and change to a divine existence. Falsehoods differ widely according to their motives. Accordingly we accept that general statement about man which the Holy Spirit uttered by the Prophet[3], 'Every man is a liar;' and this man of God, too, has not kept clear of falsehood, having chanced to give a place the name of a neighbouring district, through oversight or ignorance of its real name. But Eunomius also has told a falsehood, and what is it? Nothing less than a misstatement of Truth itself. He asserts that One who always is once was not; he demonstrates that One who is truly a Son is falsely so called; he defines the Creator to be a creature and a work; the Lord of the world he calls a servant, and ranges the Being who essentially rules with subject beings. Is the difference between falsehoods so very trifling, that one can think it matters nothing whether the falsehood is palpable[4] in this way or in that?

§ 11. *The sophistry which he employs to prove our acknowledgment that he had been tried, and that the confession of his faith had not been unimpeached, is feeble.*

He objects to sophistries in others; see the sort of care he takes himself that his proofs shall be real ones. Our Master said, in the book which he addressed to him, that at the time when our cause was ruined, Eunomius won Cyzicus as the prize of his blasphemy. What then does this detector of sophistry do? He fastens at once on that word *prize*, and declares that we on our side confess that he made an apology, that he won thereby, that he gained the prize of victory by these efforts; and he frames his argument into a syllogism consisting as he thinks of unanswerable propositions. But we will quote word for word what he has written. 'If a prize is the recognition and the crown of victory, and a trial implies a victory, and, as also inseparable from itself, an accusation, then that man who grants (in argument) the prize must necessarily allow that there was a defence.' What then is our answer to that? We do not deny that he fought this wretched battle of impiety with a most vigorous energy, and that he went a very long distance beyond his fellows in these perspiring efforts against the truth; but we will not allow that he obtained the victory over his opponents; but only that as compared with those who were running the same as himself through heresy into error he was foremost in the number of his lies and so gained the prize of Cyzicus in return for high attainments in evil, beating all who for the same prize combated the Truth; and that for this victory of blasphemy his name was blazoned loud and clear when

---

[1] ἐν ἀνωνύμῳ τινι Κορνιασπινῆς ἐσχατίᾳ. Cf. μεγὰ χρῆμα ὑὸς (Herod.) for the use of this genitive. In the next sentence εἰ ἀντι, though it gives the sense translated in the text, is not so good as ἢ ἀντὶ (i.e. ἐσχατία), which Oehler suggests, but does not adopt.
With regard to Eunomius' birthplace, Sozomen and Philostorgius give Dacora (which the former describes as on the slopes of Mt Argæus: but that it must have been on the borders of Galatia and Cappadocia is certain from what Gregory says here): 'Probably Dacora was his paternal estate: Oltiseris the village to which it belonged' (Dict. Christ. Biog.; unless indeed Corniaspa, marked on the maps as a town where Cappadocia, Galatia and Pontus join, was the spot, and Oltiseris the district. Eunomius died at Dacora. [2] Gen. xlii. 15.

[3] Psalm cxv. 11. [4] ἐψεῦσθαι δοκεῖν.

Cyzicus was selected for him by the umpires of his party as the reward of his extravagance, This is the statement of our opinion, and this we allowed; our contention now that Cyzicus was the prize of a heresy, not the successful result of a defence, shews it. Is this anything like his own mess of childish sophistries, so that he can thereby hope to have grounds for proving the fact of his trial and his defence? His method is like that of a man in a drinking bout, who has made away with more strong liquor than the rest, and having then claimed the pool from his fellow-drunkards should attempt to make this victory a proof of having won some case in the law courts. That man might chop the same sort of logic. 'If a prize is the recognition and the crown of victory, and a law-trial implies a victory and, as also inseparable from itself, an accusation, then I have won my suit, since I have been crowned for my powers of drinking in this bout.'

One would certainly answer to such a boaster that a trial in court is a very different thing from a wine-contest, and that one who wins with the glass has thereby no advantage over his legal adversaries, though he get a beautiful chaplet of flowers. No more, therefore, has the man who has beaten his equals in the advocacy of profanity anything to show in having won the prize for that, that he has won a verdict too. The testimony on our side that he is first in profanity is no plea for his imaginary 'apology.' If he did speak it before the court, and, having so prevailed over his adversaries, was honoured with Cyzicus for that, then he might have some occasion for using our own words against ourselves; but as he is continually protesting in his book that he yielded to the animus of the voters, and accepted in silence the penalty which they inflicted, not even waiting for this hostile decision, why does he impose upon himself and make this word *prize* into the proof of a successful apology? Our excellent friend fails to understand the force of this word *prize;* Cyzicus was given up to him as the reward of merit for his extravagant impiety; and as it was his will to receive such a prize, and he views it in the light of a victor's guerdon, let him receive as well what that victory implies, viz. the lion's share in the guilt of profanity. If he insists on our own words against ourselves, he must accept both these consequences, or neither.

§ 12. *His charge of cowardice is baseless: for Basil displayed the highest courage before the Emperor and his Lord-Lieutenants.*

He treats our words so; and in the rest of his presumptuous statements can there be

shown to be a particle of truth? In these he calls him 'cowardly,' 'spiritless,' 'a shirker of severer labours,' exhausting the list of such terms, and giving with laboured circumstantiality every symptom of this cowardice: 'the retired cabin, the door firmly closed, the anxious fear of intruders, the voice, the look, the tell-tale change of countenance,' everything of that sort, whereby the passion of fear is shown. If he were detected in no other lie but this, it alone would be sufficient to reveal his bent. For who does not know how, during the time when the Emperor Valens was roused against the churches of the Lord, that mighty champion of ours rose by his lofty spirit superior to those overwhelming circumstances and the terrors of the foe, and showed a mind which soared above every means devised to daunt him? Who of the dwellers in the East, and of the furthest regions of our civilized world did not hear of his combat with the throne itself for the truth? Who, looking to his antagonist, was not in dismay? For his was no common antagonist, possessed only of the power of winning in sophistic juggles, where victory is no glory and defeat is harmless; but he had the power of bending the whole Roman government to his will; and, added to this pride of empire, he had prejudices against our faith, cunningly instilled into his mind by Eudoxius [5] of Germanicia [6], who had won him to his side; and he found in all those who were then at the head of affairs allies in carrying out his designs, some being already inclined to them from mental sympathies, while others, and they were the majority, were ready from fear to indulge the imperial pleasure, and seeing the severity employed against those who held to the Faith were ostentatious in their zeal for him. It was a time of exile, confiscation, banishment, threats of fines, danger of life, arrests, imprisonment, scourging; nothing was too dreadful to put in force against those who would not yield to this sudden caprice of the Emperor; it was worse for the faithful to be caught in God's house than if they had been detected in the most heinous of crimes.

But a detailed history of that time would be too long; and would require a separate treatment; besides, as the sufferings at that sad season are known to all, nothing would be gained for our present purpose by carefully setting them forth in writing. A second drawback to such an attempt would be found to be that amidst the details of that melancholy history we should be forced to make mention

---

5 Afterwards of Antioch, and then 8th Bishop of Constantinople (360—370), one of the most influential of all the Arians. He it was who procured for Eunomius the bishopric of Cyzicus (359). (The latter must indeed have concealed his views on that occasion, for Constantius hated the Anomœans).   6 A town of Commagene.

of ourselves; and if we did anything in those struggles for our religion that redounds to our honour in the telling, Wisdom commands us to leave it to others to tell. "Let another man praise thee, and not thine own mouth [6];" and it is this very thing that our omniscient friend has not been conscious of in devoting the larger half of his book to self-glorification.

Omitting, then, all that kind of detail, I will be careful only in setting forth the achievement of our Master. The adversary whom he had to combat was no less a person than the Emperor himself; that adversary's second was the man who stood next him in the government; his assistants to work out his will were the court. Let us take into consideration also the point of time, in order to test and to illustrate the fortitude of our own noble champion. When was it? The Emperor was proceeding from Constantinople to the East, elated by his recent successes against the barbarians, and not in a spirit to brook any obstruction to his will; and his lord-lieutenant directed his route, postponing all administration of the necessary affairs of state as long as a home remained to one adherent of the Faith, and until every one, no matter where, was ejected, and others, chosen by himself to outrage our godly hierarchy, were introduced instead. The Powers then of the Propontis were moving in such a fury, like some dark cloud, upon the churches; Bithynia was completely devastated; Galatia was very quickly carried away by their stream; all in the intervening districts had succeeded with them; and now our fold lay the next to be attacked. What did our mighty Basil show like then, 'that spiritless coward,' as Eunomius calls him, 'shrinking from danger, and trusting to a retired cabin to save him?' Did he quail at this evil onset? Did he allow the sufferings of previous victims to suggest to him that he should secure his own safety? Did he listen to any who advised a slight yielding to this rush of evils [7], so as not to throw himself openly in the path of men who were now veterans in slaughter? Rather we find that all excess of language, all height of thought and word, falls short of the truth about him. None could describe his contempt of danger, so as to bring before the reader's eyes this new combat, which one might justly say was waged not between man and man, but between a Christian's firmness and courage on the one side, and a blood-stained power on the other.

The lord-lieutenant kept appealing to the commands of the Emperor, and rendering a power, which from its enormous strength was terrible enough, more terrible still by the unsparing cruelty of its vengeance. After the tragedies which he had enacted in Bithynia, and after Galatia with characteristic fickleness had yielded without a struggle, he thought that our country would fall a ready prey to his designs. Cruel deeds were preluded by words proposing, with mingled threats and promises, royal favours and ecclesiastical power to obedience, but to resistance all that a cruel spirit which has got the power to work its will can devise. Such was the enemy.

So far was our champion from being daunted by what he saw and heard, that he acted rather like a physician or prudent councillor called in to correct something that was wrong, bidding them repent of their rashness and cease to commit murders amongst the servants of the Lord; 'their plans,' he said, 'could not succeed with men who cared only for the empire of Christ, and for the Powers that never die; with all their wish to maltreat him, they could discover nothing, whether word or act, that could pain the Christian; confiscation could not touch him whose only possession was his Faith; exile had no terrors for one who walked in every land with the same feelings, and looked on every city as strange because of the shortness of his sojourn in it, yet as home, because all human creatures are in equal bondage with himself; the endurance of blows, or tortures, or death, if it might be for the Truth, was an object of fear not even to women, but to every Christian it was the supremest bliss to suffer the worst for this their hope, and they were only grieved that nature allowed them but one death, and that they could devise no means of dying many times in this battle for the Truth [8].'

When he thus confronted their threats, and looked beyond that imposing power, as if it were all nothing, then their exasperation, just like those rapid changes on the stage when one mask after another is put on, turned with all its threats into flattery; and the very man whose spirit up to then had been so determined and formidable adopted the most gentle and submissive of language; 'Do not, I beg you, think it a small thing for our mighty emperor to have communion with your people, but be willing to be called his master too: nor thwart his wish; he wishes for this peace, if only one little word in the written Creed is erased, that of Homoousios.' Our master answers that it is of the greatest importance that the emperor

---

[6] Proverbs xxvii. 2.
[7] 'The metropolitan remained unshaken. The rough threats of Modestus succeeded no better than the fatherly counsel of Enippius.' *Gwatkin's Arians.*

[8] Other words of Basil, before Modestus at Cæsarea, are also recorded: "I cannot worship any created thing, being as I am God's creation, and having been *bidden to be a God.*"

should be a member of the Church ; that is, that he should save his soul, not as an emperor, but as a mere man ; but a diminution of or addition to the Faith was so far from his (Basil's) thoughts, that he would not change even the order of the written words. That was what this 'spiritless coward, who trembles at the creaking of a door,' said to this great ruler, and he confirmed his words by what he did ; for he stemmed in his own person this imperial torrent of ruin that was rushing on the churches, and turned it aside ; he in himself was a match for this attack, like a grand immoveable rock in the sea, breaking the huge and surging billow of that terrible onset.

Nor did his wrestling stop there ; the emperor himself succeeds to the attack, exasperated because he did not get effected in the first attempt all that he wished. Just, accordingly, as the Assyrian effected the destruction of the temple of the Israelites at Jerusalem by means of the cook Nabuzardan, so did this monarch of ours entrust his business to one Demosthenes, comptroller of his kitchen, and chief of his cooks [9], as to one more pushing than the rest, thinking thereby to succeed entirely in his design. With this man stirring the pot, and with one of the blasphemers from Illyricum, letters in hand, assembling the authorities with this end in view, and with Modestus [1] kindling passion to a greater heat than in the previous excitement, every one joined the movement of the Emperor's anger, making his fury their own, and yielding to the temper of authority ; and on the other hand all felt their hopes sink at the prospect of what might happen. That same lord-lieutenant re-enters on the scene ; intimidations worse than the former are begun ; their threats are thrown out ; their anger rises to a still higher pitch ; there is the tragic pomp of trial over again, the criers, the apparitors, the lictors, the curtained bar, things which naturally daunt even a mind which is thoroughly prepared ; and again we see God's champion amidst this combat surpassing even his former glory. If you want proofs, look at the facts. What spot, where there are churches, did not that disaster reach? What nation remained unreached by these heretical commands ? Who of the illustrious in any Church was not driven from the scene of his labours? What people escaped their despiteful treatment? It reached

all Syria, and Mesopotamia up to the frontier, Phœnicia, Palestine, Arabia, Egypt, the Libyan tribes to the boundaries of the civilized world ; and all nearer home, Pontus, Cilicia, Lycia, Lydia, Pisidia, Pamphylia, Caria, the Hellespont, the islands up to the Propontis itself ; the coasts of Thrace, as far as Thrace extends, and the bordering nations as far as the Danube. Which of these countries retained its former look, unless any were · already possessed with the evil? The people of Cappadocia alone felt not these afflictions of the Church, because our mighty champion saved them in their trial.

Such was the achievement of this 'coward' master of ours ; such was the success of one who 'shirks all sterner toil.' Surely it is not that of one who 'wins renown amongst poor old women, and practises to deceive the sex which naturally falls into every snare,' and 'thinks it a great thing to be admired by the criminal and abandoned ; ' it is that of one who has proved by deeds his soul's fortitude, and the unflinching and noble manliness of his spirit. His success has resulted in the salvation of the whole country, the peace of our Church, the pattern given to the virtuous of every excellence, the overthrow of the foe, the upholding of the Faith, the confirmation of the weaker brethren, the encouragement of the zealous, everything that is believed to belong to the victorious side ; and in the commemoration of no other events but these do hearing and seeing unite in accomplished facts ; for here it is one and the same thing to relate in words his noble deeds and to show in facts the attestation of our words, and to confirm each by the other—the record from what is before our eyes, and the facts from what is being said.

§ 13. *Résumé of his dogmatic teaching. Objections to it in detail.*

But somehow our discourse has swerved considerably from the mark ; it has had to turn round and face each of this slanderer's insults. To Eunomius indeed it is no small advantage that the discussion should linger upon such points, and that the indictment of his offences against man should delay our approach to his graver sins. But it is profitless to abuse for hastiness of speech one who is on his trial for murder ; (because the proof of the latter is sufficient to get the verdict of death passed, even though hastiness of speech is not proved along with it) ; just so it seems best to subject to proof his blasphemy only, and to leave his insults alone. When his heinousness on the most important points has been detected, his other delinquencies are proved potentially

---

9 This cook is compared to Nabuzardan by Gregory Naz. also (Orat. xliii. 47). Cf. also Theodoret, iv. 19, where most of these events are recorded. The former says that 'Nabuzardan threatened Basil when summoned before him with the μαχαίρα of his trade, but was sent back to his kitchen fire.'

1 Modestus, the Lord Lieutenant or Count of the East, had sacrificed to the images under Julian, and had been re-baptized as an Arian.

without going minutely into them. Well then ; at the head of all his argumentations stands this blasphemy against the definitions of the Faith —both in his former work and in that which we are now criticizing—and his strenuous effort to destroy and cancel and completely upset all devout conceptions as to the Only-Begotten Son of God and the Holy Spirit. To show, then, how false and inconsistent are his arguments against ·these doctrines of the truth, I will first quote word for word his whole statement, and then I will begin again and examine each portion separately. "The whole account of our doctrines is summed up thus; there is the Supreme and Absolute Being, and another Being existing by reason of the First, but after It [2] though before all others ; and a third Being not ranking with either of these, but inferior to the one, as to its cause, to the other, as to the energy which produced it : there must of course be included in this account the energies that follow each Being, and the names germane to these energies. Again, as each Being is absolutely single, and is in fact and thought one, and its energies are bounded by its works, and its works commensurate with its energies, necessarily, of course, the energies which follow these Beings are relatively greater and less, some being of a higher, some of a lower order ; in a word, their difference amounts to that existing between their works : it would in fact not be lawful to say that the same energy produced the angels or stars, and the heavens or man : but a pious mind would conclude that in proportion as some works are superior to and more honourable than others. so does one energy transcend another, because sameness of energy produces sameness of work, and difference of

work indicates difference of energy. These things being so, and maintaining an unbroken connexion in their relation to each other, it seems fitting for those who make their investigation according to the order germane to the subject, and who do not insist on mixing and confusing all together, in case of a discussion being raised about Being, to prove what is in course of demonstration, and to settle the points in debate, by the primary energies and those attached to the Beings, and again to explain by the Beings when the energies are in question, yet still to consider the passage from the first to the second the more suitable and in all respects the more efficacious of the two."

Such is his blasphemy systematized ! May the Very God, Son of the Very God, by the leading of the Holy Spirit, direct our discussion to the truth ! We will repeat his statements one by one. He asserts that the "whole account of his doctrines is summed up in the Supreme and Absolute Being, and in another Being existing by reason of the First, but after It though before all others, and in a third Being not ranking with either of these but inferior to the one as to its cause, to the other as to the energy " The first point, then, of the unfair dealings in this statement to be noticed is that in professing to expound the mystery of the Faith, he corrects as it were the expressions in the Gospel, and will not make use of the words by which our Lord in perfecting our faith conveyed that mystery to us : he suppresses the names of 'Father, Son and Holy Ghost,' and speaks of a 'Supreme and Absolute Being' instead of the Father, of 'another existing through it, but after it' instead of the Son, and of 'a third ranking with neither of these two' instead of the Holy Ghost. And yet if those had been the more appropriate names, the Truth Himself would not have been at a loss to discover them, nor those men either, on whom successively devolved the preaching of the mystery, whether they were from the first eye-witnesses and ministers of the Word, or, as successors to these, filled the whole world with the Evangelical doctrines, and again at various periods after this defined in a common assembly the ambiguities raised about the doctrine ; whose traditions are constantly preserved in writing in the churches. If those had been the appropriate terms, they would not have mentioned, as they did, Father, Son, and Holy Ghost, granting indeed it were pious or safe to remodel at all, with a view to this innovation, the terms of the faith ; or else they were all ignorant men and uninstructed in the mysteries, and unacquainted with what he calls the appropriate names—those men who

---

[2] *there is the Supreme and Absolute Being, and another Being existing through the First, but after It.* The language of this exposition of Eunomius is Aristotelian : but the contents nevertheless are nothing more nor less than Gnosticism, as Rupp well points out (Gregors v. Nyssa Leben und Meinungen, p. 132 sq.). Arianism, he says, is nothing but the last attempt of Gnosticism to force the doctrine of emanations into Christian theology, clothing that doctrine on this occasion in a Greek dress. It was still an oriental heresy, not a Greek heresy like Pelagianism in the next century.

Rupp gives two reasons why Arianism may be identified with Gnosticism.

1. Arianism holds the Λόγος as the highest being after the Godhead, i.e. as the πρωτότοκος τῆς κτίσεως, and as merely the mediator between God and Man : just as it was the peculiar aim of Gnosticism to bridge over the gulf between the Creator and the Created by means of intermediate beings (the emanations).

2. Eunomius and his master adopted that very system of Greek philosophy which had always been the natural ally of Gnosticism : i.e. Aristotle is strong in divisions and differences, weak in 'identifications :' he had marked with a clearness never attained before the various stages upwards of existencies in the physical world : and this is just what Gnosticism, in its wish to exhibit all things according to their relative distances from the Ἀγέννητος, wanted.

Eunomius has in fact in this formula of his translated all the terms of Scripture straight into those of Aristotle : he has changed the ethical-physical of Christianity into the purely physical : πνεῦμα e.g. becomes οὐσία : and by thus banishing the spiritual and the moral he has made his Ἀγέννητος as completely 'single' and incommunicable as the τὸ πρῶτον κίνουν ἀκίνητον (Arist. Metaph. XII. 7).

had really neither the knowledge nor the desire to give the preference to their own conceptions over what had been handed down to us by the voice of God.

§ 14. *He did wrong, when mentioning the Doctrines of Salvation, in adopting terms of his own choosing instead of the traditional terms Father, Son, and Holy Spirit.*

The reason for this invention of new words I take to be manifest to every one—namely : that every one, when the words father and son are spoken, at once recognizes the proper and natural relationship to one another which they imply. This relationship is conveyed at once by the appellations themselves. To prevent it being understood of the Father, and the Only-begotten Son, he robs us of this idea of relationship which enters the ear along with the words, and abandoning the inspired terms, expounds the Faith by means of others devised to injure the truth.

One thing, however, that he says is true : that his own teaching, not the Catholic teaching, is summed up so. Indeed any one who reflects can easily see the impiety of his statement. It will not be out of place now to discuss in detail what his intention is in ascribing to the being of the Father alone the highest degree of that which is supreme and proper, while not admitting that the being of the Son and of the Holy Ghost is supreme and proper. For my part I think that it is a prelude to his complete denial of the 'being' of the Only-begotten and of the Holy Ghost, and that this system of his is secretly intended to effect the setting aside of all real belief in their personality, while in appearance and in mere words confessing it. A moment's reflection upon his statement will enable any one to perceive that this is so. It does not look like one who thinks that the Only-begotten and the Holy Ghost really exist in a distinct personality to be very particular about the names with which he thinks the greatness of Almighty God should be expressed. To grant the fact[3], and then go into minute distinctions about the appropriate phrases[4] would be indeed consummate folly : and so in ascribing a being that is in the highest degree supreme and proper only to the Father, he makes us surmise by this silence respecting the other two that (to him) they do not properly exist. How can that to which a proper being is denied be said to really exist? When we deny proper being to it, we must perforce affirm of it all the opposite terms. That which cannot be properly said is improperly said, so that the demonstra-

tion of its not being properly said is a proof of its not really subsisting : and it is at this that Eunomius seems to aim in introducing these new names into his teaching. For no one can say that he has strayed from ignorance into some silly fancy of separating, locally, the supreme from that which is below, and assigning to the Father as it were the peak of some hill, while he seats the Son lower down in the hollows. No one is so childish as to conceive of differences in space, when the intellectual and spiritual is under discussion. Local position is a property of the material : but the intellectual and immaterial is confessedly removed from the idea of locality. What, then, is the reason why he says that the Father alone has supreme being? For one can hardly think it is from ignorance that he wanders off into these conceptions, being one who, in the many displays he makes, claims to be wise, even "making himself overwise," as the Holy Scripture forbids us to do[5].

§ 15. *He does wrong in making the being of the Father alone proper and supreme, implying by his omission of the Son and the Spirit that theirs is improperly spoken of, and is inferior.*

But at all events he will allow that this supremacy of being betokens no excess of power, or of goodness, or of anything of that kind. Every one knows that, not to mention those whose knowledge is supposed to be very profound; viz., that the personality of the Only-begotten and of the Holy Ghost has nothing lacking in the way of perfect goodness, perfect power, and of every quality like that. Good, as long as it is incapable of its opposite, has no bounds to its goodness : its opposite alone can circumscribe it, as we may see by particular examples. Strength is stopped only when weakness seizes it ; life is limited by death alone ; darkness is the ending of light : in a word, every good is checked by its opposite, and by that alone. If then he supposes that the nature of the Only-begotten and of the Spirit can change for the worse, then he plainly diminishes the conception of their goodness, making them capable of being associated with their opposites. But if the Divine and unalterable nature is incapable of degeneracy, as even our foes allow, we must regard it as absolutely unlimited in its goodness : and the unlimited is the same as the infinite. But to suppose excess and defect in the infinite and unlimited is to the last degree unreasonable : for how can the idea of infinitude remain, if we posited increase and loss in it ? We get the idea of excess only by a comparison of limits : where

---

3 i.e. of the equality of Persons.   4 i.e. for the Persons.   5 Eccles. vii. 16.

there is no limit, we cannot think of any excess. Perhaps, however, this was not what he was driving at, but he assigns this superiority only by the prerogative of priority in time, and, with this idea only, declares the Father's being to be alone the supreme one. Then he must tell us on what grounds he has measured out more length of life to the Father, while no distinctions of time whatever have been previously conceived of in the personality of the Son.

And yet supposing for a moment, for the sake of argument, that this was so, what superiority does the being which is prior in time have over that which follows, on the score of pure being, that he can say that the one is supreme and proper, and the other is not? For while the lifetime of the elder as compared with the younger is longer, yet his being has neither increase nor decrease on that account. This will be clear by an illustration. What disadvantage, on the score of being, as compared with Abraham, had David, who lived fourteen generations after? Was any change, so far as humanity goes, effected in the latter? Was he less a human being, because he was later in time? Who would be so foolish as to assert this? The definition of their being is the same for both : the lapse of time does not change it. No one would assert that the one was more a man for being first in time, and the other less because he sojourned in life later ; as if humanity had been exhausted on the first, or as if time had spent its chief power upon the deceased. For it is not in the power of time to define for each one the measures of nature, but nature abides self-contained, preserving herself through succeeding generations : and time has a course of its own, whether surrounding, or flowing by, this nature, which remains firm and motionless within her own limits. Therefore, not even supposing, as our argument did for a moment, that an advantage were allowed on the score of time, can they properly ascribe to the Father alone the highest supremacy of being : but as there is really no difference whatever in the prerogative of time, how could any one possibly entertain such an idea about these existencies which are pre-temporal ? Every measure of distance that we could discover is beneath the divine nature : so no ground is left for those who attempt to divide this pre-temporal and incomprehensible being by distinctions of superior and inferior.

We have no hesitation either in asserting that what is dogmatically taught by them is an advocacy of the Jewish doctrine, setting forth, as they do, that the being of the Father alone has subsistence, and insisting that this only has proper existence, and reckoning that of the Son and the Spirit among non-existencies, seeing that what does not properly exist can be said nominally only, and by an abuse of terms, to exist at all. The name of man, for instance, is not given to a portrait representing one, but to so and so who is absolutely such, the original of the picture, and not the picture itself; whereas the picture is in word only a man, and does not possess absolutely the quality ascribed to it, because it is not in its nature that which it is called. In the case before us, too, if being is properly ascribed to the Father, but ceases when we come to the Son and the Spirit, it is nothing short of a plain denial of the message of salvation. Let them leave the church and fall back upon the synagogues of the Jews, proving, as they do, the Son's non-existence in denying to Him proper being. What does not properly exist is the same thing as the non-existent.

Again, he means in all this to be very clever, and has a poor opinion of those who essay to write without logical force. Then let him tell us, contemptible though we are, by what sort of skill he has detected a greater and a less in pure being. What is his method for establishing that one being is more of a being than another being,—taking being in its plainest meaning, for he must not bring forward those various qualities and properties, which are comprehended in the conception of the being, and gather round it, but are not the subject itself? Shade, colour, weight, force or reputation, distinctive manner, disposition, any quality thought of in connection with body or mind, are not to be considered here : we have to inquire only whether the actual subject of all these, which is termed absolutely the being, differs in degree of being from another. We have yet to learn that of two known existencies, which still exist, the one is more, the other less, an existence. Both are equally such, as long as they are in the category of existence, and when all notions of more or less value, more or less force, have been excluded.

If, then, he denies that we can regard the Only-begotten as completely existing,—for to this depth his statement seems to lead,—in withholding from Him a proper existence, let him deny it even in a less degree. If, however, he does grant that the Son subsists in some substantial way—we will not quarrel now about the particular way—why does he take away again that which he has conceded Him to be, and prove Him to exist not properly, which is tantamount, as we have said, to not at all ? For as humanity is not possible to that which does not possess the complete connotation of the term 'man,' and the whole conception of it is cancelled in the case of one who lacks any of the properties, so in every thing whose complete and proper existence is denied, the partial affirmation of its existence is no proof of its subsisting at all; the demonstration, in fact, of its incomplete being is a demonstration of its effacement in all points. So that if he is well-advised, he will come over to the orthodox belief, and remove from his teaching the idea of less and of incompleteness in the nature of the Son and the Spirit: but if he is determined to blaspheme, and wishes for some inscrutable reason thus to requite his Maker and God and Benefactor, let him at all events part with his conceit of possessing some amount of showy learning, unphilosophically piling, as he does, being over being, one above the other, one proper, one not such, for no discoverable reason. We have never heard that any of the infidel philosophers have committed this folly, any more than we have met with it in the inspired writings, or in the common apprehension of mankind.

I think that from what has been said it will be clear what is the aim of these newly-devised names. He drops them as the base of operations or foundation-stone of all this work of mischief to the Faith: once he can get the idea into currency that the one Being alone is supreme and proper in the highest degree, he can then assail the other two, as belonging to the inferior and not regarded as properly Being. He shows this especially in what follows, where he is discussing the belief in the Son and the Holy Spirit, and does not proceed with these names, so as to avoid bringing before us the proper characteristic of their nature by means of those appellations: they are passed over unnoticed by this man who is always telling us that minds of the hearers are to be directed by the use of appropriate names and phrases. Yet what name could be more appropriate than that which has been given by the Very Truth? He sets his views against the Gospel, and names not the Son, but 'a Being existing through the First, but after It though before all others.' That this is said to destroy the right faith in the Only-begotten will be made plainer still by his subsequent arguments. Still there is only a moderate amount of mischief in these words: one intending no impiety at all towards Christ might sometimes use them: we will therefore omit at present all discussion about our Lord, and reserve our reply to the more open blasphemies against Him. But on the subject of the Holy Spirit the blasphemy is plain and unconcealed: he says that He is not to be ranked

with the Father or the Son, but is subject to both. I will therefore examine as closely as possible this statement.

§ 16. *Examination of the meaning of 'subjection:' in that he says that the nature of the Holy Spirit is subject to that of the Father and the Son. It is shewn that the Holy Spirit is of an equal, not inferior, rank to the Father and the Son.*

Let us first, then, ascertain the meaning of this word 'subjection' in Scripture. To whom is it applied? The Creator, honouring man in his having been made in His own image, 'hath placed' the brute creation 'in subjection under his feet;' as great David relating this favour (of God) exclaimed in the Psalms[6]: "He put all things," he says, "under his feet," and he mentions by name the creatures so subjected. There is still another meaning of 'subjection' in Scripture. Ascribing to God Himself the cause of his success in war, the Psalmist says[7], "He hath put peoples and nations in subjection under our feet," and "He that putteth peoples in subjection under me." This word is often found thus in Scripture, indicating a victory. As for the future subjection of all men to the Only-begotten, and through Him to the Father, in the passage where the Apostle with a profound wisdom speaks of the Mediator between God and man as subject to the Father, impiying by that subjection of the Son who shares humanity the actual subjugation of mankind— we will not discuss it now, for it requires a full and thorough examination. But to take only the plain and unambiguous meaning of the word subjection, how can he declare the being of the Spirit to be subject to that of the Son and the Father? As the Son is subject to the Father, according to the thought of the Apostle? But in this view the Spirit is to be ranked with the Son, not below Him, seeing that both Persons are of this lower rank. This was not his meaning? How then? In the way the brute creation is subject to the rational, as in the Psalm? There is then as great a difference as is implied in the subjection of the brute creation, when compared to man. Perhaps he will reject this explanation as well. Then he will have to come to the only remaining one, that the Spirit, at first in the rebellious ranks, was afterwards forced by a superior Force to bend to a Conqueror.

Let him choose which he likes of these alternatives: whichever it is I do not see how he can avoid the inevitable crime of

<hr>

6 Psalm viii. 6–8.   7 Psalm xlvii. 3 (LXX.).

blasphemy: whether he says the Spirit is subject in the manner of the brute creation, as fish and birds and sheep, to man, or were to fetch Him a captive to a superior power after the manner of a rebel. Or does he mean neither of these ways, but uses the word in a different signification altogether to the scripture meaning? What, then, is that signification? Does he lay down that we must rank Him as inferior and not as equal, because He was given by our Lord to His disciples third in order? By the same reasoning he should make the Father inferior to the Son, since the Scripture often places the name of our Lord first, and the Father Almighty second. "I and My Father," our Lord says. "The grace of our Lord Jesus Christ, and the love of God [8]," and other passages innumerable which the diligent student of Scripture testimonies might collect: for instance, "there are differences of gifts, but it is the same Spirit: and there are differences of administration, but it is the same Lord: and there are differences of operations, but it is the same God." According to this, then, let the Almighty Father, who is mentioned third, be made 'subject' to the Son and the Spirit. However we have never yet heard of a philosophy such as this, which relegates to the category of the inferior and the dependent that which is mentioned second or third only for some particular reason of sequence: yet that is what our author wants to do, in arguing to show that the order observed in the transmission of the Persons amounts to differences of more and less in dignity and nature. In fact he rules that sequence in point of order is indicative of unlikeness of nature: whence he got this fancy, what necessity compelled him to it, is not clear. Mere numerical rank does not create a different nature: that which we would count in a number remains the same in nature whether we count it or not. Number is a mark only of the mere quantity of things: it does not place second those things only which have an inferior natural value, but it makes the sequence of the numerical objects indicated in accordance with the intention of those who are counting. 'Paul and Silvanus and Timotheus' are three persons mentioned according to a particular intention. Does the place of Silvanus, second and after Paul, indicate that he was other than a man? Or is Timothy, because he is third, considered by the writer who so ranks him a different kind of being? Not so. Each is human both before and after this arrangement. Speech,

which cannot utter the names of all three at once, mentions each separately according to an order which commends itself, but unites them by the copula, in order that the juncture of the names may show the harmonious action of the three towards one end.

This, however, does not please our new dogmatist. He opposes the arrangement of Scripture. He separates off that equality with the Father and the Son of His proper and natural rank and connexion which our Lord Himself pronounces, and numbers Him with 'subjects': he declares Him to be a work of both Persons [9], of the Father, as supplying the cause of His constitution, of the Only-begotten, as of the artificer of His subsistence: and defines this as the ground of His 'subjection,' without as yet unfolding the meaning of 'subjection.'

§ 17. *Discussion as to the exact nature of the 'energies' which, this man declares, 'follow' the being of the Father and of the Son.*

Then he says "there must of course be included in this account the energies that accompany each Being, and the names appropriate to these energies." Shrouded in such a mist of vagueness, the meaning of this is far from clear: but one might conjecture it is as follows. By the energies of the Beings, he means those powers which have produced the Son and the Holy Spirit, and by which the First Being made the Second, and the Second the Third: and he means that the names of the results produced have been provided in a manner appropriate to those results. We have already exposed the mischief of these names, and will again, when we return to that part of the question, should additional discussion of it be required.

But it is worth a moment's while now to consider how energies 'follow' beings: what these energies are essentially: whether different to the beings which they 'follow,' or part of them, and of their inmost nature: and then, if different, how and whence they arise: if the same, how they have got cut off from them, and instead of co-existing 'follow'

---

[8] John x. 30; 2 Cor. xiii. 13.

[9] *he declares Him to be a work of both Persons.* With regard to Gregory's own belief as to the procession of the Holy Spirit, it may be said once for all that there is hardly anything (but see p. 99, note 5) clear about it to be found in his writings. The question, in fact, remained undecided until the 9th century, the time of the schism of the East and West. But here, as in other points, Origen had approached the nearest to the teaching of the West: for he represents the procession as from Father and Son, just as often as from one Person or the other. Athanasius does certainly say that the Spirit 'unites the creation to the Son, and through the Son to the Father,' but with him this expression is not followed up: while in the Roman Church it led to doctrine. For why does the Holy Spirit unite the creation with God continuously and perfectly? Because, to use Bossuet's words, "proceeding from the Father and the Son He is their love and eternal union." Neither Basil, nor Gregory Nazianzen, nor Chrysostom, have anything definite about the procession of the Third Person.

them externally only. This is necessary, for we cannot learn all at once from his words, whether some natural necessity compels the 'energy,' whatever that may be, to 'follow' the being, in the way heat and vapour follow fire, and the various exhalations the bodies which produce them. Still I do not think that he would affirm that we should consider the being of God to be something heterogeneous and composite, having the energy inalienably contained in the idea of itself, like an 'accident' in some subject-matter: he must mean that the beings, deliberately and voluntarily moved, produce by themselves the desired result. But, if this be so, who would style this free result of intention as one of its external consequences? We have never heard of such an expression used in common parlance in such cases; the energy of the worker of anything is not said to 'follow' that worker. We cannot separate one from the other and leave one behind by itself: but, when one mentions the energy, one comprehends in the idea that which is moved with the energy, and when one mentions the worker one implies at once the unmentioned energy.

An illustration will make our meaning clearer. We say a man works in iron, or in wood, or in anything else. This single expression conveys at once the idea of the working and of the artificer, so that if we withdraw the one, the other has no existence. If then they are thus thought of together, i.e. the energy and he who exercises it, how in this case can there be said to "follow" upon the first being the energy which produces the second being, like a sort of go-between to both, and neither coalescing with the nature of the first, nor combining with the second: separated from the first because it is not its very nature, but only the exercise of its nature, and from that which results afterwards because it does not therein reproduce a mere energy, but an active being.

§ 18. *He has no reason for distinguishing a plurality of beings in the Trinity. He offers no demonstration that it is so.*

Let us examine the following as well. He calls one Being the work of another, the second of the first, and the third of the second. On what previous demonstration does this statement rest: what proofs does he make use of, what method, to compel belief in the succeeding Being as a result of the preceding? For even if it were possible to draw an analogy for this from created things, such conjecturing about the transcendent from lower existences would not be altogether sound, though the error in arguing from natural phenomena to

the incomprehensible might then be pardonable. But as it is, none would venture to affirm that, while the heavens are the work of God, the sun is that of the heavens, and the moon that of the sun, and the stars that of the moon, and other created things that of the stars: seeing that all are the work of One: for there is one God and Father of all, of Whom are all things. If anything is produced by mutual transmission, such as the race of animals, not even here does one produce another, for nature runs on through each generation. How then, when it is impossible to affirm it of the created world, can he declare of the transcendent existencies that the second is a work of the first, and so on? If, however, he is thinking of animal generation, and fancies that such a process is going on also amongst pure existences, so that the older produces the younger, even so he fails to be consistent: for such productions are of the same type as their progenitors: whereas he assigns to the members of his succession strange and uninherited qualities: and thus displays a superfluity of falsehood, while striving to strike truth with both hands at once, in a clever boxer's fashion. In order to show the inferior rank and diminution in intrinsic value of the Son and Holy Spirit, he declares that " one is produced from *another ;*" in order that those who understand about mutual generation might entertain no idea of family relationship here: he contradicts the law of nature by declaring that " one is produced from *another,*" and at the same time exhibiting the Son as a bastard when compared with His Father's nature.

But one might find fault with him, I think, before coming to all this. If, that is, any one else, previously unaccustomed to discussion and unversed in logical expression, delivered his ideas in this chance fashion, some indulgence might be shown him for not using the recognized methods for establishing his views. But considering that Eunomius has such an abundance of this power, that he can advance by his 'irresistible' method [1] of proof even into the

---

[1] καταληπτικῆς ἐφόδου—ἡ κατάληψις. These words are taken from the Stoic logic, and refer to the Stoic view of the standard of truth. To the question, How are true perceptions distinguished from false ones, the Stoics answered, that a true perception is one which represents a real object as it really is. To the further question, How may it be known that a perception faithfully represents a reality, they replied by pointing to a relative not an absolute test—*the degree of strength with which certain perceptions force themselves* upon our notice. Some of our perceptions are of such a kind that they at once oblige us to bestow on them assent. Such perceptions produce in us that strength of conviction which the Stoics call a conception. Whenever a perception forces itself upon us in this irresistible form, we are no longer dealing with a fiction of the imagination but with something real. The test of irresistibility (κατάληψις) was, in the first place, understood to apply to sensations from without, such sensations, according to the Stoic view, alone supplying the material for knowledge. An equal degree of certainty was, however, attached to terms deduced from originally true data, either by the universal and natural exercise of thought, or by scientific processes of proof. It is καταλέψεις obtained in this last way that Gregory refers to, and Eunomius was endeavouring to create in the supra-natural world.

supra-natural, how can he be ignorant of the starting-point from which this 'irresistible' perception of a hidden truth takes its rise in all these logical excursions. Every one knows that all such arguing must start from plain and well-known truths, to compel belief through itself in still doubtful truths : and that none of these last can be grasped without the guidance of what is obvious leading us towards the unknown. If on the other hand that which is adopted to start with for the illustration of this unknown is at variance with universal belief, it will be a long time before the unknown will receive any illustration from it.

The whole controversy, then, between the Church and the Anomœans turns on this : Are we to regard the Son and the Holy Spirit as belonging to created or uncreated existence? Our opponent declares that to be the case which all deny : he boldly lays it down, without looking about for any proof, that each being is the work of the preceding being. What method of education, what school of thought can warrant him in this, it is difficult to see. Some axiom that cannot be denied or assailed must be the beginning of every process of proof ; so as for the unknown quantity to be demonstrated from what has been assumed, being legitimately deduced by intervening syllogisms. The reasoner, therefore, who makes what ought to be the object of inquiry itself a premiss of his demonstration is only proving the obscure by the obscure, and illusion by illusion. He is making 'the blind lead the blind,' for it is a truly blind and unsupported statement to say that the Creator and Maker of all things is a creature made : and to this they link on a conclusion that is also blind : namely, that the Son is alien in nature, *unlike* in being to the Father, and quite devoid of His essential character. But of this enough. Where his thought is nakedly blasphemous, there we too can defer its refutation. We must now return to consider his words which come next in order.

§ 19. *His acknowledgment that the Divine Being is 'single' is only verbal.*

"Each Being has, in fact and in conception, a nature unmixed, single, and absolutely one as estimated by its dignity ; and as the works are bounded by the energies of each operator, and the energies by the works, it is inevitable that the energies which follow each Being are greater in the one case than the other, some being of the first, others of the second rank." The intention that runs through all this, however verbosely expressed, is one and the same ; namely, to establish that there is no connexion be-

tween the Father and the Son, or between the Son and the Holy Ghost, but that these Beings are sundered from each other, and possess natures foreign and unfamiliar to each other, and differ not only in that, but also in magnitude and in subordination of their dignities, so that we must think of one as greater than the other, and presenting every other sort of difference.

It may seem to many useless to linger over what is so obvious, and to attempt a discussion of that which to them is on the face of it false and abominable and groundless : nevertheless, to avoid even the appearance of having to let these statements pass for want of counter-arguments, we will meet them with all our might. He says, "each being amongst them is unmixed, single, and absolutely one, as estimated by its dignity, both in fact and in conception." Then premising this very doubtful statement as an axiom and valuing his own 'ipse dixit' as a sufficient substitute for any proof, he thinks he has made a point. "There are three Beings : " for he implies this when he says, 'each being amongst them :' he would not have used these words, if he meant only one. Now if he speaks thus of the mutual difference between the Beings in order to avoid complicity with the heresy of Sabellius, who applied three titles to one subject, we would acquiesce in his statement : nor would any of the Faithful contradict his view, except so far as he seems to be at fault in his names, and his mere form of expression in speaking of 'beings' instead of 'persons :' for things that are identical on the score of being will not all agree equally in definition on the score of personality. For instance, Peter, James, and John are the same viewed as beings, each was a man : but in the characteristics of their respective personalities, they were not alike. If, then, he were only proving that it is not right to confound the Persons, and to fit all the three names on to one Subject, his 'saying' would be, to use the Apostle's words, 'faithful, and worthy of all acceptation [2].' But this is not his object : he speaks so, not because he divides the Persons only from each other by their recognized characteristics, but because he makes the actual substantial being of each different from that of the others, or rather from itself: and so he speaks of a plurality of beings with distinctive differences which alienate them from each other. I therefore declare that his view is unfounded, and lacks a principle : it starts from data that are not granted, and then it constructs by mere logic a blasphemy upon them. It at-

---

[2] 1 Timothy i. 15.

tempts no demonstration that could attract towards such a conception of the doctrine : it merely contains the statement of an unproved impiety, as if it were telling us a dream. While the Church teaches that we must not divide our faith amongst a plurality of beings, but must recognize no difference of being in three Subjects or Persons, whereas our opponents posit a variety and unlikeness amongst them as Beings, this writer confidently assumes as already proved what never has been, and never can be, proved by argument : maybe he has not even yet found hearers for his talk : or he might have been informed by one of them who was listening intelligently that every statement which is made at random, and without proof, is 'an old woman's tale,' and powerless to prove the question, in itself, unaided by any plea whatever fetched from the Scriptures, or from human reasonings. So much for this.

But let us still scrutinize his words. He declares each of these Beings, whom he has shadowed forth in his exposition, to be single and absolutely one. We believe that the most boorish and simple-minded would not deny that the Divine Nature, blessed and transcendent as it is, was 'single.' That which is viewless, formless, and sizeless, cannot be conceived of as multiform and composite. But it will be clear, upon the very slightest reflection, that this view of the supreme Being as 'simple,' however finely they may talk of it, is quite inconsistent with the system which they have elaborated. For who does not know that, to be exact, simplicity in the case of the Holy Trinity admits of no degrees. In this case there is no mixture or conflux of qualities to think of ; we comprehend a potency without parts and composition ; how then, and on what grounds, could any one perceive there any differences of less and more. For he who marks differences there must perforce think of an incidence of certain qualities in the subject. He must in fact have perceived differences in largeness and smallness therein, to have introduced this conception of quantity into the question : or he must posit abundance or diminution in the matter of goodness, strength, wisdom, or of anything else that can with reverence be associated with God : and neither way will he escape the idea of composition. Nothing which possesses wisdom or power or any other good, not as an external gift, but rooted in its nature, can suffer diminution in it ; so that if any one says that he detects Beings greater and smaller in the Divine Nature, he is unconsciously establishing a composite and heterogeneous Deity, and thinking of the Subject as one thing,

and the quality, to share in which constitutes as good that which was not so before, as another. If he had been thinking of a Being really single and absolutely one, identical with goodness rather than possessing it, he would not be able to count a greater and a less in it at all. It was said, moreover, above that good can be diminished by the presence of evil alone, and that where the nature is incapable of deteriorating, there is no limit conceived of to the goodness : the unlimited, in fact, is not such owing to any relation whatever, but, considered in itself, escapes limitation. It is, indeed, difficult to see how a reflecting mind can conceive one infinite to be greater or less than another infinite. So that if he acknowledges the supreme Being to be 'single' and homogenous, let him grant that it is bound up with this universal attribute of simplicity and infinitude. If, on the other hand, he divides and estranges the 'Beings' from each other, conceiving that of the Only-begotten as another than the Father's, and that of the Spirit as another than the Only-begotten, with a 'more' and 'less' in each case, let him be exposed now as granting simplicity in appearance only to the Deity, but in reality proving the composite in Him.

But let us resume the examination of his words in order. "Each Being has in fact and conception a nature unmixed, single, and absolutely one, as estimated by its dignity." Why "as estimated by its dignity?" If he contemplates the Beings in their common dignity, this addition is unnecessary and superfluous, and dwells upon that which is obvious : although a word so out of place might be pardoned, if it was any feeling of reverence which prompted him not to reject it. But here the mischief really is not owing to a mistake about a phrase (that might be easily set right) : but it is connected with his evil designs. He says that each of the three beings is 'single, as estimated by its dignity,' in order that, on the strength of his previous definitions of the first, second, and third Being, the idea of their simplicity also may be marred. Having affirmed that the being of the Father alone is 'Supreme' and 'Proper,' and having refused both these titles to that of the Son and of the Spirit, in accordance with this, when he comes to speak of them all as 'simple,' he thinks it his duty to associate with them the idea of simplicity in proportion only to their essential worth, so that the Supreme alone is to be conceived of as at the height and perfection of simplicity, while the second, in proportion to its declension from supremacy, receives also a diminished measure of simplicity, and in the case of the third Being also, there is as much variation from the perfect simplicity, as the amount of worth is lessened in the extremes: whence it results that the Father's being is conceived as of pure simplicity, that of the Son as not so flawless in simplicity, but with a mixture of the composite, that of the Holy Spirit as still increasing in the composite, while the amount of simplicity is gradually lessened. Just as imperfect goodness must be owned to share in some measure in the reverse disposition, so imperfect simplicity cannot escape being considered composite.

§ 20. *He does wrong in assuming, to account for the existence of the Only-begotten, an 'energy' that produced Christ's Person.*

That such is his intention in using these phrases will be clear from what follows, where he more plainly materializes and degrades our conception of the Son and of the Spirit. "As the energies are bounded by the works, and the works commensurate with the energies, it necessarily follows that these energies which accompany these Beings are relatively greater and less, some being of a higher, some of a lower order." Though he has studiously wrapt the mist of his phraseology round the meaning of this, and made it hard for most to find out, yet as following that which we have already examined it will easily be made clear. "The energies," he says, "are bounded by the works." By 'works' he means the Son and the Spirit, by 'energies' the efficient powers by which they were produced, which powers, he said a little above, 'follow' the Beings. The phrase 'bounded by' expresses the balance which exists between the being produced and the producing power, or rather the 'energy' of that power, to use his own word implying that the thing produced is not the effect of the whole power of the operator, but only of a particular energy of it, only so much of the whole power being exerted as is calculated to be likely to be equal to effect that result. Then he inverts his statement: "and the works are commensurate with the energies of the operators." The meaning of this will be made clearer by an illustration. Let us think of one of the tools of a shoemaker: i. e., a leather-cutter. When it is moved round upon that from which a certain shape has to be cut, the part so excised is limited by the size of the instrument, and a circle of such a radius will be cut as the instrument possesses of length, and, to put the matter the other way, the span of the instrument will measure and cut out a corresponding circle. That is the idea which our theologian has of the divine person of the Only-begotten. He declares that a certain 'energy' which 'follows' upon

the first Being produced, in the fashion of such a tool, a corresponding work, namely our Lord: this is his way of glorifying the Son of God, Who is even now glorified in the glory of the Father, and shall be revealed in the Day of Judgment. He is a 'work commensurate with the producing energy.' But what is this energy which 'follows' the Almighty and is to be conceived of prior to the Only-begotten, and which circumscribes His being? A certain essential Power, self-subsisting, which works its will by a spontaneous impulse. It is this, then, that is the real Father of our Lord. And why do we go on talking of the Almighty as the Father, if it was not He, but an energy belonging to the things which follow Him externally that produced the Son: and how can the Son be a son any longer, when something else has given Him existence according to Eunomius, and He creeps like a bastard (may our Lord pardon the expression!) into relationship with the Father, and is to be honoured in name only as a Son? How can Eunomius rank our Lord next after the Almighty at all, when he counts Him third only, with that mediating 'energy' placed in the second place? The Holy Spirit also according to this sequence will be found not in the third, but in the fifth place, that 'energy' which follows the Only-Begotten, and by which the Holy Spirit came into existence necessarily intervening between them.

Thereby, too, the creation of all things by the Son[3] will be found to have no foundation: another personality, prior to Him, has been invented by our neologian, to which the authorship of the world must be referred, because the Son Himself derives His being according to them from that 'energy.' If, however, to avoid such profanities, he makes this 'energy' which produced the Son into something unsubstantial, he will have to explain to us how non-being can 'follow' being, and how what is not a substance can produce a substance: for, if he did that, we shall find an unreality following God, the non-existent author of all existence, the radically unsubstantial circumscribing a substantial nature, the operative force of creation contained, in the last resort, in the unreal. Such is the result of the teaching of this theologian who affirms of the Lord Artificer of heaven and earth and of all the Creation, the Word of God Who was in the beginning, through Whom are all things, that He owes His existence to such a baseless entity or conception as that unnameable 'energy' which he has just invented, and that He is circumscribed by it, as by an enclos-

---

There is of course reference here to John i. 3: and **Eunomius** is called just below the 'new theologian,' with an allusion of S. John, who was called by virtue of this passage essentially ὁ θεόλογος.

ing prison of unreality. He who 'gazes into the unseen' cannot see the conclusion to which his teaching tends. It is this: if this 'energy' of God has no real existence, and if the work that this unreality produces is also circumscribed by it, it is quite clear that we can only think of such a nature in the work, as that which is possessed by this fancied producer of the work: in fact, that which is produced from and is contained by an unreality can itself be conceived of as nothing else but a non-entity. Opposites, in the nature of things, cannot be contained by opposites: such as water by fire, life by death, light by darkness, being by non-being. But with all his excessive cleverness he does not see this: or else he consciously shuts his eyes to the truth.

Some necessity compels him to see a diminution in the Son, and to establish a further advance in this direction in the case of the Holy Ghost. "It necessarily follows," he says, "that these energies which accompany these Beings are relatively greater and less." This compelling necessity in the Divine nature, which assigns a greater and a less, has not been explained to us by Eunomius, nor as yet can we ourselves understand it. Hitherto there has prevailed with those who accept the Gospel in its plain simplicity the belief that there is no necessity above the Godhead to bend the Only-begotten, like a slave, to inferiority. But he quite overlooks this belief, though it was worth some consideration; and he dogmatizes that we must conceive of this inferiority. But this necessity of his does not stop there: it lands him still further in blasphemy: as our examination in detail has already shewn. If, that is, the Son was born, not from the Father, but from some unsubstantial 'energy,' He must be thought of as not merely inferior to the Father, and this doctrine must end in pure Judaism. This necessity, when followed out, exhibits the product of a non-entity as not merely insignificant, but as something which it is a perilous blasphemy even for an accuser to name. For as that which has its birth from an existence necessarily exists, so that which is evolved from the non-existent necessarily does the very contrary. When anything is not self-existent, how can it generate another?

If, then, this energy which 'follows' the Deity, and produces the Son, has no existence of its own, no one can be so blind as not to see the conclusion, and that his aim is to deny our Saviour's deity: and if the personality of the Son is thus stolen by their doctrine from the Faith, with nothing left of it but the name, it will be a long time before the Holy Ghost, descended as He will be from a lineage of unrealities, will be believed in again. The

energy which 'follows' the Deity has no existence of its own: then common sense requires the product of this to be unreal: then a second unsubstantial energy follows this product: then it is declared that the Holy Ghost is formed by this energy: so that their blasphemy is plain enough: it consists in nothing less than in denying that after the Ingenerate God there is any real existence: and their doctrine advances into shadowy and unsubstantial fictions, where there is no foundation of any actual subsistence. In such monstrous conclusions does their teaching strand the argument.

§ 21. *The blasphemy of these heretics is worse than the Jewish unbelief.*

But let us assume that this is not so: for they allow, forsooth, in theoretic kindness towards humanity, that the Only-begotten and the Holy Spirit have some personal existence: and if, in allowing this, they had granted too the consequent conceptions about them, they would not have been waging battle about the doctrine of the Church, nor cut themselves off from the hope of Christians. But if they have lent an existence to the Son and the Spirit, only to furnish a material on which to erect their blasphemy, perhaps it might have been better for them, though it is a bold thing to say, to abjure the Faith and apostatize to the Jewish religion, rather than to insult the name of Christian by this mock assent. The Jews at all events, though they have persisted hitherto in rejecting the Word, carry their impiety only so far as to deny that Christ has come, but to hope that He will come: we do not hear from them any malignant or destructive conception of the glory of Him Whom they expect. But this school of the new circumcision [4], or rather of "the concision," while they own that He has come, resemble nevertheless those who insulted our Lord's bodily presence by their wanton unbelief. They wanted to stone our Lord: these men stone Him with their blasphemous titles. They urged His humble and obscure origin, and rejected His divine birth before the ages: these men in the same way deny His grand, sublime, ineffable generation from the Father, and would prove that He owes His existence to a creation, just as the human race, and all that is born, owe theirs. In the eyes of the

---

4 *this school of the new circumcision.* This accusation is somewhat discounted by Gregory's comparison of Eunomius elsewhere to Bardesanes and Marcion, to the Manichees, to Nicholaus, to Philo (see Book XI. 691, 704, VI. 607, and especially VII. 645), and by his putting him down a scholar of Plato. But a momentary advantage, calculated in accordance with the character and capacities of the great mass of Gregory's audience, could not be lost. The lessons of Libanius, the rhetorician, had not been thrown away on Gregory.

Jews it was a crime that our Lord should be regarded as Son of the Supreme: these men also are indignant against those who are sincere in making this confession of Him. The Jews thought to honour the Almighty by excluding the Son from equal reverence: these men, by annihilating the glory of the Son, think to bestow more honour on the Father. But it would be difficult to do justice to the number and the nature of the insults which they heap upon the Only-begotten: they invent an 'energy' prior to the personality of the Son, and say that He is its work and product: a thing which the Jews hitherto have not dared to say. Then they circumscribe His nature, shutting Him off within certain limits of the power which made Him: the amount of this productive energy is a sort of measure within which they enclose Him: they have devised it as a sort of cloak to muffle Him up in. We cannot charge the Jews with doing this.

§ 22. *He has no right to assert a greater and less in the Divine being. A systematic statement of the teaching of the Church.*

Then they discover in His being a certain shortness in the way of deficiency, though they do not tell us by what method they measure that which is devoid of quantity and size: they are able to find out exactly by how much the size of the Only-begotten falls short of perfection, and therefore has to be classed with the inferior and imperfect: much else they lay down, partly by open assertion, partly by underhand inference: all the time making their confession of the Son and the Spirit a mere exercise-ground for their unbelieving spirit. How, then, can we fail to pity them more even than the condemned Jews, when views never ventured upon by the latter are inferred by the former? He who makes the being of the Son and of the Spirit comparatively less, seems, so far as words go perhaps, to commit but a slight profanity: but if one were to test his view stringently it will be found the height of blasphemy. Let us look into this, then, and let indulgence be shown me, if, for the sake of doctrine, and to place in a clear light the lie which they have demonstrated, I advance into an exposition of our own conception of the truth.

Now the ultimate division of all being is into the Intelligible and the Sensible. The Sensible world is called by the Apostle broadly "that which is seen." For as all body has colour, and the sight apprehends this, he calls this world by the rough and ready name of "that which is seen," leaving out all the other qualities, which are essentially inherent in its framework. The common term, again, for all the

intellectual world, is with the Apostle "that which is not seen [5]:" by withdrawing all idea of comprehension by the senses he leads the mind on to the immaterial and intellectual. Reason again divides this "which is not seen" into the uncreate and the created, inferentially comprehending it: the uncreate being that which effects the Creation, the created that which owes its origin and its force to the uncreate. In the Sensible world, then, is found everything that we comprehend by our organs of bodily sense, and in which the differences of qualities involve the idea of more and less, such differences consisting in quantity, quality, and the other properties.

But in the Intelligible world,—that part of it, I mean, which is created,—the idea of such differences as are perceived in the Sensible cannot find a place: another method, then, is devised for discovering the degrees of greater and less. The fountain, the origin, the supply of every good is regarded as being in the world that is uncreate, and the whole creation inclines to that, and touches and shares the Highest Existence only by virtue of its part in the First Good: therefore it follows from this participation in the highest blessings varying in degree according to the amount of freedom in the will that each possesses, that the greater and less in this creation is disclosed according to the proportion of this tendency in each [6]. Created intelligible nature stands on the border-line between good and the reverse, so as to be capable of either, and to incline at pleasure to the things of its choice, as we learn from Scripture; so that we can say of it that it is more or less in the heights of excellence only in proportion to its removal from the evil and its approach to the good. Whereas [7] uncreate intelligible nature is far removed from such distinctions: it does not

---

5 Colossians i. 16.
6 i.e. according as each inclines more or less to the First Good.
7 *uncreate intelligible nature is far removed from such distinctions.* This was the impregnable position that Athanasius had taken up. To admit that the Son is less than the Father, and the Spirit less than the Son, is to admit *the law of emanation* such as hitherto conceived, that is, the gradual and successive degradation of God's substance; which had conducted oriental heretics as well as the Neoplatonists to a sort of pantheistic polytheism. Arius had indeed tried to resist this tendency so far as to bring back divinity to the Supreme Being; but it was at the expense of the divinity of the Son, Who was with him just as much a created Intermediate between God and man, as one of the Æons: and Aetius and Eunomius treated the Son. But his master had treated the Son. But Arianism tended at once to Judaism and, in making creatures adorable, to Greek polytheism. There was only one way of cutting short the phantasmagoria of divine emanations, without having recourse to the contradictory hypothesis of Arius: and that was to reject the *law of emanation*, as hitherto accepted, altogether. Far from admitting that the Supreme Being is always weakening and degrading Himself in that which emanates from Him, Athanasius lays down the principle that He produces within Himself nothing but what is perfect, and first, and divine: and all that is not perfect is a work of the Divine Will, which draws it out of nothing (i.e. creates it), and not out of the Divine Substance. This was the crowning result of the teaching of Alexandria and Origen. See Denys (De la Philosophie d'Origène, p. 432, Paris, 1884).

possess the good by acquisition, or participate only in the goodness of some good which lies above it: in its own essence it is good, and is conceived as such: it is a source of good, it is simple, uniform, incomposite, even by the confession of our adversaries. But it has distinction within itself in keeping with the majesty of its own nature, but not conceived of with regard to quantity, as Eunomius supposes: (indeed the man who introduces the notion of less of good into any of the things believed to be in the Holy Trinity must admit thereby some admixture of the opposite quality in that which fails of the good: and it is blasphemous to imagine this in the case either of the Only-begotten, or of the Holy Spirit): we regard it as consummately perfect and incomprehensibly excellent, yet as containing clear distinctions within itself which reside in the peculiarities of each of the Persons: as possessing invariableness by virtue of its common attribute of uncreatedness, but differentiated by the unique character of each Person. This peculiarity contemplated in each sharply and clearly divides one from the other: the Father, for instance, is uncreate and ungenerate as well: He was never generated any more than He was created. While this uncreatedness is common to Him and the Son, and the Spirit, He is ungenerate as well as the Father. This is peculiar and uncommunicable, being not seen in the other Persons. The Son in His uncreatedness touches the Father and the Spirit, but as the Son and the Only-begotten He has a character which is not that of the Almighty or of the Holy Spirit. The Holy Spirit by the uncreatedness of His nature has contact with the Son and Father, but is distinguished from them by His own tokens. His most peculiar characteristic is that He is neither of those things which we contemplate in the Father and the Son respectively. He *is* simply, neither as ungenerate [8], nor as only-begotten: this it is that constitutes His chief peculiarity. Joined to the Father by His uncreatedness, He is disjoined from Him again by not being 'Father.' United to the Son by the bond of uncreatedness, and of deriving His existence from the Supreme, He is parted again from Him by the characteristic of not being the Only-begotten of the Father, and of having been manifested by means of the Son Himself. Again, as the creation was effected by the Only-begotten, in order to secure that the Spirit should not be considered to have something in common with this creation because of His having been manifested by means of the Son, He is distinguished from it by His unchangeableness, and independence of all external goodness. The creation does not possess in its nature this unchangeableness, as the Scripture says in the description of the fall of the morning star, the mysteries on which subject are revealed by our Lord to His disciples: "I saw Satan falling like lightning from heaven [9]." But the very attributes which part Him from the creation constitute His relationship to the Father and the Son. All that is incapable of degenerating has one and the same definition of "unchangeable."

Having stated thus much as a preface we are in a position to discuss the rest of our adversaries' teaching. "It necessarily follows," he says in his system of the Son and the Spirit, "that the Beings are relatively greater and less." Let us then inquire what is the meaning of this necessity of difference. Does it arise from a comparison formed from measuring them one with another in some material way, or from viewing them on the spiritual ground of more or less of moral excellence, or on that of pure being? But in the case of this last it has been shown by competent thinkers that it is impossible to conceive of any difference whatever, if one abstracts being from attributes and properties, and looks at it according to its bare definition. Again, to conceive of this difference as consisting in the case of the Only-begotten and the Spirit in the intensity or abatement of moral excellence, and in consequence to hint that their nature admits of change in either direction, so as to be equally capable of opposites, and to be placed in a border-land between moral beauty and its opposite—that is gross profanity. A man who thinks this will be proving that their nature is one thing in itself, and becomes something else by virtue of its participation in this beauty or its opposite: as happens with iron for example: if it is approached some time to the fire, it assumes the quality of heat while remaining iron: if it is put in snow or ice, it changes its quality to the mastering influence, and lets the snow's coldness pass into its pores.

Now just as we cannot name the material of the iron from the quality now to be observed upon it (for we do not give the name of fire or ice to that which is tempered with either of these), so the moment we grant the view of these heretics, that in the case [1] of the Life-giving Power good does not reside in It essentially, but is imparted to it only, it will become impossible to call it properly good:

---

8 But He is not *begotten*. Athanasian Creed.   9 Luke x. 18.   1 τῆς ζωοποιοῦ δυνάμεως.

such a conception of it will compel us to regard it as something different, as not eternally exhibiting the good, as not in itself to be classed amongst genuine goods, but as such that the good is at times not in it, and is at times not likely to be in it. If these existences become good only by sharing in a something superior to themselves, it is plain that before this participation they were not good, and if, being other than good, they were then coloured by the influence of good they must certainly, if again isolated from this, be considered other than good : so that, if this heresy prevails, the Divine Nature cannot be apprehended as transmissive of good, but rather as itself needing goodness : for how can one impart to another that which he does not himself possess? If it is in a state of perfection, no abatement of that can be conceived, and it is absurd to talk of less of perfection. If on the other hand its participation of good is an imperfect one, and this is what they mean by 'less,' mark the consequence that anything in that state can never help an inferior, but will be busied in satisfying its own want : so that, according to them, Providence is a fiction, and so is the judgment and the Dispensation of the Only-begotten, and all the other works believed to be done, and still doing by Him : for He will necessarily be employed in taking care of His own good, and must abandon the supervision of the Universe [2].

If, then, this surmise is to have its way, namely, that our Lord is not perfected in every kind of good, it is very easy to see the conclusion of the blasphemy. This being so, our faith is vain, and our preaching vain ; our hopes, which take their substance from our faith, are unsubstantial. Why are they baptized into Christ [3], if He has no power of goodness of His own? God forgive me for saying it ! Why do they believe in the Holy Ghost, if the same account is given of Him? How are they regenerate [4] by baptism from their mortal birth, if the regenerating Power does not possess in its own nature infallibility and independence ? How can their 'vile body' be changed, while they think that He who is to change it Himself needs change, i.e. another to change Him? For as long as a nature

is in defect as regards the good, the superior existence exerts upon this inferior one a ceaseless attraction towards itself : and this craving for more will never stop : it will be stretching out to something not yet grasped : the subject of this deficiency will be always demanding a supply, always altering into the grander nature, and yet will never touch perfection, because it cannot find a goal to grasp, and cease its impulse upward. The First Good is in its nature infinite, and so it follows of necessity that the participation in the enjoyment of it will be infinite also, for more will be always being grasped, and yet something beyond that which has been grasped will always be discovered, and this search will never overtake its Object, because its fund is as inexhaustible as the growth of that which participates in it is ceaseless [5].

Such, then, are the blasphemies which emerge from their making differences between the Persons as to the good. If on the other hand the degrees of more or less are to be understood in this case in some material sense, the absurdity of this surmise will be obvious at once, without examination in detail. Ideas of quality and distance, weight and figure, and all that goes to complete the notion of a body, will perforce be introduced along with such a surmise into the view of the Divine Nature : and where a compound is assumed, there the dissolution also of that compound must be admitted. A teaching so monstrous, which dares to discover a smaller and a larger in what is sizeless and not concrete lands us in these and suchlike conclusions, a few samples only of which are here indicated : nor indeed would it be easy to unveil all the mischief that lurks beneath it. Still the shocking absurdity that results from their blasphemous premiss will be clear from this brief notice. We now proceed to their next position, after a short defining and confirmation of our own doctrine. For an inspired testimony is a sure test of the truth of any doctrine : and so it seems to me that ours may be well guaranteed by a quotation from the divine words.

In the division of all existing things, then, we find these distinctions. There is, as appealing to our perceptions, the Sensible world :

---

[2] τοῦ παντὸς. It is worth while to mention, once for all, the distinction in the names used by the Stoics for the world, which had long since passed from them into the common parlance. Including the Empty, the world is called τὸ πᾶν, without it, ὅλον (τὸ ὅλον, τὰ ὅλα frequently occurs with the Stoics). The πᾶν, it was said, is neither material nor immaterial, since it consists of both.

[3] Τί γὰρ βαπτίζονται εἰς Χριστὸν. This throws some light on the much discussed passage, 'Why are these baptized for the dead ?' Gregory at all events seems here to take it to mean, 'Why are they baptized in the name of a dead Christ?' as he is adopting partially S. Paul's words, 1 Cor. xv. 29 ; as well as Heb. xi. 1 above.

[4] ἀναγεννῶνται.

[5] Cf. Gregory's theory of human perfection ; De anima et Resurrectione, p. 229, 230. 'The All-creating Wisdom fashioned these souls, these receptacles with free wills, as vessels as it were, for this very purpose, that there should be some capacities able to receive His blessings, and become continually larger with the inpouring of the stream. Such are the wonders that the participation in the Divine blessings works ; it makes him into whom they come larger and more capacious. . . . The fountain of blessings wells up unceasingly, and the partaker's nature, finding nothing superfluous and without a use in that which it receives, makes the whole influx an enlargement of its own proportions. . . . It is likely, therefore, that this bulk will mount to a magnitude wherein no limit checks the growth.

and there is, beyond this, the world which the mind, led on by objects of sense, can view: I mean the Intelligible: and in this we detect again a further distinction into the Created and the Uncreate: to the latter of which we have defined the Holy Trinity to belong, to the former all that can exist or can be thought of after that. But in order that this statement may not be left without a proof, but may be confirmed by Scripture, we will add that our Lord was not created, but came forth from the Father, as the Word with His own lips attests in the Gospel, in a manner of birth or of proceeding ineffable and mysterious: and what truer witness could be found than this constant declaration of our Lord all through the Gospel, that the Very Father was a father, not a creator, of Himself, and that He was not a work of God, but Son of God? Just as when He wished to name His connexion with humanity according to the flesh, He called that phase of his being Son of Man, indicating thereby His kinship according to the nature of the flesh with her from whom He was born, so also by the title of Son he expresses His true and real relationship to the Almighty, by that name of Son showing this natural connexion: no matter if there are some who, for the contradiction of the truth, do take literally and without any explanation, words used with a hidden meaning in the dark form of parable, and adduce the expression 'created,' put into the mouth of Wisdom by the author of the Proverbs[6], to support their perverted views. They say, in fact, that "the Lord created me" is a proof that our Lord is a creature, as if the Only-begotten Himself in that word confessed it. But we need not heed such an argument. They do not give reasons why we must refer that text to our Lord at all: neither will they be able to show that the idea of the word in the Hebrew leads to this and no other meaning, seeing that the other translators have rendered it by "possessed" or "constituted:" nor, finally, even if this was the idea in the original text, would its real meaning be so plain and on the surface: for these proverbial discourses do not show their aim at once, but rather conceal it, revealing it only by an indirect import, and we may judge of the obscurity of this particular passage from its context where he says, "When He set His throne upon the winds[7]," and all the similar expressions. What is God's throne? Is it material or ideal?

What are the winds? Are they these winds so familiar to us, which the natural philosophers tell us are formed from vapours and exhalations: or are they to be understood in another way not familiar to man, when they are called the bases of His throne? What is this throne of the immaterial, incomprehensible, and formless Deity? Who could possibly understand all this in a literal sense?

23. *These doctrines of our Faith witnessed to and confirmed by Scripture passages.*

It is therefore clear that these are metaphors, which contain a deeper meaning than the obvious one: so that there is no reason from them that any suspicion that our Lord was created should be entertained by reverent inquirers, who have been trained according to the grand words of the evangelist, that "all things that have been made were made by Him" and "consist in Him." "Without Him was not anything made that was made." The evangelist would not have so defined it if he had believed that our Lord was one among the things made. How could all things be made by Him and in Him consist, unless their Maker possessed a nature different from theirs, and so produced, not Himself, but them? If the creation was by Him, but He was not by Himself, plainly He is something outside the creation. And after the evangelist has by these words so plainly declared that the things that were made were made by the Son, and did not pass into existence by any other channel, Paul [8] follows and, to leave no ground at all for this profane talk which numbers even the Spirit amongst the things that were, made, he mentions one after another all the existencies which the evangelist's words imply: just as David in fact, after having said that "all things" were put in subjection to man, adds each species which that "all" comprehends, that is, the creatures on land, in water, and in air, so does Paul the Apostle, expounder of the divine doctrines, after saying that all things were made by Him, define by numbering them the meaning of "all." He speaks of "the things that are seen[9]" and "the things that are not seen:" by the first he gives a general name to all things cognizable by the senses, as we have seen: by the latter he shadows forth the intelligible world.

Now about the first there is no necessity of going into minute detail. No one is so

---

6 Proverbs viii. 22 (LXX). For another discussion of this passage, see Book II. ch. 10 (beginning) with note.
7 Proverbs viii. 27 (LXX).

8 in the Canon. (Oehler's stopping is here at fault, i.e. he begins a new paragraph with Ἐκδέχεται τὸν λόγον τοῦτον ὁ Παῦλος). We need not speculate whether Gregory was aware that the Epistle to the Colossians (quoted below) is an earlier 'Gospel' than S. John's.
9 Coloss. i. 16.

carnal, so brutelike, as to imagine that the Spirit resides in the sensible world. But after Paul has mentioned "the things that are not seen" he proceeds (in order that none may surmise that the Spirit, because He is of the intelligible and immaterial world, on account of this connexion subsists therein) to another most distinct division into the things that have been made in the way of creation, and the existence that is above creation. He mentions the several classes of these created intelligibles: " [1] thrones," "dominions," "principalities," "powers," conveying his doctrine about these unseen influences in broadly comprehensive terms: but by his very silence he separates from his list of things created that which is above them. It is just as if any one was required to name the sectional and inferior officers in some army, and after he had gone through them all, the commanders of tens, the commanders of hundreds, the captains and the colonels [2], and all the other names given to the authorities over divisions, omitted after all to speak of the supreme command which extended over all the others: not from deliberate neglect, or from forgetfulness, but because when required or intending to name only the several ranks which served under it, it would have been an insult to include this supreme command in the list of the inferior. So do we find it with Paul, who once in Paradise was admitted to mysteries, when he had been caught up there, and had become a spectator of the wonders that are above the heavens, and saw and heard "things which it is not lawful for a man to utter [3]." This Apostle proposes to tell us of all that has been created by our Lord, and he gives them under certain comprehensive terms: but, having traversed all the angelic and transcendental world, he stops his reckoning there, and refuses to drag down to the level of creation that which is above it. Hence there is a clear testimony in Scripture that the Holy Spirit is higher than the creation. Should any one attempt to refute this, by urging that neither are the Cherubim mentioned by Paul, that they equally with the Spirit are left out, and that therefore this omission must prove either that they also are above the creation, or that the Holy Spirit is not any more than they to be believed above it, let him measure the full intent of each name in the list: and he will find amongst them that which from not being actually mentioned seems, but only seems, omitted. Under "thrones" he includes the Cherubim, giving them this Greek name, as more intelligible than the Hebrew name for them. He knew that "God sits upon the Cherubim:" and so he calls these Powers the thrones of Him who sits thereon. In the same way there are included in the list Isaiah's Seraphim [4], by whom the mystery of the Trinity was luminously proclaimed, when they uttered that marvellous cry " Holy," being awestruck with the beauty in each Person of the Trinity. They are named under the title of "powers" both by the mighty Paul, and by the prophet David. The latter says, "Bless ye the Lord all ye His powers, ye ministers of His that do His pleasure [5]:" and Isaiah instead of saying " Bless ye" has written the very words of their blessing, "Holy, Holy, Holy, Lord God of hosts: the whole earth is full of His glory" and he has revealed by what one of the Seraphim did (to him) that these powers are ministers that do God's pleasure, effecting the 'purging of sin' according to the will of Him Who sent them: for this is the ministry of these spiritual beings, viz., to be sent forth for the salvation of those who are being saved.

That divine Apostle perceived this. He understood that the same matter is indicated under different names by the two prophets, and he took the best known of the two words, and called those Seraphim "powers:" so that no ground is left to our critics for saying that any single one of these beings is omitted equally with the Holy Ghost from the catalogue of creation. We learn from the existences detailed by Paul that while some existences have been mentioned, others have been passed over: and while he has taken count of the creation in masses as it were, he has (elsewhere) mentioned as units those things which are conceived of singly. For it is a peculiarity of the Holy Trinity that it is to be proclaimed as consisting of individuals: one Father, one Son, one Holy Ghost: whereas those existences aforesaid are counted in masses, "dominions," "principalities," "lordships," "powers," so as to exclude any suspicion that the Holy Ghost was one of them. Paul is wisely silent upon our mysteries; he understands how, after having heard those unspeakable words in paradise, to refrain from proclaiming those secrets when he is making mention of lower beings.

But these foes of the truth rush in upon the ineffable; they degrade the majesty of the Spirit to the level of the creation; they act as if they had never heard that the Word of God, when confiding to His disciples the secret of knowing God, Himself said that the life of

---

[1] Coloss. i. 16.

[2] ταξιάρχας καὶ λοχαγοὺς, ἐκατοντάρχους τε καὶ χιλιάρχους. The difference between the two pairs seems to be the difference between ' non-commissioned' and ' commissioned' officers.

[3] 2 Corinth. xii. 4.

[4] Isaiah vi. 6, 7.

[5] Psalm ciii. 21.

⁶the regenerate was to be completed in them and imparted in the name of Father, Son, and Holy Ghost, and, thereby ranking the Spirit with the Father and Himself, precluded Him from being confused with the creation. From both, therefore, we may get a reverential and proper conception with regard to Him: from Paul's omitting the Spirit's existence in the mention of the creation, and from our Lord's joining the Spirit with His Father and Himself in mentioning the life-giving power. Thus does our reason, under the guidance of the Scripture, place not only the Only-begotten but the Holy Spirit as well above the creation, and prompt us in accordance with our Saviour's command to contemplate Him by faith in the blessed world of life giving and uncreated existence: and so this unit, which we believe in, above creation, and sharing in the supreme and absolutely perfect nature, cannot be regarded as in any way a 'less,' although this teacher of heresy attempt to curtail its infinitude by introducing the idea of degrees, and thus contracting the divine perfection by defining a greater and a less as residing in the Persons.

§ 24. *His elaborate account of degrees and differences in 'works' and 'energies' within the Trinity is absurd.*

Now let us see what he adds, as the consequence of this. After saying that we must perforce regard the Being as greater and less, and that while ⁷the ones, by virtue of a preeminent magnitude and value, occupy a leading place, the others must be detruded to a lower place, because their nature and their value is secondary, he adds this; "their difference amounts to that existing between their works: it would in fact be impious to say that the same energy produced the angels or the stars, and the heavens or man; but one would positively maintain about this, that in proportion as some works are older and more honourable than others, so does one energy transcend another, because sameness of energy produces sameness of work, and difference of work indicates difference of energy."

I suspect that their author himself would find it difficult to tell us what he meant when he wrote those words. Their thought is obscured by the rhetorical mud, which is so thick that one can hardly see beyond any clue to interpret them. "Their difference amounts to that existing between their works" is a sentence which might be suspected of coming from some Loxias of pagan story, mystifying

his hearers. But if we may make a guess at the drift of his observations here by following out those which we have already examined, this would be his meaning, viz., that if we know the amount of difference between one work and another, we shall know the amount of that between the corresponding energies. But what "works" he here speaks of, it is impossible to discover from his words. If he means the works to be observed in the creation, I do not see how this hangs on to what goes before. For the question was about Father, Son, and Holy Ghost: what occasion was there, then, for one thinking rationally to inquire one after another into the nature of earth, and water, and air, and fire, and the different animals, and to distinguish some works as older and more honourable than others, and to speak of one energy as transcending another? But if he calls the Only-begotten and the Holy Spirit "works," what does he mean by the "differences" of the energies which produce these works: and what are ⁸those wonderful energies of this writer which transcend the others? He has neither explained the particular way in which he means them to "transcend" each other; nor has he discussed the nature of these energies: but he has advanced in neither direction, neither proving so far their real subsistence, nor their being some unsubstantial exertion of a will. Throughout it all his meaning hangs suspended between these two conceptions, and oscillates from one to the other. He adds that "it would be impious to say that the same energy produced the angels or the stars, and the heavens or man." Again we ask what necessity there is to draw this conclusion from his previous remarks? I do not see that it is proved any more ⁹because the energies vary amongst themselves as much as the works do, and because the works are not all from the same source but are stated by him to come from different sources. As for the heavens and each angel, star, and man, or anything else understood by the word "creation," we know from Scripture that they are all the work of One: whereas in their system of theology the Son and the Spirit are not the work of one and the same, the Son being the work of the energy which 'follows' the first Being, and the Spirit the further work of that work. What the connexion, then, is between that statement and the heavens, man, angel, star, which he drags in, must be revealed by himself, or some one whom he has initiated into his profound philosophy. The blasphemy intended by his words is plain

⁶ τοῖς ἀναγεννωμένοις.
⁷ τὰς μὲν, i.e. Οὐσίας. Eunomius' Arianism here degenerates into mere Emanationism: but even in this system the Substances were living: it is best on the whole to translate οὐσία 'being,' and this, as a rule, is adhered to throughout.

⁸ κἀκεῖναι αἱ ἐνεργείαι αὗται.
⁹ τῷ παρηλλάχθαι, κ.τ.λ. This is Oehler's emendation for the faulty reading τὸ of the editions

enough, but the way the profanity is stated is inconsistent with itself. To suppose that within the Holy Trinity there is a difference as wide as that which we can observe between the heavens which envelope the whole creation, and one single man or the star which shines in them, is openly profane : but still the connexion of such thoughts and the pertinence of such a comparison is a mystery to me, and I suspect also to its author himself. If indeed his account of the creation were of this sort, viz., that while the heavens were the work of some transcendent energy each star in them was the result of an energy accompanying the heavens, and that then an angel was the result of that star, and a man of that angel, his argument would then have consisted in a comparison of similar processes, and might have somewhat confirmed his doctrine. But since he grants that it was all made by One (unless he wishes to contradict Scripture downright), while he describes the production of the Persons after a different fashion, what connexion is there between this newly imported view and what went before?

But let it be granted to him that this comparison does have some connexion with proving variation amongst the Beings (for this is what he desires to establish); still let us see how that which follows hangs on to what he has just said, 'In proportion as one work is prior to another and more precious than it, so would a pious mind affirm that one energy transcends another.' If in this he alludes to the sensible world, the statement is a long way from the matter in hand. There is no necessity whatever that requires one whose subject is theological to philosophize about the order in which the different results achieved in the world-making are to come, and to lay down that the energies of the Creator are higher and lower analogously to the magnitude of each thing then made. But if he speaks of the Persons themselves, and means by works that are 'older and more honourable' those 'works' which he has just fashioned in his own creed, that is, the Son, and the Holy Ghost, it would be perhaps better to pass over in silence such an abominable view, than to create even the appearance of its being an argument by entangling ourselves with it. For can a 'more honourable' be discovered where there is not a less honourable? If he can go so far, and with so light a heart, in profanity as to hint that the expression and the idea 'less precious' can be predicated of anything whatever which we believe of the Trinity, then it were well to stop our ears, and get as quickly as possible out of hearing of such wickedness, and the contagion of reasoning which will be

transfused into the heart, as from a vessel full of uncleanness.

Can any one dare to speak of the divine and supreme Being in such a way that a less degree of honour in comparison is proved by the argument. "That all," says the evangelist, "may honour the Son, as they honour the Father[1]." This utterance (and such an utterance is a law to us) makes a law of this equality in honour : yet this man annuls both the law and its Giver, and apportions to the One more, to the Other less of honour, by some occult method for measuring its extra abundance which he has discovered. By the custom of mankind the differences of worth are the measure of the amount of honour which each in authority receives; so that inferiors do not approach the lower magistracies in the same guise exactly as they do the sovereign, and the greater or less display of fear or reverence on their part indicates the greater or the less worshipfulness in the objects of it : in fact we may discover, in this disposition of inferiors, who *are* the specially honourable; when, for instance, we see some one feared beyond his neighbours, or the recipient of more reverence than the rest. But in the case of the divine nature, because every perfection in the way of goodness is connoted with the very name of God, we cannot discover, at all events as *we* look at it, any ground for degrees of honour. Where there is no greater and smaller in power, or glory, or wisdom, or love, or of any other imaginable good whatever, but the good which the Son has is the Father's also, and all that is the Father's is seen in the Son, what possible state of mind can induce us to show the more reverence in the case of the Father? If we think of royal power and worth the Son is King: if of a judge, 'all judgment is committed to the Son[2]:' if of the magnificent office of Creation, 'all things were made by Him[2]:' if of the Author of our life, we know the True Life came down as far as our nature : if of our being taken out of darkness, we know He is the True Light, who weans us from darkness : if wisdom is precious to any, Christ is God's power and Wisdom[3].

Our very souls, then, being disposed so naturally and in proportion to their capacity, and yet so miraculously, to recognize so many and great wonders in Christ, what further excess of honour is left us to pay exclusively to the Father, as inappropriate to the Son? Human reverence of the Deity, looked at in its plainest meaning, is nothing else but

---

[1] John v. 23.   [2] John v. 22; i. 3.
[3] 1 Cor. i. 24.   "Christ the power of God, and the wisdom of God."

an attitude of love towards Him, and a confession of the perfections in Him : and I think that the precept 'so ought the Son to be honoured as the Father[4],' is enjoined by the Word in place of love. For the Law commands that we pay to God this fitting honour by *loving* Him with all our heart and strength ; and here is the equivalent of that love, in that the Word as Lawgiver thus says, that the Son ought to be *honoured* as the Father.

It was this kind of honour that the great David fully paid, when he confessed to the Lord in a prelude[5] of his psalmody that he loved the Lord, and told all the reasons for his love, calling Him his " rock " and " fortress," and " refuge," and " deliverer," and " God-helper," and " hope," and " buckler," and " horn of salvation," and " protector." If the Only-begotten Son is not all these to mankind, let the excess of honour be reduced to this extent as this heresy dictates : but if we have always believed Him to be, and to be entitled to, all this and even more, and to be equal in every operation and conception of the good to the majesty of the Father's goodness, how can it be pronounced consistent, either not to love such a character, or to slight it while we love it ? No one can say that we ought to love Him with *all* our heart and strength, but to honour Him only with half. If, then, the Son is to be honoured with the whole heart in rendering to Him all our love, by what device can anything superior to His honour be discovered, when such a measure of honour is paid Him in the coin of love as our whole heart is capable of ? Vainly, therefore, in the case of Beings essentially honourable, will any one dogmatize about a superior honour, and by comparison suggest an inferior honour.

Again ; only in the case of the creation is it true to speak of 'priority.' The sequence of works was there displayed in the order of the days ; and the heavens may be said to have preceded by so much the making of man, and that interval may be measured by the interval of days. But in the divine nature, which transcends all idea of time and surpasses all reach of thought, to talk of a "prior" and a "later" in the honours of time is a privilege only of this new-fangled philosophy. In short he who declares the Father to be 'prior' to the subsistence of the Son declares nothing short of this, viz., that the Son is later than the things made by the Son[6] (if at

least it is true to say that all the ages, and all duration of time was created after the Son, and by the Son).

§ 25. *He who asserts that the Father is 'prior' to the Son with any thought of an interval must perforce allow that even the Father is not without beginning.*

But more than this : what exposes still further the untenableness of this view is, that, besides positing a beginning in time of the Son's existence, it does not, when followed out, spare the Father even, but proves that He also had his beginning in time. For any recognizing mark that is presupposed for the generation of the Son must certainly define as well the Father's beginning.

To make this clear, it will be well to discuss it more carefully. When he pronounces that the life of the Father is prior to that of the Son, he places a certain interval between the two ; now, he must mean, either that this interval is infinite, or that it is included within fixed limits. But the principle of an intervening mean will not allow him to call it infinite ; he would annul thereby the very conception of Father and Son and the thought of anything connecting them, as long as this infinite were limited on neither side, with no idea of a Father cutting it short above, nor that of a Son checking it below. The very nature of the infinite is, to be extended in either direction, and to have no bounds of any kind.

Therefore if the conception of Father and Son is to remain firm and immoveable, he will find no ground for thinking this interval is infinite : his school must place a definite interval of time between the Only-begotten and the Father. What I say, then, is this : that this view of theirs will bring us to the conclusion that the Father is not from everlasting, but from a definite point in time. I will convey my meaning by familiar illustrations ; the known shall make the unknown clear. When we say, on the authority of the text of Moses, that man was made the fifth day after the heavens, we tacitly imply that before those same days the heavens did not exist either ; a subsequent event goes to define, by means of the interval which precedes it, the occurrence also of a previous event. If this example does not make our contention plain, we can give others. We say that 'the Law given by Moses was four hundred and thirty years later than the Promise to Abraham.' If after traversing, step by step upwards[7], the anterior time we reach

---

4 John v. 23. The Gospel enjoins honour and means love : the Law enjoins love and means honour.

5 *a prelude.* See Psalm vii. 1 and xviii. 1, "fortress," κραταίωμα ; στερέωμα, LXX.

6 The meaning is that, if the Son is later (in time) than the Father, then time must have already existed for this comparison to

be made ; i.e. the Son is later than time as well as the Father. This involves a contradiction.

7 *step by step upwards.* δι' ἀναλύσεως. This does not seem to be used in the Platonic (dialectic) sense, but in the N.T. sense of "return" or "retrogression," cf. Luke xii. 36. Gregory elsewhere

this end of that number of years, we firmly grasp as well the fact that, before that date, God's Promise was not either. Many such instances could be given, but I decline to be minute and wearisome.

Guided, then, by these examples, let us examine the question before us. Our adversaries conceive of the existences of Father, Son, and Holy Spirit as involving elder and younger, respectively. Well then ; if, at the bidding of this heresy, we journey up beyond the generation of the Son, and approach that intervening duration which the mere fancy of these dogmatists supposes between the Father and the Son, and then reach that other and supreme point of time by which they close that duration, there we find the life of the Father fixed as it were upon an apex ; and thence we must necessarily conclude that before it the Father is not to be believed to have existed always.

If you still feel difficulties about this, let us again take an illustration. It shall be that of two rulers, one shorter than the other. If we fit the bases of the two together we know from the tops the extra length of the one ; from the end of the lesser lying alongside of it we measure this excess, supplementing the deficiency of the shorter ruler by a calculation, and so bringing it up to the end of the longer ; a cubit for instance, or whatever be the distance of the one end from the other. So, if there is, as our adversaries say, an excess of some kind in the Father's life as compared with the Son's, it must needs consist in some definite interval of duration : and they will allow that this interval of excess cannot be in the future, for that Both are imperishable, even the foes of the truth will grant. No ; they conceive of this difference as in the past, and instead of equalizing the life of the Father and the Son there, they extend the conception of the Father by an interval of living. But every interval must be bounded by two ends : and so for this interval which they have devised we must grasp the two points by which the ends are denoted. The one portion takes its beginning, in their view, from the Son's generation ; and the other portion must end in some other point, from which the interval starts, and by which it limits itself. What this is, is for them to tell us ; unless, indeed, they are ashamed of the consequences of their own assumptions.

It admits not of a doubt, then, that they will not be able to find at all the other portion, corresponding to the first portion of their fancied

interval, except they were to suppose some beginning of their Ungenerate, whence the middle, that connects with the generation of the Son, may be conceived of as starting. We affirm, then, that when he makes the Son later than the Father by a certain intervening extension of life, he must grant a fixed beginning to the Father's existence also, regulated by this same interval of his devising ; and thus their much-vaunted " Ungeneracy " of the Father will be found to be undermined by its own champions' arguments ; and they will have to confess that their Ungenerate God did once not exist, but began from a starting-point : indeed, that which has a beginning of being is not inoriginate. But if we must at all risks confess this absence of beginning in the Father, let not such exactitude be displayed in fixing for the life of the Son a point which, as the term of His existence, must cut Him off from the life on the other side of it ; let it suffice on the ground of causation only to conceive of the Father as before the Son ; and let not the Father's life be thought of as a separate and peculiar one before the generation of the Son, lest we should have to admit the idea inevitably associated with this of an interval before the appearance of the Son which measures the life of Him Who begot Him, and then the necessary consequence of this, that a beginning of the Father's life also must be supposed by virtue of which their fancied interval may be stayed in its upward advance so as to set a limit and a beginning to this previous life of the Father as well : let it suffice for us, when we confess the ' coming from Him,' to admit also, bold as it may seem, the ' living along with Him ;' for we are led by the written oracles to such a belief. For we have been taught by Wisdom to contemplate the brightness [8] of the everlasting light in, and together with, the very everlastingness of that primal light, joining in one idea the brightness and its cause, and admitting no priority. Thus shall we save the theory of our Faith, the Son's life not failing in the upward view, and the Father's everlastingness being not trenched upon by supposing any definite beginning for the Son.

§ 26. *It will not do to apply this conception, as drawn out above, of the Father and Son to the Creation, as they insist on doing: but we must contemplate the Son apart with the Father, and believe that the Creation had its origin from a definite point.*

But perhaps some of the opponents of this will say, ' The Creation also has an acknowledged beginning ; and yet the things in it are

---

● *Hom. Opif.* xxv.), uses ἀναλύειν in this sense: speaking of the three examples of Christ's power of raising from the dead, he says, ' you see . . . all these equally at the command of one and the same voice returning (ἀναλύοντας) to life." 'Ἀναλύσις thus also came to mean " death," as a 'return.' Cf. Ecclesiast. xi. 7.

[8] *brightness.* Heb. i. 3, ἀπαύγασμα τῆς δόξης.

not connected in thought with the everlasting-ness of the Father, and it does not check, by having a beginning of its own, the infinitude of the divine life, which is the monstrous con-clusion this discussion has pointed out in the case of the Father and the Son. One therefore of two things must follow. Either the Creation is everlasting; or, it must be boldly admitted, the Son is later in time (than the Father). The conception of an interval in time will lead to monstrous conclusions, even when measured from the Creation up to the Creator.'

One who demurs so, perhaps from not attending closely to the meaning of our belief, fights against it with alien compari-sons which have nothing to do with the matter in hand. If he could point to any-thing above Creation which has its origin marked by any interval of time, and it were acknowledged possible by all to think of any time-interval as existing before Crea-tion, he might have occasion for endeavour-ing to destroy by such attacks that everlasting-ness of the Son which we have proved above. But seeing that by all the suffrages of the faithful it is agreed that, of all things that are, part is by creation, and part before creation, and that the divine nature is to be believed un-create (although within it, as our faith teaches, there is a cause, and there is a subsistence pro-duced, but without separation, from the cause), while the creation is to be viewed in an extension of distances,—all order and sequence of time in events can be perceived only in the ages (of this creation), but the nature pre-existent to those ages escapes all distinctions of before and after, because reason cannot see in that divine and blessed life the things which it observes, and that exclusively, in creation. The creation, as we have said, comes into existence according to a sequence of order, and is commensurate with the duration of the ages, so that if one ascends along the line of things created to their beginning, one will bound the search with the foundation of those ages. But the world above creation, being removed from all conception of distance, eludes all sequence of time : it has no commencement of that sort : it has no end in which to cease its advance, according to any discoverable method of order. Having traversed the ages and all that has been produced therein, our thought catches a glimpse of the divine nature, as of some immense ocean, but when the imagination stretches onward to grasp it, it gives no sign in its own case of any beginning ; so that one who after inquiring with curiosity into the 'priority' of the ages tries to mount to the source of all things will never be able to make a single calculation on which he may stand ; that which he seeks will always be moving on before, and no basis will be offered him for the curiosity of thought.

It is clear, even with a moderate insight into the nature of things, that there is nothing by which we can measure the divine and blessed Life. It is not in time, but time flows from it ; whereas the creation, starting from a manifest beginning, journeys onward to its proper end through spaces of time ; so that it is possible, as Solomon somewhere[9] says, to detect in it a beginning, an end, and a middle ; and mark the sequence of its history by divisions of time. But the supreme and blessed life has no time-extension accompany-ing its course, and therefore no span nor measure. Created things are confined within the fitting measures, as within a boundary, with due regard to the good adjustment of the whole by the pleasure of a wise Creator ; and so, though human reason in its weakness cannot reach the whole way to the contents of crea-tion, yet still we do not doubt that the creative power has assigned to all of them their limits and that they do not stretch beyond creation. But this creative power itself, while circumscribing by itself the growth of things, has itself no circumscribing bounds ; it buries in itself every effort of thought to mount up to the source of God's life, and it eludes the busy and ambitious strivings to get to the end of the Infinite. Every discursive effort of thought to go back beyond the ages will ascend only so far as to see that that which it seeks can never be passed through : time and its contents seem the measure and the limit of the movement and the working of human thought, but that which lies beyond remains outside its reach ; it is a world where it may not tread, unsullied by any object that can be comprehended by man. No form, no place, no size, no reckoning of time, or anything else knowable, is there : and so it is inevitable that our apprehensive faculty, seeking as it does always some object to grasp, must fall back from any side of this incomprehensible existence, and seek in the ages and in the creation which they hold its kindred and congenial sphere.

All, I say, with any insight, however moderate, into the nature of things, know that the world's Creator laid time and space as a background to receive what was to be ; on this foundation He builds the universe. It is not possible that anything which has come or is now coming into being by way of creation can be independent of space or time. But the existence which is all-suf-ficient, everlasting, world-enveloping, is not in space, nor in time : it is before these, and

<hr>

9 Compare Eccles. iii. 1—11 ; and viii. 5, "and a wise man's heart discerneth both time and judgment.'

above these in an ineffable way ; self-contained, knowable by faith alone ; immeasurable by ages ; without the accompaniment of time ; seated and resting in itself, with no associations of past or future, there being nothing beside and beyond itself, whose passing can make something past and something future. Such accidents are confined to the creation, whose life is divided with time's divisions into memory and hope. But within that transcendent and blessed Power all things are equally present as in an instant : past and future are within its all-encircling grasp and its comprehensive view.

This is the Being in which, to use the words of the Apostle, all things are formed ; and we, with our individual share in existence, live and move, and have our being [10]. It is above beginning, and presents no marks of its inmost nature : it is to be known of only in the impossibility of perceiving it. That indeed is its most special characteristic, that its nature is too high for any distinctive attribute. A very different account to the Uncreate must be given of Creation : it is this very thing that takes it out of all comparison and connexion with its Maker ; this difference, I mean, of essence, and this admitting a special account explanatory of its nature which has nothing in common with that of Him who made it. The Divine nature is a stranger to these special marks in the creation : It leaves beneath itself the sections of time, the 'before' and the 'after,' and the ideas of space : in fact 'higher' cannot properly be said of it at all. Every conception about that uncreate Power is a sublime principle, and involves the idea of what is proper in the highest degree [11].

We have shewn, then, by what we have said that the Only-begotten and the Holy Spirit are not to be looked for in the creation but are to be believed above it ; and that while the creation may perhaps by the persevering efforts of ambitious seekers be seized in its own beginning, whatever that may be, the supernatural will not the more for that come within the realm of knowledge, for no mark before the ages indicative of its nature can be found. Well, then, if in this uncreate existence those wondrous realities, with their wondrous names of Father, Son, and Holy Ghost, are to be in our thoughts, how can we imagine, of that pre-temporal world, that which our busy, restless minds perceive in things here below by comparing one of them with another and giving it precedence by an interval of time ? For there, with the Father, unoriginate, ungenerate, always

Father, the idea of the Son as coming from Him yet side by side with Him is inseparably joined ; and through the Son and yet with Him, before any vague and unsubstantial conception comes in between, the Holy Spirit is found at once in closest union ; not subsequent in existence to the Son, as if the Son could be thought of as ever having been without the Spirit ; but Himself also owning the same cause of His being, i.e. the God over all, as the Only-begotten Light, and having shone forth in that very Light, being divisible neither by duration nor by an alien nature from the Father or from the Only-begotten. There are no intervals in that pre-temporal world : and difference on the score of being there is none. It is not even possible, comparing the uncreate with the uncreated, to see differences ; and the Holy Ghost is uncreate, as we have before shewn.

This being the view held by all who accept in its simplicity the undiluted Gospel, what occasion was there for endeavouring to dissolve this fast union of the Son with the Father by means of the creation, as if it were necessary to suppose either that the Son was from everlasting along with the creation, or that He too, equally with it, was later ? For the generation of the Son does not fall within time [1], any more than the creation was before time : so that it can in no kind of way be right to partition the indivisible, and to insert, by declaring that there was a time when the Author of all existence was not, this false idea of time into the creative Source of the Universe.

Our previous contention, therefore, is true, that the everlastingness of the Son is included,

---

[10] Acts xvii. 28 ; Col. i. 17.
[11] καὶ τὸν τοῦ κυριωτάτου λόγον ἐπέχει·

[1] *The generation of the Son does not fall within time.* On this "eternal generation" Denys (*De la Philosophie d'Origène*, p. 452) has the following remarks, illustrating the probable way that Athanasius would have dealt with Eunomius : "If we do not see how God's indivisibility remains in the co-existence of the three Persons, we can throw the blame of this difficulty upon the feebleness of our reason : while it is a manifest contradiction to admit at one and the same time the simplicity of the Uncreated, and some change or inequality within His Being. I know that the defenders of the orthodox belief might be troubled with their adversaries' argument. (Eunom. Apol. 22.) 'If we admit that the Son, the energy creative of the world, is equal to the Father, it amounts to admitting that He is the actual energy of the Father in Creation, and that this energy is equal to His essence. But that is to return to the mistake of the Greeks who identified His essence and His energy, and consequently made the world coexist with God.' A serious difficulty, certainly, and one that has never yet been solved, nor will be ; as all the questions likewise which refer to the Uncreated and Created, to eternity and time. It is true we cannot explain how God's eternally active energy does prolong itself eternally. But what is this difficulty compared with those which, with the hypothesis of Eunomius, must be swallowed? We must suppose, so, that the Ἀγέννητος, since His energy is *not eternal*, *became* in a given place and moment, and that He was at that point the Γεννητός. We must suppose that this activity communicated to a creature that privilege of the Uncreated which is most incommunicable, viz. the power of creating other creatures. We must suppose that these creatures, unconnected as they are with the Ἀγέννητος (since He has not made them), nevertheless conceive of and see beyond their own creator a Being, who cannot be anything to them. [This direct intuition on our part of the Deity was a special tenet of Eunomius.] Finally we must suppose that these creatures, seeing that Eunomius agrees with orthodox believers that the end of this world will be but a commencement, will enter into new relations with this Ἀγέννητος, when the Son shall have submitted all things to the Father."

along with the idea of His birth, in the Father's ungeneracy; and that, if any interval were to be imagined dividing the two, that same interval would fix a beginning for the life of the Almighty;—a monstrous supposition. But there is nothing to prevent the creation, being, as it is, in its own nature something other than its Creator and in no point trenching on that pure pre-temporal world, from having, in our belief, a beginning of its own, as we have said. To say that the heavens and the earth and other contents of creation were out of things which are not, or, as the Apostle says, out of "things not seen,[2]" inflicts no dishonour upon the Maker of this universe; for we know from Scripture that all these things are not from everlasting nor will remain for ever. If on the other hand it could be believed that there is something in the Holy Trinity which does not coexist with the Father, if following out this heresy any thought could be entertained of stripping the Almighty of the glory of the Son and Holy Ghost, it would end in nothing else than in a God manifestly removed from every deed and thought that was good and godlike. But if the Father, existing before the ages, is always in glory, and the pre-temporal Son is His glory, and if in like manner the Spirit of Christ is the Son's glory, always to be contemplated along with the Father and the Son, what training could have led this man of learning to declare that there is a 'before' in what is timeless, and a 'more honourable' in what is all essentially honourable, and preferring, by comparisons, the one to the other, to dishonour the latter by this partiality? The term in opposition [3] to the more honourable makes it clearer still whither he is tending.

§ 27. *He falsely imagines that the same energies produce the same works, and that variation in the works indicates variation in the energies.*

Of the same strain is that which he adds in the next paragraph; "the same energies producing sameness of works, and different works indicating difference in the energies as well." Finely and irresistibly does this noble thinker plead for his doctrine. "The same energies produce sameness of works." Let us test this by facts. The energy of fire is always one and the same; it consists in heating: but what sort of agreement do its results show? Bronze melts in it; mud hardens; wax vanishes: while all other animals are destroyed by it, the salamander is preserved alive [4]; tow burns, as-

bestos is washed by the flames as if by water; so much for his 'sameness of works from one and the same energy.' How too about the sun? Is not his power of warming always the same; and yet while he causes one plant to grow, he withers another, varying the results of his operation in accordance with the latent force of each. 'That on the rock' withers; 'that in deep earth' yields an hundredfold. Investigate Nature's work, and you will learn, in the case of those bodies which she produces artistically, the amount of accuracy there is in his statement that 'sameness of energy effects sameness of result.' One single operation is the cause of conception, but the composition of that which is effected internally therein is so varied that it would be difficult for any one even to count all the various qualities of the body. Again, imbibing the milk is one single operation on the part of the infant, but the results of its being nourished so are too complex to be all detailed. While this food passes from the channel of the mouth into the secretory ducts [5], the transforming power of Nature forwards it into the several parts proportionately to their wants; for by digestion she divides its sum total into the small change of multitudinous differences, and into supplies congenial to the subject matter with which she deals; so that the same milk goes to feed arteries, veins, brain and its membranes, marrow, bones, nerves [6], sinews, tendons, flesh, surface, cartilages, fat, hair, nails, perspiration, vapours, phlegm, bile, and besides these, all useless superfluities deriving from the same source. You could not name either an organ, whether of motion or sensation, or anything else making up the body's bulk, which was not formed (in spite of startling differences) from this one and selfsame operation of feeding. If one were to compare the mechanic arts too it will be seen what is the scientific value of his statement; for there we see in them all the same operation, I mean the movement of the hands; but what have the results in common? What has building a shrine to do with a coat, though manual labour is employed on both? The house-breaker and the well-digger both move their hands: the mining of the earth, the murder of a man are results of the motion of the hands. The soldier slays the foe, and the husbandman wields the fork which breaks the clod, with his hands. How, then, can this doctrinaire lay it down that the 'same energies produce sameness of work?' But even if we were to grant that this view of his had any truth in it, the essential union of the Son with the Father, and of the

[2] Heb. xi. 1; 2 Cor. iv. 18.
[3] ἀντιδιαστολή.
[4] *is preserved alive*; ζωογονεῖται. This is the LXX., not the classical use, of the word. Cf. Exod. i. 17; Judges viii. 19, &c. It is reproduced in the speech of S. Stephen, Acts vii. 19: cf. Luke xvii. 33, "shall preserve (his life).'

[5] ἀποκριτικοὺς, *active*, so the Medical writers. The Latin 'in meatus destinato *descendit*' takes it *passive* (ἀποκριτικους).
[6] νεῦρα. So since Galen's time: not 'tendon.'

Holy Spirit with the Son, is yet again more fully proved. For if there existed any variation in their energies, so that the Son worked His will in a different manner to the Father, then (on the above supposition) it would be fair to conjecture, from this variation, a variation also in the beings which were the result of these varying energies. But if it is true that the manner of the Father's working is likewise the manner always of the Son's, both from our Lord's own words and from what we should have expected *a priori*—(for the one is not unbodied while the other is embodied, the one is not from this material, the other from that, the one does not work his will in this time and place, the other in that time and place, nor is there difference of organs in them producing difference of result, but the sole movement of their wish and of their will is sufficient, seconded in the founding of the universe by the power that can create anything)—if, I say, it is true that in all respects the Father from Whom are all things, and the Son by Whom are all things in the actual form of their operation work alike, then how can this man hope to prove the essential difference between the Son and the Holy Ghost by any difference and separation between the working of the Son and the Father? The very opposite, as we have just seen, is proved to be the case [7]; seeing that there is no manner of difference contemplated between the working of the Father and that of the Son ; and so that there is no gulf whatever between the being of the Son and the being of the Spirit, is shewn by the identity of the power which gives them their subsistence ; and our pamphleteer himself confirms this; for these are his words *verbatim*: "the same energies producing sameness of works." If sameness of works is really produced by likeness of energies, and if (as they say) the Son is the work of the Father and the Spirit the work of the Son, the likeness in manner [8] of the Father's and the Son's energies will demonstrate the sameness of these beings who each result from them.

But he adds, "variation in the works indicates variation in the energies." How, again, is this dictum of his corroborated by facts? Look, if you please, at plain instances. Is not the 'energy' of command, in Him who embodied the world and all things therein by His sole will, a single energy? "He spake and they were made. He commanded and they were created." Was not the thing commanded in every case alike given existence : did not His

single will suffice to give subsistence to the non-existent? How, then, when such vast differences are seen coming from that one energy of command, can this man shut his eyes to realities, and declare that the difference of works indicates difference of energies? If our dogmatist insists on this, that difference of works implies difference of energies, then we should have expected the very contrary to that which is the case ; viz., that everything in the world should be of one type. Can it be that he does see here a universal likeness, and detects unlikeness only between the Father and the Son?

Let him, then, observe, if he never did before, the dissimilarity amongst the elements of the world, and how each thing that goes to make up the framework of the whole hangs on to its natural opposite. Some objects are light and buoyant, others heavy and gravitating ; some are always still, others always moving ; and amongst these last some move unchangingly on one plan [9], as the heaven, for instance, and the planets, whose courses all revolve the opposite way to the universe, others are transfused in all directions and rush at random, as air and sea for instance, and every substance which is naturally penetrating [10]. What need to mention the contrasts seen between heat and cold, moist and dry, high and low position? As for the numerous dissimilarities amongst animals and plants, on the score of figure and size, and all the variations of their products and their qualities, the human mind would fail to follow them.

§ 28. *He falsely imagines that we can have an unalterable series of harmonious natures existing side by side.*

But this man of science still declares that varied works have energies as varied to produce them. Either he knows not yet the nature of the Divine energy, as taught by Scripture,—'All things were made by the word of His command,'—or else he is blind to the differences of existing things. He utters for our benefit these inconsiderate statements, and lays down the law about divine doctrines, as if he had never yet heard that anything that is merely asserted,—where no entirely undeniable and plain statement is made about the matter in hand, and where the asserter says on his own responsibility that which a cautious listener cannot assent to,—is no better than a telling of dreams or of stories over wine. Little then as this dictum of his fits facts, nevertheless,—like one who is deluded by a dream into thinking that he sees one of the objects of his waking efforts, and who grasps eagerly at this phantom and

---

7 Punctuating παρασκευάζεται, ἐπειδὴ, κ.τ.λ. instead of a full stop, as Oeuler.

8 Gregory replaces 'sameness' (in the case of the energies in Eunomius argument) by 'likeness' since the Father and the Son could not be said to be the *same*, and their energies, therefore, are not identical but similar.

with eyes deceived by this visionary desire thinks that he holds it,—he with this dream-like outline of doctrines before him imagines that his words possess force, and insists upon their truth, and essays by them to prove all the rest. It is worth while to give the passage. "These being so, and maintaining an unbroken connexion in their relation to each other, it seems fitting for those who make their investigation according to the order germane to the subject, and who do not insist on mixing and confusing all together, in case of a discussion being raised about Being, to prove what is in course of demonstration, and to settle the points in debate, by the primary energies and those attached to the Beings, and again to explain by the Being when the energies are in question." I think the actual phrases of his impiety are enough to prove how absurd is this teaching. If any one had to give a description of the way some disease mars a human countenance, he would explain it better by actually unbandaging the patient, and there would be then no need of words when the eye had seen how he looked. So some mental eye might discern the hideous mutilation wrought by this heresy: its mere perusal might remove the veil. But since it is necessary, in order to make the latent mischief of this teaching clear to the many, to put the finger of demonstration upon it, I will again repeat each word. "This being so." What does this dreamer mean? What is 'this?' How has it been stated? "The Father's being is alone proper and in the highest degree supreme; consequently the next being is dependent, and the third more dependent still." In such words he lays down the law. But why? Is it because an energy accompanies the first being, of which the effect and work, the Only-begotten, is circumscribed by the sphere of this producing cause? Or because these Beings are to be thought of as of greater or less extent, the smaller included within and surrounded by the larger, like casks put one inside the other, inasmuch as he detects degrees of size within Beings that are illimitable? Or because differences of products imply differences of producers, as if it were impossible that different effects should be produced by similar energies? Well, there is no one whose mental faculties are so steeped in sleep as to acquiesce directly after hearing such statements in the following assertion, "these being so, and maintaining an unbroken connexion in their relation to one another." It is equal madness to say such things, and to hear them without any questioning. They are placed in a 'series' and 'an unalterable relation to each other,' and yet they are parted from each other by an essential unlikeness! Either, as our own doctrine insists, they are united in being, and then they really preserve an unalterable relation to each other; or else they stand apart in essential unlikeness, as he fancies. But what series, what relationship that is unalterable can exist with alien entities? And how can they present that 'order germane to the matter' which according to him is to rule the investigation? Now if he had an eye only on the doctrine of the truth, and if the order in which he counts the differences was only that of the attributes which Faith sees in the Holy Trinity, —an order so 'natural' and 'germane' that the Persons cannot be confounded, being divided as Persons, though united in their being—then he would not have been classed at all amongst our enemies, for he would mean the very same doctrine that we teach. But, as it is, he is looking in the very contrary direction, and he makes the order which he fancies *there* quite inconceivable. There is all the difference in the world between the accomplishment of an act of the will, and that of a mechanical law of nature. Heat is inherent in fire, splendour in the sunbeam, fluidity in water, downward tendency in a stone, and so on. But if a man builds a house, or seeks an office, or puts to sea with a cargo, or attempts anything else which requires forethought and preparation to succeed, we cannot say in such a case that there is properly a rank or order inherent in his operations: their order in each case will result as an after consequence of the motive which guided his choice, or the utility of that which he achieves. Well, then; since this heresy parts the Son from any essential relationship with the Father, and adopts the same view of the Spirit as estranged from any union with the Father or the Son, and since also it affirms throughout that the Son is the work of the Father, and the Spirit the work of the Son, and that these works are the results of a purpose, not of nature, what grounds has he for declaring that this work of a will is an 'order inherent in the matter,' and what is the drift of this teaching, which makes the Almighty the manufacturer of such a nature as this in the Son and the Holy Spirit, where transcendent beings are made such as to be inferior the one to the other? If such is really his meaning, why did he not clearly state the grounds he has for presuming in the case of the Deity, that smallness of result will be evidence of all the greater power? But who really could ever allow that a cause that is great and powerful is to be looked for in this smallness of results? As if God was unable to establish His own perfection in anything that comes from Him[1]! And how can he attribute to the Deity the highest prerogative of supremacy while he exhibits His power as thus falling short of His will? Eunomius certainly seems to mean that perfection was not even proposed as the aim of God's work, for fear the honour and glory of One to Whom homage is due for His superiority might be thereby lessened. And yet is there any one so narrow-minded as to reckon the Blessed Deity Himself as not free from the passion of envy? What plausible reason, then, is left why the Supreme Deity should have constituted such an 'order' in the case of the Son and the Spirit? "But I did not mean that 'order' to come from Him," he rejoins. But whence else, if the beings to which this 'order' is connatural are not essentially related to each other? But perhaps he calls the inferiority itself of the being of the Son and of the Spirit this 'connatural order.' But I would beg of him to tell me the reason of this very thing, viz., why the Son is inferior on the score of being, when both this being and energy are to be discovered in the same characteristics and attributes. If on the other hand there is not to be the same[2] definition of being and energy, and each is to signify something different, why does he introduce a demonstration of the thing in question by means of that which is quite different from it? It would be, in that case, just as if, when it was debated with regard to man's own being whether he were a risible animal, or one capable of being taught to read, some one was to adduce the building of a house or ship on the part of a mason or a shipwright as a settling of the question, insisting on the skilful syllogism that we know beings by operations, and a house and a ship are operations of man. Do we then learn, most simple sir, by such premisses, that man is risible as well as broad-nailed? Some one might well retort; 'whether man possesses motion and energy was not the question: it was, what is the energizing principle itself; and that I fail to learn from your way of deciding the question.' Indeed, if we wanted to know something about the nature of the wind, you would not give a satisfactory answer by pointing to a heap of sand or chaff raised by the wind, or to dust which it scattered: for the account to be given of the wind is quite different: and these illustrations of yours would be foreign to the subject. What ground,

then, has he for attempting to explain beings by their energies, and making the definition of an entity out of the resultants of that entity.

Let us observe, too, what sort of work of the Father it is by which the Father's being, according to him, is to be comprehended. The Son most certainly, he will say, if he says as usual. But this Son of yours, most learned sir, is commensurate in your scheme only with the energy which produced Him, and indicates that alone, while the Object of our search still keeps in the dark, if, as you yourself confess, this energy is only one amongst the things which 'follow[3]' the first being. This energy, as you say, extends itself into the work which it produces, but it does not reveal therein its own nature, but only so much of it as we can get a glimpse of in that work. All the resources of a smith are not set in motion to make a gimlet; the skill of that artisan only operates so far as is adequate to form that tool, though it could fashion a large variety of other tools. Thus the limit of the energy is to be found in the work which it produces. But the question now is not about the amount of the energy, but about the being of that which has put forth the energy. In the same way, if he asserts that he can perceive the nature of the Only-begotten in the Spirit (Whom he styles the work of an energy which 'follows' the Son), his assertion has no foundation; for here again the energy, while it extends itself into its work, does not reveal therein the nature either of itself or of the agent who exerts it.

But let us yield in this; grant him that beings are known in their energies. The First being is known through His work; and this Second being is revealed in the work proceeding from *Him*. But what, my learned friend, is to show this Third being? No such work of this Third is to be found. If you insist that these beings are perceived by their energies, you must confess that the Spirit's nature is imperceptible; you cannot infer His nature from any energy put forth by Him to carry on the continuity. Show some substantiated work of the Spirit, through which you think you have detected the being of the Spirit, or all your cobweb will collapse at the touch of Reason. If the being is known by the subsequent energy, and substantiated energy of the Spirit there is none, such as ye say the Father shows in the Son, and the Son in the Spirit, then the nature of the Spirit must be confessed unknowable and not be apprehended through these; there is no energy conceived of in connexion with a substance to show even a side glimpse of it. But if the Spirit eludes apprehension, how

---

[1] ἐν παντὶ τῷ ἐξ αὐτοῦ.

[2] Reading αὐτός; instead of Oehler's αὐτὸς.

[3] *only one thing amongst the things which follow, &c.* The Latin translation is manifestly wrong here, "si recte a te assertum est, *iis* etiam quæ ad primam substantiam sequuntur *aliquam operationem inesse*." The Greek is εἴπερ ἡ ἐνέργεια τῶν παρεπομένων τις εἶναι τῇ πρώτῃ οὐσίᾳ μεμαρτύρηται.

by means of that which is itself imperceptible can the more exalted being be perceived? If the Son's work, that is, the Spirit according to them, is unknowable, the Son Himself can never be known; He will be involved in the obscurity of that which gives evidence of Him: and if the being of the Son in this way is hidden, how can the being who is most properly such and most supreme be brought to light by means of the being which is itself hidden; this obscurity of the Spirit is transmitted by retrogression [4] through the Son to the Father; so that in this view, even by our adversaries' confession, the unknowableness of the Father's being is clearly demonstrated. How, then, can this man, be his eye ever so 'keen to see unsubstantial entities,' discern the nature of the unseen and incomprehensible by means of itself; and how can he command us to grasp the beings by means of their works, and their works again from them?

§ 29. *He vainly thinks that the doubt about the energies is to be solved by the beings, and reversely.*

Now let us see what comes next. 'The doubt about the energies is to be solved by the beings.' What way is there of bringing this man out of his vain fancies down to common sense? If he thinks that it is possible thus to solve doubts about the energies by comprehending the beings themselves, how, if these last are not comprehended, can he change this doubt to any certainty? If the being has been comprehended, what need to make the energy of this importance, as if *it* was going to lead us to the comprehension of the being. But if this is the very thing that makes an examination of the energy necessary, viz., that we may be thereby guided to the understanding of the being that exerts it, how can this as yet unknown nature solve the doubt about the energy? The proof of anything that is doubted must be made by means of well-known truths; but when there is an equal uncertainty about both the objects of our search, how can Eunomius say that they are comprehended by means of each other, both being in themselves beyond our knowledge? When the Father's being is under discussion, he tells us that the question may be settled by means of the energy which follows Him and of the work which this energy accomplishes; but when the inquiry is about the being of the Only-begotten, whether Eunomius calls Him an energy or a product of the energy (for he does both), then he tells

us that the question may be easily solved by looking at the being of His producer!

§ 30. *There is no Word of God that commands such investigations: the uselessness of the philosophy which makes them is thereby proved.*

I should like also to ask him this. Does he mean that energies are explained by the beings which produced them only in the case of the Divine Nature, or does he recognize the nature of the produced by means of the being of the producer with regard to anything whatever that possesses an effective force? If in the case of the Divine Nature only he holds this view, let him show us how he settles questions about the works of God by means of the nature of the Worker. Take an undoubted work of God,—the sky, the earth, the sea, the whole universe. Let it be the being of one of these that, according to our supposition, is being enquired into, and let 'sky' be the subject fixed for our speculative reasoning. It is a question what the substance of the sky is; opinions have been broached about it varying widely according to the lights of each natural philosopher. How will the contemplation of the Maker of the sky procure a solution of the question, immaterial, invisible, formless, ungenerate, everlasting, incapable of decay and change and alteration, and all such things, as He is. How will anyone who entertains this conception of the Worker be led on to the knowledge of the nature of the sky? How will he get an idea of a thing which is visible from the Invisible, of the perishable from the imperishable, of that which has a date for its existence from that which never had any generation, of that which has duration but for a time from the everlasting; in fact, of the object of his search from everything which is the very opposite to it. Let this man who has accurately probed the secret of things tell us how it is possible that two unlike things should be known from each other.

§ 31. *The observations made by watching Providence are sufficient to give us the knowledge of sameness of Being.*

And yet, if he could see the consequences of his own statements, he would be led on by them to acquiesce in the doctrine of the Church. For if the maker's nature is an indication of the thing made, as he affirms, and if, according to his school, the Son is something made by the Father, anyone who has observed the Father's nature would have certainly known thereby that of the Son; if, I say, it is true that the worker's nature is a sign of that which he works. But the Only-begotten, as they say, of the Father's *unlikeness*, will be excluded from operating

---

4 κατὰ ἀνάλυσιν. So Plutarch, ii. 76 E. and see above (cap. 25, note 6.).

through Providence. Eunomius need not trouble any more about His being generated, nor force out of that another proof of the son's unlikeness. The difference of purpose will itself be sufficient to bring to light His alien nature. For the First Being is, even by our opponents' confession, one and single, and necessarily His will must be thought of as following the bent of His nature; but Providence shows that that purpose is good, and so the nature from which that purpose comes is shown to be good also. So the Father alone works good; and the Son does not purpose the same things as He, if we adopt the assumptions of our adversary; the difference, then, of their nature will be clearly attested by this variation of their purposes. But if, while the Father is provident for the Universe, the Son is equally provident for it (for 'what He sees the Father doing that also the Son does'), this sameness of their purposes exhibits a communion of nature in those who thus purpose the same things. Why, then, is all mention of Providence omitted by him, as if it would not help us at all to that which we are searching for. Yet many familiar examples make for our view of it. Anyone who has gazed on the brightness of fire and experienced its power of warming, when he approaches another such brightness and another such warmth, will assuredly be led on to think of fire; for his senses through the medium of these similar phænomena will conduct him to the fact of a kindred element producing both; anything that was not fire could not work on all occasions like fire. Just so, when we perceive a similar and equal amount of providential power in the Father and in the Son, we make a guess by means of what thus comes within the range of our knowledge about things which transcend our comprehension; we feel that causes of an alien nature cannot be detected in these equal and similar effects. As the observed phenomena are to each other, so will the subjects of those phenomena be: if the first are opposed to each other, we must reckon the revealed entities to be so too; if the first are alike, so too must those others be. Our Lord said allegorically that their fruit is the sign of the characters of trees, meaning that it does not belie that character, that the bad is not attached to the good tree, nor the good to the bad tree;—" by their fruits ye shall know them;"—so when the fruit, Providence, presents no difference, we detect a single nature from which that fruit has sprung, even though the trees be different from which the fruit is put forth. Through that, then, which is cognizable by our apprehension, viz., the scheme or Providence visible in the Son in the same way as in the Father, the common likeness of the Only-begotten and the Father is placed beyond a doubt; and it is the identity of the fruits of Providence by which we know it.

§ 32. *His dictum that 'the manner of the likeness must follow the manner of the generation' is unintelligible.*

But to prevent such a thought being entertained, and pretending to be forced somehow away from it, he says that he withdraws from all these results of Providence, and goes back to the manner of the Son's generation, because "the manner of His likeness must follow the manner of His generation." What an irresistible proof! How forcibly does this verbiage compel assent! What skill and precision there is in the wording of this assertion! Then, if we know the manner of the generation, we shall know by that the manner of the likeness. Well, then; seeing that all, or at all events most, animals born by parturition have the same manner of generation, and, according to their logic, the manner of likeness follows this manner of generation, these animals, following as they do the same model in their production, will resemble entirely those similarly generated; for things that are like the same thing are like one another. If, then, according to the view of this heresy, the manner of the generation makes every thing generated just like itself, and it is a fact that this manner does not vary at all in diversified kinds of animals but remains the same in the greatest part of them, we shall find that this sweeping and unqualified assertion of his establishes, by virtue of this similarity of birth, a mutual resemblance between men, dogs, camels, mice, elephants, leopards, and every other animal which Nature produces in the same manner. Or does he mean, not, that things brought into the world in a similar way are all like each other, but that each one of them is like that being only which is the source of its life. But if so, he ought to have declared that the child is like the parent, not that the "manner of the likeness" resembles the "manner of the generation." But this, which is so probable in itself, and is observed as a fact in Nature, that the begotten resembles the begetter, he will not admit as a truth; it would reduce his whole argumentation to a proof of the contrary of what he intended. If he allowed the offspring to be like the parent, his laboured store of arguments to prove the *unlikeness* of the Beings would be refuted as evanescent and groundless.

So he says "the manner of the likeness follows the manner of the generation." This, when tested by the exact critic of the meaning of any idea [5], will be found completely unintel-

---

[5] ἐννοίας λόγον.

ligible. It is plainly impossible to say what a "manner of generation" can mean. Does it mean the figure of the parent, or his impulse, or his disposition ; or the time, or the place, or the completing of the embryo by conception ; or the generative receptacles ; or nothing of that kind, but something else of the things observed in 'generation.' It is impossible to find out what he means. The impropriety and vagueness of the word "manner" causes perplexity as to its signification here ; every possible one is equally open to our surmises, and presents as well an equal want of connexion with the subject before us. So also with this phrase of his "manner of likeness ;" it is devoid of any vestige of meaning, if we fix our attention on the examples familiarly known to us. For the thing generated is not to be likened there to the kind or the manner of its birth. Birth consists, in the case of animal birth, in a separation of body from body, in which the animal perfectly moulded in the womb is brought forth ; but the thing born is a man, or horse, or cow, or whatever it may chance to be in its existence through birth. How, therefore, the "manner of the likeness of the offspring follows the manner of its generation" must be left to him, or to some pupil of his in midwifery, to explain. Birth is one thing : the thing born is another : they are different ideas altogether. No one with any sense would deny that what he says is perfectly untrue in the case of animal births. But if he calls the actual making and the actual fashioning a "manner of the generation," which the "manner of the likeness" of the thing produced is to "follow," even so his statement is removed from all likelihood, as we shall see from some illustrations. Iron is hammered out by the blows of the artificer into some useful instrument. How, then, the outline of its edge, if such there happen to be, can be said to be similar to the hand of the worker, or to the manner of its fashioning, to the hammers, for instance, and the coals and the bellows and the anvil by means of which he has moulded it, no one could explain. And what can be said in one case fits all, where there is any operation producing a result ; the thing produced cannot be said to be like the "manner of its generation." What has the shape of a garment got to do with the spool, or the rods, or the comb, or with the form of the weaver's instruments at all ? What has an actual seat got to do with the working of the blocks ; or any finished production with the build of him who achieved it ?—But I think even our opponents would allow that this rule of his is not in force in sensible and material instances.

It remains to see whether it contributes anything further to the proof of his blasphemy. What, then, was he aiming at ? The necessity of believing in accordance with their being in the likeness or unlikeness of the Son to the Father ; and, as we cannot know about this being from considerations of Providence, the necessity of having recourse to the "manner of the generation," whereby we may know, not indeed whether the Begotten is like the Begetter (absolutely), but only a certain "manner of likeness" between them ; and as this manner is a secret to the many, the necessity of going at some length into the being of the Begetter. Then has he forgotten his own definitions about the beings having to be known from their works ? But this begotten being, which he calls the work of the supreme being, has as yet no light thrown upon it (according to him) ; so how can its nature be dealt with ? And how can he "mount above this lower and therefore more directly comprehensible thing," and so cling to the absolute and supreme being ? Again, he always throughout his discourse lays claim to an accurate knowledge of the divine utterances ; yet here he pays them scant reverence, ignoring the fact that it is not possible to approach to a knowledge of the Father except through the Son. "No man knoweth the Father, save the Son, and he to whomsoever the Son shall reveal Him [6]." Yet Eunomius, while on every occasion, where he can insult our devout and God-adoring conceptions of the Son, he asserts in plain words the Son's inferiority, establishes His superiority unconsciously in this device of his for knowing the Deity ; for he assumes that the Father's being lends itself the more readily to our comprehension, and then attempts to trace and argue out the Son's nature from that.

§ 33. *He declares falsely that 'the manner of the generation is to be known from the intrinsic worth of the generator.'*

He goes back, for instance, to the begetting being, and from thence takes a survey of the begotten ; " for," says he, " the manner of the generation is to be known from the intrinsic worth of the generator." Again, we find this bold unqualified generalization of his causing the thought of the inquirer to be dissipated in every possible direction ; it is the nature of such general statements, to extend in their meanings to every instance, and allow nothing to escape their sweeping assertion. If then 'the manner of the generation is to be known from the intrinsic worth of the generator,' and there are many differences in the worth of gene-

6 Matt. xi. 27.

rators according to their many classifications [7] to be found (for one may be born Jew, Greek, barbarian, Scythian, bond, free), what will be the result? Why, that we must expect to find as many " manners of generation " as there are differences in intrinsic worth amongst the generators ; and that their birth will not be fulfilled with all in the same way, but that their nature will vary with the worth of the parent, and that some peculiar manner of birth will be struck out for each, according to these varying estimations. For a certain inalienable worth is to be observed in the individual parent ; the distinction, that is, of being better or worse off according as there has fallen to each race, estimation, religion, nationality, power, servitude, wealth, poverty, independence, dependence, or whatever else constitutes the life-long differences of worth. If then " the manner of the generation " is shown by the intrinsic worth of the parent, and there are many differences in worth, we shall inevitably find, if we follow this opinion-monger, that the manners of generation are various too ; in fact, this difference of worth will dictate to Nature the manner of the birth.

But if he should not [8] admit that such worth is natural, because they can be put in thought outside the nature of their subject, we will not oppose him. But at all events he will agree to this ; that man's existence is separated by an intrinsic character from that of brutes. Yet the manner of birth in these two cases presents no variation in intrinsic character ; nature brings man and the brute into the world in just the same way, i. e. by generation. But if he apprehends this native dignity only in the case of the most proper and supreme existence, let us see what he means then. In our view, the ' native dignity ' of God consists in godhead itself, wisdom, power, goodness, judgment, justice, strength, mercy, truth, creativeness, domination, invisibility, everlastingness, and every other quality named in the inspired writings to magnify his glory ; and we affirm that every one of them is properly and inalienably found in the Son, recognizing difference only in respect of unoriginateness ; and even that we do not exclude the Son from, according to *all* its meanings. But let no carp-

ing critic attack this statement as if we were attempting to exhibit the Very Son as ungenerate ; for we hold that one who maintains that is no less impious than an Anomœan. But since the meanings of ' origin ' are various, and suggest many ideas, there are some of them in which the title ' unoriginate ' is not inapplicable to the Son [9]. When, for instance, this word has the meaning of ' deriving existence from no cause whatever,' then we confess that it is peculiar to the Father ; but when the question is about ' origin ' in its other meanings (since any creature or time or order has an origin), then we attribute the being superior to origin to the Son as well, and we believe that that whereby all things were made is beyond the origin of creation, and the idea of time, and the sequence of order. So He, Who on the ground of His subsistence is not without an origin, possessed in every other view an undoubted *unoriginateness;* and while the Father is unoriginate and Ungenerate, the Son is unoriginate in the way we have said, though not ungenerate.

What, then, is that native dignity of the Father which he is going to look at in order to infer thereby the ' manner of the generation.' " His not being generated, most certainly," he will reply. If, then, all those names with which we have learnt to magnify God's glory are useless and meaningless to you, Eunomius, the mere going through the list of such expressions is a gratuitous and superfluous task ; none of these other words, you say, expresses the intrinsic worth of the God over all. But if there is a peculiar force fitting our conceptions of the Deity in each of these words, the intrinsic dignities of God must plainly be viewed in connexion with this list, and the likeness of the two beings will be thereby proved ; if, that is, the characters inalienable from the beings are an index of the subjects of those characters. The characters of each being are found to be the same ; and so the identity on the score of being of the two subjects of these identical dignities is shown most clearly. For if the variation in a single name is to be held to be the index of an alien being, how much more should the identity of these countless names avail to prove community of nature !

What, then, is the reason why the other names should all be neglected, and generation be indicated by the means of one alone ? Why do they pronounce this ' Ungeneracy ' to be the only intrinsic character in the Father, and thrust all the rest aside ? It is in order that they may establish their mischievous mode [10] of

---

[7] 'Επίνοια is the opposite of ἔννοια, ' the intuitive idea.' It means an " alterthought," and, with the notion of unnecessary addition, a ' conceit.' Here it is applied to conventional, or not purely natural difference. See Introduction to Book XIII. for the fuller meaning of 'Επίνοια.

[8] μὴ δέχοιτο. This use of the optative, where the subjunctive with ἐάν might have been expected, is one of the few instances in Gregory s Greek of declension from Classic usage ; in the latter, when εἰ with the optative does denote subjective possibility, it is only when the condition is conceived of as of frequent repetition, = g. 1 Peter iii. 14. The optative often in this Greek of the fourth century invades the province of the subjunctive.

[9] μὴ ἀπεμφαίνειν.

[10] See Note on 'Αγέννητος, p. 100.

unlikeness of Father and Son, by this contrast as regards the begotten. But we shall find that this attempt of theirs, when we come to test it in its proper place, is equally feeble, unfounded, and nugatory as the preceding attempts.

Still, that all his reasonings point this way, is shown by the sequel, in which he praises himself for having fittingly adopted this method for the proof of his blasphemy, and yet for not having all at once divulged his intention, nor shocked the unprepared hearer with his impiety, before the concatenation of his delusive argument was complete, nor displayed this Ungeneracy as God's being in the early part of his discourse, nor to weary us with talk about the difference of being. The following are his exact words: "Or was it right, as Basil commands, to begin with the thing to be proved, and to assert incoherently that the Ungeneracy is the being, and to talk about the difference or the sameness of nature?" Upon this he has a long intervening tirade, made up of scoffs and insulting abuse (such being the weapons which this thinker uses to defend his own doctrines), and then he resumes the argument, and turning upon his adversary, fixes upon him, forsooth, the blame of what he is saying, in these words; " For your party, before any others, are guilty of this offence ; having partitioned out this same being between Begetter and Begotten ; and so the scolding you have given is only a halter not to be eluded which you have woven for your own necks ; justice, as might have been expected, records in your own words a verdict against yourselves. Either you first conceive of the beings as sundered, and independent of each other [11] ; and then bring down one of them, by generation, to the rank of Son, and contend that One who exists independently nevertheless was made by means of the Other existence ; and so lay yourselves open to your own reproaches : for to Him whom you imagine as without generation you ascribe a generation by another :—or else you first allow one single causeless being, and then marking this out by an act of causation into Father and Son, you declare that this non-generated being came into existence by means of itself."

§ 34. *The Passage where he attacks the* Ὁμοούσιον, *and the contention in answer to it.*

I will omit to speak of the words which occur before this passage which has been quoted. They contain merely shameless abuse of our Master and Father in God, and nothing bearing on the matter in hand. But on the

passage itself, as he advances by the device of this terrible dilemma a double-edged refutation, we cannot be silent; we must accept the intellectual challenge, and fight for the Faith with all the power we have, and show that the formidable two-edged sword which he has sharpened is feebler than a make-believe in a scene-painting.

He attacks the community of substance with two suppositions ; he says that we either name as Father and as Son two independent principles drawn out parallel to each other, and then say that one of these existencies is produced by the other existence : or else we say that one and the same essence is conceived of, participating in both names in turn, both being [1] Father, and becoming Son, and itself produced in generation from itself. I put this in my own words, thereby not misinterpreting his thought, but only correcting the tumid exaggeration of its expression, in such a way as to reveal his meaning by clearer words and afford a comprehensive view of it. Having blamed us for want of polish and for having brought to the controversy an insufficient amount of learning, he decks out his own work in such a glitter of style, and passes the nail [2]. to use his own phrase, so often over his own sentences, and makes his periods so smart with this elaborate prettiness, that he captivates the reader at once with the attractions of language ; such amongst many others is the passage we have just recited by way of preface. We will, by leave, again recite it. "And so the scolding you have given is only a halter, not to be eluded, which you have woven for your own necks ; justice, as might have been expected, records in your own words a verdict against yourselves."

Observe these flowers of the old Attic ; what polished brilliance of diction plays over his composition ; what a delicate and subtle charm of style is in bloom there ! However, let this be as people think. Our course requires us again to turn to the thought in those words ; let us plunge once more into the phrases of this pamphleteer. " Either you conceive of the beings as separated and independent of each other, and then bring down one of them, by generation, to the rank of Son, and contend that One who exists independently nevertheless was made by means of the Other existence." That is enough for the present. He says, then, that we preach [3] two causeless Beings. How can this man, who is always accusing us of levelling and confusing, assert

---

[1] Reading οὖσαν for οὐσίαν of Oehler and Migne.

[2] ἐξουυχίζει.

[3] πρεσβεύειν. So Lucian. Diog. Laert., and Origen passim.

[11] ἀνάρχως.

this from our believing, as we do, in a single substance of Both. If two natures, alien to each other on the score of their being, were preached by our Faith, just as it is preached by the Anomœan school, then there would be good reason for thinking that this distinction óf natures led to the supposition of two causeless beings. But if, as is the case, we acknowledge one nature with the differences of Person, if, while the Father is believed in, the Son also is glorified, how can such a Faith be misrepresented by our opponents as preaching Two First Causes? Then he says, ' of these two causes, one is lowered ' by us 'to the rank of Son.' Let him point out one champion of such a doctrine; whether he can convict any single person of talking like this, or only knows of such a doctrine as taught anywhere at all in the Church, we will hold our peace. For who is so wild in his reasonings, and so bereft of reflection as, after speaking of Father and Son, to imagine in spite of that two ungenerate beings: and then again to suppose that the One of them has come into being by means of the Other? Besides, what logical necessity does he show for pushing our teaching towards such suppositions? By what arguments does he show that such an absurdity must result from it? If indeed he adduced one single article of our Faith, and then, whether as a quibble or with a real force of demonstration, made this criticism upon it, there might have been some reason for his doing so with a view to in validate that article. But when there is not, and never can be such a doctrine in the Church, when neither a teacher of it nor a hearer of it is to be found, and the absurdity cannot be shown, either, to be the strict logical consequence of anything, I cannot understand the meaning of his fighting thus with shadows. It is just as if some phenzy-struck person supposed himself to be grappling with an imaginary combatant, and then, having with great efforts thrown himself down, thought that it was his foe who was lying there; our clever pamphleteer is in the same state; he feigns suppositions which we know nothing about, and he fights with the shadows which are sketched by the workings of his own brain.

For I challenge him to say why a believer in the Son as having come into being from the Father must advance to the opinion that there are two First Causes; and let him tell us who is most guilty of this establishment of two First Causes; one who asserts that the Son is falsely so named, or one who insists that, when we call Him that, the name represents a reality? The first, rejecting a real generation of the Son, and affirming simply that He exists, would be more open to the suspicion of making Him a First Cause, if he exists indeed, but not by generation: whereas the second, making the representative sign of the Person of the Onlybegotten to consist in subsisting generatively from the Father, cannot by any possibility be drawn into the error of supposing the Son to be Ungenerate. And yet as long as, according to you thinkers, the non-generation of the Son by the Father is to be held, the Son Himself will be properly called Ungenerate in one of the many meanings of the Ungenerate; seeing that, as some things come into existence by being born and others by being fashioned, nothing prevents our calling one of the latter, which does not subsist by *generation*, an Ungenerate, looking only to the idea of generation; and this your account, defining, as it does, our Lord to be a creature, does establish about Him. So, my very learned sirs, it is in your view, not ours, when it is thus followed out, that the Only-begotten can be named Ungenerate: and you will find that " justice,"—whatever you mean by that,—records in *your own* words [4] a verdict against us.

It is easy also to find mud in his words after that to cast upon this execrable teaching. For the other horn of his dilemma partakes in the same mental delusion; he says, " or else you first allow one single causeless being, and then marking this out by an act of generation into Father and Son, you declare that this nongenerated being came into existence by means of itself." What is this new and marvellous story? How is one begotten by oneself, having oneself for father, and becoming one's own son? What dizziness and delusion is here? It is like supposing the roof to be turning down below one's feet, and the floor above one's head; it is like the mental state of one with his senses stupified with drink, who shouts out persistently that the ground does not stand still beneath, and that the walls are disappearing, and that everything he sees is whirling round and will not keep still. Perhaps our pamphleteer had such a tumult in his soul when he wrote; if so, we must pity him rather than abhor him. For who is so out of hearing of our divine doctrine, who is so far from the mysteries of the Church, as to accept such a view as this to the detriment of the Faith. Rather, it is hardly enough to say, that no one ever dreamed of such an absurdity to its detriment. Why, in the case of human nature, or any other

---

4 *your own words*, i.e. not ours, as you say. The Codex of Turin has τοῖς ἡμετέροις, and ἡμῖν above : but Oehler has wisely followed that of Venice. Eunomius had said of Basil's party (§ 34) ' justice records in your own words a verdict against yourselves.' ' No,' Gregory answers; ' *your* words (interpreting our doctrine) alone lend themselves to that.' But to change καθ' ἡμῶν of the Codd. also to καθ' ὑμῶν would supply a still better sense.

entity falling within the grasp of the senses, who, when he hears of a community of substance, dreams either that all things that are compared together on the ground of substance are without a cause or beginning, or that something comes into existence out of itself, at once producing and being produced by itself?

The first man, and the man born from him, received their being in a different way; the latter by copulation, the former from the moulding of Christ Himself; and yet, though they are thus believed to be two, they are inseparable in the definition of their being, and are not considered as two beings, without beginning or cause, running parallel to each other; nor can the existing one be said to be generated by the existing one, or the two be ever thought of as one in the monstrous sense that each is his own father, and his own son; but it is because the one and the other was a man that the two have the same definition of being; each was mortal, reasoning, capable of intuition and of science. If, then, the idea of humanity in Adam and Abel does not vary with the difference of their origin, neither the order nor the manner of their coming into existence making any difference in their nature, which is the same in both, according to the testimony of every one in his senses, and no one, not greatly needing treatment for insanity, would deny it; what necessity is there that against the divine nature we should admit this strange thought? Having heard of Father and Son from the Truth, we are taught in those two subjects the oneness of their nature; their natural relation to each other expressed by those names indicates that nature; and so do Our Lord's own words. For when He said, " I and My Father are one [5]," He conveys by that confession of a Father exactly the truth that He Himself is not a first cause, at the same time that He asserts by His union with the Father their common nature; so that these words of His secure our faith from the taint of heretical error on either side : for Sabellius has no ground for his confusion of the individuality of each Person, when the Only-begotten has so distinctly marked Himself off from the Father in those words, " I and My Father;" and Arius finds no confirmation of his doctrine of the strangeness of either nature to the other, since this oneness of both cannot admit distinction in nature. For that which is signified in these words by the oneness of Father and Son is nothing else but what belongs to them on the score of their actual being; all the other moral excellences which are to be observed in them as over and above [6] their nature may without error be set down as shared in by all created beings. For instance, Our Lord is called merciful and pitiful by the prophet [7], and He wills us to be and to be called the same ; " Be ye therefore merciful [8]," and "Blessed are the merciful [9]," and many such passages. If, then, any one by diligence and attention has modelled himself according to the divine will, and become kind and pitiful and compassionate, or meek and lowly of heart, such as many of the saints are testified to have become in the pursuit of such excellences, does it follow that they are therefore one with God, or united to Him by virtue of any one of them? Not so. That which is not in every respect the same, cannot be ' one ' with him whose nature thus varies from it. Accordingly, a man becomes 'one' with another, when in will, as our Lord says, they are 'perfected into one [1],' this union of wills being added to the connexion of nature. So also the Father and Son are one, the community of nature and the community of will running, in them, into one. But if the Son had been joined in wish only to the Father, and divided from Him in His nature, how is it that we find Him testifying to His oneness with the Father, when all the time He was sundered from Him in the point most proper to Him of all?

§ 35. *Proof that the Anomœan teaching tends to Manichæism.*

We hear our Lord saying. " I and My Father are one," and we are taught in that utterance the dependence of our Lord on a cause, and yet the absolute identity of the Son's and the Father's nature ; we do not let our idea about them be melted down into One Person, but we keep distinct the properties of the Persons, while, on the other hand, not dividing in the Persons the oneness of their substance ; and so the supposition of two diverse principles in the category of Cause is avoided, and there is no loophole for the Manichæan heresy to enter. For the created and the uncreate are as diametrically opposed to each other as their names are ; and so if the two are to be ranked as First Causes, the mischief of Manichæism will thus under cover be brought into the Church. I say this, because my zeal against our antagonists makes me scrutinize their doctrine very closely. Now I think that none would deny that we were bringing this scrutiny very near the truth, when we said, that if the created be possessed of equal power with the uncreate,

---

6 ὅσα ἐπιθεωρεῖται τῇ φύσει.
7 Psalm ciii. 8.   8 Luke vi. 36.   9 Matthew v. 7.
ɪ John xvii. 23. "I in them, and thou in Me, that they may be perfected into one." (R.V.)

5 John x. 30.

there will be some sort of antagonism between these things of diverse nature, and as long as neither of them fails in power, the two will be brought into a certain state of mutual discord : for we must perforce allow that will corresponds with, and is intimately joined to nature ; and that if two things are unlike in nature, they will be so also in will. But when power is adequate in both, neither will flag in the gratification of its wish ; and if the power of each is thus equal to its wish, the primacy will become a doubtful point with the two : and it will end in a drawn battle from the inexhaustibleness of their powers. Thus will the Manichæan heresy creep in, two opposite principles appearing with counter claims in the category of Cause, parted and opposed by reason of difference both in nature and in will. They will find, therefore, that assertion of diminution (in the Divine being) is the beginning of Manichæism ; for their teaching organizes a discord within that being, which comes to two leading principles, as our account of it has shewn ; namely the created and the uncreated.

But perhaps most will blame this as too strong .a *reductio ad absurdum*, and will wish that we had not put it down at all along with our other objections. Be it so ; we will not contradict them. It was not our impulse, but our adversaries themselves, that forced us to carry our argument into such minuteness of results. But if it is not right to argue thus, it was more fitting still that our opponents' teaching, which gave occasion to such a refutation, should never have been heard. There is only one way of suppressing the answer to bad teaching, and that is, to take away the subject-matter to which a reply has to be made. But what would give me most pleasure would be to advise those, who are thus disposed, to divest themselves a little of the spirit of rivalry, and not be such exceedingly zealous combatants on behalf of the private opinions with which they have become possessed, and, convinced that the race is for their (spiritual) life, to attend to its interests only, and to yield the victory to Truth. If, then, one were to cease from this ambitious strife, and look straight into the actual question before us, he would very soon discover the flagrant absurdity of this teaching.

For let us assume as granted what the system of our opponents demands, that the having no generation is Being, and in like manner again that generation is admitted into Being. If, then, one were to follow out carefully these statements in all their meaning, even this way the Manichæan heresy will be reconstructed ; seeing that the Manichees are wont

to take as an axiom the oppositions of good and bad, light and darkness, and all such naturally antagonistic things. I think that any who will not be satisfied with a superficial view of the matter will be convinced that I say true. Let us look at it thus. Every subject has certain inherent characteristics, by means of which the specialty of that underlying nature is known. This is so, whether we are investigating the animal kingdom, or any other. The tree and the animal are not known by the same marks ; nor do the characteristics of man extend in the animal kingdom to the brutes ; nor, again, do the same symptoms indicate life and death ; in every case, without exception, as we have said, the distinction of subjects resists any effort to confuse them and run one into another ; the marks upon each thing which we observe cannot be communicated so as to destroy that distinction. Let us follow this out in examining our opponents' position. They say that the state of having no generation is Being ; and they likewise make the having generation Being. But just as a man and a stone have not the same marks (in defining the essence of the animate and that of the inanimate you would not give the same account of each), so they must certainly grant that one who is non-generated is to be known by different signs to the generated. Let us then survey those peculiar qualities of the non-generated Deity, which the Holy Scriptures teach us can be mentioned and thought of, without doing Him an irreverence.

What are they? I think no Christian is ignorant that He is good, kind, holy, just and hallowed, unseen and immortal, incapable of decay and change and alteration, powerful, wise, beneficent, Master, Judge, and everything like that. Why lengthen our discussion by lingering on acknowledged facts? If, then, we find these qualities in the ungenerate nature, and the state of having been generated is contrary[2] in its very conception to the state of having not been generated, those who define these two states to be each of them Being, must perforce concede, that the characteristic marks of the generated being, following this opposition existing between the generated and non-generated, must be contrary to the marks observable in the non-generated being ; for if they were to declare the marks to be the same, this sameness would destroy the difference between the two beings who are the subject of

---

[2] ὑπεναντίως, i.e. as logical "contraries" differ from each other. This is not an Aristotelian, but a Neo-Platonic use of the word (i.e. Ammonius, A.D. 390, &c.). It occurs so again in this Book frequently.

these observations. Differing things must be regarded as possessing differing marks; like things are to be known by like signs. If, then, these men testify to the same marks in the Only-begotten, they can conceive of no difference whatever in the subject of the marks. But if they persist in their blasphemous position, and maintain in asserting the difference of the generated and the non-generated the variation of the natures, it is readily seen what must result: viz., that, as in following out the opposition of the names, the nature of the things which those names indicate must be considered to be in a state of contrariety to itself, there is every necessity that the qualities observed in each should be drawn out opposite each other; so that those qualities should be applied to the Son which are the reverse of those predicated of the Father, viz., of divinity, holiness, goodness, imperishability, eternity, and of every other quality that represents God to the devout mind; in fact, every negation [3] of these, every conception that ranks opposite to the good, must be considered as belonging to the generated nature.

To ensure clearness, we must dwell upon this point. As the peculiar phænomena of heat and cold—which are themselves by nature opposed to each other (let us take fire and ice as examples of each), each being that which the other is not—are at variance with each other, cooling being the peculiarity of ice, heating of fire; so if in accordance with the antithesis expressed by the names, the nature revealed by those names is parted asunder, it is not to be admitted that the faculties attending these natural "subcontraries [4]" are like each other, any more than cooling can belong to fire, or burning to ice. If, then, goodness is inseparable from the idea of the non-generated nature, and that nature is parted on the ground of being, as they declare, from the generated nature, the properties of the former will be parted as well from those of the latter: so that if the good is found in the first, the quality set against the good is to be perceived in the last. Thus, thanks to our clever systematizers, Manes lives again with his parallel line of evil in array over against the good, and his theory of opposite powers residing in opposite natures.

Indeed, if we are to speak the truth boldly, without any reserve, Manes, who for having been the first, they say, to venture to entertain the Manichæan view, gave his name to that heresy, may fairly be considered the less offensive of the two. I say this, just

as if one had to choose between a viper and an asp for the most affection towards man; still, if we consider, there is *some* difference between brutes [5]. Does not a comparison of doctrines show that those older heretics are less intolerable than these? Manes thought he was pleading on the side of the Origin of Good, when he represented that Evil could derive thence none of its causes; so he linked the chain of things which are on the list of the bad to a separate Principle, in his character of the Almighty's champion, and in his pious aversion to put the blame of any unjustifiable aberrations upon that Source of Good; not perceiving, with his narrow understanding, that it is impossible even to conceive of God as the fashioner of evil, or on the other hand, of any other First Principle besides Him. There might be a long discussion on this point, but it is beside our present purpose. We mentioned Manes' statements only in order to show, that he at all events thought it his duty to separate evil from anything to do with God. But the blasphemous error with regard to the Son, which these men systematize, is much more terrible. Like the others, they explain the existence of evil by a contrariety in respect of Being; but when they declare, besides this, that the God of the universe is actually the Maker of this alien production, and say that this "generation" formed by Him into a substance possesses a nature foreign to that of its Maker, they exhibit therein more of impiety than the aforesaid sect; for they not only give a personal existence to that which in its nature is opposed to good, but they say that a Good Deity is the Cause of another Deity who in nature diverges from His; and they all but openly exclaim in their teaching, that there is in existence something opposite to the nature of the good, deriving its personality from the good itself. For when we know the Father's substance to be good, and therefore find that the Son's substance, owing to its being unlike the Father's in its nature (which is the tenet of this heresy), is amongst the contrary predicables, what is thereby proved? Why, not only that the opposite to the good subsists, but that this contrary comes from the good itself. I declare this to be more horrible even than the irrationality of the Manichees.

But if they repudiate this blasphemy from their system, though it *is* the logical carrying out of their teaching, and if they say that the Only-begotten has inherited the excellences of the Father, not as being really His Son, but —so does it please these misbelievers —as re-

---

3 ἀπεμφαίνοντα.   4 ὑπεναντίων.   5 πλὴν ἀλλ' ἐπειδή ἐστι καὶ ἐν θηρίοις κρίσις.

ceiving His personality by an act of creation, let us look into this too, and see whether such an idea can be reasonably entertained. If, then, it were granted that it is as they think, viz., that the Lord of all things has not inherited as being a true Son, but that He rules a kindred of created things, being Himself made and created, how will the rest of creation accept this rule and not rise in revolt, being thus thrust down from kinship to subjection and condemned, though not a whit behind Him in natural prerogative (both being created), to serve and bend beneath a kinsman after all. That were like a usurpation, viz. not to assign the command to a superiority of Being, but to divide a creation that retains by right of nature equal privileges into slaves and a ruling power, one part in command, the other in subjection; as if, as the result of an arbitrary distribution [6], these same privileges had been piled at random on one who after that distribution got preferred to his equals. Even man did not share his honour with the brutes, before he received his dominion over them; his prerogative of reason gave him the title to command; he was set over them, because of a variance of his nature in the direction of superiority. And human governments experience such quickly-repeated revolutions for this very reason, that it is impracticable that those to whom nature has given equal rights should be excluded from power, but her impulse is instinct in all to make themselves equal with the dominant party, when all are of the same blood.

How, too, will it be true that "all things were made by Him," if it is true that the Son Himself is one of the things made? Either He must have made Himself, for that text to be true, and so this unreasonableness which they have devised to harm our Faith will recoil with all its force upon themselves; or else, if this is absurdly unnatural, that affirmation that the *whole* creation was made by Him will be proved to have no ground to stand on. The withdrawal of one makes "all" a false statement. So that, from this definition of the Son as a created being, one of two vicious and absurd alternatives is inevitable; either that He is not the Author of all created things, seeing that He, who, they insist, is one of those works, must be withdrawn from the "all;" or else, that He is exhibited as the maker of Himself, seeing that the preaching that 'without Him was not anything (made) that was made' is not a lie. So much for their teaching.

§ 36. *A passing repetition of the teaching of the Church.*

But if a man keeps steadfast to the sound doctrine, and believes that the Son is of the nature which is divine without admixture, he will find everything in harmony with the other truths of his religion, viz., that Our Lord is the maker of all things, that He is King of the universe, set above it not by an arbitrary act of capricious power, but ruling by virtue of a superior nature; and besides this, he will find that the one First Cause [7], as taught by us, is not divided by any unlikeness of substance into separate first causes, but one Godhead, one Cause, one Power over all things is believed in, that Godhead being discoverable by the harmony existing between these like beings, and leading on the mind through one like to another like, so that the Cause of all things, which is Our Lord, shines in our hearts by means of the Holy Spirit; (for it is impossible, as the Apostle says, that the Lord Jesus can be truly known, "except by the Holy Spirit [8]"); and then all the Cause beyond, which is God over all, is found through Our Lord, Who is the Cause of all things; nor, indeed, is it possible to gain an exact knowledge of the Archetypal Good, except as it appears in the (visible) image of that invisible. But then, after passing that summit of theology, I mean the God over all, we turn as it were back again in the racecourse of the mind, and speed through conjoint and kindred ideas from the Father, through the Son, to the Holy Ghost. For once having taken our stand on the comprehension of the Ungenerate Light, we perceive [9] that moment from that vantage ground the Light that streams from Him, like the ray co-existent with the sun, whose cause indeed is in the sun, but whose existence is synchronous with the sun, not being a later addition, but appearing at the first sight of the sun itself: or rather (for there is no necessity to be slaves to this similitude, and so give a handle to the critics to use against our teaching by reason of the inadequacy of our image), it will not be a ray of the sun that we shall perceive, but another sun blazing forth, as an offspring, out of the Ungenerate sun, and simultaneously with our conception of the First, and in every way like him, in beauty, in power, in lustre, in size,

---

6 *arbitrary distribution*, ἀποκληρώσεως: κατ' ἀποκλήρωσιν "at random," is also used by Sextus Empiric. (A.D. 200), Clem. Alex., and Greg Naz.

7 *One First Cause*, μοναρχίας. In a notable passage on the Greeks who came up to the Feast (John xii. 20), Cyrill (*Catena*, p. 307), uses the same word. "Such, seeing that some of the Jews' customs did not greatly differ from their own, as far as related to the manner of sacrifice, and the belief in a *One first Cause* . . . came up with them to worship," &c. Philo had already used the word so (*D: Charit.*). Athanasius opposes it to πολυθεία (*Quæst. ad Antioch.* I.).

8 1 Cor. xii. 3.

9 ἐνοήσαμεν: aorist of instantaneous action.

in brilliance, in all things at once that we observe in the sun. Then again, we see yet another such Light after the same fashion, sundered by no interval of time from that offspring Light, and while shining forth by means of It yet tracing the source of its being to the Primal Light ; itself, nevertheless, a Light shining in like manner as the one first conceived of, and itself a source of light and doing all that light does. There is, indeed, no difference between one light and another light, *qua light*, when the one shows no lack or diminution of illuminating grace, but by its complete perfection forms part of the highest light of all, and is beheld along with the Father and the Son, though counted after them, and by its own power gives access to the light that is perceived in the Father and Son to all who are able to partake of it. So far upon this.

§ 37. *Defence of S. Basil's statement, attacked by Eunomius, that the terms ' Father' and ' the Ungenerate' can have the same meaning.*

The stream of his abuse is very strong ; insolence is at the bottom of every principle he lays down ; and vilification is put by him in the place of any demonstration of doubtful points : so let us briefly discuss the many misrepresentations about the word Ungenerate with which he insults our Teacher himself and his treatise. He has quoted the following words of our Teacher : " For my part I should be inclined to say that this title of the Ungenerate, however fitting it may seem to express our ideas, yet, as nowhere found in Scripture and as forming the alphabet of Eunomius' blasphemy, may very well be suppressed, when we have the word Father meaning the same thing ; for One who essentially and alone is Father comes from none else ; and that which comes from none else is equivalent to the Ungenerate." Now let us hear what proof he brings of the 'folly' of these words : " Overhastiness and shameless dishonesty prompt him to put this dose of words[1] anomalously used into his attempts ; he turns completely round, because his judgment is wavering and his powers of reasoning are feeble." Notice how well-directed that blow is ; how skilfully, with all his mastery of logic, he takes Basil's words to pieces and puts a conception more consistent with piety in their place ! " Anomalous in phrase," " hasty and dishonest in judgment," " wavering and turning round from feebleness of reasoning." Why this ? what has exasperated this man, whose own judgment is so firm and reasoning so sound ? What is it that he

most condemns in Basil's words ? Is it, that he accepts the *idea* of the Ungenerate, but says that the actual word, as misused by those who pervert it, should be suppressed? Well ; is the Faith in jeopardy only as regards words and outward expressions, and need we take no account of the correctness of the thought beneath ? Or does not the Word of Truth rather exhort us first to have a heart pure from evil thoughts, and then, for the manifestation of the soul's emotions, to use any words that can express these secrets of the mind, without any minute care about this or that particular sound ? For the speaking in this way or in that is not the cause of the thought within us ; but the hidden conception of the heart supplies the motive for such and such words ; " for from the abundance of the heart the mouth speaketh." We make the words interpret the thought ; we do not by a reverse process gather[2] the thought from the words. Should both be at hand, a man may certainly be ready in both, in clever thinking and clever expression ; but if the one should be wanting, the loss to the illiterate is slight, if the knowledge in his soul is perfect in the direction of moral goodness. " This people honoureth me with their lips, but their heart is far from me[3]." What is the meaning of that ? That the right attitude of the soul towards the truth is more precious than the propriety of phrases in the sight of God, who hears the " groanings that cannot be uttered." Phrases can be used in opposite senses ; the tongue readily serving, at his will, the intention of the speaker ; but the disposition of the soul, as it is, so is it seen by Him Who sees all secrets. Why, then, does he deserve to be called " anomalous," and " hasty," and " dishonest," for bidding us suppress all in the term Ungenerate which can aid in their blasphemy those who transgress the Faith, while minding and welcoming all the meaning in the word which can be reverently held. If indeed he had said that we ought not to think of the Deity as Ungenerate, there might have been some occasion for these and even worse terms of abuse to be used against him. But if he falls in with the general belief of the faithful and admits this, and then pronounces an opinion well worthy of the Master's mind[4], viz., " Refrain from the use of the word, for into it, and from it, the subverting heresy is fetched," and bids us cherish the idea of an ungenerate Deity by means of other names,—therein he does not

---

[1] i.e. πατήρ, ἀγέννητος

[2] Putting a full stop at συναγείρομεν. Oehler otherwise.
[3] Isaiah xxix. 13 ; Matthew xv. 8.
[4] *the Master's mind.* " But whoso shall offend one of these little ones which believe in Me, it were better for him that a millstone were hanged about his neck, and that he were drowned in the depth of the sea." Matth. xviii. 6 ; Mark ix. 42.

deserve their abuse. Are we not taught by the Truth Himself to act so, and not to cling even to things exceeding precious, if any of them tend to mischief? When He thus bids us to cut away the right eye or foot or hand, if so be that one of them offends, what else does He imply by this figure, than that He would have anything, however fair-seeming, if it leads a man by an inconsiderate use to evil, remain inoperative and out of use, assuring us that it is better for us to be saved by amputation of the parts which led to sin, than to perish by retaining them?

What, too, does Paul, the follower of Christ, say? He, too, in his deep wisdom teaches the same. He, who declares that "everything is good, and nothing to be rejected, if it be received with thanks[5]," on some occasions, because of the 'conscience of the weak brother,' puts some things back from the number which he has accepted, and commands us to decline them. "If," he says, "meat make my brother to offend, I will eat no flesh while the world standeth[6]." Now this is just what our follower of Paul did. He saw that the deceiving power of those who try to teach the inequality of the Persons was increased by this word Ungenerate, taken in their mischievous, heretical sense, and so he advised that, while we cherish in our souls a devout consciousness of this ungenerate Deity, we should not show any particular love for the actual word, which was the occasion of sin to the reprobate; for that the title of Father, if we follow out all that it implies, will suggest to us this meaning of not having been generated. For when we hear the word Father, we think at once of the Author of all beings; for if He had some further cause transcending Himself, He would not have been called thus of proper right Father; for that title would have had to be transferred higher, to this pre-supposed Cause. But if He Himself is that Cause from which all comes, as the Apostle says, it is plain that nothing can be thought of beyond His existence. But this is to believe in that existence not having been generated. But this man, who claims that even the Truth shall not be considered more persuasive than himself, will not acquiesce in this; he loudly dogmatizes against it; he jeers at the argument.

§ 38. *Several ways of controverting his quibbling syllogisms.*

Let us, if you please, examine his irrefragable syllogisms, and his subtle transpositions[7] of the

terms in his own false premisses, by which he hopes to shake that argument; though, indeed. I fear lest the miserable quibbling in what he says may in a measure raise a prejudice also against the remarks that would correct it. When striplings challenge to a fight, men get more blame for pugnaciousness in closing with such foes, than honour for their show of victory. Nevertheless, what we want to say is this. We think, indeed, that the things said by him, with that well-known elocution now familiar to us, only for the sake of being insolent, are better buried in silence and oblivion; they may suit him; but to us they afford only an exercise for much-enduring patience. Nor would it be proper, I think, to insert his ridiculous expressions in the midst of our own serious controversy, and so to make this zeal for the truth evaporate in coarse, vulgar laughter; for indeed to be within hearing, and to remain unmoved, is an impossibility, when he says with such sublime and magnificient verbosity, "Where additional words amount to additional blasphemy, it is by half as much more tranquillizing to be silent than to speak." Let those laugh at these expressions who know which of them are fit to be believed, and which only to be laughed at; while we scrutinize the keenness of those syllogisms with which he tries to tear our system to pieces.

He says, "If 'Father' is the same in meaning as 'Ungenerate,' and words which have the same meaning naturally have in every respect the same force, and Ungenerate signifies by their confession that God comes from nothing, it follows necessarily that Father signifies the fact of God being of none, and not the having generated the Son." Now what is this logical necessity which prevents the having generated a Son being signified by the title "Father," if so be that that same title does in itself express to us as well the absence of beginning in the Father? If, indeed, the one idea was totally destructive of the other, it would certainly follow, from the very nature of contradictories[8], that the affirming of the one would involve the denial of the other. But if there is nothing in the world to prevent the

---

5 1 Tim. iv. 4 (R.V.).
6 1 Cor. viii. 13.
7 *Transpositions of the terms in his own false premisses;* τῶν σοφισμάτων ἀντιστροφὰς. The same as "the professional twisting of premisses," and "the hooking backward and forward and twisting

of premisses" below. The terms Father and Ἀγέννητος are transposed or twisted into each other's place in this 'irrefragable syllogism.' It is 'a reductio ad absurdum' thus:—
　　Father means Ἀγέννητος (Basil's premiss),
　∴ Ἀγέννητος means Father.
The fallacy of Eunomius consists in making 'Father' universal in his own premiss. when it was only particular in Basil's. "'Ἀγέννητος means the *whole* contents of the word Father," which therefore cannot mean having generated a son. It is a False Conversion.
This Conversion or ἀντιστροφὴ is illustrated in Aristotle's *Analytics, Prior.* I. iii. 3. It is legitimate thus:—
　　　　　Some B is A
　　　∴ Some A is (some) B.
8 κατὰ τὴν τῶν ἀντικειμένων φύσιν. If Ἀγέννητος means *not* having a son, then to affirm 'God is always Ἀγέννητος' is even to deny (its logical contradictory) 'God once had a Son.'

same Existence from being Father and also Ungenerate, when we try to think, under this title of Father, of the quality of not having been generated as one of the ideas implied in it, what necessity prevents the relation to a Son being any longer marked by the word Father? Other names which express mutual relationship are not always confined to those ideas of relationship; for instance, we call the emperor 9 autocrat and masterless, and we call the same the ruler of his subjects; and, while it is quite true that the word emperor signifies also the being masterless, it is not therefore necessary that this word, because signifying autocratic and unruled, must cease to imply the having power over inferiors; the word emperor, in fact, is midway between these two conceptions, and at one time indicates masterlessness, at another the ruling over lower orders. In the case before us, then, if there is some other Father conceivable besides the Father of Our Lord, let these men who boast of their profound wisdom show him to us, and then we will agree with him that the idea of the Ungenerate cannot be represented by the title "Father." But if the First Father has no cause transcending His own state, and the subsistence of the Son is invariably implied in the title of Father, why do they try to scare us, as if we were children, with these professional twistings of premisses, endeavouring to persuade or rather to decoy us into the belief that, if the property of not having been generated is acknowledged in the title of Father, we must sever from the Father any relation with the Son.

Despising, then, this silly superficial attempt of theirs, let us manfully own our belief in that which they adduce as a monstrous absurdity, viz., that not only does the 'Father' mean the same as Ungenerate and that this last property establishes the Father as being of none, but also that the word 'Father' introduces with itself the notion of the Only-begotten, as a relative bound to it. Now the following passage, which is to be found in the treatise of our Teacher, has been removed from the context by this clever and invincible controversialist; for, by suppressing that part which was added by Basil by way of safeguard, he thought he would make his own reply a much easier task. The passage runs thus verbatim. "For my part I should be inclined to say that this title of the Ungenerate, however readily it may seem to fall in with our own ideas, yet, as nowhere found in Scripture, and as forming the alphabet of Eunomius' blasphemy, may very well be suppressed, when we have the word Father meaning the same thing,

in addition to [1] its introducing with itself, as a relative bound to it, the notion of the Son." This generous champion of the truth, with innate good feeling [2], has suppressed this sentence which was added by way of safeguard, I mean, "in addition to introducing with itself, as a relative bound to it, the notion of the Son;" after this garbling, he comes to close quarters with what remains, and having severed the connection of the living whole [3], and thus made it, as he thinks, a more yielding and assailable victim of his logic, he misleads his own party with the frigid and feeble paralogism, that "that which has a common meaning, in one single point, with something else retains that community of meaning in every possible point;" and with this he takes their shallow intelligences by storm. For while we have only affirmed that the word Father in a *certain* signification yields the same meaning as Ungenerate, this man makes the coincidence of meanings complete in every point, quite at variance therein with the common acceptation of either word; and so he reduces the matter to an absurdity, pretending that this word Father can no longer denote any relation to the Son, if the idea of not having been generated is conveyed by it. It is just as if some one, after having acquired two ideas about a loaf,—one, that it is made of flour, the other, that it is food to the consumer—were to contend with the person who told him this, using against him the same kind of fallacy as Eunomius does, viz., that 'the being made of flour is one thing, but the being food is another; if, then, it is granted that the loaf is made of flour, this quality in it can no longer strictly be called food.' Such is the thought in Eunomius' syllogism; "if the not having been generated is implied by the word Father, this word can no longer convey the idea of having generated the Son." But I think it is time that we, in our turn, applied to this argument of his that magnificently rounded period of his own (already quoted). In reply to such words, it would be suitable to say that he would have more claim to be considered in his sober senses, if he had put the limit to such argumentative safeguards at absolute silence. For "where additional words amount to additional blasphemy," or, rather, indicate that he has utterly lost his reason, it is not only " by half as much more," but by the whole as much more " tranquillizing to be silent than to speak."

---

1 πρὸς τῷ. Cod. Ven., surely better than the common πρὸς τὸ, which Oehler has in his text.
2 ἐλευθερία; late Greek, for ἐλευθεριότης.
3 "*the living whole.*' σώματος: this is the radical meaning of σῶμα, and also the classical. Viger. (Idiom. p. 143 note) distinguishes four meanings under this. 1. Safety. 2. Individuality. 3. Living presence. 4. Life: and adduces instances of each from the Attic orators.

τὸν βασιλέα.

But perhaps a man would be more easily led into the true view by personal illustrations; so let us leave this hooking backwards and forwards and this twisting of false premises [4], and discuss the matter in a less learned and more popular way. Your father, Eunomius, was certainly a human being; but the same person was also the author of your being. Did you, then, ever use in his case too this clever quibble which you have employed; so that your own 'father,' when once he receives the true definition of his being, can no longer mean, because of being a 'man,' any relationship to yourself; 'for he must be one of two things, either a man, or Eunomius' father?'— Well, then, you must not use the names of intimate relationship otherwise than in accordance with that intimate meaning. Yet, though you would indict for libel any one who contemptuously scoffed against yourself, by means of such an alteration of meanings, are you not afraid to scoff against God; and are you safe when you laugh at these mysteries of our faith? As 'your father' indicates relationship to yourself, and at the same time humanity is not excluded by that term, and as no one in his sober senses instead of styling him who begat you 'your father' would render his description by the word 'man,' or, reversely, if asked for his genus and answering 'man,' would assert that that answer prevented him from being your father; so in the contemplation of the Almighty a reverent mind would not deny that by the title of Father is meant that He is without generation, as well as that in another meaning it represents His relationship to the Son. Nevertheless Eunomius, in open contempt of truth, does assert that the title cannot mean the 'having begotten a son' any longer, when once the word has conveyed to us the idea of 'never having been generated.'

Let us add the following illustration of the absurdity of his assertions. It is one that all must be familiar with, even mere children who are being introduced under a grammar-tutor to the study of words. Who, I say, does not know that some nouns are absolute and out of all relation, others express some relationship. Of these last, again, there are some which incline, according to the speaker's wish, either way; they have a simple intention in themselves, but can be turned so as to become nouns of relation. I will not linger amongst examples foreign to our subject. I will explain from the words of our Faith itself.

God is called Father and King and other names innumerable in Scripture. Of these names one part can be pronounced absolutely, i. e. simply as they are, and no more: viz.. "imperishable," "everlasting," "immortal," and so on. Each of these, without our bringing in another thought, contains in itself a complete thought about the Deity. Others express only relative usefulness; thus, Helper, Champion, Rescuer, and other words of that meaning; if you remove thence the idea of one in need of the help, all the force expressed by the word is gone. Some, on the other hand, as we have said, are both absolute, and are also amongst the words of relation; 'God,' for instance, and 'good,' and many other such. In these the thought does not continue always within the absolute. The Universal God often becomes the property of him who calls upon Him; as the Saints teach us, when they make that independent Being their own. 'The Lord God is Holy;' so far there is no relation; but when one adds the Lord *Our* God, and so appropriates the meaning in a relation towards oneself, then one causes the word to be no longer thought of absolutely. Again; "Abba, Father" is the cry of the Spirit; it is an utterance free from any partial reference. But we are bidden to call the Father in heaven, 'Our Father;' this is the relative use of the word. A man who makes the Universal Deity his own, does not dim His supreme dignity; and in the same way there is nothing to prevent us, when we point out the Father and Him who comes from Him, the Firstborn before all creation, from signifying by that title of Father at one and the same time having begotten that Son, and also the not being from any more transcendent Cause. For he who speaks of the First Father means Him who is presupposed before all existence, Whose is the beyond [5]. This is He, Who has nothing previous to Himself to behold, no end in which He shall cease. Whichever way we look, He is equally existing there for ever; He transcends the limit of any end, the idea of any beginning, by the infinitude of His life; whatever be His title, eternity must be implied with it.

But Eunomius, versed as he is in the contemplation of that which eludes thought, rejects this view of unscientific minds; he will not admit a double meaning in the word 'Father,' the one, that from Him are all things and in the front of all things the Only-begotten Son, the other, that He Himself has no superior Cause. He

---

4 τὸ κατηγκυλωμένον τῆς τῶν σοφισμάτων πλοκῆς. See c. 38, note 7. The false premises in the syllogisms have been—
  1. Father (partly) means 'Αγέννητος.
     Things which mean the same in part, mean the same in all (false prem s.).
     ∴. Father means 'Αγέννητος (false).
  2. Father means 'Αγέννητος (false).
     'Αγέννητος does not mean 'having a Son.'
     ∴. Father does not mean ' having a Son' (false).

5 ἐνεδείξατο, οὗ τὸ ἐπέκεινα. This is the reading of the Turin Cod., and preferable to that of the Paris edition.

may scorn the statement; but we will brave his mocking laugh, and repeat what we have said already, that the 'Father' is the same as that Ungenerate One, and both signifies the having begotten the Son, and represents the being from nothing.

But Eunomius, contending with this statement of ours, says (the very contrary now of what he said before), "If God is Father because He has begotten the Son. and 'Father' has the same meaning as Ungenerate, God is Ungenerate because He has begotten the Son, but before He begat Him He was not Ungenerate." Observe his method of turning round; how he pulls his first quibble to pieces, and turns it into the very opposite, thinking even so to entrap us in a conclusion from which there is no escape. His first syllogism presented the following absurdity, "If 'Father' means the coming from nothing, then necessarily it will no longer indicate the having begotten the Son." But this last syllogism, by turning (a premiss) into its contrary, threatens our faith with another absurdity How, then, does he pull to pieces his former conclusion [6]? "If He is 'Father' because He has begotten a Son." His first syllogism gave us nothing like that; on the contrary, its logical inference purported to show that if the Father's not having been generated was meant by the word Father, that word could *not* mean as well the having begotten a Son [7]. Thus his first syllogism contained no intimation whatever that God was Father because He had begotten a Son. I fail to understand what this argumentative and shrewdly professional reversal means.

But let us look to the thought in it below the words. 'If God is Ungenerate because He has begotten a Son, He was not Ungenerate before He begat Him.' The answer to that is plain; it consists in the simple statement of the Truth, that 'the word Father means both the having begotten a Son, and also that the Begetter is not to be thought of as Himself coming from any cause.' If you look at the effect, the Person of the Son is revealed in the word

Father; if you look for a previous Cause, the absence of any beginning in the Begetter is shown by that word. In saying that 'Before He begat a Son, the Almighty was not Ungenerate,' this pamphleteer lays himself open to a double charge; i.e. of misrepresentation of us, and of insult to the Faith. He attacks, as if there was no mistake about it, something which our Teacher never said, neither do we now assert, viz., that the Almighty became in process of time a Father, having been something else before. Moreover in ridiculing the absurdity of this fancied doctrine of ours, he proclaims his own wildness as to doctrine. Assuming that the Almighty was once something else, and then by an advance became entitled to be called Father, he would have it that before this He was not Ungenerate either, since Ungeneracy is implied in the idea of Father. The folly of this hardly needs to be pointed out; it will be abundantly clear to any one who reflects. If the Almighty was something else before He became Father, what will the champions of this theory say, if they were asked in what state they propose to contemplate Him? What name are they going to give Him in that stage of existence; child, infant, babe, or youth? Will they blush at such flagrant absurdity, and say nothing like that, and concede that He was perfect from the first? Then how can He be perfect, while as yet unable to become Father? Or will they not deprive Him of this power, but say only that it was *not fitting* that there should be Fatherhood simultaneously with His existence. But if it was not good nor fitting that He should be from the very beginning Father of such a Son, how did He go on to acquire that which was not good?

But, as it is, it *is* good and fitting to God's majesty that He should become Father of such a Son. So they will make out that at the beginning He had no share in this good thing, and as long as He did not have this Son they must assert (may God forgive me for saying it!) that He had no Wisdom, nor Power, nor Truth, nor any of the other glories which from various points of view the Only-begotten Son is and is called.

But let all this fall on the heads of those who started it. We will return whence we digressed. He says, "If God is Father because of having begotten a Son, and if Father means the being Ungenerate, then God was not this last, before He begat." Now if he could speak here as it is customary to speak about human life, where it is inconceivable that any should acquire possession of many accomplishments all at once, instead of winning each of the objects sought after in a certain order and sequence

---

6 The first syllogism was—
  'Father' means the 'coming from nothing;'
  ('Coming from nothing' does not mean 'begetting a Son')
  ∴. Father does not mean begetting a Son.
He "pulls to pieces" this conclusion by taking its logical 'contrary' as the first premiss of his second syllogism; thus—
  Father means begetting a Son;
  (Father means 'Αγέννητος)
  ∴. 'Αγέννητος means begetting a Son.
From which it follows that before that begetting the Almighty was not 'Αγέννητος.
  The conclusion of the last syllogism also involves the contrary of the 2ⁿᵈ premiss of the first.
  It is to be noticed that both syllogisms are aimed at Basil's doctrine, 'Father' means 'coming from nothing.' Eunomius strives to show that, in both, such a premiss leads to an absurdity. But Gregory ridicules both for contradicting each other.
  7 τὸ μὲν μὴ δύνασθαι. The negative, absent in Oehler, is recovered from the Turin Cod.

of time—if I say we could reason like that in the case of the Almighty, so that we could say He possessed His Ungeneracy at one time, and after that acquired His power, and then His imperishability, and then His Wisdom, and advancing so became Father, and after that Just and then Everlasting, and so came into all that enters into the philosophical conception of Him, in a certain sequence—then it would not be so manifestly absurd to think that one of His names has precedence of another name, and to talk of His being first Ungenerate, and after that having become Father.

As it is, however, no one is so earth-bound in imagination, so uninitiated in the sublimities of our Faith, as to fail, when once he has apprehended the Cause of the universe, to embrace in one collective and compact whole all the attributes which piety can give to God; and to conceive instead of a primal and a later attribute, and of another in between, supervening in a certain sequence. It is not possible, in fact, to traverse in thought amongst those attributes, and then reach another, be it a reality or a conception, which is to transcend the first in antiquity. Every name of God, every sublime conception of Him, every utterance or idea that harmonizes with our general ideas with regard to Him, is linked in closest union with its fellow; all such conceptions are massed together in our understanding into one collective and compact whole; namely, His Fatherhood, and Ungeneracy, and Power, and Imperishability, and Goodness, and Authority, and everything else. You cannot take one of these and separate it in thought from the rest by any interval of time, as if it preceded or followed something else; no sublime or adorable attribute in Him can be discovered, which is not simultaneously expressed in His everlastingness. Just, then, as we cannot say that God was ever not good, or powerful, or imperishable, or immortal, in the same way it is a blasphemy not to attribute to Him Fatherhood always, and to say that that came later. He Who is truly Father is always Father; if eternity was not included in this confession, and if a foolishly preconceived idea curtailed and checked retrospectively our conception of the Father, true Fatherhood could no longer be properly predicated of Him, because that preconceived idea about the Son would cancel the continuity and eternity of His Fatherhood. How could that which He is now called be thought of something which came into existence subsequent to these other attributes? If being first Ungenerate He then became Father, and received that name, He was not always altogether what He is

now called. But that which the God now existing is He always is; He does not become worse or better by any addition, He does not become altered by taking something from another source. He is always identical with Himself. If, then, He was not Father at first, He was not Father afterwards. But if He is confessed to be Father (now), I will recur to the same argument, that, if He is so now, He always was so; and that if He always *was*, He always will be. The Father therefore is always Father; and seeing that the Son must always be thought of along with the Father (for the title of father cannot be justified unless there is a son to make it true), all that we contemplate in the Father is to be observed also in the Son. "All that the Father hath is the Son's; and all that is the Son's the Father hath." The words are, 'The Father *hath* that which is the Son's [8],' and so a carping critic will have no authority for finding in the contents of the word "all" the ungeneracy of the Son, when it is said that the Son has all that the Father has, nor on the other hand the generation of the Father, when all that is the Son's is to be observed in the Father. For the Son *has* all the things of the Father; but He *is* not Father: and again, all the things of the Son are to be observed in the Father, but He *is* not a Son.

If, then, all that is the Father's is in the Only-begotten, and He is in the Father, and the Fatherhood is not dissociated from the 'not having been generated,' I for my part cannot see what there is to think of in connexion with the Father, by Himself, that is parted by any interval so as to precede our apprehension of the Son. Therefore we may boldly encounter the difficulties started in that quibbling syllogism; we may despise it as a mere scare to frighten children, and still assert that God is Holy, and Immortal, and Father, and Ungenerate, and Everlasting, and everything all at once; and that, if it could be supposed possible that you could withhold one of these attributes which devotion assigns to Him, all would be destroyed along with that one. Nothing, therefore, in Him is older or younger; else He would be found to be older or younger than Himself. If God is not all His attributes always, but something in Him is, and something else only becoming, following some order of sequence (we must remember God is not a compound; whatever He is is the whole of Him), and if according to this heresy He is first Ungenerate and afterwards becomes Father, then, seeing that we cannot think of Him in connexion with a heaping together of qualities,

---

[8] John xvi. 15. Oehler conjectures these words (Ἔχει ὁ πατήρ) are to be repeated; and thus obtains a good sense, which the common reading, ὁ πατὴρ εἶπον, does not give.

there is no alternative but that the whole of Him must be both older and younger than the whole of Him, the former by virtue of His Ungeneracy, the latter by virtue of His Father-hood. But if, as the prophet says of God [9], He "is the same," it is idle to say that before He begat He was not Himself Ungenerate; we cannot find either of these names, the Father and the Ungenerate One, parted from the other; the two ideas rise together, suggested by each other, in the thoughts of the devout reasoner. God is Father from everlasting, and everlasting Father, and every other term that devotion assigns to Him is given in a like sense, the mensuration and the flow of time having no place, as we have said, in the Eternal.

Let us now see the remaining results of his expertness in dealing with words; results, which he himself truly says, are at once ridiculous and lamentable. Truly one must laugh outright at what he says, if a deep lament for the error that steeps his soul were not more fitting. Whereas Father, as we teach, includes, according to one of its meanings, the idea of the Ungenerate, he transfers the full signification of the word Father to that of the Ungenerate, and declares "If Father is the same as Ungenerate, it is allowable for us to drop it, and use Ungenerate instead; thus, the Ungenerate of the Son is Ungenerate; for as the Ungenerate is Father of the Son, so reversely the Father is Ungenerate of the Son." After this a feeling of admiration for our friend's adroitness steals over me, with the conviction that the many-sided subtlety of his theological training is quite beyond the capacity of most. What our Teacher said was embraced in one short sentence, to the effect that it was possible that by the title 'Father' the Ungeneracy could be signified; but Eunomius' words depend for their number not on the variety of the thoughts, but on the way that anything within the circuit of similar names can be turned about [1]. As the cattle that run blindfold round to turn the mill remain with all their travel in the same spot, so does he go round and round the same topic, and never leaves it. Once he said, ridiculing us, that 'Father' does not signify the having begotten, but the being from nothing. Again he wove a similar dilemma, "If Father signifies Ungeneracy, before He begat He was not ungenerate." Then a third time he resorts to the same trick. "It is allowable for us to drop Father, and to use Ungenerate instead;" and then directly he repeats the logic so often vomited. "For as the Ungenerate is Father of the Son, so reversely the Father is

Ungenerate of the Son." How often he returns to his vomit; how often he blurts it out again! Shall we not, then, annoy most people, if we drag about our argument in company with this foolish display of words? It would be perhaps more decent to be silent in a case like this; still, lest any one should think that we decline discussion because we are weak in pleas, we will answer thus to what he has said. 'You have no authority, Eunomius, for calling the Father the Ungenerate of the Son, even though the title Father *does* signify that the Begetter was from no cause Himself. For as, to take the example already cited, when we hear the word 'Emperor' we understand two things, both that the one who is pre-eminent in authority is subject to none, and also that he controls his inferiors, so the title Father supplies us with two ideas about the Deity, one relating to His Son, the other to His being dependent on no preconceivable cause. As, then, in the case of 'Emperor' we cannot say that because the two things are signified by that term, viz., the ruling over subjects and the not having any to take precedence of him, there is any justification for speaking of the 'Unruled of subjects,' instead of the 'Ruler of the nation,' or allowing so much, that we may use such a juxtaposition of words, in imitation of king of a nation, as kingless of a nation, in the same way when 'Father' indicates a Son, and also represents the idea of the Ungenerate, we may not unduly transfer this latter meaning, so as to attach this idea of the Ungenerate fast to a paternal relationship, and absurdly say 'the Ungenerate is Ungenerate of the Son.'

He treads on the ground of truth, he thinks, after such utterances; he has exposed the absurdity of his adversaries' position; how boastfully he cries, "And what sane thinker, pray, ever yet wanted the natural thought to be suppressed, and welcomed the paradoxical?" No sane thinker, most accomplished sir; and therefore our argument neither, which teaches that while the term Ungenerate does suit our thoughts, and we ought to guard it in our hearts intact, yet the term Father is an adequate substitute for the one which you have perverted, and leads the mind in that direction. Remember the words which you yourself quoted; Basil did not 'want the natural thought to be suppressed, and welcome the paradoxical,' as you phrase it; but he advised us to avoid all danger by suppressing the mere word Ungenerate, that is, the expression in so many syllables, as one which had been evilly interpreted, and besides was not to be found in Scripture; as for its meaning he declares that it does most completely suit our thoughts.

1 ἐν τῇ περιόδῳ καὶ ἀναστροφῇ τῶν ὁμοίων ῥημάτων.

Thus far for our statement. But this reviler of all quibblers, who completely arms his own argument with the truth, and arraigns our sins in logic, does not blush in any of his arguing on doctrines to indulge in very pretty quibbles ; on a par with those exquisite jokes which are cracked to make people laugh at dessert. Reflect on the weight of reasoning displayed in that complicated syllogism ; which I will now again repeat. "If ‘Father’ is the same as Ungenerate, it is allowable for us to drop it, and use Ungenerate instead ; thus, the Ungenerate is Ungenerate of the Son ; for as the Ungenerate is Father of the Son, so, reversely, the Father is Ungenerate of the Son." Well, this is very like another case such as the following. Suppose some one were to state the right and sound view about Adam ; namely, that it mattered not whether we called him "father of mankind" or "the first man formed by God" (for both mean the same thing), and then some one else, belonging to Eunomius' school of reasoners, were to pounce upon this statement, and make the same complication out of it, viz.: If "first man formed by God" and "father of mankind" are the same things, it is allowable for us to drop the word "father" and use "first formed" instead ; and say that Adam was the "first formed," instead of the "father," of Abel ; for as the first formed was the father of a son, so, reversely, that father is the first formed of that son. If this had been said in a tavern, what laughter and applause would have broken from the tippling circle over so fine and exquisite a joke ! These are the arguments on which our learned theologian leans ; when he assails our doctrine, he really needs himself a tutor and a stick to teach him that all the things which are predicated of some one do not necessarily, in their meaning, have respect to one single object ; as is plain from the aforesaid instance of Abel and Adam. That one and the same Adam is Abel's father and also God's handiwork is a truth ; nevertheless it does not follow that, because he is both, he is both with respect to Abel. So the designation of the Almighty as Father has both the special meaning of that word, i.e., the having begotten a son, and also that of there being no preconceivable cause of the Very Father ; nevertheless it does not follow that when we mention the Son we must speak of the Ungenerate, instead of the Father, of that Son ; nor, on the other hand, if the absence of beginning remains unexpressed in reference to the Son, that we must banish from our thoughts about God that attribute of Ungeneracy. But he discards the usual acceptations, and like an actor in comedy, makes a joke of the whole subject, and by dint of the oddity of his quibbles makes the questions of our faith ridiculous. Again I must repeat his words : "If Father is the same as Ungenerate, it is allowable for us to drop it, and use Ungenerate instead; thus, the Ungenerate is Ungenerate of the Son ; for as the Ungenerate is Father of the Son, so, reversely, the Father is Ungenerate of the Son." But let us turn the laugh against him, by reversing his quibble ; thus: If Father is not the same as Ungenerate, the Son of the Father will not be Son of the Ungenerate ; for having relation to the Father only, he will be altogether alien in nature to that which is other than Father, and does not suit that idea ; so that, if the Father is something other than the Ungenerate, and the title Father does not comprehend that meaning, the Son, being One, cannot be distributed between these two relationships, and be at the same time Son both of the Father and of the Ungenerate ; and, as before it was an acknowledged absurdity to speak of the Deity as Ungenerate of the Son, so in this converse proposition it will be found an absurdity just as great to call the Only-begotten Son of the Ungenerate. So that he must choose one of two things ; either the Father *is* the same as the Ungenerate (which is necessary in order that the Son of the Father may be Son of the Ungenerate as well) ; and then our doctrine has been ridiculed by him without reason ; or, the Father is something different to the Ungenerate, and the Son of the Father is alienated from all relationship to the Ungenerate. But then, if it is thus to hold that the Only-begotten is not the Son of the Ungenerate, logic inevitably points to a "generated Father ;" for that which exists, but does not exist without generation, must have a generated substance. If, then, the Father, being according to these men other than Ungenerate, is therefore generated, where is their much talked of Ungeneracy ? Where is that basis and foundation of their heretical castle-building ? The Ungenerate, which they thought just now that they grasped, has eluded them, and vanished quite beneath the action of a few barren syllogisms ; their would-be demonstration of the *Unlikeness*, like a mere dream about something, slips away at the touch of criticism, and takes its flight along with this Ungenerate.

Thus it is that whenever a falsehood is welcomed in preference to the truth, it may indeed flourish for a little through the illusion which it creates, but it will soon collapse ; its own methods of proof will dissolve it. But we bring this forward only to raise a smile at the very pretty revenge we might take on their *Unlikeness*. We must now resume the main thread of our discourse.

§ 39. *Answer to the question he is always asking,*
"*Can He who is be begotten?*"

Eunomius does not like the meaning of the
Ungenerate to be conveyed by the term Father,
because he wants to establish that there was a
time when the Son was not. It is in fact a
constant question amongst his pupils, "How
can He who (always) is be begotten?" This
comes, I take it, of not weaning oneself from
the human application of words, when we
have to think about God. But let us without bitterness at once expose the actual false-
ness of this 'arrière pensée' of his[2], stating
first our conclusions upon the matter.

These names have a different meaning with
us, Eunomius; when we come to the transcendent energies they yield another sense.
Wide, indeed, is the interval in all else that
divides the human from the divine; experience cannot point here below to anything at
all resembling in amount what we may guess
at and imagine there. So likewise, as regards
the meaning of our terms, though there
may be, so far as words go, some likeness
between man and the Eternal, yet the gulf
between these two worlds is the real measure
of the separation of meanings. For instance,
our Lord calls God a 'man' that was a 'householder' in the parable[3]; but though this title is
ever so familiar to us, will the person we think
of and the person there meant be of the same
description; and will our 'house' be the same
as that large house, in which, as the Apostle
says, there are the vessels of gold, and those of
silver[4], and those of the other materials which
are recounted? Or will not *those* rather be beyond our immediate apprehension and to be
contemplated in a blessed immortality, while
ours are earthern, and to dissolve to earth?
So in almost all the other terms there is a similarity of names between things human and things
divine, revealing nevertheless underneath this
sameness a wide difference of meanings. We
find alike in both worlds the mention of bodily
limbs and senses; as with us, so with the life
of God, which all allow to be above sense,
there are set down in order fingers and arm
and hand, eye and eyelids, hearing, heart, feet
and sandals, horses, cavalry, and chariots; and
other metaphors innumerable are taken from
human life to illustrate symbolically divine things.
As, then, each one of these names has a human
sound, but not a human meaning, so also that
of Father, while applying equally to life divine
and human, hides a distinction between the
uttered meanings exactly proportionate to the

difference existing between the subjects of this
title. We think of man's generation one
way; we surmise of the divine generation in
another. A man is born in a stated time; and
a particular place must be the receptacle of
his life; without it it is not in nature that he
should have any concrete substance: whence
also it is inevitable that sections of time are
found enveloping his life; there is a Before,
and With, and After him. It *is* true to say
of any one whatever of those born into this
world that there was a time when he was
not, that he is now, and again there will be
time when he will cease to exist; but into
the Eternal world these ideas of time do not
enter; to a sober thinker they have nothing
akin to that world. He who considers what
the divine life really is will get beyond the
'sometime,' the 'before,' and the 'after,' and
every mark whatever of this extension in time;
he will have lofty views upon a subject so
lofty; nor will he deem that the Absolute is
bound by those laws which he observes to be
in force in human generation.

Passion precedes the concrete existence
of man; certain material foundations are laid
for the formation of the living creature; beneath
it all is Nature, by God's will, with her wonder-
working, putting everything under contribution
for the proper proportion of nutrition for that
which is to be born, taking from each terrestrial
element the amount necessary for the particular
case, receiving the co-operation of a measured
time, and as much of the food of the parents
as is necessary for the formation of the child:
in a word Nature, advancing through all these
processes by which a human life is built up,
brings the non-existent to the birth; and
accordingly we say that, non-existent once, it
now is born; because, at one time not being,
at another it begins to be. But when it comes
to the Divine generation the mind rejects this
ministration of Nature, and this fulness of time
in contributing to the development, and everything else which our argument contemplated
as taking place in human generation; and
he who enters on divine topics with no carnal
conceptions will not fall down again to the
level of any of those debasing thoughts,
but seeks for one in keeping with the
majesty of the thing to be expressed; he will
not think of passion in connexion with that
which is passionless, or count the Creator of
all Nature as in need of Nature's help, or
admit extension in time into the Eternal life;
he will see that the Divine generation is to be
cleared of all such ideas, and will allow to the
title 'Father' only the meaning that the Only-
begotten is not Himself without a source, but derives from That the cause of His being; though,

---

2 αὐτὸ τὸ πεπλασμένον τῆς ὑπονοίας.
3 *the parable*, i.e. of the Tares. Matthew xiii. 27; cf. v. 52.
4 2 Tim. ii. 20.

as for the actual beginning of His subsistence, he will not calculate that, because he will not be able to see any sign of the thing in question. 'Older' and 'younger' and all such notions are found to involve intervals of time; and so, when you mentally abstract time in general, all such indications are got rid of along with it.

Since, then, He who *is* with the Father, in some inconceivable category, before the ages admits not of a 'sometime,' He exists by generation indeed, but nevertheless He never begins to exist. His life is neither in time, nor in place. But when we take away these and all suchlike ideas in contemplating the subsistence of the Son, there is only one thing that we can even think of as before Him—i.e. the Father. But the Only-begotten, as He Himself has told us, is in the Father, and so, from His nature, is not open to the supposition that He ever existed not. If indeed the Father ever was not, the eternity of the Son must be cancelled retrospectively in consequence of this nothingness of the Father: but if the Father is always, how can the Son ever be non-existent, when He cannot be thought of at all by Himself apart from the Father, but is always implied silently in the name Father. This name in fact conveys the two Persons equally; the idea of the Son is inevitably suggested by that word. When was it, then, that the Son was not? In what category shall we detect His non-existence? In place? There is none. In time? Our Lord was before all times; and if so, when was He not? And if He was in the Father, in what place was He not? Tell us that, ye who are so practised in seeing things out of sight. What kind of interval have your cogitations given a shape to? What vacancy in the Son, be it of substance or of conception, have you been able to think of, which shows the Father's life, when drawn out in parallel, as surpassing that of the Only-begotten? Why, even of men we cannot say absolutely that any one was not, and then was born. Levi, many generations before his own birth in the flesh, was tithed by Melchisedech; so the Apostle says, "Levi also, who receiveth tithes, payed tithes (in Abraham),"[5] adding the proof, "for he was yet in the loins of his father, when" Abraham met the priest of the Most High. If, then, a man in a certain sense is not, and is then born, having existed beforehand by virtue of kinship of substance in his progenitor, according to an Apostle's testimony, how as to the Divine life do they dare to utter the thought that *He* was not, and then was

begotten? For He 'is in the Father,' as our Lord has told us; "I am in the Father, and the Father in Me[6]," each of course being in the other in two different senses; the Son being in the Father as the beauty of the image is to be found in the form from which it has been outlined; and the Father in the Son, as that original beauty is to be found in the image of itself. Now in all hand-made images the interval of time is a point of separation between the model and that to which it lends its form; but there the one cannot be separated from the other, neither the "express image" from the "Person," to use the Apostle's words[7], nor the "brightness" from the "glory" of God, nor the representation from the goodness; but when once thought has grasped one of these, it has admitted the associated Verity as well. "*Being*," he says (not becoming), "the brightness of His glory[8];" so that clearly we may rid ourselves for ever of the blasphemy which lurks in either of those two conceptions; viz., that the Only-begotten can be thought of as Ungenerate (for he says "the brightness of His glory," the brightness coming from the glory, and not, reversely, the glory from the brightness); or that He ever began to be. For the word "being" is a witness that interprets to us the Son's continuity and eternity and superiority to all marks of time.

What occasion, then, had our foes for proposing for the damage of our Faith that trifling question, which they think unanswerable and, so, a proving of their own doctrine, and which they are continually asking, namely, 'whether One who is can be generated.' We may boldly answer them at once, that He who is in the Ungenerate *was* generated from Him. and *does* derive His source from Him. 'I live by the Father[9]:' but it is impossible to name the 'when' of His beginning. When there is no intermediate matter, or idea, or interval of time, to separate the being of the Son from the Father, no symbol can be thought of, either, by which the Only-begotten can be unlinked from the Father's life, and shewn to proceed from some special source of His own. If, then, there is no other principle that guides the Son's life, if there is nothing that a devout mind can contemplate before (but not divided from) the subsistence of the Son, but the Father only; and if the Father is without beginning or generation, as even our adversaries admit, how can He who can be contemplated only within the Father, who is without beginning, admit Himself of a beginning?

---

5 Heb. vii. 9, 10; Genesis xiv. 18.

6 John x. 38. 7 Heb. i.
8 Heb. i. 3. (ὢν, not γενόμενος). 9 John iv. 57.

What harm, too, does our Faith suffer from our admitting those expressions of our opponents which they bring forward against us as absurd, when they ask 'whether He which is can be begotten?' We do not assert that this can be so in the sense in which Nicodemus put his offensive question[1], wherein *he* thought it impossible that one who was in existence could come to a second birth : but we assert that, having His existence attached to an Existence which is always and is without beginning, and accompanying every investigator into the antiquities of time, and forestalling the curiosity of thought as it advances into the world beyond, and intimately blended as He is with all our conceptions of the Father, He has no beginning of His existence any more than He is Ungenerate: but He was both begotten and was, evincing on the score of causation generation from the Father, but by virtue of His everlasting life repelling any moment of non-existence.

But this thinker in his exceeding subtlety contravenes this statement; he sunders the being of the Only-begotten from the Father's nature, on the ground of one being Generated, the other Ungenerate ; and although there are such a number of names which with reverence may be applied to the Deity, and all of them suitable to both Persons equally, he pays no attention to any one of them, because these others indicate that in which Both participate ; he fastens on the name Ungenerate, and that alone ; and even of this he will not adopt the usual and approved meaning; he revolutionizes the conception of it, and cancels its common associations. Whatever can be the reason of this? For without some very strong one he would not wrest language away from its accepted meaning, and innovate[2] by changing the signification of words. He knows perfectly well that if their meaning was confined to the customary one he would have no power to subvert the sound doctrine ; but that if such terms are perverted from their common and current acceptation, he will be able to spoil the doctrine along with the word. For instance (to come to the actual words which he misuses), if, according to the common thinking of our Faith he had allowed that God was to be called Ungenerate only because He was never generated, the whole fabric of his heresy would have collapsed, with the withdrawal of his quibbling about this Ungenerate. If, that is, he was to be persuaded, by following out the analogy of almost all the names of God in use for the Church, to think of the God over all as Ungen-

erate, just as He is invisible, and passionless, and immaterial ; and if he was agreed that in every one of these terms there was signified only that which in no way belongs to God— body, for instance, and passion and colour, and derivation from a cause—then, if his view of the case had been like that, his party's tenet of the *Unlikeness* would lose its meaning; for in all else (except the Ungeneracy) that is conceived concerning the God of all even these adversaries allow the likeness existing between the Only-begotten and the Father. But to prevent this, he puts the term Ungenerate in front of all these names indicating God's transcendent nature ; and he makes this one a vantage-ground from which he may sweep down upon our Faith; he transfers the contrariety between the actual expressions 'Generated' and 'Ungenerate' to the Persons themselves to whom these words apply ; and thereby, by this difference between the words he argues by a quibble for a difference between the Beings ; not agreeing with us that Generated is to be used only because the Son was generated, and Ungenerate because the Father exists without having been generated ; but affirming that he thinks the former has acquired existence by having been generated ; though what sort of philosophy leads him to such a view I cannot understand. If one were to attend to the mere meanings of those words by themselves, abstracting in thought those Persons for whom the names are taken to stand, one would discover the groundlessness of these statements of theirs. Consider, then, not that, in consequence of the Father being a conception prior to the Son (as the Faith truly teaches), the order of the names themselves must be arranged so as to correspond with the value and order of that which underlies them ; but regard them alone by themselves, to see which of them (the word, I repeat, not the Reality which it represents) is to be placed before the other as a conception of our mind ; which of the two conveys the assertion of an idea, which the negation of the same ; for instance (to be clear, I think similar pairs of words will give my meaning), Knowledge, Ignorance—Passion, Passionlessness—and suchlike contrasts, which of them possess priority of conception before the others? Those which posit the negation, or those which posit the assertion of the said quality? I take it the latter do so. Knowledge, anger, passion, are conceived of first ; and then comes the negation of these ideas. And let no one, in his excess of devotion[3], blame this argument, as if it would put the

---

[1] John iii. 4.   [2] ξενίζει, intrans. N.T. Polyb. Lucian.   [3] ἐθελοθρησκείας, "will worship."

Son before the Father. We are not making out that the Son is to be placed in conception before the Father, seeing that the argument is discriminating only the meanings of 'Generated,' and 'Ungenerate.' So Generation signifies the assertion of some reality or some idea; while Ungeneracy signifies its negation; so that there is every reason that Generation must be thought of first. Why, then, do they insist herein on fixing on the Father the second, in order of conception, of these two names; why do they keep on thinking that a negation can define and can embrace the whole substance of the term in question, and are roused to exasperation against those who point out the groundlessness of their arguments?

§ 40. *His unsuccessful attempt to be consistent with his own statements after Basil has confuted him.*

For notice how bitter he is against one who did detect the rottenness and weakness of his work of mischief; how he revenges himself all he can, and that is only by abuse and vilification: in these, however, he possesses abundant ability. Those who would give elegance of style to a discourse have a way of filling out the places that want rhythm with certain conjunctive particles [4], whereby they introduce more euphony and connexion into the assembly of their phrases; so does Eunomius garnish his work with abusive epithets in most of his passages, as though he wished to make a display of this overflowing power of invective. Again we are 'fools,' again we 'fail in correct reasoning,' and 'meddle in the controversy without the preparation which its importance requires,' and 'miss the speaker's meaning.' Such, and still more than these, are the phrases used of our Master by this decorous orator. But perhaps after all there is good reason in his anger; and this pamphleteer is justly indignant. For why should Basil have stung him by thus exposing the weakness of this teaching of his? Why should he have uncovered to the sight of the simpler brethren the blasphemy veiled beneath

his plausible sophistries? Why should he not have let silence cover the unsoundness of this view? Why gibbet the wretched man, when he ought to have pitied him, and kept the veil over the indecency of his argument? He actually finds out and makes a spectacle of one who has somehow got to be admired amongst his private pupils for cleverness and shrewdness! Eunomius had said somewhere in his works that the attribute of being ungenerate "follows" the deity. Our Master remarked upon this phrase of his that a thing which "follows" must be amongst the externals, whereas the actual Being is not one of these, but indicates the very existence of anything, so far as it does exist. Then this gentle yet unconquerable opponent is furious, and pours along a copious stream of invective, because our Master, on hearing that phrase, apprehended the sense of it as well. But what did he do wrong, if he firmly insisted only upon the meaning of your own writings. If indeed he had seized illogically on what was said, all that you say would be true, and we should have to ignore what he did; but seeing that you are blushing at his reproof, why do you not erase the word from your pamphlet, instead of abusing the reprover? 'Yes, but he did not understand the drift of the argument. Well, how do we do wrong, if being human, we guessed at the meaning from your actual words, having no comprehension of that which was buried in your heart? It is for God to see the inscrutable, and to inspect the characters of that which we have no means of comprehending, and to be cognizant of *unlikeness* [5] in the invisible world. We can only judge by what we hear.

§ 41. *The thing that follows is not the same as the thing that it follows.*

He first says, "the attribute of being ungenerate follows the Deity." By that we understood him to mean that this Ungeneracy is one of the things external to God. Then he says, "Or rather this Ungeneracy is His actual being." We fail to understand the 'sequitur' of this; we notice in fact something very queer and incongruous about it. If Ungeneracy follows God, and yet also constitutes His being, two beings will be attributed to one and the same subject in this view; so that God will be in the same way as He was before and has always been believed to be [6], but besides that will have another being accompanying, which

---

[4] *conjunctive particles*, σύνδεσμοι. In Aristotle's Poetics (xx. 6), these are reckoned as one ot the 8 'parts ot speech.' The term σύνδεσμος is illustrated by the examples μὲν, ἤτοι, δή, which leaves no doubt that it includes at all events conjunctions and particles. Its general character is defined in his Rhetoric iii. 12, 4: "It makes many (sentences) one." Harris (*Hermes* ii. c. 2), thus defines a conjunction, "A part of speech devoid of signification itself, but so formed as to help signification by making two or more significant sentences to be one significant sentence," a definition which manifestly comes from Aristotle.

The comparison here seems to be between these constantly recurring particles, themselves 'devoid of signification,' in an 'elegant' discourse, and the perpetually used epithets, "fools," &c., which, though utterly meaningless, serve to connect his dislocated paragraphs. The 'assembly' (σύναξις, always of the synagogue or the Communion. See Suicer) of his words is brought, it is ironically implied, into some sort of harmony by these means.

[5] A hit at the Anomœans. 'Your subtle distinctions, in the invisible world of your own mind, between the meanings of "following" are like the *unlikenesses* which you see between the Three Persons.'

[6] ὡς εἶναι μὲν τὸν Θεὸν κατὰ ταὐτὸν ὡς εἶναί ποτε (infinitive by attraction to preceding) καὶ εἶναι πεπίστευται.

they style Ungeneracy, quite distinct from Him Whose 'following' it is, as our Master puts it. Well, if he commands us to think so, he must pardon our poverty of ideas, in not being able to follow out such subtle speculations.

But if he disowns this view, and does not admit a double being in the Deity, one represented by the godhead, the other by the ungeneracy, let our friend, who is himself neither 'rash' nor 'malignant,' prevail upon himself not to be over partial to invective while these combats for the truth are being fought, but to explain to us, who are so wanting in culture, how that which follows is not one thing and that which leads another, but how both coalesce into one; for, in spite of what he says in defence of his statement, the absurdity of it remains; and the addition of that handful of words[7] does not correct, as he asserts, the contradiction in it. I have not yet been able to see that any explanation at all is discoverable in them. But we will give what he has written verbatim. "We say, 'or rather the Ungeneracy is His actual being,' without meaning to *contract* into the being[8] that which we have proved to follow it, but applying 'follow' to the title, but *is* to the being." Accordingly when these things are taken together, the whole resulting argument would be, that the title Ungenerate follows, because to be Ungenerate is His actual being. But what expounder of this expounding shall we get? He says "without meaning to contract into the being that which we have proved to follow it." Perhaps some of the guessers of riddles might tell us that by 'contract into' he means 'fastening together.' But who can see anything intelligible or coherent in the rest? The results of 'following' belong, he tells us, not to the being, but to the title. But, most learned sir, what *is* the title? Is it in discord with the being, or does it not rather coincide with it in the thinking? If the title is inappropriate to the being, then how can the being be represented by the title; but if, as he himself phrases it, the being is fittingly defined by the title of Ungenerate, how can there be any parting of them after that? You make the name of the being follow one thing and the being itself another. And what then is the 'construction of the entire view?' "The title Ungenerate follows God, seeing that He Himself is Ungenerate." He says that there 'follows' God, Who is something other than that which is Ungenerate, this very title. Then how can he place the definition of Godhead within the Ungeneracy?

Again, he says that this title 'follows' God as existing without a previous generation. Who will solve us the mystery of such riddles? 'Ungenerate' preceding and then following; first a fittingly attached title of the being, and then following like a stranger! What, too, is the cause of this excessive flutter about this name; he gives to it the whole contents of godhead[9]; as if there will be nothing wanting in our adoration, if God be so named; and as if the whole system of our faith will be endangered, if He is not? Now, if a brief statement about this should not be deemed superfluous and irrelevant, we will thus explain the matter.

§ 42. *Explanation of ' Ungenerate,' and a 'study' of Eternity.*

The eternity of God's life, to sketch it in mere outline, is on this wise. He is always to be apprehended as in existence; He admits not a time when He was not, and when He will not be. Those who draw a circular figure in plane geometry from a centre to the distance of the line of circumference tell us there is no definite beginning to their figure; and that the line is interrupted by no ascertained end any more than by any visible commencement: they say that, as it forms a single whole in itself with equal radii on all sides, it avoids giving any indication of beginning or ending. When, then, we compare the Infinite being to such a figure, circumscribed though it be, let none find fault with this account; for it is not on the circumference, but on the similarity which the figure bears to the Life which in every direction eludes the grasp, that we fix our attention when we affirm that such is our intuition of the Eternal. From the present instant, as from a centre and a "point," we extend thought in all directions, to the immensity of that Life. We find that we are drawn round uninterruptedly and evenly, and that we are always following a circumference where there is nothing to grasp; we find the divine life returning upon itself in an unbroken continuity, where no end and no parts can be recognized. Of God's eternity

7 ἐναριθμήτων ῥημάτων. But it is possible that the true reading may be εὐρύθμων, alluding to the 'rhythm' in the form of abuse with which Eunomius connected his arguments (preceding section).

8 οὐκ εἰς τὸ εἶναι συναιροῦντες.

9 *He gives to it the whole contents of godhead.* It was the central point in Eunomius' system that by the Ἀγεννησία we can comprehend the Divine Nature; he trusts entirely to the Aristotelian divisions (logical) and sub-divisions. A mere word (γέννητος) was thus allowed to destroy the equality of the Son. It was almost inevitable, therefore, that his opponent, as a defender of the Homoousion, should occasionally fall back so far upon Plato, as to maintain that opposites are joined and are identical with each other, i.e. that γέννησις and ἀγεννησία are not truly opposed to each other. Another method of combating this excessive insistence on the physical and logical was, to bring forward the ethical realities; and this Gregory does constantly throughout this treatise. We are to know God by Wisdom, and Truth, and Righteousness. Only occasionally (as in the next section) does he speak of the 'eternity' of God: and here only because Eunomius has obliged him, and in order to show that the idea is made up of two negations, and nothing more.

we say that which we have heard from prophecy [1]; viz.. that God is a king " of old," and rules for ages, and for ever, and beyond. Therefore we define Him to be earlier than any beginning, and exceeding any end. Entertaining, then, this idea of the Almighty, as one that is adequate, we express it by two titles ; i.e., 'Ungenerate' and 'Endless' represent this infinitude and continuity and ever-lastingness of the Deity. If we adopted only one of them for our idea, and if the remaining one was dropped, our meaning would be marred by this omission ; for it is impossible with either one of them singly [2] to express the notion residing in each of the two ; but when one speaks of the ' endless,' only the absence as regards an end has been indicated, and it does not follow that any hint has been given about a beginning ; while, when one speaks of the ' Unoriginate [3],' the fact of being beyond a beginning has been expressed, but the case as regards an end has been left quite doubtful.

Seeing, then, that these two titles equally help to express the eternity of the divine life, it is high time to inquire why our friends cut in two the complete meaning of this eternity, and declare that the one meaning, which is the negation of beginning, constitutes God's being (instead of merely forming part of the definition of eternity [4]), while they consider the other, which is the negation of end, as amongst the externals of that being. It is difficult to see the reason for thus assigning the negation of beginning to the realm of being, while they banish the negation of end outside that realm. The two are our conceptions of the same thing ; and, therefore, either both should be admitted to the definition of being, or, if the one is to be judged inadmissible, the other should be rejected also. If, however, they are determined thus to divide the thought of eternity, and to make the one fall within the realm of that being, and to reckon the other with the non-realities of Deity (for the thoughts which they adopt on this subject are grovelling, and, like birds who have shed their feathers, they are unable to soar into the sublimities of theology), I would advise them to reverse their teaching, and to count the unending as being, overlooking the unoriginate rather, and assigning the palm to that which is future and excites hope, rather than to that which is past and stale. Seeing, I say (and I speak thus owing to their narrowness of spirit, and lower the discussion to the level of a child's conception), the past period of his life is nothing to him who has lived it, and all his interest is centred on the future and on that which can be looked forward to, that which has no end will have more value than that which has no beginning. So let our thoughts upon the divine nature be worthy and exalted ones ; or else, if they are going to judge of it according to human tests, let the future be more valued by them than the past, and let them confine the being of the Deity to that, since time's lapse sweeps away with it all existence in the past, whereas expected existence gains substance from our hope [5].

Now I broach these ridiculously childish suggestions as to children sitting in the market-place and playing [6]; for when one looks into the grovelling earthliness of their heretical teaching it is impossible to help falling into a sort of sportive childishness. It would be right, however, to add this to what we have said, viz., that, as the idea of eternity is completed only by means of both (as we have already argued), by the negation of a beginning and also by that of an end, if they confine God's being to the one, their definition of this being will be manifestly imperfect and curtailed by half ; it is thought of only by the absence of beginning, and does not contain the absence of end within itself as an essential element. But if they do combine both negations, and so complete their definition of the being of God, observe, again, the absurdity that is at once apparent in this view ; it will be found, after all their efforts, to be at variance not only with the Only-begotten, but with itself. The case is clear and does not require much dwelling upon. The idea of a beginning and the idea of an end are opposed each to each ; the meanings of each differ as widely as the other diametric oppositions [7], where there is no half-way proposition below [8]. If any one is asked to define ' beginning,' he will not give a definition the same as that of end ; but will carry his definition of it to the opposite extremity. Therefore also the two

---

[5] Cf. Heb. xi. 1, of faith, ἐλπιζομένων ὑπόστασις πραγμάτων.
[6] Luke vii. 32.
[7] κατὰ διάμετρον ἀλλήλοις ἀντικειμένων, i.e. Contradictories in Logic.

[8] As in A or E, both of which have the Particular below them (I or O) as *a half-way* to the contrary Universal. Thus—
A   I   E
All men are mortal. Some men are mortal. No men are mortal.
E   O   A
No men are mortal. Some men are not mortal. All men are mortal.
But between A and O, E and I, there is no half-way.

[1] *from prophecy*. Psalm x. 16. Βασιλεύσει Κύριος εἰς τὸν αἰῶνα, καὶ εἰς τὸν αἰῶνα τοῦ αἰῶνος· xxix. 10. καθιεῖται Κύριος Βασιλεὺς εἰς τὸν αἰῶνα· lxxiv. 12. Ὁ δὲ θεὸς Βασιλεὺς ἡμῶν πρὸ αἰῶνος. [2] ἑνός τινος τούτων. [3] ἄναρχον.
[4] οὐ περὶ τὸ ἀίδιον θεωρεῖσθαι.

contraries[9] of these will be separated from each other by the same distance of opposition; and that which is without beginning, being contrary to that which is to be seen by a beginning, will be a very different thing from that which is endless, or the negation of end. If, then, they import both these attributes into the being of God, I mean the negations of end and of beginning, they will exhibit this Deity of theirs as a combination of two contradictory and discordant things, because the *contrary* ideas to beginning and end reproduce on their side also the *contradiction* existing between beginning and end. Contraries of contradictories are themselves contradictory of each other. In fact, it is always a true axiom, that two things which are naturally opposed to two things mutually opposite are themselves opposed to each other; as we may see by example. Water is opposed to fire; therefore also the forces destructive of these are opposed to each other; if moistness is apt to extinguish fire, and dryness is apt to destroy water, the opposition of fire to water is continued in those qualities themselves which are contrary to them; so that dryness is plainly opposed to moistness. Thus, when beginning and end have to be placed (diametrically) opposite each other[1], the terms contrary to these also contradict each other in their meaning, I mean, the negations of end and of beginning. Well, then, if they determine that one only of these negations is indicative of the being (to repeat my former assertion), they will bear evidence to half only of God's existence, confining it to the absence of beginning, and refusing to extend it to the absence of end; whereas, if they import both into their definition of it, they will actually exhibit it so as a combination of contradictions in the way that has been said; for these two negations of beginning and of end, by virtue of the contradiction existing between beginning and end, will part it asunder. So their Deity will be found to be a sort of patchwork compound, a conglomerate of contradictions.

But there is not, neither shall there be, in the Church of God a teaching such as that, which can make One who is single and incomposite not only multiform and patchwork, but also the combination of opposites. The simplicity of the True Faith assumes God to be that which He is, viz., incapable of being grasped by any term, or any idea, or any other device of our apprehension, remaining beyond the reach not only of the human but of the angelic and of all supramundane intelligence, unthinkable, unutterable, above all expression in words, having but one name that can represent His proper nature, the single name of being 'Above every name[2]'; which is granted to the Only-begotten also, because "all that the Father hath is the Son's." The orthodox theory allows these words, I mean "Ungenerate," "Endless," to be indicative of God's eternity, but not of His being; so that "Ungenerate" means that no source or cause lies beyond Him, and "Endless" means that His kingdom will be brought to a standstill in no end. "Thou art the same," the prophet says, "and Thy years shall not fail[3]," showing by "art" that He subsists out of no cause, and by the words following, that the blessedness of His life is ceaseless and unending.

But, perhaps, some one amongst even very religious people will pause over these investigations of ours upon God's eternity, and say that it will be difficult from what we have said for the Faith in the Only-begotten to escape unhurt. Of two unacceptable doctrines, he will say, our account[4] must inevitably be brought into contact with one. Either we shall make out that the Son is Ungenerate, which is absurd; or else we shall deny Him Eternity altogether, a denial which that *fraternity* of blasphemers make their specialty. For if Eternity is characterized by having no beginning and end, it is inevitable either that we must be impious and deny the Son Eternity, or that we must be led in our secret thoughts about Him into the idea of Ungeneracy. What, then, shall we answer? That if, in conceiving of the Father before the Son on the single score of causation, we inserted any mark of time before the subsistence of the Only-begotten, the belief which we have in the Son's eternity might with reason be said to be endangered. But, as it is, the Eternal nature, equally in the case of the Father's and the Son's life, and, as well, in what we believe about the Holy Ghost, admits not of the thought that it will ever cease to be; for where time is not, the "when" is annihilated with it. And if the Son, always ap-

---

9 Beginning (Contraries) Beginningless.

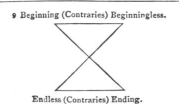

Endless (Contraries) Ending.

1 ὑπεναντίως διακειμένων. The same term has been used to express the opposition between Ungenerate and Generated: so that it means both Oppositions, i.e. Contraries and Contradictories.

2 Philip. ii. 9. ὄνομα τὸ ὑπὲρ πᾶν ὄνομα. 3 Psalm cii. 27.
4 Adopting ὁ λόγος from the Venice Cod. (ἐνὶ πάντως ὁ λόγος συνενεχθήσεται). The verb cannot be impersonal: and τις above, the only available nominative, does not suit the sense very well.
Gregory constructs this scheme of Opposition *after the analogy* of Logical Opposition. Beginning is not so opposed to Beginningless, as it is to Ending, because with the latter there is no half-way, i.e. no word of definition in common.

pearing with the thought of the Father, is always found in the category of existence, what danger is there in owning the Eternity of the Only-begotten, Who "hath neither beginning of days, nor end of life [5]." For as He is Light from Light, Life from Life, Good from Good, and Wise, Just, Strong, and all else in the same way, so most certainly is He Eternal from Eternal.

But a lover of controversial wrangling catches up the argument, on the ground that such a sequence would make Him Ungenerate from Ungenerate. Let him, however, cool his combative heart, and insist upon the proper expressions, for in confessing His 'coming from the Father' he has banished all ideas of Ungeneracy as regards the Only-begotten ; and there will be then no danger in pronouncing Him Eternal and yet not Ungenerate. On the one hand, because the existence of the Son is not marked by any intervals of time, and the infinitude of His life flows back before the ages and onward beyond them in an all-pervading tide, He is properly addressed with the title of Eternal; again, on the other hand, because the thought of Him as Son in fact and title gives us the thought of the Father as inalienably joined to it, He thereby stands clear of an ungenerate existence being imputed to Him, while He is always with a Father Who always is, as those inspired words of our Master expressed it, "bound by way of generation to His Father's Ungeneracy." Our account of the Holy Ghost will be the same also ; the difference is only in the place assigned in order. For as the Son is bound to the Father, and, while deriving existence from Him, is not substantially after Him, so again the Holy Spirit is in touch with the Only-begotten, Who is conceived of as before the Spirit's subsistence only in the theoretical light of a cause [6]. Extensions in time find no admittance in the Eternal Life ; so that, when we have removed the thought of cause, the Holy Trinity in no single way exhibits discord with itself; and to It is glory due.

[5] Heb. vii. 3.

[6] τὸν τῆς αἰτίας λόγον. This is much more probably the meaning, because of *before* above, than "on the score of the different kind of causation" (Non omne quod procedat nascitur, quamvis omne procedat quod nascitur. S. August.). It is a direct testimony to the 'Filioque' belief. "The Spirit comes forth with the Word, not begotten with Him, but being with and accompanying and proceeding from Him." Theodoret. Serm. II.

NOTE ON Ἀγέννητος (Ungenerate).

THE difference between the Father and the Son is contained in this one word. But what Gregory and what Eunomius make of that difference illustrates the gulf fixed between the Catholic Faith and Arianism.

Gregory shows (l. c. Book I. c. 33, p. 78, viii. 5 (ad fin.), ix. 2) how the Son as well as the Father can be called ἄναρχος (unoriginate or beginningless), i.e. when the ideas of time and creation are brought in ; but the Son can never be called Ungenerate. But he goes no further than this. No word can express the being of God. Gregory repeatedly maintains that He is incomprehensible. 'Ungenerate' and 'Father' only express a relation of His being (σχετικὴ ἐννοία): but of the two the latter is preferable, as Scriptural, and as lending no handle to the interpretation which from its mere form could be put upon the other.

Eunomius did actually put this interpretation upon it, and it became the watchword of his system. He made of it what many now make of the word 'Infinite.' He saw in it the expression of a positive idea which enabled the mind to comprehend the Deity, and at the same time by virtue of the logical opposition between ungenerate and generate destroyed not only the equality but also the *likeness* of the Father and the Son. As in all other dichotomies arising from privative terms (i.e. Imperishable, Unending, Uncreate, &c.), the Trinity stands apart from creation, so in this last dichotomy the First Person stands apart from the Second and the Third. It was the only distinction of this sort that Arianism could seize on for its purpose : and so this one ('Ἀγέννητος) is hypostatized and deified.

Gregory, to destroy the tyranny of a word, shows that all the conceivable attributes of Deity (the πλήρωμα of the New Testament) are still *above* the distinction of Ungenerate and Generate Deity, and are present in both : just as human nature was present equally in the 'not-born' Adam, and the 'born' Abel. Christ is Very God of Very God, Light of Light, Life of Life, and all else, ethical or spiritual, that Scripture or human intuition has ever attributed to God : only He is not Ungenerate of Ungenerate : and for the simple reason that the Generate cannot be its own opposite. But this distinction is simply dynamic, not spiritual ; and in person, not in essence.

It will be clear from this that 'Ungenerate' is the only adequate equivalent of 'Ἀγέννητος, as used in this controversy. 'Not-begotten' or 'Unbegotten' as applicable to the Father only would confuse the doctrine of the Third Person, Who is Himself also 'not made, nor created, *nor begotten.*' 'Ingenerate' is not supported by the Latin use (though ingenitus is used thus by Arnobius) ; 'Unoriginate' bears the sense of unbeginning, and can be said of the Son (see above). Lastly, 'Not-generated' does not furnish a corresponding idiomatic expression for 'Ἀγεννησία.

With regard to the form of the Greek word, "it is very well known," says Bull, *Def. Fid. Nic.* ii. 296, "that by the Greeks the words γεννητὸς and γενητὸς are used promiscuously ; although the Catholic writers of the Church for the most part, especially such as lived *after the third century*, distinguished *more accurately* between them, in the question of the divinity of the Son ;" but Lightfoot (Ignatius, vol. 2. p. 90 ff. 2nd edit.) has shewn by many citations that such writers *always* felt the distinction between ἀγέννητος and ἀγένητος. Thus 'Ἀγένητος (unmade), but not 'Ἀγέννητος, could be applied to the Son. But the instances in which the one word has been miswritten or misprinted for the other are too numerous to mention. Of course the contemporary philosophy could not enter into this distinction : still it is worth noticing that Plotinus uses ἀγέννητος of the Supreme Being : Ennead V. iii. (p. 517) ; and Celsus the Neoplatonist uses it of his eternal world (Origen, *c. Cels.* according to the text of the Philocalia, i.e. the edition of Basil and Greg. Naz.).

BOOK II

§ 1. *The second book declares the Incarnation of God the Word, and the faith delivered by the Lord to His disciples, and asserts that the heretics who endeavour to overthrow this faith and devise other additional names are of their father the devil.*

The Christian Faith, which in accordance with the command of our Lord has been preached to all nations by His disciples, is neither of men, nor by men, but by our Lord Jesus Christ Himself, Who being the Word, the Life, the Light, the Truth, and God, and Wisdom, and all else that He is by nature, for this cause above all was made in the likeness of man, and shared our nature, becoming like us in all things, yet without sin. He was like us in all things, in that He took upon Him manhood in its entirety with soul and body, so that our salvation was accomplished by means of both : —He, I say, appeared on earth and "conversed with men [1]," that men might no longer have opinions according to their own notions about the Self-existent, formulating into a doctrine the hints that come to them from vague conjectures, but that we might be convinced that God has truly been manifested in the flesh, and believe that to be the only true "mystery of godliness [2]," which was delivered to us by the very Word and God, Who by Himself spake to His Apostles, and that we might receive the teaching concerning the transcendent nature of the Deity which is given to us, as it were, "through a glass darkly [3]" from the older Scriptures,—from the Law, and the Prophets, and the Sapiential Books, as an evidence of the truth fully revealed to us, reverently accepting the meaning of the things which have been spoken, so as to accord in the faith set forth by the Lord of the whole Scriptures [4], which faith we guard as we received it, word for word, in purity, without falsification, judging even a slight divergence from the words delivered to us an extreme blasphemy and impiety. We believe, then, even as the Lord set forth the Faith to His Disciples, when He said, "Go, teach all nations, baptizing them in the name of the Father, and of the Son, and of the Holy Ghost [5]." This is the word of the mystery whereby through the new birth from above our nature is transformed from the corruptible to the incorruptible, being renewed from "the old man," "according to the image of Him who created [6]" at the beginning the likeness to the Godhead. In the Faith then which was delivered by God to the Apostles we admit neither subtraction, nor alteration, nor addition, knowing assuredly that he who presumes to pervert the Divine utterance by dishonest quibbling, the same "is of his father the devil," who leaves the words of truth and "speaks of his own," becoming the father of a lie [7]. For whatsoever is said otherwise than in exact accord with the truth is assuredly false and not true.

§ 2. *Gregory then makes an explanation at length touching the eternal Father, the Son, and the Holy Spirit.*

Since then this doctrine is put forth by the Truth itself, it follows that anything which the inventors of pestilent heresies devise besides to subvert this Divine utterance,—as, for example, calling the Father "Maker" and "Creator" of the Son instead of "Father," and the Son a "result," a "creature," a "product," instead of "Son," and the Holy Spirit the "creature of a creature," and the "product of a product," instead of His proper title the "Spirit," and whatever those who fight against God are pleased to say of Him,—all such fancies we term a denial and violation of the Godhead revealed to us in this doctrine. For once for all we have learned from the Lord, through Whom comes the transformation of our nature from mortality to immortality,—from Him, I say, we have learned to what we ought to look

---

[1] Bar. iii. 37.   [2] 1 Tim. iii. 16.   [3] 1 Cor. xiii. 12.
[4] This is perhaps the force of τῶν ὅλων: "the Lord of the Old Covenant as well as of the New." But τῶν ὅλων may mean simply "the Universe."

[5] S. Matt. xxviii. 19.   [6] Cf. Col. iii. 10.
[7] Cf. S. John viii. 44.

with the eyes of our understanding,—that is, the Father, the Son, and the Holy Spirit. We say that it is a terrible and soul-destroying thing to misinterpret these Divine utterances and to devise in their stead assertions to subvert them,—assertions pretending to correct God the Word, Who appointed that we should maintain these statements as part of our faith. For each of these titles understood in its natural sense becomes for Christians a rule of truth and a law of piety. For while there are many other names by which Deity is indicated in the Historical Books, in the Prophets and in the Law, our Master Christ passes by all these and commits to us these titles as better able to bring us to the faith about the Self-Existent, declaring that it suffices us to cling to the title, "Father, Son, and Holy Ghost," in order to attain to the apprehension of Him Who is absolutely Existent, Who is one and yet not one. In regard to essence He is one, wherefore the Lord ordained that we should look to one Name : but in regard to the attributes indicative of the Persons, our belief in Him is distinguished into belief in the Father, the Son, and the Holy Ghost [8] ; He is divided without separation, and united without confusion. For when we hear the title "Father" we apprehend the meaning to be this, that the name is not understood with reference to itself alone, but also by its special signification indicates the relation to the Son. For the term "Father" would have no meaning apart by itself, if "Son" were not connoted by the utterance of the word "Father." When, then, we learnt the name "Father" we were taught at the same time, by the selfsame title, faith also in the Son. Now since Deity by its very nature is permanently and immutably the same in all that pertains to its essence, nor did it at any time fail to be anything that it now is, nor will it at any future time be anything that it now is not, and since He Who is the very Father was named Father by the Word, and since in the Father the Son is implied,—since these things are so, we of necessity believe that He Who admits no change or alteration in His nature was always entirely what He is now, or, if there is anything which He was not, that He assuredly is not now. Since then He is named Father by the very Word, He assuredly always was Father, and is and will be even as He was. For surely it is not lawful in speaking of the Divine and unimpaired Essence to deny that what is excellent always belonged to It. For if He was not always what He now is, He certainly changed either from the better to the

worse or from the worse to the better, and of these assertions the impiety is equal either way, whichever statement is made concerning the Divine nature. But in fact the Deity is incapable of change and alteration. So, then, everything that is excellent and good is always contemplated in the fountain of excellency. But "the Only-begotten God, Who is in the bosom of the Father [9]" is excellent, and beyond all excellency :—mark you, He says, "Who is in the bosom of the Father," not "Who came to be" there.

Well then, it has been demonstrated by these proofs that the Son is from all eternity to be contemplated in the Father, in Whom He is, being Life and Light and Truth, and every noble name and conception—to say that the Father ever existed by Himself apart from these attributes is a piece of the utmost impiety and infatuation. For if the Son, as the Scripture saith, is the Power of God, and Wisdom, and Truth, and Light, and Sanctification, and Peace, and Life, and the like, then before the Son existed, according to the view of the heretics, these things also had no existence at all. And if these things had no existence they must certainly conceive the bosom of the Father to have been devoid of such excellences. To the end, then, that the Father might not be conceived as destitute of the excellences which are His own, and that the doctrine might not run wild into this extravagance, the right faith concerning the Son is necessarily included in our Lord's utterance with the contemplation of the eternity of the Father. And for this reason He passes over all those names which are employed to indicate the surpassing excellence of the Divine nature [1], and delivers to us as part of our profession of faith the title of "Father" as better suited to indicate the truth, being a title which, as has been said, by its relative sense connotes with itself the Son, while the Son, Who is in the Father, always is what He essentially is, as has been said already, because the Deity by Its very nature does not admit of augmentation. For It does not perceive any other good outside of Itself, by participation in which It could acquire any accession, but is always immutable, neither casting away what It has, nor acquiring what It has not : for none of Its properties are such as to be cast away. And if there is anything whatsoever blessed, unsullied, true and good, associated with Him and in Him, we see of necessity that the good and holy Spirit must belong to Him [2], not

---

[8] Or, somewhat more literally, "He admits of distinction into belie. in the Father, the Son, and the Holy Ghost, being divided," &c.

[9] S. John i. 18.
[1] That nature which transcends our conceptions (ὑπερκειμένῃ).
[2] Or "be conjoined with such attribute :" αὐτῷ probably refers, like περὶ αὐτὸν καὶ ἐν αὐτῷ just above, to Θεός or τὸ Θεῖον, but it may conceivably refer to εἴ τι μακάριον, κ.τ.λ.

by way of accretion. That Spirit is indisputably a princely Spirit [3], a quickening Spirit, the controlling and sanctifying force of all creation, the Spirit that "worketh all in all" as He wills [4]. Thus we conceive no gap between the anointed Christ and His anointing, between the King and His sovereignty, between Wisdom and the Spirit of Wisdom, between Truth and the Spirit of Truth, between Power and the Spirit of Power, but as there is contemplated from all eternity in the Father the Son, Who is Wisdom and Truth, and Counsel, and Might, and Knowledge, and Understanding, so there is also contemplated in Him the Holy Spirit, Who is the Spirit of Wisdom, and of Truth, and of Counsel, and of Understanding, and all else that the Son is and is called. For which reason we say that to the holy disciples the mystery of godliness was committed in a form expressing at once union and distinction,—that we should believe on the Name of the Father, and of the Son, and of the Holy Ghost. For the differentiation of the subsistences [5], makes the distinction of Persons [6] clear and free from confusion, while the one Name standing in the forefront of the declaration of the Faith clearly expounds to us the unity of essence of the Persons [6] Whom the Faith declares,—I mean, of the Father, and of the Son, and of the Holy Spirit. For by these appellations we are taught not a difference of nature, but only the special attributes that mark the subsistences [5], so that we know that neither is the Father the Son, nor the Son the Father, nor the Holy Spirit either the Father or the Son, and recognize each by the distinctive mark of His Personal Subsistence [7], in illimitable perfection, at once contemplated by Himself and not divided from that with Which He is connected.

§ 3. *Gregory proceeds to discuss the relative force of the unnameable name of the Holy Trinity and the mutual relation of the Persons, and moreover the unknowable character of the Essence, and the condescension on His part towards us, His generation of the Virgin, and His second coming, the resurrection from the dead and future retribution.*

What then means that unnameable name concerning which the Lord said, "Baptizing them into the name," and did not add the actual significant term which "the name" indicates? We have concerning it this notion, that all things that exist in the creation are defined by means of their several names. Thus whenever a man speaks of "heaven" he directs the notion of the hearer to the created object indicated by this name, and he who mentions "man" or some animal, at once by the mention of the name impresses upon the hearer the form of the creature, and in the same way all other things, by means of the names imposed upon them, are depicted in the heart of him who by hearing receives the appellation imposed upon the thing. The uncreated Nature alone, which we acknowledge in the Father, and in the Son, and in the Holy Spirit, surpasses all significance of names. For this cause the Word, when He spoke of "the name" in delivering the Faith, did not add what it is,—for how could a name be found for that which is above every name? —but gave authority that whatever name our intelligence by pious effort be enabled to discover to indicate the transcendent Nature, that name should be applied alike to Father, Son, and Holy Ghost, whether it be "the Good" or "the Incorruptible," whatever name each may think proper to be employed to indicate the undefiled Nature of Godhead. And by this deliverance the Word seems to me to lay down for us this law, that we are to be persuaded that the Divine Essence is ineffable and incomprehensible: for it is plain that the title of Father does not present to us the Essence, but only indicates the relation to the Son. It follows, then, that if it were possible for human nature to be taught the essence of God, He "Who will have all men to be saved and to come to the knowledge of the truth [8]" would not have suppressed the knowledge upon this matter. But as it is, by saying nothing concerning the Divine Essence, He showed that the knowledge thereof is beyond our power, while when we have learnt that of which we are capable, we stand in no need of the knowledge beyond our capacity, as we have in the profession of faith in the doctrine delivered to us what suffices for our salvation. For to learn that He is the absolutely existent, together with Whom, by the relative force of the term, there is also declared the majesty of the Son, is the fullest teaching of godliness; the Son, as has been said, implying in close union with Himself the Spirit of Life and Truth, inasmuch as He is Himself Life and Truth.

These distinctions being thus established, while we anathematize all heretical fancies in the sphere of divine doctrines, we believe, even as we were taught by the voice of the Lord, in the Name of the Father and of the Son and of the Holy Ghost, acknowledging together with this faith also the dispensation that has been set on foot on behalf of men

---

3 ἡγεμονικόν. Cf. Ps. li. 12 in LXX. (*Spiritus principalis* in Vulg., "*free* spirit" in the "Authorised" Version, and in the Prayer-book Version).
4 Cf. 1 Cor. xii. 6. 5 ὑποστασέων. 6 προσώπων.
7 ὑποστασεως.

8 1 Tim. ii. 4.

by the Lord of the creation. For He "being in the form of God thought it not robbery to be equal with God, but made Himself of no reputation, and took upon Him the form of a servant [9]," and being incarnate in the Holy Virgin redeemed us from death "in which we were held," "sold under sin [1]," giving as the ransom for the deliverance of our souls His precious blood which He poured out by His Cross, and having through Himself made clear for us the path of the resurrection [2] from the dead, shall come in His own time in the glory of the Father to judge every soul in righteousness, when "all that are in the graves shall hear His voice, and shall come forth, they that have done good unto the resurrection of life, and they that have done evil unto the resurrection of damnation [3]." But that the pernicious heresy that is now being sown broadcast by Eunomius may not, by falling upon the mind of some of the simpler sort and being left without investigation, do harm to guileless faith, we are constrained to set forth the profession which they circulate and to strive to expose the mischief of their teaching.

§ 4. *He next skilfully confutes the partial, empty and blasphemous statement of Eunomius on the subject of the absolutely existent.*

Now the wording of their doctrine is as follows: "We believe in the one and only true God, according to the teaching of the Lord Himself, not honouring Him with a lying title (for He cannot lie), but really existent, one God in nature and in glory, who is without beginning, eternally, without end, alone." Let not him who professes to believe in accordance with the teaching of the Lord pervert the exposition of the faith that was made concerning the Lord of all to suit his own fancy, but himself follow the utterance of the truth. Since then, the expression of the Faith comprehends the name of the Father and of the Son and of the Holy Ghost, what agreement has this construction of theirs to show with the utterances of the Lord, so as to refer such a doctrine to the teaching of those utterances? They cannot manage to show where in the Gospels the Lord said that we should believe on "the one and only true God:" unless they have

some new Gospel. For the Gospels which are read in the churches continuously from ancient times to the present day, do not contain this saying which tells us that we should believe in or baptize into "the one and only true God," as these people say, but "in the name of the Father and of the Son and of the Holy Ghost." But as we were taught by the voice of the Lord, this we say, that the word "one" does not indicate the Father alone, but comprehends in its significance the Son with the Father, inasmuch as the Lord said, "I and My Father are one [4]." In like manner also the name "God" belongs equally to the Beginning in which the Word was, and to the Word Who was in the Beginning. For the Evangelist tells us that "the Word was with God, and the Word was God [5]." So that when Deity is expressed the Son is included no less than the Father. Moreover, the true cannot be conceived as something alien from and unconnected with the truth. But that the Lord is the Truth no one at all will dispute, unless he be one estranged from the truth. If, then, the Word is in the One, and is God and Truth, as is proclaimed in the Gospels, on what teaching of the Lord does he base his doctrine who makes use of these distinctive terms? For the antithesis is between "only" and "not only," between "God" and "no God," between "true" and "untrue." If it is with respect to idols that they make their distinction of phrases, we too agree. For the name of "deity" is given, in an equivocal sense, to the idols of the heathen, seeing that "all the gods of the heathen are demons," and in another sense marks the contrast of the one with the many, of the true with the false, of those who are not Gods with Him who is God [6]. But if the contrast is one with the Only-begotten God [7], let our sages learn that truth has its opposite only in falsehood, and God in one who is not God. But inasmuch as the Lord Who is the Truth is God, and is in the Father and is one relatively to the Father [8], there is no room in the true doctrine for these distinctions of phrases. For he who truly believes in the One sees in the One Him Who is completely united with Him in truth, and deity, and essence, and life, and wisdom, and in all attributes whatsoever: or, if he does not see in the One Him Who is all these it si

---

9 Phil. ii. 6.
[1] Or, "in which we were held by sin, being sold." The reference is to Rom. vii. 7 and 14, but with the variation of ὑπὸ τῆς ἁμαρτίας for ὑπὸ τὴν ἁμαρτίαν, and a change in the order of the words.
2 A similar phrase is to be found in Book V. With both may be compared the language of the Eucharistic Prayer in the Liturgy of S. Basil (where the context corresponds to some extent with that of either passage in S. Gregory):—καὶ ἀναστὰς τῇ τρίτῃ ἡμέρᾳ, καὶ ὁδοποιήσας πάσῃ σαρκὶ τὴν ἐκ νεκρῶν ἀνάστασιν, κ.τ.λ.
3 S. John v. 29.

4 S. John x. 30.   5 S. John i. 1.
6 Or, possibly, "and the contrast he makes between the one and the many, &c. is irrelevant" (ἄλλως ἀντιδιαιρεῖ): the quotation is from Ps. xcvi. 6 (LXX.).
7 Cf. S. John i. 18, reading (as S. Gregory seems to have done) θεός for υἱός.
8 καὶ ἐν πρὸς τὸν πατέρα ὄντος. It may be questioned whether the text is sound: the phrase seems unusual; perhaps ἐν has been inserted in error from the preceding clause καὶ ἐν τῷ πατρὶ ὄντος, and we should read "is in the Father and is with the Father" (cf. the 2nd verse of the 1st Epistle, and verses 1 and 2 of the Gospel of S. John).

in nothing that he believes. For without the Son the Father has neither existence nor name, any more than the Powerful without Power, or the Wise without Wisdom. For Christ is "the Power of God and the Wisdom of God[9];" so that he who imagines he sees the One God apart from power, truth, wisdom, life, or the true light, either sees nothing at all or else assuredly that which is evil. For the withdrawal of the good attributes becomes a positing and origination of evil.

"Not honouring Him," he says, "with a lying title, for He cannot lie." By that phrase I pray that Eunomius may abide, and so bear witness to the truth that it cannot lie. For if he would be of this mind, that everything that is uttered by the Lord is far removed from falsehood, he will of course be persuaded that He speaks the truth Who says, "I am in the Father, and the Father in Me [1],"—plainly, the One in His entirety, in the Other in His entirety, the Father not superabounding in the Son, the Son not being deficient in the Father,—and Who says also that the Son should be honoured as the Father is honoured[2], and "He that hath seen Me hath seen the Father[3]," and "no man knoweth the Father save the Son[4]," in all which passages there is no hint given to those who receive these declarations as genuine, of any variation[5] of glory, or of essence, or anything else, between the Father and the Son.

"Really existent," he says, "one God in nature and in glory." Real existence is opposed to unreal existence. Now each of existing things is really existent in so far as it *is;* but that which, so far as appearance and suggestion go, seems to be, but is not, this is not really existent, as for example an appearance in a dream or a man in a picture. For these and such like things, though they exist so far as appearance is concerned, have not real existence. If then they maintain, in accordance with the Jewish opinion, that the Only-begotten God does not exist at all, they are right in predicating real existence of the Father alone. But if they do not deny the existence of the Maker of all things, let them be content not to deprive of real existence Him Who is, Who in the Divine appearance to Moses gave Himself the name of Existent, when He said, "I am that I am[6]:" even as Eunomius in his later argument agrees with this, saying that it was He Who appeared to Moses. Then he says that God is "one in nature and in glory." Whether God exists without being by nature God, he who uses these words may perhaps know : but if it be true that he who is not by nature God is not

God at all, let them learn from the great Paul that they who serve those who are not Gods do not serve God[7]." But we "serve the living and true God," as the Apostle says[8] : and He Whom we serve is Jesus the Christ[9]. For Him the Apostle Paul even exults in serving, saying, "Paul, a servant of Jesus Christ[1]." We then, who no longer serve them which by nature are no Gods[2], have come to the knowledge of Him Who by nature is God, to Whom every knee boweth "of things in heaven and things in earth and things under the earth[3]. But we should not have been His servants had we not believed that this is the living and true God, to Whom "every tongue maketh confession that Jesus is Lord to the glory of God the Father[3]."

"God," he says, "Who is without beginning, eternally, without end, alone." Once more "understand, ye simple ones," as Solomon says, "his subtlety[4]," lest haply ye be deceived and fall headlong into the denial of the Godhead of the Only-begotten Son. That is without end which admits not of death and decay : that, likewise, is called everlasting which is not only for a time. That, therefore, which is neither everlasting nor without end is surely seen in the nature which is perishable and mortal. Accordingly he who predicates "unendingness" of the one and only God, and does not include the Son in the assertion of "unendingness" and "eternity," maintains by such a proposition, that He Whom he thus contrasts with the eternal and unending is perishable and temporary. But we, even when we are told that God "only hath immortality[5]," understand by "immortality" the Son. For life is immortality, and the Lord is that life, Who said, "I am the Life[6]." And if He be said to dwell "in the light that no man can approach unto[5]," again we make no difficulty in understanding that the true Light, unapproachable by falsehood, is the Only-begotten, in Whom we learn from the Truth itself that the Father is[7]. Of these opinions let the reader choose the more devout, whether we are to think of the Only-begotten in a manner worthy of the Godhead, or to call Him, as heresy prescribes, perishable and temporary.

§ 5. *He next marvellously overthrows the unintelligible statements of Eunomius which assert that the essence of the Father is not separated or divided, and does not become anything else.*

"We believe in God," he tells us, "not separ-

9 1 Cor. i. 24.   1 S. John xiv. 10.   2 Cf. S. John v. 23.
3 S. John xiv. 9.   4 S. Matt. xi. 27.   5 παραλλαγή (Cf.
S. James i. 17).   6 Or "I am He that is," Ex. iii. 14.

7 The reference seems to be to Gal. iv. 8.   8 1 Thess. i. 10.
9 There is perhaps a reference here to Col. iii. 24.
1 Rom. i. 1.   2 Cf. Gal. iv. 8.   3 Cf. Phil. ii. 10, 11.
4 Prov. viii. 5 (Septuagint).   5 1 Tim. vi. 16.
6 S. John xiv. 6.   7 S. John xiv. 11.

ated as regards the essence wherein He is one, into more than one, or becoming sometimes one and sometimes another, or changing from being what He is, or passing from one essence to assume the guise of a threefold personality: for He is always and absolutely one, remaining uniformly and unchangeably the only God." From these citations the discreet reader may well separate first of all the idle words inserted in the statement without any meaning from those which appear to have some sense, and afterwards examine the meaning that is discoverable in what remains of his statement, to ascertain whether it is compatible with due reverence towards Christ.

The first, then, of the statements cited is completely divorced from any intelligible meaning, good or bad. For what sense there is in the words, "not separated, as regards the essence wherein He is one, into more than one, or becoming sometimes one and sometimes another, or changing from being what He is," Eunomius himself could not tell us, and I do not think that any of his allies could find in the words any shadow of meaning. When he speaks of Him as "not separated in regard to the essence wherein He is one," he says either that He is not separated from His own essence, or that His own essence is not divided from Him. This unmeaning statement is nothing but a random combination of noise and empty sound. And why should one spend time in the investigation of these meaningless expressions? For how does any one remain in existence when separated from his own essence? or how is the essence of anything divided and displayed apart? Or how is it possible for one to depart from that wherein he is, and become another, getting outside himself? But he adds, "not passing from one essence to assume the guise of three persons: for He is always and absolutely one, remaining uniformly and unchangeably the only God." I think the absence of meaning in his statement is plain to every one without a word from me: against this let any one argue who thinks there is any sense or meaning in what he says: he who has an eye to discern the force of words will decline to involve himself in a struggle with unsubstantial shadows. For what force has it against our doctrine to say "not separated or divided into more than one as regards the essence wherein He is one, or becoming sometimes one and sometimes another, or passing from one essence to assume the guise of three persons?"—things that are neither said nor believed by Christians nor understood by inference from the truths we confess. For who ever said or heard any one else say in the Church of God, that the Father

is either separated or divided as regards His essence, or becomes sometimes one, sometimes another, coming to be outside Himself, or assumes the guise of three persons? These things Eunomius says to himself, not arguing with us but stringing together his own trash, mixing with the impiety of his utterances a great deal of absurdity. For we say that it is equally impious and ungodly to call the Lord of the creation a created being and to think that the Father, in that He is, is separated or split up, or departs from Himself, or assumes the guise of three persons, like clay or wax moulded in various shapes.

But let us examine the words that follow: "He is always and absolutely one, remaining uniformly and unchangeably the only God." If he is speaking about the Father, we agree with him, for the Father is most truly one, alone and always absolutely uniform and unchangeable, never at any time present or future ceasing to be what He is. If then such an assertion as this has regard to the Father, let him not contend with the doctrine of godliness, inasmuch as on this point he is in harmony with the Church. For he who confesses that the Father is always and unchangeably the same, being one and only God, holds fast the word of godliness, if in the Father he sees the Son, without Whom the Father neither is nor is named. But if he is inventing some other God besides the Father, let him dispute with the Jews or with those who are called Hypsistiani, between whom and the Christians there is this difference, that they acknowledge that there is a God Whom they term the Highest[8] or Almighty, but do not admit that he is Father; while a Christian, if he believe not in the Father, is no Christian at all.

§ 6. *He then shows the unity of the Son with the Father and Eunomius' lack of understanding and knowledge in the Scriptures.*

What he adds next after this is as follows:—"Having no sharer," he says, "in His Godhead, no divider of His glory, none who has lot in His power, or part in His royal throne: for He is the one and only God, the Almighty, God of Gods, King of Kings, Lord of Lords." I know not to whom Eunomius refers when he protests that the Father admits none to share His Godhead with Himself. For if he uses such expressions with reference to vain idols and to the erroneous conceptions of those who worship them (even as Paul assures us that there is no agreement between Christ and Belial, and no fellowship between the temple

---

[8] ὕψιστον, whence the name of the sect.

of God and idols⁹) we agree with him. But if by these assertions he means to sever the Only-begotten God from the Godhead of the Father, let him be informed that he is providing us with a dilemma that may be turned against himself to refute his own impiety. For either he denies the Only-begotten God to be God at all, that he may preserve for the Father those prerogatives of deity which (according to him) are incapable of being shared with the Son, and thus is convicted as a transgressor by denying the God Whom Christians worship, or if he were to grant that the Son also is God, yet not agreeing in nature with the true God, he would be necessarily obliged to acknowledge that he maintains Gods sundered from one another by the difference of their natures. Let him choose which of these he will,—either to deny the Godhead of the Son, or to introduce into his creed a plurality of Gods. For whichever of these he chooses, it is all one as regards impiety : for we who are initiated into the mystery of godliness by the Divinely inspired words of the Scripture do not see between the Father and the Son a partnership of Godhead, but unity, inasmuch as the Lord hath taught us this by His own words, when He saith, "I and the Father are one ¹," and "he that hath seen Me hath seen the Father ²." For if He were not of the same nature as the Father, how could He either have had in Himself that which was different ³? or how could He have shown in Himself that which was unlike, if the foreign and alien nature did not receive the stamp of that which was of a different kind from itself? But he says, "nor has He a divider of His glory." Herein he speaks in accordance with the fact, even though he does not know what he is saying : for the Son does not divide the glory with the Father, but has the glory of the Father in its entirety, even as the Father has all the glory of the Son. For thus He spake to the Father "All Mine are Thine and Thine are Mine ³." Wherefore also He says that He will appear on the Judgment Day "in the glory of the Father ⁴," when He will render to every man according to his works. And by this phrase He shows the unity of nature that subsists between them. For as "there is one glory of the sun and another glory of the moon ⁵," because of the difference between the natures of those luminaries (since if both had the same glory there would not be deemed to be any difference in their nature), so He Who foretold of Himself that He would appear in the glory of the Father indicated by the identity of glory their community of nature.

But to say that the Son has no part in His Father's royal throne argues an extraordinary amount of research into the oracles of God on the part of Eunomius, who, after his extreme devotion to the inspired Scriptures, has not yet heard, "Seek those things which are above, where Christ sitteth on the right hand of God ⁶," and many similar passages, of which it would not be easy to reckon up the number, but which Eunomius has never learnt, and so denies that the Son is enthroned together with the Father. Again the phrase, "not having lot in his power," we should rather pass by as unmeaning than confute as ungodly. For what sense is attached to the term "having lot" is not easy to discover from the common use of the word. Those cast lots, as the Scripture tells us, for the Lord's vesture, who were unwilling to rend His garment, but disposed to make it over to that one of their number in whose favour the lot should decide ⁷. They then who thus cast lots among themselves for the "coat" may be said, perhaps, to "have had lot" in it. But here in the case of the Father, the Son, and the Holy Ghost, inasmuch as Their power resides in Their nature (for the Holy Spirit breathes "where He listeth ⁸," and "worketh all in all as He will ⁹," and the Son, by Whom all things were made, visible and invisible, in heaven and in earth, "did all things whatsoever He pleased ¹," and "quickeneth whom He will ²," and the Father put "the times in His own power ³," while from the mention of "times" we conclude that all things done in time are subject to the power of the Father), if, I say, it has been demonstrated that the Father, the Son, and the Holy Spirit alike are in a position of power to do what They will, it is impossible to see what sense there can be in the phrase "having lot in His power." For the heir of all things, the maker of the ages ⁴, He Who shines with the Father's glory and expresses in Himself the Father's person, has all things that the Father Himself has, and is possessor of all His power, not that the right is transferred from the Father to the Son, but that it at once remains in the Father and resides in the Son. For He Who is in the Father is manifestly in the Father with all His own might, and He Who has the Father in Himself includes all the power and might of the Father. For He has in Himself all the Father, and not merely a part of Him : and He Who has Him entirely assuredly has His power as well. With what meaning, then, Eunomius asserts that the Father has "none who has lot in His power," those

---

9 Cf. 2 Cor. vi. 15, 16.   ¹ S. John x. 30.   ² S. John xiv. 9.
3 S. John xvii. 10.   4 S. Mark viii. 38.   5 1 Cor. xv. 41.

6 Col. iii. 1.   7 Cf. S. John xix. 23, 24.   8 S. John iii. 8.
9 Cf. 1 Cor. xii. 6 and 11.   ¹ Ps. cxxxv. 6.   ² S. John v. 21.
3 Acts i. 7.   4 Cf. Heb. i. 2.

perhaps can tell who are disciples of his folly : one who knows how to appreciate language confesses that he cannot understand phrases divorced from meaning. The Father, he says, "has none Who has lot in His power." Why, who is there that says that the Father and Son contend together for power and cast lots to decide the matter? But the holy Eunomius comes as mediator between them and by a friendly agreement without lot assigns to the Father the superiority in power.

Mark, I pray you, the absurdity and child-ishness of this grovelling exposition of his articles of faith. What! He Who "upholds all things by the word of His power [5]," Who says what He wills to be done, and does what He wills by the very power of that command, He Whose power lags not behind His will and Whose will is the measure of His power (for " He spake the word and they were made, He commanded and they were created [6] "), He Who made all things by Himself, and made them consist in Himself [7], without Whom no existing thing either came into being or remains in being,—He it is Who waits to obtain His power by some process of allotment ! Judge you who hear whether the man who talks like this is in his senses. "For He is the one and only God, the Almighty," he says. If by the title of " Almighty" he intends the Father, the language he uses is ours, and no strange lan-guage : but if he means some other God than the Father, let our patron of Jewish doctrines preach circumcision too, if he pleases. For the Faith of Christians is directed to the Father. And the Father is all these—Highest, Almighty, King of Kings, and Lord of Lords, and in a word all terms of highest significance are proper to the Father. But all that is the Father's is the Son's also ; so that, on this understanding [8], we admit this phrase too. But if, leaving the Father, he speaks of another Almighty, he is speaking the language of the Jews or following the speculations of Plato,— for they say that that philosopher also affirms that there exists on high a maker and creator of certain subordinate gods. As then in the case of the Jewish and Platonic opinions he who does not believe in God the Father is not a Christian, even though in his creed he asserts an Almighty God, so Eunomius also falsely pretends to the name of Chris-tian, being in inclination a Jew, or asserting the doctrines of the Greeks while putting on the guise of the title borne by Chris-tians. And with regard to the next points

he asserts the same account will apply. He says He is "God of Gods." We make the declaration our own by adding the name of the Father, knowing that the Father is God of Gods. But all that belongs to the Father cer-tainly belongs also to the Son. "And Lord of Lords." The same account will apply to this. "And Most High over all the earth." Yes, for whichever of the Three Persons you are think-ing of, He is Most High over all the earth, inasmuch as the oversight of earthly things from on high is exercised alike by the Father, and the Son, and the Holy Ghost. So, too, with what follows the words above, "Most High in the heavens, Most High in the highest, Heavenly, true in being what He is, and so continuing, true in words, true in works." Why, all these things the Christian eye discerns alike in the Father, the Son, and the Holy Ghost. If Eunomius does assign them to one only of the Persons acknowledged in the creed, let him dare to call Him " not true in words" Who has said, "I am the Truth [9]," or to call the Spirit of truth " not true in words," or let him refuse to give the title of " true in works" to Him Who doeth righteousness and judgment, or to the Spirit Who worketh all in all as He will. For if he does not acknowledge that these attributes belong to the Persons delivered to us in the creed, he is absolutely cancelling the creed of Christians. For how shall any one think Him a worthy object of faith Who is false in words and untrue in works.

But let us proceed to what follows. "Above all rule, subjection and authority," he says. This language is ours, and belongs properly to the Catholic Church,—to believe that the Divine nature is above all rule, and that it has in subordination to itself everything that can be conceived among existing things. But the Father, the Son, and the Holy Ghost constitute the Divine nature. If he assigns this property to the Father alone, and if he affirms Him alone to be free from variableness and change, and if he says that He alone is undefiled, the inference that we are meant to draw is plain, namely, that He who has not these characteris-tics is variable, corruptible, subject to change and decay. This, then, is what Eunomius asserts of the Son and the Holy Spirit : for if he did not hold this opinion concerning the Son and the Spirit, he would not have em-ployed this opposition, contrasting the Father with them. For the rest, brethren, judge whether, with these sentiments, he is not a persecutor of the Christian faith. For who will allow it to be right to deem that a fitting object of reverence which varies, changes, and

---

5 Heb. i. 3.　　　6 Ps. cxlviii. 5, or xxxiii. 9 in LXX.
7 Cf. Col. i. 16 and 17.
8 " If this is so : " i.e. if Eunomius means his words in a Chris-tian sense.

9 S. John xiv. 6.

is subject to decay? So then the whole aim of one who frames such notions as these,—notions by which he makes out that neither the Truth nor the Spirit of Truth is undefiled, unvarying, or unchangeable,—is to expel from the Church the belief in the Son and in the Holy Spirit.

§ 7. *Gregory further shows that the Only-begotten being begotten not only of the Father, but also impassibly of the Virgin by the Holy Ghost, does not divide the substance; seeing that neither is the nature of men divided or severed from the parents by being begotten, as is ingeniously demonstrated from the instances of Adam and Abraham.*

And now let us see what he adds to his previous statements. "Not dividing," he says, "His own essence by begetting, and being at once begetter and begotten, at the same time Father and Son; for He is incorruptible." Of such a kind as this, perhaps, is that of which the prophet says, touching the ungodly, "They weave a spider's web [1]." For as in the cobweb there is the appearance of something woven, but no substantiality in the appearance, —for he who touches it touches nothing substantial, as the spider's threads break with the touch of a finger,—just such is the unsubstantial texture of idle phrases. "Not dividing His own essence by begetting and being at once begetter and begotten." Ought we to give his words the name of argument, or to call them rather a swelling of humours secreted by some dropsical inflation? For what is the sense of "dividing His own essence by begetting, and being at once begetter and begotten?" Who is so distracted, who is so demented, as to make the statement against which Eunomius thinks he is doing battle? For the Church believes that the true Father is truly Father of His own Son, as the Apostle says, not of a Son alien from Him. For thus he declares in one of his Epistles, "Who spared not His own Son [2]," distinguishing Him, by the addition of "own," from those who are counted worthy of the adoption of sons by grace and not by nature. But what says He who disparages this belief of ours? "Not dividing His own essence by begetting, or being at once begetter and begotten, at the same time Father and Son; for He is incorruptible." Does one who hears in the Gospel that the Word was in the beginning, and was God, and that the Word came forth from the Father, so befoul the undefiled doctrine with these base and fetid ideas, saying "He does not divide His essence by begetting?" Shame on the abomination of these base and

filthy notions! How is it that he who speaks thus fails to understand that God when manifested in flesh did not admit for the formation of His own body the conditions of human nature, but was born for us a Child by the Holy Ghost and the power of the Highest; nor was the Virgin subject to those conditions, nor was the Spirit diminished, nor the power of the Highest divided? For the Spirit is entire, the power of the Highest remained undiminished: the Child was born in the fulness of our nature [3], and did not sully the incorruption of His mother. Then was flesh born of flesh without carnal passion: yet Eunomius will not admit that the brightness of the glory is from the glory itself, since the glory is neither diminished nor divided by begetting the light. Again, the word of man is generated from his mind without division, but God the Word cannot be generated from the Father without the essence of the Father being divided! Is any one so witless as not to perceive the irrational character of his position? "Not dividing," quoth he, "His own essence by begetting." Why, whose own essence is divided by begetting? For in the case of men essence means human nature: in the case of brutes, it means, generically, brute nature, but in the case of cattle, sheep, and all brute animals, specifically, it is regarded according to the distinctions of their kinds. Which, then, of these divides its own essence by the process of generation? Does not the nature always remain undiminished in the case of every animal by the succession of its posterity? Further a man in begetting a man from himself does not divide his nature, but it remains in its fulness alike in him who begets and in him who is begotten, not split off and transferred from the one to the other, nor mutilated in the one when it is fully formed in the other, but at once existing in its entirety in the former and discoverable in its entirety in the latter. For both before begetting his child the man was a rational animal, mortal, capable of intelligence and knowledge, and also after begetting a man endowed with such qualities: so that in him are shown all the special properties of his nature; as he does not lose his existence as a man by begetting the man derived from him, but remains after that event what he was before without causing any diminution of the nature derived from him by the fact that the man derived from him comes into being.

Well, man is begotten of man, and the nature of the begetter is not divided. Yet Eunomius does not admit that the Only-begotten God, Who is in the bosom of the Father, is truly of the Father, for fear forsooth, lest he should mutilate the inviolable nature of the Father by the subsistence of the Only-begotten : but after saying " Not dividing His essence by begetting," he adds, " Or being Himself begetter and begotten, or Himself becoming Father and Son [4]," and thinks by such loose disjointed phrases to undermine the true confession of godliness or to furnish some support to his own ungodliness, not being aware that by the very means he uses to construct a *reductio ad absurdum* he is discovered to be an advocate of the truth. For we too say that He who has all that belongs to His own Father is all that He is, save being Father, and that He who has all that belongs to the Son exhibits in Himself the Son in His completeness, save being Son : so that the *reductio ad absurdum*, which Eunomius here invents, turns out to be a support of the truth, when the notion is expanded by us so as to display it more clearly, under the guidance of the Gospel. For if " he that hath seen the Son seeth the Father [5]" then the Father begat another self, not passing out of Himself, and at the same time appearing in His fulness in Him : so that from these considerations that which seemed to have been uttered against godliness is demonstrated to be a support of sound doctrine.

But he says, " Not dividing His own essence by begetting, and being at once begetter and begotten, at the same time Father and Son ; for He is incorruptible." Most cogent conclusion ! What do you mean, most sapient sir ? Because He is incorruptible, therefore He does not divide His own essence by begetting the Son : nor does He beget Himself or be begotten of Himself, nor become at the same time His own Father and His own Son, because He is incorruptible. It follows, then, that if any one is of corruptible nature, he divides his essence by begetting, and is begotten by himself, and begets himself, and is his own father and his own son, because he is not incorruptible. If this is so, then Abraham, because he was corruptible, did not beget Ishmael and Isaac, but begat himself by the bondwoman and by his lawful wife : or, to take the other mountebank tricks of the argument, he divided his essence among the sons who were begotten of him, and first, when Hagar bore him a son, he was divided into two sections, and in one of the halves became Ishmael, while in the other he remained half Abraham ; and subsequently the residue of the essence of Abraham being again divided took subsistence in Isaac. Accordingly the fourth part of the essence of Abraham was divided into the twin sons of Isaac, so that there

was an eighth in each of his grandchildren ! How could one subdivide the eighth part, cutting it small in fractions among the twelve Patriarchs, or among the threescore and fifteen souls with whom Jacob went down into Egypt ? And why do I talk thus when I really ought to confute the folly of such notions by beginning with the first man ? For if it is a property of the incorruptible only not to divide its essence in begetting, and if Adam was corruptible, to whom the word was spoken, " Dust thou art and unto dust shalt thou return [6]," then, according to Eunomius' reasoning, he certainly divided his essence, being cut up among those who were begotten of him, and by reason of the vast number of his posterity (the slice of his essence which is to be found in each being necessarily subdivided according to the number of his progeny), the essence of Adam is used up before Abraham began to subsist, being dispersed in these minute and infinitesimal particles among the countless myriads of his descendants, and the minute fragment of Adam that has reached Abraham and his descendants by a process of division, is no longer discoverable in them as a remnant of his essence, inasmuch as his nature has been already used up among the countless myriads of those who were before them by its division into infinitesimal fractions. Mark the folly of him who " understands neither what he says nor whereof he affirms [7]." For by saying " Since He is incorruptible " He neither divides His essence nor begets Himself nor becomes His own father, he implicitly lays it down that we must suppose all those things from which he affirms that the incorruptible alone are free to be incidental to generation in the case of every one who is subject to corruption. Though there are many other considerations capable of proving the inanity of his argument, I think that what has been said above is sufficient to demonstrate its absurdity. But this has surely been already acknowledged by all who have an eye for logical consistency, that, when he asserted incorruptibility of the Father alone, he places all things which are considered after the Father in the category of corruptible, by virtue of opposition to the incorruptible, so as to make out even the Son not to be free from corruption. If then he places the Son in opposition to the incorruptible, he not only defines Him to be corruptible, but also asserts of Him all those incidents from which he affirms only the incorruptible to be exempt. For it necessarily follows that, if the Father alone neither begets Himself nor is begotten of Himself, everything which is not incorruptible both begets itself

---

4 The quotation does not verbally correspond with Eunomius' words as cited above.   5 Cf. S. John xiv. 9.

6 Gen. iii. 19.   7 Cf. 1 Tim. i. 7.

and is begotten of itself, and becomes its own father and son, shifting from its own proper essence to each of these relations. For if to be incorruptible belongs to the Father alone, and if not to be the things specified is a special property of the incorruptible, then, of course, according to this heretical argument, the Son is not incorruptible, and all these circumstances, of course, find place about Him,—to have His essence divided, to beget Himself and to be begotten by Himself, to become Himself His own father and His own son.

Perhaps, however, it is waste of time to linger long over such follies. Let us pass to the next point of his statement. He adds to what he had already said, " Not standing in need, in the act of creation, of matter or parts or natural instruments : for He stands in need of nothing." This proposition, though Eunomius states it with a certain looseness of phrase, we yet do not reject as inconsistent with godly doctrine. For learning as we do that " He spake the word and they were made : He commanded and they were created [8]," we know that the Word is the Creator of matter, by that very act also producing with the matter the qualities of matter, so that for Him the impulse of His almighty will was everything and instead of everything, matter, instrument, place, time, essence, quality, everything that is conceived in creation. For at one and the same time did He will that that which ought to be should be, and His power, that produced all things that are, kept pace with His will, turning His will into act. For thus the mighty Moses in the record of creation instructs us about the Divine power, ascribing the production of each of the objects that were manifested in the creation to the words that bade them be. For " God said," he tells us, " Let there be light, and there was light [9] :" and so about the rest, without any mention either of matter or of any instrumental agency. Accordingly the language of Eunomius on this point is not to be rejected. For God, when creating all things that have their origin by creation, neither stood in need of any matter on which to operate, nor of instruments to aid Him in His construction : for the power and wisdom of God has no need of any external assistance. But Christ is " the Power of God and the Wisdom of God [1]," by Whom all things were made and without Whom is no existent thing, as John testifies [2]. If, then, all things were made by Him, both visible and invisible, and if His will alone suffices to effect the subsistence of existing things (for His will is power), Eunomius utters our doctrine though with a loose mode of expres-

sion [3]. For what instrument and what matter could He Who upholds all thinsg by the word of His power [4] need in upholding the constitution of existing things by His almighty word ? But if he maintains that what we have believed to be true of the Only-begotten in the case of the creation, is true also in the case of the Son —in the sense that the Father created Him in like manner as the creation was made by the Son,—then we retract our former statement, because such a supposition is a denial of the Godhead of the Only-begotten. For we have learnt from the mighty utterance of Paul that it is the distinguishing feature of idolatry to worship and serve the creature more than the Creator [5], as well as from David, when He says " There shall be no new God be in thee : neither shalt thou worship any alien God [6]." We use this line and rule to arrive at the discernment of the object of worship, so as to be convinced that that alone is God which is neither " new" nor " alien." Since then we have been taught to believe that the Only-begotten God is God, we acknowledge, by our belief that He is God, that He is neither " new" or " alien." If, then, He is God, He is not " new," and if He is not new, He is assuredly eternal. Accordingly, neither is the Eternal " new," nor is He Who is of the Father and in the bosom of the Father and Who has the Father in Himself "alien " from true Deity. Thus he who severs the Son from the nature of the Father either absolutely disallows the worship of the Son, that he may not worship an alien God, or bows down before an idol, making a creature and not God the object of his worship, and giving to his idol the name of Christ.

Now that this is the meaning to which he tends in his conception concerning the Only-begotten will become more plain by considering the language he employs touching the Only-begotten Himself, which is as follows. " We believe also in the Son of God, the Only-begotten God, the first-born of all creation, very Son, not ungenerate, verily begotten before the worlds, named Son not without being begotten before He existed, coming into being before all creation, not uncreate." I think that the mere reading of his exposition of his faith is quite sufficient to render its impiety plain without any investigation on our part. For though he calls Him " first-born," yet that he may not raise any

---

8 Ps. cxlviii. 5, or Ps. xxxiii. 9 in LXX.   9 Gen. i. 3.
    1 1 Cor. i. 24.   2 Cf. S. John i. 3.

3 Reading ἐν ἀτονούσῃ τῇ λέξει for ἐνατονούσῃ τῇ λέξει (the reading of the Paris edition, which Oehler follows).
4 Cf. Heb. i. 3. The quotation is not verbally exact.
5 Cf. Rom. i. 26.
6 Ps. lxxxi. 10, LXX. The words πρόσφατος ("new") and ἀλλότριος ("alien") are both represented in the A.V. by "strange," and so in R.V. The Prayer-book version expresses them by "strange" and "any other." Both words are subsequently employed by Gregory in his argument.

doubt in his readers' minds as to His not being created, he immediately adds the words, " not uncreate," lest if the natural significance of the term " Son " were apprehended by his readers, any pious conception concerning Him might find place in their minds. It is for this reason that after at first confessing Him to be Son of God and Only-begotten God, he proceeds at once, by what he adds, to pervert the minds of his readers from their devout belief to his heretical notions. For he who hears the titles " Son of God " and "Only-begotten God" is of necessity lifted up to the loftier kind of assertions respecting the Son, led onward by the significance of these terms, inasmuch as no difference of nature is introduced by the use of the title " God " and by the significance of the term " Son." For how could He Who is truly the Son of God and Himself God be conceived as something else differing from the nature of the Father? But that godly conceptions may not by these names be impressed beforehand on the hearts of his readers, he forthwith calls Him " the first-born of all creation, named Son, not without being begotten before He existed, coming into being before all creation, not uncreate." Let us linger a little while, then, over his argument, that the miscreant may be shown to be holding out his first statements to people merely as a bait to induce them to receive the poison that he sugars over with phrases of a pious tendency, as it were with honey. Who does not know how great is the difference in signification between the term "only-begotten " and " first-born?" For " first-born " implies brethren, and " only-begotten " implies that there are no other brethren. Thus the " first-born " is not " only-begotten," for certainly " first-born " is the first-born among brethren, while he who is " only-begotten " has no brother: for if he were numbered among brethren he would not be only-begotten. And moreover, whatever the essence of the brothers of the first-born is, the same is the essence of the first-born himself. Nor is this all that is signified by the title, but also that the first-born and those born after him draw their being from the same source, without the first-born contributing at all to the birth of those that come after him : so that hereby [7] is maintained the falsehood of that statement of John, which affirms that " all things were made by Him [8]." For if He is first-born, He differs from those born after Him only by priority in time, while there must be some one else by Whom the power to be at all is imparted alike to Him and to the rest. But that we may not by our objections give any unfair opponent ground for

an insinuation that we do not receive the inspired utterances of Scripture, we will first set before our readers our own view about these titles, and then leave it to their judgment which is the better.

§ 8. *He further very appositely expounds the meaning of the term " Only-begotten," and of the term " First born," four times used by the Apostle.*

The mighty Paul, knowing that the Only-begotten God, Who has the pre-eminence in all things [9], is the author and cause of all good, bears witness to Him that not only was the creation of all existent things wrought by Him, but that when the original creation of man had decayed and vanished away [1], to use his own language, and another new creation was wrought in Christ, in this too no other than He took the lead, but He is Himself the first-born of all that new creation of men which is effected by the Gospel. And that our view about this may be made clearer let us thus divide our argument. The inspired apostle on four occasions employs this term, once as here, calling Him, "first-born of all creation [2]," another time, " the first-born among many brethren [3]," again, "first-born from the dead [4]," and on another occasion he employs the term absolutely, without combining it with other words, saying, " But when again He bringeth the first-born into the world, He saith, And let all the angels of God worship Him [5]." Accordingly whatever view we entertain concerning this title in the other combinations, the same we shall in consistency apply to the phrase "first-born of all creation." For since the title is one and the same it must needs be that the meaning conveyed is also one. In what sense then does He become " the first-born among many brethren?" in what sense does He become " the first-born from the dead?" Assuredly this is plain, that because we are by birth flesh and blood, as the Scripture saith, " He Who for our sakes was born among us and was partaker of flesh and blood [6]," purposing to change us from corruption to incorruption by the birth from above, the birth by water and the Spirit, Himself led the way in this birth, drawing down upon the water, by His own baptism, the Holy Spirit; so that in all things He became the first-born of those who are spiritually born again, and gave the name of brethren to those who partook in a birth like to His own by water and the Spirit. But since it was also meet that He should

---

7 Hereby, i.e. by the use of the term προτότοκος as applicable to the Divinity of the Son.   8 S. John i. 3.

9 Cf. Col. i. 18.
1 Cf. Heb. viii. 13, whence the phrase is apparently adapted.
2 Col. i. 15.   3 Rom. viii. 29.   4 Col. i. 18 (cf. Rev. i. 5).
5 Heb. i. 6.   6 Cf. Heb. ; 14.

implant in our nature the power of rising again from the dead, He becomes the "first-fruits of them that slept [7]" and the "first-born from the dead [8]," in that He first by His own act loosed the pains of death [9], so that His new birth from the dead was made a way for us also, since the pains of death, wherein we were held, were loosed by the resurrection of the Lord. Thus, just as by having shared in the washing of regeneration [1] He became "the first-born among many brethren," and again by having made Himself the first-fruits of the resurrection. He obtains the name of the "first-born from the dead," so having in all things the pre-eminence, after that "all old things," as the apostle says, "have passed away [2]," He becomes the first-born of the new creation of men in Christ by the two-fold regeneration, alike that by Holy Baptism and that which is the consequence of the resurrection from the dead, becoming for us in both alike the Prince of Life [3], the first-fruits, the first-born. This first-born, then, hath also brethren, concerning whom He speaks to Mary, saying, "Go and tell My brethren, I go to My Father and your Father, and to My God and your God [4]." In these words He sums up the whole aim of His dispensation as Man. For men revolted from God, and "served them which by nature were no gods [5]," and though being the children of God became attached to an evil father falsely so called. For this cause the mediator between God and man [6], having assumed the first-fruits of all human nature [7], sends to His brethren the announcement of Himself not in His divine character, but in that which He shares with us, saying, "I am departing in order to make by My own self that true Father, from whom you were separated, to be your Father, and by My own self to make that true God from whom you had revolted to be your God, for by that first-fruits which I have assumed, I am in Myself presenting all humanity to its God and Father."

Since, then, the first-fruits made the true God to be its God, and the good Father to be its Father, the blessing is secured for human nature as a whole, and by means of the first-fruits the true God and Father becomes Father and God of all men. Now "if the first-fruits be holy, the lump also is holy [8]." But where

the first-fruits, Christ, is (and the first-fruits is none other than Christ), there also are they that are Christ's, as the apostle says. In those passages therefore where he makes mention of the "first-born" in connexion with other words, he suggests that we should understand the phrase in the way which I have indicated: but where, without any such addition, he says, "When again He bringeth the first-born into the world [9]," the addition of "again" asserts that manifestation of the Lord of all which shall take place at the last day. For as "at the name of Jesus every knee doth bow, of things in heaven and things in earth and things under the earth [1]," although the human name does not belong to the Son in that He is above every name, even so He says that the First-born, Who was so named for our sakes, is worshipped by all the supramundane creation, on His coming again into the world, when He "shall judge the world with righteousness and the people with equity [2]." Thus the several meanings of the titles "First-born" and "Only-begotten" are kept distinct by the word of godliness, its respective significance being secured for each name. But how can he who refers the name of "first-born" to the pre-temporal existence of the Son preserve the proper sense of the term "Only-begotten"? Let the discerning reader consider whether these things agree with one another, when the term "first-born" necessarily implies brethren, and the term "Only-begotten" as necessarily excludes the notion of brethren. For when the Scripture says, "In the beginning was the Word [3]," we understand the Only-begotten to be meant, and when it adds "the Word was made flesh [4]" we thereby receive in our minds the idea of the first-born, and so the word of godliness remains without confusion, preserving to each name its natural significance, so that in "Only-begotten" we regard the pre-temporal, and by "the first-born of creation" the manifestation of the pre-temporal in the flesh.

§ 9. *Gregory again discusses the generation of the Only-begotten, and other different modes of generation, material and immaterial, and nobly demonstrates that the Son is the brightness of the Divine glory, and not a creature.*

And now let us return once more to the precise statement of Eunomius. "We believe also in the Son of God, the only begotten God, the first-born of all creation, very Son, not Ungenerate, verily begotten before the worlds."

---

[7] 1 Cor. xv. 20.   [8] Col. i. 18.
[9] Cf. Acts ii. 24.   See note 2. p. 104, *supra.*
[1] The phrase is not verbally the same as in Tit. iii. 5.
[2] Cf. 2 Cor. v. 17.   [3] Cf. Acts iii. 15.
[4] Cf. S. John xx. 17 : the quotation is not verbal.
[5] Cf. Gal. iv. 8.   [6] Cf. 1 Tim. ii. 5.
[7] The Humanity of Christ being regarded as this "first-fruits :" unless this phrase is to be understood of the Resurrection, rather than of the Incarnation, in which case the first-fruits will be His Body, and ἀναλαβὼν should be rendered by "having *resumed.*"
[8] Rom. ix. 16.   The reference next following may be to S. John xii. 26, or xiv. 3 ; or to Col. iii. 3.

[9] Heb. i. 6.   [1] Phil. ii. 10, 11.   [2] Cf. Ps. xcviii. 10.
[3] S. John i. 1.   [4] S. John i. 14.

That he transfers, then, the sense of *generation* to indicate *creation* is plain from his expressly calling Him created, when he speaks of Him as "coming into being" and "not uncreate". But that the inconsiderate rashness and want of training which shows itself in the doctrines may be made manifest, let us omit all expressions of indignation at his evident blasphemy, and employ in the discussion of this matter a scientific division. For it would be well, I think, to consider in a somewhat careful investigation the exact meaning of the term "generation." That this expression conveys the meaning of existing as the result of some cause is plain to all, and I suppose there is no need to contend about this point : but since there are different modes of existing as the result of a cause, this difference is what I think ought to receive thorough explanation in our discussion by means of scientific division. Of things which have come into being as the results of some cause we recognize the following differences. Some are the result of material and art, as the fabrics of houses and all other works produced by means of their respective material, where some art gives direction and conducts its purpose to its proper aim. Others are the result of material and nature ; for nature orders [5] the generation of animals one from another, effecting her own work by means of the material subsistence in the bodies of the parents ; others again are by material efflux. In these the original remains as it was before, and that which flows from it is contemplated by itself, as in the case of the sun and its beam, or the lamp and its radiance, or of scents and ointments, and the quality given off from them. For these, while remaining undiminished in themselves, have each accompanying them the special and peculiar effect which they naturally produce, as the sun his ray, the lamp its brightness, and perfumes the fragrance which they engender in the air. There is also another kind of generation besides these, where the cause is immaterial and incorporeal, but the generation is sensible and takes place through the instrumentality of the body; I mean the generation of the word by the mind. For the mind being in itself incorporeal begets the word by means of sensible instruments. So many are the differences of the term generation, which we discover in a philosophic view of them, that is itself, so to speak, the result of generation.

And now that we have thus distinguished the various modes of generation, it will be time to remark how the benevolent dispensation of the Holy Spirit, in delivering to us the Divine mysteries, imparts that instruction which transcends reason by such methods as we can receive. For the inspired teaching adopts, in order to set forth the unspeakable power of God, all the forms of generation that human intelligence recognizes, yet without including the corporeal senses attaching to the words. For when it speaks of the creative power, it gives to such an energy the name of generation, because its expression must stoop to our low capacity; it does not, however, convey thereby all that we include in creative generation, as time, place, the furnishing of matter, the fitness of instruments, the design in the things that come into being, but it leaves these, and asserts of God in lofty and magnificent language the creation of all existent things, when it says, "He spake the word and they were made [6], He commanded and they were created." Again when it interprets to us the unspeakable and transcendent existence of the Only-begotten from the Father, as the poverty of human intellect is incapable of receiving doctrines which surpass all power of speech and thought, there too it borrows our language and terms Him "Son,"—a name which our usage assigns to those who are born of matter and nature. But just as Scripture, when speaking of generation by creation, does not in the case of God imply that such generation took place by means of any material, affirming that the power of God's will served for material substance, place, time and all such circumstances, even so here too, when using the term Son, it rejects both all else that human nature remarks in generation here below,—I mean affections and dispositions and the co-operation of time, and the necessity of place,—and, above all, matter, without all which natural generation here below does not take place. But when all such material, temporal and local [7] existence is excluded from the sense of the term "Son," community of nature alone is left, and for this reason by the title "Son" is declared, concerning the Only-begotten, the close affinity and genuineness of relationship which mark His manifestation from the Father. And since such a kind of generation was not sufficient to implant in us an adequate notion of the ineffable mode of subsistence of the Only-begotten, Scripture avails itself also of the third kind of generation to indicate the doctrine of the Son's Divinity, — that kind, namely, which is the result of material efflux, and speaks of Him as the "brightness of glory [8]," the "savour of ointment [9]," the "breath

5 Reading οἰκονομεῖ or οἰκοδομεῖ.

6 Or "were generated." The reference is to Ps. cxlviii. 5.
7 διαστηματικῆς seems to include the idea of extension in time as well as in space.　　8 Heb. i. 3.
9 The reference may be to the Song of Solomon i. 3.

of God [1]; " illustrations which in the scientific phraseology we have adopted we ordinarily designate as material efflux.

But as in the cases alleged neither the birth of the creation nor the force of the term "Son" admits time, matter, place, or affection, so here too the Scripture employing only the illustration of effulgence and the others that I have mentioned, apart from all material conception, with regard to the Divine fitness of such a mode of generation, shows that we must understand by the significance of this expression, an existence at once derived from and subsisting with the Father. For neither is the figure of breath intended to convey to us the notion of dispersion into the air from the material from which it is formed, nor is the figure of fragrance designed to express the passing off of the quality of the ointment into the air, nor the figure of effulgence the efflux which takes place by means of the rays from the body of the sun : but as has been said in all cases, by such a mode of generation is indicated this alone, that the Son is of the Father and is conceived of along with Him, no interval intervening between the Father and Him Who is of the Father. For since of His exceeding loving-kindness the grace of the Holy Spirit so ordered that the divine conceptions concerning the Only-begotten should reach us from many quarters, and so be implanted in us, He added also the remaining kind of generation,—that, namely, of the word from the mind. And here the sublime John uses remarkable foresight. That the reader might not through inattention and unworthy conceptions sink to the common notion of "word," so as to deem the Son to be merely a voice of the Father, he therefore affirms of the Word that He essentially subsisted in the first and blessed nature Itself, thus proclaiming aloud, "In the Beginning was the Word, and with God, and God, and Light, and Life [2]," and all that the Beginning is, the Word was also.

Since, then, these kinds of generation, those, I mean, which arise as the result of some cause, and are recognized in our every-day experience, are also employed by Holy Scripture to convey its teaching concerning transcendent mysteries in such wise as each of them may reasonably be transferred to the expression of divine conceptions, we may now proceed to examine Eunomius' statement also, to find in what sense he accepts the meaning of "generation." "Very Son," he says, "not ungenerate, verily begotten before the worlds." One may, I think, pass quickly over the violence done to logical sequence in his distinction, as being easily recognizable by all. For who does not know that while the proper opposition is between Father and Son, between generate and ungenerate, he thus passes over the term "Father" and sets "ungenerate" in opposition to "Son," whereas he ought, if he had any concern for truth, to have avoided diverting his phrase from the due sequence of relationship, and to have said, "Very Son, not Father"? And in this way due regard would have been paid at once to piety and to logical consistency, as the nature would not have been rent asunder in making the distinction between the persons. But he has exchanged in his statement of his faith the true and scriptural use of the term "Father," committed to us by the Word Himself, and speaks of the "Ungenerate" instead of the "Father," in order that by separating Him from that close relationship towards the Son which is naturally conceived of in the title of Father, he may place Him on a common level with all created objects, which equally stand in opposition to the "ungenerate [3]." "Verily begotten," he says, "before the worlds." Let him say of Whom He is begotten. He will answer, of course, "Of the Father," unless he is prepared unblushingly to contradict the truth. But since it is impossible to detach the eternity of the Son from the eternal Father, seeing that the term "Father" by its very signification implies the Son, for this reason it is that he rejects the title Father and shifts his phrase to "ungenerate," since the meaning of this latter name has no sort of relation or connection with the Son, and by thus misleading his readers through the substitution of one term for the other, into not contemplating the Son along with the Father, he opens up a path for his sophistry, paving the way of impiety by slipping in the term "ungenerate." For they who according to the ordinance of the Lord believe in the Father, when they hear the name of the Father, receive the Son along with Him in their thought, as the mind passes from the Son to the Father, without treading on an unsubstantial vacuum interposed between them. But those who are diverted to the title "ungenerate" instead of Father, get a bare notion of this name, learning only the fact that He did not at any time come into being, not that He is Father. Still, even with this mode of conception, the faith of those who read with discernment remains free from confusion. For the expression "not to come into being" is used in an identical sense of all uncreated nature : and Father, Son, and Holy Ghost are equally uncreated. For it has ever been believed by

---

[1] Wisd. vii. 25.　　[2] Cf. S. John i. 1 sqq.

[3] That is, by using as the terms of his antithesis, not "Son" and "Father," but "Son" and "Ungenerate," he avoids suggesting relationship between the two Persons, and does suggest that the Second Person stands in the same opposition to the First Person in which all created objects stand as contrasted with Him.

those who follow the Divine word that all the creation, sensible and supramundane, derives its existence from the Father, the Son, and the Holy Ghost. He who has heard that " by the word of the Lord were the heavens made, and all the host of them by the breath of His mouth [4]," neither understands by "word" mere utterance, nor by "breath" mere exhalation, but by what is there said frames the conception of God the Word and of the Spirit of God. Now to create and to be created are not equivalent, but all existent things being divided into that which makes and that which is made, each is different in nature from the other, so that neither is that uncreated which is made, nor is that created which effects the production of the things that are made. By those then who, according to the exposition of the faith given us by our Lord Himself, have believed in the Name of the Father, and of the Son, and of the Holy Ghost, it is acknowledged that each of these Persons is alike unoriginate [5], and the meaning conveyed by "ungenerate" does no harm to their sound belief: but to those who are dense and indefinite this term serves as a starting-point for deflection from sound doctrine. For not understanding the true force of the term, that "ungenerate" signifies nothing more than "not having come into being," and that "not coming into being" is a common property of all that transcends created nature, they drop their faith in the Father, and substitute for "Father" the phrase "ungenerate:" and since, as has been said, the Personal existence of the Only-begotten is not connoted in this name, they determine the existence of the Son to have commenced from some definite beginning in time, affirming (what Eunomius here adds to his previous statements) that He is called Son not without generation preceding His existence.

What is this vain juggling with words? Is he aware that it is God of Whom he speaks, Who was in the beginning and is in the Father, nor was there any time when He was not? He knows not what he says nor whereof he affirms [6], but he endeavours, as though he were constructing the pedigree of a mere man, to apply to the Lord of all creation the language which properly belongs to our nature here below. For, to take an example, Ishmael was not before the generation that brought him into being, and before his birth there was of course an interval of time. But with Him Who is " the brightness of glory [7]," "before" and "after" have no place: for before the brightness, of course neither was there any glory, for concurrently with the existence of the glory there assuredly beams forth its brightness; and it is impossible in the nature of things that one should be severed from the other, nor is it possible to see the glory by itself before its brightness. For he who says thus will make out the glory in itself to be darkling and dim, if the brightness from it does not shine out at the same time. But this is the unfair method of the heresy, to endeavour, by the notions and terms employed concerning the Only-begotten God, to displace Him from His oneness with the Father. It is to this end they say, " Before the generation that brought Him into being He was not Son :" but the "sons of rams [8]," of whom the prophet speaks,—are not they too called sons after coming into being? That quality, then, which reason notices in the " sons of rams," that they are not "sons of rams " before the generation which brings them into being,—this our reverend divine now ascribes to the Maker of the worlds and of all creation, Who has the Eternal Father in Himself, and is contemplated in the eternity of the Father, as He Himself says, " I am in the Father, and the Father in Me [9]." Those, however, who are not able to detect the sophistry that lurks in his statement, and are not trained to any sort of logical perception, follow these inconsequent statements and receive what comes next as a logical consequence of what preceded. For he says, "coming into being before all creation," and as though this were not enough to prove his impiety, he has a piece of profanity in reserve in the phrase that follows, when he terms the Son "not uncreate." In what sense then does he call Him Who is not uncreate " very Son"? For if it is meet to call Him Who is not uncreate " very Son," then of course the heaven is "very Son ; " for it too is "not uncreate." So the sun too is "very Son," and all that the creation contains, both small and great, are of course entitled to the appellation of "very Son." And in what sense does He call Him Who has come into being "Only-begotten"? For all things that come into being are unquestionably in brotherhood with each other, so far, I mean, as their coming into being is concerned. And from whom did He come into being? For assuredly all things that have ever come into being did so from the Son. For thus did John testify, saying, "All things were made by Him [1]." If then the Son also came into being, according to Eunomius' creed, He

---

4 Ps. xxxiii. 6.

5 τὸ μὴ γενέσθαι τι τούτων ἐπίσης ὁμολογεῖται. This may possibly mean "it is acknowledged that each of those alternatives" (viz. that that which comes into being is uncreate, and that that which creates should itself be created) " is equally untrue." But this view would not be confined to those who held the Catholic doctrine : the impossibility of the former alternative, indeed, was insisted upon by the Arians as an argument in their own favour.

6 Cf. 1 Tim. i. 7.

7 Cf. Heb. i. 3.   8 Ps. cxiv. 4, in Septuagint.
9 S. John xiv. 10.   1 S. John i. 3.

is certainly ranked in the class of things which have come into being. If then all things that came into being were made by Him, and the Word is one of the things that came into being, who is so dull as not to draw from these premises the absurd conclusion that our new creed-monger makes out the Lord of creation to have been His own work, in saying in so many words that the Lord and Maker of all creation is "not uncreate"? Let him tell us whence he has this boldness of assertion. From what inspired utterance? What evangelist, what apostle ever uttered such words as these? What prophet, what lawgiver, what patriarch, what other person of all who were divinely moved by the Holy Ghost, whose voices are preserved in writing, ever originated such a statement as this? In the tradition of the faith delivered by the Truth we are taught to believe in Father, Son, and Holy Spirit. If it were right to believe that the Son was created, how was it that the Truth in delivering to us this mystery bade us believe in the Son, and not in the creature? and how is it that the inspired Apostle, himself adoring Christ, lays it down that they who worship the creature besides the Creator are guilty of idolatry[2]? For, were the Son created, either he would not have worshipped Him, or he would have refrained from classing those who worship the creature along with idolaters, lest he himself should appear to be an idolater, in offering adoration to the created. But he knew that He Whom he adored was God over all[3], for so he terms the Son in his Epistle to the Romans. Why then do those who divorce the Son from the essence of the Father, and call Him creature, bestow on Him in mockery the fictitious title of Deity, idly conferring on one alien from true Divinity the name of "God," as they might confer it on Bel or Dagon or the Dragon? Let those, therefore, who affirm that He is created, acknowledge that He is not God at all, that they may be seen to be nothing but Jews in disguise, or, if they confess one who is created to be God, let them not deny that they are idolaters.

§ 10. *He explains the phrase " The Lord created Me," and the argument about the origination of the Son, the deceptive character of Eunomius' reasoning, and the passage which says, " My glory will I not give to another," examining them from different points of view.*

But of course they bring forward the passage in the book of Proverbs which says, "The Lord created Me as the beginning of His ways, for His works[4]." Now it would require a lengthy discussion to explain fully the real meaning of the passage : still it would be possible even in a few words to convey to well-disposed readers the thought intended. Some of those who are accurately versed in theology do say this, that the Hebrew text does not read "created," and we have ourselves read in more ancient copies "possessed" instead of "created." Now assuredly "possession" in the allegorical language of the Proverbs marks that slave Who for our sakes "took upon Him the form of a slave[5]." But if any one should allege in this passage the reading which prevails in the Churches, we do not reject even the expression "created." For this also in allegorical language is intended to connote the "slave," since, as the Apostle tells us, "all creation is in bondage[6]." Thus we say that this expression, as well as the other, admits of an orthodox interpretation. For He Who for our sakes became like as we are, was in the last days truly *created*,—He Who in the beginning being Word and God afterwards became Flesh and Man. For the nature of flesh is created : and by partaking in it in all points like as we do, yet without sin, He was created when He became man : and He was created "after God[7]," not after man, as the Apostle says, in a new manner and not according to human wont. For we are taught that this "new man" was *created*—albeit of the Holy Ghost and of the power of the Highest— whom Paul, the hierophant of unspeakable mysteries, bids us to "put on," using two phrases to express the garment that is to be put on, saying in one place, "Put on the new man which after God is created[7]," and in another, "Put ye on the Lord Jesus Christ[8]." For thus it is that He, Who said "I am the Way[9]," becomes to us who have put Him on the beginning of the ways of salvation, that He may make us the work of His own hands, new modelling us from the evil mould of sin once more to His own image. He is at once our foundation before the world to come, according to the words of Paul, who says, "Other foundation can no man lay than that is laid[1]," and it is true that "before the springs of the waters came forth, before the mountains were settled, before He made the depths, and before all hills, He begetteth Me[2]." For it is possible, accord-

[2] Rom. i. 25, where παρὰ τὸν κτίσαντα may be better translated "besides the Creator," or "rather than the Creator," than as in the A.V.   [3] Rom. ix. 5.

[4] Prov. viii. 22 (LXX.). The versions of Aquila, Theodotion, and Symmachus (to one or more of which perhaps § 9 refers), all render the Hebrew by ἐκτήσατο ("possessed"), not by ἔκτισε ("created"). But Gregory may be referring to MSS. of the LXX. version which read ἐκτήσατο. It is clear from what follows that Mr. Gwatkin is hardly justified in his remark (*Studies of Arianism*, p. 69), that "the whole discussion on Prov. viii. 22 (LXX.), Κύριος ἔκτισέ με, κ.τ.λ., might have been avoided by a glance at the original." The point of the controversy might have been changed, but that would have been all. Gregory seems to feel that ἐκτήσατο requires an explanation, though he has one ready.
[5] Phil. ii. 7.   [6] Rom. viii. 20-1.   [7] Eph. iv. 24.
[8] Rom. xiii. 14.   [9] S. John xiv. 6.   [1] 1 Cor iii. 11.
[2] Prov. viii. 23—25 (not quite verbal, from the LXX.).

ing to the usage of the Book of Proverbs, for each of these phrases, taken in a tropical sense, to be applied to the Word [3]. For the great David calls righteousness the "mountains of God [4]," His judgments "deeps [4]," and the teachers in the Churches " fountains," saying " Bless God the Lord from the fountains of Israel [5] "; and guilelessness he calls "hills," as he shows when he speaks of their skipping like lambs [6]. Before these therefore is born in us He Who for our sakes was created as man, that of these things also the creation may find place in us. But we may, I think, pass from the discussion of these points, inasmuch as the truth has been sufficiently pointed out in a few words to well-disposed readers ; let us proceed to what Eunomius says next.

"Existing in the beginning," he says, " not without beginning." In what fashion does he who plumes himself on his superior discernment understand the oracles of God ? He declares Him Who was in the beginning Himself to have a beginning : and is not aware that if He Who is in the beginning has a beginning, then the beginning itself must needs have another beginning. Whatever He says of the beginning he must necessarily confess to be true of Him Who was in the beginning : for how can that which is in the beginning be severed from the beginning? and how can any one imagine a " was not" as preceding the "was"? For however far one carries back one's thought to apprehend the beginning, one most certainly understands as one does so that the Word which was in the beginning (inasmuch as It cannot be separated from the beginning in which It is) does not at any point of time either begin or cease its existence therein. Yet let no one be induced by these words of mine to separate into two the one beginning we acknowledge. For the beginning is most assuredly one, wherein is discerned, indivisibly, that Word Who is completely united to the Father. He who thus thinks will never leave heresy a loophole to impair his piety by the novelty of the term "ungenerate." But in Eunomius' next propositions his statements are like bread with a large admixture of sand. For by mixing his heretical opinions with sound doctrines, he makes uneatable even that which is in itself nutritious, by the gravel which he has mingled with it. For he calls the Lord " living wisdom," " operative truth," "subsistent power," and "life " :—so far is the nutritious portion. But into these assertions he instils the poison of heresy. For when he speaks of the " life " as " generate " he makes a reservation by the implied opposition to the

"ungenerate " life, and does not affirm the Son to be the very Life. Next he says :—"As Son of God, quickening the dead, the true light, the light that lighteneth every man coming into the world [7], good, and the bestower of good things." All these things he offers for honey to the simple-minded, concealing his deadly drug under the sweetness of terms like these. For he immediately introduces, on the heels of these statements, his pernicious principle, in the words " Not partitioning with Him that begat Him His high estate, not dividing with another the essence of the Father, but becoming by generation glorious, yea, the Lord of glory, and receiving glory from the Father, not sharing His glory with the Father, for the glory of the Almighty is incommunicable, as He hath said, ' My glory will I not give to another [8].'" These are his deadly poisons, which they alone can discover who have their souls' senses trained so to do : but the mortal mischief of the words is disclosed by their conclusion :—" Receiving glory from the Father, not sharing glory with the Father, for the glory of the Almighty is incommunicable, as He hath said, ' My glory will I not give to another.'" Who is that "other " to whom God has said that He will not give His glory? The prophet speaks of the adversary of God, and Eunomius refers the prophecy to the only begotten God Himself! For when the prophet, speaking in the person of God, had said, " My glory will I not give to another," he added, "neither My praise to graven images." For when men were beguiled to offer to the adversary of God the worship and adoration due to God alone, paying homage in the representations of graven images to the enemy of God, who appeared in many shapes amongst men in the forms furnished by idols, He Who healeth them that are sick, in pity for men's ruin, foretold by the prophet the loving-kindness which in the latter days He would show in the abolishing of idols, saying, " When My truth shall have been manifested, My glory shall no more be given to another, nor My praise bestowed upon graven images : for men, when they come to know My glory, shall no more be in bondage to them that by nature are no gods." All therefore that the prophet says in the person of the Lord concerning the power of the adversary, this fighter against God, refers to the Lord Himself, Who spake these words by the prophet ! Who among the tyrants is recorded to have been such a persecutor of the faith as this? Who maintained such blasphemy as this, that He Who, as we believe, was manifested in the flesh for the salvation of our souls, is not very God, but the adversary of God, who puts his

---

3 Or "to be brought into harmony with Christian doctrine " (ἐφαρμοσθῆναι τῷ λόγῳ)　　　4 Ps. xxxvi. 6.
5 Ps. lxviii 26 (LXX.).　　　6 Cf. Ps. cxiv. 6.
7 Cf. S. John i. 9.　　　8 Is. xlii. 8.

guile into effect against men by the instrumentality of idols and graven images? For it is what was said of that adversary by the prophet that Eunomius transfers to the only-begotten God, without so much as reflecting that it is the Only-begotten Himself Who spake these words by the prophet, as Eunomius himself subsequently confesses when he says, "this is He Who spake by the prophets."

Why should I pursue this part of the subject in more detail? For the words preceding also are tainted with the same profanity—"receiving glory from the Father, not sharing glory with the Father, for the glory of the Almighty God is incommunicable." For my own part, even had his words referred to Moses who was glorified in the ministration of the Law,—not even then should I have tolerated such a statement, even if it be conceded that Moses, having no glory from within, appeared completely glorious to the Israelites by the favour bestowed on him from God. For the very glory that was bestowed on the lawgiver was the glory of none other but of God Himself, which glory the Lord in the Gospel bids all to seek, when He blames those who value human glory highly and seek not the glory that cometh from God only[9]. For by the fact that He commanded them to seek the glory that cometh from the only God, He declared the possibility of their obtaining what they sought. How then is the glory of the Almighty incommunicable, if it is even our duty to ask for the glory that cometh from the only God, and if, according to our Lord's word, "every one that asketh receiveth[1]"? But one who says concerning the Brightness of the Father's glory, that He has the glory by having received it, says in effect that the Brightness of the glory is in Itself devoid of glory, and needs, in order to become Himself at last the Lord of some glory, to receive glory from another. How then are we to dispose of the utterances of the Truth,—one which tells us that He shall be seen in the glory of the Father[2], and another which says, "All things that the Father hath are Mine[3]"? To whom ought the hearer to give ear? To him who says, "He that is, as the Apostle says, the 'heir of all things[4]' that are in the Father, is without part or lot in His Father's glory"; or to Him Who declares that all things that the Father hath, He Himself hath also? Now among the "all things," glory surely is included. Yet Eunomius says that the glory of the Almighty is incommunicable. This view Joel does not attest, nor yet the mighty Peter, who adopted, in his speech to the Jews, the language of the prophet. For both the pro-

phet and the apostle say, in the person of God,—"I will pour out of My Spirit upon all flesh[5]." He then Who did not grudge the partaking in His own Spirit to all flesh,—how can it be that He does not impart His own glory to the only-begotten Son, Who is in the bosom of the Father, Who has all things that the Father has? Perhaps one should say that Eunomius is here speaking the truth, though not intending it. For the term "impart" is strictly used in the case of one who has not his glory from within, whose possession of it is an accession from without, and not part of his own nature: but where one and the same nature is observed in both Persons, He Who is as regards nature all that the Father is believed to be stands in no need of one to impart to Him each several attribute. This it will be well to explain more clearly and precisely. He Who has the Father dwelling in Him in His entirety —what need has He of the Father's glory, when none of the attributes contemplated in the Father is withdrawn from Him?

§ 11. *After expounding the high estate of the Almighty, the Eternity of the Son, and the phrase " being made obedient," he shows the folly of Eunomius in his assertion that the Son did not acquire His sonship by obedience.*

What, moreover, is the high estate of the Almighty in which Eunomius affirms that the Son has no share? Let those, then, who are wise in their own eyes, and prudent in their own sight[6], utter their groundling opinions— they who, as the prophet says, "speak out of the ground[7]." But let us who reverence the Word and are disciples of the Truth, or rather who profess to be so, not leave even this assertion unsifted. We know that of all the names by which Deity is indicated some are expressive of the Divine majesty, employed and understood absolutely, and some are assigned with reference to the operations over us and all creation. For when the Apostle says "Now to the immortal, invisible, only wise God[8]," and the like, by these titles he suggests conceptions which represent to us the transcendent power, but when God is spoken of in the Scriptures as gracious, merciful, full of pity, true, good, Lord, Physician, Shepherd, Way, Bread, Fountain, King, Creator, Artificer, Protector, Who is over all and through all, Who is all in all, these and similar titles contain the declaration of the operations of the Divine lovingkindness in the creation. Those then who enquire precisely into the meaning of the term "Almighty" will find that it declares nothing

9 Cf. S. John v. 44.   1 S. Matt. vii. 8.
2 S. Mark viii. 38.   3 S. John xvi. 15.   4 Heb. i. 2.

5 Joel ii. 28 : Acts ii. 17.   6 Is. v. 21.
7 Is. xxix. 4.   8 Cf. 1 Tim. i. 17.

else concerning the Divine power than that that operation which controls created things and is indicated by the word "Almighty," stands in a certain relation to something. For as He would not be called a Physician, save on account of the sick, nor merciful and gracious, and the like, save by reason of one who stood in need of grace and mercy, so neither would He be styled Almighty, did not all creation stand in need of one to regulate it and keep it in being. As, then, He presents Himself as a Physician to those who are in need of healing, so He is Almighty over one who has need of being ruled: and just as "they that are whole have no need of a physician [9]," so it follows that we may well say that He Whose nature contains in it the principle of unerring and unwavering rectitude does not, like others, need a ruler over Him. Accordingly, when we hear the name "Almighty," our conception is this, that God sustains in being all intelligible things as well as all things of a material nature. For for this cause He sitteth upon the circle of the earth, for this cause He holdeth the ends of the earth in His hand, for this cause He "meteth out heaven with the span, and measureth the waters in the hollow of His hand [1]"; for this cause He comprehendeth in Himself all the intelligible creation, that all things may remain in existence controlled by His encompassing power. Let us enquire, then, Who it is that "worketh all in all." Who is He Who made all things, and without Whom no existing thing does exist? Who is He in Whom all things were created, and in Whom all things that are have their continuance? In Whom do we live and move and have our being? Who is He Who hath in Himself all that the Father hath? Does what has been said leave us any longer in ignorance of Him Who is "God over all [2]," Who is so entitled by S. Paul,—our Lord Jesus Christ, Who, as He Himself says, holding in His hand "all things that the Father hath [3]," assuredly grasps all things in the all-containing hollow of His hand and is sovereign over what He has grasped, and no man taketh from the hand of Him Who in His hand holdeth all things? If, then, He hath all things, and is sovereign over that which He hath, why is He Who is thus sovereign over all things something else and not Almighty? If heresy replies that the Father is sovereign over both the Son and the Holy Spirit, let them first show that the Son and the Holy Spirit are of mutable nature, and then over this mutability let them set its ruler, that by the help implanted from above, that which is so overruled may con-

tinue incapable of turning to evil. If, on the other hand, the Divine nature is incapable of evil, unchangeable, unalterable, eternally permanent, to what end does it stand in need of a ruler, controlling as it does all creation, and itself by reason of its immutability needing no ruler to control it? For this cause it is that at the name of Christ "every knee boweth, of things in heaven, and things in earth, and things under the earth [4]." For assuredly every knee would not thus bow, did it not recognize in Christ Him Who rules it for its own salvation. But to say that the Son came into being by the goodness of the Father is nothing else than to put Him on a level with the meanest objects of creation. For what is there that did not arrive at its birth by the goodness of Him Who made it? To what is the formation of mankind ascribed? to the badness of its Maker, or to His goodness? To what do we ascribe the generation of animals, the production of plants and herbs? There is nothing that did not take its rise from the goodness of Him Who made it. A property, then, which reason discerns to be common to all things, Eunomius is so kind as to allow to the Eternal Son! But that He did not share His essence or His estate with the Father—these assertions and the rest of his verbiage I have refuted in anticipation, when dealing with his statements concerning the Father, and shown that he has hazarded them at random and without any intelligible meaning. For not even in the case of us who are born one of another is there any division of essence. The definition expressive of essence remains in its entirety in each, in him that begets and in him who is begotten, without admitting diminution in him who begets, or augmentation in him who is begotten. But to speak of division of estate or sovereignty in the case of Him Who hath all things whatsoever that the Father hath, carries with it no meaning, unless it be a demonstration of the propounder's impiety. It would therefore be superfluous to entangle oneself in such discussions, and so to prolong our treatise to an unreasonable length. Let us pass on to what follows.

"Glorified," he says, "by the Father before the worlds." The word of truth hath been demonstrated, confirmed by the testimony of its adversaries. For this is the sum of our faith, that the Son is from all eternity, being glorified by the Father: for "before the worlds" is the same in sense as "from all eternity," seeing that prophecy uses this phrase to set forth to us God's eternity, when it speaks of Him as "He that is from before the worlds [5]." If then to exist before the worlds is beyond all begin-

---

[9] Cf. S. Matt. ix. 12, and parallel passages.
[1] Cf. Is. xl. 12 and 24. The quotation is not verbally from the LXX.
[2] Rom. ix. 5.   [3] S. John xvi. 15.   [4] Cf. Phil. ii. 10.   [5] Ps. lv. 19 (LXX.).

ning, he who confers glory on the Son before the worlds, does thereby assert His existence from eternity before that glory[6] : for surely it is not the non-existent, but the existent which is glorified. Then he proceeds to plant for himself the seeds of blasphemy against the Holy Spirit ; not with a view to glorify the Son, but that he may wantonly outrage the Holy Ghost. For with the intention of making out the Holy Spirit to be part of the angelic host, he throws in the phrase " glorified eternally by the Spirit, and by every rational and generated being," so that there is no distinction between the Holy Spirit and all that comes into being ; if, that is, the Holy Spirit glorifies the Lord in the same sense as all the other existences enumerated by the prophet, " angels and powers, and the heaven of heavens, and the water above the heavens, and all the things of earth, dragons, deeps, fire and hail, snow and vapour, wind of the storm, mountains and all hills, fruitful trees and all cedars, beasts and all cattle, worms and feathered fowls[7]." If, then, he says, that along with these the Holy Spirit also glorifies the Lord, surely his God-opposing tongue makes out the Holy Spirit Himself also to be one of them.

The disjointed incoherencies which follow next, I think it well to pass over, not because they give no handle at all to censure, but because their language is such as might be used by the devout, if detached from its malignant context. If he does here and there use some expressions favourable to devotion it is just held out as a bait to simple souls, to the end that the hook of impiety may be swallowed along with it. For after employing such language as a member of the Church might use, he subjoins, " Obedient with regard to the creation and production of all things that are, obedient with regard to every ministration, not having by His obedience attained Sonship or Godhead, but, as a consequence of being Son and being generated as the Only-begotten God, showing Himself obedient in words, obedient in acts." Yet who of those who are conversant with the oracles of God does not know with regard to what point of time it was said of Him by the mighty Paul, (and that once for all), that He " became obedient[8] " ? For it was when He came in the form of a servant to accomplish the mystery of redemption by the cross, Who had emptied Himself, Who humbled Himself by assuming the likeness and fashion of a man, being found as man in man's lowly nature—then, I say, it was that He became obedient, even He Who

" took our infirmities and bare our sicknesses[9]," healing the disobedience of men by His own obedience, that by His stripes He might heal our wound, and by His own death do away with the common death of all men,—then it was that for our sakes He was made obedient, even as He became " sin[1] " and "a curse[2] " by reason of the dispensation on our behalf, not being so by nature, but becoming so in His love for man. But by what sacred utterance was He ever taught His list of so many obediences ? Nay, on the contrary every inspired Scripture attests His independent and sovereign power, saying, " He spake the word and they were made : He commanded and they were created[3] " :—for it is plain that the Psalmist says this concerning Him Who upholds " all things by the word of His power[4]," Whose authority, by the sole impulse of His will, framed every existence and nature, and all things in the creation apprehended by reason or by sight. Whence, then, was Eunomius moved to ascribe in such manifold wise to the King of the universe the attribute of obedience, speaking of Him as " obedient with regard to all the work of creation, obedient with regard to every ministration, obedient in words and in acts " ? Yet it is plain to every one, that he alone is obedient to another in acts and words, who has not yet perfectly achieved in himself the condition of accurate working or unexceptionable speech, but keeping his eye ever on his teacher and guide, is trained by his suggestions to exact propriety in deed and word. But to think that Wisdom needs a master and teacher to guide aright Its attempts at imitation, is the dream of Eunomius' fancy, and of his alone. And concerning the Father he says, that He is faithful in words and faithful in works, while of the Son he does not assert faithfulness in word and deed, but only obedience and not faithfulness, so that his profanity extends impartially through all his statements. But it is perhaps right to pass in silence over the inconsiderate folly of the assertion interposed between those last mentioned, lest some unreflecting persons should laugh at its absurdity when they ought rather to weep over the perdition of their souls, than laugh at the folly of their words. For this wise and wary theologian says that He did not attain to being a Son as the result of His obedience ! Mark his penetration ! with what cogent force does he lay it down for us that He was not first obedient and afterwards a Son, and that we ought not to think that His obedience was prior to His generation ! Now if he had not added this defining clause, who without it would have been sufficiently silly and

6 Reading αὐτῆς. with Oehler. The general sense is the same, if αὐτῷ be read ; "does yet more strongly attest His existence from all eternity."
7 Cf. Ps. cxlviii. 2—10.   8 Phil. ii. 8.

9 Cf. S. Matt. viii. 17.   1 2 Cor. v. 21.
2 Gal. iii. 13.   3 Ps. cxlviii. 5.   4 Heb. i. 3.

idiotic to fancy that His generation was bestowed on Him by His Father, as a reward of the obedience of Him Who before His generation had showed due subjection and obedience? But that no one may too readily extract matter for laughter from these remarks, let each consider that even the folly of the words has in it something worthy of tears. For what he intends to establish by these observations is something of this kind, that His obedience is part of His nature, so that not even if He willed it would it be possible for Him not to be obedient.

For he says that He was so constituted that His nature was adapted to obedience alone [5], just as among instruments that which is fashioned with regard to a certain figure necessarily produces in that which is subjected to its operation the form which the artificer implanted in the construction of the instrument, and cannot possibly trace a straight line upon that which receives its mark, if its own working is in a curve; nor can the instrument, if fashioned to draw a straight line, produce a circle by its impress. What need is there of any words of ours to reveal how great is the profanity of such a notion, when the heretical utterance of itself proclaims aloud its monstrosity? For if He was obedient for this reason only that He was so made, then of course He is not on an equal footing even with humanity, since on this theory, while our soul is self-determining and independent, choosing as it will with sovereignty over itself that which is pleasing to it, He on the contrary exercises, or rather experiences, obedience under the constraint of a compulsory law of His nature, while His nature suffers Him not to disobey, even if He would. For it was "as the result of being Son, and being begotten, that He has thus shown Himself obedient in words and obedient in acts." Alas, for the brutish stupidity of this doctrine! Thou makest the Word obedient to words, and supposest other words prior to Him Who is truly the Word, and another Word of the Beginning is mediator between the Beginning and the Word that was in the Beginning, conveying to Him the decision. And this is not one only: there are several words, which Eunomius makes so many links of the chain between the Beginning and the Word, and which abuse His obedience as they think good. But what need is there to linger over this idle talk? Any one can see that even at that time with reference to which S. Paul says that He became obedient, (and he tells us that He became obedient in this wise, namely, by becoming for our sakes flesh, and a servant,

and a curse, and sin),—even then, I say, the Lord of glory, Who despised the shame and embraced suffering in the flesh, did not abandon His free will, saying as He does, "Destroy this temple, and in three days I will raise it up [6];" and again, "No man taketh My life from Me; I have power to lay it down, and I have power to take it again [7]"; and when those who were armed with swords and staves drew near to Him on the night before His Passion, He caused them all to go backward by saying "I am He [8]," and again, when the dying thief besought Him to remember him, He showed His universal sovereignty by saying, "To-day shalt thou be with Me in Paradise [9]." If then not even in the time of His Passion He is separated from His authority, where can heresy possibly discern the subordination to authority of the King of glory?

§ 12. *He thus proceeds to a magnificent discourse of the interpretation of "Mediator," "Like," "Ungenerate," and "generate," and of "The likeness and seal of the energy of the Almighty and of His works."*

Again, what is the manifold mediation which with wearying iteration he assigns to God, calling Him "Mediator in doctrines, Mediator in the Law [1]"? It is not thus that we are taught by the lofty utterance of the Apostle, who says that having made void the law of commandments by His own doctrines, He is the mediator between God and man, declaring it by this saying, "There is one God, and one mediator between God and man, the man Christ Jesus [2];" where by the distinction implied in the word "mediator" he reveals to us the whole aim of the mystery of godliness. Now the aim is this. Humanity once revolted through the malice of the enemy, and, brought into bondage to sin, was also alienated from the true Life. After this the Lord of the creature calls back to Him His own creature, and becomes Man while still remaining God, being both God and Man in the entirety of the two several natures, and thus humanity was indissolubly united to God, the Man that is in Christ conducting the work of mediation, to Whom, by the first-fruits assumed for us, all the lump is potentially united [3]. Since, then, a mediator is not a mediator of one [4], and God is one, not divided among the Persons in Whom we have been taught to believe (for the Godhead in the Father, the Son, and the Holy Ghost is one), the Lord, therefore, becomes a mediator once for all betwixt

---

[5] If this phrase is a direct quotation from Eunomius, it is probably from some other context: its grammatical structure does not connect it with what has gone before, nor is it quite clear where the quotation ends, or whether the illustration of the instrument is Eunomius' own, or is Gregory's exposition of the statement of Eunomius.

[6] S. John ii. 19.　　[7] S. John x. 18.
[8] S. John xviii. 5-6.　　[9] S. Luke xxiii. 43.
[1] Here again the exact connexion of the quotation from **Eunomius** with the extracts preceding is uncertain.
[2] Cf. 1. Tim. ii. 5.　　　[3] Cf. Rom. xi. 16.
[4] Gal. iii. 20.

God and men, binding man to the Deity by Himself. But even by the idea of a mediator we are taught the godly doctrine enshrined in the Creed. For the Mediator between God and man entered as it were into fellowship with human nature, not by being merely deemed a man, but having truly become so: in like manner also, being very God, He has not, as Eunomius will have us consider, been honoured by the bare title of Godhead.

What he adds to the preceding statements is characterized by the same want of meaning, or rather by the same malignity of meaning. For in calling Him "Son" Whom, a little before, he had plainly declared to be created, and in calling Him "only begotten God" Whom he reckoned with the rest of things that have come into being by creation, he affirms that He is like Him that begat Him only "by an especial likeness, in a peculiar sense." Accordingly, we must first distinguish the significations of the term "like," in how many senses it is employed in ordinary use, and afterwards proceed to discuss Eunomius' positions. In the first place, then, all things that beguile our senses, not being really identical in nature, but producing illusion by some of the accidents of the respective subjects, as form, colour, sound, and the impressions conveyed by taste or smell or touch, while really different in nature, but supposed to be other than they truly are, these custom declares to have the relation of "likeness," as, for example, when the lifeless material is shaped by art, whether carving, painting, or modelling, into an imitation of a living creature, the imitation is said to be "like" the original. For in such a case the nature of the animal is one thing, and that of the material, which cheats the sight by mere colour and form, is another. To the same class of likeness belongs the image of the original figure in a mirror, which gives appearances of motion, without, however, being in nature identical with its original. In just the same way our hearing may experience the same deception, when, for instance, some one, imitating the song of the nightingale with his own voice, persuades our hearing so that we seem to be listening to the bird. Taste, again, is subject to the same illusion, when the juice of figs mimics the pleasant taste of honey: for there is a certain resemblance to the sweetness of honey in the juice of the fruit. So, too, the sense of smell may sometimes be imposed upon by resemblance, when the scent of the herb camomile, imitating the fragrant apple itself, deceives our perception: and in the same way with touch also, likeness belies the truth in various modes, since a silver or brass coin, of equal size and similar weight with a gold one, may pass for the gold piece if our sight does not discern the truth.

We have thus generally described in a few words the several cases in which objects, because they are deemed to be different from what they really are, produce delusions in our senses. It is possible, of course, by a more laborious investigation, to extend one's enquiry through all things which are really different in kind one from another, but are nevertheless thought, by virtue of some accidental resemblance, to be like one to the other. Can it possibly be such a form of "likeness" as this, that he is continually attributing to the Son? Nay, surely he cannot be so infatuated as to discover deceptive similarity in Him Who is the Truth. Again, in the inspired Scriptures, we are told of another kind of resemblance by Him Who said, "Let us make man in our image, after our likeness [5]:" but I do not suppose that Eunomius would discern this kind of likeness between the Father and the Son, so as to make out the Only-begotten God to be identical with man. We are also aware of another kind of likeness, of which the word speaks in Genesis concerning Seth,—"Adam begat a son in his own likeness, after his image [6]": and if this is the kind of likeness of which Eunomius speaks, we do not think his statement is to be rejected. For in this case the nature of the two objects which are alike is not different, and the impress and type imply community of nature. These, or such as these, are our views upon the variety of meanings of "like." Let us see, then, with what intention Eunomius asserts of the Son that "especial likeness" to the Father, when he says that He is "like the Father with an especial likeness, in a peculiar sense, not as Father to Father, for they are not two Fathers." He promises to show us the "especial likeness" of the Son to the Father, and proceeds by his definition to establish the position that we ought not to conceive of Him as being like. For by saying, "He is not like as Father to Father," he makes out that He is not like; and again when he adds, "nor as Ungenerate to Ungenerate," by this phrase, too, he forbids us to conceive a likeness in the Son to the Father; and finally, by subjoining "nor as Son to Son," he introduces a third conception, by which he entirely subverts the meaning of "like." So it is that he follows up his own statements, and conducts his demonstration of likeness by establishing unlikeness. And now let us examine the discernment and frankness which he displays in these distinctions. After saying that the Son is like the Father, he guards the statement by adding that we ought not to think that the Son is like the Father, "as Father to Father." Why, what man on earth is such a fool as, on learning that the Son is like the Father, to be brought by any course of reasoning to think of the likeness of Father to Father? "Nor as Son to Son":—here, again, the acuteness of the distinction is equally conspicuous. When he tells us that the Son is like the Father, he adds the further definition that He must not be understood to be like Him in the same way as He would be like another Son. These are the mysteries of the awful doctrines of Eunomius, by which his disciples are made wiser than the rest of the world, by learning that the Son, by His likeness to the Father, is not like a Son, for the Son is not the Father: nor is He like "as Ungenerate to Ungenerate," for the Son is not ungenerate. But the mystery which we have received, when it speaks of the Father, certainly bids us understand the Father of the Son, and when it names the Son, teaches us to apprehend the Son of the Father. And until the present time we never felt the need of these philosophic refinements, that by the words Father and Son are suggested two Fathers or two Sons, a pair, so to say, of ungenerate beings.

Now the drift of Eunomius' excessive concern about the Ungenerate has been often explained before; and it shall here be briefly discovered yet again. For as the term Father points to no difference of nature from the Son, his impiety, if he had brought his statement to a close here, would have had no support, seeing that the natural sense of the names Father and Son excludes the idea of their being alien in essence. But as it is, by employing the terms "generate" and "ungenerate," since the contradictory opposition between them admits of no mean, just like that between "mortal" and "immortal," "rational" and "irrational," and all those terms which are opposed to each other by the mutually exclusive nature of their meaning,—by the use of these terms, I repeat, he gives free course to his profanity, so as to contemplate as existing in the "generate" with reference to the "ungenerate" the same difference which there is between "mortal" and "immortal": and even as the nature of the mortal is one, and that of the immortal another, and as the special attributes of the rational and of the irrational are essentially incompatible, just so he wants to make out that the nature of the ungenerate is one, and that of the generate another, in order to show that as the irrational nature has been created in subjection to the rational, so the generate is by a necessity of its being in a state of subordination to the ungenerate. For which reason he attaches to the ungenerate the name of "Almighty," and this he does not apply to express providential opera-

tion, as the argument led the way for him in suggesting, but transfers the application of the word to arbitrary sovereignty, so as to make the Son to be a part of the subject and subordinate universe, a fellow-slave with all the rest to Him Who with arbitrary and absolute sovereignty controls all alike. And that it is with an eye to this result that he employs these argumentative distinctions, will be clearly established from the passage before us. For after those sapient and carefully-considered expressions, that He is not like either as Father to Father, or as Son to Son,—and yet there is no necessity that father should invariably be like father or son like son: for suppose there is one father among the Ethiopians, and another among the Scythians, and each of these has a son, the Ethiopian's son black, but the Scythian white-skinned and with hair of a golden tinge, yet none the more because each is a father does the Scythian turn black on the Ethiopian's account, nor does the Ethiopian's body change to white on account of the Scythian,—after saying this, however, according to his own fancy, Eunomius subjoins that "He is like as Son to Father [7]." But although such a phrase indicates kinship in nature, as the inspired Scripture attests in the case of Seth and Adam, our doctor, with but small respect for his intelligent readers, introduces his idle exposition of the title "Son," defining Him to be the image and seal of the energy [8] of the Almighty. "For the Son," he says, "is the image and seal of the energy of the Almighty." Let him who hath ears to hear first, I pray, consider this particular point—What is "the seal of the energy"? Every energy is contemplated as exertion in the party who exhibits it, and on the completion of his exertion, it has no independent existence. Thus, for example, the energy of the runner is the motion of his feet, and when the motion has stopped there is no longer any energy. So too about every pursuit the same may be said;—when the exertion of him who is busied about anything ceases, the energy ceases also, and has no independent existence, either when a person is actively engaged in the exertion he undertakes, or when he ceases from that exertion. What then does he tell us that the energy is in itself, which is neither essence, nor image, nor person? So he speaks of the Son as the similitude of the impersonal, and that which is like the non-existent surely has itself no existence at all. This is what his juggling with idle opinions comes to,—belief in nonentity! for that which is like nonentity surely

---

[7] This is apparently a quotation from Eunomius in continuation of what has gone before.

[8] The word employed is ἐνέργεια; which might be translated by "active force," or "operation," as elsewhere.

itself is not. O Paul and John and all you others of the band of Apostles and Evangelists, who are they that arm their venomous tongues against your words? who are they that raise their frog-like croakings against your heavenly thunder? What then saith the son of thunder? "In the beginning was the Word, and the Word was with God, and the Word was God [9]." And what saith he that came after him, that other who had been within the heavenly temple, who in Paradise had been initiated into mysteries unspeakable? "Being," he says, "the Bright-ness of His glory, and the express Image of His person [1]." What, after these have thus spoken, are the words of our ventriloquist [2]? "The seal," quoth he, "of the energy of the Almighty." He makes Him third after the Father, with that non-existent energy mediating between them, or rather moulded at pleasure by non-existence. God the Word, Who was in the beginning, is "the seal of the energy":—the Only-begotten God, Who is contemplated in the eternity of the Beginning of existent things, Who is in the bosom of the Father [3], Who sustains all things by the word of His power [4], the creator of the ages, from Whom and through Whom and in Whom are all things [5], Who sitteth upon the circle of the earth, and hath meted out heaven with the span, Who measureth the water in the hollow of his hand [6], Who holdeth in His hand all things that are, Who dwelleth on high and looketh upon the things that are lowly [7], or rather did look upon them to make all the world to be His footstool [8], imprinted by the footmark of the Word—the form of God [9] is "the seal" of an "energy." Is God then an energy, not a Person? Surely Paul when expounding this very truth says He is "the express image," not of His energy, but "of His Person." Is the Brightness of His glory a seal of the energy of God? Alas for his impious ignorance! What is there intermediate between God and His own form? and Whom does the Person employ as mediator with His own express image? and what can be conceived as coming between the glory and its brightness? But while there are such weighty and numerous testimonies wherein the greatness of the Lord of the creation is proclaimed by those who were entrusted with the proclamation of the Gospel, what sort of language does this forerunner of the final apostasy hold concerning Him? What says he? "As image," he says, "and seal of all the energy and power of the Almighty." How does he take upon himself to emend the words of the mighty Paul? Paul says that the

Son is "the Power of God [1]"; Eunomius calls Him "the seal of a power," not the Power. And then, repeating his expression, what is it that he adds to his previous statement? He calls Him "seal of the Father's works and words and counsels." To what works of the Father is He like? He will say, of course, the world, and all things that are therein. But the Gospel has testified that all these things are the works of the Only-begotten. To what works of the Father, then, was He likened? of what works was He made the seal? what Scripture ever entitled Him "seal of the Father's works"? But if any one should grant Eunomius the right to fashion his words at his own will, as he de-sires, even though Scripture does not agree with him, let him tell us what works of the Father there are of which he says that the Son was made the seal, apart from those that have been wrought by the Son. All things visible and invisible are the work of the Son: in the visible are included the whole world and all that is therein; in the invisible, the supramundane creation. What works of the Father, then, are remaining to be contemplated by themselves, over and above things visible and invisible, whereof he says that the Son was made the "seal"? Will he perhaps, when driven into a corner, return once more to the fetid vomit of heresy, and say that the Son is a work of the Father? How then does the Son come to be the "seal" of these works, when He Himself, as Eunomius says, is the work of the Father? Or does he say that the same Person is at once a work and the likeness of a work? Let this be granted: let us suppose him to speak of the other works of which he says the Father was the creator, if indeed he intends us to understand likeness by the term "seal." But what other "words" of the Father does Eunomius know, besides that Word Who was ever in the Father, Whom he calls a "seal"—Him Who is and is called the Word in the absolute, true, and primary sense? And to what counsels can he possibly refer, apart from the Wisdom of God, to which the Wisdom of God is made like, in becoming a "seal" of those counsels? Look at the want of discrimination and circumspection, at the confused muddle of his statement, how he brings the mystery into ridicule, without under-standing either what he says or what he is arguing about. For He Who has the Father in His entirety in Himself, and is Himself in His entirety in the Father, as Word and Wisdom and Power and Truth, as His express image and brightness, Himself is all things in the Father, and does not come to be the image and seal and likeness of certain other things discerned in the Father prior to Himself.

---

9 S. John i. 1.   [1] Heb. i. 3.
2 Cf. the use of ἐγγαστρίμυθος in LXX. (e. g. Lev. xix. 31, Is. xliv. 25).
3 S. John i. 18.   4 Cf. Heb. i. 3.   5 Cf. Rom. xi. 36.
6 Cf. Isa. xl. 12—22.   7 Cf. Ps. cxxxviii. 6.
8 Cf. Isa. lxvi. 1.   9 Cf. Phil ii. 5.

[1] 1 Cor. i. 24.

Then Eunomius allows to Him the credit of the destruction of men by water in the days of Noah, of the rain of fire that fell upon Sodom, and of the just vengeance upon the Egyptians, as though he were making some great concessions to Him Who holds in His hand the ends of the world, in Whom, as the Apostle says, "all things consist [2]," as though he were not aware that to Him Who encompasses all things, and guides and sways according to His good pleasure all that hath already been and all that will be, the mention of two or three marvels does not mean the addition of glory, so much as the suppression of the rest means its deprivation or loss. But even if no word be said of these, the one utterance of Paul is enough by itself to point to them all inclusively—the one utterance which says that He "is above all, and through all, and in all [3]."

§ 13. *He expounds the passage of the Gospel, "The Father judgeth no man," and further speaks of the assumption of man with body and soul wrought by the Lord, of the transgression of Adam, and of death and the resurrection of the dead.*

Next he says, "He legislates by the command of the Eternal God." Who is the eternal God? and who is He that ministers to Him in the giving of the Law? Thus much is plain to all, that through Moses God appointed the Law to those that received it. Now inasmuch as Eunomius himself acknowledges that it was the only-begotten God Who held converse with Moses, how is it that the assertion before us puts the Lord of all in the place of Moses, and ascribes the character of the eternal God to the Father alone, so as, by thus contrasting Him with the Eternal, to make out the only-begotten God, the Maker of the Worlds, to be not Eternal? Our studious friend with his excellent memory seems to have forgotten that Paul uses all these terms concerning himself, announcing among men the proclamation of the Gospel by the command of God [4]. Thus what the Apostle asserts of himself, that Eunomius is not ashamed to ascribe to the Lord of the prophets and apostles, in order to place the Master on the same level with Paul, His own servant. But why should I lengthen out my argument by confuting in detail each of these assertions, where the too unsuspicious reader of Eunomius' writings may think that their author is saying what Holy Scripture allows him to say, while one who is able to unravel each statement critically will find them one and all infected

with heretical knavery. For the Churchman and the heretic alike affirm that "the Father judgeth no man, but hath committed all judgment unto the Son [5]," but to this assertion they severally attach different meanings. By the same words the Churchman understands supreme authority, the other maintains subservience and subjection.

But to what has been already said, ought to be added some notice of that position which they make a kind of foundation of their impiety in their discussions concerning the Incarnation, the position, namely, that not the whole man has been saved by Him, but only the half of man, I mean the body. Their object in such a malignant perversion of the true doctrine, is to show that the less exalted statements, which our Lord utters in His humanity, are to be thought to have issued from the Godhead Itself, that so they may show their blasphemy to have a stronger case, if it is upheld by the actual acknowledgment of the Lord. For this reason it is that Eunomius says, "He who in the last days became man did not take upon Himself the man made up of soul and body." But, after searching through all the inspired and sacred Scripture, I do not find any such statement as this, that the Creator of all things, at the time of His ministration here on earth for man, took upon Himself flesh only without a soul. Under stress of necessity, then, looking to the object contemplated by the plan of salvation, to the doctrines of the Fathers, and to the inspired Scriptures, I will endeavour to confute the impious falsehood which is being fabricated with regard to this matter. The Lord came "to seek and to save that which was lost [6]." Now it was not the body merely, but the whole man, compacted of soul and body, that was lost: indeed, if we are to speak more exactly, the soul was lost sooner than the body. For disobedience is a sin, not of the body, but of the will: and the will properly belongs to the soul, from which the whole disaster of our nature had its beginning, as the threat of God, that admits of no falsehood, testifies in the declaration that, in the day that they should eat of the forbidden fruit, death without respite would attach to the act. Now since the condemnation of man was twofold, death correspondingly effects in each part of our nature the deprivation of the twofold life that operates in him who is thus mortally stricken. For the death of the body consists in the extinction of the means of sensible perception, and in the dissolution of the body into its kindred elements: but "the soul that sinneth," he saith, "it shall die [7]." Now sin is nothing else than

---

[2] Col. i. 17.
[3] Eph. iv. 6. The application of the words to the Son is remarkable.
[4] Cf. Rom. xvi. 26.

[5] S. John v. 22.   [6] Cf. S. Luke xix. 10.
[7] Ezek. xviii. 20.

alienation from God, Who is the true and only life. Accordingly the first man lived many hundred years after his disobedience, and yet God lied not when He said, " In the day that ye eat thereof ye shall surely die [8]." For by the fact of his alienation from the true life, the sentence of death was ratified against him that self-same day : and after this, at a much later time, there followed also the bodily death of Adam. He therefore Who came for this cause, that He might seek and save that which was lost, (that which the shepherd in the parable calls the sheep,) both finds that which is lost, and carries home on His shoulders the whole sheep, not its skin only, that He may make the man of God complete, united to the deity in body and in soul. And thus He Who was in all points tempted like as we are, yet without sin, left no part of our nature which He did not take upon Himself. Now the soul is not sin, though it is capable of admitting sin into it as the result of being ill-advised : and this He sanctifies by union with Himself for this end, that so the lump may be holy along with the first fruits. Wherefore also the Angel, when informing Joseph of the destruction of the enemies of the Lord, said, " They are dead which sought the young Child's life [9]," (or " soul ") : and the Lord says to the Jews, " Ye seek to kill Me, a man that hath told you the truth [1]." Now by " Man " is not meant the body of a man only, but that which is composed of both, soul and body. And again, He says to them, " Are ye angry at Me, because I have made a man every whit whole on the Sabbath day [2]?" And what He meant by " every whit whole," He showed in the other Gospels, when He said to the man who was let down on a couch in the midst, " Thy sins be forgiven thee," which is a healing of the soul, and, " Arise and walk [3]," which has regard to the body : and in the Gospel of S. John, by liberating the soul also from its own malady after He had given health to the body, where He saith, " Thou art made whole, sin no more [4]," thou, that is, who hast been cured in both, I mean in soul and in body. For so too does S. Paul speak, " for to make in Himself of twain one new man [5]." And so too He foretells that at the time of His Passion He would voluntarily detach His soul from His body, saying, " No man taketh " my soul " from Me, but I lay it down of Myself : I have power to lay it down,

and I have power to take it again [6]." Yea, the prophet David also, according to the interpretation of the great Peter, said with foresight of Him, " Thou wilt not leave My soul in hell, neither wilt Thou suffer Thine Holy One to see corruption [7]," while the Apostle Peter thus expounds the saying, that " His soul was not left in hell, neither His flesh did see corruption." For His Godhead, alike before taking flesh and in the flesh and after His Passion, is immutably the same, being at all times what It was by nature, and so continuing for ever. But in the suffering of His human nature the Godhead fulfilled the dispensation for our benefit by severing the soul for a season from the body, yet without being Itself separated from either of those elements to which it was once for all united, and by joining again the elements which had been thus parted, so as to give to all human nature a beginning and an example which it should follow of the resurrection from the dead, that all the corruptible may put on incorruption, and all the mortal may put on immortality, our first-fruits having been transformed to the Divine nature by its union with God, as Peter said, " This same Jesus Whom ye crucified, hath God made both Lord and Christ [8] ; " and we might cite many passages of Scripture to support such a position, showing how the Lord, reconciling the world to Himself by the Humanity of Christ, apportioned His work of benevolence to men between His soul and His body, willing through His soul and touching them through His body. But it would be superfluous to encumber our argument by entering into every detail.

Before passing on, however, to what follows, I will further mention the one text, " Destroy this temple, and in three days I will raise it up [9]." Just as we, through soul and body, become a temple of Him Who " dwelleth in us and walketh in us [1]," even so the Lord terms their combination a " temple," of which the " destruction " signifies the dissolution of the soul from the body. And if they allege the passage in the Gospel, " The Word was made flesh [2]," in order to make out that the flesh was taken into the Godhead without the soul, on the ground that the soul is not expressly mentioned along with the flesh, let them learn that it is customary for Holy Scripture to imply the whole by the part. For He that said, " Unto Thee shall all flesh come [3]," does not mean that the flesh will be presented before the Judge apart from the souls : and when we read

[8] Cf. Gen. ii. 17.
[9] S. Matt. ii. 20. The word ψυχήν may be rendered by either " life " or " soul."
[1] S. John viii. 40. This is the only passage in which our Lord speaks of Himself by this term.
[2] S. John vii. 20.
[3] Cf. S. Luke v. 20, 23, and the parallel passages in S. Matt. ix. and S. Mark ii.
[4] S. John v. 14.
[5] Eph. ii. 15.

[6] Cf. S. John x. 17, 18. Here again the word ψυχήν is rendered in the A. V. by " life."
[7] Ps. xvi. 8. Acts ii. 27, 31.
[8] Acts ii. 36. A further exposition of Gregory's views on this passage will be found in Book V.
[9] S. John ii. 19.
[2] S. John i. 14.
[1] Cf. 2 Cor. vi. 16.
[3] Ps. lxv. 2.

in sacred History that Jacob went down into Egypt with seventy-five souls [4] we understand the flesh also to be intended together with the souls. So, then, the Word, when He became flesh, took with the flesh the whole of human nature ; and hence it was possible that hunger and thirst, fear and dread, desire and sleep, tears and trouble of spirit, and all such things, were in Him. For the Godhead, in its proper nature, admits no such affections, nor is the flesh by itself involved in them, if the soul is not affected co-ordinately with the body.

§ 14. *He proceeds to discuss the views held by Eunomius, and by the Church, touching the Holy Spirit ; and to show that the Father, the Son, and the Holy Ghost are not three Gods, but one God. He also discusses different senses of "Subjection," and therein shows that the subjection of all things to the Son is the same as the subjection of the Son to the Father.*

Thus much with regard to his profanity towards the Son. Now let us see what he says about the Holy Spirit. "After Him, we believe," he says, "on the Comforter, the Spirit of Truth." I think it will be plain to all who come across this passage what object he has in view in thus perverting the declaration of the faith delivered to us by the Lord, in his statements concerning the Son and the Father. Though this absurdity has already been exposed, I will nevertheless endeavour, in few words, to make plain the aim of his knavery. As in the former case, he avoided using the name "Father," that so he might not include the Son in the eternity of the Father, so he avoided employing the title Son, that he might not by it suggest His natural affinity to the Father; so here, too, he refrains from saying "Holy Spirit," that he may not by this name acknowledge the majesty of His glory, and His complete union with the Father and the Son. For since the appellation of "Spirit," and that of "Holy," are by the Scriptures equally applied to the Father and the Son (for "God is a Spirit [5]," and "the anointed Lord is the Spirit before our face [6]," and "the Lord our God is Holy [7]," and there is "one Holy, one Lord Jesus Christ [8]"), lest there should, by the use of these terms, be bred in the minds of his readers some orthodox conception of the Holy Spirit, such as would naturally arise in them from His sharing His glorious appellation with the Father and the Son, for this reason, deluding the ears of the

foolish, he changes the words of the Faith as set forth by God in the delivery of this mystery, making a way, so to speak, by this sequence, for the entrance of his impiety against the Holy Spirit. For if he had said, " We believe in the Holy Spirit," and "God is a Spirit," any one instructed in things divine would have interposed the remark, that if we are to believe in the Holy Spirit, while God is called a Spirit, He is assuredly not distinct in nature from that which receives the same titles in a proper sense. For of all those things which are indicated not unreally, nor metaphorically, but properly and absolutely, by the same names, we are necessarily compelled to acknowledge that the nature also, which is signified by this identity of names, is one and the same. For this reason it is that, suppressing the name appointed by the Lord in the formula of the faith, he says, "We believe in the Comforter." But I have been taught that this very name is also applied by the inspired Scripture to Father, Son, and Holy Ghost alike. For the Son gives the name of "Comforter" equally to Himself and to the Holy Spirit [9]; and the Father, where He is said to work comfort, surely claims as His own the name of "Comforter." For assuredly he Who does the work of a Comforter does not disdain the name belonging to the work : for David says to the Father, " Thou, Lord, hast holpen me and comforted me [1]," and the great Apostle applies to the Father the same language, when he says, " Blessed be the God and Father of our Lord Jesus Christ, Who comforteth us in all our tribulation [2] " ; and John, in one of his Catholic Epistles, expressly gives to the Son the name of Comforter [3]. Nay, more, the Lord Himself, in saying that *another* Comforter would be sent us, when speaking of the Spirit, clearly asserted this title of Himself in the first place. But as there are two senses of the word παρακαλεῖν [4],—one to *beseech*, by words and gestures of respect, to induce him to whom we apply for anything, to feel with us in respect of those things for which we apply,—the other to *comfort*, to take remedial thought for affections of body and soul,—the Holy Scripture affirms the conception of the Paraclete, in either sense alike, to belong to the Divine nature. For at one time Paul sets before us by the word παρακαλεῖν the healing power of God, as when he says, " God, Who comforteth those that are cast down, comforted us by the coming of Titus [5] "; and at another time he uses this word in its other meaning, when he says, writing to the Corinthians, " Now we are am-

[4] Acts vii. 14. Cf. Gen. xlvi. 27, and Deut. x. 22.
[5] S. John iv. 24. [6] Cf. Lam. iv. 20 in LXX.
[7] Ps. xcix. 9.
[8] Cf. the response to the words of the Priest at the elevation of the Gifts in the Greek Liturgies.

[9] S. John xiv. 16. [1] Ps. lxxvi. 17. [2] 2 Cor. i. 3-4.
[3] 1 S. John ii. 1. The word is in the A. V. rendered "advocate.")
[4] From which is derived the name Paraclete, *i.e.* Comforter or Advocate. [5] 2 Cor. vii. 6.

bassadors for Christ, as though God did beseech you by us ; we pray you in Christ's stead, be ye reconciled to God [6]." Now since these things are so, in whatever way you understand the title "Paraclete," when used of the Spirit, you will not in either of its significations detach Him from His community in it with the Father and the Son. Accordingly, he has not been able, even though he wished it, to belittle the glory of the Spirit by ascribing to Him the very attribute which Holy Scripture refers also to the Father and to the Son. But in styling Him "the Spirit of Truth," Eunomius' own wish, I suppose, was to suggest by this phrase subjection, since Christ is the Truth, and he called Him the Spirit of Truth, as if one should say that He is a possession and chattel of the Truth, without being aware that God is called a God of righteousness [7] ; and we certainly do not understand thereby that God is a possession of righteousness. Wherefore also, when we hear of the "Spirit of Truth," we acquire by that phrase such a conception as befits the Deity, being guided to the loftier interpretation by the words which follow it. For when the Lord said "The Spirit of Truth," He immediately added "Which proceedeth from the Father [8]," a fact which the voice of the Lord never asserted of any conceivable thing in creation, not of aught visible or invisible, not of thrones, principalities, powers, or dominions, nor of any other name that is named either in this world or in that which is to come. It is plain then that that, from share in which all creation is excluded, is something special and peculiar to uncreated being. But this man bids us believe in "the Guide of godliness." Let a man then believe in Paul, and Barnabas, and Titus, and Silvanus, and Timotheus, and all those by whom we have been led into the way of the faith. For if we are to believe in "that which guides us to godliness," along with the Father and the Son, all the prophets and lawgivers and patriarchs, heralds, evangelists, apostles, pastors, and teachers, have equal honour with the Holy Spirit, as they have been "guides to godliness" to those who came after them. "Who came into being," he goes on, "by the only God through the Only-begotten." In these words he gathers up in one head all his blasphemy. Once more he calls the Father "only God," who employs the Only-begotten as an instrument for the production of the Spirit. What shadow of such a notion did he find in Scripture, that he ventures upon this assertion? by deduction from what premises did he bring his profanity to such a conclusion as this?

Which of the Evangelists says it? what apostle? what prophet? Nay, on the contrary every scripture divinely inspired, written by the afflatus of the Spirit, attests the Divinity of the Spirit. For example (for it is better to prove my position from the actual testimonies), those who receive power to become children of God bear witness to the Divinity of the Spirit. Who knows not that utterance of the Lord which tells us that they who are born of the Spirit are the children of God ? For thus He expressly ascribes the birth of the children of God to the Spirit, saying, that as that which is born of the flesh is flesh,·so that which is born of the Spirit is spirit. But as many as are born of the Spirit are called the children of God [9]. So also when the Lord by breathing upon His disciples had imparted to them the Holy Spirit, John says, "Of His fulness have all we received [1]." And that "in Him dwelleth the fulness of the Godhead [2]," the mighty Paul attests : yea, moreover, through the prophet Isaiah it is attested, as to the manifestation of the Divine appearance vouchsafed to him, when he saw Him that sat "on the throne high and lifted up [3] :" the older tradition, it is true, says that it was the Father Who appeared to him, but the evangelist John refers the prophecy to our Lord, saying, touching those of the Jews who did not believe the words uttered by the prophet concerning the Lord, "These things said Esaias, when he saw His glory and spake of Him [4]." But the mighty Paul attributes the same passage to the Holy Spirit in his speech made to the Jews at Rome, when he says, "Well spake the Holy Ghost by Esaias the prophet concerning you, saying, Hearing ye shall hear and shall not understand [5]," showing, in my opinion, by Holy Scripture itself, that every specially divine vision, every theophany, every word uttered in the Person of God, is to be understood to refer to the Father, the Son, and the Holy Spirit. Hence when David says, "they provoked God in the wilderness, and grieved Him in the desert [6]," the apostle refers to the Holy Spirit the despite done by the Israelites to God, in these terms : "Wherefore, as the Holy Ghost saith, Harden not your hearts, as in the provocation, in the day of temptation in the wilderness ; when your fathers tempted me [7]," and goes on to refer all that the prophecy refers to God, to the Person of the Holy Ghost. Those who keep repeating against us the phrase "three Gods," because we hold these views, have per-

---

[6] 2 Cor. v. 20.
[7] The text reads, "that God is called righteousness," but the argument seems to require the genitive case. The reference may be to Ps. iv. 1.   [8] S. John xv. 26.

[9] With this passage cf. S. John i. 12, iii. 6; Rom. viii. 14 ; 1 S. John iii. 3.
[1] S. John xx. 21, and i. 16.   [2] Col. ii. 9.
[3] Is. vi. 1.
[4] S. John xii. 41. The "older tradition" means presumably the ancient interpretation of the Jews.
[5] Cf. Acts xxviii. 25, 26. The quotation is not verbal.
[6] Cf. Ps. lxxviii. 40.   [7] Heb. iii. 7.

haps not yet learnt how to count. For if the Father and the Son are not divided into duality, (for they are, according to the Lord's words, One, and not Two [8],) and if the Holy Ghost is also one, how can one added to one be divided into the number of three Gods? Is it not rather plain that no one can charge us with believing in the number of three Gods, without himself first maintaining in his own doctrine a pair of Gods? For it is by being added to two that the one completes the triad of Gods. But what room is there for the charge of tritheism against those by whom one God is worshipped, the God expressed by the Name of the Father and the Son and the Holy Ghost?

Let us however resume Eunomius' statement in its entirety. " Having come into being from the only God through the Only-begotten, this Spirit also—" What proof is there of the statement that " this Spirit also " is one of the things that were made by the Only-begotten? They will say of course that "all things were made by Him [9]," and that in the term " all things " " this Spirit also " is included. Our answer to them shall be this, All things were made by Him, that were made. Now the things that were made, as Paul tells us, were things visible and invisible, thrones, authorities, dominions, principalities, powers, and among those included under the head of thrones and powers are reckoned by Paul the Cherubim and Seraphim [1]: so far does the term " all things " extend. But of the Holy Spirit, as being above the nature of things that have come into being, Paul said not a word in his enumeration of existing things, not indicating to us by his words either His subordination or His coming into being ; but just as the prophet calls the Holy Spirit " good," and " right," and " guiding [2] " (indicating by the word " guiding " the power of control), even so the apostle ascribes independent authority to the dignity of the Spirit, when he affirms that He works all in all as He wills [3]. Again, the Lord makes manifest the Spirit's independent power and operation in His discourse with Nicodemus, when He says, " The Spirit breatheth where He willeth [4]." How is it then that Eunomius goes so far as to define that He also is one of the things that came into being by the Son, condemned to eternal subjection. For he describes Him as " once for all made subject," enthralling the guiding and governing Spirit in I know not what form of subjection. For this expression

of " subjection " has many significations in Holy Scripture, and is understood and used with many varieties of meaning. For the Psalmist says that even irrational nature is put in subjection [5], and brings under the same term those who are overcome in war [6], while the apostle bids servants to be in subjection to their own masters [7], and that those who are placed over the priesthood should have their children in subjection [8], as their disorderly conduct brings discredit upon their fathers, as in the case of the sons of Eli the priest. Again, he speaks of the subjection of all men to God, when we all, being united to one another by the faith, become one body of the Lord Who is in all, as the subjection of the Son to the Father, when the adoration paid to the Son by all things with one accord, by things in heaven, and things on earth, and things under the earth, redounds to the glory of the Father ; as Paul says elsewhere, "To Him every knee shall bow, of things in heaven, and things in earth, and things under the earth, and every tongue shall confess that Jesus Christ is Lord, to the glory of God the Father [9]." For when this takes place, the mighty wisdom of Paul affirms that the Son, Who is in all, is subject to the Father by virtue of the subjection of those in whom He is. What kind of " subjection once for all " Eunomius asserts of the Holy Spirit, it is thus impossible to learn from the phrase which he has thrown out,—whether he means the subjection of irrational creatures, or of captives, or of servants, or of children who are kept in order, or of those who are saved by subjection. For the subjection of men to God is salvation for those who are so made subject, according to the voice of the prophet, who says that his soul is subject to God, since of Him cometh salvation by subjection [1], so that subjection is the means of averting perdition. As therefore the help of the healing art is sought eagerly by the sick, so is subjection by those who are in need of salvation. But of what life does the Holy Spirit, that quickeneth all things, stand in need, that by subjection He should obtain salvation for Himself? Since then it is not on the strength of any Divine utterance that he asserts such an attribute of the Spirit, nor yet is it as a consequence of probable arguments that he has launched this blasphemy against the Holy Spirit, it must be plain at all events to sensible men that he vents his impiety against Him without any warrant whatsoever, unsupported as it is by any authority from Scripture or by any logical consequence.

---

[8] S. John x. 30.   [9] Cf. S. John i. 3.
[1] Cf. Col. i. 16 ; but the enumeration varies considerably.
[2] The last of these epithets is from Ps. li. 14 (πνεῦμα ἡγεμονικὸν, the " Spiritus principalis " of the Vulgate, the " free spirit " of the English version) ; the " right spirit " of ver. 12 being also applied by S. Gregory to the Holy Spirit, while the epithet " good " is from Ps cxlii. 10.
[3] Cf. 1 Cor. xii. 11.   [4] S. John iii. 8.

[5] Ps. viii. 7, 8.   [6] Ps. xlvii. 3.
[7] Tit. ii. 9.   [8] 1 Tim. iii. 4.
[9] Cf. Phil. ii. 10, 11, a passage which is apparently considered as explanatory of 1 Cor. xv. 28.
[1] Cf. Ps. lxii. 1 (LXX.).

§ 15. *Lastly he displays at length the folly of Eunomius, who at times speaks of the Holy Spirit as created, and as the fairest work of the Son, and at other times confesses, by the operations attributed to Him, that He is God, and thus ends the book.*

He goes on to add, "Neither on the same level with the Father, nor connumerated with the Father (for God over all is one and only Father), nor on an equality with the Son, for the Son is only-begotten, having none begotten with Him." Well, for my own part, if he had only added to his previous statement the remark that the Holy Ghost is not the Father of the Son, I should even then have thought it idle for him to linger over what no one ever doubted, and forbid people to form notions of Him which not even the most witless would entertain. But since he endeavours to establish his impiety by irrelevant and unconnected statements, imagining that by denying the Holy Spirit to be the Father of the Only-begotten he makes out that He is subject and subordinate, I therefore made mention of these words, as a proof of the folly of the man who imagines that he is demonstrating the Spirit to be subject to the Father on the ground that the Spirit is not Father of the Only-begotten. For what compels the conclusion, that if He be not Father, He must be subject? If it had been demonstrated that "Father" and "despot" were terms identical in meaning, it would no doubt have followed that, as absolute sovereignty was part of the conception of the Father, we should affirm that the Spirit is subject to Him Who surpassed Him in respect of authority. But if by "Father" is implied merely His relation to the Son, and no conception of absolute sovereignty or authority is involved by the use of the word, how does it follow, from the fact that the Spirit is not the Father of the Son, that the Spirit is subject to the Father? "Nor on an equality with the Son," he says. How comes he to say this? for to be, and to be unchangeable, and to admit no evil whatsoever, and to remain unalterably in that which is good, all this shows no variation in the case of the Son and of the Spirit. For the incorruptible nature of the Spirit is remote from corruption equally with that of the Son, and in the Spirit, just as in the Son, His essential goodness is absolutely apart from its contrary, and in both alike their perfection in every good stands in need of no addition. Now the inspired Scripture teaches us to affirm all these attributes of the Spirit, when it predicates of the Spirit the terms "good," and "wise," and "incorruptible," and "immortal," and all such lofty conceptions and names as are properly applied to Godhead. If then He is

inferior in none of these respects, by what means does Eunomius determine the inequality of the Son and the Spirit? "For the Son is," he tells us, "Only-begotten, having no brother begotten with Him." Well, the point, that we are not to understand the "Only-begotten" to have brethren, we have already discussed in our comments upon the phrase "first-born of all creation [2]." But we ought not to leave unexamined the sense that Eunomius now unfairly attaches to the term. For while the doctrine of the Church declares that in the Father, the Son, and the Holy Ghost there is one power, and goodness, and essence, and glory, and the like, saving the difference of the Persons, this man, when he wishes to make the essence of the Only-begotten common to the creation, calls Him "the first-born of all creation" in respect of His pre-temporal existence, declaring by this mode of expression that all conceivable objects in creation are in brotherhood with the Lord; for assuredly the first-born is not the first-born of those otherwise begotten, but of those begotten like Himself [3]. But when he is bent upon severing the Spirit from union with the Son, he calls Him "Only-begotten, not having any brother begotten with Him," not with the object of conceiving of Him as without brethren, but that by the means of this assertion he may establish touching the Spirit His essential alienation from the Son. It is true that we learn from Holy Scripture not to speak of the Holy Ghost as brother of the Son: but that we are not to say that the Holy Ghost is homogeneous [4] with the Son, is nowhere shown in the divine Scriptures. For if there does reside in the Father and the Son a life-giving power, it is ascribed also to the Holy Spirit, according to the words of the Gospel. If one may discern alike in Father, Son, and Holy Spirit the properties of being incorruptible, immutable, of admitting no evil, of being good, right, guiding, of working all in all as He wills, and all the like attributes, how is it possible by identity in these respects to infer difference in kind? Accordingly the word of godliness agrees in affirming that we ought not to regard any kind of brotherhood as attaching to the Only-begotten; but to say that the Spirit is not homogeneous with the Son, the upright with the upright, the good with the good, the life-giving with the life-giving, this has been clearly demonstrated by logical inference to be a piece of heretical knavery. Why then is the majesty of the Spirit curtailed by such arguments as these? For there is nothing

---

[2] See above, § 8 of this book.
[3] Or, "not the first-born of beings of a different race, but of those of his own stock."
[4] ὁμογενῆ, "of the same stock": the word being the same which (when coupled with ἀδελφὸν) has been translated, in the passages preceding, by "begotten with."

which can be the cause of producing in him deviation by excess or defect from conceptions such as befit the Godhead, nor, since all these are by Holy Scripture predicated equally of the Son and of the Holy Spirit, can he inform us wherein he discerns inequality to exist. But he launches his blasphemy against the Holy Ghost in its naked form, ill-prepared and unsupported by any consecutive argument. "Nor yet ranked," he says, "with any other: for He has gone above [5] all the creatures that came into being by the instrumentality of the Son in mode of being, and nature, and glory, and knowledge, as the first and noblest work of the Only-begotten, the greatest and most glorious." I will leave, however, to others the task of ridiculing the bad taste and surplusage of his style, thinking as I do that it is unseemly for the gray hairs of age, when dealing with the argument before us, to make vulgarity of expression an objection against one who is guilty of impiety. I will just add to my investigation this remark. If the Spirit has "gone above" all the creations of the Son, (for I will use his own un-grammatical and senseless phrase, or rather, to make things clearer, I will present his idea in my own language) if he transcends all things wrought by the Son, the Holy Spirit cannot be ranked with the rest of the creation; and if, as Eunomius says, he surpasses them by virtue of priority of birth, he must needs confess, in the case of the rest of creation, that the objects which are first in order of production are more to be esteemed than those which come after them. Now the creation of the irrational animals was prior to that of man. Accordingly he will of course declare that the irrational nature is more honourable than rational exist-ence. So too, according to the argument of Eunomius, Cain will be proved superior to Abel, in that he was before him in time of birth, and so the stars will be shown to be lower and of less excellence than all the things that grow out of the earth; for these last sprang from the earth on the third day, and all the stars are recorded by Moses to have been created on the fourth. Well, surely no one is such a simpleton as to infer that the grass of the earth is more to be esteemed than the marvels of the sky, on the ground of its precedence in time, or to award the meed to Cain over Abel, or to place below the irrational animals man who came into being later than they. So there is no sense in our author's con-tention that the nature of the Holy Spirit is superior to that of the creatures that came into being subsequently, on the ground that He

came into being before they did. And now let us see what he who separates Him from fellow-ship with the Son is prepared to concede to the glory of the Spirit: "For he too," he says, "being one, and first and alone, and surpassing all the creations of the Son in essence and dignity of nature, accomplishing every operation and all teaching according to the good pleasure of the Son, being sent by Him, and receiving from Him, and declaring to those who are instructed, and guiding into truth." He speaks of the Holy Ghost as "accomplishing every operation and all teaching." What operation? Does he mean that which the Father and the Son execute, ac-cording to the word of the Lord Himself Who " hitherto worketh [6]" man's salvation, or does he mean some other? For if His work is that named, He has assuredly the same power and nature as Him Who works it, and in such an one difference of kind from Deity can have no place. For just as, if anything should perform the functions of fire, shining and warming in precisely the same way, it is itself certainly fire, so if the Spirit does the works of the Father, He must assuredly be acknowledged to be of the same nature with Him. If on the other hand He operates something else than our salvation, and displays His operation in a con-trary direction, He will thereby be proved to be of a different nature and essence. But Eunomius' statement itself bears witness that the Spirit quickeneth in like manner with the Father and the Son. Accordingly, from the identity of operations it results assuredly that the Spirit is not alien from the nature of the Father and the Son. And to the statement that the Spirit accomplishes the operation and teaching of the Father according to the good pleasure of the Son we assent. For the com-munity of nature gives us warrant that the will of the Father, of the Son, and of the Holy Ghost is one, and thus, if the Holy Spirit wills that which seems good to the Son, the community of will clearly points to unity of essence. But he goes on, "being sent by Him, and receiving from Him, and declaring to those who are instructed, and guiding into truth." If he had not previously said what he has concerning the Spirit, the reader would surely have supposed that these words applied to some human teacher. For to receive a mission is the same thing as to be sent, and to have nothing of one's own, but to receive of the free favour of him who gives the mission, and to minister his words to those who are under instruction, and to be a guide into truth for those that are astray. All these things, which Eunomius is good enough to allow to the Holy Spirit, belong to the present pastors and teachers of the Church,—to be sent, to receive,

---

[5] ἀναβέβηκε : the word apparently is intended by Eunomius to have the force of "transcended"; Gregory, later on, criticizes its employment in this sense.

[6] S. John v. 17.

o announce, to teach, to suggest the truth. Now, as he had said above " He is one, and first, and alone, and surpassing all," had he but stopped there, he would have appeared as a defender of the doctrines of truth.　For He Who is indivisibly contemplated in the One is most truly One, and first Who is in the First, and alone Who is in the Only One.　For as the spirit of man that is in him, and the man himself, are but one man, so also the Spirit of God which is in Him, and God Himself, would properly be termed One God, and First and Only, being incapable of separation from Him in Whom He is.　But as things are, with his addition of his profane phrase, " surpassing all the creatures of the Son," he produces turbid confusion by assigning to Him Who " breatheth where He willeth [7]," and　" worketh all in all [8]," a mere superiority in comparison with the rest of created things.

Let us now see further what he adds to this : ' sanctifying the saints."　If any one says this also of the Father and of the Son, he will speak truly.　For those in whom the Holy One dwells, He makes holy, even as the Good One makes men good.　And the Father, the Son, and the Holy Ghost are holy and good, as has been shown. "Acting as a guide to those who approach the mystery."　This may well be said of Apollos who watered what Paul planted. For the Apostle plants by his guidance [9], and Apollos, when he baptizes, waters by Sacramental regeneration, bringing to the mystery those who were instructed by Paul.　Thus he places on a level with Apollos that Spirit Who perfects men through baptism. "Distributing every gift." With this we too agree ; for everything that is good is a portion of the gifts of the Holy Spirit. " Co-operating with the faithful for the understanding and contemplation of things appointed." As he does not add by whom they are appointed, he leaves his meaning doubtful, whether it is correct or the reverse.　But we will by a slight addition advance his statement so as to make it consistent with godliness. For since, whether it be the word of wisdom, or the word of knowledge, or faith, or help, or government, or aught else that is enumerated in the lists of saving gifts, " all these worketh that one and the self-same Spirit, dividing to every man severally as He will [1]," we therefore do not reject the statement of Eunomius when he says that the Spirit " co-operates with the faithful for understanding and contemplation of things appointed " by Him, because by Him all good teachings are appointed for us. "Sounding an accompaniment to those who pray."

It would be foolish seriously to examine the meaning of this expression, of which the ludicrous and meaningless character is at once manifest to all.　For who is so demented and beside himself as to wait for us to tell him that the Holy Spirit is not a bell nor an empty cask sounding an accompaniment and made to ring by the voice of him who prays as it were by a blow? "Leading us to that which is expedient for us."　This the Father and the Son likewise do : for " He leadeth Joseph like a sheep [2]," and, " led His people like sheep [3]," and, " the good Spirit leadeth us in a land of righteousness [4]." "Strengthening us to godliness."　To strengthen man to godliness David says is the work of God ; " For Thou art my strength and my refuge [5]," says the Psalmist, and " the Lord is the strength of His people [6]," and, " He shall give strength and power unto His people [7]." If then the expressions of Eunomius are meant in accordance with the mind of the Psalmist, they are a testimony to the Divinity of the Holy Ghost : but if they are opposed to the word of prophecy, then by this very fact a charge of blasphemy lies against Eunomius, because he sets up his own opinions in opposition to the holy prophets.　Next he says, "Lightening souls with the light of knowledge."　This grace also the doctrine of godliness ascribes alike to the Father, to the Son, and to the Holy Ghost. For He is called a light by David [8], and from thence the light of knowledge shines in them who are enlightened.　In like manner also the cleansing of our thoughts of which the statement speaks is proper to the power of the Lord. For it was " the brightness of the Father's glory, and the express image of His person," Who " purged our sins [9]."　Again, to banish devils, which Eunomius says is a property of the Spirit, this also the only-begotten God, Who said to the devil, " I charge thee [1]," ascribes to the power of the Spirit, when He says, " If I by the Spirit of God cast out devils [2]," so that the expulsion of devils is not destructive of the glory of the Spirit, but rather a demonstration of His divine and transcendent power. "Healing the sick," he says, " curing the infirm, comforting the afflicted, raising up those who stumble, recovering the distressed."　These are the words of those who think reverently of the Holy Ghost, for no one would ascribe the operation of any one of these effects to any one except to God.　If then heresy affirms that those things which it belongs to none save God alone to effect, are wrought by the power of the Spirit, we have in support of the truths for which we are contending the witness even of our adversaries.　How does the Psalmist seek his healing

---

[7] S. John iii. 8.　　　　　　[8] 1 Cor. xii. 6.
[9] If we read κατηχησέως for the καθηγησέως of Oehler's text we have a clearer sense, " the Apostle plants by his instruction."
[1] 1 Cor. xii. 11.

[2] Ps. lxxx. 1.　　[3] Ps. lxxvii. 20.　　[4] Cf. Ps. cxliii. 10.
[5] Cf. Ps. xxxi. 3.　[6] Ps. xxviii. 8.　　[7] Ps. lxviii. 35.
[8] Ps. xxvii. 1.　　　　　　　　　[9] Heb. i. 3.
[1] Cf. S. Mark ix. 25.　　　　　　[2] S. Matt. xii. 28.

from God, saying, " Have mercy upon me, O Lord, for I am weak; O Lord, heal me, for my bones are vexed [3]!" It is to God that Isaiah says, "The dew that is from Thee is healing unto them [4]." Again, prophetic language attests that the conversion of those in error is the work of God. For "they went astray in the wilderness in a thirsty land," says the Psalmist, and he adds, "So He led them forth by the right way, that they might go to the city where they dwelt [5]:" and, "when the Lord turned again the captivity of Sion [6]." In like manner also the comfort of the afflicted is ascribed to God, Paul thus speaking, "Blessed be God, even the Father of our Lord Jesus Christ, Who comforteth us in all our tribulation [7]." Again, the Psalmist says, speaking in the person of God, "Thou calledst upon Me in trouble and I delivered thee [8]." And the setting upright of those who stumble is innumerable times ascribed by Scripture to the power of the Lord: "Thou hast thrust sore at me that I might fall, but the Lord was my help [9]," and "Though he fall, he shall not be cast away, for the Lord upholdeth him with His hand [1]," and "The Lord helpeth them that are fallen [2]." And to the lovingkindness of God confessedly belongs the recovery of the distressed, if Eunomius means the same thing of which we learn in prophecy, as the Scripture says, "Thou laidest trouble upon our loins; Thou sufferedst men to ride over our heads; we went through fire and water, and Thou broughtest us out into a wealthy place [3]."

Thus far then the majesty of the Spirit is demonstrated by the evidence of our opponents, but in what follows the limpid waters of devotion are once more defiled by the mud of heresy. For he says of the Spirit that He "cheers on those who are contending": and this phrase involves him in the charge of extreme folly and impiety. For in the stadium some have the task of arranging the competitions between those who intend to show their athletic vigour; others, who surpass the rest in strength and skill, strive for the victory and strip to contend with one another, while the rest, taking sides in their good wishes with one or other of the competitors, according as they are severally disposed towards or interested in one athlete or another, cheer him on at the time of the engagement, and bid him guard against some hurt, or remember some trick of wrestling, or keep himself unthrown by the help of his art. Take note from what has been said to how low a rank Eunomius degrades the Holy Spirit. For while on the course there are some who arrange the contests, and others who settle whether the

contest is conducted according to rule, others who are actually engaged, and yet others who cheer on the competitors, who are acknowledged to be far inferior to the athletes themselves, Eunomius considers the Holy Spirit as one of the mob who look on, or as one of those who attend upon the athletes, seeing that He neither determines the contest nor awards the victory, nor contends with the adversary, but merely cheers without contributing at all to the victory. For He neither joins in the fray, nor does He implant the power to contend, but merely wishes that the athlete in whom He is interested may not come off second in the strife. And so Paul wrestles "against principalities, against powers, against the rulers of the darkness of this world, against spiritual wickedness in high places [4]," while the Spirit of power does not strengthen the combatants nor distribute to them His gifts, "dividing to every man severally as He will [5]," but His influence is limited to cheering on those who are engaged.

Again he says, "Emboldening the fainthearted." And here, while in accordance with his own method he follows his previous blasphemy against the Spirit, the truth for all that manifests itself, even through unfriendly lips. For to none other than to God does it belong to implant courage in the fearful, saying to the faint-hearted, "Fear not, for I am with thee, be not dismayed [6]," as says the Psalmist, "Yea though I walk through the valley of the shadow of death I will fear no evil, for Thou art with me [7]." Nay, the Lord Himself says to the fearful,—"Let not your heart be troubled, neither let it be afraid [8]," and, "Why are ye fearful, O ye of little faith [9]?" and, "Be of good cheer, it is I, be not afraid [1]," and again, "Be of good cheer: I have overcome the world [2]." Accordingly, even though this may not have been the intention of Eunomius, orthodoxy asserts itself by means even of the voice of an enemy. And the next sentence agrees with that which went before:—" Caring for all, and showing all concern and forethought." For in fact it belongs to God alone to care and to take thought for all, as the mighty David has expressed it, "I am poor and needy, but the Lord careth for me [3]." And if what remains seems to be resolved into empty words, with sound and without sense, let no one find fault, seeing that in most of what he says, so far as any sane meaning is concerned, he is feeble and untutored. For what on earth he means when he says, "for the onward leading of the better disposed and the guardianship of the more faithful," neither he himself, nor they who senselessly admire his follies, could possibly tell us.

3 Ps. vi. 3.   4 Is. xxvi. 19 (LXX.).   5 Ps. cviii. 4—7.
6 Ps. cxxvi. 1.   7 2 Cor. i. 3, 4.   8 Ps. lxxxi. 17.
9 Ps. cxviii. 13.   1 Ps. xxxvii. 24.
2 Ps. cxlvi. 8.   3 Ps. lxvi. 10, 11.

4 Eph. vi. 12.   5 1 Cor. xii. 11.   6 Is. xli. 10.
7 Ps. xxiii. 4.   8 S. John xiv. 27.   9 S. Matt. viii. 26.
1 S. Mark vi. 50.   2 S. John xvi. 33.   3 Ps. xl. 20.

BOOK III

§ 1. *This third book shows a third fall of Eunomius. as refuting himself, and sometimes saying that the Son is to be called Only-begotten in virtue of natural generation, and that Holy Scripture proves this from the first; at other times, that by reason of His being created He should not be called a Son, but a "product," or "creature."*

IF, when a man "strives lawfully [1]," he finds a limit to his struggle in the contest by his adversary's either refusing the struggle, and withdrawing of his own accord in favour of his conqueror from his effort for victory, or being thrown according to the rules of wrestling in three falls (whereby the glory of the crown is bestowed with all the splendour of proclamation upon him who has proved victorious in the umpire's judgment), then, since Eunomius, though he has been already twice thrown in our previous arguments, does not consent that truth should hold the tokens of her victory over falsehood, but yet a third time raises the dust against godly doctrine in his accustomed arena of falsehood with his composition, strengthening himself for his struggle on the side of deceit, our statement of truth must also be now called forth to put his falsehood to rout, placing its hopes in Him Who is the Giver and the Judge of victory, and at the same time deriving strength from the very unfairness of the adversaries' tricks of wrestling. For we are not ashamed to confess that we have prepared for our contest no weapon of argument sharpened by rhetoric, that we can bring forward to aid us in the fight with those arrayed against us, no cleverness or sharpness of dialectic, such as with inexperienced judges lays even on truth the suspicion of falsehood. One strength our reasoning against falsehood has—first the very Word Himself, Who is the might of our word,[2] and in the next place the rottenness of the arguments set against us, which is overthrown and falls by its own spontaneous action. Now in order that it may be made as clear as possible to all men, that the very efforts of Eunomius serve as means for his own overthrow to those who contend with him, I will set forth to my readers his phantom doctrine (for so I think that doctrine may be called which is quite outside the truth), and I would have you all, who are present at our struggle, and watch the encounter now taking place between my doctrine and that which is matched with it, to be just judges of the lawful striving of our arguments, that by your just award the reasoning of godliness may be proclaimed as victor to the whole theatre of the Church, having won undisputed victory over ungodliness, and being decorated, in virtue of the three falls of its enemy, with the unfading crown of them that are saved. Now this statement is set forth against the truth by way of preface to his third discourse, and this is the fashion of it :—" Preserving," he says, " natural order, and abiding by those things which are known to us from above, we do not refuse to speak of the Son, seeing He is begotten, even by the name of 'product of generation [3],' since the generated essence and [4] the appellation of Son make such a relation of words appropriate." I beg the reader to give his attention carefully to this point, that while he calls God both " begotten " and " Son," he refers the reason of such names to " natural order," and calls to witness to this conception the knowledge possessed from above: so that if anything should be found in the course of what follows contrary to the positions he has laid down, it is clear to all that he is overthrown by himself, refuted by his own arguments before ours are brought against him. And so let us consider his statement in the light of his own words. He confesses that the name of " Son " would by no means be properly applied to the Only-begotten God, did not " natural order," as he says, confirm the appellation. If, then, one were to withdraw the order of nature from the consideration of the designation of " Son," his use of this name, being deprived of its proper and natural significance, will be meaningless. And

---

[1] 2 Tim. ii. 5.
[2] The earlier editions here omit a long passage, which Oehler restores.

[3] γεννημα.
[4] Inserting καὶ, which does not appear here in Oehler's text, but is found in later quotations of the same passage : αὐτῆς is also found in the later citations.

moreover the fact that he says these statements are confirmed, in that they abide by the
knowledge possessed from above, is a strong
additional support to the orthodox view touching the designation of " Son," seeing that the
inspired teaching of the Scriptures, which comes
to us from above, confirms our argument on
these matters. If these things are so, and this
is a standard of truth that admits of no deception,
that these two concur—the "natural order," as he
says, and the testimony of the knowledge given
from above confirming the natural interpretation—it is clear, that to assert anything contrary to these, is nothing else than manifestly to
fight against the truth itself. Let us hear again
what this writer, who makes nature his instructor
in the matter of this name, and says that he
abides by the knowledge given to us from above
by the instruction of the saints, sets out at
length a little further on, after the passage I
have just quoted. For I will pretermit for the
time the continuous recital of what is set next
in order in his treatise, that the contradiction
in what he has written may not escape detection, being veiled by the reading of the intervening matter. " The same argument," he says,
" will apply also in the case of what is made and
created, as both the natural interpretation and
the mutual relation of the things, and also the
use of the saints, give us free authority for the
use of the formula : wherefore one would not be
wrong in treating the thing made as corresponding to the maker, and the thing created to the
creator." Of what product of making or of
creation does he speak, as having naturally the
relation expressed in its name towards its maker
and creator? If of those we contemplate in
the creation, visible and invisible (as Paul
recounts, when he says that by Him all things
were created, visible and invisible) [5], so that
this relative conjunction of names has a proper
and special application, that which is made
being set in relation to the maker, that which
is created to the creator,—if this is his meaning,
we agree with him. For in fact, since the
Lord is the Maker of angels, the angel is
assuredly a thing made by Him that made
him : and since the Lord is the Creator of the
world, clearly the world itself and all that is
therein are called the creature of Him that
created them. If however it is with this intention that he makes his interpretation of
"natural order," systematizing the appropriation
of relative terms with a view to their mutual
relation in verbal sense, even thus it would be
an extraordinary thing, seeing that every one is
aware of this, that he should leave his doctrinal
statement to draw out for us a system of

grammatical trivialities [6]. But if it is to the
Only-begotten God that he applies such phrases,
so as to say that He is a thing made by Him
that made Him, a creature of Him that created
Him, and to refer this terminology to "the
use of the saints," let him first of all show us in
his statement what saints he says there are who
declared the Maker of all things to be a product
and a creature, and whom he follows in this
audacity of phrase. The Church knows as
saints those whose hearts were divinely guided
by the Holy Spirit,—patriarchs, lawgivers,
prophets, evangelists, apostles. If any among
these is found to declare in his inspired words
that God over all, Who "upholds all things
with the word of His power," and grasps with
His hand all things that are, and by Himself
called the universe into being by the mere act
of His will, is a thing created and a product,
he will stand excused, as following, as he says,
the "use of the saints [7]" in proceeding to formulate such doctrines. But if the knowledge of
the Holy Scriptures is freely placed within the
reach of all, and nothing is forbidden to or hidden
from any of those who choose to share in the
divine instruction, how comes it that he endeavours to lead his hearers astray by his misrepresentation of the Scriptures, referring the
term "creature," applied to the Only-begotten,
to "the use of the saints"? For that by Him
all things were made, you may hear almost from
the whole of their holy utterance, from Moses and
the prophets and apostles who come after him,
whose particular expressions it would be tedious
here to set forth. Enough for our purpose, with
the others, and above the others, is the sublime
John, where in the preface to his discourse on
the Divinity of the Only-begotten he proclaims
aloud the fact that there is none of the things
that were made which was not made through
Him [8], a fact which is an incontestable and
positive proof of His being Lord of the creation,
not reckoned in the list of created things. For
if all things that are made exist by no other
but by Him (and John bears witness that
nothing among the things that are, throughout
the creation, was made without Him), who is
so blinded in understanding as not to see in
the Evangelist's proclamation the truth, that
He Who made all the creation is assuredly
something else besides the creation? For if
all that is numbered among the things that
were made has its being through Him, while
He Himself is "in the beginning," and is "with
God," being God, and Word, and Life, and
Light, and express Image, and Brightness, and

---

6 Oehler's punctuation here seems to admit of alteration.
7 Reading τῇ χρήσει τῶν ἁγίων for τῇ κρίσει τῶν ἁγίων. the reading of Oehler : the words are apparently a quotation from Eunomius,
from whom the phrase χρῆσις τῶν ἁγίων has already been cited.
8 Cf. S. John i. 3.

if none of the things that were made throughout creation is named by the same names—(not Word, not God, not Life, not Light, not Truth, not express Image, not Brightness, not any of the other names proper to the Deity is to be found employed of the creation)—then it is clear that He Who is these things is by nature something else besides the creation, which neither is nor is called any of these things. If, indeed, there existed in such phrases an identity of names between the creation and its Maker, he might perhaps be excused for making the name of " creation " also common to the thing created and to Him Who made it, on the ground of the community of the other names : but if the characteristics which are contemplated by means of the names, in the created and in the uncreated nature, are in no case reconcilable or common to both, how can the misrepresentation of that man fail to be manifest to all, who dares to apply the name of servitude to Him Who, as the Psalmist declares, " ruleth with His power for ever 9," and to bring Him Who, as the Apostle says, " in all things hath the preeminence 1," to a level with the servile nature, by means of the name and conception of " creation " ? For that all 2 the creation is in bondage the great Paul declares 3, — he who in the schools above the heavens was instructed in that knowledge which may not be spoken, learning these things in that place where every voice that conveys meaning by verbal utterance is still, and where unspoken meditation becomes the word of instruction, teaching to the purified heart by means of the silent illumination of the thoughts those truths which transcend speech. If then on the one hand Paul proclaims aloud, " the creation is in bondage," and on the other the Only-begotten God is truly Lord and God over all, and John bears witness to the fact that the whole creation of the things that were made is by Him, how can any one, who is in any sense whatever numbered among Christians, hold his peace when he sees Eunomius, by his inconsistent and inconsequent systematizing, degrading to the humble state of the creature, by means of an identity of name that tends to servitude, that power of Lordship which surpasses all rule and all authority ? And if he says that he has some of the saints who declared Him to be a slave, or created, or made, or any of these lowly and servile names, lo, here are the Scriptures. Let him, or some other on his behalf, produce to us one such phrase, and we will hold our peace. But if there is no such phrase (and there could never be found in those inspired Scriptures which we believe any such thought as to support this impiety), what need

is there to strive further upon points admitted with one who not only misrepresents the words of the saints, but even contends against his own definitions ? For if the " order of nature," as he himself admits, bears additional testimony to the Son's name by reason of His being begotten, and thus the correspondence of the name is according to the relation of the Begotten to the Begetter, how comes it that he wrests the significance of the word " Son " from its natural application, and changes the relation to " the thing made and its maker "—a relation which applies not only in the case of the elements of the universe, but might also be asserted of a gnat or an ant—that in so far as each of these is a thing made, the relation of its name to its maker is similarly equivalent ? The blasphemous nature of his doctrine is clear, not only from many other passages, but even from those quoted : and as for that " use of the saints " which he alleges that he follows in these expressions, it is clear that there is no such use at all.

§ 2. *He then once more excellently, appropriately, and clearly examines and expounds the passage, " The Lord created Me."*

Perhaps that passage in the Proverbs might be brought forward against us which the champions of heresy are wont to cite as a testimony that the Lord was created—the passage, " The Lord created me in the beginning of His ways, for His works 4." For because these words are spoken by Wisdom, and the Lord is called Wisdom by the great Paul 5, they allege this passage as though the Only-begotten God Himself, under the name of Wisdom, acknowledges that He was created by the Maker of all things. I imagine, however, that the godly sense of this utterance is clear to moderately attentive and painstaking persons, so that, in the case of those who are instructed in the dark sayings of the Proverbs, no injury is done to the doctrine of the faith. Yet I think it well briefly to discuss what is to be said on this subject, that when the intention of this passage is more clearly explained, the heretical doctrine may have no room for boldness of speech on the ground that it has evidence in the writing of the inspired author. It is universally admitted that the name of " proverb," in its scriptural use, is not applied with regard to the evident sense, but is used with a view to some hidden meaning, as the Gospel thus gives the name of " proverbs 6 " to dark and obscure sayings ; so that the " proverb," if one were to set forth the interpretation of the name by a

---

9 Ps. lxvi. 6 (LXX.).
2 Substituting πᾶσαν for the πᾶσιν of Oehler's text.
3 Rom. viii. 21.

1 Col. i. 18.

4 Prov. viii. 22 (LXX.). On this passage see also Book II. § 10.
5 1 Cor. i. 24.
6 E.g. S. John xvii. 25.

definition, is a form of speech which, by means of one set of ideas immediately presented, points to something else which is hidden, or a form of speech which does not point out the aim of the thought directly, but gives its instruction by an indirect signification. Now to this book such a name is especially attached as a title, and the force of the appellation is at once interpreted in the preface by the wise Solomon. For he does not call the sayings in this book "maxims," or "counsels," or "clear instruction," but "proverbs," and proceeds to add an explanation. What is the force of the signification of this word? "To know," he tells us, "wisdom and instruction [7]"; not setting before us the course of instruction in wisdom according to the method common in other kinds of learning; he bids a man, on the other hand [8], first to become wise by previous training, and then so to receive the instruction conveyed by proverb. For he tells us that there are "words of wisdom" which reveal their aim "by a turn [9]." For that which is not directly understood needs some turn for the apprehension of the thing concealed; and as Paul, when about to exchange the literal sense of the history for figurative contemplation, says that he will "change his voice [1]," so here the manifestation of the hidden meaning is called by Solomon a "turn of the saying," as if the beauty of the thoughts could not be perceived, unless one were to obtain a view of the revealed brightness of the thought by turning the apparent meaning of the saying round about, as happens with the plumage with which the peacock is decked behind. For in him, one who sees the back of his plumage quite despises it for its want of beauty and tint, as a mean sight; but if one were to turn it round and show him the other view of it, he then sees the varied painting of nature, the half-circle shining in the midst with its dye of purple, and the golden mist round the circle ringed round and glistening at its edge with its many rainbow hues. Since then there is no beauty in what is obvious in the saying (for "all the glory of the king's daughter is within [2]," shining with its hidden ornament in golden thoughts), Solomon of necessity suggests to the readers of this book "the turn of the saying," that thereby they may "understand a parable and a dark saying, words of the wise and riddles [3]." Now as this proverbial teaching embraces these elements, a reasonable man will not receive any passage cited from this book, be it never so clear and intelligible at first sight, without examination and inspection; for assuredly there is some

mystical contemplation underlying even those passages which seem manifest. And if the obvious passages of the work necessarily demand a somewhat minute scrutiny, how much more do those passages require it where even immediate apprehension presents to us much that is obscure and difficult?

Let us then begin our examination from the context of the passage in question, and see whether the reading of the neighbouring clauses gives any clear sense. The discourse describes Wisdom as uttering certain sayings in her own person. Every student knows what is said in the passage [4] where Wisdom makes counsel her dwelling-place, and calls to her knowledge and understanding, and says that she has as a possession strength and prudence (while she is herself called intelligence), and that she walks in the ways of righteousness and has her conversation in the ways of just judgement, and declares that by her kings reign, and princes write the decree of equity, and monarchs win possession of their own land. Now every one will see that the considerate reader will receive none of the phrases quoted without scrutiny according to the obvious sense. For if by her kings are advanced to their rule, and if from her monarchy derives its strength, it follows of necessity that Wisdom is displayed to us as a king-maker, and transfers to herself the blame of those who bear evil rule in their kingdoms. But we know of kings who in truth advance under the guidance of Wisdom to the rule that has no end—the poor in spirit, whose possession is the kingdom of heaven [5], as the Lord promises, Who is the Wisdom of the Gospel: and such also we recognize as the princes who bear rule over their passions, who are not enslaved by the dominion of sin, who inscribe the decree of equity upon their own life, as it were upon a tablet. Thus, too, that laudable despotism which changes, by the alliance of Wisdom, the democracy of the passions into the monarchy of reason, brings into bondage what were running unrestrained into mischievous liberty, I mean all carnal and earthly thoughts: for "the flesh lusteth against the Spirit [6]," and rebels against the government of the soul. Of this land, then, such a monarch wins possession, whereof he was, according to the first creation, appointed as ruler by the Word.

Seeing then that all reasonable men admit that these expressions are to be read in such a sense as this, rather than in that which appears in the words at first sight, it is consequently probable that the phrase we are discussing, being written in close connection with them, is not received by prudent men absolutely and

---

7 Prov. i. 2.
8 The hiatus in the Paris editions ends here.
9 Cf. Prov. i. 3 (LXX.).　　　　　1 Gal. iv. 20.
2 Ps. xlv. 13 (LXX.).　　　　　3 Prov. i. 6 (LXX.).

4 Compare with what follows Prov. viii. 12, sqq. (LXX.).
5 S. Matt. v. 3.　　　　　6 Gal. v. 17.

without examination. "If I declare to you," she says, "the things that happen day by day, I will remember to recount the things from everlasting: the Lord created me [7]." What, pray, has the slave of the literal text, who sits listening closely to the sound of the syllables, like the Jews, to say to this phrase? Does not the conjunction, "If I declare to you the things that happen day by day, the Lord created me," ring strangely in the ears of those who listen attentively? as though, if she did not declare the things that happen day by day, she will by consequence deny absolutely that she was created. For he who says, "If I declare, I was created," leaves you by his silence to understand, "I was not created, if I do not declare." "The Lord created me," she says, "in the beginning of His ways, for His works. He set me up from everlasting, in the beginning, before He made the earth, before He made the depths, before the springs of the waters came forth, before the mountains were settled, before all hills, He begetteth me [8]." What new order of the formation of a creature is this? First it is created, and after that it is set up, and then it is begotten. "The Lord made," she says, "lands, even uninhabited, and the inhabited extremes of the earth under heaven [9]." Of what Lord does she speak as the maker of land both uninhabited and inhabited? Of Him, surely, who made wisdom. For both the one saying and the other are uttered by the same person; both that which says, "the Lord created me," and that which adds, "the Lord made land, even uninhabited." Thus the Lord will be the maker equally of both, of Wisdom herself, and of the inhabited and uninhabited land. What then are we to make of the saying, "All things were made by Him, and without Him was not anything made [1]"? For if one and the same Lord creates both Wisdom (which they advise us to understand of the Son), and also the particular things which are included in the Creation, how does the sublime John speak truly, when he says that all things were made by Him? For this Scripture gives a contrary sound to that of the Gospel, in ascribing to the Creator of Wisdom the making of land uninhabited and inhabited. So, too, with all that follows [2]:—she speaks of a Throne of God set apart upon the winds, and says that the clouds above are made strong, and the fountains under the heaven sure; and the context contains many similar expressions, demanding in a marked degree that interpretation by a minute and clear-sighted intelligence, which is to be observed in the passages already quoted. What is the throne that is set apart upon the winds?

What is the security of the fountains under the heaven? How are the clouds above made strong? If any one should interpret the passage with reference to visible objects [3], he will find that the facts are at considerable variance with the words. For who knows not that the extreme parts of the earth under heaven, by excess in one direction or in the other, either by being too close to the sun's heat, or by being too far removed from it, are uninhabitable; some being excessively dry and parched, other parts superabounding in moisture, and chilled by frost, and that only so much is inhabited as is equally removed from the extreme of each of the two opposite conditions? But if it is the midst of the earth that is occupied by man, how does the proverb say that the extremes of the earth under heaven are inhabited? Again, what strength could one perceive in the clouds, that that passage may have a true sense, according to its apparent intention, which says that the clouds above have been made strong? For the nature of cloud is a sort of rather slight vapour diffused through the air, which, being light, by reason of its great subtilty, is borne on the breath of the air, and, when forced together by compression, falls down through the air that held it up, in the form of a heavy drop of rain. What then is the strength in these, which offer no resistance to the touch? For in the cloud you may discern the slight and easily dissolved character of air. Again, how is the Divine throne set apart on the winds that are by nature unstable? And as for her saying at first that she is "created," finally, that she is "begotten," and between these two utterances that she is "set up," what account of this could any one profess to give that would agree with the common and obvious sense? The point also on which a doubt was previously raised in our argument, the declaring, that is, of the things that happen day by day, and the remembering to recount the things from everlasting, is, as it were, a condition of Wisdom's assertion that she was created by God.

Thus, since it has been clearly shown by what has been said, that no part of this passage is such that its language should be received without examination and reflection, it may be well, perhaps, as with the rest, so not to interpret the text, "The Lord created me," according to that sense which immediately presents itself to us from the phrase, but to seek with all attention and care what is to be piously understood from the utterance. Now, to apprehend perfectly the sense of the passage before us, would seem to belong only to those who search out the depths by the aid of the Holy Spirit, and know how to speak in the Spirit the divine

---

7 Prov. viii. 21-22 (LXX.).   8 Prov. viii. 22 sqq. (LXX.).
9 Prov. viii. 26 (LXX.).   1 S. John i. 3.
2 Cf. Prov. viii. 27-8 (LXX.).

3 Or "according to the apparent sense."

mysteries : our account, however, will only busy itself with the passage in question so far as not to leave its drift entirely unconsidered. What, then, is our account? It is not, I think, possible that that wisdom which arises in any man from divine illumination should come alone, apart from the other gifts of the Spirit, but there must needs enter in therewith also the grace of prophecy. For if the apprehension of the truth of the things that are is the peculiar power of wisdom, and prophecy includes the clear knowledge of the things that are about to be, one would not be possessed of the gift of wisdom in perfection, if he did not further include in his knowledge, by the aid of prophecy, the future likewise. Now, since it is not mere human wisdom that is claimed for himself by Solomon, who says, "God hath taught me wisdom [4]," and who, where he says "all my words are spoken from God [5]," refers to God all that is spoken by himself, it might be well in this part of the Proverbs to trace out the prophecy that is mingled with his wisdom. But we say that in the earlier part of the book, where he says that " Wisdom has builded herself a house [6]," he refers darkly in these words to the preparation of the flesh of the Lord : for the true Wisdom did not dwell in another's building, but built for Itself that dwelling-place from the body of the Virgin. Here, however, he adds to his discourse [7] that which of both is made one—of the house, I mean, and of the Wisdom which built the house, that is to say, of the Humanity and of the Divinity that was commingled with man [8] ; and to each of these he applies suitable and fitting terms, as you may see to be the case also in the Gospels, where the discourse, proceeding as befits its subject, employs the more lofty and divine phraseology to indicate the Godhead, and that which is humble and lowly to indicate the Manhood. So we may see in this passage also Solomon prophetically moved, and delivering to us in its fulness the mystery of the Incarnation [9]. For we speak first of the eternal power and energy of Wisdom ; and here the evangelist, to a certain extent, agrees with him in his very words. For as the latter in his comprehensive [1] phrase proclaimed Him to be the cause and Maker of all things, so Solomon says that by Him were made those individual things which are included in the whole. For he tells us that God by Wisdom established the earth, and in understanding prepared the heavens, and all that follows these in order, keeping to the same sense : and that he might not seem to pass over without mention the gift of excellence in men, he again goes on to say, speaking in the person of Wisdom, the words we mentioned a little earlier ; I mean, " I made counsel my dwelling-place, and knowledge, and understanding [2]," and all that relates to instruction in intellect and knowledge.

After recounting these and the like matters, he proceeds to introduce also his teaching concerning the dispensation with regard to man, why the Word was made flesh. For seeing that it is clear to all that God Who is over all has in Himself nothing as a thing created or imported, not power nor wisdom, nor light, nor word, nor life, nor truth, nor any at all of those things which are contemplated in the fulness of the Divine bosom (all which things the Only-begotten God is, Who is in the bosom of the Father [3]), the name of " creation " could not properly be applied to any of those things which are contemplated in God, so that the Son Who is in the Father, or the Word Who is in the Beginning, or the Light Who is in the Light, or the Life Who is in the Life, or the Wisdom Who is in the Wisdom, should say, " the Lord created me." For if the Wisdom of God is created (and Christ is the Power of God and the Wisdom of God [4]), God, it would follow, has His Wisdom as a thing imported, receiving afterwards, as the result of making, something which He had not at first. But surely He Who is in the bosom of the Father does not permit us to conceive the bosom of the Father as ever void of Himself. He Who is in the beginning is surely not of the things which come to be in that bosom from without, but being the fulness of all good, He is conceived as being always in the Father, not waiting to arise in Him as the result of creation, so that the Father should not be conceived as at any time void of good, but He Who is conceived as being in the eternity of the Father's Godhead is always in Him, being Power, and Life, and Truth, and Wisdom, and the like. Accordingly the words " created me " do not proceed from the Divine and immortal nature, but from that which was commingled with it in the Incarnation from our created nature. How comes it then that the same, called wisdom, and understanding, and intelligence, establishes the earth, and prepares the heavens, and breaks up the deeps, and yet is here " created for the be-

---

[4] Prov. xxx. 3 (LXX. ch. xxiv.).

[5] Prov. xxxi. 1 (LXX. ch. xxiv.). The ordinary reading in the LXX. seems to be ὑπὸ θεοῦ, while Oehler retains in his text of Greg. Nyss. the ἀπὸ θεοῦ of the Paris editions.

[6] Prov. ix. 1, which seems to be spoken of as "earlier" in contrast, not with the main passage under examination, but with those just cited.

[7] If προστίθησι be the right reading, it would almost seem that Gregory had forgotten the order of the passages, and supposed Prov. viii. 22 to have been written *after* Prov. ix. 1. To read προτίθησι, (" presents to us") would get rid of this difficulty, but it may be that Gregory only intends to point out that the idea of the union of the two natures, from which the "communicatio idiomatum" results, is distinct from that of the preparation for the Nativity, not to insist upon the order in which, as he conceives, they are set forth in the book of Proverbs.

[8] ἀνακραθείσης τῷ ἀνθρώπῳ.　　　[9] τῆς οἰκονομίας.

[1] περιληπτῇ appears to be used as equivalent to περιληπτικῇ.

[2] Cf. Prov. viii. 12 (LXX.)

[3] S. John i. 18.　　　[4] 1 Cor. i. 24.

ginning of His works [5]"? Such a dispensation, he tells us, is not set forward without great cause. But since men, after receiving the commandment of the things we should observe, cast away by disobedience the grace of memory, and became forgetful, for this cause, "that I may declare to you the things that happen day by day for your salvation, and may put you in mind by recounting the things from everlasting, which you have forgotten (for it is no new gospel that I now proclaim, but I labour at your restoration to your first estate),—for this cause I was created, Who ever am, and need no creation in order to be; so that I am the beginning of ways for the works of God, that is for men. For the first way being destroyed, there must needs again be consecrated for the wanderers a new and living way [6], even I myself, Who am the way." And this view, that the sense of "created me" has reference to the Humanity, the divine apostle more clearly sets before us by his own words, when he charges us, "Put ye on the Lord Jesus Christ [7]," and also where (using the same word) he says, "Put on the new man which after God is created [8]." For if the garment of salvation is one, and that is Christ, one cannot say that "the new man, which after God is created," is any other than Christ, but it is clear that he who has "put on Christ" has "put on the new man which after God is created." For actually He alone is properly named "the new man," Who did not appear in the life of man by the known and ordinary ways of nature, but in His case alone creation, in a strange and special form, was instituted anew. For this reason he names the same Person, when regarding the wonderful manner of His birth [9], "the new man, which after God is created," and, when looking to the Divine nature, which was blended [1] in the creation of this "new man," he calls Him "Christ": so that the two names (I mean the name of "Christ" and the name of "the new man which after God is created") are applied to one and the same Person.

Since, then, Christ is Wisdom, let the intelligent reader consider our opponent's account of the matter, and our own, and judge which is the more pious, which better preserves in the text those conceptions which are befitting the Divine nature; whether that which declares the Creator and Lord of all to have been made, and places Him on a level with the creation that is in bondage, or that rather which looks to the Incarnation, and preserves the due proportion with regard to our conception alike of the Divinity and of the Humanity, bearing in mind that the great Paul testifies in favour of our

view, who sees in the "new man" creation, and in the true Wisdom the power of creation. And, further, the order of the passage agrees with this view of the doctrine it conveys. For if the "beginning of the ways" had not been created among us, the foundation of those ages for which we look would not have been laid; nor would the Lord have become for us "the Father of the age to come [2]," had not a Child been born to us, according to Isaiah, and His name been called, both all the other titles which the prophet gives Him, and withal "The Father of the age to come." Thus first there came to pass the mystery wrought in virginity, and the dispensation of the Passion, and then the wise master-builders of the Faith laid the foundation of the Faith: and this is Christ, the Father of the age to come, on Whom is built the life of the ages that have no end. And when this has come to pass, to the end that in each individual believer may be wrought the divine decrees of the Gospel law, and the varied gifts of the Holy Spirit—(all which the divine Scripture figuratively names, with a suitable significance, "mountains" and "hills," calling righteousness the "mountains" of God, and speaking of His judgments as "deeps [3]," and giving the name of "earth" to that which is sown by the Word and brings forth abundant fruit; or in that sense in which we are taught by David to understand peace by the "mountains," and righteousness by the "hills [4]"),—Wisdom is begotten in the faithful, and the saying is found true. For He Who is in those who have received Him, is not yet begotten in the unbelieving. Thus, that these things may be wrought in us, their Maker must be begotten in us. For if Wisdom is begotten in us, then in each of us is prepared by God both land, and land uninhabited,—the land, that which receives the sowing and the ploughing of the Word, the uninhabited land, the heart cleared of evil inhabitants,—and thus our dwelling will be upon the extreme parts of the earth. For since in the earth some is depth, and some is surface, when a man is not buried in the earth, or, as it were, dwelling in a cave by reason of thinking of things beneath (as is the life of those who live in sin, who "stick fast in the deep mire where no ground is [5]," whose life is truly a pit, as the Psalm says, "let not the pit shut her mouth upon me [6]")—if, I say, a man, when Wisdom is begotten in him, thinks of the things that are above, and touches the earth only so much as he needs must, such a man inhabits "the extreme parts of the earth under heaven," not plunging deep in earthly thought; with

5 The quotation is an inexact reproduction of Prov. viii. 22 (LXX.).
6 Cf. Heb. x. 20.
7 Rom. xiii. 14.
8 Eph. iv. 24.
9 γεννήσεως.
1 ἐγκραθεῖσαν.
2 Is. ix. 6 (LXX.). "The Everlasting Father" of the English Version.
3 Cf. Ps. xxxvi. 6.
4 Ps. lxxii. 3.
5 Ps. lxix. 2.
6 Ps. lxix. 16.

him Wisdom is present, as he prepares in himself heaven instead of earth : and when, by carrying out the precepts into act, he makes strong for himself the instruction of the clouds above, and, enclosing the great and widespread sea of wickedness, as it were with a beach, by his exact conversation, hinders the troubled water from proceeding forth from his mouth ; and if by the grace of instruction he be made to dwell among the fountains, pouring forth the stream of his discourse with sure caution, that he may not give to any man for drink the turbid fluid of destruction in place of pure water, and if he be lifted up above all earthly paths and become aerial in his life, advancing towards that spiritual life which he speaks of as "the winds," so that he is set apart to be a throne of Him Who is seated in him (as was Paul, separated for the Gospel to be a chosen vessel to bear the name of God, who, as it is elsewhere expressed, was made a throne, bearing Him that sat upon him)—when, I say, he is established in these and like ways, so that he who has already fully made up in himself the land inhabited by God, now rejoices in gladness that he is made the father, not of wild and senseless beasts, but of men (and these would be godlike thoughts, which are fashioned according to the Divine image, by faith in Him Who has been created and begotten, and set up in us ;—and faith, according to the words of Paul, is conceived as the foundation whereby wisdom is begotten in the faithful, and all the things that I have spoken of are wrought)—then, I say, the life of the man who has been thus established is truly blessed, for Wisdom is at all times in agreement with him, and rejoices with him who daily finds gladness in her alone. For the Lord rejoices in His saints, and there is joy in heaven over those who are being saved, and Christ, as the father, makes a feast for his rescued son. Though we have spoken hurriedly of these matters, let the careful man read the original text of the Holy Scripture, and fit its dark sayings to our reflections, testing whether it is not far better to consider that the meaning of these dark sayings has this reference, and not that which is attributed to it at first sight. For it is not possible that the theology of John should be esteemed true, which recites that all created things are the work of the Word, if in this passage He Who created Wisdom be believed to have made together with her all other things also. For in that case all things will not be by her, but she will herself be counted with the things that were made.

And that this is the reference of the enigmatical sayings is clearly revealed by the passage that follows, which says, "Now therefore hearken unto me, my son : and blessed is he that keepeth my ways [7]," meaning of course by "ways" the approaches to virtue, the beginning of which is the possession of Wisdom. Who, then, who looks to the divine Scripture, will not agree that the enemies of the truth are at once impious and slanderous?—impious, because, so far as in them lies, they degrade the unspeakable glory of the Only-begotten God, and unite it with the creation, striving to show that the Lord Whose power over all things is only-begotten, is one of the things that were made by Him : slanderous, because, though Scripture itself gives them no ground for such opinions, they arm themselves against piety as though they drew their evidence from that source. Now since they can by no means show any passage of the Holy Scriptures which leads us to look upon the pre-temporal glory of the Only-begotten God in conjunction with the subject creation, it is well, these points being proved, that the tokens of victory over falsehood should be adduced as testimony to the doctrine of godliness, and that sweeping aside these verbal systems of theirs by which they make the creature answer to the creator, and the thing made to the maker, we should confess, as the Gospel from heaven teaches us, the well-beloved Son—not a bastard, not a counterfeit ; but that, accepting with the name of Son all that naturally belongs to that name, we should say that He Who is of Very God is Very God, and that we should believe of Him all that we behold in the Father, because They are One, and in the one is conceived the other, not over-passing Him, not inferior to Him, not altered or subject to change in any Divine or excellent property.

§ 3. *He then shows, from the instance of Adam and Abel, and other examples, the absence of alienation of essence in the case of the "generate" and "ungenerate."*

Now seeing that Eunomius' conflict with himself has been made manifest, where he has been shown to contradict himself, at one time saying, "He ought to be called 'Son,' according to nature, because He is begotten," at another that, because He is created, He is no more called "Son," but a "product," I think it right that the careful and attentive reader, as it is not possible, when two statements are mutually at variance, that the truth should be found equally in both, should reject of the two that which is impious and blasphemous—that, I mean, with regard to the "creature" and the "product," and should assent to that only which is of orthodox tendency, which confesses that

---

[7] Prov. viii. 32 (not verbally agreeing with the LXX.).

the appellation of "Son" naturally attaches to the Only-begotten God: so that the word of truth would seem to be recommended even by the voice of its enemies.

I resume my discourse, however, taking up that point of his argument which we originally set aside. "We do not refuse," he says, "to call the Son, seeing He is generate, even by the name of 'product of generation [8],' since the generated essence itself, and the appellation of 'Son,' make such a relation of words appropriate." Meanwhile let the reader who is critically following the argument remember this, that in speaking of the "generated essence" in the case of the Only-begotten, he by consequence allows us to speak of the "ungenerate essence" in the case of the Father, so that neither absence of generation, nor generation, can any longer be supposed to constitute the essence, but the essence must be taken separately, and its being, or not being begotten, must be conceived separately by means of the peculiar attributes contemplated in it. Let us, however, consider more carefully his argument on this point. He says that an essence has been begotten, and that the name of this generated essence is "Son." Well, at this point our argument will convict out of our opponents on two grounds, first, of an attempt at knavery, secondly, of slackness in their attempt against ourselves. For he is playing the knave when he speaks of "generation of essence," in order to establish his opposition between the essences, when once they are divided in respect of a difference of nature between "generate" and "ungenerate": while the slackness of their attempt is shown by the very positions their knavery tries to establish. For he who says the essence is generate, clearly defines generation as being something else distinct from the essence, so that the significance of generation cannot be assigned to the word "essence." For he has not in this passage represented the matter as he often does, so as to say that generation is itself the essence, but acknowledges that the essence is generated, so that there is produced in his readers a distinct notion in the case of each word: for one conception arises in him who hears that it was generated, and another is called up by the name of "essence." Our argument may be made clearer by example. The Lord says in the Gospel [9] that a woman, when her travail is drawing near, is in sorrow, but afterwards rejoices in gladness because a man is born into the world. As then in this passage we derive from the Gospel two distinct conceptions,—one the birth which we conceive to be by way of generation, the other that which results from the birth (for the birth is not the man, but the man is by the birth),—so here too, when Eunomius confesses that the essence was generated, we learn by the latter word that the essence comes from something, and by the former we conceive that subject itself which has its real being from something. If then the signification of essence is one thing, and the word expressing generation suggests to us another conception, their clever contrivances are quite gone to ruin, like earthen vessels hurled one against the other, and mutually smashed to pieces. For it will no longer be possible for them, if they apply the opposition of "generate" and "ungenerate" to the essence of the Father and the Son, to apply at the same time to the things themselves the mutual conflict between these names [1]. For as it is confessed by Eunomius that the essence is generate (seeing that the example from the Gospel explains the meaning of such a phrase, where, when we hear that a man is generated, we do not conceive the man to be the same thing as his generation, but receive a separate conception in each of the two words), heresy will surely no longer be permitted to express by such words her doctrine of the difference of the essences. In order, however, that our account of these matters may be cleared up as far as possible, let us once more discuss the point in the following way. He Who framed the universe made the nature of man with all things in the beginning, and after Adam was made, He then appointed for men the law of generation one from another, saying, "Be fruitful and multiply [2]." Now while Abel came into existence by way of generation, what reasonable man would deny that, in the actual sense of human generation, Adam existed ungenerately? Yet the first man had in himself the complete definition of man's essential nature, and he who was generated of him was enrolled under the same essential name. But if the essence that was generated was made anything other than that which was not generated, the same essential name would not apply to both: for of those things whose essence is different, the essential name also is not the same. Since, then, the essential nature of Adam and of Abel is marked by the same characteristics, we must certainly agree that one essence is in both, and that the one and the other are exhibited in the same nature. For Adam and Abel are both one so far as the

8 γέννημα. This word, in what follows, is sometimes translated simply by the word "product," where it is not contrasted with ποίημα (the "product of making"), or where the argument depends especially upon its grammatical form (which indicates that the thing denoted is the *result of a process*), rather than upon the idea of the particular process.

9 Cf. S. John xvi. 21.

1 If, that is, they speak of the "generated essence" in contradistinction to "ungenerate essence" they are precluded from saying that the essence of the Son *is* that He is begotten, and that the essence of the Father *is* that He is ungenerate: that which constitutes the essence cannot be made an epithet of the essence.

2 Gen. i. 28.

definition of their nature is concerned, but are distinguished one from the other without confusion by the individual attributes observed in each of them. We cannot therefore properly say that Adam generated another essence besides himself, but rather that of himself he generated another self, with whom was produced the whole definition of the essence of him who generated him. What, then, we learn in the case of human nature by means of the inferential guidance afforded to us by the definition, this I think we ought to take for our guidance also to the pure apprehension of the Divine doctrines. For when we have shaken off from the Divine and exalted doctrines all carnal and material notions, we shall be most surely led by the remaining conception, when it is purged of such ideas, to the lofty and unapproachable heights. It is confessed even by our adversaries that God, Who is over all, both is and is called the Father of the Only-begotten, and they moreover give to the Only-begotten God, Who is of the Father, the name of "begotten," by reason of His being generated. Since then among men the word "father" has certain significances attaching to it, from which the pure nature is alien, it behoves a man to lay aside all material conceptions which enter in by association with the carnal significance of the word "father," and to form in the case of the God and Father a conception befitting the Divine nature, expressive only of the reality of the relationship. Since, therefore, in the notion of a human father there is included not only all that the flesh suggests to our thoughts, but a certain notion of interval is also undoubtedly conceived with the idea of human fatherhood, it would be well, in the case of the Divine generation, to reject, together with bodily pollution, the notion of interval also, that so what properly belongs to matter may be completely purged away, and the transcendent generation may be clear, not only from the idea of passion, but from that of interval. Now he who says that God is a Father will unite with the thought that God is, the further thought that He is something: for that which has its being from some beginning, certainly also derives from something the beginning of its being, whatever it is: but He in Whose case being had no beginning, has not His beginning from anything, even although we contemplate in Him some other attribute than simple existence. Well, God is a Father. It follows that He is what He is from eternity: for He did not become, but *is* a Father: for in God that which was, both is and will be. On the other hand, if He once was not anything, then He neither is nor will be that thing: for He is not believed to be the Father of a Being such that

it may be piously asserted that God once existed by Himself without that Being. For the Father is the Father of Life, and Truth, and Wisdom and Light, and Sanctification, and Power, and all else of a like kind that the Only-begotten is or is called. Thus when the adversaries allege that the Light "once was not," I know not to which the greater injury is done, whether to the Light, in that the Light is not, or to Him that has the Light, in that He has not the Light. So also with Life and Truth and Power, and all the other characters in which the Only-begotten fills the Father's bosom, being all things in His own fulness. For the absurdity will be equal either way, and the impiety against the Father will equal the blasphemy against the Son: for in saying that the Lord "once was not," you will not merely assert the non-existence of Power, but you will be saying that the Power of God, Who is the Father of the Power, "was not." Thus the assertion made by your doctrine that the Son "once was not," establishes nothing else than a destitution of all good in the case of the Father. See to what an end these wise men's acuteness leads, how by them the word of the Lord is made good, which says, "He that despiseth Me despiseth Him that sent Me [3]:" for by the very arguments by which they despise the existence at any time of the Only-begotten, they also dishonour the Father, stripping off by their doctrine from the Father's glory every good name and conception.

§ 4. *He thus shows the oneness of the Eternal Son with the Father, the identity of essence and the community of nature (wherein is a natural inquiry into the production of wine), and that the terms "Son" and "product" in the naming of the Only-begotten include a like idea of relationship.*

What has been said, therefore, has clearly exposed the slackness which is to be found in the knavery of our author, who, while he goes about to establish the opposition of the essence of the Only-begotten to that of the Father, by the method of calling the one "ungenerate," and the other "generate," stands convicted of playing the fool with his inconsistent arguments. For it was shown from his own words, first, that the name of "essence" means one thing, and that of "generation" another; and next, that there did not come into existence, with the Son, any new and different essence besides the essence of the Father, but that what the Father is as regards the definition of His nature, that also He is Who is of the Father, as the nature does not change into diversity in the Person of the Son,

---

3 S. Luke x. 16.

according to the truth of the argument displayed by our consideration of Adam and Abel. For as, in that instance, he that was not generated after a like sort was yet, so far as concerns the definition of essence, the same with him that was generated, and Abel's generation did not produce any change in the essence, so, in the case of these pure doctrines, the Only-begotten God did not, by His own generation, produce in Himself any change in the essence of Him Who is ungenerate, (coming forth, as the Gospel says, from the Father, and being in the Father,) but is, according to the simple and homely language of the creed we profess, "Light of Light, very God of very God," the one being all that the other is, save being that other. With regard, however, to the aim for the sake of which he carries on this system-making, I think there is no need for me at present to express any opinion, whether it is audacious and dangerous, or a thing allowable and free from danger, to transform the phrases which are employed to signify the Divine nature from one to another, and to call Him Who is generated by the name of "product of generation."

I let these matters pass, that my discourse may not busy itself too much in the strife against lesser points, and neglect the greater ; but I say that we ought carefully to consider the question whether the natural relation does introduce the use of these terms : for this surely Eunomius asserts, that with the affinity of the appellations there is also asserted an essential relationship. For he would not say, I presume, that the mere names themselves, apart from the sense of the things signified, have any mutual relation or affinity ; but all discern the relationship or diversity of the appellations by the meanings which the words express. If, therefore, he confesses that "the Son" has a natural relation with "the Father," let us leave the appellations, and consider the force that is found in their significations, whether in their affinity we discern diversity of essence, or that which is kindred and characteristic. To say that we find diversity is downright madness. For how does something without kinship or community "preserve order," connected and conformable, in the names, where "the generated essence itself," as he says, "and the appellation of 'Son,' make such a relation of words appropriate"? If, on the other hand, he should say that these appellations signify relationship, he will necessarily appear in the character of an advocate of the community of essence, and as maintaining the fact that by affinity of names is signified also the connection of subjects : and this he often does in his composition without being aware of it [4].

For, by the arguments wherewith he endeavours to destroy the truth, he is often himself unwittingly drawn into an advocacy of the very doctrines against which he is contending. Some such thing the history tells us concerning Saul, that once, when moved with wrath against the prophets, he was overcome by grace, and was found as one of the inspired, (the Spirit of prophecy willing, as I suppose, to instruct the apostate by means of himself,) whence the surprising nature of the event became a proverb in his after life, as the history records such an expression by way of wonder, "Is Saul also among the prophets [5]?"

At what point, then, does Eunomius assent to the truth? When he says that the Lord Himself, "being the Son of the living God, not being ashamed of His birth from the Virgin, often named Himself, in His own sayings, 'the Son of Man'"? For this phrase we also allege for proof of the community of essence, because the name of "Son" shows the community of nature to be equal in both cases. For as He is called the Son of Man by reason of the kindred of His flesh to her of whom He was born, so also He is conceived, surely, as the Son of God, by reason of the connection of His essence with that from which He has His existence, and this argument is the greatest weapon of the truth. For nothing so clearly points to Him Who is the "mediator between God and man [6]" (as the great Apostle called Him), as the name of "Son," equally applicable to either nature, Divine or Human. For the same Person is Son of God, and was made, in the Incarnation, Son of Man, that, by His communion with each, He might link together by Himself what were divided by nature. Now if, in becoming Son of Man, he were without participation in human nature, it would be logical to say that neither does He share in the Divine essence, though He is Son of God. But if the whole compound nature of man was in Him (for He was "in all points tempted like as we are, yet without sin [7]), it is surely necessary to believe that every property of the transcendent essence is also in Him, as the Word "Son" claims for Him both alike —the Human in the man, but in the God the Divine.

If then the appellations, as Eunomius says, indicate relationship, and the existence of relationship is observed in the things, not in the mere sound of the words (and by things I mean the things conceived in themselves, if it be not over-bold thus to speak of the Son and the Father), who would deny that the very champion of blasphemy has by his own action been dragged into the advocacy of orthodoxy, overthrowing by his own means his own arguments, and pro-

---

4 Oehler's punctuation is here slightly altered.

5 1 Sam. xix. 24.   6 1 Tim. ii. 5.   7 Heb. iv. 15.

claiming community of essence in the case of the Divine doctrines? For the argument that he unwillingly casts into the scale on the side of truth does not speak falsely as regards this point,— that He would not have been called Son if the natural conception of the names did not verify this calling. For as a bench is not called the son of the workman, and no sane man would say that the builder engendered the house, and we do not say that the vineyard is the "product [8]" of the vine-dresser, but call what a man makes his work, and him who is begotten of him the son of a man, (in order, I suppose, that the proper meaning might be attached by means of the names to the respective subjects,) so too, when we are taught that the Only-begotten is Son of God, we do not by this appellation understand a creature of God, but what the word "Son" in its signification really displays. And even though wine be named by Scripture the "product [9]" of the vine, not even so will our argument with regard to the orthodox doctrine suffer by this identity of name. For we do not call wine the "product" of the oak, nor the acorn the "product" of the vine, but we use the word only if there is some natural community between the "product" and that from which it comes. For the moisture in the vine, which is drawn out from the root through the stem by the pith, is, in its natural power, water: but, as it passes in orderly sequence along the ways of nature, and flows from the lowest to the highest, it changes to the quality of wine, a change to which the rays of the sun contribute in some degree, which by their warmth draw out the moisture from the depth to the shoots, and by a proper and suitable process of ripening make the moisture wine: so that, so far as their nature is concerned, there is no difference between the moisture that exists in the vine and the wine that is produced from it. For the one form of moisture comes from the other, and one could not say that the cause of wine is anything else than the moisture which naturally exists in the shoots. But, so far as moisture is concerned, the differences of quality produce no alteration, but are found when some peculiarity discerns the moisture which is in the form of wine from that which is in the shoots, one of the two forms being accompanied by astringency, or sweetness, or sourness, so that in substance the two are the same, but are distinguished by qualitative differences. As, therefore, when we hear from Scripture that the Only-begotten God is Son of man, we learn by the kindred expressed in the name His kinship with true man, so even, if the Son be called, in the adversaries' phrase, a "product," we none the less learn, even by this name, His kinship in essence with Him that

has "produced [1]" Him, by the fact that wine, which is called the "product" of the vine has been found not to be alien, as concerns the idea of moisture, from the natural power that resides in the vine. Indeed, if one were judiciously to examine the things that are said by our adversaries, they tend to our doctrine, and their sense cries out against their own fabrications, as they strive at all points to establish their "difference in essence." Yet it is by no means an easy matter to conjecture whence they were led to such conceptions. For if the appellation of "Son" does not merely signify "being from something," but by its signification presents to us specially, as Eunomius himself says, relationship in point of nature, and wine is not called the "product" of an oak, and those "products" or "generation of vipers [2]," of which the Gospel somewhere speaks, are snakes and not sheep, it is clear, that in the case of the Only-begotten also, the appellation of "Son" or of "product" would not convey the meaning of relationship to something of another kind: but even if, according to our adversaries' phrase, He is called a "product of generation," and the name of "Son," as they confess, has reference to nature, the Son is surely of the essence of Him Who has generated or "produced" Him, not of that of some other among the things which we contemplate as external to that nature. And if He is truly from Him, He is not alien from all that belongs to Him from Whom He is, as in the other cases too it was shown that all that has its existence from anything by way of generation is clearly of the same kind as that from whence it came.

§ 5. *He discusses the incomprehensibility of the Divine essence, and the saying to the woman of Samaria, "Ye worship ye know not what."*

Now if any one should ask for some interpretation, and description, and explanation of the Divine essence, we are not going to deny that in this kind of wisdom we are unlearned, acknowledging only so much as this, that it is not possible that that which is by nature infinite should be comprehended in any conception expressed by words. The fact that the Divine greatness has no limit is proclaimed by prophecy, which declares expressly that of His splendour, His glory, His holiness, "there is no end [3]:" and if His surroundings have no limit, much more is He Himself in His essence, whatever it may be, comprehended by no limitation in any way. If then interpretation by way of words and names implies by its meaning

---

[8] γέννημα.   [9] γέννημα. *E. g.* S. Matt. xxvi. 29.

[1] γεγεννηκότα: which, as answering to γέννημα, is here translated "produced" rather than "begotten."
[2] γεννήματα ἐχιδνῶν. *E. g.* S. Matt. iii. 7.
[3] Cf. Ps. cxlv. 3.

some sort of comprehension of the subject, and if, on the other hand, that which is unlimited cannot be comprehended, no one could reasonably blame us for ignorance, if we are not bold in respect of what none should venture upon. For by what name can I describe the incomprehensible? by what speech can I declare the unspeakable? Accordingly, since the Deity is too excellent and lofty to be expressed in words, we have learnt to honour in silence what transcends speech and thought: and if he who "thinketh more highly than he ought to think [4]," tramples upon this cautious speech of ours, making a jest of our ignorance of things incomprehensible, and recognizes a difference of unlikeness in that which is without figure, or limit, or size, or quantity (I mean in the Father, the Son, and the Holy Spirit), and brings forward to reproach our ignorance that phrase which is continually alleged by the disciples of deceit, "'Ye worship ye know not what [5],' if ye know not the essence of that which ye worship," we shall follow the advice of the prophet, and not fear the reproach of fools [6], nor be led by their reviling to talk boldly of things unspeakable, making that unpractised speaker Paul our teacher in the mysteries that transcend knowledge, who is so far from thinking that the Divine nature is within the reach of human perception, that he calls even the judgments of God "unsearchable," and His ways "past finding out [7]," and affirms that the things promised to them that love Him, for their good deeds done in this life, are above comprehension, so that it is not possible to behold them with the eye, nor to receive them by hearing, nor to contain them in the heart [8]. Learning this, therefore, from Paul, we boldly declare that, not only are the judgments of God too high for those who try to search them out, but that the ways also that lead to the knowledge of Him are even until now untrodden and impassable. For this is what we understand that the Apostle wishes to signify, when he calls the ways that lead to the incomprehensible "past finding out," showing by the phrase that that knowledge is unattainable by human calculations, and that no one ever yet set his understanding on such a path of reasoning, or showed any trace or sign of an approach, by way of perception, to the things incomprehensible.

Learning these things, then, from the lofty words of the Apostle, we argue, by the passage quoted, in this way:—If His judgments cannot be searched out, and His ways are not traced, and the promise of His good things transcends every representation that our conjectures can frame, by how much more is His actual Godhead

higher and loftier, in respect of being unspeakable and unapproachable, than those attributes which are conceived as accompanying it, whereof the divinely instructed Paul declares that there is no knowledge:—and by this means we confirm in ourselves the doctrine they deride, confessing ourselves inferior to them in the knowledge of those things which are beyond the range of knowledge, and declare that we really worship what we know. Now we know the loftiness of the glory of Him Whom we worship, by the very fact that we are not able by reasoning to comprehend in our thoughts the incomparable character of His greatness; and that saying of our Lord to the Samaritan woman, which is brought forward against us by our enemies, might more properly be addressed to them. For the words, "Ye worship ye know not what," the Lord speaks to the Samaritan woman, prejudiced as she was by corporeal ideas in her opinions concerning God: and to her the phrase well applies, because the Samaritans, thinking that they worship God, and at the same time supposing the Deity to be corporeally settled in place, adore Him in name only, worshipping something else, and not God. For nothing is Divine that is conceived as being circumscribed, but it belongs to the Godhead to be in all places, and to pervade all things, and not to be limited by anything: so that those who fight against Christ find the phrase they adduce against us turned into an accusation of themselves. For, as the Samaritans, supposing the Deity to be compassed round by some circumscription of place, were rebuked by the words they heard, "'Ye worship ye know not what,' and your service is profitless to you, for a God that is deemed to be settled in any place is no God,"—so one might well say to the new Samaritans, "In supposing the Deity to be limited by the absence of generation, as it were by some local limit, 'ye worship ye know not what,' doing service to Him indeed as God, but not knowing that the infinity of God exceeds all the significance and comprehension that names can furnish."

§ 6. *Thereafter he expounds the appellation of "Son," and of "product of generation," and very many varieties of "sons," of God, of men, of rams, of perdition, of light, and of day.*

But our discourse has diverged too far from the subject before us, in following out the questions which arise from time to time by way of inference. Let us therefore once more resume its sequence, as I imagine that the phrase under examination has been sufficiently shown, by what we have said, to be contradictory not only to the truth, but also to itself. For if,

---

[4] Rom. xii. 3. [5] S. John iv. 22. [6] Cf. Is. li. 7.
[7] Rom. xi. 33. [8] Cf. 1 Cor. ii 9.

according to their view, the natural relation to the Father is established by the appellation of " the Son," and so with that of the " product of generation " to Him Who has begotten Him (as these men's wisdom falsely models the terms significant of the Divine nature into a verbal arrangement, according to some grammatical frivolity), no one could longer doubt that the mutual relation of the names which is established by nature is a proof of their kindred, or rather of their identity of essence. But let not our discourse merely turn about our adversaries' words, that the orthodox doctrine may not seem to gain the victory only by the weakness of those who fight against it, but appear to have an abundant supply of strength in itself. Let the adverse argument, therefore, be strengthened as much as may be by us ourselves with more energetic advocacy, that the superiority of our force may be recognized with full confidence, as we bring to the unerring test of truth those arguments also which our adversaries have omitted. He who contends on behalf of our adversaries will perhaps say that the name of " Son," or " product of generation," does not by any means establish the fact of kindred in nature. For in Scripture the term " child of wrath [9] " is used, and " son of perdition [1]," and " product of a viper [2] ; " and in such names surely no community of nature is apparent. For Judas, who is called " the son of perdition," is not in his substance the same with perdition, according to what we understand by the word [3]. For the signification of the " man " in Judas is one thing, and that of " perdition " is another. And the argument may be established equally from an opposite instance. For those who are called in a certain sense " children of light," and " children of the day [4]," are not the same with light and day in respect of the definition of their nature, and the stones are made Abraham's children [5] when they claim their kindred with him by faith and works; and those who are " led by the Spirit of God," as the Apostle says, are called " Sons of God [6]," without being the same with God in respect of nature ; and one may collect many such instances from the inspired Scripture, by means of which deceit, like some image decked with the testimonies of Scripture, masquerades in the likeness of truth.

Well, what do we say to this? The divine Scripture knows how to use the word " Son " in both senses, so that in some cases such an appellation is derived from nature, in others it is adventitious and artificial. For when it speaks of " sons of men," or " sons of rams [7],"

it marks the essential relation of that which is begotten to that from which it has its being : but when it speaks of " sons of power," or " children of God," it presents to us that kinship which is the result of choice. And, moreover, in the opposite sense, too, the same persons are called " sons of Eli," and " sons of Belial [8]," the appellation of " sons " being easily adapted to either idea. For when they are called " sons of Eli," they are declared to have natural relationship to him, but in being called " sons of Belial," they are reproved for the wickedness of their choice, as no longer emulating their father in their life, but addicting their own purpose to sin. In the case, then, of this lower nature of ours, and of the things with which we are concerned, by reason of human nature being equally inclined to either side (I mean, to vice and to virtue), it is in our power to become sons either of night or of day, while our nature yet remains, so far as the chief part of it is concerned, within its proper limits. For neither is he who by sin becomes a child of wrath alienated from his human generation, nor does he who by choice addicts himself to good reject his human origin by the refinement of his habits, but, while their nature in each case remains the same, the differences of their purpose assume the names of their relationship, according as they become either children of God by virtue, or of the opposite by vice.

But how does Eunomius, in the case of the divine doctrines at least—he who " preserves the natural order " (for I will use our author's very words), " and abides by those things which are known to us from the beginning, and does not refuse to call Him that is begotten by the name of ' product of generation,' since the generated essence itself " (as he says) " and the appellation of ' Son ' makes such a relation of words appropriate ",—how does he alienate the Begotten from essential kindred with Him that begat Him ? For in the case of those who are called " sons " or " products " by way of reproach, or again where some praise accompanies such names, we cannot say that any one is called " a child of wrath," being at the same time actually begotten by wrath ; nor again had any one the day for his mother, in a corporeal sense, that he should be called its son ; but it is the difference of their will which gives occasion for names of such relationship. Here, however, Eunomius says, " we do not refuse to call the Son, seeing He is begotten, by the name of ' product of generation,' since the generated essence," he tells us, " and the appellation of ' Son,' makes such a relation of words appropriate." If, then, he confesses that such a relation of words is

9 Cf. Eph. ii. 3.　　1 S. John xvii. 12.　　2 Cf. S. Matt. iii. 7.
? Reading κατὰ τὸ νοούμενον, for κατὰ τὸν νοούμενον as the words stand in the text of Oehler, who cites no MSS. in favour of the change which he has made.
4 Cf. 1 Thess. v. 5.　　5 Cf. S. Matt. iii. 9.
6 Rom. viii. 14.　　7 Ps. xxix. 1 (LXX.).

8 1 Sam. ii. 12. The phrase is υἱοὶ λοιμοί, or "pestilent sons," as in the LXX. Gregory's argument would seem to require the reading υἱοὶ λοιμοῦ.

made appropriate by the fact that the Son is really a "product of generation," how is it opportune to assign such a rationale of names, alike to those which are used inexactly by way of metaphor, and to those where the natural relation, as Eunomius tells us, makes such a use of names appropriate? Surely such an account is true only in the case of those whose nature is a border-land between virtue and vice, where one often shares in turn opposite classes of names, becoming a child, now of light, then again of darkness, by reason of affinity to the good or to its opposite. But where contraries have no place, one could no longer say that the word "Son" is applied metaphorically, in like manner as in the case of those who by choice appropriate the title to themselves. For one could not arrive at this view, that, as a man casting off the works of darkness becomes, by his decent life, a child of light, so too the Only-begotten God received the more honourable name as the result of a change from the inferior state. For one who is a man becomes a son of God by being joined to Christ by spiritual generation : but He Who by Himself makes the man to be a son of God, does not need another Son to bestow on Him the adoption of a son, but has the name also of that which He is by nature. A man himself changes himself, exchanging the old man for the new ; but to what shall God be changed, so that He may receive what He has not? A man puts off himself, and puts on the Divine nature ; but what does He put off, or in what does He array Himself, Who is always the same? A man becomes a son of God, receiving what he has not, and laying aside what he has ; but He Who has never been in the state of vice has neither anything to receive nor anything to relinquish. Again, the man may be on the one hand truly called some one's son, when one speaks with reference to his nature ; and, on the other hand, he may be so called inexactly, when the choice of his life imposes the name. But God, being One Good, in a single and uncompounded nature, looks ever the same way, and is never changed by the impulse of choice, but always wishes what He is, and is, assuredly, what He wishes : so that He is in both respects properly and truly called Son of God, since His nature contains the good, and His choice also is never severed from that which is more excellent, so that this word is employed, without inexactness, as His name. Thus there is no room for these arguments (which, in the person of our adversaries, we have been opposing to ourselves), to be brought forward by our adversaries as a demurrer to the affinity in respect of nature.

§ 7. *Then he ends the book with an exposition of the Divine and Human names of the Only-begotten, and a discussion of the terms "generate" and "ungenerate."*

But as, I know not how or why, they hate and abhor the truth, they give Him indeed the name of "Son," but in order to avoid the testimony which this word would give to the community of essence, they separate the word from the sense included in the name, and concede to the Only-begotten the name of "Son" as an empty thing, vouchsafing to Him only the mere sound of the word. That what I say is true, and that I am not taking a false aim at the adversaries' mark, may be clearly learnt from the actual attacks they make upon the truth. Such are those arguments which are brought forward by them to establish their blasphemy, that we are taught by the divine Scriptures many names of the Only-begotten— a stone, an axe, a rock, a foundation, bread, a vine, a door, a way, a shepherd, a fountain, a tree, resurrection, a teacher, light, and many such names. But we may not piously use any of these names of the Lord, understanding it according to its immediate sense. For surely it would be a most absurd thing to think that what is incorporeal and immaterial, simple, and without figure, should be fashioned according to the apparent senses of these names, whatever they may be, so that when we hear of an axe we should think of a particular figure of iron, or when we hear of light, of the light in the sky, or of a vine, of that which grows by the planting of shoots, or of any one of the other names, as its ordinary use suggests to us to think ; but we transfer the sense of these names to what better becomes the Divine nature, and form some other conception, and if we do designate Him thus, it is not as being any of these things, according to the definition of His nature, but as being called these things while He is conceived by means of the names employed as something else than the things themselves. But if such names are indeed truly predicated of the Only-begotten God, without including the declaration of His nature, they say that, as a consequence, neither should we admit the signification of "Son," as it is understood according to the prevailing use, as expressive of nature, but should find some sense of this word also, different from that which is ordinary and obvious. These, and others like these, are their philosophical arguments to establish that the Son is not what He is and is called. Our argument was hastening to a different goal, namely to show that Eunomius' new discourse is false and inconsistent, and argues neither with the truth nor with itself. Since, however, the arguments which we employ to attack their doctrine are brought into the discussion as a sort of support for their blasphemy 9, it may be well first briefly to discusst his point, and then to proceed to the orderly examination of his writings.

What can we say, then, to such things without irrelevance? That while, as they say, the names which Scripture applies to the Only-begotten are many, we assert that none of the other names is closely connected with the reference to Him that begat Him. For we do not employ the name "Stone," or "Resurrection," or "Shepherd," or "Light," or any of the rest, as we do the name "Son of the Father," with a reference to the God of all. It is possible to make a twofold division of the signification of the Divine names, as it were by a scientific rule: for to one class belongs the indication of His lofty and unspeakable glory; the other class indicates the variety of the providential dispensation: so that, as we suppose, if that which received His benefits did not exist, neither would those words be applied with respect to them[1] which indicate His bounty. All those, on the other hand, that express the attributes of God, are applied suitably and properly to the Only-begotten God, apart from the objects of the dispensation. But that we may set forth this doctrine clearly, we will examine the names themselves. The Lord would not have been called a vine, save for the planting of those who are rooted in Him, nor a shepherd, had not the sheep of the house of Israel been lost, nor a physician, save for the sake of them that were sick, nor would He have received for Himself the rest of these names, had He not made the titles appropriate, in a manner advantageous with regard to those who were benefited by Him, by some action of His providence. What need is there to mention individual instances, and to lengthen our argument upon points that are acknowledged? On the other hand, He is certainly called "Son," and "Right Hand," and "Only-begotten," and "Word," and "Wisdom," and "Power," and all other such relative names, as being named together with the Father in a certain relative conjunction. For He is called the "Power *of God*," and the "Right Hand *of God*," and the "Wisdom *of God*," and the "Son and Only-begotten *of the Father*," and the "Word *with God*," and so of the rest. Thus, it follows from what we have stated, that in each of the names

we are to contemplate some suitable sense appropriate to the subject, so that we may not miss the right understanding of them, and go astray from the doctrine of godliness. As, then, we transfer each of the other terms to that sense in which they may be applied to God, and reject in their case the immediate sense, so as not to understand material light, or a trodden way, or the bread which is produced by husbandry, or the word that is expressed by speech, but, instead of these, all those thoughts which present to us the magnitude of the power of the Word of God,—so, if one were to reject the ordinary and natural sense of the word "Son," by which we learn that He is of the same essence as Him that begat Him, he will of course transfer the name to some more divine interpretation. For since the change to the more glorious meaning which has been made in each of the other terms has adapted them to set forth the Divine power, it surely follows that the significance of this name also should be transferred to what is loftier. But what more Divine sense could we find in the appellation of "Son," if we were to reject, according to our adversaries' view, the natural relation to Him that begat Him? I presume no one is so daring in impiety as to think that, in speech concerning the Divine nature, what is humble and mean is more appropriate than what is lofty and great. If they can discover, therefore, any sense of more exalted character than this, so that to be of the nature of the Father seems a thing unworthy to conceive of the Only-begotten, let them tell us whether they know, in their secret wisdom, anything more exalted than the nature of the Father, that, in raising the Only-begotten God to this level, they should lift Him also above His relation to the Father. But if the majesty of the Divine nature transcends all height, and excels every power that calls forth our wonder, what idea remains that can carry the meaning of the name "Son" to something greater still? Since it is acknowledged, therefore, that every significant phrase employed of the Only-begotten, even if the name be derived from the ordinary use of our lower life, is properly applied to Him with a difference of sense in the direction of greater majesty, and if it is shown that we can find no more noble conception of the title "Son" than that which presents to us the reality of His relationship to Him that begat Him, I think that we need spend no more time on this topic, as our argument has sufficiently shown that it is not proper to interpret the title of "Son" in like manner with the other names.

But we must bring back our enquiry once more to the book. It does not become the same persons "not to refuse" (for I will use

---

9 The meaning of this seems to be that the Anomoean party make the same charge of "inconsistency" against the orthodox, which Gregory makes against Eunomius, basing that charge on the fact that the title "Son" is not interpreted in the same figurative way as the other titles recited. Gregory accordingly proceeds to show why the name of "Son" stands on a different level from those titles, and is to be treated in a different way.

[1] ἐπ' αὐτῶν : perhaps "with reference to man." the plural being employed here to denote the race of men, spoken of in the preceding clause collectively as τὸ εὐεργετούμενον.

their own words) "to call Him that is generated a 'product of generation,' since both the generated essence itself and the appellation of Son make such a relation of words appropriate," and again to change the names which naturally belong to Him into metaphorical interpretations : so that one of two things has befallen them,—either their first attack has failed, and it is in vain that they fly to "natural order" to establish the necessity of calling Him that is generated a "product of generation"; or, if this argument holds good, they will find their second argument brought to nought by what they have already established. For the person who is called a "product of generation" because He is generated, cannot, for the very same reason, be possibly called a "product of making," or a "product of creation." For the sense of the several terms differs very widely, and one who uses his phrases advisedly ought to employ words with due regard to the subject, that we may not, by improperly interchanging the sense of our phrases, fall into any confusion of ideas. Hence we call that which is wrought out by a craft the work of the craftsman, and call him who is begotten by a man that man's son ; and no sane person would call the work a son, or the son a work ; for that is the language of one who confuses and obscures the true sense by an erroneous use of names. It follows that we must truly affirm of the Only-begotten one of these two things,—if He is a Son, that He is not to be called a "product of creation," and if He is created, that He is alien from the appellation of "Son [2]," just as heaven and sea and earth, and all individual things, being things created, do not assume the name of "Son." But since Eunomius bears witness that the Only-begotten God is begotten (and the evidence of enemies is of aditional value for establishing the truth), he surely testifies also, by saying that He is begotten, to the fact that He is not created. Enough, however, on these points : for though many arguments crowd upon us, we will be content, lest their number lead to disproportion, with those we have already adduced on the subject before us.

---

[2] Oehler's punctuation here seems faulty, and is accordingly not followed.

BOOK IV

§ 1. *The fourth book discusses the account of the nature of the "product of generation," and of the passionless generation of the Only-begotten, and the text, "In the beginning was the Word," and the birth of the Virgin.*

It is, perhaps, time to examine in our discourse that account of the nature of the "product of generation" which is the subject of his ridiculous philosophizing. He says, then (I will repeat word for word his beautifully composed argument against the truth):—" Who is so indifferent and inattentive to the nature of things as not to know, that of all bodies which are on earth, in their generating and being generated, in their activity and passivity, those which generate are found on examination to communicate their own essence, and those which are generated naturally receive the same, inasmuch as the material cause and the supply which flows in from without are common to both ; and the things begotten are generated by passion, and those which beget, naturally have an action which is not pure, by reason of their nature being linked with passions of all kinds?" See in what fitting style he discusses in his speculation the pre-temporal generation of the Word of God that was in the beginning! he who closely examines the nature of things, bodies on the earth, and material causes, and passion of things generating and generated, and all the rest of it,—at which any man of understanding would blush, even were it said of ourselves, if it were our nature, subject as it is to passion, which is thus exposed to scorn by his words. Yet such is our author's brilliant enquiry into nature with regard to the Only-begotten God. Let us lay aside complaints, however, (for what will sighing do to help us to overthrow the malice of our enemy?) and make generally known, as best we may, the sense of what we have quoted—concerning what sort of " product" the speculation was proposed,—that which exists according to the flesh, or that which is to be contemplated in the Only-begotten God.

As the speculation is two-fold, concerning that life which is Divine, simple, and immaterial, and concerning that existence which is material and subject to passion, and as the word "generation" is used of both, we must needs make our distinction sharp and clear, lest the ambiguity of the term " generation " should in any way pervert the truth. Since, then, the entrance into being through the flesh is material, and is promoted by passion, while that which is bodiless, impalpable, without form, and free from any material commixture, is alien from every condition that admits of passion, it is proper to consider about what sort of generation we are enquiring—that which is pure and Divine, or that which is subject to passion and pollution. Now, no one, I suppose, would deny that with regard to the Only-begotten God, it is pre-temporal existence that is proposed for the consideration [3] of Eunomius' discourse. Why, then, does he linger over this account of corporeal nature, defiling our nature by the loathsome presentment of his argument, and setting forth openly the passions that gather round human generation, while he deserts the subject. set before him? for it was not about this animal generation, that is accomplished by means of the flesh, that we had any need to learn. Who is so foolish, when he looks on himself, and considers human nature in himself, as to seek another interpreter of his own nature, and to need to be told all the unavoidable passions which are included in the thought of bodily generation—that he who begets is affected in one way, that which is begotten in another —so that the man should learn from this instruction that he himself begets by means of passion, and that passion was the beginning of his own generation? For it is all the same whether these things are passed over or spoken, and whether one publishes these secrets at length, or keeps hidden in silence things that should be left unsaid, we are not ignorant of the fact that our nature progresses by way of passion. But what we are seeking is that a clear account should be given of the exalted and unspeakable existence of the Only-begotten, whereby He is believed to be of the Father.

Now, while this is the enquiry set before him, our new theologian enriches his discourse with

---

[3] Reading, with the older editions, τῇ θεωρίᾳ. Oehler substitutes τὴν θεωρίαν (a variation which seems to give no good sense, unless θεωρία be translated as " subject of contemplation "), but alleges no MS. authority for the change.

"flowing," and "passion," and "material cause," and some "action" which "is not pure" from pollution, and all other phrases of this kind [4]. I know not under what influence it is that he who says, in the superiority of his wisdom, that nothing incomprehensible is left beyond his own knowledge, and promises to explain the unspeakable generation of the Son, leaves the question before him, and plunges like an eel into the slimy mud of his arguments, after the fashion of that Nicodemus who came by night, who, when our Lord was teaching him of the birth from above, rushed in thought to the hollow of the womb, and raised a doubt how one could enter a second time into the womb, with the words, "How can these things be?[5]" thinking that he would prove the spiritual birth impossible, by the fact that an old man could not again be born within his mother's bowels. But the Lord corrects his erroneous idea, saying that the properties of the flesh and the spirit are distinct. Let Eunomius also, if he will, correct himself by the like reflection. For he who ponders on the truth ought, I imagine, to contemplate his subject according to its own properties, not to slander the immaterial by a charge against things material. For if a man, or a bull, or any other of those things which are generated by the flesh, is not free from passion in generating or being generated, what has this to do with that Nature which is without passion and without corruption? The fact that we are mortal is no objection to the immortality of the Only-begotten, nor does men's propensity to vice render doubtful the immutability that is found in the Divine Nature, nor is any other of our proper attributes transferred to God ; but the peculiar nature of the human and the Divine life is separated, and without common ground, and their distinguishing properties stand entirely apart, so that those of the latter are not apprehended in the former, nor, conversely, those of the former in the latter.

How comes it, therefore, that Eunomius, when the Divine generation is the subject for discourse, leaves his subject, and discusses at length the things of earth, when on this matter we have no dispute with him? Surely our craftsman's aim is clear,—that by the slanderous insinuation of passion he may raise an objection to the generation of the Lord. And here I pass by the blasphemous nature of his view, and admire the man for his acuteness,—how mindful he is of his own zealous endeavour, who, having by his previous statements established the theory that the Son must be, and must be called, a "product of generation," now contends for the

view that we ought not to entertain regarding Him the conception of generation. For, if all generation, as this author imagines, has linked with it the condition of passion, we are hereby absolutely compelled to admit that what is foreign to passion is alien also from generation : for if these things, passion and generation, are considered as conjoined, He that has no share in the one would not have any participation in the other. How then does he call Him a "product" by reason of His generation, of Whom he tries to show by the arguments he now uses, that He was not generated? and for what cause does he fight against our master [6], who counsels us in matters of Divine doctrine not to presume in name-making, but to confess that He is generated without transforming this conception into the formula of a name, so as to call Him Who is generated "a product of generation," as this term is properly applied in Scripture to things inanimate, or to those which are mentioned "as a figure of wickedness [7]"? When we speak of the propriety of avoiding the use of the term "product," he prepares for action that invincible rhetoric of his, and takes also to support him his frigid grammatical phraseology, and by his skilful misuse of names, or equivocation, or whatever one may properly call his processes—by these means, I say, he brings his syllogisms to their conclusion, "not refusing to call Him Who is begotten by the name of 'product of generation.'" Then, as soon as we admit the term, and proceed to examine the conception involved in the name, on the theory that thereby is vindicated the community of essence, he again retracts his own words, and contends for the view that the "product of generation" is not generated, raising an objection by his foul account of bodily generation, against the pure and Divine and passionless generation of the Son, on the ground that it is not possible that the two things, the true relationship to the Father, and exemption of His nature from passion, should be found to coincide in God, but that, if there were no passion, there would be no generation, and that, if one should acknowledge the true relationship, he would thereby, in admitting generation, certainly admit passion also.

Not thus speaks the sublime John, not thus that voice of thunder which proclaims the mystery of the Theology, who both names Him Son of God and purges his proclamation from every idea of passion. For behold how in the very beginning of his Gospel he prepares our ears, how great forethought is shown by the teacher

---

4 Oehler's punctuation seems less clear than that of the older editions, which is here followed.
5 S. John iii. 10.

6 i.e. S. Basil.
7 The reference is to S. Basil's treatise against Eunomius (ii. 7-8 ; p. 242-4 in the Benedictine ed.). Oehler's punctuation is apparently wrong, for Gregory paraphrases not only the rule, but the reason given for it, from S. Basil, from whom the last words of the sentence are a direct quotation.

that none of his hearers should fall into low ideas on the subject, slipping by ignorance into any incongruous conceptions. For in order to lead the untrained hearing as far away as possible from passion, he does not speak in his opening words of "Son," or "Father," or "generation," that no one should either, on hearing first of all of a "Father," be hurried on to the obvious signification of the word, or, on learning the proclamation of a "Son," should understand that name in the ordinary sense, or stumble, as at a "stone of stumbling [8]," at the word "generation"; but instead of "the Father," he speaks of "the Beginning": instead of "was begotten," he says "was": and instead of "the Son," he says "the Word": and declares "In the Beginning was the Word [9]." What passion, pray, is to be found in these words, "beginning," and "was," and "Word"? Is "the beginning" passion? does "was" imply passion? does "the Word" exist by means of passion? Or are we to say, that as passion is not to be found in the terms used, so neither is affinity expressed by the proclamation? Yet how could the Word's community of essence, and real relationship, and co-eternity with the Beginning, be more strongly shown by other words than by these? For he does not say, "Of the Beginning was begotten the Word," that he may not separate the Word from the Beginning by any conception of extension in time, but he proclaims together with the Beginning Him also Who was in the Beginning, making the word "was" common to the Beginning and to the Word, that the Word may not linger after the Beginning, but may, by entering in together with the faith as to the Beginning, by its proclamation forestall our hearing, before this admits the Beginning itself in isolation. Then he declares, "And the Word was with God." Once more the Evangelist fears for our untrained state, once more he dreads our childish and untaught condition: he does not yet entrust to our ears the appellation of "Father," lest any of the more carnally minded, learning of "the Father," may be led by his understanding to imagine also by consequence a mother. Neither does he yet name in his proclamation the Son; for he still suspects our customary tendency to the lower nature, and fears lest any, hearing of the Son, should humanize the Godhead by an idea of passion. For this reason, resuming his proclamation, he again calls him "the Word," making this the account of His nature to thee in thine unbelief. For as thy word proceeds from thy mind, without requiring the intervention of passion, so here also, in hearing of the Word, thou shalt conceive that which is from some-thing, and shalt not conceive passion. Hence, once more resuming his proclamation, he says, "And the Word was with God." O, how does he make the Word commensurate with God! rather, how does he extend the infinite in comparison with the infinite! "The Word was with God"—the whole being of the Word, assuredly, with the whole being of God. Therefore, as great as God is, so great, clearly, is the Word also that is with Him; so that if God is limited, then will the Word also, surely, be subject to limitation. But if the infinity of God exceeds limit, neither is the Word that is contemplated with Him comprehended by limits and measures. For no one would deny that the Word is contemplated together with the entire Godhead of the Father, so that he should make one part of the Godhead appear to be in the Word, and another destitute of the Word. Once more the spiritual voice of John speaks, once more the Evangelist in his proclamation takes tender care for the hearing of those who are in childhood: not yet have we so much grown by the hearing of his first words as to hear of "the Son," and yet remain firm without being moved from our footing by the influence of the wonted sense. Therefore our herald, crying once more aloud, still proclaims in his third utterance "the Word," and not "the Son," saying, "And the Word was God." First he declared wherein He was, then with whom He was, and now he says what He is, completing, by his third repetition, the object of his proclamation. For he says, "It is no Word of those that are readily understood, that I declare to you, but God under the designation of the Word." For this Word, that was in the Beginning, and was with God, was not anything else besides God, but was also Himself God. And forthwith the herald, reaching the full height of his lofty speech, declares that this God Whom his proclamation sets forth is He by Whom all things were made, and is life, and the light of men, and the true light that shineth in darkness, yet is not obscured by the darkness, sojourning with His own, yet not received by His own: and being made flesh, and tabernacling, by means of the flesh, in man's nature. And when he has first gone through this number and variety of statements, he then names the Father and the Only-begotten, when there can be no danger that what has been purified by so many precautions should be allowed, in consequence of the sense of the word "Father," to sink down to any meaning tainted with pollution, for, "we beheld His glory," he says, "the glory as of the Only-begotten of the Father."

Repeat, then, Eunomius, repeat this clever objection of yours to the Evangelist: "How dost thou give the name of 'Father' in thy

---

[8] 1 S. Pet. ii. 8. [9] S. John i. 1.

discourse, how that of Only-begotten, seeing that all bodily generation is operated by passion?" Surely truth answers you on his behalf, that the mystery of theology is one thing, and the physiology of unstable bodies is another. Wide is the interval by which they are fenced off one from the other. Why do you join together in your argument what cannot blend? how do you defile the purity of the Divine generation by your foul discourse? how do you make systems for the incorporeal by the passions that affect the body? Cease to draw your account of the nature of things above from those that are below. I proclaim the Lord as the Son of God, because the gospel from heaven, given through the bright cloud, thus proclaimed Him; for "This," He saith, "is My beloved Son [1]." Yet, though I was taught that He is the Son, I was not dragged down by the name to the earthly significance of "Son," but I both know that He is from the Father, and do not know that He is from passion. And this, moreover, I will add to what has been said, that I know even a bodily generation which is pure from passion, so that even on this point Eunomius' physiology of bodily generation is proved false, if, that is to say, a bodily birth can be found which does not admit passion. Tell me, was the Word made flesh, or not? You would not, I presume, say that It was not. It was so made, then, and there is none who denies it. How then was it that "God was manifested in the flesh [2]"? "By birth," of course you will say. But what sort of birth do you speak of? Surely it is clear that you speak of that from the virginity, and that "that which was conceived in her was of the Holy Ghost [3]," and that "the days were accomplished that she should be delivered, and she brought forth [4]," and none the less was her purity preserved in her child-bearing. You believe, then, that that birth which took place from a woman was pure from passion, if you do believe, but you refuse to admit the Divine and incorruptible generation from the Father, that you may avoid the idea of passion in generation. But I know well that it is not passion he seeks to avoid in his doctrine, for that he does not discern at all in the Divine and incorruptible nature; but to the end that the Maker of all creation may be accounted a part of creation, he builds up these arguments in order to a denial of the Only-begotten God, and uses his pretended caution about passion to help him in his task.

[1] S. Matt. xvii. 5.
[2] 1 Tim. iii. 16. Here, as elsewhere in Gregory's writings, it appears that he read θεὸς in this passage.
[3] S. Matt i. 20.   [4] S. Luke ii. 6, 7.

§ 2. *He convicts Eunomius of having used of the Only-begotten terms applicable to the existence of the earth, and thus shows that his intention is to prove the Son to be a being mutable and created.*

And this he shows very plainly by his contention against our arguments, where he says that "the essence of the Son came into being from the Father, not put forth by way of extension, not separated from its conjunction with Him that generated Him by flux or division, not perfected by way of growth, not transformed by way of change, but obtaining existence by the mere will of the Generator." Why, what man whose mental senses are not closed up is left in ignorance by this utterance that by these statements the Son is being represented by Eunomius as a part of the creation? What hinders us from saying all this, word for word as it stands, about every single one of the things we contemplate in creation? Let us apply, if you will, the definition to any of the things that appear in creation, and if it does not admit the same sequence, we will condemn ourselves for having examined the definition slightingly, and not with the care that befits the truth. Let us exchange, then, the name of the Son, and so read the definition word by word. We say that the essence of the *earth* came into being from the Father, not separated by way of extension or division from its conjunction with Him Who generated it, nor perfected by way of growth, nor put forth by way of change, but obtaining existence by the mere will of Him Who generated it. Is there anything in what we have said that does not apply to the existence of the earth? I think no one would say so: for God did not put forth the earth by being extended, nor bring its essence into existence by flowing or by dissevering Himself from conjunction with Himself, nor did He bring it by means of gradual growth from being small to completeness of magnitude, nor was He fashioned into the form of earth by undergoing mutation or alteration, but His will sufficed Him for the existence of all things that were made: "He spake and they were generated [5]," so that even the name of "generation" does not fail to accord with the existence of the earth. Now if these things may be truly said of the parts of the universe, what doubt is still left as to our adversaries' doctrine, that while, so far as words go, they call Him "Son," they represent Him as being one of the things that came into existence by creation, set before the rest only in precedence of order? just as you might say about the trade of a smith, that from

[5] Cf. Ps. xxxiii. 9, and Ps. cxlviii. 5, in LXX. (reading ἐγεννήθησαν).

it come all things that are wrought out of iron; but that the instrument of the tongs and hammer, by which the iron is fashioned for use, existed before the making of the rest; yet, while this has precedence of the rest, there is not on that account any difference in respect of matter between the instrument that fashions and the iron that is shaped by the instrument, (for both one and the other are iron,) but the one form is earlier than the other. Such is the theology of heresy touching the Son,—to imagine that there is no difference between the Lord Himself and the things that were made by Him, save the difference in respect of order.

Who that is in any sense classed among Christians admits that the definition[6] of the essence of the parts of the world, and of Him Who made the world, is the same? For my own part I shudder at the blasphemy, knowing that where the definition of things is the same neither is their nature different. For as the definition of the essence of Peter and John and other men is common and their nature is one, in the same way, if the Lord were in respect of nature even as the parts of the world, they must acknowledge that He is also subject to those things, whatever they may be, which they perceive in them. Now the world does not last for ever: thus, according to them, the Lord also will pass away with the heaven and the earth, if, as they say, He is of the same kind with the world. If on the other hand He is confessed to be eternal, we must needs suppose that the world too is not without some part in the Divine nature, if, as they say, it corresponds with the Only-begotten in the matter of creation. You see where this fine process of inference makes the argument tend, like a stone broken off from a mountain ridge and rushing down-hill by its own weight. For either the elements of the world must be Divine, according to the foolish belief of the Greeks, or the Son must not be worshipped. Let us consider it thus. We say that the creation, both what is perceived by the mind, and that which is of a nature to be perceived by sense, came into being from nothing: this they declare also of the Lord. We say that all things that have been made consist by the will of God: this they tell us also of the Only-begotten. We believe that neither the angelic creation nor the mundane is of the essence of Him that made it: and they make Him also alien from the essence of the Father. We confess that all things serve Him that made them: this view they also hold of the Only-begotten. Therefore, of necessity, whatever else it may be that they conceive of the creation, all these

attributes they will also attach to the Only-begotten: and whatever they believe of Him, this they will also conceive of the creation: so that, if they confess the Lord as God, they will also deify the rest of the creation. On the other hand, if they define these things to be without share in the Divine nature, they will not reject the same conception touching the Only-begotten also. Moreover no sane man asserts Godhead of the creation. Then neither——I do not utter the rest, lest I lend my tongue to the blasphemy of the enemy. Let those say what consequence follows, whose mouth is well trained in blasphemy. But their doctrine is evident even if they hold their peace. For one of two things must necessarily happen:—either they will depose the Only-begotten God, so that with them He will no more either be, or be called so: or, if they assert Godhead of Him, they will equally assert it of all creation:—or, (for this is still left to them,) they will shun the impiety that appears on either side, and take refuge in the orthodox doctrine, and will assuredly agree with us that He is not created, that they may confess Him to be truly God.

What need is there to take time to recount all the other blasphemies that underlie his doctrine, starting from this beginning? For by what we have quoted, one who considers the inference to be drawn will understand that the father of falsehood, the maker of death, the inventor of wickedness, being created in a nature intellectual and incorporeal, was not by that nature hindered from becoming what he is by way of change. For the mutability of essence, moved either way at will, involves a capacity of nature that follows the impulse of determination, so as to become that to which its determination leads it. Accordingly they will define the Lord as being capable even of contrary dispositions, drawing Him down as it were to a rank equal with the angels, by the conception of creation[7]. But let them listen to the great voice of Paul. Why is it that he says that He alone has been called Son? Because He is *not* of the nature of angels, but of that which is more excellent. "For unto which of the angels said He at any time, 'Thou art My Son, This day have I begotten Thee'? and when again He bringeth the first-begotten into the world He saith, 'And let all the angels of God worship Him.' And of the angels He saith, 'Who maketh His angels spirits, and His

---

6 The force of λόγος here appears to be nearly equivalent to "idea," in the sense of an exact expression of the nature of a thing. Gulonius renders it by "ratio."

7 The argument appears to be this :—The Anomœans assert, on the ground that He is created, that the Son's essence is τρεπτὸν, liable to change; where there is the possibility of change, the nature must have a capacity of inclining one way or the other, according to the balance of will determining to which side the nature shall incline: and that this is the condition of the fallen angels, may be seen from the instance of the fallen angels, whose nature was inclined to evil by their προαίρεσις. It follows that to say the Son is τρεπτὸς implies that He is on a level with the angelic nature, and might fall even as the angels fell.

ministers a flame of fire': but of the Son He saith, 'Thy throne, O God, is for ever and ever ; a sceptre of righteousness is the sceptre of Thy kingdom [8],'" and all else that the prophecy recites together with these words in declaring His Godhead. And he adds also from another Psalm the appropriate words, " Thou, Lord, in the beginning hast laid the foundation of the earth, and the heavens are the works of Thine hands," and the rest, as far as " But Thou art the same, and Thy years shall not fail [9]," whereby he describes the immutability and eternity of His nature. If, then, the Godhead of the Only-begotten is as far above the angelic nature as a master is superior to his slaves, how do they make common either with the sensible creation Him Who is Lord of the creation, or with the nature of the angels Him Who is worshipped by them [1], by detailing, concerning the manner of His existence, statements which will properly apply to the individual things we contemplate in creation, even as we already showed the account given by heresy, touching the Lord, to be closely and appropriately applicable to the making of the earth ?

§ 3. *He then again admirably discusses the term* πρωτότοκος *as it is four times employed by the Apostle.*

But that the readers of our work may find no ambiguity left of such a kind as to afford any support to the heretical doctrines, it may be worth while to add to the passages examined by us this point also from Holy Scripture. They will perhaps raise a question from the very apostolic writings which we quoted : " How could He be called 'the first-born of creation [2]' if He were not what creation is ? for every first-born is the first-born not of another kind, but of its own : as Reuben, having precedence in respect of birth of those who are counted after him, was the first-born, a man the first-born of men ; and many others are called the first-born of the brothers who are reckoned with them." They say then, " We assert that He Who is 'the first-born of creation ' is of that same essence which we consider the essence of all creation. Now if the whole creation is of one essence with the Father of all, we will not deny that the first-born of creation is this also : but if the God of all differs in essence from the creation, we must of necessity say that neither has the first-born of creation community in essence with God."

The structure of this objection is not, I think, at all less imposing in the form in which it is alleged by us, than in the form in which it would probably be brought against us by our adversaries. But what we ought to know as regards this point shall now, so far as we are able, be plainly set forth in our discourse.

Four times the name of " first-born " or " first-begotten " is used by the Apostle in all his writings : but he has made mention of the name in different senses and not in the same manner. For now he speaks of " the first-born of all creation [3]," and again of " the first-born among many brethren [4]," then of " the first-born from the dead [5] ;" and in the Epistle to the Hebrews the name of " first-begotten " is absolute, being mentioned by itself : for he speaks thus, " When again He bringeth the first-begotten into the world, He saith, 'Let all the angels worship Him [6].'" As these passages are thus distinct, it may be well to interpret each of them separately by itself, how He is the " first-born of creation," how "among many brethren," how "from the dead," and how, spoken of by Himself apart from each of these, when He is again brought into the world, He is worshipped by all His angels. Let us begin then, if you will, our survey of the passages before us with the last-mentioned.

" When again He bringeth in," he says, " the first-begotten into the world." The addition of " again " shows, by the force of this word, that this event happens not for the first time : for we use this word of the repetition of things which have once happened. He signifies, therefore, by the phrase, the dread appearing of the Judge at the end of the ages, when He is seen no more in the form of a servant, but seated in glory upon the throne of His kingdom, and worshipped by all the angels that are around Him. Therefore He Who once entered into the world, becoming the first-born " from the dead," and " of His brethren," and " of all creation," does not, when He comes again into the world as He that judges the world in righteousness [7], as the prophecy saith, cast off the name of the first-begotten, which He once received for our sakes ; but as at the name of Jesus, which is above every name, every knee bows [8], so also the company of all the angels worships Him Who comes in the name of the First-begotten, in their rejoicing over the restoration of men, wherewith, by becoming the first-born among us, He restored us again to the grace which we had at the beginning [9]. For since there is joy among the angels over those who are rescued

---

[8] Cf. Heb. i. 4, and foll. It is to be noted that Gregory connects πάλιν in v. 6, with εἰσαγάγῃ, not treating it, as the A.V. does, as simply introducing another quotation. This appears from his later reference to the text   [9] Cf. Ps. cii. 25, 26.

[1] Oehler's punctuation here seems to be unsatisfactory.

[2] Cf. Col. i. 15. Πρωτότοκος may be, as it is in the Authorized Version, translated either by "first born," or by "first-begotten." Compare with this passage Book II. § 8, where the use of the word in Holy Scripture is discussed.

[3] Cf. Col. i. 15.   [4] Rom. viii. 29.
[5] Col. i. 18.   [6] Cf. Heb. i. 6.
[7] Ps. xcviii. 10.   [8] Cf. Phil. ii. 10.
[9] Oehler's punctuation, which is probably due to a printer's error, is here a good deal altered.

from sin, (because until now that creation groaneth and travaileth in pain at the vanity that affects us [1], judging our perdition to be their own loss,) when that manifestation of the sons of God takes place which they look for and expect, and when the sheep is brought safe to the hundred above, (and we surely—humanity, that is to say—are that sheep which the Good Shepherd saved by becoming the first-begotten [2],) then especially will they offer, in their intense thanksgiving on our behalf, their worship to God, Who by being first-begotten restored him that had wandered from his Father's home.

Now that we have arrived at the understanding of these words, no one could any longer hesitate as to the other passages, for what reason He is the first-born, either " of the dead," or " of the creation," or "among many brethren." For all these passages refer to the same point, although each of them sets forth some special conception. He is the first-born from the dead, Who first by Himself loosed the pains of death [3], that He might also make that birth of the resurrection a way for all men [4]. Again, He becomes "the first-born among many brethren," Who is born before us by the new birth of regeneration in water, for the travail whereof the hovering of the Dove was the midwife, whereby He makes those who share with Him in the like birth to be His own brethren, and becomes the first-born of those who after Him are born of water and of the Spirit [5]: and to speak briefly, as there are in us three births, whereby human nature is quickened, one of the body, another in the sacrament of regeneration, another by that resurrection of the dead for which we look, He is first-born in all three:—of the twofold regeneration which is wrought by two (by baptism and by the resurrection), by being Himself the leader in each of them; while in the flesh He is first-born, as having first and alone devised in His own case that birth unknown to nature, which no one in the many generations of men had originated. If these passages, then, have been rightly understood, neither will the signification of the " creation," of which He is first-born, be unknown to us. For we recognize a twofold creation of our nature, the first that whereby we were made, the second that whereby we were made anew. But there would have

been no need of the second creation had we not made the first unavailing by our disobedience. Accordingly, when the first creation had waxed old and vanished away, it was needful that there should be a new creation in Christ, (as the Apostle says, who asserts that we should no longer see in the second creation any trace of that which has waxed old, saying, " Having put off the old man with his deeds and his lusts, put on the new man which is created according to God [6]," and " If any man be in Christ," he says, " he is a new creature : the old things are passed away, behold all things are become new [7] :")—for the maker of human nature at the first and afterwards is one and the same. *Then* He took dust from the earth and formed man : again, He took dust from the Virgin, and did not merely form man, but formed man about Himself : *then*, He created ; afterwards, He was created : *then*, the Word made flesh ; afterwards, the Word became flesh, that He might change our flesh to spirit, by being made partaker with us in flesh and blood. Of this new creation therefore in Christ, which He Himself began, He was called the first-born, being the first-fruits of all, both of those begotten into life, and of those quickened by resurrection of the dead, " that He might be Lord both of the dead and of the living [8]," and might sanctify the whole lump [9] by means of its first-fruits in Himself. Now that the character of " first-born " does not apply to the Son in respect of His pre-temporal existence the appellation of " Only-begotten " testifies. For he who is truly only-begotten has no brethren, for how could any one be only-begotten if numbered among brethren ? but as He is called God and man, Son of God and Son of man,—for He has the form of God and the form of a servant [1], being some things according to His supreme nature, becoming other things in His dispensation of love to man,—so too, being the Only-begotten God, He becomes the first-born of all creation,—the Only-begotten, He that is in the bosom of the Father, yet, among those who are saved by the new creation, both becoming and being called the first-born of the creation. But if, as heresy will have it, He is called first-born because He was made before the rest of the creation, the name does not agree with what they maintain concerning the Only-begotten God. For they do not say this,—that the Son and the universe were from the Father in like manner,—but they say, that the Only-begotten God was made by the Father, and that all else was made by the Only-begotten. Therefore on the same ground on which, while they hold that the Son was created, they call God the Father of the created Being, on the same

---

[1] Cf. Rom. viii. 19—23.

[2] This interpretation is of course common to many of the Fathers, though S. Augustine, for instance, explains the "ninety and nine" otherwise, and his explanation has been often followed by modern writers and preachers. The present interpretation is assumed in a prayer, no doubt of great antiquity, which is found in the Liturgy of S. James, both in the Greek and the Syriac version, and also in the Greek form of the Coptic Liturgy of S. Basil, where it is said to be "from the Liturgy of S. James."

[3] Acts ii. 24.

[4] See Book II. §§ 4 and 8, and note on the former passage.

[5] With this passage may be compared the parallel passage in Bk. II. § 8. The interpretation of the " many brethren" of those baptized suggests that Gregory understood the " predestination" spoken of in Rom. viii. 29 to be predestination to *baptism*.

[6] Cf. Col. iii. 9, and Eph. iv. 24.　　　[7] Cf. 2 Cor. v. 17.
[8] Rom. xiv. 9.　　　[9] Cf. Rom. xi. 16.　　　[1] Cf. Phil. ii. 6.

ground, while they say that all things were made by the Only-begotten God, they give Him the name not of the "first-born" of the things that were made by Him, but more properly of their "Father," as the same relation existing in both cases towards the things created, logically gives rise to the same appellation. For if God, Who is over all, is not properly called the "First-born," but the Father of the Being He Himself created, the Only-begotten God will surely also be called, by the same reasoning, the "father," and not properly the "first-born" of His own creatures, so that the appellation of "first-born" will be altogether improper and superfluous, having no place in the heretical conception.

§ 4. *He proceeds again to discuss the impassibility of the Lord's generation; and the folly of Eunomius, who says that the generated essence involves the appellation of Son, and again, forgetting this, denies the relation of the Son to the Father: and herein he speaks of Circe and of the mandrake poison.*

We must, however, return to those who connect passion with the Divine generation, and on this account deny that the Lord is truly begotten, in order to avoid the conception of passion. To say that passion is absolutely linked with generation, and that on this account, in order that the Divine nature may continue in purity beyond the reach of passion, we ought to consider that the Son is alien to the idea of generation, may perhaps appear reasonable in the eyes of those who are easily deceived, but those who are instructed in the Divine mysteries [2] have an answer ready to hand, based upon admitted facts. For who knows not that it is generation that leads us back to the true and blessed life, not being the same with that which takes place "of blood and of the will of the flesh [3]," in which are flux and change, and gradual growth to perfection, and all else that we observe in our earthly generation: but the other kind is believed to be from God, and heavenly, and, as the Gospel says, "from above [4]," which excludes the passions of flesh and blood? I presume that they both admit the existence of this generation, and find no passion in it. Therefore not all generation is naturally connected with passion, but the material generation is subject to passion, the immaterial pure from passion. What constrains him then to attribute to the incorruptible generation of the Son what properly belongs to the flesh, and, by ridiculing the lower form of generation with his unseemly physiology, to exclude

the Son from affinity with the Father? For if, even in our own case, it is generation that is the beginning of either life,—that generation which is through the flesh of a life of passion, that which is spiritual of a life of purity, (and no one who is in any sense numbered among Christians would contradict this statement,)—how is it allowable to entertain the idea of passion in thinking of generation as it concerns the incorruptible Nature? Let us moreover examine this point in addition to those we have mentioned. If they disbelieve the passionless character of the Divine generation on the ground of the passion that affects the flesh, let them also, from the same tokens, (those, I mean, to be found in ourselves,) refuse to believe that God acts as a Maker without passion. For if they judge of the Godhead by comparison of our own conditions, they must not confess that God either begets or creates; for neither of these operations is exercised by ourselves without passion. Let them therefore either separate from the Divine nature both creation and generation, that they may guard the impassibility of God on either side, and let them, that the Father may be kept safely beyond the range of passion, neither growing weary by creation, nor being defiled by generation, entirely reject from their doctrine the belief in the Only-begotten, or, if they agree [5] that the one activity is exercised by the Divine power without passion, let them not quarrel about the other: for if He creates without labour or matter, He surely also begets without labour or flux.

And here once more I have in this argument the support of Eunomius. I will state his nonsense concisely and briefly, epitomizing his whole meaning. That men do not make materials for us, but only by their art add form to matter,—this is the drift of what he says in the course of a great quantity of nonsensical language. If, then, understanding conception and formation to be included in the lower generation, he forbids on this ground the pure notion of generation, by consequence, on the same reasoning, since earthly creation is busied with the form, but cannot furnish matter together with the form, let him forbid us also, on this ground, to suppose that the Father is a Creator. If, on the other hand, he refuses to conceive creation in the case of God according to man's measure of power, let him also cease to slander Divine generation by human imperfections. But, that his accuracy and circumspection in argument may be more clearly established, I will again return to a small point in his statements. He asserts that "things which are respectively active and passive share one another's nature," and mentions, after bodily generation,

---

[2] That is, in the sacramental doctrine with regard to Holy Baptism.   [3] S. John i. 13.
[4] S. John iii. 3, where ἄνωθεν may be interpreted either "from above" or as in A.V.

[5] Reading εἰ for εἰς, according to Oehler's suggestion.

"the work of the craftsman as displayed in materials." Now let the acute hearer mark how he here fails in his proper aim, and wanders about among whatever statements he happens to invent. He sees in things that come into being by way of the flesh the "active and passive conceived, with the same essence, the one imparting the essence, the other receiving it." Thus he knows how to discern the truth with accuracy as regards the nature of existing things, so as to separate the imparter and the receiver from the essence, and to say that each of these is distinct in himself apart from the essence. For he that receives or imparts is surely another besides that which is given or received, so that we must first conceive some one by himself, viewed in his own separate existence, and then speak of him as giving that which he has, or receiving that which he has not[6]. And when he has sputtered out this argument in such a ridiculous fashion, our sage friend does not perceive that by the next step he overthrows himself once more. For he who by his art forms at his will the material before him, surely in this operation *acts ;* and the material, in receiving its form at the hand of him who exercises the art, is passively affected : for it is not by remaining unaffected and unimpressionable that the material receives its form. If then, even in the case of things wrought by art, nothing can come into being without passivity and action concurring to produce it, how can our author think that he here abides by his own words? seeing that, in declaring community of essence to be involved in the relation of action and passion, he seems not only to attest in some sense community of essence in Him that is begotten with Him that begat Him, but also to make the whole creation of one essence [7] with its Maker, if, as he says, the active and the passive are to be defined as mutually akin in respect of nature. Thus, by the very arguments by which he establishes what he wishes, he overthrows the main object of his effort, and makes the glory of the co-essential Son more secure by his own contention. For if the fact of origination from anything shows the essence of the generator to be in the generated, and if artificial fabrication (being accomplished by means of action and passion) reduces both that which makes and that which is produced to community of essence, according to his account, our author in many places of his own writings maintains that the Lord has been begotten. Thus by the very arguments

whereby he seeks to prove the Lord alien from the essence of the Father, he asserts for Him intimate connexion. For if, according to his account, separation in essence is not observed either in generation or in fabrication, then, whatever he allows the Lord to be, whether "created" or a "product of generation," he asserts, by both names alike, the affinity of essence, seeing that he makes community of nature in active and passive, in generator and generated, a part of his system.

Let us turn however to the next point of the argument. I beg my readers not to be impatient at the minuteness of examination which extends our argument to a length beyond what we would desire. For it is not any ordinary matters on which we stand in danger, so that our loss would be slight if we should hurry past any point that required more careful attention, but it is the very sum of our hope that we have at stake. For the alternative before us is, whether we should be Christians, not led astray by the destructive wiles of heresy, or whether we should be completely swept away into the conceptions of Jews or heathen. To the end, then, that we may not suffer either of these things forbidden, that we may neither agree with the doctrine of the Jews by a denial of the verily begotten Son, nor be involved in the downfall of the idolaters by the adoration of the creature, let us perforce spend some time in the discussion of these matters, and set forth the very words of Eunomius, which run thus :—

"Now as these things are thus divided, one might reasonably say that the most proper and primary essence, and that which alone exists by the operation of the Father, admits for itself the appellations of 'product of generation,' 'product of making,' and 'product of creation':" and a little further on he says, "But the Son alone, existing by the operation of the Father, possesses His nature and His relation to Him that begat Him, without community[8]." Such are his words. But let us, like men who look on at their enemies engaged in a factious struggle among themselves, consider first our adversaries' contention against themselves, and so proceed to set forth on the other side the true doctrine of godliness. "The Son alone," he says, "existing by the operation of the Father, possesses His nature and His relation to Him that begat Him, without community." But in his previous statements, he says that he "does not refuse to call Him, that is begotten a 'product of generation,' as the generated essence itself, and the appellation of Son, make such a relation of words appropriate."

---

[6] It is not quite clear whether any of this passage, or, if so, how much of it, is a direct quotation from Eunomius. Probably only the phrase about the imparting and receiving of the essence is taken from him, the rest of the passage being Gregory's expansion of the phrase into a distinction between the essence and the thing of which it is the essence, so that the thing can be viewed apart from its own essence. [7] ὁμοούσιον.

[8] This seems to be the force of ἀκοινώνητον: it is clear from what follows that it is to be understood as denying community of essence between the Father and the Son, not as asserting only the unique character alike of the Son and of His relation to the Father.

The contradiction existing in these passages being thus evident, I am inclined to admire for their acuteness those who praise this doctrine. For it would be hard to say to which of his statements they could turn without finding themselves at variance with the remainder. His earlier statement represented that the generated essence, and the appellation of "Son," made such a relation of words appropriate. His present system says the contrary :— that "the Son possesses His relation to Him that begat Him without community." If they believe the first statement, they will surely not accept the second : if they incline to the latter, they will find themselves opposed to the earlier conception. Who will stay the combat? Who will mediate in this civil war? Who will bring this discord into agreement, when the very soul is divided against itself by the opposing statements, and drawn in different ways to contrary doctrines? Perhaps we may see here that dark saying of prophecy which David speaks of the Jews—"They were divided but were not pricked at heart 9." For lo, not even when they are divided among contrariety of doctrines have they a sense of their discordancy, but they are carried about by their ears like wine-jars, borne around at the will of him who shifts them. It pleased him to say that the generated essence was closely connected with the appellation of "Son": straightway, like men asleep, they nodded assent to his remarks. He changed his statement again to the contrary one, and denies the relation of the Son to Him that begat Him : again his well-beloved friends join in assent to this also, shifting in whatever direction he chooses, as the shadows of bodies change their form by spontaneous mimicry with the motion of the advancing figure, and even if he contradicts himself, accepting that also. This is another form of the draught that Homer tells us of, not changing the bodies of those who drink its poison into the forms of brutes, but acting on their souls to produce in them a change to a state void of reason. For of those men, the tale tells that their mind was sound, while their form was changed to that of beasts, but here, while their bodies remain in their natural state, their souls are transformed to the condition of brutes. And as there the poet's tale of wonder says that those who drank the drug were changed into the forms of various beasts, at the pleasure of her who beguiled their nature, the same thing happens now also from this Circe's cup. For they who drink the deceit of sorcery from the same writing are changed to different forms of doctrine, transformed now to one, now to another. And meanwhile these very ridiculous people, according to the revised edition of the fable, are still well pleased with him who leads them to such absurdity, and stoop to gather the words he scatters about, as if they were cornel fruit or acorns, running greedily like swine to the doctrines that are shed on the ground, not being naturally capable of fixing their gaze on those which are lofty and heavenly. For this reason it is that they do not see the tendency of his argument to contrary positions, but snatch without examination what comes in their way : and as they say that the bodies of men stupefied with mandrake are held in a sort of slumber and inability to move, so are the senses of these men's souls affected, being made torpid as regards the apprehension of deceit. It is certainly a terrible thing to be held in unconsciousness by hidden guile, as the result of some fallacious argument : yet where it is involuntary the misfortune is excusable : but to be brought to make trial of evil as the result of a kind of forethought and zealous desire, not in ignorance of what will befall, surpasses every extreme of misery. Surely we may well complain, when we hear that even greedy fish avoid the steel when it comes near them unbaited, and take down the hook only when hope of food decoys them to a bait : but where the evil is apparent, to go over of their own accord to this destruction is a more wretched thing than the folly of the fish : for these are led by their greediness to a destruction that is concealed from them, but the others swallow with open mouth the hook of impiety in its bareness, satisfied with destruction under the influence of some unreasoning passion. For what could be clearer than this contradiction—than to say that the same Person was begotten and is a thing created, and that something is closely connected with the name of "Son," and, again, is alien from the sense of "Son"? But enough of these matters.

§ 5. *He again shows Eunomius, constrained by truth, in the character of an advocate of the orthodox doctrine, confessing as most proper and primary, not only the essence of the Father, but the essence also of the Only begotten.*

It might, however, be useful to look at the sense of the utterance of Eunomius that is set before us in orderly sequence, recurring to the beginning of his statement. For the points we have now examined were an obvious incitement to us to begin our reply with the last passage, on account of the evident character of the contradiction involved in his words.

This, then, is what Eunomius says at the beginning :—

---

9 This is the LXX. version of the last part of Ps. xxxv. 15, a rendering with which the Vulgate version practically agrees.

"Now, as these things are thus divided, one might reasonably say that the most proper and primary essence, and that which alone exists by the operation of the Father, admits for itself the appellations of 'product of generation,' 'product of making,' and 'product of creation.'" First, then, I would ask those who are attending to this discourse to bear in mind, that in his first composition he says that the essence of the Father also is "most proper," introducing his statement with these words, "The whole account of our teaching is completed with the supreme and most proper essence." And here he calls the essence of the Only-begotten "most proper and primary." Thus putting together Eunomius' phrases from each of his books, we shall call him himself as a witness of the community of essence, who in another place makes a declaration to this effect, that "of things which have the same appellations, the nature also is not different" in any way. For our self-contradictory friend would not indicate things differing in nature by identity of appellation, but it is surely for this reason, that the definition of essence in Father and Son is one, that he says that the one is "most proper," and that the other also is "most proper." And the general usage of men bears witness to our argument, which does not apply the term "most proper" where the name does not truly agree with the nature. For instance, we call a likeness, inexactly, "a man," but what we properly designate by this name is the animal presented to us in nature. And similarly, the language of Scripture recognizes the appellation of "god" for an idol, and for a demon, and for the belly: but here too the name has not its proper sense; and in the same way with all other cases. A man is said to have eaten food in the fancy of a dream, but we cannot call this fancy food, in the proper sense of the term. As, then, in the case of two men existing naturally, we properly call both equally by the name of man, while if any one should join an inanimate portrait in his enumeration with a real man, one might perhaps speak of him who really exists and of the likeness, as "two men," but would no longer attribute to both the proper meaning of the word, so, on the supposition that the nature of the Only-begotten was conceived as something else than the essence of the Father, our author would not have called each of the essences "most proper." For how could any one signify things differing in nature by identity of names? Surely the truth seems to be made plain even by those who fight against it, as falsehood is unable, even when expressed in the words of the enemy, utterly to prevail over truth. Hence the doctrine of orthodoxy is proclaimed by the mouth of its opponents, without their knowing what they say, as the saving Passion of the Lord for us had been foretold in the case of Caiaphas, not knowing what he said [1]. If, therefore, true propriety of essence is common to both (I mean to the Father and the Son), what room is there for saying that their essences are mutually divergent? Or how is a difference by way of superior power, or greatness, or honour, contemplated in them, seeing that the "most proper" essence admits of no diminution? For that which is whatever it is imperfectly, is not that thing "most properly," be it nature, or power, or rank, or any other individual object of contemplation, so that the superiority of the Father's essence, as heresy will have it, proves the imperfection of the essence of the Son. If then it is imperfect, it is not proper; but if it is "most proper" it is also surely perfect. For it is not possible to call that which is deficient perfect. But neither is it possible, when, in comparing them, that which is perfect is set beside that which is perfect, to perceive any difference by way of excess or defect: for perfection is one in both cases, as in a rule, not showing a hollow by defect, nor a projection by excess. Thus, from these passages Eunomius' advocacy in favour of our doctrine may be sufficiently seen—I should rather say, not his earnestness on our behalf, but his conflict with himself. For he turns against himself those devices whereby he establishes our doctrines by his own arguments. Let us, however, once more follow his writings word for word, that it may be clear to all that their argument has no power for evil except the desire to do mischief.

§ 6. *He then exposes the argument about the "Generate," and the "product of making," and "product of creation," and shows the impious nature of the language of Eunomius and Theognostus on the "immediate" and "undivided" character of the essence, and its "relation to its creator and maker."*

Let us listen, then, to what he says. "One might reasonably say that the most proper and primary essence, and that which alone exists by the operation of the Father, admits for itself the appellations of 'product of generation,' 'product of making,' and 'product of creation.'" Who knows not that what separates the Church from heresy is this term, "product of creation," applied to the Son? Accordingly, the doctrinal difference being universally acknowledged, what would be the reasonable course for a man to take who endeavours to show that his opinions are more true than ours? Clearly, to establish his own statement, by showing, by such proofs as he could, that we ought to consider that the

---

[1] S. John xi. 51.

Lord is created. Or omitting this, should he rather lay down a law for his readers that they should speak of matters of controversy as if they were acknowledged facts? For my own part, I think he should take the former course, and perhaps all who possess any share of intelligence demand this of their opponents, that they should, to begin with, establish upon some incontrovertible basis the first principle of their argument, and so proceed to press their theory by inferences. Now our writer leaves alone the task of establishing the view that we should think He is created, and goes on to the next steps, fitting on the inferential process of his argument to this unproved assumption, being just in the condition of those men whose minds are deep in foolish desires, with their thoughts wandering upon a kingdom, or upon some other object of pursuit. They do not think how any of the things on which they set their hearts could possibly be, but they arrange and order their good fortune for themselves at their pleasure, as if it were theirs already, straying with a kind of pleasure among non-existent things. So, too, our clever author somehow or other lulls his own renowned dialectic to sleep, and before giving a demonstration of the point at issue, he tells, as if to children, the tale of this deceitful and inconsequent folly of his own doctrine, setting it forth like a story told at a drinking-party. For he says that the essence which "exists by the operation of the Father" admits the appellation of "product of generation," and of "product of making," and of "product of creation." What reasoning showed us that the Son exists by any constructive operation, and that the nature of the Father remains inoperative with regard to the Personal existence [2] of the Son? This was the very point at issue in the controversy, whether the essence of the Father begat the Son, or whether it made Him as one of the external things which accompany His nature [3]. Now seeing that the Church, according to the Divine teaching, believes the Only-begotten to be verily God, and abhors the superstition of polytheism, and for this cause does not admit the difference of essences, in order that the Godheads may not, by divergence of essence, fall under the conception of number (for this is nothing else than to introduce polytheism into our life)—seeing, I say, that the Church teaches this in plain language, that the Only-begotten is essentially God, very God of the essence of the very God, how ought one who opposes her decisions to overthrow the preconceived opinion? Should he not do so by establishing the oppos-

ing statement, demonstrating the disputed point from some acknowledged principle? I think no sensible man would look for anything else than this. But our author starts from the disputed points, and takes, as though it were admitted, matter which is in controversy as a principle for the succeeding argument. If it had first been shown that the Son had His existence through some operation, what quarrel should we have with what follows, that he should say that the essence which exists through an operation admits for itself the name of "product of making"? But let the advocates of error tell us how the consequence has any force, so long as the antecedent remains unestablished. For supposing one were to grant by way of hypothesis that man is winged, there will be no question of concession about what comes next: for he who becomes winged will fly in some way or other, and lift himself up on high above the earth, soaring through the air on his wings. But we have to see how he whose nature is not aerial could become winged, and if this condition does not exist, it is vain to discuss the next point. Let our author, then, show this to begin with, that it is in vain that the Church has believed that the Only-begotten Son truly exists, not adopted by a Father falsely so called, but existing according to nature, by generation from Him Who is, not alienated from the essence of Him that begat Him. But so long as his primary proposition remains unproved, it is idle to dwell on those which are secondary. And let no one interrupt me, by saying that what we confess should also be confirmed by constructive reasoning: for it is enough for proof of our statement, that the tradition has come down to us from our fathers, handed on, like some inheritance, by succession from the apostles and the saints who came after them. They, on the other hand, who change their doctrines to this novelty, would need the support of arguments in abundance, if they were about to bring over to their views, not men light as dust, and unstable, but men of weight and steadiness: but so long as their statement is advanced without being established, and without being proved, who is so foolish and so brutish as to account the teaching of the evangelists and apostles, and of those who have successively shone like lights in the churches, of less force than this undemonstrated nonsense?

Let us further look at the most remarkable instance of our author's cleverness; how, by the abundance of his dialectic skill, he ingeniously draws over to the contrary view the more simple sort. He throws in, as an addition to the title of "product of making," and that of "product of creation," the further phrase, "product of generation," saying that the essence of the Son "admits these names for itself"; and thinks that, so long as he harangues as if he were in some gathering of topers, his knavery in dealing with doctrine will not be detected by any one. For in joining "product of generation" with "product of making," and "product of creation," he thinks that he stealthily makes away with the difference in significance between the names, by putting together what have nothing in common. These are his clever tricks of dialectic; but we mere laymen in argument [4] do not deny that, so far as voice and tongue are concerned, we are what his speech sets forth about us, but we allow also that our ears, as the prophet says, are made ready for intelligent hearing. Accordingly, we are not moved, by the conjunction of names that have nothing in common, to make a confusion between the things they signify: but even if the great Apostle names together wood, hay, stubble, gold, silver, and precious stones [5], we reckon up summarily the number of things he mentions, and yet do not fail to recognize separately the nature of each of the substances named. So here, too, when "product of generation" and "product of making" are named together, we pass from the sounds to the sense, and do not behold the same meaning in each of the names; for "product of creation" means one thing, and "product of generation" another: so that even if he tries to mingle what will not blend, the intelligent hearer will listen with discrimination, and will point out that it is an impossibility for any one nature to "admit for itself" the appellation of "product of generation," and that of "product of creation." For, if one of these were true, the other would necessarily be false, so that, if the thing were a product of creation, it would not be a product of generation, and conversely, if it were called a product of generation, it would be alienated from the title of "product of creation." Yet Eunomius tells us that the essence of the Son "admits for itself the appellations of 'product of generation,' 'product of making,' and 'product of creation'"!

Does he, by what still remains, make at all more secure this headless and rootless statement of his, in which, in its earliest stage, nothing was laid down that had any force with regard to the point he is trying to establish? or does the rest also cling to the same folly, not deriving its strength from any support it gets from argument, but setting out its exposition of blasphemy with vague details like the recital of dreams? He says (and this he subjoins to what I have already quoted)—"Having its generation

without intervention, and preserving indivisible its relation to its Generator, Maker, and Creator." Well, if we were to leave alone the absence of intervention and of division, and look at the meaning of the words as it stands by itself, we shall find that everywhere his absurd teaching is cast upon the ears of those whom he deceives, without corroboration from a single argument. "Its Generator, and Maker, and Creator," he says. These names, though they seem to be three, include the sense of but two concepts, since two of the words are equivalent in meaning. For to make is the same as to create, but generation is another thing distinct from those spoken of. Now, seeing that the result of the signification of the words is to divide the ordinary apprehension of men into different ideas, what argument demonstrates to us that making is the same thing with generation, to the end that we may accommodate the one essence to this difference of terms? For so long as the ordinary significance of the words holds, and no argument is found to transfer the sense of the terms to an opposite meaning, it is not possible that any one nature should be divided between the conception of "product of making," and that of "product of generation." Since each of these terms, used by itself, has a meaning of its own, we must also suppose the relative conjunction in which they stand to be appropriate and germane to the terms. For all other relative terms have their connection, not with what is foreign and heterogeneous, but, even if the correlative term be suppressed, we hear spontaneously, together with the primary word, that which is linked with it, as in the case of "maker," "slave," "friend," "son," and so forth. For all names that are considered as relative to another, present to us, by the mention of them, each its proper and closely connected relationship with that which it declares, while they avoid all mixture of that which is heterogeneous [6]. For neither is the name of "maker" linked with the word "son," nor the term "slave" referred to the term "maker," nor does "friend" present to us a "slave," nor "son" a "master," but we recognize clearly and distinctly the connection of each of these with its correlative, conceiving by the word "friend" another friend; by "slave," a master; by "maker," work; by "son," a father. In the same way, then, "product of generation" has its proper relative sense; with the "product of generation," surely, is linked the *generator*, and with the "product of creation" the *creator*; and we must certainly, if we are not prepared by a substitution of names to

---

[4] This phrase seems to be quoted from Eunomius. The reference to the "prophet" may possibly be suggested by Is. vi. 9-10: but it is more probably only concerned with the words ὠτία and ἀκοήν, as applied to convey the idea of mental alertness.

[5] Cf. 1 Cor. iii. 12

[6] *E.g.* "A thing made" suggests to us the thought of a "maker," "a maker" the thought of the thing made; and they suggest also a close connection as existing between the two correlative terms of one of which the name is uttered; but neither suggests in the same way any term which is not correlative, or with which it is not, in some manner, *in pari materia*.

introduce a confusion of things, preserve for each of the relative terms that which it properly connotes.

Now, seeing that the tendency of the meaning of these words is manifest, how comes it that one who advances his doctrine by the aid of logical system failed to perceive in these names their proper relative sense? But he thinks that he is linking on the "product of generation" to "maker," and the "product of making" to "generator," by saying that the essence of the Son "admits for itself the appellations of 'product of generation,' 'product of making,' and 'product of creation,'" and "preserves indivisible its relation to its Generator, Maker, and Creator." For it is contrary to nature, that a single thing should be split up into different relations. But the Son is properly related to the Father, and that which is begotten to him that begat it, while the "product of making" has its relation to its "maker"; save if one might consider some inexact use, in some undistinguishing way of common parlance, to overrule the strict signification.

By what reasoning then is it, and by what arguments, according to that invincible logic of his, that he wins back the opinion of the mass of men, and follows out at his pleasure this line of thought, that as the God Who is over all is conceived and spoken of both as "Creator" and as "Father," the Son has a close connection with both titles, being equally called both "product of creation" and "product of generation"? For as customary accuracy of speech distinguishes between names of this kind, and applies the name of "generation" in the case of things generated from the essence itself, and understands that of "creation" of those things which are external to the nature of their maker, and as on this account the Divine doctrines, in handing down the knowledge of God, have delivered to us the names of "Father" and "Son," not those of "Creator" and "work," that there might arise no error tending to blasphemy (as might happen if an appellation of the latter kind repelled the Son to the position of an alien and a stranger), and that the impious doctrines which sever the Only-begotten from essential affinity with the Father might find no entrance—seeing all this, I say, he who declares that the appellation of "product of making" is one befitting the Son, will surely say by consequence that the name of "Son" is properly applicable to that which is the product of making; so that, if the Son is a "product of making," the heaven is called "Son," and the individual things that have been made are, according to our author, properly named by the appellation of "Son." For if He has this name, not because He shares in nature with Him that begat Him, but is called Son for this reason, that He is created, the same argument will permit that a lamb, a dog, a frog, and all things that exist by the will of their maker, should be named by the title of "Son." If, on the other hand, each of these is not a Son and is not called God, by reason of its being external to the nature of the Son, it follows, surely, that He Who is truly Son is Son, and is confessed to be God by reason of His being of the very nature of Him that begat Him. But Eunomius abhors the idea of generation, and excludes it from the Divine doctrine, slandering the term by his fleshly speculations. Well, our discourse, in what precedes, showed sufficiently on this point that, as the Psalmist says, "they are afraid where no fear is [7]." For if it was shown in the case of men that not all generation exists by way of passion, but that that which is material is by passion, while that which is spiritual is pure and incorruptible, (for that which is begotten of the Spirit is spirit and not flesh, and in spirit we see no condition that is subject to passion,) since our author thought it necessary to estimate the Divine power by means of examples among ourselves, let him persuade himself to conceive from the other mode of generation the passionless character of the Divine generation. Moreover, by mixing up together these three names, of which two are equivalent, he thinks that his readers, by reason of the community of sense in the two phrases, will jump to the conclusion that the third is equivalent also. For since the appellation of "product of making," and "product of creation," indicate that the thing made is external to the nature of the maker, he couples with these the phrase, "product of generation," that this too may be interpreted along with those above mentioned. But argument of this sort is termed fraud and falsehood and imposition, not a thoughtful and skilful demonstration. For that only is called demonstration which shows what is unknown from what is acknowledged; but to reason fraudulently and fallaciously, to conceal your own reproach, and to confound by superficial deceits the understanding of men, as the Apostle says, "of corrupt minds [8]," this no sane man would call a skilful demonstration.

Let us proceed, however, to what follows in order. He says that the generation of the essence is "without intervention," and that it "preserves indivisible its relation to its Generator, Maker, and Creator." Well, if he had spoken of the immediate and indivisible character of the essence, and stopped his discourse there, it would not have swerved from the orthodox view, since we too confess the close connection and relation of the Son with the Father, so that there is nothing inserted between them which is found to intervene in the connection of the Son with the Father, no conception of interval, not even that minute and indivisible one, which, when time is divided into past, present, and future, is conceived indivisibly by itself as the present, as it cannot be considered as a part either of the past or of the future, by reason of its being quite without dimensions and incapable of division, and unobservable, to whichever side it might be added. That, then, which is perfectly immediate, admits, we say, of no such intervention; for that which is separated by any interval would cease to be immediate. If, therefore, our author, likewise, in saying that the generation of the Son is "without intervention," excluded all these ideas, then he laid down the orthodox doctrine of the conjunction of Him Who is with the Father. When, however, as though in a fit of repentance, he straightway proceeded to add to what he had said that the essence "preserves its relation to its Generator, Maker, and Creator," he polluted his first statement by his second, vomiting forth his blasphemous utterance upon the pure doctrine. For it is clear that there too his "without intervention" has no orthodox intention, but, as one might say that the hammer is mediate between the smith and the nail, but its own making is "without intervention," because, when tools had not yet been found out by the craft, the hammer came first from the craftsman's hands by some inventive process, not [9] by means of any other tool, and so by it the others were made; so the phrase, "without intervention," indicates that this is also our author's conception touching the Only-begotten. And here Eunomius is not alone in his error as regards the enormity of his doctrine, but you may find a parallel also in the works of Theognostus [1], who says that God, wishing to make this universe, first brought the Son into existence as a sort of standard of the creation; not perceiving that in his statement there is involved this absurdity, that what exists, not for its own sake, but for the sake of something else, is surely of less value than that for the sake of which it exists: as we provide an implement of husbandry for the sake of life, yet the plough is surely not reckoned as equally valuable with life. So, if the Lord also exists on account of the world, and not all things on account of Him, the whole of the things for the sake of which they say He exists, would be more valuable than the Lord. And this is what they are here establishing by their argument, where they insist that the Son has His relation to His Creator and Maker "without intervention."

§ 7. *He then clearly and skilfully criticises the doctrine of the impossibility of comparison with the things made after the Son, and exposes the idolatry contrived by Eunomius, and concealed by the terminology of "Son" and "Only-begotten," to deceive his readers.*

In the remainder of the passage, however, he becomes conciliatory, and says that the essence "is not compared with any of the things that were made by it and after it [2]." Such are the gifts which the enemies of the truth offer to the Lord [3], by which their blasphemy is made more manifest. Tell me what else is there of all things in creation that admits of comparison with a different thing, seeing that the characteristic nature that appears in each absolutely rejects community with things of a different kind [4]? The heaven admits no comparison with the earth, nor this with the stars, nor the stars with the seas, nor water with stone, nor animals with trees, nor land animals with winged creatures, nor four-footed beasts with those that swim, nor irrational with rational creatures. Indeed, why should one take up time with individual instances, in showing that we may say of every single thing that we behold in the creation, precisely what was thrown to the Only-begotten, as if it were something special—that He admits of comparison with none of the things that have been produced after Him and by Him? For it is clear that everything which you conceive by itself is incapable of comparison with the universe, and with the individual things which compose it; and it is this, which may be truly said of any creature you please, which is allotted by the enemies of the truth, as adequate and sufficient for His honour and glory, to the Only-begotten God! And once more, putting together phrases of the same sort in the remainder of the passage, he dignifies Him with his empty honours, calling Him "Lord" and "Only-begotten": but that no orthodox meaning may be conveyed to his readers by these names, he

---

[9] It seems necessary for the sense to read οὐ δι' ἑτέρου τινὸς ὀργάνου, since the force of the comparison consists in the hammer being produced immediately by the smith: otherwise we must understand δι' ἑτέρου τινὸς ὀργάνου to refer to the employment of some tool not properly belonging to the τέχνη of the smith: but even so the parallel would be destroyed.

[1] Theognostus, a writer of the third century, is said to have been the head of the Catechetical School at Alexandria, and is quoted by S. Athanasius as an authority against the Arians. An account of his work is to be found in Photius, and this is extracted and printed with the few remaining fragments of his actual writings in the 3rd volume of Routh's *Reliquiæ Sacræ*.

[2] Oehler's proposal to read "*vel invitis libris quod sententia flagitat τῶν δι αὐτοῦ καὶ μετ' αὐτὸν*" does not seem necessary. αὐτῆς and αὐτὴν refer to οὐσία, the quotation being made (not verbally) from *Eunomius*, not from Theognostus, and following apparently the phrase about "preserving the relation," etc. If the clause were a continuation of the quotation from Theognostus, we should have to follow Oehler's proposal.

[3] Reading, according to Cotelerius' suggestion, (mentioned with approval by Oehler, though not followed by him,) δωροφοροῦσιν for δορυφοροῦσιν.

[4] That is to say, because there is no "common measure" of the distinct natures.

promptly mixes up blasphemy with the more notable of them. His phrase runs thus :—" Inasmuch," he says, "as the generated essence leaves no room for community to anything else (for it is only-begotten [5]), nor is the operation of the Maker contemplated as common." O marvellous insolence ! as though he were addressing his harangue to brutes, or senseless beings "which have no understanding [6]," he twists his argument about in contrary ways, as he pleases ; or rather he suffers as men do who are deprived of sight ; for they too behave often in unseemly ways before the eyes of those who see, supposing, because they themselves cannot see, that they are also unseen. For what sort of man is it who does not see the contradiction in his words? Because it is "generated," he says, the essence leaves other things no room for community, for it is only-begotten ; and then when he has uttered these words, really as though he did not see or did not suppose himself to be seen, he tacks on, as if corresponding to what he has said, things that have nothing in common with them, coupling " the operation of the maker" with the essence of the Only-begotten. That which is generated is correlative to the generator, and the Only-begotten, surely, by consequence, to the Father; and he who looks to the truth beholds, in co-ordination with the Son, not "the operation of the maker," but the nature of Him that begat Him. But he, as if he were talking about plants or seeds, or some other thing in the order of creation, sets "the operation of the maker" by the side of the existence [7] of the Only-begotten. Why, if a stone or a stick, or something of that sort, were the subject of consideration, it would be logical to pre-suppose " the operation of the maker" ; but if the Only-begotten God is confessed, even by His adversaries, to be a Son, and to exist by way of generation, how do the same words befit Him that befit the lowest portions of the creation? how do they think it pious to say concerning the Lord the very thing which may be truly said of an ant or a gnat? For if any one understood the nature of an ant, and its peculiarities in reference to other living things, he would not be beyond the truth in saying that "the operation of its maker is not contemplated as common" with reference to the other things. What, therefore, is affirmed of such things as these, this they predicate also of the Only-begotten, and as hunters are said to intercept the passage of their game with holes, and to conceal their design by covering over the mouths of the holes with some unsound and unsubstantial material, in order that the pit may seem level with the ground about it, so heresy contrives against men

something of the same sort, covering over the hole of their impiety with these fine-sounding and pious names, as it were with a level thatch, so that those who are rather unintelligent, thinking that these men's preaching is the same with the true faith, because of the agreement of their words, hasten towards the mere name of the Son and the Only-begotten, and step into emptiness in the hole, since the significance of these titles will not sustain the weight of their tread, but lets them down into the pitfall of the denial of Christ. This is why he speaks of the generated essence that leaves nothing room for community, and calls it "Only-begotten." These are the coverings of the hole. But when any one stops before he is caught in the gulf, and puts forth the test of argument, like a hand, upon his discourse, he sees the dangerous downfall of idolatry lying beneath the doctrine. For when he draws near, as though to God and the Son of God, he finds a creature of God set forth for his worship. This is why they proclaim high and low the name of the Only-begotten, that the destruction may be readily accepted by the victims of their deceit, as though one were to mix up poison in bread, and give a deadly greeting to those who asked for food, who would not have been willing to take the poison by itself, had they not been enticed to what they saw. Thus he has a sharp eye to the object of his efforts, at least so far as his own opinion goes. For if he had entirely rejected from his teaching the name of the Son, his falsehood would not have been acceptable to men, when his denial was openly stated in a definite proclamation ; but now leaving only the name, and changing the signification of it to express creation, he at once sets up his idolatry, and fraudulently hides its reproach. But since we are bidden not to honour God with our lips [8], and piety is not tested by the sound of a word, but the Son must first be the object of belief in the heart unto righteousness, and then be confessed with the mouth unto salvation [9], and those who say in their hearts that He is not God, even though with their mouths they confess Him as Lord, are corrupt and become abominable [1], as the prophet says,—for this cause, I say, we must look to the mind of those who put forward, forsooth, the words of the faith, and not be enticed to follow their sound. If, then, one who speaks of the Son does not by that word refer to a creature, he is on our side and not on the enemy's ; but if any one applies the name of Son to the creation, he is to be ranked among idolaters. For they too gave the name of God to Dagon and Bel and the Dragon, but they did not on that account worship God. For the wood and the brass and the monster were not God.

[5] Altering Oehler's punctuation ; it is the fact that the essence is μονογενής which excludes all other things from community with it.
[6] Ps. xxxii. 9.　　[7] ὑποστάσει.

[8] Cf. Is. xxix. 13.　　[9] Cf. Rom. x. 10.　　[1] Cf. Ps. xiii. 2.

§ 8. *He proceeds to show that there is no "variance" in the essence of the Father and the Son: wherein he expounds many forms of variation and harmony, and explains the "form," the "seal," and the "express image."*

But what need is there in our discourse to reveal his hidden deceit by mere guesses at his intention, and possibly to give our hearers occasions for objection, on the ground that we make these charges against our enemies untruly? For lo, he sets forth to us his blasphemy in its nakedness, not hiding his guile by any veil, but speaking boldly in his absurdities with unrestrained voice. What he has written runs thus:—"We, for our part," he says, "as we find nothing else besides the essence of the Son which admits of the generation, are of opinion that we must assign the appellations to the essence itself, or else we speak of 'Son' and 'begotten' to no purpose, and as a mere verbal matter, if we are really to separate them from the essence; starting from these names, we also confidently maintain that the essences are variant from each other [2]."

There is no need, I imagine, that the absurdity here laid down should be refuted by arguments from us. The mere reading of what he has written is enough to pillory his blasphemy. But let us thus examine it. He says that the essences of the Father and the Son are "variant." What is meant by "variant"? Let us first of all examine the force of the term as it is applied by itself [3], that by the interpretation of the word its blasphemous character may be more clearly revealed. The term "variance" is used, in the inexact sense sanctioned by custom, of bodies, when, by palsy or any other disease, any limb is perverted from its natural co-ordination. For we speak, comparing the state of suffering with that of health, of the condition of one who has been subjected to a change for the worse, as being a "variation" from his usual health; and in the case of those who differ in respect of virtue and vice, comparing the licentious life with that of purity and temperance, or the unjust life with that of justice, or the life which is passionate, warlike, and prodigal of anger, with

that which is mild and peaceful—and generally all that is reproached with vice, as compared with what is more excellent, is said to exhibit "variance" from it, because the marks observed in both—in the good, I mean, and the inferior—do not mutually agree. Again, we say that those qualities observed in the elements are "at variance" which are mutually opposed as contraries, having a power reciprocally destructive, as heat and cold, or dryness and moisture, or, generally, anything that is opposed to another as a contrary; and the absence of union in these we express by the term "variation"; and generally everything which is out of harmony with another in their observed characteristics, is said to be "at variance" with it, as health with disease, life with death, war with peace, virtue with vice, and all similar cases.

Now that we have thus analyzed these expressions, let us also consider in regard to our author in what sense he says that the essences of the Father and the Son are "variant from each other." What does he mean by it? Is it in the sense that the Father is according to nature, while the Son "varies" from that nature? Or does he express by this word the perversion of virtue, separating the evil from the more excellent by the name of "variation," so as to regard the one essence in a good, the other in a contrary aspect? Or does he assert that one Divine essence also is variant from another, in the manner of the opposition of the elements? or as war stands to peace, and life to death, does he also perceive in the essences the conflict which so exists among all such things, so that they cannot unite one with another, because the mixture of contraries exerts upon the things mingled a consuming force, as the wisdom of the Proverbs saith of such a doctrine, that water and fire never say "It is enough [4]," expressing enigmatically the nature of contraries of equal force and equal balance, and their mutual destruction? Or is it in none of these ways that he sees "variance" in the essences? Let him tell us, then, what he conceives besides these. He could not say, I take it, even if he were to repeat his wonted phrase [5], "The Son is variant from Him Who begat Him"; for thereby the absurdity of his statements is yet more clearly shown. For what mutual relation is so closely and concordantly engrafted and fitted together as that meaning of relation to

---

[2] The whole passage is rather obscure, and Oehler's punctuation renders it perhaps more obscure than that which is here adopted. The argument seems to be something like this:—"The generated essence is not compared with any of the things made by it, or after it, because being *only-begotten* it leaves no room for a common basis of comparison with anything else, and the operation of its maker is also peculiar to itself (since it is immediate, the operation in the case of other things being *mediate*). The essence of the Son, then, being so far isolated, it is to it that the appellations of γέννημα, ποίημα, and κτίσμα are to be assigned; otherwise the terms 'Son' and 'Only-begotten' are meaningless. Therefore the Son, being in essence a ποίημα or κτίσμα, is alien from the Father Who made or created Him." The word παρηλλάχθαι, used to express the difference of essence between the Father and the Son, is one for which it is hard to find an equivalent which shall suit all the cases of the use of the word afterwards instanced : the idea of "variation," however, seems to attach to all these cases, and the verb has been translated accordingly.

[3] Following Oehler's suggestion and reading ἐφ' ἑαυτῆς.

[4] Cf. Prov. xxx. 15 (LXX.).

[5] The sense given would perhaps be clearer if we were to read (as Gulonius seems to have done) ἀσυνήθη for συνήθη. This might be interpreted, "He could not say, I take it, even if he uses the words in an unwonted sense, that the Son is at variance with Him Who begat Him." The συνήθη would thus be the senses already considered and set aside : and the point would be that such a statement could not be made without manifest absurdity, even if some out-of-the-way sense were attached to the words. As the passage stands, it must mean that even if Eunomius repeats his wonted phrase, that can suggest no other sense of "variance" than those enumerated.

the Father expressed by the word "Son"? And a proof of this is that even if both of these names be not spoken, that which is omitted is connoted by the one that is uttered, so closely is the one implied in the other, and concordant with it: and both of them are so discerned in the one that one cannot be conceived without the other. Now that which is "at variance" is surely so conceived and so called, in opposition to that which is "in harmony," as the plumb-line is in harmony with the straight line, while that which is crooked, when set beside that which is straight, does not harmonize with it. Musicians also are wont to call the agreement of notes "harmony," and that which is out of tune and discordant "inharmonious." To speak of things as at "variance," then, is the same as to speak of them as "out of harmony." If, therefore, the nature of the Only-begotten God is at "variance," to use the heretical phrase, with the essence of the Father, it is surely not in harmony with it: and inharmoniousness cannot exist where there is no possibility of harmony [6]. For the case is as when, the figure in the wax and in the graving of the signet being one, the wax that has been stamped by the signet, when it is fitted again to the latter, makes the impression on itself accord with that which surrounds it, filling up the hollows and accommodating the projections of the engraving with its own patterns: but if some strange and different pattern is fitted to the engraving of the signet, it makes its own form rough and confused, by rubbing off its figure on an engraved surface that does not correspond with it. But He Who is "in the form of God [7]" has been formed by no impression different from the Father, seeing that He is "the express image" of the Father's Person [8], while the "form of God" is surely the same thing as His essence. For as, "being made in the form of a servant [9]," He was formed in the essence of a servant, not taking upon Him the form merely, apart from the essence, but the essence is involved in the sense of "form," so, surely, he who says that He is "in the form of God" signified essence by "form." If, therefore, He is "in the form of God," and being in the Father is sealed with the Father's glory, (as the word of the Gospel declares, which saith, "Him hath God the Father sealed [1],"—whence also "He that hath seen Me hath seen the Father [2],") then "the image of goodness" and "the brightness of glory," and all other similar titles, testify that the essence of the Son is not out of harmony with the Father. Thus by the text cited is shown the insubstantial character of the adversaries'

blasphemy. For if things at "variance" are not in harmony, and He Who is sealed by the Father, and displays the Father in Himself, both being in the Father, and having the Father in Himself [3], shows in all points His close relation and harmony, then the absurdity of the opposing views is hereby overwhelmingly shown. For as that which is at "variance" was shown to be out of harmony, so conversely that which is harmonious is surely confessed beyond dispute not to be at "variance." For as that which is at "variance" is not harmonious, so the harmonious is not at "variance." Moreover, he who says that the nature of the Only-begotten is at "variance" with the good essence of the Father, clearly has in view variation in the good itself. But as for what that is which is at variance with the good—"O ye simple," as the Proverb saith, "understand his craftiness [4]!"

§ 9. *Then, distinguishing between essence and generation, he declares the empty and frivolous language of Eunomius to be like a rattle. He proceeds to show that the language used by the great Basil on the subject of the generation of the Only-begotten has been grievously slandered by Eunomius, and so ends the book.*

I will pass by these matters, however, as the absurdity involved is evident; let us examine what precedes. He says that nothing else is found, "besides the essence of the Son, which admits of the generation." What does he mean when he says this? He distinguishes two names from each other, and separating by his discourse the things signified by them, he sets each of them individually apart by itself. "The generation" is one name, and "the essence" is another. The essence, he tells us, "admits of the generation," being therefore of course something distinct from the generation. For if the generation were the essence (which is the very thing he is constantly declaring), so that the two appellations are equivalent in sense, he would not have said that the essence "admits of the generation": for that would amount to saying that the essence admits of the essence, or the generation the generation, —if, that is, the generation were the same thing as the essence. He understands, then, the generation to be one thing, and the essence to be another, which "admits of generation": for that which is taken cannot be the same with that which admits it. Well, this is what the sage and systematic statement of our author says: but as to whether there is any sense in his words, let him consider who is expert in judging. I will resume his actual words.

He says that he finds "nothing else besides

---

6 The reading of Oehler is here followed: but the sense of the clause is not clear either in his text or in that of the Paris editions.
7 Phil. ii. 6.   8 Heb. i. 3.   9 Phil. ii. 7.
1 S. John vi 27.   2 S. John xiv. 9.

3 Cf. S. John xiv. 10.   4 Prov. viii. 5 (LXX.).

the essence of the Son which admits of the generation"; that there is no sense in his words, however, is clear to every one who hears his statement at all: the task which remains seems to be to bring to light the blasphemy which he is trying to construct by aid of these meaningless words. For he desires, even if he cannot effect his purpose, to produce in his hearers by this slackness of expression, the notion that the essence of the Son is the result of construction: but he calls its construction "generation," decking out his horrible blasphemy with the fairest phrase, that if "construction" is the meaning conveyed by the word "generation," the idea of the creation of the Lord may receive a ready assent. He says, then, that the essence "admits of generation," so that every construction may be viewed, as it were, in some subject matter. For no one would say that that is constructed which has no existence, so extending "making" in his discourse, as if it were some constructed fabric, to the nature of the Only-begotten God [5]. "If, then," he says, "it admits of this generation,"—wishing to convey some such meaning as this, that it would not have been, had it not been constructed. But what else is there among the things we contemplate in the creation which *is* without being made? Heaven, earth, air, sea, everything whatever that is, surely *is* by being made. How, then, comes it that he considered it a peculiarity in the nature of the Only-begotten, that it "admits generation" (for this is his name for making) "into its actual essence," as though the humble-bee or the gnat did not admit generation into itself [6], but into something else besides itself. It is therefore acknowledged by his own writings, that by them the essence of the Only-begotten is placed on the same level with the smallest parts of the creation: and every proof by which he attempts to establish the alienation of the Son from the Father has the same force also in the case of individual things. What need has he, then, for this varied acuteness to

establish the diversity of nature, when he ought to have taken the short cut of denial, by openly declaring that the name of the Son ought not to be confessed, or the Only-begotten God to be preached in the churches, but that we ought to esteem the Jewish worship as superior to the faith of Christians, and, while we confess the Father as being alone Creator and Maker of the world, to reduce all other things to the name and conception of the creation, and among these to speak of that work which preceded the rest as a "thing made," which came into being by some constructive operation, and to give Him the title of "First created," instead of Only-begotten and Very Son. For when these opinions have carried the day, it will be a very easy matter to bring doctrines to a conclusion in agreement with the aim they have in view, when all are guided, as you might expect from such a principle, to the consequence that it is impossible that He Who is neither begotten nor a Son, but has His existence through some energy, should share in essence with God. So long, however, as the declarations of the Gospel prevail, by which He is proclaimed as "Son," and "Only-begotten," and "of the Father," and "of God," and the like, Eunomius will talk his nonsense to no purpose, leading himself and his followers astray by such idle chatter. For while the title of "Son" speaks aloud the true relation to the Father, who is so foolish that, while John and Paul and the rest of the choir of the Saints proclaim these words,—words of truth, and words that point to the close affinity, —he does not look to them, but is led by the empty rattle of Eunomius' sophisms to think that Eunomius is a truer guide than the teaching of those who by the Spirit speak mysteries [7], and who bear Christ in themselves? Why, who is this Eunomius? Whence was he raised up to be the guide of Christians?

But let all this pass, and let our earnestness about what lies before us calm down our heart, that is swollen with jealousy on behalf of the faith against the blasphemers. For how is it possible not to be moved to wrath and hatred, while our God, and Lord, and Life-giver, and Saviour is insulted by these wretched men? If he had reviled my father according to the flesh, or been at enmity with my benefactor, would it have been possible to bear without emotion his anger against those I love? And if the Lord of my soul, Who gave it being when it was not, and redeemed it when in bondage, and gave me to taste of this present life, and prepared for me the life to come, Who calls us to a kingdom, and gives me His commands that we may escape the damnation of hell,—these are small things that I speak of, and not worthy

---

5 This whole passage, as it stands in Oehler's text, (which has here been followed without alteration,) is obscure: the connection between the clauses themselves is by no means clear; and the general meaning of the passage, in view of the succeeding sentences, seems doubtful. For it seems here to be alleged that Eunomius considered the κατασκευή to imply the previous existence of some material, so to say, which was moulded by generation—on the ground that no one would say that the essence, or anything else, was constructed without being existent. On the other hand it is immediately urged that this is just what *would* be said of all created things. If the passage might be emended thus:—ἵν', ὥσπερ ἐν ὑποκειμένῳ τινὶ πράγματι πᾶσα κατασκευὴ θεωρεῖται, (οὐ γὰρ ἄν τις εἴποι κατασκευάσθαι ὃ μὴ ὑφέστηκεν), οὕτως οἷον κατασκευάσματι τῇ τοῦ μονογενοῦς φύσει προτείη τῷ λόγῳ τὴν ποίησιν—we should have a comparatively clear sense—"in order that as all construction is observed in some subject matter, (for no one would say that that is constructed which has not existence) so he may extend the process of 'making' by his argument to the nature of the Only-begotten God, as to some product of construction." The force of this would be, that Eunomius is really employing the idea of "receiving generation," to imply that the essence of the Only-begotten is a κατασκεύασμα: and this, Gregory says, puts him at once on a level with the physical creation.

6 Oehler's punctuation seems faulty here.

7 Cf. 1 Cor. xiv. 2.

to express the greatness of our common Lord, —He that is worshipped by all creation, by things in heaven, and things on earth, and things under the earth, by Whom stand the unnumbered myriads of the heavenly ministers, to Whom is turned all that is under rule here, and that has the desire of good—if He is exposed to reviling by men, for whom it is not enough to associate themselves with the party of the apostate, but who count it loss not to draw others by their scribbling into the same gulf with themselves, that those who come after may not lack a hand to lead them to destruction, is there any one [8] who blames us for our anger against these men? But let us return to the sequence of his discourse.

He next proceeds once more to slander us as dishonouring the generation of the Son by human similitudes, and mentions what was written on these points by our father [9], where he says that while by the word "Son" two things are signified, the being formed by passion, and the true relationship to the begetter, he does not admit in discourses upon things divine the former sense, which is unseemly and carnal, but in so far as the latter tends to testify to the glory of the Only-begotten, this alone finds a place in the sublime doctrines. Who, then, dishonours the generation of the Son by human notions? He who sets far from the Divine generation what belongs to passion and to man, and joins the Son impassibly to Him that begat Him? or he who places Him Who brought all things into being on a common level with the lower creation? Such an idea, however, as it seems,—that of associating the Son in the majesty of the Father,—this new wisdom seems to regard as dishonouring; while it considers as great and

sublime the act of bringing Him down to equality with the creation that is in bondage with us. Empty complaints! Basil is slandered as dishonouring the Son, who honours Him even as he honours the Father [1], and Eunomius is the champion of the Only-begotten, who severs Him from the good nature of the Father! Such a reproach Paul also once incurred with the Athenians, being charged therewith by them as "a setter forth of strange gods [2]," when he was reproving the wandering among their gods of those who were mad in their idolatry, and was leading them to the truth, preaching the resurrection by the Son These charges are now brought against Paul's follower by the new Stoics and Epicureans, who "spend their time in nothing else," as the history says of the Athenians, "but either to tell or to hear some new thing [3]." For what could be found newer than this,—a Son of an energy, and a Father of a creature, and a new God springing up from nothing, and good at variance with good? These are they who profess to honour Him with due honour by saying that He is not that which the nature of Him that begat Him is. Is Eunomius not ashamed of the form of such honour, if one were to say that he himself is not akin in nature to his father, but has community with something of another kind? If he who brings the Lord of the creation into community with the creation declares that he honours Him by so doing, let him also himself be honoured by having community assigned him with what is brute and senseless: but, if he finds community with an inferior nature hard and insolent treatment, how is it honour for Him Who, as the prophet saith, "ruleth with His power for ever [4]," to be ranked with that nature which is in subjection and bondage? But enough of this.

---

8 Reading ἆρά τις for ἆρα τίς of Oehler's text.
9 That is, by S. Basil: the reference seems to be to the treatise *Adv. Eunomium* ii 24 (p. 260 C. in the Benedictine edition), but the quotation is not exact.

1 Cf. S. John v. 23.
3 Acts xvii. 21.
2 Acts xvii. 18.
4 Ps. lxvi. 6 (LXX.).

BOOK V

§ I. *The fifth book promises to speak of the words contained in the saying of the Apostle Peter, but delays their exposition. He discourses first of the creation, to the effect that, while nothing therein is deserving of worship, yet men, led astray by their ill-informed and feeble intelligence, and marvelling at its beauty, deified the several parts of the universe. And herein he excellently expounds the passage of Isaiah, " I am God, the first."*

It is now, perhaps, time to make enquiry into what is said concerning the words of the Apostle Peter [1], by Eunomius himself, and by our father [2] concerning the latter. If a detailed examination should extend our discourse to considerable length, the fair-minded reader will no doubt pardon this, and will not blame us for wasting time in words, but lay the blame on him who has given occasion for them. Let me be allowed also to make some brief remarks preliminary to the proposed enquiry: it may be that they too will be found not to be out of keeping with the aim of our discussion.

That no created thing is deserving of man's worship, the divine word so clearly declares as a law, that such a truth may be learned from almost the whole of the inspired Scripture. Moses, the Tables, the Law, the Prophets that follow, the Gospels, the decrees of the Apostles, all alike forbid the act of reverencing the creation. It would be a lengthy task to set out in order the particular passages which refer to this matter; but though we set out only a few from among the many instances of the inspired testimony, our argument is surely equally convincing, since each of the divine words, albeit the least, has equal force for declaration of the truth. Seeing, then, that our conception of existences is divided into two, the creation and the uncreated Nature, if the present contention of our adversaries should prevail, so that we should say that the Son of God is created, we should be absolutely compelled either to set at naught the proclamation of the Gospel, and to refuse to worship that God the Word Who was in the beginning, on the ground that we must not address worship to the creation, or, if these marvels recorded in the Gospels are too urgent for us, by which we are led to reverence and to worship Him Who is displayed in them, to place, in that case, the created and the Uncreated on the same level of honour; seeing that if, according to our adversaries' opinion, even the created God is worshipped, though having in His nature no prerogative above the rest of the creation, and if this view should get the upper hand, the doctrines of religion will be entirely transformed to a kind of anarchy and democratic independence. For when men believe that the nature they worship is not one, but have their thoughts turned away to diverse Godheads, there will be none who will stay the conception of the Deity in its progress through creation, but the Divine element, once recognized in creation, will become a stepping-stone to the like conception in the case of that which is next contemplated, and that again for the next in order, and as a result of this inferential process the error will extend to all things, as the first deceit makes its way by contiguous cases even to the very last.

To show that I am not making a random statement beyond what probability admits of, I will cite as a credible testimony in favour of my assertion the error which still prevails among the heathen [3]. Seeing that they, with their untrained and narrow intelligence, were disposed to look with wonder on the beauties of nature, not employing the things they beheld as a leader and guide to the beauty of the Nature that transcends them, they rather made their intelligence halt on arriving at the objects of its apprehension, and marvelled at each part of the creation severally—for this cause they did not stay their conception of the Deity at any single one of the things they beheld, but deemed everything they looked on in creation to be divine. And thus with the Egyptians, as the error developed its force more in respect of intellectual objects, the countless forms of spiritual beings were reckoned to be so many natures of Gods; while with the Babylonians the un-

[1] The words referred to are those in Acts ii. 36.
[2] S. Basil: the passages discussed are afterwards referred to in detail.

[3] With the following passage may be compared the parallel account in the Book of Wisdom (ch. xiii.).

erring circuit of the firmament was accounted a God, to whom they also gave the name of Bel. So, too, the foolishness of the heathen deifying individually the seven successive spheres, one bowed down to one, another to another, according to some individual form of error. For as they perceived all these circles moving in mutual relation, seeing that they had gone astray as to the most exalted, they maintained the same error by logical sequence, even to the last of them. And in addition to these, the æther itself, and the atmosphere diffused beneath it, the earth and sea and the subterranean region, and in the earth itself all things which are useful or needful for man's life,—of all these there was none which they held to be without part or lot in the Divine nature, but they bowed down to each of them, bringing themselves, by means of some one of the objects conspicuous in the creation, into bondage to all the successive parts of the creation, in such a way that, had the act of reverencing the creation been from the beginning even to them a thing evidently unlawful, they would not have been led astray into this deceit of polytheism. Let us look to it, then, lest we too share the same fate,—we who in being taught by Scripture to reverence the true Godhead, were trained to consider all created existence as external to the Divine nature, and to worship and revere that uncreated Nature alone, Whose characteristic and token is that it never either begins to be or ceases to be ; since the great Isaiah thus speaks of the Divine nature with reference to these doctrines, in his exalted utterance,—who speaks in the person of the Deity, " I am the first, and hereafter am I, and no God was before Me, and no God shall be after Me [4]." For knowing more perfectly than all others the mystery of the religion of the Gospel, this great prophet, who foretold even that marvellous sign concerning the Virgin, and gave us the good tidings [5] of the birth of the Child, and clearly pointed out to us that Name of the Son,—he, in a word, who by the Spirit includes in himself all the truth,—in order that the characteristic of the Divine Nature, whereby we discern that which really *is* from that which came into being, might be made as plain as possible to all, utters this saying in the person of God : " I am the first, and hereafter am I, and before Me no God hath been, and after Me is none." Since, then, neither is that God which was before God, nor is that God which is after God, (for that which is after God is the creation, and that which is anterior to God is

nothing, and Nothing is not God :—or one should rather say, that which is anterior to God is God in His eternal bl ssedness, defined in contradistinction to Nothing [6]) ;—since, I say, this inspired utterance was spoken by the mouth of the prophet, we learn by his means the doctrine that the Divine Nature is one, continuous with Itself and indiscerptible, not admitting in Itself priority and posteriority, though it be declared in Trinity, and with no one of the things we contemplate in it more ancient or more recent than another. Since, then, the saying is the saying of God, whether you grant that the words are the words of the Father or of the Son, the orthodox doctrine is equally upheld by either. For if it is the Father that speaks thus, He bears witness to the Son that He is not "after" Himself : for if the Son is God, and whatever is "after" the Father is not God, it is clear that the saying bears witness to the truth that the Son is in the Father, and not after the Father. If, on the other hand, one were to grant that this utterance is of the Son, the phrase, "None hath been before Me," will be a clear intimation that He Whom we contemplate "in the Beginning [7]" is apprehended together with the eternity of the Beginning. If, then, anything is "after" God, this is discovered, by the passages quoted, to be a creature, and not God : for He says, "That which is after Me is not God [8]."

§ 2. *He then explains the phrase of S. Peter, "Him God made Lord and Christ." And herein he sets forth the opposing statement of Eunomius, which he made on account of such phrase against S. Basil, and his lurking revilings and insults.*

Now that we have had presented to us this preliminary view of existences, it may be opportune to examine the passage before us. It is said, then, by Peter to the Jews, "*Him* God made Lord and Christ, this Jesus Whom ye crucified [9]," while on our part it is said that it is not pious to refer the word "made" to the Divine Nature of the Only-begotten, but that it is to be referred to that "form of a servant [1]," which came into being by the Incarnation [2], in the due time of His appearing in the flesh ; and, on the other hand, those who press the phrase the contrary way say that in the word "made" the Apostle indicates the pretemporal generation of the Son. We shall,

---

[4] Cf. Is. xli. 4, xliv. 6, xlviii. 12 (LXX.). If the whole passage is intended to be a quotation, it is not made exactly from any one of these ; the opening words are from the second passage referred to ; and perhaps this is the only portion intended to be a quotation, the second clause being explanatory ; the words of the second clause are varied in the repetition immediately afterwards.
[5] εὐαγγελισάμενος.

[6] πρὸς οὐδὲν ὁριζόμενος ; *i.e.* before the name of "God" could be applied, as now, in contradistinction to *creation*, it was applied in contradistinction to nothing, and that distinction was in a sense the definition of God. Or the words may be turned, as Gulonius turns them, "nulla re determinatus," "with no limitation"—the contradistinction to creation being regarded as a limitation by way of definition.   [7] S. John i. 1.
[8] Taking the whole phrase τὸ μετ' ἐμὲ ὂν as a loose quotation.
[9] Acts ii. 36.   [1] Phil. ii. 7.   [2] οἰκονομικῶς γενομένην.

therefore, set forth the passage in the midst, and after a detailed examination of both the suppositions, leave the judgment of the truth to our reader. Of our adversaries' view Eunomius himself may be a sufficient advocate, for he contends gallantly on the matter, so that in going through his argument word by word we shall completely follow out the reasoning of those who strive against us : and we ourselves will act as champion of the doctrine on our side as best we may, following so far as we are able the line of the argument previously set forth by the great Basil. But do you, who by your reading act as judges in the cause, "execute true judgment," as one of the prophets[3] says, not awarding the victory to contentious preconceptions, but to the truth as it is manifested by examination. And now let the accuser of our doctrines come forward, and read his indictment, as in a court of law.

"In addition, moreover, to what we have mentioned, by his refusal to take the word 'made' as referring to the essence of the Son, and withal by his being ashamed of the Cross, he ascribes to the Apostles what no one even of those who have done their best to speak ill of them on the score of stupidity, lays to their charge ; and at the same time he clearly introduces, by his doctrines and arguments, two Christs and two Lords ; for he says that it was not the Word Who was in the beginning Whom God made Lord and Christ, but He Who 'emptied Himself to take the form of a servant[4],' and 'was crucified through weakness[5].' At all events the great Basil writes expressly as follows[6] :—' Nor, moreover, is it the intention of the Apostle to present to us that existence of the Only-begotten which was before the ages (which is now the subject of our argument), for he clearly speaks, not of the very essence of God the Word, Who was in the beginning with God, but of Him Who emptied Himself to take the form of a servant, and became conformable to the body of our humiliation[7], and was crucified through weakness.' And again, ' This is known to any one who even in a small degree applies his mind to the meaning of the Apostle's words, that he is not setting forth to us the mode of the Divine existence, but is introducing the terms which belong to the Incarnation ; for he says, *Him* God made Lord and Christ, this Jesus Whom ye crucified, evidently laying stress by the demonstrative word on that in Him which was human and was seen by all[8].'

"This, then, is what the man has to say who

substitutes,—for we may not speak of it as ' application,' lest any one should blame for such madness men holy and chosen for the preaching of godliness, so as to reproach their doctrine with a fall into such extravagance,—who substitutes his own mind[9] for the intention of the Apostles ! With what confusion are they not filled, who refer their own nonsense to the memory of the saints ! With what absurdity do they not abound, who imagine that the man 'emptied himself' to become man, and who maintain that He Who by obedience ' humbled himself' to take the form of a servant was made conformable to men even before He took that form upon Him ! Who, pray, ye most reckless of men, when he *has* the form of a servant, takes the form of a servant ? and how can any one 'empty himself' to become the very thing which he is ? You will find no contrivance to meet this, bold as you are in saying or thinking things uncontrivable. Are you not verily of all men most miserable, who suppose that a man has suffered death for all men, and ascribe your own redemption to him ? For if it is not of the Word Who was in the beginning and was God that the blessed Peter speaks, but of him who was ' seen,' and who 'emptied Himself,' as Basil says, and if the man who was seen ' emptied Himself' to take ' the form of a servant,' and He Who ' emptied Himself' to take ' the form of a servant,' emptied Himself to come into being as man, then the man who was seen emptied himself to come into being as man[1]. The very nature of things is repugnant to this ; and it is expressly contradicted by that writer[2] who celebrates this dispensation in his discourse concerning the Divine Nature, when he says not that the man who was seen, but that the Word Who was in the beginning and was God took upon Him flesh, which is equivalent in other words to taking ' the form of a servant.' If, then, you hold that these things are to be believed; depart from your error, and cease to believe that the man 'emptied himself' to become man. And if you are not able to persuade those who will not be persuaded, destroy their incredulity by another saying, a second de-

---

[3] Zech. vii. 9.   [4] Cf. Phil. ii. 7.   [5] Cf. 2 Cor. xiii. 4.
[6] The quotations are from S. Basil c. Eunomius II. 3. (pp. 239-40 in the Benedictine edition.)
[7] Cf. Phil iii. 21.
[8] The latter part of the quotation from S. Basil does not exactly agree with the Benedictine text, but the variations are not material.

[9] Reading ἑαυτοῦ for the ἑαυτῶν of Oehler's text, for which no authority is alleged by the editor, and which is probably a mere misprint.
[1] The argument here takes the form of a *reductio ad absurdum* ; assuming that S. Peter's reference is to the "visible man," and bearing in mind S. Basil's words that S. Peter refers to Him Who "emptied Himself," it is said "then it was the 'visible man' who 'emptied himself.' But the purpose of that 'emptying' was the ' taking the form of a servant,' which again is the coming into being as man : therefore the ' visible ma1 ' ' emptied himself,' to come into being as man, which is absurd." The wording of S. Basil's statement makes the argument in a certain degree plausible ;—if he had said that S. Peter referred to the Son, not in regard to his actual essence, but in regard to the fact that He "emptied Himself" to become man, and as so having "emptied Himself" (which is no doubt what he intended his words to mean), then the *reductio ad absurdum* would not apply ; nor would the later arguments, by which Eunomius proceeds to prove that He Who "emptied Himself" was no mere man, but the Word Who was in the beginning, have any force as against S. Basil's statement.   [2] S. John i. 1 sqq.

cision against them. Remember him who says, 'Who being in the form of God thought it not robbery to be equal with God, but emptied Himself, taking the form of a servant.' There is none among men who will appropriate this phrase to himself. None of the saints that ever lived was the Only-begotten God and became man :—for that is what it means to 'take the form of a servant,' 'being in the form of God.' If, then, the blessed Peter speaks of Him Who 'emptied Himself' to 'take the form of a servant,' and if He Who was 'in the form of God' did 'empty Himself' to 'take the form of a servant,' and if He Who in the beginning was God, being the Word and the Only-begotten God, is He Who was 'in the form of God,' then the blessed Peter speaks to us of Him Who was in the beginning and was God, and expounds to us that it was He Who became Lord and Christ. This, then, is the conflict which Basil wages against himself, and he clearly appears neither to have 'applied his own mind to the intention of the Apostles', nor to be able to preserve the sequence of his own arguments ; for, according to them, he must, if he is conscious of their irreconcilable character, admit that the Word Who was in the beginning and was God became Lord ; or if he tries to fit together statements that are mutually conflicting, and contentiously stands by them, he will add to them others yet more hostile, and maintain that there are two Christs and two Lords. For if the Word that was in the beginning and was God be one, and He Who 'emptied Himself' and 'took the form of a servant' be another, and if God the Word, by Whom are all things, be Lord, and this Jesus, Who was crucified after all things had come into being, be Lord also, there are, according to his view, two Lords and Christs. Our author, then, cannot by any argument clear himself from this manifest blasphemy. But if any one were to say in support of him that the Word Who was in the beginning is indeed the same Who became Lord, but that He became Lord and Christ in respect of His presence in the flesh, He will surely be constrained to say that the Son was not Lord before His presence in the flesh. At all events, even if Basil and his faithless followers falsely proclaim two Lords and two Christs, for us there is one Lord and Christ, by Whom all things were made, not becoming Lord by way of promotion, but existing before all creation and before all ages, the Lord Jesus, by Whom are all things, while all the saints with one harmonious voice teach us this truth and proclaim it as the most excellent of doctrines. Here the blessed John teaches us that God the Word, by Whom all things were made, has become incarnate, saying, 'And the Word was

made flesh [3]' ; here the most admirable Paul, urging those who attend to him to humility, speaks of Christ Jesus, Who was in the form of God, and emptied Himself to take the form of a servant, and was humbled to death, even the death of the Cross [4] ; and again in another passage calls Him Who was crucified 'the Lord of Glory' : 'for had they known it,' he says, 'they would not have crucified the Lord of Glory [5]'. Indeed, he speaks far more openly than this of the very essential nature by the name of 'Lord,' where he says, 'Now the Lord is the Spirit [6]'. If, then, the Word Who was in the beginning, in that He is Spirit, is Lord, and the Lord of glory, and if God made Him Lord and Christ, it was the very Spirit and God the Word that God so made, and not some other Lord Whom Basil dreams about."

§ 3. *A remarkable and original reply to these utterances, and a demonstration of the power of the Crucified, and of the fact that this subjection was of the Human Nature, not of that which the Only-begotten has from the Father. Also an explanation of the figure of the Cross, and of the appellation "Christ," and an account of the good gifts bestowed on the Human Nature by the Godhead which was commingled with it.*

Well, such is his accusation. But I think it necessary in the first place to go briefly, by way of summary, over the points that he urges, and then to proceed to correct by my argument what he has said, that those who are judging the truth may find it easy to remember the indictment against us, which we have to answer, and that we may be able to dispose of each of the charges in regular order. He says that we are ashamed of the Cross of Christ, and slander the saints, and say that a man has "emptied himself" to become man, and suppose that the Lord had the "form of a servant" before His presence by the Incarnation, and ascribe our redemption to a man, and speak in our doctrine of two Christs and two Lords, or, if we do not do this, then we deny that the Only-begotten was Lord and Christ before the Passion. So that we may avoid this blasphemy, he will have us confess that the essence of the Son has been made, on the ground that the Apostle Peter by his own voice establishes such a doctrine. This is the substance of the accusation ; for all that he has been at the trouble of saying by way of abuse of ourselves, I will pass by in silence, as being not at all to the point. It may be that this rhetorical stroke of phrases framed according to some artificial

---

[3] S. John i. 14. [4] Cf. Phil. ii. 7. 8. [5] 1 Cor. ii. 8. [6] 2 Cor. iii. 17.

theory is the ordinary habit of those who play the rhetorician, an invention to swell the bulk of their indictment. Let our sophist then use his art to display his insolence, and vaunt his strength in reproaches against us, showing off his strokes in the intervals of the contest; let him call us foolish, call us of all men most reckless, of all men most miserable, full of confusion and absurdity, and make light of us at his good pleasure in any way he likes, and we will bear it; for to a reasonable man disgrace lies, not in hearing one who abuses him, but in making retort to what he says. There may even be some good in his expenditure of breath against us; for it may be that while he occupies his railing tongue in denouncing us he will at all events make some truce in his conflict against God. So let him take his fill of insolence as he likes: none will reply to him. For if a man has foul and loathsome breath, by reason of bodily disorder, or of some pestilential and malignant disease, he would not rouse any healthy person to emulate his misfortune, so that one should choose, by himself acquiring disease, to repay, in the same evil kind, the unpleasantness of the man's ill odour. Such men our common nature bids us to pity, not to imitate. And so let us pass by everything of this kind which by mockery, indignation, provocation, and abuse, he has assiduously mixed up with his argument, and examine only his arguments as they concern the doctrinal points at issue. We shall begin again, then, from the beginning, and meet each of his charges in turn.

The beginning of his accusation was that we are ashamed of the Cross of Him Who for our sakes underwent the Passion. Surely he does not intend to charge against us also that we preach the doctrine of dissimilarity in essence! Why, it is rather to those who turn aside to this opinion that the reproach belongs of going about to make the Cross a shameful thing. For if by both parties alike the dispensation of the Passion is held as part of the faith, while *we* hold it necessary to honour, even as the Father is honoured, the God Who was manifested by the Cross, and *they* find the Passion a hindrance to glorifying the Only-begotten God equally with the Father that begat Him, then our sophist's charges recoil upon himself, and in the words with which he imagines himself to be accusing us, he is publishing his own doctrinal impiety. For it is clear that the reason why he sets the Father above the Son, and exalts Him with supreme honour, is this,—that in Him is not seen the shame of the Cross: and the reason why he asseverates that the nature of the Son varies in the sense of inferiority is this,—that the reproach of the Cross is referred to Him alone, and does not touch the Father. And let

no one think that in saying this I am only following the general drift of his composition, for in going through all the blasphemy of his speech, which is there laboriously brought together, I found, in a passage later than that before us, this very blasphemy clearly expressed in undisguised language; and I propose to set forth, in the orderly course of my own argument, what they have written, which runs thus :—" If," he says, " he can show that the God Who is over all, Who is the unapproachable Light, was incarnate, or could be incarnate, came under authority, obeyed commands, came under the laws of men, bore the Cross, then let him say that the Light is equal to the Light." Who then is it who is ashamed of the Cross? he who, even after the Passion, worships the Son equally with the Father, or he who even before the Passion insults Him, not only by ranking Him with the creation, but by maintaining that He is of passible nature, on the ground that He could not have come to experience His sufferings had He not had a nature capable of such sufferings? We on our part assert that even the body in which He underwent His Passion, by being mingled with the Divine Nature, was made by that commixture to be that which the assuming [7] Nature is. So far are we from entertaining any low idea concerning the Only-begotten God, that if anything belonging to our lowly nature was assumed in His dispensation of love for man, we believe that even this was transformed to what is Divine and incorruptible [8]; but Eunomius makes the suffering of the Cross to be a sign of divergence in essence, in the sense of inferiority, considering, I know not how, the surpassing act of power, by which He was able to perform this, to be an evidence of weakness; failing to perceive the fact that, while nothing which moves according to its own nature is looked upon as surprisingly wonderful, all things that overpass the limitations of their own nature become especially the objects of admiration, and to them every ear is turned, every mind is attentive, in wonder at the marvel. And hence it is that all who preach the word point out the wonderful character of the mystery in this respect,—that " God was manifested in the flesh [9]," that " the Word was made flesh [1]," that " the Light shined in darkness [2]," " the Life tasted death," and all such declarations which the heralds of the faith are wont to make, whereby is increased the marvellous character

[7] Or " resuming." Cf. Book II. § 8 (*sup.* p. 113, where see note 7).
[8] With S. Gregory's language here may be compared that of S. Athanasius (*Or. adv. Arian.* iii. 53), " It was not the Wisdom, quâ Wisdom, that ' advanced '; but the humanity in the Wisdom did advance, gradually ascending above the human nature and being made Divine (θεοποιούμενον)."
[9] 1 Tim. iii. 16, where it would appear that Gregory read θεός, not ὅς.
[1] S. John i. 14.
[2] S. John i. 5 (not verbally).

of Him Who manifested the superabundance of His power by means external to his own nature. But though they think fit to make this a subject for their insolence, though they make the dispensation of the Cross a reason for partitioning off the Son from equality of glory with the Father, we believe, as those " who from the beginning were eye-witnesses and ministers of the word [3] " delivered to us by the Holy Scriptures, that the God who was in the beginning, " afterwards ", as Baruch says, " was seen upon the earth, and conversed with men [4]," and, becoming a ransom for our death, loosed by His own resurrection the bonds of death, and by Himself made the resurrection a way for all flesh [5], and being on the same throne and in the same glory with His own Father, will in the day of judgment give sentence upon those who are judged, according to the desert of the lives they have led.   These are the things which we believe concerning Him Who was crucified, and for this cause we cease not to extol Him exceedingly, according to the measure of our powers, that He Who by reason of His unspeakable and unapproachable greatness is not comprehensible by any, save by Himself and the Father and the Holy Spirit, He, I say, was able even to descend to community with our weakness.   But they adduce this proof of the Son's alienation in nature from the Father, that the Lord was manifested by the flesh and by the Cross, arguing on the ground that the Father's nature remained pure in impassibility, and could not in any way admit of a community which tended to passion, while the Son, by reason of the divergence of His nature by way of humiliation, was not incapable of being brought to experience the flesh and death, seeing that the change of condition was not great, but one which took place in a certain sense from one like state to another state kindred and homogeneous, because the nature of man is created, and the nature of the Only-begotten is created also. Who then is fairly charged with being ashamed of the Cross? he who speaks basely of it [6], or he who contends for its more exalted aspect? I know not whether our accuser, who thus abases the God Who was made known upon the Cross, has heard the lofty speech of Paul, in what terms and at what length he discourses with his exalted lips concerning that Cross.   For he, who was able to make himself known by miracles so many and so great, says, " God forbid that I should glory in anything else, than in the Cross of Christ [7]." And to the Corinthians he says that the word of the Cross is " the

power of God to them that are in a state of salvation [8]." To the Ephesians, moreover, he describes by the figure of the Cross the power that controls and holds together the universe, when he expresses a desire that they may be exalted to know the exceeding glory of this power, calling it height, and depth, and breadth, and length [9], speaking of the several projections we behold in the figure of the Cross by their proper names, so that he calls the upper part " height," and that which is below, on the opposite side of the junction, " depth," while by the name " length and breadth " he indicates the cross-beam projecting to either side, that hereby might be manifested this great mystery, that both things in heaven, and things under the earth, and all the furthest bounds of the things that are, are ruled and sustained by Him Who gave an example of this unspeakable and mighty power in the figure of the Cross.   But I think there is no need to contend further with such objections, as I judge it superfluous to be anxious about urging arguments against calumny when even a few words suffice to show the truth.   Let us therefore pass on to another charge.

He says that by us the saints are slandered. Well, if he has heard it himself, let him tell us the words of our defamation: if he thinks we have uttered it to others, let him show the truth of his charge by witnesses: if he demonstrates it from what we have written, let him read the words, and we will bear the blame.   But he cannot bring forward anything of the kind : our writings are open for examination to any one who desires it.   If it was not said to himself, and he has not heard it from others, and has no proof to offer from our writings, I think he who has to make answer on this point may well hold his peace : silence is surely the fitting answer to an unfounded charge.

The Apostle Peter says, " God made this Jesus, Whom ye crucified, Lord and Christ [1]." We, learning this from him, say that the whole context of the passage tends one way,—the Cross itself, the human name, the indicative turn of the phrase.   For the word of the Scripture says that in regard to one person two things were wrought,—by the Jews, the Passion, and by God, honour ; not as though one person had suffered and another had been honoured by exaltation : and he further explains this yet more clearly by his words in what follows, " being exalted by the right hand of God."   Who then was " exalted " ?   He that was lowly, or He that was the Highest ? and what else is the lowly, but the Humanity? what else is the Highest, but the Divinity ?   Surely, God needs not to be exalted, seeing that He is the Highest. It follows, then, that the Apostle's meaning is

---

3 S. Luke i. 2.   4 Bar. iii. 37.
5 See Note 2, p. 104, *sup.*
6 Reading αὐτοῦ (for which Oehler cites good MS. authority), for ἑαυτοῦ (the reading of his text, as well as of the Paris editions).
7 Gal. vi. 14 (not verbally).

8 Cf. 1 Cor. i. 18.   9 Cf. Eph. iii. 18.   1 Acts ii. 36.

that the Humanity was exalted : and its exaltation was effected by its becoming Lord and
Christ.   And this took place after the Passion [2].
It is not therefore the pre-temporal existence of
the Lord which the Apostle indicates by the
word " made," but that change of the lowly to
the lofty which was effected " by the right hand
of God."   Even by this phrase is declared the
mystery of godliness ; for he who says " exalted
by the right hand of God " manifestly reveals
the unspeakable dispensation of this mystery,
that the Right Hand of God, that made all
things that are, (which is the Lord, by Whom
all things were made, and without Whom
nothing that is subsists,) Itself raised to Its
own height the Man united with It, making
Him also to be what It is by nature.   Now It
is Lord and King : Christ is the King's name :
these things It made Him too.   For as He was
highly exalted by being in the Highest, so too
He became all else,—Immortal in the Immortal,
Light in the Light, Incorruptible in the Incorruptible, Invisible in the Invisible, Christ in the
Christ, Lord in the Lord.   For even in physical
combinations, when one of the combined parts
exceeds the other in a great degree, the inferior
is wont to change completely to that which is
more potent.   And this we are plainly taught by
the voice of the Apostle Peter in his mystic discourse, that the lowly nature of Him Who was
crucified through weakness, (and weakness, as
we have heard from the Lord, marks the flesh [3],)
that lowly nature, I say, by virtue of its combination with the infinite and boundless element of
good, remained no longer in its own measures
and properties, but was by the Right Hand of
God raised up together with Itself, and became
Lord instead of servant, Christ a King instead
of a subject, Highest instead of Lowly, God
instead of man.   What handle then against the
saints did he who pretends to give warning
against us in defence of the Apostles find in the
material of our writings ?   Let us pass over this
charge also in silence ; for I think it a mean
and unworthy thing to stand up against charges
that are false and unfounded.   Let us pass on
to the more pressing part of his accusation.

§ 4. *He shows the falsehood of Eunomius'*
calumnious charge that the great Basil had
said that " man was emptied to become man,"
and demonstrates that the " emptying " of the

Only-begotten took place with a view to the
restoration to life of the Man Who had
suffered [4].

He asserts that we say that man has emptied
Himself to become man, and that He Who by
obedience humbled Himself to the form of the
servant shared the form of men even before He
took that form.   No change has been made in
the wording ; we have simply transferred the
very words from his speech to our own.   Now
if there is anything of this sort in our writings,
(for I call my master's writings *ours*) let no one
blame our orator for calumny.   I ask for all
regard for the truth : and we ourselves will give
evidence.   But if there is nothing of all this in
our writings, while his language not merely lays
blame upon us, but is indignant and wrathful as
if the matter were clearly proved, calling us full
of absurdity, nonsense, confusion, inconsistency,
and so on, I am at a loss to see the right course
to take.   Just as men who are perplexed at the
groundless rages of madmen can decide upon
no plan to follow, so I myself can find no device
to meet this perplexity.   Our master says (for
I will again recite his argument verbally), " He
is not setting forth to us the mode of the
Divine existence, but the terms which belong
to the Incarnation."   Our accuser starts from
this point, and says that we maintain that man
emptied Himself to become man !   What community is there between one statement and the
other ?   If we say that the Apostle has not
set forth to us the mode of the Divine existence, but points by his phrase to the dispensation of the Passion, we are on this ground
charged with speaking of the " emptying " of
man to become man, and with saying that the
" form of the servant " had pretemporal existence, and that the Man Who was born of Mary
existed before the coming in the flesh !   Well,
I think it superfluous to spend time in discussing
what is admitted, seeing that truth itself frees
us from the charge.   In a case, indeed, where
one may have given the calumniators some
handle against oneself, it is proper to resist
accusers : but where there is no danger of being
suspected of some absurd charge, the accusation becomes a proof, not of the false charge
made against him who is calumniated, but of the
madness of the accuser.   As, however, in dealing with the charge of being ashamed of the
Cross, we showed by our examination that the
charge recoiled upon the accuser, so we shall
show how this charge too returns upon those
who make it, since it is they, and not we, who
lay down the doctrine of the change of the Son
from like to like in the dispensation of the

---

[2] It can hardly be supposed that it is intended by S. Gregory
that we should understand that, during the years of His life on earth,
our Lord's Humanity was not so united with His Divinity that "the
visible man" was then both Lord and Christ.   He probably refers
more especially to the manifestation of His Messiahship afforded by
the Resurrection and Ascension ; but he also undoubtedly dwells
on the exaltation of the Human Nature after the Passion in terms
which would perhaps imply more than he intended to convey.   His
language on this point may be compared with the more guarded and
careful statement of Hooker.   (Eccl. Pol. V. lv. 8.)   The point of
his argument is that S. Peter's words apply to the Human Nature,
not to the Divine.   [3] Cf. S. Mark xiv. 38.

[4] This seems to be the sense of the Greek title.   The Latin
version of the earlier editions appears to represent a different reading,
" contigisse, quando in passione homo Christus passus est."

Passion. We will examine briefly, bringing them side by side, the statements of each party. We say that the Only-begotten God, having by His own agency brought all things into being, by Himself [5] has full power over all things, while the nature of man is also one of the things that were made by Him: and that when this had fallen away to evil, and come to be in the destruction of death, He by His own agency drew it up once more to immortal life, by means of the Man in whom He tabernacled, taking to Himself humanity in completeness, and that He mingled His life-giving power with our mortal and perishable nature, and changed, by the combination with Himself, our deadness to living grace and power. And this we declare to be the mystery of the Lord according to the flesh, that He Who is immutable came to be in that which is mutable, to the end that altering it for the better, and changing it from the worse, He might abolish the evil which is mingled with our mutable condition, destroying the evil in Himself. For "our God is a consuming fire [6]," by whom all the material of wickedness is done away. This is our statement. What does our accuser say? Not that He Who was immutable and uncreated was mingled with that which came into being by creation, and which had therefore suffered a change in the direction of evil; but he does say that He, being Himself created, came to that which was kindred and homogeneous with Himself, not coming from a transcendent nature to put on the lowlier nature by reason of His love to man, but becoming that very thing which He was.

For as regards the general character of the appellation, the name of "creature" is one, as predicated of all things that have come into being from nothing, while the divisions into sections of the things which we contemplate as included in the term "creature", are separated one from the other by the variation of their properties: so that if He is created, and man is created, He was "emptied," to use Eunomius' phrase, to become Himself, and changed His place, not from the transcendent to the lowly, but from what is similar in kind to what (save in regard of the special character of body and the incorporeal) is similar in dignity. To whom now will the just vote of those who have to try our cause be given, or who will seem to them to be under the weight of these charges? he who says that the created was saved by the uncreated God, or he who refers the cause of our salvation to the creature? Surely the judgment of pious men is not doubtful. For any one who knows clearly the dif-

ference which there is between the created and the uncreated, (terms of which the divergence is marked by dominion and slavery, since the uncreated God, as the prophet says, "ruleth with His power for ever [7]," while all things in the creation are servants to Him, according to the voice of the same prophet, which says "all things serve Thee [8],") he, I say, who carefully considers these matters, surely cannot fail to recognize the person who makes the Only-begotten change from servitude to servitude. For if, according to Paul, the whole creation "is in bondage [9]," and if, according to Eunomius, the essential nature of the Only-begotten is created, our adversaries maintain, surely, by their doctrines, not that the master was mingled with the servant, but that a servant came to be among servants. As for our saying that the Lord was in the form of a servant before His presence in the flesh, that is just like charging us with saying that the stars are black and the sun misty, and the sky low, and water dry, and so on:—a man who does not maintain a charge on the ground of what he has heard, but makes up what seems good to him at his own sweet will, need not be sparing in making against us such charges as these. It is just the same thing for us to be called to account for the one set of charges as for the other, so far as concerns the fact that they have no basis for them in anything that we have said. How could one who says distinctly that the true Son was in the glory of the Father, insult the eternal glory of the Only-begotten by conceiving it to have been "in the form of a servant"? When our author thinks proper to speak evil of us, and at the same time takes care to present his case with some appearance of truth, it may perhaps not be superfluous or useless to rebut his unfounded accusations.

§ 5. *Thereafter he shows that there are not two Christs or two Lords, but one Christ and one Lord, and that the Divine nature, after mingling with the Human, preserved the properties of each nature without confusion, and declares that the operations are, by reason of the union, predicated of the two natures in common, in the sense that the Lord took upon Himself the sufferings of the servant, and the Humanity is glorified with Him in the honour that is the Lord's, and that by the power of the Divine Nature that is commingled with It, the Human Nature is made anew, conformably with that Divine Nature Itself.*

His next charge too has its own absurdity of the same sort. For he reproaches us with saying that there are "two Christs," and "two Lords," without being able to make good his

---

5 This seems to be the force of αὐτῷ; αὐτὸν might give a simpler construction, but the sense would not be changed. Oehler, who here restores some words which were omitted in the earlier editions, makes no mention of any variation of reading.   6 Heb. xii. 29.   7 Ps. lxvi. 6. (LXX.).   8 Ps. cxix. 91.   9 Cf. Rom. viii. 21

charge from our words, but employing falsehood at discretion to suit his fancy. Since, then, he deems it within his power to say what he likes, why does he utter his falsehood with such care about detail, and maintain that we speak but of two Christs? Let him say, if he likes, that we preach ten Christs, or ten times ten, or extend the number to a thousand, that he may handle his calumny more vigorously. For blasphemy is equally involved in the doctrine of two Christs, and in that of more, and the character of the two charges is also equally devoid of proof. When he shows, then, that we do speak of two Christs, let him have a verdict against us, as much as though he had given proof of ten thousand. But he says that he convicts us by our own statements. Well, let us look once more at those words of our master by means of which he thinks to raise his charges against us. He says "he" (he, that is, who says "Him God made Lord and Christ, this Jesus Whom ye crucified") "is not setting forth to us the mode of the Divine existence, but the terms which belong to the Incarnation . . . laying stress by the demonstrative word on that in Him which was human and was seen by all." This is what he wrote. But whence has Eunomius managed by these words to bring on the stage his "two Christs"? Does saying that the demonstrative word lays stress on that which is visible, convey the proof of maintaining "two Christs"? Ought we (to avoid being charged with speaking of "two Highests") to deny the fact that by Him the Lord was highly exalted after His Passion? seeing that God the Word, Who was in the beginning, was Highest, and was also highly exalted after His Passion, when He rose from the dead, as the Apostle says. We must of necessity choose one of two courses—either say that He was highly exalted after the Passion (which is just the same as saying that He was made Lord and Christ), and be impeached by Eunomius, or, if we avoid the accusation, deny the confession of the high exaltation of Him Who suffered.

Now at this point it seems right to put forward once more our accuser's statement in support of our own defence. We shall therefor repeat word for word the statement laid down by him, which supports our argument, as follows :— "The blessed John," he says, "teaches us that God the Word, by Whom all things were made, has become incarnate, saying 'And the Word was made flesh.'" Does he understand what he is writing when he adds this to his own argument? I can hardly myself think that the same man can at once be aware of the meaning of these words and contend against our statement. For if any one examines the words carefully, he will find that there is no mutual conflict between what is said by us and what is said by him. For we both consider the dispensation in the flesh apart, and regard the Divine power in itself : and he, in like manner with ourselves, says that the Word that was in the beginning has been manifested in the flesh : yet no one ever charged him, nor does he charge himself, with preaching "two Words", Him Who was in the beginning, and Him Who was made flesh ; for he knows, surely, that the Word is identical with the Word, He who appeared in the flesh with Him Who was with God. But the flesh was not identical with the Godhead, till this too was transformed to the Godhead, so that of necessity one set of attributes befits God the Word, and a different set of attributes befits the "form of the servant [1]." If, then, in view of such a confession, he does not reproach himself with the duality of Words, why are we falsely charged with dividing the object of our faith into "two Christs"?—we, who say that He Who was highly exalted after His Passion, was made Lord and Christ by His union [2] with Him Who is verily Lord and Christ, knowing by what we have learnt that the Divine Nature is always one and the same, and with the same mode of existence, while the flesh in itself is that which reason and sense apprehend concerning it, but when mixed [3] with the Divine no longer remains in its own limitations and properties, but is taken up to that which is overwhelming and transcendent. Our contemplation, however, of the respective properties of the flesh and of the Godhead remains free from confusion, so long as each of these is contemplated by itself [4], as, for example, "the Word was before the ages, but the flesh came into being in the last times" : but one could not reverse this statement, and say that the latter is pretemporal, or that the Word has come into being in the last times. The flesh is of a passible, the Word of an operative nature : and neither is the flesh capable of making the things that are, nor is the power possessed by the Godhead capable of suffering. The Word was

[1] This statement would seem to imply that, at some time after the Incarnation, the Humanity of Christ was transformed to the Divine Nature, and made identical with It. From other passages in what has preceded, it would seem that this change in the mutual relation of the two Natures might, according to the words of S. Gregory, be conceived as taking place *after the Passion*. Thus it might be said that S. Gregory conceived the union of the two Natures to be, since the Passion (or, more strictly, since the "exaltation"), what the Monophysites conceived it to be from the moment of the Incarnation. But other phrases, again, seem to show that he conceived the two Natures still to remain distinct (see note 4 *inf.*). There is, however, ample justification in S. Gregory's language for the remark of Bp. Hefele, that S. Gregory "cannot entirely free himself from the notion of a transmutation of the Human Nature into the Divine." (Hefele, *Hist. of the Councils*, Eng. Trans. vol. iii. p. 4.)
[2] ἐνωσέως.   [3] ἀνακραθεῖσα πρὸς τὸ θεῖον.
[4] Here S. Gregory seems to state accurately the differentiation of the two Natures, while he recognizes the possibility of the *communicatio idiomatum* : but it is not clear that he would acknowledge that the two Natures *still remain* distinct. Even this, however, seems to be implied in his citation of Phil. ii. 11, at a later point.

in the beginning with God, the man was subject to the trial of death; and neither was the Human Nature from everlasting, nor the Divine Nature mortal: and all the rest of the attributes are contemplated in the same way. It is not the Human Nature that raises up Lazarus, nor is it the power that cannot suffer that weeps for him when he lies in the grave: the tear proceeds from the Man, the life from the true Life. It is not the Human Nature that feeds the thousands, nor is it omnipotent might that hastens to the fig-tree. Who is it that is weary with the journey, and Who is it that by His word made all the world subsist? What is the brightness of the glory, and what is that that was pierced with the nails? What form is it that is buffeted in the Passion, and what form is it that is glorified from everlasting? So much as this is clear, (even if one does not follow the argument into detail,) that the blows belong to the servant in whom the Lord was, the honours to the Lord Whom the servant compassed about, so that by reason of contact and the union of Natures the proper attributes of each belong to both [5], as the Lord receives the stripes of the servant, while the servant is glorified with the honour of the Lord; for this is why the Cross is said to be the Cross of the Lord of glory [6], and why every tongue confesses that Jesus Christ is Lord, to the glory of God the Father [7].

But if we are to discuss the other points in the same way, let us consider what it is that dies, and what it is that destroys death; what it is that is renewed, and what it is that empties itself. The Godhead "empties" Itself that It may come within the capacity of the Human Nature, and the Human Nature is renewed by becoming Divine through its commixture [8] with the Divine. For as air is not retained in water when it is dragged down by some weighty body and left in the depth of the water, but rises quickly to its kindred element, while the water is often raised up together with the air in its upward rush, being moulded by the circle of air into a convex shape with a slight and membrane-like surface, so too, when the true Life that underlay the flesh sped up, after the Passion, to Itself, the flesh also was raised up with It, being forced upwards from corruption to incorruptibility by the Divine immortality. And as fire that lies in wood hidden below the surface is often unobserved by the senses of those who see, or even touch it, but is manifest when it blazes up,

so too, at His death (which He brought about at His will, Who separated His soul from His Body, Who said to His own Father "Into Thy hands I commend My Spirit [9]," Who, as He says, "had power to lay it down and had power to take it again [1]"), He Who, because He is the Lord of glory, despised that which is shame among men, having concealed, as it were, the flame of His life in His bodily Nature, by the dispensation of His death [2], kindled and inflamed it once more by the power of His own Godhead, fostering into life that which had been brought to death, having infused with the infinity of His Divine power that humble firstfruits of our nature, made it also to be that which He Himself was—making the servile form to be Lord, and the Man born of Mary to be Christ, and Him Who was crucified through weakness to be Life and power, and making all that is piously conceived to be in God the Word to be also in that which the Word assumed, so that these attributes no longer seem to be in either Nature by way of division, but that the perishable Nature being, by its commixture with the Divine, made anew in conformity with the Nature that overwhelms it, participates in the power of the Godhead, as if one were to say that mixture makes a drop of vinegar mingled in the deep to be sea, by reason that the natural quality of this liquid does not continue in the infinity of that which overwhelms it [3]. This is our doctrine, which does not, as Eunomius charges against it, preach a plurality of Christs, but the union of the Man with the Divinity, and which calls by the name of "making" the transmutation of the Mortal to the Immortal, of the Servant to the Lord, of Sin [4] to Righteousness, of the Curse [5] to the Blessing, of the Man to Christ. What further have our slanderers left to say, to show that we preach "two Christs" in our doctrine, if we refuse to say that He Who was in the beginning from the Father uncreatedly Lord, and Christ, and the Word, and God, was "made," and declare that the blessed Peter was pointing briefly and incidentally to the mystery of the Incarnation, according to the meaning now explained, that the Nature which was crucified through weakness has Itself also, as we have said, become, by the overwhelming power of Him Who dwells in It, that which the Indweller Himself is in fact and in name, even Christ and Lord?

---

[9] S. Luke xxiii. 46.   [1] S. John x. 18.

[2] Altering Oehler's punctuation, which would connect ἐν τῇ κατὰ τὸν θάνατον οἰκονομίᾳ, not with συγκαλύψας, but with ἀνῆψε.

[3] Here may be observed at once a conformity to the phraseology of the Monophysites (bearing in mind that S. Gregory is not speaking, as they were, of the union of the two Natures in the Incarnation, but of the change wrought by the "exaltation"), and a suggestion that the Natures still remain distinct, as otherwise it would be idle to speak of the Human Nature as *participating* in the power of the Divine.

[4] Cf. 2 Cor. v. 21   [5] Cf. Gal. iii. 13.

[5] Here is truly stated the ground of the *communicatio idiomatum*: while the illustrations following seem to show that S. Gregory recognized this *communicatio* as existing at the time of our Lord's humiliation, and as continuing to exist after His "exaltation"; that he acknowledged, that is, the union of the two Natures before the "exaltation," and the distinction of the two Natures after that event.

[6] 1 Cor. ii. 8.

[7] Phil. ii. 11.   [8] ἀνακράσεως

BOOK VI

§ 1. The sixth book shows that He Who came for man's salvation was not a mere man, as Eunomius, falsely slandering him, affirmed that the great Basil had said, but the Only-begotten Son of God, putting on human flesh, and becoming a mediator between God and man, on Whom we believe, as subject to suffering in the flesh, but impassible in His Godhead; and demonstrates the calumny of Eunomius.

But I perceive that while the necessities of the subject compelled me to follow this line of thought, I have lingered too long over this passage[1]. I must now resume the train of his complaints, that we may pass by none of the charges brought against us without an answer. And first I propose that we should examine this point, that he charges us with asserting that an ordinary man has wrought the salvation of the world. For although this point has been to some extent already cleared up by the investigations we have made, we shall yet briefly deal with it once more, that the mind of those who are acting as our judges on this slanderous accusation may be entirely freed from misapprehension. So far are we from referring to an ordinary man the cause of this great and unspeakable grace, that even if any should refer so great a boon to Peter and Paul, or to an angel from heaven, we should say with Paul, "let him be anathema[2]." For Paul was not crucified for us, nor were we baptized into a human name[3]. Surely the doctrine which our adversaries oppose to the truth is not thereby strengthened when we confess that the saving power of Christ is more potent than human nature[4] :—yet it may seem to be so, for their aim is to maintain at all points the difference of the essence of the Son from that of the Father, and they strive to show the dissimilarity of essence not only by the contrast of the Generated with the Ungenerate, but also by the opposition of the passible to the impassible.

And while this is more openly maintained in the last part of their argument, it is also clearly shown in their present discourse[5]. For if he finds fault with those who refer the Passion to the Human Nature, his intention is certainly to subject to the Passion the Godhead Itself. For our conception being twofold, and admitting of two developments, accordingly as the Divinity or the Humanity is held to have been in a condition of suffering, an attack on one of these views is clearly a maintaining of the other. Accordingly, if they find fault with those who look upon the Passion as concerning the Man, they will clearly approve those who say that the Godhead of the Son was subject to passion, and the position which these last maintain becomes an argument in favour of their own absurd doctrine. For if, according to their statement, the Godhead of the Son suffers, while that of the Father is preserved in absolute impassibility, then the impassible Nature is essentially different from that which admits passion. Seeing, therefore, that the dictum before us, though, so far as it is limited by number of words, is a short one, yet affords principles and hypotheses for every kind of doctrinal pravity, it would seem right that our readers should require in our reply not so much brevity as soundness. We, then, neither attribute our own salvation to a man, nor admit that the incorruptible and Divine Nature is capable of suffering and mortality : but since we must assuredly believe the Divine utterances which declare to us that the Word that was in the beginning was God[6], and that afterward the Word made flesh was seen upon the earth and conversed with men[7], we admit in our creed those conceptions which are consonant with the Divine utterance. For when we hear that He is Light, and Power, and Righteousness, and Life, and Truth, and that by Him all things were made, we account all these and such-like statements as things to be believed, referring them to God the Word : but when we hear of pain, of slumber, of need, of trouble, of bonds, of nails, of the spear, of blood, of wounds, of burial, of the sepulchre, and all else of this kind, even if they are somewhat opposed to

---

[1] The passage in S. Peter's speech (Acts ii. 36) discussed in the preceding book.   [2] Cf. Gal. i. 8, 9.   [3] 1 Cor. i. 13.
[4] The sense of this passage is rather obscure. S. Gregory intends, it would seem, to point out that, although an acknowledgment that the suffering Christ was more than man may seem at first sight to support the Eunomian view of the passibility of the Godhead of the Son, this is not its necessary effect. Apparently either οὐ μὴν must be taken as equivalent to οὐ μὴν ἀλλὰ, or a clause such as that expressed in the translation must be supplied before τοῖς μὲν γὰρ κ.τ.λ.

[5] Altering Oehler's punctuation, which here follows that of the earlier editions.   [6] Cf. S. John i. 1.   [7] Cf. Bar. iii. 37.

what has previously been stated, we none the less admit them to be things to be believed, and true, having regard to the flesh; which we receive by faith as conjoined with the Word. For as it is not possible to contemplate the peculiar attributes of the flesh as existing in the Word that was in the beginning, so also on the other hand we may not conceive those which are proper to the Godhead as existing in the nature of the flesh. As, therefore, the teaching of the Gospel concerning our Lord is mingled, partly of lofty and Divine ideas, partly of those which are lowly and human, we assign every particular phrase accordingly to one or other of these Natures which we conceive in the mystery, that which is human to the Humanity, that which is lofty to the Godhead, and say that, as God, the Son is certainly impassible and incapable of corruption : and whatever suffering is asserted concerning Him in the Gospel, He assuredly wrought by means of His Human Nature which admitted of such suffering. For verily the Godhead works the salvation of the world by means of that body which encompassed It, in such wise that the suffering was of the body, but the operation was of God ; and even if some wrest to the support of the opposite doctrine the words of the Apostle, "God spared not His own Son[8]," and, "God sent His own Son[9]," and other similar phrases which seem to refer, in the matter of the Passion, to the Divine Nature, and not to the Humanity, we shall none the less refuse to abandon sound doctrine, seeing that Paul himself declares to us more clearly the mystery of this subject. For he everywhere attributes to the Human element in Christ the dispensation of the Passion, when he says, "for since by man came death, by man came also the resurrection of the dead[1]," and, "God, sending His own Son in the likeness of sinful flesh, condemned sin in the flesh[9]" (for he says, "in the *flesh*," not "in the Godhead"); and "He was crucified through weakness" (where by "weakness" he means "the flesh"), "yet liveth by power[2]" (while he indicates by "power" the Divine Nature) ; and, "He died unto sin" (that is, with regard to the body), "but liveth unto God[3]" (that is, with regard to the Godhead, so that by these words it is established that, while the Man tasted death, the immortal Nature did not admit the suffering of death) ; and again, "He made Him to be sin for us, Who knew no sin[4]," giving once more the name of "sin" to the flesh.

§ 2. *Then he again mentions S. Peter's word, "made," and the passage in the Epistle to the Hebrews, which says that Jesus was made by* God "*an Apostle and High Priest*" : *and, after giving a sufficient answer to the charges brought against him by Eunomius, shows that Eunomius himself supports Basil's arguments, and says that the Only-begotten Son, when He had put on the flesh, became Lord.*

And although we make these remarks in passing, the parenthetic addition seems, perhaps, not less important than the main question before us. For since, when St. Peter says, "He made Him Lord and Christ[5]," and again, when the Apostle Paul says to the Hebrews that He made Him a priest[6], Eunomius catches at the word "made" as being applicable to His pretemporal existence, and thinks thereby to establish his doctrine that the Lord is a thing made[7], let him now listen to Paul when he says, "He made Him to be sin for us, Who knew not sin[4]." If he refers the word "made," which is used of the Lord in the passages from the Epistle to the Hebrews, and from the words of Peter, to the pretemporal idea, he might fairly refer the word in that passage which says that God *made* Him to be sin, to the first existence of His essence, and try to show by this, as in the case of his other testimonies, that he was "made", so as to refer the word "made" to the essence, acting consistently with himself, and to discern sin in that essence. But if he shrinks from this by reason of its manifest absurdity, and argues that, by saying, "He made Him to be sin," the Apostle indicates the dispensation of the last times, let him persuade himself by the same train of reasoning that the word "made" refers to that dispensation in the other passages also.

Let us, however, return to the point from which we digressed ; for we might gather together from the same Scripture countless other passages, besides those quoted, which bear upon the matter. And let no one think that the divine Apostle is divided against himself in contradiction, and affords by his own utterances matter for their contentions on either side to those who dispute upon the doctrines. For careful examination would find that his argument is accurately directed to one aim ; and he is not halting in his opinions : for while he everywhere proclaims the combination of the Human with the Divine, he none the less discerns in each its proper nature, in the sense that while the human weakness is changed for the better by its communion with the imperishable, the Divine power, on the other hand, is not abased by its contact with the lowly form of nature. When therefore he says, "He spared not His own Son," he contrasts the true Son with the other sons, begotten, or exalted, or

8 Rom. viii. 32.   9 Cf. Rom. viii. 3.   1 1 Cor. xv. 21.   5 Acts ii. 36.   6 Cf. Heb. v. 5.
2 2 Cor. xiii. 4.   3 Rom. vi. 10.   4 2 Cor. v. 21.   7 Altering Oehler's punctuation.

adopted [8] (those, I mean, who were brought into being at His command), marking the specialty of nature by the addition of "*own*." And, to the end that no one should connect the suffering of the Cross with the imperishable nature, he gives in other words a fairly distinct correction of such an error, when he calls Him "mediator between God and men [9]," and "man [9]," and "God [1]," that, from the fact that both are predicated of the one Being, the fit conception might be entertained concerning each Nature, —concerning the Divine Nature, impassibility, concerning the Human Nature, the dispensation of the Passion. As his thought, then, divides that which in love to man was made one, but is distinguished in idea, he uses, when he is proclaiming that nature which transcends and surpasses all intelligence, the more exalted order of names, calling Him "God over all [2]," "the great God [3]," "the power" of God, and "the wisdom ". of God [4], and the like ; but when he is alluding to all that experience of suffering which, by reason of our weakness, was necessarily assumed with our nature, he gives to the union of the Natures [5] that name which is derived from ours, and calls Him Man, not by this word placing Him Whom he is setting forth to us on a common level with the rest of nature, but so that orthodoxy is protected as regards each Nature, in the sense that the Human Nature is glorified by His assumption of it, and the Divine is not polluted by Its condescension, but makes the Human element subject to sufferings, while working, through Its Divine power, the resurrection of that which suffered. And thus the experience of death is not [6] referred to Him Who had communion in our passible nature by reason of the union with Him of the Man, while at the same time the exalted and Divine names descend to the Man, so that He Who was manifested upon the Cross is called even "the Lord of glory [7]," since the majesty implied in these names is transmitted from the Divine to the Human by the commixture of Its Nature with that Nature which is lowly. For this cause he describes Him in varied and different language, at one time as Him Who came down from heaven, at another time as Him Who was born of woman, as God from eternity, and Man in the last days ; thus too the

Only-begotten God is held to be impassible, and Christ to be capable of suffering ; nor does his discourse speak falsely in these opposing statements, as it adapts in its conceptions to each Nature the terms that belong to it. If then these are the doctrines which we have learnt from inspired teaching, how do we refer the cause of our salvation to an ordinary man ? and if we declare the word "made" employed by the blessed Peter to have regard not to the pretemporal existence, but to the new dispensation of the Incarnation, what has this to do with the charge against us ? For this great Apostle says that that which was seen in the form of the servant has been made, by being assumed, to be that which He Who assumed it was in His own Nature. Moreover, in the Epistle to the Hebrews we may learn the same truth from Paul, when he says that Jesus was made an Apostle and High Priest by God, "being faithful to him that made Him so [8]." For in that passage too, in giving the name of High Priest to Him Who made with His own Blood the priestly propitiation for our sins, he does not by the word "made" declare the first existence of the Only-begotten, but says "made" with the intention of representing that grace which is commonly spoken of in connection with the appointment of priests. For Jesus, the great High Priest (as Zechariah says [9]), Who offered up his own lamb, that is, His own Body, for the sin of the world ; Who, by reason of the children that are partakers of flesh and blood, Himself also in like manner took part with them in blood [1] (not in that He was in the beginning, being the Word and God, and being in the form of God, and equal with God, but in that He emptied Himself in the form of the servant, and offered an oblation and sacrifice for us), He, I say, became a High Priest many generations later, after the order of Melchisedech [2]. Surely a reader who has more than a casual acquaintance with the discourse to the Hebrews knows the mystery of this matter. As, then, in that passage He is said to have been *made* Priest and Apostle, so here He is said to have been *made* Lord and Christ,—the latter for the dispensation on our behalf, the former by the change and transformation of the Human to the Divine (for by "making" the Apostle means "making anew"). Thus is manifest the knavery of our adversaries, who insolently wrest the words referring to the dispensation to apply them to the pretemporal existence. For we learn from the Apostle not to know Christ in the same manner now as before, as Paul thus speaks, "Yea, though we have known Christ after the flesh, yet now know we Him no more [3]," in the sense that the one knowledge manifests

---

[8] Reading, as Gulonius seems to have done, and according to Oehler's suggestion (which he does not himself follow), υἱοθετηθεῖσι for ἀθετήσασι. In the latter reading the MSS. seem to agree, but the sense is doubtful. It may be rendered, perhaps, "Who were begotten and exalted, and who rejected Him." The quotation from S. Paul is from Rom. viii. 32.   [9] 1 Tim. ii. 5.
[1] The reference is perhaps to 1 Tim. iii. 16, but more probably to 1 Tim. ii. 5.   [2] Rom ix. 5.
[3] Tit. ii. 13.   [4] 1 Cor. i. 24.   [5] τὸ συναμφότερον.
[6] Reading οὔτε, in favour of which apparently lies the weight of MSS. The reading of the Paris edition gives an easier connection, but has apparently no MS. authority. The distinction S. Gregory draws is this :—"You may not say '*God died*,' for human weakness does not attach to the Divine Nature ; you may say ' He who d.ed is the Lord of glory,' for the Human Nature is actually made partaker of the power and majesty of the Divine."   [7] 1 Cor. ii. 8.

[8] Cf. Heb. iii. 1, 2.   [9] Cf. Zech. iii. 1.
[1] Cf. Heb. ii. 14.   [2] Cf. Heb. vii. 21.   [3] 2 Cf. Cor. v. 16.

to us His temporary dispensation, the other His eternal existence. Thus our discourse has made no inconsiderable answer to his charges :—that we neither hold two Christs nor two Lords, that we are not ashamed of the Cross, that we do not glorify a mere man as having suffered for the world, that we assuredly do not think that the word "made" refers to the formation of the essence. But, such being our view, our argument has no small support from our accuser himself, where in the midst of his discourse he employs his tongue in a flourishing onslaught upon us, and produces this sentence among others : "This, then, is the conflict that Basil wages against himself, and he clearly appears neither to have 'applied his own mind to the intention of the Apostles,' nor to be able to preserve the sequence of his own arguments ; for according to them he must, if he is conscious of their irreconcilable character, admit that the Word Who was in the beginning and was God became Lord," or he fits together "statements that are mutually conflicting." Why, this is actually our statement which Eunomius repeats, who says that "the Word that was in the beginning and was God became Lord." For, being what He was, God, and Word, and Life, and Light, and Grace, and Truth, and Lord, and Christ, and every name exalted and Divine, He did become, in the Man assumed by Him, Who was none of these, all else which the Word was, and among the rest did become Lord and Christ, according to the teaching of Peter, and according to the confession of Eunomius ;—not in the sense that the Godhead acquired anything by way of advancement, but (all exalted majesty being contemplated in the Divine Nature) He thus becomes Lord and Christ, not by arriving at any addition of grace in respect of His Godhead (for the Nature of the Godhead is acknowledged to be lacking in no good), but by bringing the Human Nature to that participation in the Godhead which is signified by the terms "Christ" and "Lord."

§ 3. *He then gives a notable explanation of the saying of the Lord to Philip, " He that hath seen Me hath seen the Father;" and herein he excellently discusses the suffering of the Lord in His love to man, and the impassibility, creative power, and providence of the Father, and the composite nature of men, and their resolution into the elements of which they were composed.*

Sufficient defence has been offered on these points, and as for that which Eunomius says by way of calumny against our doctrine, that "Christ was emptied to become Himself," there has been sufficient discussion in what has been said above, where he has been shown to be at-

tributing to our doctrine his own blasphemy.[4] For it is not one who confesses that the immutable Nature has put on the created and perishable, who speaks of the transition from like to like, but one who conceives that there is no change from the majesty of Nature to that which is more lowly. For if, as their doctrine asserts, He is created, and man is created also, the wonder of the doctrine disappears, and there is nothing marvellous in what is alleged, since the created nature comes to be in itself[5]. But we who have learnt from prophecy of "the change of the right hand of the Most High[6],"—and by the "Right Hand" of the Father we understand that Power of God, which made all things, which is the Lord (not in the sense of depending upon Him as a part upon a whole, but as being indeed from Him, and yet contemplated in individual existence),—say thus : that neither does the Right Hand vary from Him Whose Right Hand It is, in regard to the idea of Its Nature, nor can any other change in It be spoken of besides the dispensation of the Flesh. For verily the Right Hand of God was God Himself, manifested in the flesh, seen through that same flesh by those whose sight was clear ; as He did the work of the Father, being, both in fact and in thought, the Right Hand of God, yet being changed, in respect of the veil of the flesh by which He was surrounded, as regarded that which was seen, from that which He was by Nature, as a subject of contemplation. Therefore He says to Philip, who was gazing only at that which was changed, "Look through that which is changed to that which is unchangeable, and if thou seest this, thou hast seen that Father Himself, Whom thou seekest to see ; for he that hath seen Me—not Him Who appears in a state of change, but My very self, Who am in the Father—will have seen that Father Himself in Whom I am, because the very same character of Godhead is beheld in both[7]." If, then, we believe that the immortal and impassible and uncreated Nature came to be in the passible Nature of the creature, and conceive the "change" to consist in this, on what grounds are we charged with saying that He "was emptied to become Himself," by those who keep prating their own statements about our doctrines? For the participation of the created with the created is no "change of the Right Hand." To say that the Right Hand of the uncreated Nature is created belongs to Eunomius alone, and to those who adopt such opinions as he holds. For the man with an eye that looks on the truth will discern the

4 See above, Book V. § 4.
5 That is, in a nature created like itself.
6 Ps. lxxvii. 10 (LXX.). This application of the passage is also made by Michael Ayguan (the "Doctor Incognitus"), who is the only commentator mentioned by Neale and Littledale as so interpreting the text. 7 Cf. S. John xiv. 9, 10.

Right Hand of the Highest to be such as he sees the Highest to be,—Uncreated of Uncreated, Good of Good, Eternal of Eternal, without prejudice to Its eternity by Its being in the Father by way of generation. Thus our accuser has unawares been employing against us reproaches that properly fall upon himself.

But with reference [8] to those who stumble at the idea of "passion," and on this ground maintain the diversity of the Essences,—arguing that the Father, by reason of the exaltation of His Nature, does not admit passion, and that the Son on the other hand condescended, by reason of defect and divergence, to the partaking of His sufferings,—I wish to add these remarks to what has been already said :—That nothing is truly "passion" which does not tend to sin, nor would one strictly call by the name of "passion" the necessary routine of nature, regarding the composite nature as it goes on its course in a kind of order and sequence. For the mutual concurrence of heterogeneous elements in the formation of our body is a kind of a combination harmoniously conjoined out of several dissimilar elements ; but when, at the due time, the tie is loosed which bound together this concurrence of the elements, the combined nature is once more dissolved into the elements of which it was composed. This then is rather a *work* than a *passion* of the nature [9]. For we give the name of "passion" only to that which is opposed to the virtuous unimpassioned state, and of this we believe that He Who granted us salvation was at all times devoid, Who "was in all points tempted like as we are, yet without sin [1]." Of that, at least, which is truly passion, which is a diseased condition of the will, He was not a partaker ; for it says "He did no sin, neither was guile found in His mouth [2]"; but the peculiar attributes of our nature, which, by a kind of customary abuse of terms, are called by the same name of "passion," —of these, we confess, the Lord did partake,— of birth, nourishment, growth, of sleep and toil, and all those natural dispositions which the soul is wont to experience with regard to bodily inconveniences,—the desire of that which is lacking, when the longing passes from the body to the soul, the sense of pain, the dread of death, and all the like, save only such as, if followed, lead to sin. As, then, when we perceive His power extending through all things in heaven, and air, and earth, and sea, whatever there is in heaven, whatever there is beneath

the earth, we believe that He is universally present, and yet do not say that He *is* any of those things in which He is (for He is not the Heaven, Who has marked it out with His enfolding span, nor is He the earth, Who upholds the circle of the earth, nor yet is He the water, Who encompasses the liquid nature), so neither do we say that in passing through those sufferings of the flesh of which we speak He was "subject to passion," but, as we say that He is the cause of all things that are, that He holds the universe in His grasp, that He directs all that is in motion and keeps upon a settled foundation all that is stationary, by the unspeakable power of His own majesty, so we say that He was born among us for the cure of the disease of sin, adapting the exercise of His healing power in a manner corresponding to the suffering, applying the healing in that way which He knew to be for the good of that part of the creation which He knew to be in infirmity. And as it was expedient that He should heal the sufferings by touch, we say that He so healed it; yet is He not, because He is the Healer of our infirmity, to be deemed on this account to have been Himself passible. For even in the case of men, ordinary use does not allow us to affirm such a thing. We do not say that one who touches a sick man to heal him is himself partaker of the infirmity, but we say that he does give the sick man the boon of a return to health, and does not partake of the infirmity : for the suffering does not touch him, it is he who touches the disease. Now if he who by his art works any good in men's bodies is not called dull or feeble, but is called a lover of men and a benefactor and the like, why do they slander the dispensation to usward as being mean and inglorious, and use it to maintain that the essence of the Son is "divergent by way of inferiority," on the ground that the Nature of the Father is superior to sufferings, while that of the Son is not pure from passion? Why, if the aim of the dispensation of the Incarnation was not that the Son should be subject to suffering, but that He should be manifested as a lover of men, while the Father also is undoubtedly a lover of men, it follows that if one will but regard the aim, the Son is in the same case with the Father. But if it was not the Father Who wrought the destruction of death, marvel not,— for all judgment also He hath committed unto the Son, Himself judging no man [3]; not doing all things by the Son for the reason that He is unable either to save the lost or judge the sinner, but because He does these things too by His own Power, by which He works all things. Then they who were saved by the Son were saved by the Power of the Father, and they who are judged by Him undergo judgment by the

---

[8] Oehler's punctuation, while it does not exactly follow that of the earlier editions, still seems to admit of emendation here.

[9] The word πάθος, like the English word "passion," has a double sense : in one sense it connotes a tendency to evil action or evil habit—and in this sense Christ was not subject to passion. In another sense it has no such connotation, and it is in this sense (a sense, Gregory would say, somewhat inexact), that the term is used to express the sufferings of Christ :—to this case, it may be said, the inexact use of the English word is for the most part restricted.

[1] Heb. iv. 15.   [2] 1 Pet. ii. 22.

[3] Cf. S. John v. 22.

Righteousness of God. For "Christ," as the Apostle says, "is the Righteousness of God [4]," which is revealed by the Gospel; and whether you look at the world as a whole, or at the parts of the world which make up that complete whole, all these are works of the Father, in that they are works of His Power; and thus the word which says both that the Father made all things, and that none of these things that are came into being without the Son, speaks truly on both points; for the operation of the Power bears relation to Him Whose Power It is. Thus, since the Son is the Power of the Father, all the works of the Son are works of the Father. That He entered upon the dispensation of the Passion not by weakness of nature but by the power of His will, one might bring countless passages of the Gospel to show; but these, as the matter is clear, I will pretermit, that my discourse may not be prolonged by dwelling on points that are admitted. If, then, that which comes to pass is evil, we have to separate from that evil not the Father only, but the Son also; but if the saving of them that were lost is good, and if that which took place is not "passion [5]," but love of men, why do you alienate from our thanksgiving for our salvation the Father, Who by His own Power, which is Christ, wrought for men their freedom from death?

§ 4. *Then returning to the words of Peter, " God made Him Lord and Christ," he skilfully explains it by many arguments, and herein shows Eunomius as an advocate of the orthodox doctrine, and concludes the book by showing that the Divine and Human names are applied, by reason of the commixture, to either Nature.*

But we must return once more to our vehement writer of speeches, and take up again that severe invective of his against ourselves. He makes it a complaint against us that we deny that the Essence of the Son has been made, as contradicting the words of Peter, "He made Him Lord and Christ, this Jesus Whom ye crucified [6]"; and he is very forcible in his indignation and abuse upon this matter, and moreover maintains certain points by which he thinks that he refutes our doctrine. Let us see, then, the force of his attempts. "Who, pray, ye most reckless of men," he says, "when he *has* the form of a servant, takes the form of a servant?" "No reasonable man," shall be our reply to him, "would use language of this kind, save such as may be entirely alien from the hope of Christians. But to this class you belong, who charge us with recklessness because we do not admit the Creator to be created. For if the Holy Spirit does not lie, when He says by the prophet, 'All things serve Thee [7],' and the whole creation is in servitude, and the Son is, as you say [8], created, He is clearly a fellow-servant with all things, being degraded by His partaking of creation to partake also of servitude. And Him Who is in servitude you will surely invest with the servant's form: for you will not, of course, be ashamed of the aspect of servitude when you acknowledge that He is a servant by nature. Who now is it, I pray, my most keen rhetorician, who transfers the Son from the servile form to another form of a servant? he who claims for Him uncreated being, and thereby proves that He is no servant, or you, rather, who continually cry that the Son is the servant of the Father, and was actually under His dominion before He took the servant's form? I ask for no other judges; I leave the vote on these questions in your own hands. For I suppose that no one is so shameless in his dealings with the truth as to oppose acknowledged facts out of sheer impudence. What we have said is clear to any one, that by the peculiar attributes of servitude is marked that which is by nature servile, and to be created is an attribute proper to servitude. Thus one who asserts that He, being a servant, took upon Him our form, is surely the man who transfers the Only-begotten from servitude to servitude."

He tries, however, to fight against our words, and says, a little further on (for I will pass over at present his intermediate remarks, as they have been more or less fully discussed in my previous arguments), when he charges us with being "bold in saying or thinking things uncontrivable," and calls us "most miserable [9],"—he adds, I say, this:—"For if it is not of the Word Who was in the beginning and was God that the blessed Peter speaks, but of Him Who was 'seen,' and Who 'emptied Himself,' as Basil says, and if the man Who was 'seen' 'emptied Himself' to take 'the form of a servant,' and He Who 'emptied Himself' to take 'the form of a servant,' 'emptied Himself' to come into being as man, then the man who was 'seen' 'emptied himself,' to come into being as man." It may be that the judgment of my readers has immediately detected from the above citation the knavery, and, at the same time, the folly of the argument he maintains: yet a brief refutation of what he says shall be subjoined on our side, not so

---

[4] Rom. i. 17.
[5] That is, "passion" in the sense defined above, as something with evil tendency. If the γινόμενον (*i. e.* the salvation of men) is evil, then Father and Son alike must be "kept clear" from any participation in it. If it is good, and if, therefore, the means (the actual events) are not "passion" as not tending to evil, while, considered in regard to their aim, they are φιλανθρωπία, then there is no reason why a share in their fulfilment should be denied to the Father. Who, as well as the Son, is φιλάνθρωπος. and Who by His own Power (that is, by Christ) wrought the salvation of men.
[6] Acts ii. 36.

[7] Ps. cxix. 91.
[8] Reading καθ' ὑμᾶς with the earlier editions. Oehler alleges no authority for his reading καθ' ἡμᾶς, which is probably a mere misprint.
[9] Oehler's punctuation here seems to require correction.

much to overthrow his blundering sophism, which indeed is overthrown by itself for those who have ears to hear, as to avoid the appearance of passing his allegation by without discussion, under the pretence of contempt for the worthlessness of his argument. Let us accordingly look at the point in this way. What are the Apostle's words? "Be it known," he says, "that God made Him Lord and Christ[1]." Then, as though some one had asked him on *whom* such a grace was bestowed, he points as it were with his finger to the subject, saying, "this Jesus, Whom ye crucified." What does Basil say upon this? That the demonstrative word declares that *that* person was made Christ, Who had been crucified by the hearers;—for he says, "ye crucified," and it was likely that those who had demanded the murder that was done upon Him were hearers of the speech; for the time from the crucifixion to the discourse of Peter was not long. What, then, does Eunomius advance in answer to this? "If it is not of the Word Who was in the beginning and was God that the blessed Peter speaks, but of Him Who was 'seen,' and Who 'emptied Himself,' as Basil says, and if the man who was 'seen' 'emptied himself' to take 'the form of a servant'"— Hold! who says this, that the man who was seen emptied himself again to take the form of a servant? or who maintains that the suffering of the Cross took place before the manifestation in the flesh? The Cross did not precede the body, nor the body "the form of the servant." But God is manifested in the flesh, while the flesh that displayed God in itself, after having by itself fulfilled the great mystery of the Death, is transformed by commixture to that which is exalted and Divine, becoming Christ and Lord, being transferred and changed to that which He was, Who manifested Himself in that flesh. But if we should say this, our champion of the truth maintains once more that we say that He Who was shown upon the Cross "emptied Himself" to become another man, putting his sophism together as follows in its wording:—"If," quoth he, "the man who was 'seen' 'emptied himself' to take the 'form of a servant,' and He Who 'emptied Himself' to take the 'form of a servant,' 'emptied Himself' to come into being as man, then the man who was 'seen' 'emptied himself' to come into being as man."

How well he remembers the task before him! how much to the point is the conclusion of his argument! Basil declares that the Apostle said that the man who was "seen" was made Christ and Lord, and this clear and quick-witted overturner of his statements says, "If Peter does not say that the essence of Him Who was in the beginning was made, the man who was

'seen' 'emptied himself' to take the 'form of a servant,' and He Who 'emptied Himself' to take the 'form of a servant,' 'emptied Himself' to become man." We are conquered, Eunomius, by this invincible wisdom! The fact that the Apostle's discourse refers to Him Who was "crucified through weakness[2]" is forsooth powerfully disproved when we learn that if we believe this to be so, the man who was "seen" again becomes another, "emptying Himself" for another coming into being of man. Will you never cease jesting against what should be secure from such attempts? will you not blush at destroying by such ridiculous sophisms the awe that hedges the Divine mysteries? will you not turn now, if never before, to know that the Only-begotten God, Who is in the bosom of the Father, being Word, and King, and Lord, and all that is exalted in word and thought, needs not to *become* anything that is good, seeing that He *is* Himself the fulness of all good things? What then is that, by changing into which He becomes what He was not before? Well, as He Who knew not sin becomes sin[3], that He may take away the sin of the world, so on the other hand the flesh which received the Lord becomes Christ and Lord, being transformed by the commixture into that which it was not by nature: whereby we learn that neither would God have been manifested in the flesh, had not the Word been made flesh, nor would the human flesh that compassed Him about have been transformed to what is Divine, had not that which was apparent to the senses become Christ and Lord. But they treat the simplicity of what we preach with contempt, who use their syllogisms to trample on the being of God, and desire to show that He Who by creation brought into being all things that are, is Himself a part of creation, and wrest, to assist them in such an effort to establish their blasphemy, the words of Peter, who said to the Jews, "Be it known to all the house of Israel that God made Him Lord and Christ, this Jesus Whom ye crucified[4]." This is the proof they present for the statement that the essence of the Only-begotten God is created! What? tell me, were the Jews, to whom the words were spoken, in existence before the ages? was the Cross before the world? was Pilate before all creation? was Jesus in existence first, and after that the Word? was the flesh more ancient than the Godhead? did Gabriel bring glad tidings to Mary before the world was? did not the Man that was in Christ take beginning by way of birth in the days of Cæsar Augustus, while the Word that was God in the beginning is our King, as the prophet testifies, before all ages[5]? See you not what confusion you bring

---

[1] Acts ii. 36.

[2] 2 Cor. xiii. 4.
[4] Acts ii. 36.

[3] Cf. 2 Cor. v. 21.
[5] Ps. lxxiv. 12 (J.XX.).

upon the matter, turning, as the phrase goes, things upside down? It was the fiftieth day after the Passion, when Peter preached his sermon to the Jews and said, "Him Whom ye crucified, God made Christ and Lord." Do you not mark the order of his saying? which stands first, which second in his words? He did not say, "Him Whom God made Lord, ye crucified," but, "Whom ye crucified, Him God made Christ and Lord": so that it is clear from this that Peter is speaking, not of what was before the ages, but of what was after the dispensation.

How comes it, then, that you fail to see that the whole conception of your argument on the subject is being overthrown, and go on making yourself ridiculous with your childish web of sophistry, saying that, if we believe that He who was apparent to the senses has been made by God to be Christ and Lord, it necessarily follows that the Lord once more "emptied Himself" anew to become Man, and underwent a second birth? What advantage does your doctrine get from this? How does what you say show the King of creation to be created? For my own part I assert on the other side that our view is supported by those who contend against us, and that the rhetorician, in his exceeding attention to the matter, has failed to see that in pushing, as he supposed, the argument to an absurdity, he is fighting on the side of those whom he attacks, with the very weapons he uses for their overthrow. For if we are to believe that the change of condition in the case of Jesus was from a lofty state to a lowly one, and if the Divine and uncreated Nature alone transcends the creation, he will, perhaps, when he thoroughly surveys his own argument, come over to the ranks of truth, and agree that the Uncreated came to be in the created, in His love for man. But if he imagines that he demonstrates the created character of the Lord by showing that He, being God, took part in human nature, he will find many such passages to establish the same opinion which carry out their support of his argument in a similar way. For since He was the Word and was God, and "afterwards," as the prophet says, "was seen upon earth and conversed with men [6]," He will hereby be proved to be one of the creatures! And if this is held to be beside the question, similar passages too are not quite akin to the subject. For in sense it is just the same to say that the Word that was in the beginning was manifested to men through the flesh, and to say that being in the form of God He put on the form of a servant: and if one of these statements gives no help for the establishment of his blasphemy, he must needs give up the remaining one also. He is kind enough, however, to advise us to abandon our error, and to point out the truth which He himself maintains. He tells us that the Apostle Peter declares Him to have been made Who was in the beginning the Word and God. Well, if he were making up dreams for our amusement, and giving us information about the prophetic interpretation of the visions of sleep, there might be no risk in allowing him to set forth the riddles of his imagination at his pleasure. But when he tells us that he is explaining the Divine utterances, it is no longer safe for us to leave him to interpret the words as he likes. What does the Scripture say? "God made Lord and Christ this Jesus whom ye crucified [7]." When everything, then, is found to concur—the demonstrative word denoting Him Who is spoken of by the Name of His Humanity, the charge against those who were stained with blood-guiltiness, the suffering of the Cross— our thought necessarily turns to that which was apparent to the senses. But he asserts that while Peter uses these words it is the pre-temporal existence that is indicated by the word "made" [8]. Well, we may safely allow nurses and old wives to jest with children, and to lay down the meaning of dreams as they choose: but when inspired Scripture is set before us for exposition, the great Apostle forbids us to have recourse to old wives' tattle [9]. When I hear "the Cross" spoken of, I understand the Cross, and when I hear mention of a human name, I understand the nature which that name connotes. So when I hear from Peter that "this" one was made Lord and Christ, I do not doubt that he speaks of Him Who had been before the eyes of men, since the saints agree with one another in this matter as well as in others. For, as he says that He Who was crucified has been made Lord, so Paul also says that He was "highly exalted [1]," after the Passion and the Resurrection, not being exalted in so far forth as He is God. For what height is there more sublime than the Divine height, that he should say God was exalted thereunto? But he means that the lowliness of the Humanity was exalted, the word, I suppose, indicating the assimilation and union of the Man Who was assumed to the exalted state of the Divine Nature. And even if one were to allow him licence to misinterpret the Divine utterance, not even so will his argument conclude in accordance with the aim of his heresy. For be it granted that Peter does say of Him Who was in the beginning, "God made Him Lord and Christ, this Jesus Whom ye crucified," we shall find that even so his blasphemy does not gain any strength against the truth. "God made Him," he says, "Lord

---

6 Bar iii. 37.

7 Acts ii. 36.　　　　8 Altering Oehler's punctuation, which here seems certainly faulty : some lighter alterations have also been made in what precedes, and in what follows.
9 Cf. 1 Tim. iv. 7. The quotation is not verbal.
1 Cf. Phil. ii. 9.

and Christ." To which of the words are we to refer the word *made?* with which of those that are employed in this sentence are we to connect the word? There are three before us :—"this," and "Lord," and "Christ." With which of these three will he construct the word "made"? No one is so bold against the truth as to deny that "made" has reference to "Christ" and "Lord"; for Peter says that He, being already whatever He was, was "made Christ and Lord" by the Father.

These words are not mine: they are those of him who fights against the Word. For he says, in the very passage that is before us for examination, exactly thus :—"The blessed Peter speaks of Him Who was in the beginning and was God, and expounds to us that it was He Who became Lord and Christ." Eunomius, then, says that He Who was whatsoever He was became Lord and Christ, as the history of David tells us that he, being the son of Jesse, and a keeper of the flocks, was anointed to be king : not that the anointing then made him to be a man, but that he, being what he was by his own nature, was transformed from an ordinary man to a king. What follows? Is it thereby the more established that the essence of the Son was *made,* if, as Eunomius says, God made Him, when He was in the beginning and was God, both Lord and Christ? For Lordship is not a name of His *being* but of His *being in authority,* and the appellation of Christ indicates His kingdom, while the idea of His kingdom is one, and that of His Nature another. Suppose that Scripture does say that these things took place with regard to the Son of God. Let us then consider which is the more pious and the more rational view. Which can we allowably say is made partaker of superiority by way of advancement—God or man? Who has so childish a mind as to suppose that the Divinity passes on to perfection by way of addition? But as to the Human Nature, such a supposition is not unreasonable, seeing that the words of the Gospel clearly ascribe to our Lord *increase* in respect of His Humanity : for it says, "Jesus increased in wisdom and stature and favour [2]." Which, then, is the more reasonable suggestion to derive from the Apostle's words ?—that He Who was God in the beginning became Lord by way of advancement, or that the lowliness of the Human Nature was raised to the height of majesty as a result of its communion with the Divine? For the prophet David also, speaking in the person of the Lord, says, "I am established as king by Him [3]," with a meaning very close to "I was made Christ :" and again, in the person of the Father to the Lord, he says, "Be Thou Lord in the midst of Thine enemies [4]," with the same meaning as

Peter, "Be Thou *made* Lord of Thine enemies." As, then, the establishment of His kingdom does not signify the formation of His essence, but the advance to His dignity, and He Who bids Him "be Lord" does not command that which is non-existent to come into being at that particular time, but gives to Him Who *is* the rule over those who are disobedient,—so also the blessed Peter, when he says that one has been made Christ (that is, king of all) adds the word "Him" to distinguish the idea both from the essence and from the attributes contemplated in connection with it. For He made Him what has been declared when He already *was* that which He is. Now if it were allowable to assert of the transcendent Nature that it became anything by way of advancement, as a king from being an ordinary man, or lofty from being lowly, or Lord from being servant, it might be proper to apply Peter's words to the Only-begotten. But since the Divine Nature, whatever it is believed to be, always remains the same, being above all augmentation and incapable of diminution, we are absolutely compelled to refer his saying to the Humanity. For God the Word is now, and always remains, that which He was in the beginning, always King, always Lord, always God and Most High, not having become any of these things by way of advancement, but being in virtue of His Nature all that He is declared to be, while on the other hand He Who was, by being assumed, elevated from Man to the Divinity, *being* one thing and *becoming* another, is strictly and truly said to have become Christ and Lord. For He made Him to be Lord from being a servant, to be King from being a subject, to be Christ from being in subordination. He highly exalted that which was lowly, and gave to Him that had the Human Name that Name which is above every name [5]. And thus came to pass that unspeakable mixture and conjunction of human littleness commingled with Divine greatness, whereby even those names which are great and Divine are properly applied to the Humanity, while on the other hand the Godhead is spoken of by human names [6]. For it is the same Person who both has the Name which is above every name, and is worshipped by all creation in the human Name of Jesus. For he says, "at the name of Jesus every knee shall bow, of things in heaven and things in earth, and things under the earth, and every tongue shall confess that Jesus is Lord, to the glory of God the Father [7]." But enough of these matters.

---

[2] S. Luke ii. 52.　　[3] Ps. ii. 6 (LXX).　　[4] Ps. cx. 2.

[5] Cf. Phil. ii. 9.
[6] This passage may be taken as counterbalancing that in which S. Gregory seems to limit the *communicatio idiomatum* (see above, page 184, n. 6) : but he here p obably means no more than that *names* or *titles* which properly belong to the Human Nature of our Lord are applied to His Divine Personality.
[7] Cf. Phil. ii. 10.

BOOK VII

§ 1. *The seventh book shows from various statements made to the Corinthians and to the Hebrews, and from the words of the Lord, that the word " Lord" is not expressive of essence, according to Eunomius' exposition, but of dignity. And after many notable remarks concerning "the Spirit" and the Lord, he shows that Eunomius, from his own words, is found to argue in favour of orthodoxy, though without intending it, and to be struck by his own shafts.*

SINCE, however, Eunomius asserts that the word " Lord" is used in reference to the *essence* and not to the *dignity* of the Only-begotten, and cites as a witness to this view the Apostle, when he says to the Corinthians, " Now the Lord is the Spirit [1]," it may perhaps be opportune that we should not pass over even this error on his part without correction. He asserts that the word " Lord" is significative of essence, and by way of proof of this assumption he brings up the passage above mentioned. " The Lord," it says, " is the Spirit [1]." But our friend who interprets Scripture at his own sweet will calls " Lordship" by the name of " *essence*," and thinks to bring his statement to proof by means of the words quoted. Well, if it had been said by Paul, " Now the Lord is essence," we too would have concurred in his argument. But seeing that the inspired writing on the one side says, " the Lord is the Spirit," and Eunomius says on the other, " Lordship is essence," I do not know where he finds support for his statement, unless he is prepared to say again [2] that the word " Spirit" stands in Scripture for " essence." Let us consider, then, whether the Apostle anywhere, in his use of the term " Spirit," employs that word to indicate " essence." He says, " The Spirit itself beareth witness with our Spirit [3]," and " no one knoweth the things of a man save the Spirit of man which is in him [4]," and " the letter killeth, but the Spirit giveth life [5]," and " if ye through the Spirit do mortify the deeds of the body, ye shall live [6]," and " if

we live in the Spirit let us also walk in the Spirit [7]." Who indeed could count the utterances of the Apostle on this point? and in them we nowhere find " essence" signified by this word. For he who says that " the Spirit itself beareth witness with our spirit," signifies nothing else than the Holy Spirit Which comes to be in the mind of the faithful; for in many other passages of his writings he gives the name of spirit to the mind, on the reception by which of the communion of the Spirit the recipients attain the dignity of adoption. Again, in the passage, " No one knoweth the things of a man save the spirit of man which is in him," if " man" is used of the essence, and " spirit" likewise, it will follow from the phrase that the man is maintained to be of two essences. Again, I know not how he who says that " the letter killeth, but the Spirit giveth life," sets " essence" in opposition to " letter"; nor, again, how this writer imagines that when Paul says that we ought " through the Spirit" to destroy " the deeds of the body," he is directing the signification of " spirit" to express " essence"; while as for " living in the Spirit," and " walking in the Spirit," this would be quite unintelligible if the sense of the word " Spirit" referred to " essence." For in what else than in essence do all we who are alive partake of life?—thus when the Apostle is laying down advice for us on this matter that we should " live in essence," it is as though he said " partake of life by means of yourselves, and not by means of others." If then it is not possible that this sense can be adopted in any passage, how can Eunomius here once more imitate the interpreters of dreams, and bid us to take " spirit" for " essence," to the end that he may arrive in due syllogistic form at his conclusion that the word " Lord" is applied to the essence?—for if " spirit" is " essence" (he argues), and " the Lord is Spirit," the " Lord" is clearly found to be " essence." How incontestable is the force of this attempt! How can we evade or resolve this irrefragable necessity of demonstration? The word " Lord," he says, is spoken of the essence. How does he maintain it? Because the Apostle says, " The Lord is the

---

[1] 2 Cor. iii. 17.
[2] It is not quite clear whether πάλιν is to be constructed with λέγοι or with κεῖσθαι, but the difference in sense is slight.
[3] Rom. viii. 16. [4] 1 Cor. ii. 11.
[5] 2 Cor. iii. 6. [6] Rom. viii. 13.

[7] Gal. v. 25.

Spirit." Well, what has this to do with essence? He gives us the further instruction that "spirit" is put for "essence." These are the arts of his demonstrative method! These are the results of his Aristotelian science! This is why, in your view, we are so much to be pitied, who are uninitiated in this wisdom! and you of course are to be deemed happy, who track out the truth by a method like this—that the Apostle's meaning was such that we are to suppose "the Spirit" was put by him for the Essence of the Only-begotten!

Then how will you make it fit with what follows? For when Paul says, "Now the Lord is the Spirit," he goes on to say, "and where the Spirit of the Lord is, there is liberty." If then "the Lord is the Spirit," and "Spirit" means "essence," what are we to understand by "the essence of the essence"? He speaks again of another Spirit of the Lord Who is the Spirit,— that is to say, according to your interpretation, of another *essence.* Therefore in your view the Apostle, when he writes expressly of "the Lord the Spirit," and of "the Spirit of the Lord," means nothing else than an essence of an essence. Well, let Eunomius make what he likes of that which is written; what we understand of the matter is as follows. The Scripture, "given by inspiration of God," as the Apostle calls it, is the Scripture of the Holy Spirit, and its intention is the profit of men. For "every scripture," he says, "is given by inspiration of God and is profitable"; and the profit is varied and multiform, as the Apostle says—"for doctrine, for reproof, for correction, for instruction in righteousness [8]." Such a boon as this, however, is not within any man's reach to lay hold of, but the Divine intention lies hid under the body of the Scripture, as it were under a veil, some legislative enactment or some historical narrative being cast over the truths that are contemplated by the mind. For this reason, then, the Apostle tells us that those who look upon the body of the Scripture have "a veil upon their heart [9]," and are not able to look upon the glory of the spiritual law, being hindered by the veil that has been cast over the face of the law-giver. Wherefore he says, "the letter killeth, but the Spirit giveth life [5]," showing that often the obvious interpretation, if it be not taken according to the proper sense, has an effect contrary to that life which is indicated by the Spirit, seeing that this lays down for all men the perfection of virtue in freedom from passion, while the history contained in the writings sometimes embraces the exposition even of facts incongruous, and is understood, so to say, to concur with the passions of our nature, whereto if any one applies himself according to the

obvious sense, he will make the Scripture a doctrine of death. Accordingly, he says that over the perceptive powers of the souls of men who handle what is written in too corporeal a manner, the veil is cast; but for those who turn their contemplation to that which is the object of the intelligence, there is revealed, bared, as it were, of a mask, the glory that underlies the letter. And that which is discovered by this more exalted perception he says is the Lord, which is the Spirit. For he says, "when it shall turn to the Lord the veil shall be taken away: now the Lord is the Spirit [1]." And in so saying he makes a distinction of contrast between the lordship of the spirit and the bondage of the letter; for as that which gives life is opposed to that which kills, so he contrasts "the Lord" with bondage. And that we may not be under any confusion when we are instructed concerning the Holy Spirit (being led by the word "Lord" to the thought of the Only-begotten), for this reason he guards the word by repetition, both saying that "the Lord is the Spirit," and making further mention of "the Spirit of the Lord," that the supremacy of His Nature may be shown by the honour implied in lordship, while at the same time he may avoid confusing in his argument the individuality of His Person. For he who calls Him both "Lord" and "Spirit of the Lord," teaches us to conceive of Him as a separate individual besides the Only-begotten; just as elsewhere he speaks of "the Spirit of Christ [2]," employing fairly and in its mystic sense this very term which is piously employed in the system of doctrine according to the Gospel tradition. Thus we, the "most miserable of all men," being led onward by the Apostle in the mysteries, pass from the letter that killeth to the Spirit that giveth life, learning from Him Who was in Paradise initiated into the unspeakable mysteries, that all things the Divine Scripture says are utterances of the Holy Spirit. For "well did the Holy Spirit prophesy [3],"—this he says to the Jews in Rome, introducing the words of Isaiah; and to the Hebrews, alleging the authority of the Holy Spirit in the words, "wherefore as saith the Holy Spirit [4]," he adduces the words of the Psalm which are spoken at length in the person of God; and from the Lord Himself we learn the same thing,—that David declared the heavenly mysteries not "in" himself (that is, not speaking according to human nature). For how could any one, being but man, know supercelestial converse of the Father with the Son? But being "in the Spirit" he said that the Lord spoke to the Lord those words which He has uttered. For if, He says, "David *in the Spirit* calls him Lord, how is He then his

---

[8] 2 Tim. iii. 16. [9] 2 Cor. iii. 15.

[1] 2 Cor. iii. 16, 17.
[3] Cf. Acts xxviii. 25.

[2] Rom. viii. 9.
[4] Heb. iii. 7.

son [5] ?" Thus it is by the power of the Spirit that the holy men who are under Divine influence are inspired, and every Scripture is for this reason said to be "given by inspiration of God," because it is the teaching of the Divine afflatus. If the bodily veil of the words were removed, that which remains is Lord and life and Spirit, according to the teaching of the great Paul, and according to the words of the Gospel also. For Paul declares that he who turns from the letter to the Spirit no longer apprehends the bondage that slays, but the Lord which is the life-giving Spirit; and the sublime Gospel says, "the words that I speak are spirit and are life [6]," as being divested of the bodily veil. The idea, however, that "the Spirit" is the essence of the Only-begotten, we shall leave to our dreamers: or rather, we shall make use, *ex abundanti*, of what they say, and arm the truth with the weapons of the adversary. For it is allowable that the Egyptian should be spoiled by the Israelites, and that we should make their wealth an ornament for ourselves. If the essence of the Son is called "Spirit," and God also is Spirit, (for so the Gospel tells us [7]), clearly the essence of the Father is called "Spirit" also. But if it is their peculiar argument that things which are introduced by different names are different also in nature, the conclusion surely is, that things which are named alike are not alien one from the other in nature either. Since then, according to their account, the essence of the Father and that of the Son are both called "Spirit," hereby is clearly proved the absence of any difference in essence. For a little further on Eunomius says:—"Of those essences which are divergent the appellations significant of essence are also surely divergent, but where there is one and the same name, that which is declared by the same appellation will surely be one also" :—so that at all points "He that taketh the wise in their own craftiness [8]" has turned the long labours of our author, and the infinite toil spent on what he has elaborated, to the establishment of the doctrine which we maintain. For if God is in the Gospel called "Spirit," and the essence of the Only-begotten is maintained by Eunomius to be "Spirit," as there is no apparent difference in the one name as compared with the other, neither, surely, will the things signified by the names be mutually different in nature.

And now that I have exposed this futile and pointless sham-argument, it seems to me that I may well pass by without discussion what he next puts together by way of attack upon our master's statement. For a sufficient proof of the folly of his remarks is to be found in his actual argument, which of itself proclaims aloud its feebleness. To be entangled in a contest with such things as this is like trampling on the slain. For when he sets forth with much confidence some passage from our master, and treats it with preliminary slander and contempt, and promises that he will show it to be worth nothing at all, he meets with the same fortune as befalls small children, to whom their imperfect and immature intelligence, and the untrained condition of their perceptive faculties, do not give an accurate understanding of what they see. Thus they often imagine that the stars are but a little way above their heads, and pelt them with clods when they appear, in their childish folly; and then, when the clod falls, they clap their hands and laugh and brag to their comrades as if their throw had reached the stars themselves. Such is the man who casts at the truth with his childish missile, who sets forth like the stars those splendid sayings of our master, and then hurls from the ground, —from his downtrodden and grovelling understanding,—his earthy and unstable arguments. And these, when they have gone so high that they have no place to fall from, turn back again of themselves by their own weight [9]. Now the passage of the great Basil is worded as follows [1]:—

"Yet what sane man would agree with the statement that of those things of which the names are different the essences must needs be divergent also? For the appellations of Peter and Paul, and, generally speaking, of men, are different, while the essence of all is one: wherefore, in most respects we are mutually identical, and differ one from another only in those special properties which are observed in individuals: and hence also appellations are not indicative of essence, but of the properties which mark the particular individual. Thus, when we hear of Peter, we do not by the name understand the essence (and by 'essence' I here mean the material substratum), but we are impressed with the conception of the properties which we contemplate in him." These are the great man's words. And what skill he who disputes this statement displays against us, we learn,—any one, that is, who has leisure for wasting time on unprofitable matters,—from the actual composition of Eunomius.

From his writings, I say, for I do not like to insert in my own work the nauseous stuff our rhetorician utters, or to display his ignorance and folly to contempt in the midst of my own arguments. He goes on with a sort of eulogy upon the class of significant words which express the subject, and, in his accustomed style, patches and sticks together the cast-off rags of phrases: poor Isocrates is nibbled at once more, and shorn of words and figures to make out the point proposed,—here and there even the Hebrew Philo receives the same treatment, and makes him a contribution of phrases from his own labours,—yet not even thus is this much-stitched and many-coloured web of words finished off, but every assault, every defence of his conceptions, all his artistic preparation, spontaneously collapses, and, as commonly happens with the bubbles when the drops, borne down from above through a body of waters against some obstacle, produce those foamy swellings which, as soon as they gather, immediately dissolve, and leave upon the water no trace of their own formation—such are the air-bubbles of our author's thoughts, vanishing without a touch at the moment they are put forth. For after all these irrefragable statements, and the dreamy philosophizing wherein he asserts that the distinct character of the essence is apprehended by the divergence of names, as some mass of foam borne downstream breaks up when it comes into contact with any more solid body, so his argument, following its own spontaneous course, and coming unexpectedly into collision with the truth, disperses into nothingness its unsubstantial and bubble-like fabric of falsehood. For he speaks in these words:—"Who is so foolish and so far removed from the constitution of men, as, in discoursing of men to speak of one as a man, and, calling another a horse, so to compare them?" I would answer him,—"You are right in calling any one foolish who makes such blunders in the use of names. And I will employ for the support of the truth the testimony you yourself give. For if it is a piece of extreme folly to call one a horse and another a man, supposing both were really men, it is surely a piece of equal stupidity, when the Father is confessed to be God, and the Son is confessed to be God, to call the one 'created' and the other 'uncreated,' since, as in the other case humanity, so in this case the Godhead does not admit a change of name to that expressive of another kind. For what the irrational is with respect to man, that also the creature is with respect to the Godhead, being equally unable to receive the same name with the nature that is superior to it. And as it is not possible to apply the same definition to the rational animal and the quadruped alike (for each is naturally differentiated by its special property from the other), so neither can you express by the same terms the created and the uncreated essence, seeing that those attributes which are predicated of the latter essence are not discoverable in the former. For as ration-

ality is not discoverable in a horse, nor solidity of hoofs in a man, so neither is Godhead discoverable in the creature, nor the attribute of being created in the Godhead: but if He be God He is certainly not created, and if He be created He is not God; unless[2], of course, one were to apply by some misuse or customary mode of expression the mere name of Godhead, as some horses have men's names given them by their owners; yet neither is the horse a man, though he be called by a human name, nor is the created being God, even though some claim for him the name of Godhead, and give him the benefit of the empty sound of a dissyllable." Since, then, Eunomius' heretical statement is found spontaneously to fall in with the truth, let him take his own advice and stand by his own words, and by no means retract his own utterances, but consider that the man is really foolish and stupid who names the subject not according as it is, but says "horse" for "man," and "sea" for "sky," and "creature" for "God." And let no one think it unreasonable that the creature should be set in opposition to God, but have regard to the prophets and to the Apostles. For the prophet says in the person of the Father, "My Hand made all these things"[3], meaning by "Hand," in his dark saying, the power of the Only-begotten. Now the Apostle says that all things are of the Father, and that all things are by the Son[4], and the prophetic spirit in a way agrees with the Apostolic teaching, which itself also is given through the Spirit. For in the one passage, the prophet, when he says that all things are the work of the Hand of Him Who is over all, sets forth the nature of those things which have come into being in its relation to Him Who made them, while He Who made them is God over all, Who has the Hand, and by It makes all things. And again, in the other passage, the Apostle makes the same division of entities, making all things depend upon their productive cause, yet not reckoning in the number of "all things" that which produces them: so that we are hereby taught the difference of nature between the created and the uncreated, and it is shown that, in its own nature, that which makes is one thing and that which is produced is another. Since, then, all things are of God, and the Son is God, the creation is properly opposed to the Godhead; while, since the Only-begotten is something else than the nature of the universe (seeing that not even those who fight against the truth contradict this), it follows of necessity that the Son also is equally opposed to the creation, unless the words of the saints are untrue which testify that by Him all things were made.

---

[2] Altering Oehler's punctuation.
[3] Is. lxvi. 2. Not verbally from the LXX. [4] Cf. 1 Cor. viii. 6.

§ 2. *He then declares that the close relation between names and things is immutable, and thereafter proceeds accordingly, in the most excellent manner, with his discourse concerning "generated" and "ungenerate."*

Now seeing that the Only-begotten is in the Divine Scriptures proclaimed to be God, let Eunomius consider his own argument, and condemn for utter folly the man who parts the Divine into created and uncreated, as he does him who divides "man" into "horse" and "man." For he himself says, a little further on, after his intermediate nonsense, "the close relation of names to things is immutable," where he himself by this statement assents to the fixed character of the true connection of appellations with their subject. If, then, the name of God-head is properly employed in close connection with the Only-begotten God (and Eunomius, though he may desire to be out of harmony with us, will surely concede that the Scripture does not lie, and that the name of the Godhead is not inharmoniously attributed to the Only-begotten), let him persuade himself by his own reasoning that if "the close relation of names to things is immutable," and the Lord is called by the name of "God," he cannot apprehend any difference in respect of the conception of Godhead between the Father and the Son, seeing that this name is common to both,—or rather not this name only, but there is a long list of names in which the Son shares, without divergence of meaning, the appellations of the Father, — "good," "incorruptible," "just," "judge," "long-suffering," "merciful," "eternal," "everlasting," all that indicate the expression of majesty of nature and power,—without any reservation being made in His case in any of the names in regard of the exalted nature of the conception. But Eunomius passes by, as it were with closed eye, the number, great as it is, of the Divine appellations, and looks only to one point, his "generate and ungenerate,"—trusting to a slight and weak cord his doctrine, tossed and driven as it is by the blasts of error.

He asserts that "no man who has any regard for the truth either calls any generated thing 'ungenerate,' or calls God Who is over all 'Son' or 'generate.'" This statement needs no further arguments on our part for its refutation. For he does not shelter his craft with any veils, as his wont is, but treats the inversion of his absurd statement as equivalent[5], while he says

that neither is any generated thing spoken of as "ungenerate," nor is God Who is over all called "Son" or "generate," without making any special distinction for the Only-begotten Godhead of the Son as compared with the rest of the "generated," but makes his opposition of "all things that have come into being" to "God" without discrimination, not excepting the Son from "all things." And in the inversion of his absurdities he clearly separates, forsooth, the Son from the Divine Nature, when he says that neither is any generated thing spoken of as "ungenerate," nor is God called "Son" or "generate," and manifestly reveals by this contradistinction the horrid character of his blasphemy. For when he has distinguished the "things that have come into being" from the "ungenerate," he goes on to say, in that antistrophal induction of his, that it is impossible to call (not the "unbegotten," but) "God," "Son" or "generate," trying by these words to show that that which is not ungenerate is not God, and that the Only-begotten God is, by the fact of being begotten, as far removed from being God as the ungenerate is from being generated in fact or in name. For it is not in ignorance of the consequence of his argument that he makes an inversion of the terms employed thus inharmonious and incongruous : it is in his assault on the doctrine of orthodoxy that he opposes "the Godhead" to "the generate"— and this is the point he tries to establish by his words, that that which is not ungenerate is not God. What was the true sequence of his argument? that having said "no generated thing is ungenerate," he should proceed with the inference, "nor, if anything is naturally ungenerate, can it be generate." Such a statement at once contains truth and avoids blasphemy. But now by his premise that no generated thing is ungenerate, and his inference that God is not generated, he clearly shuts out the Only-begotten God from being God, laying down that because He is not ungenerate, neither is He God. Do we then need any further proofs to expose this monstrous blasphemy? Is not this enough by itself to serve for a record against the adversary of Christ, who by the arguments cited maintains that the Word, Who in the beginning was God, is not God? What need is there to engage further with such men as this? For we do not entangle ourselves in controversy with those who busy themselves with idols and with the blood that is shed upon their altars, not that we acquiesce in the destruction of those who are besotted about idols, but because their disease is too strong for our treatment. Thus, just as the fact itself declares idolatry, and the evil that men do boldly and arrogantly anticipates the reproach of those who

---

[5] That is, in making a rhetorical inversion of a proposition in itself objectionable, he so re-states it as to make it really a different proposition while treating it as equivalent. The original proposition is objectionable as classing the Son with all generated existences : the inversion of it, because the term "God" is substituted illicitly for the term "ungenerate."

accuse it, so here too I think that the advocates of orthodoxy should keep silence towards one who openly proclaims his impiety to his own discredit, just as medicine also stands powerless in the case of a cancerous complaint, because the disease is too strong for the art to deal with.

§ 3. *Thereafter he discusses the divergence of names and of things, speaking of that which is ungenerate as without a cause, and of that which is non-existent, as the Scindapsus, Minotaur, Blityri, Cyclops, Scylla, which never were generated at all, and shows that things which are essentially different, are mutually destructive, as fire of water, and the rest in their several relations. But in the case of the Father and the Son, as the essence is common, and the properties reciprocally interchangeable, no injury results to the Nature.*

Since, however, after the passage cited above, he professes that he will allege something stronger still, let us examine this also, as well as the passage cited, lest we should seem to be withdrawing our opposition in face of an overwhelming force. "If, however," he says, "I am to abandon all these positions, and fall back upon my stronger argument, I would say this, that even if all the terms that he advances by way of refutation were established, our statement will none the less be manifestly shown to be true. If, as will be admitted, the divergence of the names which are significant of properties marks the divergence of the things, it is surely necessary to allow that with the divergence of the names significant of essence is also marked the divergence of the essences. And this would be found to hold good in all cases, I mean in the case of essences, energies, colours, figures, and other qualities. For we denote by divergent appellations the different essences, fire and water, air and earth, cold and heat, white and black, triangle and circle. Why need we mention the intelligible essences, in enumerating which the Apostle marks, by difference of names, the divergence of essence?"

Who would not be dismayed at this irresistible power of attack? The argument transcends the promise, the experience is more terrible than the threat. "I will come," he says, "to my stronger argument." What is it? That as the differences of properties are recognized by those names which signify the special attributes, we must of course, he says, allow that differences of essence are also expressed by divergence of names. What then are these appellations of essences by which we learn the divergence of Nature between the Father and the son? He talks of fire and water, air and earth, cold and

heat, white and black, triangle and circle. His illustrations have won him the day: his argument carries all before it: I cannot contradict the statement that those names which are entirely incommunicable indicate difference of natures. But our man of keen and quick-sighted intellect has just missed seeing these points :—that in this case the Father is God and the Son is God; that "just," and "incorruptible," and all those names which belong to the Divine Nature, are used equally of the Father and of the Son; and thus, if the divergent character of appellations indicates difference of natures, the community of names will surely show the common character of the essence. And if we must agree that the Divine essence is to be expressed by names [6], it would behove us to apply to that Nature these lofty and Divine names rather than the terminology of "generate" and "ungenerate," because "good" and "incorruptible," "just" and "wise," and all such terms as these are strictly applicable only to that Nature which passes all understanding, whereas "generated" exhibits community of name with even the inferior forms of the lower creation. For we call a dog, and a frog, and all things that come into the world by way of generation, "generated." And moreover, the term "ungenerate" is not only employed of that whch exists without a cause, but has also a proper application to that which is non-existent. The Scindapsus [7] is called ungenerate, the Blityri [7] is ungenerate, the Minotaur is ungenerate, the Cyclops, Scylla, the Chimæra are ungenerate, not in the sense of existing without generation, but in the sense of never having come into being at all. If, then, the names more peculiarly Divine are common to the Son with the Father, and if it is the others, those which are equivocally employed either of the non-existent or of the lower animals—if it is these, I say, which are divergent, let his "generate and ungenerate" be so : Eunomius' powerful argument against us itself upholds the cause of truth in testifying that there is no divergence in respect of nature, because no divergence can be perceived in the names [8]. But if he asserts the difference of essence to exist between the "generate" and the "ungenerate," as it does between fire and water, and is of opinion that the names, like those which he has mentioned in his examples, are in the same mutual relation as "fire" and "water," the horrid character of his blasphemy will here again be brought to light, even if we hold our peace. For fire and

---

[6] On this point, besides what follows here, see the treatise against Tritheism addressed to Ablabius.
[7] These are names applied to denote existences purely imaginary ; the other names belong to classical mythology.
[8] That is, in the names more peculiarly appropriate to the Divine Nature.

water have a nature mutually destructive, and each is destroyed, if it comes to be in the other, by the prevalence of the more powerful element. If, then, he lays down the doctrine that the Nature of the Ungenerate differs thus from that of the Only-begotten, it is surely clear that he logically makes this destructive opposition to be involved in the divergence of their essences, so that their nature will be, by this reasoning, incompatible and incommunicable, and the one would be consumed by the other, if both should be found to be mutually inclusive or co-existent.

How then is the Son "in the Father" without being destroyed, and how does the Father, coming to be "in the Son," remain continually unconsumed, if, as Eunomius says, the special attribute of fire, as compared with water, is maintained in the relation of the Generate to the Ungenerate? Nor does their definition regard communion as existing between earth and air, for the former is stable, solid, resistent, of downward tendency and heavy, while air has a nature made up of the contrary attributes. So white and black are found in opposition among colours, and men are agreed that the circle is not the same with the triangle, for each, according to the definition of its figure, is precisely that which the other is not. But I am unable to discover where he sees the opposition in the case of God the Father and God the Only-begotten Son. One goodness, wisdom, justice, providence, power, incorruptibility,—all other attributes of exalted significance are similarly predicated of each, and the one has in a certain sense His strength in the other; for on the one hand the Father makes all things through the Son, and on the other hand the Only-begotten works all in Himself, being the Power of the Father. Of what avail, then, are fire and water to show essential diversity in the Father and the Son? He calls us, moreover, "rash" for instancing the unity of nature and difference of persons of Peter and Paul, and says we are guilty of gross recklessness, if we apply our argument to the contemplation of the objects of pure reason by the aid of material examples. Fitly, fitly indeed, does the corrector of our errors reprove us for rashness in interpreting the Divine Nature by material illustrations! Why then, deliberate and circumspect sir, do you talk about the elements? Is earth immaterial, fire an object of pure reason, water incorporeal, air beyond the perception of the senses? Is your mind so well directed to its aim, are you so keen-sighted in all directions in your promulgation of this argument, that your adversaries cannot lay hold of, that you do not see in yourself the faults you blame in those you are accusing? Or are we to make concessions to you when you are establishing the diversity of essence by material aid, and to be ourselves rejected when we point out the kindred character of the Nature by means of examples within our compass?

§ 4. *He says that all things that are in creation have been named by man, if, as is the case, they are called differently by every nation, as also the appellation of " Ungenerate" is conferred by us: but that the proper appellation of the Divine essence itself, which expresses the Divine Nature, either does not exist at all, or is unknown to us.*

But Peter and Paul, he says, were named by men, and hence it comes that it is possible in their case to change the appellations. Why, what existing thing has *not* been named by men? I call you to testify on behalf of my argument. For if you make change of names a sign of things having been named by men, you will thereby surely allow that every name has been imposed upon things by us, since the same appellations of objects have not obtained universally. For as in the case of Paul who was once Saul, and of Peter who was formerly Simon, so earth and sky and air and sea and all the parts of the creation have not been named alike by all, but are named in one way by the Hebrews, and in another way by us, and are denoted by every nation by different names. If then Eunomius' argument is valid when he maintains that it was for this reason, to wit, that their names had been imposed by men, that Peter and Paul were named afresh, our teaching will surely be valid also, starting as it does from like premises, which says that all things are named by us, on the ground that their appellations vary according to the distinctions of nations. Now if all things are so, surely the Generate and the Ungenerate are not exceptions, for even they are among the things that change their name. For when we gather, as it were, into the form of a name the conception of any subject that arises in us, we declare our concept by words that vary at different times, not *making*, but *signifying*, the thing by the name we give it. For the things remain in themselves as they naturally are, while the mind, touching on existing things, reveals its thought by such words as are available. And just as the essence of Peter was not changed with the change of his name, so neither is any other of the things we contemplate changed in the process of mutation of names. And for this reason we say that the term " Ungenerate" was applied by us to the true and first Father Who is the Cause of all, and that no harm would result as regards the signifying of the Subject, if we were to acknowledge the same concept under another name. For it is allowable instead of speaking of Him as "Un-generate," to call Him the "First Cause" or "Father of the Only-begotten," or to speak of Him as "existing without cause," and many such appellations which lead to the same thought; so that Eunomius confirms our doctrines by the very arguments in which he makes complaint against us, because we know no name significant of the Divine Nature. We are taught the fact of Its existence, while we assert that an appellation of such force as to include the unspeakable and infinite Nature, either does not exist at all, or at any rate is unknown to us. Let him then leave his accustomed language of fable, and show us the names which signify the essences, and then proceed further to divide the subject by the divergence of their names. But so long as the saying of the Scripture is true that Abraham and Moses were not capable of the knowledge of the Name, and that "no man hath seen God at any time[9]," and that "no man hath seen Him, nor can see[1]," and that the light around Him is unapproachable[1], and "there is no end of His greatness[2]";—so long as we say and believe these things, how like is an argument that promises any comprehension and expression of the infinite Nature, by means of the significance of names, to one who thinks that he can enclose the whole sea in his own hand! for as the hollow of one's hand is to the whole deep, so is all the power of language in comparison with that Nature which is unspeakable and incomprehensible.

§ 5. *After much discourse concerning the actually existent, and ungenerate and good, and upon the consubstantiality of the heavenly powers, showing the unvaried character of their essence, yet the difference of their ranks, he ends the book.*

Now in saying these things we do not intend to deny that the Father exists without generation, and we have no intention of refusing to agree to the statement that the Only-begotten God is generated;—on the contrary the latter has been generated, the former has not been generated. But what He *is*, in His own Nature, Who exists apart from generation, and what He *is*, Who is believed to have been generated, we do not learn from the signification of "having been generated," and "not having been generated." For when we say "this person was generated" (or "was not generated"), we are impressed with a two-fold thought, having our eyes turned to the subject by the demonstrative part of the phrase, and learning that which is contemplated in the subject by the words "was generated"

or "was not generated,"—as it is one thing to think of that which is, and another to think of what we contemplate in that which is. But, moreover, the word "*is*" is surely understood with every name that is used concerning the Divine Nature,—as "just," "incorruptible," "immortal," and "ungenerate," and whatever else is said of Him; even if this word does not happen to occur in the phrase, yet the thought both of the speaker and the hearer surely makes the name attach to "is," so that if this word were not added, the appellation would be uttered in vain. For instance (for it is better to present an argument by way of illustration), when David says, "God, a righteous judge, strong and patient[3]," if "is" were not understood with each of the epithets included in the phrase, the enumerations of the appellations will seem purposeless and unreal, not having any subject to rest upon; but when "is" is understood with each of the names, what is said will clearly be of force, being contemplated in reference to that which is. As, then, when we say "He is a judge," we conceive concerning Him some operation of judgment, and by the "is" carry our minds to the subject, and are hereby clearly taught not to suppose that the account of His being is the same with the action, so also as a result of saying, "He is generated (or ungenerate)," we divide our thought into a double conception, by "is" understanding the subject, and by "generated," or "ungenerate," apprehending that which belongs to the subject. As, then, when we are taught by David that God is "a judge," or "patient," we do not learn the Divine essence, but one of the attributes which are contemplated in it, so in this case too when we hear of His being not generated, we do not by this negative predication understand the *subject*, but are guided as to what we must not think concerning the subject, while what He essentially is remains as much as ever unexplained. So too, when Holy Scripture predicates the other Divine names of Him Who is, and delivers to Moses the Being without a name, it is for him who discloses the Nature of that Being, not to rehearse the attributes of the Being, but by his words to make manifest to us its actual Nature. For every name which you may use is an attribute of the Being, but is not the Being,—"good," "ungenerate," "incorruptible,"—but to each of these "is" does not fail to be supplied. Any one, then, who undertakes to give the account of this good Being, of this ungenerate Being, as He is, would speak in vain, if he rehearsed the attributes contemplated in Him, and were silent as to that essence which he undertakes by his

9 S. John i. 18.   1 1 Tim. vi. 16.   2 Ps. cxlv. 3.   3 Cf. Ps. vii. 8.

words to explain. To *be without generation* is one of the attributes contemplated in the Being, but the definition of " Being " is one thing, and that of " being in some particular way " is another ; and this [4] has so far remained untold and unexplained by the passages cited. Let him then first disclose to us the names of the essence, and then divide the Nature by the divergence of the appellations ;—so long as what we require remains unexplained, it is in vain that he employs his scientific skill upon names, seeing that the names [5] have no separate existence.

Such then is Eunomius' stronger handle against the truth, while we pass by in silence many views which are to be found in this part of his composition ; for it seems to me right that those who run in this armed race [6] against the enemies of the truth should arm themselves against those who are fairly fenced about with the plausibility of falsehood, and not defile their argument with such conceptions as are already dead and of offensive odour. His supposition that whatever things are united in the idea of their essence [7] must needs exist corporeally and be joined to corruption (for this he says in this part of his work), I shall willingly pass by like some cadaverous odour, since I think every reasonable man will perceive how dead and corrupt such an argument is. For who knows not that the multitude of human souls is countless, yet one essence underlies them all, and the consubstantial substratum in them is alien from bodily corruption? so that even children can plainly see the argument that

bodies are corrupted and dissolved, not because they have the same essence one with another, but because of their possessing a compound nature. The idea of the compound nature is one, that of the common nature of their essence is another, so that it is true to say, " corruptible bodies are of one essence," but the converse statement is not true at all, if it be anything like, " this consubstantial nature is also surely corruptible," as is shown in the case of the souls which have one essence, while yet corruption does not attach to them in virtue of the community of essence. And the account given of the souls might properly be applied to every intellectual existence which we contemplate in creation. For the words brought together by Paul do not signify, as Eunomius will have them do, some mutually divergent natures of the supra-mundane powers ; on the contrary, the sense of the names clearly indicates that he is mentioning in his argument, not diversities of *natures*, but the varied peculiarities of the *operations* of the heavenly host : for there are, he says, " principalities," and " thrones," and " powers," and " mights," and " dominions [8]." Now these names are such as to make it at once clear to every one that their significance is arranged in regard to some operation. For to rule, and to exercise power and dominion, and to be the throne of some one,—all these conceptions would not be held by any one versed in argument to apply to diversities of *essence*, since it is clearly *operation* that is signified by every one of the names : so that any one who says that diversities of *nature* are signified by the names rehearsed by Paul deceives himself, " understanding," as the Apostle says, " neither what he says, nor whereof he affirms [9]," since the sense of the names clearly shows that the Apostle recognizes in the intelligible powers distinctions of certain ranks, but does not by these names indicate varieties of essences.

---

4 What " this " means is not clear : it may be " the Being," but most probably is the distinction which S. Gregory is pointing out between the Being and Its attributes, which he considers has not been sufficiently recognized.

5 Reading τῶν ὀνομάτων οὐκ ὄντων with the Paris editions. Oehler reads νοημάτων, but does not give any authority for the change.

6 The metaphor seems slightly confused, being partly taken from a tournament, or gladiatorial contest, partly from a race in armour.

7 The word οὐσία seems to have had in Eunomius' mind something of the same idea of *corporeal* existence attaching to it which has been made to attach to the Latin " substantia," and to the English " substance."

8 Cf. Col. i. 16, and Eph. i. 21.   9 1 Tim. i. 7.

BOOK VIII

§ 1. The eighth book very notably overthrows the blasphemy of the heretics who say that the Only-begotten came from nothing, and that there was a time when He was not, and shows the Son to be no new being, but from everlasting, from His having said to Moses, " I am He that is," and to Manoah, " Why askest thou My name? it also is wonderful" ;—moreover David also says to God, " Thou art the same, and Thy years shall not fail ;" and furthermore Isaiah says, " I am God, the first, and hereafter am I:" and the Evangelist, " He was in the beginning, and was with God, and was God:"—and that He has neither beginning nor end: and he proves that those who say that He is new and comes from nothing are idolaters. And herein he very finely interprets " the brightness of the glory, and the express image of the Person."

THESE, then, are the strong points of Eunomius' case ; and I think that when those which promised to be powerful are proved by argument to be so rotten and unsubstantial, I may well keep silence concerning the rest, since the others are practically refuted, concurrently with the refutation of the stronger ones ; just as it happens in warlike operations that when a force more powerful than the rest has been beaten, the remainder of the army are no longer of any account in the eyes of those by whom the strong portion of it has been overcome. But the fact that the chief part of his blasphemy lies in the later part of his discourse forbids me to be silent. For the transition of the Only-begotten from nothing into being, that horrid and godless doctrine of Eunomius, which is more to be shunned than all impiety, is next maintained in the order of his argument. And since every one who has been bewitched by this deceit has the phrase, " If He was, He has not been begotten, and if He has been begotten, He was not," ready upon his tongue for the maintenance of the doctrine that He Who made of nothing us and all the creation is Himself from nothing, and since the deceit obtains much support thereby, as men of feebler mind are pressed by this superficial bit of plausibility, and led to acquiesce in the blasphemy, we

must needs not pass by this doctrinal "root of bitterness," lest, as the Apostle says, it "spring up and trouble us [1]." Now I say that we must first of all consider the actual argument itself, apart from our contest with our opponents, and thus afterwards proceed to the examination and refutation of what they have set forth.

One mark of the true Godhead is indicated by the words of Holy Scripture, which Moses learnt by the voice from heaven, when He heard Him Who said, "I am He that is [2]." We think it right, then, to believe that to be alone truly Divine which is represented as eternal and infinite in respect of being ; and all that is contemplated therein is always the same, neither growing nor being consumed ; so that if one should say of God, that formerly He was, but now is not, or that He now is, but formerly was not, we should consider each of the sayings alike to be godless : for by both alike the idea of eternity is mutilated, being cut short on one side or the other by non-existence, whether one contemplates "nothing" as preceding "being [3]," or declares that "being" ends in "nothing" ; and the frequent repetition of "first of all" or "last of all" concerning God's non-existence does not make amends for the impious conception touching the Divinity. For this reason we declare the maintenance of their doctrine as to the non-existence at some time of Him Who truly is, to be a denial and rejection of His true Godhead ; and this on the ground that, on the one hand, He Who showed Himself to Moses by the light speaks of Himself as *being*, when He says, "I am He that is [2]," while on the other, Isaiah (being made, so to say, the instrument of Him Who spoke in him) says in the person of Him that is, "I am the first, and hereafter am I [4]," so that hereby, whichever way we consider it, we conceive eternity in God. And so, too, the word that was spoken to Manoah shows the fact that the Divinity is not comprehensible by the significance of His name, because, when Manoah asks to know His name, that, when the promise has come actually to pass, he may by name glorify his benefactor,

---

[1] Cf. Heb. xii. 15.　　　　　　[2] Exod. iii. 4.
[3] Reading προθεωροίη for προσθεωροίη.
[4] See note 4 on Book V. § 1, where these words are also treated of.

He says to him, "Why askest thou this? It also is wonderful[5]"; so that by this we learn that there is one name significant of the Divine Nature—the wonder, namely, that arises unspeakably in our hearts concerning It. So, too, great David, in his discourses with himself, proclaims the same truth, in the sense that all the creation was brought into being by God, while He alone exists always in the same manner, and abides for ever, where he says, "But Thou art the same, and Thy years shall not fail[6]." When we hear these sayings, and others like them, from men inspired by God, let us leave all that is not from eternity to the worship of idolaters, as a new thing alien from the true Godhead. For that which now is, and formerly was not, is clearly new and not eternal, and to have regard to any new object of worship is called by Moses the service of demons, when he says, "They sacrificed to devils and not to God, to gods whom their fathers knew not; new gods were they that came newly up[7]." If then everything that is new in worship is a service of demons, and is alien from the true Godhead, and if what is now, but was not always, is new and not eternal, we who have regard to that which *is*, necessarily reckon those who contemplate non-existence as attaching to Him Who is, and who say that "He once was not," among the worshippers of idols. For we may also see that the great John, when declaring in his own preaching the Only-begotten God, guards his own statement in every way, so that the conception of non-existence shall find no access to Him Who is. For he says[8] that He "was in the beginning," and "was with God," and "was God," and was light, and life, and truth, and all good things at all times, and never at any time failed to be anything that is excellent, Who is the fulness of all good, and is in the bosom of the Father. If then Moses lays down as a law for us some such mark of true Godhead as this, that we know nothing else of God but this one thing, that He *is* (for to this point the words, "I am He that is[9]"); while Isaiah in his preaching declares aloud the absolute infinity of Him Who is, defining the existence of God as having no regard to beginning or to end (for He Who says "I am the first, and hereafter am I," places no limit to His eternity in either direction, so that neither, if we look to the beginning, do we find any point marked *since* which He is, and beyond which He was not, nor, if we turn our thought to the future, can we cut short by any boundary the eternal progress of Him Who is),—and if the prophet David forbids us to worship any

new and strange God[1] (both of which are involved in the heretical doctrine; "newness" is clearly indicated in that which is not eternal, and "strangeness" is alienation from the Nature of the very God),—if, I say, these things are so, we declare all the sophistical fabrication about the non-existence at some time of Him Who truly is, to be nothing else than a departure from Christianity, and a turning to idolatry. For when the Evangelist, in his discourse concerning the Nature of God, separates at all points non-existence from Him Who is, and, by his constant repetition of the word "was," carefully destroys the suspicion of non-existence, and calls Him the Only-begotten God, the Word of God, the Son of God, equal with God, and all such names, we have this judgment fixed and settled in us, that if the Only-begotten Son is God, we must believe that He Who is believed to be God is eternal. And indeed He is verily God, and assuredly is eternal, and is never at any time found to be non-existent. For God, as we have often said, if He now is, also assuredly always was, and if He once was not, neither does He now exist at all. But since even the enemies of the truth confess that the Son is and continually abides the Only-begotten God, we say this, that, being in the Father, He is not in Him in one respect only, but He is in Him altogether, in respect of all that the Father is conceived to be. As, then, being in the incorruptibility of the Father, He is incorruptible, good in His goodness, powerful in His might, and, as being in each of these attributes of special excellence which are conceived of the Father, He is that particular thing, so, also, being in His eternity, He is assuredly eternal. Now the eternity of the Father is marked by His never having taken His being from non-existence, and never terminating His being in non-existence. He, therefore, Who hath all things that are the Father's[2], and is contemplated in all the glory of the Father, even as, being in the endlessness of the Father, He has no end, so, being in the unoriginateness of the Father, has, as the Apostle says, "no beginning of days[3]," but at once is "of the Father," and is regarded in the eternity of the Father: and in this respect, more especially, is seen the complete absence of divergence in the Likeness, as compared with Him Whose Likeness He is. And herein is His saying found true which tells us, "He that hath seen Me hath seen the Father[4]." Moreover, it is in this way that those words of the Apostle, that the Son is "the brightness of His glory, and the express image of His Person[5]," are best understood to have an excellent and close application. For

[5] Cf. Judges xiii. 18 (LXX.).   [6] Ps. cii. 27.
[7] Cf. Deut. xxxii. 17 (LXX.).   The quotat on is not exact.
[8] Cf. S. John i.   [9] Exod. iii. 4.

[1] Cf. Ps. lxxxi. 10.   [2] S. John xvi. 15.   [3] Heb. vii. 3.
[4] S. John xiv. 8.   [5] Heb. i. 3.

the Apostle conveys to those hearers who are unable, by the contemplation of purely intellectual objects, to elevate their thought to the height of the knowledge of God, a sort of notion of the truth, by means of things apparent to sense. For as the body of the sun is expressly imaged by the whole disc that surrounds it, and he who looks on the sun argues, by means of what he sees, the existence of the whole solid substratum, so, he says, the majesty of the Father is expressly imaged in the greatness of the power of the Son, that the one may be believed to be as great as the other is known to be : and again, as the radiance of light sheds its brilliancy from the whole of the sun's disc (for in the disc one part is not radiant, and the rest dim), so all that glory which the Father is, sheds its brilliancy from its whole extent by means of the brightness that comes from it, that is, by the true Light ; and as the ray is of the sun (for there would be no ray if the sun were not), yet the sun is never conceived as existing by itself without the ray of brightness that is shed from it, so the Apostle delivering to us the continuity and eternity of that existence which the Only-begotten has of the Father, calls the Son " the brightness of His glory."

§ 2. *He then discusses the "willing" of the Father concerning the generation of the Son, and shows that the object of that good will is from eternity, which is the Son, existing in the Father, and being closely related to the process of willing, as the ray to the flame, or the act of seeing to the eye.*

After these distinctions on our part no one can well be longer in doubt how the Only-begotten at once is believed to be " of the Father," and *is* eternally, even if the one phrase does not at first sight seem to agree with the other,—that which declares Him to be " of the Father" with that which asserts His eternity. But if we are to confirm our statement by further arguments, it may be possible to apprehend the doctrine on this point by the aid of things cognizable by our senses. And let no one deride our statement, if it cannot find among existing things a likeness of the object of our enquiry such as may be in all respects sufficient for the presentation of the matter in hand by way of analogy and resemblance. For we should like to persuade those who say that the Father first willed and so proceeded to become a Father, and on this ground assert posteriority in existence as regards the Word, by whatever illustrations may make it possible, to turn to the orthodox view. Neither does this immediate conjunction exclude the " willing " of the Father, in the sense that He had a Son without

choice, by some necessity of His Nature, nor does the " willing " separate the Son from the Father, coming in between them as a kind of interval : so that we neither reject from our doctrine the " willing " of the Begetter directed to the Son, as being, so to say, forced out by the conjunction of the Son's oneness with the Father, nor do we by any means break that inseparable connection, when " willing " is regarded as involved in the generation. For to our heavy and inert nature it properly belongs that the wish and the possession of a thing are not often present with us at the same moment ; but now we wish for something we have not, and at another time we obtain what we do not wish to obtain. But, in the case of the simple and all-powerful Nature, all things are conceived together and at once, the willing of good as well as the possession of what He wills. For the good and the eternal will is contemplated as operating, indwelling, and co-existing in the eternal Nature, not arising in it from any separate principle, nor capable of being conceived apart from the object of will : for it is not possible that with God either the good will should not be, or the object of will should not accompany the act of will, since no cause can either bring it about that that which befits the Father should not always be, or be any hindrance to the possession of the object of will. Since, then, the Only-begotten God is by nature the good (or rather beyond all good), and since the good does not fail to be the object of the Father's will, it is hereby clearly shown, both that the conjunction of the Son with the Father is without any intermediary, and also that the will, which is always present in the good Nature, is not forced out nor excluded by reason of this inseparable conjunction. And if any one is listening to my argument in no scoffing spirit, I should like to add to what I have already said something of the following kind. Just as, if one were to grant (I speak, of course, hypothetically) the power of deliberate choice to belong to flame, it would be clear that the flame will at once upon its existence *will* that its radiance should shine forth from itself, and when it wills it will not be impotent (since, on the appearance of the flame, its natural power at once fulfils its will in the matter of the radiance), so that undoubtedly, if it be granted that the flame is moved by deliberate choice, we conceive the concurrence of all these things simultaneously—of the kindling of the fire, of its act of will concerning the radiance, and of the radiance itself ; so that the movement by way of choice is no hindrance to the dignity of the existence of the radiance,—even so, according to the illustration we have spoken of, you will not, by confessing the good act of will as existing in the Father, separate by that act of will the Son from the Father. For it is not reasonable to suppose that the act of willing that He should be, could be a hindrance to His immediately coming into being; but just as, in the eye, seeing and the will to see are, one an operation of nature, the other an impulse of choice, yet no delay is caused to the act of sight by the movement of choice in that particular direction [6],—(for each of these is regarded separately and by itself, not as being at all a hindrance to the existence of the other, but as both being somehow interexistent, the natural operation concurring with the choice, and the choice in turn not failing to be accompanied by the natural motion)—as, I say, perception naturally belongs to the eye, and the willing to see produces no delay in respect to actual sight, but one wills that it should have vision, and immediately what he wills *is*, so also in the case of that Nature which is unspeakable and above all thought, our apprehension of all comes together simultaneously—of· the eternal existence of the Father, and of an act of will concerning the Son, and of the Son Himself, Who is, as John says, "in the beginning," and is not conceived as coming after the beginning. Now the beginning of all is the Father; but in this beginning the Son also is declared to be, being in His Nature that very thing which the Beginning is. For the Beginning is God, and the Word Who "was in the Beginning." is God. As then the phrase "the beginning" points to eternity, John well conjoins "the Word in the Beginning," saying that the Word was in It; asserting, I suppose, this fact to the end that the first idea present to the mind of his hearer may not be "the Beginning" alone by itself, but that, before this has been impressed upon him, there should also be presented to his mind, together with the Beginning the Word Who was in It, entering with It into the hearer's understanding, and being present to his hearing at the same time with the Beginning.

§ 3. *Then, thus passing over what relates to the essence of the Son as having been already discussed, he treats of the sense involved in "generation," saying that there are diverse generations, those effected by matter and art, and of buildings,—and that by succession of animals, —and those by efflux, as by the sun and its beam, the lamp and its radiance, scents and ointments and the quality diffused by them,— and the word produced by the mind; and cleverly discusses generation [7] from rotten wood; and from the condensation of fire, and countless other causes.*

Now that we have thus thoroughly scrutinized our doctrine, it may perhaps be time to set forth and to consider the opposing statement, examining it side by side in comparison with our own opinion. He states it thus :—" For while there are," he says, "two statements which we have made, the one, that the essence of the Only-begotten was not before its own generation, the other that, being generated, it was before all things, he [8] does not prove either of these statements to be untrue; for he did not venture to say that He was before that supreme [9] generation and formation, seeing that he is opposed at once by the Nature of the Father, and the judgment of sober-minded men. For what sober man could admit the Son to be and to be begotten before that supreme generation? and He Who is without generation needs not generation in order to His being what He is." Well, whether he speaks truly, when he says that our master [8] opposed his antitheses to no purpose, all may surely be aware who have been conversant with that writer's works. But for my own part (for I think that the refutation of his calumny on this matter is a small step towards the exposure of his malice), I will leave the task of showing that this point was not passed over by our master without discussion, and turn my argument to the discussion, as far as in me lies, of the points now advanced. He says that he has in his own discourse spoken of two matters,—one, that the essence of the Only-begotten was not before Its own generation, the other, that, being generated, It was before all things. Now I think that by what we have already said, the fact has been sufficiently shown that no new essence was begotten by the Father besides that which is contemplated in the Father Himself, and that there is no need for us to be entangled in a contest with blasphemy of this kind, as if the argument were now propounded to us for the first time; and further, that the real force of our argument must be directed to one point, I mean to his horrible and blasphemous utterance, which clearly states concerning God the Word that "He was not." Moreover, as our argument in the foregoing discourse has already to some extent dealt with the question of his blasphemy, it would perhaps be superfluous again to establish by like considerations what we have proved already. For it was to this end that we made those former statements, that by the earlier impression upon our hearers of an orthodox mode of thought, the blasphemy

---

6 Oehler's punctuation here seems faulty.
7 To make the grammar of the sentence exact τὴν should here be substituted for τὸν, the object of the verb being apparently

γέννησιν not λόγον. The whole section of the analysis is rather confused, and does not clearly reproduce S. Gregory's division of the subject. A large part of this section, and of that which follows it, is repeated with very slight alteration from Bk. II. § 9 (see pp. 113—115 above). The resemblances are much closer in the Greek text than they appear in the present translation, in which different han·ls have been at work in the two books. 8 *i.e.* S. Basil. 9 ἀνωτάτω may be "supreme," in the sense of "ultimate" or "most remote," or in the more ordinary sense of "most exalted."

of our adversaries, who assert that non-existence preceded existence in the case of the Only-begotten God, might be more manifest.

It seems at this point well to investigate in our argument, by a more careful examination, the actual significance of "generation." That this name presents to us the fact of being as the result of some cause is clear to every one, and about this point there is, I suppose, no need to dispute. But since the account to be given of things which exist as the result of cause is various, I think it proper that this matter should be cleared up in our discourse by some sort of scientific division. Of things, then, which are the result of something, we understand the varieties to be as follows. Some are the result of matter and art, as the structure of buildings and of other works, coming into being by means of their respective matter, and these are directed by some art that accomplishes the thing proposed, with a view to the proper aim of the results produced. Others are the results of matter and nature; for the generations of animals are the building[1] of nature, who carries on her own operation by means of their material bodily subsistence. Others are the result of material efflux, in which cases the antecedent remains in its natural condition, while that which flows from it is conceived separately, as in the case of the sun and its beam, or the lamp and its brightness, or of scents and ointments and the quality they emit; for these, while they remain in themselves without diminution, have at the same time, each concurrently with itself, that natural property which they emit: as the sun its beam, the lamp its brightness, the scents the perfume produced by them in the air. There is also another species of "generation" besides these, in which the cause is immaterial and incorporeal, but the generation is an object of sense and takes place by corporeal means;—I speak of the word which is begotten by the mind: for the mind, being itself incorporeal, brings forth the word by means of the organs of sense. All these varieties of generation we mentally include, as it were, in one general view. For all the wonders that are wrought by nature, which changes the bodies of some animals to something of a different kind, or produces some animals from a change in liquids, or a corruption of seed, or the rotting of wood, or out of the condensed mass of fire transforms the cold vapour that issues from the firebrands, shut off in the heart of the fire, to produce an animal which they call the salamander,—these, even if they seem to be outside the limits we have laid down, are none the less included among the cases we have mentioned. For it is by means

of bodies that nature fashions these varied forms of animals; for it is such and such a change of body, disposed by nature in this or that particular way, which produces this or that particular animal; and this is not a distinct species of generation besides that which is accomplished as the result of nature and matter.

§ 4. *He further shows the operations of God to be expressed by human illustrations; for what hands and feet and the other parts of the body with which men work are, that, in the case of God, the will alone is, in place of these. And so also arises the divergence of generation; wherefore He is called Only-begotten, because He has no community with other generation such as is observed in creation[2], but in that He is called the " brightness of glory," and the "savour of ointment," He shows the close conjunction and co-eternity of His Nature with the Father[3].*

Now these modes of generation being well known to men, the loving dispensation of the Holy Spirit, in delivering to us the Divine mysteries, conveys its instruction on those matters which transcend language by means of what is within our capacity, as it does also constantly elsewhere, when it portrays the Divinity in bodily terms, making mention, in speaking concerning God, of His eye, His eyelids, His ear, His fingers, His hand, His right hand, His arm, His feet, His shoes[4], and the like,—none of which things is apprehended to belong in its primary sense to the Divine Nature,—but turning its teaching to what we can easily perceive, it describes by terms well worn in human use, facts that are beyond every name, while by each of the terms employed concerning God we are led analogically to some more exalted conception. In this way, then, it employs the numerous forms of generation to present to us, from the inspired teaching, the unspeakable existence of the Only-begotten, taking just so much from each as may be reverently admitted into our conceptions concerning God. For as its mention of "fingers," "hand," and "arm," in speaking of God, does not by the phrase portray the structure of the limb out of bones and sinews and flesh and ligaments, but signifies by such an expression His effective and operative power, and as it indicates by each of the other words of this kind those conceptions concerning God which correspond to them, not admitting the corporeal senses of the words, so also it speaks indeed of the forms of these modes of coming into being as applied to the Divine

---

[1] Or (reading as proposed above, p. 114, οἰκονομεῖ for οἰκοδομεῖ), "the ordering of nature."

[2] This passage is clearly corrupt: the general sense as probably intended is given here. [3] See note 7 in the last section. [4] The reference is probably to Ps. lx. 8, and Ps. cviii. 9.

Nature, yet does not speak in that sense which our customary knowledge enables us to understand. For when it speaks of the formative power, it calls that particular energy by the name of "generation," because the word expressive of Divine power must needs descend to our lowliness, yet it does not indicate all that is associated with formative generation among ourselves,—neither place nor time nor preparation of material, nor the co-operation of instruments, nor the purpose in the things produced, but it leaves these out of sight, and greatly and loftily claims for God the generation of the things that are, where it says, " He spake and they were begotten, He commanded and they were created [5]." Again, when it expounds that unspeakable and transcendent existence which the Only-begotten has from the Father, because human poverty is incapable of the truths that are too high for speech or thought, it uses our language here also, and calls Him by the name of "Son,"—a name which our ordinary use applies to those who are produced by matter and nature. But just as the word, which tells us in reference to God of the "generation" of the creation, did not add the statement that it was generated by the aid of any material, declaring that its material substance, its place, its time, and all the like, had their existence in the power of His will, so here too, in speaking of the "Son," it leaves out of sight both all other things which human nature sees in earthly generation (passions, I mean, and dispositions, and the co-operation of time and the need of place, and especially matter), without all which earthly generation as a result of nature does not occur. Now every such conception of matter and interval being excluded from the sense of the word "Son," nature alone remains, and hereby in the word "Son" is declared concerning the Only-begotten the close and true character of His manifestation from the Father. And since this particular species of generation did not suffice to produce in us an adequate idea of the unspeakable existence of the Only-begotten, it employs also another species of generation, that which is the result of efflux, to express the Divine Nature of the Son, and calls Him "the brightness of glory [6]," the "savour of ointment [7]," the "breath of God [8]," which our accustomed use, in the scientific discussion we have already made, calls material efflux. But just as in the previous cases neither the making of creation nor the significance of the word "Son" admitted time, or matter, or place, or passion, so here also the phrase, purifying the sense of "brightness" and the other terms from every material

conception, and employing only that element in this particular species of generation which is suitable to the Divinity, points by the force of this mode of expression to the truth that He is conceived as being both from Him and with Him. For neither does the word "breath" present to us dispersion into the air from the underlying matter, nor "savour" the transference that takes place from the quality of the ointment to the air, nor "brightness" the efflux by means of rays from the body of the sun; but this only, as we have said, is manifested by this particular mode of generation, that He is conceived to be of Him and also with Him, no intermediate interval existing between the Father and that Son Who is of Him. And since, in its abundant loving-kindness, the grace of the Holy Spirit has ordered that our conceptions concerning the Only-begotten Son should arise in us from many sources, it has added also the remaining species of things contemplated in generation,—that, I mean, which is the result of mind and word. But the lofty John uses especial foresight that the hearer may not by any means by inattention or feebleness of thought fall into the common understanding of "Word," so that the Son should be supposed to be the voice of the Father. For this reason he prepares us at his first proclamation to regard the Word as in essence, and not in any essence foreign to or dissevered from that essence whence It has Its being, but in that first and blessed Nature. For this is what he teaches us when he says the Word "was in the beginning [9]," and "was with God [9]," being Himself also both God and all else that the "Beginning" is. For thus it is that he makes his discourse on the Godhead, touching the eternity of the Only-begotten. Seeing then that these modes of generation (those, I mean, which are the result of cause) are ordinarily known among us, and are employed by Holy Scripture for our instruction on the subjects before us, in such a way as it might be expected that each of them would be applied to the presentation of Divine conceptions, let the reader of our argument "judge righteous judgement [1]," whether any of the assertions that heresy makes have any force against the truth.

§ 5. *Then, after showing that the Person of the Only-begotten and Maker of things has no beginning, as have the things that were made by Him, as Eunomius says, but that the Only-begotten is without beginning and eternal, and has no community, either of essence or of names, with the creation, but is co-existent with the Father from everlasting, being, as the all-excel-*

lent Wisdom says, " the beginning and end and midst of the times," and after making many observations on the Godhead and eternity of the Only-begotten, and also concerning souls and angels, and life and death, he concludes the book.

I will now once more subjoin the actual language of my opponent, word for word. It runs thus :—" While there are," he says, " two statements which we have made, the one, that the essence of the Only-begotten was not before its own generation, the other, that, being generated, it was before all things—" What kind of generation does our dogmatist propose to us? Is it one of which we may fittingly think and speak in regard to God? And who is so godless as to pre-suppose non-existence in God? But it is clear that he has in view this material generation of ours, and is making the lower nature the teacher of his conceptions concerning the Only-begotten God, and since an ox or an ass or a camel is not before its own generation, he thinks it proper to say even of the Only-begotten God that which the course of the lower nature presents to our view in the case of the animals, without thinking, corporeal theologian that he is, of this fact, that the predicate " *Only*-begotten ", applied to God, signifies by the very word itself that which is not in common with all begetting, and is peculiar to Him. How could the term " Only-begotten " be used of this "generation," if it had community and identity of meaning with other generation? That there is something unique and exceptional to be understood in His case, which is not to be remarked in other generation, is distinctly and suitably expressed by the appellation of " Only-begotten "; as, were any element of the lower generation conceived in it, He Who in respect of any of the attributes of His generation was placed on a level with other things that are begotten would no longer be " *Only*-begotten." For if the same things are to be said of Him which are said of the other things that come into being by generation, the definition will transform the sense of " Only-begotten " to signify a kind of relationship involving brotherhood. If then the sense of " Only-begotten " points to absence of mixture and community with the rest of generated things, we shall not admit that anything which we behold in the lower generation is also to be conceived in the case of that existence which the Son has from the Father. But non-existence before generation is proper to all things that exist by generation : therefore this is foreign to the special character of the Only-begotten, to which the name " Only-begotten " bears witness that there attaches nothing belonging to

the mode of that form of common generation which Eunomius misapprehends. Let this materialist and friend of the senses be persuaded therefore to correct the error of his conception by the other forms of generation. What will you say when you hear of the " brightness of glory " or of the " savour of ointment [2] ? " That the " brightness " was not before its own generation? But if you answer thus, you will surely admit that neither did the " glory " exist, nor the " ointment " : for it is not possible that the " glory " should be conceived as having existed by itself, dark and lustreless, or the " ointment " without producing its sweet breath : so that if the " brightness " " was not," the " glory " also surely " was not," and the " savour " being non-existent, there is also proved the non-existence of the " ointment." But if these examples taken from Scripture excite any man's fear, on the ground that they do not accurately present to us the majesty of the Only-begotten, because neither is essentially the same with its substratum—neither the exhalation with the ointment, nor the beam with the sun—let the true Word correct his fear, Who was in the Beginning and is all that the Beginning is, and existent before all ; since John so declares in his preaching, " And the Word was with God, and the Word was God [3]." If then the Father is God and the Son is God, what doubt still remains with regard to the perfect Divinity of the Only-begotten, when by the sense of the word " Son " is acknowledged the close relationship of Nature, by " brightness " the conjunction and inseparability, and by the appellation of " God," applied alike to the Father and the Son, their absolute equality, while the " express image," contemplated in reference to the whole Person [4] of the Father, marks the absence of any defect in the Son's proper greatness, and the " form of God " indicates His complete identity by showing in itself all those marks by which the Godhead is betokened.

Let us now set forth Eunomius' statement once more. " He was not," he says, " before His own generation." Who is it of Whom he says " He was not " ? Let him declare the Divine names by which He Who, according to Eunomius, " once was not," is called. He will say, I suppose, " light," and " blessedness," " life " and " incorruptibility," and " righteousness " and " sanctification," and " power," and " truth," and the like. He who says, then, that " He was not before His generation," absolutely proclaims this,—that when He " was not " there was no truth, no life, no light, no power, no incorruptibility, no other of those pre-eminent qualities which are conceived of Him : and,

---

[2] Heb. i. 3, and Cant. i 3, referred to above.
[3] S. John i. 1.　　　　　[4] ὑποστάσει.

what is still more marvellous and still more difficult for impiety to face, there was no "brightness," no "express image." For in saying that there was no brightness, there is surely maintained also the non-existence of the radiating power, as one may see in the illustration afforded by the lamp. For he who speaks of the ray of the lamp indicates also that the lamp shines, and he who says that the ray "is not," signifies also the extinction of that which gives light : so that when the Son is said not to be, thereby is also maintained as a necessary consequence the non-existence of the Father. For if the one is related to the other by way of conjunction, according to the Apostolic testimony— the "brightness" to the "glory," the "express image" to the "Person," the "Wisdom" to God—he who says that one of the things so conjoined "is not," surely by his abolition of the one abolishes also that which remains ; so that if the "brightness" "was not," it is acknowledged that neither did the illuminating nature exist, and if the "express image" had no existence, neither did the Person imaged exist, and if the wisdom and power of God "was not," it is surely acknowledged that He also was not, Who is not conceived by Himself without wisdom and power. If, then, the Only-begotten God, as Eunomius says, "was not before His generation," and Christ is "the power of God and the wisdom of God [5]," and the "express image" [6] and the "brightness [6]," neither surely did the Father exist, Whose power and wisdom and express image and brightness the Son is : for it is not possible to conceive by reason either a Person without express image, or glory without radiance, or God without wisdom, or a Maker without hands, or a Beginning without the Word [7], or a Father without a Son ; but all such things, alike by those who confess and by those who deny, are manifestly declared to be in mutual union, and by the abolition of one the other also disappears with it. Since then they maintain that the Son (that is, the "brightness of the glory,") "was not" before He was begotten, and since logical consequence involves also, together with the non-existence of the brightness, the abolition of the glory, and the Father is the glory whence came the brightness of the Only-begotten Light, let these men who are wise over-much consider that they are manifestly supporters of the Epicurean doctrines, preaching atheism under the guise of Christianity. Now since the logical consequence is shown to be one of two absurdities, either that we should say that God does nor exist at all, or that we should say that His being was not unoriginate, let them choose which they like of the two courses before

them,—either to be called atheist, or to cease saying that the essence of the Father is unoriginate. They would avoid, I suppose, being reckoned atheists. It remains, therefore, that they maintain that God is not eternal. And if the course of what has been proved forces them to this, what becomes of their varied and irreversible conversions of names ? What becomes of that invincible compulsion of their syllogisms, which sounded so fine to the ears of old women, with its opposition of "Generated" and "Ungenerate"?

Enough, however, of these matters. But it might be well not to leave his next point unanswered ; yet let us pass over in silence the comic interlude, where our clever orator shows his youthful conceit, whether in jest or in earnest, under the impression that he will thereby have an advantage in his argument. For certainly no one will force us to join either with those whose eyes are set askance in distorting our sight, or with those who are stricken with strange disease in being contorted, or in their bodily leaps and plunges. We shall pity them, but we shall not depart from our settled state of mind. He says, then, turning his discourse upon the subject to our master, as if he were really engaging him face to face, "Thou shalt be taken in thine own snare." For as Basil had said [8] that what is good is always present with God Who is over all, and that it is good to be the Father of such a Son,—that so what is good was never absent from Him, nor was it the Father's will to be without the Son, and when He willed He did not lack the power, but having the power and the will to be in the mode in which it seemed good to Him, He also always possessed the Son by reason of His always willing that which is good (for this is the direction in which the intention of our father's remarks tends), Eunomius pulls this in pieces beforehand, and puts forward to overthrow what has been said some such argument as this, introduced from his extraneous philosophy :—"What will become of you," he says, "if one of those who have had experience of such arguments should say, 'If to create is good and agreeable to the Nature of God, how is it that what is good and agreeable to His Nature was not present with Him unoriginately, seeing that God is unoriginate? and that when there was no hindrance of ignorance or impediment of weakness or of age in the matter of creation,"—and all the rest that he collects together and pours out upon himself,—for I may not say, upon God. Well, if it were possible for our master to answer the question in person, he would have shown Eunomius what would have become of him,

5 1 Cor. i. 24.   6 Heb. i. 3.
7 Or perhaps " or an irrational first cause," (ἄλογον ἀρχήν.)
8 The reference is to S. Basil adv. Eunomium II. 12 (p. 247 in Ben. ed.)

as he asked, by setting forth the Divine mystery with that tongue that was taught of God, and by scourging the champion of deceit with his refutations, so that it would have been made clear to all men what a difference there is between a minister of the mysteries of Christ and a ridiculous buffoon or a setter-forth of new and absurd doctrines. But since he, as the Apostle says, "being dead, speaketh [9]" to God, while the other puts forth such a challenge as though there were no one to answer him, even though an answer from us may not have equal force when compared with the words of the great Basil, we shall yet boldly say this in answer to the questioner:—Your own argument, put forth to overthrow our statement, is a testimony that in the charges we make against your impious doctrine we speak truly. For there is no other point we blame so much as this, that you [1] think there is no difference between the Lord of creation and the general body of creation, and what you now allege is a maintaining of the very things which we find fault with. For if you are bound to attach exactly what you see in creation also to the Only-begotten God, our contention has gained its end: your own statements proclaim the absurdity of the doctrine, and it is manifest to all, both that we keep our argument in the straight way of truth, and that your conception of the Only-begotten God is such as you have of the rest of the creation.

Concerning whom was the controversy? Was it not concerning the Only-begotten God, the Maker of all the creation, whether He always was, or whether He came into being afterwards as an addition to His Father? What then do our master's words say on this matter? That it is irreverent to believe that what is naturally good was not in God: for that he saw no cause by which it was probable that the good was not always present with Him Who is good, either for lack of power or for weakness of will. What does he who contends against these statements say? "If you allow that God the Word is to be believed eternal, you must allow the same of the things that have been created"—(How well he knows how to distinguish in his argument the nature of the creatures and the majesty of God! How well he knows about each, what befits it, what he may piously think concerning God, what concerning the creation!)—"if the Maker," he says, "begins from the time of His making: for there is nothing else by which we can mark the beginning of things that have been made, if time does not define by its own interval the begin-

nings and the endings of the things that come into being."

On this ground he says that the Maker of time must commence His existence from a like beginning. Well, the creation has the ages for its beginning, but what beginning can you conceive of the Maker of the ages? If any one should say, "The 'beginning' which is mentioned in the Gospel"—it is the Father Who is there signified, and the confession of the Son together with Him is there pointed to, nor can it be that He Who is in the Father [2], as the Lord says, can begin His being in Him from any particular point. And if any one speaks of another beginning besides this, let him tell us the name by which he marks this beginning, as none can be apprehended before the establishment of the ages. Such a statement, therefore, will not move us a whit from the orthodox conception concerning the Only-begotten, even if old women do applaud the proposition as a sound one. For we abide by what has been determined from the beginning, having our doctrine firmly based on truth, to wit, that all things which the orthodox doctrine assumes that we assert concerning the Only-begotten God have no kindred with the creation, but the marks which distinguish the Maker of all and His works are separated by a wide interval. If indeed the Son had in any other respect communion with the creation, we surely ought to say that He did not diverge from it even in the manner of His existence. But if the creation has no share in such things as are all those which we learn concerning the Son, we must surely of necessity say that in this matter also He has no communion with it. For the creation was not in the beginning, and was not with God, and was not, God, nor life, nor light, nor resurrection, nor the rest of the Divine names, as truth, righteousness, sanctification, Judge, just, Maker of all things, existing before the ages, for ever and ever; the creation is not the brightness of the glory, nor the express image of the Person, nor the likeness of goodness, nor grace, nor power, nor truth, nor salvation, nor redemption; nor do we find any one at all of those names which are employed by Scripture for the glory of the Only-begotten, either belonging to the creation or employed concerning it,—not to speak of those more exalted words, "I am in the Father, and the Father in Me [2]," and, "He that hath seen Me hath seen the Father [3]," and, "None hath seen the Son, save the Father [4]." If indeed our doctrine allowed us to claim for the creation things so many and so great as these, he might have been right in thinking that we ought to attach what we observe in it to our conceptions of the Only-begotten also,

---

[9] Cf. Heb. xi. 4.
[1] Reading ὑμᾶς for ἡμᾶς. If the reading ἡμᾶς, which Oehler follows, is retained, the force would seem to be "that you think we ought not to make any difference," but the construction of the sentence in this case is cumbrous.

[2] S. John xiv. 10   [3] S. John xiv. 9.
[4] Apparently an inexact quotation of S. Matt. xi. 27.

since the transfer would be from kindred subjects to one nearly allied. But if all these concepts and names involve communion with the Father, while they transcend our notions of the creation, does not our clever and sharp-witted friend slink away in shame at discussing the nature of the Lord of the Creation by the aid of what he observes in creation, without being aware that the marks which distinguish the creation are of a different sort? The ultimate division of all that exists is made by the line between "created" and "uncreated," the one being regarded as a cause of what has come into being, the other as coming into being thereby. Now the created nature and the Divine essence being thus divided, and admitting no intermixture in respect of their distinguishing properties, we must by no means conceive both by means of similar terms, nor seek in the idea of their nature for the same distinguishing marks in things that are thus separated. Accordingly, as the nature that is in the creation, as the phrase of the most excellent Wisdom somewhere tells us, exhibits "the beginning, ending, and midst of the times [5]" in itself, and extends concurrently with all temporal intervals, we take as a sort of characteristic of the subject this property, that in it we see some beginning of its formation, look on its midst, and extend our expectations to its end. For we have learnt that the heaven and the earth were not from eternity, and will not last to eternity, and thus it is hence clear that those things are both started from some beginning, and will surely cease at some end. But the Divine Nature, being limited in no respect, but passing all limitations on every side in its infinity, is far removed from those marks which we find in creation. For that power which is without interval, without quantity, without circumscription, having in itself all the ages and all the creation that has taken place in them, and overpassing at all points, by virtue of the infinity of its own nature, the unmeasured extent of the ages, either has no mark which indicates its nature, or has one of an entirely different sort, and not that which the creation has. Since, then, it belongs to the creation to have a beginning, that will be alien from the uncreated nature which belongs to the creation. For if any one should venture to suppose the existence of the Only-begotten Son to be, like the creation, from any beginning comprehensible by us, he must certainly append to his statement concerning the Son the rest also of the sequence [6]; for it is not possible to avoid acknowledging, together with the beginning, that also which

follows from it. For just as if one were to admit some person to be a man in all [7] the properties of his nature, he would observe that in this confession he declared him to be an animal and rational, and whatever else is conceived of man, so by the same reasoning, if we should understand any of the properties of creation to be present in the Divine essence, it will no longer be open to us to refrain from attaching to that pure Nature the rest of the list of the attributes contemplated therein. For the "beginning" will demand by force and compulsion that which follows it; for the "beginning," thus conceived, is a beginning of what comes after it, in such a sense, that if they are, it is, and if the things connected with it are removed, the antecedent also would not remain [8]. Now as the book of Wisdom speaks of "midst" and "end" as well as of "beginning," if we assume in the Nature of the Only-begotten, according to the heretical dogma, some beginning of existence defined by a certain mark of time, the book of Wisdom will by no means allow us to refrain from subjoining to the "beginning" a "midst" and an "end" also. If this should be done we shall find, as the result of our arguments, that the Divine word shows us that the Deity is mortal. For if, according to the book of Wisdom, the "end" is a necessary consequence of the "beginning," and the idea of "midst" is involved in that of extremes, he who allows one of these also potentially maintains the others, and lays down bounds of measure and limitation for the infinite Nature. And if this is impious and absurd, the giving a beginning to that argument which ends in impiety deserves equal, or even greater censure; and the beginning of this absurd doctrine was seen to be the supposition that the life of the Son was circumscribed by some beginning. Thus one of two courses is before them : either they must revert to sound doctrine under the compulsion of the foregoing arguments, and contemplate Him Who is of the Father in union with the Father's eternity, or if they do not like this, they must limit the eternity of the Son in both ways, and reduce the limitless character of His life to non-existence by a beginning and an end. And, granted that the nature both of souls and of the angels has no end, and is no way hindered from going on to eternity, by the fact of its being created, and having the begin-

---

[5] Wisd. vii. 18.
[6] That is, he must also acknowledge a "middle" and an "end" of the existence which has a "beginning."

[7] Oehler's emendation, for which he gives weighty MS. authority, is certainly an improvement on the earlier text, but in sense it is a little unsatisfactory. The argument seems to require the hypothesis not of some one acknowledging a person to be a man in *all*, but in *some* attributes. The defect, however, may possibly be in S. Gregory's argument, not in the text.
[8] *i. e.* "if the 'middle' and 'end' are not admitted, at the 'beginning,' which is the 'beginning' of a *sequence*, is thereby implicitly denied." Oehler's punctuation has been somewhat altered here, and at several points in the remainder of the book, where it appears to require emendation.

ning of its existence from some point of time, so that our adversaries can use this fact to assert a parallel in the case of Christ, in the sense that He is not from eternity, and yet endures everlastingly,—let any one who advances this argument also consider the following point, how widely the Godhead differs from the creation in its special attributes. For to the Godhead it properly belongs to lack no conceivable thing which is regarded as good, while the creation attains excellence by partaking in something better than itself; and further, not only had a beginning of its being, but also is found to be constantly in a state of beginning to be in excellence, by its continual advance in improvement, since it never halts at what it has reached, but all that it has acquired 9 becomes by participation a beginning of its ascent to something still greater, and it never ceases, in Paul's phrase, "reaching forth to the things that are before," and "forgetting the things that are behind 1." Since, then, the Godhead is very life, and the Only-begotten God is God, and life, and truth, and every conceivable thing that is lofty and Divine, while the creation draws from Him its supply of good, it may hence be evident that if it is in life by partaking of life, it will surely, if it ceases from this participation, cease from life also. If they dare, then, to say also of the Only-begotten God those things which it is true to say of the creation, let them say this too, along with the rest, that He has a beginning of His being like the creation, and abides in life after the likeness of souls. But if He is the very life, and needs not to have life in Himself *ab extra*, while all other things are not life, but are merely participants in life, what constrains us to cancel, by reason of what we see in creation, the eternity of the Son? For that which is always unchanged as regards its nature, admits of no contrary, and is incapable of change to any other condition : while things whose nature is on the boundary line have a tendency that shifts either way, inclining at will to what they find attractive 2. If, then, that which is truly life is contemplated in the Divine and transcendent nature, the decadence thereof will surely, as it seems, end in the opposite state 3.

Now the meaning of "life" and "death" is manifold, and not always understood in the same way. For as regards the flesh, the energy and motion of the bodily senses is called "life," and their extinction and dissolution is named "death." But in the case of the intellectual nature, approximation to the Divine is the true

life, and decadence therefrom is named "death" : for which reason the original evil, the devil, is called both "death," and the inventor of death : and he is also said by the Apostle to have the power of death 4. As, then, we obtain, as has been said, from the Scriptures, a twofold conception of death, He Who is truly unchangeable and immutable "alone hath immortality," and dwells in light that cannot be attained or approached by the darkness of wickedness 5 : but all things that participate in death, being far removed from immortality by their contrary tendency, if they fall away from that which is good, would, by the mutability of their nature, admit community with the worse condition, which is nothing else than death, having a certain correspondence with the death of the body. For as in that case the extinction of the activities of nature is called death, so also, in the case of the intellectual being, the absence of motion towards the good is death and departure from life; so that what we perceive in the bodiless creation 6 does not clash with our argument, which refutes the doctrine of heresy. For that form of death which corresponds to the intellectual nature (that is, separation from God, Whom we call Life) is, potentially, not separated even from their nature ; for their emergence from non-existence shows mutability of nature ; and that to which change is in affinity is hindered from participation in the contrary state by the grace of Him Who strengthens it : it does not abide in the good by its own nature : and such a thing is not eternal. If, then, one really speaks truth in saying that we ought not to estimate the Divine essence and the created nature in the same way, nor to circumscribe the being of the Son of God by any beginning, lest, if this be granted, the other attributes of creation should enter in together with our acknowledgment of this one, the absurd character of the teaching of that man, who employs the attributes of creation to separate the Only-begotten God from the eternity of the Father, is clearly shown. For as none other of the marks which characterize the creation appears in the Maker of the creation, so neither is the fact that the creation has its existence from some beginning a proof that the Son was not always in the Father,—that Son, Who is Wisdom, and Power, and Light, and Life, and all that is conceived of in the bosom of the Father.

---

9 Reading κτηθὲν, with the Paris ed. of 1638. Oehler's reading κτισθὲν hardly seems to give so good a sense, and he does not give his authority for it.   1 Phil. iii. 13.

2 Reading with Oehler, τοῖς κατὰ γνώμην προσκλινομένη. The reading προσκινουμένοις, found in the earlier editions, gives a tolerable sense, but appears to have no MS. authority.

3 Or (if πάντως be constructed with ἀντικείμενον), "will end, as it seems, in that state which is absolutely opposed to life."

4 Cf. Heb. ii. 14.   5 Cf. 1 Tim. iii. 16.
6 *i. e.* the order of spiritual beings, including angels and human souls. Of these S. Gregory argues that they are capable of an ἀκινησία πρὸς τὸ ἀγαθόν which is death in them, as the absence of motion and sense is *bodily* death : and that they may therefore be said to have an end, as they had a beginning : so far as they *are* eternal it is not by their own power, but by their mutable nature being upheld by grace from this state of ἀκινησία πρὸς τὸ ἀγαθόν. On both these grounds therefore—that they *have* an end, and that such eternity as they possess is not inherent, but given *ab extra*, and contingent—he says they are not properly eternal, and he therefore rejects the proposed parallel.

BOOK IX

§ 1. *The ninth book declares that Eunomius' account of the Nature of God is, up to a certain point, well stated. Then in succession he mixes up with his own argument, on account of its affinity, the expression from Philo's writings, " God is before all other things, which are generated," adding also the expression, " He has dominion over His own power." Detesting the excessive absurdity, Gregory strikingly confutes it* [1].

BUT he now turns to loftier language, and elevating himself and puffing himself up with empty conceit, he takes in hand to say something worthy of God's majesty. "For God," he says, "being the most highly exalted of all goods, and the mightiest of all, and free from all necessity—" Nobly does the gallant man bring his discourse, like some ship without ballast, driven unguided by the waves of deceit, into the harbour of truth! "God is the most highly exalted of all goods." Splendid acknowledgment! I suppose he will not bring a charge of unconstitutional conduct against the great John, by whom, in his lofty proclamation, the Only-begotten is declared to be God, Who was with God and was God [2]. If he, then, the proclaimer of the Godhead of the Only-begotten, is worthy of credit, and if "God is the most highly exalted of all goods," it follows that the Son ·is alleged by the enemies of His glory, to be "the most highly exalted of all goods." And as this phrase is also applied to the Father, the superlative force of "most highly exalted" admits of no diminution or addition by way of comparison. But· now that we have obtained from the adversary's testimony these statements for the proof of the glory of the Only-begotten, we must add in support of sound doctrine his next statement too. He says, "God, the most highly exalted of all goods, being without hindrance from nature, or constraint from cause, or impulse from need, begets and creates according to the supremacy of His own authority, having His will as power sufficient for the constitution of the things produced. If, then, all good is according to His will, He not only determines that which is made as good, but also the time of its being good, if, that is to say, as one may assume, it is an indication of weakness to make what one does not will [3]." We shall borrow so far as this, for the confirmation of the orthodox doctrines, from our adversaries' statement, percolated as that statement is by vile and counterfeit clauses. Yes, He Who has, by the supremacy of His authority, power in His will that suffices for the constitution of the things that are made, He Who created all things without hindrance from nature or compulsion from cause, does determine not only that which is made as good, but also the time of its being good. But He Who made all things is, as the gospel proclaims, the Only-begotten God. He, at that time when He willed it, did make the creation; at that time, by means of the circumambient essence, He surrounded with the body of heaven all that universe that is shut off within its compass : at that time, when He thought it well that this should be, He displayed the dry land to view, He enclosed the waters in their hollow places ; vegetation, fruits, the generation of animals, the formation of man, appeared at that time when each of these things seemed expedient to the wisdom of the Creator :—and He Who made all these things (I will once more repeat my statement) is the Only-begotten God Who made the ages. For if the interval of the ages has preceded existing things, it is proper to employ the temporal adverb, and to say "He *then* willed" and "He *then* made": but since the age was not, since no conception of interval is present to our minds in regard to that Divine Nature which is not measured by quantity or by interval, the force of temporal expressions must surely be void. Thus to say that the creation has had given to it a beginning in time, according to the good pleasure of the wisdom of Him Who made all things, does not go beyond probability : but to regard the Divine Nature itself as being in a kind of extension measured by intervals, belongs only to those who have been trained in the new

---

[1] This section of the analysis is so confused that it cannot well be literally translated. In the version given above the general sense rather than the precise grammatical construction has been followed.   [2] S. John i 1

[3] This quotation would appear from what follows not to be a consecutive extract, but one made "*omissis omittendis.*"

wisdom. What a point is this, embedded in his words, which I intentionally passed by in my eagerness to reach the subject! I will now resume it, and read it to show our author's cleverness.

"For He Who is most highly exalted in God Himself[4] before all other things that are generated," he says, "has dominion over His own power." The phrase has been transferred by our pamphleteer word for word from the Hebrew Philo to his own argument, and Eunomius' theft will be proved by Philo's works themselves to any one who cares about it. I note the fact, however, at present, not so much to reproach our speech-monger with the poverty of his own arguments and thoughts, as with the intention of showing to my readers the close relationship between the doctrine of Eunomius and the reasoning of the Jews. For this phrase of Philo would not have fitted word for word into his argument had there not been a sort of kindred between the intention of the one and the other. In the Hebrew author you may find the phrase in this form : "God, before all other things that are generated"; and what follows, "has dominion over His own power," is an addition of the new Judaism. But what an absurdity this involves an examination of the saying will clearly show. "God," he says, "has dominion over His own power." Tell me, what is He? over what has He dominion? Is He something else than His own power, and Lord of a power that is something else than Himself? Then power is overcome by the absence of power. For that which is something else than power is surely not power, and thus He is found to have dominion over power just in so far as He is not power. Or again, God, being power, has another power in Himself, and has dominion over the one by the other. And what contest or schism is there, that God should divide the power that exists in Himself, and overthrow one section of His power by the other. I suppose He could not have dominion over His own power without the assistance to that end of some greater and more violent power! Such is Eunomius' God : a being with double nature, or composite, dividing Himself against Himself, having one power out of harmony with another, so that by one He is urged to disorder, and by the other restrains this discordant motion. Again, with what intent does He dominate the power that urges

on to generation? lest some evil should arise if generation be not hindered? or rather let him explain this in the first place,—what is that which is naturally under dominion? His language points to some movement of impulse and choice, considered separately and independently. For that which dominates must needs be one thing, and that which is dominated another. Now God "has dominion over His power"—and this is—what? a self-determining nature? or something else than this, pressing on to disquiet, or remaining in a state of quiescence? Well, if he supposes it to be quiescent, that which is tranquil needs no one to have dominion over it : and if he says "He has dominion," He "has dominion" clearly over something which impels and is in motion : and this, I presume he will say, is something naturally different from Him Who rules it. What then, let him tell us, does he understand in this idea? Is it something else besides God, considered as having an independent existence? How can another existence be in God? Or is it some condition in the Divine Nature considered as having an existence not its own? I hardly think he would say so : for that which has no existence of its own is not : and that which is not, is neither under dominion, nor set free from it. What then is that power which was under dominion, and was restrained in respect of its own activity, while the due time of the generation of Christ was still about to come, and to set this power free to proceed to its natural operation? What was the intervening cause of delay, for which God deferred the generation of the Only-begotten, not thinking it good as yet to become a Father? And what is this that is inserted as intervening between the life of the Father and that of the Son, that is not time nor space, nor any idea of extension, nor any like thing? To what purpose is it that this keen and clear-sighted eye marks and beholds the separation of the life of God in regard to the life of the Son? When he is driven in all directions he is himself forced to admit that the interval does not exist at all.

§ 2. *He then ingeniously shows that the generation of the Son is not according to the phrase of Eunomius, " The Father begat Him at that time when He chose, and not before:" but that the Son, being the fulness of all that is good and excellent, is always contemplated in the Father; using for this demonstration the support of Eunomius' own arguments.*

However, though there is no interval between them, he does not admit that their communion is immediate and intimate, but condescends to the measure of our knowledge, and converses

---

[4] This seems to be the force of the phrase if we are to follow Oehler's MSS. and read ὁ γὰρ ἐξοχώτατος αὐτοῦ θεοῦ. The αὐτὸς θεὸς of the earlier editions gives a simpler sense. The phrase as read by Oehler certainly savours more of Philo than of Eunomius : but it is worth noting that S. Gregory does not dwell upon this part of the clause as being borrowed from Philo (though he may intend to include it in the general statement), but upon what follows it : and from his citation from Philo it would seem that the latter spoke (not of ὁ ἐξοχώτατος θεοῦ but) of ὁ Θεὸς πρὸ τῶν ἄλλων ὅσα γεννητά.

with us in human phrase as one of ourselves, himself quietly confessing the impotence of reasoning and taking refuge in a line of argument that was never taught by Aristotle and his school. He says, "It was good and proper that He should beget His Son at that time when He willed : and in the minds of sensible men there does not hence arise any questioning why He did not do so before." What does this mean, Eunomius? Are you too going afoot like us unlettered men? are you leaving your artistic periods and actually taking refuge in unreasoning assent? you, who so much reproached those who take in hand to write without logical skill? You, who say to Basil, "You show your own ignorance when you say that definitions of the terms that express things spiritual are an impossibility for men," who again elsewhere advance the same charge, "you make your own impotence common to others, when you declare that what is not possible for you is impossible for all"? Is this the way that you, who say such things as these, approach the ears of him who questions about the reason why the Father defers becoming the Father of such a Son? Do you think it an adequate explanation to say, "He begat Him at that time when He chose : let there be no questioning on this point"? Has your apprehensive fancy grown so feeble in the maintenance of your doctrines? What has become of your premises that lead to dilemmas? What has become of your forcible proofs? how comes it that those terrible and inevitable syllogistic conclusions of your art have dissolved into vanity and nothingness? "He begat the Son at that time when He chose : let there be no questioning on this point!" Is this the finished product of your many labours, of your voluminous undertakings? What was the question asked? "If it is good and fitting for God to have such a Son, why are we not to believe that the good is always present with Him[5]?" What is the answer he makes to us from the very shrine of his philosophy, tightening the bonds of his argument by inevitable necessity? "He made the Son at that time when He chose : let there be no questioning as to why He did not do so before." Why, if the inquiry before us were concerning some irrational being, that acts by natural impulse, why it did not sooner do whatever it may be,—why the spider did not make her webs, or the bee her honey, or the turtle-dove her nest,—what else could you have said? would not the same answer have been ready—"She did it at that time when she chose : let there be no questioning on this matter"? Nay, if it were concerning some sculptor or painter who works in paintings

or in sculptures by his imitative art, whatever it may be (supposing that he exercises his art without being subject to any authority), I imagine that such an answer would meet the case of any one who wished to know why he did not exercise his art sooner,—that, being under no necessity, he made his own choice the occasion of his operation. For men, because they do not always wish the same things[6], and commonly have not power co-operating with their will, do something which seems good to them at that time when their choice inclines to the work, and they have no external hindrance. But that nature which is always the same, to which no good is adventitious, in which all that variety of plans which arises by way of opposition, from error or from ignorance, has no place, to which there comes nothing as a result of change, which was not with it before, and by which nothing is chosen afterwards which it had not from the beginning regarded as good,—to say of this nature that it does not always possess what is good, but afterwards chooses to have something which it did not choose before,—this belongs to wisdom that surpasses us. For we were taught that the Divine Nature is at all times full of all good, or rather is itself the fulness of all goods, seeing that it needs no addition for its perfecting, but is itself by its own nature the perfection of good. Now that which is perfect is equally remote from addition and from diminution ; and therefore, we say that that perfection of goods which we behold in the Divine Nature always remains the same, as, in whatsoever direction we extend our thoughts, we there apprehend it to be such as it is. The Divine Nature, then, is never void of good : but the Son is the fulness of all good : and accordingly He is at all times contemplated in that Father Whose Nature is perfection in all good. But he says, "let there be no questioning about this point, why He did not do so before :" and we shall answer him,—"It is one thing, most sapient sir, to lay down as an ordinance some proposition that you happen to approve[7], and another to make converts by reasoning on the points of controversy. So long, therefore, as you cannot assign any reason why we may piously say that the Son was "afterwards" begotten by the Father, your ordinances will be of no effect with sensible men."

Thus it is then that Eunomius brings the truth to light for us as the result of his scientific attack. And we for our part shall apply his argument, as we are wont to do, for the establishment of the true doctrine, so that even by this

---

[5] Cf. S. Basil adv. Eun. II. 12, quoted above, p. 207.

[6] Reading ταὐτὰ for ταῦτα, which appears in the text of Oehler as well as in the earlier editions.
[7] Reading τι τῶν κατὰ γνώμην, for τι τῶν καταγνωμῶν, which is the reading of the editions, but introduces a word otherwise apparently unknown.

passage it may be clear that at every point, constrained against their will, they advocate our view. For if, as our opponent says, "He begat the Son at that time when He chose," and if He always chose that which is good, and His power coincided with His choice, it follows that the Son will be considered as always with the Father, Who always both chooses that which is excellent, and is able to possess what He chooses. And if we are to reduce his next words also to truth, it is easy for us to adapt them also to the doctrine we hold :—" Let there be no questioning among sensible men on this point, why He did not do so before "—for the word "before" has a temporal sense, opposed to what is "afterwards" and "later" : but on the supposition that time does not exist, the terms expressing temporal interval are surely abolished with it. Now the Lord was before times and before ages : questioning as to "before" or "after" concerning the Maker of the ages is useless in the eyes of reasonable men : for words of this class are devoid of all meaning, if they are not used in reference to time. Since then the Lord is antecedent to times, the words "before" and "after" have no place as applied to Him. This may perhaps be sufficient to refute arguments that need no one to overthrow them, but fall by their own feebleness. For who is there with so much leisure that he can give himself up to such an extent to listen to the arguments on the other side, and to our contention against the silly stuff? Since, however, in men prejudiced by impiety, deceit is like some ingrained dye, hard to wash out, and deeply burned in upon their hearts, let us spend yet a little time upon our argument, if haply we may be able to cleanse their souls from this evil stain. After the utterances that I have quoted, and after adding to them, in the manner of his teacher Prunicus,[8] some unconnected and ill-arranged octads of insolence and abuse, he comes to the crowning point of his arguments, and, leaving the illogical exposition of his folly, arms his discourse once more with the weapons of dialectic, and maintains his absurdity against us, as he imagines, syllogistically.

§ 3. *He further shows that the pretemporal generation of the Son is not the subject of*

influences drawn from ordinary and carnal generation, but is without beginning and without end, and not according to the fabrications constructed by Eunomius, in ignorance of His power, from the statements of Plato concerning the soul and from the sabbath rest of the Hebrews.

What he says runs thus :—" As all generation is not protracted to infinity, but ceases on arriving at some end, those who admit the origination of the Son are absolutely obliged to say that He then ceased being generated, and not to look incredulously on the beginning of those things which cease being generated, and therefore also surely *begin :* for the cessation of generation establishes a beginning of begetting and being begotten : and these facts cannot be disbelieved, on the ground at once of nature itself and of the Divine laws[9]." Now since he endeavours to establish his point inferentially, laying down his universal proposition according to the scientific method of those who are skilled in such matters, and including in the general premise the proof of the particular, let us first consider his universal, and then proceed to examine the force of his inferences. Is it a reverent proceeding to draw from "all generation" evidence even as to the pre-temporal generation of the Son? and ought we to put forward ordinary nature as our instructor on the being of the Only-begotten? For my own part, I should not have expected any one to reach such a point of madness, that any such idea of the Divine and unsullied generation should enter his fancy. "All generation," he says, "is not protracted to infinity." What is it that he understands by "generation"? Is he speaking of fleshly, bodily birth, or of the formation of inanimate objects? The affections involved in bodily generation are well known— affections which no one would think of transferring to the Divine Nature. In order therefore that our discourse may not, by mentioning the works of nature at length, be made to appear redundant, we shall pass such matters by in silence, as I suppose that every sensible man is himself aware of the causes by which generation is protracted, both in regard to its beginning and to its cessation : it would be tedious and at the same time superfluous to express them all minutely, the coming together of those who generate, the formation in the womb of that which is generated, travail, birth, place, time, without which the generation of a body cannot be brought about,—things which are all equally alien from the Divine generation of the Only-begotten : for if any one of these

---

8 So in Book I. πρῶτον μὲν τῆς Προυνίκου σοφίας γίνεται μαθητὴς, and Book XIII. p. 844 (Paris Edit.). It may be questioned whether the phrase in Books I. and XIII., and that here, refers to a supposed connection of Eunomius with Gnosticism. The Προύνικος Σοφία of the Gnostics was a " male-female," and hence the masculine τὸν παιδεύτην might properly be applied to it. If this point were cleared up, we might be more certain of the meaning to be attached to the word ὀκτάδας, which is also possibly borrowed from the Gnostic phraseology, being akin to the form ὀγδοάδας. [On the Gnostic conception of " Prunicus," see the note on the subject in Harvey's *Irenæus* (vol. I. p. 225), and Smith and Wace's *Dict. Chr. Biogr.* s. v. On the Gnostic Ogdoads, see Mansel's *Gnostic Heresies*, pp. 152 sqq., 170 sqq., and the articles on Basilides and Valentinus in *Dict. Chr. Biogr.*]

9 This quotation from Eunomius presents some difficulties, but it is quite as likely that they are due to the obscurity of his style, as that they are due to corruption of the text.

things were admitted, the rest will of necessity all enter with it. That the Divine generation, therefore, may be clear of every idea connected with passion, we shall avoid conceiving with regard to it even that extension which is measured by intervals. Now that which begins and ends is surely regarded as being in a kind of extension, and all extension is measured by time, and as time (by which we mark both the end of birth and its beginning) is excluded, it would be vain, in the case of the uninterrupted generation, to entertain the idea of end or beginning, since no idea can be formed to mark either the point at which such generation begins or that at which it ceases. If on the other hand it is the inanimate creation to which he is looking, even in this case, in like manner, place, and time, and matter, and preparation, and power of the artificer, and many like things, concur to bring the product to perfection. And since time assuredly is concurrent with all things that are produced, and since with everything that is created, be it animate or inanimate, there are conceived also bases of construction relative to the product, we can find in these cases evident beginnings and endings of the process of formation. For even the procuring of material is actually the beginning of the fabric, and is a sign of place, and is logically connected with time. All these things fix for the products their beginnings and endings; and no one could say that these things have any participation in the pretemporal generation of the Only-begotten God, so that, by the aid of the things now under consideration, we are able to calculate, with regard to that generation, any beginning or end.

Now that we have so far discussed these matters, let us resume consideration of our adversaries' argument. It says, "As all generation is not protracted to infinity, but ceases on arriving at some end." Now, since the sense of "generation" has been considered with respect to either meaning,—whether he intends by this word to signify the birth of corporeal beings, or the formation of things created (neither of which has anything in common with the unsullied Nature), the premise is shown to have no connection with the subject[1]. For it is not a matter of absolute necessity, as he maintains, that, because all making and generation ceases at some limit, therefore those who accept the generation of the Son should circumscribe it by a double limit, by supposing, as regards it, a beginning and an end. For it is only as being circumscribed in some quantitative way that things can be said either to begin or to cease on arriv-

ing at a limit, and the measure expressed by time (having its extension concomitant with the quantity of that which is produced) differentiates the beginning from the end by the interval between them. But how can any one measure or treat as extended that which is without quantity and without extension? What measure can he find for that which has no quantity, or what interval for that which has no extension? or how can any one define the infinite by "end" and "beginning?" for "beginning" and "end" are names of limits of extension, and, where there is no extension, neither is there any limit. Now the Divine Nature is without extension, and, being without extension, it has no limit; and that which is limitless is infinite, and is spoken of accordingly. Thus it is idle to try to circumscribe the infinite by "beginning" and "ending"—for what is circumscribed cannot be infinite. How comes it, then, that this Platonic Phaedrus disconnectedly tacks on to his own doctrine those speculations on the soul which Plato makes in that dialogue? For as Plato there spoke of "cessation of motion," so this writer too was eager to speak of "cessation of generation," in order to impose upon those who have no knowledge of these matters, with fine Platonic phrases. "And these facts," he tells us, "cannot be disbelieved, on the ground at once of nature itself and of the Divine laws." But nature, from our previous remarks, appears not to be trustworthy for instruction as to the Divine generation,—not even if one were to take the universe itself as an illustration of the argument: since through its creation also, as we learn in the cosmogony of Moses, there ran the measure of time, meted out in a certain order and arrangement by stated days and nights, for each of the things that came into being: and this even our adversaries' statement does not admit with regard to the being of the Only-begotten, since it acknowledges that the Lord was before the times of the ages.

It remains to consider his support of his point by "the Divine laws," by which he undertakes to show both an end and a beginning of the generation of the Son. "God," he says, "willing that the law of creation should be impressed upon the Hebrews, did not appoint the first day of generation for the end of creation, or to be the evidence of its beginning; for He gave them as the memorial of the creation, not the first day of generation, but the seventh, whereon He rested from His works." Will any one believe that this was written by Eunomius, and that the words cited have not been inserted by us, by way of misrepresenting his composition so as to make him appear ridiculous to our readers, in dragging in to prove his point

---

[1] i. e. with the subject of discussion, the generation of the Only-begotten.

matters that have nothing to do with the question? For the matter in hand was to show, as he undertook to do, that the Son, not previously existing, came into being; and that, in being generated, He took a beginning of generation, and of cessation [2],—His generation being protracted in time, as it were by a kind of travail. And what is his resource for establishing this? The fact that the people of the Hebrews, according to the Law, keep sabbath on the seventh day! How well the evidence agrees with the matter in hand! Because the Jew honours his sabbath by idleness, the fact, as he says, is proved that the Lord both had a beginning of birth and ceased being born! How many other testimonies on this matter has our author passed by, not at all of less weight than that which he employs to establish the point at issue!—the circumcision on the eighth day, the week of unleavened bread, the mystery on the fourteenth day of the moon's course, the sacrifices of purification, the observation of the lepers, the ram, the calf, the heifer, the scape-goat, the he-goat. If these things are far removed from the point, let those who are so much interested in the Jewish mysteries tell us how that particular matter is within range of the question. We judge it to be mean and unmanly to trample on the fallen, and shall proceed to enquire, from what follows in his writings, whether there is anything there of such a kind as to give trouble to his opponent. All, then, that he maintains in the next passage, as to the impropriety of supposing anything intermediate between the Father and the Son, I shall pass by, as being, in a sense, in agreement with our doctrine. For it would be alike undiscriminating and unfair not to distinguish in his remarks what is irreproachable, and what is blamable, seeing that, while he fights against his own statements, he does not follow his own admissions, speaking of the immediate character of the connection while refusing to admit its continuity, and conceiving that nothing was before the Son, and having some suspicion that the Son *was*, while yet contending that He came into being when He was not. We shall spend but a short time on these points (since the argument has already been established beforehand), and then proceed to handle the arguments proposed.

It is not allowable for the same person to set nothing above the existence of the Only-begotten, and to say that before His generation He was not, but that He was generated *then* when the Father willed. For "*then*" and "*when*" have a sense which specially and properly refers to the denoting of time, according to the common

use of men who speak soundly, and according to their signification in Scripture. One may take "*then* shall they say among the heathen [3]," and "*when* I sent you [4]," and "*then* shall the kingdom of heaven be likened [5]," and countless similar phrases through the whole of Scripture, to prove this point, that the ordinary Scriptural use employs these parts of speech to denote time. If therefore, as our opponent allows, time was not, the signifying of time surely disappears too: and if this did not exist, it will necessarily be replaced by eternity in our conception [6]. For in the phrase "was not" there is surely implied "once": as, if he should speak of "not being," without the qualification "once," he would also deny his existence *now :* but if he admits His present existence, and contends against His eternity, it is surely not "not being" *absolutely*, but "not being" *once* which is present to his mind. And as this phrase is utterly unreal, unless it rests upon the signification of time, it would be foolish and idle to say that nothing was before the Son, and yet to maintain that the Son did not always exist. For if there is neither place nor time, nor any other creature where the Word that was in the beginning is not, the statement that the Lord "once was not" is entirely removed from the region of orthodox doctrine. So he is at variance not so much with us as with himself, who declares that the Only-begotten both was and was not. For in confessing that the conjunction of the Son with the Father is not interrupted by anything, He clearly testifies to His eternity. But if he should say that the Son was not in the Father, we shall not ourselves say anything against such a statement, but shall oppose to it the Scripture which declares that the Son is in the Father, and the Father in the Son, without adding to the phrase "once" or "when" or "then," but testifying His eternity by this affirmative and unqualified utterance.

§ 4. *Then, having shown that Eunomius' calumny against the great Basil, that he called the Only-begotten " Ungenerate," is false, and having again with much ingenuity discussed the eternity, being, and endlessness of the Only-begotten, and the creation of light and of darkness, he concludes the book.*

With regard to his attempting to show that we say the Only-begotten God is ungenerate, it is as though he should say that we actually define the Father to be begotten : for either statement is of the same absurdity, or rather of the same blas-

---

[2] The genitive λήξεως is rather awkward ; it may be explained, however, as dependent upon ἀρχήν : " He began to be generated : He began to cease being generated."

phemous character. If, therefore, he has made up his mind to slander us, let him add the other charge as well, and spare nothing by which it may be in his power more violently to exasperate his hearers against us. But if one of these charges is withheld because its calumnious nature is apparent, why is the other made? For it is just the same thing, as we have said, so far as the impiety goes, to call the Son ungenerate and to call the Father generated. Now if any such phrase can found in our writings, in which the Son is spoken of as ungenerate, we shall give the final vote against ourselves : but if he is fabricating false charges and calumnies at his pleasure, making any fictitious statement he pleases to slander our doctrines, this fact may serve with sensible men for an evidence of our orthodoxy, that while truth itself fights on our side, he brings forward a lie to accuse our doctrine, and makes up an indictment for unorthodoxy that has no relation to our statements. To these charges, however, we can give a concise answer. As we judge that man accursed who says that the Only-begotten God is ungenerate, let him in turn anathematize the man who lays it down that He who was in the beginning "once was not." For by such a method it will be shown who brings his charges truly, and who calumniously. But if we deny his accusations, if, when we speak of a Father, we understand as implied in that word a Son also, and if, when we use the name "Son," we declare that He really is what He is called, being shed forth by generation from the ungenerate Light, how can the calumny of those who persist that we say the Only-begotten is ungenerate fail to be manifest? Yet we shall not, because we say that He exists by generation, therefore admit that He "once was not." For every one knows that the contradiction between "being" and "not being" is immediate, so that the affirmation of one of these terms is absolutely the destruction of the other, and that, just as "being" is the same in regard to every time at which any of the things that "are" is supposed to have its existence (for the sky, and stars, and sun, and the rest of the things that "are," are not more in a state of being now than they were yesterday, or the day before, or at any previous time), so the meaning of "not being" expresses non-existence equally at every time, whether one speaks of it in reference to what is earlier or to what is later. For any of the things that do not exist [7] is no more in a state of "not being" now than if it were

non-existent before, but the idea of "not being" is one applied to that which "is not" at any distance of time. And for this reason, in speaking of living creatures, while we use different words to denote the dissolution into a state of "not being" of that which has been, and the condition of non-existence of that which has never had an entrance into being, and say either that a thing has never come into being at all, or that that which was generated has died, yet by either form of speech we equally represent by our words "non-existence." For as day is bounded on each side by night, yet the parts of the night which bound it are not named alike, but we speak of one as "after night-fall," and of the other as "before dawn," while that which both phrases denote is night, so, if any one looks on that which *is not* in contrast to that which *is*, he will give different names to that state which is antecedent to formation and to that which follows the dissolution of what was formed, yet will conceive as one the condition which both phrases signify—the condition which is antecedent to formation and the condition following on dissolution after formation. For the state of "not being" of that which has not been generated, and of that which has died, save for the difference of the names, are the same,—with the exception of the account which we take of the hope of the resurrection. Now since we learn from Scripture that the Only-begotten God is the Prince of Life, the very life, and light, and truth, and all that is honourable in word or thought, we say that it is absurd and impious to contemplate, in conjunction with Him Who really is, the opposite conception, whether of dissolution tending to corruption, or of non-existence before formation : but as we extend our thought in every direction to what is to follow, or to what was before the ages, we nowhere pause in our conceptions at the condition of "not being," judging it to tend equally to impiety to cut short the Divine being by non-existence at any time whatever. For it is the same thing to say that the immortal life is mortal, that the truth is a lie, that light is darkness, and that that which is is not. He, accordingly, who refuses to allow that He will at some future time cease to be, will also refuse to allow that He "once was not," avoiding, according to our view, the same impiety on either hand : for, as no death cuts short the endlessness of the life of the Only-begotten, so, as we look back, no period of non-existence will terminate His life in its course towards eternity, that that which in reality *is* may be clear of all community with that which in reality *is not*. For this cause the Lord, desiring that His disciples might be far removed from this error (that they might never, by themselves searching for something antecedent to

---

7 Reading τῶν μὴ ὑφεστώτων, as the sense seems to require. unless we connect τῶν ὑφεστώτων with οὐκ ἔστιν. In this case the sense will be practically the same, but the sentence will be extremely involved. The point which S. Gregory desires to enforce is that "not being,' or "non-existence," is one and the same thing, whether it is regarded as past, present, or future, and that it is, in any of these aspects, an idea which we cannot without impiety attach to the Divine Person of the Son.

the existence of the Only-begotten, be led by their reasoning to the idea of non-existence), saith, "I am in the Father, and the Father in Me [8]," in the sense that neither is that which *is not* conceived in that which *is*, nor that which *is* in that which *is not*. And here the very order of the phrase explains the orthodox doctrine ; for because the Father is not of the Son, but the Son of the Father, therefore He says, "I am in the Father," showing the fact that He is not of another but of Him, and then reverses the phrase to, "and the Father in Me," indicating that he who, in his curious speculation, passes beyond the Son, passes also beyond the conception of the Father : for He who is in anything cannot be found outside of that in which He is : so that the man who, while not denying that the Father is in the Son, yet imagines that he has in any degree apprehended the Father as external to the Son, is talking idly. Idle too are the wanderings of our adversaries' fighting about shadows touching the matter of "ungeneracy," proceeding without solid foundation by means of nonentities. Yet if I am to bring more fully to light the whole absurdity of their argument, let me be allowed to spend a little longer on this speculation. As they say that the Only-begotten God came into existence "later," after the Father, this "unbegotten" of theirs, whatever they imagine it to be, is discovered of necessity to exhibit with itself the idea of evil. Who knows not, that, just as the non-existent is contrasted with the existent, so with every good thing or name is contrasted the opposite conception, as " bad " with " good," " falsehood " with " truth," "darkness" with "light," and all the rest that are similarly opposed to one another, where the opposition admits of no middle term, and it is impossible that the two should co-exist, but the presence of the one destroys its opposite, and with the withdrawal of the other takes place the appearance of its contrary ?

Now these points being conceded to us, the further point is also clear to any one, that, as Moses says darkness was before the creation of light, so also in the case of the Son (if, according to the heretical statement, the Father "made Him at that time when He willed"), before He made Him, that Light which the Son is was not ; and, light not yet being, it is impossible that its opposite should not be. For we learn also from the other instances that nothing that comes from the Creator is at random, but that which was lacking is added by creation to existing things. Thus it is quite clear that if. God did make the Son, He made Him by reason of a deficiency in the nature of things. As, then, while sensible light was still lacking, there was

darkness, and darkness would certainly have prevailed had light not come into being, so also, when the Son "as yet was not," the very and true Light, and all else that the Son is, did not exist. For even according to the evidence of heresy, that which exists has no need of coming into being ; if therefore He made Him, He assuredly made that which did not exist. Thus, according to their view, before the Son came into being, neither had truth come into being, nor the intelligible Light, nor the fount of life, nor, generally, the nature of any thing that is excellent and good. Now, concurrently with the exclusion of each of these, there is found to subsist the opposite conception : and if light was not, it cannot be denied that darkness *was ;* and so with the rest,—in place of each of these more excellent conceptions it is clearly impossible that its opposite did not exist in place of that which was lacking. It is therefore a necessary conclusion, that when the Father, as the heretics say, "had not as yet willed to make the Son," none of those things which the Son is being yet existent, we must say that He was surrounded by darkness instead of Light, by falsehood instead of truth, by death instead of life, by evil instead of good. For He Who creates, creates things that are not ; " That which is," as Eunomius says, " needs not generation " ; and of those things which are considered as opposed, the better cannot be non-existent, except by the existence of the worse. These are the gifts with which the wisdom of heresy honours the Father, by which it degrades the eternity of the Son, and ascribes to God and the Father, before the "production" of the Son, the whole catalogue of evils !

And let no one think to rebut by examples from the rest of creation the demonstration of the doctrinal absurdity which results from this argument. One will perhaps say that, as, when the sky was not, there was no opposite to it, so we are not absolutely compelled to admit that if the Son, Who is Truth, had not come into existence, the opposite did exist. To him we may reply that to the sky there is no corresponding opposite, unless one were to say that its non-existence is opposed to its existence. But to virtue is certainly opposed that which is vicious (and the Lord is virtue) ; so that when the sky was not, it does not follow that anything *was ;* but when good was not, its opposite *was ;* thus he who says that good was not, will certainly allow, even without intending it, that evil *was.* " But the Father also," he says [9], " is absolute virtue, and life, and light unapproachable, and all that is exalted in word or thought : so that there is no necessity to suppose, when

---

8 S. John xiv. 10.

9 The words are probably those of the imaginary objector ; but they may be a citation from Eunomius.

the Only-begotten Light was not, the existence of that darkness which is His corresponding opposite." But this is just what I say, that darkness never was; for the light never "was not," for "the light," as the prophecy says, "is always in the light [1]." If, however, according to the heretical doctrine, the "ungenerate light" is one thing, and the "generated light" another, and the one is eternal, while the other comes into existence at a later time, it follows of absolute necessity that in the eternal light we should find no place for the establishment of its opposite; (for if the light always shines, the power of darkness has no place in it;) and that in the case of the light which comes into being, as they say, afterwards, it is impossible that the light should shine forth save out of darkness; and the interval of darkness between eternal light and that which arises later will be clearly marked in every way [2]. For there would have been no need of the making of the later light, if that which was created had not been of utility for some purpose : and the one use of light is that of the dispersion by its means of the prevailing gloom. Now the light which exists without creation is what it is by nature by reason of itself; but the created light clearly comes into being by reason of something else. It must be then that its existence was preceded by darkness, on account of which the light was of necessity created, and it is not possible by any reasoning to make plausible the view that darkness did not precede the manifestation of the Only-begotten Light,—on the supposition, that is, that He is believed to have been "made" at a later time. Surely such a doctrine is beyond all impiety ! It is therefore clearly shown that the Father of truth did not make the truth at a time when it was not; but, being the fountain of light and truth, and of all good, He shed forth from Himself that Only-begotten Light of truth by which the glory of His Person is expressly imaged; so that the blasphemy of those who say that the Son was a later addition to God by way of creation is at all points refuted.

---

[1] The reference is probably to Ps. xxxvi. 9.

[2] *i. e.* the "later light" must have arisen from darkness; therefore darkness must have intervened between the "eternal light" and the "later light."

BOOK X,

LET us, however, keep to our subject. A little further on he contends against those who acknowledge that human nature is too weak to conceive what cannot be grasped, and with lofty boasts enlarges on this topic on this wise, making light of our belief on the matter in these words :—"For it by no means follows that, if some one's mind, blinded by malignity, and for that reason unable to see anything in front or above its head, is but moderately competent for the apprehension of truth, we ought on that ground to think that the discovery of reality is unattainable by the rest of mankind." But I should say to him that he who declares that the discovery of reality is attainable, has of course advanced his own intellect by some method and logical process through the knowledge of existent things, and after having been trained in matters that are comparatively small and easily grasped by way of apprehension, has, when thus prepared, flung his apprehensive fancy upon those objects which transcend all conception. Let, then, the man who boasts that he has attained the knowledge of real existence, interpret to us the real nature of the most trivial object that is before our eyes, that by what is knowable he may warrant our belief touching what is secret : let him explain by reason what is the nature of the ant, whether its life is held together by breath and respiration, whether it is regulated by vital organs like other animals, whether its body has a framework of bones, whether the hollows of the bones are filled with marrow, whether its joints are united by the tension of sinews and ligaments, whether the position of the sinews is maintained by enclosures of muscles and glands, whether the marrow extends along the vertebræ from the sinciput to the tail, whether it imparts to the limbs that are moved the power of motion by means of the enclosure of sinewy membrane; whether the creature has a liver, and in connection with the liver a gall-bladder; whether it has kidneys and heart, arteries and veins, membranes and diaphragm; whether it is externally smooth or covered with hair; whether it is distinguished by the division into male and female; in what part of its body is located the power of sight and hearing; whether it enjoys the sense of smell; whether its feet are undivided or articulated; how long it lives; what is the method in which they derive generation one from another, and what is the period of gestation; how it is that all ants do not crawl, nor are all winged, but some belong to the creatures that move along the ground, while others are borne aloft in the air. Let him, then, who boasts that he has grasped the knowledge of real existence, disclose to us awhile the nature of the ant, and then, and not till then, let him discourse on the nature of the power that surpasses all understanding. But if he has not yet ascertained by his knowledge the nature of the tiny ant, how comes he to vaunt that by the apprehension of reason he has grasped Him Who in Himself controls all creation, and to say that those who own in themselves the weakness of human nature, have the perceptions of their souls darkened, and can neither reach anything in front of them, nor anything above their head?

But now let us see what understanding he who has the knowledge of existent things possesses beyond the rest of the world. Let us listen to his arrogant utterance :—"Surely it would have been idle for the Lord to call Himself 'the door,' if there were none to pass through to the understanding and contemplation of the Father, and it would have been idle for Him to call Himself 'the way,' if He gave no facility to those who wish to come to the Father. And how could He be a light, without lightening men, without illuminating the eye of their soul to understand both Himself and the transcendent Light?" Well, if he were here enumerating some arguments from his own head, that evade the understanding of the hearers by their subtlety, there would perhaps be a possibility of being deceived by the ingenuity of the argument, as his underlying thought frequently escapes the reader's notice. But since he alleges the Divine words, of course no one blames those who believe that their inspired teaching is the common property of all. "Since then," he says, "the Lord was named 'a door,' it follows from hence that the essence of God may be comprehended by man." But the Gospel does not admit of this meaning. Let us hear the Divine utterance itself. "I am the door," Christ says; "by Me if any man enter in he shall be saved, and shall go in and out and find pasture [1]." Which then of these is the knowledge of the essence? For as several things are here said, and each of them has its own special meaning, it is impossible to refer them all to the idea of the essence, lest the Deity should be thought to be compounded of different elements; and yet it is not easy to find which of the phrases just quoted can most properly be applied to that subject. The Lord is "the door," "By Me," He says, "if any man enter in, he shall be saved, and shall go in and out and shall find pasture." Are we ·to say [2] that it is "entrance" of which he speaks in place of the essence of God, or "salvation" of those that enter in, or "going out," or "pasture," or "finding"?—for each of these is peculiar in its significance, and does not agree in meaning with the rest. For to get within appears obviously contrary to "going out," and so with the other phrases. For "pasture," in its proper meaning, is one thing, and "finding" another thing distinct from it. Which, then, of these is the essence of the Father supposed to be? For assuredly one cannot, by uttering all these phrases that disagree one with another in signification, intend to indicate by incompatible terms that Essence which is simple and uncompounded. And how can the word hold good, "No man hath seen God at any time [3]," and, "Whom no man hath seen nor can see [4]," and, "There shall no man see the face of the Lord and live [5]," if to be inside the door, or outside, or the finding pasture, denote the essence of the Father? For truly He is at the same time a "door of encompassing [6]," and a "house of defence [7]," as David calls Him, and through Himself He receives them that enter, and in Himself He saves those who have come within, and again by Himself He leads them forth to the pasture of virtues, and becomes all things to them that are in the way of salvation, that so He may make Himself that which the needs of each demand,—both way, and guide, and "door of encompassing," and "house of defence," and

"water of comfort [8]," and "green pasture [8]," which in the Gospel He calls "pasture": but our new divine says that the Lord has been called "the door" because of the knowledge of the essence of the Father. Why then does he not force into the same significance the titles, "Rock," and "Stone," and "Fountain," and "Tree," and the rest, that so he might obtain evidence for his own theory by the multitude of strange testimonies, as he is well able to apply to each of these the same account which he has given of the Way, the Door, and the Light? But, as I am so taught by the inspired Scripture, I boldly affirm that He Who is above every name has for us many names, receiving them in accordance with the variety of His gracious dealings with us [9], being called the Light when He disperses the gloom of ignorance, and the Life when He grants the boon of immortality, and the Way when He guides us from error to the truth; so also He is termed a "tower of strength [1]," and a "city of encompassing [2]," and a fountain, and a rock, and a vine, and a physician, and resurrection, and all the like, with reference to us, imparting Himself under various aspects by virtue of His benefits to us-ward. But those who are keen-sighted beyond human power, who see the incomprehensible, but overlook what may be comprehended, when they use such titles to expound the essences, are positive that they not only see, but measure Him Whom no man hath seen nor can see, but do not with the eye of their soul discern the Faith, which is the only thing within the compass of our observation, valuing before this the knowledge which they obtain from ratiocination. Just so I have heard the sacred record laying blame upon the sons of Benjamin who did not regard the law, but could shoot within a hair's breadth [3], wherein, methinks, the word exhibited their eager pursuit of an idle object, that they were far-darting and dexterous aimers at things that were useless and unsubstantial, but ignorant and regardless of what was manifestly for their benefit. For after what I have quoted, the history goes on to relate what befel them, how, when they had run madly after the iniquity of Sodom, and the people of Israel had taken up arms against them in full force, they were utterly destroyed. And it seems to me to be a kindly thought to warn young archers not to wish to shoot within a hair's-breadth, while they have no eyes for the door of the faith, but rather to drop their idle labour about the incomprehensible, and not to lose the gain that is ready to their hand, which is found by faith alone.

---

[1] S. John x. 9
[2] Reading εἴπωμεν, for which Oehler's text substitutes εἴπομεν.
[3] S. John i. 18.   [4] 1 Tim. vi. 16.
[5] Cf. Exod. xxxiii. 20.   [6] Ps. cxli. 3 (LXX.).   [7] Ps. xxxi. 3.

[8] Ps. xxiii. 2.
[9] This point has been already discussed by S. Gregory in the second and third books. See above. pp. 119, 149. It is also dealt with in the short treatise "On the Faith," addressed to Simplicius, which will be found in this volume.   [1] Ps. lxi. 3.
[2] Ps. xxxi. 21 (LXX.).   [3] Cf. Judges xx. 16.

§ 2. *He then wonderfully displays the Eternal Life, which is Christ, to those who confess Him not, and applies to them the mournful lamentation of Jeremiah over Jehoiakim, as being closely allied to Montanus and Sabellius.*

But now that I have surveyed what remains of his treatise I shrink from conducting my argument further, as a shudder runs through my heart at his words. For he wishes to show that the Son is something different from eternal life, while, unless eternal life is found in the Son, our faith will be proved to be idle, and our preaching to be vain, baptism a superfluity, the agonies of the martyrs all for nought, the toils of the Apostles useless and unprofitable for the life of men. For why did they preach Christ, in Whom, according to Eunomius, there does not reside the power of eternal life? Why do they make mention of those who had believed in Christ, unless it was through Him that they were to be partakers of eternal life? "For the intelligence," he says, "of those who have believed in the Lord, overleaping all sensible and intellectual existence, cannot stop even at the generation of the Son, but speeds beyond even this in its yearning for eternal life, eager to meet the First." What ought I most to bewail in this passage? that the wretched men do not think that eternal life is in the Son, or that they conceive of the Person of the Only-begotten in so grovelling and earthly a fashion, that they fancy they can mount in their reasonings upon His beginning, and so look by the power of their own intellect beyond the life of the Son, and, leaving the generation of the Lord somewhere beneath them, can speed onward beyond this in their yearning for eternal life? For the meaning of what I have quoted is nothing else than this, that the human mind, scrutinizing the knowledge of real existence, and lifting itself above the sensible and intelligible creation, will leave God the Word, Who was in the beginning, below itself, just as it has left below it all other things, and itself comes to be in Him in Whom God the Word was not, treading, by mental activity, regions which lie beyond the life of the Son, there searching for eternal life, where the Only-begotten God is not. "For in its yearning for eternal life," he says, "it is borne in thought beyond the Son"—clearly as though it had not in the Son found that which it was seeking. If the eternal life is not in the Son, then assuredly He Who said, "I am the life [4]," will be convicted of falsehood, or else He is life, it is true, but not eternal life. But that which is not eternal is of course limited in duration. And such a kind of life is common to the irrational animals as well as to men. Where then is the majesty of the very life, if even the irrational creation share it? and how will the Word or Divine Reason [5] be the same as the Life, if this finds a home, in virtue of the life which is but temporary, in irrational creatures? For if, according to the great John, the Word is Life [6], but that life is temporary and not eternal, as their heresy holds, and if, moreover, the temporary life has place in other creatures, what is the logical consequence? Why, either that irrational animals are rational, or that the Reason must be confessed to be irrational. Have we any further need of words to confute their accursed and malignant blasphemy? Do such statements even pretend to conceal their intention of denying the Lord? For if the Apostle plainly says that what is not eternal is temporary [7], and if these people see eternal life in the essence of the Father alone, and if by alienating the Son from the Nature of the Father they also cut Him off from eternal life, what is this but a manifest denial and rejection of the faith in the Lord? while the Apostle clearly says that those who "in this life only have hope in Christ are of all men most miserable [8]." If then the Lord is life, but not eternal life, assuredly the life is temporal, and but for a day, that which is operative only for the present time, or else [9] the Apostle bemoans those who have hope, as having missed the true life.

However, they who are enlightened in Eunomius' fashion pass the Son by, and are carried in their reasonings beyond Him, seeking eternal life in Him Who is contemplated as outside and apart from the Only-begotten. What ought one to say to such evils as these,—save whatever calls forth lamentation and weeping? Alas, how can we groan over this wretched and pitiable generation, bringing forth a crop of such deadly mischiefs? In days of yore the zealous Jeremiah bewailed the people of Israel, when they gave an evil consent to Jehoiakim who led the way to idolatry, and were condemned to captivity under the Assyrians in requital for their unlawful worship, exiled from the sanctuary and banished far from the inheritance of their fathers. Yet more fitting does it seem to me that these lamentations be chanted when the imitator of Jehoiakim draws away those whom he deceives to this new kind of idolatry, banishing them from their ancestral inheritance,—I mean the Faith. They too, in a way corresponding to the Scriptural record, are

---

[4] S. John xi. 25.

[5] ὁ λόγος: the idea of "reason" must be expressed to convey the force required for the argument following.
[6] Cf. S. John i. 4.
[7] The reference is perhaps to 2 Cor. iv. 18.
[8] Cf. 1 Cor. xv. 19.
[9] If we might read ᾖ for ἦ the sense of the passage would be materially simplified:—"His life is temporal, that life which operates only for the present time, whereon those who hope are the objects of the Apostle's pity."

carried away captive to Babylon from Jerusalem that is above,—that is from the Church of God to this confusion of pernicious doctrines,—for[1] Babylon means "confusion." And even as Jehoiakim was mutilated, so this man, having voluntarily deprived himself of the light of the truth, has become a prey to the Babylonian despot, never having learned, poor wretch, that the Gospel enjoins us to behold eternal life alike in the Father, and the Son, and the Holy Ghost, inasmuch as the Word has thus spoken concerning the Father, that to know Him is life eternal[2], and concerning the Son, that every one that believeth on Him hath eternal life[3], and concerning the Holy Spirit, that to Him that hath received His grace it shall be a well of water springing up unto eternal life[4]. Accordingly every one that yearns for eternal life, when he has found the Son,—I mean the true Son, and not the Son falsely so called—has found in Him in its entirety what he longed for, because He is life and hath life in Himself[5]. But this man, so subtle in mind, so keen-sighted of heart, does not by his extreme acuteness of vision discover life in the Son, but, having passed Him over and left Him behind as a hindrance in the way to that for which he searches, he there seeks eternal life where he thinks the true Life not to be! What could we conceive more to be abhorred than this for profanity, or more melancholy as an occasion of lamentation? But that the charge of Sabellianism and Montanism should be repeatedly urged against our doctrines, is much the same as if one should lay to our charge the blasphemy of the Anomœans. For if one were carefully to investigate the falsehood of these heresies, he would find that they have great similarity to the error of Eunomius. For each of them affects the Jew in his doctrine, admitting neither the Only-begotten God nor the Holy Spirit to share the Deity of the God Whom they call "Great," and "First." For Whom Sabellius calls God of the three names, Him does Eunomius term unbegotten: but neither contemplates the Godhead in the Trinity of Persons. Who then is really akin to Sabellius let the judgment of those who read our argument decide. Thus far for these matters.

§ 3. *He then shows the eternity of the Son's generation, and the inseparable identity of His essence with Him that begat Him, and likens the folly of Eunomius to children playing with sand.*

But since, in what follows, he is active in stirring up the ill savour of his disgusting attempts,

whereby he tries to make out that the Only-begotten God "once was not," it will be well, as our mind on this head has been made pretty clear by our previous arguments, no longer to plunge our argument also in what is likewise bad, except perhaps that it is not unseasonable to add this one point, having selected it from the multitude. He says (some one having remarked that "the property of not being begotten is equally associated with the essence of the Father[6]"), "The argument proceeds by like steps to those by which it came to a conclusion in the case of the Son." The orthodox doctrine is clearly strengthened by the attack of its adversaries, the doctrine, namely, that we ought not to think that not to be begotten or to be begotten are identical with the essence[7], but that these should be contemplated, it is true, in the subject, while the subject in its proper definition is something else beyond these, and since no difference is found in the subject, because the difference of "begotten" and "unbegotten" is apart from the essence, and does not affect it, it necessarily follows that the essence must be allowed to be in both Persons without variation. Let us moreover inquire, over and above what has been already said, into this point, in what sense he says that "generation" is alien from the Father,—whether he does so conceiving of it as an essence or an operation. If he conceives it to be an operation, it is clearly equally connected with its result and with its author, as in every kind of production one may see the operation alike in the product and the producer, appearing in the production of the effects and not separated from their artificer. But if he terms "generation" an essence separate from the essence of the Father, admitting that the Lord came into being therefrom, then he plainly puts this in the place of the Father as regards the Only-begotten, so that two Fathers are conceived in the case of the Son, one a Father in name alone, Whom he calls "the Ungenerate," Who has nothing to do with generation, and the other, which he calls "generation," performing the part of a Father to the Only-begotten.

And this is brought home even more by the statements of Eunomius himself than by our own arguments. For in what follows, he says :— "God, being without generation, is also prior to that which is generate," and a little further on, "for He Whose existence arises from being generated did not exist before He was generated." Accordingly, if the Father has nothing to do

[6] Presumably the quotation from the unknown author, if completed, would run. "as that of being begotten is associated with the essence of the Son."

[7] If the property of not being begotten is "associated with" the essence, it clearly cannot be the essence, as Eunomius elsewhere maintains it to be : hence the phrase which he here adopts concedes S. Gregory's position on this point.

[1] Altering Oehler's punctuation.   [2] Cf. S. John xvii. 3.
[3] Cf. S. John iii. 36.   [4] Cf. S. John iv. 14.
[5] Cf. S. John v. 26.

with generation, and if it is from generation that the Son derives His being, then the Father has no action in respect of the subsistence of the Son, and is apart from all connection with generation, from which the Son draws His being. If, then, the Father is alien from the generation of the Son, they either invent for the Son another Father under the name of "generation," or in their wisdom make out the Son to be self-begotten and self-generated. You see the confusion of mind of the man who exhibits his ignorance to us up and down in his own argument, how his profanity wanders in many paths, or rather in places where no path is, without advancing to its mark by any trustworthy guidance ; and as one may see in the case of infants, when in their childish sport they imitate the building of houses with sand, that what they build is not framed on any plan, or by any rules of art, to resemble the original, but first they make something at haphazard, and in silly fashion, and then take counsel what to call it,— this penetration I discern in our author. For after getting together words of impiety according to what first comes into his head, like a heap of sand, he begins to cast about to see whither his unintelligible profanity tends, growing up as it does spontaneously from what he has said, without any rational sequence. For I do not imagine that he originally proposed to invent generation as an actual subsistence standing to the essence of the Son in the place of the Father, nor that it was part of our rhetorician's plan that the Father should be considered as alien from the generation of the Son, nor was the absurdity of self-generation deliberately introduced. But all such absurdities have been emitted by our author without reflection, so that, as regards them, the man who so blunders is not even worth much refutation, as he knows, to borrow the Apostle's words, "neither what he says, nor whereof he affirms [8]."

"For He Whose existence arises from generation," he says, "did not exist before generation." If he here uses the term "generation" of the Father, I agree with Him, and there is no opponent. For one may mean the same thing by either phrase, by saying either that Abraham begat Isaac, or, that Abraham was the father of Isaac. Since then to be father is the same as to have begotten, if any one shifts the words from one form of speech to the other, paternity will be shown to be identical with generation. If, therefore, what Eunomius says is this, "He Whose existence is derived from the Father was not before the Father," the statement is sound, and we give our vote in favour of it. But if he is recurring in the phrase to that gen-eration of which we have spoken before, and says that it is separated from the Father but associated with the Son, then I think it waste of time to linger over the consideration of the unintelligible. For whether he thinks generation to be a self-existent object, or whether by the name he is carried in thought to that which has no actual existence, I have not to this day been able to find out from his language. For his fluid and baseless argument lends itself alike to either supposition, inclining to one side or to the other according to the fancy of the thinker.

§ 4. *After this he shows that the Son, who truly is, and is in the bosom of the Father, is simple and uncompounded, and that He who redeemed us from bondage is not under dominion of the Father, nor in a state of slavery: and that otherwise not He alone, but also the Father Who is in the Son and is One with Him, must be a slave; and that the word "being" is formed from the word to "be." And having excellently and notably discussed all these matters, he concludes the book.*

But not yet has the most grievous part of his profanity been examined, which the sequel of his treatise goes on to add. Well, let us consider his words sentence by sentence. Yet I know not how I can dare to let my mouth utter the horrible and godless language of him who fights against Christ. For I fear lest, like some baleful drugs, the remnant of the pernicious bitterness should be deposited upon the lips through which the words pass. "He that cometh unto God," says the Apostle, "must believe that He is [9]." Accordingly, true existence is the special distinction of Godhead. But Eunomius makes out Him Who truly is, either not to exist at all, or not to exist in a proper sense, which is just the same as not existing at all; for he who does not properly exist, does not really exist at all ; as, for example, he is said to "run" in a dream who in that state fancies he is exerting himself in the race, while, since he untruly acts the semblance of the real race, his fancy that he is running is not for this reason a race. But even though in an inexact sense it is so called, still the name is given to it falsely. Accordingly, he who dares to assert that the Only-begotten God either does not properly exist, or does not exist at all, manifestly blots out of his creed all faith in Him. For who can any longer believe in something non-existent ? or who would resort to Him Whose being has been shown by the enemies of the true Lord to be improper and unsubstantial ?

But that our statement may not be thought

---

8 1 Tim. i. 7.

9 Heb. xi. 6.

to be unfair to our opponents, I will set side by side with it the language of the impious persons, which runs as follows :—" He Who is in the bosom of the Existent, and Who is in the beginning and is with God, not being, or at all events not being in a strict sense, even though Basil, neglecting this distinction and addition, uses the title of 'Existent' interchangeably, contrary to the truth—" What do you say? that He Who is in the Father is not, and that He Who is in the beginning, and Who is in the bosom of the Father, is not, for this very reason, that He is in the beginning and is in the Father, and is discerned in the bosom of the Existent, and hence does not in a strict sense exist, because He is in the Existent? Alas for the idle and irrational tenets! Now for the first time we have heard this piece of vain babbling,—that the Lord, by Whom are all things, does not in a strict sense exist. And we have not yet got to the end of this appalling statement; but something yet more startling remains behind, that he not only affirms that He does not exist, or does not strictly speaking exist, but also that the Nature in which He is conceived to reside is various and composite. For he says "not being, or not being simple." But that to which simplicity does not belong is manifestly various and composite. How then can the same Person be at once non-existent and composite in essence? For one of two alternatives they must choose : if they predicate of Him non-existence they cannot speak of Him as composite, or if they affirm Him to be composite they cannot rob Him of existence. But that their blasphemy may assume many and varied shapes, it jumps at every godless notion when it wishes to contrast Him with the existent, affirming that, strictly speaking, He does not exist, and in His relation to the uncompounded Nature denying Him the attribute of simplicity : — "not existing, not existing simply, not existing in the strict sense." Who among those who have transgressed the word and forsworn the Faith was ever so lavish in utterances denying the Lord? He has stood up in rivalry with the divine proclamation of John. For as often as the latter has attested "was" of the Word, so often does he apply to Him Who is an opposing "was not." And he contends against the holy lips of our father Basil, bringing against him the charge that he "neglects these distinctions," when he says that He Who is in the Father, and in the beginning, and in the bosom of the Father, exists, holding the view that the addition of "in the beginning," and "in the bosom of the Father," bars the real existence of Him Who is. Vain learning! What things the teachers of deceit teach! what strange doctrines they introduce to their hearers! they instruct them that that

which is in something else does not exist! So, Eunomius, since your heart and brain are within you, neither of them, according to your distinction, exists. For if the Only-begotten God does not, strictly speaking, exist, for this reason, that He is in the bosom of the Father, then everything that is in something else is thereby excluded from existence. But certainly your heart exists in you, and not independently; therefore, according to your view, you must either say that it does not exist at all, or that it does not exist in the strict sense. However, the ignorance and profanity of his language are so gross and so glaring, as to be obvious even before our argument, at all events to all persons of sense : but that his folly as well as his impiety may be more manifest, we will add thus much to what has gone before. If one may only say that that in the strict sense exists, of which the word of Scripture attests the existence detached from all relation to anything else, why do they, like those who carry water, perish with thirst when they have it in their power to drink? Even this man, though he had at hand the antidote to his blasphemy against the Son, closed his eyes and ran past it as though fearing to be saved, and charges Basil with unfairness for having suppressed the qualifying words, and for only quoting the "was" by itself, in reference to the Only-begotten. And yet it was quite in his power to see what Basil saw and what every one who has eyes sees. And herein the sublime John seems to me to have been prophetically moved, that the mouths of those fighters against Christ might be stopped, who on the ground of these additions deny the existence, in the strict sense, of the Christ, saying simply and without qualification "The Word was God," and was Life, and was Light [1], not merely speaking of Him as being in the beginning, and with God, and in the bosom of the Father, so that by their relation the absolute existence of the Lord should be done away. But his assertion that He was God, by this absolute declaration detached from all relation to anything else, cuts off every subterfuge from those who in their reasonings run into impiety; and, in addition to this, there is moreover something else which still more convincingly proves the malignity of our adversaries. For if they make out that to exist in something is an indication of not existing in the strict sense, then certainly they allow that not even the Father exists absolutely, as they have learnt in the Gospel, that just as the Son abides in the Father, so the Father abides in the Son, according to the words of the Lord [2]. For to say that the Father is in the Son is equivalent to saying that the Son is in the

---

[1] Cf. S. John i. 1, 4.   S. John xiv. 11

bosom of the Father. And in passing let us make this further inquiry. When the Son, as they say, "was not," what did the bosom of the Father contain? For assuredly they must either grant that it was full, or suppose it to have been empty. If then the bosom was full, certainly the Son was that which filled the bosom. But if they imagine that there was some void in the bosom of the Father, they do nothing else than assert of Him perfection by way of augmentation, in the sense that He passed from the state of void and deficiency to the state of fulness and perfection. But "they knew not nor understood," says David of those that "walk on still in darkness [3]." For he who has been rendered hostile to the true Light cannot keep his soul in light. For this reason it was that they did not perceive lying ready to their hand in logical sequence that which would have corrected their impiety, smitten, as it were, with blindness, like the men of Sodom.

But he also says that the essence of the Son is controlled by the Father, his exact words being as follows:—"For He Who is and lives because of the Father, does not appropriate this dignity, as the essence which controls even Him attracts to itself the conception of the Existent." If these doctrines approve themselves to some of the sages "who are without," let not the Gospels nor the rest of the teaching of the Holy Scripture be in any way disturbed. For what fellowship is there between the creed of Christians and the wisdom that has been made foolish [4]? But if he leans upon the support of the Scriptures, let him show one such declaration from the holy writings, and we will hold our peace. I hear Paul cry aloud, "There is one Lord Jesus Christ [5]." But Eunomius shouts against Paul, calling Christ a slave. For we recognize no other mark of a slave than to be subject and controlled. The slave is assuredly a slave, but the slave cannot by nature be Lord, even though the term be applied to Him by inexact use. And why should I bring forward the declarations of Paul in evidence of the lordship of the Lord? For Paul's Master Himself tells His disciples that He is truly Lord, accepting as He does the confession of those who called Him Master and Lord. For He says, "Ye call Me Master and Lord; and ye say well, for so I am [6]." And in the same way He enjoined that the Father should be called Father by them, saying, "Call no man master upon earth: for one is your Master, even Christ: and call no man father upon earth, for one is your Father, Which is in heaven [7]." To which then ought we to give heed, as we are thus hemmed in between them? On one side the Lord Himself, and he who has Christ speaking in him [8], enjoin us not to think of Him as a slave, but to honour Him even as the Father is honoured, and on the other side Eunomius brings his suit against the Lord, claiming Him as a slave, when he says that He on Whose shoulders rests the government of the universe is under dominion. Can our choice what to do be doubtful, or is the decision which is the more advantageous course unimportant? Shall I slight the advice of Paul, Eunomius? shall I deem the voice of the Truth less trustworthy than thy deceit? But "if I had not come and spoken unto them, they had not had sin [9]." Since then, He has spoken to them, truly declaring Himself to be Lord, and that He is not falsely named Lord (for He says, "I am," not "I am called"), what need is there that they should do that, whereon the vengeance is inevitable because they are forewarned?

But perhaps, in answer to this, he will again put forth his accustomed logic, and will say that the same Being is both slave and Lord, dominated by the controlling power but lording it over the rest. These profound distinctions are talked of at the cross-roads, circulated by those who are enamoured of falsehood, who confirm their idle notions about the Deity by illustrations from the circumstances of ordinary life. For since the occurrences of this world give us examples of such arrangements [1] (thus in a wealthy establishment one may see the more active and devoted servant set over his fellow-servants by the command of his master, and so invested with superiority over others in the same rank and station), they transfer this notion to the doctrines concerning the Godhead, so that the Only-begotten God, though subject to the sovereignty of His superior, is no way hindered by the authority of His sovereign in the direction of those inferior to Him. But let us bid farewell to such philosophy, and proceed to discuss this point according to the measure of our intelligence. Do they confess that the Father is by nature Lord, or do they hold that He arrived at this position by some kind of election? I do not think that a man who has any share whatever of intellect could come to such a pitch of madness as not to acknowledge that the lordship of the God of all is His by nature. For that which is by nature simple, uncompounded, and indivisible, whatever it happens to be, that it is throughout in all its entirety, not becoming one thing after another by some process of change, but remaining eternally in the condition in which it is. What, then, is their

3 Cf. Ps. lxxxii. 5. 4 Cf. 1 Cor. i. 20.
5 Cf. 1 Cor. viii. 6. 6 Cf. S. John xiii. 13.
7 Cf. S. Matt. xxiii. 8—10.
8 Cf. 2 Cor. xiii. 3. 9 S. John xv. 22.
1 Oehler's punctuation seems here to require alteration.

belief about the Only-begotten? Do they own that His essence is simple, or do they suppose that in it there is any sort of composition? If they think that He is some multiform thing, made up of many parts, assuredly they will not concede Him even the name of Deity, but will drag down their doctrine of the Christ to corporeal and material conceptions: but if they agree that He is simple, how is it possible in the simplicity of the subject to recognize the concurrence of contrary attributes? For just as the contradictory opposition of life and death admits of no mean, so in its distinguishing characteristics is domination diametrically and irreconcilably opposed to servitude. For if one were to consider each of these by itself, one could not properly frame any definition that would apply alike to both, and where the definition of things is not identical, their nature also is assuredly different. If then the Lord is simple and uncompounded in nature, how can the conjunction of contraries be found in the subject, as would be the case if servitude mingled with lordship? But if He is acknowledged to be Lord, in accordance with the teaching of the saints, the simplicity of the subject is evidence that He can have no part or lot in the opposite condition: while if they make Him out to be a slave, then it is idle for them to ascribe to Him the title of lordship. For that which is simple in nature is not parted asunder into contradictory attributes. But if they affirm that He is one, and is called the other, that He is by nature slave and Lord in name alone, let them boldly utter this declaration and relieve us from the long labour of answering them. For who can afford to be so leisurely in his treatment of inanities as to employ arguments to demonstrate what is obvious and unambiguous? For if a man were to inform against himself for the crime of murder, the accuser would not be put to any trouble in bringing home to him by evidence the charge of blood-guiltiness. In like manner we shall no longer bring against our opponents, when they advance so far in impiety, a confutation framed after examination of their case. For he who affirms the Only-begotten to be a slave, makes Him out by so saying to be a fellow-servant with himself: and hence will of necessity arise a double enormity. For either he will despise his fellow-slave and deny the faith, having shaken off the yoke of the lordship of Christ, or he will bow before the slave, and, turning away from the self-determining nature that owns no Lord over it, will in a manner worship himself instead of God. For if he sees himself in slavery, and the object of his worship also in slavery, he of course looks at himself, seeing the whole of himself in that which he worships. But what reckoning can count up all the other mischiefs that necessarily accompany this pravity of doctrine? For who does not know that he who is by nature a slave, and follows his avocation under the constraint imposed by a master, cannot be removed even from the emotion of fear? And of this the inspired Apostle is a witness, when he says, "Ye have not received the spirit of bondage again to fear[2]." So that they will be found to attribute, after the likeness of men, the emotion of fear also to their fellow-servant God.

Such is the God of heresy. But what we, who, in the words of the Apostle, have been called to liberty by Christ[3], Who hath freed us from bondage, have been taught by the Scriptures to think, I will set forth in few words. I take my start from the inspired teaching, and boldly declare that the Divine Word does not wish even us to be slaves, our nature having now been changed for the better, and that He Who has taken all that was ours, on the terms of giving to us in return what is His, even as He took disease, death, curse, and sin, so took our slavery also, not in such a way as Himself to have what He took, but so as to purge our nature of such evils, our defects being swallowed up and done away with in His stainless nature. As therefore in the life that we hope for there will be neither disease, nor curse, nor sin, nor death, so slavery also along with these will vanish away. And that what I say is true I call the Truth Himself to witness, Who says to His disciples "I call you no more servants, but friends[4]." If then our nature will be free at length from the reproach of slavery, how comes the Lord of all to be reduced to slavery by the madness and infatuation of these deranged men, who must of course, as a logical consequence, assert that He does not know the counsels of the Father, because of His declaration concerning the slave, which tells us that "the servant knoweth not what his lord doeth[4]"? But when they say this, let them hear that the Son has in Himself all that pertains to the Father, and sees all things that the Father doeth, and none of the good things that belong to the Father is outside the knowledge of the Son. For how can He fail to have anything that is the Father's, seeing He has the Father wholly in Himself? Accordingly, if "the servant knoweth not what his lord doeth," and if He has in Himself all things that are the Father's, let those who are reeling with strong drink at last become sober, and let them now, if never before, look up at the truth, and see that He who has all things that the Father has is lord of all, and not a slave. For how can the personality that owns no lord over it bear on

---

[2] Rom. viii. 15.   [3] Cf. Gal. v. 13.   [4] Cf. S. John xv. 15.

itself the brand of slavery? How can the King of all fail to have His form of like honour with Himself? how can dishonour—for slavery is dishonour—constitute the brightness of the true glory? and how is the King's son born into slavery? No, it is not so. But as He is Light of Light, and Life of Life, and Truth of Truth, so is He Lord of Lord, King of King, God of God, Supreme of Supreme; for having in Himself the Father in His entirety, whatever the Father has in Himself He also assuredly has, and since, moreover, all that the Son has belongs to the Father, the enemies of God's glory are inevitably compelled, if the Son is a slave, to drag down to servitude the Father as well. For there is no attribute of the Son which is not absolutely the Father's. "For all Mine are Thine," He says, "and Thine are Mine 5." What then will the poor creatures say? Which is more reasonable—that the Son, Who has said, "Thine are Mine, and I am glorified in them 5," should be glorified in the sovereignty of the Father, or that insult should be offered to the Father by the degradation involved in the slavery of the Son? For it is not possible that He Who contains in Himself all that belongs to the Son, and Who is Himself in the Son, should not also absolutely be in the slavery of the Son, and have slavery in Himself. Such are the results achieved by Eunomius' philosophy, whereby he inflicts upon his Lord the insult of slavery, while he attaches the same degradation to the stainless glory of the Father.

Let us however return once more to the course of his treatise. What does Eunomius say concerning the Only-begotten? That He "does not appropriate the dignity," for he calls the appellation of "being" a "dignity." A startling piece of philosophy! Who of all men that have ever been, whether among Greeks or barbarian sages, who of the men of our own day, who of the men of all time ever gave "being" the name of "dignity"? For everything that is regarded as subsisting 6 is said, by the common custom of all who use language, to "be": and from the word "be" has been formed the term "being." But now the expression "dignity" is applied in a new fashion to the idea expressed by "being." For he says that "the Son, Who is and lives because of the Father, does not appropriate this dignity," having no Scripture to support his statement, and not conducting his statement to so senseless a conclusion by any process of logical inference, but as if he had taken into his intestines some windy food, he belches forth his blasphemy in its crude and unmethodized form, like some unsavoury breath.

"He does not appropriate this dignity." Let us concede the point of "being" being called "dignity." What then? does He Who is not appropriate being? "No," says Eunomius, "because He exists by reason of the Father." Do you not then say that He Who does not appropriate being is not? for "not to appropriate" has the same force as "to be alien from", and the mutual opposition of the ideas 7 is evident. For that which is "proper" is not "alien," and that which is "alien" is not "proper." He therefore Who does not "appropriate" being is obviously alien from being : and He Who is alien from being is non-existent.

But his cogent proof of this absurdity he brings forward in the words, "as the essence which controls even Him attracts to itself the conception of the Existent." Let us say nothing about the awkwardness of the combination here : let us examine his serious meaning. What argument ever demonstrated this? He superfluously reiterates to us his statement of the Essence of the Father having sovereignty over the Son. What evangelist is the patron of this doctrine? What process of dialectic conducts us to it. What premises support it? What line of argument ever demonstrated by any logical consequence that the Only-begotten God is under dominion? "But," says he, "the essence that is dominant over the Son attracts to itself the conception of the Existent." What is the meaning of the attraction of the existent? and how comes the phrase of "attracting" to be flung on the top of what he has said before? Assuredly he who considers the force of words will judge for himself. About this, however, we will say nothing : but we will take up again that argument that he does not grant essential being to Him to Whom he does not leave the title of the Existent. And why does he idly fight with shadows, contending about the non-existent being this or that? For that which does not exist is of course neither like anything else, nor unlike. But while granting that He is existent he forbids Him to be so called. Alas for the vain precision of haggling about the sound of a word while making concessions on the more important matter! But in what sense does He, Who, as he says, has dominion over the Son, "attract to Himself the conception of the Existent"? For if he says that the Father attracts His own essence, this process of attraction is superfluous : for existence is His already, without being attracted. If, on the other hand, his meaning is that the existence of the Son is attracted by the Father, I cannot make out how existence is to be

---

5 S. John xvii. 10. 6 ἐν ὑποστάσει θεωρούμενον.

7 The ideas of "own" implied in "appropriate," and that of incongruity implied in "alienation."

wrenched from the Existent, and to pass over to Him Who "attracts" it. Can he be dreaming of the error of Sabellius, as though the Son did not exist in Himself, but was painted on to the personal existence of the Father? is this his meaning in the expression that the conception of the Existent is attracted by the essence which exercises domination over the Son? or does he, while not denying the personal existence of the Son, nevertheless say that He is separated from the meaning conveyed by the term "the Existent"? And yet, how can "the Existent" be separated from the conception of existence? For as long as anything is what it is, nature does not admit that it should not be what it is.

BOOK XI

§ 1. *The eleventh book shows that the title of "Good" is due, not to the Father alone, as Eunomius, the imitator of Manichæus and Bardesanes, alleges, but to the Son also, Who formed man in goodness and loving-kindness, and reformed him by His Cross and death.*

LET us now go on to the next stage in his argument:—". . . . the Only-begotten Himself ascribing to the Father the title due of right to Him alone. For He Who has taught us that the appellation 'good' belongs to Him alone Who is the cause of His own [1] goodness and of all goodness, and is so at all times, and Who refers to Him all good that has ever come into being, would be slow to appropriate to Himself the authority over all things that have come into being, and the title of 'the Existent.'" Well, so long as he concealed his blasphemy under some kind of veil, and strove to entangle his deluded hearers unawares in the mazes of his dialectic, I thought it necessary to watch his unfair and clandestine dealings, and as far as possible to lay bare in my argument the lurking mischief. But now that he has stripped his falsehood of every mask that could disguise it, and publishes his profanity aloud in categorical terms, I think it superfluous to undergo useless labour in bringing logical modes of confutation to bear upon those who make no secret of their impiety. For what further means could we discover to demonstrate their malignity so efficacious as that which they themselves show us in their writings ready to our hand? He says that the Father alone is worthy of the title of "good," that to Him alone such a name is due, on the plea that even the Son Himself agrees that goodness belongs to Him alone. Our accuser has pleaded our cause for us: for perhaps in my former statements I was thought by my readers to show a certain wanton insolence when I endeavoured to demonstrate that the fighters against Christ made Him out to be alien from the goodness of the Father. But I think it has now been proved by the confession of our opponents that in bringing

such a charge against them we were not acting unfairly. For he who says that the title of "good" belongs of right to the Father only, and that such an address befits Him alone, publishes abroad, by thus disclosing his real meaning, the villainy which he had previously wrapped up in disguise. He says that the title of "good" befits the Father only. Does he mean the title with the signification which belongs to the expression, or the title detached from its proper meaning? If on the one side he merely ascribes to the Father the title of "good" in a special sense, he is to be pitied for his irrationality in allowing to the Father merely the sound of an empty name. But if he thinks that the conception expressed by the term "good" belongs to God the Father only, he is to be abominated for his impiety, reviving as he does the plague of the Manichæan heresy in his own opinions. For as health and disease, even so goodness and badness exist on terms of mutual destruction, so that the absence of the one is the presence of the other. If then he says that goodness belongs to the Father only, he cuts off these from every conceivable object in existence except the Father, so that, along with all, the Only-begotten God is shut out from good. For as he who affirms that man alone is capable of laughter implies thereby that no other animal shares this property, so he who asserts that good is in the Father alone separates all things from that property. If then, as Eunomius declares, the Father alone has by right the title of "good," such a term will not be properly applied to anything else. But every impulse of the will either operates in accordance with good, or tends to the contrary. For to be inclined neither one way nor the other, but to remain in a state of equipoise, is the property of creatures inanimate or insensible. If the Father alone is good, having goodness not as a thing acquired, but in His nature, and if the Son, as heresy will have it, does not share in the nature of the Father, then he who does not share the good essence of the Father is of course at the same time excluded also from part and lot in the title of "good." But he who has no claim either to the nature or

---

[1] That is, of the Son's goodness: for S. Gregory's comment on the awkward use of the pronoun σφετέρας, see p. 233, *inf.*

to the name of "good"—what he is is assuredly not unknown, even though I forbear the blasphemous expression. For it is plain to all that the object for which Eunomius is so eager is to import into the conception of the Son a suspicion of that which is evil and opposite to good. For what kind of name belongs to him who is not good is manifest to every one who has a share of reason. As he who is not brave is cowardly, as he who is not just is unjust, and as he who is not wise is foolish, so he who is not good clearly has as his own the opposite name, and it is to this that the enemy of Christ wishes to press the conception of the Only-begotten, becoming thereby to the Church another Manes or Bardesanes. These are the sayings in regard of which we say that our utterance would be no more effective than silence. For were one to say countless things, and to arouse all possible arguments, one could not say anything so damaging of our opponents as what is openly and undisguisedly proclaimed by themselves. For what more bitter charge could one invent against them for malice than that of denying that He is good "Who, being in the form of God, thought it not robbery to be equal with God [2]," but yet condescended to the low estate of human nature, and did so solely for the love of man? In return for what, tell me, "do ye thus requite the Lord [3]?" (for I will borrow the language of Moses to the Israelites); is He not good, Who when thou wast soulless dust invested thee with Godlike beauty, and raised thee up as an image of His own power endowed with soul? Is He not good, Who for thy sake took on Him the form of a servant, and for the joy set before Him [4] did not shrink from bearing the sufferings due to thy sin, and gave Himself a ransom for thy death, and became for our sakes a curse and sin?

§ 2. *He also ingeniously shows from the passage of the Gospel which speaks of "Good Master," from the parable of the Vineyard, from Isaiah and from Paul, that there is not a dualism in the Godhead of good and evil, as Eunomius' ally Marcion supposes, and declares that the Son does not refuse the title of "good" or "Existent," or acknowledge His alienation from the Father, but that to Him also belongs authority over all things that come into being.*

Not even Marcion himself, the patron of your opinions, supports you in this. It is true that in common with you he holds a dualism of gods, and thinks that one is different in nature from the other, but it is the more courteous

view to attribute goodness to the God of the Gospel. You however actually separate the Only-begotten God from the nature of good, that you may surpass even Marcion in the depravity of your doctrines. However, they claim the Scripture on their side, and say that they are hardly treated when they are accused for using the very words of Scripture. For they say that the Lord Himself has said, "There is none good but one, that is, God [5]." Accordingly, that misrepresentation may not prevail against the Divine words, we will briefly examine the actual passage in the Gospel. The history regards the rich man to whom the Lord spoke this word as young—the kind of person, I suppose, inclined to enjoy the pleasures of this life—and attached to his possessions; for it says that he was grieved at the advice to part with what he had, and that he did not choose to exchange his property for life eternal. This man, when he heard that a teacher of eternal life was in the neighbourhood, came to him in the expectation of living in perpetual luxury, with life indefinitely extended, flattering the Lord with the title of "good,"—flattering, I should rather say, not the Lord as we conceive Him, but as He then appeared in the form of a servant. For his character was not such as to enable him to penetrate the outward veil of flesh, and see through it into the inner shrine of Deity. The Lord, then, Who seeth the hearts, discerned the motive with which the young man approached Him as a suppliant,— that he did so, not with a soul intently fixed upon the Divine, but that it was the *man* whom he besought, calling Him "Good Master," because he hoped to learn from Him some lore by which the approach of death might be hindered. Accordingly, with good reason did He Who was thus besought by him answer even as He was addressed [6]. For as the entreaty was not addressed to God the Word, so correspondingly the answer was delivered to the applicant by the Humanity of Christ, thereby impressing on the youth a double lesson. For He teaches him, by one and the same answer, both the duty of reverencing and paying homage to the Divinity, not by flattering speeches but by his life, by keeping the commandments and buying life eternal at the cost of all possessions, and also the truth that humanity, having been sunk in depravity by reason of sin, is debarred from the title of "Good": and for this reason He says, "Why callest Thou Me good?" suggesting in His answer by the word "Me" that human nature which encompassed Him, while by attributing goodness to the Godhead He expressly declared Himself to be good, seeing that

---

[2] Cf. Phil. ii. 6.   [3] Deut. xxxii. 6.   [4] Heb. xii. 2.   [5] Cf. S. Matt. xix. 17.   [6] *i.e.* as man, and not as God.

He is proclaimed to be God by the Gospel. For had the Only-begotten Son been excluded from the title of God, it would perhaps not have been absurd to think Him alien also from the appellation of "good." But if, as is the case, prophets, evangelists, and Apostles proclaim aloud the Godhead of the Only-begotten, and if the name of goodness is attested by the Lord Himself to belong to God, how is it possible that He Who is partaker of the Godhead should not be partaker of the goodness too? For that both prophets, evangelists, disciples and apostles acknowledge the Lord as God, there is none so uninitiated in Divine mysteries as to need to be expressly told. For who knows not that in the forty-fourth [7] Psalm the prophet in his word affirms the Christ to be God, anointed by God? And again, who of all that are conversant with prophecy is unaware that Isaiah, among other passages, thus openly proclaims the Godhead of the Son, where he says: "The Sabeans, men of stature, shall come over unto thee, and shall be servants unto thee: they shall come after thee bound in fetters, and in thee shall they make supplication, because God is in thee, and there is no God beside thee; for thou art God [8]." For what other God there is Who has God in Himself, and is Himself God, except the Only-begotten, let them say who hearken not to the prophecy; but of the interpretation of Emmanuel, and the confession of Thomas after his recognition of the Lord, and the sublime diction of John, as being manifest even to those who are outside the faith, I will say nothing. Nay, I do not even think it necessary to bring forward in detail the utterances of Paul, since they are, as one may say, in all men's mouths, who gives the Lord the appellation not only of "God," but of "great God" and "God over all," saying to the Romans, "Whose are the fathers, and of whom, as concerning the flesh, Christ came, Who is over all, God blessed for ever [9]," and writing to his disciple Titus, "According to the appearing of Jesus Christ the great God and our Saviour [1]," and to Timothy, proclaims in plain terms, "God was manifest in the flesh, justified in the spirit [2]." Since then the fact has been demonstrated on every side that the Only-begotten God is God [3], how is it that he who says that goodness belongs to God, strives to show that the Godhead of the Son is alien from this

ascription, and this though the Lord has actually claimed for Himself the epithet "good" in the parable of those who were hired into the vineyard? For there, when those who had laboured before the others were dissatisfied at all receiving the same pay, and deemed the good fortune of the last to be their own loss, the just judge says to one of the murmurers [4], "Friend, I do thee no wrong: did I not agree with thee for a penny a day? Lo, there thou hast that is thine [5]: I will bestow upon this last even as upon thee. Have I not power to do what I will with mine own? Is thine eye evil because I am good?" Of course no one will contest the point that to distribute recompense according to desert is the special function of the judge; and all the disciples of the Gospel agree that the Only-begotten God is Judge; "for the Father," He saith, "judgeth no man, but hath committed all judgment unto the Son [6]." But they do not set themselves in opposition [7] to the Scriptures. For they say that the word "one" absolutely points to the Father. For He saith, "There is none good but one, that is God." Will truth then lack vigour to plead her own cause? Surely there are many means easily to convict of deception this quibble also. For He Who said this concerning the Father spake also to the Father that other word, "All Mine are Thine, and Thine are Mine, and I am glorified in them [8]." Now if He says that all that is the Father's is also the Son's, and goodness is one of the attributes pertaining to the Father, either Son has not all things if He has not this, and they will be saying that the Truth lies, or if it is impious to suspect the very Truth of being carried away into falsehood, then He Who claimed all that is the Father's as His own, thereby asserted that He was not outside of goodness. For He Who has the Father in Himself, and contains all things that belong to the Father, manifestly has His goodness with "all things." Therefore the Son is Good. But "there is none good," he says, "but one, that is God." This is what is alleged by our adversaries: nor do I myself reject the statement. I do not, however, for this cause deny the Godhead of the Son. But he who confesses that the Lord is God, by that very confession assuredly also asserts of Him goodness. For if goodness is a property of God, and if the Lord is God, then by our premises the Son is shown

---

[7] Ps. xlv. 7, 8. (The Psalm is the 44th in the LXX. numeration, and is so styled by S. Gregory.)

[8] Cf. Is. xlv. 14, 15 (LXX.). 　　　 [9] Rom. ix. 5.

[1] Cf. Tit. ii. 13. The quotation is not verbal; and here the rendering of the A. V. rather obscures the sense which it is necessary for S. Gregory's argument to bring out.

[2] 1 Tim. iii. 16 (reading Θεός, or, if the citation is to be considered as verbal. ὁ Θεός).

[3] Reading τοῦ Θεοῦ εἶναι τὸν μονογενῆ Θεὸν for τοῦ Θεοῦ εἶναι κ.τ.λ. The reading of the texts does not give the sense required for the argument.

[4] Compare with what follows S. Matt. xx. 13, 15. S. Gregory seems to be quoting from memory; his Greek is not so close to that of S. Matthew as the translation to the A. V.

[5] Cf. S. Matt. xxv. 25, from which this phrase is borrowed, with a slight variation.

[6] S. John v. 22.

[7] This seems a sense etymologically possible for καθίστανται with a genitive, a use of which Liddell and Scott give no instances. The statement must of course be taken as that of the adversaries themselves. 　　　 [8] S. John xvii. 10.

to be God. "But," says our opponent, "the word 'one' excludes the Son from participation in goodness." It is easy, however, to show that not even the word "one" separates the Father from the Son. For in all other cases, it is true, the term "one" carries with it the signification of not being coupled with anything else, but in the case of the Father and the Son "one" does not imply isolation. For He says, "I and the Father are one⁹." If, then, the good is one, and a particular kind of unity is contemplated in the Father and the Son, it follows that the Lord, in predicating goodness of "one," claimed under the term "one" the title of "good" also for Himself, Who is one with the Father, and not severed from oneness of nature.

§ 3. *He then exposes the ignorance of Eunomius, and the incoherence and absurdity of his arguments, in speaking of the Son as " the Angel of the Existent," and as being as much below the Divine Nature as the Son is superior to the things created by Himself. And in this connection there is a noble and forcible counter-statement and an indignant refutation, showing that He Who gave the oracles to Moses is Himself the Existent, the Only-begotten Son, Who to the petition of Moses, " If Thou Thyself goest not with us, carry me not up hence," said, " I will do this also that thou hast said"; Who is also called " Angel" both by Moses and Isaiah: wherein is cited the text, " Unto us a Child is born."*

But that the research and culture of our imposing author may be completely disclosed, we will consider sentence by sentence his presentment of his sentiments. "The Son," he says, "does not appropriate the dignity of the Existent," giving the name of "dignity" to the actual fact of being :—(with what propriety he knows how to adapt words to things!)—and since He is "by reason of the Father," he says that He is alienated from Himself on the ground that the essence which is supreme over Him attracts to itself the conception of the Existent. This is much the same as if one were to say that he who is bought for money, in so far as he *is* in his own existence, is not the person bought, but the purchaser, inasmuch as his essential personal existence is absorbed into the nature of him who has acquired authority over him. Such are the lofty conceptions of our divine : but what is the demonstration of his statements? . . . . "the Only-begotten," he says, " Himself ascribing to the Father the title due of right to Him alone," and then he intro-

duces the point that the Father alone is good. Where in this does the Son disclaim the title of "Existent"? Yet this is what Eunomius is driving at when he goes on word for word as follows :—"For He Who has taught us that the appellation 'good' belongs to Him alone Who is the cause of His own goodness and of all goodness, and is so at all times, and Who refers to Him all good that has ever come into being, would be slow to appropriate to Himself the authority over all things that have come into being, and the title of 'the Existent.'" What has "authority" to do with the context? and how along with this is the Son also alienated from the title of "Existent"? But really I do not know what one ought rather to do at this,—to laugh at the want of education, or to pity the pernicious folly which it displays. For the expression, "His own," not employed according to the natural meaning, and as those who know how to use language are wont to use it, attests his extensive knowledge of the grammar of pronouns, which even little boys get up with their masters without trouble, and his ridiculous wandering from the subject to what has nothing to do either with his argument or with the form of that argument, considered as syllogistic, namely, that the Son has no share in the appellation of "Existent"—an assertion adapted to his monstrous inventions ¹,—this and similar absurdities seem combined together for the purpose of provoking laughter ; so that it may be that readers of the more careless sort experience some such inclination, and are amused by the disjointedness of his arguments. But that God the Word should not exist, or that He at all events should not be good (and this is what Eunomius maintains when he says that He does not "appropriate the title" of "Existent" and "good"), and to make out that the authority over all things that come into being does not belong to him,—this calls for our tears, and for a wail of mourning.

For it is not as if he had but let fall something of the kind just once under some headlong and inconsiderate impulse, and in what followed had striven to retrieve his error : no, he dallies lingeringly with the malignity, striving in his later statements to surpass what had gone before. For as he proceeds, he says that the Son is the same distance below the Divine Nature as the nature of angels is subjected below His own, not indeed saying this in so many words, but endeavouring by what he does say to produce such an impression. The reader may judge for himself the meaning of his words : they run as follows,—"Who, by being called

---

⁹ Cf. S. John x. 30.

¹ Oehler's punctuation is here apparently erroneous. The position of συμπεραστικῷ is peculiar and the general construction of the passage a little obscure : but if the text is to be regarded as sound, the meaning must be something like that here given.

'Angel,' clearly showed by Whom He published His words, and Who is the Existent, while by being addressed also as God, He showed His superiority over all things. For He Who is the God of all things that were made by Him, is the Angel of the God over all." Indignation rushes into my heart and interrupts my discourse, and under this emotion arguments are lost in a turmoil of anger roused by words like these. And perhaps I may be pardoned for feeling such emotion. For whose resentment would not be stirred within him at such profanity, when he remembers how the Apostle proclaims that every angelic nature is subject to the Lord, and in witness of his doctrine invokes the sublime utterances of the prophets :— "When He bringeth the first-begotten into the world, He saith, And let all the angels of God worship Him," and, "Thy throne, O God, is for ever and ever," and, "Thou art the same, and Thy years shall not fail[2]"? When the Apostle has gone through all this argument to demonstrate the unapproachable majesty of the Only-begotten God, what must I feel when I hear from the adversary of Christ that the Lord of Angels is Himself only an Angel,—and when he does not let such a statement fall by chance, but puts forth his strength to maintain this monstrous invention, so that it may be established that his Lord has no superiority over John and Moses? For the word says concerning them, "This is he of whom it is written, 'Behold I send my angel before thy face[3].'" John therefore is an angel. But the enemy of the Lord, even though he grants his Lord the name of God, yet makes Him out to be on a level with the deity of Moses, since he too was a servant of the God over all, and was constituted a god to the Egyptians[4]. And yet this phrase, "over all," as has been previously observed, is common to the Son with the Father, the Apostle having expressly ascribed such a title to Him, when he says, "Of whom, as concerning the flesh, Christ came, Who is God over all[5]." But this man degrades the Lord of angels to the rank of an angel, as though he had not heard that the angels are "ministering spirits," and "a flame of fire[6]." For by the use of these distinctive terms does the Apostle make the difference between the several subjects clear and unmistakable, defining the subordinate nature to be "spirits" and "fire," and distinguishing the supreme power by the name of Godhead. And yet, though there are so many that proclaim the glory of the Only-begotten God, against them

all Eunomius lifts up his single voice, calling the Christ "an angel of the God over all," defining Him, by thus contrasting Him with the "God over all," to be one of the "all things," and, by giving Him the same name as the angels, trying to establish that He no wise differs from them in nature : for he has often previously said that all those things which share the same name cannot be different in nature. Does the argument, then, still lack its censors, as it concerns a man who proclaims in so many words that the "Angel" does not publish His own word, but that of the Existent? For it is by this means that he tries to show that the Word Who was in the beginning, the Word Who was God, is not Himself the Word, but is the Word of some other Word, being its minister and "angel." And who knows not that the only opposite to the "Existent" is the non-existent? so that he who contrasts the Son with the Existent, is clearly playing the Jew, robbing the Christian doctrine of the Person of the Only-begotten. For in saying that He is excluded from the title of the "Existent," he is assuredly trying to establish also that He is outside the pale of existence : for surely if he grants Him existence, he will not quarrel about the sound of the word.

But he strives to prop up his absurdity by the testimony of Scripture, and puts forth Moses as his advocate against the truth. For as though that were the source from which he drew his arguments, he freely sets forth to us his own fables, saying, "He Who sent Moses was the Existent Himself, but He by Whom He sent and spake was the Angel of the Existent, and the God of all else." That his statement, however, is not drawn from Scripture, may be conclusively proved by Scripture itself. But if he says that this is the sense of what is written, we must examine the original language of Scripture. Moreover let us first notice that Eunomius, after calling the Lord God of all things after Him, allows Him no superiority in comparison with the angelic nature. For neither did Moses, when he heard that he was made a god to Pharaoh[4], pass beyond the bounds of humanity, but while in nature he was on an equality with his fellows, he was raised above them by superiority of authority, and his being called a god did not hinder him from being man. So too in this case Eunomius, while making out the Son to be one of the angels, salves over such an error by the appellation of Godhead, in the manner expressed, allowing Him the title of God in some equivocal sense. Let us once more set down and examine the very words in which he delivers his blasphemy. "He Who sent Moses was the Existent Himself, but He by Whom He sent was the Angel

[2] Cf. Heb. i. 6—12. The passages there cited are Ps. xcvii. 7 ; Ps. xlv. 6 ; Ps. cii. 25, *sqq.*
[3] S. Matt. xi. 10, quoting Mal. iii. 1. The word translated "messenger" in A. V. is ἄγγελος, which the argument here seems to require should be rendered by "angel."
[4] Cf. Exod. vii. 1.   [5] Rom. ix. 5.
[6] Cf. Heb. i. 14 and 7.

of the Existent"—this, namely "Angel," being the title he gives his Lord. Well, the absurdity of our author is refuted by the Scripture itself, in the passage where Moses beseeches the Lord not to entrust an angel with the leadership of the people, but Himself to conduct their march. The passage runs thus : God is speaking, "Go, get thee down, guide this people unto the place of which I have spoken unto thee : behold Mine Angel shall go before thee in the day when I visit[7]." And a little while after He says again, "And I will send Mine Angel before thee[8]." Then, a little after what immediately follows, comes the supplication to God on the part of His servant, running on this wise, "If I have found grace in Thy sight, let my Lord go among us[9]," and again, "If Thou Thyself go not with us, carry me not up hence[1]"; and then the answer of God to Moses, "I will do for thee this thing also that thou hast spoken : for thou hast found grace in My sight, and I know thee above all men[2]." Accordingly, if Moses begs that the people may not be led by an angel, and if He Who was discoursing with him consents to become his fellow-traveller and the guide of the army, it is hereby manifestly shown that He Who made Himself known by the title of "the Existent" is the Only-begotten God.

If any one gainsays this, he will show himself to be a supporter of the Jewish persuasion in not associating the Son with the deliverance of the people. For if, on the one hand, it was not an angel that went forth with the people, and if, on the other, as Eunomius would have it, He Who was manifested by the name of the Existent is not the Only-begotten, this amounts to nothing less than transferring the doctrines of the synagogue to the Church of God. Accordingly, of the two alternatives they must needs admit one, namely, either that the Only-begotten God on no occasion appeared to Moses, or that the Son is Himself the "Existent," from Whom the word came to His servant. But he contradicts what has been said above, alleging the Scripture itself[3] which informs us that the voice of an angel was interposed, and that it was thus that the discourse of the Existent was conveyed. This, however, is no contradiction, but a confirmation of our view. For we too say plainly, that the prophet, wishing to make manifest to men the mystery concerning Christ, called the Self-Existent "Angel," that the meaning of the words might not be referred to the Father, as it would have been if the title of "Existent" alone had been found throughout the discourse. But just as our word is the revealer and messenger (or "angel") of the movements of the mind, even so we affirm that the true Word that was in the beginning, when He announces the will of His own Father, is styled "Angel" (or "Messenger"), a title given to Him on account of the operation of conveying the message. And as the sublime John, having previously called Him "Word," so introduces the further truth that the Word was God, that our thoughts might not at once turn to the Father, as they would have done if the title of God had been put first, so too does the mighty Moses, after first calling Him "Angel," teach us in the words that follow that He is none other than the Self-Existent Himself, that the mystery concerning the Christ might be foreshown, by the Scripture assuring us by the name "Angel," that the Word is the interpreter of the Father's will, and, by the title of the "Self-Existent," of the closeness of relation subsisting between the Son and the Father. And if he should bring forward Isaiah also as calling Him "the *Angel* of mighty counsel[4]," not even so will he overthrow our argument. For there, in clear and uncontrovertible terms, there is indicated by the prophecy the dispensation of His Humanity ; for "unto us," he says, "a Child is born, unto us a Son is given, and the government shall be upon His shoulder, and His name is called the Angel of mighty counsel." And it is with an eye to this, I suppose, that David describes the establishment of His kingdom, not as though He were not a King, but in the view that the humiliation to the estate of a servant to which the Lord submitted by way of dispensation, was taken up and absorbed into the majesty of His Kingdom. For he says, "I was established King by Him on His holy hill of Sion, declaring the ordinance of the Lord.[5] Accordingly, He Who through Himself reveals the goodness of the Father is called "Angel" and "Word," "Seal" and "Image," and all similar titles with the same intention. For as the "Angel" (or "Messenger") gives information from some one, even so the Word reveals the thought within, the Seal shows by Its own stamp the original mould, and the Image by Itself interprets the beauty of that whereof It is the image, so that in their signification all these terms are equivalent to one another. For this reason the title "Angel" is placed before that of the "Self-Existent," the Son being termed "Angel" as the exponent of His Father's will, and the "Existent" as having no name that could possibly give a knowledge of His essence, but transcending all the power of names to express. Wherefore also His name is testified by the

7 Cf Exod. xxxii. 34 (LXX.).
8 Cf. Exod. xxxiii. 2 ; the quotation is not verbally from LXX.
9 Cf E\od. xxxiv. 9 (LXX.).   1 Exod. xxxiii. 15 (LXX.).
2 Cf Exod. xxxiii. 17 (LXX.).   3 Cf. Exod. iii. 2.
4 Is. ix. 6 (LXX.).   5 Ps. ii. 6 (LXX.).

writing of the Apostle to be "above every name[6]," not as though it were some one name preferred above all others, though still comparable with them, but rather in the sense that He Who verily *is* is above every name.

§ 4. *After this, fearing to extend his reply to great length, he passes by most of his adversary's statements as already refuted. But the remainder, for the sake of those who deem them of much force, he briefly summarizes, and refutes the blasphemy of Eunomius, who says of the Lord also that He is what animals and plants in all creation are, non-existent before their own generation ; and so with the production of frogs ; alas for the blasphemy !*

But I must hasten on, for I see that my treatise has already extended beyond bounds, and I fear that I may be thought garrulous and inordinate in my talk, if I prolong my answer to excess, although I have intentionally passed by many parts of my adversary's treatise, that my argument might not be spun out to many myriads of words. For to the more studious even the want of conciseness gives an occasion for disparagement ; but as for those whose mind looks not to what is of use, but to the fancy of those who are idle and not in earnest, their wish and prayer is to get over as much of the journey as they can in a few steps. What then ought we to do when Eunomius' profanity draws us on ? Are we to track his every turn ? or is it perhaps superfluous and merely garrulous to spend our energies over and over again on similar encounters ? For all their argument that follows is in accordance with what we have already investigated, and presents no fresh point in addition to what has gone before. If then we have succeeded in completely overthrowing his previous statements, the remainder fall along with them. But in case the contentious and obstinate should think that the strongest part of their case is in what I have omitted, for this reason it may perhaps be necessary to touch briefly upon what remains.

He says that the Lord did not exist before His own generation—he who cannot prove that He was in anything separated from the Father. And this he says, not quoting any Scripture as a warrant for his assertion, but maintaining his proposition by arguments of his own. But this characteristic has been shown to be common to all parts of the creation. Not a frog, not a worm, not a beetle, not a blade of grass, nor any other of the most insignificant objects, existed before its own formation : so that what by aid

of his dialectic skill he tries with great labour and pains to establish to be the case with the Son, has previously been acknowleged to be true of any chance portions of the creation, and our author's mighty labour is to show that the Only-begotten God, by participation of attributes, is on a level with the lowest of created things. Accordingly the fact of the coincidence of their opinions concerning the Only-begotten God, and their view of the mode in which frogs come into being, is a sufficient indication of their doctrinal pravity. Next he urges that not to be before His generation, is equivalent in fact and meaning to not being ungenerate. Once more the same argument will fit my hand in dealing with this too,—that a man would not be wrong in saying the same thing of a dog, or a flea, or a snake, or any one you please of the meanest creatures, since for a dog not to exist before his generation is equivalent in fact and meaning to his not being ungenerate. But if, in accord with the definition they have so often laid down, all things that share in attributes share also in nature, and if it is an attribute of the dog, and of the rest severally, not to exist before generation, which is what Eunomius thinks fit to maintain also of the Son, the reader will by logical process see for himself the conclusion of this demonstration.

§ 5. [7] *Eunomius again speaks of the Son as Lord and God, and Maker of all creation intelligible and sensible, having received from the Father the power and the commission for creation, being entrusted with the task of creation as if He were an artizan commissioned by some one hiring Him, and receiving His power of creation as a thing adventitious, ab extra, as a result of the power allotted to Him in accordance with such and such combinations and oppositions of the stars, as destiny decrees their lot in life to men at their nativity. Thus, passing by most of what Eunomius had written, he confutes his blasphemy that the Maker of all things came into being in like manner with the earth and with angels, and that the subsistence of the Only-begotten differs not at all from the genesis of all things, and reproaches him with reverencing neither the Divine mystery nor the custom of the Church, nor following in his attempt to discover godliness any teacher of pious doctrine, but Manichæus, Colluthus, Arius, Aetius, and those like to them, supposing that Christianity in general is folly, and that the*

---

[7] The grammar of this section of the analysis is in parts very much confused ; the general drift of its intention, rather than its literal meaning, is given in the translation. Grammatically speaking, it appears to attribute to S. Gregory some of the opinions of Eunomius. The construction, however, is so ungrammatical that the confusion is probably in the composer's expression rather than in his interpretation of what he is summarizing.

customs of the Church and the venerable sacraments are a jest, wherein he differs in nothing from the pagans, who borrowed from our doctrine the idea of a great God supreme over all. So, too, this new idolater preaches in the same fashion, and in particular that baptism is "into an artificer and creator," not fearing the curse of those who cause addition or diminution to the Holy Scriptures. And he closes his book with showing him to be Antichrist.

Afterwards, however, he gives his discourse a more moderate turn, imparting to it even a touch of gentleness, and, though he had but a little earlier partitioned off the Son from the title of Existent, he now says,—"We affirm that the Son is not only existent, and above all existent things, but we also call Him Lord and God, the Maker of every being[8], sensible and intelligible." What does he suppose this "being" to be? created? or uncreated? For if he confesses Jesus to be Lord, God, and Maker of all intelligible being, it necessarily follows, if he says it is *uncreated*, that he speaks falsely, ascribing to the Son the making of the uncreated Nature. But if he believes it to be *created*, he makes Him His own Maker. For if the act of creation be not separated from intelligible nature in favour of Him Who is independent and uncreated, there will no longer remain any mark of distinction, as the sensible creation and the intelligible being will be thought of under one head[9]. But here he brings in the assertion that "in the creation of existent things He has been entrusted by the Father with the construction of all things visible and invisible, and with the providential care over all that comes into being, inasmuch as the power allotted to Him from above is sufficient for the production of those things which have been constructed[1]." The vast length to which our treatise has run compels us to pass over these assertions briefly: but, in a sense, profanity surrounds the argument, containing a vast swarm of notions like venomous wasps. "He was entrusted," he says, "with the construction of things by the Father." But if he had been talking about some artizan executing his work at the pleasure of his employer, would he not have used the same language? For we are not wrong in saying just the same of Bezaleel, that being entrusted by Moses with the building of the tabernacle, he became the constructor of those

things there[2] mentioned, and would not have taken the work in hand had he not previously acquired his knowledge by Divine inspiration, and ventured upon the undertaking on Moses' entrusting him with its execution. Accordingly the term "entrusted" suggests that His office and power in creation came to Him as something adventitious, in the sense that before He was entrusted with that commission He had neither the will nor the power to act, but when He received authority to execute the works, and power sufficient for the works, *then* He became the artificer of things that are, the power allotted to Him from on high being, as Eunomius says, sufficient for the purpose. Does he then place even the generation of the Son, by some astrological juggling[3], under some destiny, just as they who practise this vain deceit affirm that the appointment of their lot in life comes to men at the time of their birth, by such and such conjunctions or oppositions of the stars, as the rotation above moves on in a kind of ordered train, assigning to those who are coming into being their special faculties? It may be that something of this kind is in the mind of our sage, and he says that to Him that is above all rule, and authority, and dominion, and above every name that is named, not only in this world, but also in that which is to come, there has been allotted, as though He were pent in some hollow spaces, power from on high, measured out in accordance with the quantity of things which come into being. I will pass over this part of his treatise also summarily, letting fall from a slight commencement of investigation, for the more intelligent sort of readers, seeds to enable them to discern his profanity. Moreover, in what follows, there is ready written a kind of apology for ourselves. For we cannot any longer be thought to be missing the intention of his discourse, and misinterpreting his words to render them subject to criticism, when his own voice acknowledges the absurdity of his doctrine. His words stand as follows:—"What? did not earth and angel come into being, when before they were not?" See how our lofty theologian is not ashamed to apply the same description to earth and angels and to the Maker of all! Surely if he thinks it fit to predicate the same of earth and its Lord, he must either make a god of the one, or degrade the other to a level with it.

Then he adds to this something by which his profanity is yet more completely stripped of all disguise, so that its absurdity is obvious even

---

[8] οὐσίας.
[9] The passage is a little obscure: if the force of the dative τῷ καθ' ἑαυτὸν ἀκτίστῳ be that assigned to it, the meaning will be that, if no exception is made in the statement that the Son is the Maker of every intelligible being, the Deity will be included among the works of the Son, Who will thus be the Maker of Himself, as of the sensible creation.
[1] It is not quite clear how much of this is citation, and how much paraphrase of Eunomius' words.

[2] The reference is to Exod. xxxv. 30.
[3] Reading τερατείαν f r the otherwise unknown word περατείαν, which Oehler retains. If περατείαν is the true reading, it should probably be rendered by "fatalism," or "determination." Gulonius renders it by "determinationem." It may be connected with the name "Peratae," given to one of the Ophite sects, who held fatalist views.

to a child. For he says,—"It would be a long task to detail all the modes of generation of intelligible objects, or the essences which do not all possess the nature of the Existent in common, but display variations according to the operations of Him Who constructed them." Without any words of ours, the blasphemy against the Son which is here contained is glaring and conspicuous, when he acknowledges that that which is predicated of every mode of generation and essence in nowise differs from the description of the Divine subsistence [4] of the Only-begotten. But it seems to me best to pass over the intermediate passages in which he seeks to maintain his profanity, and to hasten to the head and front of the accusation which we have to bring against his doctrines. For he will be found to exhibit the sacrament of regeneration as an idle thing, the mystic oblation as profitless, and the participation in them as of no advantage to those who are partakers therein. For after those high-wrought æons [5] in which, by way of disparagement of our doctrine, he names as its supporters a Valentinus, a Cerinthus, a Basilides, a Montanus, and a Marcion, and after laying it down that those who affirm that the Divine nature is unknowable, and the mode of His generation unknowable, have no right or title whatever to the name of Christians, and after reckoning us among those whom he thus disparages, he proceeds to develop his own view in these terms :— "But we, in agreement with holy and blessed men, affirm that the mystery of godliness does not consist in venerable names, nor in the distinctive character of customs and sacramental tokens, but in exactness of doctrine." That when he wrote this, he did so not under the guidance of evangelists, apostles, or any of the authors of the Old Testament, is plain to every one who has any acquaintance with the sacred and Divine Scripture. We should naturally be led to suppose that by "holy and blessed men" he meant Manichæus, Nicolaus, Colluthus, Aetius, Arius, and the rest of the same band, with whom he is in strict accord in laying down this principle, that neither the confession of sacred names, nor the customs of the Church, nor her sacramental tokens, are a ratification of godliness. But we, having learnt from the holy voice of Christ that "except a man be born again of water and of the Spirit he shall not enter into the kingdom of God [6]," and that "He that eateth My flesh and drinketh My blood, shall live for ever [7]," are persuaded that the mystery of godliness is ratified by the confession of the Divine Names

—the Names of the Father, the Son, and the Holy Ghost, and that our salvation is confirmed by participation in the sacramental customs and tokens. But doctrines have often been carefully investigated by those who have had no part or lot in that mystery, and one may hear many such putting forward the faith we hold as a subject for themselves in the rivalry of debate, and some of them often even succeeding in hitting the truth, and for all that none the less estranged from the faith. Since, then, he despises the revered Names, by which the power of the more Divine birth distributes grace to them who come for it in faith, and slights the fellowship of the sacramental customs and tokens from which the Christian profession draws its vigour, let us, with a slight variation, utter to those who listen to his deceit the word of the prophet :—"How long will ye be slow of heart? Why do ye love destruction and seek after leasing [8]?" How is it that ye do not see the persecutor of the faith inviting those who consent unto him to violate their Christian profession? For if the confession of the revered and precious Names of the Holy Trinity is useless, and the customs of the Church unprofitable, and if among these customs is the sign of the cross [9], prayer, baptism, confession of sins, a ready zeal to keep the commandments, right ordering of character, sobriety of life, regard to justice, the effort not to be excited by passion, or enslaved by pleasure, or to fall short in moral excellence,—if he says that none of such habits as these is cultivated to any good purpose, and that the sacramental tokens do not, as we have believed, secure spiritual blessings, and avert from believers the assaults directed against them by the wiles of the evil one, what else does he do but openly proclaim aloud to men that he deems the mystery which Christians cherish a fable, laughs at the majesty of the Divine Names, considers the customs of the Church a jest, and all sacramental operations idle prattle and folly? What beyond this do they who remain attached to paganism bring forward in disparagement of our creed? Do not they too make the majesty of the sacred Names, in which the faith is ratified, an occasion of laughter? Do not they too deride the sacramental tokens and the customs which are observed by the initiated? And of whom is it so much a distinguishing peculiarity as of the pagans, to think that piety should consist in doctrines only? since they also say that according to their view, there is something more persuasive than the Gospel which we preach, and

---

[4] ὑποστασέως.
[5] The word seems to be used, as "octads" in Book IX. seems to be used, of sections of Eunomius' production.
[6] Cf. S. John iii. 3 and 6.   [7] Cf. S. John vi. 51 and 54.

[8] Cf. Ps. iv. 2 (LXX.). The alteration made is the substitution of ἀπώλειαν for ματαιότητα.
[9] Ἡ σφραγίς. The term is used elsewhere by Gregory in this sense, in the Life of S. Gregory Thaumaturgus, and in the Life of S. Macrina.

some of them hold that there is some one great God pre-eminent above the rest, and acknowledge some subject powers, differing among themselves in the way of superiority or inferiority, in some regular order and sequence, but all alike subject to the Supreme. This, then, is what the teachers of the new idolatry preach, and they who follow them have no dread of the condemnation that abideth on transgressors, as though they did not understand that actually to do some improper thing is far more grievous than to err in word alone. They, then, who in act deny the faith, and slight the confession of the sacred Names, and judge the sanctification effected by the sacramental tokens to be worthless, and have been persuaded to have regard to cunningly devised fables, and to fancy that their salvation consists in quibbles about the generate and the ungenerate,—what else are they than transgressors of the doctrines of salvation?

But if any one thinks that these charges are brought against them by us ungenerously and unfairly, let him consider independently our author's writings, both what we have previously alleged, and what is inferred in logical connection with our citations. For in direct contravention of the law of the Lord—(for the deliverance to us of the means of initiation constitutes a law),—he says that baptism is not into the Father, the Son, and the Holy Spirit, as Christ commanded His disciples when He delivered to them the mystery, but into an artificer and creator, and "not only Father," he says, "of the Only-begotten, but also His God[1]." Woe unto him who gives his neighbour to drink turbid mischief[2]!

---

[1] These last words are apparently a verbal quotation, those preceding more probably a paraphrase of Eunomius' statement.

[2] Cf. Hab. ii. 15 (LXX.). It is possible that the reading θολερὰν for δολερὰν, which appears both in Oehler's text and in the Paris edition, was a various reading of the passage in the LXX., and that S. Gregory intended to quote exactly.

How does he trouble and befoul the truth by flinging his mud into it! How is it that he feels no fear of the curse that rests upon those who add aught to the Divine utterance, or dare to take aught away? Let us read the declaration of the Lord in His very words—"Go," He says, "teach all nations, baptizing them in the Name of the Father, and of the Son, and of the Holy Ghost." Where did He call the Son a creature? Where did the Word teach that the Father is creator and artificer of the Only-begotten? Where in the words cited is it taught that the Son is a servant of God? Where in the delivery of the mystery is the God of the Son proclaimed? Do ye not perceive and understand, ye who are dragged by guile to perdition, what sort of guide ye have put in charge of your souls,—one who interpolates the Holy Scriptures, who garbles the Divine utterances, who with his own mud befouls the purity of the doctrines of godliness, who not only arms his own tongue against us, but also attempts to tamper with the sacred voices of truth, who is eager to invest his own perversion with more authority than the teaching of the Lord? Do ye not perceive that he stirs himself up against the Name at which all must bow, so that in time the Name of the Lord shall be heard no more, and instead of Christ Eunomius shall be brought into the Churches? Do ye not yet consider that this preaching of godlessness has been set on foot by the devil as a rehearsal, preparation, and prelude of the coming of Antichrist? For he who is ambitious of showing that his own words are more authoritative than those of Christ, and of transforming the faith from the Divine Names and the sacramental customs and tokens to his own deceit,—what else, I say, could he properly be called, but only Antichrist?

BOOK XII

BUT let us see what is the next addition that follows upon this profanity, an addition which is in fact the key of their defence of their doctrine. For those who would degrade the majesty of the glory of the Only-begotten to slavish and grovelling conceptions think that they find the strongest proof of their assertions in the words of the Lord to Mary, which He uttered after His resurrection, and before His ascension into heaven, saying, "Touch Me not, for I am not yet ascended to My Father: but go to My brethren and say unto them, I ascend unto My Father and your Father, and to My God and your God [1]." The orthodox interpretation of these words, the sense in which we have been accustomed to believe that they were spoken to Mary, is I think manifest to all who have received the faith in truth. Still the discussion of this point shall be given by us in its proper place; but meantime it is worth while to inquire from those who allege against us such phrases as "ascending," "being seen," "being recognized by touch," and moreover "being associated with men by brotherhood," whether they consider them to be proper to the Divine or to the Human Nature. For if they see in the Godhead the capacity of being seen and touched, of being supported by meat and drink, kinship and brotherhood with men, and all the attributes of corporeal nature, then let them predicate of the Only-begotten God both these and whatsoever else they will, as motive energy and local change, which are peculiar to things circumscribed by a body. But if He by Mary is discoursing with His brethren, and if the Only-begotten has no brethren, (for how, if He had brethren, could the property of being Only-begotten be preserved?) and if the same Person Who said, "God is a Spirit [2]," says to His disciples, "Handle Me [3]," that He may show that while the Human Nature is capable of being handled the Divinity is intangible, and if He Who says, "I go," indicates local change, while He who contains all things, "in Whom," as the Apostle says, "all things were created, and in Whom all things consist [4]," has nothing in existent things external to Himself to which removal could take place by any kind of motion, (for motion cannot otherwise be effected than by that which is removed leaving the place in which it is, and occupying another place instead, while that which extends through all, and is in all, and controls all, and is confined by no existent thing, has no place to which to pass, inasmuch as nothing is void of the Divine fulness,) how can these men abandon the belief that such expressions arise from that which is apparent, and apply them to that Nature which is Divine and which surpasseth all understanding, when the Apostle has in his speech to the Athenians plainly forbidden us to imagine any such thing of God, inasmuch as the Divine power is not discoverable by touch [5], but by intelligent contemplation and faith? Or, again, whom does He Who did eat before the eyes of His disciples, and promised to go before them into Galilee and there be seen of them,—whom does He reveal Him to be Who should so appear to them? God, Whom no man hath seen or can see [6]? or the bodily image, that is, the form of a servant in which God was? If then what has been said plainly proves that the meaning of the phrases alleged refers to that which is visible, expressing shape, and capable of motion, akin to the nature of His disciples, and none of these properties is discernible in Him Who is invisible, incorporeal, intangible, and formless, how do they come to degrade the very Only-begotten God, Who was in the beginning, and is in the Father, to a level with Peter, Andrew, John, and the rest of the Apostles, by calling them the brethren and fellow-servants of the Only-begotten? And yet all their exertions are directed to this aim, to show that in majesty of nature there is as great a distance between

---

[1] S. John xx. 17. [2] S. John iv. 24. [3] S. Luke xxiv. 39.

[4] Col. i. 16, 17.
[5] Cf. Acts xvii. **The precise reference is perhaps to verse 27.**
[6] The reference is perhaps to 1 Tim. vi. 16; but the quotation is not verbal. See also S. John i. 18.

the Father and the dignity, power, and essence of the Only-begotten, as there is between the Only-begotten and humanity. And they press this saying into the support of this meaning, treating the name of the God and Father as being of common significance in respect of the Lord and of His disciples, in the view that no difference in dignity of nature is conceived while He is recognized as God and Father both of Him and of them in a precisely similar manner.

And the mode in which they logically maintain their profanity is as follows;—that either by the relative term employed there is expressed community of essence also between the disciples and the Father, or else we must not by this phrase bring even the Lord into communion in the Father's Nature, and that, even as the fact [7] that the God over all is named as their God implies that the disciples are His servants, so by parity of reasoning, it is acknowledged, by the words in question, that the Son also is the servant of God. Now that the words addressed to Mary are not applicable to the Godhead of the Only-begotten, one may learn from the intention with which they were uttered. For He Who humbled Himself to a level with human littleness, He it is Who spake the words. And what is the meaning of what He then uttered, they may know in all its fulness who by the Spirit search out the depths of the sacred mystery. But as much as comes within our compass we will set down in few words, following the guidance of the Fathers. He Who is by nature Father of existent things, from Whom all things have their birth, has been proclaimed as one, by the sublime utterance of the Apostle. "For there is one God," he says, "and Father, of Whom are all things [8]." Accordingly human nature did not enter into the creation from any other source, nor grow spontaneously in the parents of the race, but it too had for the author of its own constitution none other than the Father of all. And the name of Godhead itself, whether it indicates the authority of oversight or of foresight [9], imports a certain relation to humanity. For He Who bestowed on all things that are, the power of being, is the God and overseer of what He has Himself produced. But since, by the wiles of him that sowed in us the tares of disobedience, our nature no longer preserved in itself the impress of the Father's image, but was transformed into the foul likeness of sin, for this cause it was engrafted by virtue of similarity of will into the

evil family of the father of sin: so that the good and true God and Father was no longer the God and Father of him who had been thus outlawed by his own depravity, but instead of Him Who was by Nature God, those were honoured who, as the Apostle says, "by nature were no Gods [1]," and in the place of the Father, he was deemed father who is falsely so called, as the prophet Jeremiah says in his dark saying, "The partridge called, she gathered together what she hatched not [2]." Since, then, this was the sum of our calamity, that humanity was exiled from the good Father, and was banished from the Divine oversight and care, for this cause He Who is the Shepherd of the whole rational creation, left in the heights of heaven His unsinning and supramundane flock, and, moved by love, went after the sheep which had gone astray, even our human nature [3]. For human nature, which alone, according to the similitude in the parable, through vice roamed away from the hundred of rational beings, is, if it be compared with the whole, but an insignificant and infinitesimal part. Since then it was impossible that our life, which had been estranged from God, should of itself return to the high and heavenly place, for this cause, as saith the Apostle, He Who knew no sin is made sin for us [4], and frees us from the curse by taking on Him our curse as His own [5], and having taken up, and, in the language of the Apostle, "slain" in Himself "the enmity [6]" which by means of sin had come between us and God,—(in fact sin *was* "the enmity")—and having become what we were, He through Himself again united humanity to God. For having by purity brought into closest relationship with the Father of our nature that new man which is created after God [7], in Whom dwelt all the fulness of the Godhead bodily [8], He drew with Him into the same grace all the nature that partakes of His body and is akin to Him. And these glad tidings He proclaims through the woman, not to those disciples only, but also to all who up to the present day become disciples of the Word,—the tidings, namely, that man is no longer outlawed, nor cast out of the kingdom of God, but is once more a son, once more in the station assigned to him by his God, inasmuch as along with the first-fruits of humanity the lump also is hallowed [9]. "For behold," He says, "I and the children whom God hath given Me [1]." He Who for our sakes was partaker of flesh and blood has recovered you, and brought

7 The grammar of the passage is simplified if we read τὸ θεὸν αὐτῶν ὀνομασθῆναι, but the sense, retaining Oehler's reading τὸν θεὸν, is probably the same.
8 Cf. 1 Cor. viii. 6.
9 There seems here to be an allusion to the supposed derivation of θεός from θεάομαι, which is also the basis of an argument in the treatise "On 'Not three Gods,'" addressed to Ablabius.

1 Gal. iv. 8. 2 Jer. xvii. 11 (LXX.).
3 Cf. Book IV. § 3 (p. 158 *sup.*). With the general statement may be compared the parallel passage in Book II. § 8.
4 Cf. 2 Cor. v. 21. 5 Cf. Gal. iii. 13.
6 Cf. Eph. ii. 16. 7 Cf. Eph. iv. 24.
8 Cf. Col. ii. 9. 9 Cf. Rom. xi. 16.
1 Cf. Heb. ii. 13, quoting Is. viii. 18.

you back to the place whence ye strayed away, becoming mere flesh and blood by sin[2]. And so He from Whom we were formerly alienated by our revolt has become our Father and our God. Accordingly in the passage cited above the Lord brings the glad tidings of this benefit. And the words are not a proof of the degradation of the Son, but the glad tidings of our reconciliation to God. For that which has taken place in Christ's Humanity is a common boon bestowed on mankind generally. For as when we see in Him the weight of the body, which naturally gravitates to earth, ascending through the air into the heavens, we believe according to the words of the Apostle, that we also "shall be caught up in the clouds to meet the Lord in the air[3]," even so, when we hear that the true God and Father has become the God and Father of our First-fruits, we no longer doubt that the same God has become our God and Father too, inasmuch as we have learnt that we shall come to the same place whither Christ has entered for us as our forerunner[4]. And the fact too that this grace was revealed by means of a woman, itself agrees with the interpretation which we have given. For since, as the Apostle tells us, "the woman, being deceived, was in the transgression[5]," and was by her disobedience foremost in the revolt from God, for this cause she is the first witness of the resurrection, that she might retrieve by her faith in the resurrection the overthrow caused by her disobedience, and that as, by making herself at the beginning a minister and advocate to her husband of the counsels of the serpent, she brought into human life the beginning of evil, and its train of consequences, so, by ministering[6] to His disciples the words of Him Who slew the rebel dragon, she might become to men the guide to faith, whereby with good reason the first proclamation of death is annulled. It is likely, indeed, that by more diligent students a more profitable explanation of the text may be discovered. But even though none such should be found, I think that every devout reader will agree that the one advanced by our opponents is futile, after comparing it with that which we have brought forward. For the one has been fabricated to destroy the glory of the Only-begotten, and nothing more: but the other includes in its scope the aim of the dispensation concerning man. For it has been shown that it was not the intangible, immutable, and invisible God, but the moving, visible, and tangible nature which is proper to humanity, that gave command to Mary to minister the word to His disciples.

§ 2. *Then referring to the blasphemy of Eunomius, which had been refuted by the great Basil, where he banished the Only-begotten God to the realm of darkness, and the apology or explanation which Eunomius puts forth for his blasphemy, he shows that his present blasphemy is rendered by his apology worse than his previous one; and herein he very ably discourses of the "true" and the "unapproachable" Light.*

Let us also investigate this point as well,— what defence he has to offer on those matters on which he was convicted of error by the great Basil, when he banishes the Only-begotten God to the realm of darkness, saying, "As great as is the difference between the generate and the ungenerate, so great is the divergence between Light and Light." For as he has already shown that the difference between the generate and the ungenerate is not merely one of greater or less intensity, but that they are diametrically opposed as regards their meaning; and since he has inferred by logical consequence from his premises that, as the difference between the light of the Father and that of the Son corresponds to ungeneracy and generation, we must necessarily suppose in the Son not a diminution of light, but a complete alienation from light. For as we cannot say that generation is a modified ungeneracy, but the signification of the terms γέννησις and ἀγεννησία are absolutely contradictory and mutually exclusive, so, if the same distinction is to be preserved between the Light of the Father and that conceived as existing in the Son, it will be logically concluded that the Son is not henceforth to be conceived as Light, as he is excluded alike from ungeneracy itself, and from the light which accompanies that condition,—and He Who is something different from light will evidently, by consequence, have affinity with its contrary,— since this absurdity, I say, results from his principles, Eunomius endeavours to explain it away by dialectic artifices, delivering himself as follows: "For we know, we know the true Light, we know Him who created the light after the heavens and the earth, we have heard the Life and Truth Himself, even Christ, saying to His disciples, 'Ye are the light of the world[7],' we have learned from the blessed Paul, when he gives the title of 'Light unapproachable[8]' to

[2] Cf. Heb. ii. 14.　　　　　[3] 1 Thess. iv. 16.
[4] Cf. Heb. vi. 20.　　　　　[5] 1 Tim. ii. 14.
[6] Reading διακονήσασα for the διακομίσασα of the Paris ed. and διακομήσασα of Oehler's text, the latter of which is obviously a misprint, but leaves us uncertain as to the reading which Oehler intended to adopt. The reading διακονήσασα answers to the διάκονος γενομένη above, and is to some extent confirmed by διακονήσαι occurring again a few lines further on. S. Gregory, when he has once used an unusual word or expression, very frequently repeats it in the next few sentences.

[7] S. Matt. v. 14.
[8] Cf. 1 Tim. vi. 16. **The** quotation, as S. Gregory points out, is inexact.

the God over all, and by the addition defines and teaches us the transcendent superiority of His Light; and now that we have learnt that there is so great a difference between the one Light and the other, we shall not patiently endure so much as the mere mention of the notion that the conception of light in either case is one and the same." Can he be serious when he advances such arguments in his attempts against the truth, or is he experimenting upon the dulness of those who follow his error to see whether they can detect so childish and transparent a fallacy, or have no sense to discern such a barefaced imposition? For I suppose that no one is so senseless as not to perceive the juggling with equivocal terms by which Eunomius deludes both himself and his admirers. The disciples, he says, were termed light, and that which was produced in the course of creation is also called light. But who does not know that in these only the name is common, and the thing meant in each case is quite different? For the light of the sun gives discernment to the sight, but the word of the disciples implants in men's souls the illumination of the truth. If, then, he is aware of this difference even in the case of that light, so that he thinks the light of the body is one thing, and the light of the soul another, we need no longer discuss the point with him, since his defence itself condemns him if we hold our peace. But if in that light he cannot discover such a difference as regards the mode of operation, (for it is not, he may say, the light of the eyes that illumines the flesh, and the spiritual light which illumines the soul, but the operation and the potency of the one light and of the other is the same, operating in the same sphere and on the same objects,) then how is it that from the difference between the light of the beams of the sun and that of the words of the Apostles, he infers a like difference between the Only-begotten Light and the Light of the Father? "But the Son," he says, "is called the 'true' Light, the Father 'Light unapproachable.'" Well, these additional distinctions import a difference in degree only, and not in kind, between the light of the Son and the light of the Father. He thinks that the "true" is one thing, and the "unapproachable" another. I suppose there is no one so idiotic as not to see the real identity of meaning in the two terms. For the "true" and the "unapproachable" are each of them removed in an equally absolute degree from their contraries. For as the "true" does not admit any intermixture of the false, even so the "unapproachable" does not admit the access of its contrary. For the "unapproachable" is surely unapproachable by evil. But the light of the Son is not evil; for how can any one

see in evil that which is true? Since, then, the truth is not evil, no one can say that the light which is in the Father is unapproachable by the truth. For if it were to reject the truth it would of course be associated with falsehood. For the nature of contradictories is such that the absence of the better involves the presence of its opposite. If, then, any one were to say that the Light of the Father was contemplated as remote from the presentation of its opposite, he would interpret the term "unapproachable" in a manner agreeable to the intention of the Apostle. But if he were to say that "unapproachable" signified alienation from good, he would suppose nothing else than that God was alien from, and at enmity with, Himself, being at the same time good and opposed to good. But this is impossible: for the good is akin to good. Accordingly the one Light is not divergent from the other. For the Son is the true Light, and the Father is Light unapproachable. In fact I would make bold to say that the man who should interchange the two attributes would not be wrong. For the true is unapproachable by the false, and on the other side, the unapproachable is found to be in unsullied truth. Accordingly the unapproachable is identical with the true, because that which is signified by each expression is equally inaccessible to evil. What is the difference then, that is imagined to exist in these by him who imposes on himself and his followers by the equivocal use of the term "Light"? But let us not pass over this point either without notice, that it is only after garbling the Apostle's words to suit his own fancy that he cites the phrase as if it came from him. For Paul says, "*dwelling in* light unapproachable [9]." But there is a great difference between *being* oneself something and *being in* something. For he who said, "dwelling in light unapproachable," did not, by the word "dwelling," indicate God Himself, but that which surrounds Him, which in our view is equivalent to the Gospel phrase which tells us that the Father is in the Son. For the Son is true Light, and the truth is unapproachable by falsehood; so then the Son is Light unapproachable in which the Father dwells, or in Whom the Father is.

§ 3. *He further proceeds notably to interpret the language of the Gospel, " In the beginning was the Word," and " Life" and " Light," and " The Word was made flesh," which had been misinterpreted by Eunomius ; and overthrows his blasphemy, and shows that the dispensation of the Lord took place by lovingkindness, not by lack of power, and with the co-operation of the Father.*

---

9 1 Tim. vi. 16.

But he puts his strength into his idle contention and says, "From the facts themselves, and from the oracles that are believed, I present the proof of my statement." Such is his promise, but whether the arguments he advances bear out his professions, the discerning reader will of course consider. "The blessed John," he says, "after saying that the Word was in the beginning, and after calling Him Life, and subsequently giving the Life the further title of 'Light,' says, a little later, 'And the Word was made flesh [1].' If then the Light is Life, and the Word was made flesh, it thence becomes plain that the Light was incarnate." What then? because the Light and the Life, and God and the Word, was manifested in flesh, does it follow that the true Light is divergent in any degree from the Light which is in the Father? Nay, it is attested by the Gospel that, even when it had place in darkness, the light remained unapproachable by the contrary element: for "the Light," he says, "shined in darkness, and the darkness comprehended it not [2]." If then the light when it found place in darkness had been changed to its contrary, and overpowered by gloom, this would have been a strong argument in support of the view of those who wish to show how far inferior is this Light in comparison with that contemplated in the Father. But if the Word, even though it be in the flesh, remains the Word, and if the Light, even though it shines in darkness, is no less Light, without admitting the fellowship of its contrary, and if the Life, even though it be in death, remains secure in Itself, and if God, even though He submit to take upon Him the form of a servant, does not Himself become a servant, but takes away the slavish subordination and absorbs it into lordship and royalty, making that which was human and lowly to become both Lord and Christ,— if all this be so, how does he show by this argument variation of the Light to inferiority, when each Light has in equal measure the property of being inconvertible to evil, and unalterable? And how is it that he also fails to observe this, that he who looked on the incarnate Word, Who was both Light and Life and God, recognized, through the glory which he saw, the Father of glory, and says, "We beheld His glory, the glory as of the Only-begotten of the 'Father [3]"?

But he has reached the irrefutable argument which we long ago detected lurking in the sequel of his statements [4], but which is here proclaimed aloud without disguise. For he wishes to show that the essence of the Son is subject to passion, and to decay, and in no wise differs from material nature, which is in a state of flux, that by this means he may demonstrate His difference from the Father. For he says, "If he can show that the God Who is over all, Who is the Light unapproachable, was incarnate or could be incarnate, came under authority, obeyed commands, came under the laws of men, bore the Cross, let him say that the Light is equal to the Light." If these words had been brought forward by us as following by necessary consequence from premises laid down by Eunomius, who would not have charged us with unfairness, in employing an over-subtle dialectic to reduce our adversaries' statement to such an absurdity? But as things stand, the fact that they themselves make no attempt to suppress the absurdity that naturally follows from their assumption, helps to support our contention that it was not without due reflection that, with the help of truth, we censured the argument of heresy. For behold, how undisguised and outspoken is their striving against the Only-begotten God! Nay, by His enemies His work of mercy is reckoned a means of disparaging and maligning the Nature of the Son of God, as though not of deliberate purpose, but by a compulsion of His Nature he had slipped down to life in the flesh, and to the suffering of the Cross! And as it is the nature of a stone to fall downward, and of fire to rise upward, and as these material objects do not exchange their natures one with another, so that the stone should have an upward tendency, and fire be depressed by its weight and sink downwards, even so they make out that passion was part of the very Nature of the Son, and that for this cause He came to that which was akin and familiar to Him, but that the Nature of the Father, being free from such passions, remained unapproachable by the contact of evil. For he says, that the God Who is over all, Who is Light unapproachable, neither was incarnate nor could be incarnate. The first of the two statements was quite enough, that the Father did not become incarnate. But now by his addition a double absurdity arises; for he either charges the Son with evil, or the Father with powerlessness. For if to partake of our flesh is evil, then he predicates evil of the Only-begotten God; but if the lovingkindness to man was good, then he makes out the Father to be powerless for good, by saying that it would not have been in His power to have effectually bestowed

---

[1] Cf. S. John i. 4 and 14.
[2] S. John i. 5 (A. V., following the Vulgate). The word κατέλαβε is perhaps better rendered by "overtook." "As applied to light this sense includes the further notion of overwhelming, eclipsing. The relation of darkness to light is one of essential antagonism. If the darkness is represented as pursuing the light, it can only be to overshadow and not to appropriate it." (Westcott on S. John ad loc.)
[3] S. John i. 14.

[4] The passage has already been cited by S. Gregory, Book V § 3 (p. 176 sup.).

such grace by taking flesh. And yet who in the world does not know that life-giving power proceeds to actual operation both in the Father and in the Son? "For as the Father raiseth up the dead and quickeneth them," He says, "even so the Son quickeneth whom He will [5]," —meaning obviously by "dead" us who had fallen from the true life. If then it is even so as the Father quickeneth, and not otherwise, that the Son brings to operation the same grace, how comes it that the adversary of God moves his profane tongue against both, insulting the Father by attributing to Him powerlessness for good, and the Son by attributing to Him association with evil. But "Light," he says, "is not equal to Light," because the one he calls "true," and the other "unapproachable." Is then the true considered to be a diminution of the unapproachable? Why so? and yet their argument is that the Godhead of the Father must be conceived to be greater and more exalted than that of the Son, because the one is called in the Gospel "true God [6]," the other "God [7]" without the addition of "true." How then does the same term, as applied to the Godhead, indicate an enhancement of the conception, and, as applied to Light, a diminution? For if they say that the Father is greater than the Son because He is true God, by the same showing the Son would be acknowledged to be greater than the Father, because the former is called "true Light [8]," and the latter not so. "But this Light," says Eunomius, "carried into effect the plan of mercy, while the other remained inoperative with respect to that gracious action." A new and strange mode of determining priority in dignity! They judge that which is ineffective for a benevolent purpose to be superior to that which is operative. But such a notion as this neither exists nor ever will be found amongst Christians,—a notion by which it is made out that every good that is in existent things has not its origin from the Father. But of goods that pertain to us men, the crowning blessing is held by all right-minded men to be the return to life; and it is secured by the dispensation carried out by the Lord in His human nature; not that the Father remained aloof, as heresy will have it, ineffective and inoperative during the time of this dispensation. For it is not this that He indicates Who said, "He that sent Me is with Me [9]," and "The Father that dwelleth in Me, He doeth the works [1]." With what right then does heresy attribute to the Son alone the gracious intervention on our behalf, and thereby exclude the Father from having any part or lot in our gratitude for its

successful issue? For naturally the requital of thanks is due to our benefactors alone, and He Who is incapable of benefiting us is outside the pale of our gratitude. See you how the course of their profane attack upon the Only-begotten Son has missed its mark, and is working round in natural consequence so as to be directed against the majesty of the Father? And this seems to me to be a necessary result of their method of proceeding. For if he that honoureth the Son honoureth the Father [2], according to the Divine declaration, it is plain on the other side that an assault upon the Son strikes at the Father. But I say that to those who with simplicity of heart receive the preaching of the Cross and the resurrection, the same grace should be a cause of equal thankfulness to the Son and to the Father, and now that the Son has accomplished the Father's will (and this, in the language of the Apostle, is "that all men should be saved [3]"), they ought for this boon to honour the Father and the Son alike, inasmuch as our salvation would not have been wrought, had not the good will of the Father proceeded to actual operation for us through His own power. And we have learnt from the Scripture that the Son is the power of the Father [4].

§ 4. *He then again charges Eunomius with having learnt his term* ἀγεννησία *from the hieroglyphic writings, and from the Egyptian mythology and idolatry, and with bringing in Anubis, Osiris, and Isis to the creed of Christians, and shows that, considered as admitting His sufferings of necessity and not voluntarily, the Only-begotten is entitled to no gratitude from men: and that fire has none for its warmth, nor water for its fluidity, as they do not refer their results to self-determining power, but to necessity of nature [5].*

Let us once more notice the passage cited. "If he can show," he says, "that the God Who is over all, Who is the Light unapproachable, was incarnate, or could be incarnate, ... then let him say that the Light is equal to the Light." The purport of his words is plain from the very form of the sentence, namely, that he does not think that it was by His almighty Godhead that the Son proved strong for such a form of lovingkindness, but that it was by being of a nature subject to passion that He stooped to the suffering of the Cross. Well, as I pondered and inquired how Eunomius came to stumble into such notions about the Deity, as to think that on the one side the ungenerate Light was

---

5 S. John v. 21.   6 S. John xvii. 3.
7 S. John i. 1.   8 S. John i. 9.
9 Cf. S. John v. 37, and xvi. 32.   1 S. John xiv. 10.

2 Cf. S. John v. 23.   3 1 Tim. ii. 4.   4 1 Cor. i. 24.
5 The grammar of this section of the analysis is very much confused.

unapproachable by its contrary, and entirely unimpaired and free from every passion and affection, but that on the other the generate was intermediate in its nature, so as not to preserve the Divine unsullied and pure in impassibility, but to have an essence mixed and compounded of contraries, which at once stretched out to partake of good, and at the same time melted away into a condition subject to passion, since it was impossible to obtain from Scripture premises to support so absurd a theory, the thought struck me, whether it could be that he was an admirer of the speculations of the Egyptians on the subject of the Divine, and had mixed up their fancies with his views concerning the Only-begotten. For it is reported that they say that their fantastic mode of compounding their idols, when they adapt the forms of certain irrational animals to human limbs, is an enigmatic symbol of that mixed nature which they call "dæmon," and that this is more subtle than that of men, and far surpasses our nature in power, but has the Divine element in it not unmingled or uncompounded, but is combined with the nature of the soul and the perceptions of the body, and is receptive of pleasure and pain, neither of which finds place with the "ungenerate God." For they too use this name, ascribing to the supreme God, as they imagine Him, the attribute of ungeneracy. Thus our sage theologian seems to us to be importing into the Christian creed an Anubis, Isis, or Osiris from the Egyptian shrines, all but the acknowledgment of their names : but there is no difference in profanity between him who openly makes profession of the names of idols, and him who, while holding the belief about them in his heart, is yet chary of their names. If, then, it is impossible to get out of Holy Scripture any support for this impiety, while their theory draws all its strength from the riddles of the hieroglyphics, assuredly there can be no doubt what right-minded persons ought to think of this. But that this accusation which we bring is no insulting slander, Eunomius shall testify for us by his own words, saying as he does that the ungenerate Light is unapproachable, and has not the power of stooping to experience affections, but affirming that such a condition is germane and akin to the generate : so that man need feel no gratitude to the Only-begotten God for what He suffered, if, as they say, it was by the spontaneous action of His nature that He slipped down to the experience of affections, His essence, which was capable of being thus affected, being naturally dragged down thereto, which demands no thanks. For who would welcome as a boon that which takes place by necessity, even if it be gainful and profitable?

For we neither thank fire for its warmth nor water for its fluidity, as we refer these qualities to the necessity of their several natures, because fire cannot be deserted by its power of warming, nor can water remain stationary upon an incline, inasmuch as the slope spontaneously draws its motion onwards. If, then, they say that the benefit wrought by the Son through His incarnation was by a necessity of His nature, they certainly render Him no thanks, inasmuch as they refer what He did, not to an authoritative power, but to a natural compulsion. But if, while they experience the benefit of the gift, they disparage the lovingkindness that brought it, I fear lest their impiety should work round to the opposite error, and lest they should deem the condition of the Son, that could be thus affected, worthy of more honour than the freedom from such affections possessed by the Father, making their own advantage the criterion of good. For if the case had been that the Son was incapable of being thus affected, as they affirm of the Father, our nature would still have remained in its miserable plight, inasmuch as there would have been none to lift up man's nature to incorruption by what He Himself experienced ;—and so it escapes notice that the cunning of these quibblers, by the very means which it employs in its attempt to destroy the majesty of the Only-begotten God, does but raise men's conceptions of Him to a grander and loftier height, seeing it is the case that He Who has the power to act, is more to be honoured than one who is powerless for good.

§ 5. *Then, again discussing the true Light and unapproachable Light of the Father and of the Son, special attributes, community and essence, and showing the relation of "generate" aud "ungenerate," as involving no opposition in sense[6], but presenting an opposition and contradiction admitting of no middle term, he ends the book.*

But I feel that my argument is running away with me, for it does not remain in the regular course, but, like some hot-blooded and spirited colt, is carried away by the blasphemies of our opponents to range over the absurdities of their system. Accordingly we must restrain it when it would run wild beyond the bounds of moderation in demonstration of absurd consequences. But the kindly reader will doubtless pardon what we have said, not imputing the absurdity that emerges from our investigation to us, but to those who laid down such mischievous premises. We must, however, now transfer our attention to another of his statements.

---

6 The composer of the analysis seems to have been slightly confused by the discussion on the nature of contradictory opposition.

For he says that our God also is composite, in that while we suppose the Light to be common, we yet separate the one Light from the other by certain special attributes and various differences. For that is none the less composite which, while united by one common nature, is yet separated by certain differences and conjunctions of peculiarities [7]. To this our answer is short and easily dismissed. For what he brings as matter of accusation against our doctrines we acknowledge against ourselves, if he is not found to establish the same position by his own words. Let us just consider what he has written. He calls the Lord "true" Light, and the Father Light "unapproachable." Accordingly, by thus naming each, he also acknowledges their community in respect to light. But as titles are applied to things because they fit them, as he has often insisted, we do not conceive that the name of "light" is used of the Divine Nature barely, apart from some meaning, but rather that it is predicated by virtue of some underlying reality. Accordingly, by the use of a common name, they recognize the identity of the objects signified, since they have already declared that the natures of those things which have the same name cannot be different. Since, then, the meaning of "Light" is one and the same, the addition of "unapproachable" and "true," according to the language of heresy, separates the common nature by specific differences, so that the Light of the Father is conceived as one thing, and the Light of the Son as another, separated one from the other by special properties. Let him, then, either overthrow his own positions to avoid making out by his statements that the Deity is composite, or let him abstain from charging against us what he may see contained in his own language. For our statement does not hereby violate the simplicity of the Godhead, since community and specific difference are not essence, so that the conjunction of these should render the subject composite [8]. But on the one side the essence by itself remains whatever it is in nature, being what it is, while, on the other, every one possessed of reason would say that these—community and specific difference—were among the accompanying conceptions and attributes: since even in us men there may be discerned some community with the Divine Nature, but Divinity is not the more on that account humanity, or humanity Divinity. For while we believe that God is good, we also find this character predicated of men in Scripture. But the special signification in each case estab-

lishes a distinction in the community arising from the use of the homonymous term. For He Who is the fountain of goodness is named from it; but he who has some share of goodness also partakes in the name, and God is not for this reason composite, that He shares with men the title of "good." From these considerations it must obviously be allowed that the idea of community is one thing, and that of essence another, and we are not on that account any the more to maintain composition or multiplicity of parts in that simple Nature which has nothing to do with quantity, because some of the attributes we contemplate in It are either regarded as special, or have a sort of common significance.

But let us pass on, if it seems good, to another of his statements, and dismiss the nonsense that comes between. He who laboriously reiterates against our argument the Aristotelian division of existent things, has elaborated "genera," and "species," and "differentiæ," and "individuals," and advanced all the technical language of the categories for the injury of our doctrines. Let us pass by all this, and turn our discourse to deal with his heavy and irresistible argument. For having braced his argument with Demosthenic fervour, he has started up to our view as a second Pæanian of Oltiseris [9], imitating that orator's severity in his struggle with us. I will transcribe the language of our author word for word. "Yes," he says, "but if, as the generate is contrary to the ungenerate, the Generate Light be equally inferior to the Ungenerate Light, the one will be found to be [1] light, the other darkness." Let him who has the leisure learn from his words how pungent is his mode of dealing with this opposition, and how exactly it hits the mark. But I would beg this imitator of our words either to say what we have said, or to make his imitation of it as close as may be, or else, if he deals with our argument according to his own education and ability, to speak in his own person and not in ours. For I hope that no one will so miss our meaning as to suppose that, while "generate" is contradictory in sense to "ungenerate," one is a diminution of the other. For the difference between contradictories is not one of greater or less intensity, but rests its opposition upon their being mutually exclusive in their signification: as, for example, we say that a man is asleep or not asleep, sitting or not sitting, that he was or was not, and all the rest after the same model, where the denial of one is the assertion of its

---

[7] It is not clear how far the preceding sentences are an exact reproduction of Eunomius: they are probably a summary of his argument.

[8] Oehler's punctuation seems rather to obscure the sense.

[9] That is, a new Demosthenes, with a difference. Demosthenes' native place was the Attic deme of Pæania. Eunomius, according to S. Gregory, was born at Oltiseris (see p. 38, note 6, *sup.*).

[1] Reading γενήσεται.

contradictory. As, then, to live is not a diminution of not living, but its complete opposite, even so we conceived having been generated not as a diminution of not having been generated, but as an opposite and contradictory not admitting of any middle term, so that that which is expressed by the one has nothing whatever to do with that which is expressed by the other in the way of less or more. Let him therefore who says that one of two contradictories is *defective* as compared with the other, speak in his own person, not in ours. For our homely language says that things which correspond to contradictories differ from one another even as their originals do. So that, even if Eunomius discerns in the Light the same divergence as in the generate compared with the Ungenerate, I will re-assert my statement, that as in the one case the one member of the contradiction has nothing in common with its opposite, so if "light" be placed on the same side as one of the two contradictories, the remaining place in the figure must of course be assigned to "darkness," the necessity of the antithesis arranging the term of light over against its opposite, in accordance with the analogy of the previous contradictory terms "generate" and "ungenerate." Such is the clumsy answer which we, who as our disparaging author says, have attempted to write without logical training, deliver in our rustic dialect to our new Pæanian. But to see how he contended with this contradiction, advancing against us those hot and fire-breathing words of his with Demosthenic intensity, let those who like to have a laugh study the treatise of our orator itself. For our pen is not very hard to rouse to confute the notions of impiety, but is quite unsuited to the task of ridiculing the ignorance of untutored minds.

ΕΠΙΝΟΙΑ

It is important, for the understanding of the following Book, to determine what faculty of the mind 'Επίνοια is. Eunomius, Gregory says, "makes a solemn travesty" of the word. He reduces its force to its lowest level, and makes it only "fancy the unnatural," either contracting or extending the limits of nature, or putting heterogeneous notions together. He instances colossi, pigmies, centaurs, as the result of this mental operation. "Fancy," or "notion," would thus represent Eunomius' view of it. But Gregory ascribes every art and every science to the play of this faculty. "According to my account, it is the method by which we discover things that are unknown, going on to further discoveries, by means of what adjoins and follows from our first *perception* with regard to the thing studied." He instances Ontology (!), Arithmetic, Geometry, on the one hand, Agriculture, Navigation, Horology, on the other, as the result of it. "Any one who should judge this faculty more precious than any other with the exercise of which we are gifted would not be far mistaken." "Induction" might almost represent this view of it. But then Gregory does not deny that "lying wonders are also fabricated by it." By means of it "an entertainer might amuse an audience" with fire-breathing monsters, men enfolded in the coils of serpents, &c. He calls it an inventive faculty. It must therefore be something more spontaneous than ratiocination, whether deductive or inductive; while it is more reliable than Fancy or Imagination.

This is illustrated by what S. John Damascene, in his Dialectica (c. 65), says of 'Επίνοια : "It is of two sorts. The first is the faculty which analyses and elucidates the view of things undissected and in the gross (ὁλοσχερῆ) : whereby a simple phenomenon becomes complex speculatively : for instance, man becomes a compound of soul and body. The second, by a union of perception and fancy, produces fictions out of realities, *i. e.* divides wholes into parts, and combines those parts, selected arbitrarily, into new wholes ; *e. g.* Centaurs, Sirens." Analysis (scientific) would describe the one ; fancy, the other. Basil and Gregory were thinking of the one, Eunomius of the other ; but still both parties used the same expression.

If, then, there is one word that will cover the whole meaning, it would seem to be "Conception." This word at all events, both in its outward form and in its intention, stands to perception in a way strictly analogous to that in which 'Επίνοια stands to *Ἔννοια*. Both Conception and 'Επίνοια represent some *regulated* operation of the mind upon data immediately given. In both cases the mind is led to contemplate in a new light its own contents, whether sensations or innate ideas. The fitness of Conception as an equivalent of 'Επίνοια will be clear when we consider the real point at issue between Basil and Eunomius. Their controversy rages round the term Ungenerate. Is it, or is it not, expressive of the substance (being) of the Deity ? To answer this question, it was found necessary to ascertain how such a name for the Supreme has been acquired. "By a conception," says Basil. "No," says Eunomius : "it would be dangerous to trust the naming of the Deity to a common operation of the mind. The faculty of Conception may and does play us false ; it can create monstrosities. Besides, if the names of the Father are conceptions, the names of the Son are too ; for instance, the Door, the Shepherd, the Axe, the Vine. But as our Lord Himself applied these to Himself, He would, according to you, be employing the faculty of conception ; and it is blasphemous to think that He employed names which we too might have arrived at by conceiving of Him in these particular ways. Therefore, Conception is not the Source of the Divine Names ; but rather they come from a perception or intention implanted in us directly from on High. Ungenerate is such a name ; and it reveals to us the very substance of the Deity." But Gregory defends Basil's position. He shows the entire relativity of our knowledge of the Deity. Ungenerate and every other name of God is due to a conception ; in each case we *perceive* either an operation of the Deity, or an element of evil, and then we *conceive* of Him as operating in the one, or as free from the other ; and so name Him. But there is no conception, because there is no perception, of the substance of the Deity. Scripture, which has revealed His operations, has not revealed that. "The human mind . . . feels after the unutterable Being in divers and many-sided ways ; and never chases the mystery in the light of one idea alone. Our grasping of Him would indeed be easy, if there lay before us one single assigned path to the knowledge of God ; but, as it is, from the skill apparent in the Universe, we get the idea of skill in the Ruler of the Universe ; . . . and again, when we see the execrable character of evil, we grasp His own unalterable pureness as regards this, . . . not that we split up the subject of such attributes along with them, but, believing that this Being, whatever it be in substance, is one, we still conceive that it has something in common with all these ideas."

To sum up, it had suited Eunomius to try to disparage 'Επίνοια so far as to make it appear morally impossible that any name of God, but especially 'Αγέννητος, should be derived from such a source. He scoffs at the orthodox party for treating the privative terms for the Deity as *merely privative*, embodying only a "notion," and for adhering to the truth that God's name is "above every name." He "does not see how God can be above His works simply by virtue of such things as do not belong to Him ;" this is only "giving to words the prerogative over realities." He wants, and believes in the existence of, a word for the *substance* of God, and he finds it in 'Αγέννητος, which according to him is not privative at all ; it is the single name for the single Deity, and all the others are bound up in it. "The universal Guardian thought it right to engraft these names in our minds by a *law of His creation.*" "These utterances are *from above.*" The importance of this word to the Anomœans is obvious. Gregory, as spokesman of the Nicene party, defends the efficacy of the mental operation of conception to supply terms for the Deity, which, however, can *none* of them be final. God *is* incomprehensible. At the same time there is a spiritual insight of God (an *ἔννοια* in fact) which far surpasses Eunomius' intellectual certainty (see note p. 256).

ANSWER TO EUNOMIUS' SECOND BOOK

THE first part of my contentions against Eunomius has with God's help been sufficiently established in the preceding work, as all who will may see from what I have worked out, how in that former part his fallacy has been completely exposed, and its falsehood has no further force against the truth, except in the case of those who show a very shameless animus against her. But since, like some robber's ambuscade, he has got together a second work against orthodoxy, again with God's help the truth takes up arms through me against the array of her enemies, commanding my arguments like a general and directing them at her pleasure against the foe; following whose steps I shall boldly venture on the second part of my contentions, nothing daunted by the array of falsehood, notwithstanding its display of numerous arguments. For faithful is He who has promised that "a thousand shall be chased by one," and that "ten thousand shall be put to flight by two"[2], victory in battle being due not to numbers, but to righteousness. For even as bulky Goliath, when he shook against the Israelites that ponderous spear we read of, inspired no fear in his opponent, though a shepherd and unskilled in the tactics of war, but having met him in fight loses his own head by a direct reversal of his expectations, so our Goliath, the champion of this alien system, stretching forth his blasphemy against his opponents as though his hand were on a naked sword, and flashing the while with sophisms fresh from his whetstone, has failed to inspire us, though no soldiers, with any fear of his prowess, or to find himself free to exult in the dearth of adversaries; on the contrary, he has found us warriors improvised from the Lord's sheepfold, untaught in logical warfare, and thinking it no detriment to be so, but simply slinging our plain, rude argument of truth against him. Since then, that

shepherd who is in the record, when he had cast down the alien with his sling, and broken his helmet with the stone, so that it gaped under the violence of the blow, did not confine his valour to gazing on his fallen foe, but running in upon him, and depriving him of his head, returns bearing it as a trophy to his people, parading that braggart head through the host of his countrymen; looking to this example it becomes us also to advance nothing daunted to the second part of our labours, but as far as possible to imitate David's valour, and, like him, after the first blow to plant our foot upon the fallen foe, so that that enemy of the truth may be exhibited as much as possible as a headless trunk. For separated as he is from the true faith he is far more truly beheaded than that Philistine. For since Christ is the head of every man, as saith the Apostle[3], and it is only reasonable that the believer alone should be so termed (for Christ, I take it, cannot be the head of the unbelieving also), it follows that he who is severed from the saving faith must be headless like Goliath, being severed from the true head by his own sword which he had whetted against the truth; which head it shall be our task not to cut off, but to show that it is cut off.

And let no one suppose that it is through pride or desire of human reputation that I go down to this truceless and implacable warfare to engage with the foe. For if it were allowed me to pass a peaceful life meddling with no one, it would be far enough from my disposition to wantonly disturb my tranquillity, by voluntarily provoking and stirring up a war against myself. But now that God's city, the Church, is besieged, and the great wall of the faith is shaken, battered by the encircling engines of heresy, and there is no small risk of the word of the Lord being swept into captivity through their devilish onslaught, deeming it a dreadful thing to decline taking part in the Christian conflict, I have not turned aside to repose, but have looked on the sweat of toil as more honourable than the relaxation of repose, knowing well that just as every man, as saith the Apostle, shall receive his own reward[4] according to his own

---

[1] This Book is entitled in the Munich and Venice MSS. "an Antirrhetic against Eunomius' second Essay (λόγον)": in the Paris Editions as "Essay XII. (λόγος I B) of our Father among the Saints, Gregory of Nyssa against Eunomius (1615), against Eunomius' second Essay (1638)." The discrepance of number seems to have arisen from the absence of any title to Book VI. in the Munich and Venice MSS. But the Book preceding this, i. e. Book XII., is named as such by the Paris Editt. of 1638: and cited elsewhere as such. Photius, after saying that Gregory far excelled, in these books, Theodore (of Mopsuestia), and Sophronius, who also wrote against Eunomius, particularly praises this last book.

[2] Deut. xxxii. 30; Joshua xxiii. 10.

[3] 1 Cor. xi. 2.   [4] 1 Cor. iii. 14.

labour, so as a matter of course he shall receive punishment for neglect of labour proportioned to his strength. Accordingly I supported the first encounter in the discussion with good courage, discharging from my shepherd's scrip, *i. e.* from the teaching of the Church, my natural and unpremeditated arguments for the subversion of this blasphemy, needing not at all the equipment of arguments from profane sources to qualify me for the contest; and now also I do not hang back from the second part of the encounter, fixing my hope like great David[5] on Him "Who teacheth my hands to war, and my fingers to fight," if haply the hand of the writer may in my case also be guided by Divine power to the overthrow of these heretical opinions, and my fingers may serve for the overthrow of their malignant array by directing my argument with skill and precision against the foe. But as in human conflicts those who excel in valour and might, secured by their armour and having previously acquired military skill by their training for facing danger, station themselves at the head of their column, encountering danger for those ranged behind them, while the rest of the company, though serving only to give an appearance of numbers, seem nevertheless, if only by their serried shields, to conduce to the common good, so in these our conflicts that noble soldier of Christ and vehement champion against the aliens, the mighty spiritual warrior Basil—equipped as he is with the whole armour described by the Apostle, and secured by the shield of faith, and ever holding before him that weapon of defence, the sword of the spirit —fights in the van of the Lord's host by his elaborated argument against this heresy, alive and resisting and prevailing over the foe, while we the common herd, sheltering ourselves beneath the shield of that champion of the faith, shall not hold back from any conflicts within the compass of our power, according as our captain may lead us on against the foe. As he, then, in his refutation of the false and untenable opinion maintained by this heresy, affirms that "ungenerate" cannot be predicated of God except as a mere notion or conception, whereof he has adduced proofs supported by common sense and the evidence of Scripture, while Eunomius, the author of the heresy, neither falls in with his statements nor is able to overturn them, but in his conflict with the truth, the more clearly the light of true doctrine shines forth, the more, like nocturnal creatures, does he shun the light, and, no longer able to find the sophistical hiding-places to which he is accustomed, he wanders about at random, and getting into the labyrinth of

falsehood goes round and round in the same place, almost the whole of his second treatise being taken up with this empty trifling—it is well accordingly that our battle with those opposed to us should take place on the same ground whereon our champion by his own treatise has been our leader.

First of all, however, I think it advisable to run briefly over our own doctrinal views and our opponent's disagreement with them, so that our review of the propositions in question may proceed methodically. Now the main point of Christian orthodoxy[6] is to believe that the Only-begotten God, Who is the truth and the true light, and the power of God and the life, is truly all that He is said to be, both in other respects and especially in this, that He is God and the truth, that is to say, God in truth, ever being what He is conceived to be and what He is called, Who never at any time was not, nor ever will cease to be, Whose being, such as it is essentially, is beyond the reach of the curiosity that would try to comprehend it. But to us, as saith the word of Wisdom,[7] He makes Himself known that He is "by the greatness and beauty of His creatures proportionately" to the things that are known, vouchsafing to us the gift of faith by the operations of His hands, but not the comprehension of what He is. Whereas, then, such is the opinion prevailing among all Christians, (such at least as are truly worthy of the appellation, those, I mean, who have been taught by the law to worship nothing that is not very God, and by that very act of worship confess that the Only-begotten is God in truth, and not a God falsely so called,) there arose this deadly blight of the Church, bringing barrenness on the holy seeds of the faith, advocating as it does the errors of Judaism, and partaking to a certain extent in the impiety of the Greeks. For in its figment of a created God it advocates the error of the Greeks, and in not accepting the Son it supports that of the Jews. This school, then, which would do away with the very Godhead of the Lord and teach men to conceive of Him as a created being, and not that which the Father is in essence and power and dignity, since these misty ideas find no support when exposed on all sides to the light of truth, have overlooked all those names supplied by Scripture for the glorification of God, and predicated in like manner of the Father and of the Son,

---

5 Psalm cxliv. 1.

6 εὐσεβείας. That this is the predominant idea in the word will be seen from the following definitions: "Piety is a devout life joined with *a right faith*" (Œcumenius on 1 Tim. iv. p. 754). "Piety is the looking up to the one only God, Who is believed to be and is the *true* God, and the life in accordance with this" (Eusebius, P. E. i. p. 3). "Piety is the *science* of adoration" (Suidas).

7 Wisdom of Solomon xiii. 5. "For by the greatness and beauty of the creatures proportionately (ἀναλόγως) the maker of them is seen." Compare Romans i. 20.

and have betaken themselves to the word "un-generate," a term fabricated by themselves to throw contempt on the greatness of the Only-begotten God. For whereas an orthodox con-fession teaches us to believe in the Only-be-gotten God so that all men should honour the Son even as they honour the Father, these men, rejecting the orthodox terms whereby the great-ness of the Son is signified as on a par with the dignity of the Father, draw from thence the beginnings and foundations of their heresy in regard to His Divinity. For as the Only-be-gotten God, as the voice of the Gospel teaches, came forth from the Father and is of Him, misrepresenting this doctrine by a change of terms, they make use of them to rend the true faith in pieces. For whereas the truth teaches that the Father is from no pre-existing cause, these men have given to such a view the name of "ungeneracy," and signify the sub-stance of the Only-begotten from the Father by the term "generation,"—then comparing the two terms "ungenerate" and "generate" as contradictories to each other, they make use of the opposition to mislead their senseless followers. For, to make the matter clearer by an illustration, the expressions, He was gener-ated and He was not generated, are much the same as, He is seated and He is not seated, and all such-like expressions. But they, forcing these expressions away from the natural signi-ficance of the terms, are eager to put another meaning upon them with a view to the sub-version of orthodoxy. For whereas, as has been said, the words "is seated" and "is not seated" are not equivalent in meaning (the one expression being contradictory of the other), they pretend that this formal contradiction in expression indicates an essential difference, ascribing generation to the Son and non-gener-ation to the Father as their essential attributes. Yet, as it is impossible to regard a man's sitting down or not as the essence of the man (for one would not use the same definition for a man's sitting as for the man himself), so, by the analogy of the above example, the non-generated essence is in its inherent idea some-thing wholly different from the thing expressed by "not having been generated." But our opponents, with an eye to their evil object, that of establishing their denial of the Godhead of the Only-begotten, do not say that the essence of the Father is ungenerate, but, conversely, they declare ungeneracy to be His essence, in order that by this distinction in regard to generation they may establish, by the verbal opposition, a diversity of natures. In the direction of impiety they look with ten thousand eyes, but with regard to the impracticability of their own contention they are as incapable of

vision as men who deliberately close their eyes. For who but one whose mental optics are utterly purblind can fail to discern the loose and unsubstantial character of the principle of their doctrine, and that their argument in support of ungeneracy as an essence has no-thing to stand upon? For this is the way in which their error would establish itself.

But to the best of my ability I will raise my voice to rebut our enemies' argument. They say that God is declared to be without gener-ation, that the Godhead is by nature simple, and that that which is simple admits of no composition. If, then, God Who is declared to be without generation is by His nature with-out composition, His title of Ungenerate must belong to His very nature, and that nature is identical with ungeneracy. To whom we reply that the terms incomposite and ungenerate are not the same thing, for the former represents the simplicity of the subject, the other its being without origin, and these expressions are not convertible in meaning, though both are pre-dicated of one subject. But from the appel-lation of Ungenerate we have been taught that He Who is so named is without origin, and from the appellation of simple that He is free from all admixture (or composition), and these terms cannot be substituted for each other. There is therefore no necessity that, because the Godhead is by its nature simple, that nature should be termed ungeneracy; but in that He is indivisible and without composition, He is spoken of as simple, while in that He was not generated, He is spoken of as ungenerate.

Now if the term ungenerate did not signify the being without origin, but the idea of sim-plicity entered into the meaning of such a term, and He were called ungenerate in their heretical sense, merely because He is simple and in-composite, and if the terms simple and un-generate are the same in meaning, then too must the simplicity of the Son be equivalent with ungeneracy. For they will not deny that God the Only-begotten is by His nature simple, unless they are prepared to deny that He is God. Accordingly the term simplicity will in its meaning have no such connection with being ungenerate as that, by reason of its in-composite character, His nature should be termed ungeneracy; or they draw upon them-selves one of two absurd alternatives, either denying the Godhead of the Only-begotten, or attributing ungeneracy to Him also. For if God is simple, and the term simplicity is, according to them, identical with ungenerate, they must either make out the Son to be of composite nature, by which term it is implied that neither is He God, or if they allow His Godhead, and God (as I have said) is simple, then they make Him out at the same time to be ungenerate, if the terms simple and ungenerate are convertible. But to make my meaning clearer I will recapitulate. We affirm that each of these terms has its own peculiar meaning, and that the term indivisible cannot be rendered by ungenerate, nor ungenerate by simple; but by simple we understand uncompounded, and by ungenerate we are taught to understand what is without origin. Furthermore we hold that we are bound to believe that the Son of God, being Himself God, is Himself also simple, because God is free from all compositeness; and in like manner in speaking of Him also by the appellation of Son we neither denote simplicity of substance, nor in simplicity do we include the notion of Son, but the term Son we hold to indicate that He is of the substance of the Father, and the term simple we hold to mean what the word bears upon its face. Since, then, the meaning of the term simple in regard to essence is one and the same whether spoken of the Father or of the Son, differing in no degree, while there is a wide difference between generate and ungenerate (the one containing a notion not contained in the other), for this reason we assert that there is no necessity that, the Father being ungenerate, His essence should, because that essence is simple, be defined by the term ungenerate. For neither of the Son, Who is simple, and Whom also we believe to be generated, do we say that His essence is simplicity. But as the essence is simple and not simplicity, so also the essence is ungenerate and not ungeneracy. In like manner also the Son being generated, our reason is freed from any necessity that, because His essence is simple, we should define that essence as generateness; but here again each expression has its peculiar force. For the term generated suggests to you a source whence, and the term simple implies freedom from composition. But this does not approve itself to them. For they maintain that since the essence of the Father is simple, it cannot be considered as other than ungeneracy; on which account also He is said to be ungenerate. In answer to whom we may also observe that, since they call the Father both Creator and Maker, whereas He Who is so called is simple in regard to His essence, it is high time for such sophists to declare the essence of the Father to be creation and making, since the argument about simplicity introduces into His essence any signification of any name we give Him. Either, then, let them separate ungeneracy from the definition of the Divine essence, allowing the term no more than its proper signification, or, if by reason of the simplicity of the subject they define His essence by the term ungeneracy, by

a parity of reasoning let them likewise see creation and making in the essence of the Father, not as though the power residing in the essence created and made, but as though the power itself meant creation and making. But if they reject this as bad and absurd, let them be persuaded by what logically follows to reject the other proposition as well. For as the essence of the builder is not the thing built, no more is ungeneracy the essence of the Ungenerate. But for the sake of clearness and conciseness I will restate my arguments. If the Father is called ungenerate, not by reason of His having never been generated, but because His essence is simple and incomposite, by a parity of reasoning the Son also must be called ungenerate, for He too is a simple and incomposite essence. But if we are compelled to confess the Son to be generated because He *was* generated, it is manifest that we must address the Father as ungenerate, because He was *not* generated. But if we are compelled to this conclusion by truth and the force of our premises, it is clear that the term ungenerate is no part of the essence, but is indicative of a difference of conceptions, distinguishing that which is generated from that which is ungenerate. But let us discuss this point also in addition to what I have said. If they affirm that the term ungenerate signifies the essence [8] (of the Father), and not that He has His substance without origin, what term will they use to denote the Father's being without origin, when they have set aside the term ungenerate to indicate His essence? For if we are not taught the distinguishing difference of the Persons by the term ungenerate, but are to regard it as indicating His very nature as flowing in a manner from the subject-matter, and disclosing what we seek in articulate syllables, it must follow that God is not, or is not to be called, ungenerate, there being no word left to express such peculiar significance in regard to

---

[8] Essence, substance, οὐσία. Most of this controversy might have been avoided by agreeing to banish the word οὐσία entirely from this sort of connection with the Deity. Even Celsus the Neoplatonist had said, "God does not partake of substance" (οὐσίας). "Exactly," Origen replies, "God is partaken of, viz., by those who have His spirit, rather than partakes of anything Himself. Indeed, the subject of substance involves questions complicated and difficult to decide; most especially on this point. Supposing, that is, an absolute Substance, motionless, incorporeal, is God beyond this Substance in rank and power, granting a share of it to those to whom according to His Word He chooses to communicate it? Or is He Himself this Substance, though described as invisible in that passage about the Saviour (Coloss. i. 15) 'Who is the image of the invisible God,' where invisible means incorporeal? Another point is this: is the Only-Begotten and First-Born of all Creatures to be pronounced the Substance of substances, the Original Idea of all ideas, while the Father God Himself is beyond all these?" (c. Cels. vi. 64). (Such a question as this last, however, could not have been asked a century later, when Athanasius had dispelled all traces of Neo-platonic subordination from the Christian Faith. Uncreated Spirit, not Invisible First Substance, is the mark of all in the Triune-God. But the effort of Neo-platonism to rise above every term that might seem to *include* the Deity had not been thrown away. Even "God is Spirit" is only a *conception*, not a definition, of the Deity; while "God is substance" ought to be regarded as an actual contradiction in terms.)

Him. For inasmuch as according to them the term ungenerate does not mean without origin, but indicates the Divine nature, their argument will be found to exclude it altogether, and the term ungenerate slips out of their teaching in respect of God. For there being no other word or term to represent that the Father is ungenerate, and that term signifying, according to their fallacious argument, something else, and not that He was not generated, their whole argument falls and collapses into Sabellianism. For by this reasoning we must hold the Father to be identical with the Son, the distinction between generated and ungenerate having been got rid of from their teaching, so that they are driven to one of two alternatives : either they must again adopt the view of the term as denoting a difference in the attributes proper to either Person, and not as denoting the nature, or, abiding by their conclusions as to the word, they must side with Sabellius. For it is impossible that the difference of the persons should be without confusion, unless there be a distinction between generated and ungenerate. Accordingly if the term denotes difference, essence will in no way be denoted by the appellation. For the definitions of difference and essence are by no means the same. But if they divert the meaning of the word so as to signify nature, they must be drawn into the heresy of those who are called "Son-Fathers 9," all accuracy of definition in regard to the Persons being rejected from their account. But if they say that there is nothing to hinder the distinction between generated and ungenerate from being rendered by the term ungenerate, and that that term represents the essence too, let them distinguish for us the kindred meanings of the word, so that the notion of ungenerate may properly apply to either of them taken by itself. For the expression of the difference by means of this term involves no ambiguity, consisting as it does of a verbal opposition. For as an equivalent to saying "The Son has, and the Father has not, been generated,"we too assent to the statement that the latter is ungenerate and the former generated, by a sort of verbal correlation. But from what point of view a clear manifestation of essence can be made by this appellation, this they are unable to say. But keeping silence on this head, our novel theologian weaves us a web of trifling subtleties in his former treatise. Because God, saith he, being simple, is called ungenerate, therefore God is ungeneracy. What has the notion of simplicity to do with the idea of ungenerate?

9 i. e. who hold the Father and the Son to be one and the same Person, i. e. Sabellians. " He here overthrows the heresy of Sabellius, by marking the persons of the Father and the Son : for the Church does not imagine a Son-Fatherhood (υἱοπατορίαν), such as the figment of that African" (Ammonius caten. ad Joh. I. i. p. 14).

For not only is the Only-begotten generated, but, without controversy, He is simple also. But, saith he, He is without parts also, and incomposite. But what is this to the point? For neither is the Son multiform and composite : and yet He is not on that account ungenerate.

But, saith he, He is without both quantity and magnitude. Granted : for the Son also is unlimited by quantity and magnitude, and yet is He the Son. But this is not the point. For the task set before us is this : in what signification of ungenerate is essence declared? For as this word marks the difference of the properties, so they maintain that the essence also is indicated without ambiguity by one of the things signified by the appellation.

But this thing he leaves untold, and only says that ungeneracy should not be predicated of God as a mere conception. For what is so spoken, saith he, is dissolved, and passes away with its utterance. But what is there that is uttered but is so dissolved? For we do not keep undissolved, like those who make pots or bricks, what we utter with our voice in the mould of the speech which we form once for all with our lips, but as soon as one speech has been sent forth by our voice, what we have said ceases to exist. For the breath of our voice being dispersed again into the air, no trace of our words is impressed upon the spot in which such dispersion of our voice has taken place : so that if he makes this the distinguishing characteristic of a term that expresses a mere conception, that it does not remain, but vanishes with the voice that gives it utterance, he may as well at once call every term a mere conception, inasmuch as no substance remains in any term subsequent to its utterance. No, nor will he be able to show that ungeneracy itself, which he excepts from the products of conception, is indissoluble and fixed when it has been uttered, for this expression of the voice through the lips does not abide in the air. And from this we may see the unsubstantial character of his assertions; because, even if without speech we describe in writing our mental conceptions, it is not as though the substantial objects of our thoughts will acquire their significance from the letters, while the non-substantial will have no part in what the letters express. For whatever comes into our mind, whether intellectually existing, or otherwise, it is possible for us at our discretion to store away in writing. And the voice and letters are of equal value for the expression of thought, for we communicate what we think by the latter as well as by the former. What he sees, then, to justify his making the mental conception perish with the voice only, I fail to comprehend. For in the case of all speech uttered by means of sound, the passage of the breath indeed which conveys the voice is towards its kindred element, but the sense of the words spoken is engraved by hearing on the memory of the hearer's soul, whether it be true or false. Is not this, then, a weak interpretation of this "conception" of his that our writer offers, when he characterizes and defines it by the dissolution of the voice? And for this reason the understanding hearer, as saith Isaiah, objects to this inconceivable account of mental conception, showing it, to use the man's own words, to be a veritably dissoluble and unsubstantial one, and he discusses scientifically the force inherent in the term, advancing his argument by familiar examples to the contemplation of doctrine. Against whom Eunomius exalting himself with this pompous writing, endeavours to overthrow the true account of mental conception, after this manner.

But before we examine what he has written, it may be better to enquire with what purpose it is that he refuses to admit that ungenerate can be predicated of God by way of conception. Now the tenet which has been held in common by all who have received the word of our religion is, that all hope of salvation should be placed in Christ, it being impossible for any to be found among the righteous, unless faith in Christ supply what is desired. And this conviction being firmly established in the souls of the faithful, and all honour and glory and worship being due to the Only-begotten God as the Author of life, Who doeth the works of the Father, as the Lord Himself saith in the Gospel [1], and Who falls short of no excellence in all knowledge of that which is good, I know not how they have been so perverted by malignity and jealousy of the Lord's honour, that, as though they judged the worship paid by the faithful to the Only-begotten God to be a detriment to themselves, they oppose His Divine honours, and try to persuade us that nothing that is said of them is true. For with them neither is He very God, though called so, it would seem, by Scripture, nor, though called Son, has He a nature that makes good the appellation, nor has He a community of dignity or of nature with the Father. For, say they, it is not possible for Him that is begotten to be of equal honour with Him Who made Him, either in dignity, or in power, or in nature, because the life of the latter is infinite, and His existence from eternity, while the life of the Son is in a manner circumscribed, the beginning of His being begotten limiting His life at the commencement, and preventing it from being coextensive with the eternity of the Father, so

that His life also is to be regarded as defective; and the Father was not always what He now is and is said to be, but, having been something else before, He afterwards determined that He would be a Father, or rather that He would be so called. For not even of the Son was He rightly called Father, but of a creature supposititiously invested with the title of son. And every way, say they, the younger is of necessity inferior to the elder, the finite to the eternal, that which is begotten by the will of the begetter, to the begetter himself, both in power, and dignity, and nature, and precedence due to age, and all other prerogatives of respect. But how can we justly dignify with the honours due to the true God that which is wanting in the perfection of the diviner attributes? Thus they would establish the doctrine that one who is limited in power, and wanting in the perfection of life, and subject to a superior, and doing nothing of himself but what is sanctioned by the authority of the more powerful, is in no divine honour and consideration, but that, while we call him God, we are employing a term empty of all grandeur in its significance. And since such statements as these, when stripped of their plausible dress, move indignation and make the hearer shudder at their strangeness (for who can tolerate an evil counsellor nakedly and unadvisably urging the overthrow of the majesty of Christ?), they therefore try to pervert foolish hearers with these foreign notions by enveloping their malignant and insidious arguments in a number of seductive fallacies. For after laying down such premises as might naturally lead the mind of the hearers in the desired direction, they leave the hearer to draw his conclusion for himself.

For after saying that the Only-begotten God is not the same in essence with the true Father, and after sophistically inferring this from the opposition between generate and ungenerate, they work in silence to the conclusion, their impiety prevailing by the natural course of inference. And as the poisoner makes his drug acceptable to his victim by sweetening its deadliness with honey, and, as for himself, has only to offer it, while the drug insinuating itself into the vitals without further action on the part of the poisoner does its deadly work,—so, too, do our opponents act. For qualifying their pernicious teaching with their sophistical refinements, as with honey, when they have infused into the mind of the hearer the venomous fallacy that God the Only-begotten is not very God, they cause all the rest to be inferred without saying a word. For when they are persuaded that He is not truly God, it follows as a matter of course that no other Divine

---

[1] S John x. 37.

attribute is truly applicable. For if He is truly neither Son nor God, except by an abuse of terms, then the other names which are given to Him in Holy Scripture are a divergence from the truth. For the one thing cannot be predicated of Him with truth, and the other be destitute of it; but they must needs follow one another, so that, if He be truly God, it follows that He is Judge and King, and that His several attributes are such as they are described, while, if His godhead be falsely asserted, neither will the truth hold respecting any of His other attributes. They, then, having been deceived into the persuasion that the attribute of Godhead is falsely applied to the Only-begotten, it follows that He is not rightly the object of worship and adoration, or, in fact, of any of the honours that are paid to God. In order, then, to render their attack upon the Saviour efficacious, this is the blasphemous method that they have adopted. There is no need, they urge, of looking at the collective attributes by which the Son's equality in honour and dignity with the Father is signified, but from the opposition between generate and ungenerate we must argue a distinctive difference of nature; for the Divine nature is that which is denoted by the term ungenerate. Again, since all men of sense regard it as impracticable to indicate the ineffable Being by any force of words, because neither does our knowledge extend to the comprehension of what transcends knowledge, nor does the ministry of words have such power in us as to avail for the full enunciation of our thought, where the mind is engaged on anything eminently lofty and divine,—these wise folk, on the contrary, convicting men in general of want of sense and ignorance of logic, assert their own knowledge of such matters, and their ability to impart it to whomsoever they will; and accordingly they maintain that the divine nature is simply ungeneracy *per se*, and declaring this to be sovereign and supreme, they make this word comprehend the whole greatness of Godhead, so as to necessitate the inference that if ungeneracy is the main point of the essence, and the other divine attributes are bound up with it, viz. Godhead, power, imperishableness and so on—if (I say) ungeneracy mean these, then, if this ungeneracy cannot be predicated of something, neither can the rest. For as reason, and risibility, and capacity of knowledge are proper to man, and what is not humanity may not be classed among the properties of his nature, so, if true Godhead consists in ungeneracy, then, to whatsoever thing the latter name does not properly belong, no one at all of the other distinguishing attributes of Godhead will be found in it. If, then, ungeneracy is not predicable of the Son, it follows

that no other of His sublime and godlike attributes are properly ascribed to Him. This, then, they define as a right comprehension of the divine mysteries—the rejection of the Son's Godhead—all but shouting in the ear of those who would listen to them; "To you it is given to be perfect in knowledge [2], if only you believe not in God the Only-begotten as being very God, and honour not the Son as the Father is honoured, but regard Him as by nature a created being, not Lord and Master, but slave and subject." For this is the aim and object of their design, though the blasphemy is cloaked in different terms.

Accordingly, enveloping his former special-pleading in the mazy evolutions of his sophistries, and dealing subtly with the term ungenerate, he steals away the intelligence of his dupes, saying to them, "Well, then, if neither by way of conception it is so, nor by deprivation, nor by division (for He is without parts), nor as being another in Himself [3] (for He is the one only ungenerate), He Himself must be, in essence, ungenerate.

Seeing, then, the mischief resulting to the dupes of this fallacious reasoning—that to assent to His not being very God is a departure from our confession of Him as our Lord, to which conclusion indeed his words would bring his teaching—our master does not indeed deny that ungenerate is no partial predicate of God, himself also admitting that God is without quantity, or magnitude, or parts; but the statement that this term ought not to be applied to Him by way of mental conception he impugns, and gives his proofs. But again, shifting from this position, our writer in the second of

[2] Eunomius arrived at the same conclusions as Arius, but by a different path. "The true name of God is Ἀγέννητος, and *this* name is incommunicable to other essences." He attacked both the Arians and the orthodox. The former he reproached for saying that we can know God only in part: the latter for saying that we know God only through the Universe, and the Son, the Author of the Universe. He maintained, on the contrary, that it was unworthy of a Christian to profess the impossibility of knowing the Divine Nature, and the manner in which the Son is generated. Rather, the mind of the believer rises above every sensible and intelligible essence, and does not stop even at the generation of the Son, but mounts above, aspiring to possess the First Cause. Is this bold assertion, Denys (*De la Philosophie d'Origène*, p. 446) asks, so contrary as it is to the teaching of the Fathers, a reminiscence of Origen, or a direct borrowing from Plato or the Neoplatonists? The language in which it is expressed certainly belongs to the latter (ὑποκύψας, ἐπέκεινα, πόθος, τὸ πρῶτον, γλιχόμενος): but Origen himself, less wise in this matter than Clement, was not far from believing that there was a Way above Him Whom S. John calls the Way, a Light above the Light that "lighteth every man that cometh into the world," an "Eternal Gospel" above the present Gospel; and that these were not inaccessible at once to human creatures. Only they could not be reached in themselves, and *without a Mediator*, until Christ, having vanquished His enemies, had given back the kingdom to the Father, and God was "all in all."—This doctrine of the Ἀγέννητος, then, made it necessary for Basil and Gregory to throw their whole weight against Eunomius, rather than against Macedonius, who, as inconsequent through not dealing alike with the Second and Third Person, could not be so dangerous an enemy.

[3] *As being another.* Oehler reads ὡς ἕτερον: the Paris editt. have ἐστιν ἕτερον, due to the correction of John the Franciscan, whose MS., however, (the Pithœan) had ὥστε (ὡς τι?). These words of Eunomius are found in Basil lib. i c. Eunomium, tom. i. p. 711 (Paris 1638), even more fully quoted than here: and ὡς ἕτερον is found there.

his treatises meets us with his sophistry, combating his own statements in regard to mental conception.

It will presently be time to bring to their own recollection the method of this argument. Suffice it first to say this. There is no faculty in human nature adequate to the full comprehension of the divine essence. It may be that it is easy to show this in the case of human capacity alone, and to say that the incorporeal creation is incapable of taking in and comprehending that nature which is infinite will not be far short of the truth, as we may see by familiar examples ; for as there are many and various things that have fleshly life, winged things, and things of the earth, some that mount above the clouds by virtue of their wings, others that dwell in hollows or burrow in the ground, on comparing which it would appear that there was no small difference between the inhabitants of air and of land ; while, if the comparison be extended to the stars and the fixed circumference, it will be seen that what soars aloft on wings is not less widely removed from heaven than from the animals that are on the earth ; so, too, the strength of angels compared with our own seems pre-eminently great, because, undisturbed by sensation, it pursues its lofty themes with pure naked intelligence. Yet, if we weigh even their comprehension with the majesty of Him Who really is, it may be that if any one should venture to say that even their power of understanding is not far superior to our own weakness, his conjecture would fall within the limits of probability, for wide and insurmountable is the interval that divides and fences off uncreated from created nature. The latter is limited, the former not. The latter is confined within its own boundaries according to the pleasure of its Maker. The former is bounded only by infinity. The latter stretches itself out within certain degrees of extension, limited by time and space : the former transcends all notion of degree, baffling curiosity from every point of view. In this life we can apprehend the beginning and the end of all things that exist, but the beatitude that is above the creature admits neither end nor beginning, but is above all that is connoted by either, being ever the same, self-dependent, not travelling on by degrees from one point to another in its life ; for there is no participation of other life in its life, such that we might infer end and beginning ; but, be it what it may, it is life energizing in itself, not becoming greater or less by addition or diminution. For increase has no place in the infinite, and that which is by its nature passionless excludes all notion of decrease. And as, when looking up to heaven, and in a measure apprehending by the visual

organs the beauty that is in the height, we doubt not the existence of what we see, but if asked what it is, we are unable to define its nature, but we simply admire as we contemplate the overarching vault, the reverse planetary motion [4], the so-called Zodiac graven obliquely on the pole, whereby astronomers observe the motion of bodies revolving in an opposite direction, the differences of luminaries according to their magnitude, and the specialities of their rays, their risings and settings that take place according to the circling year ever at the same seasons undeviatingly, the conjunctions of planets, the courses of those that pass below, the eclipses of those that are above, the obumbrations of the earth, the reappearance of eclipsed bodies, the moon's multiform changes, the motion of the sun midway within the poles, and how, filled with his own light, and crowned with his encircling beams, and embracing all things in his sovereign light, he himself also at times suffers eclipse (the disc of the moon, as they say, passing before him), and how, by the will of Him Who has so ordained, ever running his own particular course, he accomplishes his appointed orbit and progress, opening out the four seasons of the year in succession ; we, as I say, when we contemplate these phenomena by the aid of sight, are in no doubt of their existence, though we are as far from comprehending their essential nature as if sight had not given us any glimpse whatever of what we have seen ; and even so, with regard to the Creator of the world, we know that He exists, but of His essential nature we cannot deny that we are ignorant. But, boasting as they do that they know these things, let them first tell us about the things of inferior nature ; what they think of the body of the heavens, of the machinery which conveys the stars in their eternal courses, or of the sphere in which they move ; for, however far speculation may proceed, when it comes to the uncertain and incomprehensible it must stop. For though any one say that another body, like in fashion (to that body of the heavens), fitting to its circular shape, checks its velocity, so that, ever turning in its course, it revolves conformably to that other upon itself, being retained by the force that embraces it from flying off at a tangent, yet how can he assert that these bodies will remain unspent by their constant friction with each other? And how, again, is motion produced in the case

---

[4] Gregory here refers to the apparent "retrograde" motion of the planets, i. e. that, while passing through part of their orbits, they appear to us to move in a direction contrary to the order of the Zodiac. In what follows he represents the views of the ancient astronomy, imagining a series of concentric spheres, allotted to the several planets, the planetary motions being accomplished by the rotation of the spheres. Beyond the planetary spheres is the sphere allotted to the fixed stars, within which the others revolve. See Gale, *Opusc. Mythol.* (1688), p 550 ; and Introduction to Colet's *Lectures on Corinthians*, pp. xl—xliii.

of two coeval bodies mutually conformed, when the one remains motionless (for the inner body, one would have thought, being held as in a vice by the motionlessness of that which embraces it, will be quite unable to act); and what is it that maintains the embracing body in its fixedness, so that it remains unshaken and unaffected by the motion of that which fits into it? And if in restless curiosity of thought we should conceive of some position for it that should keep it stationary, we must go on in logical consistency to search for the base of that base, and of the next, and of the next, and so on, and so the inquiry, proceeding from like to like, will go on to infinity, and end in helpless perplexity, still, even when some body has been put for the farthest foundation of the system of the universe, reaching after what is beyond, so that there is no stopping in our inquiry after the limit of the embracing circles. But not so, say others : but (according to the vain theory of those who have speculated on these matters) there is an empty space spread over the back of the heavens, working in which vacuum the motion of the universe revolves upon itself, meeting with no resistance from any solid body capable of retarding it by opposition and of checking its course of revolution. What, then, is that vacuum, which they say is neither a body nor an idea? How far does it extend, and what succeeds it, and what relation exists between the firm, resisting body, and that void and unsubstantial one? What is there to unite things so contrary by nature? and how can the harmony of the universe consist out of elements so incongruous; and what can any one say of Heaven itself? That it is a mixture of the elements which it contains, or one of them, or something else beside them? What, again, of the stars themselves? whence comes their radiance? what is it and how is it composed? and what is the reason of their difference in beauty and magnitude? and the seven inner orbs revolving in an opposite direction to the motion of the universe, what are they, and by what influence are they propelled? Then, too, what is that immaterial and ethereal empyrean, and the intermediate air which forms a wall of partition between that element in nature which gives heat and consumes, and that which is moist and combustible? And how does earth below form the foundation of the whole, and what is it that keeps it firmly in its place? what is it that controls its downward tendency? If any one should interrogate us on these and such-like points, will any of us be found so presumptuous as to promise an explanation of them? No! the only reply that can be given by men of sense is this :—that He Who made all things in wisdom can alone furnish an

account of His creation. For ourselves, "through faith we understand that the worlds were framed by the word of God," as saith the Apostle [5].

If, then, the lower creation which comes under our organs of sense transcends human knowledge, how can He, Who by His mere will made the worlds, be within the range of our apprehension? Surely this is vanity, and lying madness, as saith the Prophet [6], to think it possible to comprehend the things which are incomprehensible. So may we see tiny children busying themselves in their play. For oft-times, when a sunbeam streams down upon them through a window, delighted with its beauty they throw themselves on what they see, and are eager to catch the sunbeam in their hands, and struggle with one another, and grasp the light in the clutch of their fingers, and fancy they have imprisoned the ray in them, but presently when they unclasp their hands and find that the sunbeam which they held has slipped through their fingers, they laugh and clap their hands. In like manner the children of our generation, as saith the parable, sit playing in the market-places; for, seeing the power of God shining in upon their souls through the dispensations of His providence, and the wonders of His creation like a warm ray emanating from the natural sun, they marvel not at the Divine gift, nor adore Him Whom such things reveal, but passing beyond the limits of the soul's capabilities, they seek with their sophistical understanding to grasp that which is intangible, and think by their reasonings to lay hold of what they are persuaded of ; but when their argument unfolds itself and discloses the tangled web of their sophistries, men of discernment see at once that what they have apprehended is nothing at all ; so pettily and so childishly labouring in vain at impossibilities do they set themselves to include the inconceivable nature of God in the few syllables of the term "ungenerate," and applaud their own folly, and imagine God to be such that human reasoning can include Him under one single term : and while they pretend to follow the teaching of the sacred writers, they are not afraid of raising themselves above them. For what cannot be shown to have been said by any of those blessed ones, any words of whose are recorded in the sacred books, these things, as saith the Apostle, "understanding neither what they say, nor whereof they affirm [7]," they nevertheless say they know, and boast of guiding others to such knowledge. And on this account they declare that they have appre-

---

5 Heb. i. 2.   6 The thought is found in Psalm xxxix. 6.
7 1 Tim. i. 7.   S. Gregory quotes from memory, viz., περὶ ὧν διατείνονται for περὶ τίνων διαβεβαιοῦνται.

hended that God the Only-begotten is not what He is called. For to this conclusion they are compelled by their premises.

How pitiable are they for their cleverness! how wretched, how fatal is their over-wise philosophy! Who is there who goes of his own accord to the pit so eagerly as these men labour and bestir themselves to dig out their lake of blasphemy? How far have they separated themselves from the hope of the Christian! What a gulf have they fixed between themselves and the faith which saves! How far have they withdrawn themselves from Abraham the father of the faith! He indeed, if in the lofty spirit of the Apostle we may take the words allegorically, and so penetrate to the inner sense of the history, without losing sight of the truth of its facts—he, I say, went out by Divine command from his own country and kindred on a journey worthy of a prophet eager for the knowledge of God[8]. For no local migration seems to me to satisfy the idea of the blessings which it is signified that he found. For going out from himself and from his country, by which I understand his earthly and carnal mind, and raising his thoughts as far as possible above the common boundaries of nature, and forsaking the soul's kinship with the senses,—so that untroubled by any of the objects of sense his eyes might be open to the things which are invisible, there being neither sight nor sound to distract the mind in its work,—"walking," as saith the Apostle, "by faith, not by sight," he was raised so high by the sublimity of his knowledge that he came to be regarded as the acme of human perfection, knowing as much of God as it was possible for finite human capacity at its full stretch to attain. Therefore also the Lord of all creation, as though He were a discovery of Abraham, is called specially the God of Abraham. Yet what saith the Scripture respecting him? That he went out not knowing whither he went, no, nor even being capable of learning the name of Him whom he loved, yet in no wise impatient or ashamed on account of such ignorance.

This, then, was the meaning of his safe guidance on the way to what he sought—that he was not blindly led by any of the means ready to hand for his instruction in the things of God, and that his mind, unimpeded by any object of sense, was never hindered from its journeying in quest of what lies beyond all that is known, but having gone by reasoning far beyond the wisdom of his countrymen, (I mean the philosophy of the Chaldees, limited as it was to the things which do appear,) and soaring above the things which are cognizable by sense, from

the beauty of the objects of contemplation, and the harmony of the heavenly wonders, he desired to behold the archetype of all beauty. And so, too, all the other things which in the course of his reasoning he was led to apprehend as he advanced, whether the power of God, or His goodness, or His being without beginning, or His infinity, or whatever else is conceivable in respect to the divine nature, using them all as supplies and appliances for his onward journey, ever making one discovery a stepping-stone to another, ever reaching forth unto those things which were before, and setting in his heart, as saith the Prophet, each fair stage of his advance[9], and passing by all knowledge acquired by his own ability as falling short of that of which he was in quest, when he had gone beyond every conjecture respecting the divine nature which is suggested by any name amongst all our conceptions of God, having purged his reason of all such fancies, and arrived at a faith unalloyed and free from all prejudice, he made this a sure and manifest token of the knowledge of God, viz. the belief that He is greater and more sublime than any token by which He may be known. On this account, indeed, after the ecstasy which fell upon him, and after his sublime meditations, falling back on his human weakness, "I am," saith he, "but dust and ashes[10]," that is to say, without voice or power to interpret that good which his mind had conceived. For dust and ashes seem to denote what is lifeless and barren; and so there arises a law of faith for the life to come, teaching those who would come to God, by this history of Abraham, that it is impossible to draw near to God, unless faith mediate, and bring the seeking soul into union with the incomprehensible nature of God. For leaving behind him the curiosity that arises from knowledge, Abraham, says the Apostle, "believed God, and it was counted unto him for righteousness[1]." "Now it was not written for his sake," the Apostle says, "but for us," that God counts to men for righteousness their faith, not their knowledge. For knowledge acts, as it were, in a commercial spirit, dealing only with what is known. But the faith of Christians acts otherwise. For it is the substance, not of things known, but of things hoped for. Now that which we have already we no longer hope for. "For what a man hath," says the Apostle, "why doth he yet hope for[2]"? But faith makes our own that which we see not, assuring us by its own certainty of that which does not appear. For so speaks the Apostle of the believer, that "he endured as seeing Him Who is invisible[3]."

---

8 Heb. xi. 8.

9 Psalm lxxxiv. 5, "in whose heart are thy ways;" but LXX. ἀναβάσεις ἐν τῇ καρδίᾳ αὐτοῦ διέθετο. 10 Gen. xviii. 27. 1 Gen. xv. 6; Rom. iv. 22. 2 Rom. viii. 24. 3 Heb. xi. 27.

Vain, therefore, is he who maintains that it is possible to take knowledge of the divine essence, by the knowledge which puffeth up to no purpose. For neither is there any man so great that he can claim equality in understanding with the Lord, for, as saith David, "Who is he among the clouds that shall be compared unto the Lord?[4]" nor is that which is sought so small that it can be compassed by the reasonings of human shallowness. Listen to the preacher exhorting not to be hasty to utter anything before God, "for God," (saith he,) "is in heaven above, and thou upon earth beneath[5]."

He shows, I think, by the relation of these elements to each other, or rather by their distance, how far the divine nature is above the speculations of human reason. For that nature which transcends all intelligence is as high above earthly calculation as the stars are above the touch of our fingers; or rather, many times more than that.

Knowing, then, how widely the Divine nature differs from our own, let us quietly remain within our proper limits. For it is both safer and more reverent to believe the majesty of God to be greater than we can understand, than, after circumscribing His glory by our misconceptions, to suppose there is nothing beyond our conception of it.

And on other accounts also it may be called safe to let alone the Divine essence, as unspeakable, and beyond the scope of human reasoning. For the desire of investigating what is obscure and tracing out hidden things by the operation of human reasoning gives an entrance to false no less than to true notions, inasmuch as he who aspires to know the unknown will not always arrive at truth, but may also conceive of falsehood itself as truth. But the disciple of the Gospels and of Prophecy believes that He Who is, is; both from what he has learnt from the sacred writers, and from the harmony of things which do appear, and from the works of Providence. But what He is and how—leaving this as a useless and unprofitable speculation, such a disciple will open no door to falsehood against truth. For in speculative enquiry fallacies readily find place. But where speculation is entirely at rest, the necessity of error is precluded. And that this is a true account of the case, may be seen if we consider how it is that heresies in the churches have wandered off into many and various opinions in regard to God, men deceiving themselves as they are swayed by one mental impulse or another; and how these very men with whom our treatise is concerned have slipped into such a pit of profanity. Would it not have been safer for all,

following the counsel of wisdom, to abstain from searching into such deep matters, and in peace and quietness to keep inviolate the pure deposit of the faith? But since, in fact, human nothingness has commenced intruding recklessly into matters that are above comprehension, and supporting by dogmatic teaching the figments of their vain imagination, there has sprung up in consequence a whole host of enemies to the truth, and among them these very men who are the subject of this treatise; dogmatizers of deceit who seek to limit the Divine Being, and all but openly idolize their own imagination, in that they deify the idea expressed by this "ungeneracy" of theirs, as not being only in a certain relation discernible in the Divine nature, but as being itself God, or the essence of God. Yet perchance they would have done better to look to the sacred company of the Prophets and Patriarchs, to whom "at sundry times, and in divers manners[6]," the Word of truth spake, and, next in order, those who were eye-witnesses and ministers of the word, that they might give honour due to the claims on their belief of the things attested by the Holy Spirit Himself, and abide within the limits of their teaching and knowledge, and not venture on themes which are not comprehended in the canon of the sacred writers. For those writers, by revealing God, so long unknown to human life by reason of the prevalence of idolatry, and making Him known to men, both from the wonders which manifest themselves in His works, and from the names which express the manifold variety of His power, lead men, as by the hand, to the understanding of the Divine nature, making known to them the bare grandeur of the thought of God; while the question of His essence, as one which it is impossible to grasp, and which bears no fruit to the curious enquirer, they dismiss without any attempt at its solution. For whereas they have set forth respecting all other things, that they were created, the heaven, the earth, the sea, times, ages, and the creatures that are therein, but what each is in itself, and how and whence, on these points they are silent; so, too, concerning God Himself, they exhort men to "believe that He is, and that He is a rewarder of them that diligently seek Him[7]," but in regard to His nature, as being above every name, they neither name it nor concern themselves about it. For if we have learned any names expressive of the knowledge of God, all these are related and have analogy to such names as denote human characteristics. For as they who would indicate some person unknown by marks of recognition speak of him as of good parentage and descent, if such happen

---

to be the case, or as distinguished for his riches or his worth, or as in the prime of life, or of such or such stature, and in so speaking they do not set forth the nature of the person indicated, but give certain notes of recognition (for neither advantages of birth, nor of wealth, nor of reputation, nor of age, constitute the man; they are considered, simply as being observable in the man), thus too the expressions of Holy Scripture devised for the glory of God set forth one or another of the things which are declared concerning Him, each inculcating some special teaching. For by these expressions we are taught either His power, or that He admits not of deterioration, or that He is without cause and without limit, or that He is supreme above all things, or, in short, something, be it what it may, respecting Him. But His very essence, as not to be conceived by the human intellect or expressed in words, this it has left untouched as a thing not to be made the subject of curious enquiry, ruling that it be revered in silence, in that it forbids the investigation of things too deep for us, while it enjoins the duty of being slow to utter any word before God. And therefore, whosoever searches the whole of Revelation will find therein no doctrine of the Divine nature, nor indeed of anything else that has a substantial existence, so that we pass our lives in ignorance of much, being ignorant first of all of ourselves, as men, and then of all things besides. For who is there who has arrived at a comprehension of his own soul? Who is acquainted with its very essence, whether it is material or immaterial, whether it is purely incorporeal, or whether it exhibits anything of a corporeal character; how it comes into being, how it is composed, whence it enters into the body, how it departs from it, or what means it possesses to unite it to the nature of the body; how, being intangible and without form, it is kept within its own sphere, what difference exists among its powers, how one and the same soul, in its eager curiosity to know the things which are unseen, soars above the highest heavens, and again, dragged down by the weight of the body, falls back on material passions, anger and fear, pain and pleasure, pity and cruelty, hope and memory, cowardice and audacity, friendship and hatred, and all the contraries that are produced in the faculties of the soul? Observing which things, who has not fancied that he has a sort of populace of souls crowded together in himself, each of the aforesaid passions differing widely from the rest, and, where it prevails, holding lordship over them all, so that even the rational faculty falls under and is subject to the predominating power of such forces, and contributes its own co-operation to such impulses, as to a despotic lord? What word, then, of the inspired Scripture has taught us the manifold and multiform character of what we understand in speaking of the soul? Is it a unity composed of them all, and, if so, what is it that blends and harmonizes things mutually opposed, so that many things become one, while each element, taken by itself, is shut up in the soul as in some ample vessel? And how is it that we have not the perception of them all as being involved in it, being at one and the same time confident and afraid, at once hating and loving and feeling in ourselves the working as well of all other emotions confused and intermingled; but, on the contrary, take knowledge only of their alternate control, when one of them prevails, the rest remaining quiescent? What in short is this composition and arrangement, and this capacious void within us, such that to each is assigned its own post, as though hindered by middle walls of partition from holding intercourse with its neighbour? And then again what account has explained whether passion is the fundamental essence of the soul, or fear, or any of the other elements which I have mentioned; and what emotions are unsubstantial? For if these have an independent subsistence, then, as I have said, there is comprehended in ourselves not one soul, but a collection of souls, each of them occupying its distinct position as a particular and individual soul. But if we must suppose these to be a kind of emotion without subsistence, how can that which has no essential existence exercise lordship over us, having reduced us as it were to slave under whichsoever of these things may have happened to prevail? And if the soul is something that thought only can grasp, how can that which is manifold and composite be contemplated as such, when such an object ought to be contemplated by itself, independently of these bodily qualities? Then, as to the soul's power of growth, of desire, of nutrition, of change, and the fact that all the bodily powers are nourished, while feeling does not extend through all, but, as in things without life, some of our members are destitute of feeling, the bones for example, the cartilages, the nails, the hair, all of which take nourishment, but do not feel,—tell me who is there that understands this only half-complete operation of the soul as to these? And why do I speak of the soul? Even the inquiry as to that thing in the flesh itself which assumes all the corporeal qualities has not been pursued to any definite result. For if any one has made a mental analysis of that which is seen into its component parts, and, having stripped the object of its qualities, has attempted to consider it by itself, I fail to see what will have been left for investigation.

For when you take from a body its colour, its shape, its degree of resistance, its weight, its quantity, its position, its forces active or passive, its relation to other objects, what remains, that can still be called a body, we can neither see of ourselves, nor are we taught it by Scripture. But how can he who is ignorant of himself take knowledge of anything that is above himself? And if a man is familiarized with such ignorance of himself, is he not plainly taught by the very fact not to be astonished at any of the mysteries that are without? Wherefore also, of the elements of the world, we know only so much by our senses as to enable us to receive what they severally supply for our living. But we possess no knowledge of their substance, nor do we count it loss to be ignorant of it. For what does it profit me to inquire curiously into the nature of fire, how it is struck out, how it is kindled, how, when it has caught hold of the fuel supplied to it, it does not let it go till it has devoured and consumed its prey; how the spark is latent in the flint, how steel, cold as it is to the touch, generates fire, how sticks rubbed together kindle flame, how water shining in the sun causes a flash; and then again the cause of its upward tendency, its power of incessant motion?—Putting aside all which curious questions and investigations, we give heed only to the subservience of this fire to life, seeing that he who avails himself of its service fares no worse than he who busies himself with inquiries into its nature.

Wherefore Holy Scripture omits all idle inquiry into substance as superfluous and unnecessary. And methinks it was for this that John, the Son of Thunder, who with the loud voice of the doctrines contained in his Gospel rose above that of the preaching which heralded them, said at the close of his Gospel, "There are also many other things which Jesus did, the which if they should be written every one, I suppose that even the world itself could not contain the books that should be written[8]." He certainly does not mean by these the miracles of healing, for of these the narrative leaves none unrecorded, even though it does not mention the names of all who were healed. For when he tells us that the dead were raised, that the blind received their sight, that the deaf heard, that the lame walked, and that He healed all manner of sickness and all manner of disease, he does not in this leave any miracle unrecorded, but embraces each and all in these general terms. But it may be that the Evangelist means this in his profound wisdom: that we are to learn the majesty of the Son of God not by the miracles alone which He did in the

flesh. For these are little compared with the greatness of His other work. "But look thou up to Heaven! Behold its glories! Transfer your thought to the wide compass of the earth, and the watery depths! Embrace with your mind the whole world, and when you have come to the knowledge of supramundane nature, learn that these are the true works of Him Who sojourned for thee in the flesh," which (saith he), "if each were written"—and the essence, manner, origin, and extent of each given—the world itself could not contain the fulness of Christ's teaching about the world itself. For since God hath made all things in wisdom, and to His wisdom there is no limit (for "His understanding," saith the Scripture, "is infinite"[9]), the world, that is bounded by limits of its own, cannot contain within itself the account of infinite wisdom. If, then, the whole world is too little to contain the teaching of the works of God, how many worlds could contain an account of the Lord of them all? For perhaps it will not be denied even by the tongue of the blasphemer that the Maker of all things, which have been created by the mere fiat of His will, is infinitely greater than all. If, then, the whole creation cannot contain what might be said respecting itself (for so, according to our explanation, the great Evangelist testifies), how should human shallowness contain all that might be said of the Lord of Creation? Let those grand talkers inform us what man is, in comparison with the universe, what geometrical point is so without magnitude, which of the atoms of Epicurus is capable of such infinitesimal reduction in the vain fancy of those who make such problems the object of their study, which of them falls so little short of non-existence, as human shallowness, when compared with the universe. As saith also great David, with a true insight into human weakness, "Mine age is as nothing unto Thee[1]," not saying that it is absolutely nothing, but signifying, by this comparison to the non-existent, that what is so exceedingly brief is next to nothing at all.

But, nevertheless, with only such a nature for their base of operations, they open their mouths wide against the unspeakable Power, and encompass by one appellation the infinite nature, confining the Divine essence within the narrow limits of the term ungeneracy, that they may thereby pave a way for their blasphemy against the Only-begotten; but although the great Basil had corrected this false opinion, and pointed out, in regard to the terms, that they have no existence in nature, but are attached as conceptions to the things signified, so far are

---

9 Ps. cxlvii. 5.
1 Ps. xxxix. 5. LXX. ὑπόστασίς μου (not αἰών, which would be the exact equivalent to the Heb.).

they from returning to the truth, that they stick to what they have once advanced, as to bird-lime, and will not loose their hold of their fallacious mode of argument, nor do they allow the term "ungeneracy" to be used in the way of a mental conception, but make it represent the Divine nature itself. Now to go through their whole argument, and to attempt to over-throw it by discussing word by word their frivolous and long-winded nonsense, would be a task requiring much leisure, and time, and freedom from calls of business. Just as I hear that Eunomius, after applying himself at his leisure, and laboriously, for a number of years exceeding those of the Trojan war, has fabricated this dream for himself in his deep slumbers, studiously seeking, not how to interpret any of the ideas which he has arrived at, but how to drag and force them into keeping with his phrases, and going round and collecting out of certain books the words in them that sound grandest. And as beggars in lack of clothing pin and tack together tunics for themselves out of rags, so he, cropping here a phrase and there a phrase, has woven together for himself the patchwork of his treatise, glueing in and fixing together the joinings of his diction with much labour and pains, displaying therein a petty and juvenile ambition for combat, which any man who has an eye to actuality would disdain, just as a steadfast wrestler, no longer in the prime of life, would disdain to play the woman by over-niceness in dress. But to me it seems that, when the scope of the whole question has been briefly run through, his roundabout flourishes may well be let alone.

I have said, then (for I make my master's words my own), that reason supplies us with but a dim and imperfect comprehension of the Divine nature; nevertheless, the knowledge that we gather from the terms which piety allows us to apply to it is sufficient for our limited capacity. Now we do not say that all these terms have a uniform significance; for some of them express qualities inherent in God, and others qualities that are not, as when we say that He is just or incorruptible, by the term "just" signifying that justice is found in Him, and by "incorruptible" that corruption is not. Again, by a change of meaning, we may apply terms to God in the way of accommodation, so that what is proper to God may be represented by a term which in no wise belongs to Him, and what is foreign to His nature may be represented by what belongs to Him. For whereas justice is the contradictory of injustice, and everlastingness the contrary of destruction, we may fitly and without impropriety employ contraries in speaking of God, as when we say that He is ever existent, or that He is not un-just, which is equivalent to saying that He is just, and that He admits not of corruption. So, too, we may say that other names of God, by a certain change of signification, may be suitably employed to express either meaning, for example "good," and "immortal," and all expressions of like formation; for each of these terms, according as it is taken, is capable of indicating what does or what does not appertain to the Divine nature, so that, notwithstanding the formal change, our orthodox opinion in regard to the object remains immovably fixed. For it amounts to the same, whether we speak of God as unsusceptible of evil, or whether we call Him good; whether we confess that He is immortal, or say that He ever liveth. For we understand no difference in the sense of these terms, but we signify one and the same thing by both, though the one may seem to convey the notion of affirmation, and the other of negation. And so again, when we speak of God as the First Cause of all things, or again, when we speak of Him as without cause, we are guilty of no con-tradiction in sense, declaring as we do by either name that God is the prime Ruler and First Cause of all. Accordingly when we speak of Him as without cause, and as Lord of all, in the former case we signify what does not attach to Him, in the latter case what does; it being possible, as I have said, by a change of the things signified, to give an opposite sense to the words that express them, and to signify a property by a word which for the time takes a negative form, and *vice versa*. For it is allow-able, instead of saying that He Himself has no primal cause, to describe Him as the First Cause of all, and again, instead of this, to hold that He alone exists ungenerately, so that while the words seem by the formal change to be at variance with each other, the sense remains one and the same. For the object to be aimed at, in questions respecting God, is not to produce a dulcet and melodious harmony of words, but to work out an orthodox formula of thought, whereby a worthy conception of God may be ensured. Since, then, it is only orthodox to infer that He Who is the First Cause of all is Him-self without cause, if this opinion is established, what further contention of words remains for men of sense and judgment, when every word whereby such a notion is conveyed to us has the same signification? For whether you say that He is the First Cause and Principle of all, or speak of Him as without origin, whether you speak of Him as of ungenerate or eternal subsistence, as the Cause of all or as alone without cause, all these words are, in a manner, of like force, and equivalent to one another, as far as the meaning of the things signified is concerned; and it is mere folly to contend for this or that vocal intonation, as if orthodoxy were a thing of sounds and syllables rather than of the mind. This view, then, has been carefully enunciated by our great master, whereby all whose eyes are not blindfolded by the veil of heresy may clearly see that, whatever be the nature of God, He is not to be apprehended by sense, and that He transcends reason, though human thought, busying itself with curious inquiry, with such help of reason as it can command, stretches out its hand and just touches His unapproachable and sublime nature, being neither keen-sighted enough to see clearly what is invisible, nor yet so far withheld from approach as to be unable to catch some faint glimpse of what it seeks to know. For such knowledge it attains in part by the touch of reason, in part from its very inability to discern it, finding that it is a sort of knowledge to know that what is sought transcends knowledge (for it has learned what is contrary to the Divine nature, as well as all that may fittingly be conjectured respecting it). Not that it has been able to gain full knowledge of that nature itself about which it reasons, but from the knowledge of those properties which are, or are not, inherent in it, this mind of man sees what alone can be seen, that that which is far removed from all evil, and is understood in all good, is altogether such as I should pronounce ineffable and incomprehensible by human reason.

But although our great master has thus cleared away all unworthy notions respecting the Divine nature, and has urged and taught all that may be reverently and fittingly held concerning it, viz. that the First Cause is neither a corruptible thing, nor one brought into being by any birth, but that it is outside the range of every conception of the kind; and that from the negation of what is not inherent, and the affirmation of what may be with reverence conceived to be inherent therein, we may best apprehend what He is—nevertheless this vehement adversary of the truth opposes these teachings, and hopes with the sounding word "ungeneracy" to supply a clear definition of the essence of God.

And yet it is plain to every one who has given any attention to the uses of words, that the word incorruption denotes by the privative particle that neither corruption nor birth appertains to God: just as many other words of like formation denote the absence of what is not inherent rather than the presence of what is; e. g. harmless, painless, guileless, undisturbed, passionless, sleepless, undiseased [2], impassible,

unblamable, and the like. For all these terms are truly applicable to God, and furnish a sort of catalogue and muster of evil qualities from which God is separate. Yet the terms employed give no positive account of that to which they are applied. We learn from them what it is not ; but what it is, the force of the words does not indicate. For if some one, wishing to describe the nature of man, were to say that it is not lifeless, not insentient, not winged, not four-footed, not amphibious, he would not indicate what it is : he would simply declare what it is not, and he would be no more making untrue statements respecting man than he would be positively defining his subject. In the same way, from the many things which are predicated of the Divine nature, we learn under what conditions we may conceive God as existing, but what He is essentially, such statements do not inform us.

While, however, we strenuously avoid all concurrence with absurd notions in our thoughts of God, we allow ourselves in the use of many diverse appellations in regard to Him, adapting them to our point of view. For whereas no suitable word has been found to express Divine nature, we address God by many names, each by some distinctive touch adding something fresh to our notions respecting Him,—thus seeking by variety of nomenclature to gain some glimmerings for the comprehension of what we seek. For when we question and examine ourselves as to what God is, we express our conclusions variously, as that He is that which presides over the system and working of the things that are, that His existence is without cause, while to all else He is the Cause of being; that He is that which has no generation or beginning, no corruption, no turning backward, no diminution of supremacy ; that He is that in which evil finds no place, and from which no good is absent.

And if any one would distinguish such notions by words, he would find it absolutely necessary to call that which admits of no changing to the worse unchanging and invariable, and to call the First Cause of all ungenerate, and that which admits not of corruption incorruptible ; and that which ceases at no limit immortal and neverfailing ; and that which presides over all Almighty. And so, framing names for all other Divine attributes in accordance with reverent conceptions of Him, we designate them now by one name, now by another, according to our varying lines of thought, as power, or strength, or goodness, or ungeneracy, or perpetuity.

I say, then, that men have a right to such

---

[2] Oehler notices that the Paris editt. have not these words, ἄϋπνον, ἄνοσον : but that John the Franciscan is a witness that they were in his codex (the Pithœan) : for he says, "after this follows ἄϋπνος ἄνθρωπος, which have crept in from the oversight of a not ἄϋπνος ω, yist, and therefore ought to be expurged :" not being aware that very ancient copies write ἄνθρωπος ανος, so that ἄνοσον is the true reading, having been changed, but not introduced, by the error of a copyist.

word-building, adapting their appellations to their subject, each man according to his judgment; and that there is no absurdity in this, such as our controversialist makes a pretence of, shuddering at it as at some gruesome hobgoblin, and that we are fully justified in allowing the use of such fresh applications of words in respect to all things that can be named, and to God Himself.

For God is not an expression, neither hath He His essence in voice or utterance. But God is of Himself what also He is believed to be, but He is named, by those who call upon Him, not what He is essentially (for the nature of Him Who alone is is unspeakable), but He receives His appellations from what are believed to be His operations in regard to our life. To take an instance ready to our hand; when we speak of Him as God, we so call Him from regarding Him as overlooking and surveying all things, and seeing through the things that are hidden. But if His essence is prior to His works, and we understand His works by our senses, and express them in words as we are best able, why should we be afraid of calling things by words of later origin than themselves? For if we stay to interpret any of the attributes of God till we understand them, and we understand them only by what His works teach us, and if His power precedes its exercise, and depends on the will of God, while His will resides in the spontaneity of the Divine nature, are we not clearly taught that the words which represent things are of later origin than the things themselves, and that the words which are framed to express the operations of things are reflections of the things themselves? And that this is so, we are clearly taught by Holy Scripture, by the mouth of great David, when, as by certain peculiar and appropriate names, derived from his contemplation of the works of God, he thus speaks of the Divine nature: "The Lord is full of compassion and mercy, long-suffering, and of great goodness [3]." Now what do these words tell us? Do they indicate His operations, or His nature? No one will say that they indicate aught but His operations. At what time, then, after showing mercy and pity, did God acquire His name from their display? Was it before man's life began? But who was there to be the object of pity? Was it, then, after sin entered into the world? But sin entered after man. The exercise, therefore, of pity, and the name itself, came after man. What then? will our adversary, wise as he is above the Prophets, convict David of error in applying names to God derived from his opportunities of knowing Him? or, in con-

tending with him, will he use against him the pretence in his stately passage as out of a tragedy, saying that "he glories in the most blessed life of God with names drawn from human imagination, whereas it gloried in itself alone, long before men were born to imagine them"? The Psalmist's advocate will readily admit that the Divine nature gloried in itself alone even before the existence of human imagination, but will contend that the human mind can speak only so much in respect of God as its capacity, instructed by His works, will allow. "For," as saith the Wisdom of Solomon, "by the greatness and beauty of the creatures proportionably the Maker of them is seen [4]."

But in applying such appellations to the Divine essence, "which passeth all understanding," we do not seek to glory in it by the names we employ, but to guide our own selves by the aid of such terms towards the comprehension of the things which are hidden. "I said unto the Lord," saith the Prophet, "Thou art my God, my goods are nothing unto Thee [5]." How then are we glorifying the most blessed life of God, as this man affirms, when (as saith the Prophet) "our goods are nothing unto Him"? Is it that he takes "call" to mean "glory in"? Yet those who employ the latter word rightly, and who have been trained to use words with propriety, tell us that the word "glory in" is never used of mere indication, but that that idea is expressed by such words as "to make known," "to show," "to indicate," or some other of the kind, whereas the word for "glory in" means to be proud of, or delight in a thing, and the like. But he affirms that by employing names drawn from human imagination we "glory in" the blessed life. We hold, however, that to add any honour to the Divine nature, which is above all honour, is more than human infirmity can do. At the same time we do not deny that we endeavour, by words and names devised with due reverence, to give some notion of its attributes. And so, following studiously in the path of due reverence, we apprehend that the first cause is that which has its subsistence not from any cause superior to itself. Which view, if so be one accepts it as true, is praiseworthy for its truth alone. But if one should judge it to be superior to other aspects of the Divine nature, and so should say that God, exulting and rejoicing in this alone, glories in it, as of paramount excellence, one would find support only from the Muse by whom Eunomius is inspired, when he says, that "ungeneracy" glories in itself, that which, mark you, he calls

---

[3] Ps. ciii. 8.

[4] Wisdom xiii. 5.
[5] Ps. xvi. 2. S. Gregory quotes the LXX. τῶν ἀγαθῶν μου οὐ χρείαν ἔχεις, which is closely followed by the Vulgate "bonorum meorum non eges," and the Arab. "Thou needest not my good actions." Heb. "I have no good beyond thee."

God's essence, and styles the blessed and Divine life.

But let us hear how, "in the way most needed, and the form that preceded" (for with such rhymes he again gives us a taste of the flowers of style), let us hear, I say, how by such means he proposes to refute the opinion formed of him, and to keep in the dark the ignorance of those whom he has deluded. For I will use our dithyrambist's own verbal inflections and phraseology. When, says he, we assert that words by which thought is expressed die as soon as they are uttered, we add that whether words are uttered or not, whether they are yet in existence or not, God was and is ungenerate. Let us learn, then, what connection there is between the conception or the formation of words, and the things which we signify by this or that mode of utterance. Accordingly, if God is ungenerate before the creation of man, we must esteem as of no account the words which indicate that thought, inasmuch as they are dispersed along with the sounds that express them, if such thought happen to be named after human notion. For to be, and to be called, are not convertible terms. But God is by His nature what He is, but He is called by us by such names as the poverty of our nature will allow us to make use of, which is incapable of enunciating thought except by means of voice and words. Accordingly, understanding Him to be without origin, we enunciate that thought by the term ungenerate. And what harm is it to Him Who indeed is, that He should be named by us as we conceive Him to be? For His ungenerate existence is not the result of His being called ungenerate, but the name is the result of the existence. But this our acute friend fails to see, nor does he take a clear view of his own positions. For if he did, he would certainly have left off reviling those who framed the word ungeneracy to express the idea in their minds. For look at what he says, "Words so spoken perish as soon as they are spoken; but God both is and was ungenerate, both after the words were spoken and before. You see that the Supreme Being is what He is, before the creation of all things, whether silent or not, being what He is neither in greater nor in less degree; while the use of words and names was not devised till after the creation of man, endowed by God with the faculty of reason and speech."

If, then, the creation is of later date than its Creator, and man is the latest in the scale of creation, and if speech is a distinctive characteristic of man, and verbs and nouns are the component elements of speech, and ungeneracy is a noun, how is it that he does not understand that he is combating his own arguments? For we, on our side, say that by human thought and intelligence words have been devised expressive of things which they represent, and he, on his side, allows that those who employ speech are demonstrably later in point of time than the Divine life, and that the Divine nature is now, and ever has been, without generation. If, then, he allows the blessed life to be anterior to man (for to that point I return), and we do not deny man's later creation, but contend that we have used forms of speech ever since we came into being and received the faculty of reason from our Maker, and if ungeneracy is a word expressive of a special idea, and every word is a part of human speech,—it follows that he who admits that the Divine nature was anterior to man must at the same time admit that the name invented by man to express that nature was itself later in being. For it was not likely that the use of speech should be exercised before the existence of creatures to use it, any more than that farming should be exercised before the existence of farmers, or navigation before that of navigators, or in fact any of the occupations of life before that of life itself. Why, then, does he contend with us, instead of following his premises to their legitimate conclusion?

He says that God was what He is, before the creation of man. Nor do we deny it. For whatsoever we conceive of God existed before the creation of the world. But we maintain that it received its name after the namer came into being. For if we use words for this purpose, that they may supply us with teaching about the things which they signify, and it is ignorance alone that requires teaching, while the Divine Nature, as comprehending all knowledge, is above all teaching, it follows that names were invented to denote the Supreme Being, not for His sake, but for our own. For He did not attach the term ungeneracy to His nature in order that He Himself might be instructed. For He Who knoweth all things has no need of syllables and words to instruct Him as to His own nature and majesty.

But that we might gain some sort of comprehension of what with reverence may be thought respecting Him, we have stamped our different ideas with certain words and syllables, labelling, as it were, our mental processes with verbal formulæ to serve as characteristic notes and indications, with the object of giving a clear and simple declaration of our mental processes by means of words attached to, and expressive of, our ideas. Why, then, does he find fault with our contention that the term ungeneracy was devised to indicate the existence of God without origin or beginning, and that, independently of all exercise of speech, or silence, or thought, and before the very idea of creation, God was and remains ungenerate? If, indeed, any one should argue that God was not ungenerate till the name ungeneracy had been found, the man might be pardonable for writing as he has written, in contravention of such an absurdity. But if no one denies that He existed before speech and reason, whereas, while the form of words by which the meaning is expressed is said by us to have been devised by mental conception, the end and aim of his controversy with us is to show that the name is not of man's device, but that it existed before our creation, though by whom it was spoken I do not know[6], what has the assertion that God existed ungenerately before all things, and the contention that[7] mental conception is posterior to God, got to do with this aim of his? For that God is not a conception has been fully demonstrated, so that we may press him with the same sort of argument, and reply, so to say, in his own words, e.g. "It is utter folly to regard understanding as of earlier birth than those who exercise it"; or again, as he proceeds a little below, "Nor as though we intended this, i. e. to make men, the latest of God's works of creation, anterior to the conceptions of their own understanding." Great indeed would be the force of the argument, if any one of us, out of sheer folly and madness, should argue that God was a conception of the mind. But if this is not so, nor ever has been, (for who would go to such a pitch of folly as to assert that He Who alone is, and Who brought all else whatsoever into being, has no substantial existence of His own, and to make Him out to be a mere conception of a name?) why does he fight with shadows, contending with imaginary propositions? Is not the cause of this unreasonable litigiousness clear, that, feeling ashamed of the fallacy respecting ungeneracy with which his dupes have been deluded (since it has been proved that the word is very far removed from the Divine essence), he is deliberately shuffling up his arguments, shifting the controversy from words to things, so that by throwing all into confusion the unwary may more easily be seduced, by imagining that God has been described by us either as a conception, or as posterior in existence to the invention of human terminology; and thus, leaving our argument unrefuted, he is shifting his position to another quarter of the field?

For our conclusion was, as I have said, that the term ungeneracy does not indicate the Divine nature, but is applicable to it as the result of a conception by which the fact that God subsists without prior cause is pointed at. But what they were for establishing was this: that the word was indicative of the Divine essence itself. Yet how has it been established that the word has this force? I suppose the handling of this question is in reserve in some other of his writings. But here he makes it his main object to show that God exists ungenerately, just as though some one were simply questioning him on such points as these—what view he held as to the term ungenerate, whether he thought it invented to show that the First Cause was without beginning and origin, or as declaring the Divine essence itself; and he, with much assumption of gravity and wisdom, were replying that he, for his part, had no doubt that God was the Maker of heaven and earth. How widely this method of proceeding differs from, and is unconnected with, his first contention, you may see, in the same way as you may see how little his fine description of his controversy with us is connected with the question at issue. For let us look at the matter in this wise.

They say that God is ungenerate, and in this we agree. But that ungeneracy itself constitutes the Divine essence, here we take exception. For we maintain that this term is declarative of God's ungenerate subsistence, but not that ungeneracy is God. But of what nature is his refutation? It is this: that before man's creation God existed ungenerately. But what has this to do with the point which he promises to establish, that the term and its Subject are identical? For he lays it down that ungeneracy is the Divine essence. But what sort of a fulfilment of his promise is it, to show that God existed before beings capable of speech? What a wonderful, what an irresistible demonstration! what perfection of logical refinement! Who that has not been initiated in the mysteries of the awful craft may venture to look it in the face? Yet in particularizing the meanings of the term "conception," he makes a solemn travesty of it. For, saith he, of words used to express a conception of the mind, some exist only in pronunciation, as for instance those which signify nonentity, while others have their peculiar meaning; and of these some have an amplifying force, as in the case of things colossal, others a diminishing, as in that of pigmies, others a multiplying, as in that of many-headed monsters, others a combinative, as in that of centaurs. After thus reducing the force of the term "conception" to its lowest value, our clever friend will allow it, you see, no further extension. He

---

6 Oehler's reading and stopping are both faulty here, viz., οὐκ οἶδα περὶ τίνος λεγόμενον τί κοινὸν ἔχει κ. τ. λ. Manifestly the stop should be at λεγόμενον, and the reading of the editt. παρὰ τίνος is right.

7 It is not necessary to change the τὸ here to τῷ as Oehler suggests. The Munich Cod. omits it altogether. But he has done good service to the text, by supplying from his Codices all that follows, down to "the same sort of argument" (except that the first διαγωνίζεσθαι is probably a gloss).

says that it is without sense and meaning, that it fancies the unnatural, either contracting or extending the limits of nature, or putting heterogeneous notions together, or juggling with strange and monstrous combinations.

With such gibes at the term "conception," he shows, to the best of his ability, that it is useless and unprofitable for the life of man. What, then, was the origin of our higher branches of learning, of geometry, arithmetic, the logical and physical sciences, of the inventions of mechanical art, of the marvels of measuring time by the brazen dial and the water-clock? What, again, of ontology, of the science of ideas, in short of all intellectual speculation as applied to great and sublime objects? What of agriculture, of navigation, and of the other pursuits of human life? how comes the sea to be a highway for man? how are things of the air brought into the service of things of the earth, wild things tamed, objects of terror brought into subjection, animals stronger than ourselves made obedient to the rein? Have not all these benefits to human life been achieved by conception? For, according to my account of it, conception is the method by which we discover things that are unknown, going on to further discoveries by means of what adjoins to and follows[8] from our first perception with regard to the thing studied. For when we have formed some idea of what we seek to know, by adapting what follows to the first result of our discoveries we gradually conduct our inquiry to the end of our proposed research.

But why enumerate the greater and more splendid results of this faculty? For every one who is not unfriendly to truth can see for himself that all else that Time has discovered for the service and benefit of human life, has been discovered by no other instrumentality than that of conception. And it seems to me, that any one who should judge this faculty more precious than any other with the exercise of which we are gifted in this life by Divine Providence would not be far mistaken in his judgment. And in saying this I am supported by Job's teaching, where he represents God as answering His servant by the tempest and the clouds, saying both other things meet for Him to say, and that it is He Who hath set man over the arts, and given to woman her skill in weaving and embroidery[9].

Now that He did not teach us such things by some visible operation, Himself presiding over the work, as we may see in matters of bodily teaching, no one would gainsay whose nature is not altogether animal and brutish. But still it has been said that our first knowledge of such arts is from Him, and, if such is the case, surely He Who endowed our nature with such a faculty of conceiving and finding out the objects of our investigation was Himself our Guide to the arts. And by the law of causation, whatever is discovered and established by conception must be ascribed to Him Who is the Author of that faculty. Thus human life invented the Art of Healing, but nevertheless he would be right who should assert that Art to be a gift from God. And whatever discovery has been made in human life, conducive to any useful purposes of peace or war, came to us from no other quarter but from an intelligence conceiving and discovering according to our several requirements; and that intelligence is a gift of God. It is to God, then, that we owe all that intelligence supplies to us. Nor do I deny the objection made by our adversaries, that lying wonders also are fabricated by this faculty. For their contention as to this makes for our own side in the argument. For we too assert that the science of opposites is the same, whether beneficial or the reverse; *e. g.* in the case of the arts of healing and navigation, and so on. For he who knows how to relieve the sick by drugs will also know, if indeed he were to turn his art to an evil purpose, how to mix some deleterious ingredient in the food of the healthy. And he who can steer a boat with its rudder into port can also steer it for the reef or the rock, if minded to destroy those on board. And the painter, with the same art by which he depicts the fairest form on his canvas, could give us an exact representation of the ugliest. So, too, the wrestling-master, by the experience which he has gained in anointing, can set a dislocated limb, or, should he wish to do so, dislocate a sound one. But why encumber our argument by multiplying instances? As in the above-mentioned cases no one would deny that he who has learned to practise an art for right purposes can also abuse it for wrong ones, so we say that the faculty of thought and conception was implanted by God in human nature for good, but, with those who abuse it as an instrument of discovery, it frequently becomes the handmaid of pernicious inventions. But although it is thus possible for this faculty to give a plausible shape to what is false and unreal, it is none the less competent to investigate what actually and in very truth subsists, and its ability for the one must in fairness be regarded as an evidence of its ability for the other.

For that one who proposes to himself to terrify or charm an audience should have plenty

8 The definition of ἐπίνοια, *i. e.* ἔφοδος εὑρετικὴ τῶν ἀγνοουμένων, διὰ τῶν προσεχῶν τε καὶ ἀκολούθων . . . τὸ ἐφέξης ἐξευρίσκουσα.

9 Job xxxviii. 36. LXX. Τίς δὲ ἔδωκε γυναιξὶν ὑφάσματος σοφίαν, ἢ ποικιλτικὴν ἐπιστήμην.

of conception to effect such a purpose, and should display to the spectators many-handed, many-headed, or fire-breathing monsters, or men enfolded in the coils of serpents, or that he should seem to increase their stature, or enlarge their natural proportions to a ridiculous extent, or that he should describe men metamorphosed into fountains and trees and birds, a kind of narrative which is not without its attraction for such as take pleasure in things of that sort;—all this, I say, is the clearest of demonstrations that it is possible to arrive at higher knowledge also by means of this inventive faculty.

For it is not the case that, while the intelligence implanted in us by the Giver is fully competent to conjure up non-realities, it is endowed with no faculty at all for providing us with things that may profit us. But as the impulsive and elective faculty of the soul is established in our nature, to incite us to what is good and noble, though a man may also abuse it for what is evil, and no one can call the fact that the elective faculty sometimes inclines to evil a proof that it never inclines to what is good—so the bias of conception towards what is vain and unprofitable does not prove its inability for what is profitable, but, on the contrary, is a demonstration of its not being unserviceable for what is beneficial and necessary to the mind. For as, in the one case, it discovers means to produce pleasure or terror, so, in the other, it does not fail to find ways for getting at truth. Now one of the objects of inquiry was whether the First Cause, viz. God, exists without beginning, or whether His existence is dependent on some beginning. But perceiving, by the aid of thought, that that cannot be a First Cause which we conceive of as the consequence of another, we devised a word expressive of such a notion, and we say that He who is without anterior cause exists without origin, or, so to say, ungenerately. And Him Who so exists we call ungenerate and without origin, indicating, by that appellation, not what He is, but what He is not.

But as far as possible to elucidate the idea, I will endeavour to illustrate it by a still plainer example. Let us suppose the inquiry to be about some tree, whether it is cultivated or wild. If the former, we call it planted, if the latter, not planted. And such a term exactly hits the truth, for the tree must needs be after this manner or that. And yet the word does not indicate the peculiar nature of the plant. From the term "not-planted" we learn that it is of spontaneous growth; but whether what is thus signified is a plane, or a vine, or some other such plant, the name applied to it does not inform us.

This example being understood, it is time to go on to the thing which it illustrates. This much

we comprehend, that the First Cause has His existence from no antecedent one. Accordingly, we call God ungenerate as existing ungenerately, reducing this notion of ungeneracy into verbal form. That He is without origin or beginning we show by the force of the term. But what that Being is which exists ungenerately, this appellation does not lead us to discern. Nor was it to be supposed that the processes of conception could avail to raise us above the limits of our nature, and open up the incomprehensible to our view, and enable us to compass the knowledge of that which no knowledge can approach [1]. Nevertheless, our adversary storms at our Master, and tries to tear to pieces his teaching respecting the faculty of thought and conception, and derides what has been said, revelling as usual in the rattle of his jingling phraseology, and saying that he (Basil) shrinks from adducing evidence respecting those things of which he presumes to be the interpreter. For, quoting certain of the Master's speculations on the faculty of conception, in which he shows that its exercise finds place, not only in reference to vain and trivial objects, but that it is competent to deal also with weightier matters, he, by means of his speculation about the corn, and seed, and other food (in Genesis), brings Basil into court with the charge, that his language is a following of pagan philosophy [2], and

---

[1] Cf. Origen c. Celsum, vi. 65. Celsus had said, "God cannot be named." "This requires a distinction to be made. If Celsus means that there is nothing in the signification of words that can express the qualities of God, what he says is true, seeing that there are many other qualities that cannot be named. Who, for instance, can express in words the difference of quality between the sweetness of a date and that of a fig? Peculiar individual qualities cannot be expressed in a word. No wonder, then, that in this absolute sense God cannot be named. But if by 'name' we only mean the possible expression of some one thing about God, by way of leading on the listener, and producing in him such a notion *about* God as human faculties can reach to, then there is nothing strange in saying that God can have **a name."**

[2] τῇ ἔξωθεν φιλοσοφίᾳ. Eunomius, in this accusation, must have been thinking, in the θέσει and φύσει controversy on the origin of language, of Dem critus, who called words "statues in sound," i. e. ascribed to them a certain amount of artificiality. But it is doubtful whether the opinion of the purely human origin of language can be ascribed to him, when we consider another expression of his, that "words were statues in sound, but statues not made by the hands of men, but by the gods themselves." Language with him was conventional, but it was not arbitrary. Again, Plato defines a word, an imitation in sound of that which it imitates (Cratylus, 423 B), and Aristotle calls words imitations (Rhet. iii. 1). But both of them were very far indeed from tracing language back to mere *onomatopœia*, i. e. ascribing it to θέσις (agreement), as opposed to φύσις in the sense of the earlier Greek philosophy, the "essence" of the thing named, rather than the "nature" of the names. Long before them Pythagoras had said, "the wisest of all things is Number, and next to Number, that which gives names." These oracular words do not countenance the idea that the origin of language was purely human. Perhaps Epicurus more definitely than any taught that in the first formation of language men acted unconsciously, moved by nature (in the modern sense), and that then as a second stage there was an agreement or understanding to use a certain sound for a certain conception. Against this Heraclitus (B.C. 503) had taught that words exist φύσει. "Words are like the shadows of things, like the pictures of trees and mountains reflected in the river, like our own images when we look into a mirror." We know at all events here what he did *not* mean, viz., that man imposed what names he pleased on the objects round him. Heraclitus' "nature" is a very different thing from the Darwinian Nature; it is the inherent fitness between the object and name. Eunomius, then, was hardly justified in calling the Greek philosophy, as a whole, atheistical in this matter, and "against Providence." This φύσις, the impalpable force in the things named, could still be represented

that he is circumscribing Divine Providence, as not allowing that words were given to things by God, and that he is fighting in the ranks of the Atheists, and taking arms against Providence, and that he admires the doctrines of the profane rather than the laws of God, and ascribes to them the palm of wisdom, not having observed in the earliest of the sacred records, that before the creation of man, the naming of fruit and seed are mentioned in Holy Writ.

Such are his charges against us; not indeed his notions as expressed in his own phraseology, for we have made such alterations as were required to correct the ruggedness and harshness of his style. What, then, is our answer to this careful guardian of Divine Providence? He asserts that we are in error, because, while we do not deny man's having been created a rational being by God, we ascribe the invention of words to the logical faculty implanted by God in man's nature. And this is the bitterest of his accusations, whereby our teacher of righteousness is charged with deserting to the tenets of the Atheists, and is denounced as partaking with and supporting their lawless company, and indeed as guilty of all the most atrocious offences. Well, then, let this corrector of our blunders tell us, *did* God give names to the things which He created? For so says our new interpreter of the mysteries: "Before the creation of man God named germ, and herb, and grass, and seed, and tree, and the like, when by the word of His power He brought them severally into being." If, then, he abides by the bare letter, and so far Judaizes, and has yet to learn that the Christian is a disciple not of the letter but of the Spirit (for the letter killeth, says the Apostle, but the Spirit giveth life [3]), and quotes to us the bare literal reading of the words as though God Himself pronounced them—if, I say, he believes this, that, after the similitude of men, God made use of fluency of speech, expressing His thoughts by voice and accent—if, I repeat, he believes this, he cannot reasonably deny what follows as its logical consequence. For our speech is uttered by the organs of speech, the windpipe, the tongue, the teeth, and the mouth, the inhalation of air from without and the breath from within working together to produce the utterance. For the windpipe, fitting into the throat like a flute, emits a sound from below; and the roof of the mouth, by reason of the void space above extending to the nostrils, like some musical instrument, gives volume from above to the voice. And the

cheeks, too, are aids to speech, contracting and expanding in accordance with their structural arrangement, or propelling the voice through a narrow passage by various movements of the tongue, which it effects now with one part of itself now with another, giving hardness or softness to the sound which passes over it by contact with the teeth or with the palate. Again, the service of the lips contributes not a little to the result, affecting the voice by the variety of their distinctive movements, and helping to shape the words as they are uttered.

If, then, God gives things their names as our new expositor of the Divine record assures us, naming germ, and grass, and tree, and fruit, He must of necessity have pronounced each of these words not otherwise than as it is pronounced; *i. e.* according to the composition of the syllables, some of which are sounded by the lips, others by the tongue, others by both. But if none of these words could be uttered, except by the operation of vocal organs producing each syllable and sound by some appropriate movement, he must of necessity ascribe the possession of such organs to God, and fashion the Divine Being according to the exigencies of speech. For each adaptation of the vocal organs must be in some form or other, and form is a bodily limitation. Further, we know very well that all bodies are composite, but where you see composition you see also dissolution, and dissolution, as the notion implies, is the same thing as destruction. This, then, is the upshot of our controversialist's victory over us; to show us the God of his imagining whom he has fashioned by the name ungeneracy—speaking, indeed, that He may not lose His share in the invention of names, but provided with vocal organs with which to utter them, and not without bodily nature to enable Him to employ them (for you cannot conceive of formal utterance in the abstract apart from a body), and gradually going on to the congenital affections of the body—through the composite to dissolution, and so finding His end in destruction.

Such is the nature of this new-fangled Deity, as deducible from the words of our new Godmaker. But he takes his stand on the Scriptures, and maintains that Moses explicitly declares this, when he says, "God said," adding His words, "Let there be light," and, "Let there be a firmament," and, "Let the waters be gathered together . . . and let the dry land appear," and, "Let the earth bring forth," and, "Let the waters bring forth," and whatsoever else is written in its order. Let us, then, examine the meaning of what is said. Who does not know, even if he be the merest simpleton, that there is a natural correlation between hearing and speech, and that, as it is impossible

as the will of the Deity. Eunomius outdoes Origen even, or any Christian writer, in contending for the sacredness of names. He makes the Deity the name-giver, but with the sole object of deifying his "Ungenerate." Perhaps Basil's teaching of the human faculty of 'Επίνοια working under God as the name-giver is the truest statement of all, and harmonizes most with modern thought.

　　　　　　　　3 2 Cor. iii. 6.

for hearing to discharge its function when no one is speaking, so speech is ineffectual unless directed to hearing? If, then, he means literally that "God said," let him tell us also to what hearing His words were addressed. Does he mean that He said them to Himself? If so, the commands which He issues, He issues to Himself. Yet who will accept this interpretation, that God sits upon His throne prescribing what He Himself must do, and employing Himself as His minister to do His bidding? But even supposing one were to allow that it was not blasphemy to say this, who has any need of words and speech for himself, even though a man? For every one's own mental action suffices him to produce choice and volition. But he will doubtless say that the Father held converse with the Son. But what need of vocal utterance for that? For it is a property of bodily nature to signify the thoughts of the heart by means of words, whence also written characters equivalent to speech were invented for the expression of thought. For we declare thought equally by speaking and by writing, but in the case of those who are not too far distant we reach their hearing by voice, but declare our mind to those who are at a distance by written characters; and in the case of those present with us, in proportion to their distance from us, we raise or lower the tones of our voice, and to those close by us we sometimes point out what they are to do simply by a nod; and such or such an expression of the eye is sufficient to convey our determination, or a movement of the hand is sufficient to signify our approval or disapproval of something going on. If, then, those who are encompassed by the body are able to make known the hidden working of their minds to their neighbours, even without voice, or speech, or correspondence by means of letters, and silence causes no hindrance to the despatch of business, can it be that in the case of the immaterial, and intangible, and, as Eunomius says, the Supreme and first Being, there is any need of words to indicate the thought of the Father and to make known His will to the Only-Begotten Son—words, which, as he himself says, are wont to perish as soon as they are uttered? No one, methinks, who has common sense will accept this as the truth, especially as all sound is poured forth into the air. For voice cannot be produced unless it takes consistence in air. Now, even they themselves must suppose some medium of communication between the speaker and him to whom he speaks. For if there were no such medium, how could the voice travel from the speaker to the hearer? What, then, will they say is the medium or interval by which they divide the Father from the Son? Between

bodies, indeed, there is an interval of atmospheric space, differing in its nature from the nature of human bodies. But God, Who is intangible, and without form, and pure from all composition, in communicating His counsels with the Only-Begotten Son, Who is similarly, or rather in the same manner, immaterial and without body—if He made His communication by voice, what medium would He have had through which the word, transmitted as in a current, might reach the ears of the Only-Begotten? For we need hardly stop to consider that God is not separable into apprehensive faculties, as we are, whose perceptions separately apprehend their corresponding objects; e.g. sight apprehends what may be seen, hearing what may be heard, so that touch does not taste, and hearing has no perception of odours and flavours, but each confines itself to that function to which it was appointed by nature, holding itself insensible, as it were, to those with which it has no natural correspondence, and incapable of tasting the pleasure enjoyed by its neighbour sense. But with God it is otherwise. All in all, He is at once sight, and hearing, and knowledge; and there we stop, for it is not permitted us to ascribe the more animal perceptions to that refined nature. Still we take a very low view of God, and drag down the Divine to our own grovelling standard, if we suppose the Father speaking with His mouth, and the Son's ear listening to His words. What, then, are we to suppose is the medium which conveys the Father's voice to the hearing of the Son? It must be created or uncreate. But we may not call it created; for the Word was before the creation of the world: and beside the Divine nature there is nothing uncreate. If, therefore, there was no creation then, and the Word spoken of in the cosmogony was older than creation, will he, who maintains that speech and a voice are meant by "the Word," suggest what medium existed between the Father and the Son, whereby those words and sounds were expressed? For if a medium exist, it must needs exist in a nature of its own, so as to differ in nature both from the Father and the Son. Being, then, something of necessity different, it divides the Father and the Son from each other, as though inserted between the two. What, then, could it be? Not created, for creation is younger than the Word. Generated we have learnt the Only-begotten (and Him alone) to be. Except the Father, none is ungenerate. Truth, therefore, obliges us to the conclusion that there is no medium between the Father and the Son. But where separation is not conceived of the closest connection is naturally implied. And what is so connected needs no medium for voice or speech. Now, by "connected," I mean here what is in all respects inseparable. For in the case of a spiritual nature the term connection does not mean corporeal connection, but the union and blending of spiritual with spiritual through identity of will. Accordingly, there is no divergence of will between the Father and the Son, but the image of goodness is after the Archetype of all goodness and beauty, and as, if a man should look at himself in a glass (for it is perfectly allowable to explain the idea by corporeal illustrations), the copy will in all respects be conformed to the original, the shape of the man who is reflected being the cause of the shape on the glass, and the reflection making no spontaneous movement or inclination unless commenced by the original, but, if it move, moving along with it,—in like manner we maintain that our Lord, the Image of the invisible God, is immediately and inseparably one with the Father in every movement of His Will. If the Father will anything, the Son Who is in the Father knows the Father's will, or rather He is Himself the Father's will. For, if He has in Himself all that is the Father's, there is nothing of the Father's that He cannot have. If, then, He has all things that are the Father's in Himself, or, say we rather, if He has the Father Himself, then, along with the Father and the things that are the Father's, He must needs have in Himself the whole of the Father's will. He needs not, therefore, to know the Father's will by word, being Himself the Word of the Father, in the highest acceptation of the term. What, then, is the word that can be addressed to Him who is the Word indeed? And how can He Who is the Word indeed require a second word for instruction?

But it may be said that the voice of the Father was addressed to the Holy Spirit. But neither does the Holy Spirit require instruction by speech, for being God, as saith the Apostle, He "searcheth all things, yea the deep things of God[4]." If, then, God utters any word, and all speech is directed to the ear, let those who maintain that God expresses Himself in the language of continuous discourse, inform us what audience He addressed. Himself He needs not address. The Son has no need of instruction by words. The Holy Ghost searcheth even the deep things of God. Creation did not yet exist. To whom, then, was God's word addressed?

But, says he, the record of Moses does not lie, and from it we learn that God spake. No! nor is great David of the number of those who lie, and he expressly says; "The heavens declare the glory of God, and the firmament showeth His handy work. Day unto day uttereth speech, and night unto night showeth know-

ledge;" and after saying that the heavens and the firmament declare, and that day and that night showeth knowledge and speech, he adds to what he has said, that "there is neither speech nor language, and that their voices are not heard[5]." Yet how can such declaring and showing forth be other than words, and how is it that no voice addresses itself to the ear? Is the prophet contradicting himself, or is he stating an impossibility, when he speaks of words without sound, and declaration without language, and announcement without voice? or, is there not rather the very perfection of truth in his teaching, which tells us, in the words which I have quoted, that the declaration of the heavens, and the word shouted forth by the day, is no articulate voice nor language of the lips, but is a revelation of the power of God to those who are capable of hearing it, even though no voice be heard?

What, then, do we think of this passage? For it may be that, if we understand it, we shall also understand the meaning of Moses. It often happens that Holy Scripture, to enable us more clearly to comprehend a matter to be revealed, makes use of a bodily illustration, as would seem to be the case in this passage from David, who teaches us by what he says that none of the things which are have their being from chance or accident, as some have imagined that our world and all that is therein was framed by fortuitous and undesigned combinations of first elements, and that no Providence penetrated the world. But we are taught that there is a cause of the system and government of the Universe, on Whom all nature depends, to Whom it owes its origin and cause, towards Whom it inclines and moves, and in Whom it abides. And since, as saith the Apostle, His eternal power and godhead are understood, being clearly seen through the creation of the world[6], therefore all creation and, before all, as saith the Scripture, the system of the heavens, declare the wisdom of the Creator in the skill displayed by His works. And this is what it seems to me that he is desirous to set forth, viz. the testimony of the things which do appear to the fact that the worlds were framed with wisdom and skill, and abide for ever by the power of Him who is the Ruler over all. The very heavens, he says, in displaying the wisdom of Him Who made them, all but shout aloud with a voice, and, though without voice, proclaim the wisdom of their Creator. For we can hear as it were words teaching us: "O men, when ye gaze upon us and behold our beauty and magnitude, and this ceaseless revolution, with its well-

---

[4] 1 Cor. ii. 10.

[5] Ps. xix. 1—3 (LXX.).

[6] Rom. i. 20.

ordered and harmonious motion, working in the same direction and in the same manner, turn your thoughts to Him Who presides over our system, and, by aid of the beauty which you see, imagine to yourselves the beauty of the invisible Archetype. For in us there is nothing without its Lord, nothing that moves of its own proper motion : but all that appears, or that is conceivable in respect to us, depends on a Power Who is inscrutable and sublime." This is not given in articulate speech, but by the things which are seen, and it instils into our minds the knowledge of Divine power more than if speech proclaimed it with a voice. As, then, the heavens declare, though they do not speak, and the firmament shows God's handy-work, yet requires no voice for the purpose, and the day uttereth speech, though there is no speaking, and no one can say that Holy Scripture is in error—in like manner, since both Moses and David have one and the same Teacher, I mean the Holy Spirit, Who says that the fiat went before the creation, we are not told that God is the Creator of words, but of things made known to us by the signification of our words. For, lest we should suppose the creation to be without its Lord, and spontaneously originated, He says that it was created by the Divine Being, and that it is established in an orderly and connected system by Him. Now it would be a work of time to discuss the order of what Moses didactically records in his historical summary respecting the creation of the world. Or (if we did) [7] each second passage would serve to prove more clearly the erroneous and futile character of our adversaries' opinion. But whoever cares to do so may read what we have written on Genesis, and judge whether our teaching or theirs is the more reasonable.

But to return to the matter in question. We assert that the words "He said" do not imply voice and words on the part of God; but the writer, in showing [8] the power of God to be concurrent with His will, renders the idea more easy of apprehension. For since by the will of God all things were created, and it is the ordinary way of men to signify their will first of all by speech, and so to bring their work into harmony with their will, and the scriptural account of the Creation is the learner's introduction, as it were, to the knowledge of God, representing to our minds the power of the Divine Being by objects more ready to our comprehension (for sensible apprehension is an aid to intellectual knowledge), on this account, Moses, by saying that God commanded all things to be, signifies to us the

inciting power of His will, and by adding, "and it was so," he shows that in the case of God there is no difference between will and performance ; but, on the contrary, that though the purposing initiates God's activity, the accomplishment keeps pace with the purpose, and that the two are to be considered together and at once, viz. the deliberate motion of the mind, and the power that effects its purpose. For the idea of the Divine purpose and action leaves no conceivable interval between them, but as light is produced along with the kindling of fire, at once coming out from it and shining forth along with it—in the same manner the existence of things created is an effect of the Divine will, but not posterior to it in time.

For the case is different from that of men endowed by nature with practical ability, where you may look at capability and execution apart from each other. For example, we say of a man who possesses the art of shipbuilding, that he is always a shipbuilder in respect of his ability to build ships, but that he operates only when he displays his skill in working. It is otherwise with God; for all that we can conceive as in Him is entirely work and action, His will passing over immediately to its object. As, then, the mechanism of the heavens testifies to the glory of their Creator and confesses Him Who made them, and needs no voice for the purpose, so on the other hand any one who is acquainted with the Mosaic Scripture will see that God speaks of the world as His creation, having brought the whole into being by the fiat of His will, and that He needs no words to make known His mind. As, then, he who heard the heavens declaring the glory of God looked not for set speech on the occasion (for, to those who can understand it, the universe speaks through the things which are being done, without regard or care for verbal explanation), so, even if any one hears Moses telling how God gave order and arrangement to each several part of Creation by name, let him not suppose the prophet to speak falsely, nor degrade the contemplation of sublime verities by mean and grovelling notions, thus, as it were, reducing God to a mere human standard, and supposing that after the manner of men he directs His operations by the instrumentality of speech; but let His fiat mean His will only, and let the names of those created things denote the mere reality of their coming into being. And thus he will learn these two things from what is recorded : (1) That God made all things by His will, and (2) that without any trouble or difficulty the Divine Will became nature.

But if any one would give a more sensuous interpretation to the words "God said," as proving that articulate speech was His creation, by a

---

7 ῏Η γαρ. Both Codd. & editt. read so ; as Oehler testifies, though he has ῏Η γὰρ.
8 Reading ἀποφαίνων as referring to Moses, with Oehler, instead of the conjecture of John the Franciscan ἀποφαίνουσα, in the Paris edit. Even the Pithœan has ἀποφαίνων.

parity of reason he must understand by the words "God saw," that He did so by faculties of perception like our own, through the organs of vision; and so again by the words "The Lord heard me and had mercy upon me," and again, "He smelled a sweet savour[9]," and whatever other sensuous expressions are employed by Scripture in reference to head, or foot, or hand, or eyes, or fingers, or sandals, as appertaining to God, taking them, I say, in their plain literal acceptation, he will present to us an anthropomorphous deity, after the similitude of what is seen among ourselves. But if any one hearing that the heavens are the work of His fingers, that He has a strong hand, and a mighty arm, and eyes, and feet, and sandals, deduces from such words ideas worthy of God, and does not degrade the idea of His pure nature by carnal and sensuous imaginations, it will follow that on the one hand he will regard the verbal utterances as indications of the Divine will, but on the other He will not conceive of them as articulate sounds, but will reason thus; that the Creator of human reason has gifted us with speech proportionally to the capacity of our nature, so that we might be able thereby to signify the thoughts of our minds; but that, so far as the Divine nature differs from ours, so great will be the degree of difference between our notions respecting it and its own inherent majesty and godhead. And as our power compared with God's, and our life with His life, is as nothing, and all else that is ours, compared with what is in Him, is "as nothing in comparison[1]" with Him, as saith the inspired Teaching, so also our word as compared with Him, Who is the Word indeed, is as nothing[2]. For this word of yours was not in the beginning, but was created along with our nature, nor is it to be regarded as having any reality of its own, but, as our master (Basil) somewhere has said, it vanishes along with the sound of the voice, nor is any operation of the word discernible, but it has its subsistence in voice only, or in written characters. But the word of God is God Himself, the Word that was in the beginning and that abideth for ever, through Whom all things were and are, Who ruleth over all, and hath all power over the things in heaven and the things on earth, being Life, and Truth, and Righteousness, and Light, and all that is good, and upholding all things in being. Such, then, and so great being the word, as we understand it, of God, our opponent allows God, as some great thing, the power of language, made up of nouns, verbs, and conjunctions, not perceiving that, as

He Who conferred practical powers on our nature is not spoken of as fabricating each of their several results, but, while He gave our nature its ability, it is by us that a house is constructed, or a bench, or a sword, or a plough, and whatsoever thing our life happens to be in need of, each of which things is our own work, although it may be ascribed to Him Who is the author of our being, and Who created our nature capable of every science,—so also our power of speech is the work of Him Who made our nature what it is, but the invention of each several term required to denote objects in hand is of our own devising. And this is proved by the fact that many terms in use are of a base and unseemly character, of which no man of sense would conceive God the inventor: so that, if certain of our familiar expressions are ascribed by Holy Scripture to God as the speaker, we should remember that the Holy Spirit is addressing us in language of our own, as e. g. in the history of the Acts we are told that each man received the teaching of the disciples in his own language wherein he was born, understanding the sense of the words by the language which he knew. And, that this is true, may be seen yet more clearly by a careful examination of the enactments of the Levitical law. For they make mention of pans, and cakes, and fine flours, and the like, in the mystic sacrifices, instilling wholesome doctrine under the veil of symbol and enigma. Mention, too, is made of certain measures then in use, such as ephah, and nebel[4], and hin, and the like. Are we, then, to suppose that God made these names and appellations, or that in the beginning He commanded them to be such, and to be so named, calling one kind of grain wheat, and its pith flour, and flat sweetmeats, whether heavy or light, cakes; and that He commanded a vessel of the kind in which a moist lump is boiled or baked to be called a pan, or that He spoke of a certain liquid measure by the name of hin or nebel, and measured dry produce by the homer? surely it is trifling and mere Jewish folly, far removed from the grandeur of Christian simplicity, to think that God, Who is the Most High and above every name and thought, Who by sole virtue of His will governs the world, which He brought into existence, and upholds it in being, should set Himself like some schoolmaster to settle the niceties of terminology. Rather let us say, that as we indicate to the deaf what we want them to do, by gestures and signs, not because we have no voice of our own, but because a verbal

9 Ps. xxx. 10 (LXX.). Gen. viii. 21.
1 Ps. xxxix. 5.
2 Or. Cat. c. 1. "For since our nature is liable to corruption, and weak, therefore is our life short, our strength unsubstantial, our word unstable (ἀπαγής);" and see note.

3 Lev. ii. 5, seqq.
4 Nebel is defined by Epiphanius de pond. et mens. c. 24. as follows, Νέβελ οἴνου, ὅπερ ἐστὶ μέτρον ξεστῶν ρ´ν´. (150 pints). The word is merely a transcription of the Hebrew for a skin. i.e. wine-skin, "bottle." Cf. Hosea iii. 2, νέβελ οἴνου (LXX.) : Symmachus has ἀσκός.

communication would be utterly useless to those who cannot hear, so, inasmuch as human nature is in a sense deaf and insensible to higher truths, we maintain that the grace of God at sundry times and in divers manners spake by the Prophets, ordering their voices conformably to our capacity and the modes of expression with which we are familiar, and that by such means it leads us, as with a guiding hand, to the knowledge of higher truths, not teaching us in terms proportioned to their inherent sublimity, (for how can the great be contained by the little?) but descending to the lower level of our limited comprehension. And as God, after giving animals their power of motion, no longer prescribes each step they take, for their nature, having once for all taken its beginning from the Creator, moves of itself, and makes its way, adapting its power of motion to its object from time to time (except in so far as it is said that a man's steps are directed by the Lord), so our nature, having received from God the power of speech and utterance and of expressing the will by the voice, proceeds on its way through things, giving them distinctive names by varying inflections of sound ; and these signs are the verbs and nouns which we use, and through which we signify the meaning of the things. And though the word "fruit" is made use of by Moses before the creation of fruit, and "seed" before that of seed, this does not disprove our assertion, nor is the sense of the lawgiver opposed to what we have said in respect to thought and conception. For that end of past husbandry which we speak of as fruit, and that beginning of future husbandry which we speak of as seed, this thing, I mean, underlying these names,—whether wheat or some other produce which is increased and multiplied by sowing—does not, he teaches us, grow spontaneously, but by the will of Him Who created them to grow with their peculiar power, so as to be the same fruit and to reproduce themselves as seed, and to support mankind with their increase. And by the Divine will the thing is produced, not the name, so that the substantial thing[5] is the work of the Creator, but the distinguishing names of things, by which speech furnishes us with a clear and accurate description of them, are the work and the invention of man's reasoning faculty, though the reasoning faculty itself and its nature are a work of God. And since all men are endowed with reason, differences of language will of necessity be found according to differences of country.

But if any one maintain that light, or heaven, or earth, or seed were named after human fashion by God, he will certainly conclude that they were named in some special language. What that was, let him show. For he who knows the one thing will not, in all probability, be ignorant of the other. For at the river Jordan, after the descent of the Holy Ghost, and again in the hearing of the Jews, and at the Transfiguration, there came a voice from heaven, teaching men not only to regard the phenomenon as something more than a figure, but also to believe the beloved Son of God to be truly God. Now that voice was fashioned by God, suitably to the understanding of the hearers, in airy substance, and adapted to the language of the day, God, "who willeth that all men should be saved and come to the knowledge of the truth [6]," having so articulated His words in the air with a view to the salvation of the hearers, as our Lord also saith to the Jews, when they thought it thundered because the sound took place in the air. "This voice came not because of Me, but for your sakes [7]." But before the creation of the world, inasmuch as there was no one to hear the word, and no bodily element capable of accentuating the articulate voice, how can he who says that God used words give any air of probability to his assertion? God Himself is without body, creation did not yet exist. Reason does not suffer us to conceive of anything material in respect to Him. They who might have been benefited by the hearing were not yet created. And if men were not yet in being, neither had any form of language been struck out in accordance with national peculiarities, by what arguments, then, can he who looks to the bare letter make good his assertion, that God spoke thus using human parts of speech?

And the futility of such assertions may be seen also by this. For as the natures of the elements, which are the work of the Creator, appear alike to all, and there is no difference to human sense in men's experience of fire, or air, or water, but the nature of each is one and unchanging, working in the same way, and suffering no modification from the differences of those who partake of it, so also the imposition of names, if applied to things by God, would have been the same for all. But, in point of fact, while the nature of things as constituted by God remains the same, the names which denote them are divided by so many differences of language, that it were no easy task even to calculate their number.

And if any one cites the confusion of tongues that took place at the building of the tower, as contradicting what I have said, not even there

---

[5] Here is the answer to Eunomius' contention above (p. 270), that "in the earliest of the sacred records before the creation of man, the naming of fruit and seed are mentioned in Holy Writ." He calls Basil, for not observing this, a pagan and atheist. So below he calls him a follower of Valentinus, "a sower of tares," for making the human faculty (ἐπίνοια) the maker of names, even of those of the Only-begotten ; apparently, as Valentinus multiplied the names of Christ.

[6] 1 Tim. ii. 4   [7] S. John xii. 30.

is God spoken of as creating men's languages, but as confounding the existing one[8], that all might not hear all. For when all lived together and were not as yet divided by various differences of race, the aggregate of men dwelt together with one language among them; but when by the Divine will it was decreed that all the earth should be replenished by mankind, then, their community of tongue being broken up, men were dispersed in various directions and adopted this and that form of speech and language, possessing a certain bond of union in similarity of tongue, not indeed disagreeing from others in their knowledge of things, but differing in the character of their names. For a stone or a stick does not seem one thing to one man and another to another, but the different peoples call them by different names. So that our position remains unshaken, that human language is the invention of the human mind or understanding. For from the beginning, as long as all men had the same language, we see from Holy Scripture that men received no teaching of God's words, nor, when men were separated into various differences of language, did a Divine enactment prescribe how each man should talk. But God, willing that men should speak different languages, gave human nature full liberty to formulate arbitrary sounds, so as to render their meaning more intelligible. Accordingly, Moses, who lived many generations after the building of the tower, uses one of the subsequent languages in his historical narrative of the creation, and attributes certain words to God, relating these things in his own tongue in which he had been brought up, and with which he was familiar, not changing the names for God by foreign peculiarities and turns of speech, in order by the strangeness and novelty of the expressions to prove them the words of God Himself[9].

But some who have carefully studied the Scriptures tell us that the Hebrew tongue is not even ancient[10] like the others, but that along with other miracles this miracle was wrought in behalf of the Israelites, that after the Exodus from Egypt, the language was hastily improvised[1]

for the use of the nation. And there is a[2] passage in the Prophet which confirms this. For he says, "when he came out of the land of Egypt he heard a strange language[3]." If, then, Moses was a Hebrew, and the language of the Hebrews was subsequent to the others, Moses, I say, who was born some thousands of years after the Creation of the world, and who relates the words of God in his own language—does he not clearly teach us that he does not attribute to God such a language of human fashion, but that he speaks as he does because it was impossible otherwise than in human language to express his meaning, though the words he uses have some Divine and profound significance?

For to suppose that God used the Hebrew tongue, when there was no one to hear and understand such a language, methinks no reasonable being will consent. We read in the Acts that the Divine power divided itself into many languages for this purpose, that no one of alien tongue might lose his share of the benefit. But if God spoke in human language before the Creation, whom was He to benefit by using it? For that His speech should have some adaptation to the capacity of the hearers, with a view to their profit, no one would conceive to be unworthy of God's love to man, for Paul the follower of Christ knew how to adapt his words suitably to the habits and disposition of his hearers, making himself milk for babes and strong meat for grown men[4]. But where no object was to be gained by such use of language, to argue that God, as it were, declaimed such words by Himself, when there was no one in need of the information they would convey—such an idea, methinks, is at once both blasphemous and absurd. Neither, then, did God speak in the Hebrew language, nor did He express Himself according to any form in use among the Gentiles. But whatsoever of God's words are recorded by Moses or the Prophets, are indications of the Divine will, flashing forth, now in one way, now in another, on the pure intellect of those holy men, according to the measure of the grace of which they were partakers. Moses, then, spoke his mother-tongue, and that in which he was educated. But he attributed these words to God, as I have said, repeatedly,

---

8 Gen. xi. 7.   9 A hit at Eunomius.
10 μηδὲ ἀρχαΐζειν : therefore, if they are not the Divine language, a fortiori this is not. The word cannot possibly mean here "to grow obsolete."
1 hastily improvised. But Origen, c. Celsum iii. 6, says—"Celsus has not shewn himself a just critic of the differing accounts of the Egyptians and the Jews. . . . He does not see that it was not possible for so large a number of rebellious Egyptians, after starting off in this way, to have changed their language at the very moment of their insurrection, and so become a separate nation, so that those who one day spoke Egyptian suddenly spoke a complete Hebrew dialect. Allow for a moment that when they left Egypt they rejected also their mother tongue ; how was it that, thereupon, they did not adopt the Syrian or Phœnician, but the Hebrew which was so different from both these? . . . For the Hebrew had been their national language before they went down into Egypt : " And, i. 16—" I wonder how Celsus can admit the Odrysians amongst the most ancient as well as the wisest people, but will admit the Jews into neither, notwithstanding that there are many books in Egypt

and Phœnicia and Greece which testify to their antiquity. Any one who likes can read Flavius Josephus' two l ooks on the antiquity of the Jews, where he makes a large collection of writers who witness to this." And yet, iii. 7, he goes on to say (what Gregory is here alluding to) that while any way the Hebrew language was never Egyptian, "yet if we look deeper, we might find it possible to say in the case of the Exodus that there was a miracle : viz. the whole mass of the Hebrew people receiving a language ; that such language was the gift of God, as one of their own prophets has expressed it, ' when he came out of Egypt, he heard a strange language.' "
2 καί τις. This reading (and not the interrogative τίς, as Oehler) is required by the context, where Gregory actually favours this theory of the lateness of the Hebrew tongue: and is confirmed by Gretser's Latin, "Et nescio quis Prophetæ sermo."
3 Ps. lxxxi. 5.   4 Heb. v. 12.

on account of the childishness of those who were being brought to the knowledge of God, in order to give a clear representation of the Divine will, and to render his hearers more obedient, as being awed by the authority of the speaker.

But this is denied by Eunomius, the author of all this contumely with which we are assailed, and the companion and adviser of this impious band. For, changing insolence into courtesy, I will present him with his own words. He maintains, in so many words, that he has the testimony of Moses himself to his assertion that men were endowed with the use of the things named, and of their names, by the Creator of nature, and that the naming of the things given was prior in time to the creation of those who should use them. Now, if he is in possession of some Moses of his own, from whom he has learned this wisdom, and, making this his base of operations, relies on such statements as these, viz. that God, as he himself says, lays down the laws of human speech, enacting that things shall be called in one way and not in another, let him trifle as much as he pleases, with his Moses in the background to support his assertions. But if there is only one Moses whose writings are the common source of instruction to those who are learned in the Divine Word, we will freely accept our condemnation if we find ourselves refuted by the law of that Moses. But where did he find this law respecting verbs and nouns? Let him produce it in the very words of the text. The account of the Creation, and the genealogy of the successive generations, and the history of certain events, and the complex system of legislation, and various regulations in regard to religious service and daily life, these are the chief heads of the writings of Moses. But, if he says that there was any legislative enactment in regard to words, let him point it out, and I will hold my tongue. But he cannot; for, if he could, he would not abandon the more striking evidences of the Deity, for such as can only procure him ridicule, and not credit, from men of sense. For to think it the essential point in piety to attribute the invention of words to God, Whose praise the whole world and the wonders that are therein are incompetent to celebrate—must it not be a proceeding of extreme folly so to neglect higher grounds of praise, and to magnify God on such as are purely human? His fiat preluded Creation, but it was recorded by Moses after human fashion, though Divinely issued. That will of God, then, which brought about the creation of the world by His Divine power, consisted, says our careful student of the Scriptures, in the teaching of words. And as though God had said, "Let there be a word," or, "Let speech be created," or, "Let this or that have such or

such an appellation," so, in advocacy of his trifling, he brings forward the fact that it was by the impulse of the Divine will that Creation took place. For with all his study and experience in the Scriptures he knows not even this, that the impulse of the mind is frequently spoken of in Scripture as a voice. And for this we have the evidence of Moses himself, whose meaning he frequently perverts, but whom on this point he simply ignores. For who is there, however slightly acquainted with the holy volume, who does not know this, that the people of Israel who had just escaped[5] from Egypt were suddenly affrighted in the wilderness by the pursuit of the Egyptians, and when dangers encompassed them on all sides, and on one side the sea cut off their passage as by a wall, while the enemy barred their flight in the rear, the people coming together to the Prophet charged him with being the cause of their helpless condition? And when he comforted them in their abject terror, and roused them to courage, a voice came from God, addressing the Prophet by name, "Wherefore criest thou unto Me?[6]" And yet before this the narrative makes no mention of any utterance on the part of Moses. But the thought which the Prophet had lifted up to God is called a cry, though uttered in silence in the hidden thought of his heart. If, then, Moses cries, though without speaking, as witnessed by Him Who hears, those "groanings which cannot be uttered[7]," is it strange that the Prophet, knowing the Divine will, so far as it was lawful for him to tell it and for us to hear it, revealed it by known and familiar words, describing God's discourse after human fashion, not indeed expressed in words, but signified by the effects themselves? "In the beginning," he says, "God created," not the names of heaven and earth, but, "the heaven and the earth[8]." And again, "God said, Let there be light," not the name Light: and having divided the light from the darkness, "God called," he says, "the light Day, and the darkness He called Night."

On these passages it is probable that our opponents will take their stand. And I will agree for them with what is said, and will myself take advantage of their positions[9] further on in our inquiry, in order that what we teach may be more firmly established, no

5 ἀποδράντες. So also the Paris editt. The Munich MS. has ἀποδράσαντες, which form of the aorist is not found at all in classic Greek, and is only used, as Oehler notices, by Epiphanius (e. g. Panar. liv. 1 ; lxviii. 4) and a few other writers of a debased style.
6 Exod. xiv. 15. 7 Rom. viii. 26. 8 Gen. i. 1, sqq.
9 τὰ παρατέθεντα παρ' ἐκείνων ἀνθυποίσω. He does this below. "And we will return to his argument that even thence we may muster reinforcements for the Truth." Gregory goes on to show that Eunomius, who attacks the doctrine that the names of God are the result of Conception, and makes their Scriptural use a proof that they are God's own direct teaching, himself seeks to overthrow this doctrine by means of the term Ungenerate, which is not in Scripture : hence, by his own showing, this theory about the Scripture names is not true. The above is the reading of the Munich MS. : Oehler has the vox nihili παρεθέντα.

point in controversy being left without due examination. "God called," he says, "the firmament Heaven, and He called the dry land Earth, and the light Day, and the darkness He called Night." How comes it, then, they will ask, when the Scripture admits that their appellations were given them by God, that you say that their names are the work of human invention? What, then, is our reply? We return to our plain statement, and we assert, that He Who brought all creation into being out of nothing is the Creator of things seen in substantial existence, not of unsubstantial words having no existence but in the sound of the voice and the lisp of the tongue. But things are named by the indication of the voice in conformity with the nature and qualities inherent in each, the names being adapted to the things according to the vernacular language of each several race.

But since the nature of most things that are seen in Creation is not simple, so as to allow of all that they connote being comprehended in one word, as, for instance, in the case of fire, the element itself is one thing in its nature, while the word which denotes it is another (for fire itself possesses the qualities of shining, of burning, of drying and heating, and consuming whatever fuel it lays hold of, but the name is but a brief word of one syllable), on this account speech, which distinguishes the powers and qualities seen in fire, gives each of them a name of its own, as I have said before. And one cannot say that only a name has been given to fire when it is spoken of as bright, or consuming, or anything else that we observe it to be. For such words denote qualities physically inherent in it. So likewise, in the case of heaven and the firmament, though one nature is signified by each of these words, their difference represents one or other of its peculiar characteristics, in looking at which we learn one thing by the appellation "heaven," and another by "firmament." For when speech would define the limit of sensible creation, beyond which it is succeeded by the transmundane void apprehended by the mind alone, in contrast with the intangible and incorporeal and invisible, the beginning and the end of all material subsistences is called the firmament. And when we survey the environment of terrestrial things, we call that which encompasses all material nature, and which forms the boundary of all things visible, by the name of heaven. In the same manner with regard to earth and dry land, since all heavy and downward-tending nature was divided into these two elements, earth and water, the appellation "dry" defines to a certain extent its opposite, for earth is called dry in opposition to moist, since having thrown off, by Divine command, the water that overspread it, it appeared

in its own character. But the name "earth" does not continue to express the signification of some one only of its qualities, but, by virtue of its meaning, it embraces all that the word connotes, e. g. hardness, density, weight, resistance, capability of supporting animal and vegetable life. Accordingly, the word "dry" was not changed by speech to the last name put upon it (for its new name did not make it cease to be called so), but while both the appellations remained, a peculiar signification attached itself to each, the one distinguishing it in nature and property from its opposite, the other embracing all its attributes collectively. And so in light and day, and again in night and darkness, we do not find a pronunciation of syllables created to suit them by the Maker of all things, but rather through these appellations we note the substance of the things which they signify. At the entrance of light, by the will of God the darkness that prevailed over the earliest creation is scattered. But the earth lying in the midst, and being upheld on all sides by its surrounding of different elements, as Job saith, "He hangeth the earth upon nothing [10]," it was necessary when light travelled over one side and the earth obstructed it on the opposite by its own bulk, that a side of darkness should be left by the obscuration, and so, as the perpetual motion of the heavens cannot but carry along with it the darkness resulting from the obscuration, God ordained this revolution for a measure of duration of time. And that measure is day and night. For this reason Moses, according to his wisdom, in his historical elucidation of these matters, named the shadow resulting from the earth's obstruction, a dividing of the light from the darkness, and the constant and measured alternation of light and darkness over the surface of the earth he called day and night. So that what was called light was not named day, but as "there was light," and not the bare name of light, so the measure of time also was created and the name followed, not created by God in a sound of words, but because the very nature of the thing assumed this vocal notation. And as, if it had been plainly said by the Lawgiver that nothing that is seen or named is of spontaneous generation or unfashioned, but that it has its subsistence from God, we might have concluded of ourselves that God made the world and all its parts, and the order which is seen in them, and the faculty of distinguishing them, so also by what he says he leads us on to understand and believe that nothing which exists is without beginning. And with this view he describes the successive events of Creation in orderly method, enumerating them one after

---

[10] Job xxvi. 7.

another. But it was impossible to represent them in language, except by expressing their signification by words that should indicate it. Since, then, it is written that God called the light day, it must be understood that God made the day from light, being something different, by the force of the term. For you cannot apply the same definition to "light" and "day," but light is what we understand by the opposite of darkness, and day is the extent of the measure of the interval of light. In the same way you may regard night and darkness by the same difference of description, defining darkness as the negation of light, and calling night the extent of the encompassing darkness. Thus in every way our argument is confirmed, though not, perhaps, drawn out in strict logical form—showing that God is the Maker of things, not of empty words. For things have their names not for His sake but for ours. For as we cannot always have all things before our eyes, we take knowledge of some of the things that are present with us from time to time, and others we register in our memories. But it would be impossible to keep memory unconfused unless we had the notation of words to distinguish the things that are stored up in our minds from one another. But to God all things are present, nor does He need memory, all things being within the range of His penetrating vision. What need, then, in His case, of parts of speech, when His own wisdom and power embraces and holds the nature of all things distinct and unconfused? Wherefore all things that exist substantially are from God; but, for our guidance, all things that exist are provided with names to indicate them. And if any one say that such names were imposed by the arbitrary usage of mankind, he will be guilty of no offence against the scheme of Divine Providence. For we do not say that the nature of things was of human invention, but only their names. The Hebrew calls Heaven by one name, the Canaanite by another, but both of them understand it alike, being in no way led into error by the difference of the sounds that convey the idea of the object. But the over-cautious and timid will-worship of these clever folk, on whose authority he asserts that, if it were granted that words were given to things by men, men would be of higher authority than God, is proved to be unsubstantial even by the example which we find recorded of Moses. For who gave Moses his name? Was it not Pharaoh's daughter who named him from what had happened [11]? For water is called Moses in the language of the Egyptians. Since, then, in consequence of the tyrant's order, his parents had placed the babe

in an ark and consigned it to the stream (for so some related concerning him), but by the will of God the ark was floated by the current and carried to the bank, and found by the princess, who happened just then to be taking the refreshment of the bath, as the child had been gained "from the water," she is said to have given him his name as a memorial of the occurrence,—a name by which God Himself did not disdain to address His servant, nor did He deem it beneath Him to allow the name given by the foreign woman to remain the Prophet's proper appellation.

In like manner before him Jacob, having taken hold of his brother's heel, was called a supplanter [1], from the attitude in which he came to the birth. For those who are learned in such matters tell us that such is the interpretation of the word "Jacob," as translated into Greek. So, too, Pharez was so named by his nurse from the incident at his birth [2], yet no one on that account, like Eunomius, displayed any jealousy of his assuming an authority above that of God. Moreover the mothers of the patriarchs gave them their names, as Reuben, and Simeon, and Levi [3], and all those who came after them. And no one started up, like our new author, as patron of Divine providence, to forbid women to usurp Divine authority by the imposition of names. And what shall we say of other particulars in the sacred record, such as the "waters of strife," and the "place of mourning," and the "hill of the foreskins," and the "valley of the cluster," and the "field of blood," and such-like names, of human imposing, but oftentimes recorded to have been uttered by the Person of God, from which we may learn that men may notify the meaning of things by words without presumption, and that the Divine nature does not depend on words for its evidence to itself?

But I will pass over his other babblings against the truth, possessing as they do no force against our doctrines, for I deem it superfluous to linger any longer over such absurdities. For who can be so wanting in the more important subjects of thought as to waste energy on silly arguments, and to contend with men who speak of us as asserting that "man's forethought is of superior weight and authority to God's guardianship," and that we "ascribe the carelessness which confuses the feebler minds to the providence of God"? These are the exact words of our calumniator. But I, for my part, think it equally as absurd to pay attention to remarks like that, as to occupy myself with old wives' dreams. For to think of securing the dignity of rule and sovereignty to the Divine

---

[11] Exod. ii. 10.

[1] Gen. xxv. 26.   [2] Gen. xxxviii. 29.   [3] Gen. xxix. 32—35.

Being by a form of words, and to show the great power of God to be dependent upon this, and on the other hand to neglect Him and disregard the providence which belongs to Him, and to lay it tó our reproach that men, having received from God the faculty of reason, make an arbitrary use of words to signify things— what is this but an old wife's fable, or a drunkard's dream? For the true power, and authority, and dominion, and sovereignty of God do not, we think, consist in syllables. Were it so, any and every inventor of words might claim equal honour with God. But the infinite ages, and the beauties of the universe, and the beams of the heavenly luminaries, and all the wonders of land and sea, and the angelic hosts and supramundane powers, and whatever else there is whose existence in the realm above is revealed to us under various figures by Holy Scripture— these are the things that bear witness to God's power over all. Whereas, to attribute the invention of vocal sound to those who are naturally endowed with the faculty of speech, this involves no impiety towards Him Who gave them their voice. Nor indeed do we hold it to be a great thing to invent words significative of things. For the being to whom Holy Scripture in the history of the creation gave the name of "man [4]" (ἄνθρωπος), a word of human devising, that same being Job calls "mortal [5]" (βροτός), while of profane writers, some call him "human being" (φώς), and others "articulate speaker" (μέροψ)—to say nothing of other varieties of the name. Do we, then, elevate them to equal honour with God, because they also invented names equivalent to that of "man," alike signifying their subject. But, as I have said before, let us leave this idle talk, and make no account of his string of revilings, in which he charges us with lying against the Divine oracles, and uttering slanders with effrontery even against God.

To pass on, then, to what remains. He brings forward once more some of the Master's words, to this effect: "And it is in precisely the same manner that we are taught by Holy Scripture the employment of a conception. Our Lord Jesus Christ, when declaring to men the nature of His Godhead, explains it by certain special characteristics, calling Himself the Door, the Bread, the Way, the Vine, the Shepherd, the Light." Now I think it seemly to pass over his insolent remarks on these words (for it is thus that his rhetorical training has taught him to contend with his opponents), nor will I suffer myself to be disturbed by his ebullitions of childish folly. Let us, however, examine one pungent and "irresistible" argument which he puts forward for our refutation.

Which of the sacred writers, he asks, gives evidence that these names were attributed to our Lord by a conception? But which of them, I reply, forbids it, deeming it a blasphemy to regard such names as the result of a conception? For if he maintains that its not being mentioned is a proof that it is forbidden, by a parity of reasoning he must admit that its not being forbidden is an argument that it is permitted. Is our Lord called by these names, or does Eunomius deny this also? If he does deny that these names are spoken of Christ, we have conquered without a battle. For what more signal victory could there be, than to prove our adversary to be fighting against God, by robbing the sacred words of the Gospel of their meaning? But if he admits that it is true that Christ is named by these names, let him say in what manner they may be applied without irreverence to the Only-begotten Son of God. Does he take "the stone" as indicative of His nature? Does he understand His essence under the figure of the Axe (not to encumber our argument by enumerating the rest)? None of these names represents the nature of the Only-begotten, or His Godhead, or the peculiar character of His essence. Nevertheless He is called by these names, and each appellation has its own special fitness. For we cannot, without irreverence, suppose anything in the words of God to be idle and unmeaning. Let him say, then, if he disallows these names as the result of a conception, how do they apply to Christ? For we on our part say this, that as our Lord provided for human life in various forms, each variety of His beneficence is suitably distinguished by His several names, His provident care and working on our behalf passing over into the mould of a name. And such a name is said by us to be arrived at by a conception. But if this is not agreeable to our opponents, let it be as each of them pleases. In his ignorance, however, of the figures of Scripture, our opponent contradicts what is said. For if he had learned the Divine names, he must have known that our Lord is called a Curse and Sin [6], and a Heifer [7], and a lion's Whelp [8], and a Bear bereaved of her whelps [9], and a Leopard [1], and such-like names, according to various modes of conception, by Holy Scripture, the sacred and inspired writers by such names, as by well-directed shafts, indicating the central point of the idea they had in view; even though these words, when taken in their literal and obvious signification, seem not above suspicion, but each single one of them, unless we allow it to be predicated of God by some process of conception, will not escape the

---

[4] Gen. i. 26.　　　[5] Job xiv. 1. βροτὸς γὰρ γεννητὸς γυναικὸς, ὀλιγόβιος καὶ πλήρης ὀργῆς.

[6] Gal. iii. 13.　　[7] Heb. ix. 13.　　[8] Gen. xlix. 9.
[9] Hosea xiii. 3.　　　[1] Hosea xiii. 7.

taint of a blasphemous suggestion. But it would be a lengthy task to bring them forward, and elucidate in every case how, in the general idea, these words have been perverted[2] out of their obvious meanings, and how it is only in connection with the conceptive faculty that the names of God can be reconciled with that reverence which is His due.

But to return. Such names are used of our Lord, and no one familiar with the inspired Scriptures can deny the fact. What then? Does Eunomius affirm that the words are indicative of His nature itself? If so, he asserts that the Divine nature is multiform, and that the variety which it displays in what is signified by the names is very complex. For the meanings of the words Bread and Lion are not the same, nor those of Axe and Water[3], but to each of them we can assign a definition of its own, of which the others do not partake. They do not, therefore, signify nature or essence, yet no one will presume to say that this nomenclature is quite inappropriate and unmeaning. If, then, these words are given us, but not as indicative of essence, and every word given in Scripture is just and appropriate, how else can these appellations be fitly applied to the Only-begotten Son of God, except in connection with the faculty of conception? For it is clear that the Divine Being is spoken of under various names, according to the variety of His operations, so that we may think of Him in the aspect so named. What harm, then, is done to our reverential ideas of God by this mental operation, instituted with a view to our thinking upon the things done, and which *we* call conception, though if any one choose to call it by some other name, we shall make no objection.

But, like a mighty wrestler, he will not relinquish his irresistible hold on us, and affirms in so many words, that "these names are the work of human thought and conception, and that, by the exercise of this operation of the mind by some, results are arrived at which no Apostle or Evangelist has taught." And after this doughty onslaught he raises that sanctimonious voice of his, spitting out his foul abuse at us with a tongue well schooled to such language. "For," says he, "to ascribe homonyms, drawn from analogy, to human thought and conception is the work of a mind that has lost all judicial sense, and that studies the words of the Lord with an en-

feebled understanding and dishonest habit of thought." Mercy on us! what a logical argument! how scientifically it proceeds to its conclusion! Who after this will dare to speak up for the cause of conception, when such a stench is poured forth from his mouth upon those who attempt speaking? I suppose, then, that we, who do attempt speaking, must forbear to examine his argument, for fear of his stirring up against us the cesspool of his abuse. And verily it is weak-minded[4] to let ourselves be irritated by childish absurdities. We will therefore allow our insolent adversary full liberty to indulge in his method as he will. But we will return to the Master's argument, that thence too we may muster reinforcements for the truth. Eunomius has been reminded of "analogy" and has perceived "the homonyms to be derived from it." Now where or from whom did he learn these terms? Not from Moses, not from the Prophets and Apostles, not from the Evangelists. It is impossible that he should have learned them from the teaching of any Scripture. How came he, then, to use them? The very word which describes this or that signification of a thought as analogy, is it not the invention of the thinking faculty of him who utters it[5]? How is it, then, that he fails to perceive that he is using the views he fights against as his allies in the war? For he makes war against our principle of words being formed by the operation of conception, and would endeavour to establish, by the aid of words formed on that very principle, that it is unlawful to use them. "It is not," says he, "the teaching of any of the sacred writers." To whom, then, or of the ancients do you yourself ascribe the term "ungenerate," and its being predicated of the essence of God? or is it allowable for you, when you want to establish some of your impious conclusions, to coin and invent terms to your own liking; but if anything is said by some one else in contravention of your impiety, to deprive your adversary of similar licence? Great indeed would be the power you would assume if you could make good your claim to such authority as this, that what you refuse to others should be allowable to you alone, and that what you yourself presume to do by virtue of it, you should prevent others from doing. You condemn, as by an edict, the doctrine that these names were applied to Christ as a result of conception, because none of the sacred writers have declared that they ought so to be applied. How, then, can you lay down the law that the Divine essence should be denoted by the word "ungenerate" —a term which none of the sacred writers can

---

[2] διαβέβληται. The Latin, "vulgo usurpata sunt," misses the force of the Greek. Or "are disliked because of their obvious meaning." Cf. above "even though these words . . . *seem not above suspicion* (διαβεβλῆσθαι δοκεῖ)." For this use of διαβάλλεσθαι (to be brought into suspicion or odium), cf. Origen c. Cels. iii. 58, διαβεβλημένῳ πρὸς ἀρετὴν καὶ καλοκἀγαθίαν, *i. e.* "who has quite broken with virtue and decency?" and vi. 42, where Celsus blasphemously says, that "the Son of God ought to have himself punished the Devil, rather than frighten with his threats that mankind which had been dragged into the quarrel by himself" (τοῖς ὑπ' αὐτοῦ διαβεβλημένοις ἀνθρώποις); a passage quite missed in the Latin. [3] S. John vii. 37.

[4] Ἡ μικροψύχων κ. τ. λ. Oehler's stopping here (and accent) is better than that of the Codices. *i. e.* ὑποκινήσειεν, ἢ κ. τ. λ.
[5] In other words, analogy implies thought (λόγος).

be shown to have handed down to us? For if this is the test of the right use of words, that only such shall be employed as the inspired word of Scripture shall authorize, the word "ungenerate" must be erased from your own writings, since none of the sacred writers has sanctioned the expression. But perhaps you accept it by reason of the sense that resides in it. Well, we ourselves in the same way accept the term "conception" by reason of the sense that resides in it. Accordingly we will either exclude both from use, or neither, and whichever alternative be adopted, we are equally masters of the field. For if the term "ungenerate" be altogether suppressed, all our adversaries' clamour against the truth is suppressed along with it, and a doctrine worthy of the Only-begotten Son of God will shine forth, inasmuch as logical opposition can furnish no name [6] to detract from the majesty of the Lord. But if both be retained, in that case also the truth will prevail, and we along with it, when we have altered the word "ungeneracy" from the substance, into a conception, of the Deity. But so long as he does not exclude the term "ungenerate" from his own writings, let our modern Pharisee admonish himself not to behold the mote that is in our eye, before he has cast out the beam that is in his own.

"But God," he says, "gave the weakest of terrestrial things a share in the most honourable names, though not giving them an equal share of dignity, and to the highest He imparted the names of the lowest, though the natural inferiority of the latter was not transferred to the former along with their names." We quote this in his very words. If they contain some deep and recondite meaning which has escaped us, let those inform us who see what is beyond our range of vision—initiated as they are by him in his esoteric and unspeakable mysteries. But if they admit of no interpretation beyond what is obvious, I scarcely know which of the two are more to be pitied, those who say such things or those who listen to them. To the weakest of terrestrial things, he says, God has given names in common with the most honourable, though not giving them an equal share of dignity. Let us examine what is meant by this. The weakest things, he says, are dignified with the bare name belonging to the honourable, their nature not corresponding with their name. And this he states to be the work of the God of truth—to dignify the worse nature with the worthier appellation! On the other hand, he says that God applies the less honourable names to things superior in their nature, the nature of the latter not being carried over to the former along with

the appellation. But that the matter may be made plainer still, the absurdity shall be shown by actual instances. If any one should call a man who is esteemed for every virtue, intemperate; or, on the other hand, a man equally in disrepute for his vices, good and moral, would sensible people think him of sound mind, or one who had any regard for truth, reversing, as would be the case, the meanings of words, and giving them a non-natural signification? I for my part think not. He speaks, then, of things relating to God, out of all keeping with our common ideas and with the holy Scriptures. For in matters of ordinary life it is only those who are unsettled by drink or madness that go wrong in names, and use them out of their proper meaning, calling, it may be, a man a dog, or vice versa. But Holy Scripture is so far from sanctioning such confusion, that we may clearly hear the voice of prophecy lamenting it. "Woe unto him," says Isaiah, "that calls darkness light, and light darkness, that calls bitter sweet, and sweet bitter [7]." Now what induces Eunomius to apply this absurdity to his God? Let those who are initiated in his mysteries say what they judge those weakest of terrestrial things to be, which God has dignified with most honourable appellations. The weakest of existing things are those animals whose generation takes place from the corruption of moist elements, as the most honourable are virtue, and holiness, and whatever else is pleasing in the sight of God. Are flies, then, and midges, and frogs, and whatever insects are generated from dung, dignified with the names of holiness and virtue, so as to be consecrated with honourable names, though not sharing in such high qualities, as saith Eunomius? But never as yet have we heard anything like this, that these weak things are called by high-sounding titles, or that what is great and honourable by nature is degraded by the name of any one of them. Noah was a righteous man, saith the Scripture, Abraham was faithful, Moses meek, Daniel wise, Joseph chaste, Job blameless, David perfect in patience. Let them say, then, whether all these had their names by contraries; or, to take the case of those who are unfavourably spoken of, as Nabal the Carmelite, and Pharaoh the Egyptian, and Abimelech the alien, and all those who are mentioned for their vices, whether they were dignified with honourable names by the voice of God. Not so! But God judges and distinguishes His creatures as they are in nature and truth, not by names contrary to them, but by such appropriate appellations as may give the clearest idea of their meaning.

This it is that our strong-minded opponent, who accuses us of dishonesty, and charges us with being irrational in judgment,—this it is that he pretends to know of the Divine nature. These are the opinions that he puts forth respecting God, as though He mocked His creatures with names untrue to their meaning, bestowing on the weakest the most honourable appellations, and pouring contempt on the honourable by making them synonymous with the base. Now a virtuous man, if carried, even involuntarily, beyond the limits of truth, is overwhelmed with shame. Yet Eunomius thinks it no shame to God that He should seem to give a false colour to things by their appellations. Not such is the testimony of the Scriptures to the Divine nature. "God is long-suffering, and plenteous in mercy and truth," says David[8]. But how can He be a God of truth Who gives false names to things, and Who perverts the truth in the meanings of their names? Again, He is called by him a righteous Lord[9]. Is it, then, a righteous thing to dignify things without honour by honourable names, and, while giving the bare name, to grudge the honour that it denotes? Such is the testimony of these Theologians to their new-fangled God. This is the end of their boasted dialectic cleverness, to display God Himself delighting in deceit, and not superior to the passion of jealousy. For surely it is no better than deceit not to name weak things, as they are in their true nature and worth, but to invest them with empty names, derived from superior things, not proportioning their value to their name ; and it is no better than jealousy if, having it in His power to bestow the more honourable appellation on things to be named for some superiority, He grudged them the honour itself, as deeming the happiness of the weak a loss to Himself personally. But I should recommend all who are wise, even if the God of these Gnostics[1] is by stress of logic shown to be of such a character, not to think thus of the true God, the Only-begotten, but to look at the truth of facts, giving each of them their due, and thence to deduce His name. "Come, ye blessed," saith our Lord ; and again, "Depart, ye cursed[2]," not honouring him who deserves cursing with the name of "blessed," nor, on the other hand, dismissing him who has treasured up for himself the blessing, along with the wicked.

But what is our author's meaning, and what is the object of this argument of his? For no one need imagine that, for lack of something to say, in order that he may seem to extend his discourse to the utmost, he has indulged in all this senseless twaddle. Its very senselessness is not without a meaning, and smacks of heresy. For to say that the most honourable names are applied to the weakest things, though not having by nature an equal apportionment of dignity, secretly paves the way, as it were, for the blasphemy to follow, that he may teach his disciples this ; that although the Only-begotten is called God, and Wisdom, and Power, and Light, and the Truth, and the Judge, and the King, and God over all, and the great God, and the Prince of peace, and the Father of the world to come, and so forth, His honour is limited to the name.

He does not, in fact, partake of that dignity which the meaning of those names indicates ; and whereas wise Daniel, in setting right the Babylonians' error of idolatry, that they should not worship the brazen image or the dragon, but reverence the name of God, which men in their folly had ascribed to them, clearly showed by what he did that the high and lofty name of God had no likeness to the reptile, or to the image of molten brass— this enemy of God exerts himself in his teaching to prove the very opposite of this in regard to the Only-begotten Son of God, exclaiming in the style which he affects, "Do not regard the names of which our Lord is a partaker, so as to infer His unspeakable and sublime nature. For many of the weakest things are likewise invested with names of honour, lofty indeed in sound, though their nature is not transformed so as to come up to the grandeur of their appellations." Accordingly he says that inferior things receive their honour from God only so far as their names go, no equality of dignity accompanying their appellations. When, therefore, we have learned all the names of the Son that are of lofty signification, we must bear in mind that the honour which they imply is ascribed to Him only so far as the words go, but that, according to the system of nomenclature which they adopt, He does not partake of the dignity implied by the words.

But in dwelling on such nonsense I fear that I am secretly gratifying our adversaries. For in setting the truth against their vain and empty words, I seem to myself to be wearing out the patience of my audience before we come to the brunt of the battle. These points, then, I will leave it to my more learned hearers to dispose of, and proceed with my task. Nor will I now notice a thing he has said, which, however, is closely connected with our inquiry ; viz. that these things have been so arranged that human thought and conception can claim no authority over names. But who is there that maintains

---

8 Ps. lxxxvi. 15.   9 Ps. xcii. 15.
1 Oehler has restored γνωστικῶν from his Codices, and notices that Cotelerius, Eccl. Gr. Monum. tom. ii. p. 622, had made the same change. Gulonius translates Gnosticorum. But the Editt. have γνωριστικῶν.   2 S. Matt. xxv. 34.

that what is not seen in its own subsistence has authority over anything? For only those creatures that are governed by their own deliberate will are capable of acting with authority. But thought and conception are an operation of the mind, which depends on the deliberate choice of those who speak, having no independent subsistence, but subsisting only in the force of the things said. But this, he says, belongs to God, the Creator of all things, who, by limitations and rules of relation, operation, and proportion, applies suitable appellations to each of the things named. But this either is sheer nonsense, or contradicts his previous assertions. For if he now professes that God affixes names suitable to their subjects, why does he argue, as we have seen, that God bestows lofty names on things without honour, not allowing them a share in the dignity which their names indicate, and again, that He degrades things of a lofty nature by names without honour, their nature not being affected by the meanness of their appellations? But perhaps we are unfair to him in subjecting his senseless collocation of phrases to such accusations as these. For they are altogether alien to any sense (I do not mean only to a sense in keeping with reverence), and they will be found to be utterly devoid of reason by all who understand how to form an accurate judgment in such matters. Since, then, like the fish called the sea-lung, what we see appears to have bulk and volume, which turns out, however, to be only viscous matter disgusting to look at, and still more disgusting to handle, I shall pass over his remarks in silence, deeming that the best answer to his idle effusions. For it would be better that we should not inquire what law governs "operation," and "proportion," and "relation," and who it is that prescribes laws to God in respect to rules and modes of proportion and relation, than that, by busying ourselves in such matters, we should nauseate our hearers, and digress from more important matters of inquiry.

But I fear that all we shall find in the discourse of Eunomius will turn out to be mere tumours and sea lungs, so that what has been said must necessarily close our argument, as his writings will supply no material to work on. For as a smoke or a mist makes the air in which it resides heavy and thick, and incapacitates the eye for the discharge of its natural function, yet does not form itself into so dense a body that he who will may grasp and hold it in his palms, and offer resistance to its stroke, so if one should say the same of his pompous piece of writing, the comparison would not be untrue. Much nonsense is worked up in his tumid and viscous discourse, and to one not gifted with over-much discernment, like a

mist to one viewing it from afar, it seems to have some substance and shape, but if you come up to it and scrutinize what is said, the theories slip from your hold like smoke, and vanish into nothing, nor have they any solidity or resistance to oppose to the stroke of your argument. It is difficult, therefore, to know what to do. For to those who like to complain either alternative will seem objectionable; whether, leaping over his empty wordiness, as over a ravine, we direct the course of our argument to the level and open country, against those points which seem to have any strength against the truth, or form our absurd battle along the whole line of his inanities. For in the latter case, to those who do not love hard work, our labour, extending over some thousands of lines to no useful purpose, will be wearisome and unprofitable. But if we attack those points only which seem to have some force against the truth, we shall give occasion to our adversaries to accuse us of passing over arguments of theirs which we are unable to refute. Since, then, two courses are open to us, either to take all their arguments seriatim, or to run through those only which are more important—the one course tedious to our hearers, the other liable to be suspected by our assailants—I think it best to take a middle course, and so, as far as possible, to avoid censure on either hand. What, then, is our method? After clearing his vain productions, as well as we can, of the rubbish they have accumulated, we will summarily run through the main points of his argument in such a way as neither to plunge needlessly into the profundities of his nonsense, nor to leave any of his statements unexamined. Now his whole treatise is an ambitious attempt to show that God speaks after the manner of men, and that the Creator of all things gives them suitable names, indicative of the things themselves. And, therefore, opposing himself to him who contended that such names are given by that rational nature which we have received from God, he accuses him of error, and of desertion from his fundamental proposition: and having brought this charge against him, he uses the following arguments in support of his position.

Basil, he says, asserts that after we have obtained our first idea of a thing, the more minute and accurate investigation of the thing under consideration is called conception. And Eunomius disproves this, as he thinks, by the following argument, that where this first, and this second notion, i. e. one more minute and accurate than the other, are not found, the operation which we call thought and conception does not find place. Here, however, he will be convicted of dishonesty by all who have ears to hear. For it was not of all thought and conception that our master (Basil) laid down this definition, but, after making a special sub-division of the objects of thought and conception (not to encumber the question with too many words), and having made this part clear, he left men of sense to reason out the whole from the part for themselves. And as, if any one should say that we get our definition of an animal from considering a number of animals of different species, he could not be convicted of missing the truth in making man an instance in point, nor would there be any need to correct him as deviating from the fact, unless he should give the same definition of a winged, or four-footed, or aquatic animal as of a man, so, when the points of view from which we may consider this conception are so many and various, it is no refutation of Basil's statement to say that it is improperly so called in one case because there is another species. Accordingly, even if another species come under consideration, it by no means follows that the one previously given is erroneously so called. Now if, says he, one of the Apostles or Prophets could be shown to have used these names of Christ, the falsehood would have something for its encouragement. To what industrious study of the word of God on the part of our opponent do not these words bear testimony! None of the Prophets or Apostles has spoken of our Lord as Bread, or a Stone, or a Fountain, or an Axe, or Light, or a Shepherd! What, then, saith David, and of whom? "The Lord shepherds me." "Thou Who shepherdest Israel, give ear[3]." What dif-ference does it make whether He is spoken of as shepherding, or as a Shepherd? And again, "With Thee is the Well of life[4]." Does he deny that our Lord is called a "Well"? And again, "The Stone which the builders rejected[5]." And John, too,—where, representing our Lord's power to uproot evil under the name of an axe, he says, "And now also the Axe is laid to the root of the trees[6]"—is he not a weighty and credible witness to the truth of our words?

And Moses, seeing God in the light, and John calling Him the true Light[7], and in the same way Paul, when our Lord first appeared to him, and a Light shone round about him, and afterwards when he heard the words of the Light saying, "I am Jesus, Whom thou per-secutest[8],"—is he not a competent witness? And as regards the name "Bread," let him read the Gospel and see how the bread given by Moses, and supplied to Israel from heaven, was taken by our Lord as a type of Himself: "For Moses gave you not that Bread, but My Father giveth you the true Bread (meaning Himself) which cometh down from heaven and giveth life unto the world[9]." But this genuine hearer of the law says that none of the Prophets or Apostles has applied these names to Christ. What shall we say, then, of what follows? "Even if our Lord Himself adopts them, yet, since in the Saviour's names there is no first or second, none more minute or accurate than another, for He knows them all at once with equal accuracy, it is not possible to accom-modate his (Basil's) account of the operation of conception to any of His names."

I have deluged my discourse with much nonsense of his, but I trust my hearers will pardon me for not leaving unnoticed even the most glaring of his inanities; not that we take pleasure in our author's indecorum, (for what advantage can we derive from the refutation of our adversaries' folly?) but that truth may be advanced by confirmation from whatever quarter. "Since," says he, "our Lord applies these ap-pellations to Himself, not deeming any one of them first, or second, or more minute and accurate than the rest, you cannot say that these names are the result of conception." Why, he has forgotten his own object! How comes he by the knowledge of the words against which he declares war? Our master and guide had made mention of an example familiar to all, in illustration of the doctrine of concep-tion, and having explained his meaning by lower illustrations, he lifts the consideration of the question to higher things. He had said that the word "corn," regarded by itself, is one thing only as to substance, but that, as to the various properties we see in it, it varies its ap-pellations, being called seed, and fruit, and food, and the like. Similarly, says he, our Lord is in respect to Himself what He is essentially, but when named according to the differences of His operations, He has not one appellation in all cases, but takes a different name according to each notion produced in us from the operation. How, then, does what he says disprove our theory that it is possible for many appellations to be attached with propriety, according to the diversity of His operations, and His relation to their effects, to the Son of God, though one in respect of the underlying force, even as corn, though one, has various names apportioned to it, according to the point of view from which we regard it? How, then, can what is said be overthrown by our saying that Christ used all these names of Himself? For the question was not, who ascribed them, but about the meaning of the names, whether they denote essence, or whether they are derived from His operations by the process of conception. But

---

[3] Ps. xxiii. 1; lxxx. 1. Cf. S. John xxi. 16, 17.
[4] Ps. xxxvi. 9.   [5] S. Matt. xxi. 42.   [6] S. Matt. iii. 10.
[7] S. John i. 9.   [8] Acts ix. 5.

[9] S. John vi. 32, sqq.

our shrewd and strong-minded opponent, over-turning our theory of conception, which declares that it is possible to find many appellations for one and the same subject, according to the significances of its operations, attacks us vigorously, asserting that such names were not given to our Lord by another. But what has this to do with the case in point? Since these names are used by our Lord, will he not allow that they are names, or appellations, or words expressive of ideas? For if he will not admit them to be names, then, in doing away with the appellations, he does away at the same time with the conception. But if he does not deny that these words are names, what harm can he do to our doctrine of conception by showing that such titles were given to our Lord, not by some one else, but by Himself? For what was said was this, that, as in the instance of corn, our Lord, though substantively One, bears epithets suitable to His operations. And as it is admitted that corn has its names by virtue of our conception of its associations, it was shown that these terms significative of our Lord are not of His essence, but are formed by the method of conception in our minds respecting Him. But our antagonist studiously avoids attacking these positions, and maintains that our Lord received these names from Himself, in the same way as, if one sought for the true interpretation of the name "Isaac," whether it means laughter[1], as some say, or something else, one of Eunomius' way of thinking should confidently reply that the name was given to him as a child by his mother: but that, one might say, was not the question, i. e. by whom the name was given, but what does it mean when translated into our language? And this being the point of the inquiry, whether our Lord's various appellations were the result of conception, instead of being indicative of His essence, he who thus seeks to demonstrate that they are not so derived because they are used by our Lord Himself,—how can he be numbered among men of sense, warring as he does against the truth, and equipping himself with such alliances for the war as serve to show the superior strength of his enemy?

Then going farther, as if his object were thus far attained, he takes up other charges against us, more difficult, as he thinks, to deal with than the former, and with many preliminary groans and attempts to prejudice his hearers against us, and to whet their appetite for his address, accusing us withal of seeking to establish doctrines savouring of blasphemy, and of ascribing to our own conception names assigned by God (though he nowhere mentions what assignment he refers to, nor when and where it

took place), and, further, of throwing everything into confusion, and identifying the essence of the Only-begotten with his operation, without arguing the matter, or showing how we prove the identity of the essence and the operation, he winds up with the same list of charges, as follows: "And now, passing beyond this, he (Basil) asperses even the Most High with the vilest blasphemies, using at the same time broken language, and illustrations wide of the mark." Now prior to inquiry, I should like to be told what our language is "broken" from, and what mark it is "wide of"; not that I want to know, except to show the confusion and obscurity of his address, which he dins into the ears of the old wives among our men, pluming himself on his nice phrases, which he mouths out to the admirers of such things, ignorant, as it would seem, that in the judgment of educated men this address of his will serve only as a memorial of his own infamy.

But all this is beside our purpose. Would that our charges against him were limited to this, and that he could be thought to err only in his delivery, and not in matters of faith; since it would have been of comparatively little importance to him to be praised or blamed for expressing himself in one style or another. But however that may be, the sequel of his charges against us contains this in addition: "Considering the case of corn (he says), and of our Lord, after exercising his conceptions in various ways upon them, he[2] declares that even in like manner the most holy essence of God admits of the same variety of conception." This is the gravest of his accusations, and it is in prosecuting this that he rehearses those heavy invectives of his, charging what we have said with blasphemy, absurdity, and so forth. What, then, is the proof of our blasphemy? "He[3] has mentioned" (says Eunomius) "certain well-known facts about corn,—perceiving how it grows, and how when ripe it affords food, growing, multiplying, and being dispensed by certain forces of nature—and, having mentioned these, he adds that it is only reasonable to suppose that the Only-begotten Son also admits of different modes of being conceived of[4], by reason of certain differences of operation, certain analogies, proportions, and relations. For he uses these terms respecting Him to satiety. And is it not absurd, or rather blasphemous, to compare the Ungenerate with such objects

---

[1] Gen. xviii. 12; xxi. 6.

[2] he, i. e. Basil. "God's nature can be looked at in as many aspects as corn can (i. e. in its growth, fructification, distribution, &c.)."

[3] He, i. e. Basil. The words ὁ Εὐνόμιος, here, are the additions of a copyist who did not understand that εἶπεν referred to Basil, or else φησὶν must be read with them. Certainly ταῦτα εἰπὼν below must refer to the same subject as εἶπεν.

[4] διαφόρους δέχεσθαι ἐπινοίας. Oehler has rightly omitted the words that follow· (διά τε τὰς ἐννοίας), both because of their irrelevancy, and from the authority of his MSS.

as these?"—What objects? Why, corn, and God the Only-begotten! You see his artfulness. He would show that insignificant corn and God the Only-begotten are equally removed from the dignity of the Ungenerate. And to show that we are not treating his words unfairly, we may learn his meaning from the very words he has written. "For," he asks, "is it not absurd, or rather blasphemous, to compare the Ungenerate with these?" And in thus speaking, he instances the case of corn and of our Lord as on a level in point of dignity, thinking it equally absurd to compare God with either. Now every one knows that things equally distant from a given object are possessed of equality as regards each other, so that according to our wise theologian the Maker of the worlds, Who holds all nature in His hand, is shown to be on a par with the most insignificant seed, since He and corn to the same degree fall short of comparison with God. To such a pitch of blasphemy has *he* come!

But it is time to examine the argument that leads to this profanity, and see how, as regards itself, it is logically connected with his whole discourse. For after saying that it is absurd to compare God with corn and with Christ, he says of God that He is not, like them, subject to change; but in respect to the Only-begotten, keeping silence on the question whether He too is not subject to change, and thereby clearly suggesting that He is of lower dignity, in that we cannot compare Him, any more than we can compare corn, with God, he breaks off his discourse without using any argument to prove that the Son of God cannot be compared with the Father, as though our knowledge of the grain were sufficient to establish the inferiority of the Son in comparison with the Father. But he discourses of the indestructibility of the Father, as not in actuality attaching to the Son. But if the True Life is an actuality, actuating itself, and if to live everlastingly means the same thing as never to be dissolved in destruction, I for myself do not as yet assent to his argument, but will reserve myself for a more proper occasion. That, however, there is but one single notion in indestructibility [5], considered in reference to the Father and to the Son alike, and that the indestructibility of the Father differs in no respect from that of the Son, no difference as to indestructibility being observable either in remission and intension, or

in any other phase of the process of destruction, this, I say, it is seasonable both now and at all times to assert, so as to preclude the doctrine that in respect of indestructibility the Son has no communion with the Father. For as this indestructibility is understood in respect of the Father, so also it is not to be disputed in respect of the Son. For to be incapable of dissolution means nearly, or rather precisely, the same thing in regard to whatever subject it is attributed to. What, then, induces him to assert, that only to the Ungenerate Deity does it belong to have this indestructibility not attaching to Him by reason of any energy, as though he would thereby show a difference between the Father and the Son? For if he supposes his own created God destructible, he well shows the essential divergence of natures by the difference between the destructible and the indestructible. But if neither is subject to destruction,—and no degrees are to be found in pure indestructibility,—how does he show that the Father cannot be compared with the Only-begotten Son, or what is meant by saying that indestructibility is not witnessed in the Father by reason of any energy? But he reveals his purpose in what follows. It is not because of His operations or energies, he says, that He is ungenerate and indestructible, but because He is Father and Creator. And here I must ask my hearers to give me their closest attention. How can he think the creative power of God and His Fatherhood identical in meaning? For he defines each alike as an energy, plainly and expressly affirming, "God is not indestructible by reason of His energy, though He is called Father and Creator by reason of energies." If, then, it is the same thing to call Him Father and Creator of the world because either name is due to an energy as its cause, the results of His energies must be homogeneous, inasmuch as it is through an energy that they both exist. But to what blasphemy this logically tends is clear to every one who can draw a conclusion. For myself, I should like to add my own deductions to my disquisition. It is impossible that an energy or operation productive of a result should subsist of itself without there being something to set the energy in motion; as we say that a smith operates or works, but that the material on which his art is exercised is operated upon, or wrought. These faculties, therefore, that of operating, and that of being operated upon, must needs stand in a certain relation to each other, so that if one be removed, the remaining one cannot subsist of itself. For where there is nothing operated upon there can be nothing operating. What, then, does this prove? If the energy which is productive of anything does not subsist of itself,

---

5 Indestructibility. Such terms ("not-composite," "indivisible," "imperishable") were the inheritance which Christian controversy received from the former struggle with Stoicism. In the hands of Origen, they had been aimed at the Stoic doctrine of the Deity as that of *corporeal* Spirit, which does not perish, only because there is no cause sufficient. "If one does not see the consequences of such an assertion, one ought to blush" (in Johann. xiii. 21). The consequences of course are that God, the Word, and our souls, made in His image, are all perishable; for all body, in that it is matter, is, by the Stoic assumption, liable to change.

there being nothing for it to operate upon, and if the Father, as they affirm, is nothing but an energy, the Only-begotten Son is thereby shown to be capable of being acted upon, in other words, moulded in accordance with the motive energy that gives Him His subsistence. For as we say that the Creator of the world, by laying down some yielding material, capable of being acted upon, gave His creative being a field for its exercise, in the case of things sensible skilfully investing the subject with various and multiform qualities for production, but in the case of intellectual essences giving shape to the subject in another way, not by qualities, but by impulses of choice, so, if any one define the Fatherhood of God as an energy, he cannot otherwise indicate the subsistence of the Son than by comparing it with some material acted upon and wrought to completion. For if it could not be operated upon, it would of necessity offer resistance to the operator : whose energy being thus hindered, no result would be produced. Either, then, they must make the essence of the Only-begotten subject to be acted upon, that the energy may have something to work upon, or, if they shrink from this conclusion, on account of its manifest impiety, they are driven to the conclusion that it has no existence at all. For what is naturally incapable of being acted upon, cannot itself admit the creative energy. He, then, who defines the Son as the effect of an energy, defines Him as one of those things which are subject to be acted upon, and which are produced by an energy. Or, if he deny such susceptibility, he must at the same time deny His existence. But since impiety is involved in either alternative of the dilemma, that of asserting His non-existence, and that of regarding Him as capable of being acted upon, the truth is made manifest, being brought to light by the removal of these absurdities. For if He verily exists, and is not subject to be acted upon, it is plain that He is not the result of an energy, but is proved to be very God of very God the Father, without liability to be acted upon, beaming from Him and shining forth from everlasting.

But in His very essence, he says, God is indestructible. Well, what other conceivable attribute of God does not attach to the very essence of the Son, as justice, goodness, eternity, incapacity for evil, infinite perfection in all conceivable goodness ? Is there one who will venture to say that any of the virtues in the Divine nature are acquired, or to deny that all good whatsoever springs from and is seen in it? "For whatsoever is good is from Him, and whatsoever is lovely is from Him[6]." But he appends to this, that He is in His very essence ungenerate too. Well, if he means by this that the Father's essence is ungenerate, I agree with what is said, and do not oppose his doctrine : for not one of the orthodox maintains that the Father of the Only-begotten is Himself begotten. But if, while the form of his expression indicates only this, he maintains that the ungeneracy itself is the essence, I say that we ought not to leave such a position unexamined, but expose his attempt to gain the assent of the unwary to his blasphemy.

Now that the idea [7] of ungeneracy and the belief in the Divine essence are quite different things may be seen by what he himself has put forward. God, he says, is indestructible and ungenerate by His very essence, as being unmixed and pure from all diversity and difference. This he says of God, Whose essence he declares to be indestructibility and ungeneracy. There are three names, then, that he applies to God, being, indestructibility, ungeneracy. If the idea of these three words in respect of God is one, it follows that the Godhead and these three are identical. Just as if any one, wanting to describe a man, should say that he was a rational, risible, and broad-nailed creature ; whereupon, because there is no essential variation from these in the individuals, we say that the terms are equivalent to each other, and that the three things seen in the subject are one thing, viz. the humanity described by these names. If, then, Godhead means this, ungeneracy, indestructibility, being, by doing away with one of these he necessarily does away with the Godhead. For just as we should say that a creature which was neither rational nor risible was not man either, so in the case of these three terms (ungeneracy, indestructibility, being), if the Godhead is described by these, should one of the three be absent, its absence destroys the definition of Godhead. Let him tell us, then, in reply, what opinion he holds of God the Only-begotten. Does he think Him generate or ungenerate ? Of course he must say generate, unless he is to contradict himself. If, then, being and indestructibility are equivalent to ungeneracy, and by all of these Godhead is denoted, to Whom ungeneracy is wanting, to Him being and indestructibility must needs be wanting also, and in that case the Godhead also must necessaríly be taken away. And thus his blasphemous logic brings him to a twofold conclusion. For if being, and indestructibility, and ungeneracy are applied to God in the same sense, our new God-maker is clearly convicted of regarding the

---

[6] Zech. ix. 17 (LXX.).

[7] τὸ νόημα. There is a lacuna in the Paris Editt., beginning here, and extending to "ungenerate," just below. Oehler's Codices have supplied it.

Son created by Him as destructible, by his not regarding Him as ungenerate, and not only so, but altogether without being, through his inability to see Him in the Godhead, as one in whom ungeneracy and indestructibility are not found, since he takes the ungeneracy and indestructibility to be identical with the being. But since in this there is manifest perdition, let some one counsel these unhappy folk to turn to the only course which is left them, and, instead of setting themselves in open opposition to the truth, to allow that each of these terms has its own proper signification, such as may be seen still better from their contraries. For we find ungenerate set against generate, and we understand the indestructible by its opposition to the destructible, and being by contrast with that which has no subsistence. For as that which was not generated is called ungenerate, and that which is not destructible is called indestructible, so that which is not non-existent we call being, and, conversely, as we do not call the generate ungenerate, nor the destructible indestructible, so that which is non-existent we do not call being. Being, then, is discernible in the being this or that, goodness or indestructibility in the being of this or of that kind, generacy or ungeneracy in the manner of the being. And thus the ideas of being, manner, and quality are distinct from each other.

But it will be well, I think, to pass over his nauseating observations (for such we must term his senseless attacks on the method of conception), and dwell more pleasurably on the subject matter of our thought. For all the venom that our disputant has disgorged with the view of overthrowing our Master's speculations in regard to conception, is not of such a kind as to be dangerous to those who come in its way, however stupid they may be and liable to be imposed on. For who is so devoid of understanding as to think that there is anything in what Eunomius says, or to see any ingenuity in his artifices against the truth when he takes our Master's reference to corn (which he meant simply by way of illustration, thereby providing his hearers with a sort of method and introduction to the study of higher instances), and applies it literally to the Lord of all? To think of his assertion that the most becoming cause for God's begetting the Son was His sovereign authority and power, which may be said not only in regard to the universe and its elements, but in regard to beasts and creeping things; and of our reverend theologian teaching that the same is becoming in our conception of God the Only-begotten—or again, of his saying that God was called ungenerate, or Father, or any other name, even before the existence of creatures to call Him such, as being afraid lest, His name not being uttered among creatures as yet unborn, He should be ignorant or forgetful of Himself, through ignorance of His own nature because of His name being unspoken! To think, again, of the insolence of his attack upon our teaching; what acrimony, what subtlety does he display, while attempting to establish the absurdity of what he (Basil) said, namely that He Who was in a manner the Father before all worlds and time, and all sensitive and intellectual nature, must somehow wait for man's creation in order to be named by means of man's conception, not having been so named, either by the Son or by any of the intelligent beings of His creation! Why no one, I imagine, can be so densely stupid as to be ignorant that God the Only-begotten, Who is in the Father [8], and Who seeth the Father in Himself, is in no need of any name or title to make Him known, nor is the mystery of the Holy Spirit, Who searcheth out the deep things of God [9], brought to our knowledge by a nominal appellation, nor can the incorporeal nature of supramundane powers name God by voice and tongue. For, in the case of immaterial intellectual nature, the mental energy is speech which has no need of material instruments of communication. For even in the case of human beings, we should have no need of using words and names if we could otherwise inform each other of our pure mental feelings and impulses. But (as things are), inasmuch as the thoughts which arise in us are incapable of being so revealed, because our nature is encumbered with its fleshly surrounding, we are obliged to express to each other what goes on in our minds by giving things their respective names, as signs of their meaning.

But if it were in any way possible by some other means to lay bare the movements of thought, abandoning the formal instrumentality of words, we should converse with one another more lucidly and clearly, revealing by the mere action of thought the essential nature of the things which are under consideration. But now, by reason of our inability to do so, we have given things their special names, calling one Heaven, another Earth, and so on, and as each is related to each, and acts or suffers, we have marked them by distinctive names, so that our thoughts in regard to them may not remain uncommunicated and unknown. But supramundane and immaterial nature being free and independent of bodily envelopment, requires no words or names either for itself or for that which is above it, but whatever utterance on the part of such intellectual nature is recorded in

---

[8] S. John xiv. 9.   [9] 1 Cor. ii. 10.

Holy Writ is given for the sake of the hearers, who would be unable otherwise to learn what is to be set forth, if it were not communicated to them by voice and word. And if David in the spirit speaks of something being said by the Lord to the Lord [1], it is David himself who is the speaker, being unable otherwise to make known to us the teaching of what is meant, except by interpreting by voice and word his own knowledge of the mysteries given him by Divine inspiration.

All his argument, then, in opposition to the doctrine of conception I think it best to pass over, though he charge with madness those who think that the name of God, as used by mankind to indicate the Supreme Being, is the result of this conception. For what he is thinking of when he considers himself bound to revile that doctrine, all who will may learn from his own words. What opinion we ourselves hold on the use of words we have already stated, viz. that, things being as they are in regard to their nature, the rational faculty implanted in our nature by God invented words indicative of those actual things. And if any one ascribe their origin to the Giver of the faculty, we would not contradict him, for we too maintain that motion, and sight, and the rest of the operations carried on by the senses are effected by Him Who endowed us with such faculties. So, then, the cause of our naming God, Who is by His nature what He is, is referable by common consent to Himself, but the liberty of naming all things that we conceive of in one way or another lies in that thing in our nature, which, whether a man wish to call it conception or something else, we are quite indifferent. And there is this one sure evidence in our favour, that the Divine Being is not named alike by all, but that each interprets his idea as he thinks best. Passing over, then, in silence his rubbishy twaddle about conception, let us hold to our tenets, and simply note by the way some of the observations that occur in the midst of his empty speeches, where he pretends that God, seating Himself by our first parents, like some pedagogue or grammarian, gave them a lesson in words and names ; wherein he says that they who were first formed by God, or those who were born from them in continuous succession, unless they had been taught how each several thing should be called and named, would have lived together in dumbness and silence, and would have been unequal to the discharge of any of the serviceable functions of life, the meaning of each being uncertain through lack of interpreters,—verbs forsooth, and nouns. Such is the infatuation of this writer ;

he thinks the faculty implanted in our nature by God insufficient for any method of reasoning, and that unless it be taught each thing severally, like those who are taught Hebrew or Latin word by word, one must be ignorant of the nature of the things, having no discernment of fire, or water, or air, or anything else, unless one have acquired the knowledge of them by the names that they bear. But we maintain that He Who made all things in His wisdom, and Who moulded this living rational creature, by the simple fact of His implanting reason in his nature, endowed him with all his rational faculties. And as naturally possessing our faculties of perception by the gift of Him Who fashioned the eye and planted the ear, we can of ourselves employ them for their natural objects, and have no need of any one to name the colours, for instance, of which the eye takes cognizance, for the eye is competent to inform itself in such matters ; nor do we need another to make us acquainted with the things which we perceive by hearing, or taste, or touch, possessing as we do in ourselves the means of discerning all of which our perception informs us. And so, again, we maintain that the intellectual faculty, made as it was originally by God, acts thenceforward by itself when it looks out upon realities, and that there be no confusion in its knowledge, affixes some verbal note to each several thing as a stamp to indicate its meaning. Great Moses himself confirms this doctrine when he says [2] that names were assigned by Adam to the brute creation, recording the fact in these words : "And out of the ground God formed every beast of the field, and every fowl of the air, and brought them unto Adam to see what he would call them, and whatsoever Adam called every living creature, that was the name thereof. And Adam gave names to all cattle, and to all the beasts of the field."

But, like some viscous and sticky clay, the nonsense he has concocted in contravention of our teaching of conception seems to hold us back, and prevent us from applying ourselves to more important matters. For how can one pass over his solemn and profound philosophy, as when he says that God's greatness is seen not only in the works of His hands, but that His wisdom is displayed in their names also, adapted as they are with such peculiar fitness to the nature of each work of His creation [3] ?

---

[1] Ps. cx. 1.

[2] Gen. ii. 19, 20.

[3] Compare with this view of Eunomius on the sacredness of names, this striking passage from Origen (c. Cels. v. 43). "We hold, then, that the origin of names is not to be found in any formal agreements on the part of those who gave them, as Aristotle thinks. Human language, in fact, did not have its beginning from man. Any one can see this who reflects upon the real nature of the incantations which in the different languages are associated with the patriarchal names of those languages. The names which have their native power in such and such a language cease to have this influence of their peculiar sound when they are changed into another

Having perchance fallen in with Plato's Cratylus, or hearing from some one who had met with it, by reason, I suppose, of his own poverty of ideas, he attached that nonsense patchwise to his own, acting like those who get their bread by begging. For just as they, receiving some trifle from each who bestows it on them, collect their bread from many and various sources, so the discourse of Eunomius, by reason of his scanty store of the true bread, assiduously collects scraps of phrases and notions from all quarters. And thus, being struck by the beauty of the Platonic style, he thinks it not unseemly to make Plato's theory a doctrine of the Church. For by how many appellations, say, is the created firmament called according to the varieties of language? For we call it Heaven, the Hebrew calls it Samaim, the Roman cœlum, other names are given to it by the Syrian, the Mede, the Cappadocian, the African, the Scythian, the Thracian, the Egyptian: nor would it be easy to enumerate the multiplicity of names which are applied to Heaven and other objects by the different nations that employ them. Which of these, then, tell me, is the appropriate word wherein the great wisdom of God is manifested? If you prefer the Greek to the rest, the Egyptian haply will confront you with his own. And if you give the first place to the Hebrew, there is the Syrian to claim precedence for his own word, nor will the Roman yield the supremacy, nor the Mede allow himself to be outdone; while of the other nations each will claim the prize. What, then, will be the fate of his dogma when torn to pieces by the claimants for so many different languages? But by these, says he, as by laws publicly promulgated, it is shown that God made names exactly suited to the nature of the things which they represent. What a grand doctrine! What grand

---

language. This has been often observed in the names given even to living men: one who from his birth has been called so and so in Greek will never, if we change his name into Egyptian or Roman, be made to feel or act as he can when called by the first name given. . . . If this is true in the case of names given to men, what are we to think of the names connected in some way or other with the Deity? For instance, there must be some change in translating Abraham's name into Greek: some new expression given to 'Isaac,' and 'Jacob': and, while he who repeats the incantation or the oath names the 'God of Abraham, of Isaac, and of Jacob,' he produces those particular effects by the mere force and working of those names: because the dæmons are mustered by him who utters them: but if on the other hand he says, 'God of the chosen Father of the Crowd,' 'of the Laughter,' 'of the Supplanter,' he can do nothing with the names so expressed, any more than with any other powerless instrument. . . . We can say the same of 'Sabaoth,' which is used in many exorcisms: if we change it to 'Lord of Powers,' or, 'Lord of Hosts,' or, 'Almighty,' we can do nothing . . ."—and (46), "This, too, is the reason why we ourselves prefer any degradation to that of owning Zeus to be Deity. We cannot conceive of Zeus as the same as Sabaoth: or as Divine in any of all possible meanings. . . . If the Egyptians offer us 'Ammon,' or death, we shall take the latter, rather than pronounce the divinity of 'Ammon.' The Scythians may tell us that their Papœus is the God of the Universe, we shall not listen: we firmly believe in the God of the Universe, but we must not call him Papœus, making that a name for absolute Deity, as the Being who occupies the desert, the nation, and the language of the Scythians would desire: although, indeed, it cannot be sin for any to use the appellation of the Deity in his own mother tongue, whether it be the Scythian way or the Egyptian."

views our theologian allows to the Divine teachings, such indeed as men do not grudge even to bathing-attendants! For we allow them to give names to the operations they engage in, and yet no one invests them with Divine honours for the invention of such names as foot-baths, depilatories, towels, and the like—words which appropriately designate the articles in question.

But I will pass over both this and their reading of Epicurus' nature-system, which he says is equivalent to our conception, maintaining that the doctrine of atoms and empty space, and the fortuitous generation of things, is akin to what we mean by conception. What an understanding of Epicurus! If we ascribe words expressive of things to the logical faculty in our nature, we thereby stand convicted of holding the Epicurean doctrine of indivisible bodies, and combinations of atoms, and the collision and rebound of particles, and so on. I say nothing of Aristotle, whom he takes as his own patron, and the ally of his system, whose opinion, he says, in his subsequent remarks, coincides with our views about conception. For he says that that philosopher taught that Providence does not extend through all nature, nor penetrate into the region of terrestrial things, and this, Eunomius contends, corresponds to our discoveries in the field of conception. Such is his idea of determining a doctrine with accuracy! But he goes on to say that we must either deny the creation of things to God, or, if we concede it, we must not deprive Him of the imposition of names. And yet even in respect to the brute creation, as we have said already, we are taught the very opposite (of both these alternatives) by Holy Scripture—that neither did Adam make the animals, nor did God name them, but the creation was the work of God, and the naming of the things created was the work of man, as Moses has recorded. Then in his own speech he gives us an encomium of speech in general (as though some one wished to disparage it), and after his eminently abusive and bombastic conglomeration of words, he says that, by a law and rule of His providence, God has combined the transmission of words with our knowledge and use of things necessary for our service; and after pouring forth twaddle of this kind in the profundity of his slumbers, he passes on in his discourse to his irresistible argument. I will not state it in so many words, but simply give the drift of it. We are not, he says, to ascribe the invention of words to poets, who are much mistaken in their notions of God. What a generous concession does he make to God in investing Him with the inventions of the poetic faculty, so that

God may thereby seem to men more sublime and august, when the disciples of Eunomius believe that such expressions as those used by Homer for "side-ways," "rang out," "aside," "mix 4," "clung to his hand," "hissed," "thumped," "rattled," "clashed," "rang terribly," "twanged," "shouted," "pondered," and many others, are not used by poets by a certain arbitrary licence, but that they introduce them into their poems by some mysterious initiation from God! Let this, too, be passed over, and withal that clever and irresistible attempt, that it is not in our power to quote Scriptural instances of holy men who have invented new terms. Now if human nature had been imperfect up to the time of such men's appearance, and not as yet completed by the gift of reason, it would have been well for them to seek that the deficiency might be supplied. But if from the very first man's nature existed self-sufficing and complete for all purposes of reason and thought, why should any one, in order to establish this doctrine of conception, humour them so far as to seek for instances where holy men initiated sounds or names? Or, if we cannot adduce any instances, why should any one regard it as a sufficient proof that such and such syllables and words were appointed by God Himself?

But, says he, since God condescends to commune with His servants, we may consequently suppose that from the very beginning He enacted words appropriate to things. What, then, is our answer? We account for God's willingness to admit men to communion with Himself by His love towards mankind. But since that which is by nature finite cannot rise above its prescribed limits, or lay hold of the superior nature of the Most High, on this account He, bringing His power, so full of love for humanity, down to the level of human weakness, so far as it was possible for us to receive it, bestowed on us this helpful gift of grace. For as by Divine dispensation the sun, tempering the intensity of his full beams with the intervening air, pours down light as well as heat on those who receive his rays, being himself unapproachable by reason of the weakness of our nature, so the Divine power, after the manner of the illustration I have used, though exalted far above our nature and inaccessible to all approach, like a tender mother who joins in the inarticulate utterances of her babe, gives to our human nature what it is capable of receiving; and thus in the various manifestations of God to man He both adapts Himself to man and speaks in human language,

and assumes wrath, and pity, and such-like emotions, so that through feelings corresponding to our own our infantile life might be led as by hand, and lay hold of the Divine nature by means of the words which His foresight has given. For that it is irreverent to imagine that God is subject to any passion such as we see in respect to pleasure, or pity, or anger, no one will deny who has thought at all about the truth of things. And yet the Lord is said to take pleasure in His servants, and to be angry with the backsliding people, and, again, to have mercy on whom He will have mercy, and to show compassion—the word teaching us in each of these expressions that God's providence helps our infirmity by using our own idioms of speech, so that such as are inclined to sin may be restrained from committing it by fear of punishment, and that those who are overtaken by it may not despair of return by the way of repentance when they see God's mercy, while those who are walking uprightly and strictly may yet more adorn their life with virtue, as knowing that by their own life they rejoice Him Whose eyes are over the righteous. But just as we cannot call a man deaf who converses with a deaf man by means of signs,—his only way of hearing,—so we must not suppose speech in God because of His employing it by way of accommodation in addressing man. For we ourselves are accustomed to direct brute beasts by clucking and whistling and the like, and yet this, by which we reach their ears, is not our language, but we use our natural speech in talking to one another, while, in regard to cattle, some suitable noise or sound accompanied with gesture is sufficient for all purposes of communication.

But our pious opponent will not allow of God's using our language, because of our proneness to evil, shutting his eyes (good man!) to the fact that for our sakes He did not refuse to be made sin and a curse. Such is the superabundance of His love for man, that He voluntarily came to prove not only our good, but our evil. And if He was partaker in our evil, why should He refuse to be partaker in speech, the noblest of our gifts? But he advances David in his support, and declares that he said that names were imposed on things by God, because it is thus written, "He telleth the number of the stars; He calleth them all by their names 5." But I think it must be obvious to every man of sense that what is thus said of the stars has nothing whatever to do with the subject. Since, however, it is not improbable that some may unwarily give their assent to his statement, I will briefly discuss the point. Holy Scripture often-

---

4 Reading κέραιρε, according to Oehler's conjecture, from Iliad ix. 203. All the Codd. and Editt., read κέκαιρε, however. The Editt., in the Homeric words which follow, show a strange ignorance, which Gulonius has reproduced, viz. Phocheiri, Poudese, Ische ! (for Θῦ χειρί, Δούπησε, Ἴαχε).

5 Ps. cxlvii 4.

times is wont to attribute expressions to God such that they seem quite accordant with our own, *e. g.* "The Lord was wroth, and it repented Him because of their sins[6]"; and again, "He repented that He had anointed Saul king[7]"; and again, "The Lord awaked as one out of sleep[8]"; and besides this, it makes mention of His sitting, and standing, and moving, and the like, which are not as a fact connected with God, but are not without their use as an accommodation to those who are under teaching. For in the case of the too unbridled, a show of anger restrains them by fear. And to those who need the medicine of repentance, it says that the Lord repenteth along with them of the evil, and those who grow insolent through prosperity it warns, by God's repentance in respect to Saul, that their good fortune is no certain possession, though it seem to come from God. To those who are not engulfed by their sinful fall, but who have risen from a life of vanity as from sleep, it says that God arises out of sleep. To those who steadfastly take their stand upon righteousness,—that He stands. To those who are seated in righteousness,—that He sits. And again, in the case of those who have moved from their steadfastness in righteousness,—that He moves or walks; as, in the case of Adam, the sacred history records God's walking in the garden in the cool of the day[9], signifying thereby the fall of the first man into darkness, and, by the moving, his weakness and instability in regard to righteousness.

But most people, perhaps, will think this too far removed from the scope of our present inquiry. This, however, no one will regard as out of keeping with our subject; the fact that many think that what is incomprehensible to themselves is equally incomprehensible to God, and that whatever escapes their own cognizance is also beyond the power of His. Now since we make number the measure of quantity, and number is nothing else than a combination of units growing into multitude in a complex way (for the decad is a unit brought to that value by the composition of units, and again the hundred is a unit composed of decads, and in like manner the thousand is another unit, and so in due proportion the myriad is another by a multiplication, the one being made up to its value by thousands, the other by hundreds, by assigning all which to their underlying class we make signs of the quantity of the things numbered), accordingly, in order that we may be taught by Holy Scripture that nothing is unknown to God, it tells us that the multitude of the stars is numbered by Him, not that their numbering takes place as I have described, (for

who is so simple as to think that God takes knowledge of things by odd and even, and that by putting units together He makes up the total of the collective quantity?) but, since in our own case the exact knowledge of quantity is obtained by number, in order, I say, that we might be taught in respect to God that all things are comprehended by the knowledge of His wisdom, and that nothing escapes His minute cognizance, on this account it represents God as "numbering the stars," counselling us by these words to understand this, viz. that we must not imagine God to take note of things by the measure of human knowledge, but that all things, however incomprehensible and above human understanding, are embraced by the knowledge of the wisdom of God. For as the stars on account of their multitude escape numbering, as far as our human conception is concerned, Holy Scripture, teaching the whole from the part, in saying that they are numbered by God attests that not one of the things unknown to us escapes the knowledge of God. And therefore it says, "Who telleth the multitude of the stars," of course not meaning that He did not know their number beforehand; for how should He be ignorant of what He Himself created, seeing that the Ruler of the Universe could not be ignorant of that which is comprehended in His power; which includes the worlds in its embrace? Why, then, should He number what He knows? For to measure quantity by number is the part of those who want information. But He Who knew all things before they were created needs not number as His informant. But when David says that He "numbers the stars," it is evident that the Scripture descends to such language in accordance with our understanding, to teach us emblematically that the things which we know not are accurately known to God. As, then, He is said to number, though needing no arithmetical process to arrive at the knowledge of things created, so also the Prophet tells us that He calleth them all by their names, not meaning, I imagine, that He does so by any vocal utterance. For verily such language would result in a conception strangely unworthy of God, if it meant that these names in common use among ourselves were applied to the stars by God. For, should any one allow that these were so applied by God, it must follow that the names of the idol gods of Greece were applied by Him also to the stars, and we must regard as true all the tales from mythological history that are told about those starry names, as though God Himself sanctioned their utterance. Thus the distribution among the Greek idols of the seven planets contained in the heavens will exempt from blame those who have erred

---

6 Ps. cvi. 40.   7 1 Sam. xv. 35.
8 Ps. lxxviii. 65.   9 Gen. iii. 8.

in respect to them, if men be persuaded that such an arrangement was God's. Thus the fables of Orion and the Scorpion will be believed, and the legends respecting the ship Argo, and the Swan, and the Eagle, and the Dog, and the mythical story of Ariadne's crown. Moreover it will pave the way for supposing God to be the inventor of the names in the zodiacal circle, devised after some fancied resemblance in the constellations, if Eunomius is right in supposing that David said that these names were given them by God.

Since, then, it is monstrous to regard God as the inventor of such names, lest the names even of these idol gods should seem to have had their origin from God, it will be well not to receive what has been said without inquiry, but to get to the meaning in this case also after the analogy of those things of which number informs us. Well, since it attests the accuracy of our knowledge, when we call one familiar to us by his name, we are here taught that He Who embraces the Universe in His knowledge not only comprehends the total of the aggregate quantity, but has an exact knowledge of the units also that compose it. And therefore the Scripture says not only that He "telleth the number of the stars," but that "He calleth them all by their names," which means that His accurate knowledge extends to the minutest of them, and that He knows each particular respecting them, just as a man knows one who is familiar to him by name. And if any one say that the names given to the stars by God are different ones, unknown to human language, he wanders far away from the truth. For if there were other names of stars, Holy Scripture would not have made mention of those which are in common use among the Greeks, Esaias saying [1], "Which maketh the Pleiads, and Hesperus, and Arcturus, and the Chambers of the South," and Job making mention of Orion and Aseroth [2]; so that from this it is clear that Holy Scripture employs for our instruction such words as are in common use. Thus we hear in Job of Amalthea's horn [3], and in Esaias of the Sirens [4], the former thus naming plenty

after the conceit of the Greeks, the latter representing the pleasure derived from hearing, by the figure of the Sirens. As, then, in these cases the inspired word has made use of names drawn from mythological fables, with a view to the advantage of the hearers, so here it freely makes use of the appellations given to the stars by human fancy, teaching us that all things whatsoever that are named among men have their origin from God—the things, not their names. For it does not say Who nameth, but "Who maketh Pleiad, and Hesperus, and Arcturus." I think, then, it has been sufficiently shown in what I have said that David supports our opinion, in teaching us by this utterance, not that God gives the stars their names, but that He has an exact knowledge of them, after the fashion of men, who have the most certain knowledge of those whom they are able, through long familiarity, to call by their names.

And if we set forth the opinion of most commentators on these words of the Psalmist, that of Eunomius regarding them will be still more convicted of foolishness. For those who have most carefully searched out the sense of the inspired Scripture, declare that not all the works of creation are worthy of the Divine reckoning. For in the Gospel narratives of feeding the multitudes in the wilderness, women and children are not thought worthy of enumeration. And in the account of the Exodus of the children of Israel, those only are enumerated in the roll who were of age to bear arms against their enemies, and to do deeds of valour. For not all names of things are fit to be pronounced by the Divine lips, but the enumeration is only for that which is pure and heavenly, which, by the loftiness of its state remaining pure from all admixture with darkness, is called a star, and the naming is only for that which, for the same reason, is worthy to be registered in the Divine tablets. For of His adversaries He says, "I will not take up their names into my lips [5]."

But the names which the Lord gives to such stars we may plainly learn from the prophecy of Esaias, which says, "I have called thee by thy name; thou art Mine [6]." So that if a man makes himself God's possession, his act becomes

---

[1] The words here attributed to Isaiah are found in Job ix. 9 (LXX.): and Orion in Isaiah xiii. 10 (LXX.), with "the stars of heaven;" and in Amos v. 8 with "the seven stars."

[2] For Aseroth perhaps Mazaroth should be read. Cf. Job xxxviii. 32, "Canst thou lead forth the Mazaroth in their season?" (R.V.) and 2 Kings xxiii. 5, "to the planets (τοῖς μαζουρώθ)," i. e. the twelve signs of the Zodiac.

[3] Ἀμαλθείας κέρας. So LXX. for the name of Job's third daughter, Keren-happuch, for which Symmachus and Aquila have Καρναφούκ, i. e. Horn of purple (fucus). The LXX. translator of Job was rather fond of classical allusions, and so brought in the Greek horn (of plenty). Amalthea's goat, that suckled Jupiter, broke its horn.

"Sustulit hoc Nymphe, cinctumque recentibus herbis
   Et plenum pomis ad Jovis ora tulit."—Ovid, *Fasti*, v. 123.

[4] Isaiah xiii. 21. καὶ ἀναπαύσονται ἐκεῖ σειρῆνες, καὶ δαιμόνια ἐκεῖ ὀρχήσονται, "and ostriches shall dwell there, and satyrs shall dance there" (R. V.). The LXX. render the Hebrew (bath-jaana)

by σειρῆνες also in Isaiah xxxiv. 13, xliii. 20: and in Micah i. 8: Jeremiah i. 39. Cyril of Alexandria has on the first passage, "Birds that have a sweet note: or, according to the Jewish interpretation, the owl." And this is followed by the majority of commentators. Cf. Gray—

   "The moping owl doth to the moon complain."

But Bochart has many and strong arguments to prove that the ostrich, i. e. the στρουθο-κάμηλος, or "large sparrow with the long neck," is meant by bath-jaana: it has a high sharp unpleasant note. Cf. Job xxx. 29, "I am a companion to ostriches" (R. V.), speaking of his bitter cry.—Jerome also translates "habitabunt ibi struthiones;" and the LXX. elsewhere than above by στρουθία. Gregory follows the traditional interpretation, of some *pleasant* note; and somehow identifies the Greek word with the Hebrew.

[5] Ps. xvi. 4.   [6] Is. xliii. 1.

his name. But be this as the reader pleases. Eunomius, however, adds to his previous statement that the beginnings of creation testify to the fact, that names were given by God to the things which He created; but I think that it would be superfluous to repeat what I have already sufficiently set forth as the result of my investigations; and he may put his own arbitrary interpretation on the word Adam, which, the Apostle tells us, points prophetically to Christ [7]. For no one can be so infatuated, when Paul, by the power of the Spirit, has revealed to us the hidden mysteries, as to count Eunomius a more trustworthy interpreter of Divine things— a man who openly impugns the words of the inspired testimony, and who by his false interpretation of the word would fain prove that the various kinds of animals were not named by Adam. We shall do well, also, to pass over his insolent expressions, and tasteless vulgarity, and foul and disgusting tongue, with its accustomed fluency going on about our Master as "a sower of tares," and about "a deceptive show [3] of grain, and the blight of Valentinus, and his grain piled in our Master's mind": and we will veil in silence the rest of his unsavoury talk as we veil putrefying corpses in the ground, that the stench may not prove injurious to many. Rather let us proceed to what remains for us to say. For once more he adduces a dictum of our Master [9], to this effect. "We call God indestructible and ungenerate, applying these words from different points of view. For when we look to the ages that are past, finding the life of God transcending all limitation, we call Him ungenerate. But when we turn our thoughts to the ages that are yet to come, Him Who is infinite, illimitable, and without end, we call indestructible. As, then, that which has no end of life is indestructible, so that which has no beginning we call ungenerate, representing things so by the faculty of conception."

I will pass over, then, the abuse with which he has prefaced his discussion of these matters, as when he uses such terms as "alteration of seed," and "teacher of sowing," and "illogical censure," and whatever other aspersions he ventures on with his foul tongue. Let us rather turn to the point which he tries to establish by his calumnious accusation. He promises to convict us of saying that God is not by His nature indestructible. But we hold only such things foreign to His nature as may be added to or subtracted from it. But, in the case of things without which the subject is incapable of being conceived by the mind, how can any one be open to the charge of separating His nature from itself? If, then, the indestructibility which we ascribe to God were adventitious, and did not always belong to Him, or might cease to belong to Him, he might be justified in his calumnious attack. But if it is always the same, and our contention is, that God is always what He is, and that He receives nothing by way of increase or addition of properties, but continues always in whatsoever is conceived and called good, why should we be slanderously accused of not ascribing indestructibility to Him as of His essential nature? But he pretends that he grounds his accusation on the words of Basil which I have already quoted, as though we *bestowed* indestructibility on God by reference to the ages. Now if our statement were put forward by ourselves, our defence might perhaps seem open to suspicion, as if we now wanted to amend or justify any questionable expressions of ours. But since our statements are taken from the lips of an adversary, what stronger demonstration could we have of their truth than the evidence of our opponents themselves? How is it, then, with the statement which Eunomius lays hold of with a view to our prejudice? When, he says, we turn our thoughts to the ages that are yet to be, we speak of the infinite, and illimitable, and unending, as indestructible. Does Eunomius count such ascription as identical with bestowing? Yet who is such a stranger to existing usage as to be ignorant of the proper meaning of these expressions? For that man *bestows* who possesses something which another has not, while that man *ascribes* who designates with a name what another has. How is it, then, that our instructor in truth is not ashamed of his plainly calumnious impeachment? But as those who, from some disease, are bereft of sight, are unseemly in their behaviour before the eyes of the seeing, supposing that what is not seen by themselves is a thing unobserved also by those whose sight is unimpaired, just such is the case of our sharp-sighted and quick-witted opponent, who supposes his hearers to be afflicted with the same blindness to the truth as himself. And who is so foolish as not to compare the words which he calumniously assails with his charge itself, and by reading them side by side to detect the malice of the writer? Our statement ascribes indestructibility; he charges it with bestowing indestructibility. What has this to do with our statement? Every man has a right to be judged by his own deeds, not to be blamed

[7] Rom. xvi. 25.—On Eunomius' knowledge of Scripture, see Socrates iv. 7. "He had a very slender knowledge of the letter of Scripture: he was wholly unable to enter into the spirit of it. Yet he abounded in words, and was accustomed to repeat the same thoughts in different terms without ever arriving at a clear explanation of what he had proposed to himself. Of this his seven books on the Apostle's Epistle to the Romans, on which he expended a quantity of vain labour, is a remarkable proof." But see c. Eunom. II. p. 107.

[8] πρόσοψιν, the reading of Oehler's MSS.: also of Pithœus' MS., which John the Franciscan changed into the vox nihili προσίψιν (putredinem), which appears in the Paris Editt. of 1638.

[9] The e words are in S. Basil's first Book against Eunomius.

for those of others; and in this present case, while he accuses us, and points his bitterness at us, in truth he is condemning no one but himself. For if it is reprehensible to bestow indestructibility on God, and this is done by no one but himself, is not our slanderer his own accuser, assailing his own statements and not ours? And with regard to the term indestructibility, we assert that as the life which is endless is rightly called indestructible, so that which is without beginning is rightly called ungenerate. And yet Eunomius says that we lend Him the primacy over all created things simply by reference to the ages.

I pass in silence his blasphemy in reducing God the Only-begotten to a level with all created things, and, in a word, allowing to the Son of God no higher honour than theirs. Still, for the sake of my more intelligent hearers, I will here give an instance of his insensate malice. Basil, he says, lends God the primacy over all things by reference to the ages. What unintelligible nonsense is this! Man is made God's patron, and gives to God a primacy owing to the ages! What is this vain flourish of baseless expressions, seeing that our Master simply says that whatever in the Divine essence transcends the measurable distances of the ages in either direction is called by certain distinctive names, in the case of Him Who, as saith the Apostle, hath neither beginning of days nor end of life [1], in order that the distinction of the conception might be marked by distinction in the names. And yet on this account Eunomius has the effrontery to write, that to call that which is anterior to all beginning ungenerate, and again that which is circumscribed by no limit, immortal and indestructible, is a bestowing or lending on our part, and other nonsense of the kind. Moreover, he says that we divide the ages into two parts, as if he had not read the words he quoted, or as if he were addressing those who had forgotten his own previous statements. For what says our Master? "If we look at the time before the Creation, and if passing in thought through the ages we reflect on the infinitude of the Eternal Life, we signify the thought by the term ungenerate. And if we turn our thoughts to what follows, and consider the being of God as extending beyond all ages, we interpret the thought by the word endless or indestructible." Well, how does such an account sever the ages in twain, if by such possible words and names we signify that eternity of God which is equally observable from every point of view, in all things the same, unbroken in continuity? For seeing that human life, moving from stage to stage, advances in its progress from a beginning to an end, and our life here is divided between that which is past and that which is expected, so that the one is the subject of hope, the other of memory; on this account, as, in relation to ourselves, we apprehend a past and a future in this measurable extent, so also we apply the thought, though incorrectly, to the transcendent nature of God; not of course that God in His own existence leaves any interval behind, or passes on afresh to something that lies before, but because our intellect can only conceive things according to our nature, and measures the eternal by a past and a future, where neither the past precludes the march of thought to the illimitable and infinite, nor the future tells us of any pause or limit of His endless life. If, then, it is thus that we think and speak, why does he keep taunting us with dividing the ages? Unless, indeed, Eunomius would maintain that Holy Scripture does so too, signifying as it does by the same idea the infinity of the Divine existence; David, for example, making mention of the "kingdom from everlasting," and Moses, speaking of the kingdom of God as "extending beyond all ages," so that we are taught by both that every duration conceivable is environed by the Divine nature, bounded on all sides by the infinity of Him Who holds the universe in His embrace. For Moses, looking to the future, says that "He reigneth from generation to generation for evermore." And great David, turning his thought backward to the past, says, "God is our King before the ages [2]," and again, "God, Who was before the ages, shall hear us." But Eunomius, in his cleverness taking leave of such guides as these, says that we talk of the life that is without beginning as one, and of that which is without end as quite another, and again, of diversities of sundry ages, effecting by their own diversity a separation in our idea of God. But that our controversy may not grow to a tedious length, we will add, without criticism or comment, the outcome of Eunomius' labours on the subject, well fitted as they are by his industry displayed in the cause of error to render the truth yet more evident to the eyes of the discerning.

For, proceeding with his discourse, he asks us what we mean by the ages. And yet we ourselves might more reasonably put such questions to him. For it is he who professes to know the essence of God, defining on his own authority what is unapproachable and incomprehensible by man. Let him, then, give us a scientific lecture on the nature of the ages, boasting as he does of his familiarity with tran-

---

[1] Heb. vii. 3.

[2] Cf. Ps. xliv. 4, and xlviii. 14, with lxxiv. 12.

scendental things, and let him not so fiercely brandish over us, poor ignorant individuals, the double danger of the dilemma involved in our reply, telling us that, whether we hold this or that view of the ages, the result must be in either case an absurdity. For if (says he) you say that they are eternal, you will be Greeks, and Valentinians [3], and uninstructed [4] : and if you say that they are generate, you will no longer be able to ascribe ungeneracy to God. What a terribly unanswerable attack! If, O Eunomius, something is held to be generate, we no longer hold the doctrine of the Divine ungeneracy! And pray what has become of your subtle distinctions between generacy and ungeneracy, by which you sought to establish the dissimilarity of the essence of the Son from that of the Father? For it seems from what we are now being taught that the Father is not dissimilar in essence when contemplated in respect of generacy, but that, in fact, if we hold His ungeneracy, we reduce Him to non-existence; since "if we speak of the ages as generate, we are driven to relinquish the Ungenerate. But let us examine the force of the argument by which he would compel us to allow this absurdity. When, says he, those things by comparison with which God is without beginning are non-existent, He Who is compared with them must be non-existent also. What a sturdy and overpowering grip is this! How tightly has this wrestler got us by the waist in his inextricable grasp! He says that God's ungeneracy is added to Him through comparison with the ages. By whom is it so added? Who is there that says that to Him Who hath no beginning ungeneracy is added as an acquisition through comparison with something else? Neither such a word nor such a sense will be found in any writings of ours. Our words indeed carry their own justification, and contain nothing like what is alleged against us; and of the meaning of what is said, who can be a more trustworthy interpreter than he who said it? Have not we, then, the better title to say what we mean when we speak of the life of God as extending beyond the ages? And what we say is what we have said already in our previous writings. But, says he, comparison with the ages being impossible, it is impossible that any addition should accrue from it to God, meaning of

course that ungeneracy is an addition. Let him tell us by whom such an addition has been made. If by himself, he becomes simply ridiculous in laying his own folly to our charge: if by us, let him quote our words, and then we will admit the force of his accusation.

But I think we must pass over this and all that follows. For it is the mere trifling of children who amuse themselves with beginning to build houses in sand. For having composed a portion of a paragraph, and not yet brought it to a conclusion, he shows that the same life is without beginning and without end, thus in his eagerness working out our own conclusion. For this is just what we say ; that the Divine life is one and continuous in itself, infinite and eternal, in no wise bounded by any limit to its infinity. Thus far our opponent devotes his labours and exertions to the truth as we represent it, showing that the same life is on no side limited, whether we look at that part of it which was before the ages, or at that which succeeds them. But in his next remarks he returns to his old confusion. For after saying that the same life is without beginning and without end, leaving the subject of life, and ranging all the ideas we entertain about the Divine life under one head, he unifies everything. If, says he, the life is without beginning and without end, ungenerate and indestructible, then indestructibility and ungeneracy will be the same thing, as will also the being without beginning and without end. And to this he adds the aid of arguments. It is not possible, he says, for the life to be one, unless indestructibility and ungeneracy are identical terms. An admirable "addition" on the part of our friend. It would seem, then, that we may hold the same language in regard to righteousness, wisdom, power, goodness, and all such attributes of God. Let, then, no word have a meaning peculiar to itself, but let one signification underlie every word in a list, and one form of description serve for the definition of all. If you are asked to define the word judge, answer with the interpretation of "ungeneracy"; if to define justice, be ready with "the incorporeal" as your answer. If asked to define incorruptibility, say that it has the same meaning as mercy or judgment. Thus let all God's attributes be convertible terms, there being no special signification to distinguish one from another. But if Eunomius thus prescribes, why do the Scriptures vainly assign various names to the Divine nature, calling God a Judge, righteous, powerful, long-suffering, true, merciful, and so on? For if none of these titles is to be understood in any special or peculiar sense, but, owing to this confusion in their meaning, they are all mixed up together, it would be useless to employ so

3 Valentinus "placed in the *pleroma* (so the Gnostics called the habitation of the Deity) thirty *æons* (ages), of which one half were male, and the other female" (Mosheim), *i.e.* these æons were co-eternal with the Deity.

4 βάρβαροι here being not opposed to "Greeks" must imply mere *inability to speak aright*: amongst those who claimed to use Catholic language another "barbarism," or "jargon," had arisen (*i.e.* that of heresy, whether Platonist or Gnostic), different from that which separated the Greeks from the Jews, Africans, Romans alike. Hesychius ; βάρβαροι οἱ ἀπαίδευτοι. So to S. Paul "the people" of Malta (Acts xxviii. 2—4), as to others the Apostles, were barbarian.

many words for the same thing, there being no difference of meaning to distinguish them from one another. But who is so much out of his wits as not to know that, while the Divine nature, whatever it is in its essence, is simple, uniform, and incomposite, and that it cannot be viewed under any form of complex formation, the human mind, grovelling on earth, and buried in this life on earth, in its inability to behold clearly the object of its search, feels after the unutterable Being in divers and many-sided ways, and never chases the mystery in the light of one idea alone. Our grasping of Him would indeed be easy, if there lay before us one single assigned path to the knowledge of God : but as it is, from the skill apparent in the Universe, we get the idea of skill in the Ruler of that Universe, from the large scale of the wonders worked we get the impression of His Power ; and from our belief that this Universe depends on Him, we get an indication that there is no cause whatever of His existence ; and again, when we see the execrable character of evil, we grasp His own unalterable pureness as regards this : when we consider death's dissolution to be the worst of ills, we give the name of Immortal and Indissoluble at once to Him Who is removed from every conception of that kind : not that we split up the subject of such attributes along with them, but believing that this thing we think of, whatever it be in substance, is One, we still conceive that it has something in common with all these ideas. For these terms are not set against each other in the way of opposites, as if, the one existing there, the other could not co-exist in the same subject (as, for instance, it is impossible that life and death should be thought of in the same subject) ; but the force of each of the terms used in connection with the Divine Being is such that, even though it has a peculiar significance of its own, it implies no opposition to the term associated with it. What opposition, for instance, is there between "incorporeal" and "just," even though the words do not coincide in meaning : and what hostility is there between goodness and invisibility? So, too, the eternity of the Divine Life, though represented under the double name and idea of "the unending" and "the unbeginning," is not cut in two by this difference of name ; nor yet is the one name the same in meaning as the other ; the one points to the absence of beginning, the other to the absence of end, and yet there is no division produced in the subject by this difference in the actual terms applied to it.

Such is our position ; our adversary's, with regard to the precise meaning of this term [5], is such as can derive no help from any reasonings ; he only spits forth at random about it these strangely unmeaning and bombastic expressions [6], in the framework of his sentences and periods. But the upshot of all he says is this ; that there is no difference in the meaning of the most varied names. But we must most certainly, as it seems to me, quote this passage of his word for word, lest we be thought to be calumniously charging him with something that does not belong to him. "True expressions," he says, "derive their precision from the subject realities which they indicate ; different expressions are applied to different realities, the same to the same : and so one or other of these two things must of necessity be held : either that the reality indicated is different (if the expressions are), or else that the indicating expressions are not different." With these and many other such-like words, he proceeds to effect the object he has before him, excluding from the expression certain relations and affinities [7], such as species, proportion, part, time, manner : in order that by the withdrawal of all these "Ungeneracy" may become indicative of the substance of God. His process of proof is in the following manner (I will express his idea in my own words). The life, he says, is not a different thing from the substance ; no addition may be thought of in connection with a simple being, by dividing our conception of him into a communicating and communicated side ; but whatever the life may be, that very thing, he insists, is the substance. Here his philosophy is excellent ; no thinking person would gainsay this. But how does he arrive at his contemplated conclusion, when he says, "when we mean the unbeginning, we mean the life, and truth compels us by this last to mean the substance"? The ungenerate, then, according to him is expressive of the very substance of God. We, on the other hand, while we agree that the life of God was not given by another, which is the meaning of "unbeginning," think that the belief that the idea expressed by the words "not generated" is the substance of God is a madman's only. Who indeed can be so beside himself as to declare the absence of any generation to be the definition of that substance (for as generation is involved in the generate, so is the absence of generation in the ungenerate)? Ungeneracy indicates that which is not in the Father ; so how shall we allow the indication of that which is absent to be His substance? Helping himself to that which neither we nor any logical conclusion from the premises allows

---

6 ἀλλοκότως αὐτοῦ τὰς τοιαύτας στομφώδεις καὶ ἀδιανοήτους φωνὰς . . . πρὸς τὸ συμβὰν ἀποπτύοντος.
7 ἐκβαλὼν τοῦ λόγου σχέσεις τινὰς καὶ παραθέσεις. Gulonius' Latin is wrong ; "protulit in medium."

him, he lays it down that God's Ungeneracy is expressive of God's life. But to make quite plain his delusion upon this subject, let us look at it in the following way; I mean, let us examine whether, by employing the same method by which he, in the case of the Father, has brought the definition of the substance to ungeneracy, we may not equally bring the substance of the Son to ungeneracy.

He says, "The Life that is the same, and thoroughly single, must have one and the same outward expression for it, even though in mere names, and manner, and order it may seem to vary. For true expressions derive their precision from the subject realities which they indicate; different expressions are applied to different realities, the same to the same; and so one or other of these two things must of necessity be held; either that the reality indicated is quite different (if the expressions are), or else that the indicating expressions are not different;" and there is in this case no other subject reality besides the life of the Son, "for one either to rest an idea upon, or to cast a different expression upon." Is there, I may ask, any unfitness in the words quoted, which would prevent them being rightly spoken or written about the Only-begotten? Is not the Son Himself also a " Life thoroughly single"? Is there not for Him also "one and the same" befitting "expression," "though in mere names, and manner, and order He may seem to vary"? Must not, for Him also, "one or other of these two things be held" fixed, "either that the reality indicated is quite different, or else that the indicating expressions are not different," there being no other subject reality, besides his life, "for one either to rest an idea upon, or to cast a different expression upon"? We mix up nothing here with what Eunomius has said about the Father; we have only passed from the same accepted premise to the same conclusion as he did, merely inserting the Son's name instead. If, then, the Son too is a single life, unadulterated, removed from every sort of compositeness or complication, and there is no subject reality besides this life of the Son (for how in that which is simple can the mixture of anything foreign be suspected? what we have to think of along with something else is no longer simple), and if the Father's substance also is a single life, and of this single life, by virtue of its very life and its very singleness, there are no differences, no increase or decrease in quantity or quality in it creating any variation, it needs must be that things thus coinciding in idea should be called by the same appellation also. If, that is, the thing that is detected both in the Father and the Son, I mean the singleness of life, is one, the very idea of single-

ness excluding, as we have said, any variation, it needs must be that the name befitting the one should be attached to the other also. For as that which reasons, and is mortal, and is capable of thought and knowledge, is called " man " equally in the case of Adam and of Abel, and this name of the nature is not altered either by the fact that Abel passed into existence by generation, or by the fact that Adam did so without generation, so, if the simplicity[1] and incompositeness of the Father's life has ungeneracy for its name, in like manner for the Son's life the same idea will necessarily have to be attached to the same utterance, if, as Eunomius says, "one or other of these two things must of necessity be held; either that the reality indicated is quite different, or else that the indicating expressions are not different."

But why do we linger over these follies, when we ought rather to put Eunomius' book itself into the hands of the studious, and so, apart from any examination of it, to prove at once to the discerning, not only the blasphemy of his opinion, but also the nervelessness of his style[2]? While in various ways, not going upon our apprehension of it, but following his own fancy, he misinterprets the word Conception, just as in a night-battle nobody can distinguish friend and foe, he does not understand that he is stabbing his own doctrine with the very weapons he thinks he is turning upon us. For the point in which he thinks he is most removed from the church of the orthodox is this; that he attempts to prove that God became Father at some later time, and that the appellation of Fatherhood is later than all those other names which attach to Him; for that He was called Father from that moment in which He purposed in Himself to become, and did become, Father. Well, then, since in this treatise he is for proving that all the names applied to the Divine Nature coincide with each other, and that there is no difference whatever between them, and since one amongst these applied names is Father (for as God is indestructible and eternal, so also He is Father), we must either sanction, in the case of this term also, the opinion he holds about the rest, and so contravene his former position, seeing that the idea of Fatherhood is found to be involved in any of these other terms (for it is plain that if the meaning of indestructible and Father is exactly the same, He will be believed to be, just as He is always indestructible, so likewise always Father, there being one single signification, he says, in all these names): or else, if he fears thus to testify to the eternal

---

[1] Reading εἴπερ τὸ ἁπλοῦν with the editt., which is manifestly required by the sense.

[2] συνηθείας, lit. usage of language. Cf. Plato, Theæt. 168 B, ἐκ συνηθείας ῥημάτων τε καὶ ὀνομάτων. It is used absolutely, by the Grammarians, for the "Vulgar dialect."

Fatherhood of God, he must perforce abandon his whole argument, and own that each of these names has a meaning peculiar to itself; and thus all this nonsense of his about the Divine names bursts like a bubble, and vanishes like smoke.

But if he should still answer with regard to this opposition (of the Divine names), that it is only the term Father, and the term Creator, that are applied to God as expressing production, both words being so applied, as he says, because of an operation, then he will cut short our long discussion of this subject, by thus conceding what it would have required a laborious argument on our part to prove. For if the word Father and the word Creator have the same meaning (for both arise from an operation), one of the things signified is exactly equivalent to the other, since if the signification is the same, the subjects cannot be different. If, then, He is called both Father and Creator because of an operation, it is quite allowable to interchange the names, and to turn one into the other and say that God is Creator of the Son, and Father of a stone, seeing that the term Father is to be devoid of any meaning of essential relation [3]. Well, the monstrous conclusion that is hereby proved cannot remain doubtful to those who reflect. For as it is absurd to deem a stone, or anything else that exists by creation, Divine, it must be agreed that there is no Divinity to be recognized in the Only-begotten either, when that one identical meaning of an operation, by which God is called both Father and Creator, assigns, according to Eunomius, both these terms to Him. But let us hold to the question before us. He abuses our assertion that our knowledge of God is formed by contributions of terms applied to different ideas, and says that the proof of His simplicity is destroyed by us so, since He must partake of the elements signified by each term, and only by virtue of a share in them can completely fill out His essence. Here I write in my own language, curtailing his wearisome prolixity; and in answer to his foolish and nerveless redundancy no sensible person, I think, would make any reply, except as regards his charging us with "senselessness." Now if anything of that description had been said by us, we ought of course to retract it if it was foolishly worded, or, if there was any doubt as to its meaning, to put an irreproachable interpretation upon it. But we have not said anything of the kind, any more than the consequences of our words lead the mind to any such necessity. Why, then, linger on that to which all assent, and weary the reader by prolonging the argument? Who

is really so devoid of reflection as to imagine, when he hears that our orthodox conceptions of the Deity are gathered from various ways of thinking of Him, that the Deity is composed of these various elements, or completes His actual fulness by participating in anything at all? A man, say, has made discoveries in geometry, and this same man, let us suppose, has made discoveries also in astronomy, and in medicine as well, and grammar, and agriculture, and sciences of that kind. Will it follow, because there are these various names of sciences viewed in connection with one single soul, that that single soul is to be considered a composite soul? Yet there is a very great difference in meaning between medicine and astronomy; and grammar means nothing in common with geometry, or seamanship with agriculture. Nevertheless it is within the bounds of possibility that the idea of each of these sciences should be associated with one soul, without that soul thereby becoming composite, or, on the other hand, without all those terms for sciences blending into one meaning. If, then, the human mind, with all such terms applied to it, is not injured as regards its simplicity, how can any one imagine that the Deity, when He is called wise, and just, and good, and eternal, and all the other Divine names, must, unless all these names are made to mean one thing, become of many parts, or take a share of all these to make up the perfection of His nature?

But let us examine a still more vehement charge of his against us; it is this: "If one must proceed to say something harsher still, he does not even keep the Divine substance pure and unadulterated from inferior and contradictory elements." This is the charge, but the proof of it is,—what? Observe the strong professional attack! "If He is imperishable only by reason of the unending in His Life, and ungenerate only by reason of the unbeginning, then wherein He is not imperishable He is perishable, and wherein He is not ungenerate He is generated." Then returning to the charge, he repeats, "He will then be, as unbeginning, at once ungenerate and perishable, and, as unending, at once imperishable and generated." Such is his "harsher" statement, which, according to his threat, he has discharged against us, to prove that we say that the Divine substance is mingled with contradictory and even inferior elements. However, I think it is plain to all who keep unimpaired within themselves the power of judging the truth, that our Master has given no handle at all, in what he has said, to this calumniator, but that the latter has garbled it at will, and then, playing at arguing, has drawn out this childish sophistry. But that

---

[3] τῆς κατὰ φύσιν σχετικῆς σημασίας.

it may be plainer still to all my readers, I will repeat that statement of the Master word for word, and then confront Eunomius' words with it. "We call the Universal Deity" (he says) "imperishable and ungenerate, using these words with different applications [4] of thought; for when we concentrate our view upon the ages behind us, we find the life of the Deity transcending every limit, and so name Him 'ungenerate'; but when we turn our thoughts upon the ages to come, we call the infinite in Him, the boundless, the absence of all end to His living, 'imperishability.' As, then, this endlessness is called imperishable, so too this beginninglessness is called ungenerate; and we arrive at these names by Conception." Such are the Master's words, and by them he teaches us this: that the Divine Life is essentially single and continuous with Itself, starting from no beginning, circumscribed by no end; and that the intuitions which we possess regarding this Life it is possible to make clear by words. That is, we express the never having come from any cause by the term unbeginning or ungenerate; and we express the not being circumscribed by any limit, and not being destroyed by any death, by the term imperishable, or unending; and this absence of cause, he defines, makes it right for us to speak of the Divine life as existing ungenerately; and this being without end we are to denote as imperishable, since anything that has ceased to exist is necessarily in a state of annihilation, and when we hear of anything annihilated, we at once think of the destruction of its substance. He says then, that One Who never ceases to exist, and is a stranger to all destruction and dissolution, is to be called imperishable.

What, then, does Eunomius say to this? "If He is imperishable only by reason of the unending in His Life, and ungenerate only by reason of the unbeginning, then wherein He is not imperishable He is perishable, and wherein He is not ungenerate He is generated." Who conceded to you this, Eunomius, that the imperishability is not to be associated with the whole life of God? Who ever divided that Life into two parts, and then put particular names to each half of the Life, so that to the division which the one name fitted the other could not be said to apply? This is the result of your dialectic sharpness; to say that the Life which has no beginning is perishable, and that what is imperishable cannot be associated with what is unbeginning! It is just as if, when one had said that man was rational, as well as capable of speculation and knowledge, attaching each phrase to the subject of them according to a

different application and idea, some one was to jeer, and to go on in the same strain, "If man is capable of speculation and knowledge, he cannot, as regards this, be rational, but wherein he is capable of such knowledge, he is this and this only, and his nature does not admit of his being the other"; and reversely, if rational were made the definition of man, he were to deny in this case his being capable of this speculation and knowledge; for "wherein he is rational, he is proved devoid of mind." But if the ridiculousness and absurdity in this case is plain to any one, neither in that former case is it at all doubtful. When you have read the passage from the Master, you will find that his childish sophistry will vanish like a shadow. In our case of the definition of man, the capability of knowledge is not hindered by the possession of reason, nor the reason by the capability of knowledge: no more is the eternity of the Divine Life deprived of imperishability, if it be unbeginning, or of beginninglessness, if we recognize its imperishability. This would-be seeker after truth, with the artifices of his dialectic shrewdness, inserts in our argument what comes from his own repertoire; and so he fights with himself and overthrows himself, without ever touching anything of ours. For our position was nothing but this; that the Life as existing without beginning is styled, by means of a fresh Conception, as ungenerate: is styled, I say, not, is made such; and that we mark the Life as going on into infinity with the appellation of imperishable; mark it, I say, as such, not, make it such; and that the result is, that while it is a property of the Divine Life, inherent in the subject, to be infinite in both views, the thoughts associated with that subject are expressed in this way or in that only as regards that particular term which indicates the thought expressed. One thought associated with that life is, that it does not exist from any cause; this is indicated by the term "ungenerate." Another thought about it is, that it is limitless and endless; this is represented by the word imperishable. Thus, while the subject remains what it is, above everything, whether name or thought, the not being from any cause, and the not changing into the non-existent, are signified by means of the Conception implied in the aforesaid words.

What, then, out of all that we have said, has stirred him up to this piece of childish folly, in which he returns to the charge and repeats himself in these words: "He will, then, be, as unbeginning, at once ungenerate and perishable, and, as unending, at once imperishable and generated." It is plain to any possessing the least reflection, without our testing this logically, how absurdly foolish it is, or rather, how con-

---

[4] ἐπιβολὰς.

demnably blasphemous. By the same argument as that whereby he establishes this union of the perishable and the unbeginning, he can make sport of any proper and worthily conceived name for the Deity. For it is not these two ideas only that we associate with the Divine Life, I mean, the being without beginning, and the not admitting of dissolution; but It is called as well immaterial and without anger, immutable and incorporeal, invisible and formless, true and just; and there are numberless other ways of thinking about the Divine Life, each one of which is announced by an expressive sound with a peculiar meaning of its own. Well, to any name—any name, I mean, expressive of some proper conception of the Deity— it is open for us to apply this method of unnatural union devised by Eunomius. For instance, immateriality and absence of anger are both predicated of the Divine Life; but not with the same thought in both cases; for by the term immaterial we convey the idea of purity from any mixture with matter, and by the term "without anger" the strangeness to any emotion of anger. Now in all probability Eunomius will run trippingly over all this, and have his dance, just as before, upon our words. Stringing together his absurdities in the same way, he will say: "If wherein He is separated from all mixture with matter He is called immaterial, in this respect He will not be without anger; and if by reason of His not indulging in anger He is without anger, it is impossible to attribute to him immateriality, but logic will compel us to admit that, in so far as He is exempt from matter, He is both immaterial and wrathful;" and so you will find the same to be the case in respect to his other attributes. And if you like we will propound another pairing of the same, i. e. His immutability and His incorporeality. For both these terms being used of the Divine Life in a distinct sense, in their case also Eunomius' skill will embellish the same absurdity. For if His being always as He is is signified by the term immutable, and if the term incorporeal represents the spirituality of His essence, Eunomius will certainly say the same here also, that the terms are irreconcilable, and alien to each other, and that the notions which our minds attach to them have no point of contact one with the other; for in so far as God is always the same He is immutable, but not incorporeal; and in regard to the spirituality and formlessness of His essence, while He possesses attributes of incorporeality, He is not immutable; so that it happens that when immutability is considered with respect to the Divine Life, along with that immutability it is established that It is corporeal; but if spirituality is the object of search,

you prove that It is at once incorporeal and mutable.

Such are the clever discoveries of Eunomius against the truth. For what need is there to go through all his argument with trifling prolixity? For in every instance you may see an attempt to establish the same futility. For instance, by an implication such as that above, what is true and what is just will be found opposed to each other; for there is a difference in meaning between truth and justice. So that by a parity of reasoning Eunomius will say about these also, that truth is not in justice, and that justice is absent from truth; and it will happen that, when in respect of God we think of His being alien to injustice, the Divine Being will be shown to be at once just and untrue, while if we regard His being alien to untruth, we prove Him to be at once true and unjust. So, too, of His being invisible and formless. For according to a wise reasoning similar to that which we have adduced, it will not be permissible to say either that the invisible exists in that which is formless, or to say that that which is formless exists in that which is invisible; but he will comprise form in that which is invisible, and so again, conversely, he will prove that that which is formless is visible, using the same language in respect of these as he devised in respect to that which is imperishable and unbeginning, to the effect that when we regard the incomposite nature of the Divine Life, we confess that it is formless, yet not invisible; and that when we reflect that we cannot see God with our bodily eyes, while thus admitting His invisibility, we cannot admit His being formless. Now if these instances seem ridiculous and foolish, much more will every sensible man condemn the absurdity of the statements, starting from which his argument has logically brought him to such a pitch of absurdity. Yet he carps at the Master's words, as wrong in seeing that which is imperishable in that which is unending, and that which is unending in that which is imperishable. Well, then, let us also have our sport, in a manner something like this cleverness of Eunomius. Let us examine his opinion about these two names aforesaid, and see what it is.

Either, he says, that which is endless is distinct in meaning from that which is imperishable, or else the two must make one. But if he call both one, he will be supporting our argument. But if he say that the meaning of the imperishable is one thing, and that that of being unending is another, then of necessity, in the case of things differing from each other, the force of the one cannot be equivalent to the force of the other. If, then, the idea of the imperishable is one, and that of being endless is another, and each of these is what the other is not, neither will he grant that the im-perishable is unending, nor that the unending is imperishable, but the unending will be perish-able, and the imperishable will be termin-able. But I must beg my readers not to turn a ridiculous method of condemnation against us. We have been compelled to adopt such a sportive vein against the mockeries of our op-ponent, that we might thereby break through the puerile toil of his sophistries. But if it would not be too wearisome to my readers, it would not be out of place again to set forth what Eunomius says in his own words. " If," says he, " God is imperishable only by reason of the unending in His Life, and ungenerate only by reason of the unbeginning, then wherein He is not imperishable He is perishable, and wherein He is not ungenerate He is generated." Then returning to the charge, he repeats, " He will then be, as unbeginning, at once ungenerate and perishable : and, as unending, at once im-perishable and generated ; " for I pass over the superfluous and unseasonable remarks which he has interspersed here, as in no way contribut-ing to the proving of his point. Now I think it is easy for any one to see, by his own words, that the drift of our argument has no connec-tion whatever with the accusation which he lays against us. " For we call the God of the uni-verse imperishable and ungenerate," says the Master, " using these words with different ap-plications." " His transcending," he continues, " every limit of the ages, and every distance in temporal extension, whether we consider the previous or the subsequent, this absence of limit or circumscription on either hand in the Eternal Life we mark in the one case with the name of imperishability, and in the other case with the name of ungeneracy." But Eunomius would make out that we say that the being without beginning is His essence, and again that the being without end is His essence, as though we brought forward two contradictory segments of essence ; and in this way he estab-lishes an absurdity, and while laying down, and then fighting against, positions of his own, and reducing notions of his own concoction to an absurdity, he lays no hold on our argument in any single point. For that God is imperishable only wherein His Life is unending, is his state-ment, not ours. In like manner, that the im-perishable is not without beginning, is an in-vention of that same subtle cleverness which would constitute a negative attribute an essence ; whereas we do not define any such negative attribute as an essence. Now it is a negative attribute of God, that neither does the Life cease in dissolution, nor did It have a com-mencement in generation ; and this we express by these two words, imperishability and un-

generacy. But Eunomius, mixing up his own folly with our teaching, does not seem to under-stand that he is publishing his own disgrace by his calumnious accusations. For, in defining ungeneracy as an essence, he will logically arrive at the same pitch of absurdity which he ascribes to our teaching. For as beginning means [5] one thing, and end means another, by virtue of an intervening extension, if any one allow the privation of the first of these to be essence, he must suppose His Life to be only half subsisting in this being without beginning, and not to extend further, by virtue of His nature, to the being without end, if ungeneracy be regarded as itself His nature. But if any one insist that both are essence, then, according to the definition put forward by Eunomius, each of these terms must necessarily, by virtue of its inherent meaning, be counted as essence, being just as much as, and no more than, is indicated by the meaning of the term ; and thus the argument of Eunomius will not be without force, inasmuch as that which is without be-ginning does not involve the notion of being without end, and vice versâ, since according to his account each of the things mentioned is an essence, and there is no confusion between the two in their relation to each other, the notion of beginning being different to that of ending, while the words which express privation of these also differ in their significations.

But that he himself also may be brought to the knowledge of his own trifling, we will convict him from his own statements. For in the course of his argument he says that God, in that He is without end, is ungener-ate, and that, in that He is ungenerate, He is without end, as if the meanings of the two terms were identical. If, then, by reason of His being without end He is ungenerate, and the being without end and ungenerate are convertible terms, and he admits that the Son also is without end, by a parity of reasoning he must necessarily admit that the Son is un-generate, if (as he has said) His being without end and His being without beginning are identical in meaning. For just as in the un-generate he sees that which is without begin-ning, so he allows that in that which is without end also he sees that which is without beginning. For otherwise he would not have made the terms wholly convertible. But God, he says, is ungenerate by nature, and not by contrast with the ages. Well, who is there that contends that God is not by nature all that He is said to be ? For we do not say that God is just, and

<hr />

5 The Latin is wrong here, " secundum rerum intellectarum dis-tinctricem significationem ; " for νοουμένων without the article must be the gen. absol. Besides this the MSS. read παράτασιν (not παράστασιν).

almighty, and Father, and imperishable, by contrast with the ages, nor by His relation to any other thing that exists. But in connection with the subject itself, whatever He may be in His nature, we entertain every idea that is a reverent idea ; so that supposing neither ages, nor any other created thing, had been made, God would no less be what we believe Him to be, being in no need of the ages to constitute Him what He is. "But," says Eunomius, "He has a Life that is not extraneous, nor composite, nor admitting of differences ; for He Himself is Life eternal, by virtue of that Life itself immortal, by virtue of that immortality imperishable." This we are taught respecting the Only-begotten as well ; nor can any one impugn this teaching without openly opposing the declaration of S. John. For life was not brought in from without upon the Son either (for He says, "I am the Life[6] "), nor is His Life either composite, nor does it admit difference, but by virtue of that life itself He is immortal (for in what else but in life can we see immortality?), and by virtue of that immortality He is imperishable. For that which is stronger than death must naturally be incapable of corruption.

Thus far our argument goes with him. But the riddle with which he accompanies his words we must leave to those trained in the wisdom of Prunicus[7] to interpret : for he seems to have produced what he has said from that system. "Being incorruptible without beginning, He is ungenerate without end, being so called absolutely, and independently of aught beside Himself." Now whoever has purged ears and an enlightened understanding knows, even without my saying it, that beyond the jingle of words produced by their extraordinary combination, there is no trace of sense in what he says ; and if any shadow of an idea could be found in such a din of words, it would prove to be either profane or ridiculous. For what do you mean when you say that He is without beginning as being without end, and without end as being without beginning? Do you think beginning identical with end, and that the two words are employed in the same sense, just as the appellations Simon and Peter represent one and the same subject, and on this account, in accordance with your thinking beginning and end the same, did you, combining under one signification these two words which denote privation of each other,—end, I mean, and beginning,—and taking the being without end as convertible with the being without end, blend and confound one word with the other ; and is this the meaning of such a mixing up of words, when

you say that He is ungenerate as being without end, and that He is without end as being ungenerate? Yet how is it that you did not see the profanity as well as the ridiculous folly of your words? For if by this novel confusion of the words they are made convertible, so that ungenerate means ungenerate without end, and that which is without end is such ungenerately, it follows by necessity that that which is without end must needs be so as being ungenerate : and thus it comes to pass, my good friend, that your much-talked-of ungeneracy, which you say is the only characteristic of the Father's essence, will be found to be shared with whatever is immortal, and to be making all things consubstantial with the Father, because it is alike apparent in all things whose life, by reason of their immortality, goes on to infinity, archangels, that is, angels, human souls, and, it may be also, in the Apostate host, the Devil and his dæmons. For if that which is without end, and imperishable, must also by your argument be ungenerately imperishable, then in whatsoever is without end and imperishable there must be connoted ungeneracy. These are the absurdities into which those men fall who, before they have learnt what it is fitting for them to learn, only publish their own ignorance by what they attempt to teach. For if he had any faculty of discernment, he would not be ignorant of the peculiar sense inherent in his terms, "without beginning," and "without end," and that the term without end is common to all things whose life we believe capable of extension to infinity, while the term without beginning belongs to Him alone Who is without originating cause. How, then, is it possible for us to regard that which is common to them all, as equivalent to that which is believed by all to be a special attribute of the Deity alone, so that we thereby either extend ungeneracy to everything that shares in immortality, or else must not allow immortality to any one of them, seeing that the being without end is to belong only to the ungenerate, and vice versâ, the being ungenerate is to belong only to that which is without end? Thus everything without end would have to be regarded as ungenerate.

But let us leave this, and along with it the usual foul deluge of calumny in his words ; and let us go on to his subsequent quotations (of Basil). But I think it would perhaps be well to pass without examination over most of these subsequent words. For in all of them he shows himself the same, not grappling with that which we have really said, but only inventing for himself points for refutation which he pretends are taken from our statement. To go carefully through these would be pronounced useless by any one

[6] S. John xi. 25.
[7] This may mean "short-hand " i. e. something difficult to decipher. See Book I. vi. note 10.

possessed of judgment; for any understanding reader of his book can from his very words perceive his scurrility. He says that God's Glory is prior to our leader's "conception." We too do not deny that. For God's glory, whatever we are to think of it, is prior not only to this present generation of ours, but to all creation; it transcends the ages. What, then, is gained for his argument from this fact, that God's glory is conceded to be superior not only to Basil, but to all the ages? "Yes, but this name *is* His glory," he says. But pray tell us, in order that we may assent to this statement, who has proved that the appellation is identical with the glory? "A law of our nature," he replies, "teaches us that, in naming realities, the dignity of the names does not depend on the will of those who give them." What is this law of nature? And how is it that it is not in force amongst all? If nature had really enacted such a law, it ought to have authority amongst all who share the common nature, just as the other things peculiar to that nature have. If, in fine, it was the law of nature that caused the appellations to spring up for us from the objects, just as her plants spring up from seeds and roots, and she did not entrust the significant naming of each of the subjects to the choice of those who had to indicate the objects, then all mankind would be of one tongue. For if the names imposed upon these objects did not vary, we should not differ from one another in the department of speech. He says it is "a holy thing, and most closely connected with the designs of Providence, that their sounds should be imposed upon realities from a source above us." How is it, then, that the Prophets were ignorant of this holy thing, and were not instructed in this design of Providence, who according to your account did not make God at all of this Ungeneracy? How, too, is it that the Deity Himself never knew of this kind of holiness, when He did not give names from above to the animals which He had formed, but gave away this power of name-giving to Adam? If it is closely connected with the designs of Providence, as Eunomius says, and a holy thing, that their sounds should be imposed from above upon realities, it is certainly an unholy thing, and an unfitting thing, that these names should have been fitted to the things that are by any here below. "But the universal Guardian," he says, "thought it right to engraft these names in our minds by a law of His creation." And how was it, then, if these were engrafted in the minds of men, that from Adam onward to your transgression no fruits of this folly were produced, grafted as they were, according to you, in those minds, so that un-

generacy should be the name of the Father's essence? Adam and all in succession after him would have pronounced this word, if such had been grafted by God in his nature. For as all that now grows upon the earth continues always, owing to a transmission of its seed from the first creation, and not one single seed at the present time innovates upon the natural form, so this word, if it had been, as you say, grafted by God in our nature, would have sprung up along with the first utterances of the first-formed human beings, and would have accompanied the line of their posterity. But seeing that this word did not exist at the first (for no one in former generations and up to the present ever uttered such a word, except this man), it is plain that it is a bastard invention, that has sprung up from the seed of tares, not from that good seed which God has sown, to use evangelic words, in the field of our nature. For all the things that characterize our common nature do not have their beginning now, but appeared with that nature at its first formation; such, for instance, as the operation of the senses, the appetitive, or contrary, instinct of the man with regard to anything, and other generally acknowledged accompaniments of his nature, none of which a particular epoch has introduced amongst those born in it; but our humanity is preserved continually, from first to last, within the same circle of qualities, losing none which it had at the beginning, any more than it acquires any which it had not then. But just as, while sight is a faculty common to our nature, scientific observation comes by training to those who have devoted themselves to some science (it is not every one, for instance, who can observe with the theodolite, or prove a theorem by means of lines in geometry, or do anything else, where art has introduced, not mere sight, but a special use of sight), so too, while one might pronounce the possession of reason to be a common property of humanity united to the very essence of our nature from above, the invention of terms significative of realities is the work of men who, possessing from above the power of reason, are continually finding out, according as they wish for them towards the elucidation of that which they plainly see, certain words expressive of these things. "But if these views are to prevail," says he, "one of two things is proved; either that conception is anterior to those who conceive, or that the names naturally befitting the Deity, and pre-existent to everything, are posterior to the beginning of man." Ought we to continue the fight against such assertions, and join issue with such manifest absurdity?

But who, pray, is so simple as to be harmed by such arguments, and to imagine that if names are once believed to be an outcome of the reasoning faculty, he must allow that the utterance of names is anterior to those who utter them, or else that he must think he is sinning against the Deity, in that every man continues to name the Deity, according as each after birth is capable of conceiving Him? As to this last supposition, it has been already explained that the Supreme Being has no need Himself of words as delivered by a voice and a tongue; and it would be superfluous to repeat what would only encumber the argument. In fine, a Being Whose nature is neither lacking nor redundant, but simply perfect, neither fails to possess anything that is necessary, nor possesses what is not necessary. Since, then, we have proved previously, and all thinking men unanimously agree, that the calling by names is not a necessity of the Deity, no one can deny the extreme profanity of thus assigning to Him what is not a necessity.

But I do not think that we need linger on this, nor minutely examine that which follows. To the more attentive reader, the argument elaborated by our opponent will itself appear in the light of a special pleader on the side of orthodoxy. He says, for instance, that imperishability and immortality are the very essence of the Deity. For my part I see no need to contend with him, no matter whether these qualities aforesaid only *accrue* to the Deity, or whether they are, by virtue of their signification, His essence; whichever of these two views is adopted, it will completely support our argument. For if the being imperishable only accrues to the essence, the not being generated will also most certainly only accrue to it; and so the idea of ungeneracy will be ejected from being the mark of the essence. If, on the other hand, because God is not subject to destruction, one affirms imperishability to be His essence, and, because He is stronger than death, one therefore defines immortality to be His very essence, and if the Son is imperishable and immortal (as He is), imperishability and immortality will also be the essence of the Only-begotten. If, then, the Father is imperishability, and the Son imperishability, and each of these imperishabilities is the essence, and no difference exists between them as regards the idea of imperishability, one essence will differ from the other essence in no way at all, seeing that in both equally the nature is a stranger to any corruption. Even if he should resume the same method as before, and place us on the horns of his dilemma from which, as he thinks, there is no escape, saying that, if we distinguish that which accrues from that which is, we make the Deity composite, whereas if we acknowledge His simplicity, then the imperishability and the

ungeneracy are seen at once to be significative of His very essence—even then again we can show that he is fighting for our side. For if he will have it that God is made composite by our saying that anything accrues to Him, then he certainly cannot eject the Fatherhood either from the essence, but must confess that He is Father by His nature as much as He is imperishable and immortal; and so without intending it he must admit the Son also to partake of that intimate nature; for it will not be possible, if God is essentially Father, to exclude the Son from a relationship to Him thus essential. But if he says that the Fatherhood accrues to God, but is outside the circle of the substance, then he must concede to us that we may say anything we like accrues to the Deity, since the Divine simplicity is in no way marred, if His quality of ungeneracy is made to mean something outside the essence. If, however, he declares that the imperishability and the ungeneracy do mean the essence, and if he insists that these two words are equivalent, since, by reason of the same meaning lying in each, there is no difference between them, and if he thus assert that the very idea of imperishability and ungeneracy is one and the same, the One who is the first of these must necessarily be the second too. But that the Son is imperishable, let us observe, even these men entertain no doubt; therefore, by Eunomius' argument, the Son also is ungenerate, if imperishability and ungeneracy are to mean the same thing. So that he must accept one of two alternatives; either he must agree with us that ungeneracy is other than imperishability, or, if he abides by his assertions, he must in various ways speak blasphemy about the Only-begotten, making Him, for instance, perishable, in order that he may not have to say that He is ungenerate; or ungenerate, in order that he may not prove Him perishable.

But now I do not know which it is best to do; to pursue step by step this subject, or to put an end here to our contest with such folly. Well, as in the case of those who are selling destructive drugs, a very slight experiment guarantees to the purchasers the destructive power latent in all the drug, and no one doubts, after he has found out by an experiment its partial deadliness, that the drug sold is entirely of this deadly character, so I think it can be no longer doubtful to reflecting persons that this poisonous dose of argument, of which a specimen has been shown in what we have already examined, will continue throughout to be such as that which we have just refuted. For this reason I think it better not to prolong this detailed dwelling upon his absurdities. Nevertheless, seeing that the champions of this error discover plausibility for it from many quarters, and there is reason to fear lest to have overlooked any of their efforts will be made a specious pretext for misrepresenting us as having shirked their strongest point, I beg for this reason those who follow us out in this work to accompany our argument still, without charging us with prolixity, while it expands itself to meet the attacks of error along the whole line. Observe, then, that he has scarcely ceased weaving in the depths of his slumber this dream about conception before he arms himself again from his storehouse with those monstrous and senseless methods, and turns his argument into another dream much more meaningless than his previous illusion. But we may best know how absurd his efforts are by observing his treatment of "privation"; though to grapple with his nonsense in all its range would require a Eunomius, or one of his school, men who have never spent a thought on serious realities. We will, however, in a concise way run over the heads of it, that while none of his charges is omitted, no meaningless item may help to prolong the discussion to an absurd length.

When, then, he is on the point of introducing this treatment of terms of "privation," he takes upon himself to show "the incurable absurdity," as he calls it, of our teaching, and its "simulated and culpable caution [8]." Such is his promise; but the proof of these accusations is, what? "Some have said that the Deity is ungenerate by virtue only of the privation of generation; but we say, in refutation of these, that neither this word nor this idea is in any way whatever applicable to the Deity." Let him point out the maintainer of such a statement, if any from the first creation of man to the present day, whether in foreign or in Greek lands, has ever committed himself to such an utterance; and we will be silent. But no one in the whole history of mankind will be found to have said such a thing, except some madman. For who was ever so reeling from intoxication, who was ever so beside himself with madness or delirium, as to say, in so many words, that generation belongs naturally to the ungenerate God, but that, deprived of this natural condition, He becomes ungenerate instead of generated? But these are the shifts of rhetoric; namely, to escape when they are refuted from the shame of their refutation by means of some supposititious characters. It was in this way that he has apologized for that celebrated "Apology" of his, transferring as he did the blame for that title to jurymen and accusers [9], though unable to show that there were any accusers, any trial, or any court at

all. Now, too, with the air of one who would correct another's folly, he pretends that he is driven by necessity to speak in this way. This is what his proof of our "incurable absurdity," and our "simulated and culpable caution," amounts to. But he goes on to say that we do not know what to do in our present position, and that to cover our perplexity we take to abusing him for his worldly learning, while we ourselves claim a monopoly of the teaching of the Holy Spirit. Here is his other dream, namely, that he has got so much of the heathen learning, that he appears by means of it a formidable antagonist to Basil. Just so there have been some men who have imagined themselves enthroned with basilicals, and of an exalted rank, because the deluded vision of their dreams, born of their waking longings, puts such fancies into their hearts. He says that Basil, not knowing what to do after what has been said, abuses him for his worldly learning. He would indeed have set a high value on such abuse, that is, on being thought formidable because of the abundance of his words even by any ordinary hearer, not to mention by Basil, and by men like him (if any are entirely like him, or ever have been). But, as for his intervening argument, if such low scurrility, and such tasteless buffoonery, can be called argument, by which he thinks he impugns our cause, I pass it all over, for I deem it an abominable and ungracious thing to soil our treatise with such pollutions; and I loathe them as men loathe some swollen and noisome ulcer, or turn from the spectacle presented by those whose skin is bloated by excess of humours, and disfigured with tuberous warts. And for a while our argument shall be allowed to expand itself freely, without having to turn to defend itself against men who are ready to scoff at and to tear to pieces everything that is said.

Every term—every term, that is, which is really such—is an utterance expressing some movement of thought. But every operation and movement of sound thinking is directed as far as it is possible to the knowledge and the contemplation of some reality. But then the whole world of realities is divided into two parts; that is, into the intelligible and the sensible. With regard to sensible phænomena, knowledge, on account of the perception of them being so near at hand, is open for all to acquire; the judgment of the senses gives occasion to no doubt about the subject before them. The differences in colour, and the differences in all the other qualities which we judge of by means of the sense of hearing, or smell, or touch, or taste, can be known and named by all possessing our common humanity; and so it is with all the other things which appear to be more

8 εὐλαβείαν τινὰ προσποίητον καὶ ἐπίληπτον.
9 See Book I. vii., ix., xi

obvious to our apprehension, the things, that is, pertaining to the age in which we live, designed for political and moral ends. But in the contemplation of the intelligible world, on account of that world transcending the grasp of the senses, we move, some in one way, some in another, around the object of our search; and then, according to the idea arising in each of us about it, we announce the result as best we can, striving to get as near as possible to the full meaning of the thing thought about through the medium of expressive phrases. In this, though it is often possible to have achieved the task in both ways, when thought does not fail to hit the mark, and utterance interprets the notion with the appropriate word, yet it may happen that we may fail even in both, or in one, at least, of the two, when either the comprehending faculty or the interpreting capacity is carried beside the proper mark. There being, then, two factors by which every term is made a correct term, the mental exactitude and the verbal utterance, the result which commands approval in both ways, will certainly be the preferable; but it will not be a lesser gain, not to have missed the right conception, even though the word itself may happen to be inadequate to that thought. Whenever, then, our thought is intent upon those high and unseen things which sense cannot reach (I mean, upon that divine and unspeakable world with regard to which it is an audacious thing to grasp in thought anything in it at random, and more audacious still to trust to any chance word the representing of the conception arising from it), then, I say, turning from the mere sound of phrases, uttered well or ill according to the mental faculty of the speaker, we search for the thought, and that alone, which is found within the phrases, to see whether that itself be sound, or otherwise; and we leave the minutiæ of phrase and name to be dealt with by the artificialities of grammarians. Now, seeing that we mark with an appellation only those things which we know, and those things which are above our knowledge it is not possible to seize by any distinctive terms (for how can one put a mark upon a thing we know nothing about?), therefore, because in such cases there is no appropriate term to be found to mark the subject adequately, we are compelled by many and differing names, as there may be opportunity, to divulge our surmises as they arise within us with regard to the Deity. But, on the other hand, all that actually comes within our comprehension is such that it must be of one of these four kinds: either contemplated as existing in an extension of distance, or suggesting the idea of a capacity in space within which its details are detected, or it comes with-

in our field of vision by being circumscribed by a beginning or an end where the non-existent bounds it in each direction (for everything that has a beginning and an end of its existence, begins from the non-existent, and ends in the non-existent), or, lastly, we grasp the phænomenon by means of an association of qualities wherein dying, and sufferance, and change, and alteration, and such-like are combined. Considering this, in order that the Supreme Being may not appear to have any connection whatever with things below, we use, with regard to His nature, ideas and phrases expressive of separation from all such conditions; we call, for instance, that which is above all times pre-temporal, that which is above beginning unbeginning, that which is not brought to an end unending, that which has a personality removed from body incorporeal, that which is never destroyed imperishable, that which is unreceptive of change, or sufferance, or alteration, passionless, changeless, and unalterable. Such a class of appellations can be reduced to any system that they like by those who wish for one; and they can fix on these actual appellations other appellations "privative," for instance, or "negative," or whatever they like. We yield the teaching and the learning of such things to those who are ambitious for it; and we will investigate the thoughts alone, whether they are within or beyond the circle of a religious and adequate conception of the Deity.

Well, then, if God did not exist formerly, or if there be a time when He will not exist, He cannot be called either unending or without beginning; and so also neither inalterable, nor incorporeal, nor imperishable, if there is any suspicion of body, or destruction, or alteration with regard to Him. But if it be part of our religion to attribute to Him none of these things, then it is a sacred duty to use of Him names privative of the things abhorrent to His Nature, and to say all that we have so often enumerated already, viz. that He is imperishable, and unending, and ungenerate, and the other terms of that class, where the sense inherent in each only informs us of the privation of that which is obvious to our perception, but does not interpret the actual nature of that which is thus removed from those abhorrent conditions. What the Deity is not, the signification of these names does point out; but what that further thing, which is not these things, is essentially, remains undivulged. Moreover, even the rest of these names, the sense of which does indicate some position or some state, do not afford that indication of the Divine nature itself, but only of the results of our reverent speculations about it. For when we have concluded generally that no single thing existing, whether an object of sense or of thought, is formed spontaneously or fortuitously, but that everything discoverable in the world is linked to the Being Who transcends all existences, and possesses there the source of its continuance, and we then perceive the beauty and the majesty of the wonderful sights in creation, we thus get from these and such-like marks a new range of thoughts about the Deity, and interpret each one of the thoughts thus arising within us by a special name, following the advice of Wisdom, who says that " by the greatness and beauty of the creatures proportionately the Maker of them is seen [1]." We address therefore as Creator Him Who has made all mortal things, and as Almighty Him Who has compassed so vast a creation, Whose might has been able to realize His wish. When too we perceive the good that is in our own life, we give in accordance with this the name of Good to Him Who is our life's first cause. Then also having learnt from the Divine writings the incorruptibility of the judgment to come, we therefore call Him Judge and Just, and to sum up in one word, we transfer the thoughts that arise within us about the Divine Being into the mould of a corresponding name; so that there is no appellation given to the Divine Being apart from some distinct intuition of Him. Even the word God ($\Theta \epsilon \grave{o} \varsigma$) we understand to have come into usage from the activity of His seeing; for our faith tells us that the Deity is everywhere, and sees ($\theta \epsilon \tilde{a} \sigma \theta a \iota$) all things, and penetrates all things, and then we stamp this thought with this name ($\Theta \epsilon \grave{o} \varsigma$), guided to it by the Holy Voice. For he who says, "O God, attend unto me [2]," and, "Look, O God [3]," and, "God knoweth the secrets of the heart plainly [4]," reveals the latent meaning of this word, viz. that $\Theta \epsilon \grave{o} \varsigma$ is so called from $\theta \epsilon \tilde{a} \sigma \theta a \iota$. For there is no difference between saying "Attend unto," "Look," and "See." Since, then, the seer must look towards some sight, God is rightly called the Seer of that which is to be seen. We are taught, then, by this word one sectional operation of the Divine Being, though we do not grasp in thought by means of it His substance itself, believing nevertheless that the Divine glory suffers no loss because of our being at a loss for a naturally appropriate name. For this inability to give expression to such unutterable things, while it reflects upon the poverty of our own nature, affords an evidence of God's glory, teaching us as it does, in the words of the Apostle, that the only name naturally appropriate to God is to believe Him to be "above every name [5]." That he transcends every effort

of thought, and is far beyond any circumscribing by a name, constitutes a proof to man of His ineffable majesty [6].

Thus much, then, is known to us about the names uttered in any form whatever in reference to the Deity. We have given a simple explanation of them, unencumbered with argument, for the benefit of our candid hearers; as for Eunomius' nerveless contentions about these names, we judge it a thing disgraceful and unbecoming to us seriously to confute them. For what could one say in answer to a man who declares that we "attach more weight to the outward form of the name than to the value of the thing named, giving to names the prerogative over realities, and equality to things unequal"? Such are the words that *he* gives utterance to. Well, let any one who can do so considerately, judge whether this calumnious charge of his against us has anything in it dangerous enough to make it worth our while to defend ourselves as to our "giving to names the prerogative over realities"; for it is plain to every one that there is no single name that has in itself any substantial reality, but that every name is but a recognizing mark placed on some reality or some idea, having of itself no existence either as a fact or a thought.

How it is possible, then, to assign one's gratuities to the non-subsistent, let this man, who claims to be using words and phrases in their natural force, explain to the followers of his error. I would not, however, have mentioned this at all, if it had not placed a necessity upon me of proving our author's weakness both in thought and expression. As for all the passages from the inspired writings which he drags in, though quite unconnected with his object, formulating thereby a difference of immortality [7] in angels and in men, I do not know what he has in his eye, or what he hopes to

---

[6] The theology of Gregory and his master Origen rises above the unconscious Stoicism of Tertullian, and even that of Clement, which has an air of materialistic pantheism about it, owing to his attempt, like that of Eunomius, to base our knowledge of God upon abstractions and analogies drawn from nature. The result, indeed, of the " abstraction process" of Clement is only a multiplication of negative terms, "immensity," "simplicity," "eternity," &c. But they will lead to nothing, if there is not already behind them all some positive idea which we have received from *a different source*. Faith is this source; it is described by Origen as "an ineffable grace of the soul which comes from God in a kind of enthusiasm;" which formula expresses the primary fact of religious consciousness such as Leibnitz demonstrated it: and the positive idea supplied by this faculty is with Origen *Goodness* (rather than the Good). He would put Will as well as Mind into the Central Idea of Metaphysics, and would have the heart governed as well as the reason. All that he says about the "incomprehensibility" of God does not militate against this: for we must have some idea of that which is incomprehensible to us: and the Goodness of the Deity is the side on which we gain this idea.
[7] But there are two meanings of $\dot{a} \theta \acute{a} \nu a \tau o \varsigma$,—and of these perhaps Eunomius was thinking,—*i. e.* 1. Not dead; 2. Immortal. In Plato's *Phædo* there is an argument for the immortality of the soul, certainly not the strongest one, drawn from this. It is assumed there that the thing, whose nature is such that *so long as it exists* it neither is nor can be dead, can never cease to exist, *i. e.* the soul by virtue of not actually dying, though capable of death, is immortal. Perhaps this accounts for Eunomius saying (lower down) that " the perishable is not opposed to the imperishable."

---

[1] Wisdom xiii. 5.   [2] Ps. lv. 2.   [3] Ps. cxix. 132.
[4] Ps. xliv. 21.   [5] Philip. ii. 9.

prove by them, and I pass them by. The immortal, as long as it is immortal, admits of no degrees of more and less arising from comparison. For if the one member of the comparison is, by the force of contrast, to suffer a diminution or privation as regards its immortality, it must needs be that such a member is not to be called immortal at all; for how can that be called absolutely immortal in which mortality is detected by this juxtaposition and comparison? And to think of that fine hairsplitting of his, in not allowing the idea of privation to be unvarying and general, but in asserting, on the contrary, that while separation from good things is privation, the absence of bad things is not to be marked by that term! If he is to get his way here, he will take the truth from the Apostle's words, which say that He "only hath immortality [8]," which He gives to others. What this newly-imported dictum of his has to do with his preceding argument, neither we nor any one else amongst reflecting people are able to understand. Yet because we have not the mental strength to take in these scientific subtleties, he calls us "unscientific both in our judgment as to objects, and in our use of terms"; those are his very words. But all this, as having no power to shake the truth, I pass over without further notice; and also how he misrepresents the view we have expounded of the imperishable, and of the unembodied, namely, that of these terms the latter signifies the undimensional, where the threefold extension belonging to all bodies is not to be found, and the former signifies that which is not receptive of destruction: and also how he says, that "we do not think it right to let the shape of these words be lost by extending them to ideas inapplicable to them, or to imagine that each of them is indicative of something not present or not accruing; but rather we think they are indicative of the actual essence"; all this I deem worthy only of silence and deep oblivion, and leave to the reader to detect for himself their mingled folly and blasphemy. He actually asserts that the perishable is not opposed to the imperishable, and that the privative sign does not mark the absence of the bad, but that the word which is the subject of our inquiry means the essence itself!

Well, if the term imperishable or indestructible is not considered by this maker of an empty system to be privative of destruction, then by a stern necessity it must follow that this shape given to the word indicates the very reverse (of the privation of destruction). If, that is, indestructibility is not the negation of destruction, it must be the assertion of some-

thing incongruous with itself; for it is the very nature of opposites that, when you take away the one, you admit the other to come in in its place. But as for the bitter task which he necessitates of proving that the Deity is unreceptive of death, as if there existed any one who held the contrary opinion, we leave it to take care of itself. For we hold that in the case of opposites, it makes no difference at all whether we say that something is A, or that it is not the opposite of A; for instance, in the present discussion, when we have said that God is Life, we implicitly forbid by this assertion the thought of death in connection with Him, even though we do not express this in speech; and when we assert that He is unreceptive of death, we in the same breath show Him to be Life.

"But I do not see," he rejoins, "how God can be above His own works simply by virtue of such things as do not belong to Him [9]." And on the strength of this clever sally he calls it a union of folly and profanity, that our great Basil has ventured on such terms. But I would counsel him not to indulge his ribaldry too freely against those who use these terms, lest he should be unconsciously at the same moment heaping insults on himself. For I think that he himself would not gainsay that the very grandeur of the Divine Nature is recognized in this, viz. in the absence of all participation in those things which the lower natures are shown to possess. For if God were involved in any of these peculiarities, He would not possess His superiority, but would be quite identified with any single individual amongst the beings who share that peculiarity. But if He is above such things, by reason, in fact, of His not possessing them, then He stands also above those who do possess them; just as we say that the Sinless is superior to those in sin. The fact of being removed from evil is an evidence of abounding in the best. But let him heap these insults on us to his heart's content. We will only remark, in passing, on a single one of the points mentioned under this head, and will then return to the discussion of the main question.

He declares that God surpasses mortal beings as immortal, destructible beings as indestructible, generated beings as ungenerate, just in the same degree. Is it not, then, plain to all

[8] 1 Tim. vi. 16.

[9] The reasoning, which precedes and follows, amounts to this. Basil had said that the terms ungenerate, imperishable, immortal, are privative, *i. e.* express the absence of a quality. Eunomius objects that—No term expressive of the absence of a quality can be God's Name: the Ungenerate (which includes the others) is God's Name, therefore It does not express a privation. You mean to say, Gregory replies, that Ungenerate, &c. does *not* mean not-generated, &c. But what is *not* not-generated is generated (by your own law of dichotomy); therefore, Ungenerate means generated: and you prove God perishable and mortal. Here, the fallacy arises from Gregory's assuming more than Eunomius' conclusion: *i. e.* "the Ungenerate means *not only* the not-generated," changes into "the Ungenerate does *not* mean," &c

what this blasphemy of a fighter against God would prove? or must we by verbal demonstration unveil the profanity? Well, who does not know the axiom, that things which are distanced to the same amount (by something else) are level with one another? If, then, the destructible and the generated are surpassed in the same degree by the Deity, and if our Lord is generated, it will be for Eunomius to draw the blasphemous conclusion resulting from these data. For it is clear that he regards generation as the same thing as destruction and death, just as in his previous discussions he declares the ungenerate to be the same thing as the indestructible. If, then, he looks upon destruction and generation as upon the same level, and asserts that the Deity is equally removed from both of them, and if our Lord is generated, let no one demand from ourselves that we should apply the logical conclusion, but let him draw it for himself; if indeed it is true, as he says, that from the generated and from the destructible God is equally removed. "But," he proceeds, "it is not allowable for us to call Him indestructible and immortal by virtue of any absence of death and destruction." Let those who are led by the nose, and turn in any direction that each successive teacher pleases, believe this, and let them declare that destruction and death do belong to God, to make it possible for Him to be called immortal and indestructible! For if these terms of privation, as Eunomius says, "do not indicate the absence of death and destruction," then the presence in Him of the things opposite to, and estranged from, these is most certainly proved by this treatment of terms. Each one amongst conceivable things is either absent from something else, or it is not absent: for instance, light, darkness; life, death; health, disease, and so on. In all these cases, if one asserts that the one conception is absent, he will necessarily demonstrate that the other is present. If, then, Eunomius denies that God can be called immortal by reason of the absence of death, he will plainly prove the presence of death in Him, and so deny any immortality in the case of the universal Deity. But perhaps some one will say that we fix unfairly on his words; for that no one is so mad as to affirm that God is not immortal. But then, when none of mankind possess any knowledge of that which certain people secretly imagine, it is by their words that we have to make our guess about those secret things.

Therefore let us again handle this dictum of his: "God is not called immortal by virtue of the absence of death." How are we to accept this statement, that death is not absent from the Deity though He be called immortal?

If he really commands us to think like this, Eunomius' God will be certainly mortal, and subject to destruction; for he from whom death is not absent is not in his essence immortal. But again; if these terms signify the absence neither of death nor of destruction, either they are applied falsely to the God over all, or else they comprise within themselves some different meaning. What this meaning is, our system-maker must explain to us. Whereas we, the people who according to Eunomius are unscientific in our judgment of objects and in our use of terms, have been taught to call sound (for instance), not the man from whom strength is absent, but the man from whom disease is absent; and unmutilated, not the man who keeps away from drinking-parties, but the man who has no mutilation upon him; and other qualities in the same way we name from the presence or the absence of something; manly, for instance, and unmanly; sleepy and sleepless; and all the other terms like that, which custom sanctions.

Still I cannot see what profit there is in deigning to examine such nonsense. For a man like myself, who has lived to gray hairs [1], and whose eyes are fixed on truth alone, to take upon his lips the absurd and flippant utterances of a contentious foe, incurs no slight danger of bringing condemnation on himself. I will therefore pass over both those words and the adjoining passage; this, for instance, "Truth gives no evidence of any union of natures with God." Well, if these words had not been spoken, who ever was there (except yourself) who mentioned a double nature in the Deity at all? You, however, unite each idea of each name with the essence of the Father, and deny that anything externally accrues to Him, centering every one of His names in that essence. Again, "Neither does she write in the statute-book of our religion any idea that is external and fabricated by ourselves." With regard to these words again I shall deprecate the idea that I have quoted them with a view of amusing the reader with their absurdity; rather I have done so with a view to show with what a slender equipment of arguments this man, after rating us for our want of system, advances to take these audacious liberties with the name of Truth. What is he in reasoning, and what is he in speech, that he should thus revel in showing himself off before his hidebound readers, who applaud him as victorious over everybody· by force of argument when he has brought these disjointed utterances

---

[1] This cannot have been written earlier than 384. The preceding twelve books, of which an instalment only was read to Gregory the Nazianzene and others during the Council of Constantinople, 381, must have occupied him a considerable time: and there may have been an interval after that before this essay was composed.

of his dry bombastic jargon to an end[2]. "Immortality," he says, "is the essence itself." But what, then, do you assert to be the essence of the Only-begotten? I ask you that: is it immortality, or is it not? For remember that in His essence also the singleness admits, as you say, of no complexity of nature. If, then Eunomius denies that immortality is the essence of the Son, it is clear what he is aiming at; for it does not require an exceedingly penetrating understanding to discover what is the direct opposite to the immortal. Just as the logic of dichotomy exhibits the destructible instead of the indestructible, and the mutable instead of the immutable, so it exhibits the mortal instead of the immortal. What, therefore, will this setter forth of new doctrine do? What proper name will he give us for the essence of the Only-begotten? Again I put this question to our author. He must either grant that it is immortality, or deny it. If, then, he will not assent to its being immortality, he must assent to the contradictory proposition; by negativing the superior term he proves that it is death. If, on the other hand, he shrinks from anything so monstrous, and names the essence of the Only-begotten also as immortality, he must perforce agree with us that there is in consequence no difference whatever, as to essence, between them. If the nature of the Father and the nature of the Son are equally immortality, and if immortality does not divide itself by any manner of difference, then it is confessed by our foes themselves, that on the score of essence no manner of difference is discoverable between the Father and the Son.

But it is time now to expose that angry accusation which he brings against us at the close of his treatise, saying that we affirm the Father to be from what is absolutely non-existent. Stealing an expression from its context, from which he drags it, as from its surrounding body, into a naked isolation, he tries to carp at it by worrying the word, or rather covering it with the slaver of his maddened teeth. I will therefore first give the meaning of the passage in which our Master explained this point to us; then I will quote it word for word: by so doing the man who intrudes upon[3] the expository work of orthodox writers, only to undermine the truth itself, will be revealed in his true colours. Our Master, in introducing us in his own treatise to the true meaning of ungenerate, suggested a way to ·arrive at a real

knowledge of the term in dispute somewhat as follows, pointing out at the same time that it had a meaning very far removed from any idea of essence. He says that the Evangelist[4], in beginning our Lord's lineage according to the flesh from Joseph, and then going back to the generation continually preceding, and then ending the genealogy in Adam, and, because there was no earthly father anterior to this first-formed creature, saying that he was "the son of God," makes it obvious to every reader's intelligence with regard to the Deity, that He, from Whom Adam was, has not Himself His subsistence from another, after the likeness of the human lives just given. When, having passed through the whole of it, we at last grasp the thought of the Deity, we perceive at the same moment the First Cause of it all. But if any such cause be found dependent on something else, then it is not a first cause. Therefore, if God is the First Cause of the Universe, there will be nothing whatever transcending this cause of all things. Such was our Master's exposition of the meaning of ungenerate; and in order that our testimony about it may not go beyond the exact truth, I will quote the passage.

"The evangelist Luke, when giving the genealogy according to the flesh of our God and Saviour Jesus Christ, and stepping up from the last to the first, begins with Joseph, saying that he was 'the son of Heli, which was the son of Matthat,' and so by ascending brings his enumeration up to Adam; but when he has come to the top and said, that Seth 'was the son of Adam, which was the son of God,' then he stops this process. As, then, he has said that Adam was the son of God, we will ask these men, 'But God, who is He the son of?' Is it not obvious to every one's intelligence that God is the son of no one? But to be the son of no one is to be without a cause, plainly; and to be without a cause is to be ungenerate. Now in the case of men, the being son of somebody is not the essence[5]; no more, in the case of the Deity Who rules the world, is it possible to say that the being ungenerate is the essence."

With what eyes will you now dare to gaze upon your guide? I speak to you, O flock[6]

[2] τὰς στομφώδεις . . . ξηροστομίας κακοσυνθέτως διαπεραίνοντα. The editt. have διαπεραίνοντες, which Gulonius' Latin follows, "arrogantes has sicci oris voces malâ compositione trajicientes," *i. e.* his hearers get through them with bad pronunciation.
[3] εἰσφθειρόμενος.

[4] S. Luke iii. 23, sqq.
[5] οὐκ ἦν οὐσία τὸ ἐκ τινος. This is Oehler's reading from the MSS.
[6] *O flock.* This could not have been written earlier than 384, and there is abundant testimony that Eunomius still had his "flock. Long before this, even soon after he had left his see of Cyzicus, and had taken up his abode with Eudoxius, he separated himself from that champion of the Homœan party, and held assemblies apart because he had repeatedly entreated that his preceptor Aetius might be received into communion (Socrates iv. 13). This must have been about 366, before his banishment by Valens for favouring the rebellion of Procopius. Sozomen says (vi. 29), "The heresy of Eunomius was spread from Cilicia and the Mountains of Taurus as far as the Hellespont and Constantinople." In 380 at Bithynia near Constantinople "multitudes resorted to him, some also gathered from other quarters, a few with the design of testing his principles, and others merely from the desire of listening to his discourses. His reputation reached the ears of the Emperor, who would gladly have had a

of perishing souls! How can you still turn to listen to this man who has reared such a monument as this of his shamelessness in argument? Are ye not ashamed now, at least, if not before, to take the hand of a man like this to lead you to the truth? Do ye not regard it as a sign of his madness as to doctrine, that he thus shamelessly stands out against the truth contained in Scripture? Is this the way to play the champion of the truth of doctrine—namely, to accuse Basil of deriving the God over all from that which has absolutely no existence? Am I to tell the way he phrases it? Am I to transcribe the very words of his shamelessness? I let the insolence of them pass; I do not blame their invective, for I do not censure one whose breath is of bad odour, because it is of bad odour; or one who has bodily mutilation, beause he is mutilated. Things such as that are the misfortunes of nature; they escape blame from those who can reflect. This strength of vituperation, then, is infirmity in reasoning; it is an affliction of a soul whose powers of sound argument are marred. No word from me, then, about his invectives. But as to that syllogism, with its stout irrefragable folds, in whose conclusion, to effect his darling object, he arrives at this accusation against us, I will write it out in its own precise words. "We will allow him to say that the Son exists by participation in the self-existent[7]; but (instead of this), he has unconsciously affirmed that the God over all comes from absolute nonentity. For if the idea of the absence of everything amounts to that of absolute nonentity[8], and the transposition of equivalents is perfectly legitimate, then the man who says that God comes from nothing says that He comes from nonentity." To which of these statements shall we first direct our attention? Shall we criticize his opinion about the Son "existing by participation" in the Deity, and his bespattering those who will not acquiesce in it with the foulness of his tongue; or shall we examine the sophism so frigidly constructed from the stuff of dreams? However, every one who possesses a spark of practical sagacity is not unaware that it is only poets and moulders of mythology who father sons "by participation" upon the Divine

Being. Those, that is, who string together the myths in their poems, fabricate a Dionysus, or a Hercules, or a Minos, and such-like, out of the combination of the superhuman with human bodies; and they exalt such personages above the rest of mankind, representing them as of greater estimation because of their participation in a superior nature. Therefore, with regard to this opinion of his, carrying as it does within itself the evidence of its own folly and profanity, it is best to be silent; and to repeat instead that irrefragable syllogism of his, in order that every poor ignoramus on our side may understand what and how many are the advantages which those who are not trained in his technical methods are deprived of. He says, "If the idea of the absence of everything amounts to that of absolute nonentity, and the transposition of equivalents is perfectly legitimate, then the man who says that God comes from nothing, says that He comes from nonentity." He brandishes over us this Aristotelian weapon, but who has yet conceded to him, that to say that any one has no father amounts to saying that he has been generated from absolute nonentity? He who enumerates those persons whose line is recorded in Scripture is plainly thinking of a father preceding each person mentioned. For what relation is Heli to Joseph? What relation is Matthat to Heli? And what relation is Adam to Seth? Is it not plain to a mere child that this catalogue of names is a list of fathers? For if Seth is the son of Adam, Adam must be the father of one thus born from him; and so tell me, who is the father of the Deity Who is over all? Come, answer this question, open your lips and speak, exert all your skill in expression to meet such an inquiry. Can you discover any expression that will elude the grasp of your own syllogism? Who *is* the father of the Ungenerate? Can you say? If you can, then He is not ungenerate. Pressed thus, you will say, what indeed necessity compels you to say,—No one is. Well, my dear sir, do you not yet find the weak seams of your sophism giving way? Do you not perceive that you have slavered upon your own lap? What says our great Basil? That the Ungenerate One is from no *father*. For the conclusion to be drawn from the mention of fathers in the preceding genealogy permits the word father, even in the silence of the evangelist, to be added to this confession of faith. Whereas, you have transformed "no one" into "nothing at all," and again "nothing at all" into "absolute nonentity," thereby concocting that fallacious syllogism of yours. Accordingly this clever result of professional shrewdness shall be turned against yourself. I ask, Who *is*

---

conference with him. But the Empress Flacilla studiously prevented an interview taking place between them; for she was the most faithful guard of the Nicene doctrines" (vii. 17). At the convention, however, of all the sects at Theodosius' palace in 382, Eunomius was present (Socrates v. 10). His ἔκθεσις τῆς πίστεως (to which he added learned notes) was laid before Theodosius in 383. It was not till 391 that the Emperor condemned him to banishment —the sole exception to Theodosius' toleration. "This heretic," says Sozomen again, "had fixed his residence in the suburbs of Constantinople, and held frequent assemblies in private houses, where he read his own writings. He induced **m**any to embrace his sentiments, so that the sectarians who were named after him became very numerous. He died not long after his banishment, and was interred at Dacora, his birthplace, a village of Cappadocia."

[7] τοῦ ὄντος.   [8] τὸ μηδὲν τῷ πάντη μὴ ὄντι ταὐτόν.

the father of the Ungenerate One? "No one,"
you will be obliged to answer; for the Ungenerate One cannot have a father.   Then, if
no one is the father of the Ungenerate, and
you have changed "no one" into "nothing at
all," and "nothing at all" is, according to your
argument, the same as "absolute nonentity,"
and the transposition of equivalents is, as you
say, perfectly legitimate, then the man (*i. e.*
you) who says that no one is the father of the
Ungenerate One, says that the Deity Who is
over all comes from absolute nonentity!

Such, to use your own words, is the "evil,"
as one might expect, not indeed "of valuing
the character for being clever before one is
really such" (for perhaps this does not amount
to a very great misfortune), but of not knowing
oneself, and how great the distance is between
the soaring Basil and a grovelling reptile.   For
if those eyes of his, with their divine penetration, still looked on this world, if he still swept
over mankind now living on the pinions of
his wisdom, he would have shown you with
the swooping rush of his words, how frail is
that native shell of folly in which you are en-
cased, how great is he whom you oppose with
your errors, while, with insults and invectives
hurled at him, you are hunting for a reputation
amongst decrepit and despicable creatures.
Still you need not give up all hope of feeling
that great man's talons 9.   For this work of
ours, while, as compared with his, it will be a
great thing for it to be judged the fraction of
one such talon, has, as regards yours, ability
enough to have broken asunder the outside
crust of your heresy, and to have detected the
deformity that hides within.

---

9 Πλὴν ἀλλ' οὐκ ἀνελπιστέον σοι καὶ τῶν ὀνύχων ἐκείνου. Viger
(De Idiotismis, p. 474), " Πλὴν ἀλλὰ interdum repellentis est, interdum *concedentis*," as here ironically, and in Book I. p. 83, πλὴν
ἀλλὰ καὶ ἐστὶν ἐν θηρίοις κρίσις, " still there is some distinction
between animals."

ON THE HOLY SPIRIT

AGAINST THE FOLLOWERS OF MACEDONIUS

It may indeed be undignified to give any answer at all to the statements that are foolish; we seem to be pointed that way by Solomon's wise advice, "not to answer a fool according to his folly." But there is a danger lest through our silence error may prevail over the truth, and so the rotting sore[2] of this heresy may invade it, and make havoc of the sound word of the faith. It has appeared to me, therefore, to be imperative to answer, not indeed according to the folly of these men who offer objections of such a description to our Religion, but for the correction of their depraved ideas. For that advice quoted above from the Proverbs gives, I think, the watchword not for silence, but for the correction of those who are displaying some act of folly; our answers, that is, are not to run on the level of their foolish conceptions, but rather to overturn those unthinking and deluded views as to doctrine.

What then is the charge they bring against us? They accuse us of profanity for entertaining lofty conceptions about the Holy Spirit. All that we, in following the teachings of the Fathers, confess as to the Spirit, they take in a sense of their own, and make it a handle against us, to denounce us for profanity[3]. We, for instance, confess that the Holy Spirit is of the same rank as the Father and the Son, so that there is no difference between them in anything, to be thought or named, that devotion can ascribe to a Divine nature. We confess that, save His being contemplated as with peculiar attributes in regard of Person, the Holy Spirit is indeed from God, and of the Christ, according to Scripture[4], but that, while not to be confounded with the Father in being never originated, nor with the Son in being the Only-begotten, and while to be regarded separately in certain distinctive properties, He has in all else, as I have just said, an exact identity[5]

[1] Macedonius had been a very eminent Semi-Arian doctor. He was deposed from the See of Constantinople, A.D. 360: and it was actually the influence of the Eunomians that brought this about. He went into exile and formed his sect. He considered the Holy Spirit as "a divine energy diffused throughout the universe: and not a person distinct from the Father and the Son" (Socrates, H. E. iv. 4). This opinion had many partizans in the Asiatic provinces, "but," says Mosheim, "the Council of Constantinople crushed it." However, that the final clauses of the Nicene Creed which express distinctly, amongst other truths, the deity and personality of the Third Person of the Trinity were added at that Council to the original form, is extremely doubtful. For—1. We find the expanded form (the Creed of Nicæa ended, "And we believe in the Holy Ghost.") which we now use in the Nicene Creed, in a work written by Epiphanius *seven years before* the Council of Constantinople. So that at all events the enlarged Creed was not prepared by the Fathers then assembled. 2. It is extremely doubtful if any symbol at all was set forth at Constantinople. Neither Socrates, nor Sozomen, nor Theodoret makes mention of one: but all speak of adherence to the evangelic faith ratified at Nicæa. It is significant too that the expanded form was entirely ignored by the Council of Ephesus, 431. But at the Council of Chalcedon, 451, it was brought forward: though even then it appears that it was far from attaining general acceptance. By 540 it had become the accepted form (according to a letter of Pope Vigilius). "It seems most likely therefore that it was a profession received amongst the churches in the patriarchate of Constantinople, but at first not more widely circulated" (J. R. Lumby, *Commentary on Prayer-Book*, S. P. C. K., p. 66). F. J. A. Hort, however, (see Two Dissertations by) regards this "Constantinopolitan" Creed as the old Creed of Jerusalem enlarged and expanded; and he suggests that S. Cyril of Jerusalem may have produced it before the Council, which gave it some sort of approval. The addition, moreover, of the later clauses was not, as Mosheim seems to imagine, the only difference between *the* Nicene Creed and this Creed.

That this lateness of accepted definition on a vital point should not excite our wonder, Neander shows "the apprehension of the idea (of the ὁμοούσιον of the Holy Spirit) had been so little permeated as yet by the Christian consciousness of the unity of God, that Gregory of Nazianzum could still say in 380, 'Some of our theologians consider the Holy Spirit to be a certain mode of the Divine energy, others a creature of God, others God Himself. Others say they do not know which opinion they ought to accept, out of reverence for the Scriptures which *have not clearly explained this point.*' Hilary of Poictiers says in his own original way that 'he was well aware that nothing could be foreign to God's nature, which searches into the deep things of that nature. Should one be displeased at being told that He exists by and through Him, by and from Whom are all things, that He is the Spirit of God, but also God's gift to believers, then will the apostles and prophets displease him; for they affirm only that He *exists*.'" There can be little doubt, however, that Gregory, in the following fragment, is defending a statement already in existence. He seems even to follow the order of the words, "Lord and giver of Life." "Who with the Father and the Son together is worshipped and glorified." Doubtless the next clause, "Who spake by the Prophets," was dealt with in what is lost. But, essentially a creed-maker as he was, his claim to have himself added these final clauses cannot be substantiated. For the MSS. of this treatise, see p. 31.

[2] σηπεδονώδης . . . γάγγραινα: both used by Galen.
[3] εἰς ἀσεβείαν γράφειν. This is Mai's reading. Cf. ἀσεβείας γραφή. The *active* (instead of middle) in this sense is found in Aristoph. Av. 1052: the passive is not infrequent in Demosthenes and Æschines.
[4] *From God, and of the Christ, according to Scripture.* This is noticeable. The Greek is ἐκ τοῦ Θεοῦ ἐστι, καὶ τοῦ Χριστοῦ ἐστι, καθὼς γέγραπται. Compare the words below "proceeding from the Father, receiving from the Son."
[5] τὸ ἀπαράλλακτον (but there is something lost before this: perhaps τὸ ἡνωμένον). This word is used to express substantial identity. Origen uses it in alluding to the "Stoic resurrection,"

with them. But our opponents aver that He is a stranger to any vital communion with the Father and the Son; that by reason of an essential variation He is inferior to, and less than they in every point; in power, in glory, in dignity, in fine in everything that in word or thought we ascribe to Deity; that, in consequence, in their glory He has no share, to equal honour with them He has no claim; and that, as for power, He possesses only so much of it as is sufficient for the partial activities assigned to Him; that with the creative force He is quite disconnected.

Such is the conception of Him that possesses them; and the logical consequence of it is that the Spirit has in Himself none of those marks which our devotion, in word or thought, ascribes to a Divine nature. What, then, shall be our way of arguing? We shall answer nothing new, nothing of our own invention, though they challenge us to it; we shall fall back upon the testimony in Holy Scripture about the Spirit, whence we learn that the Holy Spirit is Divine, and is to be called so. Now, if they allow this, and will not contradict the words of inspiration, then they, with all their eagerness to fight with us, must tell us why they are for contending with us, instead of with Scripture. We say nothing different from that which Scripture says.—But in a Divine nature, as such, when once we have believed in it, we can recognize no distinctions suggested either by the Scripture teaching or by our own common sense; distinctions, that is, that would divide that Divine and transcendent nature within itself by any degrees of intensity and remission, so as to be altered from itself by being more or less. Because we firmly believe that it is simple, uniform, incomposite, because we see in it no complicity or composition of dissimilars, therefore it is that, when once our minds have grasped the idea of Deity, we accept by the implication of that very name the perfection in it of every conceivable thing that befits the Deity. Deity, in fact, exhibits perfection in every line in which the good can be found. If it fails and comes short of perfection in any single point, in that point the conception of Deity will be impaired, so that it cannot, therein, be or be called Deity at all; for how could we apply that word to a thing that is imperfect and deficient, and requiring an addition external to itself?

We can confirm our argument by material instances. Fire naturally imparts the sense of heat to those who touch it, with all its component parts[6]; one part of it does not have the heat more intense, the other less intense; but as long as it is fire at all, it exhibits an invariable oneness with itself in an absolutely complete sameness of activity; if in any part it gets cooled at all, in that part it can no longer be called fire; for, with the change of its heat-giving activity into the reverse, its name also is changed. It is the same with water, with air, with every element that underlies the universe; there is one and the same description of the element, in each case, admitting of no ideas of excess or defect; water, for instance, cannot be called more or less water; as long as it maintains an equal standard of wetness, so long the term water will be realized by it; but when once it is changed in the direction of the opposite quality[7] the name to be applied to it must be changed also. The yielding, buoyant, "nimble"[8] nature of the air, too, is to be seen in every part of it; while what is dense, heavy, downward gravitating, sinks out of the connotation of the very term "air." So Deity, as long as it possesses perfection throughout all the properties that devotion[9] may attach to it, by virtue of this perfection in everything good does not belie its name; but if any one of those things that contribute to this idea of perfection is subtracted from it, the name of Deity is falsified in that particular, and does not apply to the subject any longer. It is equally impossible to apply to a dry substance the name of water, to that whose quality is a state of coolness the name of fire, to stiff and hard things the name of air, and to call that thing Divine which does not at once imply the idea of perfection; or rather the impossibility is greater in this last case.

If, then, the Holy Spirit is truly, and not in name only, called Divine both by Scripture and by our Fathers, what ground is left for those who oppose the glory of the Spirit? He is Divine, and absolutely good, and Omnipotent, and wise, and glorious, and eternal; He is everything of this kind that can be named to raise our thoughts to the grandeur of His being. The singleness of the subject of these properties testifies that He does not possess them in a measure only, as if we could imagine that He was one thing in His very substance, but became another by the presence of the aforesaid qualities. That condition is peculiar[1]

---

i. e. the time when the "Great Year" shall again begin, and the world's history be literally repeated, *i. e.* the "identical Socrates shall marry the identical Xantippe, and teach the identical philosophy, &c." This expression was a favourite one also with Chrysostom and Cyril of Alexandria to express the identity of Glory, of Godhead, and of Honour, in the Blessed Trinity.

6 Reading μορίοις (cf. the same word below) for μοίραν.
7 πρὸς τὴν ἐναντίαν ποιότητα.
8 *nimble,* κουφὸν ; compare Macbeth, I. vi.
"The air
Nimbly and sweetly recommends itself
Unto our senses."
9 Reading εὐσεβῶς.   1 Reading ἴδιον γὰρ τοῦτο.

to those beings who have been given a composite nature ; whereas the Holy Spirit is single and simple in every respect equally. This is allowed by all ; the man who denies it does not exist. If, then, there is but one simple and single definition of His being, the good which He possesses is not an acquired good ; but, whatever He may be besides, He is Himself Goodness, and Wisdom, and Power, and Sanctification, and Righteousness, and Everlastingness, and Imperishability, and every name that is lofty, and elevating above other names. What, then, is the state of mind that leads these men, who do not fear the fearful sentence passed upon the blasphemy against the Holy Ghost, to maintain that such a Being does not possess glory ? For they clearly put that statement forward ; that we ought not to believe that He should be glorified : though I know not for what reason they judge it to be expedient not to confess the true nature of that which is essentially glorious.

For the plea will not avail them in their self-defence, that He is delivered by our Lord to His disciples third in order, and that therefore He is estranged from our ideal of Deity. Where in each case activity in working good shows no diminution or variation whatever, how unreasonable it is to suppose the numerical order to be a sign of any diminution or essential variation[2]! It is as if a man were to see a separate flame burning on three torches (and we will suppose that the third flame is caused by that of the first being transmitted to the middle, and then kindling the end torch[3]), and were to maintain that the heat in the first exceeded that of the others ; that that next it showed a variation from it in the direction of the less ; and that the third could not be called fire at all, though it burnt and shone just like fire, and did everything that fire does. But if there is really no hindrance to the third torch being fire, though it has been kindled from a previous flame, what is the philosophy of these men, who profanely think that they can slight the dignity of the Holy Spirit because He is named by the Divine lips after the Father and the Son? Certainly, if there is in our conceptions of the substance of the Spirit anything that falls short of the Divine ideal, they do well in testifying to His not possessing glory ; but if the highness of His dignity is to be perceived in every point, why do they grudge to make the

confession of His glory? As if any one after describing some one as a man, were to consider it not safe to go on to say of him as well that he is reasoning, mortal, or anything else that can be predicated of a man, and so were to cancel what he had just allowed ; for if he is not reasoning, he is not a man at all ; but if the latter is granted, how can there be any hesitation about the conceptions already implied in "man"? So, with regard to the Spirit, if when one calls Him Divine one speaks the truth, neither when one defines Him to be worthy of honour, to be glorious, good, omnipotent, does one lie ; for all such conceptions are at once admitted with the idea of Deity. So that they must accept one of two alternatives ; either not to call Him Divine at all, or to refrain from subtracting from His Deity any one of those conceptions which are attributable to Deity. We must then, most surely, comprehend along with each other these two thoughts, viz. the Divine nature, and along with it a just idea, a devout intuition[4], of that Divine and transcendent nature.

Since, then, it has been affirmed, and truly affirmed, that the Spirit is of the Divine Essence, and since in that one word "Divine" every idea of greatness, as we have said, is involved, it follows that he who grants that Divinity has potentially granted[5] all the rest ;—the gloriousness, the omnipotence, everything indicative of superiority. It is indeed a monstrous thing to refuse to confess this in the case of the Spirit ; monstrous, because of the incongruity, as applied to Him, of the terms which in the list of opposites correspond to the above terms. I mean, if one does not grant gloriousness, one must grant the absence of gloriousness ; if one sets aside His power, one must acquiesce in its opposite. So also with regard to honour, and goodness, and any other superiority, if they are not accepted, their opposites must be conceded.

But if all must shrink from that, as going even beyond the most revolting blasphemy, then a devout mind must accept the nobler names and conceptions of the Holy Spirit, and must pronounce concerning Him all that we have already named, that He has honour, power, glory, goodness, and everything else that inspires devotion. It must own, too, that these realities do not attach to Him in imperfection or with any limit to the quality of their brilliance, but that they correspond with their names to infinity. He is not to be regarded as possessing dignity up to a certain point, and then becoming different ; but He is

---

[2] Reading ἐλαττώσεώς τινος ἢ κατὰ φύσιν παραλλαγῆς, κ. τ. λ.
[3] "The Ancient Greek Fathers, speaking of this procession, mention the Father only, and never, I think, express the Son, as sticking constantly in this to the language of the Scriptures (John xv. 26)"—Pearson. The language of the above simile of Gregory would be an illustration of this. So Greg. Naz., *Orat. I. de Filio,* "standing on our definitions, we introduce the Ungenerate, the Generated, and that which proceeds from the Father." This last expression was so known and public, that it is recorded even by Lucian in his *Philopatris,* § 12.

[4] Reading καὶ τῆς εὐσεβοῦς ἐννοίας.
[5] The edition of Cardinal Mai has ὁ ἐκεῖνο δοὺς τῇ δυνάμει, συνωμολόγησε, κ. τ. λ. But the sense requires the comma to be placed after δοὺς.

always such. If you begin to count behind the ages, or if you fix your gaze on the Hereafter [6], you will find no falling off whatever in dignity, or glory, or omnipotence, such as to constitute Him capable of increase by addition, or of diminution by subtraction. Being wholly and entirely perfect, He admits diminution in nothing. Whereinsoever, on such a supposition as theirs, He is lessened, therein He will be exposed to the inroad of ideas tending to dishonour Him. For that which is not absolutely perfect must be suspected on some one point of partaking of the opposite character. But if to entertain even the thought of this is a sign of extreme derangement of mind, it is well to confess our belief that His perfection in all that is good is altogether unlimited, uncircumscribed, in no particular diminished.

If such is the doctrine concerning Him when followed out [7], let the same inquiry be made concerning the Son and the Father as well. Do you not confess [8] a perfection of glory in the case of the one as in the case of the other? I think that all who reflect will allow it. If, then, the honour of the Father is perfect, and the honour of the Son is perfect, and they have confessed as well the perfection of honour for the Holy Spirit, wherefore do these new theorists dictate to us that we are not to allow in His case an equality of honour with the Father and the Son? As for ourselves, we follow out the above considerations and find ourselves unable to think, as well as to say, that that which requires no addition for its perfection is, as compared with something else, less dignified; for when we have something wherein, owing to its faultless perfection, reason can discover no possibility of increase, I do not see either wherein it can discover any possibility of diminution. But these men, in denying the equality of honour, really lay down the comparative absence of it; and so also when they follow out further this same line of thought, by a diminution arising from comparison they divert all the conceptions that devotion has formed of the Holy Spirit; they do not own His perfection either in goodness, or omnipotence, or in any such attribute. But if they shrink from such open profanity and allow His perfection in every attribute of good, then these clever people must tell us how one perfect thing can be more perfect or less perfect than another perfect thing; for so long as the definition of perfection applies to it, that thing can not admit of a greater and a less in the matter of perfection.

If, then, they agree that the Holy Spirit is perfect absolutely, and it has been admitted in addition that true reverence requires perfection in every good thing for the Father and the Son as well, what reasons can justify them in taking away the Father [9] when once they have granted Him? For to take away "equality of dignity" with the Father is a sure proof that they do not think that the Spirit has a share in the perfection of the Father. And as regards the idea itself of this honour in the case of the Divine Being, from which they would exclude the Spirit, what do they mean by it? Do they mean that honour which men confer on men, when by word and gesture they pay respect to them, signifying their own deference in the form of precedence and all such-like practices, which in the foolish fashion of the day are kept up in the name of "honour." But all these things depend on the goodwill of those who perform them; and if we suppose a case in which they do not choose to perform them, then there is no one amongst mankind who has from mere nature any advantage, such that he should necessarily be more honoured than the rest; for all are marked alike with the same natural proportions. The truth of this is clear; it does not admit of any doubt. We see, for instance, the man who to-day, because of the office which he holds, is considered by the crowd an object of honour, becoming to-morrow himself one of those who pay honour, the office having been transferred to another. Do they, then, conceive of an honour such as that in the case of the Divine Being, so that, as long as we please to pay it, that Divine honour is retained, but when we cease to do so it ceases too at the dictate of our will? Absurd thought, and blasphemous as well! The Deity, being independent of us, does not grow in honour; He is evermore the same; He cannot pass into a better or a worse state; for He has no better, and admits no worse.

In what sort of manner, then, can you honour the Deity? How can you heighten the Highest? How can you give glory to that which is above all glory? How can you praise the Incomprehensible? If "all the nations are as a drop of a bucket [1]," as Isaiah says, if all living humanity were to send up one united note of praise in harmony together, what addition will this gift of a mere drop be to that which is glorious essentially? The heavens are telling the glory of God [2], and yet they are counted poor heralds of His worth; because His Majesty is exalted, not as far as the heavens,

---

[9] i. e. from fellowship with the Spirit. The text is τίς ὁ λόγος καθ' ὃν εὔλογον κρίνουσιν πατέρα ἀναιρεῖν, δεδώκασι; (for which δεδωκόσι is a conjecture). But perhaps πνεῦμα ἀναιρεῖν, διδάσκωσι, or διδάξωσι, would be a more intelligible reading; though the examples of the hortatory subjunctive other than in the first person are, according to Porson (ad Eurip. Hec. 430), to be reckoned among solecisms in classical Greek.
[1] Is xl. 15. But Mai's text has σταθμὸς, not σταγὼν (LXX.).
[2] Ps. xix. 1.

but high above those heavens, which are themselves included within a small fraction of the Deity called figuratively His "span[3]." And shall a man, this frail and short-lived creature, so aptly likened to "grass," who "to-day is," and to-morrow is not, believe that he can worthily honour the Divine Being? It would be like some one lighting a thin fibre from some tow and fancying that by that spark he was making an addition to the dazzling rays of the sun. By what words, pray, will you honour the Holy Spirit, supposing you do wish to honour Him at all? By saying that He is absolutely immortal, without turning, or variableness, always beautiful, always independent of ascription from others, working as He wills all things in all, Holy, leading, direct, just, of true utterance, "searching the deep things of God," "proceeding from the Father," "receiving[4] from the Son," and all such-like things, what, after all, do you lend to Him by these and such-like terms? Do you mention what He has, or do you honour Him by what He has not? Well, if you attest what He has not, your ascription is meaningless and comes to nothing; for he who calls bitterness "sweetness," while he lies himself, has failed to commend that which is blamable. Whereas, if you mention what He has, such and such a quality is essential, whether men recognize it or not; He remains the object of faith[5], says the Apostle, if we have not faith.

What means, then, this lowering and this expanding of their soul, on the part of these men who are enthusiastic for the Father's honour, and grant to the Son an equal share with Him, but in the case of the Spirit are for narrowing down their favours; seeing that it has been demonstrated that the intrinsic worth of the Divine Being does not depend for its contents upon any will of ours, but has been always inalienably inherent in Him? Their narrowness of mind, and unthankfulness, is exposed in this opinion of theirs, while the Holy Spirit is essentially honourable, glorious, almighty, and all that we can conceive of in the way of exaltation, in spite of them.

"Yes," replies one of them, "but we have been taught by Scripture that the Father is the Creator, and in the same way that it was 'through the Son[6]' that 'all things were made'; but God's word tells us nothing of this kind about the Spirit; and how, then, can it be right to place the Holy Spirit in a position of equal dignity with One Who has displayed such magnificence of power through the Creation?"

What shall we answer so this? That the thoughts of their hearts are so much idle talk, when they imagine that the Spirit was not always with the Father and the Son, but that, as occasion varies, He is sometimes to be contemplated as alone, sometimes to be found in the closest union with Them. For if the heaven, and the earth, and all created things were really made through the Son and from the Father, but apart from the Spirit, what was the Holy Spirit doing at the time when the Father was at work with the Son upon the Creation? Was He employed upon some other works, and was this the reason that He had no hand in the building of the Universe? But, then, what special work of the Spirit have they to point to, at the time when the world was being made? Surely, it is senseless folly to conceive of a creation other than that which came into existence from the Father through the Son. Well, suppose that He was not employed at all, but dissociated Himself from the busy work of creating by reason of an inclination to ease and rest, which shrank from toil?

May the gracious Spirit Himself pardon this baseless supposition of ours.! The blasphemy of these theorists, which we have had to follow out in every step it takes, has caused us unwittingly to soil our discussion with the mud of their own imaginings. The view which is consistent with all reverence is as follows. We are not to think of the Father as ever parted from the Son, nor to look for the Son as separate from the Holy Spirit. As it is impossible to mount to the Father, unless our thoughts are exalted thither through the Son, so it is impossible also to say that Jesus is Lord except by the Holy Spirit. Therefore, Father, Son, and Holy Spirit are to be known only in a perfect Trinity, in closest consequence and union with each other, before all creation, before all the ages, before anything whatever of which we can form an idea[7]. The Father is always Father, and in Him the Son, and with the Son the Holy Spirit. If these Persons, then, are inseparate from each other, how great is the folly of these men who undertake to sunder this indivisibility by certain distinctions of time, and so far to divide the Inseparable as to assert confidently, "the Father alone, through the Son alone, made all things"; the Holy Spirit, that is, being not present at all on the occasion of this making, or else not working. Well, if He was not present, they must tell us where He was; and whether, while God embraces all things, they can imagine any separate standing-place for the Spirit, so that He could have remained in isolation during the time occupied by the process of creating. If, on the other hand, He was present, how was it

---

3 Is. xl. 12. Τίς ἐμέτρησε . . . τὸν οὐρανὸν σπιθαμῇ.
4 λαμβανόμενον. 5 πιστός. 2 Tim. ii. 13. 6 S. John i. 3.

7 πρὸ πάσης καταληπτῆς ἐπινοίας.

that He was inactive? Because He could not, or because He would not, work? Did He abstain willingly, or because some strong necessity drove Him away? Now, if He deliberately embraced this inactivity, He must reject working in any other possible way either; and He Who affirmed that "He worketh all things in all, as He wills [8]," is according to them a liar. If, on the contrary, this Spirit has the impulse to work, but some overwhelming control hinders His design, they must tell us the wherefore of this hindrance. Was it owing to his being grudged a share in the glory of those operations, and in order to secure that the admiration at their success should not extend to a third person as its object; or to a distrust of His help, as if His co-operation would result in present mischief? These clever men most certainly furnish the grounds for our holding one of these two hypotheses; or else, if a grudging spirit has no connection with the Deity, any more than a failure can be conceived of in any relation to an Infallible Being, what meaning of any kind is there in these narrow views of theirs, which isolate the Spirit's power from all world-building efficiency? Their duty rather was to expel their low human way of thinking, by means of loftier ideas, and to make a calculation more worthy of the sublimity of the objects in question. For neither did the Universal God make the universe "through the Son," as needing any help, nor does the Only-begotten God work all things "by the Holy Spirit," as having a power that comes short of His design; but the fountain of power is the Father, and the power of the Father is the Son, and the spirit of that power is the Holy Spirit; and Creation entirely, in all its visible and spiritual extent, is the finished work of that Divine power. And seeing that no toil can be thought of in the composition of anything connected with the Divine Being (for performance being bound to the moment of willing, the Plan at once becomes a Reality), we should be justified in calling all that Nature which came into existence by creation a movement of Will, an impulse of Design, a transmission of Power, beginning from the Father, advancing through the Son, and completed in the Holy Spirit.

This is the view we take, after the unprofessional way usual with us; and we reject all these elaborate sophistries of our adversaries, believing and confessing as we do, that in every deed and thought, whether in this world, or beyond this world, whether in time or in eternity, the Holy Spirit is to be apprehended as joined to the Father and Son, and is wanting in no wish or energy, or anything else that is implied in a devout conception of Supreme Goodness [9]; and, therefore, that, except for the distinction of order and Person, no variation in any point is to be apprehended; but we assert that while His place is counted third in mere sequence after the Father and Son, third in the order of the transmission, in all other respects we acknowledge His inseparable union with them; both in nature, in honour, in godhead, and glory, and majesty, and almighty power, and in all devout belief.

But with regard to service and worship, and the other things which they so nicely calculate about, and bring into prominence, we say this; that the Holy Spirit is exalted above all that we can do for Him with our merely human purpose; our worship is far beneath the honour due; and anything else that in human customs is held as honourable is somewhere below the dignity of the Spirit; for that which in its essence is measureless surpasses those who offer their all with so slight and circumscribed and paltry a power of giving. This, then, we say to those of them who subscribe to the reverential conception of the Holy Spirit that He is Divine, and of the Divine nature. But if there is any of them who rejects this statement, and this idea involved in the very name of Divinity, and says that which, to the destruction of the Spirit's greatness, is in circulation amongst the many, namely, that He belongs, not to making, but to made, beings, that it is right to regard Him not as of a Divine, but as of a created nature, we answer to a proposition such as this, that we do not understand how we can count those who make it amongst the number of Christians at all. For just as it would not be possible to style the unformed embryo a human being, but only a potential one, assuming that it is completed so as to come forth to human birth, while as long as it is in this unformed state, it is something other than a human being; so our reason cannot recognize as a Christian one who has failed to receive, with regard to the entire mystery, the genuine form of our religion [1]. We can hear Jews believing in God, and our God too: even our Lord reminds [2] them in the Gospel that they recognize no other God than the Father of the Only-begotten, "of Whom ye say that he is your God." Are we, then, to call the Jews Christians because they too agree to worship the God Whom we adore? I am aware, too, that the Manichees go about vaunting the name of Christ. Because they hold revered the Name to which we bow the knee, shall we therefore number them amongst Christians? So, too,

---

[8] 1 Cor. xiii. 6.

[9] κατὰ τὸ ἀγαθόν; probably here in its Platonic, rather than its ordinary sense.   [1] τὴν ἀληθῆ μόρφωσιν τῆς εὐσεβείας.   [2] ἐντίθεται: συντίθεται, "concedes to," would perhaps be better.

he who both believes in the Father and receives the Son, but sets aside the Majesty of the Spirit, has "denied the faith, and is worse than an infidel," and belies the name of Christ which he bears. The Apostle bids the man of God to be "perfect[3]." Now, to take only the *general* man, perfection must consist in completeness in every aspect of human nature, in having reason, capability of thought and knowledge, a share of animal life, an upright bearing, risibility, broadness of nail; and if any one were to term some individual a man, and yet were unable to produce evidence in his case of the foregoing signs of human nature, his terming him so would be a valueless honour. Thus, too, the Christian is marked by his Belief in Father, Son, and Holy Ghost; in this consists the form of him who is fashioned[4] in accordance with the mystery of the truth. But if his form is arranged otherwise, I will not recognize the existence of anything whence the form is absent; there is a blurring out of the mark, and a loss of the essential form, and an alteration of the characteristic signs of our complete humanity, when the Holy Spirit is not included in the Belief. For indeed the word of Ecclesiastes says true; your heretic is no living man, but "bones," he says[5], "in the womb of her that is with child[6]"; for how can one who does not think of the unction along with the Anointed be said to believe in the Anointed? "Him," says (Peter), "did God anoint with the Holy Spirit[7]."

These destroyers of the Spirit's glory, who relegate Him to a subject world, must tell us of what thing that unction is the symbol. Is it not a symbol of the Kingship? And what? Do they not believe in the Only-begotten as in His very nature a King? Men who have not once for all enveloped their hearts with the Jewish "vail[8]" will not gainsay that He is this. If, then, the Son is in His very nature a king, and the unction is the symbol of His kingship, what, in the way of a consequence, does your reason demonstrate? Why, that the Unction is not a thing alien to that Kingship, and so that the Spirit is not to be ranked in the Trinity as anything strange and foreign either. For the Son is King, and His living, realized, and personified Kingship is found in the Holy Spirit, Who anoints the Only-begotten, and so makes Him the Anointed, and the King of all things that exist. If, then, the Father is King, and the Only-begotten is King, and the Holy

Ghost is the Kingship, one and the same definition of Kingship must prevail throughout this Trinity, and the thought of "unction" conveys the hidden meaning that there is no interval of separation between the Son and the Holy Spirit. For as between the body's surface and the liquid of the oil nothing intervening can be detected, either in reason or in perception, so inseparable is the union of the Spirit with the Son; and the result is that whosoever is to touch the Son by faith must needs first encounter the oil in the very act of touching; there is not a part of Him devoid of the Holy Spirit. Therefore belief in the Lordship of the Son arises in those who entertain it, by means of the Holy Ghost; on all sides the Holy Ghost is met by those who by faith approach the Son. If, then, the Son is essentially a King, and the Holy Spirit is that dignity of Kingship which anoints the Son, what deprivation of this Kingship, in its essence and comparing it with itself, can be imagined?

Again, let us look at it in this way. Kingship is most assuredly shown in the rule over subjects. Now what is "subject" to this Kingly Being? The Word includes the ages certainly, and all that is in them; "Thy Kingdom," it says, "is a Kingdom of ages," and, by ages, it means every substance in them created in infinite space[9], whether visible or invisible; for in them all things were created by the Maker of those ages. If, then, the Kingship must always be thought of along with the King, and the world of subjects is acknowledged to be something other than the world of rulers, what absurdity it is for these men to contradict themselves thus, attributing as they do the unction as an expression for the worth of Him Whose very nature it is to be a King, yet degrading that unction Itself to the rank of a subject, as if wanting in such worth! If It is a subject by virtue of its nature, then why is It made the unction of Kingship, and so associated with the Kingly dignity of the Only-begotten? If, on the other hand, the capacity to rule is shown by Its being included in the majesty of Kingship, where is the necessity of having everything dragged down to a plebeian[1] and servile lower condition, and numbered with the subject creation? When we affirm of the Spirit the two conditions, we cannot be in both cases speaking the truth: *i. e.* that He is ruling, and that He is subject. If He rules, He is not under any lord, but if He is subject, then He cannot be comprehended with the Being who is a King. Men are recognized as amongst men,

3 2 Cor. xiii. 11. Cf. 1 Cor. xiv. 20.
4 Cf. 2 Tim. i. 13 (ὑποτύπωσιν); Rom. ii. 20 (μόρφωσιν); vi. 17 (τύπον), all referring to truth as contained in a formula. Cf. also Gal. iv. 19.
5 Reading καθὼς ἐκεῖνος φησίν.
6 Eccles. xi. 5 (LXX.). οὐκ ἔστι γινωσκων τίς ἡ ὁδὸς τοῦ πνεύματος, ὡς ὀστᾶ ἐν γαστρὶ κυοφορούσης.
7 Acts x. 38. Cf. iv. 27.   8 2 Cor. iii. 14, 15.

9 ἐκ τοῦ περιέχοντος. This expression of Anaxagoras is repeated more than once in the Treatise "On the Soul."
1 ἰδιωτικήν. On 1 Cor. xiv. 16, Ὁ ἀναπληρῶν τὸν τόπον τοῦ ἰδιώτου, Theodoret says, "ἰδιώτην καλεῖ τὸν ἐν τῷ λαικῷ τάγματι τεταγμένον." Theophylact also renders the word by the same equivalent.

angels amongst angels, everything amongst its kind; and so the Holy Spirit must needs be believed to belong to one only of two worlds; to the ruling, or to the inferior world; for between these two our reason can recognize nothing; no new invention of any natural attribute on the borderland of the Created and the Uncreated can be thought of, such as would participate in both, yet be neither entirely; we cannot imagine such an amalgamation and welding together of opposites by anything being blended of the Created and the Uncreated, and two opposites thus coalescing into one person, in which case the result of that strange mixture would not only be a composite thing, but composed of elements that were unlike, and disagreeing as to time; for that which receives its personality from a creation is assuredly posterior to that which subsists without a creation.

If, then, they declare the Holy Ghost to be blended of both, they must consequently view that blending as of a prior with a posterior thing; and, according to them, He will be prior to Himself; and reversely, posterior to Himself; from the Uncreated He will get the seniority, and from the Created the juniority. But, in the nature of things, this cannot be; and so it must most certainly be true to affirm of the Holy Spirit one only of these alternatives, and that is, the attribute of being Uncreated; for notice the amount of absurdity involved in the other alternative; all things that we can think of in the actual creation have, by virtue of all having received their existence by an act of creation, a rank and value perfectly equal in all cases, and so what reason can there be for separating the Holy Spirit from the rest of the creation, and ranking Him with the Father and the Son? Logic, then, will discover this about Him; That which is contemplated as part of the Uncreated, does not exist by creation; or, if It does, then It has no more power than its kindred creation, It cannot associate itself with that Transcendent Nature; if, on the other hand, they declare that He is a created being, and at the same time has a power which is above the creation, then the creation will be found at variance with itself, divided into ruler and ruled, so that part of it is the benefactor, part the benefited, part the sanctifier, part the sanctified; and all that fund of blessings which we believe to be provided for the creation by the Holy Spirit are present in Him, welling up abundantly, and pouring forth upon others, while the creation remains in need of the thence-issuing help and grace, and receives, as a mere dole, those blessings which can be passed to it from a fellow-creature! That would be like favouritism and respecting of persons; when we know that there is no

such partiality in the nature of things, as that those existences which differ in no way from each other on the score of substance should not have equal power; and I think that no one who reflects will admit such views. Either He imparts nothing to others, if He possesses nothing essentially; or, if we do believe that He does give, His possession beforehand of that gift must be granted; this capacity of giving blessings, whilst needing oneself no such extraneous help, is the peculiar and exquisite privilege of Deity, and of no other.

Then let us look to this too. In Holy Baptism, what is it that we secure thereby? Is it not a participation in a life no longer subject to death? I think that no one who can in any way be reckoned amongst Christians will deny that statement. What then? Is that life-giving power in the water itself which is employed to convey the grace of Baptism? Or is it not rather clear to every one that this element is only employed as a means in the external ministry, and of itself contributes nothing towards the sanctification, unless it be first transformed itself by the sanctification; and that what gives life to the baptized is the Spirit; as our Lord Himself says in respect to Him with His own lips, "It is the Spirit that giveth life;" but for the completion of this grace He alone, received by faith, does not give life, but belief in our Lord must precede, in order that the lively gift may come upon the believer, as our Lord has spoken, "He giveth life to whom He willeth." But further still, seeing that this grace administered through the Son is dependent on the Ungenerate Source of all, Scripture accordingly teaches us that belief in the Father Who engendereth all things is to come first; so that this life-giving grace should be completed, for those fit to receive it, after starting from that Source as from a spring pouring life abundantly, through the Only-begotten Who is the True life, by the operation of the Holy Spirit. If, then, life comes in baptism, and baptism receives its completion in the name of Father, Son, and Spirit, what do these men who count this Minister of life as nothing? If the gift is a slight one, they must tell us the thing that is more precious than this life. But if everything whatever that is precious is second to this life, I mean that higher and precious life in which the brute creation has no part, how can they dare to depreciate so great a favour, or rather the actual Being who grants the favour, and to degrade Him in their conceptions of Him to a subject world by disjoining Him from the higher world of deity[2]. Finally, if they will

---

[2] "Whether or not the Macedonians explicitly denied the Divinity of the Holy Ghost is uncertain; but they viewed Him as essentially

have it that this bestowal of life is a small thing, and that it means nothing great and awful in the nature of the Bestower, how is it they do not draw the conclusion which this very view makes inevitable, namely, that we must suppose, even with regard to the Only-begotten and the Father Himself, nothing great in Their life, the same as that which we have through the Holy Spirit, supplied as it is from the Father through the Son?

So that if these despisers and impugners of their very own life conceive of the gift as a little one, and decree accordingly to slight the Being who imparts the gift, let them be made aware that they cannot limit to one Person only their ingratitude, but must extend its profanity beyond the Holy Spirit to the Holy Trinity Itself. For like as the grace flows down in an unbroken stream from the Father, through the Son and the Spirit, upon the persons worthy of it, so does this profanity return backward, and is transmitted from the Son to the God of all the world, passing from one to the other. If, when a man is slighted, He Who sent him is slighted (yet what a distance there was between the man and the Sender!), what criminality[3] is thereby implied in those who thus defy the Holy Spirit! Perhaps this is the blasphemy against our Law-giver[4] for which the judgment without remission has been decreed ; since in Him the[5] entire Being, Blessed and Divine, is insulted also. As the devout worshipper of the Spirit sees in Him the glory of the Only-begotten, and in that sight beholds the image of the Infinite God, and by means of that image makes an outline, upon his own cognition[6], of the Original, so most plainly does this contemner[7] (of the Spirit), whenever he advances any of his bold statements against the glory of the Spirit, extend, by virtue of the same reasoning, his profanity to the Son, and beyond Him to the Father. Therefore, those who reflect must have fear lest they perpetrate an audacity the result of which will be the complete blotting out of the perpetrator of it ; and while they exalt the Spirit in the naming, they will even before the naming exalt Him in their thought, it being impossible that words can mount along with thought ; still when one shall have reached the highest limit of human faculties, the utmost height and magnificence of idea to which the mind can ever attain, even then

one must believe it is far below the glory that belongs to[8] Him, according to the words in the Psalms, that "after exalting the Lord our God, even then ye scarcely worship the footstool beneath His feet" : and the cause of this dignity being so incomprehensible is nothing else than that He is holy.

If, then, every height of man's ability falls below the grandeur of the Spirit (for that is what the Word means in the metaphor of "footstool"), what vanity is theirs who think that there is within themselves a power so great that it rests with them to define the amount of value to be attributed to a being who is invaluable ! And so they pronounce the Holy Spirit unworthy of some things which are associated with the idea of value, as if their own abilities could do far more than the Spirit, as estimated by them, is capable of. What pitiable, what wretched madness ! They understand not what they are themselves when they talk like this, and what the Holy Spirit against Whom they insolently range themselves. Who will tell these people that men are "a spirit that goeth forth and returneth not again[9]," built up in their mother's womb by means of a soiled conception, and returning all of them to a soiled earth ; inheriting a life that is likened unto grass ; blooming for a little during life's illusion[1], and then withering away, and all the bloom upon them being shed and vanishing ; they themselves not knowing with certainty what they were before their birth, nor into what they will be changed, their soul being ignorant of her peculiar destiny as long as she tarries in the flesh? Such is man.

On the contrary the Holy Spirit is, to begin with, because of qualities that are essentially holy, that which the Father, essentially Holy, is ; and such as the Only-begotten is, such is the Holy Spirit ; then, again, He is so by virtue of life-giving, of imperishability, of unvariableness, of everlastingness, of justice, of wisdom, of rectitude, of sovereignty, of goodness, of power, of capacity to give all good things, and above them all life itself, and by being everywhere, being present in each, filling the earth, residing in the heavens, shed abroad upon supernatural Powers, filling all things according to the deserts of each, Himself remaining full, being with all who are worthy, and yet not parted from the Holy Trinity. He ever "searches the deep things of God," ever "receives" from the Son, ever is being "sent," and yet not separated, and being "glorified," and yet He has always had glory. It is plain, indeed, that one who gives glory to another must be found himself in the possession of superabundant glory ; for

---

separate from, and external to, the One Indivisible Godhead. The 'Nicene' Creed declares that He is the *Lord*, or Sovereign Spirit, because the heretics considered Him to be a minister of God ; and the Supreme *Giver of Life*, because they considered Him a mere instrument by which we receive the gift."—Newman's *Arians*, note p. 420.   [3] κατάκρισιν.
[4] κατὰ τοῦ νομοθέτου is Mai's reading. Put κατὰ τὸν νομοθέτην, *i. e.* according to S. Mark iii. 29, S. Luke xii. 10, would be preferable.   Migne reads παρὰ in this sense.
[5] τὸ has probably dropped out.
[6] τῇ γνώσει ἑαυτοῦ.   [7] Something has dropped out here.

[8] ἐπιβαλλούσης. Cf. Ps. xcix. 5 ; 1 Chron. xxviii. 2.
[9] Wisdom xvi. 14.   [1] βιωτικῆς ἀπάτης.

how could one devoid of glory glorify another? Unless a thing be itself light, how can it display the gracious gift of light? So the power to glorify could never be displayed by one who was not himself glory[2], and honour, and majesty, and greatness. Now the Spirit does glorify the Father and the Son. Neither does He lie Who saith, "Them that glorify Me I glorify"[3]; and "I have glorified Thee[4]," is said by our Lord to the Father; and again He says, "Glorify Thou Me with the glory which I had with Thee before the world was[5]." The Divine Voice answers, "I have both glorified, and will glorify again[6]." You see the revolving circle of the glory moving from Like to Like. The Son is glorified by the Spirit; the Father is glorified by the Son; again the Son has His glory from the Father; and the Only-begotten thus becomes the glory of the Spirit. For with what shall the Father be glorified, but with the true glory of the Son: and with what again shall the Son be glorified, but with the majesty of the Spirit? In like manner, again, Faith completes the circle, and glorifies the Son by means of the Spirit, and the Father by means of the Son.

If such, then, is the greatness of the Spirit, and whatever is morally beautiful, whatever is good, coming from God as it does through the Son, is completed by the instrumentality of the Spirit that "worketh all in all," why do they set themselves against their own life? Why do they alienate themselves from the hope belonging to "such as are to be saved"? Why do they sever themselves from their cleaving unto God? For how can any man cleave unto the Lord unless the Spirit operates within us that union of ourselves with Him? Why do they haggle with us about the amount of service and of worship? Why do they use that word "worship" in an ironical sense, derogatory to a Divine and entirely Independent Being, supposing that they desire their own salvation? We would say to them, "Your supplication is the advantage of you who ask, and not the honouring of Him Who grants it. Why, then, do you approach your Benefactor as if you had something to give? Or rather, why do you refuse to name as a benefactor at all Him Who gives you your blessings, and slight the Life-giver while clinging to Life? Why, seeking for His sanctification, do you misconceive of the Dispenser of the Grace of sanctification; and as to the giving of those blessings, why, not denying that He has the power, do you deem Him not worthy to be asked to

give, and fail to take this into consideration, viz. how much greater a thing it is to give some blessing than to be asked to give it? The asking does not unmistakably witness to greatness in him who is asked; for it is possible that one who does not have the thing to give might be asked for it, for the asking depends only on the will of the asker. But one who actually bestows some blessing has thereby given undoubted evidence of a power residing in him. Why then, while testifying to the greater thing in Him,—I mean the power to bestow everything that is morally beautiful[7]—do you deprive Him of the asking, as of something of importance; although this asking, as we have said, is often performed in the case of those who have nothing in their power, owing to the delusion of their devotees? For instance, the slaves of superstition ask the idols for the objects of their wishes; but the asking does not, in this instance of the idols, confer any glory; only people pay that attention to them owing to the deluded expectation that they will get some one of the things they ask for, and so they do not cease to ask. But you, persuaded as you are of what and how great things the Holy Spirit is the Giver, do you neglect the asking them from Him, taking refuge in the law which bids you 'worship God and serve Him only[8]?' Well, how will you worship Him only, tell me, when you have severed Him from His intimate union with His own Only-begotten and His own Spirit? This worship is simply Jewish.

But you will say, "When I think of the Father it is the Son (alone) that I have included as well in that term." But tell me; when you have grasped the notion of the Son have you not admitted therein that of the Holy Spirit too? For how can you confess the Son except by the Holy Spirit? At what moment, then, is the Spirit in a state of separation from the Son, so that when the Father is being worshipped, the worship of the Spirit is not included along with that of the Son? And as regards their worship itself, what in the world do they reckon it to be? They bestow it, as some exquisite piece of honour, upon the God over all, and convey it over, sometimes, so as to reach the Only-begotten also; but the Holy Spirit they regard as unworthy of such a privilege. Now, in the common parlance of mankind, that self-prostration of inferiors upon the ground which they practise when they salute their betters is termed worship. Thus, it was by such a posture that the patriarch Jacob, in his self-humiliation, seems to have wished to show his inferiority when coming to

---

[2] It is worth noticing that Gregory maintains (Hom. xv. on Canticles) that Δόξα in Scripture means the Holy Ghost.
[3] Cf. 1 Sam. ii. 30.   [4] S. John xvii. 4.
[5] S. John xvii. 5.   [6] S. John xii. 28.
[7] καλόν.   [8] Deut. vi. 13; x. 20.

meet his brother and to appease his wrath; for "he bowed himself to the ground," says the Scripture, "three times"[9]; and Joseph's brethren, as long as they knew him not, and he pretended before them that he knew them not, by reason of the exaltation of his rank reverenced his sovereignty with this worship; and even the great Abraham himself " bowed himself[1] " "to the children of Heth," a stranger amongst the natives of that land, showing, I opine, by that action, how far more powerful those natives were than sojourners. It is possible to speak of many such actions both in the ancient records, and from examples before our eyes in the world now[2].

Do they too, then, mean this by their worship? Well, is it anything but absurdity to think that it is wrong to honour the Holy Spirit with that with which the patriarch honoured even Canaanites? Or do they consider their "worship" something different to this, as if one sort were fitting for men, another sort for the Supreme Being? But then, how is it that they omit worship altogether in the instance of the Spirit, not even bestowing upon Him the worship conceded in the case of men? And what kind of worship do they imagine to be reserved especially for the Deity? Is it to be spoken word, or acted gesture? Well, but are not these marks of honour shared by men as well? In their case words are spoken and gestures acted. Is it not, then, plain to every one who possesses the least amount of reflection, that any gift worthy of the Deity mankind has not got to give; for the Author of all blessings has no need of us. But it is we men who have transferred these indications of respect and admiration, which we adopt towards each other, when we would show by the acknowledgment of a neighbour's superiority that one of us is in a humbler position than another, to our attendance upon a Higher Power; out of our possessions we make a gift of what is most precious to a priceless Nature. Therefore, since men, approaching emperors and potentates for the objects which they wish in some way to obtain from those rulers, do not bring to them their mere petition only, but employ every possible means to induce them to feel pity and favour towards themselves, adopting a humble voice, and a kneeling position[3], clasping their knees, prostrating themselves on the ground, and putting forward to plead for their petition all sorts of pathetic signs, to wake that pity,—so it is that those who recognize the True Potentate, by Whom all things in existence are controlled, when they are supplicating for that which they have at heart, some lowly in spirit because of pitiable conditions in this world, some with their thoughts lifted up because of their eternal mysterious hopes, seeing that they know not how to ask, and that their humanity is not ·capable of displaying any reverence that can reach to the grandeur of that Glory, carry the ceremonial used in the case of men into the service of the Deity. And this is what "worship" is,—that, I mean, which is offered for objects we have at heart along with supplication and humiliation. Therefore Daniel too bends the knees to the Lord, when asking His love for the captive people; and He Who " bare our sicknesses," and intercedes for us, is recorded in the Gospel to have fallen on His face, because of the man that He had taken upon Him, at the hour of prayer, and in this posture to have made His petition, enjoining thereby, I think, that at the time of our petition our voice is not to be bold, but that we are to assume the attitude of the wretched ; since the Lord "resisteth the proud, but giveth grace unto the humble ;" and somewhere else (He says), " he that exalteth himself shall be abased." If, then, "worship" is a sort of suppliant state, or pleading put forward for the object of the petition, what is the intention of these new-fashioned regulations? These men do not even deign to ask of the Giver, nor to kneel to the Ruler, nor to attend upon the Potentate.

*   *   *   *   *

---

9 The LXX. has προσεκύνησεν ἐπὶ τὴν γῆν γῆν ἑπτάκις, Gen. xxxiii. 3.
1 προσεκύνησε τῷ λαῷ τῆς γῆς, τοῖς υἱοῖς τοῦ Χετ, Gen. xxiii. 7.
2 τοῦ βίου. This is a late use of βίος.

3 Still the word προσκυνεῖν became consecrated to the highest Christian worship, while θεραπεύειν was employed for address to the angels. " Every supplication, every prayer, every entreaty, and every giving of thanks must be offered to the Almighty through the High Priest who is over all the angels, the incarnate Word and God. And we shall make supplication and prayer to the Word Himself also, and we shall give Him thanks if we can distinguish prayer in its proper meaning from the wrong use of the word," Origen c. Cels. v. 4 (Cf. viii. 13, where he answers the question whether Gabriel, Michael, and the rest of the archangels should be addressed, θεραπεύεσθαι).

ON THE HOLY TRINITY, AND OF THE GODHEAD
OF THE HOLY SPIRIT
TO EUSTATHIUS

ALL you who study medicine have, one may say, humanity for your profession : and I think that one who preferred your science to all the serious pursuits of life would form the proper judgment, and not miss the right decision, if it be true that life, the most valued of all things, is a thing to be shunned, and full of pain, if it may not be had with health, and health your art supplies. But in your own case the science is in a notable degree of double efficacy ; you enlarge for yourself the bounds of its humanity, since you do not limit the benefit of your art to men's bodies, but take thought also for the cure of troubles of the mind. I say this, not only following the common reports, but because I have learnt it from experience, as in many other matters, so especially at this time in this indescribable malice of our enemies, which you skilfully dispersed when it swept like some evil flood over our life, dispelling this violent inflammation of our heart by your fomentation of soothing words. I thought it right, indeed, in view of the continuous and varied effort of our enemies against us, to keep silence, and to receive their attack quietly, rather than to speak against men armed with falsehood, that most mischievous weapon, which sometimes drives its point even through truth. But you did well in urging me not to betray the truth, but to refute the slanderers, lest, by a success of falsehood against truth, many might be injured.

I may say that those who conceived this causeless hatred for us seemed to be acting very much on the principle of Æsop's fable. For just as he makes his wolf bring some charges against the lamb (feeling ashamed, I suppose, of seeming to destroy, without just pretext, one who had done him no hurt), and then, when the lamb easily swept away all the slanderous charges brought against him, makes the wolf by no means slacken his attack, but carry the day with his teeth when he is vanquished by justice ; so those who were as keen for hatred against us as if it were something good (feeling perhaps some shame of seeming to hate without cause), make up charges and complaints against us, while they do not abide consistently by any of the things they say, but allege, now that one thing, after a little while that another, and then again that something else is the cause of their hostility to us. Their malice does not take a stand on any ground, but when they are dislodged from one charge they cling to another, and from that again they seize upon a third, and if all their charges are refuted they do not give up their hate. They charge us with preaching three Gods, and din into the ears of the multitude this slander, which they never rest from maintaining persuasively. Then truth fights on our side, for we show both publicly to all men, and privately to those who converse with us, that we anathematize any man who says that there are three Gods, and hold him to be not even a Christian. Then, as soon as they hear this, they find Sabellius a handy weapon against us, and the plague that he spread is the subject of continual attacks upon us. Once more, we oppose to this assault our wonted armour of truth, and show that we abhor this form of heresy just as much as Judaism. What then ? are they weary after such efforts, and content to rest? Not at all. Now they charge us with innovation, and frame their complaint against us in this way :—They allege that while we confess [2] three Persons we say that there is one goodness, and one power,

---

[1] The greater part of this treatise is found also among the Letters of S. Basil [Ep. 189 (80) : Ed. Gaume, Tom. iii. p. 401 (276 c.)]. The Benedictine edition of S. Basil notes that in one MS. a marginal note attributes the letter to Gregory. It may be added that those parts which appear to be found only in the MSS. of Gregory make the argument considerably clearer than it is if they are excluded, as they are from the Benedictine text of S. Basil.

[2] Reading ὁμολογοῦντας with Oehler. The Paris Edit. reads ὁμολογούντων, and so also the Benedictine S. Basil. The Latin translator of 1615, however, renders as if he had read ὁμολογοῦντας.

and one Godhead. And in this assertion they do not go beyond the truth; for we do say so. But the ground of their complaint is that their custom does not admit this, and Scripture does not support it. What then is our reply? We do not think that it is right to make their prevailing custom the law and rule of sound doctrine. For if custom is to avail for [3] proof of soundness, we too, surely, may advance our prevailing custom; and if they reject this, we are surely not bound to follow theirs. Let the inspired Scripture, then, be our umpire, and the vote of truth will surely be given to those whose dogmas are found to agree with the Divine words.

Well, what is their charge? There are two brought forward together in the accusation against us; one, that we divide the Persons; the other, that we do not employ any of the names which belong to God in the plural number, but (as I said already) speak of the goodness as one, and of the power, and the Godhead, and all such attributes in the singular. With regard to the dividing of the Persons, those cannot well object who hold the doctrine of the diversity of substances in the Divine nature. For it is not to be supposed that those who say that there are three substances do not also say that there are three Persons. So this point only is called in question: that those attributes which are ascribed to the Divine nature we employ in the singular.

But our argument in reply to this is ready and clear. For any one who condemns those who say that the Godhead is one, must necessarily support either those who say that there are more than one, or those who say that there is none. But the inspired teaching does not allow us to say that there are more than one, since, whenever it uses the term, it makes mention of the Godhead in the singular; as,— "In Him dwelleth all the fulness of the Godhead [4]"; and, elsewhere,—"The invisible things of Him from the foundation of the world are clearly seen, being understood by the things that are made, even His eternal power and Godhead [5]." If, then, to extend the number of the Godhead to a multitude belongs to those only who suffer from the plague of polytheistic error, and on the other hand utterly to deny the Godhead would be the doctrine of atheists, what doctrine is that which accuses us for saying that the Godhead is one? But they reveal more clearly the aim of their argument. As regards the Father, they admit the fact that He is God [6], and that the Son likewise is honoured

with the attribute of Godhead; but the Spirit, Who is reckoned with the Father and the Son, they cannot include in their conception of Godhead, but hold that the power of the Godhead, issuing from the Father to the Son, and there halting, separates the nature of the Spirit from the Divine glory. And so, as far as we may in a short space, we have to answer this opinion also.

What, then, is our doctrine? The Lord, in delivering the saving Faith to those who become disciples of the word, joins with the Father and the Son the Holy Spirit also; and we affirm that the union of that which has once been joined is continual; for it is not joined in one thing, and separated in others. But the power of the Spirit, being included with the Father and the Son in the life-giving power, by which our nature is transferred from the corruptible life to immortality, and in many other cases also, as in the conception of "Good," and "Holy," and "Eternal," "Wise," "Righteous," "Chief," "Mighty," and in fact everywhere, has an inseparable association with them in all the attributes ascribed in a sense of special excellence. And so we consider that it is right to think that that which is joined to the Father and the Son in such sublime and exalted conceptions is not separated from them in any. For we do not know of any differences by way of superiority and inferiority in attributes which express our conceptions of the Divine nature, so that we should suppose it an act of piety (while allowing to the Spirit community in the inferior attributes) to judge Him unworthy of those more exalted. For all the Divine attributes, whether named or conceived, are of like rank one with another, in that they are not distinguishable in respect of the signification of their subject. For the appellation of "the Good" does not lead our minds to one subject, and that of "the Wise," or "the Mighty," or "the Righteous" to another, but the thing to which all the attributes point is one; and, if you speak of God, you signify the same Whom you understood by the other attributes. If then all the attributes ascribed to the Divine nature are of equal force as regards their designation of the subject, leading our minds to the same subject in various aspects, what reason is there that one, while allowing to the Spirit community with the Father and the Son in the other attributes, should exclude Him from the Godhead alone? It is absolutely necessary either to allow to Him community in this also, or not to admit His community in the others. For if He is worthy in the case of those attributes, He is surely not less worthy in this. But if He is "less," according to their phrase [7],

---

[3] Reading εἰς ὀρθότητος ἀπόδειξιν, with Oehler and the Benedictine S. Basil. The Paris Edit. of 1615 reads εἰς ὀρθότητα λόγου.
[4] Col. ii. 9   [5] Rom. i. 20.
[6] Reading, with Oehler, τὸ θεὸν εἶναι.

[7] Reading with Oehler εἰ δέ μικρότερον . . . ἐστίν, ὥστε . . . κεχωρίσθαι The Paris Edit. and the Benedictine S. Basil read εἰ

so that He is excluded from community with the Father and the Son in the attribute of Godhead, neither is He worthy to share in any other of the attributes which belong to God. For the attributes, when rightly understood and mutually compared by that notion which we contemplate in each case, will be found to imply nothing less than the appellation of "God." And a proof of this is that many even of the inferior existences are called by this very name. Further, the Divine Scripture is not sparing in this use of the name even in the case of things incongruous, as when it names idols by the appellation of God. For it says, "Let the gods that have not made the heavens and the earth perish, and be cast down beneath the earth [8]"; and, "all the gods of the heathen are devils [9]"; and the witch in her incantations, when she brings up for Saul the spirits that he sought for, says that she "saw gods [1]." And again Balaam, being an augur and a seer, and engaging in divination, and having obtained for himself the instruction of devils and magical augury, is said in Scripture to receive counsel from God [2]. One may show by collecting many instances of the same kind from the Divine Scripture, that this attribute has no supremacy over the other attributes which are proper to God, seeing that, as has been said, we find it predicated, in an equivocal sense, even of things incongruous; but we are nowhere taught in Scripture that the names of "the Holy," "the Incorruptible," "the Righteous," "the Good," are made common to things unworthy. If, then, they do not deny that the Holy Spirit has community with the Father and the Son in those attributes which, in their sense of special excellence, are piously predicated only of the Divine nature, what reason is there to pretend that He is excluded from community in this only, wherein it was shown that, by an equivocal use, even devils and idols share?

But they say that this appellation is indicative of nature, and that, as the nature of the Spirit is not common to the Father and the Son, for this reason neither does he partake in the community of this attribute. Let them show, then, whereby they discern this diversity of nature. For if it were possible that the Divine nature should be contemplated in its absolute essence, and that we should find by appearances what is and what is not proper to it, we should surely have no need of other arguments or evidence for the comprehension of the question. But

since it is exalted above the understanding of the questioners, and we have to argue from some particular evidence about those things which evade our knowledge [3], it is absolutely necessary for us to be guided to the investigation of the Divine nature by its operations. If, then, we see that the operations which are wrought by the Father and the Son and the Holy Spirit differ one from the other, we shall conjecture from the different character of the operations that the natures which operate are also different. For it cannot be that things which differ in their very nature should agree in the form of their operation: fire does not chill, nor ice give warmth, but their operations are distinguished together with the difference between their natures. If, on the other hand, we understand that the operation of the Father, the Son, and the Holy Spirit is one, differing or varying in nothing, the oneness of their nature must needs be inferred from the identity of their operation. The Father, the Son, and the Holy Spirit alike give sanctification, and life, and light, and comfort, and all similar graces. And let no one attribute the power of sanctification in an especial sense to the Spirit, when he hears the Saviour in the Gospel saying to the Father concerning His disciples, "Father, sanctify them in Thy name [4]." So too all the other gifts are wrought in those who are worthy alike by the Father, the Son, and the Holy Spirit: every grace and power, guidance, life, comfort, the change to immortality, the passage to liberty, and every other boon that exists, which descends to us.

But the order of things which is above us, alike in the region of intelligence and in that of sense (if by what we know we may form conjectures about those things also which are above us), is itself established within the operation and power of the Holy Spirit, every man receiving the benefit according to his own desert and need. For although the arrangement and ordering of things above our nature is obscure to our sense, yet one may more reasonably infer, by the things which we know, that in them too the power of the Spirit works, than that it is banished from the order existing in the things above us. For he who asserts the latter view advances his blasphemy in a naked and unseemly shape, without being able to support his absurd opinion by any argument. But he who agrees that those things which are above us are also ordered by the power of the Spirit with the Father and the Son, makes his assertion on this point with the support of clear evidence from

---

δὲ μικρότερον . . . ἐστὶν, ἤ ὥστε . . . χωρῆσαι. "If, according to their phrase, He is too small to be capable of community," &c. Oehler's reading seems to fit better in the argument. If the new idea of "capacity" had been introduced at this point, we should expect some other phrase than μετέχειν ἄξιον at the end of the sentence. [8] Cf. Jer. x. 11. [9] Ps. xcvi. 5 (LXX.). [1] 1 Sam. xxviii. 13. [2] Num. xxii.

[3] Oehler and Migne's edit. of S. Basil here read γνῶσιν, the Paris Edit. and the Benedictine S. Basil have μνήμην.
[4] Cf. S. John xvii. 11 and 17.

his own life. For [5] as the nature of man is compounded of body and soul, and the angelic nature has for its portion life without a body, if the Holy Spirit worked only in the case of bodies, and the soul were not capable of receiving the grace that comes from Him, one might perhaps infer from this, if the intellectual and incorporeal nature which is in us were above the power of the Spirit, that the angelic life too was in no need of His grace. But if the gift of the Holy Spirit is principally a grace of the soul, and the constitution of the soul is linked by its intellectuality and invisibility to the angelic life, what person who knows how to see a consequence would not agree, that every intellectual nature is governed by the ordering of the Holy Spirit? For since it is said "the angels do alway behold the Face of My Father which is in heaven [6]," and it is not possible to behold the person of the Father otherwise than by fixing the sight upon it through His image; and the image of the person of the Father is the Only-begotten, and to Him again no man can draw near whose mind has not been illumined by the Holy Spirit, what else is shown from this but that the Holy Spirit is not separated from any operation which is wrought by the Father and the Son? Thus the identity of operation in Father, Son, and Holy Spirit shows plainly the undistinguishable character of their substance. So that even if the name of Godhead does indicate nature, the community of substance shows that this appellation is properly applied also to the Holy Spirit. But I know not how these makers-up of all sorts of arguments bring the appellation of Godhead to be an indication of nature, as though they had not heard from the Scripture that it is a matter of appointment [7], in which way nature does not arise. For Moses was appointed as a god of the Egyptians, since He Who gave him the oracles, &c., spoke thus to him, "I have given thee as a god to Pharaoh [8]." Thus the force of the appellation is the indication of some power, either of oversight or of operation. But the Divine nature itself, as it is, remains unexpressed by all the names that are conceived for it, as our doctrine declares. For in learning that He is beneficent, and a judge, good, and just, and all else of the same kind, we learn

diversities of His operations, but we are none the more able to learn by our knowledge of His operations the nature of Him Who works. For when one gives a definition of any one of these attributes, and of the nature to which the names are applied, he will not give the same definition of both: and of things of which the definition is different, the nature also is distinct. Indeed the substance is one thing which no definition has been found to express, and the significance of the names employed concerning it varies, as the names are given from some operation or accident. Now the fact that there is no distinction in the operations we learn from the community of the attributes, but of the difference in respect of nature we find no clear proof, the identity of operations indicating rather, as we said, community of nature. If, then, Godhead is a name derived from operation, as we say that the operation of the Father, and the Son, and the Holy Spirit is one, so we say that the Godhead is one: or if, according to the view of the majority, Godhead is indicative of nature, since we cannot find any diversity in their nature, we not unreasonably define the Holy Trinity to be of one Godhead [9].

But if any one were to call this appellation indicative of dignity, I cannot tell by what reasoning he drags the word to this significance. Since however one may hear many saying things of this kind, in order that the zeal of its opponents may not find a ground for attacking the truth, we go out of our way with those who take this view, to consider such an opinion, and say that, even if the name does denote dignity, in this case too the appellation will properly befit the Holy Spirit. For the attribute of kingship denotes all dignity; and "our God," it says, "is King from everlasting [1]." But the Son, having all things which are the Father's, is Himself proclaimed a King by Holy Scripture. Now the Divine Scripture says that the Holy Spirit is the unction of the Only-Begotten [2], interpreting the dignity of the Spirit by a transference of the terms commonly used in this world. For as, in ancient days, in those who were advanced to kingship, the token of this dignity was the unction which was applied to them, and when this took place there was thenceforth a change from private and humble estate to the superiority of rule, and he who was deemed worthy of this grace received after his anointing another name, being called, instead of an ordinary man, the Anointed of the Lord: for this reason, that the dignity of the Holy Spirit might be more clearly shown to men, He was called by the Scripture "the sign of the Kingdom," and "Unction," whereby we

---

[5] This sentence, and the passage following, down to the words, "is wrought by the Father and the Son," are omitted in the editions of S. Basil.
[6] S. Matt. xviii. 10.
[7] Reading ὅτι χειροτονητή, ᾗ φύσις οὐ γίνεται. The Paris Edit. and Migne's S. Basil read ὅτι χειροτονία ἡ φύσις οὐ γίνεται: the Ben. S. Basil and Oehler read ὅτι χειροτονητὴ φύσις οὐ γίνεται. The point of the argument seems to be that "Godhead" is spoken of in Scripture as being given by appointment, which excludes the idea of its being indicative of "nature." Gregory shows that it is so spoken of; but he does not show that Scripture asserts the distinction between nature and appointment, which the reading of the Benedictine text and Oehler would require him to do.
[8] Ex. vii. 1.

[9] The treatise, as it appears in S. Basil's works, ends here.
Ps. lxxiv. 12.　　　[2] Acts x. 38.

are taught that the Holy Spirit shares in the glory and kingdom of the Only-begotten Son of God. For as in Israel it was not permitted to enter upon the kingdom without the unction being previously given, so the word, by a transference of the terms in use among ourselves, indicates the equality of power, showing that not even the kingdom of the Son is received without the dignity of the Holy Spirit. And for this reason He is properly called Christ, since this name gives the proof of His inseparable and indivisible conjunction with the Holy Spirit. If, then, the Only-begotten God is the Anointed, and the Holy Spirit is His Unction, and the appellation of Anointed [3] points to the Kingly authority, and the anointing is the token of His Kingship, then the Holy Spirit shares also in His dignity. If, therefore, they say that the attribute of Godhead is significative of dignity, and the Holy Spirit is shown to share in this last quality, it follows that He Who partakes in the dignity will also partake in the name which represents it.

---

[3] Reading with Oehler Χριστοῦ in place of Θεοῦ (the reading of the Paris edition).

ON "NOT THREE GODS"

TO ABLABIUS

YE that are strong with all might in the inner man ought by rights to carry on the struggle against the enemies of the truth, and not to shrink from the task, that we fathers may be gladdened by the noble toil of our sons; for this is the prompting of the law of nature: but as you turn your ranks, and send against us the assaults of those darts which are hurled by the opponents of the truth, and demand that their "hot burning coals"[1] and their shafts sharpened by knowledge falsely so called should be quenched with the shield of faith by us old men, we accept your command, and make ourselves an example of obedience[2], in order that you may yourself give us the just requital on like commands, Ablabius, noble soldier of Christ, if we should ever summon you to such a contest.

In truth, the question you propound to us is no small one, nor such that but small harm will follow if it meets with insufficient treatment. For by the force of the question, we are at first sight compelled to accept one or other of two erroneous opinions, and either to say "there are three Gods," which is unlawful, or not to acknowledge the Godhead of the Son and the Holy Spirit, which is impious and absurd.

The argument which you state is something like this:—Peter, James, and John, being in one human nature, are called three men: and there is no absurdity in describing those who are united in nature, if they are more than one, by the plural number of the name derived from their nature. If, then, in the above case, custom admits this, and no one forbids us to speak of those who are two as two, or those who are more than two as three, how is it that in the case of our statements of the mysteries of the Faith, though confessing the Three Persons, and acknowledging no difference of nature between them, we are in some sense at variance with our confession, when we say that the Godhead of the Father and of the Son and of the Holy Ghost is one, and yet forbid men to say "there are three Gods"? The question is, as I said, very difficult to deal with: yet, if we should be able to find anything that may give support to the uncertainty of our mind, so that it may no longer totter and waver in this monstrous dilemma, it would be well: on the other hand, even if our reasoning be found unequal to the problem, we must keep for ever, firm and unmoved, the tradition which we received by succession from the fathers, and seek from the Lord the reason which is the advocate of our faith: and if this be found by any of those endowed with grace, we must give thanks to Him who bestowed the grace; but if not, we shall none the less, on those points which have been determined, hold our faith unchangeably.

What, then, is the reason that when we count one by one those who are exhibited to us in one nature, we ordinarily name them in the plural and speak of "so many men," instead of calling them all one: while in the case of the Divine nature our doctrinal definition rejects the plurality of Gods, at once enumerating the Persons, and at the same time not admitting the plural signification? Perhaps one might seem to touch the point if he were to say (speaking offhand to straightforward people), that the definition refused to reckon Gods in any number to avoid any resemblance to the polytheism of the heathen, lest, if we too were to enumerate the Deity, not in the singular, but in the plural, as they are accustomed to do, there might be supposed to be also some community of doctrine. This answer, I say, if made to people of a more guileless spirit, might seem to be of some weight: but in the case of the others who require that one of the alternatives they propose should be established (either that we should not acknowledge the Godhead in Three Persons, or that, if we do, we should speak of those who share in the same Godhead as three), this answer is not such as to furnish any solution of the difficulty. And hence we must needs make our reply at greater length, tracing out the truth as best we may; for the question is no ordinary one.

---

[1] Ps. cxx. 3; the phrase is rendered in A. V. by "coals of juniper," in the Vulg. by "carbonibus desolatoriis."
[2] Reading, with Oehler, εὐπειθείας.

We say, then, to begin with, that the practice of calling those who are not divided [3] in nature by the very name of their common nature in the plural, and saying they are "many men," is a customary abuse of language, and that it would be much the same thing to say they are "many human natures." And the truth of this we may see from the following instance. When we address any one, we do not call him by the name of his nature, in order that no confusion may result from the community of the name, as would happen if every one of those who hear it were to think that he himself was the person addressed, because the call is made not by the proper appellation but by the common name of their nature : but we separate him from the multitude by using that name which belongs to him as his own ;—that, I mean, which signifies the particular subject. Thus there are many who have shared in the nature— many disciples, say, or apostles, or martyrs— but the man in them all is one ; since, as has been said, the term "man" does not belong to the nature of the individual as such, but to that which is common. For Luke is a man, or Stephen is a man ; but it does not follow that if any one is a man he is therefore Luke or Stephen : but the idea of the persons admits of that separation which is made by the peculiar attributes considered in each severally, and when they are combined is presented to us by means of number ; yet their nature is one, at union in itself, and an absolutely indivisible unit, not capable of increase by addition or of diminution by subtraction, but in its essence being and continually remaining one, inseparable even though it appear in plurality, continuous, complete, and not divided with the individuals who participate in it. And as we speak of a people, or a mob, or an army, or an assembly in the singular in every case, while each of these is conceived as being in plurality, so according to the more accurate expression, "man" would be said to be one, even though those who are exhibited to us in the same nature make up a plurality. Thus it would be much better to correct our erroneous habit, so as no longer to extend to a plurality the name of the nature, than by our bondage to habit to transfer [4] to our statements concerning God the error which exists in the above case. But since the correction of the habit is impracticable (for how could you persuade any one not to speak of those who are exhibited in the same nature as "many men"?—indeed, in every case habit is a thing hard to change), we are not so far wrong in not going contrary to the prevailing habit in the case of the lower nature, since no harm results from the mistaken use of the name : but in the case of the statement concerning the Divine nature the various use [5] of terms is no longer so free from danger : for that which is of small account is in these subjects no longer a small matter. Therefore we must confess one God, according to the testimony of Scripture, "Hear, O Israel, the Lord thy God is one Lord," even though the name of Godhead extends through the Holy Trinity. This I say according to the account we have given in the case of human nature, in which we have learnt that it is improper to extend the name of the nature by the mark of plurality. We must, however, more carefully examine the name of "Godhead," in order to obtain, by means of the significance involved in the word, some help towards clearing up the question before us.

Most men think that the word "Godhead" is used in a peculiar degree in respect of nature : and just as the heaven, or the sun, or any other of the constituent parts of the universe are denoted by proper names which are significant of the subjects, so they say that in the case of the Supreme and Divine nature, the word "Godhead" is fitly adapted to that which it represents to us, as a kind of special name. We, on the other hand, following the suggestions of Scripture, have learnt that that nature is unnameable and unspeakable, and we say that every term either invented by the custom [6] of men, or handed down to us by the Scriptures, is indeed explanatory of our conceptions of the Divine Nature [7], but does not include the signification of that nature itself. And it may be shown without much difficulty that this is the case. For all other terms which are used of the creation may be found, even without analysis of their origin, to be applied to the subjects accidentally, because we are content to denote the things in any way by the word applied to them so as to avoid confusion in our knowledge of the things signified. But all the terms that are employed to lead us to the knowledge of God have comprehended in them each its own meaning, and you cannot find any word among the terms especially applied to God which is without a distinct sense. Hence it is clear that by any of the terms we use the Divine nature itself is not signified, but some one of its surroundings is made known. For we say, it may be, that the Deity is incorruptible, or powerful, or whatever else we are

---

[3] Reading τοὺς μὴ διῃρημένους, as Sifanus seems to have read. The Paris Edit. of 1615 reads τοὺς διῃρημένους, which Oehler leaves uncorrected.
[4] Reading with Oehler μεταβιβάζειν, for the μὴ μεταβιβάζειν of the Paris Edit.

[5] Sifanus seems to have read ἡ ἀδιάφορος χρῆσις, as he translates "promiscuus et indifferens nominum usus."
[6] Reading with Oehler συνηθείας for the οὐσίας of the Paris Edit.
[7] Reading with Oehler τῶν περὶ τὴν θείαν φύσιν νοουμένων, for τῶν τι περὶ τὴν θ. φ. νοουμένων in the Paris Edit.

accustomed to say of Him. But in each of these terms we find a peculiar sense, fit to be understood or asserted of the Divine nature, yet not expressing that which that nature is in its essence. For the subject, whatever it may be, is incorruptible : but our conception of incorruptibility is this,—that that which is, is not resolved into decay : so, when we say that He is incorruptible, we declare what His nature does not suffer, but we do not express what that is which does not suffer corruption. Thus, again, if we say that He is the Giver of life, though we show by that appellation what He gives, we do not by that word declare what that is which gives it. And by the same reasoning we find that all else which results from the significance involved in the names expressing the Divine attributes either forbids us to conceive what we ought not to conceive of the Divine nature, or teaches us that which we ought to conceive of it, but does not include an explanation of the nature itself. Since, then, as we perceive the varied operations of the power above us, we fashion our appellations from the several operations that are known to us, and as we recognize as one of these that operation of surveying and inspection, or, as one might call it, beholding, whereby He surveys all things and overlooks them all, discerning our thoughts, and even entering by His power of contemplation into those things which are not visible, we suppose that Godhead, or θεότης, is so called from θέα, or beholding, and that He who is our θεατής or beholder, by customary use and by the instruction of the Scriptures, is called θεός, or God. Now if any one admits that to behold and to discern are the same thing, and that the God Who superintends all things, both is and is called the superintender of the universe, let him consider this operation, and judge whether it belongs to one of the Persons whom we believe in the Holy Trinity, or whether the power extends [8] throughout the Three Persons. For if our interpretation of the term Godhead, or θεότης, is a true one, and the things which are seen are said to be beheld, or θεατά, and that which beholds them is called θεός, or God, no one of the Persons in the Trinity could reasonably be excluded from such an appellation on the ground of the sense involved in the word. For Scripture attributes the act of seeing equally to Father, Son, and Holy Spirit. David says, "See, O God our defender[9]" : and from this we learn that sight is a proper operation of the idea [1] of God, so far as God is conceived, since he says, "See, O God." But Jesus also sees the thoughts of those who con-

demn Him, and questions why by His own power He pardons the sins of men ? for it says, "Jesus, seeing their thoughts [2]." And of the Holy Spirit also, Peter says to Ananias, "Why hath Satan filled thine heart, to lie to the Holy Ghost ? [3]" showing that the Holy Spirit was a true witness, aware of what Ananias had dared to do in secret, and by Whom the manifestation of the secret was made to Peter. For Ananias became a thief of his own goods, secretly, as he thought, from all men, and concealing his sin : but the Holy Spirit at the same moment was in Peter, and detected his intent, dragged down as it was to avarice, and gave to Peter from Himself [4] the power of seeing the secret, while it is clear that He could not have done this had He not been able to behold hidden things.

But some one will say that the proof of our argument does not yet regard the question. For even if it were granted that the name of "Godhead" is a common name of the nature, it would not be established that we should not speak of "Gods": but by these arguments, on the contrary, we are compelled to speak of "Gods": for we find in the custom of mankind that not only those who are partakers [5] in the same nature, but even any who may be of the same business, are not, when they are many, spoken of in the singular; as we speak of "many orators," or "surveyors," or "farmers," or "shoemakers," and so in all other cases. If, indeed, Godhead were an appellation of nature, it would be more proper, according to the argument laid down, to include the Three Persons in the singular number, and to speak of "One God," by reason of the inseparability and indivisibility of the nature : but since it has been established by what has been said, that the term "Godhead" is significant of operation, and not of nature, the argument from what has been advanced seems to turn to the contrary conclusion, that we ought therefore all the more to call those "three Gods" who are contemplated in the same operation, as they say that one would speak of "three philosophers" or "orators," or any other name derived from a business when those who take part in the same business are more than one.

I have taken some pains, in setting forth this view, to bring forward the reasoning on behalf of the adversaries, that our decision may be the more firmly fixed, being strengthened by the more elaborate contradictions. Let us now resume our argument.

As we have to a certain extent shown by our

---

8 Reading with Oehler διήκει for προσήκει.
9 Ps. lxxxiv. 9.
1 Reading with Oehler ἰδέας for ἰδέαν.

2 S. Matt. ix. 4.   3 Acts v. 3.
4 Reading with Oehler παρ' ἑαυτοῦ for δι' ἑαυτοῦ.
5 Reading κοινωνοὺς for κοινωνίας, with Oehler.

statement that the word "Godhead" is not significant of nature but of operation, perhaps one might reasonably allege as a cause why, in the case of men, those who share with one another in the same pursuits are enumerated and spoken of in the plural, while on the other hand the Deity is spoken of in the singular as one God and one Godhead, even though the Three Persons are not separated from the significance expressed by the term "Godhead," —one might allege, I say, the fact that men, even if several are engaged in the same form of action, work separately each by himself at the task he has undertaken, having no participation in his individual action with others who are engaged in the same occupation. For instance, supposing the case of several rhetoricians, their pursuit, being one, has the same name in the numerous cases : but each of those who follow it works by himself, this one pleading on his own account, and that on his own account. Thus, since among men the action of each in the same pursuits is discriminated, they are properly called many, since each of them is separated from the others within his own environment, according to the special character of his operation. But in the case of the Divine nature we do not similarly learn that the Father does anything by Himself in which the Son does not work conjointly, or again that the Son has any special operation apart from the Holy Spirit; but every operation which extends from God to the Creation, and is named according to our variable conceptions of it, has its origin from the Father, and proceeds through the Son, and is perfected in the Holy Spirit. For this reason the name derived from the operation is not divided with regard to the number of those who fulfil it, because the action of each concerning anything is not separate and peculiar, but whatever comes to pass, in reference either to the acts of His providence for us, or to the government and constitution of the universe, comes to pass by the action of the Three, yet what does come to pass is not three things. We may understand the meaning of this from one single instance. From Him, I say, Who is the chief source of gifts, all things which have shared in this grace have obtained their life. When we inquire, then, whence this good gift came to us, we find by the guidance of the Scriptures that it was from the Father, Son, and Holy Spirit. Yet although we set forth Three Persons and three names, we do not consider that we have had bestowed upon us three lives, one from each Person separately; but the same life is wrought in us by the Father, and prepared by the Son, and depends on the will of the Holy Spirit. Since then the Holy Trinity fulfils every operation in a manner

similar to that of which I have spoken, not by separate action according to the number of the Persons, but so that there is one motion and disposition of the good will which is communicated from the Father through the Son to the Spirit (for as we do not call those whose operation gives one life three Givers of life, neither do we call those who are contemplated in one goodness three Good beings, nor speak of them in the plural by any of their other attributes); so neither can we call those who exercise this Divine and superintending power and operation towards ourselves and all creation, conjointly and inseparably, by their mutual action, three Gods. For as when we learn concerning the God of the universe, from the words of Scripture, that He judges all the earth [6], we say that He is the Judge of all things through the Son : and again, when we hear that the Father judgeth no man [7], we do not think that the Scripture is at variance with itself,—(for He Who judges all the earth does this by His Son to Whom He has committed all judgment; and everything which is done by the Only-begotten has its reference to the Father, so that He Himself is at once the Judge of all things and judges no man, by reason of His having, as we said, committed all judgment to the Son, while all the judgment of the Son is conformable to the will of the Father; and one could not properly say either that They are two judges, or that one of Them is excluded from the authority and power implied in judgment);—so also in the case of the word "Godhead," Christ is the power of God and the wisdom of God, and that very power of superintendence and beholding which we call Godhead, the Father exercises through the Only-begotten, while the Son perfects every power by the Holy Spirit, judging, as Isaiah says, by the Spirit of judgment and the Spirit of burning [8], and acting by Him also, according to the saying in the Gospel which was spoken to the Jews. For He says, "If I by the Spirit of God cast out devils [9]"; where He includes every form of doing good in a partial description, by reason of the unity of action : for the name derived from operation cannot be divided among many where the result of their mutual operation is one.

Since, then, the character of the superintending and beholding power is one, in Father, Son, and Holy Spirit, as has been said in our previous argument, issuing from the Father as from a spring, brought into operation by the Son, and perfecting its grace by the power of the Spirit ; and since no operation is separated in respect of the Persons, being fulfilled by each individually apart from that which is joined with

---

[6] Rom. iii. 6.   [7] S. John v. 22.
[8] Is. iv. 4.   [9] S. Matt. xii. 28.

Him in our contemplation, but all providence, care, and superintendence of all, alike of things in the sensible creation and of those of supra-mundane nature, and that power which preserves the things which are, and corrects those which are amiss, and instructs those which are ordered aright, is one, and not three, being, indeed, directed by the Holy Trinity, yet not severed by a threefold division according to the number of the Persons contemplated in the Faith, so that each of the acts, contemplated by itself, should be the work of the Father alone, or of the Son peculiarly, or of the Holy Spirit [1] separately, but while, as the Apostle says, the one and the selfsame Spirit divides His good gifts to every man severally [2], the motion of good proceeding from the Spirit is not without beginning ;—we find that the power which we conceive as preceding this motion, which is the Only-begotten God, is the maker of all things ; without Him no existent thing attains to the beginning of its being : and, again, this same source of good issues from the will of the Father.

If, then, every good thing and every good name, depending on that power and purpose which is without beginning, is brought to perfection in the power of the Spirit through the Only-begotten God, without mark of time or distinction (since there is no delay, existent or conceived, in the motion of the Divine will from the Father, through the Son, to the Spirit): and if Godhead also is one of the good names and concepts, it would not be proper to divide the name into a plurality, since the unity existing in the action prevents plural enumeration. And as the Saviour of all men, specially of them that believe [3], is spoken of by the Apostle as one, and no one from this phrase argues either that the Son does not save them who believe, or that salvation is given to those who receive it without the intervention of the Spirit ; but God who is over all, is the Saviour of all, while the Son works salvation by means of the grace of the Spirit, and yet they are not on this account called in Scripture three Saviours (although salvation is confessed to proceed from the Holy Trinity): so neither are they called three Gods, according to the signification assigned to the term "Godhead," even though the aforesaid appellation attaches to the Holy Trinity.

It does not seem to me absolutely necessary, with a view to the present proof of our argument, to contend against those who oppose us with the assertion that we are not to conceive "Godhead" as an operation. For we, believing the Divine nature to be unlimited and incomprehensible, conceive no comprehension of it, but declare that the nature is to be conceived in all respects as infinite : and that which is absolutely infinite is not limited in one respect while it is left unlimited in another, but infinity is free from limitation altogether. That therefore which is without limit is surely not limited even by name. In order then to mark the constancy of our conception of infinity in the case of the Divine nature, we say that the Deity is above every name : and "Godhead" is a name. Now it cannot be that the same thing should at once be a name and be accounted as above every name.

But if it pleases our adversaries to say that the significance of the term is not operation, but nature, we shall fall back upon our original argument, that custom applies the name of a nature to denote multitude erroneously : since according to true reasoning neither diminution nor increase attaches to any nature, when it is contemplated in a larger or smaller number. For it is only those things which are contemplated in their individual circumscription which are enumerated by way of addition. Now this circumscription is noted by bodily appearance, and size, and place, and difference in figure and colour, and that which is contemplated apart from these conditions is free from the circumscription which is formed by such categories. That which is not thus circumscribed is not enumerated, and that which is not enumerated cannot be contemplated in multitude. For we say that gold, even though it be cut into many figures, is one, and is so spoken of, but we speak of many coins or many staters, without finding any multiplication of the nature of gold by the number of staters ; and for this reason we speak of gold, when it is contemplated in greater bulk, either in plate or in coin, as "much," but we do not speak of it as "many golds" on account of the multitude of the material,—except when one says there are "many gold pieces" (Darics, for instance, or staters), in which case it is not the material, but the pieces of money to which the significance of number applies : indeed, properly, we should not call them "gold" but "golden."

As, then, the golden staters are many, but the gold is one, so too those who are exhibited to us severally in the nature of man, as Peter, James, and John, are many, yet the man in them is one. And although Scripture extends the word according to the plural significance, where it says "men swear by the greater [4]," and "sons of men," and in other phrases of the like sort, we must recognize that in using the custom of the prevailing form of speech, it does not lay down a law as to the propriety of using the

---

words in one way or another, nor does it say these things by way of giving us instruction about phrases, but uses the word according to the prevailing custom, with a view only to this, that the word may be profitable to those who receive it, taking no minute care in its manner of speech about points where no harm can result from the phrases in respect of the way they are understood.

Indeed, it would be a lengthy task to set out in detail from the Scriptures those constructions which are inexactly expressed, in order to prove the statement I have made; where, however, there is a risk of injury to any part of the truth, we no longer find in Scriptural phrases any indiscriminate or indifferent use of words. For this reason Scripture admits the naming of " men " in the plural, because no one is by such a figure of speech led astray in his conceptions to imagine a multitude of humanities, or supposes that many human natures are indicated by the fact that the name expressive of that nature is used in the plural. But the word " God " it employs studiously in the singular form only, guarding against introducing the idea of different natures in the Divine essence by the plural signification of " Gods." This is the cause why it says, "the Lord our God is one Lord [5]," and also proclaims the Only-begotten God by the name of Godhead, without dividing the Unity into a dual signification, so as to call the Father and the Son two Gods, although each is proclaimed by the holy writers as God. The Father is God : the Son is God : and yet by the same proclamation God is One, because no difference either of nature or of operation is contemplated in the Godhead. For if (according to the idea of those who have been led astray) the nature of the Holy Trinity were diverse, the number would by consequence be extended to a plurality of Gods, being divided according to the diversity of essence in the subjects. But since the Divine, single, and unchanging nature, that it may be one, rejects all diversity in essence, it does not admit in its own case the signification of multitude ; but as it is called one nature, so it is called in the singular by all its other names, " God," " Good," " Holy," " Saviour," " Just," " Judge," and every other Divine name conceivable : whether one says that the names refer to nature or to operation, we shall not dispute the point.

If, however, any one cavils at our argument, on the ground that by not admitting the difference of nature it leads to a mixture and confusion of the Persons, we shall make to such a charge this answer ;—that while we confess the invariable character of the nature, we do not deny the difference in respect of cause, and that

which is caused, by which alone we apprehend that one Person is distinguished from another ;— by our belief, that is, that one is the Cause, and another is of the Cause ; and again in that which is of the Cause we recognize another distinction. For one is directly from the first Cause, and another by that which is directly from the first Cause ; so that the attribute of being Only-begotten abides without doubt in the Son, and the interposition of the Son, while it guards His attribute of being Only-begotten, does not shut out the Spirit from His relation by way of nature to the Father.

But in speaking of " cause," and " of the cause," we do not by these words denote nature (for no one would give the same definition of " cause " and of " nature "), but we indicate the difference in manner of existence. For when we say that one is " caused," and that the other is " without cause," we do not divide the nature by the word " cause [6]", but only indicate the fact that the Son does not exist without generation, nor the Father by generation : but we must needs in the first place believe that something exists, and then scrutinize the manner of existence of the object of our belief : thus the question of existence is one, and that of the mode of existence is another. To say that anything exists without generation sets forth the mode of its existence, but what exists is not indicated by this phrase. If one were to ask a husbandman about a tree, whether it were planted or had grown of itself, and he were to answer either that the tree had not been planted or that it was the result of planting, would he by that answer declare the nature of the tree ? Surely not ; but while saying how it exists he would leave the question of its nature obscure and unexplained. So, in the other case, when we learn that He is unbegotten, we are taught in what mode He exists, and how it is fit that we should conceive Him as existing, but *what* He is we do not hear in that phrase. When, therefore, we acknowledge such a distinction in the case of the Holy Trinity, as to believe that one Person is the Cause, and another is of the Cause, we can no longer be accused of confounding the definition of the Persons by the community of nature.

Thus, since on the one hand the idea of cause differentiates the Persons of the Holy Trinity, declaring that one exists without a Cause, and another is of the Cause ; and since on the one hand the Divine nature is apprehended by every conception as unchangeable and undivided, for these reasons we properly declare the Godhead to be one, and God to be one, and employ in the singular all other names which express Divine attributes.

---

5 Deut. vi. 4.

6 The Paris Edit. omits αιτιον.

ON THE FAITH

TO SIMPLICIUS

GOD commands us by His prophet not to esteem any new God to be God, and not to worship any strange God [1]. Now it is clear that that is called new which is not from everlasting, and on the contrary, that is called everlasting which is not new. He, then, who does not believe that the Only-begotten God is from everlasting of the Father does not deny that He is new, for that which is not everlasting is confessedly new; and that which is new is not God, according to the saying of Scripture, "there shall not be in thee any new God [1]." Therefore he who says that the Son "once was not [2]," denies His Godhead. Again, He Who says "thou shalt never worship a strange God [3]," forbids us to worship another God; and the strange God is so called in contradistinction to our own God. Who, then, is our own God? Clearly, the true God. And who is the strange God? Surely, he who is alien from the nature of the true God. If, therefore, our own God is the true God, and if, as the heretics say, the Only-begotten God is not of the nature of the true God, He is a strange God, and not our God. But the Gospel says, the sheep "will not follow a stranger [4]." He that says He is created will make Him alien from the nature of the true God. What then will they do, who say that He is created? Do they worship that same created being as God [5], or do they not? For if they do not worship Him, they follow the Jews in denying the worship of Christ: and if they do worship Him, they are idolaters, for they worship one alien from the true God. But surely it is equally impious not to worship the Son, and to worship the strange God. We must then say that the Son is the true Son of the true Father, that we may both worship Him, and avoid condemnation as worshipping a strange God. But to those who quote from the Proverbs the passage, "the Lord created me [6]," and think that they hereby produce a strong argument that the Creator and Maker of all things was created, we must answer that the Only-begotten God was *made* for us many things. For He was the Word, and was made flesh; and He was God, and was made man; and He was without body, and was made a body; and besides, He was made "sin," and "a curse," and "a stone," and "an axe," and "bread," and "a lamb," and "a way," and "a door," and "a rock," and many such things; not being by nature any of these, but being made these things for our sakes, by way of dispensation. As, therefore, being the Word, He was for our sakes made flesh, and as, being God, He was made man, so also, being the Creator, He was made for our sakes a creature; for the flesh is created. As, then, He said by the prophet, "Thus saith the Lord, He that formed me from the womb to be His servant [7];" so He said also by Solomon, "The Lord created me as the beginning of His ways, for His works [6]." For all creation, as the Apostle says, is in servitude [8]. Therefore both He Who was formed in the Virgin's womb, according to the word of the prophet, is the servant, and not the Lord (that is to say, the man according to the flesh, in whom God was manifested), and also, in the other passage, He Who was created as the beginning of His ways is not God, but the man in whom God was manifested to us for the renewing again of the ruined way of man's salvation. So that, since we recognize two things in Christ, one Divine, the other human (the Divine by nature, but the human in the Incarnation), we accordingly claim for the Godhead that which is eternal, and that which is created we ascribe to His human nature. For as, according to the prophet, He was formed in the womb as a servant, so also, according to Solomon, He was manifested in

---

[1] Cf. Ps. lxxxi. 9 ; Ex. xxxiv. 14.
[2] Reading with Oehler, ὁ λέγων ὅτι ποτε οὐκ ἦν ὁ υἱὸς ; not as the Paris editions, ὁ λέγων ὅτι ποτε οὐκ ἦν, οὗτος.
[3] Cf. Ex. xx. 3.　　　　[4] S. John x. 5.
[5] Adding to the text of the Paris edit. θεὸν, with Oehler

[6] Prov. viii. 28.　　　　[7] Is. xlix 5.
[8] Cf. Rom. viii. 21. This clause is omitted in the Paris editions.

the flesh by means of this servile creation. But when they say, "if He was, He was not begotten, and if He was begotten He was not," let them learn that it is not fitting to ascribe to His Divine nature the attributes which belong to His fleshly origin [9]. For bodies which do not exist, are generated, and God makes those things to be which are not, but does not Himself come into being from that which is not. And for this reason also Paul calls Him "the brightness of glory [1]," that we may learn that as the light from the lamp is of the nature of that which sheds the brightness, and is united with it (for as soon as the lamp appears the light that comes from it shines out simultaneously), so in this place the Apostle would have us consider both that the Son is of the Father, and that the Father is never without the Son; for it is impossible that glory should be without radiance, as it is impossible that the lamp should be without brightness. But it is clear that as His being brightness is a testimony to His being in relation with the glory (for if the glory did not exist, the brightness shed from it would not exist), so, to say that the brightness "once was not [2]" is a declaration that the glory also was not, when the brightness was not; for it is impossible that the glory should be without the brightness. As therefore it is not possible to say in the case of the brightness, "If it was, it did not come into being, and if it came into being it was not," so it is in vain to say this of the Son, seeing that the Son is the brightness. Let those also who speak of "less" and "greater," in the case of the Father and the Son, learn from Paul not to measure things immeasurable. For the Apostle says that the Son is the express image of the Person of the Father [3]. It is clear then that however great the Person of the Father is, so great also is the express image of that Person; for it is not possible that the express image should be less than the Person contemplated in it. And this the great John also teaches when he says, "In the beginning was the Word, and the Word was with God [4]." For in saying that he was "in the beginning," and not "after the beginning," he showed that the beginning was never without the Word; and in declaring that "the Word was with God," he signified the absence of defect in the Son in relation to the Father; for the Word is contemplated as a whole together with the whole being of God. For if the Word were deficient in His own greatness so as not to be capable of relation with the whole being of God, we are compelled to suppose that that part of God

which extends beyond the Word is without the Word. But in fact the whole magnitude of the Word is contemplated together with the whole magnitude of God: and consequently in statements concerning the Divine nature, it is not admissible to speak of "greater" and "less."

As for those who say that the begotten is in its nature unlike the unbegotten, let them learn from the example of Adam and Abel not to talk nonsense. For Adam himself was not begotten according to the natural generation of men; but Abel was begotten of Adam. Now, surely, he who was never begotten is called unbegotten, and he who came into being by generation is called begotten [5]; yet the fact that he was not begotten did not hinder Adam from being a man, nor did the generation of Abel make him at all different from man's nature, but both the one and the other were men, although the one existed by being begotten, and the other without generation. So in the case of our statements as to the Divine nature, the fact of not being begotten, and that of being begotten, produce no diversity of nature, but, just as in the case of Adam and Abel the manhood is one, so is the Godhead one in the case of the Father and the Son.

Now touching the Holy Spirit also the blasphemers make the same statement as they do concerning the Lord, saying that He too is created. But the Church believes, as concerning the Son, so equally concerning the Holy Spirit, that He is uncreated, and that the whole creation becomes good by participation in the good which is above it, while the Holy Spirit needs not any to make Him good (seeing that He is good by virtue of His nature, as the Scripture testifies) [6]; that the creation is guided by the Spirit, while the Spirit gives guidance; that the creation is governed, while the Spirit governs; that the creation is comforted, while the Spirit comforts; that the creation is in bondage, while the Spirit gives freedom; that the creation is made wise, while the Spirit gives the grace of wisdom; that the creation partakes of the gifts, while the Spirit bestows them at His pleasure: "For all these worketh that one and the self-same Spirit, dividing to every man severally as He will [7]." And one may find multitudes of other proofs from the Scriptures that all the supreme and Divine attributes which are applied by the Scriptures to the Father and the Son are also to be contemplated in the Holy Spirit:—immortality, blessedness, goodness, wisdom, power, justice, holiness—

9 Reading γενεσέως with Oehler. The Paris editions read γεννησέως: but Oehler's reading seems to give a better sense.
1 Heb. i. 3.
2 Reading with Oehler ποτὲ for the τὲ of the Paris Editt.
3 Heb. i. 3.   4 S. John i. 1.

5 Inserting with Oehler the clause, καὶ ὁ γεννηθεὶς γεννητός, which is not in the text of the Paris Editt., though a corresponding clause appears in the Latin translation.
6 The reference may be to Ps. cxliii. 10.   7 1 Cor. xii. 11.

every excellent attribute is predicated of the Holy Spirit just as it is predicated of the Father and of the Son, with the exception of those by which the Persons are clearly and distinctly divided from each other; I mean, that the Holy Spirit is not called the Father, or the Son; but all other names by which the Father and the Son are named are applied by Scripture to the Holy Spirit also. By this, then, we apprehend that the Holy Spirit is above creation. Thus, where the Father and the Son are understood to be, there the Holy Spirit also is understood to be; for the Father and the Son are above creation, and this attribute the drift of our argument claims for the Holy Spirit. So it follows, that one who places the Holy Spirit above the creation has received the right and sound doctrine: for he will confess that uncreated nature which we behold in the Father and the Son and the Holy Spirit to be one.

But since they bring forward as a proof, according to their ideas, of the created nature of the Holy Spirit, that utterance of the prophet, which says, "He that stablisheth the thunder and createth the spirit, and declareth unto man His Christ[8]," we must consider this, that the prophet speaks of the creation of another Spirit, in the stablishing of the thunder, and not of the Holy Spirit. For the name of "thunder" is given in mystical language to the Gospel. Those, then, in whom arises firm and unshaken faith in the Gospel, pass from being flesh to become spirit, as the Lord says, "That which is born of the flesh is flesh, and that which is born of the Spirit is spirit[9]." It is God, then, Who by stablishing the voice of the Gospel makes the believer spirit: and he who is born of the Spirit and made spirit by such thunder, "declares" Christ; as the Apostle says, "No man can say that Jesus Christ is Lord but by the Holy Spirit[1]."

---

[8] Cf. Amos iv. 13 (**LXX.**).
[9] S. John iii. 6.   [1] 1 Cor. xii. 3.

II. ASCETIC AND MORAL

PREFACE

A FEW words are necessary to explain the scope and aim of this remarkable treatise. It is not the work of one who held a brief for monasticism. Gregory deals with the celibate life in a different way from other Catholic writers upon this theme. Athanasius and Basil both saw in it the means of exhibiting to the world the Christian life definitely founded on the orthodox faith ; and, for each celibate himself, this visible imitation of Christ would be more concentrated, when secular distractions and dissipations had been put aside for ever. Their aims were entirely moral and ecclesiastical. But Gregory deals with the entire human development in things spiritual. He has given the history of the struggle for moral and intellectual perfection, and the conditions of its success. He had his own inner Christian experience, the result of a recluse youth, on the one hand ; he had the systems of heathen and Christian philosophy on the other. The ideal life that he has sketched is as lofty in its aspiration as the latter, and is couched in philosophic rather than in Scriptural language ; but its scientific ground-work is entirely peculiar to himself. That groundwork is briefly this ; spirit must be freed, so as to be drawn to the Divine Spirit ; and to be so freed a "virginity" of the soul is necessary. He comes in this way to blame marriage, because in most of the marriages that he has known, this virginity of the soul is conspicuously absent. But he does not blame the married state in itself ; as he himself distinctly tells us. The virginity he seeks may exist even there ; and it is not by any means the same thing as celibacy. It is *disengagedness of heart ;* and is, as many passages in this treatise indicate, identical with philosophy, whose higher manifestations had long ago been defined as Love, called forth by the sight of the immaterial Beauty. Where this sight is not interrupted, or not treated with indifference, there Virginity exists. With Gregory philosophy had become Life, and it is virginity that keeps it so, and therein keeps it from being lost. Another word with which Gregory identifies virginity is "incorruptibility," in language sometimes which recalls the lines—

> "What, what is Virtue, but repose of mind ?
> A pure ethereal calm that knows no storm,
> Above the reach of wild ambition's wind,
> Above the passions that this world deform,
> And torture man, a proud malignant worm."

Yet no one would imagine that here the poet, any more than S. Paul in Ephes. vi. 24 (see p. 343, note 3), meant celibacy *per se*. But it may be asked, how came Gregory to use the word Virginity at all for pure disengagement of soul ? The answer seems to be, that he was very fond of metaphors and elaborate comparisons, ever since the days that he was a student of Rhetoric ; this treatise itself is full of similes from nature, and they are not so much poetry or rhetoric, as necessary means of bringing his meaning vividly before readers. Virginity, then, is one of these bold and telling figures ; and in his hands it is a very suggestive metaphor ; though certainly at times it runs away with him. The accusation, then, that when he identifies Piety and Virginity, he makes the former ·consist in a mere externality, is unfounded. He uses the one word for the other without apprising us that it is a metaphor, and he omits to give any dietary rules by which this virginity is secured. Therefore he *appears* to mean celibacy. But on the other hand no arguments can be drawn from this treatise against the monastic life ; only Gregory is busied with other matters. Rather, if the actual marriages of his time are such as he describes, it is a silent witness to the reasonableness, if not to the necessity, of such a life within the church. For this view of virginity as solving the question of Gregory's supposed marriage, see Prolegomena, p. 3.

ON VIRGINITY

INTRODUCTION.

THE object of this treatise is to create in its readers a passion for the life according to excellence. There are many distractions [1], to use the word of the Divine Apostle, incident to the secular life; and so this treatise would suggest, as a necessary door of entrance to the holier life, the calling of Virginity; seeing that, while it is not easy in the entanglements of this secular life to find quiet for that of Divine contemplation, those on the other hand who have bid farewell to its troubles can with promptitude, and without distraction, pursue assiduously their higher studies. Now, whereas all advice is in itself weak, and mere words of exhortation will not make the task of recommending what is beneficial easier to any one, unless he has first given a noble aspect to that which he urges on his hearer, this discourse will accordingly begin with the praises of Virginity; the exhortation will come at the end; moreover, as the beauty in anything gains lustre by the contrast with its opposite, it is requisite that some mention should be made of the vexations of everyday life. Then it will be quite in the plan of this work to introduce a sketch of the contemplative life, and to prove the impossibility of any one attaining it who feel's the world's anxieties. In the devotee bodily desire has become weak; and so there will follow an inquiry as to the true object of desire, for which (and which only) we have received from our Maker our power of desiring. When this has received all possible illustration, it will seem to follow naturally that we should consider some method to attain it; and the true virginity, which is free from any stain of sin, will be found to fit such a purpose. So all the intermediate part of the discourse, while it seems to look elsewhere, will be really tending to the praises of this virginity. All the particular rules obeyed by the followers of this high calling will, to avoid prolixity, be omitted here; the exhortation in the discourse will be introduced only in general terms, and for cases of wide application; but, in a way, particulars will be here included, and so nothing important will be overlooked, while prolixity is avoided. Each of us, too, is inclined to embrace some course of life with the greater enthusiasm, when he sees personalities who have already gained distinction in it; we have therefore made the requisite mention of saints who have gained their glory in celibacy. But further than this; the examples we have in biographies cannot stimulate to the attainment of excellence, so much as a living voice and an example which is still working for good; and so we have alluded to that most godly bishop [2], our father in God, who himself alone could be the master in such instructions. He will not indeed be mentioned by name, but by certain indications we shall say in cipher that he is meant. Thus, too, future readers will not think our advice unmeaning, when the candidate for this life is told to school himself by recent masters. But let them first fix their attention only on this: what such a master ought to be; then let them choose for their guidance those who have at any time by God's grace been raised up to be champions of this system of excellence; for either they will find what they seek, or at all events will be no longer ignorant what it ought to be.

CHAPTER I.

THE holy look of virginity is precious indeed in the judgment of all who make purity the test of beauty; but it belongs to those alone whose struggles to gain this object of a noble love are favoured and helped by the grace of God. Its praise is heard at once in the very name which goes with it; "Uncorrupted [3]" is the word

---

[1] περισπάσμων. The allusion must be to 1 Cor. vii. 35; but the actual word is not found in the whole of the N. T., though περιεσπᾶτο is used of Martha, S. Luke x. 40.

[2] Basil: rather than Gregory Thaumaturgus, as some have conjectured.

[3] τὸ ἄφθορον: this is connected just below with the Divine ἀφθαρσία. In commenting on the meaning of this latter word at the close of the Epistle to the Ephesians, Bishop Ellicott prefers to take it with ἀγαπώντων, "in a manner and an element that knows neither change, diminution, nor decay" ("in uncorruptness" R.V.): although in the six other passages where it occurs in S. Paul "it refers directly or indirectly to a higher sphere than the present."

commonly said of it, and this shows the kind of purity that is in it; thus we can measure by its equivalent term the height of this gift, seeing that amongst the many results of virtuous endeavour this alone has been honoured with the title of the thing that is uncorrupted. And if we must extol with laudations this gift from the great God, the words of His Apostle are sufficient in its praise; they are few, but they throw into the background all extravagant laudations; he only styles as "holy and without blemish [4]" her who has this grace for her ornament. Now if the achievement of this saintly virtue consists in making one "without blemish and holy," and these epithets are adopted in their first and fullest force to glorify the incorruptible Deity, what greater praise of virginity can there be than thus to be shown in a manner *deifying* those who share in her pure mysteries, so that they become partakers of His glory Who is in actual truth the only Holy and Blameless One; their purity and their incorruptibility being the means of bringing them into relationship with Him? Many who write lengthy laudations in detailed treatises, with the view of adding something to the wonder of this grace, unconsciously defeat, in my opinion, their own end; the fulsome manner in which they amplify their subject brings its credit into suspicion. Nature's greatnesses have their own way of striking with admiration; they do not need the pleading of words: the sky, for instance, or the sun, or any other wonder of the universe. In the business of this lower world words certainly act as a basement, and the skill of praise does impart a look of magnificence; so much so, that mankind are apt to suspect as the result of mere art the wonder produced by panegyric. So the one sufficient way of praising virginity will be to show that that virtue is above praise, and to evince our admiration of it by our lives rather than by our words. A man who takes this theme for ambitious praise has the appearance of supposing that one drop of his own perspiration will make an appreciable increase of the boundless ocean, if indeed he believes, as he does, that any human words can give more dignity to so rare a grace; he must be ignorant either of his own powers or of that which he attempts to praise.

CHAPTER II.

DEEP indeed will be the thought necessary to understand the surpassing excellence of this grace. It is comprehended in the idea of the Father incorrupt; and here at the outset is a paradox, viz. that virginity is found in Him, Who has a Son and yet without passion has begotten Him. It is included too in the nature of this Only-begotten God, Who struck the first note of all this moral innocence; it shines forth equally in His pure and passionless generation. Again a paradox; that the Son should be known to us by virginity. It is seen, too, in the inherent and incorruptible purity of the Holy Spirit; for when you have named the pure and incorruptible you have named virginity. It accompanies the whole supramundane existence; because of its passionlessness it is always present with the powers above; never separated from aught that is Divine, it never touches the opposite of this. All whose instinct and will have found their level in virtue are beautified with this perfect purity of the uncorrupted state; all who are ranked in the opposite class of character are what they are, and are called so, by reason of their fall from purity. What force of expression, then, will be adequate to such a grace? How can there be no cause to fear lest the greatness of its intrinsic value should be impaired by the efforts of any one's eloquence? The estimate of it which he will create will be less than that which his hearers had before. It will be well, then, to omit all laudation in this case; we cannot lift words to the height of our theme. On the contrary, it is possible to be ever mindful of this gift of God; and our lips may always speak of this blessing; that, though it is the property of spiritual existence and of such singular excellence, yet by the love of God it has been bestowed on those who have received their life from the will of the flesh and from blood; that, when human nature has been debased by passionate inclinations, it stretches out its offer of purity like a hand to raise it up again and make it look above. This, I think, was the reason why our Master, Jesus Christ Himself, the Fountain of all innocence, did not come into the world by wedlock. It was, to divulge by the manner of His Incarnation this great secret; that purity is the only complete indication [5] of the presence of God and of His coming, and that no one can in reality secure this for himself, unless he has altogether estranged himself from the passions of the flesh. What happened in the stainless Mary when the fulness of the Godhead which was in Christ shone out through her, that happens in every soul that leads by rule the virgin life. No longer indeed does the Master come with bodily presence; "we know Christ no longer accord-

---

[4] *i. e.* of immortality above, and might so, if the construction allowed, be taken with χάρις. This illustrates Gregory's use of ἀφθαρσία in its human relation.

[4] Eph. v. 27 (of the church).

[5] δείξασθαι. Livineius conjectures δέξασθαι; so also Cod. Reg. Cf. Sedulius:

"Domus pudici pectoris
Templum repente fit Dei."

ing to the flesh [6]"; but, spiritually, He dwells in us and brings His Father with Him, as the Gospel somewhere [7] tells. Seeing, then, that virginity means so much as this, that while it remains in Heaven with the Father of spirits, and moves in the dance of the celestial powers, it nevertheless stretches out hands for man's salvation; that while it is the channel which draws down the Deity to share man's estate, it keeps wings for man's desires to rise to heavenly things, and is a bond of union between the Divine and human, by its mediation bringing into harmony these existences so widely divided—what words could be discovered powerful enough to reach this wondrous height? But still, it is monstrous to seem like creatures without expression and without feeling; and we must choose (if we are silent) one of two things; either to appear never to have felt the special beauty of virginity, or to exhibit ourselves as obstinately blind to all beauty: we have consented therefore to speak briefly about this virtue, according to the wish of him who has assigned us this task, and whom in all things we must obey. But let no one expect from us any display of style; even if we wished it, perhaps we could not produce it, for we are quite unversed in that kind of writing. Even if we possessed such power, we would not prefer the favour of the few to the edification of the many. A writer of sense should have, I take it, for his chiefest object not to be admired above all other writers, but to profit both himself and them, the many.

CHAPTER III.

WOULD indeed that some profit might come to myself from this effort! I should have undertaken this labour with the greater readiness, if I could have hope of sharing, according to the Scripture, in the fruits of the plough and the threshing-floor; the toil would then have been a pleasure. As it is, this my knowledge of the beauty of virginity is in some sort vain and useless to me, just as the corn is to the muzzled ox that treads [8] the floor, or the water that streams from the precipice to a thirsty man when he cannot reach it. Happy they who have still the power of choosing the better way, and have not debarred themselves from it by engagements of the secular life, as we have, whom a gulf now divides from glorious virginity: no one can climb up to that who has once planted his foot upon the secular life. We are but spectators of others' blessings and witnesses to the happiness of another [9] class.

Even if we strike out some fitting thoughts about virginity, we shall not be better than the cooks and scullions who provide sweet luxuries for the tables of the rich, without having any portion themselves in what they prepare. What a blessing if it had been otherwise, if we had not to learn the good by after-regrets! Now *they* are the enviable ones, *they* succeed even beyond their prayers and their desires, who have not put out of their power the enjoyment of these delights. We are like those who have a wealthy society with which to compare their own poverty, and so are all the more vexed and discontented with their present lot. The more exactly we understand the riches of virginity, the more we must bewail the other life; for we realize by this contrast with better things, how poor it is. I do not speak only of the future rewards in store for those who have lived thus excellently, but those rewards also which they have while alive here; for if any one would make up his mind to measure exactly the difference between the two courses, he would find it well-nigh as great as that between heaven and earth. The truth of this statement may be known by looking at actual facts.

But in writing this sad tragedy what will be a fit beginning? How shall we really bring to view the evils common to life? All men know them by experience, but somehow nature has contrived to blind the actual sufferers so that they willingly ignore their condition. Shall we begin with its choicest sweets? Well then, is not the sum total of all that is hoped for in marriage to get delightful companionship? Grant this obtained; let us sketch a marriage in every way most happy; illustrious birth, competent means, suitable ages, the very flower of the prime of life, deep affection, the very best that each can think of the other [1], that sweet rivalry of each wishing to surpass the other in loving; in addition, popularity, power, wide reputation, and everything else. But observe that even beneath this array of blessings the fire of an inevitable pain is smouldering. I do not speak of the envy that is always springing up against those of distinguished rank, and the liability to attack which hangs over those who seem prosperous, and that natural hatred of superiors shown by those who do not share equally in the good fortune, which make these seemingly favoured ones pass an anxious time more full of pain than pleasure. I omit that from the picture, and will suppose that envy against them is asleep; although it would not be easy to find a single life in which both these blessings were joined, *i. e.* happiness above the common, and

---

6 2 Cor. v. 16.   7 S. John xiv. 23.
8 ἐπιστρεφομένῳ τὴν ἅλωνα. This word is used for "walking over," in Hesiod, *Theogon.* 753, γαῖαν ἐπιστρέφεται.
9 ἑτέρων, following Cod. Reg., for ἑκατέρων.

1 ὑπὲρ τοῦ ἄλλου (a *late* use of ἄλλος). This was Livineius' conjecture for τῶν ἄλλων: the interchange of υ and ν is a common mistake.

escape from envy. However, let us, if so it is to be, suppose a married life free from all such trials ; and let us see if it is possible for those who live with such an amount of good fortune to enjoy it. Why, what kind of vexation is left, you will ask, when even envy of their happiness does not reach them? I affirm that this very thing, this sweetness that surrounds their lives, is the spark which kindles pain. They are human all the time, things weak and perishing ; they have to look upon the tombs of their progenitors ; and so pain is inseparably bound up with their existence, if they have the least power of reflection. This continued expectancy of death, realized by no sure tokens, but hanging over them the terrible uncertainty of the future, disturbs their present joy, clouding it over with the fear of what is coming. If only, before experience comes, the results of experience could be learnt, or if, when one has entered on this course, it were possible by some other means of conjecture to survey the reality, then what a crowd of deserters would run from marriage into the virgin life ; what care and eagerness never to be entangled in that retentive snare, where no one knows for certain how the net galls till they have actually entered it ! You would see there, if only you could do it without danger, many contraries uniting ; smiles melting into tears, pain mingled with pleasure, death always hanging by expectation over the children that are born, and putting a finger upon each of the sweetest joys. Whenever the husband looks at the beloved face, that moment the fear of separation accompanies the look. If he listens to the sweet voice, the thought comes into his mind that some day he will not hear it. Whenever he is glad with gazing on her beauty, then he shudders most with the presentiment of mourning her loss. When he marks all those charms which to youth are so precious and which the thoughtless seek for, the bright eyes beneath the lids, the arching eyebrows, the cheek with its sweet and dimpling smile, the natural red that blooms upon the lips, the gold-bound hair shining in many-twisted masses on the head, and all that transient grace, then, though he may be little given to reflection, he must have this thought also in his inmost soul, that some day all this beauty will melt away and become as nothing, turned after all this show into noisome and unsightly bones, which wear no trace, no memorial, no remnant of that living bloom. Can he live delighted when he thinks of that? Can he trust in these treasures which he holds as if they would be always his? Nay, it is plain that he will stagger as if he were mocked by a dream, and will have his faith in life shaken, and will look upon what he sees as no longer his. You will understand, if you have a comprehensive view of things as they are, that nothing in this life looks that which it is. It shows to us by the illusions of our imagination one thing, instead of something else. Men gaze open-mouthed at it, and it mocks them with hopes ; for a while it hides itself beneath this deceitful show ; then all of a sudden in the reverses of life it is revealed as something different from that which men's hopes, conceived by its fraud in foolish hearts, had pictured. Will life's sweetness seem worth taking delight in to him who reflects on this? Will he ever be able really to feel it, so as to have joy in the goods he holds? Will he not, disturbed by the constant fear of some reverse, have the use without the enjoyment? I will but mention the portents, dreams, omens, and such-like things which by a foolish habit of thought are taken notice of, and always make men fear the worst. But her time of labour comes upon the young wife ; and the occasion is regarded not as the bringing of a child into the world, but as the approach of death ; in bearing it is expected that she will die ; and, indeed, often this sad presentiment is true, and before they spread the birthday feast, before they taste any of their expected joys, they have to change their rejoicing into lamentation. Still in love's fever, still at the height of their passionate affection, not yet having grasped life's sweetest gifts, as in the vision of a dream, they are suddenly torn away from all they possessed. But what comes next? Domestics, like conquering foes, dismantle the bridal chamber ; they deck it for the funeral, but it is death's [2] room now ; they make the useless wailings [3] and beatings of the hands. Then there is the memory of former days, curses on those who advised the marriage, recriminations against friends who did not stop it ; blame thrown on parents whether they be alive or dead, bitter outbursts against human destiny, arraigning of the whole course of nature, complaints and accusations even against the Divine government ; war within the man himself, and fighting with those who would admonish ; no repugnance to the most shocking words and acts. In some this state of mind continues, and their reason is more completely swallowed up by grief ; and *their* tragedy has a sadder ending, the victim not enduring to survive the calamity. But rather than this let us suppose a happier case. The danger of childbirth is past ; a child is born to them, the very image of its parents' beauty. Are the occasions for grief at all lessened thereby? Rather they are

---

[2] There is a play on the words θάλαμος and θάνατος : "the one is changed into the other."

[3] ἐπὶ τούτων ἀνακλήσεις : "*amongst* these", *i. e.* the domestics. Livineius reads τούτοις, and renders "Succedunt inutilis revocatio, inanis manuum plausus," *i. e.* as the last funeral act.

increased ; for the parents retain all their former fears, and feel in addition those on behalf of the child, lest anything should happen to it in its bringing up ; for instance a bad accident, or by some turn of misfortunes a sickness, a fever [4], any dangerous disease. Both parents share alike in these ; but who could recount the special anxieties of the wife ? We omit the most obvious, which all can understand, the weariness of pregnancy, the danger in childbirth, the cares of nursing, the tearing of her heart in two for her offspring, and, if she is the mother of many, the dividing of her soul into as many parts as she has children ; the tenderness with which she herself feels all that is happening to them. That is well understood by every one. But the oracle of God tells us that she is not her own mistress, but finds her resources only in him whom wedlock has made her lord ; and so, if she be for ever so short a time left alone, she feels as if she were separated from her head, and can ill bear it ; she even takes this short absence of her husband to be the prelude to her widowhood ; her fear makes her at once give up all hope ; accordingly her eyes, filled with terrified suspense, are always fixed upon the door ; her ears are always busied with what others are whispering ; her heart, stung with her fears, is well-nigh bursting even before any bad [5] news has arrived ; a noise in the doorway, whether fancied or real, acts as a messenger of ill, and on a sudden shakes her very soul ; most likely all outside is well, and there is no cause to fear at all ; but her fainting spirit is quicker than any message, and turns her fancy from good tidings to despair. Thus even the most favoured live, and they are not altogether to be envied ; their life is not to be compared to the freedom of virginity. Yet this hasty sketch has omitted many of the more distressing details. Often this young wife too, just wedded, still brilliant in bridal grace, still perhaps blushing when her bridegroom enters, and shyly stealing furtive glances at him, when passion is all the more intense because modesty prevents it being shown, suddenly has to take the name of a poor lonely widow and be called all that is pitiable. Death comes in an instant and changes that bright creature in her white and rich attire into a black-robed mourner. He takes off the bridal ornaments and clothes her with the colours of bereavement. There is darkness in the once cheerful room, and the waiting-women sing their long dirges. She hates her friends when they try to soften her grief ; she will not take food ; she wastes away, and in her

soul's deep dejection has a strong longing only for her death, a longing which often lasts till it comes. Even supposing that time puts an end to this sorrow, still another comes, whether she has children or not. If she has, they are fatherless, and, as objects of pity themselves, renew the memory of her loss. If she is childless, then the name of her lost husband is rooted up, and this grief is greater than the seeming consolation. I will say little of the other special sorrows of widowhood ; for who could enumerate them all exactly ? She finds her enemies in her relatives. Some actually take advantage of her affliction. Others exult over her loss, and see with malignant joy the home falling to pieces, the insolence of the servants, and the other distresses visible in such a case, of which there are plenty. In consequence of these, many women are compelled to risk once more the trial of the same things, not being able to endure this bitter derision. As if they could revenge insults by increasing their own sufferings ! Others, remembering the past, will put up with anything rather than plunge a second time into the like troubles. If you wish to learn all the trials of this married life, listen to those women who actually know it. How they congratulate those who have chosen from the first the virgin life, and have not had to learn by experience about the better way, that virginity is fortified against all these ills, that it has no orphan state, no widowhood to mourn ; it is always in the presence of the undying Bridegroom ; it has the offspring of devotion always to rejoice in ; it sees continually a home that is truly its own, furnished with every treasure because the Master always dwells there ; in this case death does not bring separation, but union with Him Who is longed for ; for when (a soul) departs [6], then it is with Christ, as the Apostle says. But it is time, now that we have examined on the one side the feelings of those whose lot is happy, to make a revelation of other lives, where poverty and adversity and all the other evils which men have to suffer are a fixed condition ; deformities, I mean, and diseases, and all other lifelong afflictions. He whose life is contained in himself either escapes them altogether or can bear them easily, possessing a collected mind which is not distracted from itself ; while he who shares himself with wife and child often has not a moment to bestow even upon regrets for his own condition, because anxiety for his dear ones fills his heart. But it is superfluous to dwell upon that which every one knows. If to what seems prosperity

---

[4] Reading πύρωσιν, with Galesinius : the Paris Editt. read πήρωσιν.
[5] νεώτερον, in a bad sense. So Zosimus, lib. i. p. 658, πράγματα Ῥωμαίοις νεώτερα μηχανήσασθαι.

[6] ἀναλύσῃ : Philip. i. 23. Tertullian (*De Patient.* 9) translates, " Cupis recipi (*i. e.* to flit, depart) jam et esse cum Domino." Peza, however, says that the metaphor is taken from unharnessing after a race. Chrysostom and Jerome seem to take it of loosing off the cable.

such pain and weariness is bound, what may we not expect of the opposite condition? Every description which attempts to represent it to our view will fall short of the reality. Yet perhaps we may in a very few words declare the depths of its misery. Those whose lot is contrary to that which passes as prosperous receive their sorrows as well from causes contrary to that. Prosperous lives are marred by the expectancy, or the presence, of death; but the misery of these is that death delays his coming. These lives then are widely divided by opposite feelings; although equally without hope, they converge to the same end. So many-sided, then, so strangely different are the ills with which marriage supplies the world. There is pain always, whether children are born, or can never be expected, whether they live, or die. One abounds in them but has not enough means for their support; another feels the want of an heir to the great fortune he has toiled for, and regards as a blessing the other's misfortune; each of them, in fact, wishes for that very thing which he sees the other regretting. Again, one man loses by death a much-loved [7] son; another has a reprobate son alive; both equally to be pitied, though the one mourns over the death, the other over the life, of his boy. Neither will I do more than mention how sadly and disastrously family jealousies and quarrels, arising from real or fancied causes, end. Who could go completely into all those details? If you would know what a network of these evils human life is, you need not go back again to those old stories which have furnished subjects to dramatic poets. *They* are regarded as myths on account of their shocking extravagance; there are in them murders and eating of children, husband-murders, murders of mothers and brothers, incestuous unions, and every sort of disturbance of nature; and yet the old chronicler begins the story which ends in such horrors with marriage. But turning from all that, gaze only upon the tragedies that are being enacted on this life's stage; it is marriage that supplies mankind with actors there. Go to the law-courts and read through the laws there; then you will know the shameful secrets of marriage. Just as when you hear a physician explaining various diseases, you understand the misery of the human frame by learning the number and the kind of sufferings it is liable to, so when you peruse the laws and read there the strange variety of crimes in marriage to which their penalties are attached, you will have a pretty accurate idea of its properties; for the law does not provide remedies for evils which do not exist, any more than a physician has a treatment for diseases which are never known.

CHAPTER IV.

But we need no longer show in this narrow way the drawback of this life, as if the number of its ills was limited to adulteries, dissensions, and plots. I think we should take the higher and truer view, and say at once that none of that evil in life, which is visible in all its business and in all its pursuits, can have any hold over a man, if he will not put himself in the fetters of this course. The truth of what we say will be clear thus. A man who, seeing through the illusion with the eye of his spirit purged, lifts himself above the struggling world, and, to use the words of the Apostle, slights it all as but dung, in a way exiling himself altogether from human life by his abstinence from marriage,—that man has no fellowship whatever with the sins of mankind, such as avarice, envy, anger, hatred, and everything of the kind. He has an exemption from all this, and is in every way free and at peace; there is nothing in him to provoke his neighbours' envy, because he clutches none of those objects round which envy in this life gathers. He has raised his own life above the world, and prizing virtue as his only precious possession he will pass his days in painless peace and quiet. For virtue is a possession which, though all according to their capacity should share it, yet will be always in abundance for those who thirst after it; unlike the occupation of the lands on this earth, which men divide into sections, and the more they add to the one the more they take from the other, so that the one person's gain is his fellow's loss; whence arise the fights for the lion's share, from men's hatred of being cheated. But the larger owner of *this* possession is never envied; he who snatches the lion's share does no damage to him who claims equal participation; as each is capable each has this noble longing satisfied, while the wealth of virtues in those who are already occupiers [8] is not exhausted. The man, then, who, with his eyes only on such a life, makes virtue, which has no limit that man can devise, his only treasure, will surely never brook to bend his soul to any of those low courses which multitudes tread. He will not admire earthly riches, or human power, or any of those things which folly seeks. If, indeed, his mind is still pitched so low, he is outside our band of novices, and our words

---

[7] ἠγαπημένος παῖς. Cod. Reg. has ὁ καταθύμιος, a favourite word with Gregory. Livineius reads ὁ καθήμενος, which he renders "nanus" (*i. e.* of low stature), and cites Pollux Onomast. lib. 3, c. 24 (where ἀποκαθήμενος = iners); it might also bear the meaning of "stay-at-home," in contrast to the prodigal in the next sentence.

[8] ἐν τοῖς προλαβοῦσιν. Galesinius' Latin seems wrong here, "rebus iis quas supra meminimus," though the words very often have that force in Gregory.

do not apply to him. But if his thoughts are above, walking as it were with God, he will be lifted out of the maze of all these errors; for the predisposing cause of them all, marriage, has not touched him. Now the wish to be before others is the deadly sin of pride, and one would not be far wrong in saying that this is the seed-root of all the thorns of sin; but it is from reasons connected with marriage that this pride mostly begins. To show what I mean, we generally find the grasping man throwing the blame on his nearest kin; the man mad after notoriety and ambition generally makes his family responsible for this sin: "he must not be thought inferior to his forefathers; he must be deemed a great man by the generation to come by leaving his children historic records of himself": so also the other maladies of the soul, envy, spite, hatred and such-like, are connected with this cause; they are to be found amongst those who are eager about the things of this life. He who has fled from it gazes as from some high watch-tower on the prospect of humanity, and pities these slaves of vanity for their blindness in setting such a value on bodily well-being. He sees some distinguished person giving himself airs because of his public honours, and wealth, and power, and only laughs at the folly of being so puffed up. He gives to the years of human life the longest number, according to the Psalmist's computation, and then compares this atom-interval with the endless ages, and pities the vain glory of those who excite themselves for such low and petty and perishable things. What, indeed, amongst the things here is there enviable in that which so many strive for,—honour? What is gained by those who win it? The mortal remains mortal whether he is honoured or not. What good does the possessor of many acres gain in the end? Except that the foolish man thinks his own that which never belongs to him, ignorant seemingly in his greed that "the earth is the Lord's, and the fulness thereof [9]," for "God is king of all the earth [9]." It is the passion of having which gives men a false title of lordship over that which can never belong to them. "The earth," says the wise Preacher, "abideth for ever [1]," ministering to every generation, first one, then another, that is born upon it; but men, though they are so little even their own masters, that they are brought into life without knowing it by their Maker's will, and before they wish are withdrawn from it, nevertheless in their excessive vanity think that they are her lords; that they, now born, now dying, rule that which remains continually. One who reflecting on this holds cheaply all

that mankind prizes, whose only love is the divine life, because "all flesh is grass, and all the glory of man as the flower of grass [2]," can never care for this grass which "to-day is and to-morrow is not"; studying the divine ways, he knows not only that human life has no fixity, but that the entire universe will not keep on its quiet course for ever; he neglects his existence here as an alien and a passing thing; for the Saviour said, "Heaven and earth shall pass away [3]," the whole of necessity awaits its re-fashioning. As long as he is "in this tabernacle [4]," exhibiting mortality, weighed down with this existence, he laments the lengthening of his sojourn in it; as the Psalmist-poet says in his heavenly songs. Truly, they live in darkness who sojourn in these living tabernacles; wherefore that preacher, groaning at the continuance of this sojourn, says, "Woe is me that my sojourn is prolonged [5]," and he attributes the cause of his dejection to "darkness"; for we know that darkness is called in the Hebrew language "kedar." It is indeed a darkness as of the night which envelops mankind, and prevents them seeing this deceit and knowing that all which is most prized by the living, and moreover all which is the reverse, exists only in the conception of the unreflecting, and is in itself nothing; there is no such reality anywhere as obscurity of birth, or illustrious birth, or glory, or splendour, or ancient renown, or present elevation, or power over others, or subjection. Wealth and comfort, poverty and distress, and all the other inequalities of life, seem to the ignorant, applying the test of pleasure, vastly different from each other. But to the higher understanding they are all alike; one is not of greater value than the other; because life runs on to the finish with the same speed through all these opposites, and in the lots of either class there remains the same power of choice to live well or ill, "through armour on the right hand and on the left, through evil report and good report [6]." Therefore the clear-seeing mind which measures reality will journey on its path without turning, accomplishing its appointed time from its birth to its exit; it is neither softened by the pleasures nor beaten down by the hardships; but, as is the way with travellers, it keeps advancing always, and takes but little notice of the views presented. It is the travellers' way to press on to their journey's end, no matter whether they are passing through meadows and cultivated farms, or through wilder and more rugged spots; a smiling landscape does not detain them; nor a gloomy one check their speed. So, too, that lofty mind will press straight on to its self-imposed end,

---

9 Ps. xxiv. 1; xlvii. 7.   1 Eccles. i. 4.

2 1 Pet. i. 24.   3 S. Matt. xxiv. 35.   4 2 Cor. v. 4.
5 Ps cxx 5 6 (LXX.).   6 2 Cor. vi. 7.

not turning aside to see anything on the way. It passes through life, but its gaze is fixed on heaven ; it is the good steersman directing the bark to some landmark there.   But the grosser mind looks down ; it bends its energies to bodily pleasures as surely as the sheep stoop to their pasture ; it lives for gorging and still lower pleasures [7] ; it is alienated from the life of God [8], and a stranger to the promise of the Covenants ; it recognizes no good but the gratification of the body.   It is a mind such as this that "walks in darkness [9]," and invents all the evil in this life of ours ; avarice, passions unchecked, unbounded luxury, lust of power, vain-glory, the whole mob of moral diseases that invade men's homes.   In these vices, one somehow holds closely to another ; where one has entered all the rest seem to follow, dragging each other in a natural order, just as in a chain, when you have jerked the first link, the others cannot rest, and even the link at the other end feels the motion of the first, which passes thence by virtue of their contiguity through the intervening links; so firmly are men's vices linked together by their very nature ; when one of them has gained the mastery of a soul, the rest of the train follow.   If you want a graphic picture of this accursed chain, suppose a man who because of some special pleasure it gives him is a victim to his thirst for fame ; then a desire to increase his fortune follows close upon this thirst for fame ; he becomes grasping ; but only because the first vice leads him on to this. Then this grasping after money and superiority engenders either anger with his kith and kin, or pride towards his inferiors, or envy of those above him ; then hypocrisy comes in after this envy ; a soured temper after that ; a misanthropical spirit after that ; and behind them all a state of condemnation which ends in the dark fires of hell.   You see the chain ; how all follows from one cherished passion.   Seeing, then, that this inseparable train of moral diseases has entered once for all into the world, one single way of escape is pointed out to us in the exhortations of the inspired writings ; and that is to separate ourselves from the life which involves this sequence of sufferings.   If we haunt Sodom, we cannot escape the rain of fire ; nor if one who has fled out of her looks back upon her desolation, can he fail to become a pillar of salt rooted to the spot.   We cannot be rid of the Egyptian bondage, unless we leave Egypt, that is, this life that lies under water [1], and pass, not that Red Sea, but this black and gloomy Sea of life.   But suppose we remain in this evil bondage, and, to use the Master's words, "the truth shall not have made us free," how can one who seeks a lie and wanders in the maze of this world ever come to the truth ? How can one who has surrendered his existence to be chained by nature run away from this captivity ? An illustration will make our meaning clearer. A winter torrent [2], which, impetuous in itself, becomes swollen and carries down beneath its stream trees and boulders and anything that comes in its way, is death and danger to those alone who live along its course ; for those who have got well out of its way it rages in vain. Just so, only the man who lives in the turmoil of life has to feel its force ; only he has to receive those sufferings which nature's stream, descending in a flood of troubles, must, to be true to its kind, bring to those who journey on its banks.   But if a man leaves this torrent, and these "proud waters [3]," he will escape from being "a prey to the teeth" of this life, as the Psalm goes on to say, and, as "a bird from the snare," on virtue's wings.   This simile, then, of the torrent holds ; human life *is* a tossing and tumultuous stream sweeping down to find its natural level ; none of the objects sought for in it last till the seekers are satisfied ; all that is carried to them by this stream comes near, just touches them, and passes on ; so that the present moment in this impetuous flow eludes enjoyment, for the after-current snatches it from their view.   It would be our interest therefore to keep far away from such a stream, lest, engaged on temporal things, we should neglect eternity.   How can a man keep for ever anything here, be his love for it never so passionate ?   Which of life's most cherished objects endures always ? What flower of prime ? What gift of strength and beauty ? What wealth, or fame, or power ? They all have their transient bloom, and then melt away into their opposites. Who can continue in life's prime ? Whose strength lasts for ever ? Has not Nature made the bloom of beauty even more shortlived than the shows of spring ? For they blossom in their season, and after withering for a while again revive ; after another shedding they are again in leaf, and retain their beauty of to-day to a late prime.   But Nature exhibits the human bloom only in the spring of early life ; then she kills it ; it is vanished in the frosts of age. All other delights also deceive the bodily eye for a time, and then pass behind the veil of oblivion. Nature's inevitable changes are many ; they agonize him whose love is passionate.   One way of escape is open : it is, to be attached to none of these things, and to get as far away as

7 τοῖς μετὰ γαστέρα (not, γαστέρος), Cod. Reg. ; cf. Gregor. Nazian. orat. xvi. p. 250, δοῦλος γαστρὸς, καὶ τῶν ὑπὸ γαστέρα. Euseb. lib. 7, c. 20, ταῖς ὑπὸ γαστέρα πλησμοναῖς.
8 Eph. ii. 12 ; iv. 18.   9 S. John xii. 35.
1 ὑποβρύχιον ; referring to the floods of the Nile.

2 Iliad, v. 87.
3 Ps cxxiv. 5, 6, 7 : τὸ ὕδωρ τὸ ἀνυπόστατον (LXX.), *i. e.* unsupportable.

possible from the society of this emotional and sensual world ; or rather, for a man to go outside the feelings which his own body gives rise to. Then, as he does not live for the flesh, he will not be subject to the troubles of the flesh. But this amounts to living for the spirit only, and imitating all we can the employment of the world of spirits. There they neither marry, nor are given in marriage. Their work and their excellence is to contemplate the Father of all purity, and to beautify the lines of their own character from the Source of all beauty, so far as imitation of It is possible.

CHAPTER V.

Now we declare that Virginity is man's "fellow-worker" and helper in achieving the aim of this lofty passion. In other sciences men have devised certain practical methods for cultivating the particular subject ; and so, I take it, virginity is the practical method in the science of the Divine life, furnishing men with the power of assimilating themselves with spiritual natures. The constant endeavour in such a course is to prevent the nobility of the soul from being lowered by those sensual outbreaks, in which the mind no longer maintains its heavenly thoughts and upward gaze, but sinks down to the emotions belonging to the flesh and blood. How can the soul which is riveted [4] to the pleasures of the flesh and busied with merely human longings turn a disengaged eye upon its kindred intellectual light? This evil, ignorant, and prejudiced bias towards material things will prevent it. The eyes of swine, turning naturally downward, have no glimpse of the wonders of the sky ; no more can the soul whose body drags it down look any longer upon the beauty above ; it must pore perforce upon things which though natural are low and animal. To look with a free devoted gaze upon heavenly delights, the soul will turn itself from earth ; it will not even partake of the recognized indulgences of the secular life ; it will transfer all its powers of affection from material objects to the intellectual contemplation of immaterial beauty. Virginity of the body is devised to further such a disposition of the soul ; it aims at creating in it a complete forgetfulness of natural emotions ; it would prevent the necessity of ever descending to the call of fleshly needs. Once freed from such, the soul runs no risk of becoming, through a growing habit of indulging in that which seems to a certain extent conceded by nature's law, inattentive and ignorant of Divine and undefiled delights. Purity of the heart, that master of our lives, alone can capture them.

CHAPTER VI.

This, I believe, makes the greatness of the prophet Elias, and of him who afterwards appeared in the spirit and power of Elias, than whom " of those that are born of women there was none greater [5]." If their history conveys any other mystic lesson, surely this above all is taught by their special mode of life, that the man whose thoughts are fixed upon the invisible is necessarily separated from all the ordinary events of life ; his judgments as to the True Good cannot be confused and led astray by the deceits arising from the senses. Both, from their youth upwards, exiled themselves from human society, and in a way from human nature, in their neglect of the usual kinds of meat and drink, and their sojourn in the desert. The wants of each were satisfied by the nourishment that came in their way, so that their taste might remain simple and unspoilt, as their ears were free from any distracting noise, and their eyes from any wandering look. Thus they attained a cloudless calm of soul, and were raised to that height of Divine favour which Scripture records of each. Elias, for instance, became the dispenser of God's earthly gifts ; he had authority to close at will the uses of the sky against the sinners and to open them to the penitent. John is not said indeed to have done any miracle ; but the gift in him was pronounced by Him Who sees the secrets of a man greater than any prophet's. This was so, we may presume, because both, from beginning to end, so dedicated their hearts to the Lord that they were unsullied by any earthly passion ; because the love of wife or child, or any other human call, did not intrude upon them, and they did not even think their daily sustenance worthy of anxious thought ; because they showed themselves to be above any magnificence [6] of dress, and made shift with that which chance offered them, one clothing himself in goat-skins, the other with camel's hair. It is my belief that they would not have reached to this loftiness of spirit, if marriage had softened them. This is not simple history only ; it is " written for our admonition [7]," that we might direct our lives by theirs. What, then, do we learn thereby? This : that the man who longs for union with God must, like those saints, detach his mind from all worldly business. It is impossible for the mind which is poured into many channels to win its way to the knowledge and the love of God.

---

[4] Cf. De Animâ et Resurr., p. 225, D. for the metaphor.

[5] S. Matt. xii. 11.
[6] σεμνότητος ; not as Galesinius renders, "asperitate quadam gravi."   [7] 1 Cor. x. 11.

CHAPTER VII.

An illustration will make our teaching on this subject clearer. Imagine a stream flowing from a spring and dividing itself off into a number of accidental channels. As long as it proceeds so, it will be useless for any purpose of agriculture, the dissipation of its waters making each particular current small and feeble, and therefore slow. But if one were to mass these wandering and widely dispersed rivulets again into one single channel, he would have a full and collected stream for the supplies which life demands. Just so the human mind (so it seems to me), as long as its current spreads itself in all directions over the pleasures of the sense, has no power that is worth the naming of making its way towards the Real Good; but once call it back and collect it upon itself, so that it may begin to move without scattering and wandering towards the activity which is congenial and natural to it, it will find no obstacle in mounting to higher things, and in grasping realities. We often see water contained in a pipe bursting upwards through this constraining force, which will not let it leak; and this, in spite of its natural gravitation: in the same way, the mind of man, enclosed in the compact channel of an habitual continence, and not having any side issues, will be raised by virtue of its natural powers of motion to an exalted love. In fact, its Maker ordained that it should always move, and to stop is impossible to it; when therefore it is prevented employing this power upon trifles, it cannot be but that it will speed toward the truth, all improper exits being closed. In the case of many turnings we see travellers can keep to the direct route, when they have learnt that the other roads are wrong, and so avoid them; the more they keep out of these wrong directions, the more they will preserve the straight course; in like manner the mind in turning from vanities will recognize the truth. The great prophets, then, whom we have mentioned seem to teach this lesson, viz. to entangle ourselves with none of the objects of this world's effort; marriage is one of these, or rather it is the primal root of all striving after vanities.

CHAPTER VIII.

Let no one think however that herein we depreciate marriage as an institution. We are well aware that it is not a stranger to God's blessing. But since the common instincts of mankind can plead sufficiently on its behalf, instincts which prompt by a spontaneous bias to take the high road of marriage for the procreation of children, whereas Virginity in a way thwarts this natural impulse, it is a superfluous task to compose formally an Exhortation to marriage. We put forward the pleasure of it instead, as a most doughty champion on its behalf. It may be however, notwithstanding this, that there *is* some need of such a treatise, occasioned by those who travesty the teaching of the Church. Such persons [8] "have their conscience seared with a hot iron," as the Apostle expresses it; and very truly too, considering that, deserting the guidance of the Holy Spirit for the "doctrines of devils," they have some ulcers and blisters stamped upon their hearts, abominating God's creatures, and calling them "foul," "seducing," "mischievous," and so on. "But what have I to do to judge them that are without[9]?" asks the Apostle. Truly those persons are outside the Court in which the words of our mysteries are spoken; they are not installed under God's roof, but in the monastery of the Evil One. They "are taken captive by him at his will[1]." They therefore do not understand that all virtue is found in moderation, and that any declension to either side [2] of it becomes a vice. He, in fact, who grasps the middle point between doing too little and doing too much has hit the distinction between vice and virtue. Instances will make this clearer. Cowardice and audacity are two recognized vices opposed to each other; the one the defect, the other the excess of confidence; between them lies courage. Again, piety is neither atheism nor superstition; it is equally impious to deny a God and to believe in many gods. Is there need of more examples to bring this principle home? The man who avoids both meanness and prodigality will by this shunning of extremes form the moral habit of liberality; for liberality is the thing which is neither inclined to spend at random vast and useless sums, nor yet to be closely calculating in necessary expenses. We need not go into details in the case of all good qualities. Reason, in all of them, has established virtue to be a middle state between two extremes. Sobriety itself therefore is a middle state, and manifestly involves the two declensions on either side towards vice; he, that is, who is wanting in firmness of soul, and is so easily worsted in the combat with pleasure as never even to have approached the path of a virtuous and sober life, slides into shameful indulgence; while he who goes beyond the safe ground of sobriety and overshoots the moderation of this virtue, falls as it were

---

[8] 1 Tim. iv. 2.   [9] 1 Cor. v. 12.
[1] 2 Tim. ii. 16.
[2] ἐπὶ τὰ παρακείμενα. Galesinius wrongly renders "in contrariis partes." Cf. Arist. Eth. ii. 5.

from a precipice into the "doctrines of devils," "having his conscience seared with a hot iron." In declaring marriage abominable he brands himself with such reproaches; for "if the tree is corrupt" (as the Gospel says), "the fruit also of the tree will be like it[3]"; if a man is the shoot and fruitage of the tree of marriage, reproaches cast on that turn upon him who casts them[4]. These persons, then, are like branded criminals already; their conscience is covered with the stripes of this unnatural teaching. But our view of marriage is this; that, while the pursuit of heavenly things should be a man's first care, yet if he can use the advantages of marriage with sobriety and moderation, he need not despise this way of serving the state. An example might be found in the patriarch Isaac. He married Rebecca when he was past the flower of his age and his prime was well-nigh spent, so that his marriage was not the deed of passion, but because of God's blessing that should be upon his seed. He cohabited with her till the birth of her only children[5], and then, closing the channels of the senses, lived wholly for the Unseen; for this is what seems to be meant by the mention in his history of the *dimness* of the Patriarch's eyes. But let that be as those think who are skilled in reading these meanings, and let us proceed with the continuity of our discourse. What, then, were we saying? That in the cases where it is possible at once to be true to the diviner love, and to embrace wedlock, there is no reason for setting aside this dispensation of nature and misrepresenting as abominable that which is honourable. Let us take again our illustration of the water and the spring. Whenever the husbandman, in order to irrigate a particular spot, is bringing the stream thither, but there is need before it gets there of a small outlet, he will allow only so much to escape into that outlet as is adequate to supply the demand, and can then easily be blended again with the main stream. If, as an inexperienced and easy-going steward, he opens too wide a channel, there will be danger of the whole stream quitting its direct bed and pouring itself sideways. In the same way, if (as life does need a mutual succession) a man so treats this need as to give spiritual things the first thought, and because of the shortness[6] of the time indulges but sparingly the sexual passion and keeps it under restraint, that man would

realize the character of the prudent husbandman to which the Apostle exhorts us. About the details of paying these trifling debts of nature he will not be over-calculating, but the long hours of his prayers[7] will secure the purity which is the key-note of his life. He will always fear lest by this kind of indulgence he may become nothing but flesh and blood; for in them God's Spirit does not dwell. He who is of so weak a character that he cannot make a manful stand against nature's impulse had better[8] keep himself very far away from such temptations, rather than descend into a combat which is above his strength. There is no small danger for him lest, cajoled in the valuation of pleasure, he should think that there exists no other good but that which is enjoyed along with some sensual emotion, and, turning altogether from the love of immaterial delights, should become entirely of the flesh, seeking always his pleasure only there, so that his character will be a Pleasure-lover, not a God-lover. It is not every man's gift, owing to weakness of nature, to hit the due proportion in these matters; there is a danger of being carried far beyond it, and "sticking fast in the deep mire[9]," to use the Psalmist's words. It would therefore be for our interest, as our discourse has been suggesting, to pass through life without a trial of these temptations, lest under cover of the excuse of lawful indulgence passion should gain an entrance into the citadel of the soul.

CHAPTER IX.

CUSTOM is indeed in everything hard to resist. It possesses an enormous power of attracting and seducing the soul. In the cases where a man has got into a fixed state of sentiment, a certain imagination of the good is created in him by this habit; and nothing is so naturally vile but it may come to be thought both desirable and laudable, once it has got into the fashion[1]. Take mankind now living on the earth. There are many nations, and their ambitions are not all the same. The standard of beauty and of honour is different in each, the custom of each regulating their enthusiasm and their aims. This unlikeness is seen not only amongst nations where the pursuits of the one are in no

---

3 Cf. S. Matt. vii. 18; from which it will be seen that Gregory confirms the Vulgate "malum" for σαπρόν, since he quotes it as κακὸν here.

4 τοῦ προφέροντος; not "of their Creator," or "of their father" (Livineius).

5 μέχρι μιᾶς ὠδῖνος. So perhaps Rom. ix. 10: 'Ρεβέκκα ἐξ ἑνὸς κοίτην ἔχουσα, i. e. ex uno concubitu. Below, c. 9 (p. 139, c. 11), Gregory uses the same expression of one *birth*.

6 καιροῦ συστολὴν.

7 τὴν ἐκ συμφώνου καθαρότητα τῇ σχολῇ τῶν προσευχῶν ἀφορίζων, "durch häufiges Gebet die innige Reinheit festzustellen sucht," J. Rupp. The Latin fails to give the full force, "ex convenientiâ quadam munditiam animi in orationum studio constituit:" σχολὴ is *abundant* time from the business of life.

8 κρείττων, κ. τ. λ., "melius" (Livineius), not "validior."

9 ἰλύν, a better reading than ὕλην. Cf. Ps. lxix. 2, "the mire of depth" (ἰλὺν βυθοῦ).

1 οὐδὲν οὕτω τῇ φύσει φευκτόν ἐστιν, ὡς. κ. τ. λ. Both Livineius and Galesinius have missed the meaning here. Jac. Billius has rightly interpreted, "Nihil naturâ tam turpe ac fugiendum est, quin, si," &c.

repute with the other, but even in the same nation, and the same city, and the same family; we may see in those aggregates also much difference existing owing to customary feeling. Thus brothers born from the same throe are separated widely from each other in the aims of life. Nor is this to be wondered at, considering that each single man does not generally keep to the same opinion about the same thing, but alters it as fashion influences him. Not to go far from our present subject, we have known those who have shown themselves to be in love with chastity all through the early years of puberty; but in taking the pleasures which men think legitimate and allowable they make them the starting-point of an impure life, and when once they have admitted these temptations, all the forces of their feeling are turned in that direction, and, to take again our illustration of the stream, they let it rush from the diviner channel into low material channels, and make within themselves a broad path for passion; so that the stream of their love leaves dry the abandoned channel of the higher way [2] and flows abroad in indulgence. It would be well then, we take it, for the weaker brethren to fly to virginity as into an impregnable fortress, rather than to descend into the career of life's consequences and invite temptations to do their worst upon them, entangling themselves in those things which through the lusts of the flesh war against the law of our mind; it would be well for them to consider [3] that herein they risk not broad acres, or wealth, or any other of this life's prizes, but the hope which has been their guide. It is impossible that one who has turned to the world and feels its anxieties, and engages his heart in the wish to please men, can fulfil that first and great commandment of the Master, " Thou shalt love God with all thy heart and with all thy strength [4]." How can he fulfil that, when he divides his heart between God and the world, and exhausts the love which he owes to Him alone in human affections? " He that is unmarried careth for the things of the Lord; but he that is married careth for the things that are of the world [5]." If the combat with pleasure seems wearisome, nevertheless let all take heart. Habit will not fail to produce, even in the seemingly most fretful [6], a feeling of pleasure through the very effort of their perseverance; and that pleasure will be of the noblest and purest kind; which the intelligent may well be enamoured of, rather than allow themselves, with aims narrowed by the lowness of their objects, to be estranged from the true greatness which goes beyond all thought.

[2] ἐπὶ τὰ ἄνω, Reg. Cod., better than τὸ.
[3] Reading φροντίζοντας, with Reg. Cod.
[4] S. Matt. xxii. 37.   [5] 1 Cor. vii. 32 (R.V.).
[6] τοῖς δυσκολωτάτοις; better than to take this as a neuter.

CHAPTER X.

WHAT words indeed could possibly express the greatness of that loss in falling away from the possession of real goodness? What consummate power of thought would have to be employed! Who could produce even in outline that which speech cannot tell, nor the mind grasp? On the one hand, if a man has kept the eye of his heart so clear that he can in a way behold the promise of our Lord's Beatitudes realized, he will condemn all human utterance as powerless to represent that which he has apprehended. On the other hand, if a man from the atmosphere of material indulgences has the weakness of passion spreading like a film over the keen vision of his soul, all force of expression will be wasted upon him; for it is all one whether you understate or whether you magnify a miracle to those who have no power whatever of perceiving it [7]. Just as, in the case of the sunlight, on one who has never from the day of his birth seen it, all efforts at translating it into words are quite thrown away; you cannot make the splendour of the ray shine [8] through his ears; in like manner, to see the beauty of the true and intellectual light, each man has need of eyes of his own; and he who by a gift of Divine inspiration can see it retains his ecstasy unexpressed in the depths of his consciousness; while he who sees it not cannot be made to know even the greatness of his loss. How should he? This good escapes his perception, and it cannot be represented to him; it is unspeakable, and cannot be delineated. We have not learnt the peculiar language expressive of this beauty. An example of what we want to say does not exist in the world; a comparison for it would at least be very difficult to find. Who compares the Sun to a little spark? or the vast Deep to a drop? And that tiny drop and that diminutive spark bear the same relation to the Deep and to the Sun, as any beautiful object of man's admiration does to that real beauty on the features of the First Good, of which we catch the glimpse beyond any other good. What words could be invented to show the greatness of this loss to him who suffers it? Well does the great David seem to me to express the impossibility of doing this. He has been lifted by the power of the Spirit out of himself, and sees in a blessed state of ecstacy the boundless and incomprehensible Beauty; he sees it as fully as a mortal can see who has quitted his fleshly envelopments and entered, by the mere power of thought, upon the contemplation of the spiritual and intellectual

[7] ἀναισθήτως ἐχόντων; Reg. Cod.   [8] αὐγάζειν; intrans. in N. T.

world, and in his longing to speak a word worthy of the spectacle he bursts forth with that cry, which all re-echo, " Every man a liar[9] !" I take that to mean that any man who entrusts to language the task of presenting the ineffable Light is really and truly a liar ; not because of any hatred on his part of the truth, but because of the feebleness of his instrument for expressing the thing thought of[1]. The visible beauty to be met with in this life of ours, showing glimpses of itself, whether in inanimate objects or in animate organisms in a certain choiceness of colour, can be adequately admired by our power of æsthetic feeling. It can be illustrated and made known to others by description ; it can be seen drawn in the language as in a picture. Even a perfect type[2] of such beauty does not baffle our conception. But how can language illustrate when it finds no media for its sketch, no colour, no contour[3], no majestic size, no faultlessness of feature ; nor any other commonplace of art ? The Beauty which is invisible and formless, which is destitute of qualities and far removed from everything which we recognize in bodies by the eye, can never be made known by the traits which require nothing but the perceptions of our senses in order to be grasped. Not that we are to despair of winning this object of our love, though it does seem too high for our comprehension. The more reason shows the greatness of this thing which we are seeking, the higher we must lift our thoughts and excite them with the great-ness of that object ; and we must fear to lose our share in that transcendent Good. There is indeed no small amount of danger lest, as we can base the apprehension of it on no knowable qualities, we should slip away from it altogether because of its very height and mystery. We deem it necessary therefore, owing to this weakness of the thinking faculty, to lead it towards the Unseen by stages through the cognizances of the senses. Our conception of the case is as follows.

CHAPTER XI.

Now those who take a superficial and unreflecting view of things observe the outward appearance of anything they meet, e. g. of a man, and then trouble themselves no more about him. The view they have taken of the bulk of his body is enough to make them think that they know all about him. But the pene-

trating and scientific mind will not trust to the eyes alone the task of taking the measure of reality ; it will not stop at appearances, nor count that which is not seen amongst unrealities. It inquires into the qualities of the man's soul. It takes those of its characteristics which have been developed by his bodily constitution, both in combination and singly ; first singly, by analysis, and then in that living combination which makes the personality of the subject. As regards the inquiry into the nature of beauty, we see, again, that the man of half-grown intelligence, when he observes an object which is bathed in the glow of a seeming beauty, thinks that that object is in its essence beautiful, no matter what it is that so prepossesses him with the pleasure of the eye. He will not go deeper into the subject. But the other, whose mind's eye is clear, and who can inspect such appearances, will neglect those elements which are the material only upon which the Form of Beauty works ; to him they will be but the ladder by which he climbs to the prospect of that Intellectual Beauty, in accordance with their share in which all other beauties get their existence and their name. But for the majority, I take it, who live all their lives with such obtuse faculties of thinking, it is a difficult thing to perform this feat of mental analysis and of discriminating the material vehicle from the immanent beauty, and thereby of grasping the actual nature of the Beautiful ; and if any one wants to know the exact source of all the false and pernicious conceptions of it, he would find it in nothing else but this, viz. the absence, in the soul's faculties of feeling, of that exact training which would enable them to distinguish between true Beauty and the reverse. Owing to this men give up all search after the true Beauty. Some slide into mere sensuality. Others incline in their desires to dead metallic coin. Others limit their imagination of the beautiful to worldly honours, fame, and power. There is another class which is enthusiastic about art and science. The most debased make their gluttony the test of what is good. But he who turns from all grosser thoughts and all passionate longings after what is seeming, and explores the nature of the beauty which is simple, immaterial, formless, would never make a mistake like that when he has to choose between all the objects of desire ; he would never be so misled by these attractions as not to see the transient character of their pleasures and not to win his way to an utter contempt for every one of them. This, then, is the path to lead us to the discovery of the Beautiful. All other objects that attract men's love, be they never so fashionable, be they prized never so much and embraced never so eagerly, must be

---

9 Ps. cxvi. 11.
[1] οὐχὶ τῷ μίσει τῆς ἀληθείας ἀλλὰ τῇ ἀσθενείᾳ τῆς διηγήσεως, the reading of Codd. Vatican & Reg.
[2] οὐδὲ τὸ ἀρχέτυπον, κ. τ. λ.
3 These are evidently the elements of beauty as *then* recognized by the eye ; it is still the Hellenic standard.

left below us, as too low, too fleeting, to employ the powers of loving which we possess ; not indeed that those powers are to be locked up within us unused and motionless ; but only that they must first be cleansed from all lower longings ; then we must lift them to that height to which sense can never reach. Admiration even of the beauty of the heavens, and of the dazzling sunbeams, and, indeed, of any fair phenomenon, will then cease. The beauty noticed there will be but as the hand to lead us to the love of the supernal Beauty whose glory the heavens and the firmament declare, and whose secret the whole creation sings. The climbing soul, leaving all that she has grasped already as too narrow for her needs, will thus grasp the idea of that magnificence which is exalted far above the heavens. But how can any one reach to this, whose ambitions creep below ? How can any one fly up into the heavens, who has not the wings of heaven and is not already buoyant and lofty-minded by reason of a heavenly calling ? Few can be such strangers to evangelic mysteries as not to know that there is but one vehicle on which man's soul can mount into the heavens, viz. the self-made likeness in himself to the descending Dove, whose wings [4] David the Prophet also longed for. This is the allegorical name used in Scripture for the power of the Holy Spirit ; whether it be because not a drop of gall [5] is found in that bird, or because it cannot bear any noisome smell, as close observers tell us. He therefore who keeps away from all bitterness and all the noisome effluvia of the flesh, and raises himself on the aforesaid wings above all low earthly ambitions, or, more than that, above the whole universe itself, will be the man to find that which is alone worth loving, and to become himself as beautiful as the Beauty which he has touched and entered, and to be made bright and luminous himself in the communion of the real Light. We are told by those who have studied the subject, that those gleams which follow each other so fast through the air at night and which some call shooting stars [6], are nothing but the air itself streaming into the upper regions of the sky under stress of some

particular blasts. They say that the fiery track is traced along the sky when those blasts ignite in the ether. In like manner, then, as this air round the earth is forced upwards by some blast and changes into the pure splendour of the ether, so the mind of man leaves this murky miry world, and under the stress of the spirit becomes pure and luminous in contact with the true and supernal Purity; in such an atmosphere it even itself emits light, and is so filled with radiance, that it becomes itself a Light, according to the promise of our Lord that "the righteous should shine forth as the sun [7]." We see this even here, in the case of a mirror, or a sheet of water, or any smooth surface that can reflect the light ; when they receive the sunbeam they beam themselves ; but they would not do this if any stain marred their pure and shining surface. We shall become then as the light, in our nearness to Christ's true light, if we leave this dark atmosphere of the earth and dwell above ; and we shall be light, as our Lord says somewhere to His disciples [8], if the true Light that shineth in the dark comes down even to us ; unless, that is, any foulness of sin spreading over our hearts should dim the brightness of our light. Perhaps these examples have led us gradually on to the discovery that we can be changed into something better than ourselves ; and it has been proved as well that this union of the soul with the incorruptible Deity can be accomplished in no other way but by herself attaining by her virgin state to the utmost purity possible,— a state which, being like God, will enable her to grasp that to which it is like, while she places herself like a mirror beneath the purity of God, and moulds her own beauty at the touch and the sight of the Archetype of all beauty. Take a character strong enough to turn from all that is human, from persons, from wealth, from the pursuits of Art and Science, even from whatever in moral practice and in legislation is viewed as right (for still in all of them error in the apprehension of the Beautiful comes in, sense being the criterion) ; such a character will feel as a passionate lover only towards that Beauty which has no source but Itself, which is not such at one particular time or relatively only, which is Beautiful from, and through, and in itself, not such at one moment and in the next ceasing to be such, above all increase and addition, incapable of change and alteration. I venture to affirm that, to one who has cleansed all the powers of his being from every form of vice, the Beauty which is essential, the source of every beauty and every good, will become visible. The visual eye, purged from its blinding humour, can clearly discern objects even on the

[4] Ps. lv. 6.

[5] Cf. Augustine, Tract. 6 in Joann. : "Columba fel non h·bet. Simon habebat ; ideo separatus est a columbæ visceribus." Aristotle asserts the contrary ; but even Galen denies that it possesses a bladder (*lib. de atr. bil. sub fin.*).

[6] διᾴττοντας, corrected by Livineius, the transcriber of the Vatican MS., for διατάττοντας. Cf. Arist. *Meteor.* I. iv : καὶ ὁμοίως κατὰ πλάτος καὶ βάθος οἱ δοκοῦντες ἀστέρες διᾴττειν γίνονται : and, in the same chapter, διαθέοντες ἀστέρες. Cf. Seneca. *Nat. Quæst.* iii. 14 : "Videmus ergo 'Stellarum longos a tergo albescere tractus.' Hæc velut stellæ exsiliunt et tr·nsvolant." This and much else. in the preceding and following notes to this treatise, is taken from those of Fronto Ducæus, printed in the Paris Edit. The Paris Editors, Fronto Ducæus and Claude Morell, used Livineius' edition (1574) of this treatise, which is based on the Vatican Cod. and Bricman's (of Cologne) ; and they corrected from the Cod. of F. Morell, Regius Professor of Theology ; and from the Cod. Regius.

[7] S. Matt. xiii. 43.   [8] S. John ix. 5 ; i. 9.

distant sky[9]; so to the soul by virtue of her innocence there comes the power of taking in that Light; and the real Virginity, the real zeal for chastity, ends in no other goal than this, viz. the power thereby of seeing God. No one in fact is so mentally blind as not to understand *that* without telling; viz. that the God of the Universe is the only absolute, and primal, and unrivalled[1] Beauty and Goodness. All, maybe, know that; but there are those who, as might have been expected, wish besides this to discover, if possible, a process by which we may be actually guided to it. Well, the Divine books are full of such instruction for our guidance; and besides that many of the Saints cast the refulgence of their own lives, like lamps, upon the path for those who are "walking with God[2]." But each may gather in abundance for himself suggestions towards this end out of either Covenant in the inspired writings; the Prophets and the Law are full of them; and also the Gospel and the Traditions of the Apostles. What we ourselves have conjectured in following out the thoughts of those inspired utterances is this.

CHAPTER XII.

THIS reasoning and intelligent creature, man, at once the work and the likeness of the Divine and Imperishable Mind (for so in the Creation it is written of him that "God made man in His image[3]"), this creature, I say, did not in the course of his first production have united to the very essence of his nature the liability to passion and to death. Indeed, the truth about the image could never have been maintained if the beauty reflected in that image had been in the slightest degree opposed[4] to the Archetypal Beauty. Passion was introduced afterwards, subsequent to man's first organization; and it was in this way. Being the image and the likeness, as has been said, of the Power which rules all things, man kept also in the matter of a Free-Will this likeness to Him whose Will is over all. He was enslaved to no outward necessity whatever; his feeling towards that which pleased him depended only on his own private judgment; he was free to choose whatever he liked; and so he was a free agent, though circumvented with cunning, when he drew upon himself that disaster which now overwhelms humanity. He became himself the discoverer of evil, but he did not therein discover what God had made; for God did not make death. Man became, in fact, himself the fabricator, to a certain extent, and the craftsman of evil. All who have the faculty of sight may enjoy equally the sunlight; and any one can if he likes put this enjoyment from him by shutting his eyes: in that case it is not that the sun retires and produces that darkness, but the man himself puts a barrier between his eye and the sunshine; the faculty of vision cannot indeed, even in the closing of the eyes, remain inactive[5], and so this operative sight necessarily becomes an operative darkness[6] rising up in the man from his own free act in ceasing to see. Again, a man in building a house for himself may omit to make in it any way of entrance for the light; he will necessarily be in darkness, though he cuts himself off from the light voluntarily. So the first man on the earth, or rather he who generated evil in man, had for choice the Good and the Beautiful lying all around him in the very nature of things; yet he wilfully cut out a new way for himself against this nature, and in the act of turning away from virtue, which was his own free act, he created the usage of evil. For, be it observed, there is no such thing in the world as evil irrespective of a will, and discoverable in a substance apart from that. Every creature of God is good, and nothing of His "to be rejected"; all that God made was "very good[7]." But the habit of sinning entered as we have described, and with fatal quickness, into the life of man; and from that small beginning spread into this infinitude of evil. Then that godly beauty of the soul which was an imitation of the Archetypal Beauty, like fine steel blackened[8] with the vicious rust, preserved no longer the glory of its familiar essence, but was disfigured with the ugliness of sin. This thing so great and precious[9], as the Scripture calls him, this being man, has fallen from his proud birthright. As those who have slipped and fallen heavily into mud, and have all their features so besmeared with it, that their nearest friends do not recognize them, so this creature has fallen into the mire of sin and lost the blessing of being an image of the imperishable Deity; he has clothed himself instead with a perishable and foul resemblance to something else; and this Reason

---

[9] τὰ ἐν τῷ οὐρανῷ τηλαυγῶς καθορᾶται. The same word in S. Mark viii. 25 ("clearly") evidently refers to the second stage of recovered sight, the power of seeing the *perspective*. The MSS. rea^ding is ἐν τῷ ἁγίω, for which ἀέρι and ἡλίω have been conjectured: οὐρανῷ is due to Galesinius; there is a similar place in Dio Chrys. (*de regno et tyrann.*): "impaired sight," he says, "cannot see even what is quite close, ὑγιὲς δὲ οὖσα μέχρις οὐρανοῦ τε καὶ ἀστέρων ἐξικνεῖται, *i. e.* the distant sky. Just above, ἀποῤῥυψαμένῳ (purged) is a better reading than ἀποῤῥιψαμένῳ, and supported by F. Morell's MS.
[1] μόνως.   [2] Gen. v. 24; vi. 9.
[3] Gen. i. 27.   [4] ὑπεναντίως; *i. e.* even as a sub-contrary.

[5] ἀργεῖν.   [6] σκότους ἐνέργειαν.
[7] 1 Tim. iv. 4; Gen. i. 31.   [8] κατεμελάνθη.
[9] Cf. Prov. xx. 6. μέγα ἄνθρωπος, καὶ τίμιον, ἀνὴρ ἐλεήμων; and Ambrose (*de obitu T[.] eodosii*), "Magnum et honorabile est homo misericors;" and the same on Ps. cxix. 73, "Grande homo, et preciosum vir misericors, et vere magnus est, qui divini operis interpres est, et imitator Dei."

counsels him to put away again by washing it off in the cleansing water of this calling[1]. The earthly envelopment once removed, the soul's beauty will again appear. Now the putting off of a strange accretion is equivalent to the return to that which is familiar and natural; yet such a return cannot be but by again becoming that which in the beginning we were created. In fact this likeness to the divine is not our work at all; it is not the achievement of any faculty of man; it is the great gift of God bestowed upon our nature at the very moment of our birth; human efforts can only go so far as to clear away the filth of sin, and so cause the buried beauty of the soul to shine forth again. This truth is, I think, taught in the Gospel, when our Lord says, to those who can hear what Wisdom speaks beneath a mystery, that "the Kingdom of God is within you[2]." That word[3] points out the fact that the Divine good is not something apart from our nature, and is not removed far away from those who have the will to seek it; it is in fact within each of us, ignored indeed, and unnoticed while it is stifled beneath the cares and pleasures of life, but found again whenever we can turn our power of conscious thinking towards it. If further confirmation of what we say is required, I think it will be found in what is suggested by our Lord in the searching for the Lost Drachma[4]. The thought, there, is that the widowed soul reaps no benefit from the other virtues (called drachmas in the Parable) being all of them found safe, if that one other is not amongst them. The Parable therefore suggests that a candle should first be lit, signifying doubtless our reason which throws light on hidden principles; then that in one's own house, that is, within oneself, we should search for that lost coin; and by that coin the Parable doubtless hints at the image of our King, not yet hopelessly lost, but hidden beneath the dirt; and by this last we must understand the impurities of the flesh, which, being swept and purged away by carefulness of life, leave clear to the view the object of our search. Then it is meant that the soul herself who finds this rejoices over it, and with her the neighbours, whom she calls in to share with her in this delight. Verily, all those powers which are the housemates of the soul, and which the Parable names her neighbours for this occasion[5], when so be that the image of the mighty King is revealed in all its brightness at last (that image which the Fashioner of each individual heart of us has stamped upon this our Drachma[6]), will then be converted to that

divine delight and festivity, and will gaze upon the ineffable beauty of the recovered one. "Rejoice with me," she says, "because I have found the Drachma which I had lost." The neighbours, that is, the soul's familiar powers, both the reasoning and the appetitive, the affections of grief and of anger, and all the rest that are discerned in her, at that joyful feast which celebrates the finding of the heavenly Drachma are well called her friends; and it is meet that they should all rejoice in the Lord when they all look towards the Beautiful and the Good, and do everything for the glory of God, no longer instruments of sin[7]. If, then, such is the lesson of this Finding of the lost, viz. that we should restore the divine image from the foulness which the flesh wraps round it to its primitive state, let us become that which the First Man was at the moment when he first breathed. And what was that? Destitute he was then of his covering of dead skins, but he could gaze without shrinking upon God's countenance. He did not yet judge of what was lovely by taste or sight; he found in the Lord alone all that was sweet; and he used the helpmeet given him only for this delight, as Scripture signifies when it said that "he knew her not[8]" till he was driven forth from the garden, and till she, for the sin which she was decoyed into committing, was sentenced to the pangs of childbirth. We, then, who in our first ancestor were thus ejected, are allowed to return to our earliest state of blessedness by the very same stages by which we lost Paradise. What are they? Pleasure, craftily offered, began the Fall, and there followed after pleasure shame, and fear, even to remain longer in the sight of their Creator, so that they hid themselves in leaves and shade; and after that they covered themselves with the skins of dead animals; and then were sent forth into this pestilential and exacting land where, as the compensation for having to die, marriage was instituted[9]. Now if we are destined "to depart hence, and be with Christ[1]," we must begin at the end of the route of departure (which lies nearest to ourselves); just as those who have travelled far from their friends at home, when they turn to reach again the place from which they started, first leave that district which they reached at the end of their outward journey. Marriage, then, is the last stage of our separation from the life that was led in Paradise; marriage therefore, as our discourse has been suggesting, is the first thing to be left; it is the first station as it were for our departure to Christ. Next, we must retire from all anxious toil upon the land, such as man was

---

[1] τῆς πολιτείας : used in the same sense in " On Pilgrimages."
[2] S. Luke xvii. 21.
[3] ὁ λόγος, *i. e.* Scripture. So τὸ λόγιον in Gregory passim, and Clement. Alex. (*Stromata*).   [4] S. Luke xv. 8.
[5] νῦν.   [6] ἐνεσημήνατο ἡ ἐν τῇ δραχμῇ.

[7] Rom. vi. 13.   [8] Gen. iv. 1.
[9] Gen. iii. 16.   [1] Philip. i. 23.

bound to after his sin. Next we must divest ourselves of those coverings of our nakedness, the coats of skins, namely the wisdom of the flesh; we must renounce all shameful things done in secret[2], and be covered no longer with the fig-leaves of this bitter world; then, when we have torn off the coatings of this life's perishable leaves, we must stand again in the sight of our Creator; and repelling all the illusion of taste and sight, take for our guide God's commandment only, instead of the venom-spitting serpent. That commandment was, to touch nothing but what was Good, and to leave what was evil untasted; because impatience to remain any longer in ignorance of evil would be but the beginning of the long train of actual evil. For this reason it was forbidden to our first parents to grasp the knowledge of the opposite to the good, as well as that of the good itself; they were to keep themselves from "the knowledge of good and evil[3]," and to enjoy the Good in its purity, unmixed with one particle of evil: and to enjoy *that*, is in my judgment nothing else than to be ever with God, and to feel ceaselessly and continually this delight, unalloyed by aught that could tear us away from it. One might even be bold to say that this might be found the way by which a man could be again caught up into Paradise out of this world which lieth in the Evil, into that Paradise where Paul was when he saw the unspeakable sights which it is not lawful for a man to talk of[4].

CHAPTER XIII.

But seeing that Paradise is the home of living spirits, and will not admit those who are dead in sin, and that we on the other hand are fleshly, subject to death, and sold under sin[5], how is it possible that one who is a subject of death's empire should ever dwell in this land where all is life? What method of release from this jurisdiction can be devised? Here too the Gospel teaching is abundantly sufficient. We hear our Lord saying to Nicodemus, "That which is born of the flesh is flesh; and that which is born of the Spirit is spirit[6]." We know too that the flesh is subject to death because of sin, but the Spirit of God is both incorruptible, and life-giving, and deathless. As at our physical birth there comes into the world with us a potentiality of being again turned to dust, plainly the Spirit also imparts a life-giving potentiality to the children begotten by Him-

self. What lesson, then, results from these remarks? This: that we should wean ourselves from this life in the flesh, which has an inevitable follower, death; and that we should search for a manner of life which does not bring death in its train. Now the life of Virginity is such a life. We will add a few other things to show how true this is. Every one knows that the propagation of mortal frames is the work which the intercourse of the sexes has to do; whereas for those who are joined to the Spirit, life and immortality instead of children are produced by this latter intercourse; and the words of the Apostle beautifully suit their case, for the joyful mother of such children as these "shall be saved in child-bearing[7];" as the Psalmist in his divine songs thankfully cries, "He maketh the barren woman to keep house, and to be a joyful mother of children[8]." Truly a joyful mother is the virgin mother who by the operation of the Spirit conceives the deathless children, and who is called by the Prophet barren because of her modesty only. This life, then, which is stronger than the power of death, is, to those who think, the preferable one. The physical bringing of children into the world—I speak without wishing to offend—is as much a starting-point of death as of life; because from the moment of birth the process of dying commences. But those who by virginity have desisted from this process have drawn within themselves the boundary line of death, and by their own deed have checked his advance; they have made themselves, in fact, a frontier between life and death, and a barrier too, which thwarts him. If, then, death cannot pass beyond virginity, but finds his power checked and shattered there, it is demonstrated that virginity is a stronger thing than death; and that body is rightly named undying which does not lend its service to a dying world, nor brook to become the instrument of a succession of dying creatures. In such a body the long unbroken career of decay and death, which has intervened between[9] the first man and the lives of virginity which have been led, is interrupted. It could not be indeed that death should cease working as long as the human race by marriage was working too; he walked the path of life with all preceding generations; he started with every new-born child and accompanied it to the end: but he found in virginity a barrier, to pass which was an impossible feat. Just as, in the age of Mary the mother of God, he who had reigned from Adam to her time found, when he came to her and dashed his forces against the fruit of her virginity as against a

---

[2] 2 Cor. iv. 2.   [3] Gen. ii. 17.
[4] 2 Cor. xii. 4.
[5] ὑπὸ τὴν ἁμαρτίαν should perhaps be restored from Rom. vii. 14; though the Paris Edit. has ὑπὸ τῆς ἁμαρτίας.
[6] S. John iii. 6.

[7] 1 Tim. ii. 15.   [8] Ps. cxiii. 9.
[9] διὰ μέσου οὐ γέγονεν. So Codd. Reg. Vat.; but the οὐ is manifestly a corruption arising from μέσου.

rock, that he was shattered to pieces upon her, so in every soul which passes through this life in the flesh under the protection of virginity, the strength of death is in a manner broken and annulled, for he does not find the places upon which he may fix his sting. If you do not throw into the fire wood, or straw, or grass, or something that it can consume, it has not the force to last by itself; so the power of death cannot go on working, if marriage does not supply it with material and prepare victims for this executioner. If you have any doubts left, consider the actual names of those afflictions which death brings upon mankind, and which were detailed in the first part of this discourse. Whence do they get their meaning? "Widowhood," "orphanhood," "loss of children," could they be a subject for grief, if marriage did not precede? Nay, all the dearly-prized blisses, and transports, and comforts of marriage end in these agonies of grief. The hilt of a sword is smooth and handy, and polished and glittering outside; it seems to grow to the outline of the hand[1]; but the other part is steel and the instrument of death, formidable to look at, more formidable still to come across. Such a thing is marriage. It offers for the grasp of the senses a smooth surface of delights, like a hilt of rare polish and beautiful workmanship; but when a man has taken it up and has got it into his hands, he finds the pain that has been wedded to it is in his hands as well; and it becomes to him the worker of mourning and of loss. It is marriage that has the heartrending spectacles to show of children left desolate in the tenderness of their years, a mere prey to the powerful, yet smiling often at their misfortune from ignorance of coming woes. What is the cause of widowhood but marriage? And retirement from this would bring with it an immunity from the whole burden of these sad taxes on our hearts. Can we expect it otherwise? When the verdict that was pronounced on the delinquents in the beginning is annulled, then too the mothers' "sorrows[2]" are no longer "multiplied," nor does "sorrow" herald the births of men; then all calamity has been removed from life and "tears wiped from off all faces[3];" conception is no more an iniquity, nor child-bearing a sin; and births shall be no more "of bloods," or "of the will of man," or "of the will of the flesh[4]", but of God alone. This is always happening whenever any one in a lively heart conceives all the integrity of the Spirit, and brings forth wisdom and righteousness, and sanctification and redemption too. It is possible for any one to be the mother of such a

son; as our Lord says, "He that doeth my will is my brother, my sister, and my mother[5]." What room is there for death in such parturitions? Indeed in them death is swallowed up by life. In fact, the Life of Virginity seems to be an actual representation of the blessedness in the world to come, showing as it does in itself so many signs of the presence of those expected blessings which are reserved for us there. That the truth of this statement may be perceived, we will verify it thus. It is so, first, because a man who has thus died once for all to sin lives for the future to God; he brings forth no more fruit unto death; and having so far as in him lies made an end[6] of this life within him according to the flesh, he awaits thenceforth the expected blessing of the manifestation[7] of the great God, refraining from putting any distance between himself and this coming of God by an intervening posterity: secondly, because he enjoys even in this present life a certain exquisite glory of all the blessed results of our resurrection. For our Lord has announced that the life after our resurrection shall be as that of the angels. Now the peculiarity of the angelic nature is that they are strangers to marriage; therefore the blessing of this promise has been already received by him who has not only mingled his own glory with the halo of the Saints, but also by the stainlessness of his life has so imitated the purity of these incorporeal beings. If virginity then can win us favours such as these, what words are fit to express the admiration of so great a grace? What other gift of the soul can be found so great and precious as not to suffer by comparison with this perfection?

CHAPTER XIV.

BUT if we apprehend at last the perfection of this grace, we must understand as well what necessarily follows from it; namely that it is not a single achievement, ending in the subjugation of the body, but that in intention it reaches to and pervades everything that is, or is considered, a right condition of the soul. That soul indeed which in virginity cleaves to the true Bridegroom will not remove herself merely from all bodily defilement; she will make that abstension only the beginning of her purity, and will carry this security from failure equally into everything else upon her path. Fearing lest, from a too partial heart, she should by contact with evil in any one direction give occasion for the least weakness of unfaithfulness (to suppose

---

[1] ἐμφυομένη; cf. the Homeric ἐν δ'ἄρα οἱ φῦ χειρί, κ. τ. λ.
[2] Gen. iii. 16   [3] Is. xxv. 8   [4] S. John i. 13.

[5] S. Mat·. xii. 50.
[6] συντέλειαν. Cf. S. Matt. xiii 39; and Heb. ix. 15.
[7] ἐπιφάνειαν; Tit. ii. 13.

such a case : but I will begin again what I was going to say), that soul which cleaves to her Master so as to become with Him one spirit, and by the compact of a wedded life has staked the love of all her heart and all her strength on Him alone—that soul will no more commit any other of the offences contrary to salvation, than imperil her union with Him by cleaving to fornication ; she knows that between all sins there is a single kinship of impurity, and that if she were to defile herself with but one[8], she could no longer retain her spotlessness. An illustration will show what we mean. Suppose all the water in a pool remaining smooth and motionless, while no disturbance of any kind comes to mar the peacefulness of the spot ; and then a stone thrown into the pool ; the movement in that one part[9] will extend to the whole, and while the stone's weight is carrying it to the bottom, the waves that are set in motion round it pass in circles[1] into others, and so through all the intervening commotion are pushed on to the very edge of the water, and the whole surface is ruffled with these circles, feeling the movement of the depths. So is the broad serenity and calm of the soul troubled by one invading passion, and affected by the injury of a single part. They tell us too, those who have investigated the subject, that the virtues are not disunited from each other, and that to grasp the principle of any one virtue will be impossible to one who has not seized that which underlies the rest, and that the man who shows one virtue in his character will necessarily show them all. Therefore, by contraries, the depravation of anything in our moral nature will extend to the whole virtuous life ; and in very truth, as the Apostle tells us, the whole is affected by the parts, and "if one member[2] suffer, all the members suffer with it," "if one be honoured, all rejoice."

CHAPTER XV.

But the ways in our life which turn aside towards sin are innumerable ; and their number is told by Scripture in divers manners. "Many are they that trouble me and persecute," and "Many are they that fight against me from on high[3]"; and many other texts like that. We may affirm, indeed, absolutely, that many are they who plot in the adulterer's fashion to

destroy this truly honourable marriage, and to defile this inviolate bed ; and if we must name them one by one, we charge with this adulterous spirit anger, avarice, envy, revenge, enmity, malice, hatred, and whatever the Apostle puts in the class of those things which are contrary to sound doctrine. Now let us suppose a lady, prepossessing and lovely above her peers, and on that account wedded to a king, but besieged because of her beauty by profligate lovers. As long as she remains indignant at these would-be seducers and complains of them to her lawful husband, she keeps her chastity and has no one before her eyes but her bridegroom ; the profligates find no vantage ground for their attack upon her. But if she were to listen to a single one of them, her chastity with regard to the rest would not exempt her from the retribution ; it would be sufficient to condemn her, that she had allowed that one to defile the marriage bed. So the soul whose life is in God will find her pleasure[4] in no single one of those things which make a beauteous show to deceive her. If she were, in some fit of weakness, to admit the defilement to her heart, she would herself have broken the covenant of her spiritual marriage ; and, as the Scripture tells us, "into the malicious soul Wisdom cannot come[5]." It may, in a word, be truly said that the Good Husband cannot come to dwell with the soul that is irascible, or malice-bearing, or harbours any other disposition which jars with that concord. No way has been discovered of harmonizing things whose nature is antagonistic and which have nothing in common. The Apostle tells us there is "no communion of light with darkness[6]," or of righteousness with iniquity, or, in a word, of all the qualities which we perceive and name as the essence of God's nature, with all the opposite which are perceived in evil. Seeing, then, the impossibility of any union between mutual repellents, we understand that the vicious soul is estranged from entertaining the company of the Good. What then is the practical lesson from this? The chaste and thoughtful virgin must sever herself from any affection which can in any way impart contagion to her soul ; she must keep herself pure for the Husband who has married her, "not having spot or blemish or any such thing[7]."

---

[8] The text is here due to the Vatican Codex : καὶ εἰ δι'ἑνός τινος μολυνθείη, κ. τ. λ.

[9] τῷ μέρει. This is the reading of Cod. Morell. and of the fragment used by Livineius ; preferable to τῷ μερικῷ σάλῳ συγκυματούμενον, as in Cod. Reg.   [1] κυκλοτερῶς, Plutarch, ii. 892, F.

[2] μέλος (not as Galesinius, μέρος), 1 Cor. xii. 26.

[3] Ps. lvi. 3 (from LXX. according to many MSS. : others join ἀπὸ ὕψους ἡμέρας οὐ φοβηθήσομαι, ab altitudine diei non timebo). But Aquila has ὕψιστε, agreeing with the Hebrew ; so also Jerome.

[4] οὐδενὶ ἀρεσθήσεται. The Vatican Cod. has ἐραθήσεται, which would require the genitive.

[5] Wis. i. 4.   [6] 2 Cor. vi. 14.

[7] Eph. v. 27.—Origen (c. Cels. vii. 48, 49), comparing Pagan and Christian virginity, says, "The Athenian hierophant, distrusting his power of self-control for the period of his regular religious duties, uses hemlock, and passes as pure. But you may see among the Christians men who need no hemlock. The Faith drives evil from their minds, and ever fits them to perform the service of prayer. Belonging to some of the gods now in vogue there are certainly virgins here and there—watch.d or not I care not now to inquire— who seem not to break down in the course of chastity which the honour of their god requires. But amongst Christians, for no repute

CHAPTER XVI.

THERE is only one right path. It is narrow and contracted. It has no turnings either on the one side or the other. No matter how we leave it, there is the same danger of straying hopelessly away. This being so, the habit which many have got into must be as far as possible corrected; those, I mean, who while they fight strenuously against the baser pleasures, yet still go on hunting for pleasure in the shape of worldly honour and positions which will gratify their love of power. They act like some domestic who longed for liberty, but instead of exerting himself to get away from slavery proceeded only to change his masters, and thought liberty consisted in that change. But all alike are slaves, even though they should not all go on being ruled by the same masters, as long as a dominion of any sort, with power to enforce it, is set over them. There are others again who after a long battle against all the pleasures [8], yield themselves easily on another field, where feelings of an opposite kind come in; and in the intense exactitude of their lives fall a ready prey to melancholy and irritation, and to brooding over injuries, and to everything that is the direct opposite of pleasurable feelings; from which they are very reluctant to extricate themselves. This is always happening, whenever any emotion, instead of virtuous reason, controls the course of a life. For the commandment of the Lord is exceedingly far-shining, so as to "enlighten the eyes" even of "the simple [9]," declaring that good cleaveth only unto God. But God is not pain any more than He is pleasure; He is not cowardice any more than boldness; He is not fear, nor anger, nor any other emotion which sways the untutored soul, but, as the Apostle says, He is Very Wisdom and Sanctification, Truth and Joy and Peace, and everything like that. If He is such, how can any one be said to cleave to Him, who is mastered by the very opposite? Is it not want of reason in any one to suppose that when he has striven successfully to escape the dominion of one particular passion, he will find virtue in its opposite? For instance, to suppose that when he has escaped pleasure, he will find virtue in letting pain have possession of him; or when he has by an effort remained proof against anger, in crouching with

fear. It matters not whether we miss virtue, or rather God Himself Who is the Sum of virtue, in this way, or in that. Take the case of great bodily prostration; one would say that the sadness of this failure was just the same, whether the cause has been excessive under-feeding, or immoderate eating; both failures to stop in time end in the same result. He therefore who watches over the life and the sanity of the soul will confine himself to the moderation of the truth; he will continue without touching either of those opposite states which run along-side virtue. This teaching is not mine; it comes from the Divine lips. It is clearly contained in that passage where our Lord says to His disciples, that they are as sheep wandering amongst wolves [1], yet are not to be as doves only, but are to have something of the serpent too in their disposition; and that means that they should neither carry to excess the practice of that which seems praiseworthy in simplicity [2], as such a habit would come very near to downright madness, nor on the other hand should deem the cleverness which most admire to be a virtue, while unsoftened by any mixture with its opposite; they were in fact to form another disposition, by a compound of these two seeming opposites, cutting off its silliness from the one, its evil cunning from the other; so that one single beautiful character should be created from the two, a union of simplicity of purpose with shrewdness. "Be ye," He says, "wise as serpents, and harmless as doves."

CHAPTER XVII.

LET that which was then said by our Lord be the general maxim for every life; especially let it be the maxim for those who are coming nearer God through the gateway of virginity, that they should never in watching for a perfection in one direction present an unguarded side in another and contrary one; but should in all directions realize the good, so that they may guarantee in all things their holy life against failure. A soldier does not arm himself only on some points, leaving the rest of his body to take its chance unprotected. If he were to receive his death-wound upon that, what would have been the advantage of this partial armour? Again, who would call that feature faultless, which from some accident had lost one of those requisites which go to make up the sum of beauty? The disfigurement of the mutilated part mars the grace of the part untouched. The Gospel im-

---

amongst men, for no stipend, for no mere show, they practise an absolute virginity; and as they 'liked to retain God in their knowledge,' so God has kept them in that liking mind, and in the performance of fitting works, filling them with righteousness and goodness. I say this without any depreciation of what is beautiful in Greek thought, and of what is wholesome in their teachings. I wish only to show that all they have said, and things more noble, more divine, have been said by those men of God, the prophets and apostles."

[8] τὰς ἡδονὰς s. e. the whole class.   [9] Ps. xix. 6 7, 8.

[1] S. Matt. x. 16.
[2] According to the emendation of Livineius: μήτε τὸ κατὰ τὴν ἁπλότητα δοκοῦν ἐπαινετὸν.

plies that he who undertakes the building of a tower, but spends all his labour upon the foundations without ever reaching the completion, is worthy of ridicule ; and what else do we learn from the Parable of the Tower, but to strive to come to the finish of every lofty purpose, accomplishing the work of God in all the multiform structures of His commandments? One stone, indeed, is no more the whole edifice of the Tower, than one commandment kept will raise the soul's perfection to the required height. The foundation must by all means first be laid ; but over it, as the Apostle says[3], the edifice of gold and precious gems must be built ; for so is the doing of the commandment put by the Prophet who cries, " I have loved Thy commandment above gold and many a precious stone[4]." Let the virtuous life have for its substructure the love of virginity ; but upon this let every result of virtue be reared. If virginity is believed to be a vastly precious thing and to have a divine look (as indeed is the case, as well as men believe of it), yet, if the whole life does not harmonize with this perfect note, and it be marred by the succeeding[5] discord of the soul, this thing becomes but "the jewel of gold in the swine's snout[6]," or "the pearl that is trodden under the swine's feet." But we have said enough upon this.

CHAPTER XVIII.

IF any one supposes that[7] this want of mutual harmony between his life and a single one of its circumstances is quite unimportant, let him be taught the meaning of our maxim by looking at the management of a house. The master of a private dwelling will not allow any untidiness or unseemliness to be seen in the house, such as a couch upset, or the table littered with rubbish, or vessels of price thrown away into dirty corners, while those which serve ignobler uses are thrust forward for entering guests to see. He has everything arranged neatly and in the proper place, where it stands to most advantage ; and then he can welcome his guests, without any misgivings that he need be ashamed of opening the interior of his house to receive them. The same duty, I take it, is incumbent on that master of our "tabernacle," the mind ; it has to arrange everything within us, and to put each particular faculty of the soul, which the Creator has fashioned to be our implement or our vessel, to fitting and noble uses. We will now mention in detail

the way in which any one might manage his life, with its present advantages, to his improvement, hoping that no one will accuse us of trifling[8], or over-minuteness. We advise, then, that love's passion be placed in the soul's purest shrine, as a thing chosen to be the first fruits of all our gifts, and devoted[9] entirely to God ; and when once this has been done, to keep it untouched and unsullied by any secular defilement. Then indignation, and anger, and hatred must be as watch-dogs to be roused only against attacking sins ; they must follow their natural impulse only against the thief and the enemy who is creeping in to plunder the divine treasure-chamber, and who comes only for that, that he may steal, and mangle, and destroy. Courage and confidence are to be weapons in our hands to baffle any sudden surprise and attack of the wicked who advance. Hope and patience are to be the staffs to lean upon, whenever we are weary with the trials of the world. As for sorrow, we must have a stock of it ready to apply, if need should happen to arise for it, in the hour of repentance for our sins ; believing at the same time that it is never useful, except to minister to that. Righteousness will be our rule of straightforwardness, guarding us from stumbling either in word or deed, and guiding us in the disposal of the faculties of our soul, as well as in the due consideration for every one we meet. The love of gain, which is a large, incalculably large, element in every soul, when once applied to the desire for God, will bless the man who has it ; for he will be violent[1] where it is right to be violent. Wisdom and prudence will be our advisers as to our best interests ; they will order our lives so as never to suffer from any thoughtless folly. But suppose a man does not apply the aforesaid faculties of the soul to their proper use, but reverses their intended purpose ; suppose he wastes his love upon the basest objects, and stores up his hatred only for his own kinsmen ; suppose he welcomes iniquity, plays the man only against his parents, is bold only in absurdities, fixes his hopes on emptiness, chases prudence and wisdom from his company, takes gluttony and folly for his mistresses, and uses all his other opportunities in the same fashion, he would indeed be a strange and unnatural character to a degree beyond any one's power to express. If we could imagine any one putting his armour on all the wrong way, reversing the helmet so as to cover his face while the plume nodded backward, putting his feet into the cuirass, and fitting the greaves on to his

---

3 1 Cor. iii. 12.
4 Ps. cxix. 127. LXX. (χρυσίον καὶ τοπάζιον).
5 τῇ λοιπόν.
6 For the gold, see Prov. xi. 22 ; for the pearl, S. Matt. vii. 6.
7 τὸ μὴ συνηρμόσθαι τινὶ διὰ τῶν καταλλήλων τὸν βίον.

8 ἀδολεσχίαν τοῦ λόγου τις καταγινώσκοι.
9 ὥσπερ τι ἀνάθημα ; so Gregory calls the tongue of S. Meletius the ἀνάθημα of Truth.
1 Gregory seems to allude to S. Matt. xi. 12.

breast, changing to the right side all that ought to go on the left and *vice versa*, and how such a hoplite would be likely to fare in battle, then we should have an idea of the fate in life which is sure to await him whose confused judgment makes him reverse the proper uses of his soul's faculties. We must therefore provide this balance in all feeling; the true sobriety of mind is naturally able to supply it; and if one had to find an exact definition of this sobriety, one might declare absolutely, that it amounts to our ordered control, by dint of wisdom and prudence, over every emotion of the soul. Moreover, such a condition in the soul will be no longer in need of any laborious method to attain to the high and heavenly realities; it will accomplish with the greatest ease that which erewhile seemed so unattainable; it will grasp the object of its search as a natural consequence of rejecting the opposite attractions. A man who comes out of darkness is necessarily in the light; a man who is not dead is necessarily alive. Indeed, if a man is not to have received his soul to no purpose [2], he will certainly be upon the path of truth; the prudence and the science employed to guard against error will be itself a sure guidance along the right road. Slaves who have been freed and cease to serve their former masters, the very moment they become their own masters, direct all their thoughts towards themselves; so, I take it, the soul which has been freed from ministering to the body becomes at once cognizant of its own inherent energy. But this liberty consists, as we learn from the Apostle [3], in not again being held in the yoke of slavery, and in not being bound again, like a runaway or a criminal, with the fetters of marriage. But I must return here to what I said at first; that the perfection of this liberty does not consist only in that one point of abstaining from marriage. Let no one suppose that the prize of virginity is so insignificant and so easily won as that; as if one little observance of the flesh could settle so vital a matter. But we have seen that every man who doeth a sin is the servant of sin [4]; so that a declension towards vice in any act, or in any practice whatever, makes a slave, and still more, a branded slave, of the man, covering him through sin's lashes with bruises and seared spots. Therefore it behoves the man who grasps at the transcendent aim of all virginity to be true to himself in every respect, and to manifest his purity equally in every relation of his life. If any of the inspired words are required to aid our pleading, the Truth [5] Itself will be sufficient to corroborate

the truth when It inculcates this very kind of teaching in the veiled meaning of a Gospel Parable: the good and eatable fish are separated by the fishers' skill from the bad and poisonous fish, so that the enjoyment of the good should not be spoilt by any of the bad getting into the "vessels" with them. The work of true sobriety is the same; from all pursuits and habits to choose that which is pure and improving, rejecting in every case that which does not seem likely to be useful, and letting it go back into the universal and secular life, called "the sea [6]," in the imagery of the Parable. The Psalmist [7] also, when expounding the doctrine of a full confession [8], calls this restless suffering tumultuous life, "waters coming in even unto the soul," "depths of waters," and a "hurricane"; in which sea indeed every rebellious thought sinks, as the Egyptian did, with a stone's weight into the deeps [9]. But all in us that is dear to God, and has a piercing insight into the truth (called "Israel" in the narrative), passes, but that alone, over that sea as if it were dry land, and is never reached by the bitterness and the brine of life's billows. Thus, typically, under the leadership of the Law (for Moses was a type of the Law that was coming) Israel passes unwetted over that sea, while the Egyptian who crosses in her track is overwhelmed. Each fares according to the disposition which he carries with him; one walks lightly enough, the other is dragged into the deep water. For virtue is a light and buoyant thing, and all who live in her way "fly like clouds [1]," as Isaiah says, "and as doves with their young ones"; but sin is a heavy affair, "sitting," as another of the prophets says, "upon a talent of lead [2]." If, however, this reading of the history appears to any forced and inapplicable, and the miracle at the Red Sea does not present itself to him as written for our profit, let him listen to the Apostle: "Now all these things happened unto them for types, and they are written for our admonition [3]."

CHAPTER XIX.

BUT besides other things the action of Miriam the prophetess also gives rise to these surmisings of ours. Directly the sea was crossed she took in her hand a dry and sounding timbrel and conducted the women's dance [4]. By this timbrel

---

[2] ἐπὶ ματαίῳ λάβοι. Gregory evidently alludes to Ps. xxiv. 4, and agrees with the Vulgate "in vano acceperit."
[3] Gal. v. 1.   [4] S. John viii. 34.   [5] S. John xiv. 6.

[6] S. Matt. xiii. 47, 48.   [7] Ps. lxix. 1.
[8] διδασκαλίαν ἐξομολογήσεως ὑφηγούμενος.   [9] Exod. xv. 10.
[1] Is. lx. 8. The LXX. has περιστερὰν σὺν νεοσσοῖς.
[2] Zech v. 7. "this is a woman that sitteth in the midst of the ephah:" ἐπὶ μέσον τοῦ μέτρου (LXX.). Origen and Jerome as well as Grego y make her sit upon the lead itself. Vatablus explains that the lead was in an amphora.
[3] 1 Cor. x. 11: Rom. xv. 6.   [4] Exod. xv. 20.

the story may mean to imply virginity, as first perfected by Miriam; whom indeed I would believe to be a type of Mary the mother of God [5]. Just as the timbrel emits a loud sound because it is devoid of all moisture and reduced to the highest degree of dryness, so has virginity a clear and ringing report amongst men because it repels from itself the vital sap of merely physical life. Thus, Miriam's timbrel being a dead thing, and virginity being a deadening of the bodily passions, it is perhaps not very far removed from the bounds of probability [6] that Miriam was a virgin. However, we can but guess and surmise, we cannot clearly prove, that this was so, and that Miriam the prophetess led a dance of virgins, even though many of the learned have affirmed distinctly that she was unmarried, from the fact that the history makes no mention either of her marriage or of her being a mother; and surely she would have been named and known, not as "the sister of Aaron [7]," but from her husband, if she had had one; since the head of the woman is not the brother but the husband. But if, amongst a people with whom motherhood was sought after and classed as a blessing and, regarded as a public duty, the grace of virginity, nevertheless, came to be regarded as a precious thing, how does it behove *us* to feel towards it, who do not "judge" of the Divine blessings [8] "according to the flesh"? Indeed it has been revealed in the oracles of God, on what occasion to conceive and to bring forth is a good thing, and what species of fecundity was desired by God's saints; for both the Prophet Isaiah and the divine Apostle have made this clear and certain. The one cries, "From fear of Thee, O Lord, have I conceived [9];" the other boasts that he is the parent of the largest family of any, bringing to the birth whole cities and nations; not the Corinthians and Galatians only whom by his travailings he moulded for the Lord, but all in the wide circuit from Jerusalem to Illyricum; his children filled the world, "begotten" by him in Christ through the Gospel [1]. In the same strain the womb of the Holy Virgin, which ministered to an Immaculate Birth, is pronounced blessed in the Gospel [2]; for that birth did not annul the Virginity, nor did the Virginity impede so great a birth. When the "spirit of salvation [3]," as

Isaiah names it, is being born, the willings of the flesh are useless. There is also a particular teaching of the Apostle, which harmonizes with this; viz. each man of us is a double man [4]; one the outwardly visible, whose natural fate it is to decay; the other perceptible only in the secret of the heart, yet capable of renovation. If this teaching is true,—and it must be true [5] because Wisdom is speaking there,—then there is no absurdity in supposing a double marriage also which answers in every detail to either man; and, maybe, if one was to assert boldly that the body's virginity was the co-operator and the agent of the inward marriage, this assertion would not be much beside the probable fact.

CHAPTER XX.

Now it is impossible, as far as manual exercise goes, to ply two arts at once; for instance, husbandry and sailing, or tinkering and carpentering. If one is to be honestly taken in hand, the other must be left alone. Just so, there are these two marriages for our choice, the one effected in the flesh, the other in the spirit; and preoccupation in the one must cause of necessity alienation from the other. No more is the eye able to look at two objects at once; but it must concentrate its special attention on one at a time; no more can the tongue effect utterances in two different languages, so as to pronounce, for instance, a Hebrew word and a Greek word in the same moment: no more can the ear take in at one and the same time a narrative of facts, and a hortatory discourse; if each special tone is heard separately, it will impress its ideas upon the hearers' minds; but if they are combined and so poured into the ear, an inextricable confusion of ideas will be the result, one meaning being mutually lost in the other: and no more, by analogy, do our emotional powers possess a nature which can at once pursue the pleasures of sense and court the spiritual union; nor, besides, can both those ends be gained by the same courses of life; continence, mortification of the passions, scorn of fleshly needs, are the agents of the one union; but all that are the reverse of these are the agents of bodily cohabitation. As, when two masters are before us to choose between, and we cannot be subject to both, for "no man can serve two masters [6]," he who is wise will choose the one most useful to himself, so, when two marriages are before us to choose between, and we cannot contract both, for "he that is unmarried cares for the things of

---

[5] δι' ἧς οἶμαι καὶ τὴν Θεοτόκον προδιατυποῦσθαι Μαρίαν. These words are absent from the Munich Cod. *i. e.* the German: not from Vat. and Reg. Ambrose, Ep. 25, has "Quid de alterâ Moysi sorore Mariâ loquar, quæ fœminei dux agminis pede transmisit pelagi freta," when speaking "de gloriâ virginitatis."

[6] τοῦ εἰκότος . . . ἀπεσχοίνισται. [7] Exod. xv. 20.

[8] S. John viii. 15. "Ye judge after the flesh." It is Gregory's manner to make such passing allusions to Scripture, and especially to S. Paul.

[9] Gregory here quotes from LXX. Cf. Is. xxvi. 18, and also below, ἐτέκομεν πνεῦμα σωτηρίας σου, ὃ ἐποιήσαμεν ἐπὶ τῆς γῆς.

[1] 1 Cor. iv. 15: Philemon 10. [2] S. Luke xi. 27.

[3] Is. xxvi. 18 (LXX.). See above. But R. V. "We have as it were brought forth wind: we have not wrought any deliverance in the earth."

[4] 2 Cor. iv. 16.

[5] πάντως δὲ ἀληθῆς, κ. τ. λ. So Codd. Reg. and Morell., for πάντων. Gregory alludes to 2 Cor. xiii. 3. [6] S. Matt. vi. 24.

the Lord, but he that is married careth for the things of the world [7]," I repeat that it would be the aim of a sound mind not to miss choosing the more profitable one ; and not to be ignorant either of the way which will lead it to this, a way which cannot be learnt but by some such comparison as the following. In the case of a marriage of this world a man who is anxious to avoid appearing altogether insignificant pays the greatest attention both to physical health, and becoming adornment, and amplitude of means, and the security from any disgraceful revelations as to his antecedents or his parentage ; for so he thinks things will be most likely to turn out as he wishes. Now just in the same way the man who is courting the spiritual alliance will first of all display himself, by the renewal of his mind [8], a young man, without a single touch of age upon him ; next he will reveal a lineage rich in that in which it is a noble ambition to be rich, not priding himself on worldly wealth, but luxuriating only in the heavenly treasures. As for family distinction, he will not vaunt that which comes by the mere routine of devolution even to numbers of the worthless, but that which is gained by the successful efforts of his own zeal and labours ; a distinction which only those can boast of who are "sons of the light" and children of God, and are styled "nobles from the sunrise [9]" because of their splendid deeds. Strength and health he will not try to gain by bodily training and feeding, but by all that is the contrary of this, perfecting the spirit's strength in the body's weakness. I could tell also of the suitor's gifts to the bride in such a wedding [1] ; they are not procured by the money that perishes, but are contributed out of the wealth peculiar to the soul. Would you know their names? You must hear from Paul, that excellent adorner of the Bride [2], in what the wealth of those consists who in everything commend themselves. He mentions much else that is priceless in it, and adds, "in chastity [3]" ; and besides this all the recognized fruits of the spirit from any quarter whatever are gifts of this marriage. If a man is going to carry out the advice of Solomon and take for helpmate and life-companion that true Wisdom of which he says, "Love her, and she shall keep thee," "honour her, that she may embrace thee [4]," then he will prepare himself in a manner worthy of such a love, so as to feast with all the joyous wedding guests in spotless raiment, and

not be cast forth, while claiming to sit at that feast, for not having put on the wedding garment. It is plain moreover that the argument applies equally to men and women, to move them towards such a marriage. "There is neither male nor female [5]," the Apostle says ; "Christ is all, and in all [6]" ; and so it is equally reasonable that he who is enamoured of wisdom should hold the Object of his passionate desire, Who is the True Wisdom ; and that the soul which cleaves to the undying Bridegroom should have the fruition of her love for the true Wisdom, which is God. We have now sufficiently revealed the nature of the spiritual union, and the Object of the pure and heavenly Love.

CHAPTER XXI.

It is perfectly clear that no one can come near the purity of the Divine Being who has not first himself become such ; he must therefore place between himself and the pleasures of the senses a high strong wall of separation, so that in this his approach to the Deity the purity of his own heart may not become soiled again. Such an impregnable wall will be found in a complete estrangement from everything wherein passion operates.

Now pleasure is one in kind, as we learn from the experts ; as water parted into various channels from one single fountain, it spreads itself over the pleasure-lover through the various avenues of the senses ; so that it has been on his heart that the man, who through any one particular sensation succumbs to the resulting pleasure, has received a wound from that sensation. This accords with the teaching given from the Divine lips, that "he who has satisfied the lust of the eyes has received the mischief already in his heart [7]"; for I take it that our Lord was speaking in that particular example of any of the senses ; so that we might well carry on His saying, and add, "He who hath heard, to lust after," and what follows, "He who hath touched to lust after," "He who hath lowered any faculty within us to the service of pleasure, hath sinned in his heart."

To prevent this, then, we want to apply to our own lives that rule of all temperance, never to let the mind dwell on anything wherein pleasure's bait is hid ; but above all to be specially watchful against the pleasure of taste. For that seems in a way the most deeply rooted, and to be the mother as it were of all forbidden enjoyment. The pleasures of eating and drinking, leading to boundless excess, inflict upon the body the doom of the most

---

[7] 1 Cor. vii. 32.　　　　　[8] See Eph. iv. 22, 23.
[9] See S. Matt. viii. 11 ; S. Luke xiii. 29. The same expression (εὐγενὴς τῶν ἀφ' ἡλίου ἀνατολῶν) is used of Meletius, in Gregory's funeral oration on him.
[1] τὰ ἕδνα τοῦ γάμου, i. e. given by the bridegroom. The Jurisconsults called it Donatio propter nuptias, or simply Donatio. The human soul here espouses Wisdom, i. e. Christ, as its Bride. See below, where Prov. iv. 6 is quoted.
[2] νυμφοστόλου.　　[3] 2 Cor. vi. 6.　　[4] Prov. iv. 6.

[5] Gal. iii. 28.　　[6] Col. iii. 11.　　[7] S. Matt. v. 28.

dreadful sufferings [8]; for over-indulgence is the parent of most of the painful diseases. To secure for the body a continuous tranquillity, unstirred by the pains of surfeit, we must make up our minds to a more sparing regimen, and constitute the need of it on each occasion, not the pleasure of it, as the measure and limit of our indulgence. If the sweetness will nevertheless mingle itself with the satisfaction of the need (for hunger knows how to sweeten everything [9], and by the vehemence of appetite she gives the zest of pleasure to every discoverable supply of the need), we must not because of the resulting enjoyment reject the satisfaction, nor yet make this latter our leading aim. In everything we must select the expedient quantity, and leave untouched what merely feasts the senses [1].

CHAPTER XXII.

WE see how the husbandmen have a method for separating the chaff, which is united with the wheat, with a view to employ each for its proper purpose, the one for the sustenance of man, the other for burning and the feeding of animals. The labourer in the field of temperance will in like manner distinguish the satisfaction from the mere delight, and will fling this latter nature to savages [2] "whose end is to be burned [3]," as the Apostle says, but will take the other, in proportion to the actual need, with thankfulness. Many, however, slide into the very opposite kind of excess, and unconsciously to themselves, in their over-preciseness, laboriously thwart their own design; they let their soul fall down the other side from the heights of Divine elevation to the level of dull thoughts and occupations, where their minds are so bent upon regulations which merely affect the body, that they can no longer walk in their heavenly freedom and gaze above; their only inclination is to this tormenting and afflicting of the flesh. It would be well, then, to give this also careful thought, so as to be equally on our guard against either over-amount [4], neither stifling the mind beneath the wound of the flesh, nor, on the other hand, by gratuitously inflicted weakenings

sapping and lowering the powers, so that it can have no thought but of the body's pain [5]; and let every one remember that wise precept, which warns us from turning to the right hand or to the left. I have heard a certain physician of my acquaintance, in the course of explaining the secrets of his art, say that our body consists of four elements, not of the same species, but disposed to be conflicting: yet the hot penetrated the cold, and an equally unexpected union of the wet and the dry took place, the contradictories of each pair being brought into contact by their relationship to the intervening pair. He added an extremely subtle explanation of this account of his studies in nature. Each of these elements was in its essence *diametrically* [6] opposed to its contradictory; but then it had two other qualities lying on each side of it, and by virtue of its kinship with them it came into contact with its contradictory; for example, the cold and the hot each unite with the wet, or the dry; and again, the wet and the dry each unite with the hot, or the cold: and so this sameness of quality, when it manifests itself in contradictories, is itself the agent which affects the union of those contradictories. What business of mine, however, is it to explain exactly the details of this change from this mutual separation and repugnance of nature, to this mutual union through the medium of kindred qualities, except for the purpose for which we mentioned it? And that purpose was to add that the author of this analysis of the body's constitution advised that all possible care be taken to preserve a balance between these properties, for that in fact health consisted in not letting any one of them gain the mastery within us. If his doctrine has truth in it, then, for our health's continuance, we must secure such a habit, and by no irregularity of diet produce either an excess or a defect in any member of these our constituent elements. The chariot-master, if the young horses which he has to drive will not work well together, does not urge a fast one with the whip, and rein in a slow one; nor, again, does he let a horse that

---

[8] ἀναγκὴν ἐμποιοῦσι τῶν ἀβουλητῶν κακῶν, πλησμονῆς ὡς τὰ πολλὰ ἐκτίκτουσης, κ. τ. λ., removing the comma from πλησμονῆς (Paris Edit.) to κακῶν.
[9] Cf. Cicero, 2 *De Fin. Bon.*: "Socratem audio dicentem cibi condimentum esse famem; potionis sitim;" so Antiphanes (apud Stobæum), ἀπάνθ' ὁ λιμὸς γλυκέα, πλὴν αὑτοῦ, ποιεῖ.
[1] κατὰ τὸ προηγούμενον, principaliter. Cf. Clem. Alexand. *Strom.*, τὰ ὀνόματα σύμβολα τῶν νοημάτων κατὰ τὸ προηγούμενον, *i. e.* of *general* concepts.
[2] τοῖς ἀλογωτέροις. Fronto Ducæus translates "bardis objiciat," *i. e.* "savages," not "beasts."
[3] Heb. vi. 8. "The *Apostle*" here is to be noticed. The same teaching, as to there being no necessity for pleasure, is found in Clement of Alexandria. He says it is not our σκοπός, 2 *Pæd.* c. i. and 2 *Strom.*, καθόλου γὰρ οὐκ ἀναγκαῖον τὸ τῆς ἡδονῆς πάθος, ἐπακολούθιμον δὲ χρείαις ταῖς φυσικαῖς, κ.τ.λ.
[4] ἐπιμετρίας. Cf. ἐν ἐπιμέτρῳ, Polyb., "into the bargain."

---

[5] καὶ περὶ τοὺς σωματικοὺς πόνους ἠσχολημένον (*i. e.* "busied"): Galesinius' translation must here be wrong, "ad corporis labores prorsus inutilem."

[6]

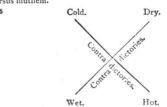

Cold.   Dry.

Wet.   Hot.

Cold can unite with Wet or Dry which "lie on each side of" it, and are "kindred" to it: and so through one or the other (which are also "kindred" to Hot) can come "in contact with" Hot. (So of all.) A wet thing becomes the medium in which both cold and heat can be manifested.

shies in the traces or is hard-mouthed gallop his own way to the confusion of orderly driving; but he quickens the pace of the first, checks the second, reaches the third with cuts of his whip, till he has made them all breathe evenly together in a straight career. Now our mind in like manner holds in its grasp the reins of this chariot of the body; and in that capacity it will not devise, in the time of youth, when heat of temperament is abundant, ways of heightening that fever; nor will it multiply the cooling and the thinning things when the body is already chilled by illness or by time; and in the case of all these physical qualities it will be guided by the Scripture, so as actually to realize it: "He that gathered much had nothing over; and he that had gathered little had no lack [7]." It will curtail immoderate lengths in either direction, and so will be careful to replenish where there is much lack. The inefficiency of the body from either cause will be that which it guards against; it will train the flesh, neither making it wild and ungovernable by excessive pampering, nor sickly and unstrung and nerveless for the required work by immoderate mortification. That is temperance's highest aim; it looks not to the afflicting of the body, but to the peaceful action of the soul's functions.

CHAPTER XXIII.

Now the details of the life of him who has chosen to live in such a philosophy as this, the things to be avoided, the exercises to be engaged in, the rules of temperance, the whole method of the training, and all the daily regimen which contributes towards this great end, has been dealt with in certain written manuals of instruction for the benefit of those who love details. Yet there is a plainer guide to be found than verbal instruction; and that is practice: and there is nothing vexatious in the maxim that when we are undertaking a long journey or voyage we should get an instructor. "But," says the Apostle [8], "the word is nigh thee;" the grace begins at home; there is the manufactory of all the virtues; there this life has become exquisitely refined by a continual progress towards consummate perfection; there, whether men are silent or whether they speak, there is large opportunity for being instructed in this heavenly citizenship through the actual practice of it. Any theory divorced from living examples, however admirably it may be dressed out, is like the

unbreathing statue, with its show of a blooming complexion impressed in tints and colours; but the man who acts as well as teaches, as the Gospel tells us, he is the man who is truly living, and has the bloom of beauty, and is efficient and stirring. It is to him that we must go, if we mean, according to the saying [9] of Scripture, to "retain" virginity. One who wants to learn a foreign language is not a competent instructor of himself; he gets himself taught by experts, and can then talk with foreigners. So, for this high life, which does not advance in nature's groove, but is estranged from her by the novelty of its course, a man cannot be instructed thoroughly unless he puts himself into the hands of one who has himself led it in perfection; and indeed in all the other professions of life the candidate is more likely to achieve success if he gets from tutors a scientific knowledge of each part of the subject of his choice, than if he undertook to study it by himself; and this particular profession [1] is not one where everything is so clear that judgment as to our best course in it is necessarily left to ourselves; it is one where to hazard a step into the unknown at once brings us into danger. The science of medicine once did not exist; it has come into being by the experiments which men have made, and has gradually been revealed through their various observations; the healing and the harmful drug became known from the attestation of those who had tried them, and this distinction was adopted into the theory of the art, so that the close observation of former practitioners became a precept for those who succeeded; and now any one who studies to attain this art is under no necessity to ascertain at his own peril the power of any drug, whether it be a poison or a medicine; he has only to learn from others the known facts, and may then practise with success. It is so also with that medicine of the soul, philosophy, from which we learn the remedy for every weakness that can touch the soul. We need not hunt after a knowledge of these remedies by dint of guess-work and surmisings; we have abundant means of learning them from him who by a long and rich experience has gained the possession which we seek. In any matter youth is generally a giddy [2] guide; and it would not be easy to

---

[7] ἐλαττονήσῃ (for LXX. Exod. xvi. 18, and also 2 Cor. viii. 15, have ἐλαττόνησεν), not ἐλαττώσῃ with Livineius.

[8] Rom. x. 8: ἐγγύς σου τὸ ῥῆμά ἐστιν, ἐν τῷ στόματί σου καὶ ἐν τῇ καρδίᾳ σου. Cf. Deut. xxx. 14.

[9] κατὰ τὸν ἐροῦντα λόγον (Codd. Reg. and Mor. αἱροῦντα). This alludes to Prov. iii. 18, rather than Prov. iv. 6.

[1] οὐ γὰρ ἐναργές ἐστι τὸ ἐπιτήδευμα τοῦτο, ὥστε κατ' ἀνάγκην, κ.τ.λ. The alternative reading is ἐν ἀρχαῖς. It has been suggested to read, ὅτε γὰρ . . . τότε (for τοῦτο), and understand an aposiopesis in the next sentence; thus—"For when our undertaking is clear and simple, then we must entrust to ourselves the decision of what is best. But when the attempt at the unknown is not unattended with risk—(then we want a guide)." Billius. But this is very awkward.

[2] Livineius had conjectured that ἐπισφαλὴς must be supplied, from a quotation of this passage in Antonius Monachus, Sententiæ, serm. 20, and in Abbas Maximus, Capita, serm. 41; and this is confirmed by Codd. Reg. and Morell.

find anything of importance succeeding, in which gray hairs have not been called in to share in the deliberations. Even in all other undertakings we must, in proportion to their greater importance, take the more precaution against failure; for in them too the thoughtless designs of youth have brought loss; on property, for instance; or have compelled the surrender of a position in the world, and even of renown. But in this mighty and sublime ambition it is not property, or secular glory lasting for its hour, or any external fortune, that is at stake; —of such things[3], whether they settle themselves well or the reverse, the wise take small account;— *here* rashness can affect the soul itself; and we run the awful hazard, not of losing any of those other things whose recovery even may perhaps be possible, but of ruining our very selves and making the soul a bankrupt. A man who has spent or lost his patrimony does not despair, as long as he is in the land of the living, of perchance coming again through contrivances into his former competence; but the man who has ejected himself from this calling, deprives himself as well of all hope of a return to better things. Therefore, since most embrace virginity while still young and unformed in understanding, this before anything else should be their employment, to search out a fitting guide and master of this way, lest, in their present ignorance, they should wander from the direct route, and strike out new paths of their own in trackless wilds[4]. "Two are better than one," says the Preacher[5]; but a single one is easily vanquished by the foe who infests the path which leads to God; and verily "woe to him that is alone when he falleth, for he hath not another to help him up[6]." Some ere now in their enthusiasm for the stricter life have shown a dexterous alacrity; but, as if in the very moment of their choice they had already touched perfection, their pride has had a shocking fall[7], and they have been tripped up from madly deluding themselves into thinking that that to which their own mind inclined them was the true beauty. In this number are those whom Wisdom calls the "slothful ones[8]," who bestrew their "way" with "thorns"; who think it a moral loss to be anxious about keeping the commandments; who erase from their own minds the Apostolic teaching, and instead of eating the bread of their own honest earning fix on that of others, and make their idleness itself into an art of living.

From this number, too, come the Dreamers, who put more faith in the illusions of their dreams[9] than in the Gospel teaching, and style their own phantasies "revelations." Hence, too, those who "creep into the houses"; and again others who suppose virtue to consist in savage bearishness, and have never known the fruits of long-suffering and humility of spirit. Who could enumerate all the pitfalls into which any one might slip, from refusing to have recourse to men of godly celebrity? Why, we have known ascetics of this class who have persisted in their fasting even unto death, as if "with such sacrifices God were well pleased[1];" and, again, others who rush off into the extreme diametrically opposite, practising celibacy in name only and leading a life in no way different from the secular; for they not only indulge in the pleasures of the table, but are openly known to have a woman in their houses[2]; and they call such a friendship a brotherly affection, as if, forsooth, they could veil their own thought, which is inclined to evil, under a sacred term. It is owing to them that this pure and holy profession of virginity is "blasphemed amongst the Gentiles[3]."

CHAPTER XXIV.

IT would therefore be to their profit, for the young to refrain from laying down[4] *for themselves* their future course in this profession; and indeed, examples of holy lives for them to follow are not wanting in the living generation[5]. Now, if ever before, saintliness abounds and penetrates our world; by gradual advances it has reached the highest mark of perfectness; and one who follows such footsteps in his daily rounds may catch this halo; one who tracks the scent of this preceding perfume may be drenched in the sweet odours of Christ Himself. As, when one torch has been fired, flame is transmitted to all the neighbouring candlesticks, without either the first light being lessened or blazing with unequal brilliance on the other points where it has been caught; so the saintliness of a life is transmitted from him who has achieved it, to those who come within his circle; for there

---

[3] ὧν καὶ κατὰ γνώμην καὶ ὡς ἑτέρως διοικουμένων ὀλίγος τοῖς σωφρονοῦσιν ὁ λόγος. The Latin here has "quas quidem res ego sane despicio, exiguamque harum tanquam extrinsecus venientium," &c.; evidently καταγνοίην must have been in the text used.
[4] ἀνοδίας τινὰς καινοτομήσωσιν (ἀνοδίᾳ, ἀνοδίαις, is frequent in Polybius; the word is not found elsewhere in other cases).
[5] Ecclesiastes iv. 9.
[6] Ecclesiastes iv. 10. Gregory supports the Vulgate, which has "quia cum ceciderit, non habet sublevantem se."
[7] ἑτέρῳ πτώματι, euphemistically. [8] Prov. xv. 19.

---

[9] The alternative reading is τῶν θηρίων; but ὀνείρων is confirmed by three of the Codd. Cf. Theodoret, lib. 4, *Hæretic. fab.*, of the Messaliani; and lib. 4, *Histor.* c. 10, ὕπνῳ δὲ σφᾶς αὐτοὺς ἐκδίδοντες τὰς τῶν ὀνείρων φαντασίας προφητείας ἀποκαλοῦσι.
[1] Heb. xiii. 16.
[2] See Chrysostom, Lib. Πρὸς τοὺς συνεισάκτους ἔχοντας.
[3] τῶν ἔξωθεν. Cf. Rom. ii. 24.
[4] The negative (μὴ νομοθετεῖν) is found in Codd. Reg. and Morell.
[5] τὴν ζωήν. So βίος also is used in Greek after 2nd century. "They (the monks) make little show in history before the reign of Valens (A.D. 364). Paul of Thebes, Hilarion of Gaza, and even the great Antony, are only characters in the novels of the day. Now, however, there was in the East a real movement towards monasticism. All parties favoured it. The Semi-arians were busy inside Mt. Taurus; and though Acacians and Anomœans held more aloof, they could not escape an influence which even Julian felt. But the Nicene party was the home of the ascetics." Gwatkin's *Arians*.

is truth in the Prophet's saying [6], that one who lives with a man who is "holy" and "clean" and "elect," will become such himself. If you would wish to know the sure signs, which will secure you the real model, it is not hard to take a sketch from life. If you see a man so standing between death and life, as to select from each helps for the contemplative course, never letting death's stupor paralyze his zeal to keep all the commandments, nor yet placing both feet in the world of the living, since he has weaned himself from secular ambitions ;—a man who remains more insensate than the dead themselves to everything that is found on examination to be living for the flesh, but instinct with life and energy and strength in the achievements of virtue, which are the sure marks of the spiritual life ;—then look to that man for the rule of your life ; let him be the leading light of your course of devotion, as the constellations that never set are to the pilot ; imitate his youth and his gray hairs : or, rather, imitate the old man and the stripling who are joined in him ; for even now in his declining years time has not blunted the keen activity of his soul, nor was his youth active in the sphere of youth's well-known employments ; in both seasons of life he has shown a wonderful combination of opposites, or rather an exchange of the peculiar qualities of each ; for in age he shows, in the direction of the good, a young man's energy, while, in the hours of youth, in the direction of evil, his passions were powerless. If you wish to know what were the passions of that glorious youth of his, you will have for your imitation the intensity and glow of his god-like love of wisdom, which grew with him from his childhood, and has continued with him into his old age. But if you cannot gaze upon him, as the weak-sighted cannot gaze upon the sun, at all events watch that band of holy men who are ranged beneath him, and who by the illu-mination of their lives are a model for this age. God has placed them as a beacon for us who live around ; many among them have been young men there in their prime, and have grown gray in the unbroken practice of continence and temperance ; they were old in reasonableness before their time, and in character outstripped their years. The only love they tasted was that of wisdom ; not that their natural instincts were different from the rest ; for in all alike "the flesh lusteth against the spirit [7] ;" but they listened to some purpose to him who said that Temperance "is a tree of life to them that lay hold upon her [8] ;" and they sailed across the swelling billows of existence upon this tree of life, as upon a skiff, and anchored in the haven of the

will of God ; enviable now after so fair a voyage, they rest their souls in that sunny cloudless calm. They now ride safe themselves at the anchor of a good hope, far out of reach of the tumult of the billows ; and for others who will follow they radiate the splendour of their lives as beacon-fires on some high watch-tower. We have indeed a mark to guide us safely over the ocean of temptations ; and why make the too curious inquiry, whether some with such thoughts as these have not fallen nevertheless, and why therefore despair, as if the achievement was be-yond your reach? Look on him who has suc-ceeded, and boldly launch upon the voyage with confidence that it will be prosperous, and sail on under the breeze of the Holy Spirit with Christ your pilot and with the oarage of good cheer [9]. For those who "go down to the sea in ships and occupy their business in great waters" do not let the shipwreck that has be-fallen some one else prevent their being of good cheer ; they rather shield their hearts in this very confidence, and so sweep on to accomplish their successful feat. Surely it is the most absurd thing in the world to reprobate him who has slipped in a course which requires the greatest nicety, while one considers those who all their lives have been growing old in failures and in errors, to have chosen the better part. If one single approach to sin is such an awful thing that you deem it safer not to take in hand at all this loftier aim, how much more awful a thing it is to make sin the practice of a whole life, and to remain thereby absolutely ignorant of the purer course ! How can you in your full life obey the Crucified? How can you, hale in sin, obey Him Who died to sin? How can you, who are not crucified to the world, and will not accept the mortification of the flesh, obey Him Who bids you follow after Him, and Who bore the Cross in His own body, as a trophy from the foe? How can you obey Paul when he exhorts you "to present your body a living sacrifice, holy, acceptable unto God [1]," when you are "conformed to this world," and not trans-formed by the renewing of your mind, when you are not "walking" in this "newness of life," but still pursuing the routine of "the old man"? How can you be a priest unto God [2], anointed though you are for this very office, to offer a gift to God ; a gift in no way another's, no counterfeited gift from sources outside yourself, but a gift that is really your own, namely, "the inner man [3]," who must be perfect and blameless, as it is required of a lamb to be without spot or blemish? How can you offer this to God, when you do not listen to the law forbidding the

6 Ps. xviii. 25, 26 (LXX.).
7 Gal. v. 17.   8 Prov. iii. 18 ; but said of *Wisdom*.

9 τῷ πηδαλίῳ τῆς εὐφροσύνης.   1 Rom. xii. 1, 2 ; vi. 4.
2 Gregory alludes to Rev. i. 6 : ἐποίησεν ἡμᾶς βασιλεῖς καὶ ἱερεῖς τῷ θεῷ καὶ πατρὶ αὐτοῦ.   3 Eph. iii. 16.

unclean to offer sacrifices? If you long for God to manifest Himself to you, why do you not hear Moses, when he commands the people to be pure from the stains of marriage, that they may take in the vision of God [4]? If this all seems little in your eyes, to be crucified with Christ, to present yourself a sacrifice to God, to become a priest unto the most high God, to make yourself worthy of the vision of the Almighty, what higher blessings than these can we imagine for you, if indeed you make light of the consequences of these as well? And the consequence of being crucified with Christ is that we shall live with Him, and be glorified with Him, and reign with Him; and the consequence of presenting ourselves to God is that we shall be changed from the rank of human nature and human dignity to that of Angels; for so speaks Daniel, that "thousand thousands stood before him [5]." He too who has taken his share in the true priesthood and placed himself beside the Great High Priest remains altogether himself a priest for ever, prevented for eternity from remaining any more in death. To say, again, that one makes oneself worthy to see God, produces no less a result than this; that one is made worthy to see God. Indeed, the crown of every hope, and of every desire, of every blessing, and of every promise of God, and of all those unspeakable delights which we believe to exist beyond our perception and our knowledge,—the crowning result of them all, I say, is this. Moses longed earnestly to see it, and many prophets and kings have desired to see the same: but the only class deemed worthy of it are the pure in heart, those who are, and are named " blessed," for this very reason, that "they shall see God [6]." Wherefore we would that you too should become crucified with Christ, a holy priest standing before God, a pure offering in all chastity, preparing yourself by your own holiness for God's coming; that you also may have a pure heart in which to see God, according to the promise of God, and of our Saviour Jesus Christ, to Whom be glory for ever and ever. Amen.

---

[4] Exod. xix. 15.   [5] Dan. vii. 10.   [6] S. Matt. v.

ON INFANTS' EARLY DEATHS

EVERY essayist and every pamphleteer will have you, most Excellent, to display his eloquence upon; your wondrous qualities will be a broad race-course wherein he may expatiate. A noble and suggestive subject in able hands has indeed a way of making a grander style, lifting it to the height of the great reality. We, however, like an aged horse, will remain outside this proposed race-course, only turning the ear to listen for the contest waged in celebrating your praises, if the sound of any literary car careering in full swing through such wonders may reach us. But though old age may compel a horse to remain away from the race, it may often happen that the din of the trampling racers rouses him into excitement, that he lifts his head with eager looks, that he shows his spirit in his breathings, and prances and paws the ground frequently, though this eagerness is all that is left to him, and time has sapped his powers of going. In the same way our pen remains outside the combat, and age compels it to yield the course to the professors who flourish now; nevertheless its eagerness to join the contest about you survives, and that it can still evince, even though these stylists who flourish now are at the height of their powers[2]. But none of this display of my enthusiasm for you has anything to do with sounding your own praises: no style, however nervous and well-balanced, would easily succeed there; so that any one, who attempted to describe that embarrassing yet harmonious mixture of opposites in your character, would inevitably be left far behind your real worth. Nature, indeed, by throwing out the shade of the eye-lashes before the glaring rays, brings to the eyes themselves a weaker light, and so the sunlight becomes tolerable to us, mingling as it does, in quantities proportionate to our need, with the shadows which the lashes cast. Just so the grandeur and the greatness of your character, tempered by your modesty and humbleness of mind, instead of blinding the beholder's eye, makes the sight on the contrary a pleasurable one; wherein this humbleness of mind does not occasion the splendour of the greatness to be dimmed, and its latent force to be overlooked; but the one is to be noticed in the other, the humility of your character in its elevation, and the grandeur reversely in the lowliness. Others must describe all this; and extol, besides, the many-sightedness of your mind. Your intellectual eyes are indeed as numerous, it may perhaps be said, as the hairs of the head; their keen unerring gaze is on everything alike; the distant is foreseen; the near is not unnoticed; they do not wait for experience to teach expedience; they see with Hope's insight, or else with that of Memory; they scan the present all over; first on one thing, then on another, but without confusing them, your mind works with the same energy and with the amount of attention that is required. Another, too, must record his admiration of the way in which poverty is made rich by you; if indeed any one is to be found in this age of ours who will make *that* a subject of praise and wonder. Yet surely now, if never before, the love of poverty will through you abound, and your *ingotten* wealth[3] will be envied above the *ingots* of Crœsus. For whom has sea and land, with all the dower of their natural produce, enriched, as thy rejection of worldly abundance has enriched thee? They wipe the stain from steel and so make it shine like silver: so has the gleam of thy life grown brighter, ever carefully cleansed from the rust of wealth. We leave that to those who can enlarge upon it, and also upon your excellent knowledge of the things in which it *is* more glorious to gain than to abstain from gain. Grant me, however, leave to say, that you do

---

[1] This treatise is written for Hierius, in Gregory's old age. It has been thought to be spurious (Oudin, p. 605), because of Fronto Ducæus' insertion (p. 374) about the Purgatorial Fire. But Tillemont, Semler, and Schroeckh have shown that there are no grounds for this opinion. Anastasius Sinaita mentions it (*Quæst.* xvi.).

[2] εἴπερ ἡβῶσιν οἱ κατὰ τοὺς νῦν τοῖς λόγοις ἀκμάζοντες. The Latin translator Laurent. Sifanus, I. U. Doct. (Basle, 1562), must have had a different text to this of the Paris Edit.: "si quidem ita floreret ut qui nunc eloquentiâ vigent."

[3] πλινθότης, playing upon πλίνθων just above; a word seemingly peculiar to Gregory. We cannot help thinking here of Plato's definition of the good man, τετράγωνος ἄνευ ψόγου: though the idea here is that of richness rather than shape.

not despise all acquisitions; that there are some which, though none of your predecessors has been able to clutch, yet you and you alone have seized with both your hands; for, instead of dresses and slaves and money, you have and hold the very souls of men, and store them in the treasure-house of your love. The essayists and pamphleteers, whose glory comes from such laudations, will go into these matters. But our pen, veteran as it now is, is to rouse itself only so far as to go at a foot's pace through the problem which your wisdom has proposed; namely, this—what we are to think of those who are taken prematurely, the moment of whose birth almost coincides with that of their death. The cultured heathen Plato spoke, in the person of one who had come to life again [4], much philosophy about the judgment courts in that other world; but he has left this other question a mystery, as ostensibly too great for human conjecture to be employed upon. If, then, there is anything in these lucubrations of ours that is of a nature to clear up the obscurities of this question, you will doubtless welcome the new account of it; if otherwise, you will at all events excuse this in old age, and accept, if nothing else, our wish to afford you some degree of pleasure. History [5] says that Xerxes, that great prince who had made almost every land under the sun into one vast camp, and roused with his own designs the whole world, when he was marching against the Greeks received with delight a poor man's gift; and that gift was water, and that not in a jar, but carried in the hollow of the palm of his hand. So do you, of your innate generosity, follow his example; to him the will made the gift, and our gift may be found in itself but a poor watery thing. In the case of the wonders in the heavens, a man *sees* their beauty equally, whether he is trained to watch them, or whether he gazes upwards with an unscientific eye; but the *feeling* towards them is not the same in the man who comes from philosophy to their contemplation, and in him who has only his senses of perception to commit them to; the latter may be pleased with the sunlight, or deem the beauty of stars worthy of his wonder, or have watched the stages of the moon's course throughout the month; but the former, who has the soul-insight, and whose training has enlightened him so as to comprehend the phenomena of the heavens, leaves unnoticed all these things which delight the senses of the more unthinking, and looks at the harmony of the whole, inspecting the concert which results even from opposite movements in the circular revolutions; how the inner circles of these turn the contrary way to

that in which the fixed stars are carried round [6]; how those of the heavenly bodies to be observed in these inner circles are variously grouped in their approachments and divergements, their disappearances behind each other and their flank movements, and yet effect always precisely in the same way that notable and never-ending harmony; of which those are conscious who do not overlook the position of the tiniest star, and whose minds, by training domiciled above, pay equal attention to them all. In the same way do you, a precious life to me, watch the Divine economy; leaving those objects which unceasingly occupy the minds of the crowd, wealth, I mean, and luxury [7] and vain-glory—things which like sunbeams flashing in their faces dazzle the unthinking—you will not pass without inquiry the seemingly most trivial questions in the world; for you do most carefully scrutinize the inequalities in human lives; not only with regard to wealth and penury, and the differences of position and descent (for you know that they are as nothing, and that they owe their existence not to any intrinsic reality, but to the foolish estimate of those who are struck with nonentities, as if they were actual things; and that if one were only to abstract from somebody who glitters with glory the blind adoration [8] of those who gaze at him, nothing would be left him after all the inflated pride which elates him, even though the whole mass of the world's riches were buried in his cellars), but it is one of your anxieties to know, amongst the other intentions of each detail of the Divine government, wherefore it is that, while the life of one is lengthened into old age, another has only so far a portion of it as to breathe the air with one gasp, and die. If nothing in this world happens without God, but all is linked to the Divine will, and if the Deity is skilful and prudential, then it follows necessarily that there is some plan in these things bearing the mark of His wisdom, and at the same time of His providential care. A blind unmeaning occurrence can never be the work of God; for it is the property of God, as the Scripture says [9], to "make all things in wisdom." What wisdom, then, can we trace in the following? A human being enters on the scene of life, draws in the air, beginning the process of living with a cry of pain, pays the tribute of a tear to Nature [1], just tastes life's sorrows, before any of its sweets have been his, before his feelings have gained

---

4 *i. e.* Er the Armenian. See Plato, *Repub.* x. § 614, &c.
5 An anecdote resembling what follows, but not quite the same, is told of Xerxes in Ælian's *Var. Hist.* xii. 40. Erasmus also refers to it in his *Adagia.*

6 τῇ ἀπλανεῖ περιφορᾷ. This is of course the Ptolemaic system which had already been in vogue two centuries. Sun, and moon, and all, were "planets" round the earth as a centre: until the 8th sphere, in which the stars were fixed, was reached; and above this was the crystalline sphere, under the *primum mobile.* Cf. Milton, *Par. Lost*, iii. 481: "They pass the planets seven, and pass the *fix'd*:" and see note p. 257.
7 Reading τρυφήν. The Paris Edit. has τύφον.
8 τὴν μύησιν. 9 Ps. civ. 24. 1 ἐλειτούργησε τὸ δάκρυον.

any strength; still loose in all his joints, tender, pulpy, unset; in a word, before he is even human (if the gift of reason is man's peculiarity, and he has never had it in him), such an one, with no advantage over the embryo in the womb except that he has seen the air, so short-lived, dies and goes to pieces again; being either exposed or suffocated, or else of his own accord ceasing to live from weakness. What are we to think about him? How are we to feel about such deaths? Will a soul such as that behold its Judge? Will it stand with the rest before the tribunal? Will it undergo its trial for deeds done in life? Will it receive the just recompense by being purged, according to the Gospel utterances, in fire, or refreshed with the dew of blessing [2]? But I do not see how we can imagine that, in the case of such a soul. The word "retribution" implies that something must have been previously given; but he who has not lived at all has been deprived of the material from which to give anything. There being, then, no retribution, there is neither good nor evil left to expect. "Retribution" purports to be the paying back of one of these two qualities; but that which is to be found neither in the category of good nor that of bad is in no category at all; for this antithesis between good and bad is an opposition that admits no middle; and neither will come to him who has not made a beginning with either of them. What therefore falls under neither of these heads may be said not even to have existed. But if some one says that such a life does not only exist, but exists as one of the good ones, and that God gives, though He does not repay, what is good to such, we may ask what sort of reason he advances for this partiality; how is justice apparent in such a view; how will he prove his idea in concordance with the utterances in the Gospels? There (the Master) says, the acquisition of the Kingdom comes to those who are deemed worthy of it, as a matter of exchange. "When ye have done such and such things, then it is right that ye get the Kingdom as a reward." But in this case there is no act of doing or of willing beforehand, and so what occasion is there for saying that these will receive from God any expected recompense? If one unreservedly accepts a statement such as that, to the effect that any so passing into life will necessarily be classed amongst the good, it will dawn upon him then that not partaking in life at all will be a happier state than living, seeing that in the one case the enjoyment of good is placed beyond a doubt even with barbarian parentage, or a conception from a union not legitimate; but he who has lived the span ordinarily possible to Nature gets the pollution of evil necessarily mingled more or less with his life, or, if he is to be quite outside this contagion, it will be at the price of much painful effort. For virtue is achieved by its seekers not without a struggle; nor is abstinence from the paths of pleasure a painless process to human nature. So that one of two probations must be the inevitable fate of him who has had the longer lease of life; either to combat here on Virtue's toilsome field, or to suffer there the painful recompense of a life of evil. But in the case of infants prematurely dying there is nothing of that sort; but they pass to the blessed lot at once, if those who take this view of the matter speak true. It follows also necessarily from this that a state of unreason is preferable to having reason, and virtue will thereby be revealed as of no value: if he who has never possessed it suffers no loss, so, as regards the enjoyment of blessedness, the labour to acquire it will be useless folly; the unthinking condition will be the one that comes out best from God's judgment. For these and such-like reasons you bid me sift the matter, with a view to our getting, by dint of a closely-reasoned inquiry, some firm ground on which to rest our thoughts about it.

For my part, in view of the difficulties of the subject proposed, I think the exclamation of the Apostle very suitable to the present case, just as he uttered it over unfathomable questions: "O the depth of the riches both of the wisdom and knowledge of God! how unsearchable are His judgments, and His ways past finding out! For who hath known the mind of the Lord [3]?" But seeing on the other hand that that Apostle declares it to be a peculiarity of him that is spiritual to "judge all things [4]," and commends those who have been "enriched [5]" by the Divine grace "in all utterance and in all knowledge," I venture to assert that it is not right to omit the

---

[2] There is introduced at these words in the text of the Paris Edition the following "Explicatio," in Greek. "Here it is manifest that the father means by the 'purging fire' the torments and agonies suffered by those who having sinned have not completed a worthy and adequate repentance, according to the Gospel parable of the Rich Man and Lazarus. For it is clear that he is thinking of this parable when he says, 'either purged in fire' (i. e. the Rich Man), 'or refreshed with the dew of blessing' (i. e. Lazarus). But that sentence of the Judgment, 'They shall go, these into everlasting punishment, but the just into life everlasting,' *has no place as yet* in these sufferings." In other words, the commentator sees here the doctrine of Purgatory, as held by the Roman Church. And when we compare the other passages in Gregory about the "cleansing fire," especially that De Animâ et Resurrectione, 247 B, we shall see that he contemplates the judgment ("the incorruptible tribunal") as coming not only after the Resurrection, but also *after* the chastising process. Not till the Judgment will the *moral* value of each life be revealed; the chastising is a purely *natural* process. But then the belief in a Judgment coming after everything rather contradicts the Universalism with which he has been charged, for what necessity would there be for it, if the chastising was successful in every instance? With regard to the nature of this "fire," it is spiritual or material with him according to the context. The invisible natures will be punished with the one, the visible (i. e. the World) with the other: although this destruction is not *always* preserved by him. See E. Moeller (on Gregory's *Doctrine on Human Nature*), p. 100.

[3] Rom. xi. 33, 34.   [4] 1 Cor. ii. 15.   [5] 1 Cor. i. 5.

examination which is within the range of our ability, nor to leave the question here raised without making any inquiries, or having any ideas about it; lest, like the actual subject of our proposed discussion, this essay should have an ineffectual ending, spoilt before its maturity by the fatal indolence of those who will not nerve themselves to search out the truth, like a new-born infant ere it sees the light and acquires any strength. I assert, too, that it is not well at once to confront and meet objections, as if we were pleading in court, but to introduce a certain order into the discussion, and to lead the view on from one point to another. What, then, should this order be? First, we want to know the whence of human nature, and the wherefore of its ever having come into existence. If we hit the answer to these questions, we shall not fail in getting the required explanation. Now, that everything that exists, after God, in the intellectual or sensible world of beings owes that existence to Him, is a proposition which it is superfluous to prove; no one, with however little insight into the truth of things, would gainsay it. For every one agrees that the Universe is linked to one First Cause; that nothing in it owes its existence to itself, so as to be its own origin and cause; but that there is on the other hand a single uncreate eternal Essence, the same for ever, which transcends all our ideas of distance, conceived of as without increase or decrease, and beyond the scope of any definition; and that time and space with all their consequences, and anything previous to these that thought can grasp in the intelligible supramundane world, are all the productions of this Essence. Well, then, we affirm that human nature is one of these productions; and a word of the inspired Teaching helps us in this, which declares that when God had brought all things else upon the scene of life, man was exhibited upon the earth, a mixture from Divine sources, the godlike intellectual essence being in him united with the several portions of earthly elements contributed towards his formation, and that he was fashioned by his Maker to be the incarnate likeness of Divine transcendent Power. It would be better however to quote the very words: "And God created man, in the image of God created He him [6]." Now the reason of the making of this animate being has been given by certain writers previous to us as follows. The whole creation is divided into two parts; that "which is seen," and that "which is not seen," to use the Apostle's words (the second meaning the intelligible and immaterial, the first, the sensible and material); and being thus divided, the

angelic and spiritual natures, which are among "the things not seen," reside in places above the world, and above the heavens, because such a residence is in correspondence with their constitution; for an intellectual nature is a fine, clear, unencumbered, agile kind of thing, and a heavenly body is fine and light, and perpetually moving, and the earth on the contrary, which stands last in the list of things sensible, can never be an adequate and congenial spot for creatures intellectual to sojourn in. For what correspondence can there possibly be between that which is light and buoyant, on the one hand, and that which is heavy and gravitating on the other? Well, in order that the earth may not be completely devoid of the local indwelling of the intellectual and the immaterial, man (these writers tell us) was fashioned by the Supreme forethought, and his earthy parts moulded over the intellectual and godlike essence of his soul; and so this amalgamation with that which has material weight enables the soul to live on this element of earth, which possesses a certain bond of kindred with the substance of the flesh. The design of all that is being born [7], then, is that the Power which is above both the heavenly and the earthly universe may in all parts of the creation be glorified by means of intellectual natures, conspiring to the same end by virtue of the same faculty in operation in all, I mean that of looking upon God. But this operation of looking upon God is nothing less than the life-nourishment appropriate, as like to like, to an intellectual nature. For just as these bodies, earthy as they are, are preserved by nourishment that is earthy, and we detect in them all alike, whether brute or reasoning, the operations of a material kind of vitality, so it is right to assume that there is an intellectual life-nourishment as well, by which such natures [8] are maintained in existence. But if bodily food, coming and going as it does in circulation, nevertheless imparts a certain amount of vital energy to those who get it, how much more does the partaking of the real thing, always remaining and always the same, preserve the eater in existence? If, then, this is the life-nourishment of an intellectual nature, namely, to have a part in God, this part will not be gained by that which is of an opposite quality; the would-be partaker must in some degree be akin to that which is to be partaken of. The eye enjoys the light by virtue of having light within itself to seize its

---

[6] Gen. i. 27.

[7] τῶν γινομένων. The Latin has overlooked this; "Hæc autem omnia huc spectant ut," &c. (Sifanus).

[8] ἡ φύσις, i. e. the intellectual φύσις mentioned above. If this were translated "Nature," it would contradict what has just been said about the body. It is plain that φύσις contains a much larger meaning always than our sole equivalent for it; φύσις is applied even to the Divine essence.

kindred light, and the finger or any other limb cannot effect the act of vision because none of this natural light is organized in any of them. The same necessity requires that in our partaking of God there should be some kinship in the constitution of the partaker with that which is partaken of. Therefore, as the Scripture says, man was made in the image of God; that like, I take it, might be able to see like; and to see God is, as was said above, the life of the soul. But seeing that ignorance of the true good is like a mist that obscures the visual keenness of the soul, and that when that mist grows denser a cloud is formed so thick that Truth's ray cannot pierce through these depths of ignorance, it follows further that with the total deprivation of the light the soul's life ceases altogether; for we have said that the real life of the soul is acted out in partaking of the Good; but when ignorance hinders this apprehension of God, the soul which thus ceases to partake of God, ceases also to live. But no one can force us to give the family history[9] of this ignorance, asking whence and from what father it is; let him be given to understand from the word itself that "ignorance" and "knowledge" indicate one of the relations of the soul;[1] but no relation, whether expressed or not, conveys the idea of substance; a relation and a substance are quite of different descriptions. If, then, knowledge is not a substance, but a perfected[2] operation of the soul, it must be conceded that ignorance must be much farther removed still from anything in the way of substance; but that which is not in that way does not exist at all; and so it would be useless to trouble ourselves about where it comes from. Now seeing that the Word[3] declares that the living in God is the life of the soul, and seeing that this living is knowledge according to each man's ability, and that ignorance does not imply the reality of anything, but is only the negation of the operation of knowing, and seeing that upon this partaking in God being no longer effected there follows at once the cancelling of the soul's life, which is the worst of evils,—because of all this the Producer of all Good would work in us the cure of such an evil. A cure is a good thing, but one who does not look to the evangelic mystery would still be ignorant of the manner of the cure. We have shown that alienation from God, Who is the Life, is an evil; the cure, then, of this infirmity is, again to be made friends with God, and so to be in life once more. When such a life, then, is always held up in hope before humanity, it cannot be said that the

winning of this life is absolutely a reward of a good life, and that the contrary is a punishment (of a bad one); but what we insist on resembles the case of the eyes. We do not say that one who has clear eyesight is rewarded as with a prize by being able to perceive the objects of sight; nor on the other hand that he who has diseased eyes experiences a failure of optic activity as the result of some penal sentence. With the eye in a natural state sight follows necessarily; with it vitiated by disease failure of sight as necessarily follows. In the same way the life of blessedness is as a familiar second nature to those who have kept clear the senses of the soul; but when the blinding stream of ignorance prevents our partaking in the real light, then it necessarily follows that we miss that, the enjoyment of which we declare to be the life of the partaker.

Now that we have laid down these premises, it is time to examine in the light of them the question proposed to us. It was somewhat of this kind. "If the recompense of blessedness is assigned according to the principles of justice, in what class shall he be placed who has died in infancy without having laid in this life any foundation, good or bad, whereby any return according to his deserts may be given him?" To this we shall make answer, with our eye fixed upon the consequences of that which we have already laid down, that this happiness in the future, while it is in its essence a heritage of humanity, may at the same time be called in one sense a recompense; and we will make clear our meaning by the same instance as before. Let us suppose two persons suffering from an affection of the eyes; and that the one surrenders himself most diligently to the process of being cured, and undergoes all that Medicine can apply to him, however painful it may be; and that the other indulges without restraint in baths[4] and wine-drinking, and listens to no advice whatever of his doctor as to the healing of his eyes. Well, when we look to the end of each of these we say that each duly receives in requital the fruits of his choice, the one in deprivation of the light, the other in its enjoyment; by a misuse of the word we do actually call that which necessarily follows, a recompense. We may speak, then, in this way also as regards this question of the infants: we may say that the enjoyment of that future life does indeed belong of right to the human being, but that, seeing the plague of ignorance has seized almost all now living in the flesh, he who has purged himself of it by means of the necessary courses of treatment receives the due reward of his diligence, when he enters on the life that is truly

9 γενεαλογεῖν.   1 τῶν πρός τί πως ἔχειν τὴν ψυχὴν.
2 περιττή. Sifanus must have had περί τι in his Cod.: "sed mentis circa aliquam rem actio."   3 S. John i. 4.

4 For an explanation of such a restriction, see Bingham, vol. viii. p. 109 (ed. 1720).

natural; while he who refuses Virtue's purgatives and renders that plague of ignorance, through the pleasures he has been entrapped by, difficult in his case to cure, gets himself into an unnatural state, and so is estranged from the truly natural life, and has no share in the existence which of right belongs to us and is congenial to us. Whereas the innocent babe has no such plague before its soul's eyes obscuring [5] its measure of light, and so it continues to exist in that natural life; it does not need the soundness which comes from purgation, because it never admitted the plague into its soul at all. Further, the present life appears to me to offer a sort of analogy to the future life we hope for, and to be intimately connected with it, thus; the tenderest infancy is suckled and reared with milk from the breast; then another sort of food appropriate to the subject of this fostering, and intimately adapted to his needs, succeeds, until at last he arrives at full growth. And so I think, in quantities continually adapted to it, in a sort of regular progress, the soul partakes of that truly natural life; according to its capacity and its power it receives a measure of the delights of the Blessed state; indeed we learn as much from Paul, who had a different sort of food for him who was already grown in virtue and for the imperfect "babe." For to the last he says, "I have fed you with milk, and not with meat: for hitherto ye were not able to bear it [6]." But to those who have grown to the full measure of intellectual maturity he says, "But strong meat belongeth to those that are of full age, even those who by reason of use have their senses exercised. . . . [7]" Now it is not right to say that the man and the infant are in a similar state, however free both may be from any contact of disease (for how can those who do not partake of exactly the same things be in an equal state of enjoyment?); on the contrary, though the absence of any affliction from disease may be predicated of both alike as long as both are out of the reach of its influence, yet, when we come to the matter of delights, there is no likeness in the enjoyment, though the percipients are in the same condition. For the man there is a natural delight in discussions, and in the management of affairs, and in the honourable discharge of the duties of an office, and in being distinguished for acts of help to the needy; in living, it may be, with a wife whom he loves, and ruling his household; and in all those amusements to be found in this life in the way of pastime, in musical pieces and theatrical spectacles, in the chase, in bathing, in gymnastics, in the mirth of banquets, and any-

thing else of that sort. For the infant, on the contrary, there is a natural delight in its milk, and in its nurse's arms, and in gentle rocking that induces and then sweetens its slumber. Any happiness beyond this the tenderness of its years naturally prevents it from feeling. In the same manner those who in their life here have nourished the forces of their souls by a course of virtue, and have, to use the Apostle's words, had the "senses" of their minds "exercised," will, if they are translated to that life beyond, which is out of the body, proportionately to the condition and the powers they have attained participate in that divine delight; they will have more or they will have less of its riches according to the capacity acquired. But the soul that has never felt the taste of virtue, while it may indeed remain perfectly free from the sufferings which flow from wickedness, having never caught the disease of evil at all, does nevertheless in the first instance [8] partake only so far in that life beyond (which consists, according to our previous definition, in the knowing and being in God) as this nursling can receive; until the time comes that it has thriven on the contemplation of the truly Existent as on a congenial diet, and, becoming capable of receiving more, takes at will more from that abundant supply of the truly Existent which is offered.

Having, then, all these considerations in our view, we hold that the soul of him who has reached every virtue in his course, and the soul of him whose portion of life has been simply nothing, are equally out of the reach of those sufferings which flow from wickedness. Nevertheless we do not conceive of the employment of their lives as on the same level at all. The one has heard those heavenly announcements, by which, in the words of the Prophet, "the glory of God is declared [9]," and, travelling through creation, has been led to the apprehension of a Master of the creation; he has taken the true Wisdom for his teacher, that Wisdom which the spectacle of the Universe suggests; and when he observed the beauty of this material sunlight he had grasped by analogy the beauty of the real sunlight; he saw in the solid firm-

---

[5] ἐπιπροσθούσης.   [6] 2 Cor. iii. 2.   [7] Heb. v. 14.

[8] παρὰ τὴν πρώτην (i. e. ὥραν).   [9] Ps. xix. 1.

[1] This mysticism of Gregory is an extension of Origen's view that there are direct affinities or analogies between the visible and invisible world. Gregory here and elsewhere proposes to find in the facts of nature nothing less than analogies with the *energies*, and so with the essence, of the Deity. The marks stamped upon the Creation translate these energies into language intelligible to us: just as the energies in their turn translate the essence, as he insists on in his treatise against Eunomius. This world, in effect, exists only in order to manifest the Divine Being. But the human soul, of all that is created, is the special field where analogies to the Creator are to be sought, because we feel both by their energies alone; both the soul and God are hid from us, in their essence. "Since," he says (*De Hom. Opif.* c. xi.), "one of the attributes we contemplate in the Divine nature is incomprehensibility of essence, it is clearly necessary that in this point 'the image' should be able to show its resemblance to the Archetype. For if, while the Archetype transcends comprehension, the essence of 'the image' were comprehended, the

ness of this earth the unchangeableness of its Creator; when he perceived the immensity of the heavens he was led on the road towards the vast Infinity of that Power which encompasses the Universe; when he saw the rays of the sun reaching from such sublimities even to ourselves he began to believe, by the means of such phenomena, that the activities of the Divine Intelligence did not fail to descend from the heights of Deity even to each one of us; for if a single luminary can occupy everything alike that lies beneath it with the force of light, and, more than that, can, while lending itself to all who can use it, still remain self-centred and undissipated, how much more shall the Creator of that luminary become "all in all," as the Apostle speaks, and come into each with such a measure of Himself as each subject of His influence can receive! Nay, look only at an ear of corn, at the germinating of some plant, at a ripe bunch of grapes, at the beauty of early autumn, whether in fruit or flower, at the grass springing unbidden, at the mountain reaching up with its summit to the height of the ether, at the springs on its slopes bursting from those swelling breasts, and running in rivers through the glens, at the sea receiving those streams from every direction and yet remaining within its limits, with waves edged by the stretches of beach and never stepping beyond those fixed boundaries of continent: look at these and such-like sights, and how can the eye of reason fail to find in them all that our education for Realities requires? Has a man who looks at such spectacles procured for himself only a slight power for the enjoyment of those delights beyond? Not to speak of the studies which sharpen the mind towards moral excellence, geometry, I mean, and astronomy, and the knowledge of the truth that the science of numbers gives, and every method that furnishes a proof of the unknown and a conviction of the known, and, before all these, the philosophy contained in the inspired Writings, which affords a complete purification to those who educate themselves thereby in the mysteries of God. But the man who has acquired the knowledge of none of these things and has not even been conducted by the material cosmos to the perception of the beauties above it, and passes through life with his mind in a kind of tender, unformed, and untrained state, he is not the man that is likely to be placed amongst the same surroundings as our argument has indicated that other man, before spoken of, to be placed; so that, in this view, it can no longer be maintained that, in the two supposed and completely opposite cases, the one who has taken no part in life is more blessed than the one who has taken a noble part in it. Certainly, in comparison with one who has lived all his life in sin, not only the innocent babe but even one who has never come into the world at all will be blessed. We learn as much too in the case of Judas, from the sentence pronounced upon him in the Gospels[2]; namely, that when we think of such men, that which never existed is to be preferred to that which has existed in such sin. For, as to the latter, on account of the depth of the ingrained evil, the chastisement in the way of purgation will be extended into infinity[3]; but as for what has never existed, how can any torment touch it?—However, notwithstanding that, the man who institutes a comparison between the infantine immature life and that of perfect virtue, must himself be pronounced immature for so judging of realities. Do you, then, in consequence of this, ask the reason why so and so, quite tender in age, is quietly taken away from amongst the living? Do you ask what the Divine wisdom contemplates in this? Well, if you are thinking of all those infants who are proofs of illicit connections, and so are made away with by their parents, you are not justified in calling to account, for such wickedness, that God Who will surely bring to judgment the unholy deeds done in this way. In the case, on the other hand, of any infant who, though his parents have nurtured him, and have with nursing and supplication spent earnest care upon him, nevertheless does not continue in this world, but succumbs to a sickness even unto death, which is unmistakably the sole cause of it, we venture upon the following considerations. It is a sign of the perfection of God's providence, that He not only heals maladies[4] that have come into existence, but also provides that some should be never mixed up at all in the things which He has forbidden; it is reasonable, that is, to expect that He Who knows the future equally with the past should check the advance of an infant to complete maturity, in order that the evil may not be developed which His foreknowledge has detected in his future life, and in order that a lifetime granted to one whose evil dispositions will be lifelong may not become the actual

<hr />

contrary character of the attributes we behold in them would prove the defect of 'the image'; but since the essence of our Mind eludes our knowledge, it has an exact resemblance to the Supreme essence, figuring as it does by its own unknowableness the incomprehensible Being." Therefore, Gregory goes to the interior facts of our nature for the actual proof of theological doctrine. God is "spirit" because of the spirituality of the soul. The "generation" of the Son is proved by the Will emanating from the Reason. Gregory follows this line even more resolutely than Origen. He was the first Father who sought to explain the Trinity by the triple divisions of the soul which Platonism offered. Cf. his treatise *De eo quod sit ad immutabilitatem*, &c., p. 26.

[2] S. Matt. xxvi. 24.
[3] εἰς ἄπειρον παρατείνεται. Such passages as these must be set against others in Gregory, such as the concluding part of the *De Animâ et Resurrectione*, in arriving at an exact knowledge of his views about a Universal Ἀποκατάστασις. [4] πάθη.

material for his vice. We shall better explain what we are thinking of by an illustration. Suppose a banquet of very varied abundance, prepared for a certain number of guests, and let the chair be taken by one of their number who is gifted to know accurately the peculiarities of constitution in each of them, and what food is best adapted to each temperament, what is harmful and unsuitable; in addition to this let him be entrusted with a sort of absolute authority over them, whether to allow as he pleases so and so to remain at the board or to expel so and so, and to take every precaution that each should address himself to the viands most suited to his constitution, so that the invalid should not kill himself by adding the fuel of what he was eating to his ailment, while the guest in robuster health should not make himself ill with things not good for him [5] and fall into discomfort from over-feeding [6]. Suppose, amongst these, one of those inclined to drink is conducted out in the middle of the banquet or even at the very beginning of it; or let him remain to the very end, it all depending on the way that the president can secure that perfect order shall prevail, if possible, at the board throughout, and that the evil sights of surfeiting, tippling, and tipsiness shall be absent. It is just so, then, as when that individual is not very pleased at being torn away from all the savoury dainties and deprived of his favourite liquors, but is inclined to charge the president with want of justice and judgment, as having turned him away from the feast for envy, and not for any forethought for him; but if he were to catch a sight of those who were already beginning to misbehave themselves, from the long continuance of their drinking, in the way of vomitings and putting their heads on the table and unseemly talk, he would perhaps feel grateful to him for having removed him, before he got into such a condition, from a deep debauch. If our illustration [7] is understood, we can easily apply the rule which it contains to the question before us. What, then, was that question? Why does God, when fathers endeavour their utmost to preserve a successor to their line, often let the son and heir be snatched away in earliest infancy [8]? To those who ask this, we shall reply with the illustration of the banquet; namely, that Life's board is as it were crowded with a vast abundance and variety of dainties; and it must, please, be noticed that, true to the practice of gastronomy, all its dishes are not sweetened with the honey of enjoyment, but in some cases an existence has a taste of some

especially harsh mischances [9] given to it: just as experts in the arts of catering desire how they may excite the appetites of the guests with sharp, or briny, or astringent dishes. Life, I say, is not in all its circumstances as sweet as honey; there are circumstances in it in which mere brine is the only relish, or into which an astringent, or vinegary, or sharp pungent flavour has so insinuated itself, that the rich sauce becomes very difficult to taste: the cups of Temptation, too, are filled with all sorts of beverages; some by the error of pride [1] produce the vice of inflated vanity; others lure on those who drain them to some deed of rashness; whilst in other cases they excite a vomiting in which all the ill-gotten acquisitions of years are with shame surrendered [2]. Therefore, to prevent one who has indulged in the carousals to an improper extent from lingering over so profusely furnished a table, he is early taken from the number of the banqueters, and thereby secures an escape out of those evils which unmeasured indulgence procures for gluttons. This is that achievement of a perfect Providence which I spoke of; namely, not only to heal evils that have been committed, but also to forestall them before they have been committed; and this, we suspect, is the cause of the deaths of new-born infants. He Who does all things upon a Plan withdraws the materials for evil in His love to the individual, and, to a character whose marks His Foreknowledge has read, grants no time to display by a pre-eminence in actual vice what it is when its propensity to evil gets free play. Often, too, the Arranger of this Feast of Life exposes by such-like dispensations the cunning device of the "constraining cause" of money-loving [3], so that this vice comes to the light bared of all specious pretexts, and no longer obscured by any misleading screen [4]. For most declare that they give play [5] to their cravings for more, in order that they may make their offspring all the richer; but that their vice belongs to their nature, and is not caused by any external necessity, is proved by that inexcusable avarice which is observed in childless persons. Many who have no heir, nor any hope of one, for the great wealth which they have laboriously gained, rear a countless brood within themselves of wants instead of children, and they are left without a channel into which to convey this incurable disease, though they cannot find an excuse in any necessity for this failing [6]. But take the case of some who, during their sojourn in life, have been fierce and domineering

---

5 Read with L. Sifanus, μὴ καταλλήλῳ τροφῇ.
6 εἰς πληθωρικὴν ἀηδίαν ἐκπίπτων. 7 θεώρημα.
8 Reading ἐν τῷ ἀτέλει τῆς ἡλικίας.

9 Reading συμπτωμάτων (for συμπομάτων. Morell).
1 τύφου (τοῦ στύφου, Paris Edit. i. e. "of their astringency")
2 διὰ τῆς αἰσχρᾶς ἀποτίσεως τὸν ἔμετον ἀνεκίνησαν.
3 τὴν σεσοφισμένην τῆς φιλαργυρίας ἀνάγκην.
4 πεπλανημένῳ. 5 ἐπιπλατύνεσθαι.
6 οὐκ ἔχοντες ποῦ τὴν ἀνάγκην τῆς ἀρρωστίας ταύτης ἐπανενέγκωσι.

in disposition, slaves to every kind of lust, passionate to madness, refraining from no act even of the most desperate wickedness, robbers and murderers, traitors to their country, and, more execrable still, patricides, mother-killers, child-murderers, mad after unnatural intercourse; suppose such characters grow old in this wickedness; how, some one may ask, does this harmonize with the result of our previous investigations? If that which is taken away before its time in order that it may not continuously glut itself, according to our illustration of the banquet, with Life's indulgences, is providentially removed from that carouse, what is the special design in so and so, who is of that disposition, being allowed to continue his revels[7] to old age, steeping both himself and his boon companions in the noxious fumes of his debauchery? In fine, you will ask, wherefore does God in His Providence withdraw one from life before his character can be perfected in evil, and leave another to grow to be such a monster that it had been better for him if he had never been born? In answer to this we will give, to those who are inclined to receive it favourably, a reason such as follows: viz. that oftentimes the existence of those whose life has been a good one operates to the advantage of their offspring; and there are hundreds of passages testifying to this in the inspired Writings, which clearly teach us that the tender care shown by God to those who have deserved it is shared in by their successors, and that even to have been an obstruction, in the path to wickedness, to any one who is sure to live wickedly, is a good result[8]. But seeing that our Reason in this matter has to grope in the dark, clearly no one can complain if its conjecturing leads our mind to a variety of conclusions. Well, then, not only one might pronounce that God, in kindness to the Founders of some Family, withdraws a member of it who is going to live a bad life from that bad life, but, even if there is no antecedent such as this in the case of some early deaths, it is not unreasonable to conjecture that *they* would have plunged into a vicious life with a more desperate vehemence than any of those who have actually become notorious for their wickedness. That nothing happens without God we know from many sources; and, reversely, that God's dispensations have no element of chance and confusion in them every one will allow, who realizes that God is Reason, and Wisdom, and Perfect Goodness, and Truth, and could not admit of that which is not good and not consistent with His Truth[9]. Whether,

then, the early deaths of infants are to be attributed to the aforesaid causes, or whether there is some further cause of them beyond these, it befits us to acknowledge that these things happen for the best. I have another reason also to give which I have learnt from the wisdom of an Apostle; a reason, that is, why some of those who have been distinguished for their wickedness have been suffered to live on in their self-chosen course. Having expanded a thought of this kind at some length in his argument to the Romans[1], and having retorted upon himself with the counter-conclusion, which thence necessarily follows, that the sinner could no longer be justly blamed, if his sinning is a dispensation of God, and that he would not have existed at all, if it had been contrary to the wishes of Him Who has the world in His power, the Apostle meets this conclusion and solves this counter-plea by means of a still deeper view of things. He tells us that God, in rendering to every one his due, sometimes even grants a scope to wickedness for good in the end. Therefore He allowed the King of Egypt, for example, to be born and to grow up such as he was; the intention was that Israel, that great nation exceeding all calculation by numbers, might be instructed by his disaster. God's omnipotence is to be recognized in every direction; it has strength to bless the deserving; it is not inadequate to the punishment of wickedness[2]; and so, as the complete removal of that peculiar people out of Egypt was necessary in order to prevent their receiving any infection from the sins of Egypt in a misguided way of living, therefore that God-defying and infamous Pharaoh rose and reached his maturity in the lifetime of the very people who were to be benefited, so that Israel might acquire a just knowledge of the two-fold energy of God, working as it did in either direction; the more beneficent they learnt in their own persons, the sterner by seeing it exercised upon those who were being scourged for their wickedness; for in His consummate wisdom God can mould even evil into co-operation with good. The artisan (if the Apostle's argument may be confirmed by any words of ours)—the artisan who by his skill has to fashion iron to some instrument for daily use, has need not only of that which owing to its natural ductility lends itself to his art, but, be the iron never so hard, be it never so difficult to soften it in the fire, be it even impossible owing to its adamantine resistance to mould it into any useful implement, his art requires the co-operation even of this; he will use it for an anvil, upon which the soft

---

[7] ἐμπαροινεῖ.   [8] κεφάλαιον; lit. "a sum total:" cf. below, ἐπὶ κεφαλαίῳ συναπτέον, "we must summarize."
[9] The text is in confusion here: but the Latin supplies: "Nothing reasonable fails in reason; nothing wise, in wisdom; neither virtue nor truth could admit of that which is not good," &c.

[1] Rom. iii. 3—9; vi. 1, 2; ix. 14—24; xi. 22—36.
[2] This sentence is not in the Greek of the Paris Edition, and is not absolutely necessary to the sense.

workable iron may be beaten and formed into something useful. But some one will say, "It is not all who thus reap in this life the fruits of their wickedness, any more than all those whose lives have been virtuous profit while living by their virtuous endeavours; what then, I ask, is the advantage of their existence in the case of these who live to the end unpunished?" I will bring forward to meet this question of yours a reason which transcends all human arguments. Somewhere in his utterances the great David declares that some portion of the blessedness of the virtuous will consist in this; in contemplating side by side with their own felicity the perdition of the reprobate. He says, "The righteous shall rejoice when he seeth the vengeance; he shall wash his hands in the blood of the ungodly[3]"; not indeed as rejoicing over the torments of those sufferers, but as then most completely realizing the extent of the well-earned rewards of virtue. He signifies by those words that it will be an addition to the felicity of the virtuous and an intensification of it, to have its contrary set against it. In saying that "he washes his hands in the blood of the ungodly" he would convey the thought that "the cleanness of his own acting in life is plainly declared in the perdition of the ungodly." For the expression "wash" represents the idea of cleanness; but no one is washed, but is rather defiled, in blood; whereby it is clear that it is a comparison with the harsher forms of punishment that puts in a clearer light the blessedness of virtue. We must now summarize our argument, in order that the thoughts which we have expanded may be more easily retained in the memory. The premature deaths of infants have nothing in them to suggest the thought that one who so terminates his life is subject to some grievous misfortune, any more than they are to be put on a level with the deaths of those who have purified themselves in this life by every kind of virtue; the more far-seeing Providence of God curtails the immensity of sins in the case of those whose lives are going to be so evil. That some of the wicked have lived on[4] does not upset this reason which we have rendered; for the evil was in their case hindered in kindness to their parents; whereas, in the case of those whose parents have never imparted to them any power of calling upon God, such a form of the Divine kindness[5], which accompanies such a power, is not transmitted to their own children; otherwise the infant now prevented by death from growing up wicked would have exhibited a far more desperate wickedness than the most notorious sinners, seeing that it would have been unhindered. Even granting that some have climbed to the topmost pinnacle of crime, the Apostolic view supplies a comforting answer to the question; for He Who does everything with Wisdom knows how to effect by means of evil some good. Still further, if some occupy a pre-eminence in crime, and yet for all that have never been a metal, to use our former illustration, that God's skill has used for any good, this is a case which constitutes an addition to the happiness of the good, as the Prophet's words suggest; it may be reckoned as not a slight element in that happiness, nor, on the other hand, as one unworthy of God's providing.

---

[3] Ps. lviii. 10.

[4] ἐπιβιῶναί τινας τῶν κακῶν : or, "That some have lived on in their sins."

[5] i. e. as letting them live, and mitigating the evil of their lives.

ON PILGRIMAGES

SINCE, my friend, you ask me a question in your letter, I think that it is incumbent upon me to answer you in their proper order upon all the points connected with it. It is, then, my opinion that it is a good thing for those who have dedicated themselves once for all to the higher life to fix their attention continually upon the utterances in the Gospel, and, just as those who correct their work in any given material by a rule, and by means of the straightness of that rule bring the crookedness which their hands detect to straightness, so it is right that we should apply to these questions a strict and flawless measure as it were,—I mean, of course, the Gospel rule of life [2],—and in accordance with that, direct ourselves in the sight of God. Now there are some amongst those who have entered upon the monastic and hermit life, who have made it a part of their devotion to behold those spots at Jerusalem where the memorials of our Lord's life in the flesh are on view; it would be well, then, to look to this Rule, and if the finger of its precepts points to the observance of such things, to perform the work, as the actual injunction of our Lord; but if they lie quite outside the commandment of the Master, I do not see what there is to command any one who has become a law of duty to himself to be zealous in performing any of them. When the Lord invites the blest to their inheritance in the kingdom of heaven, He does not include a pilgrimage to Jerusalem amongst their good deeds; when He announces the Beatitudes, He does not name amongst them that sort of devotion. But as to that which neither makes us blessed nor sets us in the path to the kingdom, for what reason it should be run after, let him that is wise consider. Even if there were some profit in what they do, yet even so, those who are perfect would do best not to be eager in practising it; but since this matter, when closely looked into, is found to inflict upon those who have begun to lead the stricter life a moral mischief, it is so far from being worth an earnest pursuit, that it actually requires the greatest caution to prevent him who has devoted himself to God from being penetrated by any of its hurtful influences. What is it, then, that is hurtful in it? The Holy Life is open to all, men and women alike. Of that contemplative Life the peculiar mark is Modesty [3]. But Modesty is preserved in societies that live distinct and separate, so that there should be no meeting and mixing up of persons of opposite sex; men are not to rush to keep the rules of Modesty in the company of women, nor women to do so in the company of men. But the necessities of a journey are continually apt to reduce this scrupulousness to a very indifferent observance of such rules. For instance, it is impossible for a woman to accomplish so long a journey without a conductor; on account of her natural weakness she has to be put upon her horse and to be lifted down again; she has to be supported [4] in difficult situations. Whichever we suppose, that she has an acquaintance to do this yeoman's service, or a hired attendant to perform it, either way the proceeding cannot escape being reprehensible; whether she leans on the help of a stranger, or on that of her own servant, she fails to keep the law of correct conduct; and as the inns and hostelries and cities of the East present many examples of licence and of indifference to vice, how will it be possible for one passing through such smoke to escape

---

[1] The modern history of this Letter is curious. Its genuineness, though suspected by Bellarmine, is admitted by Tillemont, and even by Cæsar Baronius. After having been edited by Morel in Greek and Latin, 1551, it was omitted from his son's edition of the works of Gregory by the advice of Fronto Ducæus, lest it should seem to reflect upon the practice of pilgrimages. But in 1607 it was again edited (Hannov.) by Du Moulin, with a defence of it, and a translation into French by R. Stephen : this is the only instance of a vernacular version of Gregory at this time, and shows the importance attached to this Letter. It appears in the second Paris Edition, but with the vehement protests, printed in the notes, of the Jesuit Gretser, against Du Moulin's interpretation of its scope, and even against its genuineness. He makes much of its absence from the Bavarian (Munich) Cod., and of the fact that even "heretical printers" had omitted it from the Basle Edition of 1562 : and he is very angry with Du Moulin for not having approached the Royal Library while in Paris, and while he had leisure from his "Calvinistic evening communions." But why should he, when the Librarian, no less a person than I. Casaubon (appointed 1598), had assured him that the Letter was in the Codex Regius? It is in *Migne* iii. col. 1009. See *Letter to Eustathia*, &c.

[2] πολιτείαν, "vivendi rationem." Cf. Basil, *Homil.* xiii.

[3] ἡ εὐσχημοσύνη.

[4] παρακρατουμένη ; cf. Epict. (cited by Diosc.) τὰς τρίχας ῥεούσας παρακρατεῖν, "to stop the hair from falling off."

without smarting eyes? Where the ear and the eye is defiled, and the heart too, by receiving all those foulnesses through eye and ear, how will it be possible to thread without infection such seats of contagion? What advantage, moreover, is reaped by him who reaches those celebrated spots themselves? He cannot imagine that our Lord is living, in the body, there at the present day, but has gone away from us foreigners; or that the Holy Spirit is in abundance at Jerusalem, but unable to travel as far as us. Whereas, if it is really possible to infer God's presence from visible symbols, one might more justly consider that He dwelt in the Cappadocian nation than in any of the spots outside it. For how many Altars [5] there are there, on which the name of our Lord is glorified! One could hardly count so many in all the rest of the world. Again, if the Divine grace was more abundant about Jerusalem than elsewhere, sin would not be so much the fashion amongst those that live there; but as it is, there is no form of uncleanness [6] that is not perpetrated amongst them; rascality, adultery, theft, idolatry, poisoning, quarrelling, murder, are rife; and the last kind of evil is so excessively prevalent, that nowhere in the world are people so ready to kill each other as there; where kinsmen attack each other like wild beasts, and spill each other's blood, merely for the sake of lifeless plunder. Well, in a place where such things go on, what proof, I ask, have you of the abundance of Divine grace? But I know what many will retort to all that I have said; they will say, "Why did you not lay down this rule for yourself as well? If there is no gain for the godly pilgrim in return for having been there, for what reason did you undergo the toil of so long a journey?" Let them hear from me my plea for this. By the necessities of that office in which I have been placed by the Dispenser of my life to live, it was my duty, for the purpose of the correction which the Holy Council had resolved upon, to visit the places where the Church in Arabia is; secondly, as Arabia is on the confines of the Jerusalem district, I had promised that I would confer also with the Heads of the Holy Jerusalem Churches, because matters with them were in confusion, and needed an arbiter; thirdly, our most religious Emperor had granted us facilities for the journey, by postal conveyance, so that we had to endure none of those inconveniences which in the case of others we have

noticed; our waggon was, in fact, as good as a church or monastery to us, for all of us were singing psalms and fasting in the Lord during the whole journey. Let our own case therefore cause difficulty to none; rather let our advice be all the more listened to, because we are giving it upon matters which came actually before our eyes. We confessed that the Christ Who was manifested is very God, as much before as after our sojourn at Jerusalem; our faith in Him was not increased afterwards any more than it was diminished. Before we saw Bethlehem we knew His being made man by means of the Virgin; before we saw His Grave we believed in His Resurrection from the dead; apart from seeing the Mount of Olives, we confessed that His Ascension into heaven was real. We derived only thus much of profit from our travelling thither, namely that we came to know by being able to compare them, that our own places are far holier than those abroad. Wherefore, O ye who fear the Lord, praise Him in the places where ye now are. Change of place does not effect any drawing nearer unto God, but wherever thou mayest be, God will come to thee, if the chambers of thy soul be found of such a sort that He can dwell in thee and walk in thee. But if thou keepest thine inner man full of wicked thoughts, even if thou wast on Golgotha, even if thou wast on the Mount of Olives, even if thou stoodest on the memorial-rock of the Resurrection, thou wilt be as far away from receiving Christ into thyself, as one who has not even begun to confess Him. Therefore, my beloved friend, counsel the brethren to be absent from the body to go to our Lord, rather than to be absent from Cappadocia to go to Palestine; and if any one should adduce the command spoken by our Lord to His disciples that they should not quit Jerusalem, let him be made to understand its true meaning. Inasmuch as the gift and the distribution of the Holy Spirit had not yet passed upon the Apostles, our Lord commanded them to remain in the same place, until they should have been endued with power from on high. Now, if that which happened at the beginning, when the Holy Spirit was dispensing each of His gifts under the appearance of a flame, continued until now, it would be right for all to remain in that place where that dispensing took place; but if the Spirit "bloweth" where He "listeth," those, too, who have become believers here are made partakers of that gift; and that according to the proportion of their faith, not in consequence of their pilgrimage to Jerusalem.

III. PHILOSOPHICAL WORKS

NOTE ON THE TREATISE "ON THE MAKING OF MAN."

THIS work was intended to supplement and complete the Hexaëmeron of S. Basil, and presupposes an acquaintance with that treatise. The narrative of the creation of the world is not discussed in detail: it is referred to, but chiefly in order to insist on the idea that the world was prepared to be the sphere of man's sovereignty. On the other hand, Gregory shows that man was made "with circumspection," fitted by nature for rule over the other creatures, made in the likeness of God in respect of various moral attributes, and in the possession of reason, while differing from the Divine nature in that the human mind receives its information by means of the senses and is dependent on them for its perception of external things. The body is fitted to be the instrument of the mind, adapted to the use of a reasonable being: and it is by the possession of the "rational soul," as well as of the "natural" or "vegetative" and the "sensible" soul, that man differs from the lower animals. At the same time, his mind works by means of the senses: it is incomprehensible in its nature (resembling in this the Divine nature of which it is the image), and its relation to the body is discussed at some length (chs. 12—15). The connection between mind and body is ineffable: it is not to be accounted for by supposing that the mind resides in any particular part of the body: the mind acts upon and is acted upon by the whole body, depending on the corporeal and material nature for one element of perception, so that perception requires both body and mind. But it is to the rational element that the name of "soul" properly belongs: the nutritive and sensible faculties only borrow the name from that which is higher than themselves. Man was first made "in the image of God:" and this conception excludes the idea of distinction of sex. In the first creation of man all humanity is included, according to the Divine foreknowledge: "our whole nature extending from the first to the last" is "one image of Him Who is." But for the Fall, the increase of the human race would have taken place as the increase of the angelic race takes place, in some way unknown to us. The declension of man from his first estate made succession by generation necessary: and it was because this declension and its consequences were present to the Divine mind that God "created them male and female." In this respect, and in respect of the need of nourishment by food, man is not "in the image of God," but shows his kindred with the lower creation. But these necessities are not permanent: they will end with the restoration of man to his former excellence (chs. 16— 18). Here Gregory is led to speak (chs. 19—20) of the food of man in Paradise, and of the "tree of the knowledge of good and evil." And thus, having made mention of the Fall of man, he goes on to speak of his Restoration. This, in his view, follows from the finite nature of evil: it is deferred until the sum of humanity is complete. As to the mode in which the present state of things will end, we know nothing: but that it will end is inferred from the non-eternity of matter (chs. 21— 24). The doctrine of the Resurrection is supported by our knowledge of the accuracy with which other events have been predicted in Scripture, by the experience given to us of like events in particular cases, in those whom our Lord raised to life, and especially in His own resurrection. The argument that such a restoration is impossible is met by an appeal to the unlimited character of the Divine power, and by inferences from parallels observed in nature (chs. 25—27). Gregory then proceeds to deal with the question of the pre-existence of the soul, rejecting that opinion, and maintaining that the body and the soul come into existence together, *potentially* in the Divine will, *actually* at the moment when each individual man comes into being by generation (chs. 28—29). In the course of his argument on this last point, he turns aside to discuss at some length, in the last chapter, the structure of the human body: but he returns once more, in conclusion, to his main position, that man "is generated as a living and animated being," and that the power of the soul is gradually manifested in, and by means of, the material substratum of the body; so that man is brought to perfection by the aid of the lower attributes of the soul. But the true perfection of the soul is not in these, which will ultimately be "put away," but in the higher attributes which constitute for man "the image of God."

ON THE MAKING OF MAN

Gregory, Bishop of Nyssa, to his brother Peter, the servant of God.

If we had to honour with rewards of money those who excel in virtue, the whole world of money, as Solomon says[1], would seem but small to be made equal to your virtue in the balance. Since, however, the debt of gratitude due to your Reverence is greater than can be valued in money, and the holy Eastertide demands the accustomed gift of love, we offer to your greatness of mind, O man of God, a gift too small indeed to be worthy of presentation to you, yet not falling short of the extent of our power. The gift is a discourse, like a mean garment, woven not without toil from our poor wit, and the subject of the discourse, while it will perhaps be generally thought audacious, yet seemed not unfitting. For he alone has worthily considered the creation of God who truly was created after God, and whose soul was fashioned in the image of Him Who created him,—Basil, our common father and teacher,—who by his own speculation made the sublime ordering of the universe generally intelligible, making the world as established by God in the true Wisdom known to those who by means of his understanding are led to such contemplation: but we, who fall short even of worthily admiring him, yet intend to add to the great writer's speculations that which is lacking in them, not so as to interpolate his work by insertion[2] (for it is not to be thought of that that lofty mouth should suffer the insult of being given as authority for our discourses), but so that the glory of the teacher may not seem to be failing among his disciples.

For if, the consideration of man being lacking in his Hexaëmeron, none of those who had been his disciples contributed any earnest effort to supply the defect, the scoffer would perhaps have had a handle against his great fame, on the ground that he had not cared to produce in his hearers any habit of intelligence. But now that we venture according to our powers upon the ex-position of what was lacking, if anything should be found in our work such as to be not unworthy of his teaching, it will surely be referred to our teacher: while if our discourse does not reach the height of his sublime speculation, he will be free from this charge and escape the blame of seeming not to wish that his disciples should have any skill at all, though we perhaps may be answerable to our censurers as being unable to contain in the littleness of our heart the wisdom of our instructor.

The scope of our proposed enquiry is not small: it is second to none of the wonders of the world,—perhaps even greater than any of those known to us, because no other existing thing, save the human creation, has been made like to God: thus we shall readily find that allowance will be made for what we say by kindly readers, even if our discourse is far behind the merits of the subject. For it is our business, I suppose, to leave nothing unexamined of all that concerns man,—of what we believe to have taken place previously, of what we now see, and of the results which are expected afterwards to appear (for surely our effort would be convicted of failing of its promise, if, when man is proposed for contemplation, any of the questions which bear upon the subject were to be omitted); and, moreover, we must fit together, according to the explanation of Scripture and to that derived from reasoning, those statements concerning him which seem, by a kind of necessary sequence, to be opposed, so that our whole subject may be consistent in train of thought and in order, as the statements that seem to be contrary are brought (if the Divine power so discovers a hope for what is inextricable) to one and the same end: and for clearness' sake I think it well to set forth to you the discourse by chapters, that you may be able briefly to know the force of the several arguments of the whole work.

1. Wherein is a partial inquiry into the nature of the world, and a more minute exposition of the things which preceded the genesis of man.

---

[1] Prov. xvii. 6 (LXX.). The clause is not found in the English version. [2] Reading (with Forbes' marginal note), ὑποβολῆς.

2. Why man appeared last, after the creation.

3. That the nature of man is more precious than all the visible creation.

4. That the construction of man throughout signifies his ruling power.

5. That man is a likeness of the Divine sovereignty.

6. An examination of the kindred of mind to nature: wherein by way of digression is refuted the doctrine of the Anomœans.

7. Why man is destitute of natural weapons and covering.

8. Why man's form is upright, and that hands were given him because of reason; wherein also is a speculation on the difference of souls.

9. That the form of man was framed to serve as an instrument for the use of reason.

10. That the mind works by means of the senses.

11. That the nature of mind is invisible.

·12. An examination of the question where the ruling principle is to be considered to reside; wherein also is a discussion of tears and laughter, and a physiological speculation as to the inter-relation of matter, nature, and mind.

13. A rationale of sleep, of yawning, and of dreams.

14. That the mind is not in a part of the body; wherein also is a distinction of the movements of the body and of the soul.

15. That the soul proper, in fact and name, is the rational soul, while the others are called so equivocally: wherein also is this statement, that the power of the mind extends throughout the whole body in fitting contact with every part.

16. A contemplation of the Divine utterance which said,—"Let us make man after our image and likeness;" wherein is examined what is the definition of the image, and how the passible and mortal is like to the Blessed and Impassible, and how in the image there are male and female, seeing these are not in the Prototype.

17. What we must answer to those who raise the question—"If procreation is after sin, how would souls have come into being if the first of mankind had remained sinless?"

18. That our irrational passions have their rise from kindred with irrational nature.

19. To those who say that the enjoyment of the good things we look for will again consist in meat and drink, because it is written that by these means man at first lived in Paradise.

20. What was the life in Paradise, and what was the forbidden tree.

21. That the resurrection is looked for as a consequence, not so much from the declaration of Scripture as from the very necessity of things.

22. To those who say, "If the resurrection

is a thing excellent and good, how is it that it has not happened already, but is hoped for in some periods of time?"

23. That he who confesses the beginning of the world's existence must necessarily agree also as to its end.

24. An argument against those who say that matter is co-eternal with God.

25. How one even of those who are without may be brought to believe the Scripture when teaching of the resurrection.

26. That the resurrection is not beyond probability.

27. That it is possible, when the human body is dissolved into the elements of the universe, that each should have his own body restored from the common source.

28. To those who say that souls existed before bodies, or that bodies were formed before souls: wherein there is also a refutation of the fables concerning transmigrations of souls.

29. An establishment of the doctrine that the cause of existence of soul and body is one and the same.

30. A brief consideration of the construction of our bodies from a medical point of view.

I. *Wherein is a partial inquiry into the nature of the world, and a more minute exposition of the things which preceded the genesis of man* [3].

1. "This is the book of the generation of heaven and earth [4]," saith the Scripture, when all that is seen was finished, and each of the things that are betook itself to its own separate place, when the body of heaven compassed all things round, and those bodies which are heavy and of downward tendency, the earth and the water, holding each other in, took the middle place of the universe; while, as a sort of bond and stability for the things that were made, the Divine power and skill was implanted in the growth of things, guiding all things with the reins of a double operation (for it was by rest and motion that it devised the genesis of the things that were not, and the continuance of the things that are), driving around, about the heavy and changeless element contributed by the creation that does not move, as about some fixed path, the exceedingly rapid motion of the sphere, like a wheel, and preserving the indissolubility of both by their mutual action, as the circling substance by its rapid motion compresses the compact body of the earth round about, while that which is firm and unyielding,

---

3 A Bodleian MS. of the Latin version, cited by Forbes, which gives independent titles, has here :—" Of the perfection and beauty of the world and of the harmonious discord of the four elements."
4 Gen. ii. 4 (LXX.).

by reason of its unchanging fixedness, continually augments the whirling motion of those things which revolve round it, and intensity [5] is produced in equal measure in each of the natures which thus differ in their operation, in the stationary nature, I mean, and in the mobile revolution; for neither is the earth shifted from its own base, nor does the heaven ever relax in its vehemence, or slacken its motion.

2. These, moreover, were first framed before other things, according to the Divine wisdom, to be as it were a beginning of the whole machine, the great Moses indicating, I suppose, where he says that the heaven and the earth were made by God "in the beginning [6]," that all things that are seen in the creation are the offspring of rest and motion, brought into being by the Divine will. Now the heaven and the earth being diametrically opposed to each other in their operations, the creation which lies between the opposites, and has in part a share in what is adjacent to it, itself acts as a mean between the extremes, so that there is manifestly a mutual contact of the opposites through the mean; for air in a manner imitates the perpetual motion and subtlety of the fiery substance, both in the lightness of its nature, and in its suitableness for motion; yet it is not such as to be alienated from the solid substance, for it is no more in a state of continual flux and dispersion than in a permanent state of immobility, but becomes, in its affinity to each, a kind of borderland of the opposition between operations, at once uniting in itself and dividing things which are naturally distinct.

3. In the same way, liquid substance also is attached by double qualities to each of the opposites; for in so far as it is heavy and of downward tendency it is closely akin to the earthy; but in so far as it partakes of a certain fluid and mobile energy it is not altogether alien from the nature which is in motion; and by means of this also there is effected a kind of mixture and concurrence of the opposites, weight being transferred to motion, and motion finding no hindrance in weight, so that things most extremely opposite in nature combine with one another, and are mutually joined by those which act as means between them.

4. But to speak strictly, one should rather say that the very nature of the contraries themselves is not entirely without mixture of properties, each with the other, so that, as I think, all that we see in the world mutually agree, and the creation, though discovered in properties of contrary natures, is yet at union with itself. For as motion is not conceived merely as local shifting, but is also contemplated in change and alteration, and on the other hand the immovable nature does not admit motion by way of alteration, the wisdom of God has transposed these properties, and wrought unchangeableness in that which is ever moving, and change in that which is immovable; doing this, it may be, by a providential dispensation, so that that property of nature which constitutes its immutability and immobility might not, when viewed in any created object, cause the creature to be accounted as God; for that which may happen to move or change would cease to admit of the conception of Godhead. Hence the earth is stable without being immutable, while the heaven, on the contrary, as it has no mutability, so has not stability either, that the Divine power, by interweaving change in the stable nature and motion with that which is not subject to change, might, by the interchange of attributes, at once join them both closely to each other, and make them alien from the conception of Deity; for as has been said, neither of these (neither that which is unstable, nor that which is mutable) can be considered to belong to the more Divine nature.

5. Now all things were already arrived at their own end: "the heaven and the earth [7]," as Moses says, "were finished," and all things that lie between them, and the particular things were adorned with their appropriate beauty; the heaven with the rays of the stars, the sea and air with the living creatures that swim and fly, and the earth with all varieties of plants and animals, to all which, empowered by the Divine will, it gave birth together; the earth was full, too, of her produce, bringing forth fruits at the same time with flowers; the meadows were full of all that grows therein, and all the mountain ridges, and summits, and every hill-side, and slope, and hollow, were crowned with young grass, and with the varied produce of the trees, just risen from the ground, yet shot up at once into their perfect beauty; and all the beasts that had come into life at God's command were rejoicing, we may suppose, and skipping about, running to and fro in the thickets in herds according to their kind, while every sheltered and shady spot was ringing with the chants of the song-birds. And at sea, we may suppose, the sight to be seen was of the like kind, as it had just settled to quiet and calm in the gathering together of its depths, where havens and harbours spontaneously hollowed out on the coasts made the sea reconciled with the land; and the gentle motion of the waves vied in beauty with the meadows,

---

5 ὑπερβολή apparently means "intensity" or "a high degree of force," not "excess of force," since, though the force in each is augmented, it does not exceed that in the other, which is augmented also *pari passu*.   6 Gen. i. 1.

7 Gen. ii. 1.

rippling delicately with light and harmless breezes that skimmed the surface ; and all the wealth of creation by land and sea was ready, and none was there to share it.

II. *Why man appeared last, after the creation* [8].

1. For not as yet had that great and precious thing, man, come into the world of being ; it was not to be looked for that the ruler should appear before the subjects of his rule ; but when his dominion was prepared, the next step was that the king should be manifested. When, then, the Maker of all had prepared beforehand, as it were, a royal lodging for the future king (and this was the land, and islands, and sea, and the heaven arching like a roof over them), and when all kinds of wealth had been stored in this palace (and by wealth I mean the whole creation, all that is in plants and trees, and all that has sense, and breath, and life ; and—if we are to account materials also as wealth—all that for their beauty are reckoned precious in the eyes of men, as gold and silver, and the substances of your jewels which men delight in—having concealed, I say, abundance of all these also in the bosom of the earth as in a royal treasure-house), he thus manifests man in the world, to be the beholder of some of the wonders therein, and the lord of others ; that by his enjoyment he might have knowledge of the Giver, and by the beauty and majesty of the things he saw might trace out that power of the Maker which is beyond speech and language.

2. For this reason man was brought into the world last after the creation, not being rejected to the last as worthless, but as one whom it behoved to be king over his subjects at his very birth. And as a good host does not bring his guest to his house before the preparation of his feast, but, when he has made all due preparation, and decked with their proper adornments his house, his couches, his table, brings his guest home when things suitable for his refreshment are in readiness,—in the same manner the rich and munificent Entertainer of our nature, when He had decked the habitation with beauties of every kind, and prepared this great and varied banquet, then introduced man, assigning to him as his task not the acquiring of what was not there, but the enjoyment of the things which were there ; and for this reason He gives him as foundations the instincts of a two-fold organization, blending the Divine with the earthy, that by means of both he may be naturally and properly disposed to each enjoy-ment, enjoying God by means of his more

divine nature, and the good things of earth by the sense that is akin to them.

III. *That the nature of man is more precious than all the visible creation* [9].

1. But it is right that we should not leave this point without consideration, that while the world, great as it is, and its parts, are laid as an elemental foundation for the formation of the universe, the creation is, so to say, made off-hand by the Divine power, existing at once on His command, while counsel precedes the mak-ing of man ; and that which is to be is fore-shown by the Maker in verbal description, and of what kind it is fitting that it should be, and to what archetype it is fitting that it should bear a likeness, and for what it shall be made, and what its operation shall be when it is made, and of what it shall be the ruler,—all these things the saying examines beforehand, so that he has a rank assigned him before his genesis, and possesses rule over the things that are be-fore his coming into being ; for it says, "God said, Let us make man in our image, after our likeness, and let them have dominion over the fish of the sea, and the beasts of the earth, and the fowls of the heaven, and the cattle, and all the earth [1]."

2. O marvellous ! a sun is made, and no coun-sel precedes ; a heaven likewise ; and to these no single thing in creation is equal. So great a wonder is formed by a word alone, and the saying indicates neither when, nor how, nor any such detail. So too in all particular cases, the æther, the stars, the intermediate air, the sea, the earth, the animals, the plants,—all are brought into being with a word, while only to the making of man does the Maker of all draw near with circumspection, so as to prepare be-forehand for him material for his formation, and to liken his form to an archetypal beauty, and, setting before him a mark for which he is to come into being, to make for him a nature appropriate and allied to the operations, and suitable for the object in hand.

IV. *That the construction of man throughout signifies his ruling power* [2].

1. For as in our own life artificers fashion a tool in the way suitable to its use, so the best Artificer made our nature as it were a formation fit for the exercise of royalty, preparing it at once by superior advantages of soul, and by the very form of the body, to be such as to be

---

[8] The title in the Bodleian Latin MS. is :—" That it was reason-able that man should be created last of the creatures."

[9] The title in the Bodleian Latin MS. is:—" That God created man with great deliberation."
[1] Gen. i. 26, not exactly from the LXX.
[2] The title in the Bodleian Latin MS. is :—Of the kingly dignity of the human form."

adapted for royalty : for the soul immediately shows its royal and exalted character, far removed as it is from the lowliness of private station, in that it owns no lord, and is self-governed, swayed autocratically by its own will; for to whom else does this belong than to a king? And further, besides these facts, the fact that it is the image of that Nature which rules over all means nothing else than this, that our nature was created to be royal from the first. For as, in men's ordinary use, those who make images [3] of princes both mould the figure of their form, and represent along with this the royal rank by the vesture of purple, and even the likeness is commonly spoken of as "a king," so the human nature also, as it was made to rule the rest, was, by its likeness to the King of all, made as it were a living image, partaking with the archetype both in rank and in name, not vested in purple, nor giving indication of its rank by sceptre and diadem (for the archetype itself is not arrayed with these), but instead of the purple robe, clothed in virtue, which is in truth the most royal of all raiment, and in place of the sceptre, leaning on the bliss of immortality, and instead of the royal diadem, decked with the crown of righteousness; so that it is shown to be perfectly like to the beauty of its archetype in all that belongs to the dignity of royalty.

V. *That man is a likeness of the Divine sovereignty [4].*

1. It is true, indeed, that the Divine beauty is not adorned with any shape or endowment of form, by any beauty of colour, but is contemplated as excellence in unspeakable bliss. As then painters transfer human forms to their pictures by the means of certain colours, laying on their copy the proper and corresponding tints, so that the beauty of the original may be accurately transferred to the likeness, so I would have you understand that our Maker also, painting the portrait to resemble His own beauty, by the addition of virtues, as it were with colours, shows in us His own sovereignty : and manifold and varied are the tints, so to say, by which His true form is portrayed : not red, or white [5], or the blending of these, whatever it may be called, nor a touch of black that paints the eyebrow and the eye, and shades, by some combination, the depressions in the figure, and all such arts which the hands of painters contrive,

but instead of these, purity, freedom from passion, blessedness, alienation from all evil, and all those attributes of the like kind which help to form in men the likeness of God : with such hues as these did the Maker of His own image mark our nature.

2. And if you were to examine the other points also by which the Divine beauty is expressed, you will find that to them too the likeness in the image which we present is perfectly preserved. The Godhead is mind and word : for "in the beginning was the Word [6]," and the followers of Paul "have the mind of Christ" which "speaks" in them [7] : humanity too is not far removed from these : you see in yourself word and understanding, an imitation of the very Mind and Word. Again, God is love, and the fount of love : for this the great John declares, that "love is of God," and "God is love [8]" : the Fashioner of our nature has made this to be our feature too : for "hereby," He says, "shall all men know that ye are my disciples, if ye love one another [9]" :—thus, if this be absent, the whole stamp of the likeness is transformed. The Deity beholds and hears all things, and searches all things out : you too have the power of apprehension of things by means of sight and hearing, and the understanding that inquires into things and searches them out.

VI. *An examination of the kindred of mind to nature : wherein, by way of digression, is refuted the doctrine of the Anomœans [1].*

1. And let no one suppose me to say that the Deity is in touch with existing things in a manner resembling human operation, by means of different faculties. For it is impossible to conceive in the simplicity of the Godhead the varied and diverse nature of the apprehensive operation : not even in our own case are the faculties which apprehend things numerous, although we are in touch with those things which affect our life in many ways by means of our senses ; for there is one faculty, the implanted mind itself, which passes through each of the organs of sense and grasps the things beyond : this it is that, by means of the eyes, beholds what is seen ; this it is that, by means of hearing, understands what is said ; that is content with what is to our taste, and turns from what is unpleasant ; that uses the hand for whatever it wills, taking hold or rejecting

---

3 It is not clear whether the reference here is to painting or to sculpture, of which the product was afterwards painted. The combination of ἀναμάσσονται and συμπαραγράφουσι suggests the latter.
4 In the Bodleian Latin MS. the title is :—"How the human soul is made in the image of God."
5 λαμπρότης. The old Latin version translates this by "purpurissus."

6 S. John i. 1.   7 Cf. 1 Cor. ii. 16 ; and 2 Cor. xiii. 3.
8 1 S. John iv. 7, 8.   9 S. John xiii. 35 (not verbally).
1 The Bodleian Latin MS. gives :—"That God has not human limbs, and that the image of the Father and of the Son is one, against the Eunomians."

by its means, using the help of the organ for this purpose precisely as it thinks expedient.

2. If in men, then, even though the organs formed by nature for purposes of perception may be different, that which operates and moves by means of all, and uses each appropriately for the object before it, is one and the same, not changing its nature by the differences of operations, how could any one suspect multiplicity of essence in God on the ground of His varied powers? for " He that made the eye," as the prophet says, and " that planted the ear [2]," stamped on human nature these operations to be as it were significant characters, with reference to their models in Himself: for He says, " Let us make man in our image [3]."

3. But what, I would ask, becomes of the heresy of the Anomœans? what will they say to this utterance? how will they defend the vanity of their dogma in view of the words cited? Will they say that it is possible that one image should be made like to different forms? if the Son is in nature unlike the Father, how comes it that the likeness He forms of the different natures is one? for He Who said, " Let us make after our image," and by the plural signification revealed the Holy Trinity, would not, if the archetypes were unlike one another, have mentioned the image in the singular : for it would be impossible that there should be one likeness displayed of things which do not agree with one another: if the natures were different he would assuredly have begun their images also differently, making the appropriate image for each : but since the image is one, while the archetype is not one, who is so far beyond the range of understanding as not to know that the things which are like the same thing, surely resemble one another? Therefore He says (the word, it may be, cutting short this wickedness at the very formation of human life), " Let us make man in our image, after our likeness."

VII. *Why man is destitute of natural weapons and covering* [4].

1. But what means the uprightness of his figure? and why is it that those powers which aid life do not naturally belong to his body? but man is brought into life bare of natural covering, an unarmed and poor being, destitute of all things useful, worthy, according to appearances, of pity rather than of admiration, not armed with prominent horns or sharp claws, nor with hoofs nor with teeth, nor possessing by nature

any deadly venom in a sting,—things such as most animals have in their own power for defence against those who do them harm : his body is not protected with a covering of hair: and yet possibly it was to be expected that he who was promoted to rule over the rest of the creatures should be defended by nature with arms of his own so that he might not need assistance from others for his own security. Now, however, the lion, the boar, the tiger, the leopard, and all the like have natural power sufficient for their safety : and the bull has his horn, the hare his speed, the deer his leap and the certainty of his sight, and another beast has bulk, others a proboscis, the birds have their wings, and the bee her sting, and generally in all there is some protective power implanted by nature : but man alone of all is slower than the beasts that are swift of foot, smaller than those that are of great bulk, more defenceless than those that are protected by natural arms ; and how, one will say, has such a being obtained the sovereignty over all things ?

2. Well, I think it would not be at all hard to show that what seems to be a deficiency of our nature is a means for our obtaining dominion over the subject creatures. For if man had had such power as to be able to outrun the horse in swiftness, and to have a foot that, from its solidity, could not be worn out, but was strengthened by hoofs or claws of some kind, and to carry upon him horns and stings and claws, he would be, to begin with, a wild-looking and formidable creature, if such things grew with his body : and moreover he would have neglected his rule over the other creatures if he had no need of the co-operation of his subjects ; whereas now, the needful services of our life are divided among the individual animals that are under our sway, for this reason—to make our dominion over them necessary.

3. It was the slowness and difficult motion of our body that brought the horse to supply our need, and tamed him : it was the nakedness of our body that made necessary our management of sheep, which supplies the deficiency of our nature by its yearly produce of wool: it was the fact that we import from others the supplies for our living which subjected beasts of burden to such service : furthermore, it was the fact that we cannot eat grass like cattle which brought the ox to render service to our life, who makes our living easy for us by his own labour ; and because we needed teeth and biting power to subdue some of the other animals by grip of teeth, the dog gave, together with his swiftness, his own jaw to supply our need, becoming like a live sword for man ; and there has been discovered by men iron, stronger and more penetrating than prominent horns or sharp

[2] Ps. xciv. 9.　　　　　[3] Gen. i. 26.
[4] The Bodleian Latin MS gives :—" Why man was not created with horns and other defences like certain other animals."
The argument of this and the following chapter seems to be derived to a great extent from Origen (*Contra Celsum*, iv. 75 et sqq.).

claws, not, as those things do with the beasts, always growing naturally with us, but entering into alliance with us for the time, and for the rest abiding by itself : and to compensate for the crocodile's scaly hide, one may make that very hide serve as armour, by putting it on his skin upon occasion : or, failing that, art fashions iron for this purpose too, which, when it has served him for a time for war, leaves the man-at-arms once more free from the burden in time of peace : and the wing of the birds, too, ministers to our life, so that by aid of contrivance we are not left behind even by the speed of wings : for some of them become tame and are of service to those who catch birds, and by their means others are by contrivance subdued to serve our needs :. moreover art contrives to make our arrows feathered, and by means of the bow gives us for our needs the speed of wings : while the fact that our feet are easily hurt and worn in travelling makes necessary the aid which is given by the subject animals : for hence it comes that we fit shoes to our feet.

VIII. *Why man's form is upright; and that hands were given him because of reason; wherein also is a speculation on the difference of souls* [5].

1. But man's form is upright, and extends aloft towards heaven, and looks upwards : and these are marks of sovereignty which show his royal dignity. For the fact that man alone among existing things is such as this, while all others bow their bodies downwards, clearly points to the difference of dignity between those which stoop beneath his sway and that power which rises above them : for all the rest have the foremost limbs of their bodies in the form of feet, because that which stoops needs something to support it : but in the formation of man these limbs were made hands, for the upright body found one base, supporting its position securely on two feet, sufficient for its needs.

2. Especially do these ministering hands adapt themselves to the requirements of the reason : indeed if one were to say that the ministration of hands is a special property of the rational nature, he would not be entirely wrong; and that not only because his thought turns to the common and obvious fact that we signify our reasoning by means of the natural employment of our hands in written characters. It is true that this fact, that we speak by writing, and, in a certain way, converse by the aid of our

hands, preserving sounds by the forms of the alphabet, is not unconnected with the endowment of reason; but I am referring to something else when I say that the hands co-operate with the bidding of reason.

3. Let us, however, before discussing this point, consider the matter we passed over (for the subject of the order of created things almost escaped our notice), why the growth of things that spring from the earth takes precedence, and the irrational animals come next, and then, after the making of these, comes man : for it may be that we learn from these facts not only the obvious thought, that grass·appeared to the Creator useful for the sake of the animals, while the animals were made because of man, and that for this reason, before the animals there was made their food, and before man that which was to minister to human life.

4. But it seems to me that by these facts Moses reveals a hidden doctrine, and secretly delivers that wisdom concerning the soul, of which the learning that is without had indeed some imagination, but no clear comprehension. IIis discourse then hereby teaches us that the power of life and soul may be considered in three divisions. For one is only a power of growth and nutrition supplying what is suitable for the support of the bodies that are nourished, which is called the vegetative [6] soul, and is to be seen in plants; for we may perceive in growing plants a certain vital power destitute of sense; and there is another form of life besides this, which, while it includes the form above mentioned, is also possessed in addition of the power of management according to sense; and this is to be found in the nature of the irrational animals : for they are not only the subjects of nourishment and growth, but also have the activity of sense and perception. But perfect bodily life is seen in the rational (I mean the human) nature, which both is nourished and endowed with sense, and also partakes of reason and is ordered by mind.

5. We might make a division of our subject in some such way as this. Of things existing, part are intellectual, part corporeal. Let us leave alone for the present the division of the intellectual according to its properties, for our argument is not concerned with these. Of the corporeal, part is entirely devoid of life, and part shares in vital energy. Of a living body, again, part has sense conjoined with life, and part is without sense : lastly, that which has

---

5 The Latin version divides the chapters somewhat differently at this point. The Bodleian MS. gives this section the title, "Of the dignity of the human form, and why man was created after the other creatures."

6 "Vegetative" :—reading (with several MSS. of both classes of those cited by Forbes) φυτική for φυσική (the reading which Forbes follows in his text). A similar reading has been adopted in some later passages, where the MSS. show similar variations. It seems not unlikely that the less common φυτικὸς should have been altered by copyists to φυσικός. But Gregory seems in this treatise to use the word φύσις for the *corporeal* nature : and he may have employed the adjectival form in a corresponding sense.

sense is again divided into rational and irrational. For this reason the lawgiver says that after inanimate matter (as a sort of foundation for the form of animate things), this vegetative life was made, and had earlier[7] existence in the growth of plants : then he proceeds to introduce the genesis of those creatures which are regulated by sense : and since, following the same order, of those things which have obtained life in the flesh, those which have sense can exist by themselves éven apart from the intellectual nature, while the rational principle could not be embodied save as blended with the sensitive,—for this reason mañ was made last after the animals, as nature advanced in an orderly course to perfection. For this rational animal, man, is blended of every form of soul ; he is nourished by the vegetative kind of soul, and to the faculty of growth was added that of sense, which stands midway, if we regard its peculiar nature, between the intellectual and the more material essence, being as much coarser than the one as it is more refined than the other : then takes place a certain alliance and commixture of the intellectual essence with the subtle and enlightened element of the sensitive nature : so that man consists of these three : as we are taught the like thing by the apostle in what he says to the Ephesians[8], praying for them that the complete grace of their "body and soul and spirit" may be preserved at the coming of the Lord ; using the word "body" for the nutritive part, and denoting the sensitive by the word "soul," and the intellectual by "spirit." Likewise too the Lord instructs the scribe in the Gospel that he should set before every commandment that love to God which is exercised with all the heart and soul and mind[9] : for here also it seems to me that the phrase indicates the same difference, naming the more corporeal existence "heart," the intermediate "soul," and the higher nature, the intellectual and mental faculty, "mind."

6. Hence also the apostle recognizes three divisions of dispositions, calling one "carnal," which is busied with the belly and the pleasures connected with it, another "natural[1]," which holds a middle position with regard to virtue and vice, rising above the one, but without pure participation in the other ; and another "spiritual," which perceives the perfection of godly life : wherefore he says to the Corinthians, reproaching their indulgence in pleasure and passion, "Ye are carnal[2]," and incapable of receiving the more perfect doctrine ; while else-

where, making a comparison of the middle kind with the perfect, he says, " but the natural man receiveth not the things of the Spirit : for they are foolishness unto him : but he that is spiritual judgeth all things, yet he himself is judged of no man[3]." As, then, the natural man is higher than the carnal, by the same measure also the spiritual man rises above the natural.

7. If, therefore, Scripture tells us that man was made last, after every animate thing, the lawgiver is doing nothing else than declaring to us the doctrine of the soul, considering that what is perfect comes last, according to a certaiñ necessary sequence in the order of things : for in the rational are included the others also, while in the sensitive there also surely exists the vegetative form, and that again is conceived only in connection with what is material : thus we may suppose that nature makes an ascent as it were by steps—I mean the various properties of life—from the lower to the perfect form.

8[4]. Now since man is a rational animal, the instrument of his body must be made suitable for the use of reason[5] ; as you may see musicians producing their music according to the form of their instruments, and not piping with harps nor harping upon flutes, so it must needs be that the organization of these instruments of ours should be adapted for reason, that when struck by the vocal organs it might be able to sound properly for the use of words. For this reason the hands were attached to the body ; for though we can count up very many uses in daily life for which these skilfully contrived and helpful instruments, our hands, that easily follow every art and every operation, alike in war and peace[6], are serviceable, yet nature added them to our body pre-eminently for the sake of reason. For if man were destitute of hands, the various parts of his face would certainly have been arranged like those of the quadrupeds, to suit the purpose of his feeding : so that its form would have been lengthened out and pointed towards the nostrils, and his lips would have projected from his mouth, lumpy, and stiff, and thick, fitted for taking up the grass, and his tongue would either have lain between his teeth, of a kind to match his lips, fleshy, and hard, and rough, assisting his teeth to deal with what came under his grinder, or it would have been moist and hanging out at the side like that of dogs and other carnivorous beasts, projecting through the gaps in

---

[7] *Earlier*, i. e. earlier than the animal life, or "sensitive" soul.
[8] The reference is really to 1 Thess. v. 23. Apparently all Forbes' MSS. read πρὸς τοὺς ʼΕφεσίους : but the Latin version of Dionysius Exiguus corrects the error, giving the quotation at greater length.
[9] Cf. S. Mark xii. 30.
[1] ψυχικὴν : "psychic" or "animal :"—the Authorised Version translates the word by "natural."
[2] Cf. 1 Cor. iii. 3.

[3] Cf. 1 Cor. ii. 14, 15.
[4] The Latin versions make ch. ix. begin at this point. The Bodleian MS. gives as its title :—"That the form of the human body agrees with the rationality of the mind."
[5] It is not absolutely clear whether λόγος in the following passage means *speech* or *reason*—and whether λογικὸς means "capable of speech," or "rational." But as λογικὸς in § 7 clearly has the force of "rational," it would seem too abrupt a transition to make it mean "capable of speech" in the first line of § 8, and this may determine the meaning of λόγος.
[6] Reading τῶν for τὸν, with some of Forbes' MSS.

his jagged row of teeth. If, then, our body had no hands, how could articulate sound have been implanted in it, seeing that the form of the parts of the mouth would not have had the configuration proper for the use of speech, so that man must of necessity have either bleated, or " baaed," or barked, or neighed, or bellowed like oxen or asses, or uttered some bestial sound? but now, as the hand is made part of the body, the mouth is at leisure for the service of the reason. Thus the hands are shown to be the property of the rational nature, the Creator having thus devised by their means a special advantage for reason.

IX. *That the form of man was framed to serve as an instrument for the use of reason*[7].

1. Now since our Maker has bestowed upon our formation a certain Godlike grace, by implanting in His image the likeness of His own excellences, for this reason He gave, of His bounty, His other good gifts to human nature; but mind and reason we cannot strictly say that He *gave*, but that He *imparted* them, adding to the image the proper adornment of His own nature. Now since the mind is a thing intelligible and incorporeal, its grace would have been incommunicable and isolated, if its motion were not manifested by some contrivance. For this cause there was still need of this instrumental organization, that it might, like a plectrum, touch the vocal organs and indicate by the quality of the notes struck, the motion within.

2. And as some skilled musician, who may have been deprived by some affection of his own voice, and yet wish to make his skill known, might make melody with voices of others, and publish his art by the aid of flutes or of the lyre, so also the human mind being a discoverer of all sorts of conceptions, seeing that it is unable, by the mere soul, to reveal to those who hear by bodily senses the motions of its understanding, touches, like some skilful composer, these animated instruments, and makes known its hidden thoughts by means of the sound produced upon them.

3. Now the music of the human instrument is a sort of compound of flute and lyre, sounding together in combination as in a concerted piece of music. For the breath, as it is forced up from the air-receiving vessels through the windpipe, when the speaker's impulse to utterance attunes the harmony to sound, and as it strikes against the internal protuberances which divide this flute-like passage in a circular arrangement, imitates in a way the sound

uttered through a flute, being driven round and round by the membranous projections. But the palate receives the sound from below in its own concavity, and dividing the sound by the two passages that extend to the nostrils, and by the cartilages about the perforated bone, as it were by some scaly protuberance, makes its resonance louder; while the cheek, the tongue, the mechanism of the pharynx by which the chin is relaxed when drawn in, and tightened when extended to a point—all these in many different ways answer to the motion of the plectrum upon the strings, varying very quickly, as occasion requires, the arrangement of the tones; and the opening and closing of the lips has the same effect as players produce when they check the breath of the flute with their fingers according to the measure of the tune.

X. *That the mind works by means of the senses.*

1. As the mind then produces the music of reason by means of our instrumental construction, we are born rational, while, as I think, we should not have had the gift of reason if we had had to employ our lips to supply the need of the body—the heavy and toilsome part of the task of providing food. As things are, however, our hands appropriate this ministration to themselves, and leave the mouth available for the service of reason.

2[8]. The operation of the instrument[9], however, is twofold; one for the production of sound, the other for the reception of concepts from without; and the one faculty does not blend with the other, but abides in the operation for which it was appointed by nature, not interfering with its neighbour either by the sense of hearing undertaking to speak, or by the speech undertaking to hear; for the latter is always uttering something, while the ear, as Solomon somewhere says, is not filled with continual hearing[1].

3. That point as to our internal faculties which seems to me to be even in a special degree matter for wonder, is this:—what is the extent of that inner receptacle into which flows everything that is poured in by our hearing? who are the recorders of the sayings that are brought in by it? what sort of storehouses are there for the concepts that are being put in by our hearing? and how is it, that when many of them, of varied kinds, are pressing one upon another, there arises no confusion and error in the relative position of the things

---

[7] This and part of the next chapter, according to the division of the Greek, are included in the ninth chapter of the Latin Version.

[8] Here the Latin version begins chapter x. The title in the Bodleian MS. is:—"Of the five bodily senses."
[9] That is, of the mind, in connection with reason.
[1] Cf. Eccles. i. 8. The quotation is not from the LXX.: it is perhaps not intended to be verbal.

that are laid up there? And one may have the like feeling of wonder also with regard to the operation of sight; for by it also in like manner the mind apprehends those things which are external to the body, and draws to itself the images of phenomena, marking in itself the impressions of the things which are seen.

4. And just as if there were some extensive city receiving all comers by different entrances, all will not congregate at any particular place, but some will go to the market, some to the houses, others to the churches, or the streets, or lanes, or the theatres, each according to his own inclination,—some such city of our mind I seem to discern established in us, which the different entrances through the senses keep filling, while the mind, distinguishing and examining each of the things that enters, ranks them in their proper departments of knowledge.

5. And as, to follow the illustration of the city, it may often be that those who are of the same family and kindred do not enter by the same gate, coming in by different entrances, as it may happen, but are none the less, when they come within the circuit of the wall, brought together again, being on close terms with each other (and one may find the contrary happen; for those who are strangers and mutually unknown often take one entrance to the city, yet their community of entrance does not bind them together; for even when they are within they can be separated to join their own kindred); something of the same kind I seem to discern in the spacious territory of our mind; for often the knowledge which we gather from the different organs of sense is one, as the same object is divided into several parts in relation to the senses; and again, on the contrary, we may learn from some one sense many and varied things which have no affinity one with another.

6. For instance—for it is better to make our argument clear by illustration—let us suppose that we are making some inquiry into the property of tastes—what is sweet to the sense, and what is to be avoided by tasters. We find, then, by experience, both the bitterness of gall and the pleasant character of the quality of honey; but when these facts are known, the knowledge is one which is given to us (the same thing being introduced to our understanding in several ways) by taste, smell, hearing, and often by touch and sight. For when one sees honey, and hears its name, and receives it by taste, and recognizes its odour by smell, and tests it by touch, he recognizes the same thing by means of each of his senses.

7. On the other hand we get varied and multiform information by some one sense, for as hearing receives all sorts of sounds, and our visual perception exercises its operation by be-

holding things of different kinds—for it lights alike on black and white, and all things that are distinguished by contrariety of colour,—so with taste, with smell, with perception by touch; each implants in us by means of its own perceptive power the knowledge of things of every kind.

XI. *That the nature of mind is invisible*[2]

1. What then is, in its own nature, this mind that distributes itself into faculties of sensation, and duly receives, by means of each, the knowledge of things? That it is something else besides the senses, I suppose no reasonable man doubts; for if it were identical with sense, it would reduce the proper character of the operations carried on by sense to one, on the the ground that it is itself simple, and that in what is simple no diversity is to be found. Now however, as all agree that touch is one thing and smell another, and as the rest of the senses are in like manner so situated with regard to each other as to exclude intercommunion or mixture, we must surely suppose, since the mind is duly present in each case, that it is something else besides the sensitive nature, so that no variation may attach to a thing intelligible.

2. "Who hath known the mind of the Lord[3]?" the apostle asks; and I ask further, who has understood his own mind? Let those tell us who consider the nature of God to be within their comprehension, whether they understand themselves—if they know the nature of their own mind. "It is manifold and much compounded." How then can that which is intelligible be composite? or what is the mode of mixture of things that differ in kind? Or, "It is simple, and incomposite." How then is it dispersed into the manifold divisions of the senses? how is there diversity in unity? how is unity maintained in diversity?

3. But I find the solution of these difficulties by recourse to the very utterance of God; for He says, "Let us make man in our image, after our likeness[4]." The image is properly an image so long as it fails in none of those attributes which we perceive in the archetype; but where it falls from its resemblance to the prototype it ceases in that respect to be an image; therefore, since one of the attributes we contemplate in the Divine nature is incomprehensibility of essence, it is clearly necessary that in this point the image should be able to show its imitation of the archetype.

4. For if, while the archetype transcends

---

[2] The Bodleian MS. of the Latin version gives as the title :—
" The definition of the human mind."
[3] Rom. xi. 34.　　　　[4] Gen. i. 26.

comprehension, the nature of the image were comprehended, the contrary character of the attributes we behold in them would prove the defect of the image; but since the nature of our mind, which is the likeness of the Creator, evades our knowledge, it has an accurate resemblance to the superior nature, figuring by its own unknowableness the incomprehensible Nature.

XII. *An examination of the question where the ruling principle is to be considered to reside; wherein also is a discussion of tears and laughter, and a physiological speculation as to the inter-relation of matter, nature, and mind* [5].

1. Let there be an end, then, of all the vain and conjectural discussion of those who confine the intelligible energy to certain bodily organs; of whom some lay it down that the ruling principle is in the heart, while others say that the mind resides in the brain, strengthening such opinions by some plausible superficialities. For he who ascribes the principal authority to the heart makes its local position evidence of his argument (because it seems that it somehow occupies the middle position in the body [6]), on the ground that the motion of the will is easily distributed from the centre to the whole body, and so proceeds to operation; and he makes the troublesome and passionate disposition of man a testimony for his argument, because such affections seem to move this part sympathetically. Those, on the other hand, who consecrate the brain to reasoning, say that the head has been built by nature as a kind of citadel of the whole body, and that in it the mind dwells like a king, with a body-guard of senses surrounding it like messengers and shield-bearers. And these find a sign of their opinion in the fact that the reasoning of those who have suffered some injury to the membrane of the brain is abnormally distorted, and that those whose heads are heavy with intoxication ignore what is seemly.

2. Each of those who uphold these views puts forward some reasons of a more physical character on behalf of his opinion concerning the ruling principle. One declares that the motion which proceeds from the understanding is in some way akin to the nature of fire, because fire and the understanding are alike in perpetual motion; and since heat is allowed to have its source in the region of the heart, he says on this ground that the motion of mind is compounded with the mobility of heat, and

asserts that the heart, in which heat is enclosed, is the receptacle of the intelligent nature. The other declares that the cerebral membrane (for so they call the tissue that surrounds the brain) is as it were a foundation or root of all the senses, and hereby makes good his own argument, on the ground that the intellectual energy cannot have its seat save in that part where the ear, connected with it, comes into concussion with the sounds that fall upon it, and the sight (which naturally belongs to the hollow of the place where the eyes are situated) makes its internal representation by means of the images that fall upon the pupils, while the qualities of scents are discerned in it by being drawn in through the nose, and the sense of taste is tried by the test of the cerebral membrane, which sends down from itself, by the veterbræ of the neck, sensitive nerve-processes to the isthmoidal passage, and unites them with the muscles there.

3. I admit it to be true that the intellectual part of the soul is often disturbed by prevalence of passions; and that the reason is blunted by some bodily accident so as to hinder its natural operation; and that the heart is a sort of source of the fiery element in the body, and is moved in correspondence with the impulses of passion; and moreover, in addition to this, I do not reject (as I hear very much the same account from those who spend their time on anatomical researches) the statement that the cerebral membrane (according to the theory of those who take such a physiological view), enfolding in itself the brain, and steeped in the vapours that issue from it, forms a foundation for the senses; yet I do not hold this for a proof that the incorporeal nature is bounded by any limits of place.

4. Certainly we are aware that mental aberrations do not arise from heaviness of head alone, but skilled physicians declare that our intellect is also weakened by the membranes that underlie the sides being affected by disease, when they call the disease frenzy, since the name given to those membranes is φρένες. And the sensation resulting from sorrow is mistakenly supposed to arise at the heart; for while it is not the heart, but the entrance of the belly that is pained, people ignorantly refer the affection to the heart. Those, however, who have carefully studied the affections in question give some such account as follows:—by a compression and closing of the pores, which naturally takes place over the whole body in a condition of grief, everything that meets a hindrance in its passage is driven to the cavities in the interior of the body, and hence also (as the respiratory organs too are pressed by what surrounds them), the drawing

---

5 In the Latin version chap. xii. includes only §§ 1—8 (incl.), to which the Bodleian MS. gives the title:—"That the principle of man does not all reside in the brain, but in the whole body."

6 This view of the position of the heart is perhaps shared by Gregory himself: see *e.g.* ch. xxx. § 15.

of breath often becomes more violent under the influence of nature endeavouring to widen what has been contracted, so as to open out the compressed passages; and such breathing we consider a symptom of grief and call it a groan or a shriek. That, moreover, which appears to oppress the region of the heart is a painful affection, not of the heart, but of the entrance of the stomach, and occurs from the same cause (I mean, that of the compression of the pores), as the vessel that contains the bile, contracting, pours that bitter and pungent juice upon the entrance of the stomach; and a proof of this is that the complexion of those in grief becomes sallow and jaundiced, as the bile pours its own juice into the veins by reason of excessive pressure.

5. Furthermore, the opposite affection, that, I mean, of mirth and laughter, contributes to establish the argument; for the pores of the body, in the case of those who are dissolved in mirth by hearing something pleasant, are also somehow dissolved and relaxed. Just as in the former case the slight and insensible exhalations of the pores are checked by grief, and, as they compress the internal arrangement of the higher viscera, drive up towards the head and the cerebral membrane the humid vapour which, being retained in excess by the cavities of the brain, is driven out by the pores at its base[7], while the closing of the eyelids expels the moisture in the form of drops (and the drop is called a tear), so I would have you think that when the pores, as a result of the contrary condition, are unusually widened, some air is drawn in through them into the interior, and thence again expelled by nature through the passage of the mouth, while all the viscera (and especially, as they say, the liver) join in expelling this air by a certain agitation and throbbing motion; whence it comes that nature, contriving to give facility for the exit of the air, widens the passage of the mouth, extending the cheeks on either side round about the breath; and the result is called laughter.

6. We must not, then, on this account ascribe the ruling principle any more to the liver than we must think, because of the heated state of the blood about the heart in wrathful dispositions, that the seat of the mind is in the heart; but we must refer these matters to the character of our bodily organization, and consider that the mind is equally in contact with each of the parts according to a kind of combination which is indescribable.

7. Even if any should allege to us on this

point the Scripture which claims the ruling principle for the heart, we shall not receive the statement without examination; for he who makes mention of the heart speaks also of the reins, when he says, "God trieth the hearts and reins"[8]; so that they must either confine the intellectual principle to the two combined or to neither.

8. And although I am aware that the intellectual energies are blunted, or even made altogether ineffective in a certain condition of the body, I do not hold this a sufficient evidence for limiting the faculty of the mind by any particular place, so that it should be forced out of its proper amount of free space by any inflammations that may arise in the neighbouring parts of the body[9] (for such an opinion is a corporeal one, that when the receptacle is already occupied by something placed in it, nothing else can find place there); for the intelligible nature neither dwells in the empty spaces of bodies, nor is extruded by encroachments of the flesh; but since the whole body is made like some musical instrument, just as it often happens in the case of those who know how to play, but are unable, because the unfitness of the instrument does not admit of their art, to show their skill (for that which is destroyed by time, or broken by a fall, or rendered useless by rust or decay, is mute and inefficient, even if it be breathed upon by one who may be an excellent artist in flute-playing); so too the mind, passing over the whole instrument, and touching each of the parts in a mode corresponding to its intellectual activities, according to its nature, produces its proper effect on those parts which are in a natural condition, but remains inoperative and ineffective upon those which are unable to admit the movement of its art; for the mind is somehow naturally adapted to be in close relation with that which is in a natural condition, but to be alien from that which is removed from nature.

9. [1] And here, I think there is a view of the matter more close to nature, by which we may learn something of the more refined doctrines. For since the most beautiful and supreme good of all is the Divinity Itself, to which incline all things that have a tendency towards what is beautiful and good[2], we therefore say that the

---

[7] διὰ τῶν κατὰ τὴν βάσιν πόρων. The meaning of this is obscure. If we might read τῶν κατὰ τὴν ὄψιν πόρων, we should have a parallel to τοῦ κατὰ τὸ στόμα πόρου below. But there seems to be no variation in the MSS.

[8] Ps. vii. 10.
[9] The inflammation causing swelling in the neighbouring parts, and so leaving no room for the mind.
[1] The Latin version (as well as several of the Greek MSS.) makes this the beginning of chap. xiii. The Bodleian MS. gives as the title :—"That as the mind is governed by God, so is the material life of the body by the mind."
[2] καλὸν and τὸ καλὸν seem in the following passage to be used of goodness, alike moral and æsthetic : once or twice καλὸν seems to be used as equivalent to ἀγαθὸν or as opposed to κακὸν, in a sense capable of being rendered simply by "good" ; it also seems to carry with it in other phrases the distinct idea of æsthetic goodness, or "beauty," and the use of κάλλος and καλλωπίζειν, in other phrases still, makes it necessary to preserve this idea in translation.

mind, as being in the image of the most beautiful, itself also remains in beauty and goodness so long as it partakes as far as is possible in its likeness to the archetype; but if it were at all to depart from this it is deprived of that beauty in which it was. And as we said that the mind was adorned [3] by the likeness of the archetypal beauty, being formed as though it were a mirror to receive the figure of that which it expresses, we consider that the nature which is governed by it is attached to the mind in the same relation, and that it too is adorned by the beauty that the mind gives, being, so to say, a mirror of the mirror; and that by it is swayed and sustained the material element of that existence in which the nature is contemplated.

10. Thus so long as one keeps in touch with the other, the communication of the true beauty extends proportionally through the whole series, beautifying by the superior nature that which comes next to it; but when there is any interruption of this beneficent connection, or when, on the contrary, the superior comes to follow the inferior, then is displayed the misshapen character of matter, when it is isolated from nature (for in itself matter is a thing without form or structure), and by its shapelessness is also destroyed that beauty of nature with which [4] it is adorned through the mind; and so the transmission of the ugliness of matter reaches through the nature to the mind itself, so that the image of God is no longer seen in the figure expressed by that which was moulded according to it; for the mind, setting the idea of good like a mirror behind the back, turns off the incident rays of the effulgence of the good, and it receives into itself the impress of the shapelessness of matter.

11. And in this way is brought about the genesis of evil, arising through the withdrawal of that which is beautiful and good. Now all is beautiful and good that is closely related to the First Good; but that which departs from its relation and likeness to this is certainly devoid of beauty and goodness. If, then, according to the statement we have been considering, that which is truly good is one, and the mind itself also has its power of being beautiful and good, in so far as it is in the image of the good and beautiful, and the nature, which is sustained by the mind, has the like power, in so far as it is an image of the image, it is hereby shown that our material part holds together, and is upheld when it is controlled by

nature; and on the other hand is dissolved and disorganized when it is separated from that which upholds and sustains it, and is dissevered from its conjunction with beauty and goodness.

12. Now such a condition as this does not arise except when there takes place an overturning of nature to the opposite state, in which the desire has no inclination for beauty and goodness, but for that which is in need of the adorning element; for it must needs be that that which is made like to matter, destitute as matter is of form of its own, should be assimilated to it in respect of the absence alike of form and of beauty.

13. We have, however, discussed these points in passing, as following on our argument, since they were introduced by our speculation on the point before us; for the subject of enquiry was, whether the intellectual faculty has its seat in any of the parts of us, or extends equally over them all; for as for those who shut up the mind locally in parts of the body, and who advance for the establishment of this opinion of theirs the fact that the reason has not free course in the case of those whose cerebral membranes are in an unnatural condition, our argument showed that in respect of every part of the compound nature of man, whereby every man has some natural operation, the power of the soul remains equally ineffective if the part does not continue in its natural condition. And thus there came into our argument, following out this line of thought, the view we have just stated, by which we learn that in the compound nature of man the mind is governed by God, and that by it is governed our material life, provided the latter remains in its natural state, but if it is perverted from nature it is alienated also from that operation which is carried on by the mind.

14. Let us return however once more to the point from which we started—that in those who are not perverted from their natural condition by some affection, the mind exercises its own power, and is established firmly in those who are in sound health, but on the contrary is powerless in those who do not admit its operation; for we may confirm our opinion on these matters by yet other arguments: and if it is not tedious for those to hear who are already wearied with our discourse, we shall discuss these matters also, so far as we are able, in a few words.

XIII. *A Rationale of sleep, of yawning, and of dreams* [5].

1. This life of our bodies, material and subject to flux, always advancing by way of motion,

---

The phrases "beautiful and good," or "beauty and goodness," have therefore been here adopted to express the single adjective καλὸν.

3 Omitting τοῦ, which Forbes inserts before κατακοσμεῖσθαι : it appears to be found in all the MSS., but its insertion reduces the grammar of the passage to hopeless confusion. Perhaps the true reading is τοῦ πρωτοτύπου καλλίστου.

4 Reading ᾧ, with several of Forbes' MSS., for the ᾗ of the Paris ed., and the ὅ of Forbes' text.

finds the power of its being in this, that it never rests from its motion : and as some river, flowing on by its own impulse, keeps the channel in which it runs well filled, yet is not seen in the same water always at the same place, but part of it glides away while part comes flowing on, so, too, the material element of our life here suffers change in the continuity of its succession of opposites by way of motion and flux, so that it never can desist from change, but in its inability to rest keeps up unceasingly its motion alternating by like ways [6] : and if it should ever cease moving it will assuredly have cessation also of its being.

2. For instance, emptying succeeds fulness, and on the other hand after emptiness comes in turn a process of filling : sleep relaxes the strain of waking, and, again, awakening braces up what had become slack : and neither of these abides continually, but both give way, each at the other's coming ; nature thus by their interchange so renewing herself as, while partaking of each in turn, to pass from the one to the other without break. For that the living creature should always be exerting itself in its operations produces a certain rupture and severance of the overstrained part ; and continual quiescence of the body brings about a certain dissolution and laxity in its frame : but to be in touch with each of these at the proper times in a moderate degree is a staying-power of nature, which, by continual transference to the opposed states, gives herself in each of them rest from the other. Thus she finds the body on the strain through wakefulness, and devises relaxation for the strain by means of sleep, giving the perceptive faculties rest for the time from their operations, loosing them like horses from the chariots after the race.

3. Further, rest at proper times is necessary for the framework of the body, that the nutriment may be diffused over the whole body through the passages which it contains, without any strain to hinder its progress. For just as certain misty vapours are drawn up from the recesses of the earth when it is soaked with rain, whenever the sun heats it with rays of any considerable warmth, so a similar result happens in the earth that is in us, when the nutriment within is heated up by natural warmth ; and the vapours, being naturally of upward tendency and airy nature, and aspiring to that which is above them, come to be in the region of the head like smoke penetrating the joints of a wall : then they are dispersed thence by exhalation to the passages of the organs of sense,

and by them the senses are of course rendered inactive, giving way to the transit of these vapours. For the eyes are pressed upon by the eyelids when some leaden instrument[7], as it were (I mean such a weight as that I have spoken of), lets down the eyelid upon the eyes ; and the hearing, being dulled by these same vapours, as though a door were placed upon the acoustic organs, rests from its natural operation : and such a condition is sleep, when the sense is at rest in the body, and altogether ceases from the operation of its natural motion, so that the digestive processes of nutriment may have free course for transmission by the vapours through each of the passages.

4. And for this reason, if the apparatus of the organs of sense should be closed and sleep hindered by some occupation, the nervous system, becoming filled with the vapours, is naturally and spontaneously extended so that the part which has had its density increased by the vapours is rarefied by the process of extension, just as those do who squeeze the water out of clothes by vehement wringing : and, seeing that the parts about the pharynx are somewhat circular, and nervous tissue abounds there, whenever there is need for the expulsion from that part of the density of the vapours—since it is impossible that the part which is circular in shape should be separated directly, but only by being distended in the outline of its circumference—for this reason, by checking the breath in a yawn the chin is moved downwards so as to leave a hollow to the uvula, and all the interior parts being arranged in the figure of a circle, that smoky denseness which had been detained in the neighbouring parts is emitted together with the exit of the breath. And often the like may happen even after sleep when any portion of those vapours remains in the region spoken of undigested and unexhaled.

5. Hence the mind of man clearly proves its claim[8] to connection with his nature, itself also co-operating and moving with the nature in its sound and waking state, but remaining unmoved when it is abandoned to sleep, unless any one supposes that the imagery of dreams is a motion of the mind exercised in sleep. We for our part say that it is only the conscious and sound action of the intellect which we ought to refer to mind ; and as to the fantastic nonsense which occurs to us in sleep, we suppose that some appearances of the operations of the mind are accidentally moulded in the less rational part of the soul ; for the soul, being

---

6 Life is represented as a succession of opposite states (τῶν ἐναντίων διαδοχῇ), which yet recur again and again in the same sequence (διὰ τῶν ὁμοίων). This is illustrated in the following section.

7 Reading μηχανῆς with the earlier editions and (apparently) a large number of Forbes' MSS. in place of μηχανικῆς. But μολυβδίνης may be for μολυβδαίνης.
8 Reading δείκνυσιν, as Forbes does (apparently from all the MSS. and agreeing with the earlier editt.). The Latin translation points to the reading δείκνυται.

by sleep dissociated from the senses, is also of necessity outside the range of the operations of the mind ; for it is through the senses that the union of mind with man takes place ; therefore when the senses are at rest, the intellect also must needs be inactive ; and an evidence of this is the fact that the dreamer often seems to be in absurd and impossible situations, which would not happen if the soul were then guided by reason and intellect.

6. It seems to me, however, that when the soul is at rest so far as concerns its more excellent faculties (so far, I mean, as concerns the operations of mind and sense), the nutritive part of it alone is operative during sleep, and that some shadows and echoes of those things which happen in our waking moments— of the operations both of sense and of intellect—which are impressed upon it by that part of the soul which is capable of memory, that these, I say, are pictured as chance will have it, some echo of memory still lingering in this division of the soul.

7. With these, then, the man is beguiled, not led to acquaintance with the things that present themselves by any train of thought, but wandering among confused and inconsequent delusions. But just as in his bodily operations, while each of the parts individually acts in some way according to the power which naturally resides in it, there arises also in the limb that is at rest a state sympathetic with that which is in motion, similarly in the case of the soul, even if one part is at rest and another in motion, the whole is affected in sympathy with the part ; for it is not possible that the natural unity should be in any way severed, though one of the faculties included in it is in turn supreme in virtue of its active operation. But as, when men are awake and busy, the mind is supreme, and sense ministers to it, yet the faculty which regulates the body is not dissociated from them (for the mind furnishes the food for its wants, the sense receives what is furnished, and the nutritive faculty of the body appropriates to itself that which is given to it), so in sleep the supremacy of these faculties is in some way reversed in us, and while the less rational becomes supreme, the operation of the other ceases indeed, yet is not absolutely extinguished ; but while the nutritive faculty is then busied with digestion during sleep, and keeps all our nature occupied with itself, the faculty of sense is neither entirely severed from it (for that cannot be separated which has once been naturally joined), nor yet can its activity revive, as it is hindered by the inaction during sleep of the organs of sense ; and by the same reasoning (the mind also being united to the sensitive part of the soul) it would follow that

we should say that the mind moves with the latter when it is in motion, and rests with it when it is quiescent.

8. As naturally happens with fire when it is heaped over with chaff, and no breath fans the flame—it neither consumes what lies beside it, nor is entirely quenched, but instead of flame it rises to the air through the chaff in the form of smoke ; yet if it should obtain any breath of air, it turns the smoke to flame—in the same way the mind when hidden by the inaction of the senses in sleep is neither able to shine out through them, nor yet is quite extinguished, but has, so to say, a smouldering activity, operating to a certain extent, but unable to operate farther.

9. Again, as a musician, when he touches with the plectrum the slackened strings of a lyre, brings out no orderly melody (for that which is not stretched will not sound), but his hand frequently moves skilfully, bringing the plectrum to the position of the notes so far as place is concerned, yet there is no sound, except that he produces by the vibration of the strings a sort of uncertain and indistinct hum ; so in sleep the mechanism of the senses being relaxed, the artist is either quite inactive, if the instrument is completely relaxed by satiety or heaviness ; or will act slackly and faintly, if the instrument of the senses does not fully admit of the exercise of its art.

10. For this cause memory is confused, and foreknowledge, though rendered doubtful [9] by uncertain veils, is imaged in shadows of our waking pursuits, and often indicates to us something of what is going to happen : for by its subtlety of nature the mind has some advantage, in ability to behold things, over mere corporeal grossness ; yet it cannot make its meaning clear by direct methods, so that the information of the matter in hand should be plain and evident, but its declaration of the future is ambiguous and doubtful,—what those who interpret such things call an "enigma."

11. So the butler presses the cluster for Pharaoh's cup : so the baker seemed to carry his baskets ; each supposing himself in sleep to be engaged in those services with which he was busied when awake : for the images of their customary occupations imprinted on the prescient element of their soul, gave them for a time the power of foretelling, by this sort of prophecy on the part of the mind, what should come to pass.

12. But if Daniel and Joseph and others like them were instructed by Divine power, without any confusion of perception, in the knowledge of things to come, this is nothing to the present

---

9 Reading ἐπιδιστάζουσα with several of Forbes' MSS.

statement ; for no one would ascribe this to the power of dreams, since he will be constrained as a consequence to suppose that those Divine appearances also which took place in wakefulness were not a miraculous vision but a result of nature brought about spontaneously.   As then, while all men are guided by their own minds, there are some few who are deemed worthy of evident Divine communication ; so, while the imagination of sleep naturally occurs in a like and equivalent manner for all, some, not all, share by means of their dreams in some more Divine manifestation : but to all the rest, even if a foreknowledge of anything does occur as a result of dreams, it occurs in the way we have spoken of.

13. And again, if the Egyptian and the Assyrian king were guided by God to the knowledge of the future, the dispensation wrought by their means is a different thing : for it was necessary that the hidden wisdom of the holy men[1] should be made known, that each of them might not pass his life without profit to the state.   For how could Daniel have been known for what he was, if the soothsayers and magicians had not been unequal to the task of discovering the dream ?   And how could Egypt have been preserved while Joseph was shut up in prison, if his interpretation of the dream had not brought him to notice ?   Thus we must reckon these cases as exceptional, and not class them with common dreams.

14. But this ordinary seeing of dreams is common to all men, and arises in our fancies in different modes and forms : for either there remain, as we have said, in the reminiscent part of the soul, the echoes of daily occupations ; or, as often happens, the constitution of dreams is framed with regard to such and such a condition of the body : for thus the thirsty man seems to be among springs, the man who is in need of food to be at a feast, and the young man in the heat of youthful vigour is beset by fancies corresponding to his passion.

15. I also knew another cause of the fancies of sleep, when attending one of my relations attacked by frenzy ; who being annoyed by food being given him in too great quantity for his strength, kept crying out and finding fault with those who were about him for filling intestines with dung and putting them upon him : and when his body was rapidly tending to perspire he blamed those who were with him for having water ready to wet him with as he lay : and he did not cease calling out till the result showed the meaning of these complaints : for all at once a copious sweat broke out over

his body, and a relaxation of the bowels explained the weight in the intestines.   The same condition then which, while his sober judgment was dulled by disease, his nature underwent, being sympathetically affected by the condition of the body—not being without perception of what was amiss, but being unable clearly to express its pain, by reason of the distraction resulting from the disease—this, probably, if the intelligent principle of the soul were lulled to rest, not from infirmity but by natural sleep, might appear as a dream to one similarly situated, the breaking out of perspiration being expressed by water, and the pain occasioned by the food, by the weight of intestines.

16. This view also is taken by those skilled in medicine, that according to the differences of complaints the visions of dreams appear differently to the patients : that the visions of those of weak stomach are of one kind, those of persons suffering from injury to the cerebral membrane of another, those of persons in fevers of yet another ; that those of patients suffering from bilious and from phlegmatic affections are diverse, and those again of plethoric patients, and of patients in wasting disease, are different ; whence we may see that the nutritive and vegetative faculty of the soul has in it by commixture some seed of the intelligent element, which is in some sense brought into likeness to the particular state of the body, being adapted in its fancies according to the complaint which has seized upon it.

17. Moreover, most men's dreams are conformed to the state of their character : the brave man's fancies are of one kind, the coward's of another ; the wanton man's dreams of one kind, the continent man's of another ; the liberal man and the avaricious man are subject to different fancies ; while these fancies are nowhere framed by the intellect, but by the less rational disposition of the soul, which forms even in dreams the semblances of those things to which each is accustomed by the practice of his waking hours.

XIV. *That the mind is not in a part of the body ; wherein also is a distinction of the movements of the body and of the soul[2].*

1. But we have wandered far from our subject, for the purpose of our argument was to show that the mind is not restricted to any part of the body, but is equally in touch with the whole, producing its motion according to the nature of the part which is under its influence.

---

[1] "The holy men," Joseph and Daniel, who were enabled, by the authority they obtained through their interpretation of dreams, to benefit the state.

[2] This is chapter xv. in the Latin version and some Greek MSS. The Bodleian MS. of the Latin gives the title :—"That the mind is sometimes in servitude to the body, and of its three differences, vital, spiritual, and rational."

There are cases, however, in which the mind even follows the bodily impulses, and becomes, as it were, their servant; for often the bodily nature takes the lead by introducing either the sense of that which gives pain or the desire for that which gives pleasure, so that it may be said to furnish the first beginnings, by producing in us the desire for food, or, generally, the impulse towards some pleasant thing; while the mind, receiving such an impulse, furnishes the body by its own intelligence with the proper means towards the desired object. Such a condition, indeed, does not occur in all, save in those of a somewhat slavish disposition, who bring the reason into bondage to the impulses of their nature and pay servile homage to the pleasures of sense by allowing them the alliance of their mind; but in the case of more perfect men this does not happen; for the mind takes the lead, and chooses the expedient course by reason and not by passion, while their nature follows in the tracks of its leader.

2. But since our argument discovered in our vital faculty three different varieties—one which receives nourishment without perception, another which at once receives nourishment and is capable of perception, but is without the reasoning activity, and a third rational, perfect, and co-extensive with the whole faculty—so that among these varieties the advantage belongs to the intellectual,—let no one suppose on this account that in the compound nature of man there are three souls welded together, contemplated each in its own limits, so that one should think man's nature to be a sort of conglomeration of several souls. The true and perfect soul is naturally one, the intellectual and immaterial, which mingles with our material nature by the agency of the senses; but all that is of material nature, being subject to mutation and alteration, will, if it should partake of the animating power, move by way of growth: if, on the contrary, it should fall away from the vital energy, it will reduce its motion to destruction.

3. Thus, neither is there perception without material substance, nor does the act of perception take place without the intellectual faculty.

XV. *That the soul proper, in fact and name, is the rational soul, while the others are called so equivocally; wherein also is this statement, that the power of the mind extends throughout the whole body in fitting contact with every part* [3].

1. Now, if some things in creation possess the nutritive faculty, and others again are regulated by the perceptive faculty, while the former have no share of perception nor the latter of the intellectual nature, and if for this reason any one is inclined to the opinion of a plurality of souls, such a man will be positing a variety of souls in a way not in accordance with their distinguishing definition. For everything which we conceive among existing things, if it be perfectly that which it is, is also properly called by the name it bears: but of that which is not in every respect what it is called, the appellation also is vain. For instance :—if one were to show us true bread, we say that he properly applies the name to the subject: but if one were to show us instead that which had been made of stone to resemble the natural bread, which had the same shape, and equal size, and similarity of colour, so as in most points to be the same with its prototype, but which yet lacks the power of being food, on this account we say that the stone receives the name of " bread," not properly, but by a misnomer, and all things which fall under the same description, which are not absolutely what they are called, have their name from a misuse of terms.

2. Thus, as the soul finds its perfection in that which is intellectual and rational, everything that is not so may indeed share the name of " soul," but is not really soul, but a certain vital energy associated with the appellation of " soul [4]." And for this reason also He Who gave laws on every matter, gave the animal nature likewise, as not far removed from this vegetative life [5], for the use of man, to be for those who partake of it instead of herbs :—for He says, " Ye shall eat all kinds of flesh even as the green herb [6] ; " for the perceptive energy seems to have but a slight advantage over that which is nourished and grows without it. Let this teach carnal men not to bind their intellect closely to the phenomena of sense, but rather to busy themselves with their spiritual advantages, as the true soul is found in these, while sense has equal power also among the brute creation.

3. The course of our argument, however, has diverged to another point : for the subject of our speculation was not the fact that the energy of mind is of more dignity among the attributes we conceive in man than the material element of his being, but the fact that the mind is not confined to any one part of us, but is equally in all and through all, neither surrounding anything without, nor being enclosed within any-

---

3 Otherwise chap. xvi. The Bodleian MS. of the Latin version gives the title :—" That the vital energy of the irrational creatures is not truly but equivocally called ' soul ', and of the unspeakable communion of body and soul."

4 τῇ τῆς ψυχῆς κλήσει συγκεκριμένη. The meaning is apparently something like that given ; but if we might read συγκεχρημένη the sense of the passage would be much plainer.
5 Reading φυτικῆς for φυσικῆς as before, ch. 8, § 4 (where see note).
6 Cf. Gen. ix. 3. The quotation, except the last few words, is not verbally from the LXX.

thing : for these phrases are properly applied to casks or other bodies that are placed one inside the other ; but the union of the mental with the bodily presents a connection unspeakable and inconceivable,—not being *within* it (for the incorporeal is not enclosed in a body), nor yet surrounding it without (for that which is incorporeal does not include [7] anything), but the mind approaching our nature in some inexplicable and incomprehensible way, and coming into contact with it, is to be regarded as both in it and around it, neither implanted in it nor enfolded with it, but in a way which we cannot speak or think, except so far as this, that while the nature prospers according to its own order, the mind is also operative ; but if any misfortune befalls the former, the movement of the intellect halts correspondingly.

XVI. *A contemplation of the Divine utterance which said—" Let us make man after our image and likeness " ; wherein is examined what is the definition of the image, and how the possible and mortal is like to the Blessed and Impassible, and how in the image there are male and female, seeing these are not in the Prototype* [8].

1. Let us now resume our consideration of the Divine word, " Let us make man in our image, after our likeness [9]." How mean and how unworthy of the majesty of man are the fancies of some heathen writers, who magnify humanity, as they supposed, by their comparison of it to this world ! for they say that man is a little world, composed of the same elements with the universe. Those who bestow on human nature such praise as this by a high-sounding name, forget that they are dignifying man with the attributes of the gnat and the mouse : for they too are composed of these four elements,—because assuredly about the animated nature of every existing thing we behold a part, greater or less, of those elements without which it is not natural that any sensitive being should exist. What great thing is there, then, in man's being accounted a representation and likeness of the world,—of the heaven that passes away, of the earth that changes, of all things that they contain, which pass away with the departure of that which compasses them round?

2. In what then does the greatness of man consist, according to the doctrine of the Church?

Not in his likeness to the created world, but in his being in the image of the nature of the Creator.

3. What therefore, you will perhaps say, is the definition of the image? How is the incorporeal likened to body? how is the temporal like the eternal? that which is mutable by change like to the immutable ? that which is subject to passion and corruption to the impassible and incorruptible? that which constantly dwells with evil, and grows up with it, to that which is absolutely free from evil? there is a great difference between that which is conceived in the archetype, and a thing which has been made in its image : for the image is properly so called if it keeps its resemblance to the prototype ; but if the imitation be perverted from its subject, the thing is something else, and no longer an image of the subject.

4. How then is man, this mortal, passible, shortlived being, the image of that nature which is immortal, pure, and everlasting? The true answer to this question, indeed, perhaps only the very Truth knows : but this is what we, tracing out the truth so far as we are capable by conjectures and inferences, apprehend concerning the matter. Neither does the word of God lie when it says that man was made in the image of God, nor is the pitiable suffering of man's nature like to the blessedness of the impassible Life : for if any one were to compare our nature with God, one of two things must needs be allowed in order that the definition of the likeness may be apprehended in both cases in the same terms,—either that the Deity is passible, or that humanity is impassible : but if neither the Deity is passible nor our nature free from passion, what other account remains whereby we may say that the word of God speaks truly, which says that man was made in the image of God?

5. We must, then, take up once more the Holy Scripture itself, if we may perhaps find some guidance in the question by means of what is written. After saying, " Let us make man in our image," and for what purposes it was said " Let us make him," it adds this saying :—" and God created man ; in the image of God created He him; male and female created He them [1]." We have already said in what precedes, that this saying was uttered for the destruction of heretical impiety, in order that being instructed that the Only-begotten God made man in the image of God, we should in no wise distinguish the Godhead of the Father and the Son, since Holy Scripture gives to each equally the name of God,—to Him Who made man, and to Him in Whose image he was made.

---

[7] It does not seem of much consequence whether we read περιλαμβάνεται with Forbes and the MSS., and treat it as of the middle voice, or περιλαμβάνει τι with the Paris Editt. The reading περιλαμβάνεται, taken *passively*, obscures the sense of the passage.

[8] Otherwise chap. xvii. The title in the Latin Version is :—" That the excellence of man does not consist in the fact that, according to philosophers, he is made after the image of the world, but in the fact that he is made in the image of God, and how he is made in the image of God." [9] Gen. i. 26.

[1] Gen. i. 27.

6. However, let us pass by our argument upon this point : let us turn our inquiry to the question before us,—how it is that while the Deity is in bliss, and humanity is in misery, the latter is yet in Scripture called "like" the former?

7. We must, then, examine the words carefully : for we find, if we do so, that that which was made "in the image" is one thing, and that which is now manifested in wretchedness is another. "God created man," it says ; "in the image of God created He him[3]." There is an end of the creation of that which was made "in the image" : then it makes a resumption of the account of creation, and says, "male and female created He them." I presume that every one knows that this is a departure from the Prototype : for "in Christ Jesus," as the apostle says, "there is neither male nor female[2]." Yet the phrase declares that man is thus divided.

8. Thus the creation of our nature is in a sense twofold : one made like to God, one divided according to this distinction : for something like this the passage darkly conveys by its arrangement, where it first says, "God created man, in the image of God created He him[3]," and then, adding to what has been said, "male and female created He them[3],"—a thing which is alien from our conceptions of God.

9. I think that by these words Holy Scripture conveys to us a great and lofty doctrine ; and the doctrine is this. While two natures—the Divine and incorporeal nature, and the irrational life of brutes—are separated from each other as extremes, human nature is the mean between them : for in the compound nature of man we may behold a part of each of the natures I have mentioned,—of the Divine, the rational and intelligent element, which does not admit the distinction of male and female ; of the irrational, our bodily form and structure, divided into male and female : for each of these elements is certainly to be found in all that partakes of human life. That the intellectual element, however, precedes the other, we learn as from one who gives in order an account of the making of man; and we learn also that his community and kindred with the irrational is for man a provision for reproduction. For he says first that "God created man in the image of God" (showing by these words, as the Apostle says, that in such a being there is no male or female): then he adds the peculiar attributes of human nature, "male and female created He them[3]."

10. What, then, do we learn from this? Let no one, I pray, be indignant if I bring from far an argument to bear upon the present subject.

God is in His own nature all that which our mind can conceive of good ;—rather, transcending all good that we can conceive or comprehend. He creates man for no other reason than that He is good ; and being such, and having this as His reason for entering upon the creation of our nature, He would not exhibit the power of His goodness in an imperfect form, giving our nature some one of the things at His disposal, and grudging it a share in another : but the perfect form of goodness is here to be seen by His both bringing man into being from nothing, and fully supplying him with all good gifts : but since the list of individual good gifts is a long one, it is out of the question to apprehend it numerically. The language of Scripture therefore expresses it concisely by a comprehensive phrase, in saying that man was made "in the image of God" : for this is the same as to say that He made human nature participant in all good ; for if the Deity is the fulness of good, and this is His image, then the image finds its resemblance to the Archetype in being filled with all good.

11. Thus there is in us the principle of all excellence, all virtue and wisdom, and every higher thing that we conceive : but pre-eminent among all is the fact that we are free from necessity, and not in bondage to any natural power, but have decision in our own power as we please ; for virtue is a voluntary thing, subject to no dominion : that which is the result of compulsion and force cannot be virtue.

12. Now as the image bears in all points the semblance of the archetypal excellence, if it had not a difference in some respect, being absolutely without divergence it would no longer be a likeness, but will in that case manifestly be absolutely identical with the Prototype. What difference then do we discern between the Divine and that which has been made like to the Divine? We find it in the fact that the former is uncreate, while the latter has its being from creation : and this distinction of property brings with it a train of other properties ; for it is very certainly acknowledged that the uncreated nature is also immutable, and always remains the same, while the created nature cannot exist without change ; for its very passage from non-existence to existence is a certain motion and change of the non-existent transmuted by the Divine purpose into being.

13. As the Gospel calls the stamp upon the coin "the image of Cæsar[4]," whereby we learn that in that which was fashioned to resemble Cæsar there was resemblance as to outward look, but difference as to material, so also in the present saying, when we consider the attri-

---

[2] Cf. Gal. iii. 28.   [3] Gen. i. 27.   [4] Cf. S. Matt. xxii. 20, 21.

butes contemplated both in the Divine and human nature, in which the likeness consists, to be in the place of the features, we find in what underlies them the difference which we behold in the uncreated and in the created nature.

14. Now as the former always remains the same, while that which came into being by creation had the beginning of its existence from change, and has a kindred connection with the like mutation, for this reason He Who, as the prophetical writing says, "knoweth all things before they be [5]," following out, or rather perceiving beforehand by His power of foreknowledge what, in a state of independence and freedom, is the tendency of the motion of man's will,—as He saw, I say, what would be, He devised for His image the distinction of male and female, which has no reference to the Divine Archetype, but, as we have said, is an approximation to the less rational nature.

15. The cause, indeed, of this device, only those can know who were eye-witnesses of the truth and ministers of the Word; but we, imagining the truth, as far as we can, by means of conjectures and similitudes, do not set forth that which occurs to our mind authoritatively, but will place it in the form of a theoretical speculation before our kindly hearers.

16. What is it then which we understand concerning these matters? In saying that "God created man" the text indicates, by the indefinite character of the term, all mankind; for was not Adam here named together with the creation, as the history tells us in what follows [6]? yet the name given to the man created is not the particular, but the general name: thus we are led by the employment of the general name of our nature to some such view as this—that in the Divine foreknowledge and power all humanity is included in the first creation; for it is fitting for God not to regard any of the things made by Him as indeterminate, but that each existing thing should have some limit and measure prescribed by the wisdom of its Maker.

17. Now just as any particular man is limited by his bodily dimensions, and the peculiar size which is conjoined with the superficies of his body is the measure of his separate existence, so I think that the entire plenitude of humanity was included by the God of all, by His power of foreknowledge, as it were in one body, and that this is what the text teaches us which says, "God created man, in the image of God created He him." For the image is not in part of our nature, nor is the grace in any one of the things found in that nature, but this power extends equally to all the race: and a sign of this is that mind is implanted alike in all: for all have the power of understanding and deliberating, and of all else whereby the Divine nature finds its image in that which was made according to it: the man that was manifested at the first creation of the world, and he that shall be after the consummation of all, are alike: they equally bear in themselves the Divine image [7].

18. For this reason the whole race was spoken of as one man, namely, that to God's power nothing is either past or future, but even that which we expect is comprehended, equally with what is at present existing, by the all-sustaining energy. Our whole nature, then, extending from the first to the last, is, so to say, one image of Him Who is; but the distinction of kind in male and female was added to His work last, as I suppose, for the reason which follows [8].

XVII. *What we must answer to those who raise the question—"If procreation is after sin, how would souls have come into being if the first of mankind had remained sinless [9]?"*

1. It is better for us however, perhaps, rather to inquire, before investigating this point, the solution of the question put forward by our adversaries; for they say that before the sin there is no account of birth, or of travail, or of the desire that tends to procreation, but when they were banished from Paradise after their sin, and the woman was condemned by the sentence of travail, Adam thus entered with his consort upon the intercourse of married life, and then took place the beginning of procreation. If, then, marriage did not exist in Paradise, nor travail, nor birth, they say that it follows as a necessary conclusion that human souls would not have existed in plurality had not the grace of immortality fallen away to mortality, and marriage preserved our race by means of descendants, introducing the offspring of the departing to take their place, so that in a certain way the sin that entered into the world was profitable for the life of man: for the human

---

[5] Hist. Sus. 42.

[6] The punctuation followed by Forbes here does not seem to give a good sense, and also places S. Gregory in the position of formally stating that one passage of Genesis contradicts another. By substituting an interrogation after ἡ ἱστορία φησίν, the sense given is this:—we know from a later statement in Genesis that the name Adam was given "in the day that they were created" (Gen. v. 2), but here the name given is *general*, not *particular*. There must be a reason for this, and the reason is, that the race of man, and not the individual, is that spoken of as "created in the image of God." With this view that all humanity is included in the first creation may be compared a passage near the end of the *De Anima*, where the first man is compared to a full ear of corn, afterwards "divided into a multitude of bare grain."

[7] With this passage, again, may be compared the teaching of the *De Anima* on the subject of the Resurrection.

[8] The explanation of the reason, however, is deferred; see xvii. 4.

[9] Otherwise Chap. xviii. The Bodleian MS. of the Latin version has the title:—"Against those who say that sin was a useful introduction for the propagation of the human race; and that by sin it deserved animal generation."

race would have remained in the pair of the first-formed, had not the fear of death impelled their nature to provide succession.

2. Now here again the true answer, whatever it may be, can be clear to those only who, like Paul, have been instructed in the mysteries of Paradise ; but our answer is as follows. When the Sadducees once argued against the doctrine of the resurrection, and brought forward, to establish their own opinion, that woman of many marriages, who had been wife to seven brethren, and thereupon inquired whose wife she will be after the resurrection, our Lord answered their argument so as not only to instruct the Sadducees, but also to reveal to all that come after them the mystery of the resurrection-life : " for in the resurrection," He says, "they neither marry, nor are given in marriage ; neither can they die any more, for they are equal to the angels, and are the children of God, being the children of the resurrection [1]." Now the resurrection promises us nothing else than the restoration of the fallen to their ancient state ; for the grace we look for is a certain return to the first life, bringing back again to Paradise him who was cast out from it. If then the life of those restored is closely related to that of the angels, it is clear that the life before the transgression was a kind of angelic life, and hence also our return to the ancient condition of our life is compared to the angels. Yet while, as has been said, there is no marriage among them, the armies of the angels are in countless myriads ; for so Daniel declared in his visions : so, in the same way, if there had not come upon us as the result of sin a change for the worse, and removal from equality with the angels, neither should we have needed marriage that we might multiply ; but whatever the mode of increase in the angelic nature is (unspeakable and inconceivable by human conjectures, except that it assuredly exists), it would have operated also in the case of men, who were "made a little lower than the angels [2]," to increase mankind to the measure determined by its Maker.

3. But if any one finds a difficulty in an inquiry as to the manner of the generation of souls, had man not needed the assistance of marriage, we shall ask him in turn, what is the mode of the angelic existence, how they exist in countless myriads, being one essence, and at the same time numerically many ; for we shall be giving a fit answer to one who raises the question how man would have been without marriage, if we say, "as the angels are without marriage ; " for the fact that man was in a like condition with them before the transgression is shown by the restoration to that state.

4. Now that we have thus cleared up these matters, let us return to our former point,— how it was that after the making of His image God contrived for His work the distinction of male and female. I say that the preliminary speculation we have completed is of service for determining this question ; for He Who brought all things into being and fashioned Man as a whole by His own will to the Divine image, did not wait to see the number of souls made up to its proper fulness by the gradual additions of those coming after ; but while looking upon the nature of man in its entirety and fulness by the exercise of His foreknowledge, and bestowing upon it a lot exalted and equal to the angels, since He saw beforehand by His all-seeing power the failure of their will to keep a direct course to what is good, and its consequent declension from the angelic life, in order that the multitude of human souls might not be cut short by its fall from that mode by which the angels were increased and multiplied,—for this reason, I say, He formed for our nature that contrivance for increase which befits those who had fallen into sin, implanting in mankind, instead of the angelic majesty of nature, that animal and irrational mode by which they now succeed one another.

5. Hence also, it seems to me, the great David pitying the misery of man mourns over his nature with such words as these, that, " man being in honour knew it not " (meaning by " honour " the equality with the angels), therefore, he says, " he is compared to the beasts that have no understanding, and made like unto them [3]." For he truly was made like the beasts, who received in his nature the present mode of transient generation, on account of his inclination to material things.

XVIII. *That our irrational passions have their rise from kindred with irrational nature .*[4]

1. For I think that from this beginning all our passions issue as from a spring, and pour their flood over man's life ; and an evidence of my words is the kinship of passions which appears alike in ourselves and in the brutes ; for it is not allowable to ascribe the first beginnings of our constitutional liability to passion to that human nature which was fashioned in the Divine likeness ; but as brute life first entered into the world, and man, for the reason already mentioned, took something of their nature (I mean the mode of generation), he accordingly took at the same time a share of the other

---

[1] S. Luke xx. 35, 36.   [2] Ps viii. 6.

[3] Ps. xlix. 13 (LXX.)
[4] Otherwise Chap. xix. The Bodleian MS. of the Latin version has the title :—" That our other passions also are common to us and to the irrational animals, and that by the restraint of them we are said to be like to God."

attributes contemplated in that nature; for the likeness of man to God is not found in anger, nor is pleasure a mark of the superior nature; cowardice also, and boldness, and the desire of gain, and the dislike of loss, and all the like, are far removed from that stamp which indicates Divinity.

2. These attributes, then, human nature took to itself from the side of the brutes; for those qualities with which brute life was armed for self-preservation, when transferred to human life, became passions; for the carnivorous animals are preserved by their anger, and those which breed largely by their love of pleasure; cowardice preserves the weak, fear that which is easily taken by more powerful animals, and greediness those of great bulk; and to miss anything that tends to pleasure is for the brutes a matter of pain. All these and the like affections entered man's composition by reason of the animal mode of generation.

3. I may be allowed to describe the human image by comparison with some wonderful piece of modelling. For, as one may see in models those carved[5] shapes which the artificers of such things contrive for the wonder of beholders, tracing out upon a single head two forms of faces; so man seems to me to bear a double likeness to opposite things—being moulded in the Divine element of his mind to the Divine beauty, but bearing, in the passionate impulses that arise in him, a likeness to the brute nature; while often even his reason is rendered brutish, and obscures the better element by the worse through its inclination and disposition towards what is irrational; for whenever a man drags down his mental energy to these affections, and forces his reason to become the servant of his passions, there takes place a sort of conversion of the good stamp in him into the irrational image, his whole nature being traced anew after that design, as his reason, so to say, cultivates the beginnings of his passions, and gradually multiplies them; for once it lends its co-operation to passion, it produces a plenteous and abundant crop of evils.

4. Thus our love of pleasure took its beginning from our being made like to the irrational creation, and was increased by the transgressions of men, becoming the parent of so many varieties of sins arising from pleasure as we cannot find among the irrational animals. Thus the rising of anger in us is indeed akin to the impulse of the brutes; but it grows by the alliance of thought: for thence come malignity, envy, deceit, conspiracy, hypocrisy; all these are the

result of the evil husbandry of the mind; for if the passion were divested of the aid it receives from thought, the anger that is left behind is short-lived and not sustained, like a bubble, perishing straightway as soon as it comes into being. Thus the greediness of swine introduces covetousness, and the high spirit of the horse becomes the origin of pride; and all the particular forms that proceed from the want of reason in brute nature become vice by the evil use of the mind.

5. So, likewise, on the contrary, if reason instead assumes sway over such emotions, each of them is transmuted to a form of virtue; for anger produces courage, terror caution, fear obedience, hatred aversion from vice, the power of love the desire for what is truly beautiful; high spirit in our character raises our thought above the passions, and keeps it from bondage to what is base; yea, the great Apostle, even, praises such a form of mental elevation when he bids us constantly to "think those things that are above[6];" and so we find that every such motion, when elevated by loftiness of mind, is conformed to the beauty of the Divine image.

6. But the other impulse is greater, as the tendency of sin is heavy and downward; for the ruling element of our soul is more inclined to be dragged downwards by the weight of the irrational nature than is the heavy and earthy element to be exalted by the loftiness of the intellect; hence the misery that encompasses us often causes the Divine gift to be forgotten, and spreads the passions of the flesh, like some ugly mask, over the beauty of the image.

7. Those, therefore, are in some sense excusable, who do not admit, when they look upon such cases, that the Divine form is there; yet we may behold the Divine image in men by the medium of those who have ordered their lives aright. For if the man who is subject to passion, and carnal, makes it incredible that man was adorned, as it were, with Divine beauty, surely the man of lofty virtue and pure from pollution will confirm you in the better conception of human nature.

8. For instance (for it is better to make our argument clear by an illustration), one of those noted for wickedness—some Jechoniah, say, or some other of evil memory—has obliterated the beauty of his nature by the pollution of wickedness; yet in Moses and in men like him the form of the image was kept pure. Now where the beauty of the form has not been obscured, there is made plain the faithfulness of the saying that man is an image of God.

9. It may be, however, that some one feels

---

5 Reading with Forbes διαγλύφους. The reading διγλύφους of the earlier editt. gives a better sense, but is not supported by any of Forbes' MSS.

6 Col. iii. 2.

shame at the fact that our life, like that of the brutes, is sustained by food, and for this reason deems man unworthy of being supposed to have been framed in the image of God; but he may expect that freedom from this function will one day be bestowed upon our nature in the life we look for; for, as the Apostle says, "the Kingdom of God is not meat and drink[7];" and the Lord declared that "man shall not live by bread alone, but by every word that proceedeth out of the mouth of God[8]." Further, as the resurrection holds forth to us a life equal with the angels, and with the angels there is no food, there is sufficient ground for believing that man, who will live in like fashion with the angels, will be released from such a function.

XIX. *To those who say that the enjoyment of the good things we look for will again consist in meat and drink, because it is written that by these means man at first lived in Paradise[9].*

1. But some one perhaps will say that man will not be returning to the same form of life, if, as it seems, we formerly existed by eating, and shall hereafter be free from that function. I, however, when I hear the Holy Scripture, do not understand only bodily meat, or the pleasure of the flesh; but I recognize another kind of food also, having a certain analogy to that of the body, the enjoyment of which extends to the soul alone: "Eat of my bread[1]," is the bidding of Wisdom to the hungry; and the Lord declares those blessed who hunger for such food as this, and says, "If any man thirst, let him come unto Me, and drink": and "drink ye joy[2]," is the great Isaiah's charge to those who are able to hear his sublimity. There is a prophetic threatening also against those worthy of vengeance, that they shall be punished with famine; but the "famine" is not a lack of bread and water, but a failure of the word:— "not a famine of bread, nor a thirst for water, but a famine of hearing the word of the Lord ."

2. We ought, then, to conceive that the fruit in Eden was something worthy of God's planting (and Eden is interpreted to mean "delight"), and not to doubt that man was hereby nourished: nor should we at all conceive, concerning the mode of life in Paradise, this transitory and perishable nutriment: "of every tree of the garden," He says, "thou mayest freely eat[4]."

3. Who will give to him that has a healthful hunger that tree that is in Paradise, which in-cludes all good, which is named "every tree," in which this passage bestows on man the right to share? for in the universal and transcendent saying every form of good is in harmony with itself, and the whole is one. And who will keep me back from that tasting of the tree which is of mixed and doubtful kind? for surely it is clear to all who are at all keen-sighted what that "every" tree is whose fruit is life, and what again that mixed tree is whose end is death: for He Who presents ungrudgingly the enjoy-ment of "every" tree, surely by some reason and forethought keeps man from participation in those which are of doubtful kind.

4. It seems to me that I may take the great David and the wise Solomon as my instructors in the interpretation of this text: for both under-stand the grace of the permitted delight to be one,—that very actual Good, which in truth is "every" good;—David, when he says, "Delight thou in the Lord[5]," and Solomon, when he names Wisdom herself (which is the Lord) "a tree of life[6]."

5. Thus the "every" tree of which the pas-sage gives food to him who was made in the likeness of God, is the same with the tree of life; and there is opposed to this tree another tree, the food given by which is the knowledge of good and evil:—not that it bears in turn as fruit each of these things of opposite signifi-cance, but that it produces a fruit blended and mixed with opposite qualities, the eating of which the Prince of Life forbids, and the serpent counsels, that he may prepare an en-trance for death: and he obtained credence for his counsel, covering over the fruit with a fair appearance and the show of pleasure, that it might be pleasant to the eyes and stimulate the desire to taste.

XX. *What was the life in Paradise, and what was the forbidden tree[7]?*

1. What then is that which includes the knowledge of good and evil blended together, and is decked with the pleasures of sense? I think I am not aiming wide of the mark in employing, as a starting-point for my specula-tion, the sense of "knowable[8]." It is not, I think, "science" which the Scripture here means by "knowledge"; but I find a certain distinc-tion, according to Scriptural use, between "knowledge" and "discernment": for to "dis-

---

[7] Rom. xiv. 17.　　　　　[8] S. Matt. iv. 4.
[9] Otherwise Chap. xx. The Bodleian MS. of the Latin version has the title:—"How the food ought to be understood with which man was fed in Paradise and from which he was prohibited."
[1] Prov. ix. 5.　　　　　[2] Cf. Is. xii. 3.
Amos viii. 11.　　　　　[4] Gen. ii. 16.

[5] Ps. xxxvii. 4.　　　　[6] Prov. iii. 18.
[7] Otherwise Chap. xxi. The Bodleian MS. of the Latin version gives as the title:—"Why Scripture calls the tree, 'the tree of the knowledge of good and evil.'"
[8] The reference is to Gen. ii. 9 (in LXX.), where the tree is called, τὸ ξύλον τοῦ εἰδέναι γνωστὸν καλοῦ καὶ πονηροῦ. S. Gregory proceeds to ascertain the exact meaning of the word γνωστὸν in the text; the eating is the "knowing," but what is "knowing"? He answers, "desiring."

cern" skilfully the good from the evil, the Apostle says is a mark of a more perfect condition and of "exercised senses [9]," for which reason also he bids us "prove all things [1]," and says that "discernment" belongs to the spiritual man [2] : but "knowledge" is not always to be understood of skill and acquaintance with anything, but of the disposition towards what is agreeable,—as "the Lord knoweth them that are His [3]"; and He says to Moses, "I knew thee above all [4]"; while of those condemned in their wickedness He Who knows all things says, "I never knew you [5]."

2. The tree, then, from which comes this fruit of mixed knowledge, is among those things which are forbidden ; and that fruit is combined of opposite qualities, which has the serpent to commend it, it may be for this reason, that the evil is not exposed in its nakedness, itself appearing in its own proper nature—for wickedness would surely fail of its effect were it not decked with some fair colour to entice to the desire of it him whom it deceives—but now the nature of evil is in a manner mixed, keeping destruction like some snare concealed in its depths, and displaying some phantom of good in the deceitfulness of its exterior. The beauty of the substance seems good to those who love money : yet "the love of money is a root of all evil [6]" : and who would plunge into the unsavoury mud of wantonness, were it not that he whom this bait hurries into passion thinks pleasure a thing fair and acceptable? so, too, the other sins keep their destruction hidden, and seem at first sight acceptable, and some deceit makes them earnestly sought after by unwary men instead of what is good.

3. Now since the majority of men judge the good to lie in that which gratifies the senses, and there is a certain identity of name between that which is, and that which appears to be "good,"—for this reason that desire which arises towards what is evil, as though towards good, is called by Scripture "the knowledge of good and evil;" "knowledge," as we have said, expressing a certain mixed disposition. It speaks of the fruit of the forbidden tree not as a thing absolutely evil (because it is decked with good), nor as a thing purely good (because evil is latent in it), but as compounded of both, and declares that the tasting of it brings to death those who touch it ; almost proclaiming aloud the doctrine that the very actual good is in its nature simple and uniform, alien from all duplicity or conjunction with its opposite, while evil is many-coloured and fairly adorned, being esteemed to

be one thing and revealed by experience as another, the knowledge of which (that is, its reception by experience) is the beginning and antecedent of death and destruction.

4. It was because he saw this that the serpent points out the evil fruit of sin, not showing the evil manifestly in its own nature (for man would not have been deceived by manifest evil), but giving to what the woman beheld the glamour of a certain beauty, and conjuring into its taste the spell of a sensual pleasure, he appeared to her to speak convincingly : "and the woman saw," it says, "that the tree was good for food, and that it was pleasant to the eyes to behold, and fair to see ; and she took of the fruit thereof and did eat [7]," and that eating became the mother of death to men. This, then, is that fruit-bearing of mixed character, where the passage clearly expresses the sense in which the tree was called "capable of the knowledge of good and evil," because, like the evil nature of poisons that are prepared with honey, it appears to be good in so far as it affects the senses with sweetness : but in so far as it destroys him who touches it, it is the worst of all evil. Thus when the evil poison worked its effect against man's life, then man, that noble thing and name, the image of God's nature, was made, as the prophet says, "like unto vanity [8]."

5. The image, therefore, properly belongs to the better part of our attributes ; but all in our life that is painful and miserable is far removed from the likeness to the Divine.

XXI. *That the resurrection is looked for as a consequence, not so much from the declaration of Scripture as from the very necessity of things [9].*

1. Wickedness, however, is not so strong as to prevail over the power of good ; nor is the folly of our nature more powerful and more abiding than the wisdom of God : for it is impossible that that which is always mutable and variable should be more firm and more abiding than that which always remains the same and is firmly fixed in goodness : but it is absolutely certain that the Divine counsel possesses immutability, while the changeableness of our nature does not remain settled even in evil.

2. Now that which is always in motion, if its progress be to good, will never cease moving onwards to what lies before it, by reason of the infinity of the course to be traversed :—for it will not find any limit of its object such that when it has apprehended it, it will at last cease

---

9 Cf. Heb. v. 14.
2 Cf. 1 Cor. ii. 15.
4 Ex. xxxiii. 12 (LXX.).
6 1 Tim. vi. 10.

1 1 Thess. v. 21.
3 2 Tim. ii. 19.
5 S. Matt. vii. 23.

7 Gen. iii. 5, 6 (LXX.).   8 Ps. cxliv. 4 (LXX.).
9 Otherwise Chap. xxii.   The Bodleian MS. of the Latin version gives as the title :—" That the Divine counsel is immutable."

its motion : but if its bias be in the opposite direction, when it has finished the course of wickedness and reached the extreme limit of evil, then that which is ever moving, finding no halting point for its impulse natural to itself, when it has run through the lengths that can be run in wickedness, of necessity turns its motion towards good : for as evil does not extend to infinity, but is comprehended by necessary limits, it would appear that good once more follows in succession upon the limit of evil ; and thus, as we have said, the ever-moving character of our nature comes to run its course at the last once more back towards good, being taught the lesson of prudence by the memory of its former misfortunes, to the end that it may never again be in like case.

3. Our course, then, will once more lie in what is good, by reason of the fact that the nature of evil is bounded by necessary limits. For just as those skilled in astronomy tell us that the whole universe is full of light, and that darkness is made to cast its shadow by the inter-position of the body formed by the earth ; and that this darkness is shut off from the rays of the sun, in the shape of a cone, according to the figure of the sphere-shaped body, and be-hind it ; while the sun, exceeding the earth by a size many times as great as its own, enfolding it round about on all sides with its rays, unites at the limit of the cone the concurrent streams of light ; so that if (to suppose the case) any one had the power of passing beyond the measure to which the shadow extends, he would certainly find himself in light unbroken by dark-ness ;—even so I think that we ought to under-stand about ourselves, that on passing the limit of wickedness we shall again have our con-versation in light, as the nature of good, when compared with the measure of wickedness, is incalculably superabundant.

4. Paradise therefore will be restored, that tree will be restored which is in truth the tree of life ;—there will be restored the grace of the image, and the dignity of rule. It does not seem to me that our hope is one for those things which are now subjected by God to man for the necessary uses of life, but one for another kingdom, of a description that belongs to unspeakable mysteries.

XXII. *To those who say, " If the resurrection is a thing excellent and good, how is it that it has not happened already, but is hoped for in some periods of time ? "* [1]

1. Let us give our attention, however, to the next point of our discussion. It may be that some one, giving his thought wings to soar towards the sweetness of our hope, deems it a burden and a loss that we are not more speedily placed in that good state which is above man's sense and knowledge, and is dissatisfied with the extension of the time that intervenes be-tween him and the object of his desire. Let him cease to vex himself like a child that is discontented at the brief delay of something that gives him pleasure ; for since all things are governed by reason and wisdom, we must by no means suppose that anything that happens is done without reason itself and the wisdom that is therein.

2. You will say then, What is this reason, in accordance with which the change of our pain-ful life to that which we desire does not take place at once, but this heavy and corporeal existence of ours waits, extended to some de-terminate time, for the term of the consumma-tion of all things, that then man's life may be set free as it were from the reins, and revert once more, released and free, to the life of blessedness and impassibility ?

3. Well, whether our answer is near the truth of the matter, the Truth Itself may clearly know ; but at all events what occurs to our intelligence is as follows. I take up then once more in my argument our first text :—God says, " Let us make man in our image, after our likeness, and God created man, in the image of God created He him [2]." Accordingly, the Image of God, which we behold in universal humanity, had its consummation then [3] ; but Adam as yet was not ; for the thing formed from the earth is called Adam, by etymological nomenclature, as those tell us who are acquainted with the Hebrew tongue—wherefore also the apostle, who was specially learned in his native tongue, the tongue of the Israelites, calls the man " of the earth [4] " χοϊκός, as though trans-lating the name Adam into the Greek word.

4. Man, then, was made in the image of God ; that is, the universal nature, the thing like God ; not part of the whole, but all the fulness of the nature together was so made by omnipotent wisdom. He saw, Who holds all limits in His grasp, as the Scripture tells us which says, " in His hand are all the corners of the earth [5]," He saw, " Who knoweth all things " even " before they be [6]," comprehending them in His knowledge, how great in number humanity will be in the sum of its individuals. But as He perceived in our created nature the bias towards evil, and the fact that after its voluntary fall from equality with the angels it would acquire a fellowship with the lower

---

[1] Otherwise Chap. xxiii. The title in the Bodleian MS. of the Latin version is :—"That when the generation of man is finished, time also will come to an end." Some MSS. of the Latin version make the first few words part of the preceding chapter.

[2] Gen. i. 26, 27.
[3] This Realism is expressed even more strongly in the *De Animâ et Resurrectione*.   [4] 1 Cor. xv. 47.
[5] Ps. xcv. 4.   [6] Cf. Hist. Sus. 42.

nature, He mingled, for this reason, with His own image, an element of the irrational (for the distinction of male and female does not exist in the Divine and blessed nature) ;—transferring, I say, to man the special attribute of the irrational formation, He bestowed increase upon our race not according to the lofty character of our creation ; for it was not when He made that which was in His own image that He bestowed on man the power of increasing and multiplying ; but when He divided it by sexual distinctions, then He said, "Increase and multiply, and replenish the earth[7]." For this belongs not to the Divine, but to the irrational element, as the history indicates when it narrates that these words were first spoken by God in the case of the irrational creatures ; since we may be sure that, if He had bestowed on man, before imprinting on our nature the distinction of male and female, the power for increase conveyed by this utterance, we should not have needed this form of generation by which the brutes are generated.

5. Now seeing that the full number of men pre-conceived by the operation of foreknowledge will come into life by means of this animal generation, God, Who governs all things in a certain order and sequence,—since the inclination of our nature to what was beneath it (which He Who beholds the future equally with the present saw before it existed) made some such form of generation absolutely necessary for mankind,—therefore also foreknew the time coextensive with the creation of men, so that the extent of time should be adapted for the entrances of the pre-determined souls, and that the flux and motion of time should halt at the moment when humanity is no longer produced by means of it ; and that when the generation of men is completed, time should cease together with its completion, and then should take place the restitution of all things, and with the World-Reformation humanity also should be changed from the corruptible and earthly to the impassible and eternal.

6. And this it seems to me the Divine apostle considered when he declared in his epistle to the Corinthians the sudden stoppage of time, and the change of the things that are now moving on back to the opposite end where he says, "Behold, I show you a mystery ; we shall not all sleep, but we shall all be changed, in a moment, in the twinkling of an eye, at the last trump[8]." For when, as I suppose, the full complement of human nature has reached the limit of the pre-determined measure, because there is no longer anything to be made up in the way of increase to the number of souls, he

teaches us that the change in existing things will take place in an instant of time, giving to that limit of time which has no parts or extension the names of "a moment," and "the twinkling of an eye" ; so that it will no more be possible for one who reaches the verge of time (which is the last and extreme point, from the fact that nothing is lacking to the attainment of its extremity) to obtain by death this change which takes place at a fixed period, but only when the trumpet of the resurrection sounds, which awakens the dead, and transforms those who are left in life, after the likeness of those who have undergone the resurrection change, at once to incorruptibility ; so that the weight of the flesh is no longer heavy, nor does its burden hold them down to earth, but they rise aloft through the air—for, "we shall be caught up," he tells us, "in the clouds to meet the Lord in the air ; and so shall we ever be with the Lord[9]."

7. Let him therefore wait for that time which is necessarily made co-extensive with the development of humanity. For even Abraham and the patriarchs, while they had the desire to see the promised good things, and ceased not to seek the heavenly country, as the apostle says, are yet even now in the condition of hoping for that grace, "God having provided some better thing for us," according to the words of Paul, "that they without us should not be made perfect[1]." If they, then, bear the delay who by faith only and by hope saw the good things "afar off" and "embraced them[2]," as the apostle bears witness, placing their certainty of the enjoyment of the things for which they hoped in the fact that they "judged Him faithful Who has promised[3]," what ought most of us to do, who have not, it may be, a hold upon the better hope from the character of our lives ? Even the prophet's soul fainted with desire, and in his psalm he confesses this passionate love, saying that his "soul hath a desire and longing to be in the courts of the Lord[4]," even if he must needs be rejected[5] to a place amongst the lowest, as it is a greater and more desirable thing to be last there than to be first among the ungodly tents of this life ; nevertheless he was patient of the delay, deeming, indeed, the life there blessed, and accounting a brief participation in it more desirable than "thousands" of time—for he says, "one day in Thy courts is better than thousands[6]"—yet he did not repine at the necessary dispensation concerning existing things, and thought it sufficient bliss for man to have those good things even by way of hope ; wherefore he says at the end of the

---

7 Gen. i. 28.   8 1 Cor. xv. 51, 52.

9 1 Thess. iv. 17.   1 Heb. xi. 40.   2 Heb. xi. 13.
3 Heb. xi. 11.   4 Ps. lxxxiv. 3.
5 Ps. lxxxiv. 11 (LXX.).   6 Ps. lxxxiv. 10.

Psalm, "O Lord of hosts, blessed is the man that hopeth in Thee [7]."

8. Neither, then, should we be troubled at the brief delay of what we hope for, but give diligence that we may not be cast out from the object of our hopes; for just as though, if one were to tell some inexperienced person beforehand, "the gathering of the crops will take place in the season of summer, and the stores will be filled, and the table abundantly supplied with food at the time of plenty," it would be a foolish man who should seek to hurry on the coming of the fruit-time, when he ought to be sowing seeds and preparing the crops for himself by diligent care; for the fruit-time will surely come, whether he wishes or not, at the appointed time; and it will be looked on differently by him who has secured for himself beforehand abundance of crops, and by him who is found by the fruit-time destitute of all preparation. Even so I think it is one's duty, as the proclamation is clearly made to all that the time of change will come, not to trouble himself about times (for He said that "it is not for us to know the times and the seasons [8]"), nor to pursue calculations by which he will be sure to sap the hope of the resurrection in the soul; but to make his confidence in the things expected as a prop to lean on, and to purchase for himself, by good conversation, the grace that is to come.

XXIII. *That he who confesses the beginning of the world's existence must necessarily also agree as to its end [9].*

But if some one, beholding the present course of the world, by which intervals of time are marked, going on in a certain order, should say that it is not possible that the predicted stoppage of these moving things should take place, such a man clearly also does not believe that in the beginning the heaven and the earth were made by God; for he who admits a beginning of motion surely does not doubt as to its also having an end; and he who does not allow its end, does not admit its beginning either; but as it is by believing that "we understand that the worlds were framed by the word of God," as the apostle says, "so that things which are seen were not made of things which do appear [1]," we must use the same faith as to the word of God when He foretells the necessary stoppage of existing things.

2. The question of the "how" must, however, be put beyond the reach of our meddling; for even in the case mentioned it was "by faith" that we admitted that the thing seen was framed from things not yet apparent, omitting the search into things beyond our reach. And yet our reason suggests difficulties on many points, offering no small occasions for doubt as to the things which we believe.

3. For in that case too, argumentative men might by plausible reasoning upset our faith, so that we should not think that statement true which Holy Scripture delivers concerning the material creation, when it asserts that all existing things have their beginning of being from God. For those who abide by the contrary view maintain that matter is co-eternal with God, and employ in support of their own doctrine some such arguments as these. If God is in His nature simple and immaterial, without quantity [2], or size, or combination, and removed from the idea of circumscription by way of figure, while all matter is apprehended in extension measured by intervals, and does not escape the apprehension of our senses, but becomes known to us in colour, and figure, and bulk, and size, and resistance, and the other attributes belonging to it, none of which it is possible to conceive in the Divine nature,—what method is there for the production of matter from the immaterial, or of the nature that has dimensions from that which is unextended? for if these things are believed to have their existence from that source, they clearly come into existence after being in Him in some mysterious way; but if material existence was in Him, how can He be immaterial while including matter in Himself? and similarly with all the other marks by which the material nature is differentiated; if quantity exists in God, how is God without quantity? if the compound nature exists in Him, how is He simple, without parts and without combination? so that the argument forces us to think either that He is material, because matter has its existence from Him as a source; or, if one avoids this, it is necessary to suppose that matter was imported by Him *ab extra* for the making of the universe.

4. If, then, it was external to God, something else surely existed besides God, conceived, in respect of eternity, together with Him Who exists ungenerately; so that the argument supposes two eternal and unbegotten existences, having their being concurrently with each other

---

[7] Ps. lxxxiv. 12.   [8] Acts i. 7.
[9] Otherwise Chap. xxiv. The Bodleian MS. of the Latin version has a title corresponding to that of the following chapter in the other MSS.:—"Against those who say that matter is co-eternal with God."
[1] Cf. Heb. xi. 3. The MSS. give somewhat the same variations which are observable in the N. T. Codices. The reading which Forbes adopts coincides with the Textus Receptus

[2] Reading, with some of Forbes' MSS., ἄποσος, which seems on the whole the better reading so far as sense is concerned. ἄποιος may be the result of a sense of the awkwardness of employing both ἄποσος and ἀμεγέθης: but further on in the section we find ἄποσος where the MSS. seem to agree. Further, the connecting particles seem to show a closer connection of sense between ἄποσος and ἀμεγέθης than between ἀμεγέθης and ἀσύνθετος.

—that of Him Who operates as an artificer, and that of the thing which admits this skilled operation; and if any one under pressure of this argument should assume a material substratum for the Creator of all things, what a support will the Manichæan find for his special doctrine, who opposes by virtue of ungenerateness a material existence to a Good Being. Yet we do believe that all things are of God, as we hear the Scripture say so; and as to the question how they were in God, a question beyond our reason, we do not seek to pry into it, believing that all things are within the capacity of God's power—both to give existence to what is not, and to implant qualities at His pleasure in what is.

5. Consequently, as we suppose the power of the Divine will to be a sufficient cause to the things that are, for their coming into existence out of nothing, so too we shall not repose our belief on anything beyond probability in referring the World-Reformation to the same power. Moreover, it might perhaps be possible, by some skill in the use of words, to persuade those who raise frivolous objections on the subject of matter not to think that they can make an unanswerable attack on our statement.

XXIV. *An argument against those who say that matter is co-eternal with God* [3].

1. For after all that opinion on the subject of matter does not turn out to be beyond what appears consistent, which declares that it has its existence from Him Who is intelligible and immaterial. For we shall find all matter to be composed of certain qualities, of which if it is divested it can, in itself, be by no means grasped by idea. Moreover in idea each kind of quality is separated from the substratum; but idea is an intellectual and not a corporeal method of examination. If, for instance, some animal or tree is presented to our notice, or any other of the things that have material existence, we perceive in our mental discussion of it many things concerning the substratum, the idea of each of which is clearly distinguished from the object we contemplate: for the idea of colour is one, of weight another; so again that of quantity and of such and such a peculiar quality of touch: for "softness," and "two cubits long," and the rest of the attributes we spoke of, are not connected in idea either with one another or with the body: each of them has conceived concerning it its own explanatory definition according to its being, having nothing in common with any other of the qualities that are contemplated in the substratum.

2. [4] If, then, colour is a thing intelligible, and resistance also is intelligible, and so with quantity and the rest of the like properties, while if each of these should be withdrawn from the substratum, the whole idea of the body is dissolved; it would seem to follow that we may suppose the concurrence of those things, the absence of which we found to be a cause of the dissolution of the body, to produce the material nature: for as that is not a body which has not colour, and figure, and resistance, and extension, and weight, and the other properties, while each of these in its proper existence is found to be not the body but something else besides the body, so, conversely, whenever the specified attributes concur they produce bodily existence. Yet if the perception of these properties is a matter of intellect, and the Divinity is also intellectual in nature, there is no incongruity in supposing that these intellectual occasions for the genesis of bodies have their existence from the incorporeal nature, the intellectual nature on the one hand giving being to the intellectual potentialities, and the mutual concurrence of these bringing to its genesis the material nature.

3. Let this discussion, however, be by way of digression: we must direct our discourse once more to the faith by which we accept the statement that the universe took being from nothing, and do not doubt, when we are taught by Scripture, that it will again be transformed into some other state.

XXV. *How one even of those who are without may be brought to believe the Scripture when teaching of the resurrection* [5].

1. Some one, perhaps, having regard to the dissolution of bodies, and judging the Deity by the measure of his own power, asserts that the idea of the resurrection is impossible, saying that it cannot be that both those things which are now in motion should become stationary, and those things which are now without motion should rise again.

2. Let such an one, however, take as the first and greatest evidence of the truth touching the resurrection the credibility of the herald who proclaims it. Now the faith of what is said derives its certainty from the result of the other predictions: for as the Divine Scripture delivers statements many and various, it is possible by examining how the rest of the utterances stand in the matter of falsehood and truth to survey also, in the light of them, the doctrine concerning the resurrection. For if in the other

---

3 Otherwise Chap. xxv. The Bodleian MS. of the Latin version has the title:—" That all matter exists in certain quantities."

4 With this passage may be compared the idealistic doctrine of the *De Anim. et Resurr.*
5 Otherwise Chap. xxvi. The title in the Bodleian MS. of the Latin version is:—" Of faith in the resurrection, and of the three dead persons whom the Lord Jesus raised."

matters the statements are found to be false and to have failed of true fulfilment, neither is this out of the region of falsehood; but if all the others have experience to vouch for their truth, it would seem logical to esteem as true, on their account, the prediction concerning the resurrection also. Let us therefore recall one or two of the predictions that have been made, and compare the result with what was foretold, so that we may know by means of them whether the idea has a truthful aspect.

3. Who knows not how the people of Israel flourished of old, raised up against all the powers of the world ; what were the palaces in the city of Jerusalem, what the walls, the towers, the majestic structure of the Temple? things that seemed worthy of admiration even to the disciples of the Lord, so that they asked the Lord to take notice of them, in their disposition to marvel, as the Gospel history shows us, saying, "What works, and what buildings[6]!" But He indicates to those who wondered at its present state the future desolation of the place and the disappearance of that beauty, saying that after a little while nothing of what they saw should be left. And, again, at the time of His Passion, the women followed, bewailing the unjust sentence against Him,—for they could not yet see into the dispensation of what was being done :—but He bids them be silent as to what is befalling Him, for it does not demand their tears, but to reserve their wailing and lamentation for the true time for tears, when the city should be compassed by besiegers, and their sufferings reach so great a strait that they should deem him happy who had not been born : and herein He foretold also the horrid deed of her who devoured her child, when He said that in those days the womb should be accounted blest that never bare[7]. Where then are those palaces? where is the Temple? where are the walls? where are the defences of the towers? where is the power of the Israelites? were not they scattered in different quarters over almost the whole world? and in their overthrow the palaces also were brought to ruin.

4. Now it seems to me that the Lord foretold these things and others like them not for the sake of the matters themselves—for what great advantage to the hearers, at any rate, was the prediction of what was about to happen? they would have known by experience, even if they had not previously learnt what would come ;—but in order that by these means faith on their part might follow concerning more important matters : for the testimony of facts in the former cases is also a proof of truth in the latter.

5. For just as though, if a husbandman were explaining the virtue of seeds, it were to happen that some person inexperienced in husbandry should disbelieve him, it would be sufficient as proof of his statement for the agriculturist to show him the virtue existing in one seed of those in the bushel and make it a pledge of the rest—for he who should see the single grain of wheat or barley, or whatever might chance to be the contents of the bushel, grow into an ear after ·being cast into the ground, would by the means of the one cease also to disbelieve concerning the others—so the truthfulness which confessedly belongs to the other statements seems to me to be sufficient also for evidence of the mystery of the resurrection.

6. Still more, however, is this the case with the experience of actual resurrection which we have learnt not so much by words as by actual facts : for as the marvel of resurrection was great and passing belief, He begins gradually by inferior instances of His miraculous power, and accustoms our faith, as it were, for the reception of the greater.

7. For as a mother who nurses her babe with due care for a time supplies milk by her breast to its mouth while still tender and soft ; and when it begins to grow and to have teeth she gives it bread, not hard or such as it cannot chew, so that the tender and unpractised gums may not be chafed by rough food ; but softening it with her own teeth, she makes it suitable and convenient for the powers of the eater ; and then as its power increases by growth she gradually leads on the babe, accustomed to tender food, to more solid nourishment ; so the Lord, nourishing and fostering with miracles the weakness of the human mind, like some babe not fully grown, makes first of all a prelude of the power of the resurrection in the case of a desperate disease, which prelude, though it was great in its achievement, yet was not such a thing that the statement of it would be disbelieved : for by "rebuking the fever." which was fiercely consuming Simon's wife's mother, He produced so great a removal of the evil as to enable her who was already expected to be near death, to "minister[8]" to those present.

8. Next He makes a slight addition to the power, and when the nobleman's son lies in acknowledged danger of death (for so the history tells us, that he was about to die, as his father cried, "come down, ere my child die[9]"), He again brings about the resurrection of one who was believed about to die; accomplishing the miracle with a greater act of power in that He did not even approach the place, but sent life from afar off by the force of His command.

---

6 Cf. S. Mark xiii. 1.　　　　7 Cf. S. Luke xxiii. 27—29.　　　　8 S. Luke iv. 39.　　　　9 S. John iv. 49.

9. Once more in what follows He ascends to higher wonders. For having set out on His way to the ruler of the synagogue's daughter, he voluntarily made a halt in His way, while making public the secret cure of the woman with an issue of blood, that in this time death might overcome the sick. When, then, the soul had just been parted from the body, and those who were wailing over the sorrow were making a tumult with their mournful cries, He raises the damsel to life again, as if from sleep, by His word of command, leading on human weakness, by a sort of path and sequence, to greater things.

10. Still in addition to these acts He exceeds them in wonder, and by a more exalted act of power prepares for men the way of faith in the resurrection. The Scripture tells us of a city called Nain in Judæa : a widow there had an only child, no longer a child in the sense of being among boys, but already passing from childhood to man's estate : the narrative calls him "a young man." The story conveys much in few words : the very recital is a real lamentation : the dead man's mother, it says, "was a widow." See you the weight of her misfortune, how the text briefly sets out the tragedy of her suffering? for what does the phrase mean? that she had no more hope of bearing sons, to cure the loss she had just sustained in him who had departed ; for the woman was a widow : she had not in her power to look to another instead of to him who was gone ; for he was her only child ; and how great a grief is here expressed any one may easily see who is not an utter stranger to natural feeling. Him alone she had known in travail, him alone she had nursed at her breast ; he alone made her table cheerful, he alone was the cause of brightness in her home, in play, in work, in learning, in gaiety, at processions, at sports, at gatherings of youth ; he alone was all that is sweet and precious in a mother's eyes. Now at the age of marriage, he was the stock of her race, the shoot of its succession, the staff of her old age. Moreover, even the additional detail of his time of life is another lament : for he who speaks of him as "a young man" tells of the flower of his faded beauty, speaks of him as just covering his face with down, not yet with a full thick beard, but still bright with the beauty of his cheeks. What then, think you, were his mother's sorrows for him? how would her heart be consumed as it were with a flame ; how bitterly would she prolong her lament over him, embracing the corpse as it lay before her, lengthening out her mourning for him as far as possible, so as not to hasten the funeral of the dead, but to have her fill of sorrow ! Nor does the narrative pass this by : for Jesus "when He saw her," it says, "had compassion" ; "and He

came and touched the bier ; and they that bare him stood still ;" and He said to the dead, "Young man, I say unto thee, arise [1]," "and He delivered him to his mother" alive. Observe that no short time had intervened since the dead man had entered upon that state, he was all but laid in the tomb ; the miracle wrought by the Lord is greater, though the command is the same.

11. His miraculous power proceeds to a still more exalted act, that its display may more closely approach that miracle of the resurrection which men doubt. One of the Lord's companions and friends is ill (Lazarus is the sick man's name) ; and the Lord deprecates any visiting of His friend, though far away from the sick man, that in the absence of the Life, death might find room and power to do his own work by the agency of disease. The Lord informs His disciples in Galilee of what has befallen Lazarus, and also of his own setting out to him to raise him up when laid low. They, however, were exceedingly afraid on account of the fury of the Jews, thinking it a difficult and dangerous matter to turn again towards Judæa, in the midst of those who sought to slay Him : and thus, lingering and delaying, they return slowly from Galilee : but they do return, for His command prevailed, and the disciples were led by the Lord to be initiated at Bethany in the preliminary mysteries of the general resurrection. Four days had already passed since the event ; all due rites had been performed for the departed ; the body was hidden in the tomb : it was probably already swollen and beginning to dissolve into corruption, as the body mouldered in the dank earth and necessarily decayed : the thing was one to turn from, as the dissolved body under the constraint of nature changed to offensiveness [2]. At this point the doubted fact of the general resurrection is brought to proof by a more manifest miracle ; for one is not raised from severe sickness, nor brought back to life when at the last breath—nor is a child just dead brought to life, nor a young man about to be conveyed to the tomb released from his bier ; but a man past the prime of life, a corpse, decaying, swollen, yea already in a state of dissolution, so that even his own kinsfolk could not suffer that the Lord should draw near the tomb by reason of the offensiveness of the decayed body there enclosed, brought into life by a single call, confirms the proclamation of the resurrection, that is to say, that expectation of it as universal, which we learn by a par-

---

[1] Cf. S. Luke vii. 13—15.

[2] Omitting, as several of Forbes' MSS. do, and as the MS. employed by Dionysius seems to have done, the words ἀποδίδοναι πάλιν τῷ ζῆν. If these words are retained, βιαζομένης must be taken passively, and the πρᾶγμα φευκτόν understood not of the condition of the corpse, but of the *resurrection* of Lazarus.

ticular experience to entertain. For as in the regeneration of the universe the Apostle tells us that "the Lord Himself will descend with a shout, with the voice of the archangel [3]," and by a trumpet sound raise up the dead to incorruption—so now too he who is in the tomb, at the voice of command, shakes off death as if it were a sleep, and ridding himself from the corruption that had come upon his condition of a corpse, leaps forth from the tomb whole and sound, not even hindered in his egress by the bonds of the grave-cloths round his feet and hands.

12. Are these things too small to produce faith in the resurrection of the dead? or dost thou seek that thy judgment on this point should be confirmed by yet other proofs? In truth the Lord seems to me not to have spoken in vain to them of Capernaum, when He said to Himself, as in the person of men, "Ye will surely say unto me this proverb, 'Physician, heal thyself [4].'" For it behoved Him, when He had accustomed men to the miracle of the resurrection in other bodies, to confirm His word in His own humanity. Thou sawest the thing proclaimed working in others—those who were about to die, the child which had just ceased to live, the young man at the edge of the grave, the putrefying corpse, all alike restored by one command to life. Dost thou seek for those who have come to death by wounds and bloodshed? does any feebleness of life-giving power hinder the grace in them? Behold Him Whose hands were pierced with nails : behold Him Whose side was transfixed with a spear ; pass thy fingers through the print of the nails ; thrust thy hand into the spear-wound [5] ; thou canst surely guess how far within it is likely the point would reach, if thou reckonest the passage inwards by the breadth of the external scar ; for the wound that gives admission to a man's hand, shows to what depth within the iron entered. If He then has been raised, well may we utter the Apostle's exclamation, "How say some that there is no resurrection of the dead [6]?"

13. Since, then, every prediction of the Lord is shown to be true by the testimony of events, while we not only have learnt this by His words, but also received the proof of the promise in deed, from those very persons who returned to life by resurrection, what occasion is left to those who disbelieve? Shall we not bid farewell to those who pervert our simple faith by "philosophy and vain deceit [7]," and hold fast to our confession in its purity, learning briefly through the prophet the mode of the grace, by his words, "Thou shalt take away their breath

and they shall fail, and turn to their dust. Thou shalt send forth Thy Spirit and they shall be created, and Thou shalt renew the face of the earth [8] ;" at which time also he says that the Lord rejoices in His works, sinners having perished from the earth : for how shall any one be called by the name of sin, when sin itself exists no longer?

XXVI. *That the resurrection is not beyond probability* [9].

1. There are, however, some who, owing to the feebleness of human reasoning, judging the Divine power by the compass of our own, maintain that what is beyond our capacity is not possible even to God. They point to the disappearance of the dead of old time, and to the remains of those who have been reduced to ashes by fire ; and further, besides these, they bring forward in idea the carnivorous beasts, and the fish that receives in its own body the flesh of the shipwrecked sailor, while this again in turn becomes food for men, and passes by digestion into the bulk of him who eats it : and they rehearse many such trivialities, unworthy of God's great power and authority, for the overthrow of the doctrine, arguing as though God were not able to restore to man his own, by return [1] through the same ways.

2. But we briefly cut short their long circuits of logical folly by acknowledging that dissolution of the body into its component parts does take place, and not only does earth, according to the Divine word, return to earth, but air and moisture also revert to the kindred element, and there takes place a return of each of our components to that nature to which it is allied ; and although the human body be dispersed among carnivorous birds, or among the most savage beasts by becoming their food, and although it pass beneath the teeth of fish, and although it be changed by fire into vapour and dust, wheresoever one may in argument suppose the man to be removed, he surely remains in the world ; and the world, the voice of inspiration tells us, is held by the hand of God. If thou, then, art not ignorant of any of the things in thy hand, dost thou then deem the knowledge of God to be feebler than thine own power, that it should fail to discover the most minute of the things that are within the compass of the Divine span?

---

[8] Ps. civ. 29, 30 (LXX.). Cf. also with what follows vv. 31—35.
[9] Otherwise Chap. xxvii. The Bodleian MS. of the Latin version has the title :—"That however much the human body may have been consumed, the Divine power can easily bring it together."
[1] ἀναλυσέως, in S. Gregory, seems to be frequently used in the sense of "return." Cf. Phil. i. 23, εἰς τὸ ἀναλῦσαι, καὶ σὺν Χριστῳ εἶναι, where Tertullian translates "cupio *recipi*", (*De Patientia*).

---

[3] 1 Thess. iv. 16.   [4] S. Luke iv. 23.
[5] Cf. S. John xx. 27.   [6] 1 Cor. xv. 12.
[7] Col. ii. 8.

XXVII. *That it is possible, when the human body is dissolved into the elements of the universe, that each should have his own body restored from the common source* [2].

1. Yet it may be thou thinkest, having regard to the elements of the universe, that it is a hard thing when the air in us has been resolved into its kindred element, and the warmth, and moisture, and the earthy nature have likewise been mingled with their own kind, that from the common source there should return to the individual what belongs to itself.

2. Dost thou not then judge by human examples that even this does not surpass the limits of the Divine power? Thou hast seen surely somewhere among the habitations of men a common herd of some kind of animals collected from every quarter: yet when it is again divided among its owners, acquaintance with their homes and the marks put upon the cattle serve to restore to each his own. If thou conceivest of thyself also something like to this, thou wilt not be far from the right way: for as the soul is disposed to cling to and long for the body that has been wedded to it, there also attaches to it in secret a certain close relationship and power of recognition, in virtue of their commixture, as though some marks had been imprinted by nature, by the aid of which the community remains unconfused, separated by the distinctive signs. Now as the soul attracts again to itself that which is its own and properly belongs to it, what labour, I pray you, that is involved for the Divine power, could be a hindrance to concourse of kindred things when they are urged to their own place by the unspeakable attraction of nature, whatever it may be? For that some signs of our compound nature remain in the soul even after dissolution, is shown by the dialogue in Hades [3], where the bodies had been conveyed to the tomb, but some bodily token still remained in the souls by which both Lazarus was recognized and the rich man was not unknown.

3. There is therefore nothing beyond probability in believing that in the bodies that rise again there will be a return from the common stock to the individual, especially for any one who examines our nature with careful attention. For neither does our being consist altogether in flux and change—for surely that which had by nature no stability would be absolutely incomprehensible—but according to the more accurate statement some one of our constituent parts is stationary while the rest goes through a process

of alteration: for the body is on the one hand altered by way of growth and diminution, changing, like garments, the vesture of its successive statures, while the form, on the other hand, remains in itself unaltered through every change, not varying from the marks once imposed upon it by nature, but appearing with its own tokens of identity in all the changes which the body undergoes.

4. We must except, however, from this statement the change which happens to the form as the result of disease: for the deformity of sickness takes possession of the form like some strange mask, and when this is removed by the word [4], as in the case of Naaman the Syrian, or of those whose story is recorded in the Gospel, the form that had been hidden by disease is once more by means of health restored to sight again with its own marks of identity.

5. Now to the element of our soul which is in the likeness of God it is not that which is subject to flux and change by way of alteration, but this stable and unalterable element in our composition that is allied: and since various differences of combination produce varieties of forms (and combination is nothing else than the mixture of the elements—by elements we mean those which furnish the substratum for the making of the universe, of which the human body also is composed), while the form necessarily remains in the soul as in the impression of a seal, those things which have received from the seal the impression of its stamp do not fail to be recognized by the soul, but at the time of the World-Reformation, it receives back to itself all those things which correspond to the stamp of the form: and surely all those things would so correspond which in the beginning were stamped by the form; thus it is not beyond probability that what properly belongs to the individual should once more return to it from the common source [5].

6. It is said also that quicksilver, if poured out from the vessel that contains it down a dusty slope, forms small globules and scatters itself over the ground, mingling with none of those bodies with which it meets: but if one should collect at one place the substance dispersed in many directions, it flows back to its kindred substance, if not hindered by anything intervening from mixing with its own kind. Something of the same sort, I think, we ought to understand also of the composite nature of

---

[2] Otherwise Chap. xxviii. The title in the Bodleian MS. of the Latin version is :—" That although bodies rise together they will yet receive their own souls."
[3] Cf. S. Luke xvi. 24—31.

[4] The word, that is of the Prophet, or of the Saviour, as in the cases cited.
[5] The "form" seems to be regarded as a seal, which, while taking its pattern from the combination of elements, yet marks those elements which have been grouped together under it ; and which at the same time leaves an impression of itself upon the soul. The soul is thus enabled to recognize the elemental particles which make up that body which belonged to it, by the τύπος imprinted on them as well as on itself.

man, that if only the power were given it of God, the proper parts would spontaneously unite with those belonging to them, without any obstruction on their account arising to Him Who reforms their nature.

7. Furthermore, in the case of plants that grow from the ground, we do not observe any labour on the part of nature spent on the wheat or millet or any other seed of grain or pulse, in changing it into stalk or spike or ears ; for the proper nourishment passes spontaneously, without trouble, from the common source to the individuality of each of the seeds. If, then, while the moisture supplied to all the plants is common, each of those plants which is nourished by it draws the due supply for its own growth, what new thing is it if in the doctrine of the resurrection also, as in the case of the seeds, it happens that there is an attraction on the part of each of those who rise, of what belongs to himself ?

8. So that we may learn on all hands, that the preaching of the resurrection contains nothing beyond those facts which are known to us experimentally.

9. And yet we have said nothing of the most notable point concerning ourselves ; I mean the first beginning of our existence. Who knows not the miracle of nature, what the maternal womb receives—what it produces ? Thou seest how that which is implanted in the womb to be the beginning of the formation of the body is in a manner simple and homogeneous : but what language can express the variety of the composite body that is framed ? and who, if he did not learn such a thing in nature generally, would think that to be possible which does take place—that that small thing of no account is the beginning of a thing so great ? Great, I say, not only with regard to the bodily formation, but to what is more marvellous than this, I mean the soul itself, and the attributes we behold in it.

XXVIII. *To those who say that souls existed before bodies, or that bodies were formed before souls ; wherein there is also a refutation of the fables concerning transmigration of souls* [6].

1. For it is perhaps not beyond our present subject to discuss the question which has been raised in the churches touching soul and body. Some of those before our time who have dealt with the question of " principles " think it right to say that souls have a previous existence as a people in a society of their own, and that among them also there are standards of vice and of virtue, and that the soul there, which

abides in goodness, remains without experience of conjunction with the body ; but if it does depart from its communion with good, it falls down to this lower life, and so comes to be in a body. Others, on the contrary, marking the order of the making of man as stated by Moses, say, that the soul is second to the body in order of time, since God first took dust from the earth and formed man, and then animated the being thus formed by His breath [7] : and by this argument they prove that the flesh is more noble than the soul ; that which was previously formed than that which was afterwards infused into it : for they say that the soul was made for the body, that the thing formed might not be without breath and motion ; and that everything that is made for something else is surely less precious than that for which it is made, as the Gospel tells us that " the soul is more than meat and the body than raiment [8]," because the latter things exist for the sake of the former— for the soul was not made for meat nor our bodies for raiment, but when the former things were already in being the latter were provided for their needs.

2. Since then the doctrine involved in both these theories is open to criticism—the doctrine alike of those who ascribe to souls a fabulous pre-existence in a special state, and of those who think they were created at a later time than the bodies, it is perhaps necessary to leave none of the statements contained in the doctrines without examination : yet to engage and wrestle with the doctrines on each side completely, and to reveal all the absurdities involved in the theories, would need a large expenditure both of argument and of time ; we shall, however, briefly survey as best we can each of the views mentioned, and then resume our subject.

3. Those who stand by the former doctrine, and assert that the state of souls is prior to their life in the flesh, do not seem to me to be clear from the fabulous doctrines of the heathen which they hold on the subject of successive incorporation : for if one should search carefully, he will find that their doctrine is of necessity brought down to this. They tell us that one of their sages said that he, being one and the same person, was born a man, and afterwards assumed the form of a woman, and flew about with the birds, and grew as a bush, and obtained the life of an aquatic creature ;—and he who said these things of himself did not, so far as I can judge, go far from the truth : for such doctrines as this of saying that one soul passed through so many changes are really fitting for the chatter of frogs or jackdaws, or the stupidity of fishes, or the insensibility of trees.

---

[6] Otherwise Chap. xxix. The title in the Bodleian MS. of the Latin version is :—" Of different views of the origin of the soul."

[7] Cf. Gen. ii. 7. [8] S. Matt. vi. 25.

4. And of such absurdity the cause is this—the supposition of the pre-existence of souls: for the first principle of such doctrine leads on the argument by consequence to the next and adjacent stage, until it astonishes us by reaching this point. For if the soul, being severed from the more exalted state by some wickedness, after having once, as they say, tasted corporeal life, again becomes a man, and if the life in the flesh is, as may be presumed, acknowledged to be, in comparison with the eternal and incorporeal life, more subject to passion, it naturally follows that that which comes to be in a life such as to contain more occasions of sin, is both placed in a region of greater wickedness and rendered more subject to passion than before (now passion in the human soul is a conformity to the likeness of the irrational); and that being brought into close connection with this, it descends to the brute nature: and that when it has once set out on its way through wickedness, it does not cease its advance towards evil even when found in an irrational condition: for a halt in evil is the beginning of the impulse towards virtue, and in irrational creatures virtue does not exist. Thus it will of necessity be continually changed for the worse, always proceeding to what is more degraded and always finding out what is worse than the nature in which it is: and just as the sensible nature is lower than the rational, so too there is a descent from this to the insensible.

5. Now so far in its course their doctrine, even if it does overstep the bounds of truth, at all events derives one absurdity from another by a kind of logical sequence: but from this point onwards their teaching takes the form of incoherent fable. Strict inference points to the complete destruction of the soul; for that which has once fallen from the exalted state will be unable to halt at any measure of wickedness, but will pass by means of its relation with the passions from rational to irrational, and from the latter state will be transferred to the insensibility of plants; and on the insensible there borders, so to say, the inanimate; and on this again follows the non-existent, so that absolutely by this train of reasoning they will have the soul to pass into nothing: thus a return once more to the better state is impossible for it: and yet they make the soul return from a bush to the man: they therefore prove that the life in a bush is more precious than an incorporeal state [9].

6. It has been shown that the process of deterioration which takes place in the soul will probably be extended downwards; and lower than the insensible we find the inanimate, to

which, by consequence, the principle of their doctrine brings the soul: but as they will not have this, they either exclude the soul from insensibility, or, if they are to bring it back to human life, they must, as has been said, declare the life of a tree to be preferable to the original state—if, that is, the fall towards vice took place from the one, and the return towards virtue takes place from the other.

7. Thus this doctrine of theirs, which maintains that souls have a life by themselves before their life in the flesh, and that they are by reason of wickedness bound to their bodies, is shown to have neither beginning nor conclusion: and as for those who assert that the soul is of later creation than the body, their absurdity was already demonstrated above [1].

8. The doctrine of both, then, is equally to be rejected; but I think that we ought to direct our own doctrine in the way of truth between these theories: and this doctrine is that we are not to suppose, according to the error of the heathen that the souls that revolve with the motion of the universe weighed down by some wickedness, fall to earth by inability to keep up with the swiftness of the motion of the spheres.

XXIX. *An establishment of the doctrine that the cause of the existence of soul and body is one and the same.* [2]

1. Nor again are we in our doctrine to begin by making up man like a clay figure, and to say that the soul came into being for the sake of this; for surely in that case the intellectual nature would be shown to be less precious than the clay figure. But as man is one, the being consisting of soul and body, we are to suppose that the beginning of his existence is one, common to both parts, so that he should not be found to be antecedent and posterior to himself, if the bodily element were first in point of time, and the other were a later addition; but we are to say that in the power of God's foreknowledge (according to the doctrine laid down a little earlier in our discourse), all the fulness of human nature had pre-existence (and to this the prophetic writing bears witness, which says that God "knoweth all things before they be [3]"), and in the creation of individuals not to place the one element before the other, neither the soul before the

---

[1] In the discourse that is contained in the next chapter. The point has been mentioned, but the conclusions were not drawn from it in the opening section of this chapter.

[2] Otherwise Chap. xxx. But in the Latin translation of Dionysius, the new chapter does not begin till the end of the first sentence of the Greek text. As Forbes remarks, either place is awkward: a better beginning would be found at § 8 of the preceding chapter. The Bodleian MS. of the Latin version gives as the title :—"That God equally made the soul and the body of man."

[3] Hist. Sus. 42.

body, nor the contrary, that man may not be at strife against himself, by being divided by the difference in point of time.

2. For as our nature is conceived as twofold, according to the apostolic teaching, made up of the visible man and the hidden man, if the one came first and the other supervened, the power of Him that made us will be shown to be in some way imperfect, as not being completely sufficient for the whole task at once, but dividing the work, and busying itself with each of the halves in turn.

3. But just as we say that in wheat, or in any other grain, the whole form of the plant is potentially included—the leaves, the stalk, the joints, the grain, the beard—and do not say in our account of its nature that any of these things has pre-existence, or comes into being before the others, but that the power abiding in the seed is manifested in a certain natural order, not by any means that another nature is infused into it—in the same way we suppose the human germ to possess the potentiality of its nature, sown with it at the first start of its existence, and that it is unfolded and manifested by a natural sequence as it proceeds to its perfect state, not employing anything external to itself as a stepping-stone to perfection, but itself advancing its own self in due course to the perfect state; so that it is not true to say either that the soul exists before the body, or that the body exists without the soul, but that there is one beginning of both, which according to the heavenly view was laid as their foundation in the original will of God; according to the other, came into existence on the occasion of generation.

4. For as we cannot discern the articulation of the limbs in that which is implanted for the conception of the body before it begins to take form, so neither is it possible to perceive in the same the properties of the soul before they advance to operation; and just as no one would doubt that the thing so implanted is fashioned into the different varieties of limbs and interior organs, not by the importation of any other power from without, but by the power which resides in it transforming [4] it to this manifestation of energy,—so also we may by like reasoning equally suppose in the case of the soul that even if it is not visibly recognized by any manifestations of activity it none the less is there; for even the form of the future man is there potentially, but is concealed because it is not possible that it should be made visible before the necessary sequence of events allows it; so also the soul is there, even though it is not visible, and will be manifested by means of its own proper and natural operation, as it advances concurrently with the bodily growth.

5. For since it is not from a dead body that the potentiality for conception is secreted, but from one which is animate and alive, we hence affirm that it is reasonable that we should not suppose that what is sent forth from a living body to be the occasion of life is itself dead and inanimate; for in the flesh that which is inanimate is surely dead; and the condition of death arises by the withdrawal of the soul. Would not one therefore in this case be asserting that withdrawal is antecedent to possession—if, that is, he should maintain that the inanimate state which is the condition of death is antecedent to the soul [5]? And if any one should seek for a still clearer evidence of the life of that particle which becomes the beginning of the living creature in its formation, it is possible to obtain an idea on this point from other signs also, by which what is animate is distinguished from what is dead. For in the case of men we consider it an evidence of life that one is warm and operative and in motion, but the chill and motionless state in the case of bodies is nothing else than deadness.

6. Since then we see that of which we are speaking to be warm and operative, we thereby draw the further inference that it is not inanimate; but as, in respect of its corporeal part, we do not say that it is flesh, and bones, and hair, and all that we observe in the human being, but that potentially it is each of these things, yet does not visibly appear to be so; so also of the part which belongs to the soul, the elements of rationality, and desire, and anger, and all the powers of the soul are not yet visible; yet we assert that they have their place in it, and that the energies of the soul also grow with the subject in a manner similar to the formation and perfection of the body.

7. For just as a man when perfectly developed has a specially marked activity of the soul, so at the beginning of his existence he shows in himself that co-operation of the soul which is suitable and conformable to his existing need, in its preparing for itself its proper dwelling-place by means of the implanted matter; for we do not suppose it possible that the soul is adapted to a strange building, just as it is not possible that the seal impressed on wax should be fitted to an engraving that does not agree with it.

8. For as the body proceeds from a very small original to the perfect state, so also the operation of the soul, growing in correspondence with the subject, gains and increases with it.

---

4 The reading αὐτῆς μεθισταμένης, "itself being transformed," seems to give a better sense, but the weight of MS. authority seems to be against it.

5 Altering Forbes' punctuation.

For at its first formation there comes first of all its power of growth and nutriment alone, as though it were some root buried in the ground ; for the limited nature of the recipient does not admit of more ; then, as the plant comes forth to the light and shows its shoot to the sun, the gift of sensibility blossoms in addition, but when at last it is ripened and has grown up to its proper height, the power of reason begins to shine forth like a fruit, not appearing in its whole vigour all at once, but by care increasing with the perfection of the instrument, bearing always as much fruit as the powers of the subject allow.

9. If, however, thou seekest to trace the operation of the soul in the formation of the body, "take heed to thyself[6]," as Moses says, and thou wilt read, as in a book, the history of the works of the soul ; for nature itself expounds to thee, more clearly than any discourse, the varied occupations of the soul in the body, alike in general and in particular acts of construction.

10. But I deem it superfluous to declare at length in words what is to be found in ourselves, as though we were expounding some wonder that lay beyond our boundaries :—who that looks on himself needs words to teach him his own nature ? For it is possible for one who considers the mode of his own life, and learns how closely concerned the body is in every vital operation, to know in what the vegetative[7] principle of the soul was occupied on the occasion of the first formation of that which was beginning its existence ; so that hereby also it is clear to those who have given any attention to the matter, that the thing which was implanted by separation from the living body for the production of the living being was not a thing dead or inanimate in the laboratory of nature.

11. Moreover we plant in the ground the kernels of fruits, and portions torn from roots, not deprived by death of the vital power which naturally resides in them, but preserving in themselves, hidden indeed, yet surely living, the property of their prototype ; the earth that surrounds them does not implant such a power from without, infusing it from itself (for surely then even dead wood would proceed to growth), but it makes that manifest which resides in them, nourishing it by its own moisture, perfecting the plant into root, and bark, and pith, and shoots of branches, which could not happen were not a natural power implanted with it, which drawing to itself from its surroundings its kindred and proper nourishment, becomes a bush, or a tree, or an ear of grain, or some plant of the class of shrubs.

XXX. *A brief examination of the construction of our bodies from a medical point of view*[8].

1. Now the exact structure of our body each man teaches himself by his experiences of sight and light and perception, having his own nature to instruct him ; any one too may learn everything accurately who takes up the researches which those skilled in such matters have worked out in books. And of these writers some learnt by dissection the position of our individual organs ; others also considered and expounded the reason for the existence of all the parts of the body ; so that the knowledge of the human frame which hence results is sufficient for students. But if any one further seeks that the Church should be his teacher on all these points, so that he may not need for anything the voice of those without (for this is the wont of the spiritual sheep, as the Lord says, that they hear not a strange voice[9]), we shall briefly take in hand the account of these matters also.

2. We note concerning our bodily nature three things, for the sake of which our particular parts were formed. Life is the cause of some, good life of others, others again are adapted with a view to the succession of descendants. All things in us which are of such a kind that without them it is not possible that human life should exist, we consider as being in three parts ; in the brain, the heart, and the liver. Again, all that are a sort of additional blessings, nature's liberality, whereby she bestows on man the gift of living well, are the organs of sense ; for such things do not constitute our life, since even where some of them are wanting man is often none the less in a condition of life ; but without these forms of activity it is impossible to enjoy participation in the pleasures of life. The third aim regards the future, and the succession of life. There are also certain other organs besides these, which help, in common with all the others, to subserve the continuance of life, importing by their own means the proper supplies, as the stomach and the lungs, the latter fanning by respiration the fire at the heart, the former introducing the nourishment for the internal organs.

3. Our structure, then, being thus divided, we have carefully to mark that our faculty for life is not supported in any one way by some single organ, but nature, while distributing the means for our existence among several parts, makes the contribution of each individual necessary for the whole ; just as the things which nature contrives for the security and beauty of life are also numerous, and differ much among themselves.

---

6 Deut. iv. 23.
7 Reading φυτικὸν for φυσικόν, see note 6 on ch. 8, § 4.

8 Otherwise Chap. xxxi. The Bodleian MS. of the Latin version gives the title :—" Of the threefold nature of the body."
9 Cf. S. John x. 5.

4. We ought, however, I think, first to discuss briefly the first beginnings of the things which contribute to the constitution of our life. As for the material of the whole body which serves as a common substratum for the particular members, it may for the present be left without remark; for a discussion as to natural substance in general will not be of any assistance to our purpose with regard to the consideration of the parts.

5. As it is then acknowledged by all that there is in us a share of all that we behold as elements in the universe—of heat and cold, and of the other pair of qualities of moisture and dryness—we must discuss them severally.

6. We see then that the powers which control life are three, of which the first by its heat produces general warmth, the second by its moisture keeps damp that which is warmed, so that the living being is kept in an intermediate condition by the equal balance of the forces exerted by the quality of each of the opposing natures (the moist element not being dried up by excess of heat, nor the hot element quenched by the prevalence of moisture); and the third power by its own agency holds together the separate members in a certain agreement and harmony, connecting them by the ties which it itself furnishes, and sending into them all that self-moving and determining force, on the failure of which the member becomes relaxed and deadened, being left destitute of the determining spirit.

7. Or rather, before dealing with these, it is right that we should mark the skilled workmanship of nature in the actual construction of the body. For as that which is hard and resistent does not admit the action of the senses (as we may see in the instance of our own bones, and in that of plants in the ground, where we remark indeed a certain form of life in that they grow and receive nourishment, yet the resistent character of their substance does not allow them sensation), for this reason it was necessary that some wax-like formation, so to say, should be supplied for the action of the senses, with the faculty of being impressed with the stamp of things capable of striking them, neither becoming confused by excess of moisture (for the impress would not remain in moist substance), nor resisting by extraordinary solidity (for that which is unyielding would not receive any mark from the impressions), but being in a state between softness and hardness, in order that the living being might not be destitute of the fairest of all the operations of nature—I mean the motion of sense.

8. Now as a soft and yielding substance, if it had no assistance from the hard parts, would certainly have, like molluscs, neither motion nor articulation, nature accordingly mingles in the body the hardness of the bones, and uniting these by close connection one to another, and knitting their joints together by means of the sinews, thus plants around them the flesh which receives sensations, furnished with a somewhat harder and more highly-strung surface than it would otherwise have had.

9. While resting, then, the whole weight of the body on this substance of the bones, as on some columns that carry a mass of building, she did not implant the bone undivided through the whole structure: for in that case man would have remained without motion or activity, if he had been so constructed, just like a tree that stands on one spot without either the alternate motion of legs to advance its motion or the service of hands to minister to the conveniences of life: but now we see that she contrived that the instrument should be rendered capable of walking and working by this device, after she had implanted in the body, by the determining spirit which extends through the nerves, the impulse and power for motion. And hence is produced the service of the hands, so varied and multiform, and answering to every thought. Hence are produced, as though by some mechanical contrivance, the turnings of the neck, and the bending and raising of the head, and the action of the chin, and the separation of the eyelids, that takes place with a thought, and the movements of the other joints, by the tightening or relaxation of certain nerves. And the power that extends through these exhibits a sort of independent impulse, working with the spirit of its will by a sort of natural management, in each particular part; but the root of all, and the principle of the motions of the nerves, is found in the nervous tissue that surrounds the brain.

10. We consider, then, that we need not spend more time in inquiring in which of the vital members such a thing resides, when the energy of motion is shown to be here. But that the brain contributes to life in a special degree is shown clearly by the result of the opposite conditions: for if the tissue surrounding it receives any wound or lesion, death immediately follows the injury, nature being unable to endure the hurt even for a moment; just as, when a foundation is withdrawn, the whole building collapses with the part; and that member, from an injury to which the destruction of the whole living being clearly follows, may properly be acknowledged to contain the cause of life.

11. But as furthermore in those who have ceased to live, when the heat that is implanted in our nature is quenched, that which has become dead grows cold, we hence recognize the

vital cause also in heat : for we must of necessity acknowledge that the living being subsists by the presence of that, which failing, the condition of death supervenes. And of such a force we understand the heart to be as it were the fountain-head and principle, as from it pipe-like passages, growing one from another in many ramifications, diffuse in the whole body the warm and fiery spirit.

12. And since some nourishment must needs also be provided by nature for the element of heat—for it is not possible that the fire should last by itself, without being nourished by its proper food—therefore the channels of the blood, issuing from the liver as from a fountain-head, accompany the warm spirit everywhere in its way throughout the body, that the one may not by isolation from the other become a disease and destroy the constitution. Let this instruct those who go beyond the bounds of fairness, as they learn from nature that covetousness is a disease that breeds destruction.

13. But since the Divinity alone is free from needs, while human poverty requires external aid for its own subsistence, nature therefore, in addition to those three powers by which we said that the whole body is regulated, brings in imported matter from without, introducing by different entrances that which is suitable to those powers.

14. For to the fount of the blood, which is the liver, she furnishes its supply by food : for that which from time to time is imported in this way prepares the springs of blood to issue from the liver, as the snow on the mountain by its own moisture increases the springs in the low ground, forcing its own fluid deep down to the veins below.

15. The breath in the heart is supplied by means of the neighbouring organ, which is called the lungs, and is a receptacle for air, drawing the breath from without through the windpipe inserted in it, which extends to the mouth. The heart being placed in the midst of this organ (and itself also moving incessantly in imitation of the action of the ever-moving fire), draws to itself, somewhat as the bellows do in the forges, a supply from the adjacent air, filling its recesses by dilatation, and while it fans its own fiery element, breathes upon the adjoining tubes ; and this it does not cease to do, drawing the external air into its own recesses by dilatation, and by compression infusing the air from itself into the tubes.

16. And this seems to me to be the cause of this spontaneous respiration of ours ; for often the mind is occupied in discourse with others, or is entirely quiescent when the body is relaxed in sleep, but the respiration of air does not cease, though the will gives no co-operation to

this end. Now I suppose, since the heart is surrounded by the lungs, and in the back part of its own structure is attached to them, moving that organ by its own dilatations and compressions, that the inhaling and exhaling[1] of the air is brought about by the lungs : for as they are a lightly built and porous body, and have all their recesses opening at the base of the windpipe, when they contract and are compressed they necessarily force out by pressure the air that is left in their cavities ; and, when they expand and open, draw the air, by their distention, into the void by suction.

17. This then is the cause of this involuntary respiration—the impossibility that the fiery element should remain at rest : for as the operation of motion is proper to heat, and we understand that the principle of heat is to be found in the heart, the continual motion going on in this organ produces the incessant inspiration and exhalation of the air through the lungs : wherefore also when the fiery element is unnaturally augmented, the breathing of those fevered subjects becomes more rapid, as though the heart were endeavouring to quench the flame implanted in it by more violent[2] breathing.

18. But since our nature is poor and in need of supplies for its own maintenance from all quarters, it not only lacks air of its own, and the breath which excites heat, which it imports from without for the preservation of the living being, but the nourishment it finds to fill out the proportions of the body is an importation. Accordingly, it supplies the deficiency by food and drink, implanting in the body a certain faculty for appropriating that which it requires, and rejecting that which is superfluous, and for this purpose too the fire of the heart gives nature no small assistance.

19. For since, according to the account we have given, the heart which kindles by its warm breath the individual parts, is the most important of the vital organs, our Maker caused it to be operative with its efficacious power at all points, that no part of it might be left ineffectual or unprofitable for the regulation of the whole organism. Behind, therefore, it enters the lungs, and, by its continuous motion, drawing that organ to itself, it expands the passages to inhale the air, and compressing them again it brings about the exspiration of the imprisoned air ; while in front, attached to the space at the upper extremity of the stomach, it warms it and makes it respond by motion to its own activity, rousing it, not to inhale air, but to receive its appropriate food : for the entrances for breath

---

[1] Reading (with Forbes' marginal suggestion) ἐκπνοήν.

[2] Or perhaps " fresher," the heart seeking as it were for fresher and cooler air, and the breath being thus accelerated in the effort to obtain it.

and food are near one another, extending lengthwise one alongside the other, and are terminated in their upper extremity by the same boundary, so that their mouths are contiguous and the passages come to an end together in one mouth, from which the entrance of food is effected through the one, and that of the breath through the other.

20. Internally, however, the closeness of the connection of the passages is not maintained throughout; for the heart intervening between the base of the two, infuses in the one the powers for respiration, and in the other for nutriment. Now the fiery element is naturally inclined to seek for the material which serves as fuel, and this necessarily happens with regard to the receptacle of nourishment; for the more it becomes penetrated by fire through the neighbouring warmth, the more it draws to itself what nourishes the heat. And this sort of impulse we call appetite.

21. But if the organ which contains the food should obtain sufficient material, not even so does the activity of the fire become quiescent: but it produces a sort of melting of the material just as in a foundry, and, dissolving the solids, pours them out and transfers them, as it were from a funnel, to the neighbouring passages: then separating the coarser from the pure substance, it passes the fine part through certain channels to the entrance of the liver, and expels the sedimentary matter of the food to the wider passages of the bowels, and by turning it over in their manifold windings retains the food for a time in the intestines, lest if it were easily got rid of by a straight passage it might at once excite the animal again to appetite, and man, like the race of irrational animals, might never cease from this sort of occupation.

22. As we saw, however, that the liver has especial need of the co-operation of heat for the conversion of the fluids into blood, while this organ is in position distant from the heart (for it would, I imagine, have been impossible that, being one principle or root of the vital power, it should not be hampered by vicinity with another such principle), in order that the system may suffer no injury by the distance at which the heat-giving substance is placed, a muscular passage (and this, by those skilled in such matters, is called the artery) receives the heated air from the heart and conveys it to the liver, making its opening there somewhere beside the point at which the fluids enter, and, as it warms the moist substance by its heat, blends with the liquid something akin to fire, and makes the blood appear red with the fiery tint it produces.

23. Issuing thence again, certain twin channels, each enclosing its own current like a pipe, disperse air and blood (that the liquid substance may have free course when accompanied and lightened by the motion of the heated substance) in divers directions over the whole body, breaking at every part into countless branching channels; while as the two principles of the vital powers mingle together (that alike which disperses heat, and that which supplies moisture to all parts of the body), they make, as it were, a sort of compulsory contribution from the substance with which they deal to the supreme force in the vital economy.

24. Now this force is that which is considered as residing in the cerebral membranes and the brain, from which it comes that every movement of a joint, every contraction of the muscles, every spontaneous influence that is exerted upon the individual members, renders our earthen statue active and mobile as though by some mechanism. For the most pure form of heat and the most subtle form of liquid, being united by their respective forces through a process of mixture and combination, nourish and sustain by their moisture the brain, and hence in turn, being rarefied to the most pure condition, the exhalation that proceeds from that organ anoints the membrane which encloses the brain, which, reaching from above downwards like a pipe, extending through the successive vertebræ, is (itself and the marrow which is contained in it) conterminous with the base of the spine, itself giving like a charioteer the impulse and power to all the meeting-points of bones and joints, and to the branches of the muscles, for the motion or rest of the particular parts.

25. For this cause too it seems to me that it has been granted a more secure defence, being distinguished, in the head, by a double shelter of bones round about, and in the vertebræ of the neck by the bulwarks formed by the projections of the spine as well as by the diversified interlacings of the very form of those vertebræ, by which it is kept in freedom from all harm, enjoying safety by the defence that surrounds it.

26. So too one might suppose of the heart, that it is itself like some safe house fitted with the most solid defences, fortified by the enclosing walls of the bones round about; for in rear there is the spine, strengthened on either side by the shoulder-blades, and on each flank the enfolding position of the ribs makes that which is in the midst between them difficult to injure; while in front the breast-bone and the juncture of the collar-bone serve as a defence, that its safety may be guarded at all points from external causes of danger.

27. As we see in husbandry, when the rainfall from the clouds or the overflow from the river channels causes the land beneath it to be saturated with moisture (let us suppose for

our argument a garden, nourishing within its own compass countless varieties of trees, and all the forms of plants that grow from the ground, and whereof we contemplate the figure, quality, and individuality in great variety of detail); then, as these are nourished by the liquid element while they are in one spot, the power which supplies moisture to each individual among them is one in nature; but the individuality of the plants so nourished changes the liquid element into different qualities; for the same substance becomes bitter in wormwood, and is changed into a deadly juice in hemlock, and becomes different in different other plants, in saffron, in balsam, in the poppy: for in one it becomes hot, in another cold, in another it obtains the middle quality: and in laurel and mastick it is scented, and in the fig and the pear it is sweetened, and by passing through the vine it is turned into the grape and into wine; while the juice of the apple, the redness of the rose, the radiance of the lily, the blue of the violet, the purple of the hyacinthine dye, and all that we behold in the earth, arise from one and the same moisture, and are separated into so many varieties in respect of figure and aspect and quality; the same sort of wonder is wrought in the animated soil of our being by Nature, or rather by Nature's Lord. Bones, cartilages, veins, arteries, nerves, ligatures, flesh, skin, fat, hair, glands, nails, eyes, nostrils, ears, —all such things as these, and countless others in addition, while separated from one another by various peculiarities, are nourished by the one form of nourishment in ways proper to their own nature, in the sense that the nourishment, when it is brought into close relation with any of the subjects, is also changed according to that to which it approaches, and becomes adapted and allied to the special nature of the part. For if it should be in the neighbourhood of the eye, it blends with the visual part and is appropriately distributed by the difference of the coats round the eye, among the single parts; or, if it flow to the auditory parts, it is mingled with the auscultatory nature, or if it is in the lip, it becomes lip; and it grows solid in bone, and grows soft in marrow, and is made tense with the sinew, and extended with the surface, and passes into the nails, and is fined down for the growth of the hair, by correspondent exhalations, producing hair that is somewhat curly or wavy if it makes its way through winding passages, while, if the course of the exhalations that go to form the hair lies straight, it renders the hair stiff and straight.

28. Our argument, however, has wandered far from its purpose, going deep into the works of nature, and endeavouring to describe how and from what materials our particular organs are formed, those, I mean, intended for life and for good life, and any other class which we included with these in our first division.

29. For our purpose was to show that the seminal cause of our constitution is neither a soul without body, nor a body without soul, but that, from animated and living bodies, it is generated at the first as a living and animate being, and that our humanity takes it and cherishes it like a nursling with the resources she herself possesses, and it thus grows on both sides and makes its growth manifest correspondingly in either part:—for it at once displays, by this artificial and scientific process of formation, the power of soul that is interwoven in it, appearing at first somewhat obscurely, but afterwards increasing in radiance concurrently with the perfecting of the work.

30. And as we may see with stone-carvers— for the artist's purpose is to produce in stone the figure of some animal; and with this in his mind, he first severs the stone from its kindred matter, and then, by chipping away the superfluous parts of it, advances somehow by the intermediate step of his first outline to the imitation which he has in his purpose, so that even an unskilled observer may, by what he sees, conjecture the aim of his art; again, by working at it, he brings it more nearly to the semblance of the object he has in view; lastly, producing in the material the perfect and finished figure, he brings his art to its conclusion, and that which a little before was a shapeless stone is a lion, or a man, or whatsoever it may be that the artist has made, not by the change of the material into the figure, but by the figure being wrought upon the material. If one supposes the like in the case of the soul he is not far from probability; for we say that Nature, the all-contriving, takes from its kindred matter the part that comes from the man, and moulds her statue within herself. And as the form follows upon the gradual working of the stone, at first somewhat indistinct, but more perfect after the completion of the work, so too in the moulding of its instrument the form of the soul is expressed in the substratum, incompletely in that which is still incomplete, perfect in that which is perfect; indeed it would have been perfect from the beginning had our nature not been maimed by evil. Thus our community in that generation which is subject to passion and of animal nature, brings it about that the Divine image does not at once shine forth at our formation, but brings man to perfection by a certain method and sequence, through those attributes of the soul which are material, and belong rather to the animal creation.

31. Some such doctrine as this the great apostle also teaches us in his Epistle to the

Corinthians, when he says, "When I was a child, I spake as a child, I understood as a child, I thought as a child; but when I became a man I put away childish things [3]"; not that the soul which arises in the man is different from that which we know to be in the boy, and the childish intellect fails while the manly intellect takes its being in us; but that the same soul displays its imperfect condition in the one, its perfect state in the other.

32. For we say that those things are alive which spring up and grow, and no one would deny that all things that participate in life and natural motion are animate, yet at the same time one cannot say that such life partakes of a perfect soul,—for though a certain animate operation exists in plants, it does not attain to the motions of sense; and on the other hand, though a certain further animate power exists in the brutes, neither does this attain perfection, since it does not contain in itself the grace of reason and intelligence.

33. And even so we say that the true and perfect soul is the human soul, recognized by every operation; and anything else that shares in life we call animate by a sort of customary misuse of language, because in these cases the soul does not exist in a perfect condition, but only certain parts of the operation of the soul, which in man also (according to Moses' mystical account of man's origin) we learn to have accrued when he made himself like this sensuous world. Thus Paul, advising those who were able to hear him to lay hold on perfection, indicates also the mode in which they may attain that object, telling them that they must "put off the old man," and put on the man "which is renewed after the image of Him that created him [4]."

34. Now may we all return to that Divine grace in which God at the first created man, when He said, "Let us make man in our image and likeness"; to Whom be glory and might for ever and ever. Amen.

---

[3] 1 Cor. xiii. 11.

[4] Col. iii. 9, 10.

ON THE SOUL AND THE RESURRECTION

ARGUMENT

THE mind, in times of bereavement, craves a certainty gained by reasoning as to the existence of the soul after death.

First, then : Virtue will be impossible, if deprived of the life of eternity, her only advantage. But this is a moral argument. The case calls for speculative and scientific treatment.

How is the objection that the nature of the soul, as of real things, is material, to be met?

Thus ; the truth of this doctrine would involve the truth of Atheism ; whereas Atheism is refuted by the fact of the wise order that reigns in the world. In other words, the spirituality of God cannot be denied : and this proves the possibility of spiritual or immaterial existence : and therefore, that of the soul.

But is God, then, the same thing as the soul?

No : but man is "a little world in himself ;" and we may with the same right conclude from this Microcosm to the actual existence of an immaterial soul, as from the phenomena of the world to the reality of God's existence.

A Definition of the soul is then given, for the sake of clearness in the succeeding discussion. It is *a created, living, intellectual being,* with the power, as long as it is provided with organs, of sensuous perception. For "the mind sees," not the eye ; take, for instance, the meaning of the phases of the moon. The objection that the "organic machine" of the body produces all thought is met by the instance of the water-organ. Such machines, if thought were really an attribute of matter, ought to build themselves spontaneously : whereas they are a direct proof of an *invisible* thinking power in man. A work of Art means mind : there is a thing perceived, and a thing not perceived.

But still, what *is* this thing not perceived?

If it has no sensible quality whatever—Where is it?

The answer is, that the same question might be asked about the Deity (Whose existence is not denied).

Then the Mind and the Deity are identical?

Not so : in its substantial existence, as separable from matter, the soul is *like* God ; but this likeness does not extend to sameness ; it resembles God as a copy the original.

As being "simple and uncompounded" the soul survives the dissolution of the composite body, whose scattered elements it will continue to accompany, as if watching over its property till the Resurrection, when it will clothe itself in them anew.

The soul was defined "an *intellectual* being." But anger and desire are not of the body either. Are there, then, two or three souls?—Answer. Anger and desire do *not* belong to the essence of the soul, but are only among its varying states ; they are not originally part of ourselves, and we can and must rid ourselves of them, and bring them, as long as they continue to mark our community with the brute creation, into the service of the good. They are the "tares" of the heart, while they serve any other purpose.

But where will the soul "accompany its elements"?—Hades is not a particular spot ; it means the Invisible ; those passages in the Bible in which the regions under the earth are alluded to are explained as allegorical, although the partizans of the opposite interpretation need not be combated.

But how will the soul know the scattered elements of the once familiar form? This is answered by two illustrations (not analogies). The skill of the painter, the force that has united numerous colours to form a single tint, will, if (by some miracle) that actual tint was to fall back into those various colours, be cognizant of each one of these last, *e. g.* the tone and size of the drop of gold, of red, &c.; and could at will recombine them. The owner of a cup of clay would know its fragments (by their shape) amidst a mass of fragments of clay vessels of other shapes, or even if they were plunged again into their native clay. So the soul knows its elements amidst their "kindred dust"; or when each one has flitted back to its own primeval source on the confines of the Universe.

But how does this harmonize with the Parable of the Rich Man and Lazarus?

The bodies of both were in the grave : and so all that is said of them is in a *spiritual* sense. But the *soul* can suffer still, being cognizant, not only of the elements of the whole body, but of those that formed each member, *e. g.* the tongue. By the relations of the Rich Man are meant the impressions made on his soul by the things of flesh and blood.

But if we must have no emotions in the next world, how shall there be virtue, and how shall there be love of God? For anger, we saw, contributed to the one, desire to the other.

We shall be like God so far that we shall always contemplate the Beautiful in Him. Now, God, in contemplating Himself, has no desire and hope, no regret and memory. The moment of fruition is always present, and so His Love is perfect, without the need of any emotion. So will it be with us. God draws "that which belongs to Him" to this blessed passionlessness; and in this very drawing consists the torment of a passion-laden soul. Severe and long-continued pains in eternity are thus decreed to sinners, not because God hates them, nor for the sake alone of punishing them; but "because what belongs to God must *at any cost* be preserved for Him." The degree of pain which must be endured by each one is necessarily proportioned to the measure of the wickedness.

God will thus be "all in all"; yet the loved one's form will then be woven, though into a more ethereal texture, of the same elements as before. (This is not Nirvana.)

Here the doctrine of the Resurrection is touched. The Christian Resurrection and that of the heathen philosophies coincide in that the soul is reclothed from *some* elements of the Universe. But there are fatal objections to the latter under its two forms:

Transmigration pure and simple;
The Platonic Soul-rotation.

The first—1. Obliterates the distinction between the mineral or vegetable, and the spiritual, world.
2. Makes it a sin to eat and drink.
Both—3. Confuse the moral choice.
4. Make heaven the cradle of vice, and earth of virtue.
5. Contradict the truth that they assume, that there is no change in heaven.
6. Attribute every birth to a vice, and therefore are either Atheist or Manichæan.
7. Make a life a chapter of accidents.
8. Contradict facts of moral character.

God *is* the cause of our life, both in body and soul.

But *when* and *how* does the soul come into existence?

The *how* we can never know.

There are objections to seeking the material for any created thing either in God, or outside God. But we may regard the whole Creation as the *realized thoughts* of God. (Anticipation of Malebranche.)

The *when* may be determined. Objections to the existence of soul *before* body have been given above. But soul is necessary to life, and the embryo lives.

Therefore soul is not born *after* body. So body and soul are born together.

As to the number of souls, Humanity itself is a thought of God not yet completed, as these continual additions prove. When it is completed, this "progress of Humanity" will cease, by there being no more births : and no births, no deaths.

Before answering objections to the Scriptural doctrine of the Resurrection, the passages that contain it are mentioned : especially Psalm cxviii. 27 (LXX.).

The various objections to it, to the Purgatory *to follow*, and to the Judgment, are then stated; especially that

A man is not the same being (physically) two days together. Which phase of him, then, is to rise again, be tortured (if need be), and judged?

They are all answered by a Definition of the Resurrection, i. e. *the restoration of man to his original state*. In that, there is neither age nor infancy; and the "coats of skins" are laid aside.

When the process of purification has been completed, the better attributes of the soul appear— imperishability, life, honour, grace, glory, power, and, in short, all that belongs to human nature as the image of Deity.

ON THE SOUL AND THE RESURRECTION

BASIL, great amongst the saints, had departed from this life to God; and the impulse to mourn for him was shared by all the churches. But his sister the Teacher was still living; and so I journeyed to her [1], yearning for an interchange of sympathy over the loss of her brother. My soul was right sorrow-stricken by this grievous blow, and I sought for one who could feel it equally, to mingle my tears with. But when we were in each other's presence the sight of the Teacher awakened all my pain; for she too was lying in a state of prostration even unto death. Well, she gave in to me for a little while, like a skilful driver, in the ungovernable violence of my grief; and then she tried to check me by speaking, and to correct with the curb of her reasonings the disorder of my soul. She quoted the Apostle's words about the duty of not being "grieved for them that sleep"; because only "men without hope" have such feelings. With a heart still fermenting with my pain, I asked—

[2] How can that ever be practised by mankind?

There is such an instinctive and deep-seated abhorrence of death in all! Those who look on a death-bed can hardly bear the sight; and those whom death approaches recoil from him all they can. Why, even the law that controls us puts death highest on the list of crimes, and highest on the list of punishments. By what device, then, can we bring ourselves to regard as nothing a departure from life even in the case of a stranger, not to mention that of relations, when so be they·cease to live? We see before us the whole course of human life aiming at this one thing, viz. how we may continue in this life; indeed it is for this that houses have been invented by us to live in; in order that our bodies may not be prostrated in their environment [3] by cold or heat. Agriculture, again, what is it but the providing of our sustenance? In fact all thought about how we are to go on living is occasioned by the fear of dying. Why is medicine so honoured amongst men? Because it is thought to carry on the combat with death to a certain extent by its methods. Why do we have corslets, and long shields, and greaves, and helmets, and all the defensive armour, and inclosures of fortifications, and iron-barred gates, except that we fear to die? Death then being naturally so terrible to us, how can it be easy for a survivor to obey this command to remain unmoved over friends departed?

Why, what is the especial pain you feel, asked the Teacher, in the mere necessity itself of dying? This common talk of unthinking persons is no sufficient accusation.

What! is there no occasion for grieving, I replied to her, when we see one who so lately lived and spoke becoming all of a sudden lifeless and motionless, with the sense of every bodily organ extinct, with no sight or hearing in operation, or any other faculty of apprehension that sense possesses; and if you apply

---

[1] Gregory himself tells us, in his life of S. Macrina, that he went to see her after the Council of Antioch. (This and Basil's death occurred in the year 379 : so that this Dialogue was probably composed in 380.) "The interval during which the circumstances of our times of trials prevented any visits had been long." He goes on to say (p. 189 B.) ; " And that she might cause me no depression of spirits, she somehow subdued the noise and concealed the difficulty of her breathing, and assumed perfect cheerfulness: she not only started pleasant topics herself, but suggested them as well by the questions which she asked. The conversation led naturally to the mention of our great Basil. While my very soul sank and my countenance was saddened and fell, she herself was so far from going with me into the depths of mourning, that she made the mention of that saintly name an opportunity for the most sublime philosophy. Examining human nature in a scientific way, disclosing the divine plan that underlies all afflictions, and dealing, as if inspired by the Holy Spirit, with all the questions relating to a future life, she maintained such a discourse that my soul seemed to be lifted along with her words almost beyond the compass of humanity, and, as I followed her argument, to be placed within the sanctuary of heaven." Again (p. 190 B) : " And if my tract would not thereby be extended to an endless length, I would have reported everything in its order ; i. e. how her argument lifted her as she went into the philosophy both of the soul, and of the causes of our life in the flesh, and of the final cause of Man and his mortality, and of death and the return thence into life again. In all of it her reasoning continued clear and consecutive : it flowed on so easily and naturally that it was like the water from some spring falling unimpeded downwards."

[2] Two grounds are here given why this practice of grief for the departed is difficult to give up. One lies in the natural abhorrence of death, showing itself in two ways, viz. in our grief over others dying, and in recoiling from our own death, expressed by two evenly balanced sentences, οὔτε τῶν ὁρώντων . . . οἷς τε ἄν . . .; in the latter a second οὔτε might have been expected ; but such an

anacoluthon is frequent in dialogue. Oehler is wrong in giving to the second τε an intensive force, i. e. "much more." The other ground lies in the attitude of the law towards death.

[3] Reading περιέχοντι : the same word is used below, " as long as the breath within was held in by the enveloping substance " (see p. 432, note 8). Here it means "the air" : as in Marcus Antoninus, Lib. iv. 39.

fire or steel to him, even if you were to plunge a sword into the body, or cast it to the beasts of prey, or if you bury it beneath a mound, that dead man is alike unmoved at any treatment? Seeing, then, that this change is observed in all these ways, and that principle of life, whatever it might be, disappears all at once out of sight, as the flame of an extinguished lamp which burnt on it the moment before neither remains upon the wick nor passes to some other place, but completely disappears, how can such a change be borne without emotion by one who has no clear ground to rest upon? We *hear* the departure of the spirit, we *see* the shell that is left; but of the part that has been separated we are ignorant, both as to its nature, and as to the place whither it has fled; for neither earth, nor air, nor water, nor any other element can show as residing within itself this force that has left the body, at whose withdrawal a corpse only remains, ready for dissolution.

Whilst I was thus enlarging on the subject, the Teacher signed to me with her hand [4], and said: Surely what alarms and disturbs your mind is not the thought that the soul, instead of lasting for ever, ceases with the body's dissolution!

I answered rather audaciously, and without due consideration of what I said, for my passionate grief had not yet given me back my judgment. In fact, I said that the Divine utterances seemed to me like mere commands compelling us to believe that the soul lasts for ever; not, however, that we were led by them to this belief by any reasoning. Our mind within us appears slavishly to accept the opinion enforced, but not to acquiesce with a spontaneous impulse. Hence our sorrow over the departed is all the more grievous; we do not exactly know whether this vivifying principle is anything by itself; where it is, or how it is; whether, in fact, it exists in any way at all anywhere. This uncertainty [5] about the real state of the case balances the opinions on either side; many adopt the one view, many the other; and indeed there are certain persons, of no small philosophical reputation amongst the Greeks, who have held and maintained this which I have just said.

Away, she cried, with that pagan nonsense!

For therein the inventor of lies fabricates false theories only to harm the Truth. Observe this, and nothing else; that such a view about the soul amounts to nothing less than the abandoning of virtue, and seeking the pleasure of the moment only; the life of eternity, by which alone virtue claims the advantage, must be despaired of.

And pray how, I asked, are we to get a firm and unmovable belief in the soul's continuance? I, too, am sensible of the fact that human life will be bereft of the most beautiful ornament that life has to give, I mean virtue, unless an undoubting confidence with regard to this be established within us. What, indeed, has virtue to stand upon in the case of those persons who conceive of this present life as the limit of their existence, and hope for nothing beyond?

Well, replied the Teacher, we must seek where we may get a beginning for our discussion upon this point; and if you please, let the defence of the opposing views be undertaken by yourself; for I see that your mind is a little inclined to accept such a brief. Then, after the conflicting belief has been stated, we shall be able to look for the truth.

When she made this request, and I had deprecated the suspicion that I was making the objections in real earnest, instead of only wishing to get a firm ground for the belief about the soul by calling into court [6] first what is aimed against this view, I began—

Would not the defenders of the opposite belief say this: that the body, being composite, must necessarily be resolved into that of which it is composed? And when the coalition of elements in the body ceases, each of those elements naturally gravitates towards its kindred element with the irresistible bias of like to like; the heat in us will thus unite with heat, the earthy with the solid, and each of the other elements also will pass towards its like. Where, then, will the soul be after that? If one affirm that it is in those elements, one will be obliged to admit that it is identical with them, for this fusion could not possibly take place between two things of different natures. But this being granted, the soul must necessarily be viewed as a complex thing, fused as it is with qualities so opposite. But the complex is not simple, but must be classed with the composite, and the composite is necessarily dissoluble; and

---

[4] Reading κατασείσασα τῇ χειρί, instead of the vox nihili μετασείσασα of the two Paris Editions, which can be accounted for by μετα being repeated in error from μεταξύ. The question which this gesture accompanied is one to which it would be very appropriate. The reading adopted is that of the Codex Uffenbach, and this phrase, κατασείειν τῇ χειρί, is unimpeachable for "commanding silence," being used by Polybius, and Xenophon (without χειρί). Wolf and Krabinger prefer this reading to that of most of the Codd., κατασιγήσασα: and doubtless Sifanus read it ("manu silentio imperato").

[5] ἴσας . . . ἀδηλία. This is Krabinger's reading (for ἴσως . . . ἡ δειλία in the Parisian Editions) with abundant MS. authority.

[6] ἀντιπιπτόντων πρὸς τὸν σκοπὸν τοῦτον ὑποκληθέντων: he reading of the Parisian Editions. But the preponderance of MS. authority is in favour of ὑπεκλυθέντων, "si quæ ad hoc propositum opponuntur soluta fuerint," Krabinger. The force of ὑπό will then be "by way of rejoinder." The idea in σκοπὸν seems to be that of a butt set up to be shot at. All the MSS., but not the Paris Editions, have the article before ἀντιπιπτόντων: but it is not absolutely necessary, for Gregory not unfrequently omits it before participles, when his meaning is general, i. e. "Everything that," &c.

dissolution means the destruction of the compound; and the destructible is not immortal, else the flesh itself, resolvable as it is into its constituent elements, might so be called immortal. If, on the other hand, the soul is something other than these elements, where can our reason suggest a place for it to be, when it is thus, by virtue of its alien nature, not to be discovered in those elements, and there is no other place in the world, either, where it may continue, in harmony with its own peculiar character, to exist? But, if a thing can be found nowhere, plainly it has no existence.

The Teacher sighed gently at these words of mine, and then said; Maybe these were the objections, or such as these, that the Stoics and Epicureans collected at Athens made in answer to the Apostle. I hear that Epicurus carried his theories in this very direction. The framework of things was to his mind a fortuitous[7] and mechanical affair, without a Providence penetrating its operations; and, as a piece with this, he thought that human life was like a bubble, existing only as long as the breath within was held in by the enveloping substance[8], inasmuch as our body was a mere membrane, as it were, encompassing a breath; and that on the collapse of the inflation the imprisoned essence was extinguished. To him the visible was the limit of existence; he made our senses the only means of our apprehension of things; he completely closed the eyes of his soul, and was incapable of seeing anything in the intelligible and immaterial world, just as a man, who is imprisoned in a cabin whose walls and roof obstruct the view outside, remains without a glimpse of all the wonders of the sky. Verily, everything in the universe that is seen to be an object of sense is as an earthen wall, forming in itself a barrier between the narrower souls and that intelligible world which is ready for their contemplation; and it is the earth and water and fire alone that such behold; whence comes each of these elements, in what and by what they are encompassed, such souls because of their narrowness cannot detect. While the

sight of a garment suggests to any one the weaver of it, and the thought of the shipwright comes at the sight of the ship, and the hand of the builder is brought to the mind of him who sees the building, these little souls gaze upon the world, but their eyes are blind to Him whom all this that we see around us makes manifest; and so they propound their clever and pungent doctrines about the soul's evanishment;—body from elements, and elements from body, and, besides, the impossibility of the soul's self-existence (if it is not to be one of these elements, or lodged in one); for if these opponents suppose that by virtue of the soul not being akin to the elements it is nowhere after death, they must propound, to begin with, the absence of the soul from the fleshly life as well, seeing that the body itself is nothing but a concourse of those elements; and so they must not tell us that the soul is to be found there either, independently vivifying their compound. If it is not possible for the soul to exist *after* death, though the elements do, then, I say, according to this teaching our life as well is proved to be nothing else but death. But if on the other hand they do not make the existence of the soul now in the body a question for doubt, how can they maintain its evanishment when the body is resolved into its elements? Then, secondly, they must employ an equal audacity against the God in this Nature too. For how can they assert that the intelligible and immaterial Unseen can be dissolved and diffused into the wet and the soft, as also into the hot and the dry, and so hold together the universe in existence through being, though not of a kindred nature with the things which it penetrates, yet not thereby incapable of so penetrating them? Let them, therefore, remove from their system the very Deity Who upholds the world.

That is the very point, I said, upon which our adversaries cannot fail to have doubts; viz. that all things depend on God and are encompassed by Him, or, that there is any divinity at all transcending the physical world.

It would be more fitting, she cried, to be silent about such doubts, and not to deign to make any answer to such foolish and wicked propositions; for there is a Divine precept forbidding us to answer a fool in his folly; and he must be a fool, as the Prophet declares, who says that there is no God. But since one needs must speak, I will urge upon you an argument which is not mine nor that of any human being (for it would then be of small value, whosoever spoke it), but an argument which the whole Creation enunciates by the medium of its wonders to the audience[9] of the eye, with a

---

7 ὡς τυχαία, κ. τ. λ. It is better to connect this directly with Epicurus himself, than to refer it, by bracketing the preceding sentence (with Oehler), to his followers. Macrina infers from the opinions known to her of Epicurus, what he must have said about the human soul: *i. e.* that it was a bubble; and then what his followers probably said. There is no evidence that Epicurus used this actual figure: still Gregory *may* be recording his very words.— Lucian (*Charon*, 68) enlarges on such a simile: and his ὠκύμορον φύσημα, as a description of man, is reproduced by Gregory himself in *Orat. de Beatitud.* p. 768 D.

8 τῷ περιέχοντι. Sifanus takes this of the surrounding atmosphere. So also Krabinger, "aere circumfuso," just as above (182 A.) it does certainly mean the air, and Wolf quotes a passage to that effect from Marcus Antoninus and the present instance also. Still there is no reason that it should not here mean the body of the man, which is as it were a case retentive of the vital breath within; and the sense seems to require it. As to the construction, although πομφόλυξ is sometimes masculine in later Greek, yet it is much more likely that περιταθέντος (not περιτεθέντος of the Paris Editt.) is the genitive absolute with τοῦ σώματος: τῷ περιέχοντι would then very naturally refer to this.

9 But Dr. Hermann Schmidt sees even more than this in this bold figure. The Creation preaches, as it were, and its tones are first

skilful and artistic utterance that reaches the heart. The Creation proclaims outright the Creator; for the very heavens, as the Prophet says, declare the glory of God with their unutterable words. We see the universal harmony in the wondrous sky and on the wondrous earth; how elements essentially opposed to each other are all woven together in an ineffable union to serve one common end, each contributing its particular force to maintain the whole; how the unmingling and mutually repellent do not fly apart from each other by virtue of their peculiarities, any more than they are destroyed, when compounded, by such contrariety; how those elements which are naturally buoyant move downwards, the heat of the sun, for instance, descending in the rays, while the bodies which possess weight are lifted by becoming rarefied in vapour, so that water contrary to its nature ascends, being conveyed through the air to the upper regions; how too that fire of the firmament so penetrates the earth that even its abysses feel the heat; how the moisture of the rain infused into the soil generates, one though it be by nature, myriads of differing germs, and animates in due proportion each subject of its influence; how very swiftly the polar sphere revolves, how the orbits within it move the contrary way, with all the eclipses, and conjunctions, and measured intervals [1] of the planets. We see all this with the piercing eyes of mind, nor can we fail to be taught by means of such a spectacle that a Divine power, working with skill and method, is manifesting itself in this actual world, and, penetrating each portion, combines those portions with the whole and completes the whole by the portions, and encompasses the universe with a single all-controlling force, self-centred and self-contained, never ceasing from its motion, yet never altering the position which it holds.

And pray how, I asked, does this belief in the existence of God prove along with it the existence of the human soul? For God, surely, is not the same thing as the soul, so that, if the one were believed in, the other must necessarily be believed in.

She replied: It has been said by wise men that man is a little world [2] in himself and contains all the elements which go to complete the universe. If this view is a true one (and so it seems), we perhaps shall need no other ally than it to establish the truth of our conception

of the soul. And our conception of it is this; that it exists, with a rare and peculiar nature of its own, independently of the body with its gross texture. We get our exact knowledge of this outer world from the apprehension of our senses, and these sensational operations themselves lead us on to the understanding of the super-sensual world of fact and thought, and our eye thus becomes the interpreter of that almighty wisdom which is visible in the universe, and points in itself to the Being Who encompasses it. Just so, when we look to our inner world, we find no slight grounds there also, in the known, for conjecturing the unknown; and the unknown there also is that which, being the object of thought and not of sight, eludes the grasp of sense.

I rejoined, Nay, it may be very possible to infer a wisdom transcending the universe from the skilful and artistic designs observable in this harmonized fabric of physical nature; but, as regards the soul, what knowledge is possible to those who would trace, from any indications the body has to give, the unknown through the known?

Most certainly, the Virgin replied, the soul herself, to those who wish to follow the wise proverb and know themselves, is a competent [3] instructress; of the fact, I mean, that she is an immaterial and spiritual thing, working and moving in a way corresponding to her peculiar nature, and evincing these peculiar emotions through the organs of the body. For this bodily organization exists the same even in those who have just been reduced by death to the state of corpses, but it remains without motion or action because the force of the soul is no longer in it. It moves only when there is sensation in the organs, and not only that, but the mental force by means of that sensation penetrates with its own impulses and moves whither it will all those organs of sensation.

What then, I asked, is the soul? Perhaps there may be some possible means of delineating its nature; so that we may have some comprehension of this subject, in the way of a sketch.

Its definition, the Teacher replied, has been attempted in different ways by different writers, each according to his own bent; but the following is our opinion about it. The soul is an essence created, and living, and intellectual, transmitting from itself to an organized and sentient body the power of living and of grasping objects of sense, as long as a natural constitution capable of this holds together.

Saying this she pointed to the physician [4]

---

heard in our hearts (ἐνηχοῦντος τῇ καρδίᾳ): and these tones are then reflected back from the heart to the contemplating eye, which thus becomes not a seeing only, but a hearing (ἀκροατὴς γίνεται) organ, in its external activity.

[1] ἐναρμονίους ἀποστάσεις, i. e. to which the music of the spheres was due: see Macrobius, *Somnium Scipionis*, c. 4: for the "retrograde" motion of the planets above, see Joannes de Sacro Bosco, *Sphæra* (1564), p. 47, sqq.

[2] See *On the Making of Man*, c. viii. 5.

[3] ἱκανή. This is the reading of Codd. A and B (of Krabinger, but the common reading is εἰ κἂν ᾖ!

[4] It may be noticed that besides the physician several others were present. Cf. 242 D, τοῖς πολλοῖς παρακαθημένοις.

who was sitting to watch her state, and said : There is a proof of what I say close by us. How, I ask, does this man, by putting his fingers to feel the pulse, hear in a manner, through this sense of touch, Nature calling loudly to him and telling him of her peculiar pain ; in fact, that the disease in the body is an inflammatory one [5], and that the malady originates in this or that internal organ ; and that there is such and such a degree of fever ? How too is he taught by the agency of the eye other facts of this kind, when he looks to see the posture of the patient and watches the wasting of the flesh ? As, too, the state of the complexion, pale somewhat and bilious, and the gaze of the eyes, as is the case with those in pain, involuntarily inclining to sadness, indicate the internal condition, so the ear gives information of the like, ascertaining the nature of the malady by the shortness of the breathing and by the groan that comes with it. One might say that even the sense of smell in the expert is not incapable of detecting the kind of disorder, but that it notices the secret suffering of the vitals in the particular quality of the breath. Could this be so if there were not a certain force of intelligence present in each organ of the senses ? What would our hand have taught us of itself, without thought conducting it from feeling to understanding the subject before it ? What would the ear, as separate from mind, or the eye or the nostril or any other organ have helped towards the settling of the question, all by themselves ? Verily, it is most true what one of heathen culture is recorded to have said, that it is the mind that sees and the mind that hears [6]. Else, if you will not allow this to be true, you must tell me why, when you look at the sun, as you have been trained by your instructor to look at him, you assert that he is not in the breadth of his disc of the size he appears to the many, but that he exceeds by many times the measure of the entire earth. Do you not confidently maintain that it is so, because you have arrived by reasoning through phenomena at the conception of such and such a movement, of such distances of time and space, of such causes of eclipse ? And when you look at the waning and waxing moon you are taught

other truths by the visible figure of that heavenly body, viz. that it is in itself devoid of light, and that it revolves in the circle nearest to the earth, and that it is lit by light from the sun ; just as is the case with mirrors, which, receiving the sun upon them, do not reflect rays of their own, but those of the sun, whose light is given back from their smooth flashing surface. Those who see this, but do not examine it, think that the light comes from the moon herself. But that this is not the case is proved by this ; that when she is diametrically facing the sun she has the whole of the disc that looks our way illuminated ; but, as she traverses her own circle of revolution quicker from moving in a narrower space, she herself has completed this more than twelve times before the sun has once travelled round his ; whence it happens that her substance is not always covered with light. For her position facing him is not maintained in the frequency of her revolutions ; but, while this position causes the whole side of the moon which looks to us to be illumined, directly she moves sideways her hemisphere which is turned to us necessarily becomes partially shadowed, and only that which is turned to him meets his embracing rays ; the brightness, in fact, keeps on retiring from that which can no longer see the sun to that which still sees him, until she passes right across the sun's disc and receives his rays upon her hinder part ; and then the fact of her being in herself totally devoid of light and splendour causes the side turned to us to be invisible while the further hemisphere is all in light ; and this is called the completion[7] of her waning. But when again, in her own revolution, she has passed the sun and she is transverse to his rays, the side which was dark just before begins to shine a little, for the rays move from the illumined part to that so lately invisible. You see what the eye does teach ; and yet it would never of itself have afforded this insight, without something that looks through the eyes and uses the data of the senses as mere guides to penetrate from the apparent to the unseen. It is needless to add the methods of geometry that lead us step by step through visible delineations to truths that lie out of sight, and countless other instances which all prove that apprehension is the work of an intellectual essence deeply seated in our nature, acting through the operation of our bodily senses.

But what, I asked, if, insisting on the great

---

[5] Krabinger's Latin " in intentione," though a literal translation, hardly represents the full force of this passage, which is interesting because, the terms being used specially, if not only, of fevers or inflammation, it is evident that the speaker has her own illness in mind, and her words are thus more natural than if she spoke of patients generally. If ἐν ἐπίτασει is translated " at its height," this will very awkwardly anticipate what follows, ἐπὶ τοσόνδε . . . . ἡ ἐπίτασις. The doctor is supposed simply to class the complaint as belonging to the order of those which manifest themselves δι' ἐπιτάσεως, as opposed to those which do so δι' ἀνέσεως : he then descends to particulars, i. e. ἐπὶ τοσόνδε. The demonstrative in τῶνδε τῶν σπλάγχνων has the same force as in τὸ ἐν τῷδε θέρμον, 214 C, " such and such : " the nobler organs (viscera thoracis) of course are here meant. Gregory himself gives a list of them, 250 C.

[6] A trochaic line to this effect from the comedian Epicharmus is quoted by Theodoret, De Fide, p. 15.

[7] ὅπερ δὴ παντελὴς τοῦ στοιχείου μείωσις λέγεται, "perfecta elementi diminutio ; " ὅπερ referring to the dark " new " moon just described, which certainly is the consummation of the waning of the moon : though it is not itself a μείωσις.—This last consideration, and the use of δὴ, and the introduction of τοῦ στοιχείου, favour another meaning which might be given, i. e., by joining παντελὴς with τοῦ στοιχείου, and making ὅπερ refer to the whole passage of the moon from full to new, " which indeed is commonly (but erroneously) spoken of as a substantial diminution of the elementary body itself," as if it were a true and real decrease of bulk.

differences which, in spite of a certain quality of matter shared alike by all elements in their visible form, exist between each particular kind of matter (motion, for instance, is not the same in all, some moving up, some down; nor form, nor quality either), some one were to say that there was in the same manner incorporated in, and belonging to, these elements a certain force [8] as well which effects these intellectual insights and operations by a purely natural effort of their own (such effects, for instance, as we often see produced by the mechanists, in whose hands matter, combined according to the rules of Art, thereby imitates Nature, exhibiting resemblance not in figure alone but even in motion, so that when the piece of mechanism sounds in its resonant part it mimics a human voice, without, however, our being able to perceive anywhere any mental force working out the particular figure, character, sound, and movement); suppose, I say, we were to affirm that all this was produced as well in the organic machine of our natural bodies, without any intermixture of a special thinking substance, but owing simply to an inherent motive power of the elements within us accomplishing [9] by itself these operations—to nothing else, in fact, but an impulsive movement working for the cognition of the object before us; would not then the fact stand proved of the absolute non-existence [1] of that intellectual and impalpable Being, the soul, which you talk of?

Your instance, she replied, and your reasoning upon it, though belonging to the counter-argument, may both of them be made allies of our statement, and will contribute not a little to the confirmation of its truth.

Why, how can you say that?

Because, you see, so to understand, manipulate, and dispose the soulless matter, that the art which is stored away in such mechanisms becomes almost like a soul to this material, in all the various ways in which it mocks movement, and figure, and voice, and so on, may be turned into a proof of there being something in man whereby he shows an innate fitness to think out within himself, through the contemplative and inventive faculties, such thoughts, and having prepared such mechanisms in theory, to put them into practice by manual skill, and exhibit in matter the product of his mind. First, for instance, he saw, by dint of thinking, that to produce any sound there is need of some wind; and then, with a view to produce wind in the mechanism, he previously ascertained by a course of reasoning and close observation of the nature of elements, that there is no vacuum at all in the world, but that the lighter is to be considered a vacuum only by comparison with the heavier; seeing that the air itself, taken as a separate subsistence, is crowded quite full. It is by an abuse of language that a jar is said to be "empty"; for when it is empty of any liquid it is none the less, even in this state, full, in the eyes of the experienced. A proof of this is that a jar when put into a pool of water is not immediately filled, but at first floats on the surface, because the air it contains helps to buoy up its rounded sides; till at last the hand of the drawer of the water forces it down to the bottom, and, when there, it takes in water by its neck; during which process it is shown not to have been empty even before the water came; for there is the spectacle of a sort of combat going on in the neck between the two elements, the water being forced by its weight into the interior, and therefore streaming in; the imprisoned air on the other hand being straitened for room by the gush of the water along the neck, and so rushing in the contrary direction; thus the water is checked by the strong current of air, and gurgles and bubbles against it. Men observed this, and devised in accordance with this property of the two elements a way of introducing air to work their mechanism [2]. They made a kind of cavity of some hard stuff, and prevented the air in it from escaping in any direction; and then introduced water into this cavity through its mouth, apportioning the quantity of water according to requirement; next they allowed an exit in the opposite direction to the air, so that it passed into a pipe placed ready to hand, and in so doing, being violently constrained by the water, became a blast; and this, playing on the structure of the pipe, produced a note. Is it not clearly proved by such visible results that there is a mind of some kind in man, something other than that which is visible, which, by virtue of an invisible thinking nature of its own, first prepares by inward invention such devices, and then, when they have been so matured, brings them to the light and exhibits them in the subservient matter? For if

---

[8] εἴ τινα τούτων κατὰ τὸν αὐτὸν λόγον συνουσιωμένην τις εἶναι λέγοι δύναμιν, κ. τ. λ. The difficulty here is in τούτων, which Krabinger takes as a partitive genitive after εἶναι, and refers to the "elements"; and this is perhaps the best way of taking it. But still, as Schmidt points out, it is rather the human body than the elements themselves that ought here to be spoken of as the efficient cause of thought: and so he would either refer τούτων to τὸν αὐτὸν ("in the same way as these instances just given"), and compares Eurip. *Helen.*, ὄνομα δὲ ταὐτὸν τῆς ἐμῆς ἔχουσά τις δάμαρτος ἄλλη (Matt. Gr. p. 706); or else would join τούτων with the preceding διάφορος (with Codd. Mon. D, E).

[9] Cod. Mon. D, ἀποτελούσης. This seems a better reading than that preferred by Krabinger, ἀποτέλεσμα εἶναι: for ἀποτέλεσμα must be pressed to mean, in order to preserve the sense, "a mere result," *i. e.* something secondary, and not itself a principle or cause: the following ἤ, besides, cannot without awkwardness be referred to ἐνέργειαν.

[1] Reading οὐσίαν οὐκ ἂν ἀποδεικνύοιτο ἢ τὸ μηδ' ὅλως εἶναι;

[2] According to an author quoted by Athenæus (iv. 75), the first organist (ὑδραύλης), or rather organ-builder, was Ctesibius of Alexandria, about B.C. 200.

it were possible to ascribe such wonders, as the theory of our opponents does, to the actual constitution of the elements, we should have these mechanisms building themselves spontaneously; the bronze would not wait for the artist, to be made into the likeness of a man, but would become such by an innate force; the air would not require the pipe, to make a note, but would sound spontaneously by its own fortuitous flux and motion; and the jet of the water upwards would not be, as it now is, the result of an artificial pressure forcing it to move in an unnatural direction, but the water would rise into the mechanism of its own accord, finding in that direction a natural channel. But if none of these results are produced spontaneously by elemental force, but, on the contrary, each element is employed at will by artifice; and if artifice is a kind of movement and activity of mind, will not the very consequences of what has been urged by way of objection show us Mind as something other than the thing perceived?

That the thing perceived, I replied, is not the same as the thing not perceived, I. grant; but I do not discover any answer to our question in such a statement; it is not yet clear to me what we are to think that thing not-perceived to be; all I have been shown by your argument is that it is not anything material; and I do not yet know the fitting name for it. I wanted especially to know what it is, not what it is not.

We do learn, she replied, much about many things by this very same method, inasmuch as, in the very act of saying a thing is "not so and so," we by implication interpret the very nature of the thing in question[3]. For instance, when we say a "guileless," we indicate a good man; when we say "unmanly," we have expressed that a man is a coward; and it is possible to suggest a great many things in like fashion, wherein we either convey the idea of goodness by the negation of badness[4], or *vice versâ*. Well, then, if one thinks so with regard to the matter now before us, one will not fail to gain a proper conception of it. The question is,— What are we to think of Mind in its very essence? Now granted that the inquirer has had his doubts set at rest as to the existence of the thing in question, owing to the activities which it displays to us, and only wants to know what it is, he will have adequately discovered it

by being told that it is not that which our senses perceive, neither a colour, nor a form, nor a hardness, nor a weight, nor a quantity, nor a cubic dimension, nor a point, nor anything else perceptible in matter; supposing, that is,[5] that there does exist a something beyond all these.

Here I interrupted her discourse: If you leave all these out of the account I do not see how you can possibly avoid cancelling along with them the very thing which you are in search of. I cannot at present conceive to what, as apart from these, the perceptive activity is to cling. For on all occasions in investigating with the scrutinizing intellect the contents of the world, we must, so far as we put our hand[6] at all on what we are seeking, inevitably touch, as blind men feeling along the walls for the door, some one of those things aforesaid; we must come on colour, or form, or quantity, or something else on your list; and when it comes to saying that the thing is none of them, our feebleness of mind induces us to suppose that it does not exist at all.

Shame on such absurdity! said she, indignantly interrupting. A fine conclusion this narrow-minded, grovelling view of the world brings us to! If all that is not cognizable by sense is to be wiped out of existence, the all-embracing Power that presides over things is admitted by this same assertion not to be; once a man has been told about the non-material and invisible nature of the Deity, he must perforce with such a premise reckon it as absolutely non-existent. If, on the other hand, the absence of such characteristics in His case does not constitute any limitation of His existence, how can the Mind of man be squeezed out of existence along with this withdrawal one by one of each property of matter?

Well, then, I retorted, we only exchange one paradox for another by arguing in this way; for our reason will be reduced to the conclusion that the Deity and the Mind of man are identical, if it be true that neither can be thought of, except by the withdrawal of all the data of sense.

Say not so, she replied; to talk so also is blasphemous. Rather, as the Scripture tells you, say that the one is *like* the other. For that which is "made in the image" of the Deity necessarily possesses a likeness to its prototype in every respect; it resembles it in being intellectual, immaterial, unconnected

---

3 Remove comma after ζητουμένου, in Paris Editt.

4 *or vice versâ*, i. e. the idea of badness by the negation of goodness. Krabinger appositely quotes a passage from Plotinus : "Who could picture to himself evil as a specific thing, appearing as it does only in the absence of each good ? . . . it will be necessary for all who are to know what evil is to have a clear conception about good : since even in dealing with real species the better take precedence of the worse ; and evil is not even a species, but rather a negation." Cf. Origen, *In Johan.* p. 66 A, πᾶσα ἡ κακία οὐδέν ἐστιν, ἐπεὶ καὶ οὐκ ὂν τυγχάνει. See also Gregory s *Great Catechism*, cap. v. and vii.

5 *supposing, that is.* This only repeats what was said above : "granted that the inquirer has had his doubts set at rest as to the existence of the thing." It is the reading of Krabinger (εἰ δή τι), and the best. Sifanus follows the less supported reading οἶδεν ὅτι, which is open to the further objection that it would be absurd to say, "when a man learns that A is not B he knows that it is something else." The reading of the Paris. Editt. ἴδη is unintelligible.

6 (καθ') ὅσον τε . . . θιγγάνομεν.

with any notion of weight [7], and in eluding any measurement of its dimensions [8]; yet as regards its own peculiar nature it is something different from that other. Indeed, it would be no longer an "image," if it were altogether identical with that other; but [9] where we have *A* in that uncreate prototype we have *a* in the image; just as in a minute particle of glass, when it happens to face the light, the complete disc of the sun is often to be seen, not represented thereon in proportion to its proper size, but so far as the minuteness of the particle admits of its being represented at all. Thus do the reflections of those ineffable qualities of Deity shine forth within the narrow limits of our nature; and so our reason, following the leading of these reflections, will not miss grasping the Mind in its essence by clearing away from the question all corporeal qualities; nor on the other hand will it bring the pure [1] and infinite Existence to the level of that which is perishable and little; it will regard this essence of the Mind as an object of thought only, since it is the "image" of an Existence which is such; but it will not pronounce this image to be identical with the prototype. Just, then, as we have no doubts, owing to the display of a Divine mysterious wisdom in the universe, about a Divine Being and a Divine Power existing in it all which secures its continuance (though if you required a definition of that Being you would therein find the Deity completely sundered from every object in creation, whether of sense or thought, while in these last, too, natural distinctions are admitted), so, too, there is nothing strange in the soul's separate existence as a substance (whatever we may think that substance to be) being no hindrance to her actual existence, in spite of the elemental atoms of the world not harmonizing with her in the definiton of her being. In the case of our living bodies, composed as they are from the blending of these atoms, there is no sort of communion, as has been just said, on the score of substance, between the simplicity and invisibility of the soul, and the grossness of those bodies; but, notwithstanding that, there is not a doubt that there is in them the soul's vivifying influence exerted by a law which it is beyond the human understanding to comprehend [2]. Not even then, when those atoms have again been dissolved [3] into themselves, has that bond of a vivifying influence vanished; but as, while the framework of the body still holds together, each individual part is possessed of a soul which penetrates equally every component member, and one could not call that soul hard and resistent though blended with the solid, nor humid, or cold, or the reverse, though it transmits life to all and each of such parts, so, when that framework is dissolved, and has returned to its kindred elements, there is nothing against probability that that simple and incomposite essence which has once for all by some inexplicable law grown with the growth of the bodily framework should continually remain beside the atoms with which it has been blended, and should in no way be sundered from a union once formed. For it does not follow that because the composite is dissolved the incomposite must be dissolved with it [4].

That those atoms, I rejoined, should unite and again be separated, and that this constitutes the formation and dissolution of the body, no one would deny. But we have to consider this. There are great intervals between these atoms; they differ from each other, both in position, and also in qualitative distinctions and peculiarities. When, indeed, these atoms have all converged upon the given subject, it is reasonable that that intelligent and undimensional essence which we call the soul should cohere with that which is so united; but once these atoms are separated from each other, and have gone whither their nature impels them, what is to become of the soul when her vessel [5] is thus scattered in many directions? As a sailor, when his ship has been wrecked and gone to pieces, cannot float upon all the pieces at once [6] which have been scattered this way

---

[2] λόγῳ τινὶ κρείττονι τῆς ἀνθρωπίνης κατανοήσεως. So just below ἀρρήτῳ τινὶ λόγῳ. The *mode* of the union of soul and body is beyond our comprehension. To refer these words to the Deity Himself ("incomprehensible cause"), as Oehler, would make of them, as Schmidt well remarks, a "mere showy phrase."

[3] ἀναλυθέντων. Krabinger reads ἀναλυσάντων, *i. e.* "returning"; as frequently in this treatise, and in N. T. usage.

[4] *i. e.* as we have already seen (p. 433). The fact of the continuity of the soul was there deduced from its being incomposite. So that the γὰρ here does not give the ground for the statement immediately preceding.

Gregory (p. 431) had suggested two alternatives:—1. That the soul dissolves with the body. This is answered by the soul's "incompositeness." 2. That the union of the immaterial soul with the still material atoms after death cannot be maintained. This is answered by the analogy given in the present section, of God's presence in an uncongenial universe, and that of the soul in the still living body. The γὰρ therefore refers to the answer to 1, without which the question of the soul continuing in the atoms could not have been discussed at all.

[5] *her vessel.* Of course this is not the "vehicle" of the soul (after death) which the later Platonists speak of, but the body itself. The word ὄχημα is used in connection with a ship, Soph. *Trach.* 656; and though in Plato (*Timæus*, p. 69), whose use of this word for the body was afterwards followed, it is not clear whether a car or a ship is most thought of, yet that the latter is Gregory's meaning appears from his next words.

[6] *at once.* Reading (with Codd. A, B, C, and Uff.) κατὰ ταὐτόν.

---

[7] *weight* (ὄγκου). This is a Platonic word: it means the weight, and then (morally) the burden, of the body: *not* necessarily connected with the idea of swelling, even in Empedocles, v. 220; its Latin equivalent is "onus" in both meanings. Cf. Heb. xii. 1; ὄγκον ἀποθέμενοι πάντα, "every weight," or "all cumbrance."

[8] Reading διαστηματικήν. Cf. 239 A.

[9] ἀλλ' ἐν οἷς . . . ἐκεῖνο . . . τοῦτο.

[1] *pure* (ἀκηράτῳ). *perishable* (ἐπίκηρον). The first word is a favourite one with the Platonists; such as Plotinus, and Synesius. Gregory uses it in his funeral speech over Flacilla, "she passes with a soul unstained to the pure and perfect life"; and both in his treatise *De Mortuis*, "that man's grief is real, who becomes conscious of the blessings he has lost; and contrasts this perishing and soiled existence with the perfect blessedness above."

and that over the surface of the sea (for he seizes any bit that comes to hand, and lets all the rest drift away), in the same way the soul, being by nature incapable of dissolution along with the atoms, will, if she finds it hard to be parted from the body altogether, cling to some one of them ; and if we take this view, consistency will no more allow us to regard her as immortal for living in one atom than as mortal for not living in a number of them.

But the intelligent and undimensional, she replied, is neither contracted nor diffused [7] (contraction and diffusion being a property of body only) ; but by virtue of a nature which is formless and bodiless it is present with the body equally in the contraction and in the diffusion of its atoms, and is no more narrowed by the compression which attends the uniting of the atoms than it is abandoned by them when they wander off to their kindred, however wide the interval is held to be which we observe between alien atoms. For instance, there is a great difference between the buoyant and light as contrasted with the heavy and solid ; between the hot as contrasted with the cold ; between the humid as contrasted with its opposite ; nevertheless it is no strain to an intelligent essence to be present in each of those elements to which it has once cohered ; this blending with opposites does not split it up. In locality, in peculiar qualities, these elemental atoms are held to be far removed from each other ; but an undimensional nature finds it no labour to cling to what is locally divided, seeing that even now it is possible for the mind at once to contemplate the heavens above us and to extend its busy scrutiny beyond the horizon, nor is its contemplative power at all distracted by these excursions into distances so great. There is nothing, then, to hinder the soul's presence in the body's atoms, whether fused in union or decomposed in dissolution. Just as in the amalgam of gold and silver a certain methodical force is to be observed which has fused the metals, and if the one be afterwards smelted out of the other, the law of this method nevertheless continues to reside in each, so that while the amalgam is separated this method does not suffer division along with it (for you cannot make fractions out of the indivisible), in the same way this intelligent essence of the soul is observable in the concourse of the atoms, and does not undergo division when they are dissolved ; but it remains with them, and even in their separation it is co-extensive with them, yet

not itself dissevered nor discounted[8] into sections to accord with the number of the atoms. Such a condition belongs to the material and spacial world, but that which is intelligent and undimensional is not liable to the circumstances of space. Therefore the soul exists in the actual atoms which she has once animated, and there is no force to tear her away from her cohesion with them. What cause for melancholy, then, is there herein, that the visible is exchanged for the invisible ; and wherefore is it that your mind has conceived such a hatred of death?

Upon this I recurred to the definition which she had previously given of the soul, and I said that to my thinking her definition had not indicated[9] distinctly enough all the powers of the soul which are a matter of observation. It declares the soul to be an intellectual essence which imparts to the organic body a force of life by which the senses operate. Now the soul is not thus operative only in our scientific and speculative intellect ; it does not produce results in that world only, or employ the organs of sense only for this their natural work. On the contrary, we observe in our nature many emotions of desire and many of anger ; and both these exist in us as qualities of our kind, and we see both of them in their manifestations displaying further many most subtle differences. There are many states, for instance, which are occasioned by desire ; many others which on the other hand proceed from anger ; and none of them are of the body ; but that which is not of the body is plainly intellectual. Now [1] our definition exhibits the soul as something intellectual ; so that one of two alternatives, both absurd, must emerge when we follow out this

---

[8] κατακερματίζεται.
[9] ἐνδεδεῖχθαι. Gregory constantly uses ἐνδείκνυσθαι (middle) transitively, e. g. 202 C, 203 A, C, 208 B, and above, 189 A, so that it is possible that we have here, in the passive form, a deponent (transitive) perfect ; moreover the sense seems to require it. Gregory objects that in what has been said *all* the powers which analysis finds in the soul have not been set forth with sufficient fulness : an *exhaustive* account of them has not been given ; and he immediately proceeds to name other δυνάμεις and ἐνέργειαι which have not been taken into consideration. That this view of the passage is correct is further shown by 202 C, where, the present objection having been treated at length, it is concluded that there is no real ground for quarrelling with the definition of soul ὡς ἐλλειπῶς ἐνδειξαμένῃ τὴν φύσιν. Krabinger therefore is right in dropping ἐννοουμένῳ, which two of his MSS. exhibit, and which Sifanus translates as governing τὰς . . . δυνάμεις, as if the sense were, "When I consider all the powers of the soul, I do not think that your definition has been made good."
[1] The syllogism implied in the following words is this :—
The emotions are something intellectual (because incorporeal).
Therefore the emotions are soul (or souls).
This conclusion is obviously false ; logically, by reason of the fallacy of "the undistributed middle" ; ontologically, because it requires a false premise additional (*i. e.* "everything intellectual is soul") to make it true. Macrina directly after this piece of bad logic deprecates the use of the syllogism. Is this accidental? It looks almost like an excuse for not going into technicalities and exposing this fallacy, which she has detected in her opponent's statement. Macrina actually answers as if Gregory had urged his objection thus. "The emotions are not purely intellectual, but are conditioned by the bodily organism : but they do belong to the expression and the substance of the soul : the soul therefore is dependent on the organism and will perish along with it."

---

[7] οὔτε διαχεῖται. Oehler translates wrongly "noch dehnt es sich aus" ; because the faculty of *extension* is ascribed to the intelligence (cf. ἐκτείνεσθαι, διατεινόμενον, παρεκτεινομένη, below), but *diffusion* is denied of it, both here, and in the words διασχίζεται (above and below), διάκρισις, and διασπᾶται, *i. e.* separation in space.

view to this end; either anger and desire are both second souls in us, and a plurality of souls must take the place of the single soul, or the thinking faculty in us cannot be regarded as a soul either (if *they* are not), the intellectual element adhering equally to all of them and stamping them all as souls, or else excluding every one of them equally from the specific qualities of soul.

You are quite justified, she replied, in raising this question, and it has ere this been discussed by many elsewhere; namely, what we are to think of the principle of desire and the principle of anger within us. Are they consubstantial with the soul, inherent in the soul's very self from her first organization[2], or are they something different, accruing to us afterwards? In fact, while all equally allow that these principles are to be detected in the soul, investigation has not yet discovered exactly what we are to think of them so as to gain some fixed belief with regard to them. The generality of men still fluctuate in their opinions about this, which are as erroneous as they are numerous. As for ourselves, if the Gentile philosophy, which deals methodically with all these points, were really adequate for a demonstration, it would certainly be superfluous to add[3] a discussion on the soul to those speculations. But while the latter proceeded, on the subject of the soul, as far in the direction of supposed consequences as the thinker pleased, we are not entitled to such licence, I mean that of affirming what we please; we make the Holy Scriptures the rule and the measure of every tenet; we necessarily fix our eyes upon that, and approve that alone which may be made to harmonize with the intention of those writings. We must therefore neglect the Platonic chariot and the pair of horses of dissimilar forces yoked to it, and their driver, whereby the philosopher allegorizes these facts about the soul; we must neglect also all that is said by the philosopher who succeeded him and who followed out probabilities by rules of art[4], and diligently investigated the very question now before us, declaring that the soul was mortal[5] by reason of these two principles; we

must neglect all before and since their time, whether they philosophized in prose or in verse, and we will adopt, as the guide of our reasoning, the Scripture, which lays it down as an axiom that there is no excellence in the soul which is not a property as well of the Divine nature. For he who declares the soul to be God's likeness asserts that anything foreign to Him is outside the limits of the soul; similarity cannot be retained in those qualities which are diverse from the original. Since, then, nothing of the kind we are considering is included in the conception of the Divine nature, one would be reasonable in surmising that such things are not consubstantial with the soul either. Now to seek to build up our doctrine by rule of dialectic and the science which draws and destroys conclusions, involves a species of discussion which we shall ask to be excused from, as being a weak and questionable way of demonstrating truth. Indeed, it is clear to every one that that subtle dialectic possesses a force that may be turned both ways, as well for the overthrow of truth[6] as for the detection of falsehood; and so we begin to suspect even truth itself when it is advanced in company with such a kind of artifice, and to think that the very ingenuity of it is trying to bias our judgment and to upset the truth. If on the other hand any one will accept a discussion which is in a naked unsyllogistic form, we will speak upon these points by making our study of them so far as we can follow the chain[7] of Scriptural tradition. What is it, then, that we assert? We say that the fact of the reasoning animal man being capable of understanding and knowing is most surely[8] attested by those outside our faith; and that this definition would never have sketched our nature so, if it had viewed anger and desire and all such-like emotions as consubstantial with that nature. In any other case, one would not give a definition of the subject in hand by putting a generic instead of a specific quality; and so, as the principle of desire and the principle of anger are observed equally in rational and irrational natures, one could not

---

[2] παρὰ τὴν πρώτην (*i. e.* ὥραν understood). This is the reading of all the Codd. for the faulty παρὰ τὴν αὐτὴν of the Editions.

[3] προστιθέναι. Sifanus translates "illorum commentationi de animâ adjicere sermonem," which Krabinger wonders at. The Greek could certainly bear this meaning: but perhaps the other reading is better, *i. e.* προτιθέναι, "to propose for consideration."

[4] *i. e.* the syllogism.

[5] *that the soul was mortal.* Aristotle, guided only by probabilities as discoverable by the syllogism, does indeed define the soul, "*the first entelechy of a physical, potentially living, and organic body*." Entelechy is more than mere potentiality: it is "developed force" ("dormant activity;" see W. Archer Butler's *Lectures*, ii. p. 393), capable of manifestation. The human soul, uniting in itself all the faculties of the other orders of animate existence, is a Microcosm. The other parts of the soul are inseparable from the body, and are hence perishable (*De Animâ*, ii. 2); but the νοῦς exists before the body, into which it enters from without as something divine and immortal (*De Gen. Animal.* ii. 3). But he makes a distinction between the form-receiving, and the

form-giving νοῦς: substantial eternal existence belongs only to the latter (*De Animâ*, iii. 5). The secret of the difference between him and Plato, with whom "all the soul is immortal" (*Phædrus*, p. 245 C), lies in this; that Plato regarded the soul as always in motion, while Aristotle denied it, in itself, any motion at all. "It is one of the things that are impossible that motion should exist in it" (*De Animâ*, i. 4). It cannot be moved at all; therefore it cannot move itself. Plotinus and Porphyry, as well as Nemesius the Platonizing Bishop of Emesa (whose treatise *De Animâ* is wrongly attributed to Gregory), attacked this teaching of an "entelechy." Cf. also Justin Martyr (ad *Græc. cohort*, c. 6, p. 12); "Plato declares that all the soul is immortal; Aristotle calls her an 'entelechy,' and not immortal. The one says she is ever-moving, the other that she is never-moving, but prior to all motion." Also Gregory Naz., *Orat.* xxvii. "Away with Aristotle's calculating Providence, and his art of logic, and his dead reasonings about the soul, and purely human doctrine!"

[6] *for the overthrow of the truth.* So'c. Eunom. iii. (ii. 500).

[7] εἱρμόν.

[8] *most surely*, ᾗ. This is the common reading: but the Codd. have mostly καί.

rightly mark the specific quality by means of this generic one. But how can that which, in defining a nature, is superfluous and worthy of exclusion be treated as a part of that nature, and, so, available for falsifying the definition? Every definition of an essence looks to the specific quality of the subject in hand; and whatever is outside that speciality is set aside as having nothing to do with the required definition. Yet, beyond question, these faculties of anger and desire are allowed to be common to all reasoning and brute natures; anything common is not identical with that which is peculiar; it is imperative therefore that we should not range these faculties amongst those whereby humanity is exclusively meant: but just as one may perceive the principle[9] of sensation, and that of nutrition and growth in man, and yet not shake thereby the given definition of his soul (for the quality A being in the soul does not prevent the quality B being in it too), so, when one detects in humanity these emotions of anger and desire, one cannot on that account fairly quarrel with this definition, as if it fell short of a full indication of man's nature.

What then, I asked the Teacher, are we to think about this? For I cannot yet see how we can fitly repudiate faculties which are actually within us.

You see, she replied, there is a battle of the reason with them and a struggle to rid the soul of them; and there are men in whom this struggle has ended in success; it was so with Moses, as we know; he was superior both to anger and to desire; the history testifying of him in both respects, that he was meek beyond all men (and by meekness it indicates the absence of all anger and a mind quite devoid of resentment), and that he desired none of those things about which we see the desiring faculty in the generality so active. This could not have been so, if these faculties were nature, and were referable to the contents of man's essence[1]. For it is impossible for one who has come quite outside of his nature to be in Existence at all. But if Moses was at one and the same time in Existence and not in these conditions, then[2] it follows that these conditions are something other than nature and not nature itself. For if, on the one hand, that is truly nature in which the essence of the being is found, and, on the other,

the removal of these conditions is in our power, so that their removal not only does no harm, but is even beneficial to the nature, it is clear that these conditions are to be numbered amongst externals, and are affections, rather than the essence, of the nature; for the essence is that thing only which it is. As for anger, most think it a fermenting of the blood round the heart; others an eagerness to inflict pain in return for a previous pain; we would take it to be the impulse to hurt one who has provoked us. But none of these accounts of it tally with the definition of the soul. Again, if we were to define what desire is in itself, we should call it a seeking for that which is wanting, or a longing for pleasurable enjoyment, or a pain at not possessing that upon which the heart is set, or a state with regard to some pleasure which there is no opportunity of enjoying. These and such-like descriptions all indicate desire, but they have no connection with the definition of the soul. But it is so with regard to all those other conditions also which we see to have some relation to the soul, those, I mean, which are mutually opposed to each other, such as cowardice and courage, pleasure and pain, fear and contempt, and so on; each of them seems akin to the principle of desire or to that of anger, while they have a separate definition to mark their own peculiar nature. Courage and contempt, for instance, exhibit a certain phase of the irascible impulse; the dispositions arising from cowardice and fear exhibit on the other hand a diminution and weakening of that same impulse. Pain, again, draws its material both from anger and desire. For the impotence of anger, which consists in not being able to punish one who has first given pain, becomes itself pain; and the despair of getting objects of desire and the absence of things upon which the heart is set create in the mind this same sullen state. Moreover, the opposite to pain, I mean the sensation of pleasure[3], like pain, divides itself between anger and desire; for pleasure is the leading motive of them both. All these conditions, I say, have some relation to the soul, and yet they are not the soul[4], but only like warts growing out of the soul's thinking part, which are reckoned as parts of it because they adhere to it, and yet are not that actual thing which the soul is in its essence.

And yet, I rejoined to the virgin, we see no slight help afforded for improvement to the

---

9 Aristotle, *Ethic.* i. 13, dwells upon these principles. Of the last he says, *i. e.* the common vegetative, the principle of nutrition and growth: "One would assume such a power of the soul in everything that grows, even in the embryo, and just this very same power in the perfect creatures: for this is more likely than that it should be a different one." Sleep, in which this power almost alone is active, levels a[i]l.

1 οὐσία.

2 It is best to keep ἄρα: ἄρα is Krabinger's correction from four Codd.: and he reads ὁ for εἰ above: but only one class of Codd. support these alterations.

3 *I mean the sensation of pleasure.* This (νόημα) is Krabinger's reading: but Oehler reads from his Codd. νόσημα: and H. Schmidt suggests κίνημα, comparing (205 A) below, "any other such-like emotion of the soul."

4 *have some relation to the soul, and yet they are not the soul.* Macrina does not mean that the Passions are altogether severed from the soul, as the following shows: and so Oehler cannot be right in reading and translating "Das Alles hat nichts mit der Seele zu schaffen." The Greek περὶ τὴν ψυχὴν is to be parallelled by οἱ περὶ τὸν Περικλέα, "Pericles' belongings," or "party"; passing, in later Greek, almost into "Pericles himself."

virtuous from all these conditions. Daniel's desire was his glory; and Phineas' anger pleased the Deity. We have been told, too, that fear is the beginning of wisdom, and learnt from Paul that salvation is the goal of the "sorrow after a godly sort." The Gospel bids us have a contempt for danger; and the "not being afraid with any amazement" is nothing else but a describing of courage, and this last is numbered by Wisdom amongst the things that are good. In all this Scripture shows that such conditions are not to be considered weaknesses; weaknesses would not have been so employed for putting virtue into practice.

I think, replied the Teacher, that I am myself responsible for this confusion arising from different accounts of the matter; for I did not state it as distinctly as I might have, by introducing a certain order of consequences for our consideration. Now, however, some such order shall, as far as it is possible, be devised, so that our essay may advance in the way of logical sequence and so give no room for such contradictions. We declare, then, that the speculative, critical, and world-surveying faculty of the soul is its peculiar property by virtue of its very nature [5], and that thereby the soul preserves within itself the image of the divine grace; since our reason surmises that divinity itself, whatever it may be in its inmost nature, is manifested in these very things,—universal supervision and the critical discernment between good and evil. But all those elements of the soul which lie on the border-land [6] and are capable from their peculiar nature of inclining to either of two opposites (whose eventual determination to the good or to the bad depends on the kind of use they are put to), anger, for instance, and fear, and any other such-like emotion of the soul divested of which human nature [7] cannot be studied—all these we reckon as accretions from without, because in the Beauty which is man's prototype no such characteristics are to be found. Now let the following statement [8] be offered

as a mere exercise (in interpretation). I pray that it may escape the sneers of cavilling hearers. Scripture informs us that the Deity proceeded by a sort of graduated and ordered advance to the creation of man. After the foundations of the universe were laid, as the history records, man did not appear on the earth at once; but the creation of the brutes preceded his, and the plants preceded them. Thereby Scripture shows that the vital forces blended with the world of matter according to a gradation; first, it infused itself into insensate nature; and in continuation of this advanced into the sentient world; and then ascended to intelligent and rational beings. Accordingly, while all existing things must be either corporeal or spiritual, the former are divided into the animate and inanimate. By animate, I mean possessed of life: and of the things possessed of life, some have it with sensation, the rest have no sensation. Again, of these sentient things, some have reason, the rest have not. Seeing, then, that this life of sensation could not possibly exist apart from the matter which is the subject of it, and the intellectual life could not be embodied, either, without growing in the sentient, on this account the creation of man is related as coming last, as of one who took up into himself every single form of life, both that of plants and that which is seen in brutes. His nourishment and growth he derives from vegetable life; for even in vegetables such processes are to be seen when aliment is being drawn in by their roots and given off in fruit and leaves. His sentient organization he derives from the brute creation. But his faculty of thought and reason is incommunicable [9], and is a peculiar gift in our nature, to be considered by itself. However, just as this nature has the instinct acquisitive of the necessaries to material existence—an instinct which, when manifested in us men, we call Appetite—and as we admit this appertains to the vegetable form of life, since we can notice it there too like so many impulses working naturally to satisfy themselves with their kindred aliment and to issue in germination, so all the peculiar conditions of the brute creation are blended with the intellectual part of the soul. To them, she continued, belongs anger; to them belongs fear; to them all those other opposing activities within us;

---

[5] Reading κατὰ φύσιν αὐτήν, καὶ τῆς θεοειδοῦς χάριτος, κ. τ. λ. with Sifanus.

[6] ὅσα δὲ τῆς ψυχῆς ἐν μεθορίῳ κεῖται. Möller (*Gregorii Nysseni doctrina de hominis naturâ*) remarks rightly that Krabinger's translation is here incorrect: "quæcunque autem in animæ confinio posita sunt"; and that τῆς ψυχῆς should on the contrary be joined closely to ὅσα. The opposition is not between elements which lie in, and on the confines of, the soul, but between the divine and adventitious elements *within* the soul: μεθορίῳ refers therefore to "good and bad," below.

[7] This is no contradiction of the passage above about Moses: there it was stated that the Passions did not belong to the *essence* (οὐσία) of man.

[8] ὅδε δή. The Teacher introduces this λόγος with some reserve. "We do not lay it down ex cathedrâ, we put it forward as open to challenge and discussion as we might do in the schools (ὡς ἐν γυμνασίῳ)." It is best then to take διαφύγοι as a pure optative. Gregory appears in his answer to congratulate her on the success of this "exercise." "To any one that reflects . . . your exposition . . . bears sufficiently upon it the stamp of correctness, and hits the truth." But he immediately asks for Scripture authority. So that this λόγος, though it refers to Genesis, is not yet based upon Scripture. It is a "consecutive" and consistent account of human nature: but it is virtually identical with that advanced at the end of

Book I. of Aristotle's *Ethics*. It is a piece of secular theorizing. The sneers of cavillers may well be deprecated. Consistent, however, with this view of the λόγος here offered by Macrina, there is another possible meaning in ὡς ἐν γυμνασίῳ, κ. τ. λ., *i.e.* "Let us put forward the following account with all possible care and circumspection, as if we were disputing in the schools; so that cavillers may have nothing to find fault with": ὡς ἂν expressing purpose, not a wish. The cavillers will thus refer to sticklers for Greek method and metaphysics: and Gregory's congratulation of his sister's lucidity and grasp of the truth will be all the more significant.

[9] Following the order and stopping of Krabinger, ἄμικτόν ἐστι καὶ ἰδιάζον ἐπὶ ταύτης τῆς φύσεως, ἐφ᾽ ἑαυτοῦ, κ. τ. λ.

everything except the faculty of reason and thought. That alone, the choice product, as has been said, of all our life, bears the stamp of the Divine character. But since, according to the view which we have just enunciated, it is not possible for this reasoning faculty to exist in the life of the body without existing by means of sensations, and since sensation is already found subsisting in the brute creation, necessarily as it were, by reason of this one condition, our soul has touch with the other things which are knit up with it[1]; and these are all those phænomena within us that we call "passions"; which have not been allotted to human nature for any bad purpose at all (for the Creator would most certainly be the author of evil, if in *them*, so deeply rooted as they are in our nature, any necessities of wrong-doing were found), but according to the use which our free will puts them to, these emotions of the soul become the instruments of virtue or of vice. They are like the iron which is being fashioned according to the volition of the artificer, and receives whatever shape the idea which is in his mind prescribes, and becomes a sword or some agricultural implement. Supposing, then, that our reason, which is our nature's choicest part, holds the dominion over these imported emotions (as Scripture allegorically declares in the command to men to rule over the brutes), none of them will be active in the ministry of evil; fear will only generate within us obedience[2], and anger fortitude, and cowardice caution; and the instinct of desire will procure for us the delight that is Divine and perfect. But if reason drops the reins and is dragged behind like a charioteer who has got entangled in his car, then these instincts are changed into fierceness, just as we see happens amongst the brutes. For since reason does not preside over the natural impulses that are implanted[3] in them, the more irascible animals, under the generalship of their anger, mutually destroy each other; while the bulky and powerful animals get no good themselves from their strength, but become by their want of reason slaves of that which has reason. Neither are the activities of their desire for pleasure employed on any of the higher objects; nor does any other instinct to be observed in them result in any profit to themselves. Thus too, with ourselves, if these instincts are not turned by reasoning into the right direction, and if our feelings get the mastery of our mind, the man is changed from a reasoning into an unreasoning being, and from godlike intelligence sinks by the force of these passions to the level of the brute.

Much moved by these words, I said : To any one who reflects indeed, your exposition, advancing as it does in this consecutive manner, though plain and unvarnished, bears sufficiently upon it the stamp of correctness and hits the truth. And to those who are expert only in the technical methods of proof a mere demonstration suffices to convince ; but as for ourselves, we were agreed[4] that there is something more trustworthy than any of these artificial conclusions, namely, that which the teachings of Holy Scripture point to: and so I deem that it is necessary to inquire, in addition to what has been said, whether this inspired teaching harmonizes with it all.

And who, she replied, could deny that truth is to be found only in that upon which the seal of Scriptural testimony is set? So, if it is necessary that something from the Gospels should be adduced in support of our view, a study of the Parable of the Wheat and Tares will not be here out of place. The Householder there sowed good seed; (and we are plainly the "house"). But the "enemy," having watched for the time when men slept, sowed that which was useless in that which was good for food, setting the tares in the very middle of the wheat. The two kinds of seed grew up together ; for it was not possible that seed put into the very middle of the wheat should fail to grow up with it. But the Superintendent of the field forbids the servants to gather up the useless crop, on account of their growing at the very root of the contrary sort; so as not to root up[5] the nutritious along with that foreign growth. Now we think that Scripture means by the good seed the corresponding impulses of the soul, each one of which, if only they are cultured for good, necessarily puts forth the fruit of virtue within us. But since there has been scattered[6] amongst these the bad seed of the error of judgment as to the true Beauty which is alone in its intrinsic nature such, and since this last has been thrown into the shade by the growth of delusion which springs up along with it (for the active principle

---

[1] Reading διὰ τοῦ ἑνὸς καὶ πρὸς τὰ συνημμένα τούτῳ (for τούτων), with Sifanus.

[2] Cf. *De Hom. Opif.* c. xviii. 5. "So, on the contrary, if reason instead assumes sway over such emotions, each of them is transmuted to a form of virtue : for anger produces courage ; terror, caution ; fear, obedience ; hatred, aversion from vice ; the power of love, the desire for what is truly beautiful, &c." Just below, the allusion is to Plato's charioteer, *Phædrus*, p. 253 C, and the old custom of having the reins round the driver's waist is to be noticed.

[3] *are implanted.* All the Codd. have ἐγκειμένης here, instead of the ἐγκωμιαζομένης of the Paris Edition, which must be meant for ἐγκωμαζομένης (itself a vox nihili), "run riot in them."

[4] *we were agreed.* ὡμολογεῖτο : cf. 201 D, "If on the other hand any one will accept a discussion which is in a naked unsyllogistic form, we will speak upon these points by making our study of them as far as we can follow the chain of Scriptural tradition."

[5] There is a variety of readings from the Codd. here ; συνεγκαταλείη, συνεκτάλῃ, συνεκταλείη, συνεκταλαίη, συγκαταλύη in two (and on the margins of two others), συνεκτίλῃ, which Krabinger has adopted. The Paris Editt. have συνεκτίνει.

[6] παρενεσπάρη, the idea of badness being contained in παρά, which in such cases is always the first compound. One Cod. has the curious inversion ἐνπαρεσπάρη.

of desire does not germinate and increase in the direction of that natural Beauty which was the object of its being sown in us, but it has changed its growth so as to move towards a bestial and unthinking state, this very error as to Beauty carrying its impulse towards this result ; and in the same way the seed of anger does not steel us to be brave, but only arms us to fight with our own people ; and the power of loving deserts its intellectual objects and becomes completely mad for the immoderate enjoyment of pleasures of sense ; and so in like manner our other affections put forth the worse instead of the better growths),—on account of this the wise Husbandman leaves this growth that has been introduced amongst his seed to remain there, so as to secure our not being altogether stripped of better hopes by desire having been rooted out along with that good-for-nothing growth. If our nature suffered such a mutilation, what will there be to lift us up to grasp the heavenly delights ? If love is taken from us, how shall we be united to God ? If anger is to be extinguished, what arms shall we possess against the adversary ?   Therefore the Husbandman leaves those bastard seeds within us, not for them always to overwhelm the more precious crop, but in order that the land itself (for so, in his allegory, he calls the heart) by its native inherent power, which is that of reasoning, may wither up the one growth and may render the other fruitful and abundant : but if that is not done, then he commissions the fire to mark the distinction in the crops. If, then, a man indulges these affections in a due proportion and holds them in his own power instead of being held in theirs, employing them for an instrument as a king does his subjects' many hands, then efforts towards excellence more easily succeed for him. But should he become theirs, and, as when any slaves mutiny against their master, get enslaved[7] by those slavish thoughts and ignominiously bow before them, a prey to his natural inferiors, he will be forced to turn to those employments which his imperious masters command. This being so, we shall not pronounce these emotions of the soul, which lie in the power of their possessors for good or ill, to be either virtue or vice. But, whenever their impulse is towards what is noble, then they become matter for praise, as his desire did to Daniel, and his anger to Phineas, and their grief to those who nobly mourn. But if they incline to baseness, then these are, and they are called, bad passions.

She ceased after this statement and allowed the discussion a short interval, in which I reviewed mentally all that had been said ; and reverting to that former course of proof in

her discourse, that it was not impossible that the soul after the body's dissolution should reside in its atoms, I again addressed her. Where is that much-talked-of and renowned Hades[8], then ?   The word is in frequent circulation both in the intercourse of daily life, and in the writings of the heathens and in our own ; and all think that into it, as into a place of safe-keeping, souls migrate from here. Surely you would not call your atoms that Hades.

Clearly, replied the ·Teacher, you have not quite attended to the argument.   In speaking of the soul's migration from the seen to the unseen, I thought I had omitted nothing as regards the question about Hades.   It seems to me that, whether in the heathen or in the Divine writings, this word for a place in which souls are said to be means nothing else but a transition to that Unseen world of which we have no glimpse.

And how, then, I asked, is it that some think that by the underworld[9] is meant an actual place, and that it harbours within itself[1] the souls that have at last flitted away from human life, drawing them towards itself as the right receptacle for such natures ?

Well, replied the Teacher, our doctrine will be in no ways injured by such a supposition. For if it *is* true, what you say[2], and also that the vault of heaven prolongs itself so uninterruptedly that it encircles all things with itself, and that the earth and its surroundings are poised in the middle, and that the motion of all the revolving bodies[3] is round this fixed and solid centre, then, I say, there is an absolute necessity that, whatever may happen to each one of the atoms on the upper side of the earth, the same will happen on the opposite side, seeing that one single substance encompasses its entire bulk.   As, when the sun shines *above* the earth, the shadow is spread over its lower part, because its spherical shape makes it impossible for it to be clasped all round at one and the same time by the rays, and necessarily, on whatever side the sun's rays may fall on some particular point of the globe, if we follow a straight diameter, we shall find shadow upon the opposite point, and so, continuously, at the opposite end of the direct line of the rays

---

7 ἐξανδραποδισθείη ; this is adopted by Krabinger from the Haselman Cod. for the common ἐξ ὧν δραποδισθείη.

8 ᾅδου ὄνομα.   9 τὸν ὑποχθόνιον.
1 κἀκεῖνον ἐν αὐτῷ, H. Schmidt's reading, on the authority of 3 Codd.   The reading of Krabinger is ἐν ἑαυτῷ τε κἀκεῖνον.   But the underworld is the *only* habitation in question.—οὕτω λέγεσθαι, above, must mean, " is rightly so named."
2 εἰ γὰρ ἀληθὴς ὁ λόγος ὁ κατὰ σέ, καὶ τὸ συνεχῆ τε πρὸς, κ. τ. λ., Krabinger's reading, following the majority of Codd. ; ὁ κατὰ σέ being thus opposed to the next words, which others say.   But Schmidt points out that the conclusion introduced below by ἀνάγκη πᾶσα does not follow at all from the first, but only from the second of these suppositions, and he would await the evidence of fresh Codd. Sifanus and Augentius would read εἰ καὶ . . . κατὰ σέ.   Τῷ γὰρ, κ.τ.λ., which would certainly express the sense required.
3 πάντων τῶν κυκλοφορουμένων, *i. e.* the heavenly bodies moving as one (according to the ancient astronomy) round the central earth.

shadow moves round that globe, keeping pace with the sun, so that equally in their turn both the upper half and the under half of the earth are in light and darkness; so, by this analogy, we have reason to be certain that, whatever in our hemisphere is observed to befall the atoms, the same will befall them in that other. The environment of the atoms being one and the same on every side of the earth, I deem it right neither to contradict nor yet to favour those who raise the objection that we must regard either this or the lower region as assigned to the souls released. As long as this objection does not shake our central doctrine of the existence of those souls after the life in the flesh, there need be no controversy about the whereabouts, to our mind, holding as we do that place is a property of body only, and that soul, being immaterial, is by no necessity of its nature detained in any place.

But what, I asked, if your opponent should shield himself[4] behind the Apostle, where he says that every reasoning creature, in the restitution of all things, is to look towards Him Who presides over the whole? In that passage in the Epistle to the Philippians[5] he makes mention of certain things that are "under the earth"; "every knee shall bow" to Him "of things in heaven, and things in earth, and things under the earth."

We shall stand by our doctrine, answered the Teacher, even if we should hear them adducing these words. For the existence of the soul (after death) we have the assent of our opponent, and so we do not make an objection as to the place, as we have just said.

But if some were to ask the meaning of the Apostle in this utterance, what is one to say? Would you remove all signification of place from the passage?

I do not think, she replied, that the divine Apostle divided the intellectual world into localities, when he named part as in heaven, part as on earth, and part as under the earth. There are three states in which reasoning creatures can be: one from the very first received an immaterial life, and we call it the angelic: another is in union with the flesh, and we call it the human: a third is released by death from fleshly entanglements, and is to be found in souls pure and simple. Now I think that the divine Apostle in his deep wisdom looked to this, when he revealed the future concord of all these reasoning beings in the work of goodness; and that he puts the unembodied angel-world "in heaven," and that still involved with a body "on earth," and that released from a

body "under the earth"; or, indeed, if there is any other world to be classed under that which is possessed of reason (it is not left out); and whether any one choose to call this last "demons" or "spirits," or anything else of the kind, we shall not care. We certainly believe, both because of the prevailing opinion, and still more of Scripture teaching, that there exists another world of beings besides, divested of such bodies as ours are, who are opposed to that which is good and are capable of hurting the lives of men, having by an act of will lapsed from the nobler view[6], and by this revolt from goodness personified in themselves the contrary principle; and this world is what, some say, the Apostle adds to the number of the "things under the earth," signifying in that passage that when evil shall have been some day annihilated in the long revolutions of the ages, nothing shall be left outside the world of goodness, but that even from those evil spirits[7] shall rise in harmony the confession of Christ's Lordship. If this is so, then no one can compel us to see any spot of the underworld in the expression, "things under the earth"; the atmosphere spreads equally over every part of the earth, and there is not a single corner of it left unrobed by this circumambient air.

When she had finished, I hesitated a moment, and then said: I am not yet satisfied about the thing which we have been inquiring into; after all that has been said my mind is still in doubt; and I beg that our discussion may be allowed to revert to the same line of reasoning as before[8], omitting only that upon which we are thoroughly agreed. I say this, for I think that all but the most stubborn controversialists will

---

[6] *lapsed from 'he nobler view* (ὑπολήψεως). This is the common reading: but Krabinger prefers λήξεως, which is used by Gregory (*De Hom. Opif.* c. 17, "the sublime angelic lot "), and is a Platonic word. The other word, "lapsed," is also Platonic.

[7] *from those evil spirits.* So *Great Catechism,* c. 26 (fin.). Here too Gregory follows Origen (*c. Cels.* vi. 44), who declares that the Powers of evil are for a purpose (in answer to Celsus' objection that the Devil himself, instead of humanity, ought to have been punished). "Now it is a thing which can in no way cause surprise, that the Almighty, Who knows how to use wicked apostates for His own purposes, should assign to such a certain place in the universe, and should thus open an arena, as it were, of virtue, for those to contend in who wish to "strive lawfully" for her prize: those wicked ones were to try them, as the fire tries the gold, that, having done their utmost to prevent the admission of any alloy into their spiritual nature, and having proved themselves worthy to mount to heaven, they might be drawn by the bands of the Word to the highest blessedness and the summit of all Good." These Powers, as reasoning beings, shall then themselves be "mastered by the Word." See *c. Cels.* viii. 72.

[8] The conclusion of which was drawn, 199 C. "Therefore the soul exists in the actual atoms which she has once animated, and there is no force to tear her away from her cohesion with them." It is to the line of reasoning (ἀκολουθία) leading up to this conclusion that Gregory would revert, in order to question this conclusion. What both sides are agreed on is, the existence merely of the soul after death. All between this conclusion and the present break in the discussion has been a digression on the Passions and on Hades. Now Gregory asks, how can the soul possibly recognize the atoms that once belonged to her? Oehler therefore does not translate aright, "ich bitte nur den geführten Beweis . . . in derselben Folge zu wiederholen:" but Krabinger expresses the true sense, "ut rursus mihi ad eandem consequentiam reducatur oratio," *i. e.* the discussion (not the proof), which is here again, almost in Platonic fashion, personified.

---

[4] προβάλλοιτο. This is the proper meaning of the middle: "should object," as Oehler translates (einwerfen wollte), would require the active.   [5] Philip. ii. 10.

have been sufficiently convinced by our debate not to consign the soul after the body's dissolution to annihilation and nonentity, nor to argue that because it differs substantially from the atoms it is impossible for it to exist anywhere in the universe; for, however much a being that is intellectual and immaterial may fail to coincide with these atoms, it is in no ways hindered (so far) from existing in them; and this belief of ours rests on two facts: firstly, on the soul's existing in our bodies in this present life, though fundamentally different from them: and secondly, on the fact that the Divine being, as our argument has shown, though distinctly something other than visible and material substances, nevertheless pervades each one amongst all existences, and by this penetration of the whole keeps the world in a state of being; so that following these analogies we need not think that the soul, either, is out of existence, when she passes from the world of forms to the Unseen. But how, I insisted, after the united whole of the atoms has assumed[9], owing to their mixing together, a form quite different—the form in fact with which the soul has been actually domesticated—by what mark, when this form, as we should have expected, is effaced along with the resolution of the atoms, shall the soul follow along (them), now that that familiar form ceases to persist?

She waited a moment and then said: Give me leave to invent a fanciful simile in order to illustrate the matter before us: even though that which I suppose may be outside the range of possibility. Grant it possible, then, in the art of painting not only to mix opposite colours, as painters are always doing, to represent a particular tint[1], but also to separate again this mixture and to restore to each of the colours its natural dye. If then white, or black, or red, or golden colour, or any other colour that has been mixed to form the given tint, were to be again separated from that union with another and remain by itself, we suppose that our artist will none the less remember the actual nature of that colour, and that in no case will he show forgetfulness, either of the red, for instance, or the black, if after having become quite a differ-

ent colour by composition with each other they each return to their natural dye. We suppose, I say, that our artist remembers the manner of the mutual blending of these colours, and so knows what sort of colour was mixed with a given colour and what sort of colour was the result, and how, the other colour being ejected from the composition, (the original colour) in consequence of such release resumed its own peculiar hue; and, supposing it were required to produce the same result again by composition, the process will be all the easier from having been already practised in his previous work. Now, if reason can see any analogy in this simile, we must search the matter in hand by its light. Let the soul stand for this Art of the painter[2]; and let the natural atoms stand for the colours of his art; and let the mixture of that tint compounded of the various dyes, and the return of these to their native state (which we have been allowed to assume), represent respectively the concourse, and the separation of the atoms. Then, as we assume in the simile that the painter's Art tells him the actual dye of each colour, when it has returned after mixing to its proper hue, so that he has an exact knowledge of the red, and of the black, and of any other colour that went to form the required tint by a specific way of uniting with another kind—a knowledge which includes its appearance both in the mixture, and now when it is in its natural state, and in the future again, supposing all the colours were mixed over again in like fashion—so, we assert, does the soul know the natural peculiarities of those atoms whose concourse makes the frame of the body in which it has itself grown, even after the scattering of those atoms. However far from each other their natural propensity and their inherent forces of repulsion urge them, and debar each from mingling with its opposite, none the less will the soul be near each by its power of recognition, and will persistently cling to the familiar atoms, until their concourse after this division again takes place in the same way, for that fresh formation of the dissolved body which will properly be, and be called, resurrection.

You seem, I interrupted, in this passing remark to have made an excellent defence of the faith in the Resurrection. By it, I think, the opponents of this doctrine might be gradually led to consider it not as a thing absolutely impossible that the atoms should again coalesce and form the same man as before.

That is very true, the Teacher replied. For we may hear these opponents urging the following difficulty. "The atoms are resolved, like

9 *has assumed*, ἀναλαβόντων. The construction is accommodated to the sense, not the words; τῆς τῶν στοιχείων ἐνώσεως having preceded.

1 *tint*, μορφῆς. Certainly in earlier Greek μορφή is strictly used of "form," "shape" (or the beauty of it) only, and colours cannot be said to be mixed in imitation of form. It seems we have here a late use of μορφή as = "outward appearance"; so that we may even speak of the μορφή of a colour, or combinations of colours. So (214 A) the painter "works up (on his palette) a particular tint of colour" (μορφήν). Here it is the particular hue, in person or picture, which it is desired to imitate. Akin to this question is that of the proper translation of πρὸς τὴν ὁμοιότητα τοῦ προκειμένου, which Sifanus and Krabinger translate "ad similitudinem *argumenti*," and which may either mean (1) "to make the analogy to the subject matter of our question as perfect as possible," *i. e.* as a parenthesis. or (2) "in imitation of the thing or colour (lying before the painter) to be copied." The last seems preferable ("to form the given tint").

2 γραφικῆς τέχνης.

to like, into the universe; by what device, then, does the warmth, for instance, residing in such and such a man, after joining the universal warmth, again dissociate itself from this connection with its kindred [3], so as to form this man who is being 'remoulded'? For if the identical individual particle does not return and only something that is homogeneous but not identical is fetched, you will have something else in the place of that first thing, and such a process will cease to be a resurrection and will be merely the creation of a new man. But if the same man is to return into himself, he must be the same entirely, and regain his original formation in every single atom of his elements."

Then to meet such an objection, I rejoined, the above opinion about the soul will, as I said, avail; namely, that she remains after dissolution in those very atoms in which she first grew up, and, like a guardian placed over private property, does not abandon them when they are mingled with their kindred atoms, and by the subtle ubiquity of her intelligence makes no mistake about them, with all their subtle minuteness, but diffuses herself along with those which belong to herself when they are being mingled with their kindred dust, and suffers no exhaustion in keeping up with the whole number of them when they stream back into the universe, but remains with them, no matter in what direction or in what fashion Nature may arrange them. But should the signal be given by the All-disposing Power for these scattered atoms to combine again, then, just as when every one of the various ropes that hang from one block answer at one and the same moment [4] to the pull from that centre, so, following this force of the soul which acts upon the various atoms, all these, once so familiar with each other, rush simultaneously together and form the cable of the body by means of the soul, each single one of them being wedded to its former neighbour and embracing an old acquaintance.

The following illustration also, the Teacher went on, might be very properly added to those already brought forward, to show that the soul has not need of much teaching in order to distinguish its own from the alien amongst the atoms. Imagine a potter with a supply of clay; and let the supply be a large one; and let part of it have been already moulded to form finished vessels, while the rest is still waiting to be moulded; and suppose the vessels themselves not to be all of similar shape, but one to be a jug, for instance, and another a wine-jar, another a plate, another a cup or any other useful vessel; and further, let not one owner possess them all, but let us fancy for each a special owner. Now as long as these vessels are unbroken they are of course recognizable by their owners, and none the less so, even should they be broken in pieces; for from those pieces each will know, for instance, that this belongs to a jar [5], and, again, what sort of fragment belongs to a cup. And if they are plunged again into the unworked clay, the discernment between what has been already worked and that clay will be a more unerring one still. The individual man is as such a vessel; he has been moulded out of the universal matter, owing to the concourse of his atoms; and he exhibits in a form peculiarly his own a marked distinction from his kind; and when that form has gone to pieces the soul that has been mistress of this particular vessel will have an exact knowledge of it, derived even from its fragments; nor will she leave this property, either, in the common blending with all the other fragments, or if it be plunged into the still formless part of the matter from which the atoms have come [6]; she always remembers her own as it was when compact in bodily form, and after dissolution she never makes any mistake about it, led by marks still clinging to the remains.

I applauded this as well devised to bring out the natural features of the case before us; and I said: It is very well to speak like this and to believe that it is so; but suppose some one were to quote against it our Lord's narrative about those who are in hell, as not harmonizing with the results of our inquiry, how are we to be prepared with an answer?

The Teacher answered: The expressions of that narrative of the Word are certainly material; but still many hints are interspersed in it to rouse the skilled inquirer to a more discriminating study of it. I mean that He Who parts the good from the bad by a great gulf, and makes the man in torment crave for a drop to be conveyed by a finger, and the man who has been ill-treated in this life rest on a patriarch's bosom, and Who relates their previous death and consignment to the tomb, takes an intelligent searcher of His meaning far beyond a superficial interpretation. For what sort of eyes has the

---

3 ἀμιγὲς τοῦ συγγενοῦς πάλιν ἀποκριθῆναι. Krabinger's and Oehler's reading. But Krabinger, more correctly than Oehler, opposes ἐν τῷ δε to ἐν τῷ καθ' ὅλου (quod est hic calidum, si fuerit in universo): though neither he, nor Oehler, nor Schmidt himself appears to have any suspicion that τῷδε may mean "so and so": and yet it is quite in accordance with Gregory's usage, and makes better sense, as contrasting the particular and universal heat more completely. Ἀμιγὲς is proleptic: the genitive may depend either on it or on the verb. Just below ἀναπλασσόμενον is read by 5 of Krabinger's Codd. (including the Hasselmann). This is better than Migne's ἀπαλλασσόμενον, which is hardly supported by 1 Cor. xv. 51.

4 same moment. κατὰ ταὐτὸν : on the authority of 2 Codd. Mon.

5 Reading ὅτι τὸ μὲν τὸ ἐκ τοῦ πίθου, ποῖον δὲ τὸ ἐκ τοῦ ποτηρίου, κ.τ.λ.

6 πρὸς τὸ ἀκατέργαστον τῆς τῶν στοιχείων ὕλης. There is the same sort of distinction above, 215 A, i. e. between the kindred dust first, and then the universe (τὸ πᾶν) into which the atoms may stream back.

Rich Man to lift up in hell, when he has left his bodily eyes in that tomb? And how can a disembodied spirit feel any flame? And what sort of tongue can he crave to be cooled with the drop of water, when he has lost his tongue of flesh? What is the finger that is to convey to him this drop? What sort of place is the "bosom" of repose? The bodies of both of them are in the tomb, and their souls are disembodied, and do not consist of parts either; and so it is impossible to make the framework of the narrative correspond with the truth, if we understand it literally; we can do that only by translating each detail into an equivalent in the world of ideas. Thus we must think of the gulf as that which parts ideas which may not be confounded from running together, not as a chasm of the earth. Such a chasm, however vast it were, could be traversed with no difficulty by a disembodied intelligence; since intelligence can in no time [7] be wherever it will.

What then, I asked, *are* the fire and the gulf and the other features in the picture? Are they not that which they are said to be?

I think, she replied, that the Gospel signifies by means of each of them certain doctrines with regard to our question of the soul. For when the patriarch first says to the Rich Man, "Thou in thy lifetime receivedst thy good things," and in the same way speaks of the Poor Man, that he, namely, has done his duty in bearing his share of life's evil things, and then, after that, adds with regard to the gulf that it is a barrier between them, he evidently by such expressions intimates a very important truth; and, to my thinking, it is as follows. Once man's life had but one character; and by that I mean that it was to be found only in the category of the good and had no contact with evil. The first of God's commandments attests the truth of this; that, namely, which gave to man unstinted enjoyment of all the blessings of Paradise, forbidding only that which was a mixture of good and evil and so composed of contraries, but making death the penalty for transgressing in that particular. But man, acting freely by a voluntary impulse, deserted the lot that was unmixed with evil, and drew upon himself that which was a mixture of contraries. Yet Divine Providence did not leave that recklessness of ours without a corrective. Death indeed, as the fixed penalty for breaking the law, necessarily fell upon its transgressors; but God divided the life of man into two parts, namely, this present life, and that "out of the body" hereafter; and He placed on the first a limit of the briefest possible time, while He prolonged the other into eternity; and in His love

for man He gave him his choice, to have the one or the other of those things, good or evil, I mean, in which of the two parts he liked: either in this short and transitory life, or in those endless ages, whose limit is infinity. Now these expressions "good" and "evil" are equivocal; they are used in two senses, one relating to mind and the other to sense; some classify as good whatever is pleasant to feeling: others are confident that only that which is perceptible by intelligence is good and deserves that name. Those, then, whose reasoning powers have never been exercised and who have never had a glimpse of the better way soon use up on gluttony in this fleshly life the dividend of good which their constitution can claim, and they reserve none of it for the after life; but those who by a discreet and sober-minded calculation economize the powers of living are afflicted by things painful to sense here, but they reserve their good for the succeeding life, and so their happier lot is lengthened out to last as long as that eternal life. This, in my opinion, is the "gulf"; which is not made by the parting of the earth, but by those decisions in this life which result in a separation into opposite characters. The man who has once chosen pleasure in this life, and has not cured his inconsiderateness by repentance, places the land of the good beyond his own reach; for he has dug against himself the yawning impassable abyss of a necessity that nothing can break through. This is the reason, I think, that the name of Abraham's bosom is given to that good situation of the soul in which Scripture makes the athlete of endurance repose. For it is related of this patriarch first, of all up to that time born, that he exchanged the enjoyment of the present for the hope of the future; he was stripped of all the surroundings in which his life at first was passed, and resided amongst foreigners, and thus purchased by present annoyance future blessedness. As then figuratively [8] we call a particular circuit of the ocean a "bosom," so does Scripture seem to me to express the idea of those measureless blessings above by the word "bosom," meaning a place into which all virtuous voyagers of this life are, when they have put in from hence, brought to anchor in the waveless harbour of that gulf of blessings [9]. Meanwhile the denial of these blessings which they witness becomes in the others a flame, which burns the soul and causes the craving for the refreshment of one drop out of that ocean of blessings wherein the saints are affluent; which nevertheless they do not get. If, too,

---

[7] ἀχρόνως.

[8] ἐκ καταχρήσεώς τινος : not, as usually, "by a misuse of words."
[9] There is an anacoluthon here, for τῷ ἀγάθῳ κόλπῳ follows ᾧ above; designed no doubt to bring the things compared more closely together. Oehler, however, would join ἀγάθῳ with the relative, and translates as if τῷ = καί.

you consider the "tongue," and the "eye," and the "finger," and the other names of bodily organs, which occur in the conversation between those disembodied souls, you will be persuaded that this conjecture of ours about them chimes in with the opinion we have already stated about the soul. Look closely into the meaning of those words. For as the concourse of atoms forms the substance of the entire body, so it is reasonable to think that the same cause operates to complete the substance of each member of the body. If, then, the soul is present with the atoms of the body when they are again mingled with the universe, it will not only be cognizant of the entire mass which once came together to form the whole body, and will be present with it, but, besides that, will not fail to know the particular materials of each one of the members, so as to remember by what divisions amongst the atoms our limbs were completely formed. There is, then, nothing improbable in supposing that what is present in the complete mass is present also in each division of the mass. If one, then, thinks of those atoms in which each detail of the body potentially inheres, and surmises that Scripture means a "finger" and a "tongue" and an "eye" and the rest as existing, after dissolution, only in the sphere of the soul, one will not miss the probable truth. Moreover, if each detail carries the mind away from a material acceptation of the story, surely the "hell" which we have just been speaking of cannot reasonably be thought a place so named; rather we are there told by Scripture about a certain unseen and immaterial situation in which the soul resides. In this story of the Rich and the Poor Man we are taught another doctrine also, which is intimately connected with our former discoveries. The story makes the sensual pleasure-loving man, when he sees that his own case is one that admits of no escape, evince forethought for his relations on earth; and when Abraham tells him that the life of those still in the flesh is not unprovided with a guidance, for they may find it at hand, if they will, in the Law and the Prophets, he still continues entreating that Just [1] Patriarch, and asks that a sudden and convincing message, brought by some one risen from the dead, may be sent to them.

What then, I asked, is the doctrine here?

Why, seeing that Lazarus' soul is occupied [2] with his present blessings and turns round to look at nothing that he has left, while the rich man is still attached, with a cement as it were, even after death, to the life of feeling, which he does not divest himself of even when he has

ceased to live, still keeping as he does flesh and blood in his thoughts (for in his entreaty that his kindred may be exempted from his sufferings he plainly shows that he is not freed yet from fleshly feeling),—in such details of the story (she continued) I think our Lord teaches us this; that those still living in the flesh must as much as ever they can separate and free themselves in a way from its attachments by virtuous conduct, in order that after death they may not need a second death to cleanse them from the remnants that are owing to this cement[3] of the flesh, and, when once the bonds are loosed from around the soul, her soaring[4] up to the Good may be swift and unimpeded, with no anguish of the body to distract her. For if any one becomes wholly and thoroughly carnal in thought, such an one, with every motion and energy of the soul absorbed in fleshly desires, is not parted from such attachments, even in the disembodied state; just as those who have lingered long in noisome places do not part with the unpleasantness contracted by that lengthened stay, even when they pass into a sweet atmosphere. So[5] it is that, when the change is made into the impalpable Unseen, not even then will it be possible for the lovers of the flesh to avoid dragging away with them under any circumstances some fleshly foulness; and thereby their torment will be intensified, their soul having been materialized by such surroundings. I think too that this view of the matter harmonizes to a certain extent with the assertion made by some persons that around their graves shadowy phantoms of the departed are often seen[6]. If this is really so, an inordinate attachment of that particular soul to the life in the flesh is proved to have existed, causing it to be unwilling, even when expelled from the flesh, to fly clean away and to admit the com-

---

[1] τὸν δίκαιον. Most of Krabinger's Codd. read τὸν πλούσιον.
[2] is occupied with his present blessings (ἄσχολος τοῖς παροῦσιν); surely not, with Oehler, " is not occupied with the present world " !

[3] κόλλης. The metaphor is Platonic. "The soul . . . absolutely bound and glued to the body " (Phædo, p. 82 E).
[4] her soaring. Plato first spoke (Phædrus, p. 248 C) of "that growth of wing, by which the soul is lifted." Once these natural wings can get expanded, her flight upwards is a matter of course. This image is reproduced by Plotinus p. 769 A (end of Enneads) ; Libanius, Pro Socrate, p. 258 ; Synesius, De Providentiâ, p. 90 D, and Hymn i. 111, where he speaks of the ἄλμα κοῦφον of the soul, and Hymn iii. 42. But there is mixed here with the idea of a flight upwards (i. e. ἀναδρομή), that of the running-ground as well (cf. Greg. De scopo Christian. III. p. 299, τοῖς τῆς ἀρετῆς δρόμοις), which, as sanctioned in the New Testament. Chrysostom so often uses. [5] οὕτως answers to καθάπερ, not to ὡς above.
[6] shadowy phantoms of the departed are often seen. Cf. Origen c. Cels. ii. 60 (in answer to Celsus' " Epicurean " opinion that ghosts are pure illusion) : "He who does believe this (i. e. in ghosts) necessarily believes in the immortality, or at all events the long continuance of the soul : as Plato does in his treatise on the soul (i. e. the Phædo) when he says that the shadowy apparitions of the dead hover round their tombs. These apparitions, then, have some substance : it is the so-called ' radiant' frame in which the soul exists. But Celsus, not liking this, would have us believe that people have waking dreams and ' imagine as real, in accordance with their wishes, a wild piece of unreality.' In sleep we may well believe that this is the case : not so in waking hours, unless some one is quite out of his senses, or is melancholy mad." But Origen here quotes Plato in connection with the reality of the Resurrection body of Christ ; Gregory refers to ghosts only, with regard to the φιλοσώματοι, whose whole condition after death he represents very much in Plato's words. See Phædo, p. 81 B.

plete change of its form into the impalpable; it remains near the frame even after the dissolution of the frame, and though now outside it, hovers regretfully over the place where its material is, and continues to haunt it.

Then, after a moment's reflection on the meaning of these latter words, I said: I think that a contradiction now arises between what you have said and the result of our former examination of the passions. For if, on the one hand, the activity of such movements within us is to be held as arising from our kinship with the brutes, such movements I mean as were enumerated in our previous discussion [7], anger, for instance, and fear, desire of pleasure, and so on, and, on the other hand, it was affirmed that virtue consists in the good employment of these movements, and vice in their bad employment, and in addition to this we discussed the actual contribution of each of the other passions to a virtuous life, and found that through desire above all we are brought nearer God, drawn up, by its chain as it were, from earth towards Him,—I think (I said) that that part of the discussion is in a way opposed to that which we are now aiming at.

How so? she asked.

Why, when every unreasoning instinct is quenched within us after our purgation, this principle of desire will not exist any more than the other principles; and this being removed, it looks as if the striving after the better way would also cease, no other emotion remaining in the soul that can stir us up to the appetence of Good.

To that objection, she replied, we answer this. The speculative and critical faculty is the property of the soul's godlike part; for it is by these that we grasp the Deity also. If, then, whether by forethought here, or by purgation hereafter, our soul becomes free from any emotional connection with the brute creation, there will be nothing to impede its contemplation of the Beautiful; for this last is essentially capable of attracting in a certain way every being that looks towards it. If, then, the soul is purified of every vice, it will most certainly be in the sphere of Beauty. The Deity is in very substance Beautiful; and to the Deity the soul will in its state of purity have affinity, and will embrace It as like itself. Whenever this happens, then, there will be no longer need of the impulse of Desire to lead the way to the Beautiful. Whoever passes his time in darkness, he it is who will be under the influence of a desire for the light; but whenever he comes into the light, then enjoyment takes the place of desire, and the power to enjoy renders desire useless

and out of date. It will therefore be no detriment to our participation in the Good, that the soul should be free from such emotions, and turning back upon herself should know herself accurately what her actual nature is, and should behold the Original Beauty reflected in the mirror and in the figure of her own beauty. For truly herein consists the real assimilation to the Divine; viz. in making our own life in some degree a copy of the Supreme Being. For a Nature like that, which transcends all thought and is far removed from all that we observe within ourselves, proceeds in its existence in a very different manner to what we do in this present life. Man, possessing a constitution whose law it is to be moving, is carried in that particular direction whither the impulse of his will directs: and so his soul is not affected in the same way towards what lies before it [8], as one may say, as to what it has left behind; for hope leads the forward movement, but it is memory that succeeds that movement when it has advanced to the attainment of the hope; and if it is to something intrinsically good that hope thus leads on the soul, the print that this exercise of the will leaves upon the memory is a bright one; but if hope has seduced the soul with some phantom only of the Good, and the excellent way has been missed, then the memory that succeeds what has happened becomes shame, and an intestine war is thus waged in the soul between memory and hope, because the last has been such a bad leader of the will. Such in fact is the state of mind that shame gives expression to; the soul is stung as it were at the result; its remorse for its ill-considered attempt is a whip that makes it feel to the quick, and it would bring in oblivion to its aid against its tormentor. Now in our case nature, owing to its being indigent of the Good, is aiming always at this which is still wanting to it, and this aiming at a still missing thing is this very habit of Desire, which our constitution displays equally, whether it is baulked of the real Good, or wins that which it is good to win. But a nature that surpasses every idea that we can form of the Good and transcends all other power, being in no want of anything that can be regarded as good, is itself the plenitude of every good; it does not move in the sphere of the good by way of participation in it only, but if is itself the substance of the Good (whatever we imagine the Good to be); it neither gives scope for any rising hope (for hope manifests activity in the direction of something absent; but "what a man has, why doth he yet hope for?" as the Apostle asks), nor is it in want of the activity of the memory for the knowledge

---

[7] προλαβὼν; on the authority of five Codd., for προσλαβών.
VOL. V.

[8] κατὰ τὸ ἔμπροσθεν αὐτῆς.

of things; that which is actually seen has no need of being remembered. Since, then, this Divine nature is beyond any particular good[9], and to the good the good is an object of love, it follows that when It looks within Itself[1], It wishes for what It contains and contains that which It wishes, and admits nothing external. Indeed there is nothing external to It, with the sole exception of evil, which, strange as it may seem to say, possesses an existence in not existing at all. For there is no other origin of evil except the negation of the existent, and the truly-existent forms the substance of the Good. That therefore which is not to be found in the existent must be in the non-existent. Whenever the soul, then, having divested itself of the multifarious emotions incident to its nature, gets its Divine form and, mounting above Desire, enters within that towards which it was once incited by that Desire, it offers no harbour within itself either for hope or for memory. It holds the object of the one; the other is extruded from the consciousness by the occupation in enjoying all that is good: and thus the soul copies the life that is above, and is conformed to the peculiar features of the Divine nature; none of its habits are left to it except that of love, which clings by natural affinity to the Beautiful. For this is what love is; the inherent affection towards a chosen object. When, then, the soul, having become simple and single in form and so perfectly godlike, finds that perfectly simple and immaterial good which is really worth enthusiasm and love[2], it attaches itself to it and blends with it by means of the movement and activity of love, fashioning itself according to that which it is continually finding and grasping. Becoming by this assimilation to the Good all that the nature of that which it participates is, the soul will consequently, owing to there being no lack of any good in that thing itself which it participates, be itself also in no lack of anything, and so will expel from within the activity and the habit of Desire; for this arises only when the thing missed is not found. For this teaching we have the authority of God's own Apostle, who announces a subduing[3] and a ceasing of all other activities, even for the good, which are within us, and finds no limit for love alone. Prophecies, he says, shall fail; forms of knowledge shall cease; but "charity never faileth;" which is equivalent to its being always as it is: and though[4] he says that

faith and hope have endured so far by the side of love, yet again he prolongs its date beyond theirs, and with good reason too; for hope is in operation only so long as the enjoyment of the things hoped for is not to be had; and faith in the same way is a support[5] in the uncertainty about the things hoped for; for so he defines it—"the substance[6] of things hoped for"; but when the thing hoped for actually comes, then all other faculties are reduced to quiescence[7], and love alone remains active, finding nothing to succeed itself. Love, therefore, is the foremost of all excellent achievements and the first of the commandments of the law. If ever, then, the soul reach this goal, it will be in no need of anything else; it will embrace that plenitude of things which are, whereby alone[8] it seems in any way to preserve within itself the stamp of God's actual blessedness. For the life of the Supreme Being is love, seeing that the Beautiful is necessarily lovable to those who recognize it, and the Deity does recognize it, and so this recognition becomes love, that which He recognizes being essentially beautiful. This True Beauty the insolence of satiety cannot touch[9]; and no satiety interrupting this continuous capacity to love the Beautiful, God's life will have its activity in love; which life is thus in itself beautiful, and is essentially of a loving disposition towards the Beautiful, and receives no check to this activity of love. In fact, in the Beautiful no limit is to be found so that love should have to cease with any limit of the Beautiful. This last can be ended only by its opposite; but when you have a good, as here, which is in its essence incapable of a change for the worse, then that good will go on unchecked into infinity. Moreover, as every being is capable of attracting its like, and humanity is, in a way, like God, as bearing within itself some resemblances to its Prototype, the soul is by a strict necessity attracted to the kindred Deity. In fact what belongs to God must by all means and at any cost be preserved

---

9 any particular good, not as Oehler, "jenseits alles Guten." The Divine Being is the complement, not the negation, of each single good.
1 ἐν ἑαυτῇ βλέπουσα. But Augentius and Sifanus seem to have read ἑαυτὴν: and this is supported by three Codd.
2 τὸ μόνον τῷ ὄντι ἀγαπητὸν καὶ ἐράσμιον.
3 καταστολὴν. Cf. 1 Cor. xiii. 8—13.
4 Schmidt well remarks that there lies in λέγων here not a causal but only a concessive force: and he puts a stop before εἰκότως.

Oehler has not seen that ἀγάπη is governed by the preposition σὺν in the verb "by the side of love," and quite mistranslates the passage.
5 ἔρεισμα.   6 ὑπόστασις. Heb. xi. 1.
7 reduced to quiescence, ἀτρεμούντων. This is the reading adopted by Krabinger, from four Codd., instead of the vox nihili of the editions, εὐτρεμεόντων. The contrast must be between "remaining in activity (ἐνεργεία)," and "becoming idle," and he quotes a passage from Plotinus to show that ἀτρεμεῖν has exactly this latter sense. Cf. 1 Cor. xiii. 8, 10, καταργηθήσονται, κατοργηθήσεται.
8 whereby alone, καθ' ὃ δοκεῖ μόνον πως αὐτῆς, κ. τ. λ, the reading of Sifanus.
9 the insolence of satiety cannot touch. Krabinger quotes from two of his Codd. a scholium to this effect: "Then this proves to be nonsense what Origen has imagined about the satiety of minds, and their consequent fall and recall, on which he bases his notorious teaching about the pre-existence and restoration of souls that are always revolving in endless motion, determined as he is, like a retailer of evil, to mingle the Grecian myths with the Church's truth." Gregory, more sober in his idealism, certainly does not follow on this point his great Master. The phrase ὑβριστὴς κόρος is used by Gregory Naz. also in his Poems (p. 32 A), and may have been suggested to both by some poet, now lost. "Familiarity breeds contempt" is the modern equivalent.

for Him. If, then, on the one hand, the soul is unencumbered with superfluities and no trouble connected with the body presses it down, its advance towards Him Who draws it to Himself is sweet and congenial. But suppose[1], on the other hand, that it has been transfixed with the nails of propension[2] so as to be held down to a habit connected with material things, —a case like that of those in the ruins caused by earthquakes, whose bodies are crushed by the mounds of rubbish ; and let us imagine by way of illustration that these are not only pressed down by the weight of the ruins, but have been pierced as well with some spikes and splinters discovered with them in the rubbish. What, then, would naturally be the plight of those bodies, when they were being dragged by relatives from the ruins to receive the holy rites of burial, mangled and torn entirely, disfigured in the most direful manner conceivable, with the nails beneath the heap harrowing them by the very violence necessary to pull them out ?— Such I think is the plight of the soul as well, when the Divine force, for God's very love of man, drags that which belongs to Him from the ruins of the irrational and material. Not in hatred or revenge for a wicked life, to my thinking, does God bring upon sinners those painful dispensations ; He is only claiming and drawing to Himself whatever, to please Him, came into existence. But while He for a noble end is attracting the soul to Himself, the Fountain of all Blessedness, it is the occasion necessarily to the being so attracted of a state of torture. Just as those who refine gold from the dross which it contains not only get this base alloy to melt in the fire, but are obliged to melt the pure gold along with the alloy, and then while this last is being consumed the gold remains, so, while evil is being consumed in the purgatorial[3] fire, the soul that is welded to this evil must inevitably be in the fire too, until the spurious material alloy is consumed and annihilated by this fire. If a clay of the more tenacious kind is deeply plastered round a rope, and then the end of the rope is put through a narrow hole, and then some one on the further side violently pulls it by that end, the result must be that, while the rope itself obeys the force exerted, the clay that has been plastered upon it is scraped off it with this violent pulling and is left outside the hole, and, moreover, is the cause why the rope does not run easily through the passage, but has to undergo a violent tension at the hands of the puller. In such a manner, I think, we may figure to ourselves the agonized struggle of that soul which has wrapped itself up in earthy material passions, when God is drawing it, His own one, to Himself, and the foreign matter, which has somehow grown into its substance, has to be scraped from it by main force, and so occasions it that keen intolerable anguish.

Then it seems, I said, that it is not punishment chiefly and principally that the Deity, as Judge, afflicts sinners with ; but He operates, as your argument has shown, only to get the good separated from the evil and to attract it into the communion of blessedness.

That, said the Teacher, is my meaning ; and also that the agony will be measured by the amount of evil there is in each individual. For it would not be reasonable to think that the man who has remained so long as we have supposed in evil known to be forbidden, and the man who has fallen only into moderate sins, should be tortured to the same amount in the judgment upon their vicious habit ; but according to the quantity of material will be the longer or shorter time that that agonizing flame will be burning ; that is, as long as there is fuel to feed it. In the case of the man who has acquired a heavy weight of material, the consuming fire must necessarily be very searching ; but where that which the fire has to feed upon[4] has spread less far, there the penetrating fierceness of the punishment is mitigated, so far as the subject itself, in the amount of its evil, is diminished. In any and every case evil must be removed out of existence, so that, as we said above, the absolutely non-existent should cease to be at all. Since it is not in its nature that evil should exist outside the will, does it not follow that when it shall be that every will rests in God, evil will be reduced to complete annihilation, owing to no receptacle being left for it ?

But, said I, what help can one find in this devout hope, when one considers the greatness of the evil in undergoing torture even for a single year ; and if that intolerable anguish be prolonged for the interval of an age, what grain of comfort is left from any subsequent expectation to him whose purgation is thus commensurate with an entire age ?[5]

---

[1] *But suppose*, &c. Möller (*Gregorii doctrina de hom. natur.*, p. 99) shows that the following view of Purgatory is not that taught by the Roman Church.

[2] *by the nails of propension.* This metaphor is frequently used by Gregory. Cf. *De Virginit.* c 5 : " How can the soul which is riveted (προσηλωθεῖσα) to the pleasures of the flesh, and busied with merely human longings, turn a disengaged eye upon its kindred intellectual light ?" So *De Beatitud.* Or. viii. (I. p. 833), &c.

[3] *purgatorial*, καθαρσίῳ. Five of Krabinger's Codd. and the versions of Augentius and Sifanus approve this reading. That of the Editions is ἀκοιμήτῳ. [This last epithet is applied to God's justice (δικῇ) by Isidore of Pelusium, *Ep.* 90 : and to the " worm," and, on the other hand, the Devil, by Cyril Alexand. *Act. Ephes.*, p. 252. Cf. S. Math. iii. 12 ; S. Mark ix. 48.] It is the same with αἰωνίῳ before πυρὶ just below. The Editions have it ; the Codd. and Latin versions have not : Krabinger therefore has not hesitated to expunge t.

[4] ἡ τοῦ πυρὸς δαπανή These words can have no other meaning to suit the sense. Krabinger's reproduction of Sifanus' Latin, " ignis ille consumens," makes the sentence a tautology.

[5] πρὸς ὅλον αἰῶνα. But cf. Plato, *Timæus*, 37, 39 D.

Why[6], either we must plan to keep the soul absolutely untouched and free from any stain of evil; or, if our passionate nature makes that quite impossible, then we must plan that our failures in excellence consist only in mild and easily-curable derelictions. For the Gospel in its teaching distinguishes between[7] a debtor of ten thousand talents and a debtor of five hundred pence, and of fifty pence and of a farthing[8], which is "the uttermost" of coins; it proclaims that God's just judgment reaches to all, and enhances the payment necessary as the weight of the debt increases, and on the other hand does not overlook the very smallest debts. But the Gospel tells us that this payment of debts was not effected by the refunding of money, but that the indebted man was delivered to the tormentors until he should pay the whole debt; and that means nothing else than paying in the coin of torment[9] the inevitable recompense, the recompense, I mean, that consists in taking the share of pain incurred during his lifetime, when he inconsiderately chose mere pleasure, undiluted with its opposite; so that having put off from him all that foreign growth which sin is, and discarded the shame of any debts, he might stand in liberty and fearlessness. Now liberty is the coming up to a state which owns no master and is self-regulating[1]; it is that with which we were gifted by God at the beginning, but which has been obscured by the feeling of shame arising from indebtedness. Liberty too is in all cases one and the same essentially; it has a natural attraction to itself. It follows, then, that as everything that is free will be united with its like, and as virtue is a thing that has no master, that is, is free, everything that is free will be united with virtue. But, further, the Divine Being is the fountain of all virtue.

Therefore, those who have parted with evil will be united with Him; and so, as the Apostle says, God will be "all in all[2]"; for this utterance seems to me plainly to confirm the opinion we have already arrived at, for it means that God will be instead of all other things, and in all. For while our present life is active amongst a variety of multiform conditions, and the things we have relations with are numerous, for instance, time, air, locality, food and drink, clothing, sunlight, lamplight, and other necessities of life, none of which, many though they be, are God,—that blessed state which we hope for is in need of none of these things, but the Divine Being will become all, and instead of all, to us, distributing Himself proportionately to every need of that existence. It is plain, too, from the Holy Scripture that God becomes, to those who deserve it, locality, and home, and clothing, and food, and drink, and light, and riches, and dominion, and everything thinkable and nameable that goes to make our life happy. But He that becomes "all" things will be "in all" things too; and herein it appears to me that Scripture teaches the complete annihilation of evil[3]. If, that is, God will be "in all" existing things, evil, plainly, will not then be amongst them; for if any one was to assume that it did exist then, how will the belief that God will be "in all" be kept intact? The excepting of that one thing, evil, mars the comprehensiveness of

---

6 Macrina's answer must begin here, though the Paris Editt. take no notice of a break. Krabinger on the authority of one of his Codd. has inserted φησὶν ἡ διδάσκαλος after προνοητέον.

7 *distinguishes between.* The word here is οἶδεν, which is used of "teaching," "telling," after the fashion of the later Greek writers, in making a quotation.

8 *of a farthing.* No mention is made of this in the Parable (S. Matt. xviii. 23; S. Luke vii. 41). The "uttermost farthing" of S. Matt. v. 26 does not apply here.

9 διὰ τῆς βασάνου. Of course διὰ cannot go with ὀφειλὴν, though Krabinger translates "per tormenta debita." He has. however, with Oehler, pointed the Greek right, so as to take ὀφλημα as in opposition to ὀφειλὴν.

1 *a state which owns no master and is self-regulating,* &c. He repeats this, *De Hom. Opif.* c. 4 : " For the soul immediately shows its royal and exalted character, far removed from the lowliness of private station, in that it owns no master, and is self-governed, swayed autocratically by its own will,—for to whom else does this belong than to a king?" and c. 16 : "Thus, there is in us the principle of all excellence, all virtue, and every higher thing that we conceive : but pre-eminent among all is the fact that we are free from necessity, and not in bondage to any natural force, but have decision in our power as we please : for virtue is a voluntary thing, subject to no dominion :" and *Orat. Catech.* c. 5 : "Was it not, then, most right that that which is in every detail made like the Divine should possess in its nature a self-ruling and independent principle, such as to enable the participation of the good to be the reward of its virtue?" It would be possible to quote similar language from the Neoplatonists (e. g. Plotinus vi. 83-6) : but Gregory learnt the whole bearing and meaning of moral liberty from none but Origen, whose so-called "heresies" all flowed from his constant insistence on its reality.

2 This (1 Cor. xv. 28) is a text much handled by the earlier Greek Fathers. Origen especially has made it one of the Scripture foundations upon which he has built up theology. This passage in Gregory should be compared with the following in Origen, *c. Cels.* iv. 69, where he has been speaking of evil and its origin, and its disappearance : " God checks the wider spread of evil, and banishes it altogether in a way that is conducive to the good of the whole. Whether or not there is reason to believe that after the banishment of evil it will again appear is a separate question. By later corrections, then, God does put right some defects : for although in the creation of the whole all the work was fair and strong, nevertheless a certain healing process is needed for those whom evil has infected, and for the world itself which it has as it were tainted; and God is never negligent in interfering on certain occasions in a way suitable to a changeful and alterable world," &c. " He is like a husbandman performing different work at different times upon the land, for a final harvest." Also viii. 72 : 'This subject requires much study and demonstration : still a few things must and shall be said at once tending to shew that it is not only possible, but an actual truth, that every being that reasons 'shall agree in one law (quoting Celsus' words). Now while the Stoics hold that when the strongest of the elements has by its nature prevailed over the rest, there shall be the Conflagration, when all things will fall into the fire, we hold that the Word shall some day master the whole of 'reasoning nature,' and shall transfigure it to its own perfection, when each with pure spontaneity shall will what it wishes, and act what it wills. We hold that there is no analogy to be drawn from the case of bodily diseases, and wounds, where some things are beyond the power of any art of healing. We do not hold that there are any of the results of sin which the universal Word, and the universal God, cannot heal. The healing power of the Word is greater than any of the maladies of the soul, and, *according to the will*, He does draw it to Himself : and so the aim of things is that evil should be annihilated : whether with no possibility whatever of the soul ever turning to it again, is foreign to the present discussion. It is sufficient now to quote Zephaniah " (iii. 7—13, LXX.).

3 But, when A. Jahn, as quoted by Krabinger, asserts that Gregory and Origen derived their denial of the eternity of punishment from a source "merely extraneous," *i. e.* the Platonists, we must not forget that Plato himself in the *Phædo,* 113 F (cf. also *Gorgias,* 525 C, and *Republic,* x. 615), expressly teaches the eternity of punishment hereafter, for he uses there not the word αἰών or αἰώνιος, but οὔποτε. They were influenced rather by the later Platonists.

the term "all." But He that will be "in all" will never be in that which does not exist.

What then, I asked, are we to say to those whose hearts fail at these calamities [4]?

We will say to them, replied the Teacher, this. "It is foolish, good people, for you to fret and complain of the chain of this fixed sequence of life's realities; you do not know the goal towards which each single dispensation of the universe is moving. You do not know that all things have to be assimilated to the Divine Nature in accordance with the artistic plan of their author, in a certain regularity and order. Indeed, it was for this that intelligent beings came into existence; namely, that the riches of the Divine blessings should not lie idle. The All-creating Wisdom fashioned these souls, these receptacles with free wills, as vessels as it were, for this very purpose, that there should be some capacities able to receive His blessings and become continually larger with the inpouring of the stream. Such are the wonders [5] that the participation in the Divine blessings works : it makes him into whom they come. larger and more capacious; from his capacity to receive it gets for the receiver an actual increase in bulk as well, and he never stops enlarging. The fountain of blessings wells up unceasingly, and the partaker's nature, finding nothing superfluous and without a use in that which it receives, makes the whole influx an enlargement of its own proportions, and becomes at once more wishful to imbibe the nobler nourishment and more capable of containing it; each grows along with each, both the capacity which is nursed in such abundance of blessings and so grows greater, and the nurturing supply which comes on in a flood answering to the growth of those increasing powers. It is likely, therefore, that this bulk will mount to such a magnitude as [6] there is no limit to check, so that we should not grow into it. With such a prospect before us, are you angry that our nature is ad-vancing to its goal along the path appointed for us ? Why, our career cannot be run thitherward, except that which weighs us down, I mean this encumbering load of earthiness, be shaken off the soul; nor can we be domiciled in Purity with the corresponding part of our nature, unless we have cleansed ourselves by a better training from the habit of affection which we have contracted in life towards this earthiness. But if there be in you any clinging to this body [7], and the being unlocked from this darling thing give you pain, let not this, either, make you despair. You will behold this bodily envelopment, which is now dissolved in death, woven again out of the same atoms, not indeed into this organization with its gross and heavy texture, but with its threads worked up into something more subtle and ethereal, so that you will not only have near you that which you love, but it will be restored to you with a brighter and more entrancing beauty [8]."

But it somehow seems to me now, I said, that the doctrine of the Resurrection necessarily comes on for our discussion; a doctrine which I think is even at first sight true as well as credible [9], as it is told us in Scripture ; so that that will not come in question between us : but since the weakness of the human understanding is strengthened still farther by any arguments that are intelligible to us, it would be well not to leave this part of the subject, either, without philosophical examination. Let us consider, then, what ought to be said about it.

As for the thinkers, the Teacher went on, outside our own system of thought, they have, with all their diverse ways of looking at things, one in one point, another in another, approached and touched the doctrine of the Resurrection : while they none of them exactly coincide with us, they have in no case wholly abandoned such an expectation. Some indeed make human nature vile in their comprehensiveness, maintaining that a soul becomes alternately that of a man and of something irrational; that it transmigrates into various bodies, changing at pleasure from the man into fowl, fish, or beast, and then returning to human kind. While some extend this absurdity even to trees [1] and shrubs,

---

4 Reading συμφοραῖς, i. e. death especially.

5 *Such are the wonders.* There is here, Denys (*De la Philosophie d' Origène,* p. 484) remarks, a great difference between Gregory and Origen. Both speak of an "eternal sabbath," which will end the circle of our destinies. But Origen, after all the progress and peregrinations of the soul, which he loves to describe, establishes "the reasoning nature" at last in an unchangeable quiet and repose ; while Gregory sets before the soul an endless career of perfections and ever-increasing happiness. This is owing to their different conceptions of the Deity. Origen cannot understand how He can know Himself or be accessible to our thought, if He is Infinite : Gregory on the contrary conceives Him as Infinite, as beyond all real or imaginable boundaries, πασῆς περιγραφῆς ἐκτός (*Orat. Cat.* viii. 65); this is the modern, rather than the Greek view. In the following description of the life eternal Gregory hardly merits the censure of Ritter that he "introduces absurdity" into it.

6 *such a magnitude as.* Reading, ἐφ' ὃ, with Schmidt. The "limit" is the present body, which must be laid aside in order to cease to be a hindrance to such a growth. Krabinger reads ἐφ ὧν on the authority of six Codd., and translates "ii in quibus nullus terminus interrumpit incrementum." But τοσοῦτον can answer to nothing before, and manifestly refers to the relative clause.

7 Macrina may be here alluding to Gregory's brotherly affection for her.

8 But on high
A record lives of thine identity !
Thou shalt not lose one charm of lip or eye ;
The hues and liquid lights shall wait for thee,
And the fair tissues, wheresoe'er they be !
Daughter of heaven ! our grieving hearts repose
On the dear thought that we once more shall see
Thy beauty—like Himself our Master rose.
C. TENNYSON TURNER.—*Anastasis.*

9 ἰδεῖν . . . ἵνα μὴ ἀμφιβάλλῃ. This is the reading of the Paris Editt. : ἰδεῖν seems to go closely with ἀληθὲς : so that Krabinger's δεῖν is not absolutely necessary.

1 *some extend this absurdity even to trees :* Empedocles for instance. Cf. *Philosophumena* (of Hippolytus, falsely attributed to

so that they consider their wooden life as corresponding and akin to humanity, others of them hold only thus much—that the soul exchanges one man for another man, so that the life of humanity is continued always by means of the same souls, which, being exactly the same in number, are being born perpetually first in one generation, then in another. As for ourselves, we take our stand upon the tenets of the Church, and assert that it will be well to accept only so much of these speculations as is sufficient to show that those who indulge in them are to a certain extent in accord with the doctrine of the Resurrection. Their statement, for instance, that the soul after its release from this body insinuates itself into certain other bodies is not absolutely out of harmony with the revival which we hope for. For our view, which maintains that the body, both now, and again in the future, is composed of the atoms of the universe, is held equally by these heathens. In fact, you cannot imagine any constitution of the body independent of a concourse [2] of these atoms. But the divergence lies in this : we assert that the same body again as before, composed of the same atoms, is compacted around the soul ; they suppose that the soul alights on other bodies, not only rational, but irrational and even insensate ; and while all are agreed that these bodies which the soul resumes derive their substance from the atoms of the universe, they part company from us in thinking that they are not made out of identically the same atoms as those which in this mortal life grew around the soul. Let, then, this external testimony stand for the fact that it is not contrary to probability that the soul should again inhabit a body; after that, however, it is incumbent upon us to make a survey of the inconsistencies of their position, and it will be easy thus, by means of the consequences that arise as we follow out the consist-

ent view, to bring the truth to light. What, then, is to be said about these theories? This that those who would have it that the soul migrates into natures divergent from each other seem to me to obliterate all natural distinctions; to blend and confuse together, in every possible respect, the rational, the irrational, the sentient, and the insensate ; if, that is, all these are to pass into each other, with no distinct natural order[3] secluding them from mutual transition. To say that one and the same soul, on account of a particular environment of body, is at one time a rational and intellectual soul, and that then it is caverned along with the reptiles, or herds with the birds, or is a beast of burden, or a carnivorous one, or swims in the deep ; or even drops down to an insensate thing, so as to strike out roots or become a complete tree, producing buds on branches, and from those buds a flower, or a thorn, or a fruit edible or noxious—to say this, is nothing short of making all things the same and believing that one single nature runs through all beings ; that there is a connexion between them which blends and confuses hopelessly all the marks by which one could be distinguished from another. The philosopher who asserts that the same thing may be born in anything intends no less than that all things are to be one ; when the observed differences in things are for him no obstacle to mixing together things which are utterly incongruous. He makes it necessary that, even when one sees one of the creatures that are venom-darting or carnivorous, one should regard it, in spite of appearances, as of the same tribe, nay even of the same family, as oneself. With such beliefs a man will look even upon hemlock as not alien to his own nature, detecting, as he does, humanity in the plant. The grape-bunch itself[4], produced though it be by cultivation for the purpose of sustaining life, he will not regard without suspicion ; for it too comes from a plant[5] : and we find even the fruit of the ears of corn upon which we live are plants ; how, then, can one put in the sickle to cut them down ; and how can one squeeze the bunch, or pull up the thistle from the field, or gather flowers, or hunt birds, or set fire to the logs of the funeral pyre : it being all the while

---

Origen), p. 50, where two lines of his are quoted. Chrysostom's words (I. iv. p. 196), "There are those amongst them who carry souls into plants, into shrubs, and into dogs," are taken by Matthæus to refer to Empedocles. Cf. Celsus also (quoted in Origen, c. Cels. viii. 53), "Seeing then men are born bound to a body—no matter whether the economy of the world required this, or that they are paying the penalty for some sin, or that the soul is weighted with certain emotions till it is purified from them at the end of its destined cycle, three myriad hours, according to Empedocles, being the necessary period of its wanderings far away from the Blessed Ones, during which it passes successively into every perishable shape—we must believe any way that there exist certain guardians of this prison-house." See *De Hom. Opif.* c. 28. Empedocles can be no other, then, than "the philosopher who asserts that the same thing may be born in anything :" below (p. 232 D). Anaxagoras, however, seems to have indulged in the same dictum (πᾶν ἐν παντὶ), but with a difference ; as Nicetas explains in his commentary on Gregory Naz., *Orations* : "That everything is contained in everything Empedocles asserted, and Anaxagoras asserted also: but not with the same meaning. Empedocles said it of the four elements, namely, that they are not only divided and self-centred, but are also mingled with each other. This is clear from the fact that every animal is engendered by all four. But Anaxagoras, finding an old proverb that nothing can be produced out of nothing, did away with creation. and introduced 'differentiation' instead, &c." See also Greg. Naz., *Poems*, p. 170.
[2] συνδρομῆς.

---

[3] εἰρμῷ, *i. e.* as links in a chain which cannot be altered. Sifanus' "carcere et claustro" is due to εἰργμῷ against all the MSS. Krabinger's six have διατειχιζόμενα for διαστοιχιζόμενα of the Editt.
[4] οὐδὲ . . . τὸν βότρυν. The intensive need not surprise us, though a grape-bunch does seem a more fitting body for a human soul than a stalk of hemlock : it is explained by the sentence in apposition, "produced . . . for the purpose of sustaining life," *i. e.* it is eaten, and so a soul might be eaten ; which increases the horror.
[5] καὶ γὰρ καὶ αὐτὸς τῶν φυομένων ἐστίν, *i. e.* the fruit, and not the tree only. belongs to the kingdom of plants : φυτὰ in the next sentence is exactly equivalent to τὰ φυόμενα, *i. e.* plants. The probability that this is the meaning is strengthened by Krabinger's reading οὗτος, from five of his Codd. But still if αὐτὸς be retained, it might have been taken to refer to the *man* who must needs look suspiciously at a bunch of grapes; "for what, according to this theory, is he himself, but a vegetable !" since all things are mixed, πάντα ὁμοῦ.

uncertain whether we are not laying violent hands on kinsmen, or ancestors, or fellow-country-men, and whether it is not through the medium of some body of theirs that the fire is being kindled, and the cup mixed, and the food prepared? To think that in the case of any single one of these things a soul of a man has become a plant or animal [6], while no marks are stamped upon them to indicate what sort of plant or animal it is that has been a man, and what sort has sprung from other beginnings,— such a conception as this will dispose him who has entertained it to feel an equal amount of interest in everything : he must perforce either harden himself against actual human beings who are in the land of the living, or, if his nature inclines him to love his kindred, he will feel alike towards every kind of life, whether he meet it in reptiles or in wild beasts. Why, if the holder of such an opinion go into a thicket of trees, even then he will regard the trees as a crowd of men. What sort of life will his be, when he has to be tender towards everything on the ground of kinship, or else hardened towards mankind on account of his seeing no difference between them and the other creatures? From what has been already said, then, we must reject this theory : and there are many other considerations as well which on the grounds of mere consistency lead us away from it. For I have heard persons who hold these opinions[7] saying that whole nations of souls are hidden away somewhere in a realm of their own, living a life analogous to that of the embodied soul; but such is the fineness and buoyancy of their substance that they themselves roll round along with the revolution of the universe ; and that these souls, having individually lost their wings through some gravitation towards evil, become embodied ; first this takes place in men ; and after that, passing from a human life, owing to brutish affinities of their passions, they are reduced [8] to the level of brutes ; and, leaving that, drop down to this insensate life of pure nature [9] which you have been hearing so much of; so that that inherently fine and buoyant thing that the soul is first becomes weighted and downward tending in consequence of some vice, and so migrates to a human body; then its reasoning powers are extinguished, and it goes on living in some brute ; and then even this gift of sensation is withdrawn, and it changes into the insensate plant life ; but after that mounts up again by the same gradations until it is restored to its place in heaven. Now this doctrine will at once be found, even after a very cursory survey, to have no coherency with itself. For, first, seeing that the soul is to be dragged down from its life in heaven, on account of evil there, to the condition of a tree, and is then from this point, on account of virtue exhibited there, to return to heaven, their theory will be unable to decide which is to have the preference, the life in heaven, or the life in the tree. A circle, in fact, of the same sequences will be perpetually traversed, where the soul, at whatever point it may be, has no resting-place. If it thus lapses from the disembodied state to the embodied, and thence to the insensate, and then springs back to the disembodied, an inextricable confusion of good and evil must result in the minds of those who thus teach. For the life in heaven will no more preserve its blessedness (since evil can touch heaven's denizens), than the life in trees will be devoid of virtue (since it is from this, they say, that the rebound of the soul towards the good begins, while from there it begins the evil life again). Secondly [1], seeing that the soul as it moves round in heaven is there entangled with evil and is in consequence dragged down to live in mere matter, from whence, however, it is lifted again into its residence on high, it follows that those philosophers establish the very contrary [2] of their own views ; they establish, namely, that the life in matter is the purgation of evil, while that undeviating revolution along with the stars [3] is the foundation and cause of evil in every soul : if it is here that the soul by means of virtue grows its wing and then soars upwards, and there that those wings by reason of evil fall off, so that it descends and clings to this lower world and is commingled with the grossness of material nature. But the untenableness of this view does not stop even in this,

---

6 Two Codd. Mon. (D, E) omit φυτὸν ἢ ζῷον, which is repeated below.

7 *i. e.* Pythagoreans and later Platonists. Cf. Origen, *c. Cels.* iii. 80. For the losing of the wings, cf. *c. Cels* iii. 40 : "The coats of skins also, which God made for those sinners, the man and the woman cast forth from the garden, have a mystical meaning far deeper than Plato's fancy about the soul shedding its wings, and moving downward till it meets some spot upon the solid earth."

8 ἀποκτηνοῦσθαι.

9 τῆς φυσικῆς ταύτης. This is the common reading : but φύσις and φυσικὸς have a rather higher meaning than our equivalent for them : cf. just below, "that inherently (τῇ φύσει) fine and buoyant thing" : and Krabinger is probably right in reading φυτικῆς from four Codd.

1 With the γὰρ here (unlike the three preceding) begins the second "incoherency" of this view. The *first* is,—"it confuses the ideas of good and evil." The *second*,—"it is inconsistent with a view already adopted by these teachers." The *third* (beginning with καὶ οὐ μέχρι τούτων, κ. τ. λ.),—"it contradicts the truth which it assumes, *i. e.* that there is no change in heaven."

2 See just above : "For I have heard persons who hold these opinions saying that whole nations of souls are hidden away somewhere in a realm of their own," &c., and see next note.

3 *that undeviating revolution along with the stars,* τὴν ἀπλανῆ περιφοράν. Cf. Origen, *De Princip.* ii. 3—6 (Rufinus' translation), "Sed et ipsum supereminentem, quem dicunt ἀπλανῆ, globum proprie nihilominus mundum appellari volunt :" Cicero, *De Repub.* vi. 17 : "Novem tibi orbibus vel potius globis connexa sunt omnia : quorum unus est cœlestis, extimus, qui reliquos omnes complectitur ; in quo infixi sunt illi, qui volvuntur, stellarum cursus sempiterni," *i. e.* they roll, not on their axes, but only as turning round with the general revolution. They are literally *fixed* in that heaven (cf. Virg. : "tacito volvuntur sidera lapsu") : and the spiritual beings in it are as fixed and changeless : in fact, with Plato it is the abode only of Divine intelligences, not of the δαίμονες : but the theorists, whom Gregory is refuting, confuse this distinction which their own master drew.

namely, that it contains assertions diametrically opposed to each other. Beyond this, their fundamental conception [4] itself cannot stand secure on every side. They say, for instance, that a heavenly nature is unchangeable. How, then, can there be room for any weakness in the unchangeable? If, again, a lower nature is subject to infirmity, how in the midst of this infirmity can freedom from it be achieved? They attempt to amalgamate two things that can never be joined together: they descry strength in weakness, passionlessness in passion. But even to this last view they are not faithful throughout; for they bring home the soul from its material life to that very place whence they had exiled it because of evil there, as though the life in that place was quite safe and uncontaminated; apparently quite forgetting the fact that the soul was weighted with evil *there*, before it plunged down into this lower world. The blame thrown on the life here below, and the praise of the things in heaven, are thus interchanged and reversed; for that which was once blamed conducts in their opinion to the brighter life, while that which was taken for the better state gives an impulse to the soul's propensity to evil. Expel, therefore, from amongst the doctrines of the Faith all erroneous and shifting suppositions about such matters! We must not follow, either, as though they had hit the truth, those who suppose that souls pass from women's bodies to live in men [5], or, reversely [6], that souls that have parted with men's bodies exist in women: or even if they only say that they pass from men into men, or from women into women. As for the former theory [7], not only has it been rejected for being shifting and illusory, and for landing us in opinions diametrically opposed to each other; but it must be rejected also because it is a godless theory, maintaining as it does that nothing amongst the things in nature is brought into existence without deriving its peculiar constitution from evil as its source. If, that is, neither men nor plants nor cattle can be born unless some soul from above has fallen into them, and if this fall is owing to

some tendency to evil, then they evidently think that evil controls the creation of all beings. In some mysterious way, too, both events are to occur at once; the birth of the man in consequence of a marriage, and the fall of the soul (synchronizing as it must with the proceedings at that marriage). A greater absurdity even than this is involved: if, as is the fact, the large majority of the brute creation copulate in the spring, are we, then, to say that the spring brings it about that evil is engendered in the revolving world above, so that, at one and the same moment, *there* certain souls are impregnated with evil and so fall, and *here* certain brutes conceive? And what are we to say about the husbandman who sets the vine-shoots in the soil? How does his hand manage to have covered in a human soul along with the plant, and how does the moulting of wings last simultaneously with his employment in planting? The same absurdity, it is to be observed, exists in the other of the two theories as well; in the direction, I mean, of thinking that the soul must be anxious about the intercourses of those living in wedlock, and must be on the look-out for the times of bringing forth, in order that it may insinuate itself into the bodies then produced. Supposing the man refuses the union, or the woman keeps herself clear of the necessity of becoming a mother, will evil then fail to weigh down that particular soul? Will it be marriage, in consequence, that sounds up above the first note of evil in the soul, or will this reversed state invade the soul quite independently of any marriage? But then, in this last case, the soul will have to wander about in the interval like a houseless vagabond, lapsed as it has from its heavenly surroundings, and yet, as it may happen in some cases, still without a body to receive it. But how, after that, can they imagine that the Deity exercises any superintendence over the world, referring as they do the beginnings of human lives to this casual and meaningless descent of a soul. For all that follows must necessarily accord with the beginning; and so, if a life begins in consequence of a chance accident, the whole course of it [8] becomes at once a chapter of accidents, and the attempt to make the whole world depend on a Divine power is absurd, when it is made by these men, who deny to the individualities in it a birth from the fiat of the Divine Will and refer the several origins of beings to encounters that come of evil, as though there could never have existed such a thing as a human life, unless a vice had struck, as it were, its leading note. If the beginning is like that, a sequel will most certainly be set in motion in accord-

---

[4] ὑπόνοια.

[5] Such theories are developed in the *Phædo* of Plato; and constitute ὁ ἕτερος τῶν λόγων, criticized more fully below.

[6] Reading δοκεῖ, ἢ τὸ ἔμπαλιν, instead of the corrupt δοκείη τὸ ἔμπαλιν.

[7] ὁ πρότερος (λόγος). The second is mentioned below. "The same absurdity exists in the other of the two theories as well." Obviously these two theories are those alluded to at the beginning of this last speech of Macrina, where, speaking of the heathen transmigration, she says, "While some of them extend this absurdity even to trees and shrubs, so that they consider their wooden life as corresponding and akin to humanity (*i. e.* ὁ πρότερος λόγος), others of them opine only thus much, that the soul exchanges one man for another man," &c. (*i. e.* ὁ ἕτερος). In either case the soul is supposed to return from the dead body to heaven, and then by a fresh fall into sin there, to sink down again. The absurdity and the godlessness is just as glaring, Macrina says, in the last case (the Platonic soul-rotation) as in the first (Transmigration pure and simple). But the one point in both in contact with the Christian Resurrection is this, that the soul of the departed *does assume another body.*

[8] ἡ κατ' αὐτὸν (*i. e.* βίον) διέξοδος. The Editions have κατ' αὐτῶν. Krabinger well translates by "percursatio." Cf. *Phædrus*, p. 247 A.

ance with that beginning. None would dare to maintain that what is fair can come out of what is foul, any more than from good can come its opposite. We expect fruit in accordance with the nature of the seed. Therefore this blind movement of chance is to rule the whole of life, and no Providence is any more to pervade the world.

Nay, even the forecasting by our calculations will be quite useless; virtue will lose its value; and to turn from evil will not be worth the while. Everything will be entirely under the control of the driver, Chance; and our lives will differ not at all from vessels devoid of ballast, and will drift on waves of unaccountable circumstances, now to this, now to that incident of good or of evil. The treasures of virtue will never be found in those who owe their constitution to causes quite contrary to virtue. If God really superintends our life, then, confessedly, evil cannot begin it. But if we do owe our birth to evil, then we must go on living in complete uniformity with it. Thereby it will be shown that it is folly to talk about the "houses of correction" which await us after this life is ended, and the "just recompences," and all the other things there asserted, and believed in too, that tend to the suppression of vice: for how can a man, owing, as he does, his birth to evil, be outside its pale? How can he, whose very nature has its rise in a vice, as they assert, possess any deliberate impulse towards a life of virtue? Take any single one of the brute creation; it does not attempt to speak like a human being, but in using the natural kind of utterance sucked in, as it were, with its mother's milk[9], it deems it no loss to be deprived of articulate speech. Just in the same way those who believe that a vice was the origin and the cause of their being alive will never bring themselves to have a longing after virtue, because it will be a thing quite foreign to their nature. But, as a fact[1], they who by reflecting have cleansed the vision of their soul do all of them desire and strive after a life of virtue. Therefore it is by that fact clearly proved that vice is not prior in time to the act of beginning to live, and that our nature did not thence derive its source, but that the all-disposing wisdom of God was the Cause of it: in short, that the soul issues on the stage of life in the manner which is pleasing to its Creator, and then (but not before), by virtue of its power of willing, is free to choose that which is to its mind, and so, whatever it may wish to be, becomes that very thing. We may understand this truth by the example of the eyes. To see

is their natural state; but to fail to see results to them either from choice or from disease. This unnatural state may supervene instead of the natural, either by wilful shutting of the eyes or by deprivation of their sight through disease. With the like truth we may assert that the soul derives its constitution from God, and that, as we cannot conceive of any vice in Him, it is removed from any necessity of being vicious; that nevertheless, though this is the condition in which it came into being, it can be attracted of its own free will in a chosen direction, either wilfully shutting its eyes to the Good, or letting them be damaged[2] by that insidious foe whom we have taken home to live with us, and so passing through life in the darkness of error; or, reversely, preserving undimmed its sight of the Truth and keeping far away from all weaknesses that could darken it. —But then some one will ask, "When and how did it come into being?" Now as for the question, how any single thing came into existence, we must banish it altogether from our discussion. Even in the case of things which are quite within the grasp of our understanding and of which we have sensible perception, it would be impossible for the speculative reason[3] to grasp the "how" of the production of the phenomenon; so much so, that even inspired and saintly men have deemed such questions insoluble. For instance, the Apostle says, "Through faith we understand that the worlds were framed by the word of God, so that things which are seen are not made of things which do appear[4]." He would not, I take it, have spoken like that, if he had thought that the question could be settled by any efforts of the reasoning powers. While the Apostle affirms that it is an object of his faith[5] that it was by the will of God that the world itself and all which is therein was framed (whatever this "world" be that involves the idea of the whole visible and invisible creation), he has on the other hand left out of the investigation the "how" of this framing. Nor do I think that this point can ever be reached by any inquirers. The question presents, on the face of it, many insuperable difficulties. How, for instance, can a world of movement come from one that is at rest? how from the simple and undimensional that which shows dimension and compositeness? Did it come actually out of the Supreme Being? But the fact that this world presents a difference in kind to that Being militates against[6] such a

---

[9] συντρόφῳ.
[1] ἀλλὰ μὴν introduces a fact into the argument (cf. καὶ μὴν); Lat. "verum enimvero."

[2] τὸν ὀφθαλμὸν βλαπτομένην.   [3] λόγῳ.   [4] Heb. xi. 3.
[5] *that it is an object of his faith*, &c. In the Greek the μὲν contrasts the Apostle's declaration on this point with his silence as to the "how."
[6] *militates against*, &c. 'Αλλ' οὐχ ὁμολογεῖται (reading then, ὅτι τὸ ἑτερογενὲς ἔχει πρὸς ἐκείνην τὰ ὄντα). Cf. Plato, *Tim.* 29 C, αὐτοὶ αὐτοῖς οὐχ ὁμολογούμενοι λόγοι, "theories that *contradict* each other." This world cannot come out of the Supreme Being: its

supposition. Did it then come from some other quarter? Yet Faith[7] can contemplate nothing as quite outside the Divine Nature; for we should have to believe in two distinct and separate Principles, if outside the Creative Cause we are to suppose something else, which the Artificer, with all His skill, has to put under contribution for the formative processes of the Universe. Since, then, the Cause of all things is one, and one only, and yet the existences produced by that Cause are not of the same nature as its transcendent quality, an inconceivability of equal magnitude[8] arises in both our suppositions, i. e. both that the creation comes straight out of the Divine Being, and that the universe owes its existence to some cause other than Him; for if created things are to be of the same nature as God, we must consider Him to be invested with the properties belonging to His creation; or else a world of matter, outside the circle of God's substance, and equal, on the score of the absence in it of all beginning, to the eternity of the Self-existent One, will have to be ranged against Him : and this is in fact what the followers of Manes, and some of the Greek philosophers who held opinions of equal boldness with his, did imagine ; and they raised this imagination into a system. In order, then, to avoid falling into either of these absurdities, which the inquiry into the origin of things involves, let us, following the example of the Apostle, leave the question of the "how" in each created thing, without meddling with it at all, but merely observing incidentally that the movement of God's Will becomes at any moment that He pleases a fact, and the intention becomes at once realized in Nature[9] ; for Omnipotence does not leave the plans of its far-seeing skill in the state of unsubstantial wishes : and the actualizing of a wish is Substance. In short, the whole world of existing things falls into two divisions : i. e. that of the intelligible, and that of the corporeal : and the intelligible creation does not, to begin with, seem to be in any way at variance with a spiritual Being, but on the contrary to verge closely upon Him, exhibiting as it does that absence of tangible form and of dimension which we rightly attribute to His transcendent nature. The corporeal creation[1],

on the other hand, must certainly be classed amongst specialities that have nothing in common with the Deity ; and it does offer this supreme difficulty to the Reason ; namely, that the Reason cannot see *how* the visible comes out of the invisible, *how* the hard solid comes out of the intangible, *how* the finite comes out of the infinite, *how* that which is circumscribed by certain proportions, where the idea of quantity comes in, can come from that which has no size, no proportions, and so on through each single circumstance of body. But even about this we can say so much : i. e. that not one of those things which we attribute to body is itself body ; neither figure, nor colour, nor weight, nor extension, nor quantity, nor any other qualifying notion whatever ; but every one of them is a category ; it is the combination of them all into a single whole that constitutes body. Seeing, then, that these several qualifications which complete the particular body are grasped by thought alone, and not by sense, and that the Deity is a thinking being, what trouble can it be to such a thinking agent to produce the thinkables whose mutual combination generates *for us* the substance of that body ? All this discussion, however, lies outside our present business. The previous question was,— If some souls exist anterior to their bodies, *when* and *how* do they come into existence ? and of this question[2], again, the part about the *how* has been left out of our examination and has not been meddled with, as presenting impenetrable difficulties. There remains the question of the *when* of the soul's commencement of existence : it follows immediately on that which we have already discussed. For if we were to grant that the soul has lived previous to its body[3] in some place of resort peculiar to itself, then we cannot avoid seeing some force in all that fantastic teaching lately discussed, which would explain the soul's habitation of the body as a consequence of some vice. Again, on the other hand, no one who can reflect will imagine an after-birth of the soul, i. e. that it is younger than the moulding of the body ; for every one can see for himself that not one amongst all the things that are inanimate or

---

alien nature contradicts that. Krabinger's translation is therefore wrong, "sed non constat :" and Oehler's, "Aber das ist nicht angemacht."   [7] ὁ λόγος.
  [8] Reading ἴση δή.   [9] ἡ φύσις.
  [1] The long Greek sentence, which begins here with a genitive absolute (τῆς δὲ σωματικῆς κτίσεως, κ. τ. λ.), leading up to nothing but the anacoluthon περὶ ὧν τοσοῦτον, κ. τ. λ., has been broken up in translating. Doubtless this anacoluthon can be explained by the sentences linked on to the last words (τῷ λόγῳ) of the genitive clause, which are so long as to throw that clause quite into the background. There is no need therefore to take the words where this anacoluthon begins, down to σῶμα γίνεται, as a parenthesis, with Krabinger and Oehler ; especially as the words that follow γίνεται are a direct recapitulation of what immediately precedes.

[2] Reading, as Dr. H. Schmidt conjectures, καὶ τούτου πάλιν, cf. 205 C.
[3] Origen, Gregory's master in most of his theology, did teach this very thing, the pre-existence of the soul : nor did he attempt to deny that *some* degree of transmigration was a necessary accompaniment of such teaching ; only he would adjust the moral meaning of it. Cf. c. *Celsum*, Lib. iii. 75. "And even if we should treat (i. e. medically) those who have caught the folly of the transmigration of souls from doctors who push down a reasoning nature into any of the unreasoning natures, or even into that which is insensate, how can any say that we shall not work improvement in their souls by teaching them that the bad do not have allotted to them by way of punishment that insensate or unreasoning state, but that what is inflicted by God upon the bad, be it pain or affliction, is only in the way of a very efficacious cure for them ? This is the teaching of the wise Christian : he attempts to teach the simpler of his flock as fathers do the merest infants." Not the theory itself, but the exaggeration of it, is here combated.

soulless possesses any power of motion or of growth; whereas there is no question about that which is bred in the uterus both growing and moving from place to place. It remains therefore that we must think that the point of commencement of existence is one and the same for body and soul. Also we affirm that, just as the earth receives the sapling from the hands of the husbandman and makes a tree of it, without itself imparting the power of growth to its nursling, but only lending it, when placed within itself, the impulse to grow, in this very same way that which is secreted from a man for the planting of a man is itself to a certain extent a living being as much gifted with a soul and as capable of nourishing itself as that from which it comes [4]. If this offshoot, in its diminutiveness, cannot contain at first all the activities and the movements of the soul, we need not be surprised; for neither in the seed of corn is there visible all at once the ear. How indeed could anything so large be crowded into so small a space? But the earth keeps on feeding it with its congenial aliment, and so the grain becomes the ear, without changing its nature while in the clod, but only developing it and bringing it to perfection under the stimulus of that nourishment. As, then, in the case of those growing seeds the advance to perfection is a graduated one [5], so in man's formation the forces of his soul show themselves in proportion to the size to which his body has attained. They dawn first in the fœtus, in the shape of the power of nutrition and of development: after that, they introduce into the organism that has come into the light the gift of perception: then, when this is reached, they manifest a certain measure of the reasoning faculty, like the fruit of some matured plant, not growing all of it at once, but in a continuous progress along with the shooting up of that plant. Seeing, then, that that which is secreted from one living being to lay the foundations of another living being cannot itself be dead (for a state of deadness arises from the privation of life, and it cannot be that privation should precede the having), we grasp from these considerations the fact that in the compound which results from the joining of both (soul and body) there is a simultaneous passage of both into existence; the one does not come first, any more than the other comes after. But as to the number of souls, our reason must necessarily contemplate a stopping some day of its increase; so that Nature's stream may not flow on for ever, pouring forward in her successive births and never staying that onward movement. The reason for our race having some day to come to a

standstill is as follows, in our opinion : since every intellectual reality is fixed in a plenitude of its own, it is reasonable to expect that humanity [6] also will arrive at a goal (for in this respect also humanity is not to be parted from the intellectual world [7]); so that we are to believe that it will not be visible for ever only in defect, as it is now : for this continual addition of after generations indicates that there is something deficient in our race.

Whenever, then, humanity shall have reached the plenitude that belongs to it, this on-streaming movement of production will altogether cease; it will have touched its destined bourn, and a new order of things quite distinct from the present procession of births and deaths will carry on the life of humanity. If there is no birth, it follows necessarily that there will be nothing to die. Composition must precede dissolution (and by composition I mean the coming into this world by being born); necessarily, therefore, if this synthesis does not precede, no dissolution will follow. Therefore, if we are to go upon probabilities, the life after this is shown to us beforehand as something that is fixed and imperishable, with no birth and no decay to change it.

The Teacher finished her exposition; and to the many persons sitting by her bedside the whole discussion seemed now to have arrived at a fitting conclusion. Nevertheless, fearing that if the Teacher's illness took a fatal turn (such as did actually happen), we should have no one amongst us to answer the objections of the unbelievers to the Resurrection [8], I still insisted.

The argument has not yet touched the most vital of all the questions relating to our Faith. I mean, that the inspired Writings, both in the New and in the Old Testament, declare most emphatically not only that, when our race has completed the ordered chain of its existence as the ages lapse through their complete circle [9], this current streaming onward as generation succeeds generation will cease altogether, but also that then, when the completed Universe no longer admits of further increase, all the souls in their entire number will come back out of their invisible and scattered condition into tangibility and light, the identical

---

[4] ἐκ τρεφομένου τρεφόμενον.   [5] κατὰ λόγον.

[6] This seems like a prelude to the Realism of the Middle Ages.
[7] Each individual soul represents, to Gregory's view, a "thought" of God, which becomes visible by the soul being born. There will come a time when all these "thoughts," which complete, and do not destroy, each other, will have completed the πλήρωμα (Humanity) which the Deity contemplates. This immediate apparition of a soul, as a "thought" of God, is very unlike the teaching of his master Origen : and yet more sober, and more scriptural.
[8] The situation here is, as Dr. H. Schmidt points out, just like that in the *Phædo* of Plato, where all are satisfied with Socrates' discourse, except Kebes and Simmias, who seize the precious moments still left, to bring forward an objection which none but their great Teacher could remove.
[9] περιοδικὴν : a better reading than παροδικὴν, which most Codd. have.

atoms (belonging to each soul) reassembling together in the same order as before; and this reconstitution of human life is called, in these Writings which contain God's teaching, the Resurrection, the entire movement of the atoms receiving the same term as the raising up of that which is actually prostrate on the ground [1].

But, said she, which of these points has been left unnoticed in what has been said?

Why, the actual doctrine of the Resurrection, I replied.

And yet, she answered, much in our long and detailed discussion pointed to that.

Then are you not aware, I insisted, of all the objections, a very swarm of them, which our antagonists bring against us in connection with that hope of yours?

And I at once tried to repeat all the devices hit upon by their captious champions to upset the doctrine of the Resurrection.

She, however, replied, First, I think, we must briefly run over the scattered proclamations of this doctrine in Holy Scripture; they shall give the finishing touch to our discourse. Observe, then, that I can hear David, in the midst of his praises in the Divine Songs, saying at the end of the hymnody of the hundred and third (104th) Psalm, where he has taken for his theme God's administration of the world, "Thou shalt take away their breath, and they shall die, and return to their dust: Thou shalt send forth Thy Spirit, and they shall be created: and Thou shalt renew the face of the earth." He says that a power of the Spirit which works in all vivifies the beings into whom it enters, and deprives those whom He abandons of their life. Seeing, then, that the dying is declared to occur at the Spirit's departure, and the renewal of these dead ones at His appearance, and seeing moreover that in the order of the statement the death of those who are to be thus renewed comes first, we hold that in these words that mystery of the Resurrection is proclaimed to the Church, and that David in the spirit of prophecy expressed this very gift which you are asking about. You will find this same prophet in another place [2] also saying

that "the God of the world, the Lord of everything that is, hath showed Himself to us, that we may keep the Feast amongst the decorators;" by that mention of "decoration" with boughs, he means the Feast of Tabernacle-fixing, which, in accordance with Moses' injunction, has been observed from of old. That lawgiver, I take it, adopting a prophet's spirit, predicted therein things still to come; for though the decoration was always going on it was never finished. The truth indeed was foreshadowed under the type and riddle of those Feasts that were always occurring, but the true Tabernacle-fixing was not yet come; and on this account "the God and Lord of the whole world," according to the Prophet's declaration, "hath showed Himself to us, that the Tabernacle-fixing of this our tenement that has been dissolved may be kept for human kind"; a material decoration, that is, may be begun again by means of the concourse of our scattered atoms. For that word πυκασμὸς in its peculiar meaning signifies the Temple-circuit and the decoration which completes it. Now this passage from the Psalms runs as follows: "God and Lord hath showed Himself to us; keep the Feast amongst the decorators even unto the horns of the altar;" and this seems to me to proclaim in metaphors the fact that one single feast is to be kept by the whole rational creation, and that in that assembly of the saints the inferiors are to join the dance with their superiors. For in the case of the fabric of that Temple which was the Type it was not allowed to all who were on the outside of its circuit [3] to come within, but everything that was Gentile and alien was prohibited from entering; and of those, further, who had entered, all were not equally privileged to advance towards the centre; but only those who had consecrated themselves by a holier manner of life, and by certain sprinklings; and, again, not every one amongst these last might set foot within the interior of the Temple; the priests alone had the right of entering within the curtain, and that only for the service of the sanctuary; while even to the priests the darkened shrine of the Temple, where stood the beautiful Altar with its jutting horns, was forbidden, except to one of them, who held the highest office of the

---

[1] receiving the same term (συνονομαζομένης) as the raising up of that which is actually prostrate on the ground (τοῦ γεώδους), i. e. the term ἀνάστασις is extended by analogy to embrace the entire movement of the atoms. Though there is here of course an *allusion* to the elevation of the nature from the "earthly" to the "heavenly," and perhaps to the raising of the body from the tomb, yet the primary meaning is that the term ἀνάστασις is derived from its special use of raising from the ground one who lies prostrate (as a suppliant). *Some* of the elements of the body are supposed to be γεώδη, *i. e.* mingled with their kindred earth. But though strictly the word ἀνάστασις should apply to them alone, it does not do so, but denotes more generally the movement of *all* the atoms to reform the body.

[2] Gregory quotes as usual the LXX. for this Psalm (cxviii. 27): Θεὸς κύριος, καὶ ἐπέφανεν ἡμῖν· συστήσασθε τὴν ἑορτὴν ἐν τοῖς πυκάζουσιν ἕως τῶν κεράτων τοῦ θυσιαστηρίου. [Krabinger has replaced συστήσασθε from one of his Codd. for the common συστήσασθαι;

but if this is retained ὥστε must be understood. Cf. Matt., Gr. Gr. § 532.] The LXX. is rendered by the Psalterium Romanum "constitute diem in *confrequentationibus.*" So also Eusebius, Theodoret, and Chrysostom interpret. But the Psalterium Gallicanum reproduces the LXX. otherwise, *i. e.* in *condensis*, as Apollinaris and Jerome (in *frondosis*) also understand it. "Adorn the feast with green boughs, even to the horns of the altar": Luther. "It is true that during the time of the second temple the altar of burnt offering was planted round about at the Feast of Tabernacles with large branches of osiers, which leaned over the edge of that altar": Delitzsch (who however says that this is, *linguistically*, untenable). Gregory's rendering differs from this only in making πυκάζουσιν masculine.

[3] Reading τοῖς ἕξωθεν περιβολῆς.

priesthood, and who once a year, on a stated day, and unattended, passed within it, carrying an offering more than usually sacred and mystical. Such being the differences in connection with this Temple which you know of, it was clearly [4] a representation and an imitation of the condition of the spirit-world, the lesson taught by these material observances being this, that it is not the whole of the rational creation that can approach the temple of God, or, in other words, the adoration of the Almighty; but that those who are led astray by false persuasions are outside the precinct of the Deity; and that from the number of those who by virtue of this adoration have been preferred to the rest and admitted within it, some by reason of sprinklings and purifications have still further privileges; and again amongst these last those who have been consecrated priests have privileges further still, even to being admitted to the mysteries of the interior. And, that one may bring into still clearer light the meaning of the allegory, we may understand the Word here as teaching this, that amongst all the Powers endued with reason some have been fixed like a Holy Altar in the inmost shrine of the Deity; and that again of these last some jut forward like horns, for their eminence, and that around them others are arranged first or second, according to a prescribed sequence of rank; that the race of man, on the contrary, on account of indwelling evil was excluded from the Divine precinct, but that purified with lustral water it re-enters it; and, since all the further barriers by which our sin has fenced us off from the things within the veil are in the end to be taken down, whenever the time comes that the tabernacle of our nature is as it were to be fixed up again in the Resurrection, and all the inveterate corruption of sin has vanished from the world, then a universal feast will be kept around the Deity by those who have decorated themselves in the Resurrection; and one and the same banquet will be spread for all, with no differences cutting off any rational creature from an equal participation in it; for those who are now excluded by reason of their sin will at last be admitted within the Holiest places of God's blessedness, and will bind themselves to the horns of the Altar there, that is, to the most excellent of the transcendental Powers. The Apostle says the same thing more plainly when he indicates the final accord of the whole Universe with the Good: "That" to Him "every knee should bow, of things in heaven, and things in earth, and things under the earth: And that every tongue

should confess that Jesus Christ is Lord, to the glory of God the Father": instead of the "horns," speaking of that which is angelic and "in heaven," and by the other terms signifying ourselves, the creatures whom we think of next to that; one festival of united voices shall occupy us all; that festival shall be the confession and the recognition of the Being Who truly Is. One might (she proceeded) select many other passages of Holy Scripture to establish the doctrine of the Resurrection. For instance, Ezekiel leaps in the spirit of prophecy over all the intervening time, with its vast duration; he stands, by his powers of foresight, in the actual moment of the Resurrection, and, as if he had really gazed on what is still to come, brings it in his description before our eyes. He saw a mighty plain [5], unfolded to an endless distance before him, and vast heaps of bones upon it flung at random, some this way, some that; and then under an impulse from God these bones began to move and group themselves with their fellows that they once owned, and adhere to the familiar sockets, and then clothe themselves with muscle, flesh, and skin (which was the process called "decorating" in the poetry of the Psalms); a Spirit in fact was giving life and movement to everything that lay there. But as regards our Apostle's description of the wonders of the Resurrection, why should one repeat it, seeing that it can easily be found and read? how, for instance, "with a shout" and the "sound of trumpets" (in the language of the Word) all dead and prostrate things shall be "changed [6] in the twinkling of an eye" into immortal beings. The expressions in the Gospels also I will pass over; for their meaning is quite clear to every one; and our Lord does not declare in word alone that the bodies of the dead shall be raised up again; but He shows in action the Resurrection itself, making a beginning of this work of wonder from things more within our reach and less capable of being doubted. First, that is, He displays His life-giving power in the case of the deadly forms of disease, and chases those maladies by one word of command; then He raises a little girl just dead; then He makes a young man, who is already being carried out, sit up on his bier, and delivers him to his mother; after that He calls forth from his tomb the four-days-dead and already decomposed Lazarus, vivifying the prostrate body with His commanding voice; then after three days He raises from the dead His own human body, pierced though it was

---

[4] Reading δηλόνοτι.

[5] Ezek. xxxvii. 1–10.

[6] Gregory, as often, seems to quote from memory (ὑπαμειφθήσεσθαι, but 1 Cor. xv. 52 ἀλλαγησόμεθα; and St. Paul says ἡμεῖς δὲ, i. e. "we shall be changed," in distinction from the dead *generally*, who "shall be raised incorruptible"). But the doctrine of a *general* resurrection, with or without change, is quite in harmony with the end of this treatise. Cf. p. 468.

with the nails and spear, and brings the print of those nails and the spear-wound to witness to the Resurrection. But I think that a detailed mention of these things is not necessary; for no doubt about them lingers in the minds of those who have accepted the written accounts of them.

But that, said I, was not the point in question. Most of your hearers will assent to the fact that there will some day be a Resurrection, and that man will be brought before the incorruptible tribunal [7]; on account both of the Scripture proofs, and also of our previous examination of the question. But still the question remains [8] : Is the state which we are to expect to be like the present state of the body? Because if so, then, as I was saying [9], men had better avoid hoping for any Resurrection at all. For if our bodies are to be restored to life again in the same sort of condition as they are in when they cease to breathe, then all that man can look forward to in the Resurrection is an unending calamity. For what spectacle is more piteous than when in extreme old age our bodies shrivel up [1] and change into something repulsive and hideous, with the flesh all wasted in the length of years, the skin dried up about the bones till it is all in wrinkles, the muscles in a spasmodic state from being no longer enriched with their natural moisture, and the whole body consequently shrunk, the hands on either side powerless to perform their natural work, shaken with an involuntary trembling? What a sight again are the bodies of persons in a long consumption! They differ from bare bones only in giving the appearance of being covered with a worn-out veil of skin. What a sight too are those of persons swollen with the disease of dropsy! What words could describe the unsightly disfigurement of sufferers from leprosy [2]? Gradually over all their limbs

and organs of sensation rottenness spreads and devours them. What words could describe that of persons who have been mutilated in earthquake, battle, or by any other visitation, and live on in such a plight for a long time before their natural deaths? Or of those who from an injury have grown up from infancy with their limbs awry! What can one say of them? What is one to think about the bodies of new-born infants who have been either exposed, or strangled, or died a natural death, if they are to be brought to life again just such as they were? Are they to continue in that infantine state? What condition could be more miserable than that? Or are they to come to the flower of their age? Well, but what sort of milk has Nature got to suckle them again with? It comes then to this : that, if our bodies are to live again in every respect the same as before, this thing that we are expecting is simply a calamity; whereas if they are not the same, the person raised up will be another than he who died. If, for instance, a little boy was buried, but a grown man rises again, or reversely, how can we say that the dead in his very self is raised up, when he has had some one substituted for him by virtue of this difference in age? Instead of the child, one sees a grown-up man. Instead of the old man, one sees a person in his prime. In fact, instead of the one person another entirely. The cripple is changed into the able-bodied man; the consumptive sufferer into a man whose flesh is firm; and so on of all possible cases, not to enumerate them for fear of being prolix. If, then, the body will not come to life again just such in its attributes as it was when it mingled with the earth, that dead body will not rise again; but on the contrary the earth will be formed into another man. How, then, will the Resurrection affect myself, when instead of me some one else will come to life? Some one else, I say; for how could I recognize myself when, instead of what was once myself, I see some one not myself? It cannot really be I, unless it is in every respect the same as myself. Suppose, for instance, in this life I had in my memory the traits of some one; say he was bald, had prominent lips, a somewhat flat nose, a fair complexion, grey eyes, white hair, wrinkled skin; and then went to look for such an one, and met a young man with a fine head of hair, an aquiline nose, a dark complexion, and in all other respects quite different in his type of countenance; am I likely in seeing the latter to think of the former? But why dwell longer on these the less forcible objections to the Resurrection, and neglect the strongest one of all? For who has not heard that human life is like a stream, moving from birth to death at

---

[7] *the incorruptible tribunal.* The Judgment comes *after* the Resurrection (cf. 250 A, 254 A, 258 D), and *after* the purifying and chastising detailed above. The latter is represented by Gregory as a necessary process of *nature* : but not till the Judgment will the *moral* value of each life be revealed. There is no contradiction, such as Möller tries to find, between this Dialogue and Gregory's *Oratio Catechetica.* There too he is speaking of chastisement *after* the Resurrection and *before* the Judgment. "For not everything that is granted in the resurrection means a return to existence will return to the same kind of life. There is a wide interval between those who have been purified (*i. e.* by baptism) and those who still need purification." . . . "But as for those whose weaknesses have become inveterate, and to whom no purgation of their defilement has been applied, no mystic water, no invocation of the Divine power, no amendment by repentance, it is absolutely necessary that they should be submitted to something proper to their case," *i. e.* to compensate for Baptism, which they have never received (c. 35).

[8] φῆσιν should probably be struck out (as the insertion of a copyist encouraged by εἶπον below) : five of Krabinger's Codd. omit it.

[9] εἶπον. Cf. 243 C : καὶ ἅμα λεγειν ἐπεχείρουν ὅσα πρὸς ἀνατρο-πὴν τῆς ἀναστάσεως παρὰ τῶν ἐριστικῶν ἐφευρίσκεται. So that this is not the first occasion on which objections to the Resurrection have been started by Gregory, and there is no occasion to adopt the conjecture of Augentius and Sifanus, ἀν εἴποιμι, "dixerim", especially as εἶπον is found in all Codd. without exception.

[1] Reading καταρρικνωθέντα.

[2] ἱερᾷ νόσῳ. That these words can mean leprosy, as well as epilepsy, seems clear from Eusebius.

a certain rate of progress, and then only ceasing from that progressive movement when it ceases also to exist? This movement indeed is not one of spacial change; our bulk never exceeds itself; but it makes this advance by means of internal alteration; and as long as this alteration is that which its name implies, it never remains at the same stage (from moment to moment); for how can that which is ·being altered be kept in any sameness? The fire on the wick, as far as appearance goes, certainly seems always the same, the continuity of its movement giving it the look of being an uninterrupted and self-centred whole; but in reality it is always passing itself along and never remains the same; the moisture which is extracted by the heat is burnt up and changed into smoke the moment it has burst into flame, and this alterative force effects the movement of the flame, working by itself the change of the subject-matter into smoke; just, then, as it is impossible for one who has touched that flame twice on the same place, to touch twice the very same flame [3] (for the speed of the alteration is too quick; it does not wait for that second touch, however rapidly it may be effected; the flame is always fresh and new; it is always being produced, always transmitting itself, never remaining at one and the same place), a thing of the same kind is found to be the case with the constitution of our body. There is influx and efflux going on in it in an alterative progress until the moment that it ceases to live; as long as it is living it has no stay; for it is either being replenished, or it is discharging in vapour, or it is being kept in motion by both of these processes combined. If, then, a particular man is not the same even as he was yesterday [4], but is made different by this transmutation, when so be that the Resurrection shall restore our body to life again, that single man will become a crowd of human beings, so that with his rising again there will be found the babe, the child, the boy, the youth, the man, the father, the old man, and all the intermediate persons that he once was.

But further [5]; chastity and profligacy are both carried on in the flesh; those also who endure the most painful tortures for their religion, and those on the other hand who shrink from such, both one class and the other reveal their character in relation to fleshly sensations; how, then, can justice be done at the Judgment [6]? Or take the case of one and the same man first sinning and then cleansing himself by repentance, and then, it might so happen, relapsing into his sin; in such a case both the defiled and the undefiled body alike undergoes a change, as his nature changes, and neither of them continue to the end the same; which body, then, is the profligate to be tortured in? In that which is stiffened with old age and is near to death? But this is not the same as that which did the sin. In that, then, which defiled itself by giving way to passion? But where is the old man, in that case? This last, in fact, will not rise again, and the Resurrection will not do a complete work; or ·else he will rise, while the criminal will escape. Let me say something else also from amongst the objections made by unbelievers to this doctrine. No part, they urge, of the body is made by nature without a function. Some parts, for instance, are the efficient causes within us of our being alive; without them our life in the flesh could not possibly be carried on; such are the heart, liver, brain, lungs, stomach, and the other vitals; others are assigned to the activities of sensation; others to those of handing and walking [7]; others are adapted for the transmission of a posterity. Now if the life to come is to be in exactly the same circumstances as this, the supposed change in us is reduced to nothing; but if the report is true, as indeed it is, which represents marriage as forming no part of the economy of that after-life, and eating and drinking as not then preserving its continuance, what use will there be for the members of our body, when we are no longer to expect in that existence any of the activities for which our members now exist? If, for the sake of marriage, there are now certain organs adapted for marriage, then, whenever the latter ceases to be, we shall not need those organs: the same may be said of the

---

3 *to touch twice the very same flame.* Albert Jahn (quoted by Krabinger) here remarks that Gregory's comparison rivals that of Heraclitus: and that there is a deliberate intention of improving on the expression of the latter, "you cannot step twice into the same stream." Above (p. 459), Gregory has used directly Heraclitus' image, "so that Nature's stream may not flow on for ever, pouring forward in her successive births," &c. See also *De Hom. Opif.* c. 13 (beginning).

4 *not the same even as he was yesterday.* Cf. Gregory's *Oratio de Mortuis,* t. III. p. 633 A. "It is not exaggeration to say that death is woven into our life. Practically such an idea will be found by any one to be based on a reality: for experiment would confirm this belief that the man of yesterday is not the same as the man of to-day in material substance, but that something of him must be alway becoming dead, or be growing, or being destroyed, or ejected: . . . Wherefore, according to the expression of the mighty Paul, 'we die daily': we are not always the same people remaining in the same homes of the body, but each moment we change from what we were by reception and ejectment, altering continually into a fresh body."

5 A fresh objection is here started. It is answered (254 A, B).
6 Which succeeds (and is bound up with) the Resurrection. The argument is, "the *flesh* has behaved differently in *different persons* here; how then can it be treated alike in all by being allowed to rise again? Even before the judgment an injustice has been done by all rising in the same way to a new life."—In what follows, ἡ τοῦ αὐτοῦ νῦν μὲν, κ.τ.λ., the difficulty of different dispositions in the *same* person is considered.
7 παρεκτικῆς καὶ μεταβατικῆς ἐνεργείας. To the latter expression, which simply means walking, belong the words below, καὶ πρὸς τὸν δρομον οἱ πόδες (p. 464). Schmidt well remarks that a simpler form than μεταβατικός does not exist, because in all walking the notion of putting one foot in the place of the other (μετά) is implied; and shows that Krabinger's translation "transeundi officium" makes too much of the word.

hands for working with, the feet for running with, the mouth for taking food with, the teeth for grinding it with, the organs of the stomach for digesting, the evacuating ducts for getting rid of that which has become superfluous. When, therefore, all those operations will be no more, how or wherefore will their instruments exist? So that necessarily, if the things that are not going to contribute in any way to that other life are not to surround the body, none of the parts which at present constitute the body would[8] exist either. That life[9], then, will be carried on by other instruments; and no one could call such a state of things a Resurrection, where the particular members are no longer present in the body, owing to their being useless to that life. But if on the other hand our Resurrection will be represented in every one of these, then the Author of the Resurrection will fashion things in us of no use and advantage to that life. And yet we must believe, not only that there is a Resurrection, but also that it will not be an absurdity. We must, therefore, listen attentively to the explanation of this, so that, for every part of this truth we may have its probability saved to the last[10].

When I had finished, the Teacher thus replied, You have attacked the doctrines connected with the Resurrection with some spirit, in the way of rhetoric as it is called; you have coursed round and round the truth with plausibly subversive arguments; so much so, that those who have not very carefully considered this mysterious truth might possibly be affected in their view of it by the likelihood of those arguments, and might think that the difficulty started against what has been advanced was not altogether beside the point. But, she proceeded, the truth does not lie in these arguments, even though we may find it impossible to give a rhetorical answer to them, couched in equally strong language. The true explanation of all these questions is still stored up in the hidden treasure-rooms of Wisdom, and will not come to the light until that moment when we shall be taught the mystery of the Resurrection by the reality of it; and then there will be no more need of phrases to explain the things which we

now hope for. Just as many questions might be started for debate amongst people sitting up at night as to the kind of thing that sunshine is, and then the simple appearing of it in all its beauty would render any verbal description superfluous, so every calculation that tries to arrive conjecturally at the future state will be reduced to nothingness by the object of our hopes, when it comes upon us. But since it is our duty not to leave the arguments brought against us in any way unexamined, we will expound the truth as to these points as follows. First let us get a clear notion as to the scope of this doctrine; in other words, what is the end that Holy Scripture has in view in promulgating it and creating the belief in it. Well, to sketch the outline of so vast a truth and to embrace it in a definition, we will say that the Resurrection is "*the reconstitution of our nature in its original form*[1]." But in that form of life, of which God Himself was the Creator, it is reasonable to believe that there was neither age nor infancy nor any of the sufferings arising from our present various infirmities, nor any kind of bodily affliction whatever. It is reasonable, I say, to believe that God was the Creator of none of these things, but that man was a thing divine before his humanity got within reach of the assault of evil; that then, however, with the inroad of evil, all these afflictions also broke in upon him. Accordingly a life that is free from evil is under no necessity whatever of being passed amidst the things that result from evil. It follows that when a man travels through ice he must get his body chilled; or when he walks in a very hot sun that he must get his skin darkened; but if he has kept clear of the one or the other, he escapes these results entirely, both the darkening and the chilling; no one, in fact, when a particular cause was removed, would be justified in looking for the effect of that particular cause. Just so our nature, becoming passional, had to encounter all the necessary results of a life of passion: but when it shall have started back to that state of passionless blessedness, it will no longer encounter the inevitable results of evil tendencies. Seeing, then, that all the infusions of the life of the brute into our nature were not in us before our humanity descended through the touch of evil into passions, most certainly, when we abandon those passions, we shall abandon all their visible results. No one, therefore, will be justified in seeking in that other life for the consequences in us of any passion. Just as if a man, who, clad in a ragged tunic, has divested himself of the garb, feels no

---

8 Reading ὡς ἂν ἀνάγκην εἶναι, εἰ μὴ εἴη περὶ τὸ σῶμα τὰ πρὸς οὐδὲν, κ.τ.λ. The ἂν seems required by the protasis εἰ μὴ εἴη, and two Codd. supply it. The interrogative sentence ends with ἔσται.—Below (ὥστε παθεῖν ἂν), ἂν is found with the same force with the infinitive; "so that those . . . might possibly be affected."

9 Reading ἐν ἄλλοις ἄρ᾽ ἡ ζωή, as Schmidt suggests, and as the sense seems to require, although there is no MS. authority except for γὰρ.

10 *saved to the last.* The word here is διασώζειν; lit. to "preserve through danger," but it is used by later writers mostly of dialectic battles, and Plato himself uses it so (e. g. *Timæus*, p. 56, 68, *Polit.* p. 395) always of "probability." It is used by Gregory, literally, in his letter to Flavian, "we at last *arrived alive* in our own district," and, with a slight difference, *On Pilgrimages*, "it is impossible for a woman to accomplish so long a journey without a *conductor*, on account of her natural weakness." Hence the late word διασώστης, dux itineris.

---

1 The actual language of this definition is Platonic (cf. *Sympos.* p. 193 D), but it is Gregory's constant formula for the Christian Resurrection; see *De Hom. Opif.* c. 17; *In Ecclesiast.* I. p. 385 A; *Funeral Oration for Pulcheria*, III. p. 523 C; *Orat. de Mortuis*, III. p. 632 C; *De Virginitate*, c. xii. p. 358.

more its disgrace upon him, so we too, when we have cast off that dead unsightly tunic made from the skins of brutes and put upon us (for I take the "coats of skins" to mean that conformation belonging to a brute nature with which we were clothed when we became familiar with passionate indulgence), shall, along with the casting off of that tunic, fling from us all the belongings that were round us of that skin of a brute; and such accretions are sexual intercourse, conception, parturition, impurities, suckling, feeding, evacuation, gradual growth to full size, prime of life, old age, disease, and death. If that skin is no longer round us, how can its resulting consequences be left behind within us? It is folly, then, when we are to expect a different state of things in the life to come, to object to the doctrine of the Resurrection on the ground of something that has nothing to do with it. I mean, what has thinness or corpulence, a state of consumption or of plethora, or any other condition supervening in a nature that is ever in a flux, to do with the other life, stranger as it is to any fleeting and transitory passing such as that? One thing, and one thing only, is required for the operation of the Resurrection; viz. that a man should have lived, by being born; or, to use rather the Gospel words, that "a man should be born[2] into the world"; the length or briefness of the life, the manner, this or that, of the death, is an irrelevant subject of inquiry in connection with that operation. Whatever instance we take, howsoever we suppose this to have been, it is all the same; from these differences in life there arises no difficulty, any more than any facility, with regard to the Resurrection. He who has once begun to live must necessarily go on having once lived[3], after his intervening dissolution in death has been repaired in the Resurrection. As to the *how* and the *when* of his dissolution, what do *they* matter to the Resurrection? Consideration of such points belongs to another line of inquiry altogether. For instance, a man may have lived in bodily comfort, or in affliction, virtuously or viciously, renowned or disgraced; he may have passed his days miserably, or happily. These and such-like results must be obtained from the length of his life and the manner of his living; and to be able to pass a judgment on the things done in his life, it *will* be necessary for the judge to scrutinize his indulgences, as the case may be, or his losses, or his disease, or his old age, or his prime, or his youth, or his wealth, or his poverty: how well

or ill a man, placed in either of these, concluded his destined career; whether he was the recipient of many blessings, or of many ills in a length of life; or tasted neither of them at all, but ceased to live before his mental powers were formed. But whenever the time come that God shall have brought our nature back to the primal state of man, it will be useless to talk of such things then, and to imagine that objections based upon such things can prove God's power to be impeded in arriving at His end. His end is one, and one only; it is this: when the complete whole of our race shall have been perfected from the first man to the last,—some having at once in this life been cleansed from evil, others having afterwards in the necessary periods been healed by the Fire, others having in their life here been unconscious equally of good and of evil,—to offer to every one of us participation in the blessings which are in Him, which, the Scripture tells us, "eye hath not seen, nor ear heard," nor thought ever reached. But this is nothing else, as I at least understand it, but to be in God Himself; for the Good which is above hearing and eye and heart must be that Good which transcends the universe. But the difference between the virtuous and the vicious life led at the present time[4] will be illustrated in this way; viz. in the quicker or more tardy participation of each in that promised blessedness. According to the amount of the ingrained wickedness of each will be computed the duration of his cure. This cure consists in the cleansing of his soul, and that cannot be achieved without an excruciating condition, as has been expounded in our previous discussion. But any one would more fully comprehend the futility and irrelevancy of all these objections by trying to fathom the depths of our Apostle's wisdom. When explaining this mystery to the Corinthians, who, perhaps, themselves were bringing forward the same objections to it as its impugners to-day bring forward to overthrow our faith, he proceeds on his own authority to chide the audacity of their ignorance, and speaks thus: "Thou wilt say, then, to me, How are the dead raised up, and with what body do they come? Thou fool, that which thou sowest is not quickened, except it die; And that which thou sowest, thou sowest not that body that shall be, but bare grain, it may chance of wheat or of some other grain; But God giveth it a body as it hath pleased Him." In that passage, as it seems to

---

[2] ἐγεννήθη. S. John xvi. 21.
[3] τὸν γὰρ τοῦ ζῆν ἀρξάμενον, ζῆσαι χρὴ πάντως. The present infinitive here expresses only a new state of existence, the aorist a continued act. The aorist may have this force, if (as a whole) it is viewed as a *single event* in past time. Cf. Appian, *Bell. Civ.* ii. 91, ἦλθον, εἶδον, ἐνίκησα.

[4] Reading with Krabinger, ἐν τῷ νῦν καιρῷ instead of ἐν τῷ μετὰ ταῦτα, which cannot possibly refer to what immediately precedes, *i. e.* the union with God, by means of the Resurrection. If μετὰ ταῦτα is retained, it must = μετὰ τοῦτον τὸν βίον. Gregory here implies that the Resurrection is not a single contemporaneous act, but differs in time, as individuals differ; carrying out the Scriptural distinction of a first and second Resurrection.

me, he gags the mouths of men who display their ignorance of the fitting proportions in Nature, and who measure the Divine power by their own strength, and think that only so much is possible to God as the human understanding can take in, but that what is beyond it surpasses also the Divine ability. For the man who had asked the Apostle, "how are the dead raised up?" evidently implies that it is impossible when once the body's atoms have been scattered that they should again come in concourse together; and this being impossible, and no other possible form of body, besides that arising from such a concourse, being left, he, after the fashion of clever controversialists, concludes the truth of what he wants to prove, by a species of syllogism, thus: If a body is a concourse of atoms, and a second assemblage of these is impossible, what sort of body will those get who rise again? This conclusion, involved seemingly in this artful contrivance of premisses, the Apostle calls "folly," as coming from men who failed to perceive in other parts of the creation the masterliness of the Divine power. For, omitting the sublimer miracles of God's hand, by which it would have been easy to place his hearer in a dilemma (for instance he might have asked "how or whence comes a heavenly body, that of the sun for example, or that of the moon, or that which is seen in the constellations; whence the firmament, the air, water, the earth?"), he, on the contrary, convicts the objectors of inconsiderateness by means of objects which grow alongside of us and are very familiar to all. "Does not even husbandry teach thee," he asks, "that the man who in calculating the transcendent powers of the Deity limits them by his own is a fool?" Whence do seeds get the bodies that spring up from them? What precedes this springing up? Is it not a death that precedes[5]? At least, if

---

[5] Dr. H. Schmidt has an admirable note here, pointing out the great and important difference between S. Paul's use of this analogy of the grain of wheat, and that of our Saviour in S. John xii. 23, whence S. Paul took it. In the words, "The hour is come that the Son of man should be glorified. Verily, verily I say unto you, Except a corn of wheat fall into the ground and die, it abideth alone: but if it die, it bringeth forth much fruit" (A. V.), the fact and the similitude exactly correspond. To the corn with its life-engendering shoot, answers the man with his vivifying soul. The shoot, when the necessary conditions are fulfilled, breaks through the corn, and mounts up into an ear, exquisitely developed: so the soul, when the due time is come, bursts from the body into a nobler form. Again, through the death of the integument a number of new corns are produced: so through the death of the body that encases a perfect soul (*i. e.* that of Jesus), an abundance of blessings is produced for mankind. Everything here exactly corresponds; the principle of life, on the one hand in the corn, on the other hand in the human body, breaks, by dying, into a more beautiful existence. But this comparison in S. Paul becomes a *similitude* rather than an *analogy*. With him the lifeless body is set over against the life-containing corn; he does not compare the lifeless body with the lifeless corn: because out of the latter no stalk and ear would ever grow. The comparison, therefore, is not exact: it is not pretended that the rising to life of the dead human body is not a process transcendently above the natural process of the rising of the ear of wheat. But the similitude serves to illustrate the *form* and the *quality* of the risen body, which has been in question since v. 35 (1 Cor. xv.), "with what body do they come?" and the salient point is that the risen body will be as little like the buried body, *as the ear*

---

the dissolution of a compacted whole is a death; for indeed it cannot be supposed that the seed would spring up into a shoot unless it had been dissolved in the soil, and so become spongy and porous to such an extent as to mingle its own qualities with the adjacent moisture of the soil, and thus become transformed into a root and shoot; not stopping even there, but changing again into the stalk with its intervening knee-joints that gird it up like so many clasps, to enable it to carry with figure erect the ear with its load of corn. Where, then, were all these things belonging to the grain before its dissolution in the soil? And yet this result sprang from that grain; if that grain had not existed first, the ear would not have arisen. Just, then, as the "body" of the ear comes to light out of the seed, God's artistic touch of power producing it all out of that single thing, and just as it is neither entirely the same thing as that seed nor something altogether different, so (she insisted) by these miracles performed on seeds you may now interpret the mystery of the Resurrection. The Divine power, in the superabundance of Omnipotence, does not only restore you that body once dissolved, but makes great and splendid additions to it, whereby the human being is furnished in a manner still more magnificent. "It is sown," he says, "in corruption; it is raised in incorruption: it is sown in weakness; it is raised in power: it is sown in dishonour; it is raised in glory: it is sown a natural body; it is raised a spiritual body." The grain of wheat, after its dissolution in the soil, leaves behind the slightness of its bulk and the peculiar quality of its shape, and yet it has not left and lost itself, but, still self-centred, grows into the ear, though in many points it has made an advance upon itself, viz. in size, in splendour, in complexity, in form. In the same fashion the human being deposits in death all those peculiar surroundings which it has acquired from passionate propensities; dishonour, I mean, and corruption and weakness and characteristics of age; and yet the human being does not lose itself. It changes into an ear of corn as it were; into incorruption, that is, and glory and honour and power and absolute perfection; into a condition in which its life is no longer carried on in the ways peculiar to mere nature, but has passed into a spiritual and passionless existence. For it is the peculiarity of the natural body to be always moving on a stream, to be always altering from its state for the moment and changing into something else; but none of these processes, which we observe

---

of wheat is like its corn. The possibility of the Resurrection has been *already* proved by S. Paul in this chapter by Christ's own Resurrection, which he states from the very commencement as a fact: it is not proved by this similitude.

not in man only but also in plants and brutes, will be found remaining in the life that shall be then. Further, it seems to me that the words of the Apostle in every respect harmonize with our own conception of what the Resurrection is. They indicate the very same thing that we have embodied in our own definition of it, wherein we said that the Resurrection is no other thing than "*the re-constitution of our nature in its original form.*" For, whereas we learn from Scripture in the account of the first Creation [6], that first the earth brought forth "the green herb" (as the narrative says), and that then from this plant seed was yielded, from which, when it was shed on the ground, the same form of the original plant again sprang up, the Apostle, it is to be observed, declares that this very same thing happens in the Resurrection also; and so we learn from him the fact, not only [7] that our humanity will be then changed into something nobler, but also that what we have therein to expect is nothing else than that which was at the beginning. In the beginning, we see, it was not an ear rising from a grain, but a grain coming from an ear, and, after that, the ear grows round the grain: and so the order indicated in this similitude [8] clearly shows that all that blessed state which arises for us by means of the Resurrection is only a return to our pristine state of grace. We too, in fact, were once in a fashion a full ear [9]; but the burning heat of sin withered us up, and then on our dissolution by death the earth received us: but in the spring of the Resurrection she will reproduce this naked grain [1] of our body in the form of an ear, tall, well-proportioned, and erect, reaching to the heights of heaven, and, for blade and beard, resplendent in incorruption, and with all the other godlike marks. For "this corruptible must put on incorruption"; and this incorruption and glory and honour and power are those distinct and acknowledged marks of Deity which once belonged to him who was created in God's image, and which we hope for hereafter. The first man Adam, that is, was the first ear; but with the arrival of evil human nature was diminished into a mere multitude [2]; and, as happens to the grain [3] on the ear, each individual man was denuded of the beauty of that primal ear, and mouldered in the soil: but in the Resurrection we are born again in our original splendour; only instead of that single primitive ear we become the countless myriads of ears in the cornfields. The virtuous life as contrasted with that of vice is distinguished thus: those who while living have by virtuous conduct exercised husbandry on themselves are at once revealed in all the qualities of a perfect ear, while those whose bare grain (that is the forces of their natural soul) has become through evil habits degenerate, as it were, and hardened by the weather (as the so-called "hornstruck" seeds [4], according to the experts in such things, grow up), will, though they live again in the Resurrection, experience very great severity from their Judge, because they do not possess the strength to shoot up into the full proportions of an ear, and thereby become that which we were before our earthly fall [5]. The remedy offered by the Over-

---

[6] The Resurrection being the second. The ἐπειδὴ here does not give the reason for what precedes: that is given in the words, φησὶ δὴ τοῦτο ὁ ἀπόστολος, to which the leading γὰρ therefore belongs: the colon should be replaced (after ἀνέδραμεν) by a comma.

[7] Reading οὐ μόνον δὲ τοῦτο, κ.τ.λ. The δὲ is not found in two Codd.

[8] *i. e.* of grain, adopted by the Apostle.

[9] στάχυς here might be the nom. plur. Any way it is a "nominativus pendens."

[1] This "*naked* grain" is suggested by the words of S. Paul, not so much 1 Cor. xv. 37, as 2 Cor. v. 4: "For we that are in this tabernacle do groan, being burdened: not for that we would be unclothed, but clothed upon." Tertullian's words (*de resurr. carnis* c. 52) deserve to be quoted, "Seritur granum sine folliculi veste, sine fundamento spicæ, sine munimento aristæ, sine superbiâ culmi. Exsurgit copiâ feneratum, compagine ædificatum, ordine structum, cultu munitum, et usquequaque vestitum." In allusion to this passage (2 Cor. v. 4), Origen says, "Our theory of the Resurrection teaches that the relations of a seed attach to that which the Scriptures call the 'tabernacle of the soul,' in which the righteous 'do groan being burdened,' not wishing to put it off, but 'to be clothed upon' (with something else). We do not, as Celsus thinks, mean by the resurrection anything like the transmigration of souls. The soul, in its essence unbodied and invisible, when it comes into material space, requires a body fitted to the conditions of that particular space: which body it wears, having either put off a former body, or else having put it on over its former body. . . For instance, when it comes to the actual birth into this world, it lays aside the environment (χωρίον) which was needed as long as it is in the womb of her that is with child: and it clothes itself with that which is necessary for one destined to pass through life. Then there is a 'tabernacle,' and 'an earthly house,' as well: and the Scriptures tell us that this 'earthly house' of the tabernacle is to be dissolved, but that the tabernacle itself is to surround itself with another house not made with hands. The men of God declare that the corruptible must put on incorruption (which is a different thing from the incorruptible), and the mortal must put on immortality (which is different from the immortal: just as the relative quality of wisdom is different from that which is absolutely wise). Observe, then, where this system leads us. It says that the souls put on incorruption and immortality like garments which keep their wearer from corruption, and their inmate (τὸν περικείμενον αὐτὰ) from death" (*c. Cels.* vii. 32). We see at once this is another explanation of the Resurrection, by the σπερματικὸς λόγος of the soul, and not Gregory's; with him the soul re-collects its scattered atoms, and he thus saves the true scriptural view.

[2] This connection of "evil" and "multitude" is essentially Platonic. Cf. also Plotinus, vi. 6. 1: "Multitude, then, is a revolt from unity, and infinity a more complete revolt by being infinite multitude: and so infinity is bad, and we are bad, when we are a multitude" (cf. "Legion" in the parable).

[3] *as happens to the grain*, i. e. to become bare, as compared with the beautiful envelopments of the entire ear.

[4] "*hornstruck*" *seeds*, i. e. those which have been struck by, or have struck, the horns of the oxen, in the process of sowing: according to the rustic superstition, which Gregory Nazianz. in some very excellent hexameters alludes to (*Opp.* t. II. pp. 66—163): "There is," he says, "a dry upsoakable seed, which never sinks into the ground, or fattens with the rain; it is harder than horn; its horn has struck the horn of the ox, what time the ploughman's hand is scattering the grain over his land." Ruhnken (ad *Timæum*, p. 155) has collected the ancient authorities on this point. The word is used by Plato of a "hard," "intractable" person. The "bare grain" of the wicked is here compared to these hard seeds, which even though they may sink into the earth and rise again, yet have a poor and stunted blade, which may never grow.

[5] Reading ἐπὶ τῆς γῆς, instead of τὴν γῆν: for a fall "on to the earth," instead of "on the earth," agrees neither with what Gregory (speaking by Macrina) has urged against the heathen doctrine of Transmigration, nor with the words of Scripture which he follows. The "earthly fall" is compared with the heavenly rising: κατάπτωσις, in the sense of a "moral fall," is used in 3 Maccab. ii. 14 (quoted by Schmidt.

seer of the produce is to collect together the tares and the thorns, which have grown up with the good seed, and into whose bastard life all the secret forces that once nourished its root have passed, so that it not only has had to remain without its nutriment, but has been choked and so rendered unproductive by this unnatural growth. When from the nutritive part within them everything that is the reverse or the counterfeit of it has been picked out, and has been committed to the fire that consumes everything unnatural, and so has disappeared, then in this class also their humanity will thrive and will ripen into fruit-bearing, owing to such husbandry, and some day after long courses of ages will get back again that universal form which God stamped upon us at the beginning. Blessed are they, indeed, in whom the full beauty of those ears shall be developed directly they are born in the Resurrection. Yet we say this without implying that any merely bodily distinctions will be manifest between those who have lived virtuously and those who have lived viciously in this life, as if we ought to think that one will be imperfect as regards his material frame, while another will win perfection as regards it. The prisoner and the free, here in this present world, are just alike as regards the constitutions of their two bodies ; though as regards enjoyment and suffering the gulf is wide between them. In this way, I take it, should we reckon the difference between the good and the bad in that intervening time [6].

---

[6] Between the Resurrection and the Ἀποκατάστασις.

For the perfection of bodies that rise from that sowing of death is, as the Apostle tells us, to consist in incorruption and glory and honour and power ; but any diminution in such excellences does not denote a corresponding bodily mutilation of him who has risen again, but a withdrawal and estrangement from each one of those things which are conceived of as belonging to the good. Seeing, then, that one or the other of these two diametrically opposed ideas, I mean good and evil, must any way attach to us, it is clear that to say a man is not included in the good is a necessary demonstration that he is included in the evil. But then, in connection with evil, we find no honour, no glory, no incorruption, no power ; and so we are forced to dismiss all doubt that a man who has nothing to do with these last-mentioned things must be connected with their opposites, viz. with weakness, with dishonour, with corruption, with everything of that nature, such as we spoke of in the previous parts of the discussion, when we said how many were the passions, sprung from evil, which are so hard for the soul to get rid of, when they have infused themselves into the very substance of its entire nature and become one with it. When such, then, have been purged from it and utterly removed by the healing processes worked out by the Fire, then every one of the things which make up our conception of the good will come to take their place ; incorruption, that is, and life, and honour, and grace, and glory, and everything else that we conjecture is to be seen in God, and in His Image, man as he was made.

IV. APOLOGETIC

THE GREAT CATECHISM

SUMMARY

The Trinity

PROLOGUE and Chapter I.—The belief in God rests on the art and wisdom displayed in the order of the world : the belief in the *Unity* of God, on the *perfection* that must belong to Him in respect of power, goodness, wisdom, etc. Still, the Christian who combats polytheism has need of care lest in contending against Hellenism he should fall unconsciously into Judaism. For God has a Logos : else He would be without reason. And this Logos cannot be merely an attribute of God. We are led to a more exalted conception of the Logos by the consideration that in the measure in which God is greater than we, all His predicates must also be higher than those which belong to us. Our logos is limited and transient ; but the subsistence (ὑπόστασις) of the Divine Logos must be indestructible ; and at the same time living, since the rational cannot be lifeless, like a stone. It must also have an independent life, not a participated life, else it would lose its simplicity ; and, as living, it must also have the faculty of will. This will of the Logos must be equalled by his power : for a mixture of choice and impotence would, again, destroy the simplicity. His will, as being Divine, must be also good. From this ability and will to work there follows the realization of the good ; hence the bringing into existence of the wisely and artfully adjusted world. But since, still further, the logical conception of the Word is in a certain sense a relative one, it follows that together with the Word He Who speaks it, *i. e.* the Father of the Word, must be recognized as existing. Thus the mystery of the faith avoids equally the absurdity of Jewish monotheism, and that of heathen polytheism. On the one hand, we say that the Word has *life and activity ;* on the other, we affirm that we find in the Λόγος, whose existence is derived from the Father, *all* the attributes of the Father's nature.

Chapter II.—By the analogy of human breath, which is nothing but inhaled and exhaled fire, *i. e.* an object foreign to us, is demonstrated the community of the Divine Spirit with the essence of God, and yet the independence of Its existence.

Chapter III.—From the Jewish doctrine, then, the unity of the Divine nature has been retained : from Hellenism the distinction into hypostases.

Chapter IV.—The Jew convicted from Scripture.

Reasonableness of the Incarnation.

Chapters V. and VI.—God created the world by His reason and wisdom ; for He cannot have proceeded irrationally in that work ; but His reason and wisdom are, as above shown, not to be conceived as a spoken word, or as the mere possession of knowledge, but as a personal and willing potency. If the entire world was created by this second Divine hypostasis, then certainly was man also thus created ; yet not in view of any necessity, but *from superabounding love,* that there might exist a being who should participate in the Divine perfections. If man was to be receptive of these, it was necessary that his nature should contain an element akin to God ; and, in particular, that he should be immortal. Thus, then, man was created in the image of God.

---

[1] It is not exactly clear why this Instruction for Catechizers is called the " Great " : perhaps with reference to some lesser manual. For its apologetic intention, see *Prolegomena*, p. 12. Its genuineness, which has been called in question by a few merely on the ground of opinions in it Origenistic and even Eutychian, is confirmed by Theodoret, *Dial.* ii. 3, *contr. Eutych.* Aubertin and Casaubon both recognize Gregory as its author. The division, however, of the chapters, by whoever made, is far from a correct guide to the contents ; but, by grouping them, the main argument can be made clear.

He could not therefore be without the gifts of freedom, independence, self-determination ; and his participation in the Divine gifts was consequently made dependent on his virtue. Owing to this *freedom* he could decide in favour of evil, which cannot have its origin in the Divine will, but only in our inner selves, where it arises in the form of a deviation from good, and so a privation of it. Vice is opposed to virtue only as the absence of the better. Since, then, all that is created is subject to change, it was possible that, in the first instance, one of the created spirits should turn his eye away from the good, and become envious, and that from this envy should arise a leaning towards badness, which should, in natural sequence, prepare the way for all other evil. He seduced the first men into the folly of turning away from goodness, *by disturbing the Divinely ordered harmony between their sensuous and intellectual natures ;* and guilefully tainting their wills with evil.

Chapters VII. and VIII.—God did not, on account of His foreknowledge of the evil that would result from man's creation, leave man uncreated ; for it was better to bring back sinners to original grace by the way of repentance and physical suffering than not to create man at all. The raising up of the fallen was a work befitting the Giver of life, Who is the wisdom and power of God ; and for this purpose He became man.

Chapter IX.—The Incarnation was not unworthy of Him ; for *only evil brings degradation.*

Chapter X.—The objection that the finite cannot contain the infinite, and that therefore the human nature could not receive into itself the Divine, is founded on the false supposition that the Incarnation of the Word means that the infinity of God was contained in the limits of the flesh, as in a vessel.—Comparison of the flame and wick.

Chapters XI., XII., XIII.—For the rest, the manner in which the Divine nature was united to the human surpasses our power of comprehension ; although we are not permitted to doubt the fact of that union in Jesus, *on account of the miracles which He wrought.* The supernatural character of those miracles bears witness to their Divine origin.

Chapters XIV., XV., XVI., XVII.—The scheme of the Incarnation is still further drawn out, to show that this way for man's salvation was preferable to a single fiat of God's will. Christ took human *weakness* upon Him ; but it was physical, not moral, weakness. In other words the Divine goodness did not change to its opposite, which is only vice. In Him soul and body were united, and then separated, according to the course of nature ; but after He had thus purged human life, He reunited them *upon a more general scale,* for all, and for ever, in the Resurrection.

Chapter XVIII.—The ceasing of demon-worship, the Christian martyrdoms, and the devastation of Jerusalem, are accepted by some as proofs of the Incarnation—

Chapters XIX., XX.—But not by the Greek and the Jew. To return, then, to its *reasonableness.* Whether we regard the goodness, the power, the wisdom, or the justice of God, it displays a combination of all these acknowledged attributes, which, if one be wanting, cease to be Divine. It is therefore true to the Divine perfection.

Chapters XXI., XXII., XXIII.—What, then, is the *justice* in it ? We must remember that man was necessarily created subject to change (to better or to worse). Moral beauty was to be the direction in which his free will was to move ; but then he was deceived, to his ruin, by an illusion of that beauty. After we had thus *freely* sold ourselves to the deceiver, He who of His goodness sought to restore us to liberty could not, because He was just too, for this end have recourse to measures of arbitrary violence. It was necessary therefore that a ransom should be paid, which should exceed in value that which was to be ransomed ; and hence it was necessary that the Son of God should surrender Himself to the power of death. God's *justice* then impelled Him to choose a method of exchange, as His *wisdom* was seen in executing it.

Chapters XXIV., XXV.—But how about the *power ?* That was more conspicuously displayed in Deity descending to lowliness, than in all the natural wonders of the universe. It was like flame being made to stream downwards. Then, after such a birth, Christ conquered death.

Chapter XXVI.—A certain deception was indeed practised upon the Evil one, by concealing the Divine nature within the human ; but for the latter, as himself a deceiver, it was only a just recompense that he should be deceived himself : the great adversary must himself at last find that what has been done is just and salutary, when he also shall experience the benefit of the Incarnation. He, as well as humanity, will be purged.

Chapters XXVII., XXVIII.—A patient, to be healed, must be *touched ;* and humanity had to be touched by Christ. It was not in "heaven" ; so only through the Incarnation could it be healed.—It was, besides, no more inconsistent with His Divinity to assume a human than a "heavenly" body ; all created beings are on a level beneath Deity. Even "abundant honour" is due to the instruments of human birth.

Chapters XXIX., XXX., XXXI.—As to the delay of the Incarnation. it was necessary that human degeneracy should have reached the lowest point, before the work of salvation could enter in. That, however, grace through faith has not come to all must be laid to the account of human freedom ; if God were to break down our opposition by violent means, the praise-worthiness of human conduct would be destroyed.

Chapter XXXII.—Even the death on the Cross was sublime : for it was the culminating and necessary point in that scheme of Love in which death was to be followed by blessed resurrection for the whole "lump" of humanity : and the Cross itself has a mystic meaning.

The Sacraments.

Chapters XXXIII., XXXIV., XXXV., XXXVI.—The saving nature of Baptism depends on three things ; Prayer, Water, and Faith. 1. It is shown how Prayer secures the Divine Presence. God is a God of truth ; and He has promised to come (as Miracles prove that He has come already) if invoked *in a particular way.* 2. It is shown how the Deity gives life from water. In human generation, even without prayer, He gives life from a small beginning. In a higher generation He transforms matter, not into soul, but into spirit. 3. Human freedom, as evinced in faith and repentance, is also necessary to Regeneration. Being thrice dipped in the water is our earliest mortification ; coming out of it is a forecast of the ease with which the pure shall rise in a *blessed* resurrection : the whole process is an imitation of Christ.

Chapter XXXVII.—The Eucharist unites the body, as Baptism the soul, to God. Our bodies, having received poison, need an Antidote ; and only by eating and drinking can it enter. One Body, the receptacle of Deity, is this Antidote, thus received. But how can it enter whole into each one of the Faithful ? This needs an illustration. Water gives its own body to a skin-bottle. So nourishment (bread and wine) by becoming flesh and blood gives bulk to the human frame : the nourishment *is* the body. Just as in the case of other men, our Saviour's nourishment (bread and wine) *was* His Body ; but these, nourishment and Body, were in Him changed into the Body of God by the Word indwelling. So now repeatedly the bread and wine, sanctified by the Word (the sacred Benediction), is *at the same time* changed into the Body of that Word ; and this Flesh is disseminated amongst all the Faithful.

Chapters XXXVIII., XXXIX.—It is essential for Regeneration to believe that the Son and the Spirit are not created spirits, but of like nature with God the Father ; for he who would make his salvation dependent (in the baptismal Invocation) on anything created would trust to an imperfect nature, and one itself needing a saviour.

Chapter XL.—He alone has truly become a child of God who gives evidence of his regeneration by putting away from himself all vice

---

PROLOGUE.

THE presiding ministers of the "mystery of godliness"[2] have need of a system in their in-structions, in order that the Church may be replenished by the accession of such as should be saved[3], through the teaching of the word of Faith being brought home to the hearing of un-believers. Not that the same method of in-struction will be suitable in the case of all who approach the word. The catechism must be adapted to the diversities of their religious worship ; with an eye, indeed, to the one aim and end of the system, but not using the same method of preparation in each individual case. The Judaizer has been preoccupied with one set of notions, one conversant with Hellenism, with others ; while the Anomœan,

and the Manichee, with the followers of Marcion[4], Valentinus, and Basilides[5], and the rest on the list of those who have wandered

---

[4] Marcion, a disciple of Cerdo, added a third Principle to the two which his master taught. The first is an unnamed, invisible, and good God, but no creator ; the second is a visible and creative God, *i. e.* the Demiurge ; the third intermediate between the invisible and visible God, *i. e.* the Devil. The Demiurge is the God and Judge of the Jews. Marcion affirmed the Resurrection of the soul alone. He rejected the Law and the Prophets as proceeding from the Demiurge ; only Christ came down from the unnamed and invisible Father to save the soul, and to confute this God of the Jews. The only Gospel he acknowledged was S. Luke's, omitting the beginning which details our Lord's Conception and Incarnation. Other portions also both in the middle and the end he curtailed. Besides this broken Gospel of S. Luke he retained ten of the Apostolic letters, but garbled even them. Gregory says elsewhere, that the followers of Eunomius got their "duality of Gods" from Marcion, but went beyond him in denying essential goodness to the Only-begotten, the "God of the Gospel."
[5] Of the Gnostics Valentinus and Basilides the truest and best account is given in H. L. Mansel's *Gnostics,* and in the articles upon them in the *Dictionary of Christian Biography.* It is there shown how all their visions of celestial Hierarchies, and the romances connected with them, were born of the attempt to solve the insoluble problem, *i. e.* how that which in modern philosophy would be called the Infinite is to pass into the Finite. They fell into the fatalism of the Emanationist view of the Deity. but still the attempt was an honest one.

---

[2] 1 Tim. iii. 16. [3] Acts ii. 47.

into heresy, each of them being prepossessed with their peculiar notions, necessitate a special controversy with their several opinions. The method of recovery must be adapted to the form of the disease. You will not by the same means cure the polytheism of the Greek, and the unbelief of the Jew as to the Only-begotten God: nor as regards those who have wandered into heresy will you, by the same arguments in each case, upset their misleading romances as to the tenets of the Faith. No one could set Sabellius[6] right by the same instruction as would benefit the Anomœan[7]. The controversy with the Manichee is profitless against the Jew[8]. It is necessary, therefore, as I have said, to regard the opinions which the persons have taken up, and to frame your argument in accordance with the error into which each has fallen, by advancing in each discussion certain principles and reasonable propositions, that thus, through what is agreed upon on both sides, the truth may conclusively be brought to light. When, then, a discussion is held with one of those who favour Greek ideas, it would be well to make the ascertaining of this the commencement of the reasoning, *i. e.* whether he presupposes the existence of a God, or concurs with the atheistic view. Should he say there is no God, then, from the consideration of the skilful and wise economy of the Universe he will be brought to acknowledge that there is a certain overmastering power manifested through these channels. If, on the other hand, he should have no doubt as to the existence of Deity, but should be inclined to entertain the presumption of a plurality of Gods, then we will adopt against him some such train of reasoning as this: "does he think Deity is perfect or defective?" and if, as is likely, he bears testimony to the perfection in the Divine nature, then we will demand of him to grant a perfection throughout in everything that is observable in that divinity, in order that Deity may not be regarded as a mixture of opposites, defect and perfection. But whether as respects power, or the conception of goodness, or wisdom and imperishability and eternal existence, or any other notion besides suitable to the nature of Deity, that is found to lie close to the subject of our contemplation, in all he will agree that perfection is the idea to be entertained of the Divine nature, as being a just inference from these premises. If this, then, be granted us, it would not be difficult to bring round these scattered notions of a plurality of Gods to the acknowledgment of a unity of Deity. For if he admits that perfection is in every respect to be ascribed to the subject before us, though there is a plurality of these perfect things which are marked with the same character, he must be required by a logical necessity, either to point out the particularity in each of these things which present no distinctive variation, but are found always with the same marks, or, if (he cannot do that, and) the mind can grasp nothing in them in the way of particular, to give up the idea of any distinction. For if neither as regards "more and less" a person can detect a difference (in as much as the idea of perfection does not admit of it), nor as regards "worse" and "better" (for he cannot entertain a notion of Deity at all where the term "worse" is not got rid of), nor as regards "ancient" and "modern" (for what exists not for ever is foreign to the notion of Deity), but on the contrary the idea of Godhead is one and the same, no peculiarity being on any ground of reason to be discovered in any one point, it is an absolute necessity that the mistaken fancy of a plurality of Gods would be forced to the acknowledgment of a unity of Deity. For if goodness, and justice, and wisdom, and power may be equally predicated of it, then also imperishability and eternal existence, and every orthodox idea would be in the same way admitted. As then all distinctive difference in any aspect whatever has been gradually removed, it necessarily follows that together with it a plurality of Gods has been removed from his belief, the general identity bringing round conviction to the Unity.

CHAPTER I.

BUT since our system of religion is wont to observe a distinction of persons in the unity of the Nature, to prevent our argument in our contention with Greeks sinking to the level of Judaism there is need again of a distinct technical statement in order to correct all error on this point.

For not even by those who are external to

---

[6] Sabellius. The Sabellian heresy was rife in the century preceding; *i. e.* that Personality is attributed to the Deity only from the exigency of human language, that consequently He is sometimes characterized as the Father, when operations and works more appropriate to the paternal relation are spoken of; and so in like manner of the Son, and the Holy Ghost; as when Redemption is the subject, or Sanctification. In making the Son the Father, it is the opposite pole to Arianism.

[7] "We see also the rise (*i.e.* A.D. 350) of a new and more defiant Arian school, more in earnest than the older generation, impatient of their shuffling diplomacy, and less pliant to court influences. Aetius . . . . came to rest in a clear and simple form of Arianism. Christianity without mystery seems to have been his aim. The Anomœan leaders took their stand on the doctrine of Arius himself, and dwelt with emphasis on its most offensive aspects. Arius had long ago laid down the absolute unlikeness of the Son to the Father, but for years past the Arianizers had prudently softened it down. Now, however, 'unlike' became the watchword of Aetius and Eunomius": Gwatkin's *Arians*. For the way in which this school treated the Trinity see *Against Eunomius*, p. 50.

[8] *I.e.* an argument against Dualism would only confirm the Jew in his stern monotheism. Manes had taught also that "those souls who believe Jesus Christ to be the Son of God renounce the worship of the God of the Jews, who is the Prince of Darkness," and that "the Old Testament was the work of this Prince, who was substituted by the Jews in the place of the true God."

our doctrine is the Deity held to be without Logos [9]. Now this admission of theirs will quite enable our argument to be unfolded. For he who admits that God is not without Logos, will agree that a being who is not without Logos (or word) certainly possesses Logos. Now it is to be observed that the utterance of man is expressed by the same term. If, then, he should say that he understands what the Logos of God is according to the analogy of things with us, he will thus be led on to a loftier idea, it being an absolute necessity for him to believe that the utterance, just as everything else, corresponds with the nature. Though, that is, there is a certain sort of force, and life, and wisdom, observed in the human subject, yet no one from the similarity of the terms would suppose that the life, or power, or wisdom, were in the case of God of such a sort as that, but the significations of all such terms are lowered to accord with the standard of our nature. For since our nature is liable to corruption and weak, therefore is our life short, our strength unsubstantial, our word unstable [1]. But in that transcendent nature, through the greatness of the subject contemplated, every thing that is said about it is elevated with it. Therefore though mention be made of God's Word it will not be thought of as having its realization in the utterance of what is spoken, and as then vanishing away, like our speech, into the non-existent. On the contrary, as our nature, liable as it is to come to an end, is endued with speech which likewise comes to an end, so that imperishable and ever-existing nature has eternal and substantial speech. If, then, logic requires him to admit this eternal subsistence of God's Word, it is altogether necessary to admit also that the subsistence [2] of that word

consists in a living state; for it is an impiety to suppose that the Word has a soulless subsistence after the manner of stones. But if it subsists, being as it is something with intellect and without body, then certainly it lives, whereas if it be divorced from life, then as certainly it does not subsist; but this idea that the Word of God does not subsist, has been shown to be blasphemy. By consequence, therefore, it has also been shown that the Word is to be considered as in a living condition. And since the nature of the Logos is reasonably believed to be simple, and exhibits in itself no duplicity or combination, no one would contemplate the existence of the living Logos as dependent on a mere participation of life, for such a supposition, which is to say that one thing is within another, would not exclude the idea of compositeness; but, since the simplicity has been admitted, we are compelled to think that the Logos has an independent life, and not a mere participation of life. If, then, the Logos, as being life, lives [3], it certainly has the faculty

---

[9] *the Deity . . . without Logos.* In another treatise (*De Fide,* p. 40) Gregory bases the argument for the eternity of the Λόγος on S John i. 1, where it is not said, "after the beginning," but "in the beginning." The beginning, therefore, never was without the Λόγος.

[1] *unstable*: ἀπαγὴς (the reading ἄρπαγις is manifestly wrong). So afterwards human speech is called ἐπίκηρος. Cf. Athanasius (*Contr. Arian.* 3): "Since man came from the non-existent, therefore his 'word' also has a pause, and does not last. From man we get, day after day, many different words, because the first abide not, but are forgotten."

[2] ὑπόστασιν. About this oft repeated word the question arises whether we are indebted to Christians or to Platonists for the first skilful use of it in expressing that which is *neither substance nor quality.* Abraham Tucker (*Light of Nature,* ii. p. 191) hazards the following remark with regard to the Platonic Triad, *i. e.* Goodness, Intelligence, Activity, viz. that *quality* would not do as a general name for these principles, because the ideas and abstract essences existed in the Intelligence, &c., and qualities cannot exist in one another, *e. g.* yellowness cannot be soft : nor could *substance* be the term, for then they must have been component parts of the Existent, which would have destroyed the unity of the Godhead : "therefore, he (Plato) styled them Hypostases or Subsistencies, which is something between substance and quality, inexisting in the one, and serving as a receptacle for the other's inexistency within it." But he adds, " I do not recommend this explanation to anybody"; nor does he state the authority for this Platonic use, so lucidly explained, of the word. Indeed, if the word had ever been applied to the principles of the Platonic triad, to express in the case of each of them "the distinct subsistence in a common οὐσία," it would have falsified the very conception of the first, *i. e.* Goodness, which was *never relative.* So that this very word seems to emphasize, so far, the antagonism

between Christianity and Platonism. Socrates (*E. H.* iii. 7) bears witness to the absence of the word from the ancient Greek philosophy : "it appears to us that the Greek philosophers have given us various definitions of οὐσία, but have not taken the slightest notice of ὑπόστασις. . . . it is not found in any of the ancients except occasionally in a sense quite different from that which is attached to it at the present day (*i. e.* fifth century). Thus Sophocles in his tragedy entitled *Phœnix* uses it to signify 'treachery'; in Menander it implies 'sauces' (*i. e.* sediment). But although the ancient philosophical writers scarcely noticed the word, the more modern ones have frequently used it *instead of* οὐσία." But it was, as far as can be traced, the unerring genius of Origen that first threw around the Λόγος that atmosphere of a new term, *i. e.* ὑπόστασις, as well as ὁμοούσιος, αὐτόθεος, which afterward made it possible to present the Second Person to the Greek-speaking world as the member of an equal and indivisible Trinity. It was he who first selected such words and saw what they were capable of ; though he did not insist on that fuller meaning which was put upon them when all danger within the Church of Sabellianism had disappeared, and error passed in the guise of Arianism to the opposite extreme.

[3] *lives.* This doctrine is far removed from that of Philo, *i. e.* from the Alexandrine philosophy. The very first statement of S. John represents the Λόγος as having a backward movement towards the Deity, as well as a forward movement from Him ; as held there, and yet sent thence by a force which he calls Love, so that the primal movement towards the world does not come from the Λόγος, but from the Father Himself. The Λόγος here is the Word, and *not the Reason ;* He is the living effect of a living cause, not a theory or hypothesis standing at the gateway of an insoluble mystery. The Λόγος speaks because the Father speaks, not because the Supreme cannot and will not speak ; for the Father becomes at times the mediator between the Λόγος and the world drawing men towards Him and subduing portions of the Creation before His path. Psychology seems to pour a light straight into the Council-chamber of the Eternal ; while Metaphysics had turned away from it, with her finger on her lips. Philo may have used, as Tholuck thinks, those very texts of the Old Testament which support the Christian doctrine of the Word, and in the translation of which the LXX. supplied him with the Greek word. But, however derived, his theology eventually ranged itself with those pantheistic views of the universe which subdued all thinking minds not Christianized, for more than three centuries after him. The majority of recent critics certainly favour the supposition that the Λόγος of Philo is a being numerically distinct from the Supreme ; but when the relation of the Supreme is attentively traced in each, the actual antagonism of the Christian system and his begins to be apparent. The Supreme of Philo is not and can never be related to the world. The Λόγος is a logical necessity as a mediator between the two ; a spiritual being certainly, but only the head of a long series of such beings, who succeed at last in filling the passage between the finite and the infinite. In this system there is no mission of love and of free will ; such beings are but as the milestones to mark the distance between man and the Great Unknown. It is significant that Vacherot, the leading historian of the Alexandrine school of philosophy, doubts whether John the Evangelist ever even heard of the Jewish philosopher of Alexandria. It is pretty much the same with the members of the Neoplatonic Triad as with the Λόγος of Philo. The

of will, for no one of living creatures is without such a faculty. Moreover that such a will has also capacity to act must be the conclusion of a devout mind. For if you admit not this potency, you prove the reverse to exist. But no; impotence is quite removed from our conception of Deity. Nothing of incongruity is to be observed in connection with the Divine nature, but it is absolutely necessary to admit that the power of that word is as great as the purpose, lest mixture, or concurrence, of contradictions be found in an existence that is incomposite, as would be the case if, in the same purpose, we were to detect both impotence and power, if, that is, there were power to do one thing, but no power to do something else. Also we must suppose that this will in its power to do all things will have no tendency to anything that is evil (for impulse towards evil is foreign to the Divine nature), but that whatever is good, this it also wishes, and, wishing, is able to perform, and, being able, will not fail to perform[4]; but that it will bring all its proposals for good to effectual accomplishment. Now the world *is* good, and all its contents are seen to be wisely and skilfully ordered. All of them, therefore, are the works of the Word, of one who, while He lives and subsists, in that He is God's Word, has a will too, in that He lives; of one too who has power to effect what He wills, and who wills what is absolutely good and wise and all else that connotes superiority. Whereas, then, the world is admitted to be something good, and from what has been said the world has been shown to be the work of the Word, who both wills and is able to effect the good, this Word is other than He of whom He is the Word. For this, too, to a certain extent is a term of "relation," inasmuch as the Father of the

Word must needs be thought of with the Word, for it would not be word were it not a word of some one. If, then, the mind of the hearers, from the relative meaning of the term, makes a distinction between the Word and Him from whom He proceeds, we should find that the Gospel mystery, in its contention with the Greek conceptions, would not be in danger of coinciding with those who prefer the beliefs of the Jews. But it will equally escape the absurdity of either party, by acknowledging both that the living Word of God is an effective and creative being, which is what the Jew refuses to receive, and also that the Word itself, and He from whom He is, do not differ in their nature. As in our own case we say that the word is from the mind, and no more entirely the same as the mind, than altogether other than it (for, by its being from it, it is something else, and not it; still by its bringing the mind in evidence it can no longer be considered as something other than it; and so it is in its essence one with mind, while as a subject it is different), in like manner, too, the Word of God by its self-subsistence is distinct from Him from whom it has its subsistence; and yet by exhibiting in itself those qualities which are recognized in God it is the same in nature with Him who is recognizable by the same distinctive marks. For whether one adopts goodness[5], or power, or wisdom, or eternal existence, or the incapability of vice, death, and decay, or an entire perfection, or anything whatever of the kind, to mark one's conception of the Father, by means of the same marks he will find the Word that subsists from Him.

CHAPTER II.

As, then, by the higher mystical ascent[6] from matters that concern ourselves to that

---

God of Plotinus and Proclus is not a God in three hypostases: he is simply one, Intelligence and Soul being his necessary emanations; they are not in God, but they are not God: Soul is but a hypostasis of a hypostasis. The One is not a hypostasis, but above it. This "Trinity" depends on the distinction and succession of the *necessary* movements of the Deity; it consists of three distinct and separate principles of things. The Trinity is really peculiar to Christianity. Three inseparable Hypostases make equally a part of the Divine nature, so that to take away one would be to destroy the whole. The Word and Spirit are Divine, not intermediaries disposed in a hierarchy on the route of the world to God. As Plotinus reproached the Gnostics, the Christian mysticism despises the world, and suppressing the intermediaries who in other doctrines serve to elevate the soul gradually to God, it transports it by one impulse as it were into the Divine nature. The Christian goes straight to God by Faith. The Imagination, Reason, and Contemplation of the Neoplatonists, *i. e.* the three movements of the soul which correspond to their lower "trinity" of Nature, Soul, Intelligence, are no longer necessary. There is an antipathy profound between the two systems. How then could the one be said to influence the other? Neoplatonism may have tinged Christianity, while it was still seeking for language in which to express its inner self: but it never influenced the intrinsically moral character of the Christian Creeds. The Alexandrine philosophy is all metaphysics, and its rock was pantheism; all, even matter, proceeds from God necessarily and eternally. The Church never hesitated: she saw the abyss that opens upon that path; and by severe decrees she has closed the way to pantheism.

[4] *will not fail to perform;* μὴ ἀνενέργητον εἶναι. This is a favourite word with Gregory, and the Platonist Synesius.

[5] *goodness.* "God is love;" but how is this love above or equal to the Power? "Infinite Goodness, according to our apprehension, requires that it should exhaust omnipotence: that it should give capacities of enjoyment and confer blessings until there were no more to be conferred: but our idea of omnipotence requires that it should be inexhaustible; that nothing should limit its operation, so that it should do no more than it has done. Therefore, it is much easier to conceive an imperfect creature completely good, than a perfect Being who is so. . . . Since, then, we find our understanding incapable of comprehending *infinite* goodness joined with *infinite* power, we need not be surprised at finding our thoughts perplexed concerning them . . . we may presume that the obscurity rises from something wrong in our ideas, *not from any inconsistencies in the subjects themselves.*" Abraham Tucker, *L. of N.*, i. 355.

[6] *by the higher mystical ascent,* ἀναγωγικῶς. The common reading was ἀναλογικῶς, which Hervetus and Morell have translated. But Krabinger, from all his Codd. but one, has rightly restored ἀναγωγικῶς. It is not "analogy," but rather "induction," that is here meant; *i. e.* the arguing from the known to the unknown, from the facts of human nature (τὰ καθ' ἡμᾶς) to those of the Godhead, or from history to spiritual events. Ἀναγωγή is the chief instrument in Origen's interpretation of the Bible; it is more important than allegory. It alone gives the "heavenly" meaning, as opposed to the moral and practical though *still mystical* (cf. Guericke, *Hist. Schol. Catech.* ii. p. 60) meaning. Speaking of the Tower of Babel, he says that there is a "riddle" in the account. "A competent exposition will have a more convenient season for dealing with this, when there is a direct necessity to explain the passage in its higher mystical meaning" (*c. Cels.* iv. p. 173). Gregory imitates

transcendent nature we gain a knowledge of the Word, by the same method we shall be led on to a conception of the Spirit, by observing in our own nature certain shadows and resemblances of His ineffable power. Now in us the spirit (or breath) is the drawing of the air, a matter other than ourselves, inhaled and breathed out for the necessary sustainment of the body. This, on the occasion of uttering the word, becomes an utterance which expresses in itself the meaning of the word. And in the case of the Divine nature it has been deemed a point of our religion that there is a Spirit of God, just as it has been allowed that there is a Word of God, because of the inconsistency of the Word of God being deficient as compared with our word, if, while this word of ours is contemplated in connection with spirit, that other Word were to be believed to be quite unconnected with spirit. Not indeed that it is a thought proper to entertain of Deity, that after the manner of our breath something foreign from without flows into God, and in Him becomes the Spirit; but when we think of God's Word we do not deem the Word to be something unsubstantial, nor the result of instruction, nor an utterance of the voice, nor what after being uttered passes away, nor what is subject to any other condition such as those which are observed in our word, but to be essentially self-subsisting, with a faculty of will ever-working, all-powerful. The like doctrine have we received as to God's Spirit; we regard it as that which goes with the Word and manifests its energy, and not as a mere effluence of the breath; for by such a conception the grandeur of the Divine power would be reduced and humiliated, that is, if the Spirit that is in it were supposed to resemble ours. But we conceive of it as an essential power, regarded as self-centred in its own proper person, yet equally incapable of being separated from God in Whom it is, or from the Word of God whom it accompanies, as from melting into nothingness; but as being, after the likeness of God's Word, existing as a person[7], able to will, self-moved, efficient, ever choosing the good, and

for its every purpose having its power concurrent with its will.

CHAPTER III.

AND so one who severely studies the depths of the mystery, receives secretly in his spirit, indeed, a moderate amount of apprehension of the doctrine of God's nature, yet he is unable to explain clearly in words the ineffable depth of this mystery. As, for instance, how the same thing is capable of being numbered and yet rejects numeration, how it is observed with distinctions yet is apprehended as a monad, how it is separate as to personality yet is not divided as to subject matter[8]. For, in personality, the Spirit is one thing and the Word another, and yet again that from which the Word and Spirit is, another. But when you have gained the conception of what the distinction is in these, the oneness, again, of the nature admits not division, so that the supremacy of the one First Cause is not split and cut up into differing Godships, neither does the statement harmonize with the Jewish dogma, but the truth passes in the mean between these two conceptions, destroying each heresy, and yet accepting what is useful to it from each. The Jewish dogma is destroyed by the acceptance of the Word, and by the belief in the Spirit; while the polytheistic error of the Greek school is made to vanish by the unity of the Nature abrogating this imagination of plurality. While yet again, of the Jewish conception, let the unity of the Nature stand; and of the Hellenistic, only the distinction as to persons; the remedy against a profane view being thus applied, as required, on either side. For it is as if the number of the triad were a remedy in the case of those who are in error as to the One, and the assertion of the unity for those whose beliefs are dispersed among a number of divinities.

CHAPTER IV.

BUT should it be the Jew who gainsays these arguments, our discussion with him will no

---

his master in constantly thus dealing with the Old Testament, *i.e.* making inductions about the highest spiritual truths from the "history." So Basil would treat the prophecies (in *Isai.* v. p. 948). Chrysostom, on the Songs of "Degrees" in the Psalms, says that they are so called because they speak of the going up from Babylon, according to history; but, according to their high mysticism, because they lift us into the way of excellence. Here Gregory uses the facts of human nature neither in the way of mere analogy nor of allegory: he argues straight from them, as one reality, to another reality almost of the same *class*, as it were, as the first, man being "in the image of God"; and so ἀναγωγή here comes nearer induction than anything else.

[7] καθ' ὑπόστασιν. Ueberweg (*Hist. of Philosophy*, vol. i. 329) remarks: "That the same argumentation, which in the last analysis reposes only on the double sense of ὑπόστασις (viz.: (*a*) real subsistence; (*b*) individually independent, not attributive subsistence), could be used with reference to each of the Divine attributes, and so for the complete restoration of polytheism, Gregory leaves unnoticed." Yet Gregory doubtless was well aware of this, for he

says, just below, that even a severe study of the mystery can only result in a moderate amount of apprehension of it.

[8] *it is separate as to personality yet is not divided as to subject matter.* The words are respectively ὑπόστασις and ὑποκείμενον. The last word is with Gregory, whose clearness in philosophical distinctions makes his use of words very observable, always equivalent to οὐσία, and οὐσία generally to φύσις. The following note of Casaubon (*Epist. ad Eustath.*) is valuable: In the Holy Trinity there is neither "confusion," nor "composition," nor "coalescing"; neither the Sabellian "contraction," any more than the Arian "division," neither on the other hand "estrangement," or "difference." There is "distinction" or "distribution" without division. This word "distribution" is used by Tertullian and others to express the effect of the "persons" (ἰδιότητες, ὑποστάσεις, πρόσωπα) upon the Godhead which forms the definition of the substance (ὁ τῆς οὐσίας λόγος).

longer present equal difficulty[9], since the truth will be made manifest out of those doctrines on which he has been brought up. For that there is a Word of God, and a Spirit of God, powers essentially subsisting, both creative of whatever has come into being, and comprehensive of things that exist, is shown in the clearest light out of the Divinely-inspired Scriptures. It is enough if we call to mind one testimony, and leave the discovery of more to those who are inclined to take the trouble. "By the Word of the Lord," it is said, "the heavens were established, and all the power of them by the breath of His mouth[1]." What word and what breath? For the Word is not mere speech, nor that breath mere breathing. Would not the Deity be brought down to the level of the likeness of our human nature, were it held as a doctrine that the Maker of the universe used such word and such breath as this? What power arising from speech or breathing could there be of such a kind as would suffice for the establishment of the heavens and the powers that are therein? For if the Word of God is like our speech, and His Breath is like our breath, then from these like things there must certainly come a likeness of power; and the Word of God has just so much force as our word, and no more. But the words that come from us and the breath that accompanies their utterance are ineffective and unsubstantial. Thus, they who would bring down the Deity to a similarity with the word as with us render also the Divine word and spirit altogether ineffective and unsubstantial. But if, as David says, "By the Word of the Lord were the heavens established, and their powers had their framing by His breath," then has the mystery of the truth been confirmed, which instructs us to speak of a word as in essential being, and a breath as in personality.

CHAPTER V.

THAT there is, then, a Word of God, and a Breath of God, the Greek, with his "innate ideas"[2], and the Jew, with his Scriptures, will perhaps not deny. But the dispensation as regards the Word of God, whereby He became man, both parties would perhaps equally reject, as being incredible and unfitting to be told of God. By starting, therefore, from another point we will bring these gainsayers to a belief in this fact. They believe that all things came into

being by thought and skill on the part of Him Who framed the system of the universe; or else they hold views that do not conform to this opinion. But should they not grant that reason and wisdom guided the framing of the world, they will install unreason and unskilfulness on the throne of the universe. But if this is an absurdity and impiety, it is abundantly plain that they must allow that thought and skill rule the world. Now in what has been previously said, the Word of God has been shown not to be this actual utterance of speech, or the possession of some science or art, but to be a power essentially and substantially existing, willing all good, and being possessed of strength to execute all its will; and, of a world that is good, this power appetitive and creative of good is the cause. If, then, the subsistence of the whole world has been made to depend on the power of the Word, as the train of the argument has shown, an absolute necessity prevents us entertaining the thought of there being any other cause of the organization of the several parts of the world than the Word Himself, through whom all things in it passed into being. If any one wants to call Him Word, or Skill, or Power, or God, or anything else that is high and prized, we will not quarrel with him. For whatever word or name be invented as descriptive of the subject, one thing is intended by the expressions, namely the eternal power of God which is creative of things that are, the discoverer of things that are not, the sustaining cause of things that are brought into being, the foreseeing cause of things yet to be. This, then, whether it be God, or Word, or Skill, or Power, has been shown by inference to be the Maker of the nature of man, not urged to framing him by any necessity, but in the superabundance of love operating the production of such a creature. For needful it was that neither His light should be unseen, nor His glory without witness, nor His goodness unenjoyed, nor that any other quality observed in the Divine nature should in any case lie idle, with none to share it or enjoy it. If, therefore, man comes to his birth upon these conditions, namely to be a partaker of the good things in God, necessarily he is framed of such a kind as to be adapted to the participation of such good. For as the eye, by virtue of the bright ray which is by nature wrapped up in it, is in fellowship with the light, and by its innate capacity draws to itself that which is akin to it, so was it needful that a certain affinity with the Divine should be mingled with the nature of man, in order that by means of this correspondence it might aim at that which was native to it. It is thus even with the nature of the unreasoning creatures, whose lot is cast in water or

---

[9] *i. e.* as with the Greek.
[1] Ps. xxxiii. 4, Septuagint version.
[2] *innate ideas* (κοινῶν ἐννοιῶν). There is a Treatise of Gregory introducing Christianity to the Greeks "from innate ideas." This title has been, wrongly, attributed by some to a later hand.

in air; each of them has an organization adapted to its kind of life, so that by a peculiar formation of the body, to the one of them the air, to the other the water, is its proper and congenial element. Thus, then, it was needful for man, born for the enjoyment of Divine good, to have something in his nature akin to that in which he is to participate. For this end he has been furnished with life, with thought, with skill, and with all the excellences that we attribute to God, in order that by each of them he might have his desire set upon that which is not strange to him. Since, then, one of the excellences connected with the Divine nature is also eternal existence, it was altogether needful that the equipment of our nature should not be without the further gift of this attribute, but should have in itself the immortal, that by its inherent faculty it might both recognize what is above it, and be possessed with a desire for the divine and eternal life[3]. In truth this has been shown in the comprehensive utterance of one expression, in the description of the cosmogony, where it is said that man was made "in the image of God"[4]. For in this likeness, implied in the word image, there is a summary of all things that characterize Deity; and whatever else Moses relates, in a style more in the way of history, of these matters, placing doctrines before us in the form of a story, is connected with the same instruction. For that Paradise of his, with its peculiar fruits, the eating of which did not afford to them who tasted thereof satisfaction of the appetite, but knowledge and eternity of life, is in entire agreement with what has been previously considered with regard to man, in the view that our nature at its beginnings was good, and in the midst of good. But, perhaps, what has been said will be contradicted by one who looks only to the present condition of things, and thinks to convict our statement of untruthfulness, inasmuch as man is seen no longer under those primeval circumstances, but under almost entirely opposite ones. "Where is the divine resemblance in the soul? Where the body's freedom from suffering? Where the eternity of life? Man is of brief existence, subject to passions, liable to decay, and ready both in body and mind for every form of suffering." By these and the like assertions, and by directing the attack against human nature, the opponent will think that he upsets the account that has been offered respecting man. But to secure that our argument may not have to be diverted from its course at any future stage, we will briefly discuss these points. That the life of man is at present subject to abnormal conditions is no proof that man was not created in the midst of good. For since man is the work of God, Who through His goodness brought this creature into being, no one could reasonably suspect that he, of whose constitution goodness is the cause, was created by his Maker in the midst of evil. But there is another reason for our present circumstances being what they are, and for our being destitute of the primitive surroundings: and yet again the starting-point of our answer to this argument against us is not beyond and outside the assent of our opponents. For He who made man for the participation of His own peculiar good, and incorporated in him the instincts for all that was excellent, in order that his desire might be carried forward by a corresponding movement in each case to its like, would never have deprived him of that most excellent and precious of all goods; I mean the gift implied in being his own master, and having a free will. For if necessity in any way was the master of the life of man, the "image" would have been falsified in that particular part, by being estranged owing to this unlikeness to its archetype. How can that nature which is under a yoke and bondage to any kind of necessity be called an image of a Master Being? Was it not, then, most right that that which is in every detail made like the Divine should possess in its nature a self-ruling and independent principle, such as to enable the participation of good to be the reward of its virtue? Whence, then, comes it, you will ask, that he who had been distinguished throughout with most excellent endowments exchanged these good things for the worse? The reason of this also is plain. No growth of evil had its beginning in the Divine will. Vice would have been blameless were it inscribed with the name of God as its maker and father. But the evil is, in some way or other, engendered[5] from within, springing up in the will at that moment when there is a retrocession of the soul from the beautiful[6]. For as sight is an activity of nature, and blindness a deprivation of that natural operation, such is the kind of opposition between virtue and vice. It is, in fact, not possible to form any other notion of the origin of vice than as the absence of virtue. For as when the light has been removed the darkness supervenes, but as long as it is present there is

---

3 Cf. Cato's Speech in Addison's *Cato*:—
It must be so : Plato, thou reasonest well !—
Else whence this pleasing hope, this fond desire
This longing after immortality?
*   *   *   *   *
'Tis the divinity that stirs within us :
'Tis heaven itself that points out an hereafter,
And intimates eternity to man.
4 Gen i. 27

5 S. James i. 15 : ἡ ἐπιθυμία τίκτει . . . ἁμαρτίαν.
6 τὸ καλὸν. The Greek word for moral perfection, according to one view of its derivation (καίειν), refers to "brightness"; according to another (cf. κεκαδμενος), to "finish" or perfection.

no darkness, so, as long as the good is present in the nature, vice is a thing that has no inherent existence; while the departure of the better state becomes the origin of its opposite. Since, then, this is the peculiarity of the possession of a free will, that it chooses as it likes the thing that pleases it, you will find that it is not God Who is the author of the present evils, seeing that He has ordered your nature so as to be its own master and free; but rather the recklessness that makes choice of the worse in preference to the better.

CHAPTER VI.

But you will perhaps seek to know the cause of this error of judgment; for it is to this point that the train of our discussion tends. Again, then, we shall be justified in expecting to find some starting-point which will throw light on this inquiry also. An argument such as the following we have received by tradition from the Fathers; and this argument is no mere mythical narrative, but one that naturally invites our credence. Of all existing things there is a twofold manner of apprehension, the consideration of them being divided between what appertains to intellect and what appertains to the senses; and besides these there is nothing to be detected in the nature of existing things, as extending beyond this division. Now these two worlds have been separated from each other by a wide interval, so that the sensible is not included in those qualities which mark the intellectual, nor this last in those qualities which distinguish the sensible, but each receives its formal character from qualities opposite to those of the other. The world of thought is bodiless, impalpable, and figureless; but the sensible is, by its very name, bounded by those perceptions which come through the organs of sense. But as in the sensible world itself, though there is a considerable mutual opposition of its various elements, yet a certain harmony maintained in those opposites has been devised by the wisdom that rules the Universe, and thus there is produced a concord of the whole creation with itself, and the natural contrariety does not break the chain of agreement; in like manner, owing to the Divine wisdom, there is an admixture and interpenetration of the sensible with the intellectual department, in order that all things may equally have a share in the beautiful, and no single one of existing things be without its share in that superior world. For this reason the corresponding locality of the intellectual world is a subtile and mobile essence, which, in accordance with its supramundane habitation, has in its peculiar nature large affinity with the intellectual part. Now, by a

provision of the supreme Mind there is an intermixture of the intellectual with the sensible world, in order that nothing in creation may be thrown aside [7] as worthless, as says the Apostle, or be left without its portion of the Divine fellowship. On this account it is that the com mixture of the intellectual and sensible in man is effected by the Divine Being, as the description of the cosmogony instructs us. It tells us that God, taking dust of the ground, formed the man, and by an inspiration from Himself He planted life in the work of His hand, that thus the earthy might be raised up to the Divine, and so one certain grace of equal value might pervade the whole creation, the lower nature being mingled with the supramundane. Since, then, the intellectual nature had a previous existence, and to each of the angelic powers a certain operation was assigned, for the organization of the whole, by the authority that presides over all things, there was a certain power ordained to hold together and sway the earthly region [8], constituted for this purpose by the power that administers the Universe. Upon that there was fashioned that thing moulded of earth, an "image" copied from the superior Power. Now this living being was man. In him, by an ineffable influence, the godlike beauty of the intellectual nature was mingled. He to whom the administration of the earth has been consigned takes it ill and thinks it not to be borne, if, of that nature which has been subjected to him, any being shall be exhibited bearing likeness to his transcendent dignity. But the question, how one who had been created for no evil purpose by Him who framed the system of the Universe in goodness fell away, nevertheless, into this passion of envy, it is not a part of my present business minutely to discuss; though it would not be difficult, and it would not take long, to offer an account to those who are amenable to persuasion. For the distinctive difference between virtue and vice is not to be contemplated as that between two actually subsisting phenomena; but as there is a logical opposition between that which is and that

---

[7] 1 Tim. iv. 4; "rejected" (R.V.), better than "refused" (A.V.).
[8] This is not making the Devil the Demiurge, but only the "angel of the Earth." And as the celestial regions and atmosphere of the earth were assigned to "angelic powers," so the Earth itself and her nations were assigned to subordinate angels. Origen had already developed, or rather christianized, this doctrine. Speaking of the Confusion of Tongues, he says, "And so each (nation) had to be handed over to the keeping of angels more or less severe, and or this character or of that, according as each had moved a greater or less distance from the East, and had prepared more or less bricks for stone, and more or less slime for mortar; and had built up more or less. This was that they might be punished for their boldness. These angels who had already created for each nation its peculiar tongue, were to lead their charges into various parts according to their deserts: one for instance to some burning clime, another to one which would chastise the dwellers in it with its freezing: . . . those who retained the original speech through not having moved from the East are the only ones that became 'the portion of the Lord.' . . . They, too, alone are to be considered as having been under a ruler who did not take them in hand to be punished as the others were ' (c. Cels. v. 30-1).

which is not, and it is not possible to say that, as regards subsistency, that which is not is distinguished from that which is, but we say that nonentity is only *logically* opposed to entity, in the same way also the word vice is opposed to the word virtue, not as being any existence in itself, but only as becoming thinkable by the absence of the better. As we say that blindness is logically opposed to sight, not that blindness has of itself a natural existence, being only a deprivation of a preceding faculty, so also we say that vice is to be regarded as the deprivation of goodness, just as a shadow which supervenes at the passage of the solar ray. Since, then, the uncreated nature is incapable of admitting of such movement as is implied in turning or change or alteration, while everything that subsists through creation has connection with change, inasmuch as the subsistence itself of the creation had its rise in change, that which was not passing by the Divine power into that which is; and since the above-mentioned power was created too, and could choose by a spontaneous movement whatever he liked, when he had closed his eyes to the good and the ungrudging like one who in the sunshine lets his eyelids down upon his eyes and sees only darkness, in this way that being also, by his very unwillingness to perceive the contrary to goodness, became cognisant of the contrary to goodness. Now this is Envy. Well, it is undeniable that the beginning of any matter is the cause of everything else that by consequence follows upon it, as, for instance, upon health there follows a good habit of body, activity, and a pleasurable life, but upon sickness, weakness, want of energy, and life passed in distaste of everything; and so, in all other instances, things follow by consequence their proper beginnings. As, then, freedom from the agitation of the passions is the beginning and groundwork of a life in accordance with virtue, so the bias to vice generated by that Envy is the constituted road to all these evils which have been since displayed. For when once he, who by his apostacy from' goodness had begotten in himself this Envy, had received this bias to evil[9], like a rock, torn asunder from a mountain ridge, which is driven down headlong by its own weight, in like manner he, dragged away from his original natural propension to goodness and gravitating with all his weight in the direction of vice, was

deliberately forced and borne away as by a kind of gravitation to the utmost limit of iniquity; and as for that intellectual power which he had received from his Creator to co-operate with the better endowments, this he made his assisting instrument in the discovery of contrivances for the purposes of vice, while by his crafty skill he deceives and circumvents man, persuading him to become his own murderer with his own hands. For seeing that man by the commission of the Divine blessing had been elevated to a lofty pre-eminence (for he was appointed king over the earth and all things on it; he was beautiful in his form, being created an image of the archetypal beauty; he was without passion in his nature, for he was an imitation of the unimpassioned; he was full of frankness, delighting in a face-to-face manifestation of the personal Deity),—all this was to the adversary the fuel to his passion of envy. Yet could he not by any exercise of strength or dint of force accomplish his purpose, for the strength of God's blessing over-mastered his own force. His plan, therefore, is to withdraw man from this enabling strength, that thus he may be easily captured by him and open to his treachery. As in a lamp when the flame has caught the wick and a person is unable to blow it out, he mixes water with the oil and by this device-will dull the flame, in the same way the enemy, by craftily mixing up badness in man's will, has produced a kind of extinguishment and dulness in the blessing, on the failure of which that which is opposed necessarily enters. For to life is opposed death, to strength weakness, to blessing curse, to frankness shame, and to all that is good whatever can be conceived as opposite. Thus it is that humanity is in its present evil condition, since that beginning introduced the occasions for such an ending.

CHAPTER VII.

YET let no one ask, "How was it that, if God foresaw the misfortune that would happen to man from want of thought, He came to create him, since it was, perhaps, more to his advantage not to have been born than to be in the midst of such evils?" This is what they who have been carried away by the false teaching of the Manichees put forward for the establishment of their error, as thus able to show that the Creator of human nature is evil. For if God is not ignorant of anything that is, and yet man is in the midst of evil, the argument for the goodness of God could not be upheld; that is, if He brought forth into life the man who was to be in this evil. For if the operating force which is in accordance with the good is entirely

---

[9] "We affirm that it is not easy, or perhaps possible, even for a philosopher to know the origin of evil without its being made known to him by an inspiration of God, whence it comes, and how it shall vanish. Ignorance of God is itself in the list of evils; ignorance of His way of healing and of serving Him aright is itself the greatest evil : we affirm that no one whatever can possibly know the origin of evil, who does not see that the standard of piety recognized by the average of established laws is itself an evil. No one, either can know it who has not grasped the truth about the Being who is called the Devil; what he was at the first, and how he became such as he is."—Origen (*c. Cels.* iv. 65).

that of a nature which is good, then this painful and perishing life, they say, can never be referred to the workmanship of the good, but it is necessary to suppose for such a life as this another author, from whom our nature derives its tendency to misery. Now all these and the like assertions seem to those who are thoroughly imbued with the heretical fraud, as with some deeply ingrained stain, to have a certain force from their superficial plausibility. But they who have a more thorough insight into the truth clearly perceive that what they say is unsound, and admits of speedy demonstration of its fallacy. In my opinion, too, it is well to put forward the Apostle as pleading with us on these points for their condemnation. In his address to the Corinthians he makes a distinction between the carnal and spiritual dispositions of souls ; showing, I think, by what he says that it is wrong to judge of what is morally excellent, or, on the other hand, of what is evil, by the standard of the senses ; but that, by withdrawing the mind from bodily phenomena, we must decide by itself and from itself the true nature of moral excellence and of its opposite. "The spiritual man," he says, "judgeth all things[1]." This, I think, must have been the reason of the invention of these deceptive doctrines on the part of those who propound them, viz. that when they define the good they have an eye only to the sweetness of the body's enjoyment, and so, because from its composite nature and constant tendency to dissolution that body is unavoidably subject to suffering and sicknesses, and because upon such conditions of suffering there follows a sort of sense of pain, they decree that the formation of man is the work of an evil deity. Since, if their thoughts had taken a loftier view, and, withdrawing their minds from this disposition to regard the gratifications of the senses, they had looked at the nature of existing things dispassionately, they would have understood that there is no evil other than wickedness. Now all wickedness has its form and character in the deprivation of the good ; it exists not by itself, and cannot be contemplated as a subsistence. For no evil of any kind lies outside and independent of the will ; but it is the non-existence of the good that is so denominated. Now that which is not has no substantial existence, and the Maker of that which has no substantial existence is not the Maker of things that have substantial existence. Therefore the God of things that are is external to the causation of things that are evil, since He is not the Maker of things that are non-existent. He Who formed the sight did not make blindness.

He Who manifested virtue manifested not the deprivation thereof. He Who has proposed as the prize in the contest of a free will the guerdon of all good to those who are living virtuously, never, to please Himself, subjected mankind to the yoke of a strong compulsion, as if he would drag it unwilling, as it were his lifeless tool, towards the right. But if, when the light shines very brightly in a clear sky, a man of his own accord shuts his eyelids to shade his sight, the sun is clear of blame on the part of him who sees not.

CHAPTER VIII.

NEVERTHELESS one who regards only the dissolution of the body is greatly disturbed, and makes it a hardship that this life of ours should be dissolved by death ; it is, he says, the extremity of evil that our being should be quenched by this condition of mortality. Let him, then, observe through this gloomy prospect the excess of the Divine benevolence. He may by this, perhaps, be the more induced to admire the graciousness of God's care for the affairs of man. To live is desirable to those who partake of life, on account of the enjoyment of things to their mind ; since, if any one lives in bodily pain, not to be is deemed by such an one much more desirable than to exist in pain. Let us inquire, then, whether He Who gives us our outfit for living has any other object in view than how we may pass our life under the fairest circumstances. Now since by a motion of our self-will we contracted a fellowship with evil, and, owing to some sensual gratification, mixed up this evil with our nature like some deleterious ingredient spoiling the taste of honey, and so, falling away from that blessedness which is involved in the thought of passionlessness, we have been viciously transformed—for this reason, Man, like some earthen potsherd, is resolved again into the dust of the ground, in order to secure that he may part with the soil which he has now contracted, and that he may, through the resurrection, be reformed anew after the original pattern ; at least if in this life that now is he has preserved what belongs to that image. A doctrine such as this is set before us by Moses under the disguise of an historical manner[2]. And yet this disguise of history contains a teaching which is most plain. For after, as he tells us, the earliest of mankind were brought into contact with what was forbidden, and thereby were stripped naked of that primal blessed condition, the Lord clothed these, His first-formed creatures, with coats of skins. In my opinion we are not bound to take these

---

[1] 1 Cor. ii. 15.

[2] ἱστορικώτερον καὶ δι' αἰνιγμάτων.

skins in their literal meaning. For to what sort of slain and flayed animals did this clothing devised for these humanities belong? But since all skin, after it is separated from the animal, is dead, I am certainly of opinion that He Who is the healer of our sinfulness, of His foresight invested man subsequently with that capacity of dying which had been the special attribute of the brute creation. Not that it was to last for ever; for a coat is something external put on us, lending itself to the body for a time, but not indigenous to its nature. This liability to death, then, taken from the brute creation, was, provisionally, made to envelope the nature created for immortality. It enwrapped it externally, but not internally. It grasped the sentient part of man, but laid no hold upon the Divine image. This sentient part, however, does not disappear, but is dissolved. Disappearance is the passing away into non-existence, but dissolution is the dispersion again into those constituent elements of the world of which it was composed. But that which is contained in them perishes not, though it escapes the cognisance of our senses.

Now the cause of this dissolution is evident from the illustration we have given of it. For since the senses have a close connection with what is gross and earthy, while the intellect is in its nature of a nobler and more exalted character than the movements involved in sensation, it follows that as, through the estimate which is made by the senses, there is an erroneous judgment as to what is morally good, and this error has wrought the effect of substantiating a contrary condition, that part of us which has thus been made useless is dissolved by its reception of this contrary. Now the bearing of our illustration is as follows. We supposed that some vessel has been composed of clay, and then, for some mischief or other, filled with melted lead, which lead hardens and remains in a non-liquid state; then that the owner of the vessel recovers it, and, as he possesses the potter's art, pounds to bits the ware which held the lead, and then remoulds the vessel after its former pattern for his own special use, emptied now of the material which had been mixed with it: by a like process the maker of our vessel, now that wickedness has intermingled with our sentient part, I mean that connected with the body, will dissolve the material which has received the evil, and, remoulding it again by the Resurrection without any admixture of the contrary matter, will recombine the elements into the vessel in its original beauty. Now since both soul and body have a common bond of fellowship in their participation of the sinful affections, there is also an analogy between the soul's and body's

death. For as in regard to the flesh we pronounce the separation of the sentient life to be death, so in respect of the soul we call the departure of the real life death. While, then, as we have said before, the participation in evil observable both in soul and body is of one and the same character, for it is through both that the evil principle advances into actual working, the death of dissolution which came from that clothing of dead skins does not affect the soul. For how can that which is uncompounded be subject to dissolution? But since there is a necessity that the defilements which sin has engendered in the soul as well should be removed thence by some remedial process, the medicine which virtue supplies has, in the life that now is, been applied to the healing of such mutilations as these. If, however, the soul remains unhealed [3], the remedy is dispensed in the life that follows this. Now in the ailments of the body there are sundry differences, some admitting of an easier, others requiring a more difficult treatment. In these last the use of the knife, or cauteries, or draughts of bitter medicines are adopted to remove the disease that has attacked the body. For the healing of the soul's sicknesses the future judgment announces something of the same kind, and this to the thoughtless sort is held out as the threat of a terrible correction [4], in order that through fear of this painful retribution they may gain the wisdom of fleeing from wickedness: while by those of more intelligence it is believed to be a remedial process ordered by God to bring back man, His peculiar creature, to the grace of his primal condition. They who use the knife or cautery to remove certain unnatural excrescences in the body, such as wens or warts, do not bring to the person they are serving a method of healing that is painless, though certainly they apply the knife without any intention of injuring the patient. In like manner whatever material excrescences are hardening on our souls, that have been sensualized by fellowship with the body's affections, are, in the day of the judgment [5], as it were cut and scraped away by the ineffable wisdom and power of Him Who, as the Gospel says, "healeth those that are sick [6]." For, as He says again, "they that are whole have no need of

3 "Here," says Semler, "our Author reveals himself as a scholar of Origen, and other doctors, who had imbibed the heathen thoughts of Plato, and wished to rest their system upon a future (purely) moral improvement." There is certainly too little room left here for the application to the soul and body in this life of Christ's atonement.

4 σκυθρωπῶν ἐπανόρθωσις, lit. "a correction consisting in terrible (processes)" (subjective genitive). The following passage will illustrate this: "Now this requires a deeper investigation, before it can be decided whether some evil powers have had assigned them . . . certain duties, like the State-executioners, who hold a melancholy (τεταγμένοι ἐπὶ τῶν σκυθρωπῶν . . . πραγμάτων) but necessary office in the Constitution." Origen, c. Cels. vii. 70.

5 in the day of the judgment. The reading κτίσεως, which Hervetus has followed, must be wrong here.   6 S. Matt. ix. 12.

the physician, but they that are sick [7]." Since, then, there has been inbred in the soul a strong natural tendency to evil, it must suffer, just as the excision of a wart [8] gives a sharp pain to the skin of the body; for whatever contrary to the nature has been inbred in the nature attaches itself to the subject in a certain union of feeling, and hence there is produced an abnormal intermixture of our own with an alien quality, so that the feelings, when the separation from this abnormal growth comes, are hurt and lacerated. Thus when the soul pines and melts away under the correction of its sins, as prophecy somewhere tells us [9], there necessarily follow, from its deep and intimate connection with evil, certain unspeakable and inexpressible pangs, the description of which is as difficult to render as is that of the nature of those good things which are the subjects of our hope. For neither the one nor the other is capable of being expressed in words, or brought within reach of the understanding. If, then, any one looks to the ultimate aim of the Wisdom of Him Who directs the economy of the universe, he would be very unreasonable and narrow-minded to call the Maker of man the Author of evil; or to say that He is ignorant of the future, or that, if He knows it and has made him, He is not uninfluenced by the impulse to what is bad. He knew what was going to be, yet did not prevent the tendency towards that which actually happened. That humanity, indeed, would be diverted from the good, could not be unknown to Him Who grasps all things by His power of foresight, and Whose eyes behold the coming equally with the past events. As, then, He had in sight the perversion, so He devised man's recall to good. Accordingly, which was the better way?—never to have brought our nature into existence at all, since He foresaw that the being about to be created would fall away from that which is morally beautiful; or to bring him back by repentance, and restore his diseased nature to its original beauty? But, because of the pains and sufferings of the body which are the necessary accidents of its unstable nature, to call God on that account the Maker of evil, or to think that He is not the Creator of man at all, in hopes thereby to prevent the supposition of His being the Author

of what gives us pain,—all this is an instance of that extreme narrow-mindedness which is the mark of those who judge of moral good and moral evil by mere sensation. Such persons do not understand that that only is intrinsically good which sensation does not reach, and that the only evil is estrangement from the good. But to make pains and pleasures the criterion of what is morally good and the contrary, is a characteristic of the unreasoning nature of creatures in whom, from their want of mind and understanding, the apprehension of real goodness has no place. That man is the work of God, created morally noble and for the noblest destiny, is evident not only from what has been said, but from a vast number of other proofs; which, because they are so many, we shall here omit. But when we call God the Maker of man we do not forget how carefully at the outset [1] we defined our position against the Greeks. It was there shown that the Word of God is a substantial and personified being, Himself both God and the Word; Who has embraced in Himself all creative power, or rather Who is very power with an impulse to all good; Who works out effectually whatever He wills by having a power concurrent with His will; Whose will and work is the life of all things that exist; by Whom, too, man was brought into being and adorned with the highest excellences after the fashion of Deity. But since that alone is unchangeable in its nature which does not derive its origin through creation, while whatever by the uncreated being is brought into existence out of what was non-existent, from the very first moment that it begins to be, is ever passing through change, and if it acts according to its nature the change is ever to the better, but if it be diverted from the straight path, then a movement to the contrary succeeds,—since, I say, man was thus conditioned, and in him the changeable element in his nature had slipped aside to the exact contrary, so that this departure from the good introduced in its train every form of evil to match the good (as, for instance, on the defection of life there was brought in the antagonism of death; on the deprivation of light darkness supervened; in the absence of virtue vice arose in its place, and against every form of good might be reckoned a like number of opposite evils), by whom, I ask, was man, fallen by his recklessness into this and the like evil state (for it was not possible for him to retain even his prudence when he had estranged himself from prudence, or to take any wise counsel when he had severed himself from wisdom),—by whom was man to be recalled to the grace of his

[7] S. Mark ii. 17.

[8] *of a wart*; μυρμηκίας. Gregory uses the same simile in his treatise *On the Soul* (iii. p. 204). The following "scholium" in Greek is found in the margin of two MSS. of that treatise, and in that of one MS. of this treatise: "There is an affection of the skin which is called a wart. A small fleshy excrescence projects from the skin, which seems a part of it, and a natural growth upon it: but this is not really so; and therefore it requires removal for its cure. This illustration made use of by Gregory is exceedingly appropriate to the matter in hand."

[9] Ps. xxxix. (xxxviii.) 11: "When thou with rebukes dost correct man for iniquity, thou makest his beauty to consume away" (A. V).

[1] *i. e.* Chapter I., throughout.

original state ? To whom belonged the restoration of the fallen one, the recovery of the lost, the leading back the wanderer by the hand ? To whom else than entirely to Him Who is the the Lord of his nature? For Him only Who at the first had given the life was it possible, or fitting, to recover it when lost. This is what we are taught and learn from the Revelation of the truth, that God in the beginning made man and saved him when he had fallen.

CHAPTER IX.

Up to this point, perhaps, one who has followed the course of our argument will agree with it, inasmuch as it does not seem to him that anything has been said which is foreign to the proper conception of the Deity. But towards what follows and constitutes the strongest part of this Revelation of the truth, he will not be similarly disposed ; the human birth, I mean, the growth of infancy to maturity, the eating and drinking, the fatigue and sleep, the sorrow and tears, the false accusation and judgment hall, the cross of death and consignment to the tomb. All these things, included as they are in this revelation, to a certain extent blunt the faith of the more narrow-minded, and so they reject the sequel itself in consequence of these antecedents. They will not allow that in the Resurrection from the dead there is anything consistent with the Deity, because of the unseemly circumstances of the Death. Well, I deem it necessary first of all to remove our thoughts for a moment from the grossness of the carnal element, and to fix them on what is morally beautiful in itself, and on what is not, and on the distinguishing marks by which each of them is to be apprehended. No one, I think, who has reflected will challenge the assertion that, in the whole nature of things, one thing only is disgraceful, and that is vicious weakness ; while whatever has no connection with vice is a stranger to all disgrace ; and whatever has no mixture in it of disgrace is certainly to be found on the side of the beautiful ; and what is really beautiful has in it no mixture of its opposite. Now whatever is to be regarded as coming within the sphere of the beautiful becomes the character of God. Either, then, let them show that there was viciousness in His birth, His bringing up, His growth, His progress to the perfection of His nature, His experience of death and return from death ; or, if they allow that the aforesaid circumstances of His life remain outside the sphere of viciousness, they will perforce admit that there is nothing of disgrace in this that is foreign to viciousness. Since,

then, what is thus removed from every disgraceful and vicious quality is abundantly shown to be morally beautiful, how can one fail to pity the folly of men who give it as their opinion that what is morally beautiful is not becoming in the case of God ?

CHAPTER X.

" But the nature of man," it is said, " is narrow and circumscribed, whereas the Deity is infinite. How could the infinite be included in the atom [2] ? " But who is it that says the infinitude of the Deity is comprehended in the envelopment of the flesh as if it were in a vessel ? Not even in the case of our own life is the intellectual nature shut up within the boundary of the flesh. On the contrary, while the body's bulk is limited to the proportions peculiar to it, the soul by the movements of its thinking faculty can coincide [3] at will with the whole of creation. It ascends to the heavens, and sets foot within the deep. It traverses the breadth of the world, and in the restlessness of its curiosity makes its way into the regions that are beneath the earth ; and often it is occupied in the scrutiny of the wonders of heaven, and feels no weight from the appendage [4] of the body. If, then, the soul of man, although by the necessity of its nature it is transfused through the body, yet presents itself everywhere at will, what necessity is there for saying that the Deity is hampered by an environment of fleshly nature, and why may we not, by examples which we are capable of understanding, gain some reasonable idea of God's plan of salvation ? There is an analogy, for instance, in the flame of a lamp, which is seen to embrace the material with which it is supplied [5]. Reason makes a distinction between the flame upon the material, and the material that kindles the flame, though in fact it is not possible to cut off the one from the other so as to exhibit the flame separate from the material, but they both united form one single thing. But let no one, I beg, associate also with this illustration the idea of the perishableness of the flame ; let him accept only what is apposite in the

---

[2] τῷ ἀτόμῳ : here, the individual body of man : "individuo corpusculo," Zinus translates. Theodoret in his second (" Unconfused ") Dialogue quotes this very passage about the " infiniteness of the Deity," and a " vessel," to prove the *two* natures of Christ.
[3] ἐφαπλοῦται.   [4] ἐφολκίῳ.
[5] There is a touch of Eutychianism in this illustration of the union of the Two Natures ; as also in Gregory's answer (*c. Eunom.* iii. 265 ; v. 589) to Eunomius' charge of Two Persons against the Nicene party, viz. that "the flesh with all its peculiar marks and properties is taken up and transformed into the Divine nature " ; whence arose that ἀντιμεθίστασις τῶν ὀνομάτων, i. e. *reciprocal* interchange of the properties human and Divine, which afterwards occasioned the Monophysite controversy. But Origen had used language still more incautious : " with regard to his mortal body and his human soul, we believe that owing to something more than communion with Him, to actual union and intermingling, it has acquired the highest qualities, and partakes of His Divinity, and so has changed into God " (*c. Cels.* iii. 41).

image; what is irrelevant and incongruous let him reject. What is there, then, to prevent our thinking (just as we see flame fastening on the material [6], and yet not inclosed in it) of a kind of union or approximation of the Divine nature with humanity, and yet in this very approximation guarding the proper notion of Deity, believing as we do that, though the Godhead be in man, it is beyond all circumscription?

CHAPTER XI.

SHOULD you, however, ask in what way Deity is mingled with humanity, you will have occasion for a preliminary inquiry as to what the coalescence is of soul with flesh. But supposing you are ignorant of the way in which the soul is in union with the body, do not suppose that that other question is bound to come within your comprehension; rather, as in this case of the union of soul and body, while we have reason to believe that the soul is something other than the body, because the flesh when isolated from the soul becomes dead and inactive, we have yet no exact knowledge of the method of the union, so in that other inquiry of the union of Deity with manhood, while we are quite aware that there is a distinction as regards degree of majesty between the Divine and the mortal perishable nature, we are not capable of detecting how the Divine and the human elements are mixed up together. The miracles recorded permit us not to entertain a doubt [7] that God was born in the nature of man. But how— this, as being a subject unapproachable by the processes of reasoning, we decline to investigate. For though we believe, as we do, that all the corporeal and intellectual creation derives its subsistence from the incorporeal and uncreated Being, yet the *whence* or the *how*, these we do not make a matter for examination along with our faith in the thing itself. While we accept the fact, we pass by the manner of the putting together of the Universe, as a subject which must not be curiously handled, but one altogether ineffable and inexplicable.

CHAPTER XII.

IF a person requires proofs of God's having been manifested to us in the flesh, let him look at the Divine activities. For of the existence of the Deity at all one can discover no other demonstration than that which the testimony

of those activities supplies. When, that is, we take a wide survey of the universe, and consider the dispensations throughout the world, and the Divine benevolences that operate in our life, we grasp the conception of a power overlying all, that is creative of all things that come into being, and is conservative of them as they exist. On the same principle, as regards the manifestation of God in the flesh, we have established a satisfactory proof of that apparition of Deity, in those wonders of His operations; for in all his work as actually recorded we recognize the characteristics of the Divine nature. It belongs to God to give life to men, to uphold by His providence all things that exist. It belongs to God to bestow meat and drink on those who in the flesh have received from Him the boon of life, to benefit the needy, to bring back to itself, by means of renewed health, the nature that has been perverted by sickness. It belongs to God to rule with equal sway the whole of creation; earth, sea, air, and the realms above the air. It is His to have a power that is sufficient for all things, and above all to be stronger than death and corruption. Now if in any one of these or the like particulars the record of Him had been wanting, they who are external to the faith had reasonably taken exception [8] to the gospel revelation. But if every notion that is conceivable of God is to be traced in what is recorded of Him, what is there to hinder our faith?

CHAPTER XIII.

BUT, it is said, to be born and to die are conditions peculiar to the fleshly nature. I admit it. But what went before that Birth and what came after that Death escapes the mark of our common humanity. If we look to either term of our human life, we understand both from what we take our beginning, and in what we end. Man commenced his existence in a weakness and in a weakness completes it. But in the instance of the Incarnation neither did the birth begin with a weakness, nor in a weakness did the death terminate; for neither did sensual pleasure go before the birth, nor did corruption follow upon the death. Do you disbelieve this marvel? I quite welcome your incredulity. You thus entirely admit that those marvellous facts are supernatural, in the very way that you think that what is related is above belief. Let this very fact, then, that the proclamation of the mystery did not proceed

---

[6] *fastening on the material.* The word (ἅπτεσθαι) could mean either "fastening on," or "depending on," or "kindled from" (it has been used in this last sense just above). Krabinger selects the second, "quæ a subjecto dependet."

[7] διὰ τῶν ἱστορουμένων θαυμάτων οὐκ ἀμφιβάλλομεν.

[8] παρεγράφοντο.

in terms that are natural, be a proof to you of the manifestation of the Deity. For if what is related of Christ were within the bounds of nature, where were the Godhead? But if the account surpasses nature, then the very facts which you disbelieve are a demonstration that He who was thus proclaimed was God. A man is begotten by the conjunction of two persons, and after death is left in corruption. Had the Gospel comprised no more than this, you certainly would not have deemed *him* to be God, the testimony to whom was conveyed in terms peculiar only to our nature. But when you are told that He was born, and yet transcended our common humanity both in the manner of His birth, and by His incapacity of a change to corruption, it would be well if, in consequence of this, you would direct your incredulity upon the other point, so as to refuse to suppose Him to be one of those who have manifestly existed as mere men; for it follows of necessity that a person who does not believe that such and such a being is mere man, must be led on to the belief that He is God. Well, he who has recorded that He was born *has* related also that He was born of a Virgin. If, therefore, on the evidence stated, the fact of His being born is established as a matter of faith, it is altogether incredible, on the same evidence, that He was not born in the manner stated. For the author who mentions His birth adds also, that it was of a Virgin; and in recording His death bears further testimony to His resurrection from the dead. If, therefore, from what you are told, you grant that He both was born and died, on the same grounds you must admit that both His birth and death were independent of the conditions of human weakness,—in fact, were above nature. The conclusion, therefore, is that He Who has thus been shown to have been born under supernatural circumstances was certainly Himself not limited by nature.

CHAPTER XIV.

"THEN why," it is asked, "did the Deity descend to such humiliation? Our faith is staggered to think that God, that incomprehensible, inconceivable, and ineffable reality, transcending all glory of greatness, wraps Himself up in the base covering of humanity, so that His sublime operations as well are debased by this admixture with the grovelling earth."

CHAPTER XV.

EVEN to this objection we are not at a loss for an answer consistent with our idea of God. You ask the reason why God was born among men. If you take away from life the benefits that come to us from God, you would not be able to tell me what means you have of arriving at any knowledge of Deity. In the kindly treatment of us we recognize the benefactor; that is, from observation of that which happens to us, we conjecture the disposition of the person who operates it. If, then, love of man be a special characteristic of the Divine nature, here is the reason for which you are in search, here is the cause of the presence of God among men. Our diseased nature needed a healer. Man in his fall needed one to set him upright. He who had lost the gift of life stood in need of a life-giver, and he who had dropped away from his fellowship with good wanted one who would lead him back to good. He who was shut up in darkness longed for the presence of the light. The captive sought for a ransomer, the fettered prisoner for some one to take his part, and for a deliverer he who was held in the bondage of slavery. Were these, then, trifling or unworthy wants to importune the Deity to come down and take a survey of the nature of man, when mankind was so miserably and pitiably conditioned? "But," it is replied, "man might have been benefited, and yet God might have continued in a passionless state. Was it not possible for Him Who in His wisdom framed the universe, and by the simple impulse of His will brought into subsistence that which was not, had it so pleased Him, by means of some direct Divine command to withdraw man from the reach of the opposing power, and bring him back to his primal state? Whereas He waits for long periods of time to come round, He submits Himself to the condition of a human body, He enters upon the stage of life by being born, and after passing through each age of life in succession, and then tasting death, at last, only by the rising again of His own body, accomplishes His object,—as if it was not optional to Him to fulfil His purpose without leaving the height of His Divine glory, and to save man by a single command 9, letting those long periods of time alone.

---

9 Origen answering the same objections says, "I know not what sort of alteration of mankind it is that Celsus wants, when he doubts whether it were not possible to improve man by a display of Divine power, without any one being sent in the course of nature (φύσει) for that purpose. Does he want this to take place among mankind by a sudden appearance of God destroying evil in their hearts at a blow, and causing virtue to spring up there? One might well inquire if it were fitting or possible that such a thing should happen. But we will suppose that it is so. What then? How will our assent to the truth be (in that case) praiseworthy? You yourself profess to recognize a special Providence: therefore you ought just as

Needful, therefore, is it that in answer to objections such as these we should draw out the counter-statement of the truth, in order that no obstacle may be offered to the faith of those persons who will minutely examine the reasonableness of the gospel revelation. In the first place, then, as has been partially discussed before [1], let us consider what is that which, by the rule of contraries, is opposed to virtue. As darkness is the opposite of light, and death of life, so vice, and nothing else besides, is plainly the opposite of virtue. For as in the many objects in creation there is nothing which is distinguished by its opposition to light or life, but only the peculiar ideas which are their exact opposites, as darkness and death—not stone, or wood, or water, or man, or anything else in the world,— so, in the instance of virtue, it cannot be said that any created thing can be conceived of as contrary to it, but only the idea of vice. If, then, our Faith preached that the Deity had been begotten under vicious circumstances, an opportunity would have been afforded the objector of running down our belief, as that of persons who propounded incongruous and absurd opinions with regard to the Divine nature. For, indeed, it were blasphemous to assert that the Deity, Which is very wisdom, goodness, incorruptibility, and every other exalted thing in thought or word, had undergone change to the contrary. If, then, God is real and essential virtue, and no mere existence [2] of any kind is logically opposed to virtue, but only vice is so ; and if the Divine birth was not into vice, but into human existence ; and if only vicious weakness is unseemly and shameful— and with such weakness neither was God born, nor had it in His nature to be born,— why are they scandalized at the confession that God came into touch with human nature, when in relation to virtue no contrariety whatever is observable in the organization of man? For neither Reason, nor Understanding [3], nor Receptivity for science, nor any other like quality proper to the essence of man, is opposed to the principle of virtue.

CHAPTER XVI.

"But," it is said, "this change in our body by birth is a weakness, and one born under such condition is born in weakness. Now the Deity is free from weakness. It is, therefore, a strange idea in connection with God," they say, "when people declare that one who is essentially free from weakness thus comes into fellowship with weakness." Now in reply to this let us adopt the same argument as before, namely that the word "weakness" is used partly in a proper, partly in an adapted sense. Whatever, that is, affects the will and perverts it from virtue to vice is really and truly a weakness ; but whatever in nature is to be seen proceeding by a chain peculiar to itself of successive stages would be more fitly called a work than a weakness. As, for instance, birth, growth, the continuance of the underlying substance through the influx and efflux of the aliments, the meeting together of the component elements of the body, and, on the other hand, the dissolution of its component parts and their passing back into the kindred elements. Which "weakness," then, does our Mystery assert that the Deity came in contact with? That which is properly called weakness, which is vice, or that which is the result of natural movements? Well, if our Faith affirmed that the Deity was born under forbidden circumstances, then it would be our duty to shun a statement which gave this profane and unsound description of the Divine Being. But if it asserts that God laid hold on this nature of ours, the production of which in the first instance and the subsistence afterwards had its origin in Him, in what way does this our preaching fail in the reverence that befits Him? Amongst our notions of God no disposition tending to weakness goes along with our belief in Him. We do not say that a physician is in weakness when he is employed in healing one who is so [4]. For though he touches the infirmity he is himself unaffected by it. If birth is not regarded in itself as a weakness, no one can call life such. But the feeling of sensual pleasure does go before the human birth, and as to the impulse to vice in all living men, this *is* a disease of our nature. But then the Gospel mystery asserts that He Who took our nature was pure from both these feelings. If, then, His birth had no connection with sensual pleasure, and His life none with vice, what "weakness" is there left which the mystery of our religion asserts that God participated in? But should any one call the separation of body and soul a weakness [5], far more justly might he term the

---

much to have told *us*, as we you, why it is that God, knowing the affairs of men, does not correct them, and by a single stroke of His power rid Himself of the whole family of evil. But we confidently assert that He does send messengers for this very purpose : for His words appealing to men's noblest emotions are amongst them. But whereas there had been already great differences between the various ministers of the Word, the reformation of Jesus went beyond them all in greatness ; for He did not mean to heal the men of one little corner only of the world, but He came to save all ;" *c. Cels.* iv. 3, 4.
[1] Ch. v.   [2] φύσις.   [3] τὸ διανοητικόν.

[4] So Origen (*c. Cels.* iv. 15) illustrates the κένωσις and συγκατάβασις of Christ : "Nor was this change one from the heights of excellence to the depths of baseness (τὸ πονηρότατον), for how can goodness and love be baseness ? If they were, it would be high time to declare that the surgeon who inspects or touches grievous and unsightly cases in order to heal them undergoes such a change from good to bad."
[5] There is no one word in English which would represent the full meaning of πάθος. "Sufferance" sometimes comes nearest to it, but not here, where Gregory is attempting to express that which in no way whatever attached to the Saviour, *i. e.* moral weakness, as opposed to physical infirmity.

meeting together of these two elements such. For if the severance of things that have been connected is a weakness, then is the union of things that are asunder a weakness also. For there is a feeling of movement in the uniting of things sundered as well as in the separation of what has been welded into one. The same term, then, by which the final movement is called, it is proper to apply to the one that initiated it. If the first movement, which we call birth, is not a weakness, it follows that neither the second, which we call death, and by which the severance of the union of the soul and body is effected, is a weakness. Our position is, that God was born subject to both movements of our nature; first, that by which the soul hastens to join the body, and then again that by which the body is separated from the soul; and that when the concrete humanity was formed by the mixture of these two, I mean the sentient and the intelligent element, through that ineffable and inexpressible conjunction, this result in the Incarnation followed, that after the soul and body had been once united the union continued for ever. For when our nature, following its own proper course, had even in Him been advanced to the separation of soul and body, He knitted together again the disunited elements, cementing them, as it were, together with the cement of His Divine power, and recombining what has been severed in a union never to be broken. And this is the Resurrection, namely the return, after they have been dissolved, of those elements that had been before linked together, into an indissoluble union through a mutual incorporation; in order that thus the primal grace which invested humanity might be recalled, and we restored to the everlasting life, when the vice that has been mixed up with our kind has evaporated through our dissolution, as happens to any liquid when the vessel that contained it is broken, and it is spilt and disappears, there being nothing to contain it. For as the principle of death took its rise in one person and passed on in succession through the whole of human kind, in like manner the principle of the Resurrection-life extends from one person to the whole of humanity. For He Who reunited to His own proper body the soul that had been assumed by Himself, by virtue of that power which had mingled with both of these component elements at their first framing, then, upon a more general scale as it were [6],

conjoined the intellectual to the sentient nature, the new principle freely progressing to the extremities by natural consequence. For when, in that concrete humanity which He had taken to Himself, the soul after the dissolution returned to the body, then this uniting of the several portions passes, as by a new principle, in equal force upon the whole human race. This, then, is the mystery of God's plan with regard to His death and His resurrection from the dead; namely, instead of preventing the dissolution of His body by death and the necessary results of nature, to bring both back to each other in the resurrection; so that He might become in Himself the meeting-ground both of life and death, having re-established in Himself that nature which death had divided, and being Himself the originating principle of the uniting those separated portions.

CHAPTER XVII.

But it will be said that the objection which has been brought against us has not yet been solved, and that what unbelievers have urged has been rather strengthened by all we have said. For if, as our argument has shown, there is such power in Him that both the destruction of death and the introduction of life resides in Him, why does He not effect His purpose by the mere exercise of His will, instead of working out our salvation in such a roundabout way, by being born and nurtured as a man, and even, while he was saving man, tasting death; when it was possible for Him to have saved man without subjecting Himself to such conditions? Now to this, with all candid persons, it were sufficient to reply, that the sick do not dictate to their physicians the measures for their recovery, nor cavil with those who do them good as to the method of their healing; why, for instance, the medical man felt the diseased part and devised this or that particular remedy for the removal of the complaint, when they expected another; but the patient looks to the end and aim of the good work, and receives the benefit with gratitude. Seeing, however, as says the Prophet [7], that God's abounding goodness

---

6 *upon a more general scale as it were.* The Greek here is somewhat obscure; the best reading is Krabinger's; γενικωτέρῳ τινι λόγῳ τὴν νοερὰν οὐσίαν τῇ αἰσθητῇ συγκατέμιξεν. Hervetus' translation is manifestly wrong; "Is generosiorem quandam intelligentem essentiam commiscuit sensili principio."—Soul and body have been reunited by the Resurrection, on a larger scale and to a wider extent (λόγῳ), than in the former instance of a single Person (in the Incarnation), the new principle of life progressing to the extremities of humanity by natural consequence : γενικωτέρῳ will thus

refer by comparison to "the *first* framing of these component elements." Or else it contrasts the amount of life with that of death : and is to be explained by Rom. v. 15, "But not as the offence, so also is the free gift. For if through the offence of one many be dead, *much more* the grace of God, and the gift by grace, which is by one man, Jesus Christ, hath *abounded* unto many." Krabinger's translation, "generaliori quâdam ratione," therefore seems correct. The mode of the union of soul and body is described in Gregory's Treatise on the Soul as κρείττων λόγος, and in his *Making of Man* as ἄφραστος λόγος, but in neither is there any comparison but with other less perfect modes of union ; *i. e.* the reference is to *quality*, not to *quantity*, as here.

7 *the Prophet*, i. e. David ; Ps. xxxi. 19 : ὡς πολὺ τὸ πλῆθος τῆς χρηστότητός σου, κ.τ.λ. Hervetus translates Gregory here "divitiæ benignitatis," as if he had found πλοῦτος in the text, which does not appear. Jerome twice translates the χρηστότης οἱ

keeps its utility concealed, and is not seen in complete clearness in this present life—otherwise, if the eyes could behold all that is hoped for, every objection of unbelievers would be removed,—but, as it is, abides the ages that are coming, when what is at present seen only by the eye of faith must be revealed, it is needful accordingly that, as far as we may, we should by the aid of arguments, the best within our reach, attempt to discover for these difficulties also a solution in harmony with what has gone before.

CHAPTER XVIII.

AND yet it is perhaps straining too far for those who do believe that God sojourned here in life to object to the manner of His appearance[8], as wanting wisdom or conspicuous reasonableness. For to those who are not vehemently antagonistic to the truth there exists no slight proof of the Deity having sojourned here; I mean that which is exhibited now in this present life before the life to come begins, the testimony which is borne by actual facts. For who is there that does not know that every part of the world was overspread with demoniacal delusion which mastered the life of man through the madness of idolatry; how this was the customary rule among all nations, to worship demons under the form of idols, with the sacrifice of living animals and the polluted offerings on their altars? But from the time when, as says the Apostle, "the grace of God that bringeth salvation to all men appeared[9]," and dwelt among us in His human nature, all these things passed away like smoke into nothingness, the madness of their oracles and prophesyings ceased, the annual pomps and pollutions of their bloody hecatombs came to an end, while among most nations altars entirely disappeared, together with porches, precincts, and shrines, and all the ritual besides which was followed out by the attendant priest of those demons, to the deception both of themselves and of all who came in their way. So that in many of these places no memorial exists of these things having ever been. But, instead, throughout the whole world there have arisen in the name of Jesus temples and altars and a

holy and unbloody Priesthood[1], and a sublime philosophy, which teaches, by deed and example more than by word, a disregard of this bodily life and a contempt of death, a contempt which they whom tyrants have tried to force to apostatize from the faith have manifestly displayed, making no account of the cruelties done to their bodies or of their doom of death: and yet, plainly, it was not likely that they would have submitted to such treatment unless they had had a clear and indisputable proof of that Divine Sojourn among men. And the following fact is, further, a sufficient mark, as against the Jews, of the presence among them[2] of Him in Whom they disbelieve; up to the time of the manifestation of Christ the royal palaces in Jerusalem were in all their splendour: there was their far-famed Temple; there was the customary round of their sacrifices throughout the year: all the things, which had been expressed by the Law in symbols to those who knew how to read its secrets, were up to that point of time unbroken in their observance, in accordance with that form of worship which had been established from the beginning. But when at length they saw Him Whom they were looking for, and of Whom by their Prophets and the Law they had before been told, and when they held in more estimation than faith in Him Who had so manifested Himself that which for the future became but a degraded superstition, because they took it in a wrong sense[3], and clung to the mere phrases of the Law in obedience to the dictates of custom rather than of intelligence, and when they had

---

[1] unbloody Priesthood, ἀναίμακτον ἱερωσύνην, i. e. "sacerdotium," not "sacrificium." This, not θυσίαν, is supported by the Codd. The Eucharist is often called by the Fathers "the unbloody sacrifice" (e. g. Chrysost. in Ps. xcv., citing Malachi), and the Priesthood which offers it can be called "unbloody" too. Cf. Greg. Naz. in Poem. xi. 1—

*Ω θυσίας πέμποντες ἀναιμάκτους ἱερῆες.

While these terms assert the sacrificial nature of the Eucharist, might they not at the same time supply an argument against the Roman view of Transubstantiation, which teaches that the actual blood of Christ is received, and makes it still a bloody sacrifice?

[2] of the presence among them, &c. Cf. a striking passage in Origen: "One amongst the convincing proofs that Jesus was something Divine and holy is this; that the Jews after what they did to Him have suffered so many terrible afflictions for his sake. And we shall be bold to say that they never will be restored again. They have committed the most impious of crimes. They plotted against the Saviour of mankind in that city where the ceremonies they continually performed for God enshrined great mysteries. It was right that that city where Jesus suffered should be utterly destroyed, and the Jewish nation expelled, and that God's call to blessedness should be made to others, I mean the Christians, to whom have passed the doctrines of a religion of stainless purity, and who have received new laws fitted for any form of government that exists" (c. Celsum, iv. 22). The Jews, he says, will even "suffer more than others in the judgment which they anticipate, in addition to what they have suffered already," ii. 8. But he says, v. 43, "Would that they had not committed the error of having broken their own law; first killing their prophets, and at last taking Jesus by stealth; for then we should still have amongst us the model of that heavenly city which Plato attempted to sketch, though I cannot say that his powers came up to those of Moses and his successors."

[3] they took it (i. e. the religion, which for the future, &c.) in a wrong sense: κακῶς ἐκλαβόντες (Hasius, ad Leon. Diacon.), shows how λαμβάνειν and μεταλαμβάνειν also have this meaning "interpret," "accipere"). This is a better reading than ἐκβαλόντες, and is supported by two MSS.

LXX. by "bonitas"; Aquila and Symmachus have τί πολὺ τὸ ἀγαθόν σου. This is the later sense of χρηστότης, which originally meant "serviceableness" and then "uprightness" (Psalm xiii. 2, 4, xxxvi. 3, cxix. 66), rather than "kindness."

[8] appearance, παρουσίαν. Casaubon in his notes to Gregory's Ep. to Eustathia, gives a list of the various terms applied by the Greek Fathers to the Incarnation, viz. (besides παρουσία),—ἡ τοῦ Χριστοῦ ἐπιφάνεια; ἡ δεσποτικὴ ἐπιδημία; ἡ διὰ σαρκὸς ὁμιλία; ἡ τοῦ λόγου ἐνσάρκωσις; ἡ ἐνανθρώπησις; ἡ ἔλευσις; ἡ κένωσις; ἡ συγκατάβασις; ἡ οἰκονομία (none more frequent than this); and others.

[9] Tit. ii. 11. This is the preferable rendering; not as in the A.V., "appeared to all men."

thus refused the grace which had appeared,— then even [4] those holy monuments of their religion were left standing, as they do, in history alone; for no traces even of their Temple can be recognized, and their splendid city has been left in ruins, so that there remains to the Jews nothing of the ancient institutions; while by the command of those who rule over them the very ground of Jerusalem which they so venerated is forbidden to them.

CHAPTER XIX.

NEVERTHELESS, since neither those who take the Greek view, nor yet the leaders of Jewish opinions, are willing to make such things the proofs of that Divine manifestation, it may be as well, as regards these demurrers to our statement, to treat more particularly the reason by virtue of which the Divine nature is combined with ours, saving, as it does, humanity by means of itself, and not working out its proposed design by means of a mere command. With what, then, must we begin, so as to conduct our thinking by a logical sequence to the proposed conclusion? What but this,* viz. with a succinct detail of the notions that can religiously be entertained of God [5]?

CHAPTER XX.

IT is, then, universally acknowledged that we must believe the Deity to be not only almighty, but just, and good, and wise, and everything else that suggests excellence. It follows, therefore, in the present dispensation of things, that it is not the case that some particular one [6] of these Divine attributes freely displays itself in creation, while there is another that is not present there; for, speaking once for all, no one of those exalted terms, when disjoined from the rest, is by itself alone a virtue, nor is the good really good unless allied with what is just, and wise, and mighty (for what is unjust, or unwise, or powerless, is not good, neither is power, when disjoined from the principle of justice and of wisdom, to be considered in the light of virtue; such species of power is brutal and tyrannous; and so, as to

the rest, if what is wise be carried beyond the limits of what is just, or if what is just be not contemplated along with might and goodness, cases of that sort one would more properly call vice; for how can what comes short of perfection be reckoned among things that are good?). If, then, it is fitting that all excellences should be combined in the views we have of God, let us see whether this Dispensation as regards man fails in any of those conceptions which we should entertain of Him. The object of our inquiry in the case of God is before all things the indications of His goodness. And what testimony to His goodness could there be more palpable than this, viz. His regaining to Himself the allegiance of one who had revolted to the opposite side, instead of allowing the fixed goodness of His nature to be affected by the variableness of the human will? For, as David says, He had not come to save us had not "goodness" created in Him such a purpose [7]; and yet His goodness had not advanced His purpose had not wisdom given efficacy to His love for man. For, as in the case of persons who are in a sickly condition, there are probably many who wish that a man were not in such evil plight, but it is only they in whom there is some technical ability operating in behalf of the sick, who bring their good-will on their behalf to a practical issue, so it is absolutely needful that wisdom should be conjoined with goodness. In what way, then, is wisdom contemplated in combination with goodness; in the actual events, that is, which have taken place? because one cannot observe a good purpose in the abstract; a purpose cannot possibly be revealed unless it has the light of some events upon it. Well, the things accomplished, progressing as they did in orderly series and sequence, reveal the wisdom and the skill of the Divine economy. And since, as has been before remarked, wisdom, when combined with justice, then absolutely becomes a virtue, but, if it be disjoined from it, cannot in itself alone be good, it were well moreover in this discussion of the Dispensation in regard to man, to consider attentively in the light of each other these two qualities; I mean, its wisdom and its justice.

CHAPTER XXI.

WHAT, then, is justice? We distinctly remember what in the course of our argument

---

[4] *then even.* The apodosis begins here, and ὥστε must be understood after ὑπολέλειπται, to govern μεῖναι, "were left standing, &c. . . . so that there remains."

[5] The Greek Fathers and the English divines for the most part confine themselves to showing their moral fitness and consonance with God's nature in the Incarnation, and do not attempt to prove its absolute necessity. Cf. Athanasius, *De Incarn. Verb.* c. 6; Hooker, *Eccles. Pol.* V. li. 3; Butler's *Analogy*, pt. ii. c. 5.

[6] τὸ μέν τι (for τοι). There is the same variety of reading in c. i. and xxi., where Krabinger has preserved the τι: he well quotes Synesius, *de Prov.* ii. 2; 'Ο μέν τις ἀποθνήσκει πληγείς, ὁ δὲ κ.τ.λ. (and refers to his note there).

[7] Ps. cvi. (cv.) 4, 5; cxix. (cxviii.) 65, 66, 68. In the first passage the LXX. has τοῦ ἰδεῖν ἐν τῇ χρηστότητι τῶν ἐκλεκτῶν σου (Heb. "the felicity of Thy chosen"): evidently referring to *God's εὐδοκία* in them; He, good Himself (χρηστὸς, v. 1), will save them, "in order to approve their goodness." The second passage mentions four times this χρηστότης (bonitas).

we said in the commencement of this treatise; namely, that man was fashioned in imitation of the Divine nature, preserving his resemblance to the Deity as well in other excellences as in possession of freedom of the will, yet being of necessity of a nature subject to change. For it was not possible that a being who derived his origin from an alteration should be altogether free from this liability. For the passing from a state of non-existence into that of existence is a kind of alteration; when being, that is, by the exercise of Divine power takes the place of nonentity. In the following special respect, too, alteration is necessarily observable in man, namely, because man was an imitation of the Divine nature, and unless some distinctive difference had been occasioned, the imitating subject would be entirely the same as that which it resembles; but in this instance, it is to be observed, there is a difference between that which "was made in the image" and its pattern; namely this, that the one is not subject to change, while the other is (for, as has been described, it has come into existence through an alteration), and being thus subject to alteration does not always continue in its existing state. For alteration is a kind of movement ever advancing from the present state to another; and there are two forms of this movement; the one being ever towards what is good, and in this the advance has no check, because no goal of the course to be traversed[8] can be reached, while the other is in the direction of the contrary, and of it this is the essence, that it has no subsistence; for, as has been before stated, the contrary state to goodness conveys some such notion of opposition, as when we say, for instance, that that which is is logically opposed to that which is not, and that existence is so opposed to non-existence. Since, then, by reason of this impulse and movement of changeful alteration it is not possible that the nature of the subject of this change should remain self-centred and unmoved, but there is always something towards which the will is tending, the appetency for moral beauty naturally drawing it on to movement, this beauty is in one instance really such in its nature, in another it is not so, only blossoming with an illusive appearance of beauty; and the criterion of these two kinds is the mind that dwells within us. Under these circumstances it is a matter of risk whether we happen to choose the real beauty, or whether we are diverted from its choice by some de-

ception arising from appearance, and thus drift away to the opposite; as happened, we are told in the heathen fable, to the dog which looked askance at the reflection in the water of what it carried in its mouth, but let go the real food, and, opening its mouth wide to swallow the image of it, still hungered. Since, then, the mind has been disappointed in its craving for the real good, and diverted to that which is not such, being persuaded, through the deception of the great advocate and inventor of vice, that that was beauty which was just the opposite (for this deception would never have succeeded, had not the glamour of beauty been spread over the hook of vice like a bait),—the man, I say, on the one hand, who had enslaved himself by indulgence to the enemy of his life, being of his own accord in this unfortunate condition,—I ask you to investigate, on the other hand, those qualities which suit and go along with our conception of the Deity, such as goodness, wisdom, power, immortality, and all else that has the stamp of superiority. As good, then, the Deity entertains pity for fallen man; as wise He is not ignorant of the means for his recovery; while a just decision must also form part of that wisdom; for no one would ascribe that genuine justice to the absence of wisdom.

CHAPTER XXII.

WHAT, then, under these circumstances is justice? It is the not exercising any arbitrary sway over him who has us in his power[9], nor, by tearing us away by a violent exercise of force from his hold, thus leaving some colour for a just complaint to him who enslaved man through sensual pleasure. For as they who have bartered away their freedom for money are the slaves of those who have purchased them (for they have constituted themselves their own sellers, and it is not allowable either for themselves or any one else in their behalf to call freedom to their aid, not even though those who have thus reduced themselves to this sad state are of noble birth; and, if any one out of regard for the person who has so sold himself should use violence against him who has bought him, he will clearly be acting un-

---

[8] *of the course to be traversed*: τοῦ διεξοδευομένου. Glauber remarks that the Latin translation here, "ejus qui transit," gives no sense. and rightly takes the word as a passive. Krabinger also translates, "ejus quod evolvitur." Here again there is unconscious Platonism: αὐτὸ τὸ καλόν is eternal.

[9] Compare a passage in Dionysius Areop. (*De eccles. hierarch.* c. iii. p. 297). "The boundless love of the Supreme Goodness did not refuse a personal providing for us, but perfectly participating in all that belongs to us, and united to our lowliness, along with an undiluted and unimpaired possession of its own qualities, has gifted us for ever with a communion of kinship with Itself, and exhibited us as partners in Its glories: undoing the adverse power of the Rebel throng, as the secret Tradition says, "*not by might, as if it was domineering, but, according to the oracle secretly delivered to us, by right and justice*" (quoted by Krabinger). To the words "not by might," S. Maximus has added the note, "This is what Gregory of Nyssa says in the Catechetic." See next note.

justly in thus arbitrarily rescuing one who has been legally purchased as a slave, whereas, if he wishes to pay a price to get such a one away, there is no law to prevent that), on the same principle, now that we had voluntarily bartered away our freedom, it was requisite that no arbitrary method of recovery, but the one consonant with justice [1] should be devised by Him Who in His goodness had undertaken our rescue. Now this method is in a measure this; to make over to the master of the slave whatever ransom he may agree to accept for the person in his possession.

CHAPTER XXIII.

WHAT, then, was it likely that the master of the slave would choose to receive in his stead? It is possible in the way of inference to make a guess as to his wishes in the matter, if, that is, the manifest indications of what we are seeking for should come into our hands. He then, who, as we before stated in the beginning of this treatise, shut his eyes to the good in his envy of man in his happy condition, he who generated in himself the murky cloud of wickedness, he who suffered from the disease of the love of rule, that primary and fundamental cause of propension to the bad and the mother, so to speak, of all the wickedness that follows,—what would he accept in exchange for the thing which he held, but something, to be sure, higher and better, in the way of ransom, that thus, by receiving a gain in the exchange, he might foster the more his own special passion of pride? Now unquestionably in not one of those who had lived in history from the beginning of the world had he been conscious of any such circumstance as he observed to surround Him Who then manifested Himself, i. e. conception without carnal connection, birth without impurity, motherhood with virginity, voices of the unseen testifying from above to a transcendent worth, the healing of natural disease, without the use of means and of an extraordinary character, proceeding from Him by the mere utterance of a word and exercise of His will, the restoration of the dead to life, the absolution of the damned [2], the fear with which

He inspired devils, His power over tempests, His walking through the sea, not by the waters separating on either side, and, as in the case of Moses' miraculous power, making bare its depths for those who passed through, but by the surface of the water presenting solid ground for His feet, and by a firm and hard resistance supporting His steps; then, His disregard for food as long as it pleased Him to abstain, His abundant banquets in the wilderness wherewith many thousands were fully fed (though neither did the heavens pour down manna on them, nor was their need supplied by the earth producing corn for them in its natural way, but that instance of munificence [3] came out of the ineffable store-houses of His Divine power), the bread ready in the hands of those who distributed it, as if they were actually reaping it, and becoming more, the more the eaters were filled; and then, the banquet on the fish; not that the sea supplied their need, but He Who had stocked the sea with its fish. But how is it possible to narrate in succession each one of the Gospel miracles? The Enemy, therefore, beholding in Him such power, saw also in Him an opportunity for an advance, in the exchange, upon the value of what he held. For this reason he chooses Him as a ransom [4] for those who were shut up in the prison of death. But it was out of his power to look on the unclouded aspect of God; he must see in Him some portion of that fleshly nature which through sin he had so long held in bondage. Therefore it was that the Deity was invested with the flesh, in order, that is, to secure that he, by looking upon something congenial and kindred to himself, might have no fears in approaching that supereminent power; and might yet by perceiving that power, showing as it did, yet only gradually, more and more splendour in the miracles, deem what was seen an object of desire rather than of fear. Thus, you see how goodness was conjoined with justice, and how wisdom was not divorced from them. For to have devised that the Divine power should have been containable in the envelopment of a body, to the end that the Dispensation in our behalf might not be thwarted through any fear inspired by the Deity actually appearing, affords a demonstration of all these qualities at once—goodness, wisdom, justice. His choosing to save man is a testimony of his goodness; His making the redemption of the captive a matter of exchange exhibits His justice, while the

---

[1] *one consonant with justice.* This view of Redemption, as a coming to terms with Satan and making him a party or defender in the case, is rather remarkable. The Prologue to the Book of Job furnishes a basis for it, where Satan enters into terms with God. It appears to be the Miltonic view: as also that Envy was the first sin of Satan.

[2] *the absolution of the damned.* These words, wanting in all others, Krabinger has restored from the Codex B. Morell translates "damnatorum absolutio." The Greek is τὴν τῶν καταδίκων ἀνάρρυσιν. "Hæc Origenem sapiunt, qui damnatorum pœnis finem statuit:" Krabinger. But here at all events it is not necessary to accuse Gregory of this, since he is clearly speaking only of Christ's forgiveness of sins during His earthly ministry.

[3] φιλοτιμία.

[4] *he chooses Him as a ransom.* This peculiar teaching of Gregory of Nyssa, that it was to the Devil, not God the Father, that the ransom, *i. e.* Christ's blood, was paid, is shared by Origen, Ambrose, and Augustine. The latter says, "Sanguine Christi diabolus non ditatus est, sed ligatus," *i. e.* bound by compact. On the other hand Gregory Naz. (tom. I. *Orat.* 42) and John Damascene (*De Fid. Orthod.* iii. c. 27) give the ransom to the Father.

invention whereby He enabled the Enemy to apprehend that of which he was before incapable, is a manifestation of supreme wisdom.

CHAPTER XXIV.

But possibly one who has given his attention to the course of the preceding remarks may inquire : "wherein is the power of the Deity, wherein is the imperishableness of that Divine power, to be traced in the processes you have described?" In order, therefore, to make this also clear, let us take a survey of the sequel of the Gospel mystery, where that Power conjoined with Love is more especially exhibited. In the first place, then, that the omnipotence of the Divine nature should have had strength to descend to the humiliation of humanity, furnishes a clearer proof of that omnipotence than even the greatness and supernatural character of the miracles. For that something pre-eminently great should be wrought out by Divine power is, in a manner, in accordance with, and consequent upon the Divine nature ; nor is it startling to hear it said that the whole of the created world, and all that is understood to be beyond the range of visible things, subsists by the power of God, His will giving it existence according to His good pleasure. But this His descent to the humility of man is a kind of superabundant exercise of power, which thus finds no check even in directions which contravene nature. It is the peculiar property of the essence of fire to tend upwards ; no one, therefore, deems it wonderful in the case of flame to see that natural operation. But should the flame be seen to stream downwards, like heavy bodies, such a fact would be regarded as a miracle ; namely, how fire still remains fire, and yet, by this change of direction in its motion, passes out of its nature by being borne downward. In like manner, it is not the vastness of the heavens, and the bright shining of its constellations, and the order of the universe, and the unbroken administration over all existence that so manifestly displays the transcendent power of the Deity, as this condescension to the weakness of our nature ; the way, in fact, in which sublimity, existing in lowliness, is actually seen in lowliness, and yet descends not from its height, and in which Deity, entwined as it is with the nature of man, becomes this, and yet still is that. For since, as has been said before, it was not in the nature of the opposing power to come in contact with the undiluted presence of God, and to undergo His unclouded manifestation, therefore, in order to secure that the ransom in our behalf might be easily accepted by him who required it, the Deity was hidden under the veil of our nature,

that so, as with ravenous fish [5], the hook of the Deity might be gulped down along with the bait of flesh, and thus, life being introduced into the house of death, and light shining in darkness, that which is diametrically opposed to light and life might vanish ; for it is not in the nature of darkness to remain when light is present, or of death to exist when life is active. Let us, then, by way of summary take up the train of the arguments for the Gospel mystery, and thus complete our answer to those who question this Dispensation of God, and show them on what ground it is that the Deity by a personal intervention works out the salvation of man. It is certainly most necessary that in every point the conceptions we entertain of the Deity should be such as befit the subject, and not that, while one idea worthy of His sublimity should be retained, another equally belonging to that estimate of Deity should be dismissed from it ; on the contrary, every exalted notion, every devout thought, must most surely enter into our belief in God, and each must be made dependent on each in a necessary sequence. Well, then ; it has been pointed out that His goodness, wisdom, justice, power, incapability of decay, are all of them in evidence in the doctrine of the Dispensation in which we are. His goodness is caught sight of in His election to save lost man ; His wisdom and justice have been displayed in the method of our salvation ; His power, in that, though born in the likeness and fashion of a man, on the lowly level of our nature, and in accordance with that likeness raising the expectation that he could be overmastered by death, he, after such a birth, nevertheless produced the effects peculiar and natural to Him. Now it is the peculiar effect of light to make darkness vanish, and of life to destroy death. Since, then, we have been led astray from the right path, and diverted from that life which was ours at the beginning, and brought under the sway of death, what is there improbable in the lesson we are taught by the Gospel mystery, if it be this ; that cleansing reaches those who are befouled with sin, and life the dead, and guidance the wanderers, in order that defilement may be cleansed, error corrected, and what was dead restored to life?

CHAPTER XXV.

That Deity should be born in our nature, ought not reasonably to present any strangeness

5 *as with ravenous fish.* The same simile is found in John of Damascus (*De Fid.* iii. 27), speaking of Death. "Therefore Death will advance, and, gulping down the bait of the Body, be transfixed with the hook of the Divinity : tasting that sinless and life-giving Body, he is undone, and disgorges all whom he has ever engulphed : for as darkness vanishes at the letting in of light, so corruption is chased away by the onset of life, and while there is life given to all else, there is corruption only for the Corrupter."

to the minds of those who do not take too narrow a view of things. For who, when he takes a survey of the universe, is so simple as not to believe that there is Deity in everything, penetrating it, embracing it, and seated in it? For all things depend on Him Who is [6], nor can there be anything which has not its being in Him Who is. If, therefore, all things are in Him, and He in all things, why are they scandalized at the plan of Revelation, when it teaches that God was born among men, that same God Whom we are convinced is even now not outside mankind? For although this last form of God's presence amongst us is not the same as that former presence, still His existence amongst us equally both then and now is evidenced; only now He Who holds together Nature in existence is transfused in *us;* while at that other time He was transfused throughout *our nature*, in order that our nature might by this transfusion of the Divine become itself divine, rescued as it was from death, and put beyond the reach of the caprice of the antagonist. For His return from death becomes to our mortal race the commencement of our return to the immortal life.

CHAPTER XXVI.

STILL, in his examination of the amount of justice and wisdom discoverable in this Dispensation a person is, perhaps, induced to entertain the thought that it was by means of a certain amount of deceit that God carried out this scheme on our behalf. For that not by pure Deity alone, but by Deity veiled in human nature, God, without the knowledge of His enemy, got within the lines of him who had man in his power, is in some measure a fraud and a surprise; seeing that it is the peculiar way with those who want to deceive to divert in another direction the expectations of their intended victims, and then to effect something quite different from what these latter expected. But he who has regard for truth will agree that the essential qualities of justice and wisdom are before all things these; viz. of justice, to give to every one according to his due; of wisdom, not to pervert justice, and yet at the same time not to dissociate the benevolent aim of the love of mankind from the verdict of justice, but skilfully to combine both these requisites together, in regard to justice [7] returning the due recompense, in regard to kindness not swerving from the aim of that love of man. Let us see, then,

whether these two qualities are not to be observed in that which took place. That repayment, adequate to the debt, by which the deceiver was in his turn deceived, exhibits the justice of the dealing, while the object aimed at is a testimony to the goodness of Him who effected it. It is, indeed, the property of justice to assign to every one those particular results of which he has sunk already the foundations and the causes, just as the earth returns its harvests according to the kinds of seeds thrown into it; while it is the property of wisdom, in its very manner of giving equivalent returns, not to depart from the kinder course. Two persons may both mix poison with food, one with the design of taking life, the other with the design of saving that life; the one using it as a poison, the other only as an antidote to poison; and in no way does the manner of the cure adopted spoil the aim and purpose of the benefit intended; for although a mixture of poison with the food may be effected by both of these persons alike, yet looking at their intention we are indignant with the one and approve the other; so in this instance, by the reasonable rule of justice, he who practised deception receives in return that very treatment, the seeds of which he had himself sown of his own free will. He who first deceived man by the bait of sensual pleasure is himself deceived by the presentment of the human form. But as regards the aim and purpose of what took place, a change in the direction of the nobler is involved; for whereas he, the enemy, effected his deception for the ruin of our nature, He Who is at once the just, and good, and wise one, used His device, in which there was deception, for the salvation of him who had perished, and thus not only conferred benefit on the lost one, but on him, too, who had wrought our ruin. For from this approximation of death to life, of darkness to light, of corruption to incorruption, there is effected an obliteration of what is worse, and a passing away of it into nothing, while benefit is conferred on him who is freed from those evils. For it is as when some worthless material has been mixed with gold, and the gold-refiners [8] burn up the foreign and refuse part in the consuming fire, and so restore the precious substance to its natural lustre : (not that the separation is effected without difficulty, for it takes time for the fire by its melting force to cause the baser matter to disappear; but for all that, this melting away of the actual thing that was embedded in it to the injury of its beauty is a kind of healing of the gold.) In

---

6 Exod. iii. 14.

7 τῇ μὲν δικαιοσύνῃ. The dative is not governed by ἀντιδιδόντα but corresponds to τῇ δὲ ἀγαθότητι (a dative of reference), which has no such verb after it. Krabinger therefore hardly translates correctly "justitiæ quod datur, pro meritis tribuendo."

8 οἱ θεραπευταὶ τοῦ χρυσίου On the margin of one of Krabinger's Codd. is written here in Latin, "This must be read with caution : it seems to savour of Origen's opinion," *i. e.* the curing of Satan.

the same way when death, and corruption, and darkness, and every other offshoot of evil had grown into the nature of the author of evil, the approach of the Divine power, acting like fire [9], and making that unnatural accretion to disappear, thus by purgation [1] of the evil becomes a blessing to that nature, though the separation is agonizing. Therefore even the adversary himself will not be likely to dispute that what took place was both just and salutary, that is, if he shall have attained to a perception of the boon. For it is now as with those who for their cure are subjected to the knife and the cautery; they are angry with the doctors, and wince with the pain of the incision; but if recovery of health be the result of this treatment, and the pain of the cautery passes away, they will feel grateful to those who have wrought this cure upon them. In like manner, when, after long periods of time, the evil of our nature, which now is mixed up with it and has grown with its growth, has been expelled, and when there has been a restoration of those who are now lying in Sin to their primal state, a harmony of thanksgiving will arise from all creation [2], as well from those who in the process of the purgation have suffered chastisement, as from those who needed not any purgation at all. These and the like benefits the great mystery of the Divine incarnation bestows. For in those points in which He was mingled with humanity, passing as He did through all the accidents proper to human nature, such as birth, rearing, growing up, and advancing even to the taste of death, He accomplished all the results before mentioned, freeing both man from evil, and healing even the introducer of evil himself. For the chastisement, however painful, of moral disease is a healing of its weakness.

CHAPTER XXVII.

IT is, then, completely in keeping with this, that He Who was thus pouring Himself into our nature should accept this commixture in all its accidents. For as they who wash clothes do not pass over some of the dirt and cleanse the rest, but clear the whole cloth from all its stains,

from one end to the other, that the cloak by being uniformly brightened from washing may be throughout equal to its own standard of cleanness, in like manner, since the life of man was defiled by sin, in its beginning, end, and all its intermediate states, there needed an abstergent force to penetrate the whole, and not to mend some one part by cleansing, while it left another unattended to. For this reason it is that, seeing that our life has been included between boundaries on either side, one, I mean, at its beginning, and the other at its ending, at each boundary the force that is capable of correcting our nature is to be found, attaching itself to the beginning, and extending to the end, and touching all between those two points [3]. Since, then, there is for all men only one way of entrance into this life of ours, from whence was He Who was making His entrance amongst us to transport Himself into our life? From heaven, perhaps some one will say, who rejects with contempt, as base and degraded, this species of birth, *i. e.* the human. But there was no humanity in heaven: and in that supramundane existence no disease of evil had been naturalized; but He Who poured Himself into man adopted this commixture with a view to the *benefit* of it. Where, then, evil was not and the human life was not lived, how is it that any one seeks *there* the scene of this wrapping up of God in man, or, rather, not man, but some phantom resemblance of man? In what could the recovery of our nature have consisted if, while this earthly creature was diseased and needed this recovery, something else, amongst the heavenly beings, had experienced the Divine sojourning? It is impossible for the sick man to be healed, unless his suffering member receives the healing. If, therefore, while this sick part was on earth, omnipotence had touched it not, but had regarded only its own dignity, this its pre-occupation with matters with which we had nothing in common would have been of no benefit to man. And with regard to the undignified in the case of Deity we can make no distinction; that is, if it is allowable to conceive at all of anything beneath the dignity of Deity beside evil. On the contrary, for one who forms such a narrow-minded view of the greatness of the Deity as to make it consist in inability to admit of fellowship with the peculiarities of our nature, the degradation is in no point lessened by the Deity

---

9 Mal. iii. 2, 3.

1 τῇ καθάρσει. This is the reading of three of Krabinger's Codd. and that of Hervetus and Zinus; "purgatione," "purgationis": the context too of the whole chapter seems to require it. But Morell's Cod. had τῇ ἀφθαρσίᾳ, and Ducæus approved of retaining it. For this κάθαρσις see especially Origen, *c. Cels.* vi. 44.

2 "Far otherwise was it with the great thinkers of the early Church. . . . They realized that redemption was a means to an end, and that end the reconsecration of the whole universe to God. And so the very completeness of their grasp upon the Atonement led them to dwell upon the cosmical significance of the Incarnation, its purpose to 'gather together all things in one.' For it was an age in which the problems of the universe were keenly felt."—*Lux Mundi*, p. 134.

3 "In order that the sacrifice might be representative, He took upon Him the whole of our human nature, and became flesh, conditioned though that fleshly nature was throughout by sin. It was not only in His death that we contemplate Him as the sin-bearer: but throughout His life He was as it were conditioned by the sinfulness of those with whom His human nature brought Him into close and manifold relations."—*Lux Mundi*, p. 217 (Augustine, *de Musicâ*, vi. 4, quoted in note, "Hominem sine peccato, non sine peccatoris conditione, suscepit ").

being conformed to the fashion of a heavenly rather than that of an earthly body. For every *created* being is distant, by an equal degree of inferiority, from that which is the Highest, Who is unapproachable by reason of the sublimity of His Being: the whole universe is in value the same distance beneath Him. For that which is absolutely inaccessible does not allow access to some one thing while it is unapproachable by another, but it transcends all existences by an equal sublimity. Neither, therefore, is the earth further removed from this dignity, nor the heavens closer to it, nor do the things which have their existence within each of these elemental worlds differ at all from each other in this respect, that some are allowed to be in contact with the inaccessible Being, while others are forbidden the approach. Otherwise we must suppose that the power which governs the Universe does not equally pervade the whole, but in some parts is in excess, in others is deficient. Consequently, by this difference of less or more in quantity or quality, the Deity will appear in the light of something composite and out of agreement with itself; if, that is, we could suppose it, as viewed in its essence, to be far away from us, whilst it is a close neighbour to some other creature, and from that proximity easily apprehended. But on this subject of that exalted dignity true reason looks neither downward nor upward in the way of comparison; for all things sink to a level beneath the power which presides over the Universe: so that if it shall be thought by them that any earthly nature is unworthy of this intimate connection with the Deity, neither can any other be found which has such worthiness. But if all things equally fall short of this dignity, one thing there is that is not beneath the dignity of God, and that is, to do good to him that needed it. If we confess, then, that where the disease was, there the healing power attended, what is there in this belief which is foreign to the proper conception of the Deity?

CHAPTER XXVIII.

BUT they deride our state of nature, and din into our ears the manner of our being born, supposing in this way to make the mystery ridiculous, as if it were unbecoming in God by such an entrance into the world as this to connect Himself with the fellowship of the human life. But we touched upon this point before, when we said that the only thing which is essentially degraded is moral evil or whatever has an affinity with such evil; whereas the orderly process of Nature, arranged as it has been by the Divine will and law, is beyond the reach

of any misrepresentation on the score of wickedness: otherwise this accusation would reach up to the Author of Nature, if anything connected with Nature were to be found fault with as degraded and unseemly. If, then, the Deity is separate only from evil, and if there is no nature in evil, and if the mystery declares that God was born in man but not in evil, and if, for man, there is but one way of entrance upon life, namely that by which the embryo passes on to the stage of life, what other mode of entrance upon life would they prescribe for God? these people, I mean, who, while they judge it right and proper that the nature which evil had weakened should be visited by the Divine power, yet take offence at this special method of the visitation, not remembering that the whole organization of the body is of equal value throughout, and that nothing in it, of all the elements that contribute to the continuance of the animal life, is liable to the charge of being worthless or wicked. For the whole arrangement of the bodily organs and limbs has been constructed with one end in view, and that is, the continuance in life of humanity; and while the other organs of the body conserve the present actual vitality of men, each being apportioned to a different operation, and by their means the faculties of sense and action are exercised, the generative organs on the contrary involve a forecast of the future, introducing as they do, by themselves, their counteracting transmission for our race. Looking, therefore, to their utility, to which of those parts which are deemed more honourable are these inferior[4]? Nay, than which must they not in all reason be deemed more worthy of honour? For not by the eye, or ear, or tongue, or any other sense, is the continuation of our race carried on. These, as has been remarked, pertain to the enjoyment of the present. But by those other organs the immortality of humanity is secured, so that death, though ever operating against us, thus in a certain measure becomes powerless and ineffectual, since Nature, to baffle him, is ever as it were throwing herself into the breach through those who come successively into being. What unseemliness, then, is contained in our revelation of God mingled with the life of humanity through those very means by which Nature carries on the combat against death?

CHAPTER XXIX.

BUT they change their ground and endeavour to vilify our faith in another way. They ask, if what took place was not to the dishonour of

---

[4] Cf. 1 Cor xii. 14—24

God or unworthy of Him, why did He delay the benefit so long? Why, since evil was in the beginning, did He not cut off its further progress?—To this we have a concise answer; viz. that this delay in conferring the benefit was owing to wisdom and a provident regard for that which would be a gain for our nature. In diseases, for instance, of the body, when some corrupt humour spreads unseen beneath the pores, before all the unhealthy secretion has been detected on the skin, they who treat diseases by the rules of art do not use such medicines as would harden the flesh, but they wait till all that lurks within comes out upon the surface, and then, with the disease unmasked, apply their remedies. When once, then, the disease of evil had fixed itself in the nature of mankind, He, the universal Healer, waited for the time when no form of wickedness was left still hidden in that nature. For this reason it was that He did not produce his healing for man's disease immediately on Cain's hatred and murder of his brother; for the wickedness of those who were destroyed in the days of Noah had not yet burst into a flame, nor had that terrible disease of Sodomite lawlessness been displayed, nor the Egyptians' war against God [5], nor the pride of Assyria, nor the Jews' bloody persecution of God's saints, nor Herod's cruel murder of the children, nor whatever else is recorded, or if unrecorded was done in the generations that followed, the root of evil budding forth in divers manners in the wilful purposes of man. When, then, wickedness had reached its utmost height, and there was no form of wickedness which men had not dared to do, to the end that the healing remedy might pervade the whole of the diseased system, He, accordingly, ministers to the disease; not at its beginning, but when it had been completely developed.

CHAPTER XXX.

IF, however, any one thinks to refute our argument on this ground, that even after the application of the remedial process the life of man is still in discord through its errors, let us lead him to the truth by an example taken from familiar things. Take, for instance, the case of a serpent; if it receives a deadly blow on the head, the hinder part of the coil is not at once deadened along with it; but, while the head is dead, the tail part is still animated with its own particular spirit, and is not deprived of its vital motion: in like manner we may see Sin struck its deadly blow and yet in its remainders still

vexing the life of man. But then they give up finding fault with the account of Revelation on these points, and make another charge against it; viz. that the Faith does not reach all mankind. "But why is it," they ask, "that all men do not obtain the grace, but that, while some adhere to the Word, the portion who remain unbelieving is no small one; either because God was unwilling to bestow his benefit ungrudgingly upon all, or because He was altogether unable to do so?" Now neither of these alternatives can defy criticism. For it is unworthy of God, either that He should not will what is good, or that He should be unable to do it. "If, therefore, the Faith is a good thing, why," they ask, "does not its grace come upon all men?" Now [6], if in our representation of the Gospel mystery we had so stated the matter as that it was the Divine will that the Faith should be so granted away amongst mankind that some men should be called, while the rest had no share in the calling, occasion would be given for bringing such a charge against this Revelation. But if the call came with equal meaning to all and makes no distinction as to worth, age, or different national characteristics (for it was for this reason that at the very first beginning of the proclamation of the Gospel they who ministered the Word were, by Divine inspiration, all at once enabled to speak in the language of any nation, viz. in order that no one might be destitute of a share in the blessings of evangelical instruction), with what reasonableness can they still charge it upon God that the Word has not influenced all mankind? For He Who holds the sovereignty of the universe, out of the excess of this regard for man, permitted something to be under our own control, of which each of us alone is master. Now this is the will, a thing that cannot be enslaved, and of self-determining power, since it is seated in the liberty of thought and mind. Therefore such a charge might more justly be transferred to those who have not attached themselves to the Faith, instead of resting on Him Who has called them to believe. For even when Peter at the beginning preached the Gospel in a crowded assembly of the Jews, and three thousand at once received the Faith, though those who disbelieved were more in number than the believers, they did not attach blame to the Apostle on the ground of their disbelief. It was, indeed, not in reason, when the grace of the Gospel had been publicly set forth, for one who had absented himself

---

[5] θεομαχία, a word often applied by the Greek Fathers to the conduct of the Egyptians, in reference, of course, to Pharaoh.

[6] The following passage is anti-Calvinistic. Gregory here, as continually elsewhere, asserts the freedom of the will; and is strongly supported by Justin Martyr, i. 43: "If it has been fixed by fate that one man shall be good, and another bad, the one is not praiseworthy, the other not culpable. And again, if mankind has not power by a free choice to flee the evil and to choose the good, it is not responsible for any results, however shocking."

from it of his own accord to lay the blame of his exclusion on another rather than himself.

CHAPTER XXXI.

YET, even in their reply to this, or the like, they are not at a loss for a contentious rejoinder. For they assert that God, if He had been so pleased, might have forcibly drawn those, who were not inclined to yield, to accept the Gospel message. But where then would have been their free will? Where their virtuous merit? Where their meed of praise from their moral directors? It belongs only to inanimate or irrational creatures to be brought round by the will of another to his purpose; whereas the reasoning and intelligent nature, if it lays aside its freedom of action, loses at the same time the gracious gift of intellect. For upon what is he to employ any faculty of thought, if his power of choosing anything according to his inclination lies in the will of another? But then, if the will remains without the capacity of action, virtue necessarily disappears, since it is shackled by the enforced quiescence of the will. Then, if virtue does not exist, life loses its value, reason moves in accordance with fatalism, the praise of moral guardians [7] is gone, sin may be indulged in without risk, and the difference between the courses of life is obliterated. For who, henceforth, could with any reason condemn profligacy, or praise sobriety? since [8] every one would have this ready answer, that nothing of all the things we are inclined to is in our own power, but that by some superior and ruling influence the wills of men are brought round to the purpose of one who has the mastery over them. The conclusion, then, is that it is not the goodness of God that is chargeable with the fact that the Faith is not engendered in all men, but rather the disposition of those by whom the preaching of the Word is received.

CHAPTER XXXII.

WHAT other objection is alleged by our adversaries? This; that (to take the preferable view [9]) it was altogether needless that that transcendent Being should submit to the experience of death, but He might independently of this, through the superabundance of His power, have wrought with ease His purpose; still, if for some ineffable reason or other it was absolutely necessary that so it should be,

at least He ought not to have been subjected to the contumely of such an ignominious kind of death. What death, they ask, could be more ignominious than that by crucifixion? What answer can we make to this? Why, that the death is rendered necessary by the birth, and that He Who had determined once for all to share the nature of man must pass through all the peculiar conditions of that nature. Seeing, then, that the life of man is determined between two boundaries, had He, after having passed the one, not touched the other that follows, His proposed design would have remained only half fulfilled, from His not having touched that second condition of our nature. Perhaps, however, one who exactly understands the mystery would be justified rather in saying that, instead of the death occurring in consequence of the birth, the birth on the contrary was accepted by Him for the sake of the death; for He Who lives for ever did not sink down into the conditions of a bodily birth from any need to live, but to call us back from death to life. Since, then, there was needed a lifting up from death for the whole of our nature, He stretches forth a hand as it were to prostrate man, and stooping down to our dead corpse He came so far within the grasp of death as to touch a state of deadness, and then in His own body to bestow on our nature the principle of the resurrection, raising as He did by His power along with Himself the whole man. For since from no other source than from the concrete lump of our nature [1] had come that flesh, which was the receptacle of the Godhead and in the resurrection was raised up together with that Godhead, therefore just in the same way as, in the instance of this body of ours, the operation of one of the organs of sense is felt at once by the whole system, as one with that member, so also the resurrection principle of this Member, as though the whole of mankind was a single living being, passes through the entire race, being imparted from the Member to the whole by virtue of the continuity and oneness of the nature. What, then, is there beyond the bounds of probability in what this Revelation teaches us; viz. that He Who stands upright stoops to one who has fallen, in order to lift him up from his prostrate condition? And as to the Cross, whether it possesses some other and deeper meaning, those who are skilled in mysticism may explain; but, however that may be, the traditional teaching which has reached us is as follows. Since all things in the Gospel, both

---

[7] τῶν κατορθούντων.

[8] This is an answer to modern "Ethical Determinants."

[9] μάλιστα μεν.

[1] Cf. Rom. ix. 21: φύραμα is used for the human body often in the Greek Fathers, i. e. Athanasius, Chrysostom, John Damascene: by all of whom Christ is called ἀπαρχὴ τοῦ ἡμετέρου φυράματος. Cf. Gen. ii. 7; Job x. 9: Epictetus also calls the human body πηλοκομψῶς πεφυραμένον

deeds and words, have a sublime and heavenly meaning, and there is nothing in it which is not such, that is, which does not exhibit a complete mingling of the human with the Divine, where the utterance exerted and the deeds enacted are human but the secret sense represents the Divine, it would follow that in this particular as well as in the rest we must not regard only the one element and overlook the other; but in the *fact* of this death we must contemplate the human feature, while in the *manner* of it we must be anxious to find the Divine [2]. For since it is the property of the Godhead to pervade all things, and to extend itself through the length and breadth of the substance of existence in every part—for nothing would continue to be if it remained not within the existent; and that which is this existent properly and primarily is the Divine Being, Whose existence in the world the continuance of all things that are forces us to believe in,—this is the very thing we learn from the figure of the Cross; it is divided into four parts, so that there are the projections, four in number, from the central point where the whole converges upon itself; because He Who at the hour of His pre-arranged death was stretched upon it is He Who binds together all things into Himself, and by Himself brings to one harmonious agreement the diverse natures of actual existences. For in these existences there is the idea either of something above, or of something below, or else the thought passes to the confines sideways. If, therefore, you take into your consideration the system of things above the heavens, or of things below the earth, or of things at the boundaries of the universe on either side, everywhere the presence of Deity anticipates your thought as the sole observable power that in every part of existing things holds in a state of being all those things. Now whether we ought to call this Existence Deity, or Mind, or Power, or Wisdom, or any other lofty term which might be better able to express Him Who is above all, our argument has no quarrel with the appellation or name or form of phrase used. Since, then, all creation looks to Him, and is about and around Him, and through Him is coherent with itself, things above being through Him conjoined to things below and things lateral to themselves, it was right that not by hearing only we should be conducted to the full understanding of the Deity, but that sight also should be our teacher in these sublime subjects for thought; and it is from sight that the mighty Paul starts when he initiates [3] the people of Ephesus in the mysteries, and imbues them through his instructions with the power of knowing what is that "depth and height and breadth and length." In fact he designates each projection of the Cross by its proper appellation. The upper part he calls height, the lower depth, and the side extensions breadth and length; and in another passage [4] he makes his thought still clearer to the Philippians, to whom he says, "that at the name of Jesus every knee should bow, of things in heaven, and things in earth, and things under the earth." In that passage he includes in one appellation the centre and projecting arms [5], calling "things in earth" all that is in the middle between things in heaven and things under the earth. Such is the lesson we learn in regard to the mystery of the Cross. And the subsequent events which the narrative contains follow so appropriately that, as even unbelievers must admit, there is nothing in them adverse to the proper conceptions of the Deity. That He did not abide in death, that the wounds which His body had received from the iron of the nails and spear offered no impediment to His rising again, that after His resurrection He showed Himself as He pleased to His disciples, that when He wished to be present with them He was in their midst without being seen, as needing no entrance through open doors, and that He strengthened the disciples by the inspiration of the Holy Ghost, and that He promised to be amongst them, and that no partition wall should intervene between them and Him, and that to the sight He ascended to Heaven while to the mind He was everywhere; all these, and whatever like facts the history of Him comprises, need no assistance from arguments to show that they are signs of deity and of a sublime and supereminent power. With regard to them therefore I do not deem it necessary to go into any detail, inasmuch as their description of itself shows the supernatural character. But since the dispensation of the washing (whether we choose to call it baptism, or illumination, or regeneration; for we make the name no subject of controversy) is a part of our revealed doctrines, it may be as well to enter on a short discussion of this as well.

---

[2] ἐν μὲν τῷ θανάτῳ καθορᾶν τὸ ἀνθρώπινον, ἐν δὲ τῷ τρόπῳ πολυπραγμονεῖν τὸ θειότερον. This is Krabinger's reading (for ἐν τῷ ἀθανάτῳ . . . ἐν δὲ τῷ ἀνθρώπῳ) on the authority of Theodoret's quotation and two Codd. for the first, and of all his Codd. for the second. Hervetus also seems to have read the same, "in *morte* quidem quod est humanum intueri, in *modo* autem perscrutari quod est divinius." Glauber, however, translates the common text, "Man muss *bei dem Unsterblichen* zwar das Menschliche betrachten, aber *bei dem Menschen* auch das Göttliche hervorsuchen:" notwithstanding that he hints his preference for another reading, σκοπῷ, for this last; cf. just above, "but the secret sense represents the Divine," which would then be parallel to this last sentence.

[3] Eph. iii. 18. [4] Philip. ii. 10.
[5] κεφαλαίαν. The Fathers were fond of tracing similitudes to the form of the Cross, in nature and art: in the sail-yards of a ship, as here, and in the flight of birds on the wing. This is the reading of Codd. Morell., Reg., and three of Krabinger's: but γαῖαν in the margin of that of J. Vulcobius (Abbot of Belpré) has got into the text of both Paris Editt., though the second asterisks it. Hervetus ("et fastigium") seems to have read καὶ ἄκραν.

CHAPTER XXXIII.

FOR when they have heard from us something to this effect—that when the mortal passes into life it follows necessarily that, as that first birth leads only to the existence of mortality, another birth should be discovered, a birth which neither begins nor ends with corruption, but one which conducts the person begotten to an immortal existence, in order that, as what is begotten of a mortal birth has necessarily a mortal subsistence, so from a birth which admits not corruption that which is born may be superior to the corruption of death; when, I say, they have heard this and the like from us, and are besides instructed as to the process,— namely that it is prayer and the invocation of heavenly grace, and water, and faith, by which the mystery of regeneration is accomplished,— they still remain incredulous and have an eye only for the outward and visible, as if that which is operated corporeally [6] concurred not with the fulfilment of God's promise. How, they ask, can prayer and the invocation of Divine power over the water be the foundation of life in those who have been thus initiated? In reply to them, unless they be of a very obstinate disposition, one single consideration suffices to bring them to an acquiescence in our doctrine. For let us in our turn ask them about that process of the carnal generation which every one can notice. How does that something which is cast for the beginnings of the formation of a living being become a Man? In that case, most certainly, there is no method whatever that can discover for us, by any possible reasoning, even the probable truth. For what correlation is there between the definition of man and the quality observable in that something? Man, when once he is put together, is a reasoning and intellectual being, capable of thought and knowledge; but that something is to be observed only in its quality of humidity, and the mind grasps nothing in it beyond that which is seen by the sense of sight. The reply, therefore, which we might expect to receive from those whom we questioned as to how it is credible that a man is compounded from that humid element, is the very reply which we make when questioned about the regeneration that takes place through the water. Now in that other case any one so questioned has this reply ready at hand, that that élément becomes a man by a Divine power, wanting which, the element is motionless and inoperative. If, therefore, in that instance the subordinate matter does not make the man, but the Divine power changes that visible thing into a man's nature, it would be utterly unfair for them, when in the one case they testify to such power in God, in this other department to suppose that the Deity is too weak to accomplish His will. What is there common, they ask, between water and life? What is there common, we ask them in return, between humidity and God's image? In that case there is no paradox if, God so willing, what is humid changes into the most rare creature [7]. Equally, then, in this case we assert that there is nothing strange when the presence of a Divine influence transforms what is born with a corruptible nature into a state of incorruption.

CHAPTER XXXIV.

BUT they ask for proof of this presence of the Deity when invoked for the sanctification of the baptismal process [8]. Let the person who requires this evidence recall to mind the result of our inquiries further back. The reasoning by which we established that the power which was manifested to us through the flesh was really a Divine power, is the defence of that which we now say. For when it has been shown that He Who was manifested in the flesh, and then exhibited His nature by the miracles which He wrought, was God, it is also at the same time shown that He is present in that process, as often as He is invoked. For, as of everything that exists there is some peculiarity which indicates its nature, so truth is the distinctive peculiarity of the Divine nature. Well, then, He has promised that He will always be present with those that call upon Him, that He is in the midst of those that believe, that He remains among them collectively and has special intercourse with each one. We can no longer, then, need any other proof of the presence of the Deity in the things that are done in Baptism, believing as we do that He is God by reason of the miracles which He wrought, and knowing as we do that it is the peculiarity of the Godhead to be free from any touch of falsehood, and confidently holding as we do that the thing promised was involved in the truthfulness of its announcement. The invocation by prayer, then, which precedes this Divine Dispensation constitutes an abundance of proof that what is effected is done by God. For if in the case of that other kind of man-formation the impulses of the parents, even though they

---

[6] σωματικῶς : with a general reference both to the recipient, the words (the "form"), and the water (the "matter," in the Aristotelian sense). Cf. questions in *Private Baptism of Infants* : and Hampden's *Bampton Lectures*, p. 336 *n.*

[7] τιμιώτατον (τιμή = "price") ζῷον. So Plato, *Laws*, p. 766 : "Man, getting right training and a happy organization, is wont to become a most godlike and cultivated creature."
[8] τῶν γινομένων.

do not invoke the Deity, yet by the power of God, as we have before said, mould the embryo, and if this power is withheld their eagerness is ineffectual and useless, how much more will the object be accomplished in that spiritual mode of generation, where both God has promised that He will be present in the process and, as we have believed, has put power from Himself into the work, and, besides, our own will is bent upon that object; supposing, that is, that the aid which comes through prayer has at the same time been duly called in? For as they who pray God that the sun may shine on them in no way blunt the promptitude of that which is actually going to take place, yet no one will say that the zeal of those who thus pray is useless on the ground that they pray God for what must happen, in the same way they who, resting on the truthfulness of His promise, are firmly persuaded that His grace is surely present in those who are regenerate in this mystical Dispensation, either themselves make [9] an actual addition to that grace, or at all events do not cause the existing grace to miscarry. For that the grace is there is a matter of faith, on account of Him Who has promised to give it being Divine; while the testimony as to His Divinity comes through the Miracles [1]. Thus, then, that the Deity is present in all the baptismal process [2] admits of no question.

CHAPTER XXXV

BUT the descent into the water, and the trine immersion of the person in it, involves another mystery. For since the method of our salvation was made effectual not so much by His precepts in the way of teaching [3] as by the deeds of Him Who has realized an actual fellowship with man, and has effected life as a living fact, so that by means of the flesh which He has assumed, and at the same time deified [4], everything kindred

and related may be saved along with it, it was necessary that some means should be devised by which there might be, in the baptismal process, a kind of affinity and likeness between him who follows and Him Who leads the way. Needful, therefore, is it to see what features are to be observed in the Author of our life, in order that the imitation on the part of those that follow may be regulated, as the Apostle says, after the pattern of the Captain of our salvation [5]. For, as it is they who are actually drilled into measured and orderly movements in arms by skilled drill-masters, who are advanced to dexterity in handling their weapons by what they see with their eyes, whereas he who does not practise what is shown him remains devoid of such dexterity, in the same way it is imperative on all those who have an equally earnest desire for the Good as He has, to be followers by the path of an exact imitation of Him Who leads the way to salvation, and to carry into action what He has shown them. It is, in fact, impossible for persons to reach the same goal unless they travel by the same ways. For as persons who are at a loss how to thread the turns of mazes, when they happen to fall in with some one who has experience of them, get to the end of those various misleading turnings in the chambers by following him behind, which they could not do, did they not follow him their leader step by step, so too, I pray you mark, the labyrinth of this our life cannot be threaded by the faculties of human nature unless a man pursues that same path as He did Who, though

---

[9] ποιοῦνται (middle), i. e. by their prayers.
[1] ἡ δὲ τῆς θεότητος μαρτυρία διὰ τῶν θαυμάτων ἐστίν: a noteworthy sentence. [2] τῶν γινομένων (cf. above) being understood.
[3] ἐκ τῆς κατὰ διδαχὴν ὑφηγήσεως. This is what Krabinger finds in three Codd., and Morell and Hervetus have rendered in the Latin. But the editions have διαδοχήν. Ὑφήγησις does not refer to any "preceding" ("præeunte," Hervetus) teaching; but to "instruction" of any kind, whether "in the way of teaching," or of example, as below.
[4] the flesh which He has assumed, and at the same time deified. "Un terme cher aux Pères du IVe siècle, de nous déifier" (Denis, Philosophie d'Origène, p. 458). This θεοποίησις or θέωσις is more than a metaphor even from the first; "vere fideles vocantur θεοί, non naturâ quidem, sed τῇ ὁμοιώσει, ait Athanasius;" Casaubon, In Epist. ad Eustath. "We become 'gods' by grasping the Divine power and substance;" Clement, Stromata, iv. That the Platonists had thus used the word of τὸ πρὸς μείζονα δόξαν ἀνυψωθὲν is clear. Synesius in one of his Hymns says to his soul :—

"Soon commingled with the Father
Thou shalt dance a 'god' with God."

Just as elsewhere (in Dione, p. 50) he says, "it is not sufficient not to be bad ; each must be even a 'god.'" Cf. also Gregory Thaum. Panegyr Origenis, § 142 When we come to the Fathers of the 4th century and later, these words are used more especially of the work of the Holy Spirit upon man. Cf. Cyrill. Alex. : "If to be

able to 'deify' is a greater thing than a creature can do, and if the Spirit does 'deify,' how can he be created or anything but God, seeing that he 'deifies'?" "If the Spirit is not God," says Gregory Naz., "let him first be deified, and then let him deify me his equal;" where two things are implied, 1. that the recognized work of the Holy Spirit is to 'deify,' 2. that this "deification" is not Godhead. It is "the comparative god-making" of Dionysius Areopag. whereby we are "partakers of the Divine nature" (2 Pet. i. 4). On the word as applied to the human nature of our Saviour Himself, Huet (Origeniana, ii. 3, c. 17), in discussing the statement of Origen, in his Commentary on S. Matthew (Tract 27), that "Christ after His resurrection 'deified' the human nature which He had taken," remarks, "If we take this word so as to make Origen mean that the Word was changed into the human nature, and that the flesh itself was changed into God and made of the same substance as the Word, he will clearly be guilty of that deadly error which Apollinaris brought into the Church (i. e. that the Saviour's soul is not 'reasonable,' nor His flesh human) ; or rather of the heresy perpetrated by some sects of the Eutychians, who asserted that the human nature was changed into the Divine after the Resurrection. But if we take him to mean that Christ's human nature, after being divested of weakness after death, assumed a certain Divine quality, we shall be doing Him no wrong." He then quotes a line from Gregory's Iambics :—

"The thing 'deifying,' and the thing 'deified,' are one God :"

and this is said even of Christ's Incarnation ; how much more then can it be said of His Resurrection state, as in this passage of the Great Catechism? Huet adds one of Origen's answers to Celsus: "His mortal body and the human soul in Him, by virtue of their junction or rather union and blending with that (deity), assumed, we assert, qualities of the very greatest kind. . . . What incredibility is there in the quality of mortality in the body of Jesus changing, when God so planned and willed it, into an ethereal and Divine" (i. e. the matter, as the receptacle of these qualities, remaining the same)? It is in this sense that Chrysostom can say that "Christ came to us, and took upon Him our nature and deified it;" and Augustine, "your humanity received the name of that deity" (contr. Arian.).
[5] Heb. ii. 10; xii. 2.

once in it, yet got beyond the difficulties which hemmed Him in. I apply this figure of a labyrinth to that prison of death, which is without an egress[6] and environs the wretched race of mankind. What, then, have we beheld in the case of the Captain of our salvation? A three days' state of death and then life again. Now some sort of resemblance in us to such things has to be planned. What, then, is the plan by which in us too a resemblance to that which took place in Him is completed? Everything that is affected by death has its proper and natural place, and that is the earth in which it is laid and hidden. Now earth and water have much mutual affinity. Alone of the elements they have weight and gravitate downwards; they mutually abide in each other; they are mutually confined. Seeing, then, the death of the Author of our life subjected Him to burial in earth and was in accord with our common nature, the imitation which we enact of that death is expressed in the neighbouring element. And as He, that Man from above[7], having taken deadness on Himself, after His being deposited in the earth, returned back to life the third day, so every one who is knitted to Him by virtue of his bodily form, looking forward to the same successful issue, I mean this arriving at life by having, instead of earth, water poured on him[8], and so submitting to that element, has represented for him in the three movements the three-days-delayed grace of the resurrection. Something like this has been said in what has gone before, namely, that by the Divine providence death has been introduced as a dispensation into the nature of man, so that, sin having flowed away at the dissolution of the union of soul and body, man, through the resurrection, might be refashioned, sound, passionless, stainless, and removed from any touch of evil. In the case however of the Author of our Salvation this dispensation of death reached its fulfilment, having entirely accomplished its special purpose. For in His death, not only were things that once were one put asunder, but also things that had been disunited were again brought together; so that in this dissolution of things that had naturally grown together, I mean, the soul and body, our nature might be purified, and this return to union of these severed elements might secure freedom from the contamination of any foreign admixture. But as regards those who follow this Leader, their nature does not admit of an exact and entire imitation, but it receives now as much as it is capable of receiving, while it reserves the remainder for the time that comes

after. In what, then, does this imitation consist? It consists in the effecting the suppression of that admixture of sin, in the figure of mortification that is given by the water, not certainly a complete effacement, but a kind of break in the continuity of the evil, two things concurring to this removal of sin—the penitence of the transgressor and his imitation of the death. By these two things the man is in a measure freed from his congenital tendency to evil; by his penitence he advances to a hatred of and averseness from sin, and by his death he works out the suppression of the evil. But had it been possible for him in his imitation to undergo a complete dying, the result would be not imitation but identity; and the evil of our nature would so entirely vanish that, as the Apostle says, "he would die unto sin once for all[9]." But since, as has been said, we only so far imitate the transcendent Power as the poverty of our nature is capable of, by having the water thrice poured on us and ascending again up from the water, we enact that saving burial and resurrection which took place on the third day, with this thought in our mind, that as we have power over the water both to be in it and arise out of it, so He too, Who has the universe at His sovereign disposal, immersed Himself in death, as we in the water, to return[1] to His own blessedness. If, therefore, one looks to that which is in reason, and judges of the results according to the power inherent in either party, one will discover no disproportion in these results, each in proportion to the measure of his natural power working out the effects that are within his reach. For, as it is in the power of man, if he is so disposed, to touch the water and yet be safe, with infinitely greater ease may death be handled by the Divine Power so as to be in it and yet not to be changed by it injuriously. Observe, then, that it is necessary for us to rehearse beforehand in the water the grace of the resurrection, to the intent that we may understand that, as far as facility goes, it is the same thing for us to be baptized with water and to rise again from death. But as in matters that concern our life here, there are some which take precedence of others, as being those without which the result could not be achieved, although if the beginning be compared with the end, the beginning so contrasted will seem of no account (for what equality, for instance, is there between the man and that which is laid as a foundation for the constitution of his animal being? And yet if that had never been, neither would this be which we see), in like manner that which happens in the great resurrection, essentially vaster

---

6 ἀδιέξοδον . . . φρουράν. Krabinger s excellent reading. Cf. Plato, *Phæd.* p. 62 B, "We men are in a sort of prison."

7 S. John iii. 31 : 1 Cor. xv. 47 (ἄνωθεν = ἐξ οὐρανοῦ).

8 ἐπιχεύμενος. This may be pressed to imply that immersion was not absolutely necessary. So below τὸ ὕδωρ τρὶς ἐπιχεαμενοι.

9 ἐφάπαξ. So Rom. vi. 10, "He died unto sin once" (A. V.) ; *i. e.* once for all.

1 ἀναλύειν. Cf. Philip. i. 23 (ἀναλῦσαι)

though it be, has its beginnings and its causes here; it is not, in fact, possible that that should take place, unless this had gone before; I mean, that without the laver of regeneration it is impossible for the man to be in the resurrection; but in saying this I do not regard the mere remoulding and refashioning of our composite body; for towards this it is absolutely necessary that human nature should advance, being constrained thereto by its own laws according to the dispensation of Him Who has so ordained, whether it have received the grace of the laver, or whether it remains without that initiation: but I am thinking of the restoration to a blessed and divine condition, separated from all shame and sorrow. For not everything that is granted in the resurrection a return to existence will return to the same kind of life. There is a wide interval between those who have been purified, and those who still need purification. For those in whose life-time here the purification by the laver has preceded, there is a restoration to a kindred state. Now, to the pure, freedom from passion is that kindred state, and that in this freedom from passion blessedness consists, admits of no dispute. But as for those whose weaknesses have become inveterate [2], and to whom no purgation of their defilement has been applied, no mystic water, no invocation of the Divine power, no amendment by repentance, it is absolutely necessary that they should come to be in something proper to their case,—just as the furnace is the proper thing for gold alloyed with dross,—in order that, the vice which has been mixed up in them being melted away after long succeeding ages, their nature may be restored pure again to God. Since, then, there is a cleansing virtue in fire and water, they who by the mystic water have washed away the defilement of their sin have no further need of the other form of purification, while they who have not been admitted to that form of purgation must needs be purified by fire.

CHAPTER XXXVI.

FOR common sense as well as the teaching of Scripture shows that it is impossible for one who has not thoroughly cleansed himself from all the stains arising from evil to be admitted amongst the heavenly company. This is a thing which, though little in itself, is the beginning and foundation of great blessings. I call it little on account of the facility of the means of amendment. For what difficulty is there in this matter? viz. to believe that God is everywhere, and that being in all things He is also present

with those who call upon Him for His life-supporting power, and that, thus present, He does that which properly belongs to Him to do. Now, the work properly belonging to the Divine energy is the salvation of those who need it; and this salvation proves effectual [3] by means of the cleansing in the water; and he that has been so cleansed will participate in Purity; and true Purity is Deity. You see, then, how small a thing it is in its beginning, and how easily effected; I mean, faith and water; the first residing within the will, the latter being the nursery companion of the life of man. But as to the blessing which springs from these two things, oh! how great and how wonderful it is, that it should imply relationship with Deity itself!

CHAPTER XXXVII.

BUT since the human being is a twofold creature, compounded of soul and body, it is necessary that the saved should lay hold of [4] the Author of the new life through both their component parts. Accordingly, the soul being fused into Him through faith derives from that the means and occasion of salvation; for the act of union with the life implies a fellowship with the life. But the body comes into fellowship and blending with the Author of our salvation in another way. For as they who owing to some act of treachery have taken poison, allay its deadly influence by means of some other drug (for it is necessary that the antidote should enter the human vitals in the same way as the deadly poison, in order to secure, through them, that the effect of the remedy may be distributed through the entire system), in like manner we, who have tasted the solvent of our nature [5], necessarily need something that may combine what has been so dissolved, so that such an antidote entering within us may, by its own counter-influence, undo the mischief introduced into the body by the poison. What, then, is this remedy to be? Nothing else than that very Body which has been shown to be superior to death, and has been the First-fruits of our life. For, in the manner that, as the Apostle says [6], a little leaven assimilates to itself the whole lump, so in like manner that body to which immortality has been given it by God, when it is in ours,

[2] οἷς δὲ προσεπωρώθη τὰ πάθη.

[3] S. John iii. 5.
[4] ἐφάπτεσθαι. Krabinger prefers this to ἐφέπεσθαι (Paris Edit.), as more suitable to what follows.
[5] Gregory seems here to refer to Eve's eating the apple, wh'ch introduced a moral and *physical* poison into our nature. General Gordon's thoughts ("in Palestine") took the same direction as the whole of this passage; which Fronto Ducæus (as quoted by Krabinger) would even regard as a proof of transubstantiation.
[6] 1 Cor. v. 6.

translates and transmutes the whole into itself. For as by the admixture of a poisonous liquid with a wholesome one the whole draught is deprived of its deadly effect, so too the immortal Body, by being within that which receives it, changes the whole to its own nature. Yet in no other way can anything enter within the body but by being transfused through the vitals by eating and drinking. It is, therefore, incumbent on the body to admit this life-producing power in the one way that its constitution makes possible. And since that Body only which was the receptacle of the Deity received this grace of immortality, and since it has been shown that in no other way was it possible for our body to become immortal, but by participating in incorruption through its fellowship with that immortal Body, it will be necessary to consider how it was possible that that one Body, being for ever portioned to so many myriads of the faithful throughout the whole world, enters, through that portion, whole into each individual, and yet remains whole in itself. In order, therefore, that our faith, with eyes fixed on logical probability, may harbour no doubt on the subject before us, it is fitting to make a slight digression in our argument, to consider the physiology of the body. Who is there that does not know that our bodily frame, taken by itself, possesses no life in its own proper subsistence, but that it is by the influx of a force or power from without that it holds itself together and continues in existence, and by a ceaseless motion that it draws to itself what it wants, and repels what is superfluous? When a leathern bottle is full of some liquid, and then the contents leak out at the bottom, it would not retain the contour of its full bulk unless there entered in at the top something else to fill up the vacuum ; and thus a person, seeing the circumference of this bottle swollen to its full size, would know that this circumference did not really belong to the object which he sees, but that what was being poured in, by being in it, gave shape and roundness to the bulk. In the same way the mere framework of our body possesses nothing belonging to itself that is cognizable by us, to hold it together, but remains in existence owing to a force that is introduced into it. Now this power or force both is, and is called, nourishment. But it is not the same in all bodies that require aliment, but to each of them has been assigned a food adapted to its condition by Him who governs Nature. Some animals feed on roots which they dig up. Of others grass is the food, of others different kinds of flesh, but for man above all things bread ; and, in order to continue and preserve the moisture of his body, drink, not simply water, but water frequently sweetened with wine, to join forces

with our internal heat. He, therefore, who thinks of these things, thinks by implication[7] of the particular bulk of our body. For those things by being within me became my blood and flesh, the corresponding nutriment by its power of adaptation being changed into the form of my body. With these distinctions we must return to the consideration of the question before us. The question was, how can that one Body of Christ vivify the whole of mankind, all, that is, in whomsoever there is Faith, and yet, though divided amongst all, be itself not diminished? Perhaps, then, we are now not far from the probable explanation. If the subsistence of every body depends on nourishment, and this is eating and drinking, and in the case of our eating there is bread and in the case of our drinking water sweetened with wine, and if, as was explained at the beginning, the Word of God, Who is both God and the Word, coalesced with man's nature, and when He came in a body such as ours did not innovate on man's physical constitution so as to make it other than it was, but secured continuance for His own body by the customary and proper means, and controlled its subsistence by meat and drink, the former of which was bread,—just, then, as in the case of ourselves, as has been repeatedly said already, if a person sees bread he also, in a kind of way, looks on a human body, for by the bread being within it the bread becomes it, so also, in that other case, the body into which God entered, by partaking of the nourishment of bread, was, in a certain measure, the same with it ; that nourishment, as we have said, changing itself into the nature of the body. For that which is peculiar to all flesh is acknowledged also in the case of that flesh, namely, that that Body too was maintained by bread ; which Body also by the indwelling of God the Word was transmuted to the dignity of Godhead. Rightly, then, do we believe that now also the bread which is consecrated by the Word of God is changed into the Body of God the Word. For that Body was once, by implication, bread, but has been consecrated by the inhabitation of the Word that tabernacled in the flesh. Therefore, from the same cause as that by which the bread that was transformed in that Body was changed to a Divine potency, a similar result takes place now. For as in that case, too, the grace of the Word used to make holy the Body, the substance of which came of the bread, and in a manner was itself bread, so also in this case the bread, as says the Apostle[8], "is sanctified by the Word of God and prayer" ; not that it advances by the process of eating[9]

---

[7] δυνάμει. [8] 1 Tim. iv. 5.
[9] *by the process of eating*, διὰ βρώσεως. There is very little authority for καὶ πόσεως which follows in some Codd. If Krabinger's text is here correct, Gregory distinctly teaches a transmutation of the elements very like the later transubstantiation : he

to the stage of passing into the body of the Word, but it is at once changed into the body by means of the Word, as the Word itself said, "This is My Body." Seeing, too, that all flesh is nourished by what is moist (for without this combination our earthly part would not continue to live), just as we support by food which is firm and solid the solid part of our body, in like manner we supplement the moist part from the kindred element; and this, when within us, by its faculty of being transmitted, is changed to blood, and especially if through the wine it receives the faculty of being transmuted into heat. Since, then, that God-containing flesh partook for its substance and support of this particular nourishment also, and since the God who was manifested infused Himself into perishable humanity for this purpose, viz. that by this communion with Deity mankind might at the same time be deified, for this end it is that, by dispensation of His grace, He disseminates Himself in every believer through that flesh, whose substance comes from bread and wine, blending Himself with the bodies of believers, to secure that, by this union with the immortal, man, too, may be a sharer in incorruption. He gives these gifts by virtue of the benediction through which He transelements [1] the natural quality of these visible things to that immortal thing.

CHAPTER XXXVIII.

THERE is now, I think, wanting in these remarks no answer to inquiries concerning the Gospel mystery, except that on Faith [2]; which we give briefly in the present treatise. For those who require a more elaborate account we have already published it in other works of ours, in which we have explained the subject with all the earnestness and accuracy in our power. In those treatises we have both fought [3] controversially with our opponents, and also have taken private consultation with ourselves as to the questions which have been brought against us. But in the present discussion we have thought it as well only to say just so much on the subject of faith as is involved in the language of the Gospel, namely, that one who is begotten by the spiritual regeneration may know who it is that begets him, and what sort of creature he becomes. For it is only this form of generation which has in it the power to become what it chooses to be.

CHAPTER XXXIX.

FOR, while all things else that are born are subject to the impulse of those that beget them, the spiritual birth is dependent on the power of him who is being born. Seeing, then, that here lies the hazard, namely, that he should not miss what is for his advantage, when to every one a free choice is thus open, it were well, I think, for him who is moved towards the begetting of himself, to determine by previous reasoning what kind of father is for his advantage, and of what element it is better for him that his nature should consist. For, as we have said, it is in the power of such a child as this to choose its parents. Since, then, there is a twofold division of existences, into created and uncreated, and since the uncreated world possesses within itself immutability and immobility, while the created is liable to change and alteration, of which will he, who with calculation and deliberation is to choose what is for his benefit, prefer to be the offspring; of that which is always found in a

---

also distinctly teaches that the words of consecration effect the change. There seems no reason to doubt that the text is correct. The three Latin interpretations, "a verbo transmutatus," "statim a verbo transmutatus," "per verbum mutatus," of Hervetus, Morell, and Zinus, all point to their having found πρὸς τὸ σῶμα διὰ τοῦ λόγου μεταποιούμενος in the text: and this is the reading of Cod. Reg. (the other reading is πρὸς τὸ σῶμα τοῦ λόγου). A passage from Justin Mart., *Apol.* ii. p. 77, also supports Krabinger's text. Justin says, "so we are taught that that food which has been blessed by the pronouncing of the word that came from Him, which food by changing nourishes our blood and flesh, is the flesh and blood of that Incarnate Jesus." As to the nature of the change (πρὸς τὸ σῶμα μεταποιούμενος), another passage in Gregory (*In Baptism. Christi*, 370 A) should be compared: "The bread, again, was for a while common bread, but when the mystic word shall have consecrated it (ἱερουργήσῃ), it is called, *and moreover is*, the body of Christ." He says also at the end of this chapter, "He gives these gifts by virtue of the benediction through which He *transelements* (μεταστοιχειώσας) the natural quality of these visible things to that immortal thing." Harnack does not attempt to weaken the force of these and other passages, but only points out that the idea of this change does not exactly correspond (how could it?) with the mediæval scholastically-philosophical "transubstantiation." Gregory's belief is that, just as the Word, when Christ was here in the flesh, rendered holy His body that assimilated bread, which still *in a manner remained bread*, so now the bread is sanctified by the Word of God and by prayer. "The idea," says Neander, "of the repetition of the consecration of the Λόγος had taken hold of his mind." The construction is προϊὼν (ὥστε) γενέσθαι εἰς τὸ σῶμα τοῦ λόγου, "eo progrediens, ut verbi corpus evadat."

[1] μεταστοιχειώσας. Suicer labours, without success, to show that the word is not equivalent to *transelementare* or *μετουσιοῦν*, but only to *substantiam convertere*, i. e. to change by an addition of grace into another *mode* or *use*. In the passages from Epiphanius which Suicer adduces for "figure," "mode," as a meaning of στοιχεῖον itself, that word means a sign of the zodiac (as in our Gregory's *De Animâ et Resurr.*, it means the moon), only because the heavenly bodies are the *elements or first principles* as it were of the celestial alphabet. The other meaning of μεταστοιχειοῦν which he gives, i. e. to unteach, with a view to obscure the literal meaning here, is quite inapplicable. Gregory defines more clearly than Chrysostom (μεταρρυθμίζεσθαι), Theophylact (μεταποιεῖσθαι), and John Damascene (μεταβάλλεσθαι), the change that takes place : but all go beyond Theodoret's (*Dial.* ii.), "not changing nature, but adding grace to the nature," which Suicer endeavours to read into this word of Gregory's. It is to be noticed, too, that in Philo the word is used of Xerxes changing in his march one element into another, i. e. *earth into water*, not the mere use of the one into the use of the other.

[2] *Faith*. Cf. Church Catechism; "Faith whereby they steadfastly believe the promises of God made to them in that Sacrament (of Baptism)."

[3] συνεπλάκημεν, *i. e.* against Eunomius, in defence of the equality of the Trinity in the Baptismal symbol. Often as Gregory in that treatise opposes Eunomius for placing the essence of Christianity in mere γνῶσις and δογμάτων ἀκρίβεια, as against God's incomprehensibility, and knowledge only by the heart, he had yet spent his whole life in showing the supreme importance of accuracy in the formulas upon which the Faith rested. This helps to give a date for the *Great Catechism*.

state of change, or of that which possesses a nature that is changeless, steadfast, and ever consistent and unvarying in goodness? Now there have been delivered to us in the Gospel three Persons and names through whom the generation or birth of believers takes place, and he who is begotten by this Trinity is equally begotten of the Father, and of the Son, and of the Holy Ghost—for thus does the Gospel speak of the Spirit, that "that which is born of Spirit is spirit [4]," and it is "in Christ [5]" that Paul begets, and the Father is the " Father of all ;" here, then, I beg, let the mind of the hearer be sober in its choice, lest it make itself the offspring of some inconstant nature, when it has it in its power to make the steadfast and unalterable nature the founder of its life. For according to the disposition of heart in one who comes to the Dispensation will that which is begotten in him exhibit its power ; so that he who confesses that the Holy Trinity is uncreate enters on the steadfast unalterable life; while another, who through a mistaken conception sees only a created nature in the Trinity and then is baptized in *that*, has again been born into the shifting and alterable life. For that which is born is of necessity of one kindred with that which begets. Which, then, offers the greater advantage ; to enter on the unchangeable life, or to be again tossed about by the waves of this lifetime of uncertainty and change? Well, since it is evident to any one of the least understanding that what is stable is far more valuable than what is unstable, what is perfect than what is deficient, what needs not than what needs, and what has no further to advance, but ever abides in the perfection of all that is good, than what climbs by progressive toil, it is incumbent upon every one, at least upon every one who is possessed of sense, to make an absolute choice of one or other of these two conditions, either to believe that the Holy Trinity belongs to the uncreated world, and so through the spiritual birth to make It the foundation of his own life, or, if he thinks that the Son or the Holy Ghost is external to the being of the first, the true, the good, God, I mean, of the Father, not to include these Persons in the belief which he takes upon him at the moment of his new birth, lest he unconsciously make himself over to that imperfect nature [6] which itself needs some one to make it good, and in a manner bring himself back again to something of the same nature as his own by thus removing his faith [7] from that higher world. For whoever

has bound himself to any created thing forgets that, as from the Deity, he has no longer hope of salvation. For all creation, owing to the whole equally proceeding from non-existence into being, has an intimate connection with itself ; and as in the bodily organization all the limbs have a natural and mutual coherence, though some have a downward, some an upward direction, so the world of created things is, viewed as the creation, in oneness with itself, and the differences in us, as regards abundance or deficiency, in no wise disjoint it from this natural coherence with itself. For in things which equally imply the idea of a previous non-existence, though there be a difference between them in other respects, as regards this point we discover no variation of nature. If, then, man, who is himself a created being, thinks that the Spirit and the Only-begotten God [8] are likewise created, the hope which he entertains of a change to a better state will be a vain one ; for he only returns to himself [9]. What happens then is on a par with the surmises of Nicodemus ; he, when instructed by our Lord as to the necessity of being born from above, because he could not yet comprehend the meaning of the mystery, had his thoughts drawn back to his mother's womb [1]. So that if a man does not conduct himself towards the uncreated nature, but to that which is kindred to, and equally in bondage with, himself, he is of the birth which is from below, and not of that which is from above. But the Gospel tells us that the birth of the saved is from above.

CHAPTER XL.

BUT, as far as what has been already said, the instruction of this Catechism does not seem to me to be yet complete. For we ought, in my opinion, to take into consideration the sequel of this matter ; which many of those who come to the grace of baptism [2] overlook, being led astray, and self-deceived, and indeed only seemingly, and not really, regenerate. For that change in our life which takes place through regeneration will not be change, if we continue in the state in which we were. I do not see

---

[4] S. John iii. 6.   [5] 1 Cor. iv. 15.
[6] *imperfect nature* : i. e. of a creature (κτιστός) ; for instance, of a merely human Christ, which himself needs, and therefore cannot give, perfection.
[7] *removing his faith* : i. e. as he would do, if he placed it on beings whom he *knew* were not of that higher, uncreated. world

[8] *and the Only-begotten God.* One Cod. reads here υἱόν (not θεόν), as it is in S. John i. 18, though even there "many very ancient authorities" (R.V.) read θεόν. The Latin of Hervetus implies an οὐκ here ; "et unigenitum Deum *non* esse existimant :" and Glauber would retain it, making κτιστὸν = θεὸν οὐκ εἶναι. But Krabinger found no οὐκ in any of his Codd.
[9] πρὸς ἑαυτὸν ἀναλύων, as explained above, *i. e.* εἰς τὸ ὁμογενὲς ἑαυτὸν εἰσαγάγῃ.   [1] S. John iii. 4.
[2] We need not consider this passage about Regeneration as an interpolation, with Aubertin, *De Sacram. Eucharist.* lib. ii. p. 487, because Gregory has already dealt with Baptism in ch. xxxv.—xxxvi.; and then with the Eucharist : his view of the relation between the two Sacraments, that the Eucharist unites the body, as Baptism the soul. to God, quite explains this return to the preliminaries of this double union.

how it is possible to deem one who is still in the same condition, and in whom there has been no change in the distinguishing features of his nature, to be any other than he was, it being palpable to every one that it is for a renovation and change of our nature that the saving birth is received. And yet human nature does not of itself admit of any change in baptism; neither the reason, nor the understanding, nor the scientific faculty, nor any other peculiar characteristic of man is a subject for change. Indeed the change would be for the worse if any one of these properties of our nature were exchanged away [3] for something else. If, then, the birth from above is a definite refashioning of the man, and yet these properties do not admit of change, it is a subject for inquiry what that is in him, by the changing of which the grace of regeneration is perfected. It is evident that when those evil features which mark our nature have been obliterated a change to a better state takes place. If, then, by being "washed," as says the Prophet [4], in that mystic bath we become "clean" in our wills and "put away the evil" of our souls, we thus become better men, and are changed to a better state. But if, when the bath has been applied to the body, the soul has not cleansed itself from the stains of its passions and affections, but the life after initiation keeps on a level with the uninitiate life, then, though it may be a bold thing to say, yet I will say it and will not shrink; in these cases the water is but water, for the gift of the Holy Ghost in no ways appears in him who is thus baptismally born; whenever, that is, not only the deformity of anger [5], or the passion of greed, or the unbridled and unseemly thought, with pride, envy, and arrogance, disfigures the Divine image, but the gains, too, of injustice abide with him, and the woman he has procured by adultery still even after that ministers to his pleasures. If these and the like vices, after, as before, surround the life of the baptized, I cannot see in what respects he has been changed; for I observe him the same man as he was before. The man whom he has unjustly treated, the man whom he has falsely accused, the man whom he has forcibly deprived of his property, these, as far as they are concerned, see no change in him though he has been washed in the laver of baptism. They do not hear the cry of Zacchæus from him as well: "If I have taken any thing from any man by false accusation, I restore fourfold [6]." What they said of him before his baptism, the same they now more fully declare; they call him

by the same names, a covetous person, one who is greedy of what belongs to others, one who lives in luxury at the cost of men's calamities. Let such an one, therefore, who remains in the same moral condition as before, and then babbles to himself of the beneficial change he has received from baptism, listen to what Paul says: "If a man think himself to be something, when he is nothing, he deceiveth himself [7]." For what you have not become, that you are not. "As many as received Him," thus speaks the Gospel of those who have been born again, "to them gave He power to become the sons of God [8]." Now the child born of any one is entirely of a kindred nature with his parent. If, then, you have received God, if you have become a child of God, make manifest in your disposition the God that is in you, manifest in yourself Him that begot you. By the same marks whereby we recognize God, must this relationship to God of the son so born be exhibited. "He openeth His hand and filleth every living thing with His good pleasure." "He passeth over transgressions." "He repenteth Him of the evil." "The Lord is good to all, and bringeth not on us His anger every day." "God is a righteous Lord, and there is no injustice in Him [9];" and all other sayings of the like kind which are scattered for our instruction throughout the Scripture;—if you live amidst such things as these, you are a child of God indeed; but if you continue with the characteristic marks of vice in you, it is in vain that you babble to yourself of your birth from above. Prophecy will speak against you and say, "You are a 'son of man,' not a son of the Most High. You 'love vanity, and seek after leasing.' Know you not in what way man is 'made admirable [1]'? In no other way than by becoming holy."

It will be necessary to add to what has been said this remaining statement also; viz. that those good things which are held out in the Gospels to those who have led a godly life, are not such as can be precisely described. For how is that possible with things which "eye hath not seen, neither ear heard, neither have entered into the heart of man [2]"? Indeed, the sinner's life of torment presents no equivalent to anything that pains the sense here. Even if some one of the punishments in that other world be named in terms that are well known here, the distinction is still

---

[3] ὑπαμειφθείη. A word almost peculiar to this Gregory.
[4] Is. i. 16.
[5] τὸ κατὰ τὸν θυμὸν αἶσχος. Quite wrongly the Latin translators, "animi turpitudo," i. e. baseness of *mind*, which is mentioned just below. [6] S. Luke xix. 8

[7] Gal. vi. 3. [8] S. John i. 12.
[9] These quotations are from the LXX. of Ps. cxlv. 16; ciii 12 (Is. xliii. 25); Joel ii. 13; Ps. vii. 11 (Heb. "God is angry every day"); xcii. 15.
[1] Ps. iv. 2, 3. In the last verse the LXX. has ἐθαυμάστωσε; which the Vulgate follows, i. e. "He hath made his Saint wonderful" (the Hebrew implies, "hath wonderfully separated"). That θαυμαστοῦται (three of Krabinger's Codd., and Morell's) is the reading here (omitted in Editt.), is clear from the whole quotation from the LXX. of this Psalm. [2] Is. lxiv. 4; 1 Cor. ii. 9.

not small. When you hear the word fire, you have been taught to think of a fire other than the fire we see, owing to something being added to that fire which in this there is not; for that fire is never quenched, whereas experience has discovered many ways of quenching this; and there is a great difference between a fire which can be extinguished, and one that does not admit of extinction. That fire, therefore, is something other than this. If, again, a person hears the word "worm," let not his thoughts, from the similarity of the term, be carried to the creature here that crawls upon the ground; for the addition that it "dieth not" suggests the thought of another reptile than that known here. Since, then, these things are set before us as to be expected in the life that follows this, being the natural out-growth according to the righteous judgment of God, in the life of each, of his particular disposition, it must be the part of the wise not to regard the present, but that which follows after, and to lay down the foundations for that unspeakable blessedness during this short and fleeting life, and by a good choice to wean themselves from all experience of evil, now in their lifetime here, hereafter in their eternal recompense [3].

3 The section beginning here, which one Cod. (Vulcobius'), used by Hervetus, exhibits, is "evidently the addition of some blundering copyist." P. Morell considers it the portion of a preface to a treatise against Severus, head of the heretics called Acephali. But Severus was condemned under Justinian, A.D. 536: and the Acephali themselves were no recognized party till after the Council of Ephesus (those who would follow neither S. Cyril, nor John of Damascus, in one meaning of the term, i. e. "headless"), or after the Council of Chalcedon (those who rejected the Henoticon of the Emperor Zeno, addressed to the orthodox and the Monophysites, in the other meaning). It is quoted by Krabinger, none of whose Codd. recognize it.

V. ORATORICAL

FUNERAL ORATION ON MELETIUS

THE number of the Apostles has been enlarged for us by this our late Apostle being reckoned among their company. These Holy ones have drawn to themselves one of like conversation ; those athletes a fellow athlete ; those crowned ones another crowned like them ; the pure in heart one chaste in soul : those ministers of the Word another herald of that Word. Most blessed, indeed, is our Father for this his joining the Apostolic band and his departure to Christ. Most pitiable we ! for the unseasonableness of our orphaned condition does not permit us to congratulate ourselves on our Father's happy lot. For him, indeed, better it was by his departure hence to be with Christ, but it was a grievous thing for us to be severed from his fatherly guidance. Behold, it is a time of need for counsel ; and our counsellor is silent. War, the war of heresy, encompasses us, and our Leader is no more. The general body of the Church labours under disease, and we find not the physician. See in what a strait we are. Oh ! that it were possible I could nerve my weakness, and rising to the full proportions of our loss, burst out with a voice of lamentation adequate to the greatness of the distress, as these excellent preachers of yours have done,

who have bewailed with loud voice the misfortune that has befallen them in this loss of their father. But what can I do ? How can I force my tongue to the service of the theme, thus heavily weighted, and shackled, as it were, by this calamity ? How shall I open my mouth thus subdued to speechlessness ? How shall I give free utterance to a voice now habitually sinking to the pathetic tone of lamentations ? How can I lift up the eyes of my soul, veiled as I am with this darkness of misfortune ? Who will pierce for me this deep dark cloud of grief, and light up again, as out of a clear sky, the bright ray of peace ? From what quarter will that ray shine forth, now that our star has set ? Oh ! evil moonless night that gives no hope of any star ! With what an opposite meaning, as compared with those of late, are our words uttered in this place now ! Then we rejoiced with the song of marriage, now we give way to piteous lamentation for the sorrow that has befallen us ! Then we chanted an epithalamium, but now a funeral dirge ! You remember the day when we entertained you at the feast of that spiritual marriage, and brought home the virgin bride to the house of her noble bridegroom ; when to the best of our ability we proffered the wedding gifts of our praises, both giving and receiving joy in turn [2]. But now our delight has been changed to lamentation, and our festal garb become sackcloth. It were better, maybe, to suppress our woe, and to hide our grief in silent seclusion, so as not to disturb the children of the bride-chamber, divested as we are of the bright marriage garment, and clothed instead with the black robe of the preacher. For since that noble bridegroom has been taken from us, sorrow has all at once clothed us in the garb of black ; nor is it possible for us to indulge in the usual cheerfulness of our conversation, since Envy [3] has stripped us of our proper and be-

[1] Meletius, Bishop of Antioch, died at Constantinople, whither he had gone to attend the second Œcumenical Council, A.D. 381. Of the "translation" of the remains to his own metropolis, described in this oration, Sozomen (vii. 10) says, "The remains of Meletius were at the same time conveyed to Antioch ; and deposited near the tomb of Babylas the Martyr. It is said that by the command of the Emperor, the relics were received with honour in every city through which they had to be conveyed, and that psalms were sung on the occasion, a practice that was quite contrary to the usual Roman customs. After the pompous interment of Meletius, Flavian was ordained in his stead. . . . This gave rise to fresh troubles." The rationale of the rising relic-worship, at all events of the sanctity of tombs, is thus given by Origen : " A feeling such as this (of bodies differing, as tenanted by different souls) has prompted some to go so far as to treat as Divine the remains of uncommon men ; they feel that great souls have been there, while they would cast forth the bodies of the morally worthless without the honour of a funeral (ἀτιμάσαι). This perhaps is not the right thing to do : still it proceeds from a right instinct (ἐννοίας ὑγιοῦς). For it is not to be expected of a thinking man that he would take the same pains over the burial of an Anytus, as he would over a Socrates, and that he would place the same barrow or the same sepulchre over each " (c. Cels. iv. 59). Again, " The dwelling-place of the reasoning soul is not to be flung irreverently aside, like that of the irrational soul ; and more than this, we Christians believe that the reverence paid to a body that has been tenanted by a reasoning soul passes to him also who has received a soul which by means of such an instrument has fought a good fight," viii. 30.

[2] This all refers to the very recent installation of Gregory of Nazianzum in the episcopal chair of Constantinople : on which occasion also Gregory of Nyssa seems to have preached.

[3] Casaubon very strongly condemns the sentiment here expressed, as savouring more of heathenism than Christianity. He gives other instances, in which the loss from the death of friends and good men is

coming dress. Rich in blessings we came to you; now we leave you bare and poor. The lamp we held right above our head, shining with the rich fulness of light, we now carry away quenched, its bright flame all dissolved into smoke and dust. We held our great treasure in an earthen vessel. Vanished is the treasure, and the earthen vessel, emptied of its wealth, is restored to them who gave it [4]. What shall we say who have consigned it? What answer will they make by whom it is demanded back? Oh! miserable shipwreck! How, even with the harbour around us, have we gone to pieces with our hopes! How has the vessel, fraught with a thousand bales of goods, sunk with all its cargo, and left us destitute who were once so rich! Where is that bright sail which was ever filled by the Holy Ghost? Where is that safe helm of our souls which steered us while we sailed unhurt over the swelling waves of heresy? Where that immovable anchor of intelligence which held us in absolute security and repose after our toils? Where that excellent pilot [5] who steered our bark to its heavenly goal? Is, then, what has happened of small moment, and is my passionate grief unreasoning? Is it not rather that I reach not the full extent of our loss, though I exceed in the loudness of my expression of grief? Lend me, oh lend me, my brethren, the tear of sympathy. When you were glad we shared your gladness. Repay us, therefore, this sad recompense. "Rejoice with them that do rejoice [6]." This *we* have done. It is for *you* to return it by "weeping with them that weep." It happened once that a strange people bewailed the loss of the patriarch Jacob, and made the misfortune of another people their own, when his united family transported their father out of Egypt, and lamented in another land the loss that had befallen them. They all prolonged their mourning over him for thirty days and as many nights [7]. Ye, therefore, that are brethren, and of the same kindred, do as they who were of another kindred did. On that occasion the tear of strangers was shed in common with that of countrymen; be it shed in common now, for common is the grief. Behold these your patriarchs. All these are children of our Jacob. All these are children

of the free-woman [8]. No one is base born, no one supposititious. Nor indeed would it have become that Saint to introduce into the nobility of the family of Faith a bond-woman's kindred. Therefore is he our father because he was the father of our father [9]. Ye have just heard what and how great things an Ephraim and a Manasses [1] related of their father, and how the wonders of the story surpassed description. Give me also leave to speak on them. For this beatification of him from henceforth incurs no risk. Neither fear I Envy; for what worse evil can it do me? Know, then, what the man was; one of the nobility of the East, blameless, just, genuine, devout, innocent of any evil deed. Indeed the great Job will not be jealous if he who imitated him be decked with the like testimonials of praise. But Envy, that has an eye for all things fair, cast a bitter glance upon our blessedness; and one who stalks up and down the world also stalked in our midst, and broadly stamped the foot-mark of affliction on our happy state. It is not herds of oxen or sheep [2] that he has maltreated, unless in a mystical sense one transfers the idea of a flock to the Church. It is not in these that we have received injury from Envy; it is not in asses or camels that he has wrought us loss, neither has he excruciated our bodily feelings by a wound in the flesh; no, but he has robbed us of our very head. And with that head have gone away from us the precious organs of our senses. That eye which beheld the things of heaven is no longer ours, nor that ear which listened to the Divine voice, nor that tongue with its pure devotion to truth [3]. Where is that sweet serenity of his eyes? Where that bright smile upon his lips? Where that courteous right hand with fingers outstretched to accompany the benediction of the mouth. I feel an impulse, as if I were on the stage, to shout aloud for our calamity. Oh! Church, I pity you. To you, the city of Antioch, I address my words. I pity you for this sudden reversal. How has your beauty been despoiled! How have you been robbed of your ornaments! How suddenly has the flower faded! "Verily the grass withereth and the flower thereof falleth away [4]." What evil eye, what witchery of drunken malice has intruded on that distant Church? What is there to compensate her loss? The fountain has failed. The stream has dried up. Again has water been turned into blood [5]. Oh! the sad tidings which tell the Church of her calamity!

---

attributed by Christian writers to the envy of a Higher Power. That the disturbed state of the Church should be attributed by Gregory Nazianzen to "Envy" is well enough, but he in the same strain as his namesake speaks thus in connection with the death of his darling brother Cæsarius, and of Basil. Our Gregory uses the word also in lamenting Pulcheria and Flacilla. It only proves, however, how strong the habit still was of using heathen expressions.

[4] The text is τοῖς δεδωκόσιν ἐπανασώζεται. The people of Antioch must here be referred to, if the text is to stand.

[5] Meletius was president of the Council.

[6] Rom. xii. 15.

[7] According to Gen. l. 3, the Egyptian mourning was seventy days, but there is no precise mention of the length of the Israelites' mourning, except that at Atad, beyond the Jordan, they appear to have rested, on their way up, and mourned for seven days.

[8] Gal. iv. 31.

[9] *i. e.* the spiritual father of Basil, the "father" (brother really) of Gregory.

[1] *i. e.* preachers (perhaps of the *Egyptian* Church) who had preceded Gregory, spiritual sons of Basil, and so of Meletius, in the direct line of blessing. See Gen. xlviii. 5.

[2] *i. e.* as those of Job. [3] τὸ ἁγνὸν ἀνάθημα τῆς ἀληθείας.

[4] 1 Pet. i. 24; Is. xl. 8. [5] Exod. vii. 17.

Who shall say to the children that they have no more a father? Who shall tell the Bride she is a widow? Alas for their woes! What did they send out? What do they receive back? They sent forth an ark, they receive back a coffin. The ark, my brethren, was that man of God; an ark containing in itself the Divine and mystic things. There was the golden vessel full of Divine manna, that celestial food [6]. In it were the Tables of the Covenant written on the tablets of the heart, not with ink but by the Spirit of the living God [7]. For on that pure heart no gloomy or inky thought was imprinted. In it, too, were the pillars, the steps, the chapters, the lamps, the mercy-seat, the baths, the veils of the entrances. In it was the rod of the priesthood, which budded in the hands of our Saint; and whatever else we have heard the Ark contained [8] was all held in the soul of that man. But in their stead what is there now? Let description cease. Cloths of pure white linen, scarves of silk, abundance of perfumes and spices; the loving munificence of a modest and beautiful lady [9]. For it must be told, so as to be for a memorial of her [1], what *she* did for that Priest when, without stint, she poured the alabaster box of ointment on his head. But the treasure preserved within, what is it? Bones, now dead, and which even before dissolution had rehearsed their dying, the sad memorials of our affliction. Oh! what a cry like that of old will be heard in Rama, Rachel weeping [2], not for her children but for a husband, and admitting not of consolation. Let alone, ye that would console; let alone; force not on us your consolation [3]. Let the widow indulge the deepness of her grief. Let her feel the loss that has been inflicted on her. Yet she is not without previous practice in separation. In those contests in which our athlete was engaged she had before been trained to bear to be left. Certainly you must remember how a previous sermon to ours related to you the contests of the man; how throughout, even in the very number of his contests, he had maintained the glory of the Holy Trinity, which he ever glorified; for there were three trying attacks that he had to repel. You have heard the whole series of his labours, what he was in the first, what in the middle, and what in the last. I deem it

superfluous to repeat what has been so well described. Yet it may not be out of place to add just so much as this. When that Church, so sound in the faith, at the first beheld the man, she saw features truly formed [4] after the image of God, she saw love welling forth, she saw grace poured around his lips, a consummate perfection of humility beyond which it is impossible to conceive any thing further, a gentleness like that of David, the understanding of Solomon, a goodness like that of Moses, a strictness as of Samuel, a chastity as of Joseph, the skill of a Daniel, a zeal for the faith such as was in the great Elijah, a purity of body like that of the lofty-minded John [5], an unsurpassable love as of Paul. She saw the concurrence of so many excellences in one soul, and, thrilled with a blessed affection, she loved him, her own bridegroom, with a pure and virtuous passion. But ere she could accomplish her desire, ere she could satisfy her longing, while still in the fervour of her passion, she was left desolate, when those trying times called the athlete to his contests. While, then, he was engaged in these toilsome struggles for religion, she remained chaste and kept the marriage vow. A long time intervened, during which one, with adulterous intent [6], made an attempt upon the immaculate bridal-chamber. But the Bride remained undefiled; and again there was a return, and again an exile. And thus it happened thrice, until the Lord dispelled the gloom of that heresy, and sending forth a ray of peace gave us the hope of some respite from these lengthened troubles [7]. But when at length they had seen each other, when there was a renewal of those chaste joys and spiritual desires, when the flame of love had again been lit, all at once his last departure breaks off the enjoyment. He came to adorn you as his bride, he failed not in the eagerness of his zeal, he placed on this fair union the chaplets of blessing, in imitation of his Master. As did the Lord at Cana of Galilee [8], so here did this imitator of Christ. The Jewish waterpots, which were filled with the water of heresy, he filled with genuine wine, changing its nature by the power of his faith. How often did he set before you a chalice, but not of wine, when with that sweet

---

[6] Ps. lxxviii. 25; Wisd. xvi. 20: but τρυφῆς, not τροφῆς, must have been the reading in the MS. which Sifanus used, "plena cœlestium deliciarum."
[7] Jer. xxxi. 33; Heb. x. 16.
[8] The above description enumerates the whole furniture of the Tabernacle. According to Heb. ix. 4, all that was actually in the Ark was, the pot of manna, Aaron's rod that budded, and the Tables of the Covenant. See also Exod. xvi. 33; xxv. 37—40.
[9] Flacilla, the wife of the Emperor Theodosius.
[1] S. Matt. xxvi. 13: S. Mark xiv. 9.
[2] Jer. xxxi. 15.
[3] This is from the LXX. of Is. xxii. 4, μὴ κατισχύσητε παρακαλεῖν με ἐπὶ τὸ σύντριμμα, κ.τ.λ.: "Nolite contendere ut me consolemini super contritione:" S. Jerome. Ducæus has rightly restored this, for κατισχύσηται.

[4] πρόσωπον ἀληθῶς μεμορφωμένον. This is the reading of the best MSS. Morell has ἀλιέως.
[5] κατὰ τὸν ὑψηλὸν Ἰωάννην ἐν τῇ ἀφθορίᾳ τοῦ σώματος. Sifanus translates "integritate corporis ornatum." Rupp rejects the idea that the John who "should not die" is here meant: and thinks that the epithet, and ἀφθορία (= the more technical ἀφθαρσία) point to the monasticism of John the Baptist.
[6] He alludes here to Paulinus and Demophilus, two Arians mentioned by Socrates and Sozomen.
[7] In 379 the Council of Antioch settled the schism of Antioch, which seemed as if it would disturb the whole East, and even the West. Even the Catholics of Antioch had been divided, between Meletius and Paulinus, since the days of Julian. It was settled that, at the death of either, the other should succeed to his "diocese." Gregory himself was present, the ninth month after his brother Basil's death. [8] S. John ii.

voice he poured out in rich abundance the wine of Grace, and presented to you the full and varied feast of reason! He went first with the blessing of his words, and then his illustrious disciples were employed in distributing his teaching to the multitude.

We, too, were glad, and made our own the glory of your nation [9]. Up to this point how bright and happy is our narrative. What a blessed thing it were with this to bring our sermon to an end. But after these things what follows? "Call for the mourning women [1]," as says the prophet Jeremiah. In no other way can the burning heart cool down, swelling as it is with its affliction, unless it relieves itself by sobs and tears. Formerly the hope of his return consoled us for the pang of separation, but now he has been torn from us by that final separation. A huge intervening chasm is fixed between the Church and him. He rests indeed in the bosom of Abraham, but there exists not one who might bring the drop of water to cool the tongue of the agonized. Gone is that beauty, silent is that voice, closed are those lips, fled that grace. Our happy state has become a tale that is told. Elijah of old time caused grief to the people of Israel when he soared from earth to God. But Elisha [2] consoled them for the loss by being adorned with the mantle of his master. But now our wound is beyond healing; our Elijah has been caught up, and no Elisha left behind in his place. You have heard certain mournful and lamenting words of Jeremiah, with which he bewailed Jerusalem as a deserted city, and how among other expressions of passionate grief he added this, "The ways of Zion do mourn [3]." These words were uttered then, but now they have been realized. For when the news of our calamity shall have been spread abroad, then will the ways be full of mourning crowds, and the sheep of his flock will pour themselves forth, and like the Ninevites utter the voice of lamentation [4], or, rather, will lament more bitterly than they. For in their case their mourning released them from the cause of their fear, but with these no hope of release from their distress removes their need of mourning. I know, too, of another utterance of Jeremiah, which is reckoned among the books of the Psalms [5]; it is that which he made over

the captivity of Israel. The words run thus: "We hung our harps upon the willows, and condemned ourselves as well as our harps to silence." I make this song my own. For when I see the *confusion* of heresy, this *confusion* is Babylon [6]. And when I see the flood of trials that pours in upon us from this confusion, I say that these are "the waters of Babylon by which we sit down, and weep" because there is no one to guide us over them. Even if you mention the *willows*, and the *harps* that hung thereon, that part also of the figure shall be mine. For in truth our life is among willows [7], the willow being a fruitless tree, and the sweet fruit of our life having all withered away. Therefore have we become fruitless willows, and the harps of love we hung upon those trees are idle and unvibrating. "If I forget thee, oh Jerusalem," he adds, "may my right hand be forgotten." Suffer me to make a slight alteration in that text. It is not we who have forgotten the *right hand*, but the *right hand* that has forgotten us: and the "tongue has cleaved to the roof of" his own "mouth," and barred the passage of his words, so that we can never again hear that sweet voice. But let me have all tears wiped away, for I feel that I am indulging more than is right in this womanish sorrow for our loss.

Our Bridegroom has not been taken from us. He stands in our midst, though we see him not. The Priest is within the holy place. He is entered into that within the veil, whither our forerunner Christ has entered for us [8]. He has left behind him the curtain of the flesh. No longer does he pray to the type or shadow of the things in heaven, but he looks upon the very embodiment of these realities. No longer through a glass darkly does he intercede with God, but face to face he intercedes with Him: and he intercedes for us [9], and for the "negligences and ignorances" of the people. He has put away the coats of skin [1]; no need is there now for the dwellers in paradise of such garments as these; but he wears the raiment which the purity of his life has woven into a glorious dress. "Precious in the sight of the Lord is the death [2]" of such a man, or rather it is not death, but the breaking of bonds, as it is said, "Thou hast broken my bonds asunder."

---

[9] Gregory is here addressing men of Antioch, though he said before that that city was too distant yet to have heard the news. They must have been the bishops of the neighbourhood of Antioch and other Christians from the diocese of Meletius, then present in the capital. [1] Jer. ix. 17. [2] 2 Kings ii.
[3] Lam. i. 4. "The ways of Zion do mourn." The best of the three readings here is ἠκούσατε, adopted by Krabinger.
[4] Jonah iii. 5.
[5] Ps. cxxxvii. The title of this Psalm in LXX., Τῷ Δαυὶδ (διὰ) Ιερεμίου (which the Vulgate follows), implies that it is "a Davidic song springing from Jeremiah's heart." But "beginning with perfects, this Psalm is evidently not written during the time of the Exile, but in recollection of it:" Delitzsch. Some see resemblances to Ezekiel in it. The poplar is meant, not the weeping-willow, which is not met with wild in anterior Asia.

[6] Gen. xi. 9.
[7] ἐν ἰτέαις. The best MSS. support this reading, so that Krabinger has not dared to alter it to ἰτέα, as Morell's MS. Sifanus has "plane enim in salicibus vita consistit;" but Rupp, "Unser Leben ist in der That ein Weidengebüsche." In Bellarmine's mystical interpretation the willows are the citizens of Babylon, who resemble willows "in being unfruitful, bitter in themselves, and dwelling by choice in the midst of Babylon," to whom the instruments of worldly mirth are left.
[8] Heb. vi. 20.
[9] Doubtless an allusion to Rom. xi. 2; "how he (Elias) maketh intercession to God against Israel;" but here Meletius *departed* intercedes *for* the people, and the Intercession of Saints is clearly intimated.
[1] Gen. iii. 21. [2] Ps. cxvi. 15. 16.

Simeon has been let depart [3]. He has been freed from the bondage of the body. The "snare is broken and the bird hath flown away [4]." He has left Egypt behind, this material life. He has crossed [5], not this Red Sea of ours, but the black gloomy sea of life. He has entered upon the land of promise, and holds high converse with God upon the mount. He has loosed the sandal of his soul, that with the pure step of thought he may set foot upon that holy land where there is the Vision of God. Having therefore, brethren, this consolation, do ye, who are conveying the bones of our Joseph to the place of blessing, listen to the exhortation of Paul: "Sorrow not as others who have no hope [6]." Speak to the people there; relate the glorious tale; speak of the incredible wonder, how the people in their myriads, so densely crowded together as to look like a sea of heads, became all one continuous body, and like some watery flood surged around the procession bearing his remains. Tell them how the fair [7] David distributed himself, in divers ways and manners, among innumerable ranks of people, and danced before that ark [8] in the midst of men of the same and of different language [9]. Tell them how the streams of fire, from the succession of the lamps, flowed along in an unbroken track of light, and extended so far that the eye could not reach them. Tell them of the eager zeal of all the people, of his joining "the company of Apostles [1]," and how the napkins that bound his face were plucked away to make amulets for the faithful. Let it be added to your narration how the Emperor [2] showed in his countenance his sorrow for this misfortune, and rose from his throne, and how the whole city joined the funeral procession of the Saint. Moreover console each other with the following words; it is a good medicine that Solomon [3] has for sorrow; for he bids wine be given to the sorrowful; saying this to us, the labourers in the vineyard: "Give," therefore, "your wine to those that are in sorrow [4]," not that wine which produces drunkenness, plots against the senses, and destroys the body, but such as gladdens the heart, the wine which the Prophet recommends when he says: "Wine maketh glad the heart of man [5]." Pledge each other in that liquor undiluted [6] and with the unstinted goblets of the word, that thus our grief may be turned to joy and gladness, by the grace of the Only-begotten Son of God, through Whom be glory to God, even the Father, for ever and ever. Amen.

---

3 Gen. xliii. 23: S. Luke ii. 30. 4 Ps. cxxiv. 7.

5 Morell reads here, "Moses has left," "Moses has crossed;" but Krabinger has no doubt that this word is due to a gloss upon the text. The Scholiast Nicetas (on Gregory Naz., *Orat.* 28) well explains this use of "Egypt": "Egypt is sometimes taken for this present world, sometimes for the flesh, sometimes for sin, sometimes for ignorance, sometimes for mischief."

6 1 Thess. iv. 13.

7 καλὸς. "Atticæ urbanitatis proprium," Krabinger. But David is described as "of a fair countenance."

8 2 Sam. vi. 14. "That ark," very probably refers to the *remains* of Meletius, not to the coffin or bier. The human body is called by this very term (σκῆνος, tabernacle), 2 Cor. v. 1 and 4, nor was the word in this sense unknown to Plato. The body of Meletius has been already called a κιβωτός.

9 ἑτερογλώσσοις: καὶ ἐν χείλεσιν ἑτέροις is added (cf. 1 Cor. xiv. 21: Is. xxviii. 11), in the text of Morell, but none of Krabinger's MSS. recognize these words.

---

1 τῶν ἀποστόλων τὴν συσκηνίαν (εἴπατε): "Thirteenth Apostle!" was in these times a usual expression of the highest praise. It was even heard in the applause given to living preachers. But if εἴπατε cannot bear so extended a meaning, some funeral banquet of the "apostles" assembled at the Council ts alluded to: or else (remembering the use of σκῆνος just above) "the lying in state in an Apostle's Church," in the capital: cf. above, "his joining the Apostolic band *and* his departure to Christ." 2 Theodosius.

3 It is only the Rabbis that make Lemuel, the author of the last chapter of Proverbs, the same as Solomon: Grotius identifies him with Hezekiah. Some German commentators regard him as the chief of an Arab tribe, on the borders of Palestine, and brother of Agur, author of ch. xxx. But the suggestion of Eichhorn and Ewald is the more probable, that Lemuel is an ideal name signifying "for God," the true King who leads a life consecrated to Jehovah.

4 Prov. xxxi. 6. Just above πρὸς ἡμᾶς is the reading of Krabinger's MSS. and of the Paris Editt.: Sifanus and Ducæus have rendered ὑμᾶς.

5 S. Gregory has misapplied both this passage from Ps. civ. 15 and the previous one from Prov. xxxi. 6. An attentive consideration of them shows that they do not lend themselves to the use he has made of them.

6 Ζωροτέρῳ. For the comparative see Lobeck, *Ad Phrynich.* p. 146: μειζοτέρῳ is the common faulty reading. These words are joined closely to what precedes in the MSS. Then, in what follows, "the unstinted goblets of the word," πνευματικοῦ is rightly omitted before λόγου: "and gladness" (καὶ ἀγαλλίασις) is rightly added, as it is joined with εὐφροσύνη in Ps. xlv. 15; and by Gregory himself, *In Diem Nat. Christ.* (pp. 340 and 352), and *In Bapt. Christi* (p. 377).

ON THE BAPTISM OF CHRIST

A SERMON FOR THE DAY OF THE LIGHTS.[1]

Now I recognize my own flock: to-day I behold the wonted figure of the Church, when, turning with aversion from the occupation even of the cares of the flesh, you come together in your undiminished numbers for the service of God — when the people crowds the house, coming within the sacred sanctuary, and when the multitude that can find no place within fills the space outside in the precincts like bees. For of them some are at their labours within, while others outside hum around the hive. So do, my children: and never abandon this zeal. For I confess that I feel a shepherd's affections, and I wish, when I am set upon this watch-tower, to see the flock gathered round about the mountain's foot: and when it so happens to me, I am filled with wonderful earnestness, and work with pleasure at my sermon, as the shepherds do at their rustic strains. But when things are otherwise, and you are straying in distant wanderings, as you did but lately, the last Lord's Day, I am much troubled, and glad to be silent; and I consider the question of flight from hence, and seek for the Carmel of the prophet Elijah, or for some rock without inhabitant; for men in depression naturally choose loneliness and solitude. But now, when I see you thronging here with all your families, I am reminded of the prophetic saying, which Isaiah proclaimed from afar off, addressing by anticipation the Church with her fair and numerous children :—" Who are these that fly as a cloud, and as doves with their young to me[2]"? Yes, and he adds moreover this also, "The place is too strait for me; give place that I may dwell[3]." For these predictions the power of the Spirit made with reference to the populous Church of God, which was afterwards to fill the whole world from end to end of the earth.

The time, then, has come, and bears in its course the remembrance of holy mysteries, purifying man, — mysteries which purge out from soul and body even that sin which is hard to cleanse away, and which bring us back to that fairness of our first estate which God, the best of artificers, impressed upon us. Therefore it is that you, the initiated people, are gathered together; and you bring also that people who have not made trial of them, leading, like good fathers, by careful guidance, the uninitiated to the perfect reception of the faith. I for my part rejoice over both;—over you that are initiated, because you are enriched with a great gift : over you that are uninitiated, because you have a fair expectation of hope—remission of what is to be accounted for, release from bondage, close relation to God, free boldness of speech, and in place of servile subjection equality with the angels. For these things, and all that follow from them, the grace of Baptism secures and conveys to us. Therefore let us leave the other matters of the Scriptures for other occasions, and abide by the topic set before us, offering, as far as we may, the gifts that are proper and fitting for the feast : for each festival demands its own treatment. So we welcome a marriage with wedding songs; for mourning we bring the due offering with funeral strains; in times of business we speak seriously, at times of festivity we relax the concentration and strain of our minds; but each time we keep free from disturbance by things that are alien to its character.

Christ, then, was born as it were a few days ago—He Whose generation was before all things, sensible and intellectual. To-day He is baptized by John that He might cleanse him who was defiled, that He might bring the Spirit from above, and exalt man to heaven, that he who had fallen might be raised up and he who had cast him down might be put to shame. And marvel not if God showed so great earnestness in our cause : for it was with care on the part of him who did us wrong that the plot was laid against us; it is with forethought

---

[1] That is, for the Festival of the Epiphany or Theophany, when the Eastern Church commemorates especially the Baptism of our Lord.   [2] Is. lx. 8 (LXX.).   [3] Is. xlix. 20.

on the part of our Maker that we are saved. And he, that evil charmer, framing his new device of sin against our race, drew along his serpent train, a disguise worthy of his own intent, entering in his impurity into what was like himself,— dwelling, earthly and mundane as he was in will, in that creeping thing. But Christ, the repairer of his evil-doing, assumes manhood in its fulness, and saves man, and becomes the type and figure of us all, to sanctify the first-fruits of every action, and leave to His servants no doubt in their zeal for the tradition. Baptism, then, is a purification from sins, a remission of trespasses, a cause of renovation and regeneration. By regeneration, understand regeneration conceived in thought, not discerned by bodily sight. For we shall not, according to the Jew Nicodemus and his somewhat dull intelligence, change the old man into a child, nor shall we form anew him who is wrinkled and gray-headed to tenderness and youth, if we bring back the man again into his mother's womb: but we do bring back, by royal grace, him who bears the scars of sin, and has grown old in evil habits, to the innocence of the babe. For as the child new-born is free from accusations and from penalties, so too the child of regeneration has nothing for which to answer, being released by royal bounty from accountability [4]. And this gift it is not the water that bestows (for in that case it were a thing more exalted than all creation), but the command of God, and the visitation of the Spirit that comes sacramentally to set us free. But water serves to express the cleansing. For since we are wont by washing in water to render our body clean when it is soiled by dirt or mud, we therefore apply it also in the sacramental action, and display the spiritual brightness by that which is subject to our senses. Let us however, if it seems well, persevere in enquiring more fully and more minutely concerning Baptism, starting, as from the fountain-head, from the Scriptural declaration, "Except a man be born of water and of the Spirit, he cannot enter into the kingdom of God [5]." Why are both named, and why is not the Spirit alone accounted sufficient for the completion of Baptism? Man, as we know full well, is compound, not simple: and therefore the cognate and similar medicines are assigned for healing to him who is twofold and conglomerate:—for his visible body, water, the sensible element,— for his soul, which we cannot see, the Spirit invisible, invoked by faith, present unspeakably. For "the Spirit breathes where He wills, and thou hearest His voice, but canst not tell whence

He cometh or whither He goeth [6]." He blesses the body that is baptized, and the water that baptizes. Despise not, therefore, the Divine laver, nor think lightly of it, as a common thing, on account of the use of water. For the power that operates is mighty, and wonderful are the things that are wrought thereby. For this holy altar, too, by which I stand, is stone, ordinary in its nature, nowise different from the other slabs of stone that build our houses and adorn our pavements; but seeing that it was consecrated to the service of God, and received the benediction, it is a holy table, an altar undefiled, no longer touched by the hands of all, but of the priests alone, and that with reverence. The bread again is at first [7] common bread, but when the sacramental action consecrates it, it is called, and becomes, the Body of Christ. So with the sacramental oil; so with the wine: though before the benediction they are of little value, each of them, after the sanctification bestowed by the Spirit, has its several operation. The same power of the word, again, also makes the priest venerable and honourable, separated, by the new blessing bestowed upon him, from his community with the mass of men. While but yesterday he was one of the mass, one of the people, he is suddenly rendered a guide, a president, a teacher of righteousness, an instructor in hidden mysteries; and this he does [8] without being at all changed in body or in form; but, while continuing to be in all appearance the man he was before, being, by some unseen power and grace, transformed in respect of his unseen soul to the higher condition. And so there are many things, which if you consider you will see that their appearance is contemptible, but the things they accomplish are mighty: and this is especially the case when you collect from the ancient history [9] instances cognate and similar to the subject of our inquiry. The rod of Moses was a hazel wand. And what is that, but common wood that every hand cuts and carries, and fashions to what use it chooses, and casts as it will into the fire? But when God was pleased to accomplish by that rod those wonders, lofty, and passing the power of language to express, the wood was changed into a serpent. And again, at another time, he smote the waters, and now made the water blood, now made to issue forth a countless brood of frogs: and again he divided the sea, severed to its depths without flowing together again. Likewise the mantle of one of the prophets, though it was but a goat's skin, made Elisha renowned in the whole world. And the wood of the Cross is of saving

---

[4] The language of this passage, if strictly taken, seems to imply a denial of original sin; but it is perhaps not intended to be so understood.   [5] S. John iii. 3.

[6] S. John iii. 8.   [7] Or "up to a certain point of time."
[8] That is, "these functions he fulfils."
[9] i. e. from the Old Testament Scriptures.

efficacy [1] for all men, though it is, as I am informed, a piece of a poor tree, less valuable than most trees are. So a bramble bush showed to Moses the manifestation of the presence of God: so the remains of Elisha raised a dead man to life; so clay gave sight to him that was blind from the womb. And all these things, though they were matter without soul or sense, were made the means for the performance of the great marvels wrought by them, when they received the power of God. Now, by a similar train of reasoning, water also, though it is nothing else than water, renews the man to spiritual regeneration [2], when the grace from above hallows it. And if any one answers me again by raising a difficulty, with his questions and doubts, continually asking and inquiring *how* water and the sacramental act that is performed therein regenerate, I most justly reply to him, "Show me the mode of that generation which is after the flesh, and I will explain to you the power of regeneration in the soul." You will say perhaps, by way of giving an account of the matter, "It is the cause of the seed which makes the man." Learn then from us in return, that hallowed water cleanses and illuminates the man. And if you again object to me your "How?" I shall more vehemently cry in answer, "How does the fluid and formless substance become a man?" and so the argument as it advances will be exercised on everything through all creation. How does heaven exist? how earth? how sea? how every single thing? For everywhere men's reasoning, perplexed in the attempt at discovery, falls back upon this syllable "how," as those who cannot walk fall back upon a seat. To speak concisely, everywhere the power of God and His operation are incomprehensible, and incapable of being reduced to rule, easily producing whatever He wills, while concealing from us the minute knowledge of His operation. Hence also the blessed David, applying his mind to the magnificence of creation, and filled with perplexed wonder in his soul, spake that verse which is sung by all, "O Lord, how manifold are Thy works: in wisdom hast Thou made them all [3]." The wisdom he perceived: but the art of the wisdom he could not discover. Let us then leave the task of searching into

what is beyond human power, and seek rather that which shows signs of being partly within our comprehension:—what is the reason why the cleansing is effected by water? and to what purpose are the three immersions received? That which the fathers taught, and which our mind has received and assented to, is as follows:—We recognize four elements, of which the world is composed, which every one knows even if their names are not spoken; but if it is well, for the sake of the more simple, to tell you their names, they are fire and air, earth and water. Now our God and Saviour, in fulfilling the Dispensation for our sakes, went beneath the fourth of these, the earth, that He might raise up life from thence. And we in receiving Baptism, in imitation of our Lord and Teacher and Guide, are not indeed buried in the earth (for this is the shelter of the body that is entirely dead, covering the infirmity and decay of our nature), but coming to the element akin to earth, to water, we conceal ourselves in that as the Saviour did in the earth: and by doing this thrice we represent for ourselves that grace of the Resurrection which was wrought in three days: and this we do, not receiving the sacrament in silence, but while there are spoken over us the Names of the Three Sacred Persons on Whom we believed, in Whom we also hope, from Whom comes to us both the fact of our present and the fact of our future existence. It may be thou art offended, thou who contendest boldly against the glory of the Spirit, and that thou grudgest to the Spirit that veneration wherewith He is reverenced by the godly. Leave off contending with me: resist, if thou canst, those words of the Lord which gave to men the rule of the Baptismal invocation. What says the Lord's command? "Baptizing them in the Name of the Father and of the Son and of the Holy Ghost [4]." How in the Name of the Father? Because He is the primal cause of all things. How in the Name of the Son? Because He is the Maker of the Creation. How in the Name of the Holy Ghost? Because He is the power perfecting all. We bow ourselves therefore before the Father, that we may be sanctified: before the Son also we bow, that the same end may be fulfilled: we bow also before the Holy Ghost, that we may be made what He is in fact and in Name. There is not a distinction in the sanctification, in the sense that the Father sanctifies more, the Son less, the Holy Spirit in a less degree than the other Two. Why then dost thou divide the Three Persons into fragments of different natures, and make Three Gods, unlike one to another, whilst from all thou dost receive one and the same grace?

---

[1] The reference appears to be not to the Cross as the instrument of that Death which was of saving efficacy, but to miraculous cures, real or reputed, effected by means of the actual wood of the Cross. The argument seems to require that we should understand the *Cross* itself, and not only the sacrifice offered upon it, to be the means of producing wondrous effects: and the grammatical construction favours this view. S. Cyril of Jerusalem mentions the extensive distribution of fragments of the Cross (Cat. x. 19), but this is probably one of the earliest references to miracles worked by their means.

[2] *i. e.* regeneration perceived by the mind (νοητὴν) as distinct from any regeneration of which the senses could take cognizance.

[3] Ps. civ. 24. The Psalm is the prefatory Psalm at Vespers in the present service of the Eastern Church. S. Gregory seems to indicate some such daily use in his own time.

[4] S. Matt. xxviii. 19.

As, however, examples always render an argument more vivid to the hearers, I propose to instruct the mind of the blasphemers by an illustration, explaining, by means of earthly and lowly matters, those matters which are great, and invisible to the senses. If it befel thee to be enduring the misfortune of captivity among enemies, to be in bondage and in misery, to be groaning for that ancient freedom which thou once hadst—and if all at once three men, who were notable men and citizens in the country of thy tyrannical masters, set thee free from the constraint that lay upon thee, giving thy ransom equally, and dividing the charges of the money in equal shares among themselves, wouldst thou not then, meeting with this favour, look upon the three alike as benefactors, and make repayment of the ransom to them in equal shares, as the trouble and the cost on thy behalf was common to them all—if, that is, thou wert a fair judge of the benefit done to thee? This we may see, so far as illustration goes[5], for our aim at present is not to render a strict account of the Faith. Let us return to the present season, and to the subject it sets before us.

I find that not only do the Gospels, written after the Crucifixion, proclaim the grace of Baptism, but, even before the Incarnation of our Lord, the ancient Scripture everywhere prefigured the likeness of our regeneration; not clearly manifesting its form, but foreshowing, in dark sayings, the love of God to man. And as the Lamb was proclaimed by anticipation, and the Cross was foretold by anticipation, so, too, was Baptism shown forth by action and by word. Let us recall its types to those who love good thoughts—for the festival season of necessity demands their recollection.

Hagar, the handmaid of Abraham (whom Paul treats allegorically in reasoning with the Galatians[6]), being sent forth from her master's house by the anger of Sarah—for a servant suspected. in regard to her master is a hard thing for lawful wives to bear—was wandering in desolation to a desolate land with her babe Ishmael at her breast. And when she was in straits for the needs of life, and was herself nigh unto death, and her child yet more so— for the water in the skin was spent (since it was not possible that the Synagogue, she who once dwelt among the figures of the perennial Fountain, should have all that was needed to support life), an angel unexpectedly appears, and shows her a well of living water, and drawing thence, she saves Ishmael. Behold, then, a sacramental type : how from the very first it is by the means of living water that salvation comes to him that was perishing—water that was not before, but was given as a boon by an angel's means. Again, at a later time, Isaac—the same for whose sake Ishmael was driven with his mother from his father's home—was to be wedded. Abraham's servant is sent to make the match, so as to secure a bride for his master, and finds Rebekah at the well : and a marriage that was to produce the race of Christ had its beginning and its first covenant in water[7]. Yes, and Isaac himself also, when he was ruling his flocks, digged wells at all parts of the desert, which the aliens stopped and filled up[8], for a type of all those impious men of later days who hindered the grace of Baptism, and talked loudly in their struggle against the truth. Yet the martyrs and the priests overcame them by digging the wells, and the gift of Baptism overflowed the whole world. According to the same force of the text, Jacob also, hastening to seek a bride, met Rachel unexpectedly at the well. And a great stone lay upon the well, which a multitude of shepherds were wont to roll away when they came together, and then gave water to themselves and to their flocks. But Jacob alone rolls away the stone, and waters the flocks of his spouse[9]. The thing is, I think, a dark saying, a shadow of what should come. For what is the stone that is laid but Christ Himself? for of Him Isaiah says, "And I will lay in the foundations of Sion a costly stone, precious, elect[1] :" and Daniel likewise, "A stone was cut out without hands[2]," that is, Christ was born without a man. For as it is a new and marvellous thing that a stone should be cut out of the rock without a hewer or stone-cutting tools, so it is a thing beyond all wonder that an offspring should appear from an unwedded Virgin. There was lying, then, upon the well the spiritual[3] stone, Christ, concealing in the deep and in mystery the laver of regeneration which needed much time—as it were a long rope—to bring it to light. And none rolled away the stone save Israel, who is mind seeing God. But he both draws up the water and gives drink to the sheep of Rachel ; that is, he reveals the hidden mystery, and gives living water to the flock of the Church. Add to this also the history of the three rods of Jacob[4]. For from the time when the three rods were laid by the well, Laban the polytheist thenceforth became poor, and Jacob became rich and wealthy in

---

[5] The meaning of this clause may be, either that Gregory does not propose to follow this point out, as the subject of his discourse is Baptism, not the doctrine of the Trinity ; or, that the example he has given is not to be so pressed as to imply tritheism, being merely an illustration of moral obligation, not a parallel from which anything is to be inferred as to the exact relation between the Three Persons.
[6] Cf. Gal. iv. 22, &c. See Gen. xxi.

[7] See Gen. xxiv.   [8] See Gen. xxvi. 15, sqq.
[9] See Gen. xxix.   [1] Is. xxviii. 16 (not exactly from LXX.).
[2] Cf. Dan. ii. 45.   [3] νοητὸς.   [4] Cf. Gen. xxx. 37, sqq.

herds. Now let Laban be interpreted of the devil, and Jacob of Christ. For after the institution of Baptism Christ took away all the flock of Satan and Himself grew rich. Again, the great Moses, when he was a goodly child, and yet at the breast, falling under the general and cruel decree which the hard-hearted Pharaoh made against the men-children, was exposed on the banks of the river—not naked, but laid in an ark, for it was fitting that the Law should typically be enclosed in a coffer [5]. And he was laid near the water; for the Law, and those daily sprinklings of the Hebrews which were a little later to be made plain in the perfect and marvellous Baptism, are near to grace. Again, according to the view of the inspired Paul [6], the people itself, by passing through the Red Sea, proclaimed the good tidings of salvation by water. The people passed over, and the Egyptian king with his host was engulfed, and by these actions this Sacrament was foretold. For even now, whensoever the people is in the water of regeneration, fleeing from Egypt, from the burden of sin, it is set free and saved; but the devil with his own servants (I mean, of course, the spirits of evil), is choked with grief, and perishes, deeming the salvation of men to be his own misfortune.

Even these instances might be enough to confirm our present position; but the lover of good thoughts must yet not neglect what follows. The people of the Hebrews, as we learn, after many sufferings, and after accomplishing their weary course in the desert, did not enter the land of promise until it had first been brought, with Joshua for its guide and the pilot of its life, to the passage of the Jordan [7]. But it is clear that Joshua also, who set up the twelve stones in the stream [8], was anticipating the coming of the twelve disciples, the ministers of Baptism. Again, that marvellous sacrifice of the old Tishbite [9], that passes all human understanding, what else does it do but prefigure in action the Faith in the Father, the Son, and the Holy Ghost, and redemption? For when all the people of the Hebrews had trodden underfoot the religion of their fathers, and fallen into the error of polytheism, and their king Ahab was deluded by idolatry, with Jezebel, of ill-omened name, as the wicked partner of his life, and the vile prompter of his impiety, the prophet, filled with the grace of the Spirit, coming to a meeting with Ahab, withstood the priests of Baal in a marvellous and wondrous contest in the sight of the king and all the people; and by proposing to them the task of sacrificing the bullock without fire, he displayed them

in a ridiculous and wretched plight, vainly praying and crying aloud to gods that were not. At last, himself invoking his own and the true God, he accomplished the test proposed with further exaggerations and additions. For he did not simply by prayer bring down the fire from heaven upon the wood when it was dry, but exhorted and enjoined the attendants to bring abundance of water. And when he had thrice poured out the barrels upon the cleft wood, he kindled at his prayer the fire from out of the water, that by the contrariety of the elements, so concurring in friendly co-operation, he might show with superabundant force the power of his own God. Now herein, by that wondrous sacrifice, Elijah clearly proclaimed to us the sacramental rite of Baptism that should afterwards be instituted. For the fire was kindled by water thrice poured upon it, so that it is clearly shown that where the mystic water is, there is the kindling, warm, and fiery Spirit, that burns up the ungodly, and illuminates the faithful. Yes, and yet again his disciple Elisha, when Naaman the Syrian, who was diseased with leprosy, had come to him as a suppliant, cleanses the sick man by washing him in Jordan [1], clearly indicating what should come, both by the use of water generally, and by the dipping in the river in particular. For Jordan alone of rivers, receiving in itself the first-fruits of sanctification and benediction, conveyed in its channel to the whole world, as it were from some fount in the type afforded by itself, the grace of Baptism. These then are indications in deed and act of regeneration by Baptism. Let us for the rest consider the prophecies of it in words and language. Isaiah cried saying, "Wash you, make you clean, put away evil from your souls [2];" and David, "Draw nigh to Him and be enlightened, and your faces shall not be ashamed [3]." And Ezekiel, writing more clearly and plainly than them both, says, "And I will sprinkle clean water upon you, and ye shall be cleansed: from all your filthiness, and from all your idols, will I cleanse you. A new heart also will I give you, and a new spirit will I give you: and I will take away the stony heart out of your flesh, and I will give you an heart of flesh, and my Spirit will I put within you [4]." Most manifestly also does Zechariah prophesy of Joshua [5], who was clothed with the filthy garment (to wit, the flesh of a servant, even ours), and stripping him of his ill-favoured raiment adorns him with the clean and fair apparel; teaching us by the figurative illustration that verily in

---

[1] See 2 Kings v.
[2] Is. i. 16 (LXX.).　　　　[3] Ps. xxxiv. 5 (LXX.).
[4] Ez. xxxvi. 25—27 (not exactly as LXX.).
[5] Cf. Zech. iii. 3. It is to be remembered, of course, that the form of the name in the Septuagint is not Joshua but Jesus.

[5] Cf. Ex. ii.　　　[6] Cf. 1 Cor. x. 1, 2; and see Ex. xiv.
[7] See Josh. iii.　　[8] See Josh. iv.　　[9] See 1 Kings xviii.

the Baptism of Jesus[6] all we, putting off our sins like some poor and patched garment, are clothed in the holy and most fair garment of regeneration. And where shall we place that oracle of Isaiah, which cries to the wilderness, "Be glad, O thirsty wilderness: let the desert rejoice and blossom as a lily: and the desolate places of Jordan shall blossom and shall rejoice[7]"? For it is clear that it is not to places without soul or sense that he proclaims the good tidings of joy: but he speaks, by the figure of the desert, of the soul that is parched and unadorned, even as David also, when he says, "My soul is unto Thee as a thirsty land[8]," and, "My soul is athirst for the mighty, for the living God[9]." So again the Lord says in the Gospels, "If any man thirst, let him come unto Me and drink[1];" and to the woman of Samaria, "Whosoever drinketh of this water shall thirst again: but whosoever drinketh of the water that I shall give him shall never thirst[2]." And "the excellency of Carmel"[3] is given to the soul that bears the likeness to the desert, that is, the grace bestowed through the Spirit. For since Elijah dwelt in Carmel, and the mountain became famous and renowned by the virtue of him who dwelt there, and since moreover John the Baptist, illustrious in the spirit of Elijah, sanctified the Jordan, therefore the prophet foretold that "the excellency of Carmel" should be given to the river. And "the glory of Lebanon[3]," from the similitude of its lofty trees, he transfers to the river. For as great Lebanon presents a sufficient cause of wonder in the very trees which it brings forth and nourishes, so is the Jordan glorified by regenerating men and planting them in the Paradise of God: and of them, as the words of the Psalmist say, ever blooming and bearing the foliage of virtues, "the leaf shall not wither[4]," and God shall be glad, receiving their fruit in due season, rejoicing, like a good planter, in his own works. And the inspired David, foretelling also the voice which the Father uttered from heaven upon the Son at His Baptism, that He might lead the hearers, who till then had looked upon that low estate of His Humanity which was perceptible by their senses, to the dignity of nature that belongs to the Godhead, wrote in his book that passage, "The voice of the Lord is upon the waters, the voice of the Lord in majesty[5]." But here we must make an end of the testimonies from the Divine

Scriptures: for the discourse would extend to an infinite length if one should seek to select every passage in detail, and set them forth in a single book.

But do ye all, as many as are made glad, by the gift of regeneration, and make your boast of that saving renewal, show me, after the sacramental grace, the change in your ways that should follow it, and make known by the purity of your conversation the difference effected by your transformation for the better. For of those things which are before our eyes nothing is altered: the characteristics of the body remain unchanged, and the mould of the visible nature is nowise different. But there is certainly need of some manifest proof, by which we may recognize the new-born man, discerning by clear tokens the new from the old. And these I think are to be found in the intentional motions of the soul, whereby it separates itself from its old customary life, and enters on a newer way of conversation, and will clearly teach those acquainted with it that it has become something different from its former self, bearing in it no token by which the old self was recognized. This, if you be persuaded by me, and keep my words as a law, is the mode of the transformation. The man that was before Baptism was wanton, covetous, grasping at the goods of others, a reviler, a liar, a slanderer, and all that is kindred with these things, and consequent from them. Let him now become orderly, sober, content with his own possessions, and imparting from them to those in poverty, truthful, courteous, affable—in a word, following every laudable course of conduct. For as darkness is dispelled by light, and black disappears as whiteness is spread over it, so the old man also disappears when adorned with the works of righteousness. Thou seest how Zacchaeus also by the change of his life slew the publican, making fourfold restitution to those whom he had unjustly damaged, and the rest he divided with the poor—the treasure which he had before got by ill means from the poor whom he oppressed. The Evangelist Matthew, another publican, of the same business with Zacchaeus, at once after his call changed his life as if it had been a mask. Paul was a persecutor, but after the grace bestowed on him an Apostle, bearing the weight of his fetters for Christ's sake, as an act of amends and repentance for those unjust bonds which he once received from the Law, and bore for use against the Gospel. Such ought you to be in your regeneration: so ought you to blot out your habits that tend to sin; so ought the sons of God to have their conversation: for after the grace bestowed we are called His children. And therefore we ought narrowly to scrutinize

---

6 If "the Baptism of Jesus" here means (as seems most likely) the Baptism of our Lord by S. John, not the Baptism instituted by our Lord, then we are apparently intended to understand that our Lord, summing up humanity in Himself, represented by His Baptism that of all who should thereafter be baptized.
7 Is. xxxv. 1, 2 (LXX.). 8 Ps. cxliii. 6 (LXX.).
9 Ps. xlii. 2 (not as LXX.). 1 S. John vii. 37.
2 S John iv. 13, 14. 3 Is. xxxv. 2.
4 Ps. i. 4. 5 Ps. xxix. 3, 4 (LXX.).

our Father's characteristics, that by fashioning and framing ourselves to the likeness of our Father, we may appear true children of Him Who calls us to the adoption according to grace. For the bastard and the supposititious son, who belies his father's nobility in his deeds, is a sad reproach. Therefore also, methinks, it is that the Lord Himself, laying down for us in the Gospels the rules of our life, uses these words to His disciples, "Do good to them that hate you, pray for them that despitefully use you and persecute you; that ye may be the children of your Father which is in heaven: for He maketh His sun to rise on the evil and on the good, and sendeth rain on the just and on the unjust [6]." For *then* He says they are sons when in their own modes of thought they are fashioned in loving kindness towards their kindred, after the likeness of the Father's goodness.

Therefore, also, it is that after the dignity of adoption the devil plots more vehemently against us, pining away with envious glance, when he beholds the beauty of the new-born man, earnestly tending towards that heavenly city, from which he fell: and he raises up against us fiery temptations, seeking earnestly to despoil us of that second adornment, as he did of our former array. But when we are aware of his attacks, we ought to repeat to ourselves the apostolic words, "As many of us as were baptized into Christ were baptized into His death [7]." Now if we have been conformed to His death, sin henceforth in us is surely a corpse, pierced through by the javelin of Baptism, as that fornicator was thrust through by the zealous Phinehas [8]. Flee therefore from us, ill-omened one! for it is a corpse thou seekest to despoil, one long ago joined to thee, one who long since lost his senses for pleasures. A corpse is not enamoured of bodies, a corpse is not captivated by wealth, a corpse slanders not, a corpse lies not, snatches not at what is not its own, reviles not those who encounter it. My way of living is regulated for another life: I have learnt to despise the things that are in the world, to pass by the things of earth, to hasten to the things of heaven, even as Paul expressly testifies, that the world is crucified to him, and he to the

world [9]. These are the words of a soul truly regenerated: these are the utterances of the newly-baptized man, who remembers his own profession, which he made to God when the sacrament was administered to him, promising that he would despise for the sake of love towards Him all torment and all pleasure alike.

And now we have spoken sufficiently for the holy subject of the day, which the circling year brings to us at appointed periods. We shall do well in what remains to end our discourse by turning it to the loving Giver of so great a boon, offering to Him a few words as the requital of great things. For Thou verily, O Lord, art the pure and eternal fount of goodness, Who didst justly turn away from us, and in loving kindness didst have mercy upon us. Thou didst hate, and wert reconciled; Thou didst curse, and didst bless; Thou didst banish us from Paradise, and didst recall us; Thou didst strip off the fig-tree leaves, an unseemly covering, and put upon us a costly garment; Thou didst open the prison, and didst release the condemned; Thou didst sprinkle us with clean water, and cleanse us from our filthiness. No longer shall Adam be confounded when called by Thee, nor hide himself, convicted by his conscience, cowering in the thicket of Paradise. Nor shall the flaming sword encircle Paradise around, and make the entrance inaccessible to those that draw near; but all is turned to joy for us that were the heirs of sin: Paradise, yea, heaven itself may be trodden by man: and the creation, in the world and above the world, that once was at variance with itself, is knit together in friendship: and we men are made to join in the angels' song, offering the worship of their praise to God. For all these things then let us sing to God that hymn of joy, which lips touched by the Spirit long ago sang loudly: "Let my soul be joyful in the Lord: for He hath clothed me with a garment of salvation, and hath put upon me a robe of gladness: as on a bridegroom He hath set a mitre upon me, and as a bride hath He adorned me with fair array [1]." And verily the Adorner of the bride is Christ, Who is, and was, and shall be, blessed now and for evermore. Amen.

---

[6] S. Matt. v. 44.   [7] Rom. vi. 3.   [8] Num. xxv. 7, 8.   [9] Cf. Gal. vi. 14.   [1] Is. lxi. 10 (not exactly from LXX.).

VI. LETTERS

LETTERS

LETTER I.

TO EUSEBIUS[2].

WHEN the length of the day begins to expand in winter-time, as the sun mounts to the upper part· of his course, we keep the feast of the appearing of the true Light divine, that through the veil of flesh has cast its bright beams upon the life of men : but now when that luminary has traversed half the heaven in his course, so that night and day are of equal length, the upward return of human nature from death to life is the theme of this great and universal festival, which all the life of those who have embraced the mystery of the Resurrection unites in celebrating. What is the meaning of the subject thus suggested for my letter to you ? Why, since it is the custom in these general holidays for us to take every way to show the affection harboured in our hearts, and some, as you know, give proof of their good will by presents of their own, we thought it only right not to leave you without the homage of our gifts, but to lay before your lofty and high-minded soul the scanty offerings of our poverty. Now our offering which is tendered for your acceptance in this letter is the letter itself, in which there is not a single word wreathed with the flowers of rhetoric or adorned with the graces of composition, to make it to be deemed a gift at all in literary circles, but the mystical gold, which is wrapped up in the faith of Christians, as in a packet[3], must be my present

to you, after being unwrapped, as far as possible, by these lines, and showing its hidden brilliancy. Accordingly we must return to our prelude. Why is it that then only, when the night has attained its utmost length, so that no further addition is possible, that He appears in flesh to us, Who holds the Universe in His grasp, and controls the same Universe by His own power, Who cannot be contained even by all intelligible things, but includes the whole, even at the time that He enters the narrow dwelling of a fleshly tabernacle, while His mighty power thus keeps pace with His beneficent purpose, and shows itself even as a shadow wherever the will inclines, so that neither in the creation of the world was the power found weaker than the will, nor when He was eager to stoop down to the lowliness of our mortal nature did He lack power to that very end, but actually did come to be in that condition, yet without leaving the universe unpiloted[4]? Since, then, there is some account to be given of both those seasons, how it is that it is winter-time when He appears in the flesh, but it is when the days are as long as the nights that He restores to life man, who because of his sins returned to the earth from whence he came, —by explaining the reason of this, as well as I can in few words, I will make my letter my present to you. Has your own sagacity, as of course it has, already divined the mystery hinted at by these coincidences; that the advance of night is stopped by the accessions to the light, and the period of darkness begins to be shortened, as the length of the day is increased by the successive additions? For thus much perhaps would be plain enough even to the uninitiated, that sin is near akin to darkness ; and in fact evil is so termed by the Scripture. Accordingly the season in which our mystery of godliness begins is a kind of exposition of the Divine dispensation on behalf of our souls. For meet and right it was that, when vice was shed abroad[5] without bounds, [upon this night of evil the Sun of righteousness should rise, and

---

[1] The first fourteen of these Letters have been once edited ; *i. e.* by Zacagni (Rome, 1638), from the Vatican MS. See *Prolegomena,* p. 30. They are found also in the Medicean MS., of which Bandinus gives an accurate account, and which is much superior, on the authority of Caraccioli, who saw both, to the Vatican. Zacagni did not see the Medicean : but many of his felicitous emendations of the Vatican lacunæ correspond with it. They are here translated by the late Reverend Harman Chaloner Ogle, Fellow of Magdalen College, Oxford (Ireland Scholar), who died suddenly (1887), to the grief of very many, and the irreparable loss to scholarship, on the eve of his departure to aid the Mission of the Archbishop of Canterbury to the Armenian Church. The notes added by him are signed with his initials.
[2] Sent as an Easter present to Eusebius, bishop of Chalcis, in Cœle-Syria, a staunch Catholic, who attended the Council of Constantinople. For this custom amongst the Eastern Christians of exchanging presents at the great festivals, cf. *On the Making of Man* (p. 387), which Gregory sent to his brother Peter : Gregory Naz. *Letter* 54 *to Helladius,* and *Letter* 87 *to Theodore of Tyana.*
[3] ἀποδέσμῳ.

[4] Evidently an allusion to the myth in Plato.
[5] The χύσις τῆς κακίας is a frequent expression in Origen.

that in us who have before walked in darkness [6]] the day which we receive from Him Who placed that light in our hearts should increase more and more; so that the life which is in the light should be extended to the greatest length possible, being constantly augmented by additions of good; and that the life in vice should by gradual subtraction be reduced to the smallest possible compass; for the increase of things good comes to the same thing as the diminution of things evil. But the feast of the Resurrection, occurring when the days are of equal length, of itself gives us this interpretation of the coincidence, namely, that we shall no longer fight with evils only upon equal terms, vice grappling with virtue in indecisive strife, but that the life of light will prevail, the gloom of idolatry melting as the day waxes stronger. For this reason also, after the moon has run her course for fourteen days, Easter exhibits her exactly opposite to the rays of the sun, full with all the wealth of his brightness, and not permitting any interval of darkness to take place in its turn [7]: for, after taking the place of the sun at its setting, she does not herself set, before she mingles her own beams with the genuine rays of the sun, so that one light remains continuously, throughout the whole space of the earth's course by day and night, without any break whatsoever being caused by the interposition of darkness. This discussion, dear one, we contribute by way of a gift from our poor and needy hand; and may your whole life be a continual festival and a high day, never dimmed by a single stain of nightly gloom.

LETTER II.

TO THE CITY OF SEBASTEIA [8].

SOME of the brethren whose heart is as our heart told us of the slanders that were being propagated to our detriment by those who hate

peace, and privily backbite their neighbour, and have no fear of the great and terrible judgment-seat of Him Who has declared that account will be required even of idle words in that trial of our life which we must all look for: they say that the charges which are being circulated against us are such as these; that we entertain opinions opposed to those who at Nicæa set forth the right and sound faith, and that without due discrimination and inquiry we received into the communion of the Catholic Church those who formerly assembled at Ancyra under the name of Marcellus. Therefore, that falsehood may not overpower the truth, in another letter we made a sufficient defence against the charges levelled at us, and before the Lord we protested that we had neither departed from the faith of the Holy Fathers, nor had we done anything without due discrimination and inquiry in the case of those who came over from the communion of Marcellus to that of the Church: but all that we did we did only after the orthodox in the East, and our brethren in the ministry had entrusted to us the consideration of the case of these persons, and had approved our action. But inasmuch as, since we composed that written defence of our conduct, again some of the brethren who are of one mind with us begged us to make separately [9] with our own lips a profession of our faith, which we entertain with full conviction [10], following as we do the utterances of inspiration and the tradition of the Fathers, we deemed it necessary to discourse briefly of these heads as well. We confess that the doctrine of the Lord, which He taught His disciples, when He delivered to them the mystery of godliness, is the foundation and root of right and sound faith, nor do we believe that there is aught else loftier or safer than that tradition. Now the doctrine of the Lord is this: "Go," He said, "teach all nations, baptizing them in the name of the Father, and of the Son, and of the Holy Ghost." Since, then, in the case of those who are regenerate from death to eternal life, it is through the Holy Trinity that the life-giving power is bestowed on those who with faith are deemed worthy of the grace, and in like manner the grace is imperfect, if any one, whichever it be, of the names of the Holy Trinity be omitted in the saving baptism—for the sacrament of regenera-

[6] A corrupt passage. Probably some lines have been lost. A double opposition seems intended; (1) between the night of evil and our Saviour's coming like the Sun to disperse it; and (2) between walking in darkness and walking in light on the part of the individual (H. C. O.).

[7] ἐν τῷ μέρει, or "on her part," or "at that particular season." To support this last, Col. ii. 16, ἐν μέρει ἑορτῆς, may be compared, as Origen interprets it, "in a particular feast," c. Cels. viii. 23: "Paul alludes to this, when he names the feast selected in preference to others only 'part of a feast,' hinting that the life everlasting with the Word of God is not 'in the part of a feast, but in a complete and continuous one.' Modern commentators on that passage, it is true, interpret ἐν μέρει "with regard to," "on the score of." But has Origen's meaning been sufficiently considered?

[8] Marcellus of Ancyra had been deposed in the Council of Constantinople in 336, for teaching the doctrine of Paul of Samosata. Basil and Athanasius successively separated from their communion all who were united to Marcellus: and these, knowing that Valens the Emperor had exiled several bishops of Egypt to Diocæsarea, went to find them (375) and were admitted to their communion. Armed with letters from them, they demanded to be received into that of the other bishops of the East, and at length Basil and others, having examined the matter closely, admitted them. Gregory followed Basil's example, being assured of their Catholicity: and to justify himself wrote this letter to the Catholics of Sebasteia.

[9] ἰδίως, i. e. as a distinct matter from the previous ἀπολογία; or perhaps "privately."

[10] πεπληροφορήμεθα; a deponent, the same use as in Rom. iv. 21, of Abraham, πληροφορηθεὶς ὅτι ὃ ἐπήγγελται, κ.τ.λ.: cf. πληροφορία πίστεως, Heb. x. 22: πληροφορία τῆς ἐλπίδος, Heb. vi. 11. The other N. T. use of this word, as an active and passive, is found 2 Tim. iv. 5, "fulfil thy ministry;" 2 Tim. iv. 17; S. Luke i. 1, πεπληροφορημένων, "most surely believed" (A. V.): in all which the R.V. follows the Vulgate interpretation. In the Latin translation of this passage in Gregory, "(professionem) quâ sacris nos Scripturis ac Patrum traditioni penitus inhærere persuasum omnibus foret," the meaning put upon πληροφορεῖσθαι by A. V. in the last text is adopted, "we are fully believed to follow," with a very harsh construction.

tion is not completed in the Son and the Father alone without the Spirit : nor is the perfect boon of life imparted to Baptism in the Father and the Spirit, if the name of the Son be suppressed : nor is the grace of that Resurrection accomplished in the Father and the Son, if the Spirit be left out [1] :—for this reason we rest all our hope, and the persuasion of the salvation of our souls, upon the three Persons, recognized [2] by these names ; and we believe in the Father of our Lord Jesus Christ, Who is the Fountain of life, and in the Only-begotten Son of the Father, Who is the Author of life, as saith the Apostle, and in the Holy Spirit of God, concerning Whom the Lord hath spoken, "It is the Spirit that quickeneth". And since on us who have been redeemed from death the grace of immortality is bestowed, as we have said, through faith in the Father, and the Son, and the Holy Spirit, guided by these we believe that nothing servile, nothing created, nothing unworthy of the majesty of the Father is to be associated in thought with the Holy Trinity; since, I say, our life is one which comes to us by faith in the Holy Trinity, taking its rise from the God of all, flowing through the Son, and working in us by the Holy Spirit. Having, then, this full assurance, we are baptized as we were commanded, and we believe as we are baptized, and we hold as we believe ; so that with one accord our baptism, our faith, and our ascription of praise are to [3] the Father, and to the Son, and to the Holy Ghost. But if any one makes mention of two or three Gods, or of three Godheads, let him be accursed. And if any, following the perversion of Arius, says that the Son or the Holy Spirit were produced from things that are not, let him be accursed. But as many as walk by the rule of truth and acknowledge the three Persons, devoutly recognized in Their several properties, and believe that there is one Godhead, one goodness, one rule, one authority and power, and neither make void the supremacy of the Sole-sovereignty [4], nor fall away into polytheism, nor confound the Persons, nor make up the Holy Trinity of heterogeneous and unlike elements, but in simplicity receive the doctrine of the faith, grounding all their hope of salvation upon the Father, the Son, and the Holy Spirit,—these according to our judgment are of the same mind as we, and with them we also trust to have part in the Lord.

---

[1] There is some repetition and omission here. Gregory ought to have said in one of the clauses, " Nor is Baptism in the name of the Son and Holy Ghost sufficient, without the name of the Father " (H. C. O.).
[2] γνωριζομένην looks as if it ought to be γνωριζομέναις, and the Latin translator renders accordingly (H. C. O.).
[3] The same preposition εἰς is used after βάπτισμα, πίστις, and δόξα.
[4] μοναρχία, i. e. the One First Cause or Principle. See p. 84, note 7.

LETTER III.

TO ABLABIUS [5].

THE Lord, as was meet and right, brought us safe through, accompanied as we had been by your prayers, and I will tell you a manifest token of His loving kindness. For when the sun was just over the spot which we left behind Earsus [6], suddenly the clouds gathered thick, and there was a change from clear sky to deep gloom. Then a chilly breeze blowing through the clouds, bringing a drizzling with it, and striking upon us with a very damp feeling, threatened such rain as had never yet been known, and on the left there were continuous claps of thunder, and keen flashes of lightning alternated with the thunder, following one crash and preceding the next, and all the mountains before, behind, and on each side were shrouded in clouds. And already a heavy [7] cloud hung over our heads, caught by a strong wind and big with rain, and yet we, like the Israelites of old in their miraculous passage of the Red Sea, though surrounded on all sides by rain, arrived unwetted at Vestena. And when we had already found shelter there, and our mules had got a rest, then the signal for the down-pour was given by God to the air. And when we had spent some three or four hours there, and had rested enough, again God stayed the down-fall, and our conveyance moved along more briskly than before, as the wheel easily slid through the mud just moist and on the surface. Now the road from that point to our little town is all along the river side, going down stream with the water, and there is a continuous string of villages along the banks, all close upon the road, and with very short distances between them. In consequence of this unbroken line of habitations all the road was full of people, some coming to meet us, and others escorting us, mingling tears in abundance with their joy. Now there was a little drizzle, not unpleasant, just enough to moisten the air ; but a little way before we

---

[5] This Letter must have been written, either (1) After the first journey of Gregory to Constantinople, i. e. after the Council, 381 ; or (2) On his return from exile at the death of Valens, 378. The words at the end, " rejoiced and wept with my people," are against the first view.
[6] Ἐαρσοῦ. The distance prevents us conjecturing "Tarsus" here, though, Gregory was probably coming from the sea (and the Holy Land). But "Garsaura" is marked on the maps as about 40 miles south of Nyssa with the "Morimene" mountains (Erjash Dagh) intervening. (Nyssa lay on a southern tributary of the Halys, N.W. of Nazianzum.) The Medicean MS. is said by Migne to read ἑαυτῶν here—"we left behind us." Nothing is known of Vestena below.
[7] Adopting the conjecture of the Latin translator, βαρεῖα for βραχεῖα. His translation, however, though ingenious, would require something different in the Greek. It runs "jamque nubes, quæ nostro impendebat capiti, postquam acri vehementique vento abrepta alio delata fuit, hiemem peperit." As the text stands ὑποληφθεῖσα cannot bear this translation (H. C. O.)

got home the cloud that overhung us was condensed into a more violent shower, so that our entrance was quite quiet, as no one was aware beforehand of our coming. But just as we got inside our portico, as the sound of our carriage wheels along the dry hard ground was heard, the people turned up in shoals, as though by some mechanical contrivance, I know not whence nor how, flocking round us so closely that it was not easy to get down from our conveyance, for there was not a foot of clear space. But after we had persuaded them with difficulty to allow us to get down, and to let our mules pass, we were crushed on every side by folks crowding round, insomuch that their excessive kindness all but made us faint. And when we were near the inside of the portico, we see a stream of fire flowing into the church; for the choir of virgins, carrying their wax torches in their hands, were just marching in file along the entrance of the church, kindling the whole into splendour with their blaze. And when I was within and had rejoiced and wept with my people —for I experienced both emotions from witnessing both in the multitude,—as soon as I had finished the prayers, I wrote off this letter to your Holiness as fast as possible, under the pressure of extreme thirst, so that I might when it was done attend to my bodily wants.

LETTER IV.

TO CYNEGIUS [8].

WE have a law that bids us "rejoice with them that rejoice, and weep with them that weep": but of these commandments it often seems that it is in our power to put only one into practice. For there is a great scarcity in the world of "them that rejoice," so that it is not easy to find with whom we may share our blessings, but there are plenty who are in the opposite case. I write thus much by way of preface, because of the sad tragedy which some spiteful power has been playing among people of long-standing nobility. A young man of good family, Synesius by name, not unconnected

with myself, in the full flush of youth, who has scarcely begun to live yet, is in great dangers, from which God alone has power to rescue him, and next to God, you, who are entrusted with the decisions of all questions of life and death. An involuntary mishap has taken place. Indeed, what mishap is voluntary? And now those who have made up this suit against him, carrying with it the penalty of death, have turned his mishap into matter of accusation. However, I will try by private letters to soften their resentment and incline them to pity; but I beseech your kindliness to side with justice and with us, that your benevolence may prevail over the wretched plight of the youth, hunting up any and every device by which the young man may be placed out of the reach of danger, having conquered the spiteful power which assails him by the help of your alliance. I have said all that I want in brief; but to go into details, in order that my endeavour may be successful, would be to say what I have no business to say, nor you to hear from me.

LETTER V.

A TESTIMONIAL.

THAT for which the king of the Macedonians is most admired by people of understanding,— for he is admired not so much for his famous victories [9] over the Persians and Indians, and his penetrating as far as the Ocean, as for his saying that he had his treasure in his friends;—in this respect I dare to compare myself with his marvellous exploits, and it will be right for me to utter such a sentiment too. Now because I am rich in friendships, perhaps I surpass in that kind of property even that great man who plumed himself upon that very thing. For who was such a friend to him as you are to me, perpetually endeavouring to surpass yourself in every kind of excellence? For assuredly no one would ever charge me with flattery, when I say this, if he were to look at my age and your life: for grey hairs are out of season for flattery, and old age is ill-suited for complaisance, and as for you, even if you are ever in season for flattery, yet praise would not fall under the suspicion of flattery, as your life shows forth your praise before words. But since, when men are rich in blessings, it is a special gift to know how to use what one has, and the best use of superfluities is to let one's friends share them with one, and since my be-

---

[8] Cynegius was "prefect of the prætorium," from 384 to 390. Cod. Medic. has on the title, Ἰερίῳ Ἡγέμονι : but this must be wrong. It was this Cynegius, not then Prefect of the East, whom Libanius was to lead, however unwilling, to the study of eloquence (see end of Letter xi.). The four Prætorian Prefects remained, after Diocletian's institution of the four Princes, under whom they served, had been abolished by Constantine. The Prefect of the East stretched his jurisdiction "from the cataracts of the Nile to the banks of the Phasis, and from the mountains of Thrace to the frontiers of Persia." From all inferior jurisdictions an *appeal* in every matter of importance, either civil or criminal, might be brought before the tribunal of the Prefect ; but *his* sentence was final : the emperors themselves refused to dispute it. Hence Gregory says, that, " next to God, Cynegius had the power to remove his young relative from danger." How intimate Gregory was, not only with the highest officers, but at the Court itself, is shown in his orations on Pulcheria and Flacilla. He must have been over sixty when this letter was written.

[9] διηγήμασιν. "He believed in fidelity, and was capable of the sublimest, most intimate friendships. He loved Hephæstion so fervently, that . . . . he remained inconsolable for his loss."—F. Schlegel. Achilles was his hero : for he too knew the delight of a constant friendship.

loved son Alexander is most of all a friend united to me in all sincerity, be persuaded to show him my treasure, and not only to show it to him, but also to put it at his disposal to enjoy abundantly, by extending to him your protection in those matters about which he has come to you, begging you to be his patron. He will tell you all with his own lips. For it is better so than that I should go into details in a letter.

LETTER VI.

TO STAGIRIUS.

THEY say that conjurors [10] in theatres contrive some such marvel as this which I am going to describe. Having taken some historical narrative, or some old story as the ground-plot of their sleight of hand, they relate the story to the spectators in action. And it is in this way that they make their representations of the narrative [1]. They put on their dresses and masks, and rig up something to resemble a town on the stage with hangings, and then so associate the bare scene with their life-like imitation of action that they are a marvel to the spectators —both the actors themselves of the incidents of the play, and the hangings, or rather their imaginary city. What do I mean, do you think, by this allegory? Since we must needs show to those who are coming together that which is not a city as though it were one, do you let yourself be persuaded to become for the nonce the founder of our city [2], by just putting in an appearance there; I will make the desert-place seem to be a city; now it is no great distance for you, and the favour which you will confer is very great; for we wish to show ourselves more splendid to our companions here, which we shall do if, in place of any other ornament, we are adorned with the splendour of your party.

LETTER VII.

TO A FRIEND.

WHAT flower in spring is so bright, what voices of singing birds are so sweet, what breezes that soothe the calm sea are so light and mild, what glebe is so fragrant to the husbandman— whether it be teeming with green blades, or waving with fruitful ears—as is the spring of

the soul, lit up with your peaceful beams, from the radiance which shone in your letter, which raised our life from despondency to gladness? For thus, perhaps, it will not be unfitting to adapt the word of the prophet to our present blessings : "In the multitude of the sorrows which I had in my heart, the comforts of God," by your kindness, "have refreshed my soul," [3] like sunbeams, cheering and warming our life nipped by frost. For both reached the highest pitch—the severity of my troubles, I mean, on the one side, and the sweetness of your favours on the other. And if you have so gladdened us, by only sending us the joyful tidings of your coming, that everything changed for us from extremest woe to a bright condition, what will your precious and benign coming, even the sight of it, do? what consolation will the sound of your sweet voice in our ears afford our soul? May this speedily come to pass, by the good help of God, Who giveth respite from pain to the fainting, and rest to the afflicted. But be assured, that when we look at our own case we grieve exceedingly at the present state of things, and men cease not to tear us in pieces [4] : but when we turn our eyes to your excellence, we own that we have great cause for thankfulness to the dispensation of Divine Providence, that we are able to enjoy in your neighbourhood [5] your sweetness and good-will towards us, and feast at will on such food to satiety, if indeed there is such a thing as satiety of blessings like these.

LETTER VIII [6].

TO A STUDENT OF THE CLASSICS.

WHEN I was looking for some suitable and proper exordium, I mean of course from Holy Scripture, to put at the head of my letter, according to my usual custom, I did not know which to choose, not from inability to find what was suitable, but because I deemed it superfluous to write such things to those who knew nothing about the matter. For your eager pursuit of profane literature proved incontestably to us that you did not care about sacred. Accordingly I will say nothing about Bible texts, but will select a prelude adapted to your literary tastes taken from the poets you love so well. By the great master of your education there is introduced one, showing all an old man's joy, when after long affliction he once more beheld his son, and his son's son as well.

---

[10] θαυματοποιοῦντας . . . . θαυματοποιΐας : something more than ordinary mime playing, or than the optical illusion of tableaux-vivants, but less than what we should call conjuring seems to be meant (H. C. O.).
[1] τὰ κατάλληλα τῶν ἱστορουμένων.   [2] οἰκίστης αὐτοσχέδιος.

[3] Ps. xciv. 19.
[4] διαφοροῦντας. This letter is probably written during his exile, (375-8) and to Otreius, the bishop of Melitene. See Letter 14, note.
[5] ἐκ γειτόνων.   [6] Perhaps to Eupatrius (Cod. Medic.).

And the special theme of his exultation is the rivalry between the two, Ulysses and Telemachus, for the highest meed of valour, though it is true that the recollection of his own exploits against the Cephallenians adds to the point of his speech [7]. For you and your admirable father, when you welcomed me, as they did Laertes, in your affection, contended in most honourable rivalry for the prize of virtue, by showing us all possible respect and kindness; he in numerous ways which I need not here mention, and you by pelting me with [8] your letters from Cappadocia. What, then, of me the aged one? I count that day one to be blessed, in which I witness such a competition between father and son. May you, then, never cease from accomplishing the rightful prayer of an excellent and admirable father, and surpassing in your readiness to all good works the renown which from him you inherit. I shall be a judge acceptable to both of you, as I shall award you the first prize against your father, and the same to your father against you. And we will put up with rough Ithaca, rough not so much with stones as with the manners of the inhabitants, an island in which there are many suitors, who are suitors [9] most of all for the possessions of her whom they woo, 'and insult their intended bride by this very fact, that they threaten her chastity with marriage, acting in a way worthy of a Melantho, one might say, or some other such person; for nowhere is there a Ulysses to bring them to their senses with his bow. You see how in an old man's fashion I go maundering off into matters with which you have no concern. But pray let indulgence be readily extended to me in consideration of my grey hairs; for garrulity is just as characteristic of old age as to be blear-eyed, or for the limbs to fail [1]. But you by entertaining us with your brisk and lively language, like a bold young man as you are, will make our old age young again, supporting the feebleness of our length of days with this kind attention which so well becomes you.

---

[7] The text here seems hopelessly corrupt. Or the meaning may be, "Our main text shall be his exultation at the generous rivalry between Ulysses and Telemachus, though his mention of his exploits against the Cephallenians shall also contribute to illustrate our discussion;" but this can hardly be got out of the Greek. The reference is to *Odyssey*, xxiv. 514. Gregory was evidently fond of Homer: the comparison of Diomede to a winter torrent (*Iliad*, v. 87) is used *De Virginit.* c. 4: and Menelaus' words about the young and old (*Iliad*, iii. 108), c. 23: and in Letter II. of the seven edited by Caraccioli (Letter XV.) describing the gardens of Vanota, *Od.* vii. 115, xiii. 589. For other quotations from the classics see Letters XI. and XII. of this Series (H. C. O.).

[8] βάλλοντες, with allusion to the darts hurled by Ulysses and Telemachus (H. C. O.).

[9] Reading μνηστῆρες, for the unmeaning κρατῆρες; "they are suitors not so much for the hand of Penelope as for her money" (H. C. O.). The Medicean has βρωστῆρες, "devourers." Just below the allusion is to Melantho's rudely threatening Ulysses, and getting hanged for it.

[1] ὑπὸ τῆς τοῦ γήρως ἀπονοίας, an irrelevant phrase, and, as not necessary to the sense, here omitted in translation (H. C. O.).

LETTER IX.

AN INVITATION.

It is not the natural wont of spring to shine forth in its radiant beauty all at once, but there come as preludes of spring the sunbeam gently warming earth's frozen surface, and the bud half hidden beneath the clod, and breezes blowing over the earth, so that the fertilizing and generative power of the air penetrates deeply into it. One may see the fresh and tender grass, and the return of birds which winter had banished, and many such tokens, which are rather signs of spring, not spring itself. Not but that these are sweet, because they are indications of what is sweetest. What is the meaning of all that I have been saying? Why, since the expression of your kindness which reached us in your letters, as a forerunner of the treasures contained in you, with a goodly prelude brings the glad tidings of the blessing which we expect at your hands, we both welcome the boon which those letters convey, like some first-appearing flower of spring, and pray that we may soon enjoy in you the full beauty of the season. For, be well assured, we have been deeply, deeply distressed by the passions and spite of the people here, and their ways; and just as ice forms in cottages after the rains that come in—for I will draw my comparison from the weather of our part of the world [2],—and so moisture, when it gets in, if it spreads over the surface that is already frozen, becomes congealed about the ice, and an addition is made to the mass already existing, even so one may notice much the same kind of thing in the character of most of the people in this neighbourhood, how they are always plotting and inventing something spiteful, and a fresh mischief is congealed on the top of that which has been wrought before, and another one on the top of that, and then again another, and this goes on without intermission, and there is no limit to their hatred and to the increase of evils; so that we have great need of many prayers that the grace of the Spirit may speedily breathe upon them, and thaw the bitterness of their hatred, and melt the frost that is hardening upon them from their malice. For this cause the spring, sweet as it is by nature, becomes yet more to be desired than ever to those

---

[2] For the climate, cf. Sozomen, *H. E.* vi. 34: "I suppose that Galatia, Cappadocia, and the neighbouring provinces contained many other ecclesiastical philosophers at that time (*i. e.* reign of Valens). These monks, for the most part, dwelt in communities in cities and villages, for they did not habituate themselves to the tradition of their predecessors. The severity of the winter, which is always a natural feature of that country, would probably make a hermit life impracticable."

who after such storms look for you. Let not the boon, then, linger. Especially as our great holiday[3] is approaching, it would be more reasonable that the land which bare you should exult in her own treasures than that Pontus should in ours. Come then, dear one, bringing us a multitude of blessings, even yourself; for this will fill up the measure of our beatitude.

LETTER X[4].

TO LIBANIUS.

I ONCE heard a medical man tell of a wonderful freak of nature. And this was his story. A man was ill of an unmanageable complaint, and began to find fault with the medical faculty, as being able to do far less than it professed; for everything that was devised for his cure was ineffectual. Afterwards when some good news beyond his hopes was brought him, the occurrence did the work of the healing art, by putting an end to his disease. Whether it were that the soul by the overflowing sense of release from anxiety, and by a sudden rebound, disposed the body to be in the same condition as itself, or in some other way, I cannot say : 'for I have no leisure to enter upon such disquisitions, and the person who told me did not specify the cause. But I have just called to mind the story very seasonably, as I think : for when I was not as well as I could wish—now I need not tell you exactly the causes of all the worries which befel me from the time I was with you to the present,—after some one told me all at once of the letter which had arrived from your unparalleled Erudition, as soon as I got the epistle and ran over what you had written, forthwith, first my soul was affected in the same way as though I had been proclaimed before all the world as the hero of most glorious achievements—so highly did I value the testimony which you favoured me with in your letter,—and then also my bodily health immediately began to improve : and I afford an example of the same marvel as the story which I told you just now, in that I was ill when I read one half of the letter, and well when I read the other half of the same. Thus much for those matters. But now, since Cynegius was

the occasion of that favour, you are able, in the overflowing abundance of your ability to do good, not only to benefit us, but also our benefactors ; and he is a benefactor of ours, as has been said before, by having been the cause and occasion of our having a letter from you; and for this reason he well deserves both our good offices. But if you ask who are our teachers,—if indeed we are thought to have learned anything,—you will find that they are Paul and John, and the rest of the Apostles and Prophets ; if I do not seem to speak too boldly in claiming any knowledge of that art in which you so excel, that competent judges declare[5] that the rules of oratory stream down from you, as from an overflowing spring, upon all who have any pretensions to excellence in that department. This I have heard the admirable Basil say to everybody, Basil, who was your disciple, but my father and teacher. But be assured, first, that I found no rich nourishment in the precepts of my teachers[6], inasmuch as I enjoyed my brother's society only for a short time, and got only just enough polish from his diviner tongue to be able to discern the ignorance of those who are uninitiated in oratory ; next, however, that whenever I had leisure, I devoted my time and energies to this study, and so became enamoured of your beauty, though I never yet obtained the object of my passion. If, then, on the one side we never had a teacher, which I deem to have been our case, and if on the other it is improper to suppose that the opinion which you entertain of us is other than the true one—nay, you are correct in your statement, and we are not quite contemptible in your judgment,—give me leave to presume to attribute to you the cause of such proficiency as we may have attained. For if Basil was the author of our oratory, and if his wealth came from your treasures, then what we possess is yours, even though we received it through others. But if our attainments are scanty, so is the water in a jar; still it comes from the Nile.

LETTER XI.

TO LIBANIUS.

IT was a custom with the Romans[7] to celebrate a feast in winter-time, after the custom of

---

3 For such invitations, cf. Greg. Naz. *Epist.* 99, 100, 102.

4 This and the following letter appear to have been written when Gregory still publicly professed *belles lettres*. They are addressed to one of the masters whom Basil had had at Athens. For these see Socrates, *H. E.* iv. 26 : it was probably Libanius ; rather than Prohæresius, who did not live in Asia Minor, or Himærius, who (according to Eunapius, *Philosoph. Vit.* p. 126) had become a Christian before the reign of Julian, and it is clear that this Letter is written to a pagan. The Cod. Medic. has Libanius' name as a title to both Letters. No Letter to Gregory certainly is to be found amongst Libanius' unpublished Letters in the Vatican Library, as Zacagni himself testifies : but no conclusion can be drawn from this.

5 This passage as it stands is unmanageable. The Latin translator appears to give the sense required, but it is hard to see how it can be got out of the words (H. C. O.).

6 ἴσθι με μηδὲν ἔχοντα λιπαρὸν (MS. λυπρὸν) ἐν τοῖς τῶν διδασκάλων διηγήμασιν : but τοῦ διδασκάλου perhaps should be read instead of τῶν διδασκάλων (H. C. O.).

7 The custom of New Year's gifts (strenarum commercium) had been discontinued by Tiberius, because of the trouble it involved to himself, and abolished by Claudius : but in these times it had been revived. We find mention of it in the reigns of Theodosius, and of Arcadius ; Auson. *Ep.* xviii. 4 ; Symmach. *Ep.* x. 28.

their fathers, when the length of the days begins to draw out, as the sun climbs to the upper regions of the sky. Now the beginning of the month is esteemed holy, and by this day auguring the character of the whole year, they devote themselves to forecasting lucky accidents, gladness, and wealth [8]. What is my object in beginning my letter in this way? Why, I do so because I too kept this feast, having got my present of gold as well as any of them; for then there came into my hands as well as theirs gold, not like that vulgar gold, which potentates treasure and which those that have it give,— that heavy, vile, and soulless possession,—but that which is loftier than all wealth, as Pindar says [9], in the eyes of those that have sense, being the fairest presentation, I mean your letter, and the vast wealth which it contained. For thus it happened; that on that day, as I was going to the metropolis of the Cappadocians, I met an acquaintance, who handed me this present, your letter, as a new year's gift. And I, being overjoyed at the occurrence, threw open my treasure to all who were present; and all shared in it, each getting the whole of it, without any rivalry, and I was none the worse off. For the letter by passing through the hands of all, like a ticket for a feast, is the private wealth of each, some by steady continuous reading engraving the words upon their memory, and others taking an impression [10] of them upon tablets; and it was again in my hands, giving me more pleasure than the hard [1] metal does to the eyes of the rich. Since, then, even to husbandmen—to use a homely comparison—approbation of the labours which they have already accomplished is a strong stimulus to those which follow, bear with us if we treat what you have yourself given as so much seed, and if we write that we may provoke you to write back. But I beg of you a public and general boon for our life; that you will no longer entertain the purpose which you expressed to us in a dark hint at the end of your letter. For I do not think that it is at all a fair decision to come to, that,—because there are some who disgrace themselves by deserting from the Greek language to the barbarian, becoming mercenary soldiers and choosing a soldier's rations instead of the renown of eloquence,—you should therefore condemn oratory altogether, and sentence human life to be as voiceless as that of beasts. For who is he who will open his lips, if you carry into effect this severe sentence against oratory? But perhaps it will be well to remind you of a passage in our Scriptures. For our Word bids those that can to do good,

not looking at the tempers of those who receive the benefit, so as to be eager to benefit only those who are sensible of kindness, while we close our beneficence to the unthankful, but rather to imitate the Disposer of all, Who distributes the good things of His creation alike to all, to the good and to the evil. Having regard to this, admirable Sir, show yourself in your way of life such an one as the time past has displayed you. For those who do not see the sun do not thereby hinder the sun's existence. Even so neither is it right that the beams of your eloquence should be dimmed, because of those who are purblind as to the perceptions of the soul. But as for Cynegius, I pray that he may be as far as possible from the common malady, which now has seized upon young men; and that he will devote himself of his own accord to the study of rhetoric. But if he is otherwise disposed, it is only right, even if he be unwilling, he should be forced to it; so as to avoid the unhappy and discreditable plight in which they now are, who have previously abandoned the pursuit of oratory.

LETTER XII [2].

ON HIS WORK AGAINST EUNOMIUS.

WE Cappadocians are poor in well-nigh all things that make the possessors of them happy, but above all we are badly off for people who are able to write. This, be sure, is the reason why I am so slow about sending you a letter: for, though my reply to the heresy (of Eunomius) had been long ago completed, there was no one to transcribe it. Such a dearth of writers it was that brought upon us the suspicion of sluggishness or of inability to frame an answer. But since now at any rate, thank God, the writer and reviser have come, I have sent this treatise to you; not, as Isocrates says [3], as a present, for I do not reckon it to be such that it should be received in lieu of something of substantial value, but that it may be in our power to cheer on those who are in the full vigour of youth to do battle with the enemy, by stirring up the naturally sanguine temperament of early life. But if any portion of the treatise should appear worthy of serious consideration, after examining some parts, especially those prefatory to the "trials," [4] and those which are of the same cast, and perhaps also some

---

[8] Or, not improbably, " they contrive lucky meetings, festivities, and contributions."

[9] Pindar, *Ol.* i. 1: ὁ δὲ χρυσὸς, αἰθόμενον πῦρ ἅτε διαπρέπει νυκτὸς, μεγαλάνορος ἔξοχα πλούτου.

[10] ἐναπομορξαμένων.　　　　[1] ἀπόκροτον.

[2] The Cod. Medic. has "to John and Maximinian." In this letter but one person seems to be addressed. Gregory here speaks, without doubt, of his books against Eunomius: not of his *Antirrhetic against Apollinaris*, which could have been transcribed in a very short time. Therefore we can place the date about 383, some months after Gregory's twelve Books against Eunomius, according to Hermantius, were published.　　[3] *Oratio ad Demonicum*.

[4] See *Against Eunomius*, I. 1—9.

of the doctrinal parts of the book, you will think them not ungracefully composed. But to whatever conclusion you come, you will of course read them, as to a teacher and corrector, to those who do not act like the players at ball[5], when they stand in three different places and throw it from one to the other, aiming it exactly and catching one ball from one and one from another, and they baffle the player who is in the middle, as he jumps up to catch it, pretending that they are going to throw with a made-up expression of face, and such and such a motion of the hand to left or right, and whichever way they see him hurrying, they send the ball just the contrary way, and cheat his expectation by a trick. This holds even now in the case of most of us, who, dropping all serious purpose, play at being good-natured[6], as if at ball, with men, instead of realizing the favourable hope which we hold out, beguiling to sinister[7] issues the souls of those who repose confidence in us. Letters of reconciliation, caresses, tokens, presents, affectionate embrace by letters—these are the making as if to throw with the ball to the right. But instead of the pleasure which one expects therefrom, one gets accusations, plots, slanders, disparagement, charges brought against one, bits of a sentence torn from their context, caught up, and turned to one's hurt. Blessed in your hopes are ye, who through all such trials exercise confidence towards God. But we beseech you not to look at our words, but to the teaching of our Lord in the Gospel. For what consolation to one in anguish can another be, who surpasses him in the extremity of his own anguish, to help his luckless fortunes to obtain their proper issue? As He saith, "Vengeance is Mine; I will repay, saith the Lord." But do you, best of men, go on in a manner worthy of yourself, and trust in God, and do not be hindered by the spectacle of our misfortunes from being good and true, but commit to God that judgeth righteously the suitable and just issue of events, and act as Divine wisdom guides you. Assuredly Joseph had in the result no reason to grieve at the envy of his brethren, inasmuch as the malice of his own kith and kin became to him the road to empire.

---

5 *i. e.* the game of φαινίνδα : called also ἐφετίνδα by Hesychius.
6 ἐν εὐφυΐα.
7 It is difficult to reproduce the play upon words in δεξιᾶς, and σκαιότητι, which refer to the κατὰ τὸ δέξιον ἢ εὐώνυμον in the description of the game of ball : the words having both a local meaning, "right," and "left," and a metaphorical one, "favourable," and "sinister" (H. C. O.).

LETTER XIII.

TO THE CHURCH AT NICOMEDIA[8].

MAY the Father of mercies and the God of all comfort, Who disposeth all things in wisdom for the best, visit you by His own grace, and comfort you by Himself, working in you that which is well-pleasing to Him, and may the grace of our Lord Jesus Christ come upon you, and the fellowship of the Holy Spirit, that ye may have healing of all tribulation and affliction, and advance towards all good, for the perfecting of the Church, for the edification of your souls, and to the praise of the glory of His name. But in making here a defence of ourselves before your charity, we would say that we were not neglectful to render an account of the charge entrusted to us, either in time past, or since the departure hence of Patricius of blessed memory; but we insist that there were many troubles in our Church, and the decay of our bodily powers was great, increasing, as was natural, with advancing years; and great also was the remissness of your Excellency towards us, inasmuch as no word ever came by letter to induce us to undertake the task, nor was any connection kept up between your Church and ourselves, although Euphrasius, your Bishop of blessed memory, had in all holiness bound together our Humility to himself and to you with love, as with chains. But even though the debt of love has not been satisfied before, either by our taking charge of you, or your Piety's encouragement of us, now at any rate we pray to God, taking your prayer to God as an ally to our own desire, that we may with all speed possible visit you, and be comforted along with you, and along with you show diligence, as the Lord may direct us; so as to discover a means of rectifying the disorders which have already found place, and of securing safety for the future, so that you may no longer be distracted by this discord, one withdrawing himself from the Church in one direction, another in another, and be thereby exposed as a laughing-stock to the Devil, whose desire and business it is (in direct contrariety to the Divine will) that no one should be saved, or come to the knowledge of the truth. For how do you think, brethren, that we were afflicted upon hearing from those who reported to us your state, that there was no return to better things[9]; but that the resolution

---

8 Euphrasius, mentioned in this Letter, had subscribed to the *first* Council of Constantinople, as Bishop of Nicomedia. On his death, clergy and laity proceeded to a joint election of a successor. The date of this is uncertain; Zacagni and Page think that the dispute here mentioned is to be identified with that which Sozomen records, and which is placed by Baronius and Basnage in 400, 401. But we have no evidence that Gregory's life was prolonged so far.
9 οὐδεμία γέγονε τῶν ἐφεστώτων ἐπιστροφή, literally, "no return

of those who had once swerved aside is ever carried along in the same course ; and—as water from a conduit often overflows the neighbouring bank, and streaming off sideways, flows away, and unless the leak is stopped, it is almost impossible to recall it to its channel, when the submerged ground has been hollowed out in accordance with the course of the stream,—even so the course of those who have left the Church, when it has once through personal motives deflected from the straight and right faith, has sunk deep in the rut of habit, and does not easily return to the grace it once had. For which cause your affairs demand a wise and strong administrator, who is skilled to guide such wayward tempers aright, so as to be able to recall to its pristine beauty the disorderly circuit of this stream, that the corn-fields of your piety may once again flourish abundantly, watered by the irrigating stream of peace. For this reason great diligence and fervent desire on the part of you all is needed for this matter, that such an one may be appointed your President by the Holy Spirit, who will have a single eye to the things of God alone, not turning his glance this way or that to any of those things that men strive after. For for this cause I think that the ancient law gave the Levite no share in the general inheritance of the land; that he might have God alone for the portion of his possession, and might always be engaged about the possession in himself, with no eye to any material object.

[What follows is unintelligible, and something has probably been lost.]

For it is not lawful that the simple should meddle with that with which they have no concern, but which properly belongs to others. For you should each mind your own business, that so that which is most expedient may come about [and that your Church may again prosper], when those who have been dispersed have returned again to the unity of the one body, and spiritual peace is established by those who devoutly glorify God. To this end it is well, I think, to look out for high qualifications in your election, that he who is appointed to the Presidency may be suitable for the post. Now the Apostolic injunctions do not direct us to look to high birth, wealth, and distinction in the eyes of the world among the virtues of a Bishop; but if all this should, unsought, accompany your spiritual chiefs, we do not reject it, but consider it merely as a shadow accidentally [10] following the body; and none the less

shall we welcome the more precious endowments, even though they happen to be apart from those boons of fortune. The prophet Amos was a goat-herd; Peter was a fisherman, and his brother Andrew followed the same employment; so too was the sublime John; Paul was a tentmaker, Matthew a publican, and the rest of the Apostles in the same way—not consuls, generals, prefects, or distinguished in rhetoric and philosophy, but poor, and of none of the learned professions, but starting from the more humble occupations of life : and yet for all that their voice went out into all the earth, and their words unto the ends of the world. "Consider your calling, brethren, that not many wise after the flesh, not many mighty, not many noble are called, but God hath chosen the foolish things of the world [11]." Perhaps even now it is thought something foolish, as things appear to men, when one is not able to do much from poverty, or is slighted because of meanness of extraction [1], not of character. But who knows whether the horn of anointing is not poured out by grace upon such an one, even though he be less than the lofty and more illustrious? Which was more to the interest of the Church at Rome, that it should at its commencement be presided over by some high-born and pompous senator, or by the fisherman Peter, who had none of this world's advantages to attract men to him [2]? What house had he, what slaves, what property ministering luxury, by wealth constantly flowing in? But that stranger, without a table, without a roof over his head, was richer than those who have all things, because through having nothing he had God wholly. So too the people of Mesopotamia, though they had among them wealthy satraps, preferred Thomas above them all to the presidency of their Church; the Cretans preferred Titus, the dwellers at Jerusalem James, and we Cappadocians the centurion, who at the Cross acknowledged the Godhead of the Lord, though there were many at that time of splendid lineage, whose fortunes enabled them to maintain a stud, and who prided themselves upon having the first place in the Senate. And in all the Church one may see those who are great according to God's standard preferred above worldly magnificence. You too, I think, ought to have an eye to these spiritual qualifications at this time present, if you really mean to revive the ancient glory of your Church. For nothing is better known to you than your own history, that anciently, before the city near you [3] flourished,

---

from existing (or besetting) evils." The words might possibly mean something very different; "no concern shown on the part of those set over you " (H. C. O.).

[10] The shadow may be considered as an accidental appendage to the body, inasmuch as it does not always appear, but only when there is some light, e. g. of the sun, to cast it (H. C. O.).

[11] 1 Cor. i. 26, 27.

[1] σώματος δυσγένειαν, might possibly mean "bodily deformity ; " but less probably (H. C. O.).

[2] Reading ἐφολκόν: if ἐφόλκιον, "a boat taken in tow," perhaps still regarding S. Peter as the master of a ship : or "an appendage;" Gregory so uses it in his De Animâ. Some suggest ἐφόδιον, meaning "resource," but ἐφολκόν is simpler.

[3] i. e. Nicæa. "The whirligig of time has brought about its

the seat of government was with you, and among Bithynian cities there was nothing pre-eminent above yours. And now, it is true, the public buildings that once graced it have dis-appeared, but the city that consists in men—whether we look to numbers or to quality—is rapidly rising to a level with its former splendour. Accordingly it would well become you to enter-tain thoughts that shall not fall below the height of the blessings that now are yours, but to raise your enthusiasm in the work before you to the height of the magnificence of your city, that you may find such a one to preside over the laity as will prove himself not unworthy of you [4]. For it is disgraceful, brethren, and utterly monstrous, that while no one ever becomes a pilot unless he is skilled in navigation, he who sits at the helm of the Church should not know how to bring the souls of those who sail with him safe into the haven of God. How many wrecks of Churches, men and all, have ere now taken place by the inexperience of their heads! Who can reckon what disasters might not have been avoided, had there been aught of the pilot's skill in those who had command? Nay, we entrust iron, to make vessels with, not to those who know nothing about the matter, but to those who are acquainted with the art of the smith; ought we not therefore to trust souls to him who is well-skilled to soften them by the fervent heat of the Holy Spirit, and who by the impress of rational implements may fashion each one of you to be a chosen and useful vessel? It is thus that the inspired Apostle bids us to take thought, in his Epistle to Timothy [5], laying injunction upon all who hear, when he says that a Bishop must be without reproach. Is this all that the Apostle cares for, that he who is advanced to the priesthood should be irreproachable? and what is so great an advantage as that all possible qualifications should be included in one? But he knows full well that the subject is moulded by the character of his superior, and that the upright walk of the guide becomes that of his followers too. For what the Master is, such does he make the disciple to be. For it is impossible that he who has been apprenticed to the art of the smith should practise that of the weaver, or that one who has only been taught to work at the loom should turn out an orator or a mathematician: but on the contrary that which the disciple sees in his master he adopts and transfers to himself. For this reason it is that the Scripture says, "Every disciple that is perfect shall be as his master [6]." What then, brethren? Is it possible to be lowly and subdued in character, moderate, superior to the love of lucre, wise in things divine, and trained to virtue and considerateness in works and ways, without seeing those quali-ties in one's master? Nay, I do not know how a man can become spiritual, if he has been a disciple in a worldly school. For how can they who are striving to resemble their master fail to be like him? What advantage is the magnificence of the aqueduct to the thirsty, if there is no water in it, even though the symmetrical disposition of columns [7] variously shaped rear aloft the pedi-ment [8]? Which would the thirsty man rather choose for the supply of his own need, to see marbles beautifully disposed or to find good spring water, even if it flowed through a wooden pipe, as long as the stream which it poured forth was clear and drinkable? Even so, brethren, those who look to godliness should neglect the trappings of outward show, and whether a man exults in powerful friends, or plumes himself on the long list of his dignities, or boasts that he receives large annual revenues, or is puffed up with the thought of his noble ancestry, or has his mind on all sides clouded [9] with the fumes of self-esteem, should have nothing to do with such an one, any more than with a dry aqueduct, if he display not in his life the primary and essential qualities for high office. But, employing the lamp of the Spirit for the search [10], you should, as far as is possible, seek for "a garden enclosed, a fountain sealed [11]," that, by your election the garden of delight having been opened and the water of the fountain having been unstopped, there may be a common acquisition to the Catholic Church. May God grant that there may soon be found among you such an one, who shall be a chosen vessel, a pillar of the Church. But we trust in the Lord that so it will be, if you are minded by the grace of con-cord with one mind to see that which is good, preferring to your own wills the will of the Lord, and that which is approved of Him, and perfect, and well-pleasing in His eyes; that there may be such a happy issue among you, that therein

---

revenge," and Nicomedia (Ismid) is now more important than Nicæa (Isnik). Nicomedia had, in fact, been the residence of the Kings of Bithynia; and Diocletian had intended to make it the rival of Rome (cf. Lactantius, *De Mort. Persec.* c. 7). But it had been destroyed by an earthquake in the year 368: Socrates, ii. 39.

[4] Reading ὑμῶν for ὑμῖν.   [5] 1 Tim. iii. 2.

[6] S. Luke vi. 40. Cf. Gregory's Treatises *On Perfection, What is the Christian name and profession, Sketch of the aim of True Asceticism.*
[7] ἡ τῶν κιόνων ἐπάλληλος θέσις.   [8] πέτασον.   [9] περιαυτίζεται.
[10] For humility and spirituality required in prelates, cf. Origen, c. *Cels.* viii. 75. "We summon to the magistracies of these churches men of ability and good life: but instead of selecting the ambitious amongst these we put compulsion upon those whose deep humility makes them backward in accepting this general charge of the Church. Our best rulers then, are like consuls compelled to rule by a mighty Emperor: no other, we are persuaded, than the Son of God, Who is the Word of God. If, then, these magistrates in the assembly of God's nation rule well, or at all events strictly in accordance with the Divine enactment, they are not because of that to meddle with the secular law-making. It is not that the Christians wish to escape all public responsibility, that they keep themselves away from such things: but they wish to reserve themselves for the higher and more urgent responsibilities (ἀναγκαιοτέρᾳ λειτουργίᾳ) of God's Church." [11] Song of Songs, iv. 12.

we may rejoice, and you triumph, and the God of all be glorified, Whom glory becometh for ever and ever.

LETTER XIV [12].

TO THE BISHOP OF MELITENE.

How beautiful are the likenesses of beautiful objects, when they preserve in all its clearness the impress of the original beauty! For of your soul, so truly beautiful, I saw a most clear image in the sweetness of your letter, which, as the Gospel says, "out of the abundance of the heart" you filled with honey. And for this reason I fancied I saw you in person, and enjoyed your cheering company. from the affection expressed in your letter; and often taking your letter into my hands and going over it again from beginning to end, I only came more vehemently to crave for the enjoyment, and there was no sense of satiety. Such a feeling can no more put an end to my pleasure, than it can to that derived from anything that is by nature beautiful and precious. For neither has our constant participation of the benefit blunted the edge of our longing to behold the sun, nor does the unbroken enjoyment of health prevent our desiring its continuance; and we are persuaded that it is equally impossible for our enjoyment of your goodness, which we have often experienced face to face and now by letter, ever to reach the point of satiety. But our case is like that of those who from some circumstance are afflicted with unquenchable thirst; for just in the same way, the more we taste your kindness, the more thirsty we become. But unless you suppose our language to be mere blandishment and unreal flattery—and assuredly you will not so suppose, being what you are in all else, and to us especially good and staunch, if any one ever was,—you will certainly believe what I say; that the favour of your letter, applied to my eyes like some medical prescription, stayed my ever-flowing "fountain of tears," and that fixing our hopes on the medicine of your holy prayers, we expect that soon and completely the disease of our soul will be healed : though, for the present at any rate, we are in such a case, that we spare the ears of one who is fond of us, and bury the truth in silence, that we may not drag those who loyally love us into partnership with our

troubles. For when we consider that, bereft of what is dearest to us, we are involved in wars, and that it is our children that we were compelled to leave behind, our children whom we were counted worthy to bear to God in spiritual pangs, closely joined to us by the law of love, who at the time of their own trials amid their afflictions extended their affection to us ; and over and above these, a fondly-loved [1] home, brethren, kinsmen, companions, intimate associates, friends, hearth, table, cellar, bed, seat, sack, converse, tears—and how sweet these are, and how dearly prized from long habit, I need not write to you who know full well—but not to weary you further, consider for yourself what I have in exchange for those blessings. Now that I am at the end of my life, I begin to live again, and am compelled to learn the graceful versatility of character which is now in vogue : but we are late learners in the shifty school of knavery; [2] so that we are constantly constrained to blush at our awkwardness and inaptitude for this new study. But our adversaries, equipped with all the training of this wisdom, are well able to keep what they have learned, and to invent what they have not learned. Their method of warfare accordingly is to skirmish at a distance, and then at a preconcerted signal to form their phalanx in solid order ; they utter by way of prelude [3] whatever suits their interests, they execute surprises by means of exaggerations, they surround themselves with allies from every quarter. But a vast amount of cunning invincible in power [4] accompanies them, advanced before them to lead their host, like some right-and-left-handed combatant, fighting with both hands in front of his army, on one side levying tribute upon his subjects, on the other smiting those who come in his way. But if you care to inquire into the state of our internal affairs, you will find other troubles to match; a stifling hut, abundant in cold, gloom, confinement, and all such advantages; a life the mark of every one's censorious observation, the voice, the look, the way of wearing one's cloak, the movement of the hands, the position of one's feet, and everything else, all a subject for busy-bodies. And unless one from time to time emits a deep breathing, and unless a continuous groaning is uttered with the breathing, and unless the tunic passes gracefully through the girdle (not to mention the very disuse of the girdle itself), and unless our cloak flows aslant down our backs—the omission of any one of these niceties is a pretext for war against

---

[12] To Otreius, Bishop of Melitene (in eastern Cappadocia, on or near the upper Euphrates), to whose successor Letoius Gregory addressed his *Canonical Epistle* about Penitents (Cod. Medic.). Written when Gregory was in exile under Valens. Zacagni thinks that the "war," and the carping criticisms here complained of, refer to the followers of Eustathius of Sebasteia or of Macedonius, who had plenty to find fault with, even in the gestures and dress of the Catholics (cf. Basil, *De Spiri. S.*, end).

[1] κεχαριτωμένος.
[2] This passage is very corrupt, and I have put the best sense I could on the fragmentary words preserved to us (H. C. O.).
[3] προλογίζοντας. But προλοχίζοντας would suit the context better ; *i. e.* "they lay an ambush wherever their interests are concerned" (H. C. O.).
[4] Or "accompanies their power :" τῇ δυνάμει may go with ὁμαρτεῖ, or with ἀκαταγώνιστος (H. C. O.).

us. And on such grounds as these, they gather together to battle against us, man by man [5], township by township, even down to all sorts of out-of-the-way places. Well, one cannot be always faring well or always ill, for every one's life is made up of contraries. But if by God's grace your help should stand by us steadily, we will bear the abundance of annoyances, in the hope of being always a sharer in your goodness. May you, then, never cease bestowing on us such favours, that by them you may refresh us, and prepare for yourself in ampler measure the reward promised to them that keep the commandments.

LETTER XV.

TO ADELPHIUS THE LAWYER [6].

I WRITE you this letter from the sacred Vanota, if I do not do the place injustice by giving it its local title :—do it injustice, I say, because in its name it shows no polish. At the same time the beauty of the place, great as it is, is not conveyed by this Galatian epithet : eyes are needed to interpret its beauty. For I, though I have before this seen much, and that in many places, and have also observed many things by means of verbal description in the accounts of old writers, think both all I have seen, and all of which I have heard, of no account in comparison with the loveliness that is to be found here. Your Helicon is nothing : the Islands of the Blest are a fable : the Sicyonian plain is a trifle : the accounts of the Peneus are another case of poetic exaggeration—that river which they say by overflowing with its rich current the banks which flank its course makes for the Thessalians their far-famed Tempe. Why, what beauty is there in any one of these places I have mentioned, such as Vanota can show us of its own? For if one seeks for natural beauty in the place, it needs none of the adorn-

ments of art : and if one considers what has been done for it by artificial aid, there has been so much done, and that so well, as might overcome even natural disadvantages. The gifts bestowed upon the spot by Nature who beautifies the earth with unstudied grace are such as these : below, the river Halys makes the place fair to look upon with his banks, and gleams like a golden ribbon through their deep purple, reddening his current with the soil he washes down. Above, a mountain densely overgrown with wood stretches with its long ridge, covered at all points with the foliage of oaks, worthy of finding some Homer to sing its praises more than that Ithacan Neritus, which the poet calls "far-seen with quivering leaves [7]." But the natural growth of wood, as it comes down the hill-side, meets at the foot the planting of men's husbandry. For forthwith vines, spread out over the slopes, and swellings, and hollows at the mountain's base, cover with their colour, like a green mantle, all the lower ground : and the season at this time even added to their beauty, displaying its grape-clusters wonderful to behold. Indeed this caused me . yet more surprise, that while the neighbouring country shows fruit still unripe, one might here enjoy the full clusters, and be sated with their perfection. Then, far off, like a watch-fire from some great beacon, there shone before our eyes the fair beauty of the buildings. On the left as we entered was the chapel built for the martyrs, not yet complete in its structure, but still lacking the roof, yet making a good show notwithstanding. Straight before us in the way were the beauties of the house, where one part is marked out from another by some delicate invention. There were projecting towers, and preparations for banqueting among the wide and high-arched rows of trees crowning the entrance before the gates [8]. Then about the buildings are the Phaeacian gardens ; rather, let not the beauties of Vanota be insulted by comparison with those Homer never saw "the apple with bright fruit [9]" as we have it here, approaching to the hue of its own blossom in the exceeding brilliancy of its colouring : he never saw the pear whiter than new-polished ivory. And what can one say of the varieties of the peach, diverse and multiform, yet blended and compounded out of different species? For just as with those who paint "goat-stags," and "centaurs," and the like, commingling things of different kind, and making themselves wiser than Nature, so it is in the case of this fruit : Nature, under the despotism of art, turns one to an almond, an-

---

[5] κατ' ἄνδρας, καὶ δήμους, καὶ ἐσχατίας. But the Latin, having "solitudines," shows that ἐρήμους was read for δήμους. We seem to get here a glimpse of Gregory's activity during his exile (376-78). Rupp thinks that Macrina's words to her brother also refer to this period : "Thee the Churches call to help them and correct them." He moved from place to place to strengthen the Catholic cause ; "we," he says in the longer *Antirrhetic*, "who have sojourned in many spots, and have had serious conversation upon the points in dispute both with those who hold and those who reject the Faith." Gregory of Nazianzum consoles him during these journeys, so exhausting and discouraging to one of his spirit, by comparing him to the comet which is ruled while it seems to wander, and by seeing in the seeming advance of heresy only the last hiss of the dying snake. His travels probably ended in a visit to Palestine : for his Letter *On Pilgrimages* certainly presupposes former visits in which he had learnt the manners of Jerusalem. His love of Origen, too, makes it likely that he made a private pilgrimage (distinct from the visit of 379) to the land where Origen had chiefly studied.

[6] σχολαστικὸς, or possibly "student," but the title of λογιστής, afterwards employed of the person to whom the letter is addressed, rather suggests the profession of an "advocate," than the occupation of a scholar.

---

[7] Cf. Hom. *Odyss.* ix. 22.

[8] The text is clearly erroneous, and perhaps στεφανοῦσι is the true reading : it seems clearer in construction than στεφανοῦσαι suggested by Caraccioli.   [9] Cf. Hom. *Od.* vii. 115.

other to a walnut, yet another to a " Doracinus [1]," mingled alike in name and in flavour. And in all these the number of single trees is more noted than their beauty; yet they display tasteful arrangement in their planting, and that harmonious form of drawing—drawing, I call it, for the marvel belongs rather to the painter's art than to the gardener's. So readily does Nature fall in with the design of those who arrange these devices, that it seems impossible to express this by words. Who could find words worthily to describe the road under the climbing vines, and the sweet shade of their cluster, and that novel wall-structure where roses with their shoots, and vines with their trailers, twist themselves together and make a fortification that serves as a wall against a flank attack, and the pond at the summit of this path, and the fish that are bred there? As regards all these, the people who have charge of your Nobility's house were ready to act as our guides with a certain ingenuous kindliness, and pointed them out to us, showing us each of the things you had taken pains about, as if it were yourself to whom, by our means, they were showing courtesy. There too, one of the lads, like a conjuror, showed us such a wonder as one does not very often find in nature: for he went down to the deep water and brought up at will such of the fish as he selected; and they seemed no strangers to the fisherman's touch, being tame and submissive under the artist's hands, like well-trained dogs. Then they led me to a house as if to rest—a house, I call it, for such the entrance betokened, but, when we came inside, it was not a house but a portico which received us. The portico was raised up aloft to a great height over a deep pool: the basement supporting the portico of triangular shape, like a gateway leading to the delights within, was washed by the water. Straight before us in the interior a sort of house occupied the vertex of the triangle, with lofty roof, lit on all sides by the sun's rays, and decked with varied paintings; so that this spot almost made us forget what had preceded it. The house attracted us to itself; and again, the portico on the pool was a unique sight. For the excellent fish would swim up from the depths to the surface, leaping up into the very air like winged things, as though purposely mocking us creatures of the dry land. For showing half their form and tumbling through the air, they plunged once more into the depth. Others, again, in shoals, following one another in order, were a sight for unaccustomed eyes: while in another place one might see another shoal packed in a cluster round a morsel of bread, pushed aside

one by another, and here one leaping up, there another diving downwards. But even this we were made to forget by the grapes that were brought us in baskets of twisted shoots, by the varied bounty of the season's fruit, the preparation for breakfast, the varied dainties, and savoury dishes, and sweetmeats, and drinking of healths, and wine-cups. So now since I was sated and inclined to sleep, I got a scribe posted beside me, and sent to your Eloquence, as if it were a dream, this chattering letter. But I hope to recount in full to yourself and your friends, not with paper and ink, but with my own voice and tongue, the beauties of your home.

LETTER XVI.

TO AMPHILOCHIUS.

I AM well persuaded that by God's grace the business of the Church of the Martyrs is in a fair way. Would that you were willing in the matter. The task we have in hand will find its end by the power of God, Who is able, wherever He speaks, to turn word into deed. Seeing that, as the Apostle says, "He Who has begun a good work will also perform it [2]", I would exhort you in this also to be an imitator of the great Paul, and to advance our hope to actual fulfilment, and send us so many workmen as may suffice for the work we have in hand.

Your Perfection might perhaps be informed by calculation of the dimensions to which the total work will attain: and to this end I will endeavour to explain the whole structure by a verbal description. The form of the chapel is a cross, which has its figure completed throughout, as you would expect, by four structures. The junctions of the buildings intercept one another, as we see everywhere in the cruciform pattern. But within the cross there lies a circle, divided by eight angles (I call the octagonal figure a circle in view of its circumference), in such wise that the two pairs of sides of the octagon which are diametrically opposed to one another, unite by means of arches the central circle to the adjoining blocks of building; while the other four sides of the octagon, which lie between the quadrilateral buildings, will not themselves be carried to meet the buildings, but upon each of them will be described a semicircle like a shell [3], terminating in an arch above: so that the arches will be eight in all, and by their means the quadrilateral and semicircular buildings will be connected, side by side, with the central

---

[1] The word seems otherwise unknown. It may be a Græcizing of the Latin "*duracinus*," for which cf. *Plin.* XV. xii. 11.

[2] Cf. Phil. i. 6.　　　[3] Reading κογχοειδῶς.

structure. In the blocks of masonry formed by the angles there will be an equal number of pillars, at once for ornament and for strength, and these again will carry arches built of equal size to correspond with those within[4]. And above these eight arches, with the symmetry of an upper range of windows, the octagonal building will be raised to the height of four cubits : the part rising from it will be a cone shaped like a top, as the vaulting[5] narrows the figure of the roof from its full width to a pointed wedge. The dimensions below will be,—the width of each of the quadrilateral buildings, eight cubits, the length of them half as much again, the height as much as the proportion of the width allows. It will be as much in the semicircles also. The whole length between the piers extends in the same way to eight cubits, and the depth will be as much as will be given by the sweep of the compasses with the fixed point placed in the middle of the side[6] and extending to the end. The height will be determined in this case too by the proportion to the width. And the thickness of the wall, an interval of three feet from inside these spaces, which are measured internally, will run round the whole building.

I have troubled your Excellency with this serious trifling, with this intention, that by the thickness of the walls, and by the intermediate spaces, you may accurately ascertain what sum the number of feet gives as the measurement ; because your intellect is exceedingly quick in all matters, and makes its way, by God's grace, in whatever subject you will, and it is possible for you, by subtle calculation, to ascertain the sum made up by all the parts, so as to send us masons neither more nor fewer than our need requires. And I beg you to direct your attention specially to this point, that some of them may be skilled in making vaulting[7] without supports : for I am informed that when built in this way it is more durable than what is made to rest on props. It is the scarcity of wood that brings us to this device of roofing the whole fabric with stone ; because the place supplies no timber for roofing. Let your unerring mind be persuaded, because some of the people here contract with me to furnish thirty workmen for a stater, for the dressed stonework, of course with a specified ration along with the

stater. But the material of our masonry is not of this sort[8], but brick made of clay and chance stones, so that they do not need to spend time in fitting the faces of the stones accurately together. I know that so far as skill and fairness in the matter of wages are concerned, the workmen in your neighbourhood are better for our purpose than those who follow the trade here. The sculptor's work lies not only in the eight pillars, which must themselves be improved and beautified, but the work requires altar-like base-mouldings[9], and capitals carved in the Corinthian style. The porch, too, will be of marbles wrought with appropriate ornaments. The doors set upon these will be adorned with some such designs as are usually employed by way of embellishment at the projection of the cornice. Of all these, of course, we shall furnish the materials ; the form to be impressed on the materials art will bestow. Besides these there will be in the colonnade not less than forty pillars : these also will be of wrought stone. Now if my account has explained the work in detail, I hope it may be possible for your Sanctity, on perceiving what is needed, to relieve us completely from anxiety so far as the workmen are concerned. If, however, the workman were inclined to make a bargain favourable to us, let a distinct measure of work, if possible, be fixed for the day, so that he may not pass his time doing nothing, and then, though he has no work to show for it, as having worked for us so many days, demand payment for them. I know that we shall appear to most people to be higglers, in being so particular about the contracts. But I beg you to pardon me ; for that Mammon about whom I have so often said such hard things, has at last departed from me as far as he can possibly go, being disgusted, I suppose, at the nonsense that is constantly talked against him, and has fortified himself against me by an impassable gulf—to wit, poverty—so that neither can he come to me, nor can I pass to him[10]. This is why I make a point of the fairness of the workmen, to the end that we may be able to fulfil the task before us, and not be hindered by poverty—that laudable and desirable evil. Well, in all this there is a certain admixture of jest. But do you, man of God, in such ways as are possible and legitimate, boldly promise in bargaining with the men that they will all meet with fair treatment at our hands, and full payment of their wages : for we shall give all and keep back nothing, as God also opens to us, by your prayers, His hand of blessing.

[4] That is, on an inner line ; the upper row having their supports at the *angles* of the inscribed octagon, and therefore at a point further removed from the centre of the circle than those of the lower tier, which correspond to the *sides* of the octagon. Or, simply, "those inside the building," the upper tier showing in the outside view of the structure, while the lower row would only be visible from the interior. There is apparently a corresponding row of windows *above* the upper row of arches, carrying the central tower four cubits higher. This at least seems the sense of the clause immediately following.

[5] Reading εἰλησέως, of which this seems to be the meaning.

[6] *i. e.* of the side of the octagon.

[7] Reading εἴλησιν.

[8] *i. e.* not dressed stone.

[9] The σπεῖρα is a moulding at the base of the column, equivalent to the Latin *torus*.

[10] Cf. S. Luke xvi. 26.

LETTER XVII.

TO EUSTATHIA, AMBROSIA, AND BASILISSA [1].

To the most discreet and devout Sisters, Eustathia and Ambrosia, and to the most discreet and noble Daughter, Basilissa, Gregory sends greeting in the Lord.

THE meeting with the good and the beloved, and the memorials of the immense love of the Lord for us men, which are shown in your localities, have been the source to me of the most intense joy and gladness. Doubly indeed have these shone upon divinely festal days; both in beholding the saving tokens [2] of the God who gave us life, and in meeting with souls in whom the tokens of the Lord's grace are to be discerned spiritually in such clearness, that one can believe that Bethlehem, and Golgotha, and Olivet, and the scene of the Resurrection are really in the God-containing heart. For when through a good conscience Christ has been formed in any, when any has by dint of godly fear nailed down the promptings of the flesh and become crucified to Christ, when any has rolled away from himself the heavy stone of this world's illusions, and coming forth from the grave of the body has begun to walk as it were in a newness of life, abandoning this low-lying valley of human life, and mounting with a soaring desire to that heavenly country [3] with all its elevated thoughts, where Christ is, no longer feeling the body's burden, but lifting it by chastity, so that the flesh with cloud-like lightness accompanies the ascending soul—such an one, in my opinion, is to be counted in the number of those famous ones in whom the memorials of the Lord's love for us men are to be seen. When, then, I not only saw with the sense of sight those Sacred Places, but I saw the tokens of places like them, plain in yourselves as well, I was filled with joy so great that the description of its blessing is beyond the power of utterance. But because it is a difficult, not to say an impossible

thing for a human being to enjoy unmixed with evil any blessing, therefore something of bitterness was mingled with the sweets I tasted : and by this, after the enjoyment of those blessings, I was saddened in my journey back to my native land, estimating now the truth of the Lord's words, that "the whole world lieth in wickedness [4]," so that no single part of the inhabited earth is without its share of degeneracy. For if the spot itself that has received the footprints of the very Life is not clear of the wicked thorns, what are we to think of other places where communion with the Blessing has been inculcated by hearing and preaching alone [5]. With what view I say this, need not be explained more fully in words ; facts themselves proclaim more loudly than any speech, however intelligible, the melancholy truth.

The Lawgiver of our life has enjoined upon us one single hatred. I mean, that of the Serpent : for no other purpose has He bidden us exercise this faculty of hatred, but as a resource against wickedness. "I will put enmity," He says, "between thee and him." Since wickedness is a complicated and multifarious thing, the Word allegorizes it by the Serpent, the dense array of whose scales is symbolic of this multiformity of evil. And we by working the will of our Adversary make an alliance with this serpent, and so turn this hatred against one another [6], and perhaps not against ourselves alone, but against Him Who gave the commandment ; for He says, "Thou shalt love thy neighbour and hate thine enemy," commanding us to hold the foe to our humanity as our only enemy, and declaring that all who share that humanity are the neighbours of each one of us. But this grosshearted age has disunited us from our neighbour, and has made us welcome the serpent, and revel in his spotted scales [7]. I affirm, then, that it is a lawful thing to hate God's enemies, and that this kind of hatred is pleasing to our Lord : and by God's enemies I mean those who deny the glory of our Lord, be they Jews, or downright idolaters, or those who through Arius' teaching idolize the creature, and so adopt the error of the Jews. Now when the Father, the Son, and the Holy Ghost, are with orthodox devotion being glorified and adored by those who believe that in a distinct and unconfused Trinity there is One Substance, Glory, Kingship, Power, and Universal Rule, in such a case as this what good excuse for fighting can there be ? At the time, certainly, when

---

[1] This Letter was published, Paris 1606, by R. Stephens (not the great lexicographer), who also translated *On Pilgrimages* into French for Du Moulin (see p. 382): and this edition was reprinted a year after at Hanover, with notes by Isaac Casaubon, "viro docto, sed quod dolendum, in castris Calvinianis militanti" (Gretser). Heyns places it in 382, and Rupp also.

[2] σωτήρια σύμβολα. Casaubon remarks "hoc est τοῦ σωτῆρος, Salvatoris, non autem σωτηρίας ποιητικὰ." This is itself doubtful; and he also makes the astounding statement that both Jerome, Augustine, and the whole primitive Church felt that visits to the Sacred Places contributed nothing to the alteration of character. But see especially Jerome, *De Peregrinat.*, and *Epistle to Marcella*. Fronto Ducæus adds, "At, velis nolis, σωτήρια sunt illa loca : tum quia aspectu sui corda ad pœnitentiam et salutares lacrymas non raro commovent, ut patet de Mariâ Ægyptiacâ ; tum quia . . ."

[3] ἐπουράνιον πολίτειαν. Even Casaubon (against Du Moulin here) allows this to mean the ascetic or monastic Life ; "sublimius propositum." Cf. Macarius, *Hom.* v. p. 85, ἐνάρετος πολιτεία: Isidore of Pelusium, lib. I, c. xiv, πνευματικὴ πολιτεία.

[4] 1 S. John v. 19.

[5] ψιλῆς : this word expresses the absence of something, without implying any contempt: cf. ψιλὸς ἄνθρωπος, ψιλὸς λόγος (prose).

[6] κατ' ἀλλήλων.

[7] τοῖς τῶν φολίδων στίγμασιν. For στίγμα with this meaning and connexion, see Hesiod, *Scutum*, 166

the heretical views prevailed, to try issues with the authorities, by whom the adversaries' cause was seen to be strengthened, was well; there was fear then lest our saving Doctrine should be over-ruled by human rulers. But now, when over the whole world from one end of heaven to the other the orthodox Faith is being preached, the man who fights with them who preach it, fights not with them, but with Him Who is thus preached. What other aim, indeed, ought that man's to be, who has the zeal for God, than in every possible way to announce the glory of God? As long, then, as the Only-begotten is adored with all the heart and soul and mind, believed to be in everything that which the Father is, and in like manner the Holy Ghost is glorified with an equal amount of adoration, what plausible excuse for fighting is left these over-refined disputants, who are rending the seamless robe, and parting the Lord's name between Paul and Cephas, and undisguisedly abhorring contact with those who worship Christ, all but exclaiming in so many words, "Away from me, I am holy"?

Granting that the knowledge which they believe themselves to have acquired is somewhat greater than that of others : yet can they possess more than the belief that the Son of the Very God is Very God, seeing that in that article of the Very God every idea that is orthodox, every idea that is our salvation, is included? It includes the idea of His Goodness, His Justice, His Omnipotence : that He admits of no variableness nor alteration, but is always the same; incapable of changing to worse or changing to better, because the first is not His nature, the second He does not admit of; for what can be higher than the Highest, what can be better than the Best? In fact, He is thus associated with all perfection, and, as to every form of alteration, is unalterable ; He did not on occasions display this attribute, but was always so, both before the Dispensation that made Him man, and during it, and after it; and in all His activities in our behalf He never lowered any part of that changeless and unvarying character to that which was out of keeping with it. What is essentially imperishable and changeless is always such ; it does not follow the variation of a lower order of things, when it comes by dispensation to be there ; just as the sun, for example, when he plunges his beam into the gloom, does not dim the brightness of that beam ; but instead, the dark is changed by the beam into light ; thus also the True Light, shining in our gloom, was not itself overshadowed with that shade, but enlightened it by means of itself. Well, seeing that our humanity was in darkness, as it is written, 'They know not, neither will they understand,

they walk on in darkness [8]," the Illuminator of this darkened world darted the beam of His Divinity through the whole compound of our nature, through soul, I say, and body too, and so appropriated humanity entire by means of His own light, and took it up and made it just that thing which He is Himself. And as this Divinity was not made perishable, though it inhabited a perishable body, so neither did it alter in the direction of any change, though it healed the changeful in our soul : in medicine, too, the physician of the body, when he takes hold of his patient, so far from himself contracting the disease, thereby perfects the cure of the suffering part. Let no one, either, putting a wrong interpretation on the words of the Gospel, suppose that our human nature in Christ was transformed to something more divine by any gradations and advance : for the increasing in stature and in wisdom and in favour, is recorded in Holy Writ only to prove that Christ really was present in the human compound, and so to leave no room for their surmise, who propound that a phantom, or form in human outline, and not a real Divine Manifestation, was there. It is for this reason that Holy Writ records unabashed with regard to Him all the accidents of our nature, even eating, drinking, sleeping, weariness, nurture, increase in bodily stature, growing up—everything that marks humanity, except the tendency to sin. Sin, indeed, is a miscarriage, not a quality of human nature : just as disease and deformity are not congenital to it in the first instance, but are its unnatural accretions, so activity in the direction of sin is to be thought of as a mere mutilation of the goodness innate in us ; it is not found to be itself a real thing, but we see it only in the absence of that goodness. Therefore He Who transformed the elements of our nature into His divine abilities, rendered it secure from mutilation and disease, because He admitted not in Himself the deformity which sin works in the will. "He did no sin," it says, "neither was guile found in his mouth [9]." And this in Him is not to be regarded in connection with any interval of time : for at once the man in Mary (where Wisdom built her house), though naturally part of our sensuous compound, along with the coming upon her of the Holy Ghost, and her overshadowing with the power of the Highest, became that which that overshadowing power in essence was : for, without controversy, it is the Less that is blest by the Greater. Seeing, then, that the power of the Godhead is an immense and immeasurable thing, while man is a weak atom, at the moment when the Holy Ghost came upon the Virgin, and the power of the Highest over-

---

[8] Ps. lxxxii. 5.　　　　[9] 1 Pet. ii. 22.

shadowed her, the tabernacle formed by such an impulse was not clothed with anything of human corruption; but, just as it was first constituted, so it remained, even though it was man, Spirit nevertheless, and Grace, and Power; and the special attributes of our humanity derived lustre from this abundance of Divine Power [1].

There are indeed two limits of human life: the one we start from, and the one we end in: and so it was necessary that the Physician of our being should enfold us at both these extremities, and grasp not only the end, but the beginning too, in order to secure in both the raising of the sufferer. That, then, which we find to have happened on the side of the finish we conclude also as to the beginning. As at the end He caused by virtue of the Incarnation that, though the body was disunited from the soul, yet the indivisible Godhead which had been blended once for all with the subject (who possessed them) was not stripped from that body any more than it was from that soul, but while it was in Paradise along with the soul, and paved an entrance there in the person of the Thief for all humanity, it remained by means of the body in the heart of the earth, and therein destroyed him that had the power of Death (wherefore His *body* too is called "the Lord [2]" on account of that inherent Godhead)— so also, at the beginning, we conclude that the power of the Highest, coalescing with our entire nature by that coming upon (the Virgin) of the Holy Ghost, both resides in our soul, so far as reason sees it possible that it should reside there, and is blended with our body, so that our salvation throughout every element may be perfect, that heavenly passionlessness which is peculiar to the Deity being nevertheless preserved both in the beginning and in the end of this life as Man [3]. Thus the beginning was not as our beginning, nor the end as our end. Both in the one and in the other He evinced His

Divine independence; the beginning had no stain of pleasure upon it, the end was not the end in dissolution.

Now if we loudly preach all this, and testify to all this, namely that Christ is the power of God and the wisdom of God, always changeless, always imperishable, though He comes in the changeable and the perishable; never stained Himself, but making clean that which is stained; what is the crime that we commit, and wherefore are we hated? And what means this opposing array [4] of new Altars? Do we announce another Jesus? Do we hint at another? Do we produce other scriptures? Have any of ourselves dared to say "Mother of Man" of the Holy Virgin, the Mother of God [5]: which is what we hear that some of them say without restraint? Do we romance about three Resurrections [6]? Do we promise the gluttony of the Millennium? Do we declare that the Jewish animal-sacrifices shall be restored? Do we lower men's hopes again to the Jerusalem below, imagining its rebuilding with stones of a more brilliant material? What charge like these can be brought against us, that our company should be reckoned a thing to be avoided, and that in some places another altar should be erected in opposition to us, as if we should defile their sanctuaries? My heart was in a state of burning indignation about this: and now that I have set foot in the City [7] again, I am eager to unburden my soul of its bitterness, by appealing, in a letter, to your love. Do ye, whithersoever the Holy Spirit shall lead you, there remain; walk with God before you; confer not with flesh and blood; lend no occasion to any of them for glorying, that they may not glory in you, enlarging their ambition by anything in your lives. Remember the Holy Fathers, into whose hands ye were commended by your Father now in bliss [8], and to whom we

---

[1] Compare Gregory against Apollinaris (*Ad Theophil.* iii. 265): "The first-fruits of humanity assumed by omnipotent Deity were, like a drop of vinegar merged in a boundless ocean, found still in that Deity, but not in their own distinctive properties: otherwise we should be obliged to think of a duality of Sons." In *Orat. Cat.* c. 10, he says that the Divine nature is to be conceived as having been so united with the human, as flame is with its fuel, the former extending beyond the latter, as our souls also overstep the limits of our bodies. The first of these passages appeared to Hooker (V. liii. 2) to be "so plain and direct for Eutyches," that he doubted whether the words were Gregory's. But at the Council of Ephesus, S. Cyril (of Alexandria), in his contest with the Nestorians, had showed that these expressions were capable of a Catholic interpretation, and pardonable in discussing the difficult and mysterious question of the union of the Two Natures.

[2] S Matt. xxviii. 6. "Come see the place where the Lord lay." Cf. S. John xx. 2, 13.

[3] "Here is the true vicariousness of the Atonement, which consisted not in the substitution of His punishment for ours, but in His offering the sacrifice which man had neither the purity nor the power to offer. From out of the very heart or centre of human nature . . . there is raised the sinless sacrifice of perfect humanity by the God Man. . . . It is a representative sacrifice, for it consists of no unheard-of experience, of no merely symbolic ceremony, but of just those universal incidents of suffering, which, though he must have felt them with a bitterness unknown to us, are intensely human." *Lux Mundi*, p. 218.

[4] ἀντεξαγωγή.

[5] As early as 250, Dionysius of Alexandria, in his letter to Paul of Samosata, frequently speaks of ἡ θεοτόκος Μαρία. Later, in the Council of Ephesus (430), it was decreed that "the immaculate and ever-Virgin mother of our Lord should be called properly (κυρίως) and really θεοτόκος," against the Nestorian title χριστοτόκος. Cf. Theodoret. *Anath.* I. tom. iv. p. 709. "We call Mary not Mother of Man, but Mother of God;" and Greg. Naz. *Or.* li. p. 738. "If any one call not Mary Mother of God he is outside 'divinity.'"

[6] μὴ τρεῖς ἀναστάσεις μυθοποιοῦμεν; For the first Resurrection (of the Soul in Baptism) and the second (of the Body), see Rev. xx. 5, with Bishop Wordsworth's note.

[7] *i. e.* Cæsarea in Cappadocia.

[8] Basil, probably: who after Cyril's exile had been called in to heal the heresy of Apollinaris, which was spreading in the convents at Jerusalem. The factious purism, however, which Gregory deplores here, and which led to rival altars, seems to have evinced itself amongst the orthodox themselves. "quo majorem apud omnes opinionem de suâ præstantiâ belli isti cathari excitarent" (Casaubon). Cyril, it is true, had returned this year, 382; and spent the last years of his life in his see; but with more than twenty years interval of Arian rule (Herennius, Heraclius, and Hilarius, according to Sozomen) the communities of the Catholics must have suffered from want of a constant control: and unity was always difficult to maintain in a city frequented by all the ecclesiastics of the world. Gregory must have "succeeded" to this charge in his visit to Jerusalem after the Council of Antioch in 379, to which he refers in his letter *On Pilgrimages*: but it is possible that he had paid even an earlier visit: see Letter XIV. p. 539, note 5.

by God's grace were deemed worthy to succeed : and remove not the boundaries which our Fathers have laid down, nor put aside in any way the plainness of our simpler proclamation in favour of their subtler school. Walk by the primitive rule of the Faith : and the God of peace shall be with you, and ye shall be strong in mind and body. May God keep you uncorrupted, is our prayer.

LETTER XVIII.

TO FLAVIAN 9.

THINGS with us, O man of God, are not in a good way. The development of the bad feeling existing amongst certain persons who have conceived a most groundless and unaccountable hatred of us is no longer a matter of mere conjecture ; it is now evinced with an earnestness and openness worthy only of some holy work. You meanwhile, who have hitherto been beyond the reach of such annoyance, are too remiss in stifling the devouring conflagration on your neighbour's land ; yet those who are well-advised for their own interests really do take pains to check a fire close to them, securing themselves, by this help given to a neighbour, against ever needing help in like circumstances. Well, you will ask, what do I complain of? Piety has vanished from the world ; Truth has fled from our midst ; as for Peace, we used to have the name at all events going the round upon men's lips ; but now not only does she herself cease to exist, but we do not even retain the word that expresses her. But that you may know more exactly the things that move our indignation, I will briefly detail to you the whole tragic story.

Certain persons had informed me that the Right Reverend Helladius had unfriendly feelings towards me, and that he enlarged in conversation to every one upon the troubles that I had brought upon him. I did not at first believe what they said, judging only from myself, and the actual truth of the matter. But when every one kept bringing to us a tale of the same strain, and facts besides corroborated their report, I thought it my duty not to continue to overlook this ill-feeling, while it was still without root and development. I therefore wrote by letter to your piety, and to many others who could help me

in my intention, and stimulated your zeal in this matter. At last, after I had concluded the services at Sebasteia in 10 commemoration of Peter 1 of most blessed memory, and of the holy martyrs, who had lived in his times, and whom the people were accustomed to commemorate with him, I was returning to my own See, when some one told me that Helladius himself was in the neighbouring mountain district, holding martyrs' memorial services. At first I held on my journey, judging it more proper that our meeting should take place in the metropolis itself. But when one of his relations took the trouble to meet me, and to assure me that he was sick, I left my carriage at the spot where this news arrested me ; I performed on horse-back the intervening journey over a road that was like a precipice, and well-nigh impassable with its rocky ascents. Fifteen milestones measured the distance we had to traverse. Painfully travelling, now on foot, now mounted, in the early morning, and even employing some part of the night, I arrived between twelve and one o'clock at Andumocina ; for that was the name of the place where, with two other bishops, he was holding his conference. From a shoulder of the hill overhanging this village, we looked down, while still at a distance, upon this out-door assemblage of the Church. Slowly, and on foot, and leading the horses, I and my company passed over the intervening ground, and we arrived at the chapel 2 just as he had retired to his residence.

Without any delay a messenger was despatched to inform him of our being there ; and a very short while after, the deacon in attendance on him met us, and we requested him to tell Helladius at once, so that we might spend as much time as possible with him, and so have an opportunity of leaving nothing in the misunderstanding between us unhealed. As for myself, I then remained sitting, still in the open air, and waited for the invitation indoors ; and at a most inopportune time I became, as I sat there, a gazing stock to all the visitors at the conference. The time was long ; drowsiness came on, and languor, intensified by the fatigue of the journey and the excessive heat of the day ; and all these things, with people staring at me, and pointing me out to others, were so very distressing that in me the words of the prophet were realized : "My spirit within me was desolate 3." I was kept

---

9 The date of this letter is probably as late as 393. Flavian's authority at Antioch was now undisputed, by his reconciliation, after the deaths of Paulinus and Evagrius, with the Bishops of Alexandria and Rome, and, through them, with all his people. Gregory writes to him not only as his dear friend, but one who had known how to appease wrath, and to check opposition from the Emperor downward. He died in 404. The litigiousness of Helladius is described by Greg. Naz., *Letter* ccxv. He it was who a few years later, against Ambrose's authority, and for mere private interest, consecrated the physician Gerontius (Sozomen, viii. 6).

10 Sebasteia (*Sivâs*) was in Pontus on the upper Halys : and the "mountain district" between this and Helladius' "metropolis" (Cæsarea, ad Argæum) must have been some offshoots of the Anti-Taurus.
1 His brother, who had urged him to write the books against Eunomius, and to whom he sent *On the Making of Man*.
2 μαρτυρίῳ, i. e. dedicated to Peter ; but the word is used even of a chapel dedicated to Christ.
3 ἠκηδίασεν. Ps. cxliii. 4 (LXX.).

in this state till noon, and heartily did I repent of this visit, and that I had brought upon myself this piece of discourtesy ; and my own reflection vexed me worse than this injury done me by my enemies [4], warring as it did against itself, and changing into a regret that I had made the venture. At last the approach to the Altars was thrown open, and we were admitted to the sanctuary ; the crowd, however, were excluded, though my deacon entered along with me, supporting with his arm my exhausted frame. I addressed his Lordship, and stood for a moment, expecting from him an invitation to be seated ; but when nothing of the kind was heard from him, I turned towards one of the distant seats, and rested myself upon it, still expecting that he would utter something that was friendly, or at all events kind ; or at least give one nod of recognition.

Any hopes I had were doomed to complete disappointment. There ensued a silence dead as night, and looks as downcast as in tragedy, and daze, and dumbfoundedness, and perfect dumbness. A long interval of time it was, dragged out as if it were in the blackness of night. So struck down was I by this reception, in which he did not deign to accord me the merest utterance even of those common salutations by which you discharge the courtesies of a chance meeting [5],—"welcome," for instance, or "where do you come from?" or "to what am I indebted for this pleasure?" or "on what important business are you here?" —that I was inclined to make this spell of silence into a picture of the life led in the underworld. Nay, I condemn the similitude as inadequate. For in that underworld the equality of conditions is complete, and none of the things that cause the tragedies of life on earth disturb existence. Their glory, as the Prophet says, does not follow men down there ; each individual soul, abandoning the things so eagerly clung to by the majority here, his petulance, and pride, and conceit, enters that lower world in simple unencumbered nakedness ; so that none of the miseries of this life are to be found among them. Still [6], notwithstanding this reservation, my condition then did appear to me like an underworld, a murky dungeon, a gloomy torture-chamber ; the more so, when I reflected what treasures of social courtesies we have inherited from our fathers, and what recorded deeds of it we shall leave to our descendants. Why, indeed, should I speak at all of that affectionate disposition of our fathers towards each other ? No wonder that, being all naturally equal [7], they wished for no advantage over one another, but thought to exceed each other only in humility. But my mind was penetrated most of all with this thought ; that the Lord of all creation, the Only-begotten Son, Who was in the bosom of the Father, Who was in the beginning, Who was in the form of God, Who upholds all things by the word of His power, humbled Himself not only in this respect, that in the flesh He sojourned amongst men, but also that He welcomed even Judas His own betrayer, when he drew near to kiss Him, on His blessed lips ; and that when He had entered into the house of Simon the leper He, as loving all men, upbraided his host, that He had not been kissed by him : whereas I was not reckoned by him as equal even to that leper ; and yet what was I, and what was he? I cannot discover any difference between us. If one looks at it from the mundane point of view, where was the height from which he had descended, where was the dust in which I lay? If, indeed, one must regard things of this fleshly life, thus much perhaps it will hurt no one's feelings to assert that, looking at our lineage, whether as noble or as free, our position was about on a par ; though, if one looked in either for the true freedom and nobility, i. e. that of the soul, each of us will be found equally a bondsman of Sin ; each equally needs One Who will take away his sins ; it was Another Who ransomed us both from Death and Sin with His own blood, Who redeemed us, and yet showed no contempt of those whom He has redeemed, calling them though He does from deadness to life, and healing every infirmity of their souls and bodies.

Seeing, then, that the amount of this conceit and overweening pride was so great, that even the height of heaven was almost too narrow limits for it (and yet I could see no cause or occasion whatever for this diseased state of mind, such as might make it excusable in the case of some who in certain circumstances contract it ; when, for instance, rank or education, or pre-eminence in dignities of office may have happened to inflate the vainer minds), I had no means whereby to advise myself to keep quiet : for my heart within me was swelling with indignation at the absurdity of the whole proceeding, and was rejecting all the reasons for enduring it. Then, if ever, did I feel admiration for that divine Apostle who so vividly depicts the civil war that rages within us, declaring that there is a certain "law of sin in the members, warring against the law of the

---

[4] χαλεπώτερον τῆς παρὰ τῶν ἐχθρῶν μοι γενομένης ὕβρεως. The Latin does not express this, "quam si ab hostibus profecta fuisset."

[5] τῶν κατημαξευμένων (so Paris Editt. and Migne, but it must be καθημαξευμένων, from ἅμαξα) τούτων τὴν συντυχίαν ἀφοσιουμένων.

[6] πλὴν ἀλλ' ἐμοὶ, κ. τ. λ. See note, p. 313.

[7] ἐν ὁμοτίμῳ τῇ φύσει. Cf. οἱ ὁμότιμοι, the peers of the Persian kingdom.

mind," and often making the mind a captive, and a slave as well, to itself. This was the very array, in opposition, of two contending feelings that I saw within myself: the one, of anger at the insult caused by pride, the other prompting to appease the rising storm. When, by God's grace, the worse inclination had failed to get the mastery, I at last said to him, "But is it, then, that some one of the things required for your personal comfort is being hindered by our presence, and is it time that we withdrew?" On his declaring that he had no bodily needs, I spoke to him some words calculated to heal, so far as in me lay, his ill-feeling. When he had, in a very few words, declared that the anger he felt towards me was owing to many injuries done him, I for my part answered him thus: "Lies possess an immense power amongst mankind to deceive: but in the Divine Judgment there will be no place for the misunderstandings thus arising. In my relations towards yourself, my conscience is bold enough to prompt me to hope that I may obtain forgiveness for all my other sins, but that, if I have acted in any way to harm you, this may remain for ever unforgiven." He was indignant at this speech, and did not suffer the proofs of what I had said to be added.

It was now past six o'clock, and the bath had been well prepared, and the banquet was being spread, and the day was the sabbath [8], and a martyr's commemoration. Again observe how this disciple of the Gospel imitates the Lord of the Gospel: He, when eating and drinking with publicans and sinners, answered to those who found fault with Him that He did it for love of mankind: this disciple considers it a sin and a pollution to have us at his board, even after all that fatigue which we underwent on the journey, after all that excessive heat out of doors, in which we were baked while sitting at his gates; after all that gloomy sullenness with which he treated us to the bitter end, when we had come into his presence. He sends us off to toil painfully, with a frame now thoroughly exhausted with the over-fatigue, over the same

distance, the same route: so that we scarcely reached our travelling company at sunset, after we had suffered many mishaps on the way. For a storm-cloud, gathered into a mass in the clear air by an eddy of wind, drenched us to the skin with its floods of rain; for owing to the excessive sultriness, we had made no preparation against any shower. However, by God's grace we escaped, though in the plight of shipwrecked sailors from the waves: and right glad were we to reach our company.

Having joined our forces we rested there that night, and at last arrived alive in our own district; having reaped in addition this result of our meeting him, that the memory of all that had happened before was revived by this last insult offered to us; and, you see, we are positively compelled to take measures, for the future, on our own behalf, or rather on his behalf; for it was because his designs were not checked on former occasions that he has proceeded to this unmeasured display of vanity. Something, therefore, I think, must be done on our part, in order that he may improve upon himself, and may be taught that he is human, and has no authority to insult and to disgrace those who possess the same beliefs and the same rank as himself. For just consider; suppose we granted for a moment, for the sake of argument, that it is true that I have done something that has annoyed him, what trial [9] was instituted against us, to judge either of the fact or the hearsay? What proofs were given of this supposed injury? What Canons were cited against us? What legitimate episcopal decision confirmed any verdict passed upon us? And supposing any of these processes had taken place, and that in the proper way, my standing [1] in the Church might certainly have been at stake, but what Canons could have sanctioned insults offered to a free-born person, and disgrace inflicted on one of equal rank with himself? "Judge righteous judgment," you who look to God's law in this matter; say wherein you deem this disgrace put upon us to be excusable. If our dignity is to be estimated on the ground of priestly jurisdiction, the privilege of each recorded by the Council [2] is one and the same; or rather the oversight of Catholic correction [3], from the fact that we possess an equal share of it, is so. But if some are inclined to regard each of us by himself, divested of any priestly dignity, in

---

[8] Cf. *Dies Dominica* (by Thomas Young, tutor of Milton the poet): 'It's without controversie that the Oriental Christians, and others, did at that time hold assemblies on the Sabbath day. . . . Yet did they not hold the Sabbath day holy," p. 35. Again, "Socrates doth not record that they of Alexandria and Rome did celebrate those mysteries on the Sabbath. While Chrysostom requireth it of the rich Lords of Villages, that they build Churches in them (*Hom.* 18 *in Act.*), he distinguisheth those congregations that were on other days from those that were held upon the Lord's day. 'Upon those congregations (συνάξεις) Prayers and hymns were had, in these an oblation was made on every Lord's day,' and for that cause the Lord's day is in Chrysostom called, 'dies panis'. Athanasius purgeth himself of a calumny imputed to him, for breaking the cup, because it was not the time of administering the holy mysteries; 'for it is not,' saith he, 'the Lord's day.'" A law of Constantine had enacted that the first day of the week, "the Lord's day," should be observed with greater solemnity than formerly; which shows that the seventh day, the Sabbath, still held its place; and it does not follow that in remoter places, as here, both were kept. The hour of service was generally "in the evening after sunset; or in the morning before the dawn," Mosheim.

[9] κριτήριον.
[1] τὸν βαθμὸν *i.e.* "a grade of honour": cf. 1 Tim. iii. 13. βαθμὸν ἑαυτοῖς καλὸν περιποιοῦνται. So in the Canons often.
[2] The Council of Constantinople.
[3] *the oversight of Catholic correction.* "On July 30. 381, the Bishop of Nyssa received the supreme honour of being named by Theodosius as one of the acknowledged authorities in all matters of theological orthodoxy: and he was appointed to regulate the affairs of the Church in Asia Minor, conjointly with Helladius of Cæsarea, and Otreius of Melitene:" Farrar's *Lives of the Fathers*, 1889.

what respect has one any advantage over the other; in education for instance, or in birth connecting with the noblest and most illustrious lineage, or in theology? These things will be found either equal, or at all events not inferior, in me. "But what about revenue?" he will say. I would rather not be obliged to speak of this in his case; thus much only it will suffice to say, that our own was so much at the beginning, and is so much now; and to leave it to others to enquire into the causes of this increase of our revenue[4], nursed as it is up till now, and growing almost daily by means of noble under-

takings. What licence, then, has he to put an insult upon us, seeing that he has neither superiority of birth to show, nor a rank exalted above all others, nor a commanding power of speech, nor any previous kindness done to me? While, even if he had all this to show, the fault of having slighted those of gentle birth would still be inexcusable. But he has not got it; and therefore I deem it right to see that this malady of puffed-up pride is not left without a cure; and it will be its cure to put it down to its proper level, and reduce its inflated dimensions, by letting off a little of the conceit with which he is bursting. The manner of effecting this we leave to God

---

[4] He is speaking of the funds of his Diocese, which at one period certainly he had been accused of mismanaging.

APPENDIX

THE other Treatises of Gregory are as follows (the order is that of the first Paris Edition, 1615, and Gretser's Appendix, 1618).

1. **Apologetic on the Seven Days.**
   So called because it was a defence of the words of Moses; and also an explanation of Basil's "Seven Days."
   It was translated into Latin by L. Sifanus (Basle, 1562), and P. F. Zinus (Venice, 1553). It is in 9 Paris MSS. and one at Leyden (not older than cent. 15).

2. **On the words "Let us make man in our image and likeness."**
   Two Homilies. He explains what this creation was, and thence proves the pre-eminence of man; lastly, some moral truths are based on this manner of creation, different to that of brutes.
   They are found after Basil's "Seven Days," and on the strength of this Tilman edited them under his name (Paris, 1666). But this work of Basil's was itself incomplete, as Jerome, Photius, Suidas, testify; and Fabricius defends these homilies as Gregory's: so also Zinus (who translated them) and others.

3. **On the Life of Moses.**
   A mystical treatise, exhorting to Christian Perfection, the type of which is to be found in Moses; but perfection is infinite, and in this life unattainable. There is a fine passage at the end on the disinterested love of God.
   It was translated by G. Trapezuntius, and edited by J. Gremperius (Basle, 1517): translated by J. Leunclavius, and edited with notes by D. Hoeschel (Leyden, 1593).

4. **On the titles of the Psalms.**
   "Contains subtle allegorizing and fancies" (Du Pin).
   It was translated by Jacob Gretser, the Jesuit (Ingoldstadt, 1600, 1617): and had been previously edited by Maximus Margunius (Venice, 1585), Bishop of Cythera. Many MSS. of the Escurial have it.

5. **Homily on the Eighth Day (Circumcision), and Sixth Psalm.**
   Sifanus and Maximus Margunius translated it.

6. **An accurate exposition of Ecclesiastes.**
   Eight Homilies (the last imperfect). Partly practical, partly allegorical. Septuagint used.
   A translation by Gentian Hervetus is corrected by F. Ducæus in his notes.
   P. Possinus asserts (Prologue to *Thesaur. Ascetic.* Paris, 1684), that he has ready for publishing this Commentary of Gregory complete, copied from the Roman MS., much superior to the Paris: but this edition never appeared.

7. **An accurate exposition of the Song of Songs.**
   Fifteen Homilies. In the Preface he determines that the sense must be allegorical.

Translated by Hervetus and Leunclavius. Zinus and Livineius translated an exposition of the Song of Songs, collected from the commentaries of Gregory, Nilus, and Maximus.

8. **On Prayer.**
   Five Homilies. The last four are a careful explanation of the Lord's Prayer ("lectu dignissimæ," Fabricius).
   Translated by Sifanus; and by Galesinius, with a Preface (Rome, 1565). Translated and edited by J. Krabinger (Munich, 1832). Leo Allatius thinks a passage in them on the Procession of the Holy Ghost has been corrupted by the Greeks.

9. **On the Beatitudes.**
   These Homilies are cited in the acts of the Council of Ephesus, by Theodoret, and by John of Damascus.
   Translated by Sifanus and Galesinius.

10. **On 1 Corinthians xv. 28.**
    Written at the request of a friend. He defends the "subjection of the Son" from any Arian interpretation. Oudin judges the treatise spurious, or interpolated, because it is full of Origen's thought, and seems inconsistent with Gregory's other treatises; but without reason.
    Translated by Hervetus.

11. **On Genesis i. 26 (See No. 2).**
    It explains why the Angels are not said to be created in the 'image' of God. Methodius' opinions about Adam and Eve, and about the origin of souls are cited. Some have attributed it to Anastasius Sinaïta.
    Translated by Fronto Ducæus with notes (Ingoldstadt, 1596).

12. **To Theodosius (the Bishop), on the Ventriloquist.**
    He asserts that a demon, and not Samuel (there is a gulf between the good and bad), appeared to Saul. This was an opinion of many ancient Doctors.
    Translated by Ducæus (Ingoldstadt, 1596).

13. **On his Ordination.**
    This title is wrong. He was made bishop in 372: this was preached in 394. John of Damascus cites it as "On the appointment of Gregory in Constantinople," i.e. to have the rights of a Metropolitan. See 'Prolegomena,' p. 7.
    Translated by Ducæus.

14. **Against Apollinaris.**
    A fragment. Refutes the charge of Apollinaris, that the orthodox make the Trinity quadruple; and defends the Angels serving man.

15. **On love of the Poor.**
    A pathetic description of the vagabond poor, and a moving exhortation to liberality.
    Translated by Zinus; and edited by Gretser (from the Vienna MS.), Ingoldstadt, 1617, with notes by Fronto Ducæus.

16. Against Fate.

A dispute with a heathen philosopher in 382 at Constantinople. Gregory shows that if Fate is the influence of the. stars, which are always changing their position, on a man's natal hour, then that influence ought to change when their position is changed. A reduction to an absurdity.

It was edited in Latin at Strasbourg, 1512 ; and at Ingoldstadt (by Fronto Ducæus), 1600.

17. To the Greeks, from Universal Ideas.

It deals with all the expressions used in explaining the Trinity.

F. Morel's Latin accompanies it in the Paris Editions.

18. *On the Soul.*

This is the second and third chapters of Nemesius "On the Nature of Man." Christ. F. Matthæus, in his edition of Nemesius, has collected many authorities to show that it is not Gregory's. Schroeckh, in his history, contradicts himself on this point. It was inserted in Gregory by some copyist who thought his Making of Man was not complete without it.

19. Letter to Letoius, Bishop of Melitene (in Cappadocia).

"A canonical Epistle." So called because it gives eight rules for as many classes of penitents. Letoius is exhorted to ascertain above all things the disposition and behaviour of the penitent.

This has been more than once edited, with or without the canonical Epistles of the Fathers, with the scholia of Balsamon, Zonaras, and Aristenus (Paris, 1561, 1618, 1620).

It was edited separately by Antonius Augustinus, with notes (Venice, 1589) ; and with Hervetus' translation (Augsburg, 1591).

20. Against those who defer Baptism.

An earnest effort to dissuade Catechumens from the danger of dying in their sins.

Translated by Hervetus.

21. On 1 Corinthians vi. 18.

Translated by Hervetus.

22. *On the Woman who was a sinner.*

This, according to Fabricius, is the work of Asterius of Amasea, not Gregory's. It is so cited by Photius (Codex cclxxi.).

Translated by Zinus.

23. On Pentecost.

Only in the Latin of Zinus, in Paris Editions. Zacagni first edited the Greek (Collectanea Monument. vet., Rome, 1699), with his own version ; from three Vatican MSS.

24. Against the Usurers.

The Divine prohibitions of usury cited : usury breaks all the laws of charity.

25. *Against the Jews, on the Trinity.*

All the critics pronounce this spurious, for the single reason that the name of Chrysostom is found in it. Zacagni has nevertheless reported from the inspection of *one* Vatican MS., that the words about Chrysostom are imported into the text. If, then, the witness of MSS. is doubtful, the question must still be decided by the evidence of style : and this is distinctly too poor and meagre to be Gregory's.

In Latin only, in Paris Editions : the Greek edited by Zacagni (as above, No. 23).

26. *On the Difference of* Ὀυσία *and* Ὑπόστασις.

"The style proclaims that it is Basil's" (Fabricius).

Three Paris MSS., one Venice, and one Vienna also attest this. The Council of Chalcedon also acknowledged it to be Basil's. Basil sent it to his brother (Basil, T. iii. p. 23. Letter 38).

It was translated by Johan. Cono (Cologne, 1537), and by Sifanus.

27. Ten Syllogisms against the Manichees.

To prove that evil is not an οὐσία, but a nonentity; and that its father the Devil is not Ungenerate (Ἀγέννητος).

Translated with notes by Fronto Ducæus.

28. Against Apollinaris.

To Theophilus of Alexandria. Proves that the Word, who appeared to the Patriarchs, really became flesh : in such a manner that the Divine properties were *ascribed* to the complete human nature.

Translated with notes by Fronto Ducæus.

29. What is the Christian name and profession?

He defines it the "imitation of God," and answers the objection that we cannot imitate God.

Translation by Maximus Margunius (Venice, 1585), and Sifanus (Leyden, 1593).

30. On Perfection.

To the monk Olympius. A distinction, in passing, is drawn between First-born and Only-begotten.

Translation by Maximus Margunius. It was edited with Zinus' translation (Venice, 1574; Leyden, 1593).

31. Sketch of the aim of true Ascetism.

The Christian virtues are enumerated and shown to be intimately united. Mutual intercourse is especially dwelt upon.

This sketch was first edited and translated by F. Morel, separately (Paris, 1606).

32. To those who resent reproof.

A bishop's severity must not be complained of. It proceeds from the whole Church. He (Gregory) had to suffer many injuries himself from the reprobate.

Translated by Hervetus ; first edited, Paris, Sebast. Nivell., 1573.

33. On the Birth of Christ.

The Sermon begins upon the way to keep the Day. Old Testament prophecies noticed : and also some apocryphal legends, about the Virgin's mother, and her own training by the Priests : also about Zacharias' death. The murder of the Innocents vividly described. Reproduced in parts in Cyril against the Anthropomorphites.

Translated by Zinus ; Joach. Camerarius' translation (Leipsic, 1564) appeared in Hoeschel's edition (Leipsic, 1587). Notes by Ducæus in Paris Editions.

34. On St. Stephen.

The Divinity of the Holy Spirit cleared from the objection that the Martyr, at the moment of his death, saw only the Two Persons : the Divinity of the Son, from the objection that He was seen "*standing* at the right hand of God." Suidas defends the authenticity of this striking sermon.

Translated by Zinus and Sifanus. Edited by Hoeschel (Augsburg, 1587) ; notes by Ducæus in Paris Editions.

35. On the Holy Passover.

On the great importance of the Feast (of Easter). The "three days" discussed, and allegorized from Isaiah. An account of the Resurrection.

Translated by Sifanus and Ducæus. Edited by Joach. Camerarius (Leipsic, 1564).

36. **On Christ's Resurrection.**
Reconciles the Evangelists' accounts of the Resurrection. An early instance of a Harmony. Combeficius thought it must be by another hand than the preceding sermon, because ὀψὲ σαββάτων (S. Matt. xxviii. 1) is, as he thought, differently explained in the two. But Gregory does not in the first, any more than in the second, explain ὀψὲ by ἑσπέρας.
Translated by Ducæus.

37. **On the Great Lord's Day.**
A fine discourse on the importance of Easter. The possibility, and then the necessity of the Resurrection shown.

38. **On the Passover.**
An exhortation to the right keeping of Easter. Translated by Sifanus. Edited by Joach. Camerarius (Lelpsic, 1563), and by Henric. Oeschlegel, with explanatory and theological notes (Dresden, 1628).

39. **On the Light-bringing and Holy Resurrection.**
The humility of Christ expounded from Isaiah; and then His triumph. From the way in which the subject is handled Tillemont (p. 275) has thought that this Homily was written by a late Greek academic; but all the MSS. give it to Gregory.
Translated by F. Morel: edited separately (Paris, 1600).

40. **On the Ascension.**
Quotes from Psalms xxiii. and xxiv., and praises the Sacred Poet for his help in the right keeping of the Great Feasts.
Translated by Sifanus and Zinus.

41. *On the Meeting of the Lord.*
This is spurious, because this Festival (of the ὑπαπαντὴ, or "meeting of the Lord," by Simeon in the Temple) was not instituted till the year 542, under Justinian; Cedrenus (p. 366) is the authority for this. See Bingham's 'Origines,' vol. ix. p. 184 (1722).

42. **On the Deity of the Son, and of the Spirit.**
He compares some men of his own time to the Athenians who were eager "to tell, or to hear some new thing;" and Heretics, to the Stoics and Epicureans of S. Paul's time, refuting some of their opinions upon the Trinity, and ending with an encomium of Abraham (quoted by Theodoret, John Damasc, Adrian I., and Euthymius). Preached at Constantinople.
Translated by Sifanus, Joach. Camerarius, and Hervetus (Augsburg, 1591).

43. **Funeral Oration on Basil.**
He compares his great brother to S. John the Baptist, and S. Paul. Though extravagant at times in its language, this oration contributes much to the knowledge of Basil's character.

44. **Praise of the Forty Martyrs.**
Two Sermons. The first does not deal with the subject, but is an address to the overflowing congregation in the Martyrium. The second, next day in the Cathedral of Nyssa, tells the story of these Martyrs, and calls their mothers blest. The Day of these Martyrs is connected with an incident in Gregory's early life.

45. **Funeral Oration on Pulcheria.**
He consoles Theodosius and Flacilla for the loss of their daughter, universally beloved. It is clear from this that Gregory was very intimate with the Emperor and Empress.

46. **Funeral Oration on Flaccilla.**
Bewails "the shrine of chastity, the majestic gentleness, the noble humility, the free-spoken modesty (ἡ πεπαρρησιασμένη αἰδὼς) . . . the ornament of the Altars . . . the common refuge of the afflicted," lost in the Empress. She died 384.

47. **On the Life of Saint Gregory Thaumaturgus.**
Mentions his great attainments in theology, philosophy, and rhetoric; his integrity of life; his education by Firmilian. Compares him to Moses, except only in celibacy. Narrates his visions, and the wonders that he worked. This Life was written as a counterfoil to the Neoplatonic 'Lives of Saints,' and must not be judged altogether by a modern standard. It is called by Suidas "a very admirable encomium," and for the facts about Thaumaturgus, see Socrates, *H. E.* iv. 27.
Gerard Voss' translation and notes on this are found in the Works of Thaumaturgus (Mayence, 1604). Hervetus also translated it.

48. **Praise of Theodore the Martyr.**
The Martyr, a soldier who suffered under Diocletian, is called upon to save the Empire from another "Scythian" invasion, as he had already done in the past. This is certainly an Invocation, not a mere Apostrophe, of the Saint. For this invasion (of Armenia) in the time of Gregory, which has been doubted, see Jerome, Letter 30. Tillemont (l. c. p. 275) answers objections rising from difference of style.
Translated by Sifanus and Zinus.

49. **Praise of our Holy Father Ephraëm.**
He extols this illustrious saint of an obscure country for his excellences both of mind and heart; and compares him to Basil.
Asseman, in his preface to Ephraëm Syrus' Works, has gone carefully into the question of genuineness. A translation with the notes of G. Voss was prefixed to Ephraëm's Works (Rome, 1589).

50. **To Mourners for the Departed.**
Death is only a change to a Life that is really blest; its good things are infinite; Death is not an evil.

51. *On Repentance.*
This is considered spurious on the authority of Photius, who attributes it to Asterius of Amasea (Cod. cclxxi.).

52. **On the Life of the Holy Macrina.**
A letter to Olympius. It describes his sister's girlhood, and her care for her brother's education; her docility and piety, and her death.
Written about 380. Translated by Zinus.

53. **Praise of the Forty Martyrs.**
Narrates further details (see No. 44) of the dreadful treatment which they received from the Emperor. Seems part of the former Sermons; but Fabricius says "In addition to the two former."

54. *On the Beginning of the Fasts.*
Cited by Photius under the name of Asterius of Amasea (Cod. cclxxi.).

The Paris Editions omit the longer—

55. **Antirrhetic against Apollinaris.**
Begins with a vehement invective against his book on the Incarnation of the Word. This Antirrhetic sees the light in order to refute the charges made by the people of Sebaste against their Bishop, Gregory's brother; and to avert the danger to the true Faith.

It ranks Apollinaris with Arius and Eunomius; he even surpasses them in blasphemy. The fragment above (No. 14) seems part of this.

Zacagni edited this (Collect. Monum. vet. pp. 123—237. Rome, 1699) from a Vatican MS. of the 7th century. The style, the thoughts, the very same words as in other Polemics of Gregory, prove it to be his. It is also quoted as his. There is no clue to the date, except that the author says (c. iv.) that he had heard, by travelling (probably during his exile, 374-78) in various localities, the religious opinions of many orthodox, and of many heretics. Zacagni places it between 373 and the Council of Constantinople; Schroeckh much later. This work also exists in two Florence MSS. "A remarkable work" (Fabricius).

56. Another Praise of St. Stephen.

It begins with a tribute to the surpassing excellence of the First Martyr; and finds many allegories in his name. It goes on to commemorate SS. Peter, James, and John. "Bodily weakness did not allow of the completion" of the discourse on S. Stephen the day before (No. 32); and so, on the Day of these three Apostles, he completes it. S. Stephen's Day, therefore, just preceded this Saints' Day.

Edited by Zacagni from the Vatican MS.

57. Letter to the Monk Evagrius.

A discourse on 'Deity.' Commonly attributed to the Nazianzene; but many Vienna MSS. give it to the Nyssene; and Euthymius in his Panoplia cites it as his.

58. Letter to a certain John on certain Questions, and on the Life and Disposition of his sister Macrina, so much beloved.

There are no words sufficient to describe his present misery; troubles in Galatia; discord and immorality at Babylon. He exhorts John (probably a bishop), together with his people, to have services of intercession. Macrina's death delayed the sending of this letter: her life described.

This and the four following were edited by J. B. Caraccioli. See 'Prolegomena,' p. 31.

59. Letter to Bishop Ablabius.

A most courteous exhortation that he should alter his licentious life.

60 and 61. To the Bishops.

Two very short letters in which he complains of some men of the time: and calls upon one to give an account of himself.

62. To the Heretic Heracleanus.

Expounds the nature of the Trinity: without separation, difference, confusion. Opinions about the Faith must harmonize with the truths of Holy Baptism. The Divine properties enumerated.

63. Against Arius and Sabellius.

Edited by Angelo Mai from the Vatican MS. (Script. Vet. Nova Collectio, Rome, 1833).

64. *On the Procession of the Holy Spirit from the Son* (see No. 63).

The style throws doubts upon its genuineness. Edited by A. Mai.

The *chief* groups, then, of these translations and editions which *preceded* the two Paris Editions, are as follows. It will be seen that it was long before the complete works of Gregory were collected.

1. Several Moral Treatises, translated by Zinus, were printed by Vascosanus (Venice, 1550).

2. Several Treatises translated by Sifanus were printed at Basle, 1562: and, with the Canticles and Letter to Flavian, reprinted at Basle, 1567.

3. Some Orations were edited by Hoeschel (Augsburg, 1564).

4. Almost all Gregory's Works, with the versions (Sebast. Nivell., Paris, 1573).

5. Eight Treatises, including the Antirrhetic against Apollinaris, and against Fate, translated by Fronto Ducæus (Ingoldstadt, 1600).

The Editions of parts or whole, *after* the Paris, are as follows:—

6. Zacagni's collection, viz. Fourteen Letters, the Antirrhetic against Apollinaris, and Another Praise of St. Stephen (Rome, 1698).

7. Caraccioli's collection, viz. Seven Letters (Florence, 1731).

8. Cardinal Angelo Mai's edition, viz. Against Macedonius, and Against Arius and Sabellius (Rome, 1833).

9. Krabinger's Editions: On the Soul and the Resurrection, Leipsic, 1837; Great Catechism, and On Meletius (see Edit.), Munich, 1838; On Prayer, Landshut, 1840.

10. Forbes's Edition: Hexaëmeron and The Making of Man (Burntisland, 1855, 1861).

11. Opera Omnia. Migne. Paris, 1858. 3 Vols.

12. Opera Omnia. Ceillier. Paris, 1860.

13. Oehler published in four vols (1858, 1859) an Edition of the Greek text, with a German version of the following treatises:—On the Soul and the Resurrection; Life of Macrina; The Great Catechism; On Father, Son, and Holy Ghost; To Simplicius; On the Trinity; To Eustathius; On Universal Ideas; On the Making of Man; five sermons on Prayer; On Virginity, and On the Beatitudes. This is independent of his First Vol. of all the Works, published at Halle, 1865.

GENERAL INDEX TO GREGORY OF NYSSA

Abel, 81, 92, 145, 299.
Abimelech, 282.
Ablabius, question put by, 331.
Abraham, 52, 94; history of, allegorized, 259; faithful, 282; "father of the crowd," 291; a sojourner, 325, 447; bosom of, 447.
Acephali, 509.
Activities (see *Energies*).
Adam, 81, 92, 145, 290 *sq.*, 299, 313; Humanity created in, 411 *sq.*,467.
Adelphius, 439.
Adoption, son of God by, 163, 183 *sq.*
Æon, 50, 297.
Aetius, a serf, 39; avocations of, 39 *sq.*; an Aristotelian. 39; with Gallus, 40; with George, 40; Eunomius compared to, 238; his aim, 474.
Affusion, 503.
Ahab, 522.
Alexander the Great, his love of friendship, 530.
Alexandria, synod of, 24.
Alexandrine philosophy, 475.
Allegory, higher and lower, 476.
Altar, "horns" of the, 461; consecrated, 519.
Amalthea, horn of, 294.
Ambrosia, 542.
Ancyra (Angora), 5.
Andumocina, 545.
Angel, name of, used of Moses and John the Baptist, 234; in what sense used of the Son, 235; the Angel "of the earth," 480.
Angels, perfections of, 11; place of, 444; "guardian," 480; lapsed, 444, 480; orders of, 199; the Son placed on a level with, by Eunomius, 156, 237; in what sense eternal, 209 *sq.*; immortal, 309; address to the, 325; equality with, 360, 371, 518; the Son superior to, 235; how multiplied, 407.
Anger, uses of, 363, 443; is it a second soul? 439; definitions of, 440, 441.
Animals, kinds of, 76.
Annesi, 6, 7.
Anointed, the, 321
Anomœans, 39, 47, 56, 75, 80 *sq.*, 96, 474.
Anthropomorphic language in Scripture, 63, 93, 204, 274, 293.
Antioch, burial of Meletius at, 513; Church of, 514 *sq.*; Council of, 430, 544.

Ants, questions as to the nature of, 220.
Apollinaris, 18, 544.
Apology, the "Great Catechism" an, 12; why Eunomius wrote his, 41.
Apostle, author of the epistle to the Hebrews called the, 94.
Aquinas, 9.
Arabia, church in, 6, 383.
Architecture of a church described, 540-41.
Argæus, Mt., 46.
Ariadne, crown of, 294.
Arianism, akin to Gnosticism, 50; the later, 474; repudiated, 529; alliance of world-powers with, 543.
Aristotle, 39, 50, 96, 97, 269, 291, 439, 441.
Arius, 39, 81, 238, 542.
Ark, contents of the, 515; use of the word, 517.
Armenia, 33.
Art implies mind, 436.
Asceticism, Elijah and the Baptist, models of, 351.
Aseroth, 294.
Assyria, pride of, 498.
Astringent flavour in Life, 379
Astronomy, the Ptolemaic, 257, 373, 433, 434.
Athanasius, bishop of Ancyra, 39.
Athanasius, bishop of Alexandria, 17, 24, 28 *sq.*, 54, 60, 70, 547.
Atheist, 270; how to deal with an, 474.
Athenians, Anomœans compared to, 171.
Athens, 2.
Atonement, too little room in this life left by Gregory for the, 483.
Attic Greek, Eunomius attempts, 41, 79.
Attributes, the Divine, common to the Three Persons, 51, 57, 60 *sq.*, 69, 78, 82 *sq.*, 131, 317, 327, 542; in reference to God's dealing with the Creation, 119 *sq.*, 298, 476; and human, 180 *sq.*; expressive of operation, 329; not expressive of the Divine Nature, 333; perfection in all, proves the Unity, 474; evinced in the Incarnation, 491.
Augentius, 32, 450.
Augustine, S., 23, 356.
Avarice, a sign that Baptism has effected no change, 508.

Babylon, 6, 516.
Babylonians, the religion of, 172 *sq.*, 283.
Bandinus, 31.
Baptism, the Holy Spirit in, 12, 322, 507, 519; why not to be deferred, 13; why trine immersion in, 502-3, 520; "for the dead," 62; of Christ, 158, 322; Eunomius on, 239; terms expressive of, 500; regeneration in analogous or bodily generation, 501; proof of the presence of Deity in, 501-2; a mortification, 503, 519; necessary cause of a *blessed* Resurrection, 504; faith at, 506; free choice in, 506; not the faculties of mind, but the bad will changed in, 508; effect of, 519, 520; types and prophecies of; in O. T., 521 *sq.*
Baptismal regeneration, 62, 65, 159, 501, 508, 519, 520.
Baptismal formula, the, a rule of saving doctrine, 101 *sq.*, 117, 321, 507, 528, 529.
Baronius, 382.
Baruch, 101.
Basil the Great, author of Gregory'; style, 2, 533; his prophecy about his brother, 3; defends him, 3; of the newer Nicene school, 24; defines ὑπόστασις, 25; treatises of, sometimes attributed to Gregory, 32; attempts to save Eunomius, 35; "no deep divine," 43; charges the jury against Eunomius, 43; courage against Valens, 48, 49; rejects the term Ungenerate, 85, 86; objects to Eunomius' term "follow," 96; Liturgy of, apparently cited, 104, 113, 177; defence of, by S. Gregory, 172 *sq.*, 175 *sq.*, 187 *sq.*, 249; his exposition of Acts ii. 36, 171 *sq.*, 187 *sq.*; his teaching on essence and individuals, 193; his argument on the eternal generation, 207; fights in the van, 251; on the significance of the names of God, 263, 301, 303; accused of being a pagan as to the origin of language, 269; his account of a certain species of mental conception, 284, 285; illustrates the Divine nature by the analogies of "corn," 286, 289; shows the true meaning of Ungenerate, 312, 313; compared to an eagle, 314; his character.

INDEX OF SCRIPTURES CITED

A. *Old Testament Books.*

III

INDEX OF GREEK WORDS DISCUSSED OR ILLUSTRATED

INDEX OF GREEK WORDS DISCUSSED OR ILLUSTRATED

ERRATA.

Page 33, col. 2, line 31, *for* arms, *read* aims,
,, 38, ,, 2, note 4, ,, iv. 23, ,, iv. 23),
,, 46, ,, 1, ,, 7, ,, Enippius. *read* Euippius.
,, 58, ,, 2, line 51, ,, Creation ,, Creation,
,, 59, ,, 2, ,, 9, ,, Ingenerate ,, Ungenerate
,, 75, ,, 1, note 4, ,, ἀνάλυοιν. ,, ἀνάλυσιν.
,, 87, ,, 1, ,, 9, *add* 9
,, 88, ,, 1, ,, 4, *for* συφισμάτων *read* σοφισμάτων
,, 94, ,, 2, ,, 7, ,, Heb. i. ,, Heb. i. 3.